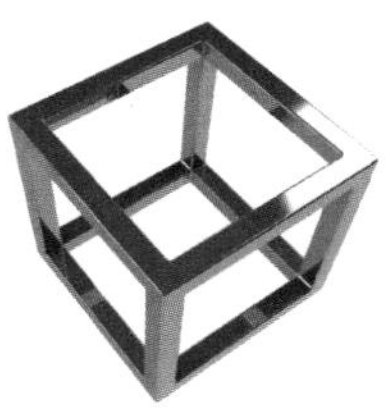

KEY CORNERSTONE	MANAGERIAL FOCUS
Understanding the Difference between Financial Accounting and Managerial Accounting	Organizational structures
Calculating Product Cost in Total and Per Unit	Different costs for different purposes
Creating and Using a Cost Formula	Differentiating between fixed and variable costs
Solving for the Number of Units to Be Sold (or Sales Revenue) to Earn a Target Operating Income	First stage of feasibility analysis
Calculating Predetermined Departmental Overhead Rates and Applying Overhead to Production	Understanding and applying manufacturing overhead
Preparing a Production Report: Weighted Average Method	Costing in a different environment
Calculating Activity-Based Units Costs	More precise allocation of costs to products
Explaining the Difference between Absorption and Variable Costing	GAAP reporting
Defining and Preparing the Financial Budget, Identifying Its Major Components, and Explaining the Interrelationships of Its Various Components	Planning and control—at an organizational level
Describing the Basic Concepts Underlying Variance Analysis, and Explaining When Variances Should Be Investigated	Planning and control—at a product level
Preparing a Flexible Budget, and Using It for Performance Reporting	Performance reporting based on actual activity levels
Explaining How and Why Firms Choose to Decentralize	Decision making and accountability
Applying Relevant Costing and Decision Making Concepts in a Variety of Business Situations	Short-run decision making
Using Net Present Value Analysis and the Profitability Index for Capital Investment Decisions Involving Independent Projects	Investing in long-term assets

THIRD CANADIAN EDITION

CORNERSTONES
OF MANAGERIAL ACCOUNTING

THIRD CANADIAN EDITION

CORNERSTONES
OF MANAGERIAL ACCOUNTING

Maryanne M. Mowen
Oklahoma State University

Don R. Hansen
Oklahoma State University

Dan L. Heitger
Miami University

David J. McConomy
Queen's University

Bradley D. Witt
Humber Institute of Technology and Advanced Learning

Jeffrey A. Pittman
Memorial University of Newfoundland

NELSON

NELSON

Cornerstones of Managerial Accounting, Third Canadian Edition

by Maryanne M. Mowen, Don R. Hansen, Dan L. Heitger, David J. McConomy, Bradley D. Witt, and Jeffrey A. Pittman

VP, Product Solutions, K–20:
Claudine O'Donnell

Publisher:
Anne-Marie Taylor

Executive Marketing Manager:
Amanda Henry

Technical Reviewer:
Ross Meacher

Content Manager:
Lisa Peterson

Photo and Permissions Researcher:
Jessica Freedman

Senior Production Project Manager:
Natalia Denesiuk Harris

Production Service:
MPS Limited

Copy Editor:
Laurel Sparrow

Proofreader:
Shilbhadra Maity

Indexer:
Edwin Durbin

Design Director:
Ken Phipps

Higher Education Design PM:
Pamela Johnston

Interior Design:
Brian Malloy

Cornerstones Icon:
Karpiyon/iStockphoto

Cover Design:
Trinh Truong

Cover Image:
Mina De La O/Getty Images

Compositor:
MPS Limited

Printed and bound in Canada
2 3 4 5 21 20 19 18

For more information contact Nelson Education Ltd., 1120 Birchmount Road, Toronto, Ontario, M1K 5G4. Or you can visit our Internet site at nelson.com

Library and Archives Canada Cataloguing in Publication

Mowen, Maryanne M., author

Cornerstones of managerial accounting / Maryanne M. Mowen, Oklahoma State University, Don R. Hansen, Oklahoma State University, Dan L. Heitger, Miami University, David J. McConomy, Queen's University, Bradley D. Witt, Humber Institute of Technology and Advanced Learning, Jeffrey A. Pittman, Memorial University of Newfoundland. — Third Canadian edition.

Includes bibliographical references and index.
Issued in print and electronic formats.
ISBN 978-0-17-672123-7 (hardcover).
—ISBN 978-0-17-685377-8 (PDF)

1. Managerial accounting—Textbooks. 2. Textbooks. I. Hansen, Don R., author II. Heitger, Dan L. (Dan Lester), author III. McConomy, David J., author IV. Witt, Bradley D., author V. Pittman, Jeffrey A., author VI. Title.

HF5657.4.M69 2017 658.15'11
C2017-905994-7
C2017-905995-5

ISBN-13: 978-0-17-672123-7
ISBN-10: 0-17-672123-1

This book is dedicated to our students—past, present, and future—who are at the heart of our passion for teaching.

Maryanne Mowen, Don Hansen, and Dan Heitger

This book is dedicated to my wife, Candace, whose love, support, and encouragement have always been there and have helped me to accomplish whatever I have done.

David McConomy

This book is dedicated to my students, whose energy and drive continue to feed my passion for teaching.

Brad Witt

This book is dedicated to my wife, Tracey, and our three children, Jack, Sophie, and Rachel, whose love and support have made it all possible.

Jeffrey Pittman

BRIEF CONTENTS

CONTENTS

CHAPTER 3

Cost Behaviour 76

CHAPTER 4

Cost–Volume–Profit Analysis: A Managerial Planning Tool 126

CHAPTER 5

Job-Order Costing 186

Get there with CORNERSTONES AND CENGAGENOWv2

Cornerstones is a complete text and technology solution that helps you and your students reach course goals and objectives. The Cornerstone pedagogy incorporates step-by-step coverage of important concepts throughout each chapter by utilizing the familiar Cornerstone examples and exercises throughout. The approach provides students with a solid foundation of the core concepts, which allows them to build on that knowledge to get to a higher understanding of managerial accounting. The integration of the *Cornerstones* text and unique features in CengageNOWv2™ will get students thinking like managers! The goal of this text is to solidify homework concepts so that students can spend more time learning how to analyze business situations and become good decision makers.

The *Cornerstones* approach focuses on three core needs:

BUILDING A STRONG FOUNDATION

Students simply cannot move forward in this course until they have built and practised the foundational aspects of accounting. With *Cornerstones*, students learn the foundations of managerial accounting FASTER, so that they can easily transition into applying and analyzing business information in a conceptual manner.

ANALYZING RELATIONSHIPS

Students also need to be able to analyze and interpret the interrelationships between the numbers and how they affect one another in order to make sound business decisions. Because accounting is an interrelated accounting system, *Cornerstones* incorporates digital technology to allow students to see actual results.

DECISION MAKING

Cornerstones has a plethora of tools to give students practice in decision making. Armed with the foundational knowledge and interrelationship understanding, students should now feel comfortable analyzing the data in order to make sound business decisions.

BUILDING A STRONG FOUNDATION

Students need to obtain a solid understanding of the foundations of accounting to set the stage for thinking like a manager.

Where other texts bury their examples in blocks of text, **Cornerstone examples** are easy to find, clear, and consistently formatted to help students digest material faster. Students value step-by-step, clear examples more than any other feature in a text.

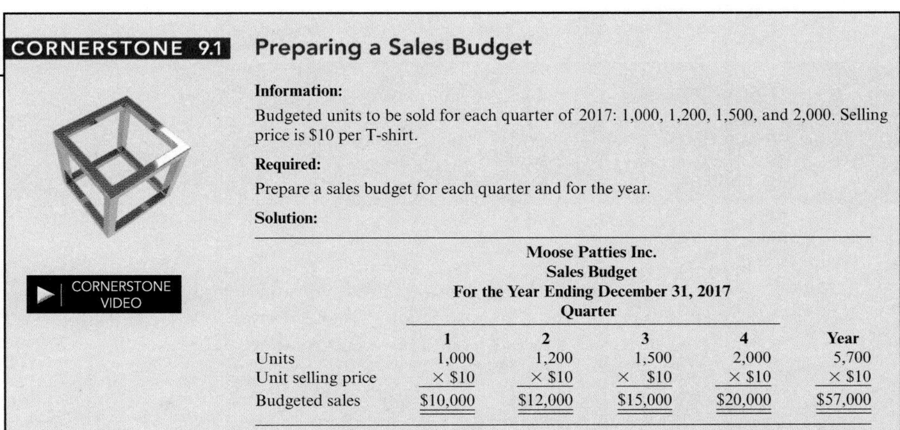

CORNERSTONE 9.1 **Preparing a Sales Budget**

CORNERSTONE VIDEO

Information:

Budgeted units to be sold for each quarter of 2017: 1,000, 1,200, 1,500, and 2,000. Selling price is $10 per T-shirt.

Required:

Prepare a sales budget for each quarter and for the year.

Solution:

Moose Patties Inc.
Sales Budget
For the Year Ending December 31, 2017

	Quarter				
	1	**2**	**3**	**4**	**Year**
Units	1,000	1,200	1,500	2,000	5,700
Unit selling price	× $10	× $10	× $10	× $10	× $10
Budgeted sales	$10,000	$12,000	$15,000	$20,000	$57,000

CORNERSTONE EXERCISES

OBJECTIVE 2
CORNERSTONE 9.1

Cornerstone Exercise 9-1 **Preparing a Sales Budget**

Memorsave Inc. makes and sells picture frames and expects the following units to be sold from July to September of the coming year:

July	56,000
August	59,000
September	61,000

The average price for a unit is $52.

Required:

Prepare a sales budget for the third quarter of the coming year, showing units and sales revenue by month and in total for the quarter.

OBJECTIVE 2
CORNERSTONE 9.2

Cornerstone Exercise 9-2 **Preparing a Production Budget**

Memorsave Inc. makes and sells picture frames. From July to October of the coming year, Memorsave expects the following unit sales:

July	56,000
August	59,000
September	61,000

Each end-of-chapter **Cornerstone Exercise** references the corresponding Cornerstone example from the text that will aid students in completing that particular exercise. This makes getting started with the homework less intimidating and encourages students to learn independently.

As further reinforcement, newly revised **Cornerstone Videos** are available for every Cornerstone example and are linked to the Cornerstone Exercises in CengageNOWv2. These videos further solidify concepts as they walk through Cornerstone examples in a way that appeals to visual and auditory learners!

ANALYZING RELATIONSHIPS

Students need to be able to get beyond just understanding the individual pieces of an accounting system and be able to connect concepts and see the relationships between the parts.

INTEGRATIVE CASE 1

Cost Behaviour and Cost–Volume–Profit Analysis for Many Glacier Hotel

Located on Swiftcurrent Lake in Glacier National Park, Many Glacier Hotel was built in 1915 by the Great Northern Railway. In an effort to supplement its lodging revenue, the hotel decided in 2001 to begin manufacturing and selling small wooden canoes decorated with symbols hand-painted by First Nations people living near the park. Due to the great success of the canoes, the hotel began manufacturing and selling paddles as well in 2003. Many hotel guests purchase a canoe and paddles for use in self-guided tours of Swiftcurrent Lake. Because production of the two products began in different years, the canoes and paddles are produced in separate production facilities and employ different labourers. Each canoe sells for $500, and each paddle sells for $50. A 2012 fire destroyed the hotel's accounting records. However, a new system put into place before the 2013 season provides the following aggregated data for the hotel's canoe and paddle manufacturing and marketing activities:

Manufacturing Data:

Number	Total Canoe	Number	Total Paddle

The chapter-spanning **Integrative Cases** present opportunities to integrate concepts from several chapters in order to analyze managerial accounting information in a broader context.

The end-of-chapter materials also contain exercises and problems that challenge students to think backward, to give students a better understanding of the different accounting interrelationships.

> "The cases give an excellent summative analysis of concepts learned in the preceding chapters. In addition, they are progressive in requiring critical thinking."
>
> —Deirdre Fitzpatrick, George Brown College

> "The *Cornerstones of Managerial Accounting* textbook is one of the best contemporary managerial accounting textbooks. It provides you with the fundamental concepts, business experience, and techniques of managerial accounting in an understandable way."
>
> —Sameer Alrishani, Seneca College

DECISION MAKING

Students need concrete ways to practise how to use accounting information to make sound business decisions.

You Decide takes *Cornerstones'* concepts beyond the foundations. Students must put themselves in the shoes of a manager or business owner and consider the different implications and outcomes of their "company's" decisions. *Cornerstones* gives students a chance to actually *practise* making decisions.

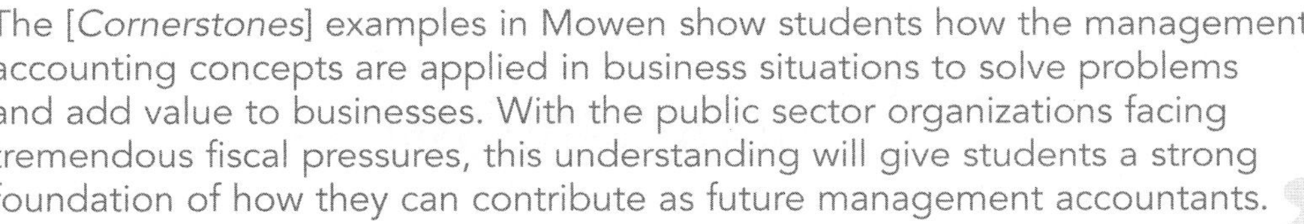

YOU DECIDE Using Contribution Margin Income Statements to Consider Varying Scenarios

You are the chief accountant for Boyne Resorts winter sports. Early in the year, you budgeted sales prices (lift tickets, restaurant prices), costs, and expected quantity to be sold. However, once the season starts, from week to week you will know more about the actual weather conditions.

How can you use this information about current weather conditions to better predict operating results for Boyne?

You can recast the budgeted statements according to how the weather will affect skiing. If the snow is good, some costs will go down. For example, you will lower the predicted cost of running the snow-making machines. However, good weather and more skiers will require additional seasonal hiring as more direct labour will be needed to run the lifts, operate ski equipment rental shops and restaurants, and so on. You can put together contribution margin budgeted income statements under various scenarios, increasing volume with good ski weather, and decreasing it with poor weather.

Having the ability to recast budgets will help managers respond quickly to the changing conditions and be able to raise or lower some prices as needed.

"The [*Cornerstones*] examples in Mowen show students how the management accounting concepts are applied in business situations to solve problems and add value to businesses. With the public sector organizations facing tremendous fiscal pressures, this understanding will give students a strong foundation of how they can contribute as future management accountants."

—Ranil Mendis CPA, CMA, CGMA, City of Toronto, Budget Coordinator

OBJECTIVE 2
CORNERSTONE 4.6

Cornerstone Exercise 4-6 Sales Needed to Earn Target Income

Head-First Company plans to sell 5,000 bicycle helmets at $70 each in the coming year. Variable cost is 70 percent of the sales price; contribution margin is 30 percent of sales price. Total fixed cost equals $29,400 (includes fixed factory overhead and fixed selling and administrative expense).

Required:

1. Calculate the sales revenue that Head-First must make to earn operating income of $81,900.
2. Check your answer by preparing a contribution margin income statement based on the sales dollars calculated in Requirement 1.
3. CONCEPTUAL CONNECTION How does a contribution margin income statement help managers make better decisions?

OBJECTIVE 4
CORNERSTONE 4.7

Cornerstone Exercise 4-7 Break-Even Point in Units for a Multiple-Product Firm

Suppose that Head-First Company now sells both bicycle helmets and motorcycle helmets. The bicycle helmets are priced at $70 and have variable costs of $49 each. The motorcycle helmets are priced at $220 and have variable costs of $143 each. Total fixed costs for Head-First as a whole equal

Conceptual Connection requirements within many end-of-chapter assignments ask students to go beyond the calculations and analyze the conceptual context of the problem. Students will better understand how companies use the calculations to make sound business decisions.

"A very comprehensive text covering all the major topic areas of managerial accounting in an easy-to-read format with some interesting cases and videos that students may enjoy and benefit from."

—Scott Laing, Dalhousie University

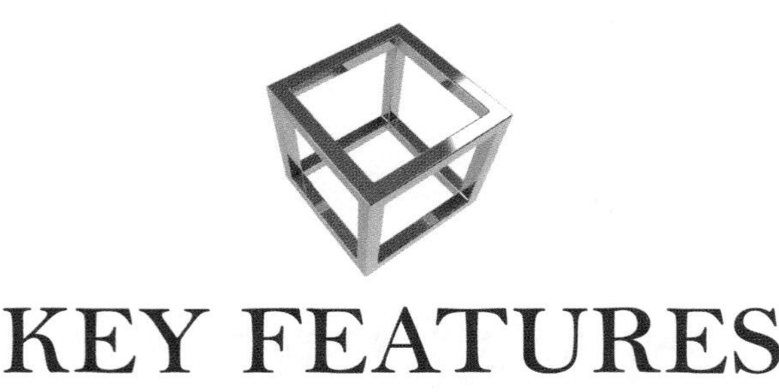

KEY FEATURES

- **Experience Managerial Decisions** vignettes offer a relational approach to teaching and learning materials through the use of chapter-opening cases that show how real businesses deal with managerial accounting issues.
- The **You Decide** feature helps students actively practise decision making. Students play the part of a manager or business owner, then consider the different factors in their decisions and how they will affect outcomes. You Decide helps students prepare for work in the real world.
- **Conceptual Connection** requirements within many end-of-chapter assignments ask students to go beyond the calculations and analyze the conceptual context of the problem. Students will better understand how companies use the calculations to make sound business decisions.
- The **Concept Q&A** boxes throughout the text challenge students to use higher-level reasoning skills. Students are prompted to go beyond the procedures and understand the broader business implications.
- The chapter-spanning **Integrative Cases** present opportunities to integrate concepts from several chapters in order to analyze managerial accounting information in a broader context.
- The **Integrated Learning System (ILS)** anchors chapter concepts, provides a framework for study, and links all the instructor resources. Learning objectives with number icons are listed at the start of each chapter. These icons reappear throughout the text and end-of-chapter materials, linking them to the chapter learning objectives. The ILS provides structure for instructors preparing lectures and exams, and helps students learn quickly and study efficiently.

- **CengageNOWv2™** is an online learning resource that provides students with access to the tools that will help them get the most out of their course. Interactive learning resources include the Adaptive Study Plan, Animated Activities, and the Blueprint Problems and Cornerstone Video resources detailed below.
- **Check My Work Feedback:** CengageNOWv2 helps students progress further outside the classroom and keeps them from getting stuck in their studies by providing them with meaningful guidance and tips as they work through their homework assignments. Feedback is consistent with material presented in the text.
- **Post-submission Feedback:** Also available in CengageNOWv2 is the ability to show the full solution in addition to newly added source calculations to enhance the learning process. Now students can see where they may have gone wrong so that they can correct their work through further practice.
- **Animated Activities:** Animated Activities in CengageNOWv2 are the perfect pre-lecture assignment to expose students to concepts before class! These cartoon-like illustrations visually guide students through selected core topics. A realistic company example illustrates how the concepts relate to the everyday activities of a business. Animated Activities are assignable or available for self-study and review.
- **Blueprint Connections:** These scenario-based teaching problems solidify concepts and demonstrate their interrelationships as well as promoting critical thinking. Blueprint Connections combine multiple topics, allowing students to explore a larger concept more fully.

UPDATED FOR THIS EDITION

- **Improved end-of-chapter content:** This edition features a revision of approximately 25 percent of the end-of-chapter content, including an average per chapter of one new case and three to four new exercises or problems.
- **New real-company references:** The Experience Managerial Decisions opening vignettes have been updated to reflect additional Canadian companies or multinational corporations that have prominent operations in Canada. These companies are then appropriately referenced within the chapters to reinforce the connections between key concepts and their applications in real-world business situations.
- **Highlights of content updates:** Chapter 1 has been amended to reflect changes to the CPA in 2015. Chapter 2 includes additional content support in the "Why" section of the Cornerstone boxes. Chapter 3 features a fully revised discussion of relevant range as well as one new exhibit. Chapter 4 has been expanded to include new sections on cost–volume–profit relationships and cost structure. Chapter 6 includes a revised Cornerstone box and updated revenue statistics in the opening vignette. Chapter 8 features a new opening vignette and one new Cornerstone box. Chapter 11 has been reorganized to feature one new appendix. Chapter 12 features a new opening vignette. All chapters have been revised for currency.

- Newly released **CengageNOWv2™** connects students to assignable content matched to their text. CengageNOWv2 is an interactive learning solution that helps students focus on what they need to learn. It improves academic performance by increasing students' time on task and giving them prompt feedback. With a focus on active learning, concept mastery, and automatic grading, CengageNOWv2 is an easy-to-use digital resource designed to get students involved in their learning progress and be better prepared for class participation and assessment. CengageNOWv2 for *Cornerstones of Managerial Accounting* can be used for self-study or assigned as homework. Each student's unique needs are identified with a pre-test that generates an Adaptive Study Plan for each chapter. Platform enhancements in CengageNOWv2 allow for more advanced types of questions, providing students with an even richer learning experience.
- **Blueprint Problems:** These have been fully revised for this edition and are author-written specifically for this text. Blueprint Problems are teaching-type problems that are based on the Cornerstones from within the chapter. Each chapter contains two to four Blueprint Problems written to help students understand the fundamental accounting concepts and their associated building blocks—not just memorize the formulas. They are written in a step-by-step format, from an overview to application of the concepts.
- **Analyzing Cornerstones Using Excel:** These have also been revised for this edition and are designed as an alternative to the Blueprint Problems as a way to incorporate Microsoft Excel in greater detail. Students build their own spreadsheets and create their own formulas rather than simply inputting numbers into a template. The unique Blueprint format starts as a conceptual overview and is followed by application of the chapter concepts using Excel.
- **Cornerstone Videos:** Revised and updated Cornerstone videos provide clear examples. Additional hints and tips have been added to guide students through each Cornerstone problem.

SUPERIOR SUPPLEMENTS

Inspired Instruction at Nelson

The **Nelson Education Teaching Advantage (NETA)** program delivers research-based instructor resources that promote student engagement and higher order thinking to enable the success of Canadian students and educators. Be sure to visit Nelson Education's **Inspired Instruction** website at **nelson .com/inspired** to find out more about NETA. Don't miss the testimonials of instructors who have used NETA supplements and seen student engagement increase!

Instructor's Resources

Key instructor ancillaries are provided on the Instructor's Website: **nelson.com/instructor**.

- **NETA Test Bank:** This resource was revised by Tamara Ebl of the University of British Columbia. It includes over 1,100 multiple-choice questions written according to NETA guidelines for effective construction and development of higher-order questions. Also included are over 400 true/false questions, over 300 problems, over 100 essay questions, over 250 fill-in-the-blank exercises, and over 450 matching questions.

The NETA Test Bank is available in a new cloud-based platform. **Nelson Testing Powered by Cognero®** is a secure online testing system that allows instructors to author, edit, and manage Test Bank content from anywhere Internet access is available. No special installations or downloads are needed, and the desktop-inspired interface, with its drop-down menus and familiar, intuitive tools, allows instructors to create and manage tests with ease. Multiple test versions can be created in an instant, and content can be imported or exported into other systems. Tests can be delivered from a learning management system, the classroom, or wherever an instructor chooses. Nelson Testing Powered by Cognero for *Cornerstones of Managerial Accounting* can be accessed through **nelson.com/instructor**.

- **NETA Presentation:** Microsoft® PowerPoint® lecture slides for every chapter feature key concepts, exhibits, and tables from *Cornerstones of Managerial Accounting*. NETA principles of clear design and engaging content have been incorporated throughout.
- **Instructor's Manual:** The Instructor's Manual to accompany *Cornerstones of Managerial Accounting* contains learning objectives, chapter outlines, suggested Cornerstone exercises, and suggested application exercises.
- **Instructor's Solutions Manual:** This manual, prepared by the authors, has been independently checked for accuracy by Ross Meacher. It contains complete solutions to discussion questions, multiple-choice exercises, Cornerstone exercises, exercises, problem sets, and cases.
- **Spreadsheet Solutions:** The complete solutions to the Excel-based spreadsheet exercises are provided.
- **Image Library:** This resource consists of digital copies of exhibits, Cornerstones, Concept Q&As, and You Decide boxes used in the book. Instructors may use these jpegs to create their own PowerPoint presentations.

This resource was revised by Rosalie Harms of the University of Winnipeg and Douglas Kong of the University of Toronto. With its engaging learning and assessment tools, CengageNOWv2 supports the entire student workflow, from motivation to mastery. For instructors, CengageNOWv2 provides control and customization with the opportunity to tailor the learning experience to improve outcomes. Class-tested and student-praised, CengageNOWv2 offers a variety of features that support course objectives and interactive learning. These features include:

- Multipanel View
- Adaptive Study Plan
- Animated Activities
- Cornerstones Videos
- Blueprint Problems
- Blueprint Connections

Ask your Nelson Education learning solutions consultant for more information about integrating CengageNOWv2 into your course.

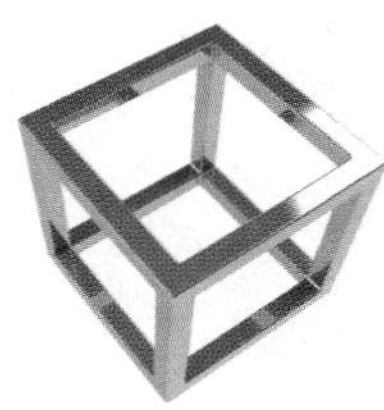

ACKNOWLEDGMENTS AND THANKS

We have received assistance from many people who have contributed to this book.

We are grateful for the assistance and support provided by Memorial University's Faculty of Business Administration and the Queen's University School of Business.

Our appreciation is also extended to CPA Canada and CPA Ontario and their predecessor organizations—the Canadian Institute of Chartered Accountants (CICA), the Institute of Chartered Accountants of Ontario (ICAO), the Society of Management Accountants of Canada (SMAC), and the Certified General Accountants' Association of Canada (CGAC)—and to the other sources as indicated for their generous permission to use or adapt problems from their publications.

We would like to thank the reviewers of this text for their insights and suggestions. The following people helped shape the Third Canadian Edition:

Anthony Chan, *Ryerson University*
Andrea Chance, *University of Guelph* (Humber)
Deirdre Fitzpatrick, *George Brown College*
Saththiyabama Kumaravel, *George Brown College*
Scott Laing, *Dalhousie University*
Howard Leaman, *University of Guelph* (Humber)
Eddie Lombardi CPA (CMA), ACMA
Alexandra McMullen, *University of Winnipeg*
Ranil Mendis CPA, CMA, CGMA
Michael Meehan, *Pilon School of Business*
Humayun Qadri, *MacEwan University*
Helen Vallee, *Kwantlen Polytechnic University*

The Third Canadian Edition of this book was adapted from the U.S. Sixth Edition by Mowen, Hansen, and Heitger. We appreciate the U.S. authors' willingness to share their work with us. This book has certainly benefited from their experience and contribution.

Many people at Nelson Education also earn our deepest thanks for their thoughtful contributions. Special thanks go to Anne-Marie Taylor, Publisher; Lisa Peterson, Content Manager; Natalia Denesiuk Harris, Senior Production Project Manager; Laurel Sparrow, Copy Editor; and Charu Verma, Project Manager at MPS. We are most grateful to Ross Meacher for taking extraordinary care in the technical check of the manuscript and solutions.

Finally, special recognition is due to our families for understanding the demands of our work and supporting our efforts.

David J. McConomy
Bradley D. Witt
Jeffrey A. Pittman
August 2017

ABOUT THE AUTHORS

David J. McConomy is an Assistant Professor at the Queen's University School of Business. He graduated with an MBA from Queen's University with a major in finance and accounting in 1969 after receiving a BA (Econ) from Loyola College (now part of Concordia University) in Montreal. Since qualifying as a chartered accountant with Arthur Andersen & Co. in Toronto, he has focused on the finance and accounting requirements of small- to medium-sized companies during his 30-year career in business.

Mr. McConomy has gained considerable experience assisting young companies, mainly in the technology field, in strategic planning and corporate finance. As chief financial officer of Systemhouse Ltd. (which was later sold to MCI and subsequently to EDS), he was instrumental in taking that company public. During his tenure with Systemhouse, revenues rose from $16.5 million to in excess of $100 million.

With Antares Electronics Inc., Mr. McConomy raised $20 million (through venture capital investments, sale-and-leaseback transactions, and the restructuring of bank lines of credit) to enable the company to become one of *Profit* magazine's fastest growing companies, as revenues increased over a three-year period from $36 million to $100 million. Later, he helped CommnetiX Computer Systems Inc. to become a public company and to raise funds from a variety of sources to fund its growth.

Since joining the faculty of the Queen's University School of Business in 2001, Mr. McConomy has won numerous Faculty Teaching Awards. He prides himself on engaging with students both within the classroom and outside of it.

Mr. McConomy has taught accounting, financial management, and business strategy (at the undergraduate and MBA levels) on both a full-time and part-time basis at Queen's University, the University of Ottawa, and internationally with the Academy of Economic Studies in Bucharest, Romania, and in Beijing, China.

Bradley D. Witt is Professor of Accounting at Humber Institute of Technology and Advanced Learning. He graduated with an MBA from Central Michigan University with a major in finance in 1998, and is a graduate of Wilfrid Laurier University in Waterloo, Ontario. He holds the CPA (Chartered Professional Accountant) designation. Most of his 20-year business career is in manufacturing, in accounting and finance roles, with a *Fortune* 500 company. While in Minneapolis, Mr. Witt was the treasurer for a start-up company, Natureworks (a joint venture between The Dow Chemical Company and Cargill), that was introducing a new biodegradable polymer (poly lactic acid (PLA)) into the plastics industry.

Mr. Witt has taught accounting and finance on a part-time basis in Michigan (at an undergraduate level) and has been active in the Canadian CMA strategic leadership professional program as a marker and an evaluator for candidate board reports. His scholarly research is in the areas of management accounting and the effectiveness of various pedagogical techniques.

Dr. Jeffrey A. Pittman was recently appointed Memorial University's Chair in Corporate Governance and Transparency as well as its CMA Professor of Accounting. Dr. Pittman has been an editor of *Contemporary Accounting Research* since 2010. Although he primarily publishes his research in such major accounting journals as *The Accounting Review*, the *Journal of Accounting Research*, the *Journal of Accounting and Economics*, and *Contemporary*

Accounting Research, Dr. Pittman's papers also appear in top finance (e.g., the *Journal of Financial Economics*) and ethics (e.g., the *Journal of Business Ethics*) outlets. Apart from a two-year visit at the Hong Kong University of Science and Technology (HKUST), Dr. Pittman has taught at Memorial University since graduating from the University of Waterloo's accounting PhD program in 2001. He has received numerous research and teaching honours, including the Dean's Teaching Award at Memorial's Faculty of Business Administration in 2010. Dr. Pittman, who is a chartered accountant and certified management accountant, has been a moderator in the CMA professional program for several years.

Dr. Maryanne M. Mowen is Associate Professor Emerita of Accounting at Oklahoma State University. She currently teaches online classes in cost and management accounting for Oklahoma State University. She received her PhD from Arizona State University. Dr. Mowen brings an interdisciplinary perspective to teaching and writing in cost and management accounting, as she has degrees in history and economics. She has taught classes in ethics and the impact of the Sarbanes-Oxley Act on accountants. Her scholarly research is in the areas of management accounting, behavioural decision theory, and compliance with the Sarbanes-Oxley Act. She has published articles in journals such as *Decision Sciences*, the *Journal of Economics and Psychology*, and the *Journal of Management Accounting Research*. Dr. Mowen has served as a consultant to mid-sized and *Fortune* 100 companies and works with corporate controllers on management accounting issues. She is a member of the Northern New Mexico chapter of SCORE and serves as a mentor, assisting small and start-up businesses. Outside the classroom, she enjoys hiking, travelling, reading mysteries, and working crossword puzzles.

Dr. Don R. Hansen is Professor Emeritus of Accounting at Oklahoma State University. He received his PhD from the University of Arizona in 1977. He has an undergraduate degree in mathematics from Brigham Young University. Dr. Hansen's research interests include activity-based costing and mathematical modelling. He has published articles in both accounting and engineering journals including *The Accounting Review*, the *Journal of Management Accounting Research*, *Accounting Horizons*, and *Accounting, Organizations and Society*. He has served on the editorial board of *The Accounting Review*. His outside interests include family, church activities, reading, movies, and watching sports.

Dr. Dan L. Heitger is Professor of Accounting and Co-Director of the Center for Business Excellence at Miami University. He received his PhD from Michigan State University and his undergraduate degree in accounting from Indiana University. He actively works with executives and students of all levels in developing and teaching courses in managerial and cost accounting, business sustainability, risk management, and business reporting. He co-founded an organization that provides executive education for large international organizations. Dr. Heitger's interactions with business professionals, through executive education and the Center, allow him to bring a current and real-world perspective to his writing. His published research focuses on managerial accounting and risk management issues and has appeared in *Harvard Business Review*, *Behavioral Research in Accounting*, *Accounting Horizons*, *Issues in Accounting Education*, *Journal of Accountancy*, and *Management Accounting Quarterly*. His outside interests include hiking with his family in the national park system.

1

Introduction to Managerial Accounting

After studying Chapter 1, you should be able to:

1. Explain the meaning of managerial accounting.
2. Explain the differences between financial accounting and managerial accounting.
3. Identify and explain the current focus of managerial accounting.
4. Describe the role of managerial accountants in an organization.
5. Explain the importance of ethical behaviour for managers and managerial accountants.
6. Identify three accounting designations formerly available in Canada.

ColobusYeti/iStock by Getty Images

EXPERIENCE MANAGERIAL DECISIONS

with BuyCostumes.com

The greatest benefit of managerial accounting is also its biggest challenge—to provide managers with information that improves decisions and creates organizational value. This information helps inform managers about the impact of various strategic and operational decisions on key performance measures, both financial and nonfinancial, and their eventual impact on the organization's success. The information is challenging to prepare and analyze because it requires an understanding of all the value chain components that affect the organization, including production, marketing, distribution, customer service, and research and development (R&D).

Since its inception in 1999, BuyCostumes.com has blended the right managerial accounting information and an innovative business model to provide costumes to customers in over 50 countries. Using the Internet and marketing creativity, BuyCostumes.com serves a market of 150 million consumers that spend $3.6 billion on costumes each year! According to former CEO Jalem Getz, BuyCostumes.com measures key performance indicators to guide its decision making. For example, managerial accountants analyze measures of customer satisfaction, average time between order placement and costume arrival for each shipping method, and the profitability of individual customer types. As customer trends change, competitors emerge, and technological advances occur, BuyCostumes.com's managerial accounting information adapts to provide crucial insight into the company's performance and how its strategy must evolve for it to remain the world's largest Internet costume retailer.

In writing this textbook, we wanted to show our readers the importance and relevance of managerial accounting to decision making. Therefore, each chapter begins with a quick look at how different companies—ones that you likely recognize—use the managerial accounting topics studied in that particular chapter (e.g., "Experience Managerial Decisions with BuyCostumes.com"). Throughout the textbook, we have used references to real companies and real situations to make the learning process much more relevant. It is our belief that this will enhance the learning process and allow you, the reader, to identify more closely how managerial accountants can impact the success of various businesses.

buycostumes.com©
the web's most popular costume store!

WHAT IS MANAGERIAL ACCOUNTING?

OBJECTIVE 1

Explain the meaning of managerial accounting.

What do we mean by managerial accounting? Quite simply, **managerial accounting** is the provision of accounting information for a company's internal users. It uses the firm's accounting system, and formats the information in a way to support the information needs of managers. Unlike financial accounting, managerial accounting is not bound by any formal criteria such as generally accepted accounting principles (GAAP) or International Financial Reporting Standards (IFRS). Managerial accounting has three broad objectives:

- To provide information for planning the organization's actions.
- To provide information for controlling the organization's actions.
- To provide information for making effective decisions.

Using recent examples from many companies in both the for-profit and not-for-profit sectors, this textbook explains how all manufacturing (e.g., aircraft producer Bombardier), merchandising (e.g., clothing retailer lululemon), and service (e.g., public accounting firm KPMG) organizations use managerial accounting information and concepts. For instance, hospital administrators, presidents of corporations, dentists, educational administrators, and city managers all can improve their managerial skills by being well grounded in the basic concepts and use of managerial accounting information for planning, controlling, and decision making.

It should be noted that many companies (currently over 2,500 large multinationals in total) increasingly are deciding to publicly release large quantities of managerial accounting information, typically given only to internal users, through optional reports known as corporate sustainability reports (e.g., BC Hydro and TELUS), social responsibility reports (e.g., Canada Post), or citizenship reports (e.g., Proctor & Gamble). The release of these reports—typically referred to as CSR reports—often occurs because firms want to manage their reputations by preparing and releasing such information themselves, rather than having Internet bloggers, newspapers, and 24-hour cable news networks publish their own estimates of such information. Some leading companies (e.g., PepsiCo) have even moved so far as to combine their CSR report with their annual report, resulting in a single, integrated report containing both traditional financial accounting information and managerial accounting information. Clearly, the demand for managerial accounting information continues to grow.

Information Needs for Planning, Controlling, and Decision Making

Accounting is the language of business, and so it is essential that every manager—whatever their prime responsibility—have a firm understanding of how the numbers are generated and what they mean. Managerial accounting information is needed by a variety of individuals. In particular, managers and empowered workers need comprehensive, up-to-date information for the following activities: (1) planning, (2) controlling, and (3) decision making. Exhibit 1.1 shows how these activities relate to one another.

EXHIBIT 1.1

Uses of Managerial Accounting Information

The detailed formulation of action to achieve a particular end is the management activity called **planning**. Planning requires setting objectives and identifying methods to achieve those objectives. For example, a firm may set the objective of increasing its short-term and long-term profitability by improving the overall quality of its products. Fiat Chrysler Automobiles drastically improved the quality and profitability of its Chrysler automobile division during the beginning of the 21st century to the point where its quality surpassed that of Mercedes-Benz.[1] By improving product quality, firms like Fiat Chrysler should be able to reduce scrap and rework, decrease the number of customer complaints and warranty work, reduce the resources currently assigned to inspection, and so on, thus increasing profitability. To realize these benefits, management must develop some specific methods that, when implemented, will lead to the achievement of the desired objective. A plant manager, for example, may start a supplier evaluation program to identify and select suppliers that are willing and able to supply defect-free parts. Empowered workers may be able to identify production processes that cause defects and to develop new methods to eliminate such defects, resulting in reduced scrap and rework.

Planning is only half the battle. Once a plan is created, it must be implemented and its implementation monitored by managers and workers to ensure that the plan is being carried out as intended. The managerial activity of monitoring a plan's implementation and taking corrective action as needed is referred to as **controlling**. Control is usually achieved by comparing actual performance with expected performance. This information can be used to evaluate the steps being taken to implement a plan. Based on the feedback, a manager (or worker) may decide to let the plan continue as is, take corrective action of some type to put the actions back into harmony with the original plan, or do some midstream replanning.

The managerial accounting information used for planning and control purposes can be either financial or nonfinancial in nature. For example, by redesigning operations, a firm may be able to reduce production time, downtime, and energy consumed, while increasing output per hour. All of these relate to nonfinancial performance. Yet they will have a positive impact on financial results.

The process of choosing among competing alternatives is called **decision making**. This managerial function is intertwined with planning and control in that a manager cannot successfully plan or control the organization's actions without making decisions regarding competing alternatives. For instance, suppose BMW plans to offer a car that runs on gasoline and hydrogen. Decisions can be improved if information about the alternatives (e.g., pertaining to gasoline vs. hydrogen vs. hybrid combinations of these two automobile fuel options) is gathered and made available to managers. Ultimately, the information they gather will assist managers in deciding if this is a good idea or not. One of the major roles of the managerial accounting information system is to supply information that facilitates and improves decision making. For example, a company's vice-president of sales and marketing wondered whether to hold tent sales in certain cities in the current year. If she had information on expected sales and the related expenses of holding each tent sale, this information, along with her knowledge of competitive conditions and customers' needs, would improve her ability to select appropriate cities for the tent sales.

YOU DECIDE What Constitutes Managerial Accounting Information?

You are the Second Cup executive who has been chosen to decide whether the company should continue its policy of sourcing only Fair Trade coffee.

What types of information should you consider as you decide how best to structure and analyze this important long-term strategic decision? What challenges do you expect to face in making this decision?

What constitutes managerial accounting information is growing considerably as organizations must make decisions that include the global consequences of their actions, as well as the impact

(Continued)

[1] Sarah A. Webster and Joe Guy Collier, "Fixing a Car Company: Zetsche on Mercedes: 'A Lot of Work Is Ahead,'" *Detroit Free Press*. Taken from http://forums.mbworld.org/forums/showthread.php?t121650 on April 8, 2008.

on an increasingly large number of vocal, well-informed, and powerful stakeholders. Stakeholders include the company's customers, suppliers, employees, regulators, politicians, lawmakers, and local community members. Generally speaking, managerial accounting information can be *financial* in nature, such as sales revenue or cost of sales, or *nonfinancial* in nature, such as the number of quality defects or the percentage of manufacturing plants that are inspected for compliance with human rights policies. One of the most exciting—and yet daunting—aspects of managerial accounting is that one can choose to measure *anything*, assuming the resources, information technology, and creativity exist to capture the desired performance measure.

As a Second Cup executive, one of the first nonfinancial factors you likely would consider measuring is the quality of the Fair Trade coffee to ensure that it fulfills Second Cup's strategic goal of creating a competitive advantage by providing premium coffee to customers. Quality could be defined by the beans' taste, shelf life longevity, or other factors valued by customers. Other important nonfinancial performance measures might include the time required to ship the harvested beans from the Fair Trade suppliers to the Second Cup distribution centre, and the presence of a local farming workforce growing and harvesting Fair Trade coffee critical to successfully sustaining a long-term supply chain between the growers and the company.

One of the most important financial items to measure would be the importance to Second Cup's customers of consuming Fair Trade premium quality coffee, which could be measured by the additional price they are willing to pay for the current coffee offering over and above more average quality coffee. Other financial measures might include the cost of harvesting, inspecting, and shipping beans, as well as investments in Fair Trade farming communities (e.g., physical infrastructure and schools) that ensure the relationship is sustainable for future generations.

Finally, you should consider how the decision to continue sourcing premium Fair Trade coffee will be perceived by Second Cup's important stakeholders, including its customers who buy the coffee, suppliers who provide the coffee beans, and government officials in Canada who set trading policies between countries. Accurately measuring issues like stakeholder perceptions of such decisions can be difficult because the managerial accountant often must invent new measures, determine where the data to create such measures might come from, and estimate how accurate these measures will be once collected.

The managerial accountant's ability to inform executive decision makers by providing innovative, accurate, and timely performance measures can create an important competitive advantage for the organization by improving its key decisions. Each company will require different information for this purpose, as can be seen for BuyCostumes.com at the beginning of the chapter compared to Fiat Chrysler.

COMPARISON OF MANAGERIAL AND FINANCIAL ACCOUNTING

OBJECTIVE 

Explain the differences between financial accounting and managerial accounting.

There are two basic kinds of accounting information systems: financial accounting and managerial accounting. **Financial accounting** is primarily concerned with producing information (financial statements) for *external* users, including investors, creditors, customers, suppliers, government agencies (e.g., Canada Revenue Agency), and labour unions. This information has historical orientation and is used for such things as investment decisions, stewardship evaluation, monitoring activity, and regulatory measures. Financial statements must conform to certain rules and conventions that are defined by various bodies, such as the Accounting Standards Board (AcSB) of CPA Canada, the Financial Accounting Standards Board in the United States, or the International Accounting Standards Board (IASB) internationally. These rules, referred to as GAAP or IFRS, pertain to issues such as the recognition of revenues; timing of expenses; and recording of assets, liabilities, and shareholders' equity.

The managerial accounting system produces information for *internal* users, such as managers, executives, and workers. Thus, managerial accounting could be properly called *internal accounting*, and financial accounting could be called *external accounting*. Specifically, managerial accounting identifies, collects, measures, classifies, and reports financial and nonfinancial information that is useful to internal users in planning, controlling, and decision making. Managerial accounting consists of tools to help the accountant to formulate, analyze, and report this information to the managers in the company.

When comparing managerial accounting to financial accounting, several differences can be identified. Some of the more important differences follow and are summarized in Exhibit 1.2.

- *Targeted users.* As mentioned, managerial accounting focuses on providing information for internal users, while financial accounting focuses on providing information for external users.

EXHIBIT 1.2

Comparison of Managerial and Financial Accounting

Managerial Accounting	Financial Accounting
• Internally focused	• Externally focused
• No mandatory rules	• Must follow externally imposed rules
• Financial and nonfinancial information; subjective information possible	• Objective financial information
• Emphasis on the future	• Historical orientation
• Internal information and decision making based on decisions, departments, products, and jobs	• Information about the firm as a whole
• Broad, multidisciplinary	• More self-contained

- *Restrictions on inputs and processes.* Managerial accounting is not subject to the requirements of GAAP. The inputs and processes of financial accounting are well defined and, in fact, restricted. Only certain kinds of economic events qualify as inputs, and processes must follow generally accepted methods. Unlike financial accounting, managerial accounting has no official body that prescribes the format, content, and rules for selecting inputs and processes, and for preparing internal financial reports. Also, whereas financial accounting information is historical (i.e., looking into the rearview mirror), managerial accounting information is both backward-looking and forward-looking (i.e., looking through the front windshield). Managers are free to choose whatever information they want and will choose different information for different purposes—provided it can be justified on a cost–benefit basis.
- *Type of information.* The restrictions imposed by financial accounting tend to produce objective and verifiable financial information. For managerial accounting, information may be financial or nonfinancial and may be much more subjective in nature.
- *Time orientation.* Financial accounting has a historical orientation. It records and reports events that have already happened. Although managerial accounting also records and reports events that have already occurred, it strongly emphasizes providing information about future events. Management may, for example, want to know what it will cost to produce a product next year. Knowing this information helps in planning purchases and making pricing decisions, among other things. This future orientation is needed to support the managerial functions of planning and decision making.
- *Degree of aggregation.* Managerial accounting provides measures and internal reports used to evaluate the performance of entities, product lines, departments, and managers. Essentially, detailed information is needed and provided. Financial accounting, on the other hand, focuses on overall firm performance, providing a more aggregated viewpoint.
- *Breadth.* Managerial accounting is much broader than financial accounting. It includes aspects of managerial economics, industrial engineering, and management science as well as numerous other areas.

The accounting system should be designed to provide both financial and managerial accounting information. The key point here is flexibility—the system should be able to supply different information for different purposes.

Triple Bottom Line

Many companies have expanded the definition of "bottom line" to include a measure of activities not simply related to increasing profits. The **Triple Bottom Line** is a reference to establishing objectives within the organization that reflect the company's concern for its social and environmental impact. Companies have often been criticized for having too narrow a focus on making money, sometimes to the detriment of their workers or with no regard to the impact on the environment. We have all heard horror stories about the contamination of soil by manufacturing plants disposing of their waste materials in an unsafe manner. For many years, little, if any, attention was paid to the implications of heavy manufacturing on the surrounding areas. Today, however, the environmental impact of businesses and their activities is under much closer scrutiny. Laws have been passed to prevent unsafe waste disposal and to restrict corporate operations that will damage the surrounding areas. To understand the importance of these issues, one need only to follow the debate about running a pipeline from the oilfields of Alberta through the United States to the gulf ports of Texas or across the Rocky Mountains to the coast of British Columbia. There is no question of the economic value of the pipelines, but at what cost?

The same can be said of the implications of the impact of business on various members of society. Discussions about minimum wage rates being paid to workers in developed countries, let alone to subsistence wages being paid by companies in the developed world to workers in underdeveloped countries, highlight the disparity that tends to undermine the social values that we all say we hold true. Concern about social inequalities has become so severe that many organizations allow their employees to take time off, with pay, to do charitable work in the community. Habitat for Humanity recognized the work of Home Depot Canada in supporting its efforts to provide affordable housing to as many Canadian families as possible. In a press release, Habitat for Humanity said "In 2012, THDC [The Home Depot Canada] and THDCF [The Home Depot Canada Foundation] donated more than $9.3 million in cash and building materials to Habitat and its ReStores in Canada. Since 1996, THDC and THDCF have donated more than $40 million in cash and product to Habitat for Humanity Canada—along with countless volunteers on Habitat Build sites—in support of the shared vision of building a world where everyone has a safe and decent place to live."[2]

Many companies have developed a formal approach to evaluating how they are performing in the areas of social and environmental activities by introducing the Triple Bottom Line rather than focusing simply on the financial performance. These measures are often embodied in the annual report as a means of illustrating the commitment of the company to being a good corporate citizen as well as a profitable company.

CURRENT FOCUS OF MANAGERIAL ACCOUNTING

OBJECTIVE 3

Identify and explain the current focus of managerial accounting.

The business environment in which companies operate has changed dramatically over the past several decades. For instance, advances in technology, the Internet, globalization, increased competitive pressures, and increased complexity of strategies (e.g., the acquisition of Shoppers Drug Mart by Loblaw Companies) and operations all have combined to produce a much more complex business environment. Effective managerial accounting systems also have changed in order to provide information that helps improve companies' planning, control, and decision-making effectiveness in such a complex environment. Several important uses of managerial accounting resulting from these advances include new methods of estimating product and service cost and profitability, understanding customer requirements, evaluating the business from a cross-functional perspective, and providing information useful in improving total quality.

New Methods of Costing Products and Services

Today's companies need focused, accurate information on the cost of their products and services. Years ago, a company might have produced a few products that were roughly

[2] Habitat for Humanity, press release, retrieved from http://www.habitat.ca/hfhcnewsp4237.php?ID=169&command=viewArticle¤tFeed= on April 15, 2014. Reprinted with permission from Habitat for Humanity Canada.

similar, with only the cost of materials and labour differing from one product to another. Figuring out the cost of each unit was relatively easy. Now, however, with the increase in technology and automation, and the proliferation of products, it is more difficult to generate the costing information needed by management to make a wide variety of decisions. As Peter Drucker, the internationally respected management guru, points out:

> *Traditional cost accounting in manufacturing does not record the cost of nonproducing, such as the cost of faulty quality, or of a machine being out of order, or of needed parts not being on hand. Yet these unrecorded and uncontrolled costs in some plants run as high as the costs that traditional accounting does record. By contrast, a new method of cost accounting developed in the past 10 years—called "activity-based" accounting—records all costs. And it relates them, as traditional accounting cannot, to value added.*[3]

Activity-based costing (ABC) is a more detailed approach to determining the cost of goods and services. ABC improves costing accuracy by emphasizing the cost of the many activities or tasks that must be done to produce a product or offer a service. United Parcel Service (UPS) used ABC to discover and manage the cost of each of the activities involved with shipping packages by truck, as opposed to by plane, in order to compete effectively with FedEx in its overnight delivery business in quick mid-distance (up to 800 kilometres) overnight deliveries.[4] The objective of every manager is to find ways to perform necessary activities more efficiently and to eliminate those activities that do not create customer value.

Customer Orientation

Customer value is a key focus because firms can establish a competitive advantage by creating better customer value for the same cost as competitors or creating equivalent value for lower cost than that of competitors. Customer value is the difference between what a customer receives and what the customer gives up when buying a product or service. When we talk about customer value, we consider the complete range of tangible and intangible benefits that a customer receives from a purchased product.

Strategic Positioning Effective cost information can help the company identify strategies that increase customer value and create a sustainable competitive advantage.[5] Generally, firms choose one of two general strategies: (1) cost leadership or (2) superior products through differentiation (highest performance quality, most desired product features, best customer service, etc.). The objective of the cost leadership strategy is to provide the same or better value to customers at a *lower* cost than competitors. A differentiation strategy, on the other hand, strives to increase customer value by providing something to customers not provided by competitors. For example, Best Buy's Geek Squad of computer technicians creates a competitive advantage for Best Buy by providing 24-hour in-home technical assistance for its customers. Accurate cost information is important to see whether the additional service provided by the Geek Squad adds more to revenue than it does to cost.

Product Life Cycles New products progress through a series of stages: conception, introduction into the market, growth, maturity, and, finally, decline and eventual withdrawal from the market. This sequence is known as the **product life cycle**, and it is associated with different marketing strategies and product mixes that require different planning and control decisions.

[3] From "We Need to Measure, Not Count" by Peter F. Drucker. Reprinted with permission of *The Wall Street Journal*.
[4] Charles Haddad and Jack Ewing, "Ground Wars: UPS's Rapid Ascent Leaves FedEx Scrambling," *Business Week* (May 21, 2001): 64–68.
[5] C. Rutledge and R. Williams, "A Seat at the Table," *Outlook Journal* (June 2004). Taken from http://www.accenture.com/xd/xd.asp?it=enweb&xd=ideas%5Coutlook%5C2_2004%5Cm on October 6, 2005.

Product life cycles range from a few months for trendy goods to many years for appliances and automobiles. Similarly, each stage of the product life cycle may be long or short depending on the product. For example, technology-based products usually have a long development stage and a relatively short market life. Other products, such as airplanes, have market lives many times longer than their development stage. To effectively plan and control the production of goods or services, management accountants must consider the product's life cycle. The key element for planning and control purposes is that managers identify and track revenues and costs over the product's entire life cycle.

The Value Chain Successful pursuit of cost leadership and/or differentiation strategies requires an understanding of a firm's value chain. The **value chain** refers to the set of business functions that add value to an organization's products or services. For the company to succeed, all stages of the various functions—such as R&D, product design, production, marketing, distribution, and customer service—need to add value to the customer experience.

The value chain analysis is a systematic way to examine the development of a firm's competitive advantage. The concept was introduced by M.E. Porter in his book *Competitive Advantage* (1985). When value is built into each stage of a product or service, this increases the total value delivered by the organization to its customers.

Clearly, not all functions are equally important to the success of a company. However, no matter what product or service an organization produces, it must try to create goods and services that are valued by its customers. According to Porter, *value chain primary activities* include the following:

- *Inbound logistics*—receiving raw materials and goods from the company's suppliers.
- *Operations*—manufacturing or assembling goods. This includes "individual" operations, such as room service for a hotel chain.
- *Outbound logistics*—sending finished goods to wholesalers, retailers, or the final consumer.
- *Marketing and sales*—developing a marketing, communications, and promotions strategy to meet the needs of targeted customers.
- *Service*—providing customers with installation, after-sales service, complaint handling, and so on.

Also, the value chain includes a number of *support activities:*

- *Procurement*—securing the lowest prices for inputs of the highest quality, and deciding which components or operations will be provided in-house or obtained from external sources.
- *Technology development*—innovating to reduce costs. This includes sustaining competitive advantage through lean manufacturing, customer relationship management, Internet marketing activities, the use of social media, and so on.
- *Human resources management*—effectively managing recruitment, selection, training, development, and remuneration of employees, who are a vital resource.
- *Developing infrastructure*—which includes structuring the firm's reporting, planning, control, management information systems, and so on.

Management accountants play a key role in delivering all value chain functions as they provide estimated revenue and cost data for each stage of a product's life. The information provided by managerial accountants will help line managers to devise methods for reducing costs and production time, and to make marketing decisions that will have a significant impact on sales. Decisions such as whether a company sells its products directly to a chain of retail stores or indirectly through a wholesaler, and at what price, cannot be made without the detailed analysis of projected revenues and costs. These data also influence the decision of which transportation system should be used (e.g., air cargo, trucks, or trains), and whether a product warranty should be offered.

Many companies will focus on one aspect of the value chain and improve performance in that area to such an extent that it will stand out from all other competitors in the field. It can be argued that Apple has spent an inordinate amount of time on the design and development of its products, but the introduction of every new product from Apple is a huge event. The unique designs set Apple products apart from every one of the company's competitors.

Exhibit 1.3 illustrates the value chain. A managerial accounting system must track information about a wide variety of activities that span every facet of the value chain. For example, prior to issuing final approval for its most recent version of the iPhone, Apple spent considerable effort researching the cost of developing and manufacturing the new iPhone, as well as the amount of money potential customers would be willing to spend to purchase it. Also, customer value can be increased by improving the speed of delivery and response. FedEx exploited this part of the value chain to develop a service that was not being offered by any postal service in the world. Today, many customers believe that delivery delayed is delivery denied, which indicates that a good managerial accounting system must develop and measure indicators of customer satisfaction.

The Value Chain

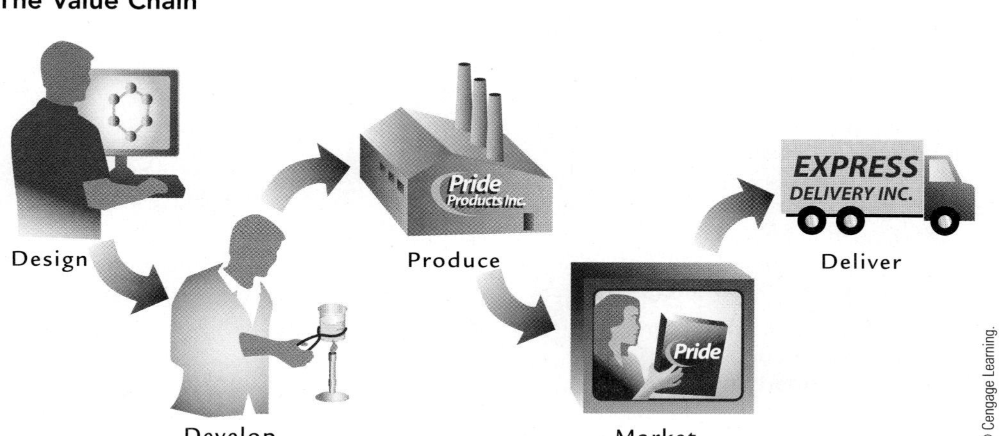

© Cengage Learning.

Assume a company has two departments: assembling and finishing. The value-added and non-value-added activities may be classified as shown in Exhibit 1.4. Note the difference between the value-added time and the non-value-added time. Anything that can be done to reduce non-value-added time will benefit the company.

It is important to note that companies have internal customers as well. For example, the procurement process acquires and delivers parts and materials to producing departments. Providing high-quality parts on a timely basis to managers of internal producing departments is just as vital as providing high-quality goods to external customers. The emphasis on managing the internal value chain and servicing internal customers has revealed the importance of a *cross-functional perspective.*

Cross-Functional Perspective

In managing the value chain, a management accountant must understand and measure many functions of the business. Contemporary approaches to costing may include initial design and engineering costs, as well as manufacturing costs, and the costs of distribution, sales, and service. Understanding the various definitions of cost—including the shifting definitions of cost from the short run to the long run—can be invaluable in determining what information is relevant in decision making. In a long-run decision environment, a company may spend many millions of dollars to perform customer profitability analyses

EXHIBIT 1.4

Value-Added and Non-Value-Added Activities

Operations	Average Time (days)
1. Assembling department	
Receiving	4
Quality control	2
Storage	20–30
Move to production	1
Waiting for use	6
Setup of machinery	1
Assembly process	**6**
Move to inspection	1
Move to finishing	1
Total time in assembling:	42–52
2. Finishing department	
Receiving	1
Move to production	1
Waiting for use	10–24
Setup of machinery	1
Finishing process	**4**
Inspection	1
Packaging process	**1**
Move to dockside	1
Storage	3
Ship to customer	2–8
Total time in finishing:	25–45
Total processing time:	67–97
Total non-value-added time:	56–86
Assembling value-added time:	**6**
Finishing value-added time:	**5**
Total value-added time:	**11**

that identify its most and least profitable customers. However, a short-run decision to determine the profitability of a special order (e.g., Canadian Tire Corporation's order for extra snow tires) may require minimal effort and expense to identify only the incremental costs of a special order in a single functional area.

Why try to relate managerial accounting to marketing, management, engineering, finance, and other business functions? When a value chain approach is taken and customer value is emphasized, we see that these disciplines are all interrelated; a decision affecting one affects the others. For example, salespeople may offer deep discounts at the end of the year to meet their sales targets. Customers, of course, buy more products. The company's factories may have to work double shifts, with a great deal of overtime pay, to meet this sudden increase in demand. A **cross-functional perspective** allows us to see the big picture—to see that the increased revenue may come at the expense of much higher product costs. By having a broader vision, managers may be able to plan ahead, knowing that additional orders will probably result from the deeper discounts and they can produce extra inventory in advance to maintain product quality, deliver on a timely basis, and reduce overall costs. The result would be increased efficiency and higher profits.

Total Quality Management

Continuous improvement is the continual search for ways to increase the overall efficiency and productivity of activities by reducing waste, increasing quality, and managing costs. Managerial accounting information about the costs of products, customers, processes, and other objects of management interest can be the basis for identifying ways to achieve continuous improvement. Continuous improvement is fundamental to establishing excellence in a company.

Providing products with little waste and ensuring that they perform according to specifications are the twin objectives of world-class firms. A philosophy of **total quality management**, in which manufacturers strive to create an environment that will enable workers to manufacture perfect (zero-defect) products, has replaced the "acceptable quality" attitudes of the past. This emphasis on quality has also created a demand for a managerial accounting system that provides financial and nonfinancial information about quality, including cost measurement of quality, and reporting for both manufacturing and service industries. For example, in response to increasing customer complaints regarding its laptop computer repair process, Toshiba formed an alliance with UPS in which UPS picks up the broken laptop, fixes it, and returns the repaired laptop to the customer. In order for this alliance to work effectively, both Toshiba and UPS require relevant managerial accounting information regarding the cost of existing poor quality and efforts to improve future quality.[6]

Many companies, such as Fiat Chrysler Automobiles, are increasingly using techniques such as Six Sigma and Design for Six Sigma (DFSS), together with various types of cost information, to achieve improved quality performance. Specifically, Chrysler's goal is "to meet customer requirements and improve vehicle and system reliability while reducing development costs and cultivating innovation."[7] On a related note, many companies attempt to increase organizational value by eliminating wasteful activities that exist throughout the value chain. In eliminating such waste, companies usually find that their accounting must also change to **lean accounting**, which organizes costs according to the value chain and collects both financial and nonfinancial information. The objective is to provide information to managers that supports their waste reduction efforts and to provide financial statements that better reflect overall performance, using both financial and nonfinancial information.

Finally, one of the more recent tasks of management accountants is to help carry out the company's enterprise risk management (ERM) approach. ERM is a formal way for companies to identify and respond to the most important threats and business opportunities facing the organization. ERM is becoming increasingly important for long-term success. For example, it is well recognized that Walmart's expert crisis management processes and teams repeatedly responded to the aftermath of Hurricane Katrina throughout Louisiana and Mississippi better and faster than did either local or federal government agencies. The results of many public accounting firm surveys highlight the growing importance that organizations place on effective risk management practices.[8]

Time as a Competitive Element

Time is a crucial element in all phases of the value chain. World-class firms reduce time to market by compressing design, implementation, and production cycles. These firms deliver products or services quickly by eliminating non-value-added time, which is time of no value to the customer (e.g., the time a product spends on the loading dock). Interestingly, decreasing non-value-added time appears to go hand in hand with increasing quality.[9]

What about the relationship between time and product life cycles? The rate of technological innovation has increased for many industries, and the life of a particular product

[6] T. Friedman, *The World Is Flat: A Brief History of the Twenty-First Century*. Farrar, Straus and Giroux: New York, New York, 2005.

[7] Kevin Kelly, "Chrysler Continues Quality Push," WardsAuto.Com. Taken from http://wardsauto.com/microsites/news-article.asp on September 30, 2005.

[8] *Enterprise Risk Management: Tools and Techniques for Effective Implementation*. Institute of Management Accountants, Montvale, New Jersey, 2007: 1–31.

[9] An excellent analysis of time as a competitive element is contained in A. Faye Borthick and Harold P. Roth, "Accounting for Time: Reengineering Business Processes to Improve Responsiveness," *Journal of Cost Management* (Fall 1993): 4–14.

can be quite short. Managers must be able to respond quickly and decisively to changing market conditions. Information allowing them to accomplish this must be available. For example, Hewlett-Packard found that it is better to be 50 percent over budget in new product development than to be six months late. This correlation between cost and time is the kind of information that should be available from a managerial accounting information system.

Efficiency

Improving efficiency is also a vital concern as it will have a direct impact on profitability. Both financial and nonfinancial measures of efficiency are needed to indicate to managers whether they are accomplishing their objectives. Cost is a critical measure of efficiency, and cost trends and changes in measures of productivity over time can be important indicators of the success of continuous improvement decisions. For these efficiency measures to be of value, costs must be properly defined, measured, and assigned; furthermore, production of output must be related to the inputs required, and the overall financial effect of productivity changes must be calculated.

Management Accounting for Service and Not-for-Profit Organizations

Management accounting was primarily developed for manufacturing firms, however, management accounting concepts have evolved over the years and today apply to all types of organizations, including service and not-for-profit organizations.

Service organizations—such as hotels, real estate agencies, insurance companies, law firms, consultants of all kinds, libraries, government agencies, schools, and hospitals—do not make or sell tangible goods but instead provide services. Unlike products, services cannot be stored and can differ from one establishment to another or from one service provider to another. Services are sometimes difficult to define. For example, schools offer a service, but the output of education is not easy to measure. The same can be said for hospitals, where patient care and health are also difficult to quantify and measure.

Western countries, including Canada, have moved from a manufacturing-based economy to a service- and knowledge-based economy. Innovation- and technology-based industries are also service-based. Increasingly more people work for the service industries than for manufacturing industries. For example, in terms of the number of employees, the travel industry—clearly a service industry—is larger than the North American automotive industry (i.e., GM, Chrysler, and Ford), which has recently declined to a much smaller workforce than it once had.

Management accounting applies also to not-for-profit organizations. Much like for-profit firms, not-for-profit organizations need to prepare budgets and performance evaluations, assess the efficiency and effectiveness of various programs and services, raise funds, and invest wisely.

Contemporary not-for-profit leaders and managers, though they may have noble social objectives that go beyond the maximization of profit, still have to develop at least basic skills in management accounting. Expecting someone else to manage finances and do the "number crunching" is clearly asking for trouble. Basic skills in management accounting should be developed according to appropriate plans and controls in order to ensure the integrity of procedures and processes. Managers should learn how to generate financial reports, analyze data, and really understand the organization's financial condition. Management accounting shows the "reality" of the situation at hand; as such, it is one of the most important tools for those who manage healthy not-for-profit organizations.

In all organizations, managers and administrators are better equipped to deal with work issues when they understand management accounting concepts.

THE ROLE OF THE MANAGEMENT ACCOUNTANT

OBJECTIVE 4

Describe the role of managerial accountants in an organization.

Today's business press writes about world-class firms. Often these are firms at the cutting edge of customer support. They know their markets and their products. They strive to continually improve product design, manufacture, and delivery. These companies can compete with the best of the best in a global environment. Management accountants must support management in all phases of business decision making. As specialists in accounting, they must be intelligent, well prepared, up-to-date with new developments, and familiar with the customs and practices of all countries in which their firms operate.

Structure of the Company

The role of management accountants in an organization is one of support. They assist those individuals who are responsible for carrying out an organization's basic objectives. Positions that have direct responsibility for the basic objectives of an organization are referred to as **line positions**. Positions that are supportive in nature and have only indirect responsibility for an organization's basic objectives are called **staff positions**.

For example, assume that the basic mission of an organization is to produce and sell laser printers. The vice-presidents of manufacturing and marketing, the factory manager, and the assemblers are all line positions. The vice-presidents of finance and human resources, the cost accountant, and the purchasing manager are all staff positions.

A typical organization chart is shown in Exhibit 1.5. Although management accountants, such as controllers and cost accounting managers, may wield considerable influence in the organization, they have no authority over the managers in the production area. The managers in line positions are the ones who set policy and make the decisions that impact the company. However, by supplying and interpreting accounting information, management accountants can have significant input into policies and decisions.

EXHIBIT 1.5

Typical Organizational Chart

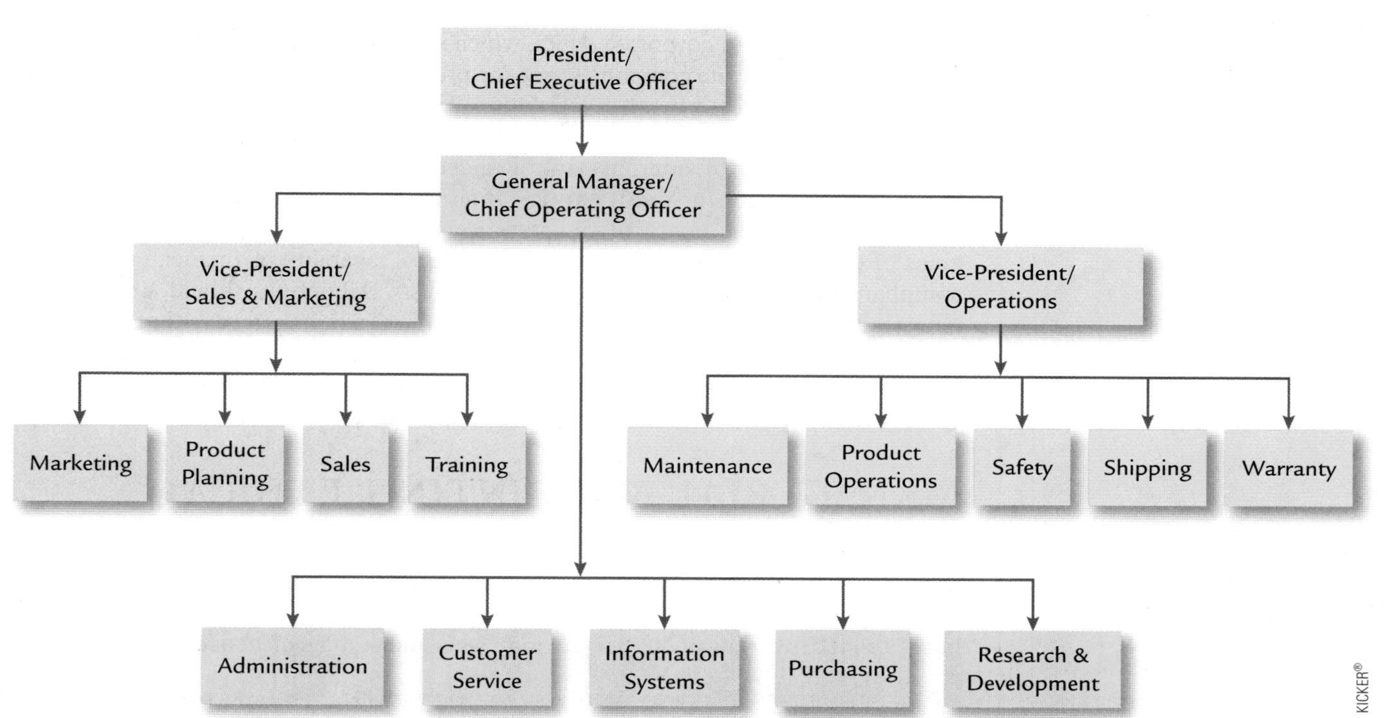

The **controller**, or chief accounting officer, is in the administration department. She supervises all accounting functions and reports directly to the general manager and chief operating officer (COO). Because of the critical role that managerial accounting plays in the operation of an organization, the controller is often viewed as a member of the top management team and is encouraged to participate in planning, controlling, and decision-making activities. As the chief accounting officer, the controller has responsibility for both internal and external accounting requirements. In larger firms, this charge may include direct responsibility for internal auditing, cost accounting, financial accounting (including government reports and financial statements), accounting systems (including analysis, design, and internal controls), and taxes. The duties and organization of the controller's office vary from firm to firm. For example, in some firms, the internal audit department may report directly to the financial vice-president; similarly, the systems department may report directly to the financial vice-president or some other vice-president.

In larger companies, the controller is separate from the treasury department. The **treasurer** is responsible for the finance function. Specifically, the treasurer raises capital and manages cash and investments. The treasurer may also be in charge of credit and collection, and insurance. Both the controller and the treasurer would report to the vice-president finance.

Sarbanes-Oxley Act of 2002

In June 2002, the United States Congress passed the **Sarbanes-Oxley Act (SOX)**. This legislation was passed in response to the collapse of Enron and the revelations of securities fraud and accounting misconduct associated with companies such as WorldCom, Adelphia, and HealthSouth. SOX established stronger government control and regulation of public companies in the United States. SOX applies to **publicly traded companies**, which issue shares traded on U.S. stock exchanges. Major sections of SOX relate to (among other things) enhanced auditor independence, tightened regulation of corporate governance, control over management, and management/auditor assessment of the firm's internal controls. In Canada, **Ontario Bill 198** was enacted to amend the Securities Act (Ontario) and took effect on April 7, 2003. These amendments parallel many of the provisions of SOX in the U.S. and apply to the vast majority of Canadian public companies, as they trade on the Toronto Stock Exchange (TSX). SOX and Bill 198 also led to increased attention to corporate ethics, which is discussed in the next section.

Importantly, private companies, not-for-profit entities, and governmental agencies or entities are not covered by such legislation. However, these entities have been affected through their dealings with constituents and their boards of directors. In particular, the intense scrutiny of internal control under SOX is a feature that many would like to see applied to not-for-profit entities. Internal control is a process put into place by management and the board of directors to ensure that objectives are achieved in the areas of effectiveness and efficiency of operations, reliability of financial reporting, and compliance with applicable laws and regulations.[10] All entities should strive to achieve their legitimate objectives, and good internal control can help ensure that. Management accountants, through the offices of internal auditing or the chief financial officer (CFO), are the people in the organization who are expected to ensure that their organizations comply with whatever legislation they are subject to.

OBJECTIVE 5

Explain the importance of ethical behaviour for managers and managerial accountants.

MANAGERIAL ACCOUNTING, ETHICAL CONDUCT, AND SOCIAL RESPONSIBILITY

Virtually all managerial accounting practices were developed to assist managers in maximizing profits. Traditionally, actions regarding the economic performance of the firm have been the overriding concern. Yet managers and management accountants should not

[10] Definition taken from COSO Internal Control Integrated Framework, http://www.coso.org/publications/executive_summary_integrated_framework.htm.

become so focused on profits that they develop a belief that the only goal of a business is to maximize its net worth. The objective of profit maximization should be constrained by the requirement that profits be achieved through legal and ethical means. While this has always been an implicit assumption of managerial accounting, recent experience has shown that this assumption should be made explicit. To help illustrate this objective, many of the problems in this textbook require explicit consideration of ethical issues.

Ethical Behaviour

Ethical behaviour involves choosing actions that are right, proper, and just. Behaviour can be right or wrong; it can be proper or improper; and the decisions we make can be fair or unfair. Though people often differ in their views of the meaning of the ethical terms cited, there seems to be a common principle underlying all ethical systems, expressed by the belief that each member of a group bears some responsibility for the well-being of other members. Willingness to sacrifice one's self-interest for the well-being of the group is at the heart of all ethical action.

This notion of sacrifice produces some core values—values that describe what is meant by right and wrong in more concrete terms. James W. Brackner, writing for the "Ethics Column" in *Management Accounting,* made the following observation:

> *For moral or ethical education to have meaning, there must be agreement on the values that are considered "right." Ten of these values are identified and described by Michael Josephson in* Teaching Ethical Decision Making and Principled Reasoning. *The study of history, philosophy, and religion reveals a strong consensus as to certain universal and timeless values essential to the ethical life.*
>
> *These 10 core values yield a series of principles that delineate right and wrong in general terms. Therefore, they provide a guide to behavior.*[11]

The 10 core values referred to in the quotation are the following:

1. Honesty
2. Integrity
3. Promise keeping
4. Fidelity
5. Fairness
6. Caring for others
7. Respect for others
8. Responsible citizenship
9. Pursuit of excellence
10. Accountability

Many of the well-known accounting scandals—such as those involving Enron, Adelphia, WorldCom, HealthSouth, Livent, Hollinger, and Parmalat—provide evidence of the pressures faced by top managers and accountants to produce large net income numbers, especially in the short term. Unfortunately, such individuals often acquiesce to these pressures when faced with questionable revenue- and expense-related judgments. For example, the scandal at Livent involved the two most senior executives—Garth Drabinsky and Myron Gottlieb—browbeating accounting managers within the company to falsify accounting records to record as revenue certain items that should have been shown as advance payments and to capitalize certain costs that should have been expensed. The fraudulent activities were so pervasive that the company prepared a separate software program to keep track of the false entries. The total fraud amounted to a $98 million

[11] James W. Brackner, "Consensus Values Should Be Taught," *Management Accounting* (August 1992): 19. For a more complete discussion of the 10 core values, see also Michael Josephson, "Teaching Ethical Decision Making and Principled Reasoning," *Ethics Easier Said Than Done* (The Josephson Institute, Los Angeles, CA: Winter 1988): 29–30.

overstatement of net income. Drabinsky and Gottlieb, the two main perpetrators, both received jail sentences and several of the accounting personnel were disciplined by their professional bodies. The subprime mortgage crisis also highlights the importance of ethical considerations as some banks tried to increase their profits either by lending individuals more money than they could reasonably afford or using terms that were intentionally less clear, or transparent, than many outsiders thought they should be.[12]

As some of these examples point out, though it may seem contradictory, sacrificing self-interest for the collective good might not only be right and bring a sense of individual worth but also make good business sense. Companies with a strong code of ethics can create strong customer and employee loyalty. While liars and cheats may win on occasion, their victories often are short-lived. Companies in business for the long term find that it pays to treat all of their constituents with honesty and loyalty. The Triple Bottom Line, discussed earlier in this chapter, indicates the focus that some companies have adopted to meeting the needs of ethical behaviour.

Company Codes of Ethical Conduct

To promote ethical behaviour by managers and employees, organizations commonly establish standards of conduct often referred to as *company codes of conduct*. One needs only to read the business press to be reminded of the importance of ethical conduct. Bell Canada publishes a 36-page Code of Business Conduct for all of its employees, executives, and directors in which it emphasizes that everyone should conduct their business with integrity and act in a dynamic, straightforward, honest, and fair manner. Power Corporation of Canada, one of Canada's largest non-bank financial institutions, is very explicit about the importance of ethical behaviour. In the preamble to its Code of Business Conduct and Ethics, it states: "The Corporation is committed to the principles set out in the Code and considers any violation to be a very serious matter. An individual who violates the Code may face disciplinary action up to and including termination of office or employment with the Corporation without notice."[13]

In 2012, Loblaw Companies outlined its approach to social responsibility and expressed its achievements and core values in a Corporate Social Responsibility Report (CSR). That document linked the company to five core values:

- Respect the Environment
- Sourcing with Integrity
- Making a Positive Difference in Our Community
- Reflect Our Nation's Diversity
- Being a Great Place to Work

Reflecting those values, Loblaw highlighted the following:

Respect the Environment:

- Reduced the number of plastic shopping bags from our stores by more than five billion since 2007
- Diverted 81% of waste from our distribution centres
- Diverted approximately 1,135,000 pounds of plastic plant pots and flats from landfill, for a total of 5,235,000 pounds diverted since 2008
- To date, converted more than 72,000 light fixtures in our corporate stores, resulting in energy savings sufficient to power 9,923 homes for a year

(Continued)

[12] Jane Sasseen, "FBI Widens Net Around Subprime Industry: With 14 Companies Under Investigation, the Bureau's Scope Is the Entire Securitization Process," *Business Week Online* (January 30, 2008). Taken from http://www.businessweek.com/bwdaily/dnflash/content/jan2008/db20080129_728982.htm?chan=search on February 12, 2008.
[13] Power Corporation of Canada, Code of Business Conduct and Ethics, retrieved from http://www.powercorporation.com/media/upload/documents/pages_doc/PCC-Code_of_Conduct-Eng-incl_BF_Rev.pdf on April 15, 2014.

- Installed a fleet tracking system in all corporate trucks to help reduce our carbon footprint

Source with Integrity:

- We now offer 108 Marine Stewardship Council (MSC) certified products in our stores—more than any other Canadian food retailer
- Sourced 100% of fresh pork from Canada
- Sourced 31% of the produce sold in our stores year-round from Canadian growers
- Sourced 100% of non-tropical outdoor Garden Centre plants and Christmas trees from Canadian growers

Make a Positive Difference in Our Community:

- Together with our customers, colleagues, vendors, franchisees and their employees, donated more than $45 million to charities and non-profit organizations across Canada
- President's Choice Children's Charity has granted more than $86 million to more than 15,000 families and 13,000 nutrition programs across Canada since its inception in 1989
- Reduced 117.6 metric tonnes of sodium in 428 control brand processed products since 2010
- We now offer 319 PC Organics products in our stores—the largest organics line in Canada
- Rolled out Guiding Stars nutrition rating system in Loblaws banner stores in Ontario—first Canadian retailer to introduce this rating system
- Added 22 dietitians in 50 corporate stores

Reflect Our Nation's Diversity:

- 45% of management positions are held by women
- Five Loblaw executives received Women of Influence Distinction
- Named one of Canada's Best Employers for New Canadians and one of Canada's Best Diversity Employers
- We now offer 101 T&T brand products
- Launched *Sufra*, our new control brand line of Halal products

Be a Great Place to Work:

- Named one of Canada's Top 100 Employers
- Named one of Canada's Top Employers for Young People
- Received the Défi Employeurs Inspirants award, recognizing the most inspiring employers in Quebec
- Reduced the number of workplace accidents by 52% over the past five years

Source: From 2012 Loblaw Corporate Social Responsibility Report. Reprinted with permission from Loblaw Companies Limited.

Unfortunately, Loblaw was implicated in the collapse of a manufacturing facility in Bangladesh in early 2013 where hundreds of workers were killed. Concern was expressed about the unsafe conditions and the lack of oversight of these locations by companies for whom goods were being produced. In keeping with its expressed code of behaviour, Loblaw has been a leader in enacting more stringent oversight of its foreign manufacturing subcontractors to try to avoid such tragedies in the future.

Important parts of corporate codes of conduct are integrity, performance of duties, and compliance with the rule of law. They also uniformly prohibit the acceptance of kickbacks and improper gifts, insider trading, and misappropriation of corporate information and assets.

Standards of Ethical Conduct for Management Accountants

Organizations commonly establish standards of conduct for their managers and employees. Professional associations also establish ethical standards. All three Canadian accounting bodies—governing **Chartered Accountant (CA)**, **Certified Management Accountant (CMA)**, and **Certified General Accountant (CGA)** designation holders—had established ethical standards for accountants, before their amalgamation in 2011. Professional accountants, now operating as a single body in Canada as CPAs, are bound by these codes of conduct, which stress the importance of competence, confidentiality, integrity, and credibility or objectivity.

To illustrate an application of the code, suppose a manager's bonus is linked to reported profits, with the bonus increasing as profits increase. Thus, the manager has an incentive to find ways to increase profits, including unethical approaches. For example, a manager could increase profits by delaying promotions of deserving employees or by using cheaper parts to produce a product. In either case, if the motive is simply to increase the bonus, the behaviour could be labelled as unethical. Neither action is in the best interest of the company or its employees. Yet where should the blame be assigned? After all, the reward system strongly encourages the manager to increase profits. Is the reward system at fault, or is the manager who chooses to increase profits at fault? Or both?

In reality, both the manager and reward system are probably at fault. It is important to design evaluation and reward systems so that incentives to pursue undesirable behaviour are minimized, yet designing a perfect reward system is not a realistic expectation. Managers also have an obligation to avoid abusing the system.

Can ethics be taught? Philosophers and ethicists from Socrates to those studying business ethics today agree that ethics can be taught and, even more importantly, learned. Students know that they have been taught about ethical conduct from preschool on. When they encounter new situations, ethical behaviour must be defined and reinforced. When you came to university, you were no doubt advised of the importance of doing your own work (not cheating) and of properly citing sources used in your papers and presentations. Clearly, individual rules were not intrinsically a part of you—they were taught. Similarly, accountants and businesspeople must be advised of the finer points of business ethics and of the behaviour appropriate to the job. Codes of conduct are intended to spell out, in general terms, what is deemed acceptable and unacceptable behaviour. Adherence to the code, both in exact legal terms and in the spirit in which it was intended, is of paramount importance. An example of a code of conduct of a professional organization can be found in Exhibit 1.6.

Rather than attempt to study numerous ethical issues in one place, each chapter of this textbook includes an ethical dilemma or situation designed to increase student awareness of the types of conduct considered unethical in business.

EXHIBIT 1.6

Excerpts from the CPA Code of Professional Conduct

Characteristics of a Profession

The CPA Code presumes the existence of a profession. Since the word "profession" has lost some of its earlier precision, through widespread application, it is worthwhile reviewing the characteristics which mark a calling as professional in the traditional sense. Much has been written on the subject and court cases have revolved around it. The weight of the authorities, however, identifies the following distinguishing elements:

- there is mastery of a particular intellectual skill, acquired by lengthy training and education;

(Continued)

- the traditional foundation of the calling rests in the provision of services to others through the application of the acquired skill to their affairs;
- the calling centres on the provision of personal services rather than entrepreneurial dealing in goods;
- there is an outlook, in the practice of the calling, which is essentially objective;
- there is acceptance of a responsibility to subordinate personal interests to those of the public good;
- there exists a developed and independent body, comprising the members of the calling, which sets and maintains standards of qualification, attests to the competence of the individual members and safeguards and develops the skills and standards of the calling;
- there is a specialized code of ethical conduct, laid down and enforced by that body designed principally for the protection of the public;
- there is a belief, on the part of those engaged in the calling, in the virtue of interchange of views, and in a duty to contribute to the development of their profession, adding to its knowledge and sharing advances in knowledge and technique with their fellow professionals.

By these criteria chartered professional accountancy is a profession.

Fundamental Principles Governing Conduct

Members and firms have a fundamental responsibility to act in the public interest. The public's trust and reliance on sound and fair financial and management reporting and competent advice on business affairs—and the economic importance of that reporting and advice—impose these special obligations on the profession. They also establish, firmly, the profession's social usefulness. The CPA Code is derived from five fundamental principles of ethics—statements of accepted conduct for all members and firms whose soundness is, for the most part, self-evident. These principles are fundamental to the conduct of all members and firms and are as follows:

Professional Behaviour
Chartered Professional Accountants conduct themselves at all times in a manner which will maintain the good reputation of the profession and its ability to serve the public interest.

Integrity and Due Care
Chartered Professional Accountants perform professional services with integrity and due care.

Objectivity
Chartered Professional Accountants do not allow their professional or business judgment to be compromised by bias, conflict of interest or the undue influence of others.

Professional Competence
Chartered Professional Accountants maintain their professional skills and competence by keeping informed of, and complying with, developments in their area of professional service.

Confidentiality
Chartered Professional Accountants protect confidential information acquired as a result of professional, employment and business relationships and do not disclose it without proper and specific authority, nor do they exploit such information for their personal advantage or the advantage of a third party.

ACCOUNTING DESIGNATIONS AND CAREER OPPORTUNITIES

OBJECTIVE 6

Identify three accounting designations formerly available in Canada.

As with the legal and medical professions, the accounting profession relies on certification to provide evidence that the holder has achieved a minimum level of professional competence, as well as to promote and enforce ethical behaviour.

Accounting embraces all management functions, including purchasing, manufacturing, wholesaling, retailing, and a variety of marketing and transportation activities. It deals with all facets of an organization and provides an excellent opportunity for gaining a broad range of knowledge. Thus, accountants acquire many necessary general management skills. This is why today, probably more than ever before, more CEOs come from accounting than from any other area, such as marketing, production, or engineering. Because some of you may want to pursue a career in accounting, you would find it helpful to know your career options in accounting.

Canada has undergone a major restructuring of the professional bodies for the certification and regulation of professional accountants. On January 4, 2013, **CPA Canada** was formed to be the body that brings together all three professional accounting groups across Canada. New members will all receive the **Chartered Professional Accountant (CPA)** designation, but will have specific skills and capabilities as formerly developed by the individual groups. Members of each group at the time of amalgamation must use both the CPA designation and the one they previously held for a period of ten years. Since accreditation is a provincial matter, each of the ten provincial and three territorial groups had to vote on provincial amalgamation. In June 2014, the final approval was given so that all former bodies have now merged into CPA bodies on a provincial basis.

The primary reason for amalgamation is to ensure that Canadian professional accountants have a strong voice in the international community. This has become increasingly important as globalization has become the norm for many companies in both their production operations and their marketing. We will outline below the individual strengths and opportunities for each of the three professional accounting designations in Canada as they were before amalgamation to give a sense of their differences. Now they are constituted as three separate subsets of the CPA designation in Canada.

Society of Management Accountants of Canada—CMA Canada

This society confers the internationally recognized Certified Management Accountant (CMA) designation. CMAs are strategic and financial management professionals who combine accounting expertise with professional management skills to provide leadership, innovation, and an integrating perspective to organizational decision making. CMAs use their management skills to foster an organization's growth and their accounting skills to track its progress. They add value to a business by developing total business solutions, identifying new market opportunities, and protecting and maximizing shareholder value.

Canadian Institute of Chartered Accountants (CICA)

The CICA confers the Chartered Accountant (CA) designation. The CA education program focuses on external financial reports and, in particular, the auditing functions. The CA is one of Canada's most valued designations and is recognized internationally. It prepares leaders in senior financial, tax, advisory, and assurance roles. Chartered Accountants are valued for their integrity and expertise as practitioners of public accounting.

Certified General Accountants Association of Canada (CGAAC)

The CGAAC confers the Certified General Accountant (CGA) designation. The CGA program provides a broad-based education in accounting and financial management.

The CGAAC ensures that its members merit the confidence and trust of all who rely on their professional knowledge, skills, judgment, and integrity. It does so by regulating qualification, performance, and discipline standards. Competence and currency are cornerstones of a CGA's skill set.

Pursuing an Accounting Designation

Education in Canada is a provincial or territorial jurisdiction. Therefore, accounting students wishing to pursue an accounting designation need to register with the appropriate provincial or territorial organization. In Ontario, for example, the provincial professional accounting association is CPA Ontario. Students who qualify for admission and who pass a national examination are awarded a professional accounting designation from the corresponding provincial or territorial accounting organization.

For further information, visit the website of CPA Canada and/or one of the provincial or territorial CPA organizations.

SUMMARY OF LEARNING OBJECTIVES

LO1. Explain the meaning of managerial accounting.

- Managerial accounting information is used to identify problems, solve problems, and evaluate performance.
- Managerial accounting information helps managers in planning, controlling, and decision making.
- Planning is the detailed formulation of action to achieve a particular end.
- Controlling is the monitoring of a plan's implementation.
- Decision making is choosing among competing alternatives.

LO2. Explain the differences between financial accounting and managerial accounting.

- Financial accounting is
  - Directed toward external users
  - Subject to externally imposed rules (e.g., GAAP and IFRS)
  - Able to provide audited, objective financial information
- Managerial accounting is
  - Intended for internal users
  - Not subject to rules for external financial reporting (e.g., GAAP and IFRS)
  - Subjective
  - Able to use both financial and nonfinancial measures of performance
  - Able to give a broader, interdisciplinary perspective

LO3. Identify and explain the current focus of managerial accounting.

- It supports management focus on customer value, total quality management, and time-based competition.
- Information about value chain activities and customer implications (such as post-purchase costs) is collected and made available.
- Activity-based management is a major innovative response to the demand for more accurate and relevant managerial accounting information.
- The nature of a managerial accounting information system may depend on the strategic position of the firm:
  - Cost leadership strategy
  - Product differentiation strategy
  - Lean accounting

LO4. Describe the role of management accountants in an organization.

- They are responsible for identifying, collecting, measuring, analyzing, preparing, interpreting, and communicating information.

- They must be sensitive to the information needs of managers.
- They serve as staff members of the organization and are part of the management team.

LO5. Explain the importance of ethical behaviour for managers and management accountants.

- A strong ethical sense is needed to resist efforts to change economic information that may present an untrue picture of firm performance.
- Many firms have a written code of ethics or code of conduct.
- With the amalgamation of the professional accounting bodies in each province, there is now a single Code of Conduct in each province covering all Chartered Professional Accountants in that province.

LO6. Identify three accounting designations formerly available in Canada.

- Certified Management Accountant (CMA)
- Chartered Accountant (CA)
- Certified General Accountant (CGA)

GLOSSARY

Activity-based costing (ABC) A method of costing goods and services that emphasizes the cost of the many activities or tasks that must be done to produce a product or offer a service. (p. 9)

Certified General Accountant (CGA) A certified accountant who is permitted (by law) to serve as an external auditor. (p. 20)

Certified Management Accountant (CMA) A certified management accountant who has passed a rigorous qualifying examination, has met an experience requirement, and participates in continuing education. (p. 20)

Chartered Accountant (CA) An accountant who works as a business professional in public practice, industry, government, or education. CAs must pass a rigorous national examination and be licensed by the province in which they practise. (p. 20)

Chartered Professional Accountant (CPA) CPA is the designation for professional accountants in Canada. Recently, all three professional bodies for accountants in Canada merged into a single body to accredit professional accountants as CPAs. CPAs must pass a national examination and be licensed by the province in which they practise. (p. 22)

Continuous improvement Searching for ways to increase the overall efficiency and productivity of activities by reducing waste, increasing quality, and managing costs. (p. 12)

Controller The chief accounting officer in an organization. (p. 16)

Controlling The managerial activity of monitoring a plan's implementation and taking corrective action as needed. (p. 5)

CPA Canada As of June 2014, the body that brings together all three professional accounting groups across Canada and confers on members the designation of Chartered Professional Accountant (CPA) through its provincial or territorial counterparts. (p. 22)

Cross-functional perspective Seeing the interrelation in the disciplines of managerial accounting, marketing, management, engineering, finance, and other business functions. (p. 12)

Decision making The process of choosing among competing alternatives. (p. 5)

Ethical behaviour Choosing actions that are right, proper, and just. (p. 17)

Financial accounting A type of accounting that is primarily concerned with producing information for external users. (p. 6)

Lean accounting An accounting practice that organizes costs according to the value chain by focusing primarily on the elimination of waste. The objective is to provide information to managers that supports this effort and to provide financial statements that better reflect overall performance, using financial and nonfinancial information. (p. 13)

Line positions Positions that have direct responsibility for the basic objectives of an organization. (p. 15)

Managerial accounting The provision of accounting information for a company's internal users. (p. 4)

Ontario Bill 198 A bill passed by the Ontario Legislature in response to a variety of financial scandals in Canada and the United States. It enacts legislation similar to the Sarbanes-Oxley Act in the United States. (p. 16)

Planning A management activity that involves the detailed formulation of action to achieve a particular end. (p. 5)

Product life cycle New products' series of stages: conception, introduction into the market, growth, maturity, and decline and eventual withdrawal from the market. (p. 9)

Publicly traded companies Companies that issue shares traded on a stock exchange which are subject to regulation. (p. 16)

Sarbanes-Oxley Act (SOX) Passed in 2002 in response to revelations of misconduct and fraud by several well-known firms, this legislation established stronger governmental control and regulation of public companies in the United States, from enhanced oversight (PCAOB), to increased auditor independence and tightened regulation of corporate governance. (p. 16)

Staff positions Positions that are supportive in nature and have only indirect responsibility for an organization's basic objectives. (p. 15)

Total quality management A management philosophy in which manufacturers strive to create an environment that will enable workers to manufacture perfect (zero-defect) products. (p. 13)

Treasurer The individual responsible for the finance function; raises capital and manages cash and investments. (p. 16)

Triple Bottom Line Performance measures for companies that include financial, social, and environmental factors. (p. 7)

Value chain The set of activities required to design, develop, produce, market, and deliver products and services to customers. (p. 10)

DISCUSSION QUESTIONS

1. What is managerial accounting?
2. What are the three broad objectives of managerial accounting?
3. Who are the users of managerial accounting information?
4. Should a managerial accounting system provide both financial and nonfinancial information? Explain.
5. What is meant by controlling?
6. Describe the connection between planning, feedback, and controlling.
7. How do managerial accounting and financial accounting differ?
8. Explain the role of financial reporting in the development of managerial accounting. Why has this changed in recent years?
9. Explain the meaning of customer value. How is focusing on customer value changing managerial accounting?
10. Explain why today's management accountant must have a cross-functional perspective.
11. Briefly explain the practice of enterprise risk management and the role that can be played by management accountants in enterprise risk management.
12. What is the value chain? Why is it important?
13. What is the difference between a staff position and a line position?
14. "The controller should be a member of the top management staff." Do you agree or disagree? Explain.
15. What is ethical behaviour? Is it possible to teach ethical behaviour in a managerial accounting course?

16. Briefly describe some of the common themes or pressures faced by executives who commit corporate fraud.
17. What is the professional accounting designation in Canada? Which three previous accounting bodies have been merged to form this Canadian professional accounting body?

EXERCISES

OBJECTIVE 1

Exercise 1-1 The Managerial Process

Each of the following scenarios requires the use of accounting information to carry out one or more of the three managerial objectives: planning, controlling (including performance evaluation), or decision making.

a. **Laboratory Manager:** A medical laboratory approached me recently and offered us its entire range of blood tests. It provided a price list revealing the amount it is willing to pay for each test. In many cases, the prices are below what we normally charge. I need to know the costs of the individual tests to assess the feasibility of accepting its offer and perhaps suggest some price adjustments on some of the tests.
b. **Operating Manager:** This report indicates that we have 30 percent more defects than originally targeted. An investigation into the cause has revealed the problem: We were using a lower-quality material than expected, and the waste has been higher than normal. By switching to the quality level originally specified, we can reduce the defects to the planned level.
c. **Divisional Manager:** Our market share has increased because of higher-quality products. Current projections indicate that we should sell 25 percent more units than last year. I want a projection of the effect that this increase in sales will have on profits. I also want to know our expected cash receipts and cash expenditures on a month-by-month basis. I have a feeling that some short-term borrowing may be necessary.
d. **Plant Manager:** Foreign competitors are producing goods with lower costs and delivering them more rapidly than we can to customers in our markets. We need to decrease the cycle time and increase the efficiency of our manufacturing process. There are two proposals that should help us accomplish these goals, both of which involve investing in computer-aided manufacturing. I need to know the future cash flows associated with each system and the effect each system has on unit costs and cycle time.
e. **Senior Executive:** At the last board meeting, we established an objective of earning a 25 percent return on sales. I need to know how many units of our product we need to sell to meet this objective. Once I have the estimated sales in units, we need to outline a promotional campaign that will take us where we want to be. However, in order to compute the targeted sales in units, I need to know the expected unit price and a lot of cost information.
f. **Manager:** Perhaps the Hippocrates Medical Clinic should not offer a full range of medical services. Some services seem to be having a difficult time showing any kind of profit. I am particularly concerned about the mental health service. It has not shown a profit since the clinic opened. I want to know what costs can be avoided if I drop the service. I also want some assessment of the impact on the other services we offer. Some of our patients may choose this clinic because we offer a full range of services.

Required:

Select the managerial accounting objective(s) that are applicable for each scenario: planning, controlling, or decision making.

OBJECTIVE 2

Exercise 1-2 Differences between Managerial Accounting and Financial Accounting

Jenna Monera, the controller for Excelsior Company, has faced the following situations in the past two weeks:

a. Ben Heald, the head of production, wondered whether it would be more cost effective to buy parts partially assembled or to buy individual parts and assemble them at the Excelsior factory.

b. The president of Excelsior reminded Jenna that the shareholders' meeting was coming up, and he needed her to prepare a presentation showing the income statement and balance sheet information for last year.
c. Ellen Johnson, the vice-president of sales, has decided to expand the sales offices for next year. She sent Jenna the information on next year's rent and depreciation information for budgeting purposes.
d. Jenna's assistant, Mike, received the information from Ellen on depreciation and added it to depreciation expenses and accumulated depreciation on office equipment.
e. Jenna compared the budgeted spending on materials used in production with the actual spending on materials used in production. Materials spending was significantly higher than expected. She set up a meeting to discuss this outcome with Ben Heald so that he could explain it.

Required:

Determine whether each request is relatively more managerial accounting oriented or financial accounting oriented.

Exercise 1-3 Customer Value, Strategic Positioning

OBJECTIVE 3

Adriana Alvarado has decided to purchase a laptop computer. She has narrowed the choices to two: Drantex and Confiar. Both brands have the same processing speed, 12 gigabytes of hard-disk capacity, two USB ports, a DVD drive, identical battery life, and the same basic software support package. Both come from mail-order companies with good reputations. The selling prices are identical. After some review, Adriana discovers that the cost of operating and maintaining Drantex over a three-year period is estimated to be $300, while for the Confiar system, the operating and maintenance cost is $600 over the same period. The sales agent for Drantex emphasized the lower operating and maintenance costs. The agent for Confiar, however, emphasized the service reputation of the product and the faster delivery time (Confiar can be purchased and delivered one week sooner than Drantex). Based on all the information, Adriana has decided to buy Confiar.

Required:

1. What is the total product purchased by Adriana?
2. How does the strategic positioning differ for the two companies?
3. When asked why she decided to buy Confiar, Adriana responded, "I think that Confiar offers more value than Drantex." What are the possible sources of this greater value? What implications does this have for the managerial accounting information system?
4. Suppose that Adriana's decision was prompted mostly by the desire to receive the laptop quickly. Informed that it was losing sales because of the longer time to produce and deliver its products, the management of Drantex decided to improve delivery performance by upgrading its internal assembly processes. These improvements decreased the number of defective units and the time required to produce its product. Consequently, delivery time and costs both decreased, allowing the company to lower its prices on Drantex. Explain how these actions translate into strengthening the competitive position of the Drantex laptop relative to the Confiar laptop. Also discuss the implications for the managerial accounting information system.

Exercise 1-4 Line versus Staff

OBJECTIVE 4

The following describes the job responsibilities of two employees of Sparrow Manufacturing.

Joan Dennison, Cost Accounting Manager. Joan is responsible for measuring and collecting costs associated with the manufacture of the garden hose product line. She is also responsible for preparing periodic reports that compare the actual costs with planned costs. These reports are provided to the production line managers and the plant manager. Joan helps to explain and interpret the reports.

Steven Swasey, Production Manager. Steven is responsible for the manufacture of the high-quality garden hose. He supervises the line workers, helps to develop the production schedule, and is responsible for seeing that production quotas are met. He is also held accountable for controlling manufacturing costs.

(Continued)

Required:

1. Identify Joan and Steven as line or staff and explain your reasons.
2. CONCEPTUAL CONNECTION Explain the differences between line and staff functions in a manner that will have universal applicability.

OBJECTIVE 5

Exercise 1-5 Ethical Behaviour

Consider the following conversation between Mary, a self-employed printer, and Peter, an assistant in the athletics and recreation department of a local university.

Peter: Mary, we have been customers of yours for several years and we currently need 10,000 posters for the upcoming basketball season. Here is the mock-up and we will need them in one month. What price can you give us?

Mary: Based on my costs for card stock and supplies, I think I can do them for about $5,000 and have them to you in the required timeframe. I think this is the best price you are going to get anywhere.

Peter: We have always been satisfied with your work and reliability. I like your price, but I have a better idea. Send me an invoice for $7,500, which is our budget for this job and when it is paid, give me back $2,000, preferably in cash. I'll make sure you get the job and we will continue our relationship.

Required:

Would it be ethical for Mary to go along with what Peter is proposing? What should she do?

OBJECTIVE 5

Exercise 1-6 Ethical Behaviour

Brad Taylor has just reviewed his internal financial statements for the month of November and is dismayed that he might not achieve his profit targets for the year, which ends in a month. As a result, he might miss out on a $10,000 bonus for surpassing his target for the year. After consulting with the managers reporting to him, he concludes that something dramatic must happen if he is going to meet his numbers. An idea occurs to him: he can postpone the start of the marketing campaign that was to start in mid-December to mid-January and avoid having to recognize the expense of developing the campaign until the next fiscal year.

He realizes that delaying the marketing campaign by one month might impact his sales for the following year, but he is willing to deal with that issue next year at this time. The bonus is really important to him as he promised his wife a January cruise.

Required:

1. Is Brad behaving ethically in how he is approaching the problem? Why or why not?
2. What suggestions do you have for Brad in arriving at a satisfactory solution to his dilemma?

OBJECTIVE 5

Exercise 1-7 Ethical Issues

The following statements have appeared in newspaper editorials:

a. "Business students come from all segments of society. If they have not been taught ethics by their families and by their elementary and secondary schools, a business school can have little effect."
b. "Sacrificing self-interest for the collective good won't happen unless a majority of people also accept this premise."
c. "Competent executives manage people and resources for the good of society. Monetary benefits and titles are simply the by-products of doing a good job."
d. "Unethical firms and individuals, like high rollers in Las Vegas, are eventually wiped out financially."

Required:

1. Assess and comment on each of the statements.
2. CONCEPTUAL CONNECTION Why do you think we have experienced so many financial scandals in the past ten years?

Exercise 1-8 Ethical Behaviour

OBJECTIVE 5

PaperTigers is a software development company operating in Waterloo, Ontario. The company specializes in developing applications for the healthcare industry relating to controlling the distribution of drugs to patients. Several years ago, the company went public and has been trading on the Toronto Stock Exchange, but the stock has languished. Recently, senior management has been in discussions with a private equity firm about the possibility of taking the company private and investing heavily in new applications to enhance its market position.

John Magnum is the chief technology officer of the company and has been in meetings with the private equity people and the executive committee where discussions of the proposed transaction are taking place. The private equity people are considering offering a price for all of the outstanding shares that is 40 percent higher than the current trading price.

At his Monday morning technology update meeting with his development team, someone asks John how the discussions are going. John responds that the deal has moved from the possible stage to the probable stage and the price will likely be a minimum of a 40 percent premium. He encourages all of his developers to quietly acquire as many of the shares as they can before the announcement of the deal takes place.

Required:

Comment on John's actions in telling his staff the details of the transaction. Should the developers take advantage of this knowledge and buy shares immediately?

Exercise 1-9 Ethical Issues

OBJECTIVE 5

Gross and Company is a major consulting firm located in three provinces in Canada. In its Vancouver office, Reginald Shuttleworth is a senior manager, reporting to a partner who is in charge of a major project. Reginald has been with the firm for seven years and believes that he is in line for a promotion to partner based on his excellent performance over the past two years as a manager. One very significant performance measure for managers is their ability to bring projects to a conclusion on time and within budget.

In the very competitive consulting field, firms have a great deal of difficulty receiving payment from their clients for any amounts incurred for services above and beyond the amount quoted for the job, even though the quotes are clearly marked as being estimates. As a result, most firms are forced to absorb any cost overruns on jobs rather than billing and collecting from their clients. In evaluating performance of individuals, most firms look very closely at the recovery rate of the amount of costs incurred and the amount recovered from the client.

Reginald believes that he has an advantage over all other managers in the firm since he ensures that his budget overruns are minimized on every job because he insists that his team does not report any excess hours that they have to work to complete the job over and above the estimated number of hours. This has resulted in his being able to report excellent performance, but his team has become very disgruntled because they receive neither pay nor recognition for the extra hours that they work. Since Reginald is a very hands-on manager, he has been able to intimidate them to remain silent about his management style.

Required:

Discuss the ethical implications and the potential performance implications of the approach that Reginald is using to make himself look good to his superiors.

Exercise 1-10 Company Codes of Conduct

OBJECTIVE 5

Using the Internet, locate the codes of conduct for three different companies. Briefly describe each code of conduct. How are they similar? How are they different?

Exercise 1-11 Professional Ethics

OBJECTIVE 5

After studying the corporate codes of conduct for the companies in **Exercise 1-10**, do you believe that members of professional organizations such as CPA Canada should be held to a higher ethical standard than the rest of the general population? Does this higher standard apply only to their professional life or to their private life as well?

2

Basic Managerial Accounting Concepts

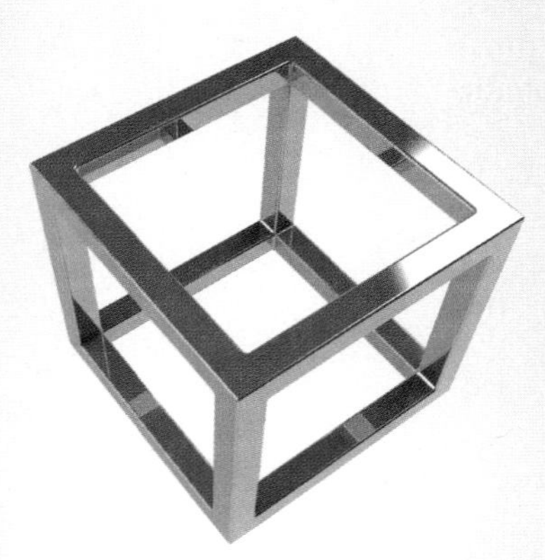

After studying Chapter 2, you should be able to:

1. Explain the meaning of cost and how costs are assigned to products and services.
2. Define the various costs of manufacturing products and providing services as well as the costs of selling and administration.
3. Prepare income statements for manufacturing and service organizations.

Cammeraydave/Dreamstime.com

EXPERIENCE MANAGERIAL DECISIONS

with Canada's Worst Cellphone Bill

It is likely that you own a cellphone. About 75 percent of Canadians—some 25 million people—have a cellphone. Worldwide, there are some 5 billion cellphones. This makes the cellphone industry one of the most lucrative in the world.

The first mobile phone was produced by Motorola in 1973. It took about 10 years for the first cellphone (the Motorola Dyna TAC) to become commercially available. In the 1990s, commercially viable cellular networks mushroomed and cellphone usage took off, penetrating not only developed nations' markets but also the developing economies.

The modern cellphone is not just a phone. It is also, among other things, a watch, a camera, a calculator, a calendar, and an alarm clock. Modern mobile phones also support many other services such as email, Internet access, and gaming. Bluetooth and infrared technology offer more advanced computing ability through so-called "smart phones."

"Canada's Worst Cell Bill" (CBC *Marketplace* video) offers insight into the exorbitant and questionable billing practices of many cell service providers—practices that will make you reconsider the details of your own cell plan.

How Does Your Plan Work?

- If it is a pay-as-you-go plan, do you have to add more money so that the unused minutes you have paid for do not expire?
- If you are using your cellphone abroad, what are the roaming charges?
- If you have signed a contract, are you sure you know what you have signed up for? And what are your cancellation fees?
- Are incoming calls and texts really free?
- Overall, why do cellphone customers seem to be so confused and unhappy about the myriad charges they face?

What Is the *Real* Cost of a Cellphone?

- How much does it cost you? And how little does it cost the phone company?
- Is your cell company charging too much?
- What is the true cost of the service your cell company is providing?
- What drives the costs of cell usage?
- If the cost to you is 15 cents per minute and the cost to the company is only one-third of a cent, is the markup of 4,400 percent justified?

These and many such questions are dealt with throughout this textbook. Through your managerial accounting studies, you will soon become a cost expert and be able to answer these questions yourself.

THE MEANING AND USES OF COST

OBJECTIVE 

Explain the meaning of cost and how costs are assigned to products and services.

One of the most important tasks of managerial accounting is to determine the cost of products, services, customers, and other items of interest to managers. Therefore, we need to understand the meaning of cost and the ways in which costs can be used to make decisions, both for small entrepreneurial businesses and for large international businesses. For example, consider a small gourmet restaurant and its owner, Courtney, who is also the head chef. In addition to understanding the complexities of gourmet food preparation, Courtney needs to understand the breakdown of the restaurant's costs into various categories in order to make effective operating decisions. Cost categories of particular interest include direct costs (food and beverages) and indirect costs (laundering of linens). On a larger scale, banks operating in university communities often look at the cost of providing basic chequing account services to students. These accounts typically lose money—that is, the accounts cost more to service than they yield in fees and interest revenue. However, the banks find that if students begin banking with them, they are more likely to take out student loans through the same bank, and these loans can be very profitable. As a result, a bank may actually decide to make it easier for a student to open an account and offer enhanced services when the profits on the related loan business are considered. Now, let's define *cost* and more fully describe its importance to managers and their decision making.

Cost

Cost is the amount of cash or cash equivalent sacrificed for goods and/or services that are expected to bring a current or future benefit to the organization. If a furniture manufacturer buys lumber in cash for $10,000, then the cost of that lumber is $10,000. Sometimes, one asset is traded for another asset. Then the cost of the new asset is measured by the value of the asset given up (the cash equivalent). If the same manufacturer trades office equipment valued at $8,000 for a forklift, then the cost of the forklift is the $8,000 value of the office equipment traded for it. Cost is a dollar measure of the resources used to achieve a given benefit. Managers strive to minimize the cost of achieving benefits. Reducing the cost required to achieve a given benefit means that a firm is becoming more efficient.

Costs are incurred to produce future benefits. In a profit-making firm, these benefits usually mean revenues. As costs are used up in the production of revenues, they are said to expire. Expired costs are called **expenses**. On the income statement, expenses are deducted from revenues to determine net income (also called net *profit*). For a company to remain viable, revenues must be greater than expenses. Also, the net income earned must be large enough to satisfy the objectives of the owners of the firm.

We can look more closely at the relationship between cost and revenue by focusing on the units sold. The revenue per unit is called **price**. In our everyday conversation, we have a tendency to use *cost* and *price* to mean the same thing, because the price of an item (e.g., a cellphone) is the cost to us. However, accounting courses take the viewpoint of the owner of the company. In that case, *cost* and *price* are not the same. Instead, for the company, *revenue* and *price* are the same. Price must be greater than cost in order for the firm to earn income. Hence, managers need to know cost and future trends in cost. For example, the price a customer pays for a fleece jacket from Roots might be $200, while the total cost that the company incurs to design, manufacture, deliver, and service that jacket is much lower than the $200 price it charges its customers.

The cost to a customer is the revenue charged by the company supplying the product or service. As we saw in "Experience Managerial Decisions with Canada's Worst Cellphone Bill," the understanding of what cost a customer will incur and how the company is recovering this cost is crucial to having a productive relationship with your customer.

Accumulating and Assigning Costs

Accumulating costs is the way that costs are measured and recorded. The accounting system typically does this job quite well. When a telephone bill comes to the company, the bookkeeper records an addition to the telephone expense account and an addition to the liability account, Accounts Payable. In this way, the cost is *accumulated*. It would be easy to tell, at the end of the year, the total spending on the telephone expense. Accumulating costs tells the company what was spent. However, that usually is not enough information. The company also wants to know *why* the money was spent. In other words, it wants to know how costs were assigned to cost objects.

Assigning costs is the way that a cost is linked to some cost object. A cost object is something for which a company wants to measure the cost. For example, of the total telephone expense, how much was for the sales department, and how much was for manufacturing? *Assigning* costs tells the company why the money was spent. In this case, cost assignment tells whether the money spent on telephone expense was to support the manufacturing or the selling of the product. As we will discuss in later chapters, cost assignment typically is more difficult than cost accumulation.

Cost Objects

Managerial accounting systems are structured to measure and assign costs to entities called *cost objects*. A **cost object** is any item such as a product, service, customer, department, project, geographic region, plant, and so on, for which costs are measured and assigned. For example, if the Royal Bank of Canada wants to determine the cost of a platinum credit card, then the cost object is the platinum credit card. All costs related to the platinum card are added in, such as the cost of mailings to potential customers, the cost of customer service telephone lines dedicated to the card, the portion of the computer department that processes platinum card transactions and bills, and so on. In a more personal example, suppose that you are considering taking a course during the summer session. Taking the course is the cost object, and the cost would include tuition, books, fees, transportation, and (possibly) housing. Notice that you could also include the forgone earnings from a summer job (assuming that you cannot work while taking summer classes), which would be an **opportunity cost** (a benefit given up or sacrificed when one alternative is chosen over another).

Different companies will have different cost objects and accumulate costs differently, as can be seen by comparing a gourmet restaurant and a cellphone supplier. The various methods of determining and assigning costs to cost objects are the heart of managerial accounting and are the focus of much of the material in this textbook.

YOUDECIDE For Which Business Activities Do We Need an Estimate of Cost?

You are the chief financial officer for a major airline company. Managing the company's numerous costs is critically important in this fiercely competitive industry. Therefore, one of your major tasks is deciding which costs to manage in order to achieve the company's profitability targets. In other words, you must identify the airline's most important cost objects to track, measure, and control.

Which cost objects would you select as critical to the company's success?

Certain airline cost objects are obvious, such as the cost of operating a flight, which includes jet fuel (Air Canada spent over $3.7 billion in 2014 for jet fuel) and labour costs, which include pilots, flight crews, and maintenance staff ($2.3 billion in 2014 for wages and benefits). However, even the costs of these obvious cost objects can become challenging. For example, when an airline operates multiple types of aircraft, it incurs additional costs to train workers and store spare parts for each aircraft type (i.e., the total cost of training and maintaining 100 aircraft of two different types is greater than for the same number of aircraft all of one type). Airlines might be even more specific with certain cost objects, such as when they focus on the cost per available seat mile (or CASM, as industry experts refer to it), which typically falls in the 6–10 cent range for most airlines.

Other airline cost objects are even more challenging. For example, you likely did not include the cost of managing crises as an important cost object. However, according to the International Air Transit Association, the airline industry took an estimated $1.7 billion hit from disrupted airline travel resulting from the volcanic ash cloud caused by the eruption of the Icelandic volcano Eyjafjallajökull.[1]

(Continued)

[1] Graeme Wearden, "Airline Industry Takes $1.7bn Hit from Volcanic Ash Disruption," *The Guardian*, www.guardian.co.uk/business/2010/apr/21/airline-industry-cost-volcanic-ash (accessed on May 8, 2010).

Finally, you might consider the cost object of processing customers, such as loading and unloading passengers and their baggage on to and off of flights. For example, airlines have charged fees for using curbside check-in services, consuming beverages during flight, using pillows and blankets while onboard, selecting seats prior to the day of the flight, and checking bags. Spirit Airlines raised many customers' (and even regulators') eyebrows by being the first airline to charge passengers ($45) for their carry-on bags.[2]

Like any company, an airline can identify and manage any cost objects it so desires. Sometimes the most difficult part of effective cost management is the first step—deciding on the exact items for which one needs to understand the cost. Mistakes in selecting the cost objects almost always lead to poor decisions and subpar performance.

Assigning Costs to Cost Objects

Costs can be assigned to cost objects in a number of ways. By comparison, some methods are more accurate, while others are simpler. The choice of a method depends on a number of factors, such as the importance of accuracy. The notion of accuracy is a relative concept and has to do with the reasonableness and logic of the cost assignment methods used. The objective is to measure and assign costs as well as possible, given management's priorities. For example, suppose you and three of your friends go out to dinner at a local pizza parlour. When the bill comes, everything has been added together for a total of $36. How much is each person's share? One easy way to find the share is to divide the bill evenly among you and your friends. In that case, you each owe $9 (= $36 ÷ 4). But suppose that one of you had a small salad and a drink (totalling $5), while another had a specialty pizza, an appetizer, and a beer (totalling $15). Clearly, it is possible to identify what each person had and assign costs that way. The second method is more accurate, but also more work. Which method you choose will depend on how important it is to you to assign the specific meal costs to each individual and the additional effort required to be more accurate. It is the same way in accounting. There are a number of ways to assign costs to cost objects. Some methods are quick and easy, but may not be totally accurate. Other methods are much more accurate, but involve much more work (in business, more work equals more expense).

Cost Classification

A cost is a payment of cash or the commitment to pay cash in the future for the purpose of generating revenues. For example, cash paid or a signed note payable to purchase supplies is the cost of supplies. In managerial accounting, costs are classified according to the decision-making needs of management.

Different costs are used for different purposes. Cost definitions can vary according to the objective being served. Thus costs can be classified into groups using a variety of criteria. The classification of costs helps make sense of the great variety of costs, which facilitates decision making and strategic planning.

The following cost groups and terms will be defined later in this chapter:

- direct costs (materials and labour)
- indirect costs (manufacturing overhead)
- prime costs
- conversion costs
- product costs
- period costs
- variable costs
- fixed costs
- mixed costs
- selling costs
- administrative costs

[2] Joan Lowy, "Spirit CEO Says Carry-On Fees Will Be Disclosed," NBCNews.com (May 6, 2010), retrieved from www.msnbc.msn.com/id/37004725/ns/travel-news/ on April 16, 2014.

It should be emphasized that there is only one pool of costs. Using different criteria, we can "break out" this single pool into various categories. So a pool of costs can be categorized as—for example—direct or indirect costs, prime or conversion costs, product or period costs, selling or administrative costs, or variable, fixed, or mixed costs.

To facilitate accountability and control, selling and administrative expenses may be reported by level of responsibility. For example, selling expenses may be reported in terms of products, salespersons, departments, divisions, or territories. Likewise, administrative expenses may be reported in terms of areas such as human resources, computer services, legal, accounting, or finance. Therefore, we must be very specific in terms of which costs we are talking about.

Tracing Direct Costs **Direct costs** are those costs that can be easily and accurately traced to a cost object. When we say that a cost is easy to trace, we often mean that the relationship between the cost and the object can be physically observed and is easy to track. The more costs that can be traced to the object, the more accurate are the cost assignments. For example, suppose that our chef, Courtney, from the earlier discussion, wants to know the cost of emphasizing fresh, in-season fruits and vegetables in her entrées. The purchase cost of the fresh fruits and vegetables would be relatively easy to determine. Some costs, however, are harder to trace.

Indirect costs are costs that cannot be easily, accurately, or economically traced to a cost object. For example, Courtney incurs additional costs in scouting the outlying farms and farmers' markets (as opposed to simply ordering fruits and vegetables from a distributor). She must use her own time and automobile to make the trips. Farmers' markets may not deliver, so Courtney must arrange for a co-worker with a van to pick up the produce. By definition, fruits and vegetables that are currently in season will be out of season (i.e., unavailable) in a few weeks. This seasonality means that Courtney must spend more time revising menus and developing new recipes that can be adapted to restaurant conditions. In addition, waste and spoilage may increase until Courtney and the kitchen staff learn just how much to order. These costs are difficult to assign to each meal prepared and sold. Therefore, we treat these costs as indirect costs. Exhibit 2.1 shows direct and indirect costs being assigned to cost objects. Exhibit 2.2 provides another schematic for classifying costs.

EXHIBIT 2.1

Assigning to Cost Objects

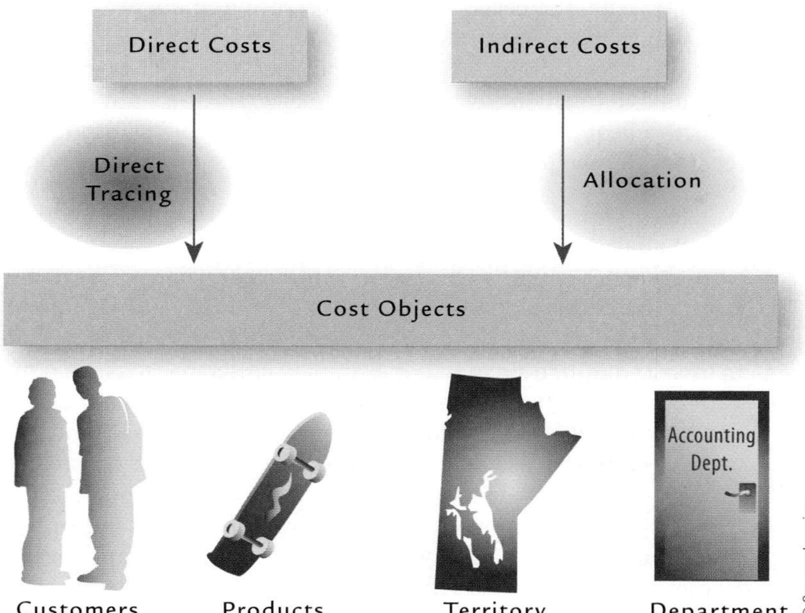

EXHIBIT 2.2

Cost Classification

Cost Classification	Types of Costs
A. In relation to cost object	Direct (easily traceable) Indirect (not easily or economically traceable; need to be allocated)
B. In relation to changes in activity levels	Fixed (total cost remains constant) Variable (total cost varies according to the level of activity) Mixed (part variable, part fixed)
C. In relation to the classification in the financial statements	Product (inventoriable) Period (expensed immediately) Prime (direct material and direct labour) Conversion (direct labour and manufacturing overhead)

Assigning Indirect Costs Even though indirect costs cannot be traced to cost objects, we must consider them in determining the cost of a cost object. This assignment is usually accomplished by using cost allocation.

Allocation means that an indirect cost is assigned to a cost object by using a reasonable and convenient method. Since no clearly observable causal relationship exists, allocating indirect costs is based on observation and/or some assumed causal linkage. For example, consider the cost of heating and lighting a plant in which five products are manufactured. Suppose that this utility cost is to be assigned to these five products. It may be difficult to see any direct causal relationship between utility costs and each unit of product manufactured. Therefore, a convenient way to allocate this cost may be to assign it in proportion to the direct labour hours used by each product. This method is relatively easy to measure and accomplishes the purpose of ensuring that all costs are assigned to units produced. Allocating indirect costs is important for a variety of reasons. For example, allocating indirect costs to products is needed to determine the value of inventory and the amount of cost of goods sold. Perhaps more importantly, as companies automate their manufacturing operations and become more complex in the number and types of products and services they offer to customers, the need to understand, allocate, and effectively control indirect costs, which are increasing dramatically, becomes more critical to sound management and strategic planning.

Direct and indirect costs occur in service businesses as well. For example, a bank's cost of printing and mailing monthly statements to chequing account holders is a direct cost of the product—chequing accounts. However, the cost of office furniture in the bank is an indirect cost for the chequing accounts.

Other Categories of Costs In addition to being categorized as either direct or indirect, costs are often analyzed with respect to their behaviour patterns, or the way in which a cost changes when the level of the output changes.

A **variable cost** is one that, in total, varies in direct proportion to changes in output. In other words, it increases in total as output increases, and decreases in total as output decreases. For example, the denim used in making jeans is a variable cost. As the company makes more jeans, it uses more denim.

A **fixed cost** is a cost that does not increase in total as output increases, and does not decrease in total as output decreases. For example, the cost of property taxes on the factory building stays the same no matter how many pairs of jeans the company makes. How can that be, since property taxes can and do change? While the cost changes, it is not because output changes. Rather, it changes because the city or local government decides to raise taxes. Variable and fixed costs are covered more extensively in Chapter 3.

concept Q&A

Make a list of the costs you are incurring for your classes this term. Which costs are direct costs for your courses? Which costs are indirect? Now, from your list of total costs, which ones are direct costs of this course? Which are indirect?

Answers on pages 734 to 738.

Many costs are neither fixed nor variable; they are *mixed*, having both variable and fixed components.

The various methods of assigning costs to cost objects will be the subject of the succeeding chapters.

PRODUCT AND SERVICE COSTS

OBJECTIVE 

Define the various costs of manufacturing products and providing services as well as the costs of selling and administration.

Output represents one of the most important cost objects. There are two types of output: products and services.

Products are goods produced by converting raw materials through the use of labour and other manufacturing resources, such as the manufacturing plant, land, and machinery. Flat screen TVs, hamburgers, automobiles, computers, clothes, and furniture are examples of products.

Services are tasks or activities performed for a customer, or an activity performed by a customer using an organization's products or facilities. Insurance coverage, medical care, dental care, funeral care, and accounting are examples of service activities performed for customers. Car rental, video rental, and skiing are examples of services where the customer uses an organization's products or facilities to receive the service.

Organizations that produce products are called **manufacturing organizations**, while organizations that provide services are called **service organizations**. Managers of both types of organizations need to know the cost of individual products or services. Accurate cost information is vital for profitability analysis and strategic decisions concerning product design, pricing, and product mix. Incidentally, retail organizations, such as La Senza, buy finished products from other organizations, such as manufacturers, and then sell them to customers. The accounting for inventory and cost of goods sold for retail organizations (often referred to as merchandisers) is much simpler than for manufacturing organizations and is usually covered extensively in introductory financial accounting courses. Therefore, the focus in most managerial accounting textbooks is on manufacturing and service organizations, rather than retail operations.

Services differ from products in many ways. First, a service is intangible, that is, the buyers of services cannot see, feel, hear, or taste a service before it is bought. Second, services are perishable; they cannot be stored for future use by a consumer but must be consumed when the service is performed. Inventory valuation, so important for products, is not an issue for services. In other words, because service organizations do not produce and sell products as part of their regular operations, they do not have an inventory asset on their balance sheet. Third, providers of services and buyers of services must usually be in direct contact for an exchange to take place. For example, an eye examination requires both the patient and the optometrist to be present. However, producers of products need not have direct contact with the buyers of their goods. Thus, buyers of automobiles never need to have contact with the engineers and assembly line workers that produced their automobiles. How a company costs services, in terms of classifying related costs as either direct or indirect, is very similar to how it would cost products. The main difference in costing is that products have inventories, and services do not.

Corporate and Social Responsibility

Tracking costs can also act as an early warning system for unauthorized activity and possible ethical problems. For example, Metropolitan Life Insurance Company was dismayed to learn that some of its agents were selling policies as retirement plans. This practice is illegal, and it cost the company more than $20 million in fines as well as $50 million in refunds to policyholders.[3] More accurate and comprehensive data tracking regarding sales, individual agents, types of policies, and policyholders could have alerted Metropolitan Life much earlier to a potential problem. Thus, we can see that tracking costs can serve many different and important purposes.

Similar things happened in the finance industry during 2000–2008, which led to a virtual meltdown of world economies. People behaving badly led to very serious issues.

[3] Chris Roush, "Fields of Green—and Disaster Areas," *Business Week* (January 9, 1995): 94.

Product Costs

Management accountants will decide what types of managerial accounting information to provide to managers, how to measure such information, and when and to whom to communicate the information. For example, when making most strategic and operating decisions, managers typically rely on managerial accounting information that is prepared in whatever manner the management accountant believes provides the best analysis for the decision at hand. Therefore, when we examine the information and the methodology of gathering the information for managerial decision making, there are no rules to be followed. Every company will determine for itself what information is relevant to the particular decision or situation being analyzed.

However, there is one major exception: Management accountants must follow specific external reporting rules (i.e., GAAP) when their companies provide outside parties with cost information about the amount of ending inventory on the balance sheet and the **cost of goods sold (COGS)** on the income statement. In order to calculate these two amounts, management accountants must subdivide costs into functional categories: production and period (i.e., nonproduction) costs. The following section describes the process for categorizing costs as either product or period in nature.

Product (manufacturing) costs are those costs, both direct and indirect, of producing a product in a manufacturing firm, or of acquiring a product in a merchandising firm and preparing it for sale. Therefore, only costs in the *production* section of the value chain are included in product costs. A key feature of product costs is that they form the value of inventory (or are inventoried). Product costs initially are added to an inventory account and remain in inventory until they are sold, at which time they are transferred to COGS. Product costs can be further classified as direct materials, direct labour, and manufacturing overhead, which are the three cost elements that *must* be assigned to products for external financial reporting (e.g., inventories or COGS). Exhibit 2.3 illustrates how direct materials, direct labour, and factory (manufacturing) overhead become product costs.

EXHIBIT 2.3

Product Costs Include Direct Materials, Direct Labour, and Factory Overhead

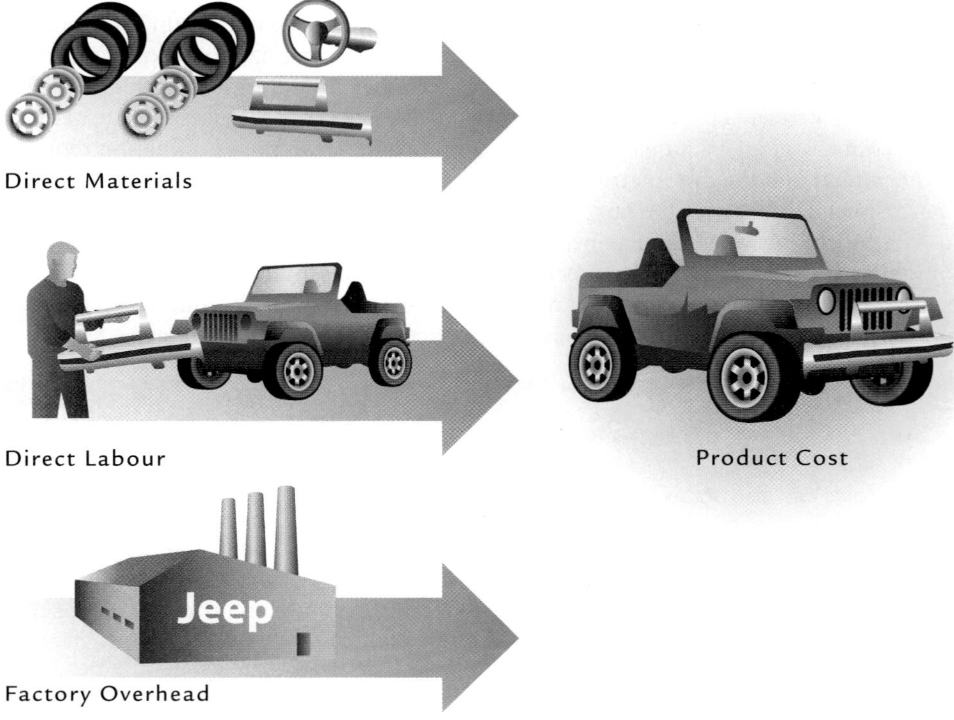

Direct Materials **Direct materials** are those materials that are part of the final product and can be directly traced to the goods being produced. The cost of these materials can be directly charged to products because physical observation can be used to measure the quantity used by each product. Materials that become part of a product usually are classified as direct materials. For example, tires on a new Porsche automobile, alcohol in an Estée Lauder cologne, and denim in a pair of Diesel jeans are all part of direct materials for manufacturers of these products.

A closely related term is *raw materials*. Often, the inventory of materials is called the *raw materials account*. Materials in the raw materials account do not become *direct materials* until they are withdrawn from inventory for use in production. The raw materials inventory account can include indirect materials as well as direct materials. Indirect materials are used in the production process but the amount used by each unit cannot be easily determined and, as a result, these costs are treated as indirect costs (as discussed later).

Direct Labour **Direct labour** is the labour that can be directly traced to the goods being produced. Physical observation can be used to measure the amount of labour used to produce a product. Those employees who convert direct materials into a product are classified as direct labour. For example, workers on an assembly line at Pratt & Whitney Canada are classified as direct labour.

Just as there were indirect materials in a company, there may also be indirect labour. This labour is not direct labour since these workers do not actually make the product. However, their contribution is necessary to production. An example of indirect labour in a production setting is the maintenance crew that performs regularly scheduled preventative maintenance every week at AbitibiBowater in Thunder Bay, Ontario. Indirect labour is included in manufacturing overhead and, therefore, is allocated as an indirect cost rather than traced as a direct cost.

Manufacturing Overhead All product costs, other than direct materials and direct labour, are put into a category called **manufacturing overhead**. In a manufacturing firm, manufacturing overhead is also known as *factory burden* or *indirect* manufacturing costs. Costs are included as manufacturing overhead if they cannot be easily traced to the cost object of interest (e.g., unit of product). The manufacturing overhead cost category contains a wide variety of items such as depreciation on plant buildings and equipment, janitorial and maintenance labour, plant supervision labour, materials handling, power for plant utilities, and plant property taxes. The important thing to remember is that all costs related to the factory are classified as direct materials, direct labour, or manufacturing overhead. No element of product cost can be omitted from classification, no matter how far removed you might think it is from the actual production of a product. Earlier we mentioned that indirect materials and indirect labour are included in overhead. In manufacturing, the glue used in furniture or toys is an example, as is the cost of oil to grease cookie sheets for producing cookies.

Total Product Cost The total product cost equals the sum of direct materials, direct labour, and manufacturing overhead. The unit product cost equals total product cost divided by the number of units produced. Cornerstone 2.1 shows how to calculate total product cost and per unit product cost.

Product costs include direct materials, direct labour, and manufacturing overhead. Once the product is finished, no more costs attach to it. That is, any costs associated with storing, selling, and delivering the product are not product costs, but instead are period costs.

concept Q&A

Focus on any object in the room. What do you think the direct materials for that object might include? What kind of direct labour might have worked on that object? Finally, what types of overhead costs might have been incurred by the company that produced it?

Answers on pages 734 to 738.

analytical Q&A

A company produced and sold 1,000 units last month. Direct materials totalled $4,000, direct labour totalled $5,000, and overhead amounted to $10,000. (1) What is total prime cost for last month? (2) What is conversion cost per unit?

Answers on pages 734 to 738.

CORNERSTONE 2.1

Calculating Product Cost in Total and Per Unit

CORNERSTONE VIDEO

Information:

BlueDenim Company makes blue jeans. Last week, direct materials (denim, thread, zippers, and rivets) costing $48,000 were put into production. Direct labour of $30,000 (= 50 workers × 40 hours × $15 per hour) was incurred. Overhead equalled $72,000. By the end of the week, the company had manufactured 30,000 pairs of jeans.

Required:

1. Calculate the total product cost for last week.
2. Calculate the cost of one pair of jeans that was produced last week.

Solution:

1.

Direct materials	$ 48,000
Direct labour	30,000
Overhead	72,000
Total product cost	$150,000

2. Per-unit product cost = $150,000/30,000 = $5
   Therefore, one pair of jeans costs $5 to produce.

Why:

1. The accumulation of product costs ensures that all manufacturing costs incurred are properly assigned to the products produced.
2. Proper cost assignment ensures that inventories are accurately valued.
3. Proper product costing will ensure that managers can accurately determine profitability.

Prime and Conversion Costs

Product costs of direct materials, direct labour, and manufacturing overhead are sometimes grouped into prime cost and conversion cost. **Prime cost** is the sum of direct materials cost and direct labour cost. **Conversion cost** is the sum of direct labour cost and manufacturing overhead cost. For a manufacturing firm, conversion cost can be interpreted as the cost of converting raw materials into a final product. Cornerstone 2.2 shows how to calculate prime cost for a manufactured product.

CORNERSTONE 2.2

Calculating Prime Cost and Conversion Cost in Total and Per Unit

Information:

BlueDenim Company makes blue jeans. Last week, direct materials (denim, thread, zippers, and rivets) costing $48,000 were put into production. Direct labour of $30,000 (=50 workers × 40 hours × $15 per hour) was incurred. Overhead equalled $72,000. By the end of the week, the company had manufactured 30,000 pairs of jeans.

(Continued)

CORNERSTONE

2.2

(Continued)

Required:

1. Calculate the total prime cost for last week.
2. Calculate the per-unit prime cost.
3. Calculate the total conversion cost for last week.
4. Calculate the per-unit conversion cost.

Solution:

1.

Direct materials	$48,000
Direct labour	30,000
Total prime cost	$78,000

2. Per-unit prime cost = $78,000/30,000 = $2.60

3.

Direct labour	$ 30,000
Overhead	72,000
Total conversion cost	$102,000

4. Per-unit conversion cost = $102,000/30,000 = $3.40

Note: Remember that prime cost and conversion cost do NOT equal total product cost. This is because direct labour is part of BOTH prime cost and conversion cost.

Why:

To accurately accumulate costs in a manner consistent with the definition of each category of costs. These costs will be used in further analysis and for managerial decision making.

Period Costs

The costs of production are assets that are carried in inventories until the goods are sold. There are other costs of running a company, referred to as *period costs*; these costs do not form part of the costs carried in inventory.

Period costs are all costs that are not product costs (i.e., all areas of the value chain except for production). The costs of office supplies, research and development activities, the CEO's salary, and advertising are examples of period costs. For example, according to *Forbes* magazine, a 30-second advertisement during widely watched shows such as the Super Bowl can cost up to $5.5 million. The Super Bowl's ratings are high, with many millions of people watching; even so, there are some who question the wisdom of spending such exorbitant sums of money for 30 seconds of advertising exposure. Management accountants help executives at companies like Canadian apparel maker Canada Goose determine whether such costly advertising campaigns generate enough additional sales revenue over the long run to make them worthwhile.

Period costs cannot be assigned to products or appear as part of the reported values of inventories on the balance sheet. Instead, period costs typically are expensed in the period in which they are incurred. However, if a period cost is expected to provide an economic benefit (i.e., revenues) beyond the next year, then it may be recorded as an asset (i.e., capitalized) and allocated to expense through depreciation or amortization throughout its useful life. The cost associated with the purchase of a delivery truck is an example of a period cost that would be capitalized when incurred and then recognized as an expense over the useful life of the truck. Exhibit 2.4 illustrates the distinction between

EXHIBIT 2.4

The Impact of Product vs. Period Costs on the Financial Statements

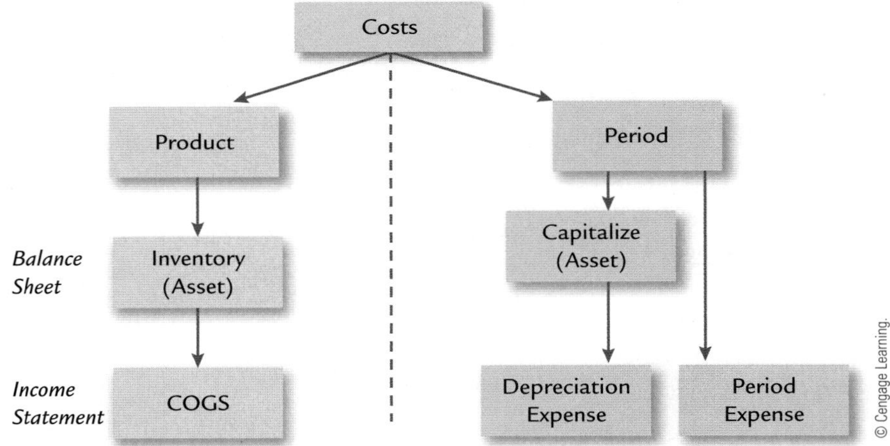

product and period costs and how each type of cost eventually becomes an expense on the income statement. As shown in the exhibit, product costs, which are carried as an inventory asset, are expensed on the income statement as COGS to match against the revenues generated from the sale of the inventory. However, capitalized period costs are depreciated to expense on the income statement over the useful life of the asset to match against the revenues generated by utilization of the asset over its useful life.

In a manufacturing organization, the level of period costs can be significant (often greater than 25 percent of sales revenue), and controlling them may bring greater cost savings than using the same effort to control production costs. For example, in fiscal 2013, BlackBerry's period expenses were 42 percent of its revenue ($4,669 million/$11,073 million), while in 2015 they were 61 percent of revenues($2,027/$3,335) due to massive restructuring. For service organizations, the relative importance of selling and administrative costs depends on the nature of the service produced. Physicians and dentists, for example, do relatively little marketing and thus have very low selling costs. On the other hand, a grocery chain may incur substantial marketing costs. Period costs often are divided into selling costs and administrative costs.

Selling Costs Those costs necessary to market, distribute, and service a product or service are **selling costs**. They are often referred to as *order-getting* and *order-filling* costs. Examples of selling costs include salaries and commissions of sales personnel, advertising, warehousing, shipping, and customer service. The first two items are examples of order-getting costs; the last three are order-filling costs.

Administrative Costs All costs associated with research, development, and general administration of the organization that cannot reasonably be assigned to either selling or production are **administrative costs**. General administration has the responsibility of ensuring that the various activities of the organization are properly integrated so that the overall mission of the firm is realized. The president of the firm, for example, is concerned with the efficiency of selling, production, and research and development activities. Proper integration of these activities is essential to maximizing the overall profits of a firm. Examples of general administrative costs are executive salaries, legal fees, printing the annual report, and general accounting. Research and development costs are the costs associated with designing and developing new products.

As with product costs, it is often helpful to distinguish between direct period costs and indirect period costs. Service companies also make this important distinction. For example, a surgical centre would show that surgical gauze and anesthesia are direct costs used for an operation because it could be determined how much gauze or anesthesia was used for each procedure or patient. Other examples of direct costs in service industries include the chef in a restaurant, a surgical nurse attending an open heart operation, and a pilot for WestJet.

Alternatively, though shampoo and hair spray are used in a hair salon, the exact amount used in each individual's appointment is not easily determinable. As a result, the costs associated with shampoo and hair spray would be considered indirect, or overhead, costs and allocated, rather than traced, to individual appointment. Examples of indirect labour costs in a service setting include the surgical assistants in a hospital who clean up the operating room after surgery, dispose of certain used materials, and sterilize the reusable instruments. Indirect labour is included in overhead. Though these costs do not affect the valuation of inventories or COGS (i.e., because they are service companies), their correct classification nonetheless affects numerous decisions and planning and control activities for managers, as we will discuss in detail in future chapters.

PREPARING FINANCIAL STATEMENTS FOR MANUFACTURING OPERATIONS

OBJECTIVE 

Prepare income statements for manufacturing and service organizations.

The earlier definitions of product, selling, and administrative costs provide a good conceptual overview of these important costs. However, the actual calculation of these costs in practice is a bit more complicated. Let's take a closer look at just how costs are calculated for purposes of preparing the external financial statements, focusing first on manufacturing firms.

Financial Statements for Manufacturing Operations

The operations of a business can be classified as one of the following:

- service
- merchandising
- manufacturing

The accounting for service and merchandising businesses is described and illustrated in basically all financial accounting courses. This textbook focuses mainly on manufacturing businesses; however, most of the managerial accounting concepts discussed here also apply to service and merchandising businesses, as illustrated in some of the exercises and problems at the end of the chapters.

The cost of a manufactured product includes the cost of materials used in making the product as well as the cost of converting those materials into a finished product. Thus, the cost of a finished product includes the following:

- direct materials cost
- direct labour cost
- manufacturing overhead cost

Direct Materials Cost Manufactured products begin with raw materials, which are converted into finished products. The cost of any materials that are an integral part of the finished product is classified as a **direct materials cost**. Direct materials costs include, for example, the cost of the electronic components in a television, and the tires on an automobile. To be classified as a direct materials cost, the materials must:

- be easily traceable and recognizable, as well as integral to the finished product, *and*
- reflect a significant portion of the total cost of the product.

Insignificant costs such as the glue used to produce a TV or the lubricants used to make automobile tires shine would be classified as **indirect materials**, and form a part of manufacturing overhead costs.

Direct Labour Cost Most manufacturing companies use employee labour to convert materials into finished products. The wages of employees who are integral to the finished product are classified as a **direct labour cost**. For example, machine operators' wages for assembling a TV are direct labour costs, and so are assembly line workers' wages for manufacturing an automobile. As with direct materials cost, a direct labour cost must:

- be easily traceable to production, as well as an integral part of the finished product; *and*
- reflect a significant portion of the total cost of the product.

The wages of the cleaning staff who clean the factory are not a direct labour cost, nor are those of the security staff who guard the factory at night. Cleaning and security costs are not an integral part of, or a significant cost of, each TV or car produced. Instead, such costs are classified as **indirect labour**, a part of factory overhead cost.

Manufacturing Overhead (Factory Overhead Cost) Costs other than direct materials cost and direct labour cost that are incurred in the manufacturing process are combined and classified as **manufacturing overhead cost**. All manufacturing overhead costs are indirect costs of the product. These may include the following:

- heat and light for the factory
- power to run the machines
- salaries for factory supervisors (indirect labour)
- factory caretaking wages (indirect labour)
- equipment repair and maintenance
- property taxes on factory buildings and land
- insurance on factory buildings
- depreciation of factory plant and equipment

Manufacturing overhead cost also includes indirect materials cost, covering materials that are not easily traced to the finished product. Examples include lubricants, glue, buffing compounds, and machine coolants.

When you total direct materials, direct labour, and manufacturing overhead, you arrive at **manufacturing costs**.

The retained earnings and cash flow statements for a manufacturing business are similar to those illustrated in financial accounting courses for service and merchandising businesses. However, the balance sheet and income statement for a manufacturing business are more complex.

Balance Sheet for a Manufacturing Business

A manufacturing business reports three types of inventory on its balance sheet. **Materials inventory** consists of the costs of the direct and indirect materials that have not yet entered the manufacturing process. **Work-in-process (WIP) inventory** consists of the direct materials, direct labour, and manufacturing overhead costs for products that have entered the manufacturing process but are not yet completed. WIP inventory includes all products still being made, regardless of the level of completion (e.g., they could be 10, 20, 30, or 90 percent complete). **Finished goods inventory** consists of completed (or finished) products that have not been sold. Exhibit 2.5 illustrates how inventories are reported on the balance sheets of a merchandising and a manufacturing business respectively.

Income Statement for a Manufacturing Business

The income statements for merchandising and manufacturing businesses differ mainly in how they report the cost of goods purchased and the cost of goods manufactured during the period. These differences are shown in Exhibit 2.6.

EXHIBIT 2.5

Balance Sheet Reporting of Inventories

Merchandising Business		Manufacturing Business	
Current assets:		Current assets:	
Cash	$100,000	Cash	$100,000
Accounts receivable	300,000	Accounts receivable	300,000
Merchandise inventory	**80,000**	**Finished goods inventory**	**80,000**
Supplies	50,000	**WIP inventory**	**80,000**
Total current assets	$530,000	**Raw materials inventory**	**45,000**
		Supplies	50,000
		Total current assets	$655,000

EXHIBIT 2.6

Income Statements: Merchandising and Manufacturing

Merchandising Business		Manufacturing Business	
Sales	$700,000	Sales	$700,000
Beginning inventory	100,000	Beginning **finished goods** inventory	100,000
Plus **net purchases**	370,000	Plus **cost of goods manufactured**	370,000
Cost of goods available for sale	470,000	Cost of finished goods available for sale	470,000
Less ending inventory	80,000	Less ending finished goods inventory	80,000
Cost of goods sold	390,000	Cost of goods sold	390,000
Gross margin	310,000	Gross margin	310,000
Operating expenses:		Operating expenses:	
Selling expenses	120,000	Selling expenses	120,000
Administrative expenses	90,000	Administrative expenses	90,000
Total operating expenses	210,000	Total operating expenses	210,000
Net income	$100,000	Net income	$100,000

A merchandising business purchases merchandise ready for resale to customers. The total cost of *goods available for sale* during the period is determined by adding beginning inventory to net purchases. The *cost of goods sold* is determined by subtracting ending inventory from cost of merchandise available for sale.

A manufacturer makes the products it sells, using direct materials, direct labour, and manufacturing overhead. The total cost of making products that are available for sale during the period is called the **cost of goods manufactured (COGM)**.

To determine the COGS, and thus to prepare the income statement, first the COGM needs to be calculated. The COGM is often determined by preparing a *statement of cost of goods manufactured*.

Statement of Cost of Goods Manufactured

The statement of COGM is prepared using these three steps:

Step 1. Determine the cost of direct materials used.

Materials inventory, January 1, 2018	$ 65,000
Plus materials purchased	100,000
Cost of materials available for use	165,000
Less materials inventory, December 31, 2018	45,000
Cost of direct materials used	$120,000

Step 2. Determine the total manufacturing costs incurred.

Cost of direct materials used in production (step 1)	$120,000
All direct labour	210,000
All factory overhead	70,000
Total manufacturing costs incurred	$400,000

The total manufacturing costs incurred in 2018 of $400,000 are determined by adding the direct materials used in production (step 1), the direct labour cost, and the factory overhead costs.

Step 3. Determine the cost of goods manufactured.

Total manufacturing costs incurred (step 2)	$400,000
Work-in-process inventory, January 1, 2018	50,000
Total manufacturing costs	450,000
Less work-in-process inventory, December 31, 2018	80,000
Cost of goods manufactured	$370,000

The COGM of $370,000 is determined by taking the manufacturing costs, adding the WIP beginning inventory, and subtracting the WIP ending inventory. Thus the statement of COGM is shaped as follows:

Statement of Cost of Goods Manufactured
For the Year Ended December 31, 2018

Materials inventory, January 1, 2018	$ 65,000
Plus materials purchased	100,000
Cost of materials available for use	165,000
Less materials inventory, December 31, 2018	45,000
Cost of direct materials used	120,000
Plus direct labour	210,000
Plus factory overhead	70,000
Total manufacturing costs incurred	400,000
Plus work-in-process inventory, January 1, 2018	50,000
Total manufacturing costs	450,000
Less work-in-process inventory, December 31, 2018	80,000
Cost of goods manufactured	$370,000

Income Statement
For the Year Ended December 31, 2018

Sales	$700,000
Cost of goods sold:	
Finished goods inventory, January 1, 2018	100,000
Cost of goods manufactured	370,000
Cost of finished goods available for sale	470,000
Less finished goods inventory, December 31, 2018	80,000
Cost of goods sold	390,000
Gross margin	310,000
Operating expenses:	
Selling expenses	120,000
Administrative expenses	90,000
Total operating expenses	210,000
Net income	$100,000

The *cost of finished goods available for sale* is determined by adding the beginning finished goods inventory to the COGM during the period. The COGS is determined by subtracting the ending finished goods inventory from the cost of finished goods available for sale.

Cost of Goods Manufactured: A Second Look

The *COGM* represents the total product cost of goods *completed* during the current period and transferred to finished goods inventory. The only costs assigned to goods completed are the manufacturing costs of direct materials, direct labour, and manufacturing overhead. So, why don't we just add together the current period's costs of direct materials, direct labour, and manufacturing overhead to arrive at COGS? The reason is inventories of materials and work in process. For instance, some of the materials purchased in the current period likely were used in production (i.e., transferred from materials inventory to WIP inventory during the period). However, other materials likely were not used in production, and thus remain in materials inventory at period-end. Also, some of the units that were worked on (and thus allocated labour and manufacturing overhead costs) in the current period likely were completed during the period (i.e., transferred from WIP inventory to finished goods inventory during the period). However, other units worked on during the period likely were not completed during the period, and thus remain in WIP inventory at period-end. In calculating COGS, we need to distinguish between the total manufacturing cost for the current period and the manufacturing costs associated with the units that were completed during the current period (i.e., COGM).

Let's take a look at direct materials. Suppose a company had no materials on hand at the beginning of the month, then bought $15,000 of direct materials during the month and used all of them in production. The entire $15,000 would be properly called *direct materials*. Usually, though, the company has some materials on hand at the beginning of the month. These materials are the beginning inventory of materials. Let's say that this beginning inventory of materials cost $2,500. Then during the month, the company would have a total of $17,500 of materials that could be used in production ($2,500 from beginning inventory and $15,000 purchased during the month). Typically, the company would not use the entire amount of materials on hand in production. Perhaps it uses only $12,000 of materials. Then, the cost of direct materials used in production this month is $12,000 and the remaining $5,500 of materials is the ending inventory of materials, an asset account on the balance sheet. This reasoning can be easily expressed in a formula.

Beginning inventory of materials + Purchases − Direct materials used in production = Ending inventory of materials

While this computation is logical and simple, it does not express the result for which we usually are looking. We are usually trying to figure out the amount of direct materials used in production—not the amount of ending inventory. Cornerstone 2.3 shows how to compute the amount of direct materials used in production.

Once the direct materials used are calculated, the direct labour and manufacturing overhead *for the time period* can be added to get the total manufacturing cost for the period. Now we need to consider the second type of inventory—WIP.

WIP inventory is the cost of the partially completed goods that are still on the factory floor at the end of an accounting period. These are units that have been started but are not finished. They have value, but not as much as they will when they are completed. Just as there are beginning and ending inventories of materials, there are

CORNERSTONE 2.3

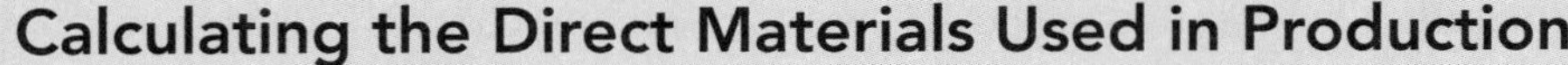

Calculating the Direct Materials Used in Production

CORNERSTONE VIDEO

Information:

BlueDenim Company makes blue jeans. On May 1, BlueDenim had $68,000 of materials in inventory. During the month of May, the company purchased $210,000 of materials. On May 31, materials inventory equalled $22,000.

Required:

Calculate the direct materials used in production for the month of May.

Solution:

Materials inventory, May 1	$ 68,000
Purchases	210,000
Materials inventory, May 31	(22,000)
Direct materials used in production	$256,000

Why:

Because direct materials are an element of manufacturing costs and we must determine how much of the materials were actually used in production during the period.

beginning and ending inventories of WIP. We must adjust the total manufacturing cost for the time period for the inventories of WIP. When that is done, we will have the total cost of the goods that were completed and transferred from WIP inventory to finished goods inventory during the accounting period. Cornerstone 2.4 shows how to calculate the COGM for a particular accounting period.

CORNERSTONE 2.4

Calculating Cost of Goods Manufactured (COGM)

CORNERSTONE VIDEO

Information:

BlueDenim Company makes blue jeans. During the month of May, the company purchased $210,000 of materials. On May 31, materials inventory equalled $22,000. During the month of May, BlueDenim Company incurred direct labour cost of $135,000 and manufacturing overhead of $150,000. Inventory information is as follows:

	May 1	May 31
Materials	$68,000	$22,000
Work in process	50,000	16,000

Required:

1. Calculate the cost of goods manufactured for the month of May.
2. Calculate the cost of one pair of jeans, assuming that 115,000 pairs of jeans were completed during May.

(Continued)

CORNERSTONE

2.4

(Continued)

Solution:

Direct materials*	$256,000
Direct labour	135,000
Manufacturing overhead	150,000
Total manufacturing cost for May	541,000
WIP, May 1	50,000
WIP, May 31	(16,000)
Cost of goods manufactured	$575,000

* Direct materials = $68,000 + $210,000 – $22,000 = $256,000. This amount was calculated in Cornerstone 2.3.

Per-unit cost of goods manufactured = $575,000/115,000 units = $5.

Why:

Because this calculation allows the determination of what it costs (direct materials, direct labour, and overhead) to manufacture completed units of a product in the current period. The costs of incomplete units (ending work in process [EWIP]) are passed on to the next accounting period. This accounting treatment is in compliance with the requirement to report only current costs in the current period.

Cost of Goods Sold

To meet external reporting requirements, costs must be classified into three categories: production, selling, and administration. Remember that product costs are initially put into inventory. They become expenses only when the products are sold, which matches the expenses of manufacturing the product to the sales revenue generated by the product at the time it is sold. Therefore, the expense of manufacturing is not the COGM; instead it is the cost of the goods that are sold, with the balance remaining in inventory to be sold in future periods.

COGS represents the cost of goods that were sold during the period and, therefore, transferred from finished goods inventory on the balance sheet to COGS on the income statement (i.e., as an expense). Cornerstone 2.5 shows how to calculate the COGS.

Calculating Cost of Goods Sold (COGS)

CORNERSTONE 2.5

Information:

BlueDenim Company makes blue jeans. During the month of May, 115,000 pairs of jeans were completed at a COGM of $575,000. Suppose that on May 1, BlueDenim had 10,000 units in the finished goods inventory costing $50,000, and on May 31, the company had 26,000 units in the finished goods inventory costing $130,000.

Required:

1. Prepare a COGS sold statement for the month of May.
2. Calculate the number of pairs of jeans that were sold during May.

(Continued)

CORNERSTONE
2.5

(Continued)

Solution:

1.

BlueDenim Company
Cost of Goods Sold Statement
For the Month of May

Cost of goods manufactured	$ 575,000
Finished goods inventory, May 1	50,000
Finished goods inventory, May 31	(130,000)
Cost of goods sold	$ 495,000

2.

Number of units sold:	
Finished goods inventory, May 1	10,000
Units finished during May	115,000
Finished goods inventory, May 31	(26,000)
Units sold during May	99,000

Why:

Because we need to know the cost of what was sold to accurately determine the profit for the accounting period by subtracting it from revenue. Knowing the number of units sold during the period will allow us to calculate the average cost of each unit sold.

The ending inventories of materials, WIP, and finished goods are important because they are assets and appear on the balance sheet (as current assets). The COGS is an expense that appears on the income statement. Selling and administrative costs are period costs and also appear on the income statement as an expense. Collectively, Cornerstones 2.3, 2.4, and 2.5 depict the flow of costs through the three inventories (materials, WIP, and finished goods) and finally into COGS.

Income Statement: Manufacturing Firm

The income statement for a manufacturing firm is displayed in Cornerstone 2.6. This income statement follows the traditional format taught in an introductory financial accounting course. Notice that the income statement covers a certain period of time (i.e., the month

CORNERSTONE 2.6

Preparing an Income Statement for a Manufacturing Firm

Information:

BlueDenim Company sold 99,000 pairs of jeans during the month of May at a total cost of $495,000. Each pair sold at a price of $8. BlueDenim also incurred two types of selling costs: commissions equal to 10 percent of the sales price, and other selling expenses of $120,000. Administrative expense totalled $85,000.

Required:

Prepare an income statement for BlueDenim for the month of May.

(Continued)

CORNERSTONE
2.6
(Continued)

Solution:

BlueDenim Company
Income Statement
For the Month of May

Sales revenue (99,000 × $8)		$792,000
Cost of goods sold		495,000
Gross margin		297,000
Less:		
Selling expense		
Commissions (0.10 × $792,000)	$ 79,200	
Fixed selling expense	120,000	199,200
Administrative expense		85,000
Operating income		$ 12,800

Why:

An income statement is a fundamental method of determining the profitability of a company and reporting these results to stakeholders (shareholders, CRA, suppliers, and employees). Once operating income is determined, the income tax liability can be calculated.

of May in Cornerstone 2.6). However, the time period may vary. The key point is that all sales revenue and expenses related to that period of time appear on the income statement.

Look at the income statement in Cornerstone 2.6. First, the heading tells us what type of statement it is, for what firm, and for what period of time. Then, the income statement itself always begins with "sales revenue" (or "sales" or "revenue"). The sales revenue is the price multiplied by the units sold. After the sales revenue is determined, the firm must calculate expenses for the period.

Notice that the expenses are separated into three categories: production (COGS), selling, and administrative. The first type of expense is the cost of producing the units sold, or the COGS. This amount was computed and explained in Cornerstone 2.5. Remember that the COGS is the cost of producing the units that were sold during the time period. It includes direct materials, direct labour, and manufacturing overhead. It does *not* include any selling or administrative expenses. In the case of a retail (i.e., merchandising) firm, the COGS represents the total cost of the goods that were sold when they were purchased from an outside supplier. Therefore, the COGS for a retailer equals the purchase costs adjusted for the beginning and ending balances in its single inventory account. A merchandising firm such as Canadian Tire has only one inventory account because it does not transform the purchased good into a different form by adding materials, labour, and overhead, as does a manufacturing firm.

Gross margin is the difference between sales revenue and COGS. It shows how much the firm is making over and above the cost of the units sold. Gross margin does *not* equal operating income or profit. Selling and administrative expenses must be deducted. However, gross margin does provide useful information. If gross margin is positive, the firm at least charges prices that cover the product cost. In addition, the firm can calculate its gross margin percentage (gross margin divided by sales revenue), as shown in Cornerstone 2.7, and compare it with the average gross margin percentage for the industry to see if its experience is consistent with other firms in the industry. Gross margin percentage varies significantly by industry. Grocery stores such as Sobeys traditionally have low

CORNERSTONE 2.7

Calculating the Percentage of Sales Revenue for Each Line on the Income Statement

Information:

BlueDenim Company's income statement for the month of May was shown in Cornerstone 2.6.

Required:

Calculate the percentage of sales revenue represented by each line of the income statement.

Solution:

BlueDenim Company
Income Statement
For the Month of May

			Percent*
Sales revenue (99,000 × $8)		$792,000	100.0
Cost of goods sold		495,000	62.5
Gross margin		297,000	37.5
Less:			
Selling expense			
Commissions (0.10 × $792,000)	$ 79,200		
Fixed selling expense	120,000	199,200	25.2
Administrative expense		85,000	10.7
Operating income		$ 12,800	1.6

* Steps in calculating the percentages:

1. Sales revenue percent = $792,000/$792,000 = 1.00, or 100 percent (sales revenue is always 100 percent of itself)
2. Cost of goods sold percent = $495,000/$792,000 = 0.625, or 62.5 percent
3. Gross margin percent = $297,000/$792,000 = 0.375, or 37.5 percent
4. Selling expense percent = $199,200/$792,000 = 0.252, or 25.2 percent (this has been rounded)
5. Administrative expense percent = $85,000/$792,000 = 0.107, or 10.7 percent (this has been rounded)
6. Operating income percent = $12,800/$792,000 = 0.016, or 1.6 percent (this has been rounded)

Why:

Because the absolute amounts do not always tell the full story. The percentage of sales revenue allows for comparisons to other companies, no matter how big or small the absolute amounts.

analytical Q&A

Your friend Ted mentioned that Mark's department store marks up sweaters by 100 percent. "Wow," said Ted. "So a sweater that costs them $25 is sold for $50—they're making $25 in profit!" Is Ted correct? Refer to the income statement from Cornerstone 2.7. What line would include the $50 price of the sweater? What line would include the $25 original cost (to the store) of the sweater? What line would include the $25 that is over and above the cost?

Answers on pages 734 to 738.

profit margins. They earn only a few pennies per food item (e.g., a bag of sugar). Luxury stores such as jewellery stores can enjoy a high gross profit margin of 75 percent and more. The overall profitability of low-margin companies is driven by high turnover, that is, high sales (a grocery store sells many bags of sugar). The overall profitability of a high-margin company is driven by the high profit margin on individual items since a jewellery store sells fewer pieces of jewellery than a grocery store sells grocery items.

Finally, selling expense and administrative expense for the period are subtracted from gross margin to arrive at operating income. Operating income is the key figure from the income statement; it is profit, and shows how much the owners are actually earning from the company. Again, calculating the percentage of operating income (i.e., operating income divided by sales revenue) and comparing it to the average for the industry gives the owners valuable information about relative profitability. For simplicity, we are ignoring income taxes, which are also an expense of the business.

The income statement can be analyzed further by calculating the percentage of sales revenue represented by each line of the statement, as was done in Cornerstone 2.7. How can management use this information? The first thing that jumps out is that operating income is less than 2 percent of sales revenue. That's a very small percentage. Unless this is common for the blue jeans manufacturing business, BlueDenim's management should work hard to increase the percentage. Selling expense is a whopping 25.2 percent of sales! Do commissions really need to be that high? Or is the price too low (compared to competitors' prices)? Can COGS be reduced? Is 62.5 percent reasonable? These are questions that are suggested by Cornerstone 2.7, but not answered. Answering the questions is the job of management.

Income Statement: Service Firm

In a service organization, there is no product to purchase (e.g., a merchandiser like RONA) or to manufacture (e.g., BlackBerry), and, therefore, there are no beginning or ending inventories. As a result, there is no COGS or gross margin on the income statement. Instead, the cost of providing services appears along with the other operating expenses of the company. For example, WestJet's 2016 income statement begins with total revenues of $4,122,859,000 and subtracts total expenses of $3,682,762,000 to arrive at operating earnings of $440,097,000. An income statement for a service firm is shown in Cornerstone 2.8.

Preparing an Income Statement for a Service Organization

CORNERSTONE 2.8

Information:

Komala Information Systems designs and installs human resources software for small companies. Last month, Komala had software licensing costs of $5,000, service technicians' costs of $35,000, and research and development costs of $55,000. Selling expenses were $5,000, and administrative expenses equalled $7,000. Sales totalled $130,000.

Required:

Prepare an income statement for Komala Information Systems for the past month.

Solution:

Komala Information Systems
Income Statement
For the Past Month

Sales revenues:		$130,000
Less operating expenses:		
Software licensing	$ 5,000	
Service technicians	35,000	
Research and development	55,000	
Selling expenses	5,000	
Administrative expenses	7,000	107,000
Operating income		$ 23,000

Why:

An income statement is a fundamental means of determining the profitability of a company and reporting these results to stakeholders (shareholders, CRA, suppliers, and employees). Once operating income is determined, the income tax liability can be calculated. A service firm's income statement is significantly different from the income statement of a manufacturing firm.

FLOW OF COSTS THROUGH THE GENERAL LEDGER

For every company, the flow of costs through the general ledger is a critical accounting procedure. In the above analysis, we have shown how various statements are prepared and amounts calculated. Exhibit 2.7 shows how this information flows through the various accounts in the general ledger during the accounting period.

Cost Flow for Manufacturing Company

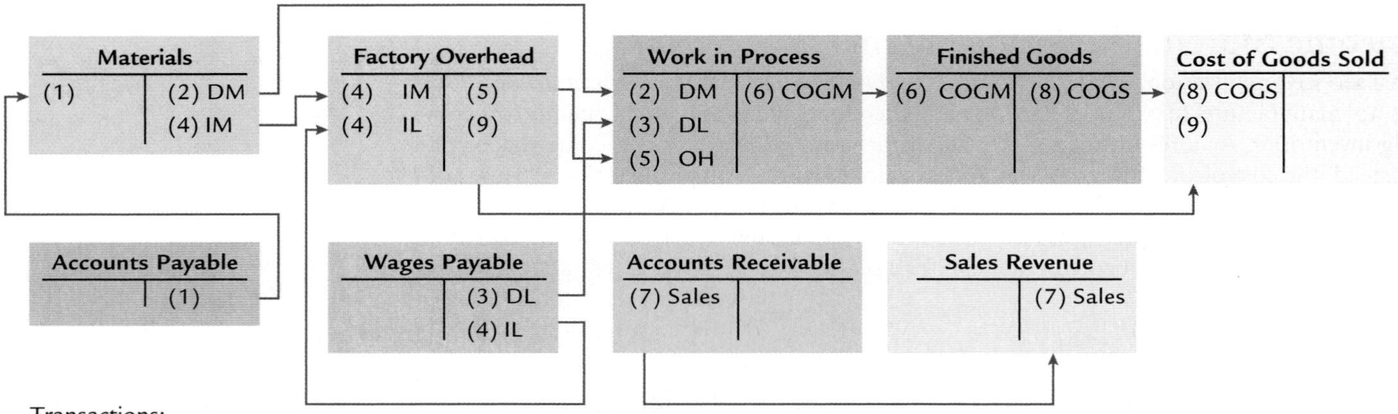

Transactions:
(1) Materials purchased.
(2) Materials requisitioned to jobs.
(3) Direct labour used in production of jobs.
(4) Factory overhead incurred in production of jobs.
(5) Factory overhead applied to jobs by the predetermined overhead rate.
(6) Jobs completed.
(7) Units of the completed jobs that were sold.
(8) Cost of the units sold.
(9) Close underapplied factory overhead to cost of goods sold.

SUMMARY OF LEARNING OBJECTIVES

LO1. Explain the meaning of cost and how costs are assigned to products and services.

- Cost is the cash or cash-equivalent value sacrificed for goods and services that are expected to bring a current or future benefit to the organization.
- Managers use cost information to determine the cost of objects such as products, projects, plants, and customers.
- Direct costs are traced to cost objects based on cause-and-effect relationships.
- Indirect (i.e., overhead) costs are allocated to cost objects based on assumed relationships and convenience.

LO2. Define the various costs of manufacturing products and providing services as well as the costs of selling and administration.

- Products are goods that are either purchased or produced by converting raw materials through the use of labour and indirect manufacturing resources, such as plants, land, and machinery. Services are tasks performed for a customer, or activities performed by a customer using an organization's products or facilities.
- Product costs are those costs, both direct and indirect, of acquiring a product in a merchandising business and preparing it for sale, or of producing a product in a manufacturing business. Product costs are classified as inventory on the balance sheet and then expensed as COGS on the income statement when the inventory is sold.

- Selling costs are the costs of marketing and distributing goods and services, and administrative costs are the costs of organizing and running a company.
- Both selling and administrative costs are period costs.

LO3. Prepare income statements for manufacturing and service organizations.

- The COGM represents the total product cost of goods *completed* during the period and transferred to finished goods inventory. The COGS represents the cost of goods that were sold during the period and, therefore, transferred from finished goods inventory to COGS. For a retailer, there is no COGM, and COGS equals the beginning inventory plus net purchases minus ending inventory.
- For manufacturing and merchandising firms, COGS is subtracted from sales revenue to arrive at gross margin. In addition, for manufacturing firms, COGM must first be calculated before calculating COGS.
- Service firms do not calculate gross margin because they do not purchase or produce inventory for sale and, as a result, do not have a COGS (i.e., inventory expense).
- All firms next subtract selling and administrative expense to arrive at operating income.

SUMMARY OF IMPORTANT EQUATIONS

1. $\text{Total product cost} = \text{Direct materials} + \text{Direct labour} + \text{Manufacturing overhead}$
2. $\text{Unit product cost} = \dfrac{\text{Total product cost}}{\text{Number of units}}$
3. $\text{Prime cost} = \text{Direct materials} + \text{Direct labour}$
4. $\text{Conversion cost} = \text{Direct labour} + \text{Manufacturing overhead}$
5. $\text{Direct materials used in production} = \text{Beginning inventory of materials} + \text{Purchases} - \text{Ending inventory of materials}$
6. $\text{Cost of goods manufactured} = \text{Direct materials used in production} + \text{Direct labour used in production} + \text{Manufacturing overhead costs used in production} + \text{Beginning WIP inventory} - \text{Ending WIP inventory}$
7. $\text{Cost of goods sold} = \text{Beginning finished goods inventory} + \text{Cost of goods manufactured} - \text{Ending finished goods inventory}$

CORNERSTONES

GLOSSARY

Accumulating costs The way that costs are measured and recorded. (p. 32)

Administrative costs All costs associated with research, development, and general administration of the organization that cannot reasonably be assigned to either selling or production. (p. 42)

Allocation When an indirect cost is assigned to a cost object using a reasonable and convenient method. (p. 36)

Assigning costs The way that a cost is linked to some cost object. (p. 33)

Conversion cost The sum of direct labour cost and overhead cost. (p. 40)

Cost The amount of cash or cash equivalent sacrificed for goods and/or services that are expected to bring a current or future benefit to the organization. (p. 32)

Cost object Any item such as a product, customer, department, project, and so on, for which costs are measured and assigned. (p. 33)

Cost of goods manufactured The total product cost of goods completed during the current period. (p. 45)

Cost of goods sold The total product cost of goods sold during the period. (p. 38)

Direct costs Costs that can be easily and accurately traced to a cost object. (p. 35)

Direct labour The labour that can be directly traced to the goods or services being produced. (p. 39)

Direct labour cost The wages of employees who are integral to the finished product. (p. 44)

Direct materials Materials that are a part of the final product and can be directly traced to the goods or services being produced. (p. 39)

Direct materials cost The cost of any materials that are an integral part of the finished product. (p. 43)

Expenses Costs that are used up (expired) in the production of revenue. (p. 32)

Finished goods inventory Completed products that have not yet been sold. (p. 44)

Fixed cost Cost that, in total, is constant as the level of output increases or decreases. (p. 36)

Gross margin The difference between sales revenue and cost of goods sold. (p. 51)

Indirect costs Costs that cannot be easily and accurately traced to a cost object. (p. 35)

Indirect labour Labour costs incurred in the manufacturing process that cannot easily be traced to a product and are, therefore, part of manufacturing overhead and are allocated to products as part of manufacturing overhead. (p. 44)

Indirect materials Materials that are consumed in the manufacturing process that cannot be easily traced to a product and are included in manufacturing overhead and allocated to the product. (p. 43)

Manufacturing costs The total product cost of goods completed during the current period, equal to direct materials cost plus direct labour cost plus manufacturing overhead cost. (p. 44)

Manufacturing organizations Organizations that produce products. (p. 37)

Manufacturing overhead All product costs other than direct materials and direct labour. In a manufacturing firm, manufacturing overhead is also known as *factory burden* or *indirect* manufacturing costs. Costs are included in manufacturing overhead if they cannot be traced to the cost object of interest (e.g., unit of product). (p. 39)

Manufacturing overhead cost Combined costs that are incurred in the manufacturing process other than direct materials cost and direct labour cost. (p. 44)

Materials inventory The costs of direct and indirect materials that have not entered the manufacturing process. (p. 44)

Opportunity cost The benefit given up or sacrificed when one alternative is chosen over another. (p. 33)

Period costs Costs that are expensed in the period in which they are incurred; they are not inventoried. (p. 41)

Price The revenue per unit. (p. 32)

Prime cost The sum of direct materials cost and direct labour cost. (p. 40)

Product (manufacturing) costs Costs associated with the manufacture of goods or the provision of services. Product costs include direct materials, direct labour, and overhead. (p. 38)

Products Goods produced by converting raw materials through the use of labour and indirect manufacturing resources, such as the manufacturing plant, land, and machinery. (p. 37)

Selling costs Those costs necessary to market, distribute, and service a product or service. (p. 42)

Service organizations Organizations that produce intangible products. (p. 37)

Services Tasks or activities performed for a customer, or an activity performed by a customer using an organization's products or facilities. (p. 37)

Variable cost Cost that, in total, varies in direct proportion to changes in output. (p. 36)

Work-in-process (WIP) inventory The cost of the partially completed goods that are still being worked on at the end of a time period. (p. 44)

REVIEW PROBLEM

Product Costs, Cost of Goods Manufactured Statement, and the Income Statement

Brody Company makes industrial cleaning solvents. Various chemicals, detergent, and water are mixed together and then bottled in 10-litre drums. Brody provided the following information for last year:

Raw materials purchases	$250,000
Direct labour	140,000
Depreciation on factory equipment	45,000
Depreciation on factory building	30,000
Depreciation on headquarters building	50,000
Factory insurance	15,000
Property taxes:	
Factory	20,000
Headquarters	18,000
Utilities for factory	34,000
Utilities for sales office	1,800
Administrative salaries	150,000
Indirect labour salaries	156,000
Sales office salaries	90,000
Beginning balance, raw materials	124,000
Beginning balance, WIP	124,000
Beginning balance, finished goods	84,000
Ending balance, raw materials	102,000
Ending balance, WIP	130,000
Ending balance, finished goods	82,000

Last year, Brody completed 100,000 units. Sales revenue equalled $1,200,000, and Brody paid a sales commission of 5 percent of sales.

Required:

1. Calculate the direct materials used in production for last year.
2. Calculate total prime cost.
3. Calculate total conversion cost.
4. Prepare a cost of goods manufactured statement for last year. Calculate the unit product cost.
5. Prepare a cost of goods sold statement for last year.
6. Prepare an income statement for last year. Show the percentage of sales that each line item represents.

Solution:

1. Direct materials = $124,000 + $250,000 − $102,000 = $272,000
2. Prime cost = $272,000 + $140,000 = $412,000
3. First, calculate total manufacturing overhead cost:

Depreciation on factory equipment	$ 45,000
Depreciation on factory building	30,000
Factory insurance	15,000
Factory property taxes	20,000
Factory utilities	34,000
Indirect labour salaries	156,000
Total manufacturing overhead	$300,000

Conversion cost = $140,000 + $300,000 = $440,000

4.

Direct materials	$272,000
Direct labour	140,000
Manufacturing overhead	300,000
Total manufacturing cost	712,000
+ Beginning WIP	124,000
− Ending WIP	130,000
Cost of goods manufactured	$706,000

$$\text{Unit product cost} = \frac{\$706{,}000}{100{,}000 \text{ units}} = \$7.06$$

5.

Cost of goods manufactured	$706,000
+ Beginning inventory, finished goods	84,000
− Ending inventory, finished goods	82,000
Cost of goods sold	$708,000

6. First, compute selling expense and administrative expense:

Utilities, sales office	$ 1,800
Sales office salaries	90,000
Sales commissions ($1,200,000 × 0.05)	60,000
Selling expense	$151,800

Depreciation on headquarters building	$ 50,000
Property taxes, headquarters	18,000
Administrative salaries	150,000
Administrative expense	$218,000

Brody Company
Income Statement
For Last Year

		Percent
Sales	$1,200,000	100.00
Cost of goods sold	708,000	59.00
Gross margin	492,000	41.00
Less:		
Selling expense	151,800	12.65
Administrative expense	218,000	18.17
Operating income	$ 122,200	10.18

DISCUSSION QUESTIONS

1. What is a cost object? Give some examples.
2. What is the difference between accumulating costs and assigning costs?
3. What is a direct cost? An indirect cost? Can the same cost be direct for one purpose and indirect for another? Give an example.
4. What is the cost of goods manufactured?
5. Define *prime cost* and *conversion cost*. Why can't prime cost be added to conversion cost to get total product cost?
6. What is the difference between a product and a service? Give an example of each.
7. Explain the difference between cost and expense.
8. How does a period cost differ from a product cost?
9. What is allocation?
10. Define *manufacturing overhead.*
11. Explain the difference between direct materials purchases in a month and direct materials for the month.
12. Why do firms like to calculate a percentage column on the income statement (in which each line item is expressed as a percentage of sales)?
13. What is the difference between the income statement for a manufacturing firm and the income statement for a service firm?
14. Define *selling costs*. Give five examples of selling costs.
15. What is the difference between cost of goods manufactured and cost of goods sold?

CORNERSTONE EXERCISES

Cornerstone Exercise 2-1 **Total Product Cost and Per-Unit Product Cost**

OBJECTIVE 2
CORNERSTONE 2.1

Slapshot Company makes ice hockey sticks. Last week, direct materials (wood, paint, Kevlar, and resin) costing $48,000 were put into production. Direct labour of $80,000 (= 100 workers × 40 hours × $20 per hour) was incurred. Manufacturing overhead equalled $112,000. By the end of the week, the company had manufactured 8,000 hockey sticks.

Required:

Calculate the total product cost for last week. Also calculate the per-unit cost of one hockey stick that was produced last week.

Cornerstone Exercise 2-2 **Prime Cost and Conversion Cost**

OBJECTIVE 2
CORNERSTONE 2.2

Slapshot Company makes ice hockey sticks. Last week, direct materials (wood, paint, Kevlar, and resin) costing $48,000 were put into production. Direct labour of $80,000 (= 100 workers × 40 hours × $20 per hour) was incurred. Manufacturing overhead equalled $112,000. By the end of the week, the company had manufactured 8,000 hockey sticks.

Required:

Calculate the total prime cost for last week. Calculate the per-unit prime cost. Also calculate the total conversion cost for last week. Calculate the per-unit conversion cost.

Cornerstone Exercise 2-3 **Direct Materials Used in Production**

Slapshot Company makes ice hockey sticks. On June 1, Slapshot had $42,000 of materials in inventory. During the month of June, the company purchased $180,000 of materials. On June 30, materials inventory equalled $51,000.

(Continued)

Required:

Calculate the direct materials used in production for the month of June.

OBJECTIVE 3
CORNERSTONE 2.4

Cornerstone Exercise 2-4 Cost of Goods Manufactured

Slapshot Company makes ice hockey sticks. During the month of June, the company purchased $180,000 of materials. Also during the month of June, Slapshot Company incurred direct labour cost of $165,000 and manufacturing overhead of $215,000. Inventory information is as follows:

	June 1	June 30
Materials	$42,000	$51,000
Work in process	60,000	71,000

Required:

Calculate the cost of goods manufactured for the month of June. Calculate the cost of one hockey stick assuming that 18,000 sticks were completed during June.

OBJECTIVE 3
CORNERSTONE 2.5

Cornerstone Exercise 2-5 Cost of Goods Sold

Slapshot Company makes ice hockey sticks. During the month of June, 18,000 sticks were completed at a cost of goods manufactured of $540,000. Suppose that on June 1, Slapshot had 5,000 units in finished goods inventory costing $160,000 and on June 30, 7,000 units in finished goods inventory costing $215,000.

Required:

Prepare a cost of goods sold statement for the month of June. Calculate the number of sticks that were sold during June.

OBJECTIVE 3
CORNERSTONE 2.6

Cornerstone Exercise 2-6 Manufacturing Firm Income Statement

Slapshot Company makes ice hockey sticks and sold 16,000 sticks during the month of June at a total cost of $485,000. Each stick sold at a price of $90. Slapshot also incurred two types of selling costs: commissions equal to 15 percent of the sales price, and other selling expense of $200,000. Administrative expense totalled $115,000.

Required:

Prepare an income statement for Slapshot for the month of June.

OBJECTIVE 3
CORNERSTONE 2.7

Cornerstone Exercise 2-7 Income Statement Percentages

Slapshot Company makes ice hockey sticks and sold 16,000 sticks during the month of June at a total cost of $485,000. Each stick sold at a price of $90. Slapshot also incurred two types of selling costs: commissions equal to 15 percent of the sales price, and other selling expense of $200,000. Administrative expense totalled $115,000.

Required:

Prepare an income statement for Slapshot for the month of June and calculate the percentage of sales revenue represented by each line of the income statement. Round answers to one decimal place.

OBJECTIVE 3
CORNERSTONE 2.8

Cornerstone Exercise 2-8 Service Organization Income Statement

Allstar Exposure designs and sells advertising services to small, relatively unknown companies. Last month, Allstar had sales commission costs of $50,000, technology costs of $75,000, and research and development costs of $200,000. Selling expenses were $10,000, and administrative expenses equalled $35,000. Sales totalled $410,000.

Required:

Prepare an income statement for Allstar for the past month.

EXERCISES

Exercise 2-9 Cost Assignment

OBJECTIVE 1

An analysis of costs for a small media company in Cornwall, Ontario, revealed that the sales team for the company consists of three different individuals: Peter Piper, Lauren McCarthy, and Elizabeth Alldred. Each of them is deeply involved in selling advertising space in the company's community newspaper as well as on the local community cable channel.

Many tasks must be done to keep the office running efficiently. Lauren is responsible for ensuring that the office runs smoothly and that all ads are properly formatted and placed in the appropriate media. Elizabeth handles all of the accounting in the office. Lauren divides her time, with 75 percent in selling and 25 percent in administration. Elizabeth devotes 40 percent of her time to accounting and the rest to selling. The costs of each are as follows:

	Salary	Commissions
Peter Piper	$ 40,000	$ 40,000
Lauren McCarthy	50,000	35,000
Elizabeth Alldred	50,000	25,000
	$140,000	$100,000

Required:

1. Categorize the costs of the sales team between sales and administrative costs.
2. CONCEPTUAL CONNECTION Why do you think Lauren and Elizabeth are paid more salary than Peter?

Exercise 2-10 Assigning Costs to a Cost Object, Direct and Indirect Costs

OBJECTIVE 1

Hummer Company uses manufacturing cells to produce its products (a cell is a manufacturing unit dedicated to the production of subassemblies or products). One manufacturing cell produces small motors for lawn mowers. Suppose that the motor manufacturing cell is the cost object. Assume that all or a portion of the following costs must be assigned to the cell.

a. Salary of cell supervisor
b. Power to heat and cool the plant in which the cell is located
c. Materials used to produce the motors
d. Maintenance for the cell's equipment (provided by the maintenance department)
e. Labour used to produce motors
f. Cafeteria that services the plant's employees
g. Depreciation on the plant
h. Depreciation on equipment used to produce the motors
i. Ordering costs for materials used in production
j. Engineering support (provided by the engineering department)
k. Cost of maintaining the plant and grounds
l. Cost of the plant's personnel office
m. Property tax on the plant and land

Required:

Classify each of the costs as a direct cost or an indirect cost to the motor manufacturing cell.

Exercise 2-11 Total and Unit Product Cost

Martinez Manufacturing Inc. showed the following costs for last month:

Direct materials	$17,000
Direct labour	13,000
Manufacturing overhead	12,000
Selling expense	18,000

Last month, 6,000 units were produced and sold.

Required:

1. Classify each of the costs as product cost or period cost.
2. What is the total product cost for last month?
3. What is the unit product cost for last month?

Exercise 2-12 Cost Classification

Frontenac Company incurred the following costs last year:

Direct materials	$324,000
Factory rent	36,000
Direct labour	180,000
Factory utilities	9,450
Supervision in the factory	75,000
Indirect labour in the factory	45,000
Depreciation on factory equipment	13,500
Sales commissions	40,500
Sales salaries	97,500
Advertising	55,500
Depreciation on the headquarters building	15,000
Salary of the corporate receptionist	45,000
Other administrative costs	262,500
Salary of the factory receptionist	42,000

Required:

1. Classify each of the costs using the following table format. Be sure to total the amounts in each column.
   Example: Direct materials, $324,000.

	Product Cost			Period Cost	
Costs	**Direct Materials**	**Direct Labour**	**Manufacturing Overhead**	**Selling Expense**	**Administrative Expense**
Direct materials	$324,000				

2. What was the total product cost for last year?
3. What was the total period cost for last year?
4. If 30,000 units were produced last year, what was the unit product cost?
5. CONCEPTUAL CONNECTION Why are certain costs contained in the cost of the product and others are not?

Exercise 2-13 Classifying Cost of Production

A factory manufactures jelly. The jars of jelly are packed six to a box, and the boxes are sold to grocery stores. The following types of costs were incurred in the factory:

Jars
Sugar
Fruit
Pectin (thickener used in jams and jellies)
Boxes
Depreciation on the factory building
Cooking equipment operators' wages
Filling equipment operators' wages
Packers' wages
Janitors' wages
Receptionist's wages
Telephone
Utilities
Rental of Santa Claus suit (for the Christmas party for factory employees' children)
Supervisory labour salaries
Insurance on factory building
Depreciation on factory equipment
Oil to lubricate filling equipment

Required:

Classify each of the costs as direct materials, direct labour, or manufacturing overhead by using the following table. The row for "Jars" is filled in as an example.

Costs	Direct Materials	Direct Labour	Manufacturing Overhead
Jars	X		

Exercise 2-14 Cost Definitions

OBJECTIVE 2

SureShot Company manufactures digital cameras. In January, SureShot produced 19,200 cameras with the following costs:

Direct materials	$1,200,000
Direct labour	240,000
Manufacturing overhead	960,000

There were no beginning or ending inventories of WIP.

Required:

1. What was the total product cost in January?
2. What was the product cost per unit in January?

Exercise 2-15 Prime Cost and Conversion Cost

OBJECTIVE 2

SureShot Company manufactures digital cameras. In January, SureShot produced 19,200 cameras with the following costs:

Direct materials	$1,200,000
Direct labour	240,000
Manufacturing overhead	960,000

There were no beginning or ending inventories of WIP. In addition to these manufacturing costs, the company incurred administrative costs of $2,600,000 and marketing and selling costs of $1,600,000.

Required:

1. What was the total prime cost in January?
2. What was the prime cost per unit in January?
3. What was the total conversion cost in January?
4. What was the conversion cost per unit in January?
5. What is the full cost of a single unit during this accounting period?
6. CONCEPTUAL CONNECTION How would the full cost be used rather than the product costs referred to above?

Exercise 2-16 Direct Materials Used

OBJECTIVE 3

Hannah Bakers makes chocolate chip cookies for cafés and restaurants. In June, Hannah purchased $38,750 of materials. On June 1, the materials inventory was $9,250. On June 30, $4,000 of materials remained in materials inventory.

Required:

What is the cost of the direct materials used in production during June?

Exercise 2-17 Cost of Goods Sold

OBJECTIVE 3

Allyson Ashley makes jet skis. During the year, Allyson manufactured 54,000 jet skis. Finished goods inventory had the following units:

January 1	2,100
December 31	2,750

Required:

1. How many jet skis did Allyson sell during the year?
2. If each jet ski had a product cost of $1,125, what was the cost of goods sold last year?

OBJECTIVE 3

Exercise 2-18 Direct Materials Used, Cost of Goods Manufactured

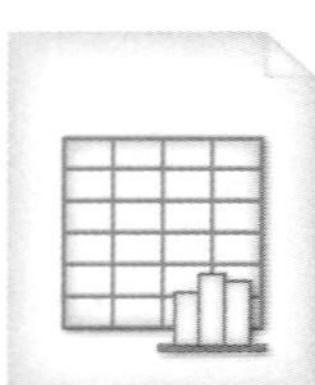

In March, AEK Company purchased materials costing $14,000 and incurred direct labour cost of $20,000. Overhead totalled $36,000 for the month. Information on inventories was as follows:

	March 1	March 31
Materials	$8,600	$2,300
Work in process	1,700	9,000
Finished goods	7,000	6,500

Required:

1. What was the cost of direct materials for March?
2. What was the total manufacturing cost in March?
3. What was the cost of goods manufactured for March?

OBJECTIVE 3

Exercise 2-19 Cost of Goods Sold

Refer to the data provided in **Exercise 2-18**.

Required:

1. What was the cost of goods sold for March?
2. CONCEPTUAL CONNECTION Why was the cost of goods sold different from the cost of goods manufactured?

OBJECTIVE 3

Exercise 2-20 Income Statement Analysis

Jasper Company provided the following information for last year:

Sales in units	280,000
Selling price	$ 12
Direct materials	180,000
Direct labour	505,000
Manufacturing overhead	110,000
Selling expense	437,000
Administrative expense	854,000

Last year, beginning and ending inventories of work in process and finished goods equalled zero.

Required:

1. Prepare an income statement for Jasper for last year.
2. Calculate the percentage of sales for each line item on the income statement. (*Note:* Round percentages to the nearest tenth of a percent.)
3. CONCEPTUAL CONNECTION Briefly explain how a manager could use the income statement created above to better control costs.

OBJECTIVE 3

Exercise 2-21 Income Statement Preparation

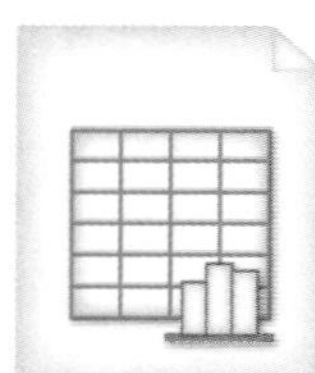

Packers' Nation, an NFL franchise company, generates $62,500,000 in revenues each year. Its gross margin is 37.5 percent. Selling expenses account for two-thirds of its operating expenses and administration costs account for the balance. The income tax rate for the company is 24 percent and the company was able to generate net income of $3,250,000.

Required:

Prepare the income statement for the company.

PROBLEMS

Problem 2-22 Manufacturing, Cost Classification, Income Statement, Product Costs, and Selling and Administrative Costs

OBJECTIVE 2 3

Pop's Drive-Thru Burger Haven produces and sells hamburgers. Each burger is wrapped and put in a "burger bag," which also includes a serving of fries and a soft drink. The price for the burger bag is $3.50. During December, 10,000 burger bags were sold. The restaurant employs students part-time to cook and fill orders. There is one supervisor, the owner, Andrew "Pop" Gallant. Pop's maintains a pool of part-time employees so that the number of employees scheduled can be adjusted to the changes in demand. Demand varies on a weekly as well as a monthly basis.

A janitor is hired to clean the building early each morning. Cleaning supplies are used by the janitor, as well as the staff, to wipe counters, wash cooking equipment, and so on. The building is leased from a local real estate company; it has no seating capacity. All orders are filled on a drive-through basis.

The supervisor schedules work, opens the building, counts the cash, advertises, and is responsible for hiring and firing. The following costs were incurred during December:

Hamburger meat	$4,500	Rent	$1,800
Buns, lettuce, pickles, and onions	800	Depreciation, cooking equipment and fixtures	600
Frozen potato strips	1,250		
Wrappers, bags, and condiment packages	600	Advertising	500
Other ingredients	660	Janitor's wages	520
Part-time employees' wages	7,250	Janitorial supplies	150
Andrew Gallant's salary	3,000	Accounting fees	1,500
Utilities	1,500	Taxes	4,250

Pop's accountant, Elena DeMarco, does the bookkeeping, handles payroll, and files all necessary taxes. She noted that there were no beginning or ending inventories of materials. To simplify accounting for costs, Elena assumed that all part-time employees are production employees and that Andrew Gallant's salary is a selling and administrative expense. She further assumed that all rent and depreciation expenses are part of product cost. Finally, she decided to put all taxes into one category, taxes, and to treat them as an administrative expense.

Required:

1. Classify each of the costs for Pop's December operations using the table format given below. Be sure to total the amounts in each column.

   Example: Hamburger meat, $4,500.

Cost	Direct Materials ($)	Direct Labour ($)	Manufacturing Overhead ($)	Selling and Administrative Expense ($)
Hamburger meat	4,500			
Total				

2. Prepare an income statement for the month of December.
3. Elena made some simplifying assumptions. Were those reasonable? Suppose a good case could be made that the portion of the employees' time spent selling the burger bags was really a part of sales. In that case, would it be better to divide their time between production and selling? Should Andrew Gallant's time be divided between production, and selling and administrative duties? What difference (if any) would that make on the income statement?

Check figures:
1. Total direct materials = $7,810
2. Net income = $6,120

Problem 2-23 Direct and Indirect Costs

OBJECTIVE 

Austen Marner manufactures and sells hockey sticks. During the year, he incurred a variety of costs, including composite materials ($632,000), salaries for 10 workers ($500,000), the salary for one supervisor ($70,000), labelling ink ($12,500), disposable stencils for labelling ($27,500), strapping for packaging sticks in bundles of 10 ($6,250), factory rent ($18,000), and a machine with a cost of $25,000, which has a life of five years.

(*Continued*)

Check figures:

1. Direct cost = $1,144,500
2. Total cost = $1,271,250
3. Per unit = $150
4. Selling price = $250

Required:

1. Categorize the costs into direct and indirect costs of manufacture.
2. Determine the cost of manufacturing the sticks during the year.
3. If 8,475 sticks were manufactured, what is the unit cost?
4. To make a gross margin of 40 percent, how much should he charge per stick?

OBJECTIVE 3

Problem 2-24 Cost of Direct Materials, Cost of Goods Manufactured, Cost of Goods Sold

Kintrix Company manufactures fishing rods. At the beginning of July, the following information was supplied by its accountant:

Raw materials inventory	$120,000
Work-in-process inventory	63,000
Finished goods inventory	69,600

During July, the direct labour cost was $130,500, raw materials purchases were $192,000, and the total overhead cost was $326,250. The inventories at the end of July were:

Raw materials inventory	$59,400
Work-in-process inventory	97,500
Finished goods inventory	66,300

Check figures:

2. Cost of goods manufactured = $674,850
3. Cost of goods sold = $678,150

Required:

1. What is the cost of the direct materials used in production during July?
2. What is the cost of goods manufactured for July?
3. What is the cost of goods sold for July?

OBJECTIVE 3

Problem 2-25 Preparation of Income Statement: Manufacturing Firm

Infinity Inc. manufactures small camping tents. Last year, 200,000 tents were made and sold for $60 each. Each tent includes the following costs:

Direct materials	$18
Direct labour	12
Manufacturing overhead	16

The only selling expenses were a commission of $2 per unit sold and advertising totalling $100,000. Administrative expenses, all fixed, equalled $300,000. There were no beginning or ending finished goods inventories. There were no beginning or ending work-in-process inventories.

Check figures:

1. Total product cost = $9,200,000
2. Operating income = $2,000,000
3. Gross margin = $2,860,000

Required:

1. Calculate the product cost for one tent. Calculate the total product cost for last year.
2. Prepare an income statement for external users. Did you need to prepare a supporting statement of cost of goods manufactured? Explain.
3. CONCEPTUAL CONNECTION Suppose 200,000 tents were produced (and 200,000 sold) but that the company had a beginning finished goods inventory of 10,000 tents produced in the prior year at a cost of $40 per unit. The company follows a first-in, first-out policy for its inventory (meaning that the units produced first are sold first for purposes of cost flow). What effect does this have on the income statement? Show the new statement.

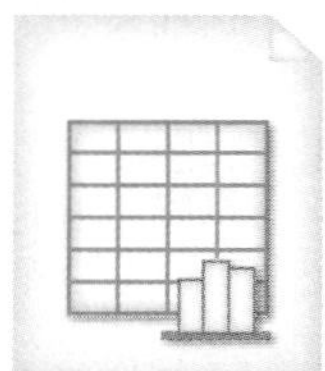

Problem 2-26 Cost of Goods Manufactured, Cost of Goods Sold

Hayward Company, a manufacturing firm, has supplied the following information from its accounting records for the month of May:

Direct labour cost	$10,500
Purchases of raw materials	15,000
Supplies used	675
Factory insurance	350

Commissions paid	2,500
Factory supervision	2,225
Advertising	800
Materials handling	3,750
Materials inventory, May 1	3,475
Work-in-process inventory, May 1	12,500
Finished goods inventory, May 1	6,685
Materials inventory, May 31	9,500
Work-in-process inventory, May 31	14,250
Finished goods inventory, May 31	4,250

Check figures:
1. Cost of goods manufactured = $24,725
2. Cost of goods sold = $27,160

Required:

1. Prepare a statement of cost of goods manufactured.
2. Prepare a statement of cost of goods sold.

OBJECTIVE 1 2

Problem 2-27 Cost Identification

Following is a list of cost items described in the chapter as well as a list of brief descriptive settings for each item.

Cost terms:

a. Opportunity cost
b. Period cost
c. Product cost
d. Direct labour cost
e. Selling cost
f. Conversion cost
g. Prime cost
h. Direct materials cost
i. Manufacturing overhead cost
j. Administrative cost

Settings:

1. Marcus Burbosa, manager of Timmins Optical, estimated that the cost of plastic, wages of the technician producing the lenses, and overhead totalled $30 per pair of single-vision lenses.
2. Linda was having a hard time deciding whether to return to school. She was concerned about the salary she would have to give up for the next four years.
3. Randy Harris is the finished goods warehouse manager for a medium-sized manufacturing firm. He is paid a salary of $90,000 per year. As he studied the financial statements prepared by a local CPA, he wondered how his salary was treated.
4. Jamie Young is in charge of the legal department at company headquarters. Her salary is $95,000 per year. She reports to the chief executive officer.
5. This category includes all factory costs that are not classified as direct materials or direct labour.
6. The new product required machining, assembly, and painting. The design engineer asked the accounting department to estimate the labour cost of each of the three operations. The engineer supplied the estimated labour hours for each operation.
7. After obtaining the estimate of direct labour cost, the design engineer estimated the cost of the materials that would be used for the new product.
8. The design engineer totalled the costs of materials and direct labour for the new product.
9. The design engineer also estimated the cost of converting the raw materials into their final form.
10. The auditor for a soft drink bottling plant pointed out that the depreciation on the delivery trucks had been incorrectly assigned to product cost (through overhead). Accordingly, the depreciation charge was reallocated on the income statement.

Required:

1. Match the items with the settings. More than one cost classification may be associated with each setting; however, select the setting that seems to fit the item best. When you are done, each cost term will be used just once.
2. CONCEPTUAL CONNECTION Explain how there can be so many different types of costs even though there aren't that many different items of cost.

OBJECTIVE 2 3

Problem 2-28 Income Statement, Cost of Services Provided, Service Attributes

Berry Company is an architectural firm located in Toronto, Ontario. The company works with small and medium-sized construction businesses to prepare building plans according to client contracts. Berry employs 10 professionals and 5 staff. The following data are provided for last year:

Number of designs completed and sold	700
Beginning inventory of direct materials	$ 20,000
Beginning inventory of designs in process	60,000
Ending inventory of direct materials	0
Ending inventory of designs in process	100,000
Purchases, direct materials	40,000
Direct labour	800,000
Manufacturing overhead	100,000
Administrative expense	150,000
Selling expense	60,000

Required:

1. Calculate the cost of services sold.
2. Assume that the average fee for a design is $2,100. Prepare an income statement for Berry Company.
3. Refer to the cost of services sold (calculated in Requirement 1). What is the dominant cost? Will this always be true of service organizations? If not, provide an example of an exception.
4. CONCEPTUAL CONNECTION Why does Berry Company show a zero inventory of finished plans? What change(s) in the company could result in a positive finished goods inventory?

Check figure:
1. Cost of services sold = $920,000

OBJECTIVE 3

Problem 2-29 Cost of Goods Manufactured, Income Statement

W.W. Phillips Company produced 4,000 leather recliners during the year. These recliners sell for $400 each. Phillips had 500 recliners in finished goods inventory at the beginning of the year. At the end of the year, there were 700 recliners in finished goods inventory. Phillips' accounting records provide the following information:

Purchases of raw materials	$320,000	Salary, sales supervisor	$ 90,000
Beginning materials inventory	46,800	Commissions, salespersons	180,000
Ending materials inventory	66,800	General administration	300,000
Direct labour	200,000	Beginning work-in-process inventory	13,040
Indirect labour	40,000	Ending work-in-process inventory	14,940
Rent, factory building	42,000	Beginning finished goods inventory	80,000
Depreciation, factory equipment	60,000	Ending finished goods inventory	114,100
Utilities, factory	11,900		

Required:

1. Prepare a statement of cost of goods manufactured.
2. Compute the average cost of producing one unit of product in the year.
3. Prepare an income statement for external users.

Check figure:
3. Operating income = $332,100

OBJECTIVE 1

Problem 2-30 Cost Definitions

Luisa Giovanni is a student at Niagara University. To help pay her way through university, Luisa started a dog walking service. She has 12 client dogs—six are walked on the first shift (6:30 a.m. and 5:00 p.m.), and six are walked on the second shift (7:30 a.m. and 6:00 p.m.).

Last month, Luisa noted the following:

a. Purchase of three leashes at $10 each (she carries these with her in case a leash breaks during a walk).
b. Internet service cost of $40 a month. This enables her to keep in touch with the owners, bill them by email, and so on.

c. Dog treats of $50 to reward each dog at the end of each walk.
d. A heavy-duty raincoat and hat for $100.
e. Partway through the month, Luisa's friend Jason offered her a chance to play a bit role in a movie that was shooting on location in Toronto. The job paid $100 and would have required Luisa to be on location at 6:00 a.m. and to remain for 12 hours. Regretfully, Luisa turned it down.
f. The owners pay Luisa $250 per month per dog for her services.

Required:

1. At the end of the month, how would Luisa classify her Internet payment of $40—as a cost on the balance sheet or as an expense on the income statement?
2. Which of the above is an opportunity cost? Why?
3. What price is charged? What is Luisa's total revenue for a month?

Problem 2-31 Cost Identification and Analysis, Cost Assignment, Income Statement

OBJECTIVE 1 2 3

Peter Kanakarian has decided to open a printing shop. He has secured two contracts: (1) a five-year contract to print a popular regional magazine (5,000 copies each month), and (2) a three-year agreement to print tourist brochures for the province (10,000 brochures per month).

Peter has rented a building for $1,400 per month. His printing equipment was purchased for $40,000 and has a life expectancy of 20,000 hours with no salvage value. Depreciation is assigned to a period based on the hours of usage. Peter has scheduled the delivery of the products so that two production runs are needed. In the first run, the equipment is prepared for the magazine printing. In the second run, the equipment is reconfigured for brochure printing. It takes twice as long to configure the equipment for the magazine setup as it does for the brochure setup. The total setup costs per month are $600.

Insurance costs for the building and equipment are $140 per month. Power to operate the printing equipment is strongly related to machine usage. The printing equipment causes virtually all the power costs. Power costs will run $350 per month. Printing materials will cost $0.40 per copy for the magazine and $0.08 per copy for the brochure. Peter will hire workers to run the presses as needed (part-time workers are easy to hire). He must pay $10 per hour. Each worker can produce 20 copies of the magazine per printing hour or 100 copies of the brochure. Distribution costs are $500 per month. Peter will receive a salary of $1,500 per month. He is responsible for personnel, accounting, sales, and production—in effect, he is responsible for administering all aspects of the business.

Required:

1. What are the total monthly manufacturing costs?
2. What are the total monthly prime costs? Total monthly prime costs for the regional magazine? For the brochure?
3. What are the total monthly conversion costs? Suppose Peter wants to determine monthly conversion costs for each product. Assign monthly conversion costs to each product using direct tracing and relationship tracing whenever possible. For those costs that cannot be assigned using a tracing approach, you may assign them using direct labour hours.
4. Peter receives $1.80 per copy of the magazine and $0.45 per brochure. Prepare an income statement for the first month of operations.

Check figures:
2. Magazine total prime costs = $4,500
4. Income before taxes = $2,010

Problem 2-32 Cost Analysis, Income Statement

Stampede Automotive Sound Systems puts on tent sales five to six times a year in various cities throughout Alberta. The tent sales are designed to show customers new products, engender enthusiasm about those products, and sell soon-to-be out-of-date products at greatly reduced prices. Each tent sale lasts one day and requires parking lot space to set up the Stampede semitrailer; a couple of show cars; a deejay playing music; and a tent to sell sound system merchandise, distribute brochures, and so on.

(Continued)

Last year, the Edmonton tent sale was held in a far corner of the parking lot outside the city exhibition hall where the automotive show was in progress. Because most customers were interested more in the new model cars than in the refurbishment of their current cars, foot traffic was low. In addition, customers did not want to carry speakers and amplifiers all the way back to where they had originally parked. Total direct costs for this tent sale were $14,300. Direct costs included gasoline and fuel for three pickup trucks and the semitrailer; wages and per diem for the five Stampede personnel who travelled to the show; rent on the parking lot space; and depreciation on the semitrailer, pickups, tent, tables (in tent), and sound equipment. Revenue was $20,000. Cost of goods sold for the sound systems was $7,000.

Required:

1. How do you suppose Stampede accounts for the costs of the tent sales? What income statement items are affected by the tent sales?
2. What was the profit (loss) from the Edmonton tent sale? What do you think Stampede might do to make it more profitable in the future?

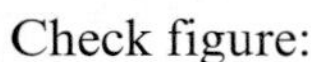
Check figure:

2. Tent sale loss = $(1,300)

OBJECTIVE 1 2

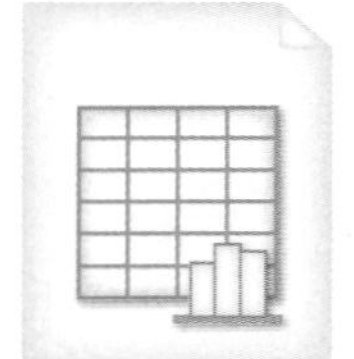

Problem 2-33 Cost Analysis, Income Statement, Manufacturing Firm

Quadrant Corporation, a major producer of machine parts, recorded the following information for its year ended September 30, 2018 (all figures in thousands of dollars):

Cash	$ 15,000
Accounts Receivable (October 1, 2017)	24,642
Accounts Receivable (September 30, 2018)	28,768
Finished Goods Inventory (October 1, 2017)	36,555
Finished Goods Inventory (September 30, 2018)	38,775
Work-in-Process Inventory (October 1, 2017)	9,624
Work-in-Process Inventory (September 30, 2018)	10,007
Raw Materials Inventory (October 1, 2017)	2,685
Raw Materials Inventory (September 30, 2018)	2,992
Property, Plant, and Equipment (October 1, 2017)	88,374
Property, Plant, and Equipment (September 30, 2018)	96,052
Goodwill (October 1, 2017)	24,327
Goodwill (September 30, 2018)	16,378
Accounts Payable (October 1, 2017)	8,627
Accounts Payable (September 30, 2018)	8,997
Accrued Liabilities (October 1, 2017)	4,339
Accrued Liabilities (September 30, 2018)	5,685
Taxes Payable (October 1, 2017)	19,727
Taxes Payable (September 30, 2018)	20,654
Long-Term Debt (October 1, 2017)	50,789
Long-Term Debt (September 30, 2018)	37,852
Common Shares (October 1, 2017)	91,627
Common Shares (September 30, 2018)	97,687
Retained Earnings (October 1, 2017)	67,698
Retained Earnings (September 30, 2018)	81,327
Revenues	296,844
Raw Materials Purchases	36,699
Factory Wages Paid	45,772
Factory Overhead	27,556
Selling Expenses	76,251
Administrative Expenses	68,728
Other Corporate Overhead	11,785
Income Tax Expense	8,240

Required:

1. Prepare a cost of goods manufactured statement for 2018.
2. Prepare an income statement for 2018. Calculate the percentage of sales for each line item on the income statement. Round percentages to the nearest tenth of a percent.

Problem 2-34 Cost Analysis and Profitability

OBJECTIVE 1 2

Healy & Sons is a law firm in Red Deer, Alberta. During the past year, the firm experienced some difficulty achieving its hoped-for profitability. The four partners were paid $150,000 each during the year, with an anticipation of adding an additional $125,000 each to their compensation through profit sharing. Each partner receives an equal share of profits after all expenses are paid.

The firm employed two research lawyers, who performed much of the support required for the various cases but did not work directly with clients. Each was paid $125,000 per year. Other support salaries for legal assistants (four at $60,000 per year) and receptionists and clerks (two at $50,000 per year) were treated as indirect costs. All other administrative costs totalled $500,000 for the year.

Peter Healy, the father of the other three lawyers in the firm, had practised for many years, early in his career, with a large firm in Eastern Canada where the billing practice was to charge three times the salary of the person performing the services. He was informed that this worked on the basis of one-third covering the direct cost of salaries, one-third covering the indirect cost of running the office, and one-third representing profit. This was the billing arrangement that he adopted in his firm and it worked very well in the early years.

However, as each of his sons joined the firm, even though revenues increased, profits declined and he couldn't figure out why. He realized that, as the firm expanded, more support costs were required, but he couldn't determine how to change his approach to achieve better profits.

Required:

Advise Peter Healy on how to increase profitability and achieve the objectives he has set.

Problem 2-35 Cost Analysis and Profitability

Miller and Just is a law firm located in Smiths Falls, Ontario. The firm was founded by Samuel Miller and Blaney Just 15 years ago. Both lawyers love the fact that they own and run their own business with little or no need to be involved in the normal office politics of a large law firm. Over the years, they have hired two junior lawyers who work for them at a salary. The firm has hired two secretaries, two administrative assistants, and one receptionist. These jobs are viewed as being well paying jobs in this small community so turnover has been minimal.

Each partner takes out $175,000 each year as salary and they share any profits equally after all expenses have been paid. Since the firm is a partnership, the firm does not pay any taxes but the profits are taxed in the hands of the partners. The two other lawyers are paid a salary of $135,000 each as well as sharing a combined 20 percent of the profits.

The secretaries are each paid $62,500 per year and the administrative assistants are paid $40,000 each. The receptionist receives $32,500 a year. The firm covers all of the professional costs of all four lawyers, including their liability insurance. This amounts to $75,000 per year. Rent, utilities, and office supplies total $250,000 per year.

Required:

1. How much revenue must the firm generate if the partners hope to double their income after profit sharing?
2. If the average per hour fee is $250, how many billable hours must they have among the four lawyers?

PROFESSIONAL EXAMINATION PROBLEMS*

Professional Examination Problem 2-36 Manufacturing Cost—Princeton Manufacturing

The following information pertains to Princeton Manufacturing for 2018:

Direct labour	$ 30,000
Sales	400,000
Selling expenses	50,000
Raw (direct) materials on hand:	
January 1	8,000
December 31	4,000
General and administrative expenses	18,000
Finished goods:	
January 1	25,000
Work-in-process:	
January 1	19,000
December 31	18,000
Direct materials purchases	47,000
Depreciation: factory	20,000
Indirect labour	3,000
Indirect materials used	7,000
Marketing promotions	1,500
Factory taxes	11,000
Utilities	20,000
Courier costs (office)	900
Miscellaneous plant overhead	4,000
Plant repairs and maintenance	9,000
Customer service costs	3,000
Fire insurance: factory equipment	3,000
Materials handling costs	8,000

Additional Information:

a. The gross profit margin is 73.25 percent.
b. Depreciation is charged to production at 70 percent.
c. Utilities are charged to production at 90 percent.

Required:

1. Prepare a schedule of cost of goods manufactured for the year ended December 31.
2. Prepare a schedule of cost of goods sold.
3. Prepare an income statement for the year ended December 31.

Professional Examination Problem 2-37 Cost Classification and Behaviour—Multiple Choice

1. Consider a single hard copy of this textbook as a cost object. What would be the best two labels to classify the relation between this cost object and the following two costs of producing the cost object respectively: (1) the paper; and (2) the one-time fees paid to the authors (i.e., not royalties)?

   a. (1) direct cost; (2) variable cost
   b. (1) variable cost; (2) unavoidable cost
   c. (1) fixed cost; (2) variable cost
   d. (1) direct cost; (2) fixed cost
   e. (1) avoidable cost; (2) variable cost

2. Given a cost has already been identified as a variable cost, which of the following additional descriptions of the cost is incompatible with that identification?
   a. The cost, in total, does not change with changes in the volume of the cost item.
   b. The cost can be traced directly to the cost object.
   c. The cost, in total, does change with changes in the volume of the cost item.
   d. The cost cannot be traced directly to the cost object.
   e. The cost is not a prime cost.

3. The total direct labour cost of producing 100 units of Product X is $50. The direct materials cost of producing the 100 units is perfectly variable and the cost item is the number of units produced. The cost of the direct materials traced to each unit is $1.25. Indirect costs are completely fixed at $75 for the production of the 100 units. What are the total conversion costs for the 100 units of Product X?
   a. $125
   b. $175
   c. $200
   d. $250
   e. $275

CASES

Case 2-38 Cost Classification, Income Statement

Gateway Construction Company is a family-operated business that was founded in 1950 by Samuel Gateway. In the beginning, the company consisted of Gateway and three employees laying gas, water, and sewage pipelines as subcontractors. Currently, the company employs 25 to 30 people; Jack Gateway, Samuel's son, directs it. The main line of business continues to be laying pipeline.

Most of Gateway's work comes from contracts with city and provincial agencies. All of the company's work is located in Manitoba. The company's sales volume averages $3 million, and profits vary between 0 and 10 percent of sales.

Sales and profits have been somewhat below average for the past three years due to a recession and intense competition. Because of this competition, Jack Gateway is constantly reviewing the prices that other companies bid for jobs; when a bid is lost, he makes every attempt to analyze the reasons for the differences between his bid and those of his competitors. He uses this information to increase the competitiveness of future bids.

Jack has become convinced that Gateway's current accounting system is deficient. Currently, all expenses are simply deducted from revenues to arrive at operating income. No effort is made to distinguish among the costs of laying pipe, obtaining contracts, and administering the company. Yet all bids are based on the costs of laying pipe.

With these thoughts in mind, Jack began a careful review of the income statement for the previous year (see below). First, he noted that jobs were priced on the basis of equipment hours, with an average price of $165 per equipment hour. However, when it came to classifying and assigning costs, he decided that he needed some help. One thing that really puzzled him was how to classify his own salary of $114,000. About half of his time was spent in bidding and securing contracts, and the other half was spent in general administrative matters.

Gateway Construction
Income Statement
For the Year Ended December 31, 2018

Sales (18,200 equipment hours @ $165 per hour)		$3,003,000
Less expenses:		
Utilities	$ 24,000	
Machine operators	218,000	
Rent, office building	24,000	
CPA fees	20,000	

(Continued)

Other direct labour	265,700	
Administrative salaries	114,000	
Supervisory salaries	70,000	
Pipe	1,401,340	
Tires and fuel	418,600	
Depreciation, equipment	198,000	
Salaries of mechanics	50,000	
Advertising	15,000	
Total expenses		2,818,640
Income before income taxes		$ 184,360

Required:

1. Classify the costs in the income statement as (1) costs of laying pipe (production costs), (2) costs of securing contracts (selling costs), or (3) costs of general administration. For production costs, identify direct materials, direct labour, and overhead costs. The company never has significant work in process (most jobs are started and completed within a week).
2. Assume that a significant reason for costs to change is equipment hours. Identify the expenses that would likely be traced to jobs using this driver. Explain why you feel these costs are traceable using equipment hours. What is the cost per equipment hour for these traceable costs?

OBJECTIVE 1 2 3

Case 2-39 Cost Information and Decision Making

Peter Boking has worked as a muffler mechanic for several years and believes that he could make more money by starting his own muffler shop. He has the commitment from his father to finance the business. Peter must decide whether to sell high-quality mufflers intended for the automobile enthusiast or target the regular automobile owner. He has done quite a bit of investigation and believes that he could sell 900 high-quality mufflers a year at $2,000 each. On the other hand, he believes that he could sell 1,200 mufflers if he concentrated on standard mufflers at $1,000 each. The high-end mufflers would cost him $1,050 each while the standard ones would be $400 each. He would spend half his time installing mufflers and would need to hire six mechanics at $20 per hour. The mechanics would work an average of 2,000 hours per year. He has located a place that would be a suitable location, no matter which alternative he chose, at a rent of $120,000 per year. Utilities would be $18,000 per year.

He would need to acquire equipment such as hoists, tools, and storage racks. The nature of the equipment would differ depending on the choice he made with respect to the quality of mufflers being sold. The depreciation would be $105,000 per year for the high-end mufflers and $65,000 per year for the standard mufflers. He has found a person to handle all of the administration of the business at a cost of $50,000 per year, including all administration expenses. Advertising, which would be his only additional selling cost, would be either $15,000 per month for the high-end mufflers or $10,000 per month for the standard mufflers.

He hopes to be able to pay himself a salary of $100,000 for his own efforts in the business, half installation and half selling.

Required:

1. Prepare income statements for each alternative, separating costs into direct and indirect costs.
2. Is the business profitable enough for Peter to justify quitting his job and starting his own business?
3. Which alternative should Peter choose?

Case 2-40 Cost Information and Ethical Behaviour, Service Organization

Sydney Malkin, an architect in a small town in Saskatchewan, was asked to bid on a major project to build a new arena for the city. While he had never been involved in such a project, he had played hockey in the junior leagues and felt that he could design a beautiful arena. In addition to being a skilled architect, he was a close friend of Freddie Sacic, the chief administrative officer of the city. They played hockey together, lived close to each other, and had kids on the same hockey team.

From a professional point of view, this project could position Sydney and his growing firm as a potential leader in the region for other similar projects. Success in winning the job would have major financial and professional benefits for Sydney.

Sydney knew that Freddie, a professional accountant, would be involved in reviewing the submissions for the new arena and could significantly influence the final decision. Over a period of several months, whenever he had a chance Sydney would speak to Freddie, on an unofficial basis, about the project. Freddie always encouraged him to prepare the best possible bid and to ensure that his cost estimates were as accurate as possible.

Sydney was becoming frustrated because, as much as he talked to Freddie, he could not get any specific guidance on how to formulate his bid. Finally, as the bid deadline got very close, Sydney visited Freddie at home and began to talk about the bid for the new arena. Sydney told Freddie that winning the job would put him in a very good position, both financially and professionally. He told Freddie that, if he was successful, he would make sure that Freddie and his wife could join Sydney and his wife on a holiday to Hawaii at Sydney's expense. They had holidayed together on one other occasion and no one needed to know that Sydney would pay all the expenses of the holiday for both couples.

Required:

What should Freddie do? Explain.

3

Cost Behaviour

After studying Chapter 3, you should be able to:

1. Explain the meaning of cost behaviour, and define and describe fixed and variable costs.
2. Define and describe mixed costs and step costs.
3. Separate mixed costs into their fixed and variable components using the high–low method and the scattergraph method.
4. (*Appendix 3A*) Separate mixed costs into their fixed and variable components using the method of least squares.
5. (*Appendix 3A*) Use a personal computer spreadsheet program to perform the method of least squares.

Smontgom65/Dreamstime.com

EXPERIENCE MANAGERIAL DECISIONS
with Zingerman's

Often people think of income statements in the form learned in financial accounting—with all of the sales and expenses shown for the company as a whole. This may be sufficient for external parties, such as investors and banks. However, companies with more than one business segment need to know how each segment is performing as well. Zingerman's Delicatessen has eight separate businesses. Seven of these segments—the Delicatessen, Mail Order, Bakehouse, ZingTrain, Roadhouse Restaurant, Creamery, and Coffee Company—sell to external customers. The eighth segment, ZingNet, provides payroll, accounting, and human resources services to the other seven segments.

In looking at the segments, it is easy to see that each has both variable and fixed costs. For example, Roadhouse Restaurant has variable costs of food, beverages, paper products, and some labour. Direct fixed costs for Roadhouse include rent/depreciation for the building, furniture, and equipment. In addition, there are common costs.

All seven external customer-oriented Zingerman businesses use ZingNet (part of the Zingerman conglomerate of businesses) to provide support services, such as human resources, payroll, organizational marketing, graphics brand design, information technology, administration, accounting, and office rental. The allocation of the ZingNet costs is done on the basis of revenues for each business. Zingerman executives note that this method of allocation can occasionally cause problems among the other businesses– especially those that do not use much of the ZingNet services, but have high sales (thereby getting a larger share of ZingNet cost allocation). The use of variable costing and segmented income statements can help to overcome this kind of problem, since a properly developed segmented income statement separates direct fixed costs from common fixed costs. Treating the ZingNet costs as common fixed costs would also be consistent with Zingerman's belief that ZingNet costs are an investment in future profitability.

Zingerman's®

© Ryan Stiner

In Chapter 2, we discussed various types of costs and took a close look at manufacturing and service costs. However, the primary concern of the chapter was organizing costs into production, selling, and administrative costs. Related schedules of the cost of goods manufactured, cost of goods sold, and income statements were built. Now it is time to focus on cost behaviour—the way costs change as the related activity changes.

Cost behaviour represents the foundation on which managerial accounting is built, much like the critical role played by accounting principles in financial accounting. Financial accounting contains critical assumptions (e.g., the economic entity assumption) and principles (e.g., matching principle), in order to help financial accountants properly record transactions and prepare financial statements. In much the same way, managers must properly understand cost behaviour in order to make wise decisions. For example, a Grant Thornton survey of 300 business leaders and senior executives reported that 79 percent of CEOs focus on understanding and managing costs in an attempt to increase company value.[1] This textbook provides numerous examples of how understanding cost behaviour improves managerial decision making.

Costs can be variable, fixed, or mixed. Knowing how costs change as output changes is essential for managers in planning, controlling, and decision making. For example, suppose that BlueDenim Company expects demand for its jeans to increase by 10 percent next year. How will that affect the total costs budgeted for the factory? Clearly, BlueDenim will need 10 percent more raw materials (denim, thread, zippers, and so on). In addition, it will need more cutting and sewing labour because someone will need to make the additional jeans, so these costs are variable in nature. But the factory building will probably not need to be expanded. Neither will the factory need an additional receptionist or plant manager. So those costs are fixed in nature. As long as BlueDenim's accountant understands the behaviour of the fixed and variable costs, it will be possible to develop a fairly accurate budget for the next year.

Budgeting, deciding to keep or drop a product line, and evaluating the performance of each segment all benefit from knowledge of cost behaviour. (For example, in 2001, Canadian Tire Corporation, Limited bought Mark's Work Wearhouse; in 2009, it decided to get out of the online sales business; in 2011, it acquired The Forzani Group Ltd. All of these decisions were based on an understanding of the costs and benefits involved.) In fact, failure to know and understand cost behaviour can lead to poor—even disastrous—decisions. This chapter discusses cost behaviour in depth so that a proper foundation can be laid for its use in studying other cost management topics.

BASICS OF COST BEHAVIOUR

OBJECTIVE 1

Explain the meaning of cost behaviour, and define and describe fixed and variable costs.

Cost behaviour is the general term to describe how a cost changes when the level of activity changes. A cost that does not change in total as activity changes is a *fixed cost*. A *variable cost*, on the other hand, increases in total with an increase in activity and decreases in total with a decrease in activity. Let's first review the basics of cost and output measures. Then we will look at fixed and variable costs.

Measures of Output

In order to determine the behaviour of a cost, we need to have a good grasp of the cost under consideration and a measure of the output associated with the activity. The terms *fixed cost* and *variable cost* do not exist in a vacuum; they only have meaning when related to some output measure. In other words, a cost is fixed or variable with respect to some output measure or cost driver. In order to understand the behaviour of costs, we must first determine the underlying business activity and ask ourselves "What causes the cost

[1] Grant Thornton LLP Survey of U.S. Business Leaders, 12th Edition, 2006.

of this particular activity to go up (or down)?" A **cost driver** is a causal measurement that causes costs to change. Identifying and managing cost drivers helps managers to better predict and control costs.

Let's look at some examples. Suppose that BlueDenim Company wants to classify its product costs as either variable or fixed with respect to the number of jeans produced. In this case, the number of jeans produced is the cost driver. Clearly, the use of raw materials (denim, thread, zippers, and buttons) varies with the number of jeans produced. So, we would say that materials costs are variable with respect to the number of units produced. How about direct labour to operate the sewing machines? That, too, is variable with respect to the number of jeans produced because the more jeans that are produced, the more operators we need to use the sewing machines. Finally, what about the cost of supervision for the sewing department? Whether the company produces many pairs of jeans or fewer pairs of jeans, the cost of supervision is unchanged. So, we would say that supervision is fixed with respect to the number of jeans produced.

Fixed Costs

Fixed costs are costs that *in total* are constant as the level of output increases or decreases. For example, a fleet of airplanes represents a fixed cost to an airline because the cost does not change as the number of flights or the number of passengers changes. Similarly, the rental cost of warehouse space by a wholesaler is fixed for the term of the lease. If the wholesaler's sales go up or down, the cost of the leased warehouse stays the same.

To illustrate fixed cost behaviour, consider a factory operated by Custom Bicycles, a British Columbia company that produces high-quality bicycles. The assembly department of the factory assembles components into completed bicycles. Assume that Custom Bicycles wants to look at the cost relationship between supervision cost and the number of bicycles assembled. The assembly department can assemble up to 50,000 bicycles per year. The assemblers (direct labour) are supervised by a production line manager who is paid $32,000 per year. The factory was established five years ago. Currently, the factory assembles 40,000 to 50,000 bicycles per year. Since inception, production has never fallen below 20,000 bicycles in a year. The cost of supervision for several levels of production is as follows:

Custom Bicycles
Cost of Supervision

Number of Bicycles Assembled	Total Cost of Supervision ($)	Unit Cost ($)
20,000	32,000	1.60
30,000	32,000	1.07
40,000	32,000	0.80
50,000	32,000	0.64

The cost relationship considered is between supervision cost and the number of bicycles assembled. The number of bicycles assembled is called the *output measure*, or *cost driver*. Notice that the *total* cost of supervision remains constant within this range as more bicycles are assembled. Custom Bicycles pays $32,000 for supervision regardless of whether it assembles 20,000, 40,000, or 50,000 bicycles.

Pay particular attention to the words *in total* in the definition of fixed costs. While the total cost of supervision remains unchanged as more bicycles are assembled, the unit cost per bicycle does change as the level of output changes. As the example in the table shows, the unit cost of supervision decreases from $1.60 to $0.64. Because of the behaviour of per-unit fixed costs, it is easy to get the impression that the fixed costs themselves are affected by changes in the level of output. But that is not true. Instead, higher output means that the fixed costs can be spread over more units and are thus smaller on a per-unit basis. Unit fixed costs can often be misleading and may lead to poor decisions. It is often safer to work with total fixed costs.

Let's take a look at the graph of fixed costs given in Exhibit 3.1. We see that fixed cost behaviour is described by a horizontal line. Notice that at 40,000 bicycles assembled, supervision cost is $32,000; at 50,000 bicycles assembled, supervision is also $32,000. This line visually demonstrates that cost remains unchanged as the level of the activity driver varies. Total fixed costs are simply an amount. For the company, supervision cost amounted to $32,000 for any level of output between 20,000 and 50,000 bicycles assembled. Thus, supervision is a fixed cost and can be expressed as:

$$\text{Supervision cost} = \$32{,}000$$

Strictly speaking, this equation assumes that the fixed costs are $32,000 for all levels (as if the line extends to the vertical axis as indicated by the dashed portion in Exhibit 3.1). Though this assumption is not strictly true, it is harmless if the operating decisions are confined to the normal operating level.

EXHIBIT 3.1

Fixed Cost of Supervision

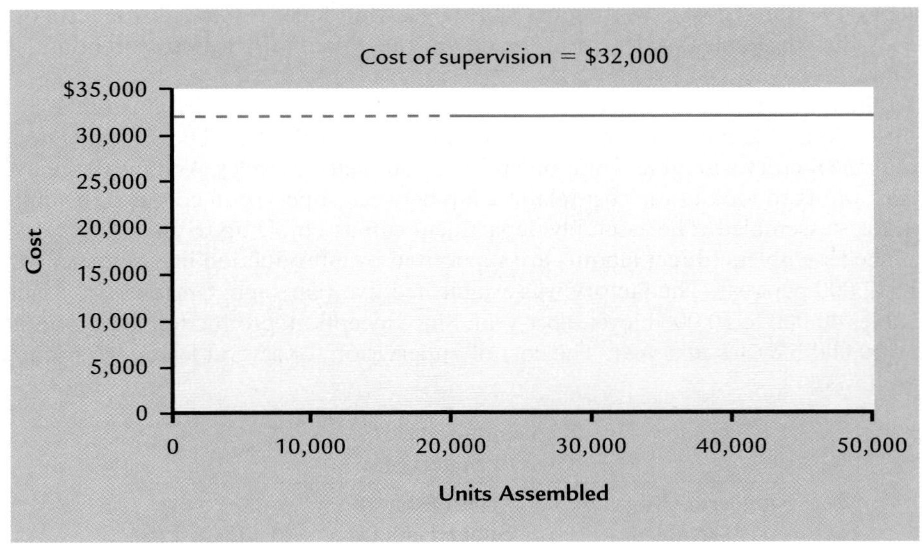

Can fixed costs change? Of course, but this possibility does not make them variable. They are fixed at a new higher (or lower) rate. Going back to Custom Bicycles, suppose that the company gives a raise to the assembly department supervisor. Instead of $32,000 per year, the salary is $34,000 per year. The cost of supervision is now $34,000 per year. However, supervision cost is still *fixed* with respect to the number of bicycles assembled.

By their nature, fixed costs are usually difficult to change quickly—that is why they are considered fixed. Two types of fixed costs are commonly recognized: discretionary fixed costs and committed fixed costs.

Discretionary fixed costs are fixed costs that can be changed or avoided relatively easily at management's discretion. For example, advertising is a discretionary fixed cost. Advertising cost depends on the decision by management to purchase print, radio, or video advertising. This cost might depend on the size of the ad or the number of times it runs, but it does *not*

analytical Q&A

In Exhibit 3.1, the fixed cost of supervision is drawn at $32,000. If the supervisor's salary is raised to $34,000 per year, can you draw in the new fixed cost line on Exhibit 3.1?

Answers on pages 734 to 738.

depend on the number of units produced and sold. Management can easily decide to increase or decrease dollars spent on advertising.

As an example of cutting discretionary costs, on April 30, 2013, FP Tech Desk reported in an article entitled "Postmedia eliminates publisher positions as part of a wider restructuring" that Postmedia Network Canada Corp., the owner of 16 daily newspapers across Canada, including the *National Post*, was eliminating the role of publisher at each of its currently owned newspapers. The publishers would be replaced by three regional senior executives who would each perform the tasks of the publisher for several of the company's papers. This would result in significant savings as part of the company's effort to cut operating costs by 15–20 percent. As a result, three of the current publishers—from the *Saskatoon StarPhoenix*, the *Regina Leader-Post*, the *Calgary Herald*, and the *Edmonton Journal*—would be leaving the company. The cost of the publishers is a discretionary cost because it can be eliminated by changing the strategy for the company in delivering these services.

> **concept Q&A**
>
> Consider the cost of a wedding reception. What costs are fixed? What costs are variable? What output measure did you use in classifying the costs as fixed or variable?
>
> Answers on pages 734 to 738.

Committed fixed costs, on the other hand, are fixed costs that cannot easily be changed. Often, committed fixed costs are those that involve a long-term contract (e.g., leasing of machinery or warehouse space) or the purchase of property, plant, and equipment. For example, a construction company may lease heavy-duty earth-moving equipment for a period of three years. The lease cost is a committed fixed cost.

Variable Costs

Variable costs are costs that in total vary in direct proportion to changes in output. The costs of producing and assembling the propeller on each boat manufactured by Evinrude (of Bombardier Recreational Products) represent variable costs for the manufacturer. In a dentist's office, certain supplies—such as dental floss, X-ray film, and disposable bibs—will vary with the number of procedures performed. The cost of fruits, such as blueberries and strawberries that Yogen Früz uses to top its frozen yogurt, varies with the number of treats sold.

To illustrate, let's expand the Custom Bicycles example to include the cost of the gear assembly that is added to each bicycle. Here the cost is the cost of direct materials—the gear assembly—and the output measure is the number of bicycles produced. Each bicycle requires one gear assembly costing $20. The cost of gear assemblies for various levels of production is as follows:

Custom Bicycles
Cost of Gear Assemblies

Number of Bicycles Produced	Total Cost of Gear Assemblies ($)	Unit Cost ($)
20,000	400,000	20
30,000	600,000	20
40,000	800,000	20
50,000	1,000,000	20

As more bicycles are produced, the total cost of gear assemblies increases in direct proportion to the number produced. For example, as production doubles from 20,000 to 40,000 units, the *total* cost of gear assemblies doubles from $400,000 to $800,000. Notice also that the unit cost of this direct material is constant.

Variable costs can also be represented by a linear equation. Here, total variable costs depend on the level of output. This relationship can be described by the following equation:

Total variable costs = Variable rate per unit × Units of output

The relationship that describes the cost of gear assemblies is:

Total variable cost = \$20 × Number of bicycles

Exhibit 3.2 shows graphically that variable cost behaviour is represented by a straight line extending out from the origin. Notice that at zero units produced, total variable cost is zero. However, as units produced increase, the total variable cost also increases. It can be seen that total cost increases in direct proportion to increases in the number of bicycles assembled; the rate of increase is measured by the slope of the line. At 50,000 bicycles assembled, the total cost of gear assemblies is \$1,000,000 (or \$20 × 50,000 bicycles assembled); at 30,000 bicycles assembled, the total cost would be \$600,000. Exhibit 3.2 illustrates variable cost behaviour for the gear assemblies.

EXHIBIT 3.2

Custom Bicycles Variable Cost of Gear Assemblies

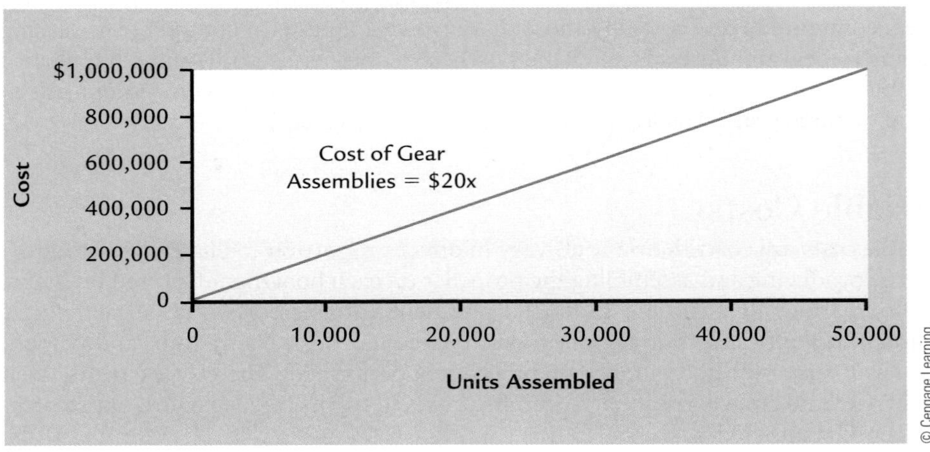

OBJECTIVE 2

Define and describe mixed costs and step costs.

While strictly fixed and variable costs are easy to handle, many costs do not fall into these categories. Often, costs are a combination of fixed and variable costs (mixed costs) or have an increased fixed component at specified intervals (step costs).

Mixed Costs

Mixed costs (sometimes called **semi-variable costs)** are costs that have both a fixed and a variable component. For example, sales representatives are often paid a salary plus a commission on sales. Suppose that Custom Bicycles has 10 sales representatives, each earning a salary of \$30,000 per year plus a commission of \$25 per bicycle sold. The activity is selling, and the output measure is units sold. If 50,000 bicycles are sold, then the total cost associated with the sales representatives is \$1,550,000—the sum of the fixed salary cost of \$300,000 (=10 × \$30,000) and the variable cost of \$1,250,000 (=\$25 × 50,000).

The formula for a mixed cost is as follows:

Total cost = Total fixed cost + Total variable cost

For Custom Bicycles, the cost of the sales representatives is given by the following equation:

Total cost = \$300,000 + (\$25 × Number of bicycles sold)

The following table shows the selling cost for different levels of sales activity:

Custom Bicycles

Fixed Cost of Selling ($)	Variable Cost of Selling ($)	Total Cost ($)	Bicycles Sold	Selling Cost per Unit ($)
300,000	500,000	800,000	20,000	40.00
300,000	750,000	1,050,000	30,000	35.00
300,000	1,000,000	1,300,000	40,000	32.50
300,000	1,250,000	1,550,000	50,000	31.00

The graph for our mixed-cost example is given in Exhibit 3.3. Mixed costs are represented by a line that intercepts the vertical axis (at $300,000 for this example). The vertical axis intercept corresponds to the fixed cost, and the slope of the line gives the variable cost per unit of the activity driver (slope is $25 for this example).

EXHIBIT 3.3

Mixed Cost Behaviour

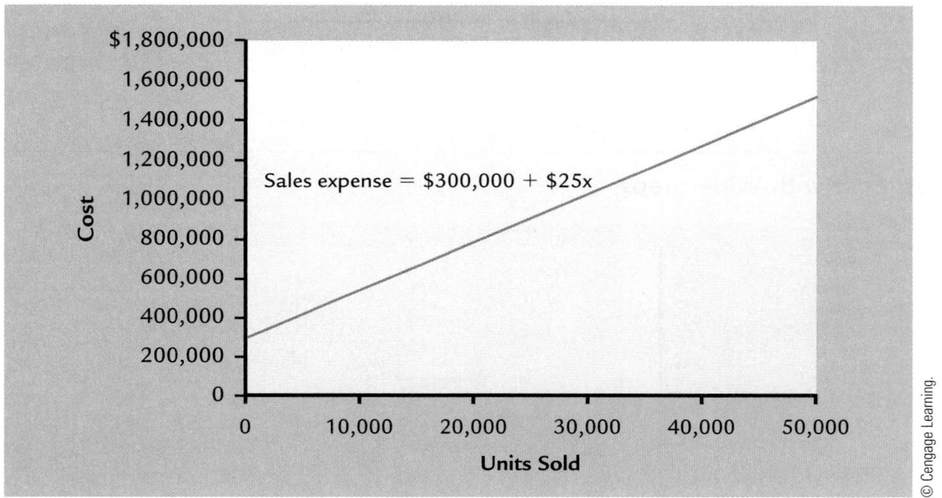

Step Cost Behaviour

So far in our discussion of cost behaviour, we have assumed that the cost function is continuous. In reality, some cost functions may be discontinuous; these costs are known as step costs (or semi-fixed).

A **step cost** displays a constant level of cost for a range of output and then jumps to a higher level of cost at some point, where it remains for a similar range of output. Items that display a step cost behaviour must be purchased in chunks. The width of the step defines the range of output for which a particular amount of the resource applies.

Exhibits 3.4A and B illustrate step costs. Exhibit 3.4A shows a step cost with relatively narrow steps. These narrow steps mean that the cost changes in response to fairly small changes in output. Often, if the steps are very narrow, we can approximate the step cost as a strictly variable cost. For example, Epicurean Delight, a high-end restaurant in London, Ontario, prides itself in serving its patrons quickly and efficiently. It requires waiters to come to work on the basis of number of expected patrons each day. On a weekend it will have more waiters than on a weekday. Exhibit 3.4B, however, shows a step cost with relatively wide steps. An example of this type of cost is a factory that leases production machinery. Suppose that each machine can produce 1,000 units per month.

EXHIBIT 3.4A

Step Cost with Narrow Steps

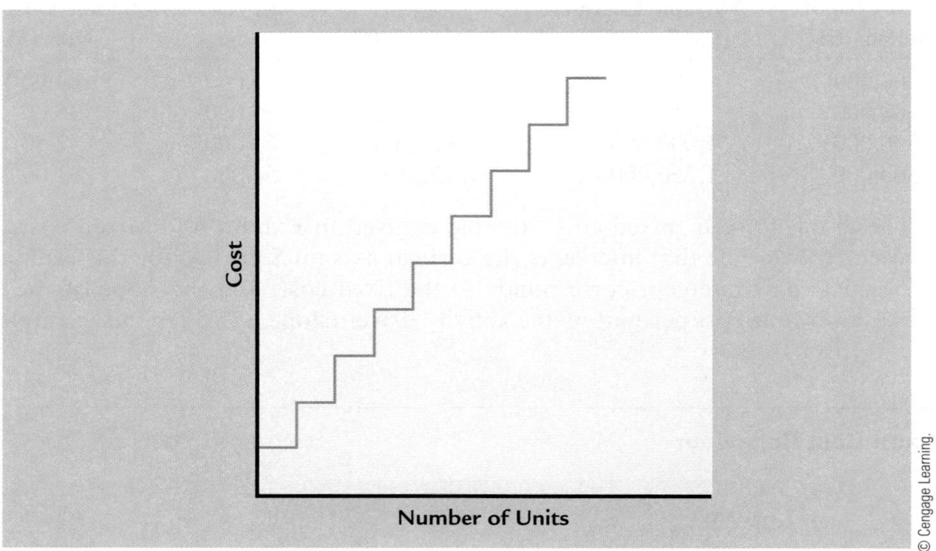

EXHIBIT 3.4B

Step Cost with Wide Steps

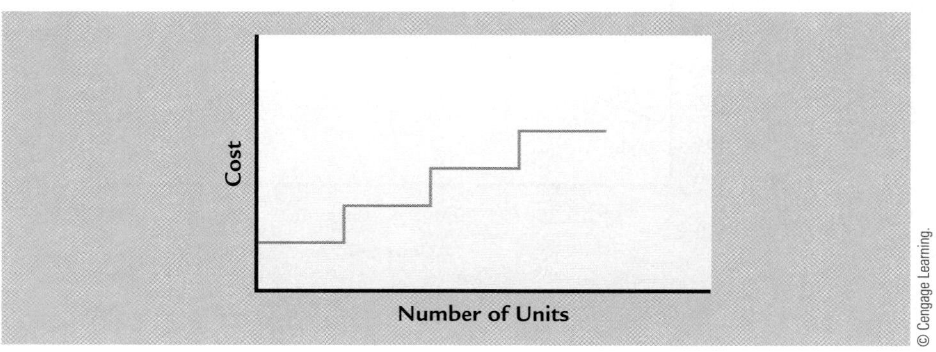

If production ranges from 0 to 1,000 units, only one machine is needed. However, if production increases to amounts between 1,001 and 2,000 units, a second machine must be leased. Many so-called fixed costs may be, in reality, step costs.

Exhibit 3.5 contrasts variable cost behaviour with fixed cost behaviour.

EXHIBIT 3.5

Variable–Fixed–Mixed Cost

	Total Cost	Unit Cost
Variable Cost	Varies in direct proportion to changes in activity	Is fixed throughout the relevant range
Fixed Cost	Remains fixed throughout the relevant range	Varies inversely with changes in activity throughout the relevant range
Mixed Cost	Is a combination of both fixed and variable cost	Varies in total as activity increases, but not at a given rate

The **relevant range** is the range of output over which an assumed cost relationship is valid for the normal operations of a firm. The relevant range limits the cost relationship to the range of operations that the firm normally expects to occur. Let's consider BlueDenim's cost relationships more carefully. We said that the salary of the supervisor is fixed. But is that true? If the company produced just a few pairs of jeans a year, it would not even need a supervisor. Surely the owner could handle that task (and probably a good number of other tasks as well). On the other hand, suppose that BlueDenim increased its current production by two or three times, perhaps by adding a second and third shift. One supervisor could not possibly handle all three shifts. If production expanded, the company would need to hire an additional supervisor and the cost of supervision would double. So, when we talk about supervision cost, we are implicitly talking about it for the range of production that normally occurs, the relevant range. Likewise outside the relevant range, variable costs per unit may be different. As more products are produced, the company may be able to receive volume discounts. We now take a closer look at fixed, variable, and a combination of the two, mixed costs. In each case, the cost is related to only one driver and is defined within the relevant range. Therefore, if we look at our cost behaviour graphs in Exhibit 3.6, we will see that, in the relevant range, the assumptions about costs being fixed or variable can be assumed to be valid. If the company intends to operate outside the boundaries of the relevant range, we can no longer assume that the cost assumptions will hold.

EXHIBIT 3.6

Relevant Range/Cost Behaviour

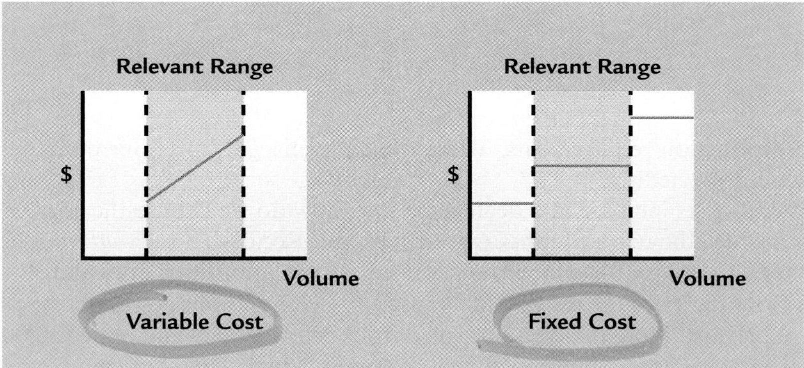

Discussion of Relevant Range: Are Real-World Cost Relationships Linear?

The graphs of fixed and variable costs that were just reviewed show cost relationships that are straight lines. Is this reasonable? Are real-world cost relationships linear?

In the Custom Bicycles example, the gear assemblies cost \$20 each—no matter how many were purchased. However, if only a few assemblies were bought, surely the per-unit cost would be higher—perhaps more than double. So, there are economies of scale in producing larger quantities of output. For example, at extremely low levels of output workers often use more materials per unit or require more time per unit than they do at higher levels of output. Then, as the level of output increases, economies of scale arise as workers experience a learning curve and figure out how to use materials and time more efficiently such that the variable cost per unit decreases as more and more units are produced. Therefore, when economies of scale are present, the true total cost function is increasing at a decreasing rate, as shown in Exhibit 3.7.

Another example of nonlinear cost behaviour would be when production in a certain period must be increased due to unexpected demand. Under these circumstances, assembly workers probably have to be paid overtime to work the extra hours to meet the

EXHIBIT 3.7

Nonlinearity of Variable Costs

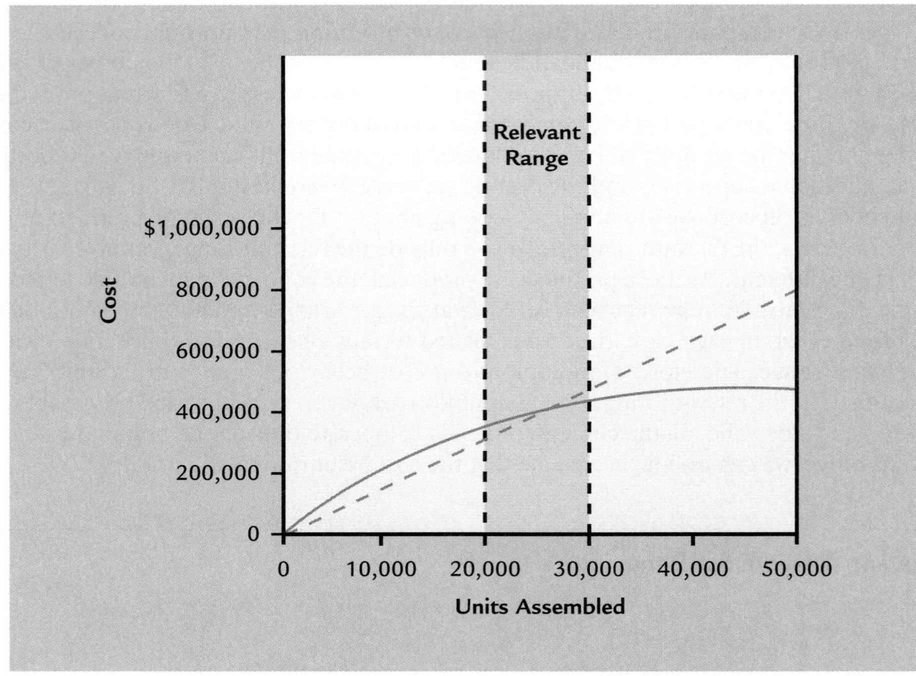

increased production requirements. These overtime charges cause our direct labour bill to increase unexpectedly.

When unit costs increase at a decreasing rate, how do we choose the correct variable rate? Fortunately, the relevant range can help us out. Recall that *relevant range* is defined as the range of activity for which the assumed cost relationships are valid. Exhibit 3.7 shows us how the relevant range can be used to see how well a straight line approximates variable cost. Note that for units of output below 20,000 and above 30,000 on the horizontal axis, the approximation appears to break down. Therefore, managers must be extremely careful in applying cost behaviour assumptions to decision making whenever the output level falls outside of the company's relevant range of operations.

METHODS FOR SEPARATING MIXED COSTS INTO FIXED AND VARIABLE COMPONENTS

Accounting Records and Mixed Costs

OBJECTIVE 3

Separate mixed costs into their fixed and variable components using the high–low method and the scattergraph method.

Sometimes it is easy to identify the variable and fixed components of a mixed cost, as in the example given earlier for Custom Bicycles' sales representatives. Many times, however, the only information available is the total cost and the measure of output. For example, the accounting system will usually record both the total cost of maintenance and the number of maintenance hours provided during a given period of time. How much of the total maintenance cost represents a fixed cost and how much represents a variable cost is not revealed by the accounting records. (In fact, the accounting records may not even reveal the breakdown of costs in the sales representative example.) Often, the total cost is simply recorded with no attempt to segregate the fixed and variable components of costs.

Need for Cost Separation into Fixed and Variable Costs

Accounting records typically show only the total cost. Therefore, for detailed analysis purposes, it is necessary to separate the total cost into its fixed and variable components. Only through a formal effort to separate costs can all costs be classified into the appropriate cost behaviour categories. As we saw in the opening vignette on Zingerman's, many decisions hinge on an understanding of how much of the total cost is fixed and how much is variable. Commitments to fixed costs are often more carefully considered as they may be more difficult to reverse than increasing variable costs.

If mixed costs are a very small percentage of total costs, formal cost separation may be more trouble than it's worth. In this case, mixed costs could be assigned to either the fixed or variable cost category without much concern for the classification error or its effect on decision making. Alternatively, the total mixed cost could be arbitrarily divided between the two cost categories. Mixed costs for many firms are large enough to call for putting in the extra time and effort to make an accurate separation.

Methods for Cost Separation into Fixed and Variable Costs

Three methods of separating a mixed cost into the fixed and variable components are commonly used: the high–low method, the scattergraph method, and the method of least squares (see Appendix 3A). Each method requires the simplifying assumption of a linear cost relationship. Therefore, before we examine each of these methods more closely, let's review the expression of cost as an equation for a straight line.

$$\text{Total cost} = \text{Fixed cost} + (\text{Variable rate} \times \text{Output})$$

The **dependent variable** is a variable whose value depends on the value of another variable. In this equation, total cost is the dependent variable; it is the cost we are trying to predict. The **independent variable** is a variable that measures output and is used to explain changes in the cost of a dependent variable. A good independent variable is one that causes changes in, or is closely associated with changes in, the dependent variable. Therefore, many managers refer to an independent variable as a cost driver. The **intercept** corresponds to the level of fixed cost. Graphically, the intercept is the point at which the cost line intercepts the cost (vertical) axis. The **slope** corresponds to the variable rate (the variable cost per unit of output); it is the slope of the cost line. Cornerstone 3.1 shows how to create and use a cost formula.

Creating and Using a Cost Formula

CORNERSTONE 3.1

Information:

The art and graphics department of Wolftown College decided to equip each faculty office with an inkjet colour printer (computers were already in place). The appropriate colour printers had monthly depreciation of $25. The department purchased paper in boxes of 10,000 sheets (20 reams of 500 sheets each) for $35 per box. Ink cartridges cost $30 and will print, on average, 300 pages.

Required:

1. Create a formula for the monthly cost of inkjet printing in the art and graphics department.
2. If the department expects to print 4,400 pages next month, what is the expected fixed cost? Total variable cost? Total printing cost?

(Continued)

CORNERSTONE
3.1
(Continued)

Solution:

1. The cost formula takes the following form:

Total cost = Fixed cost + (Variable rate × Number of pages)

The monthly fixed cost is $25 (the cost of printer depreciation), as it does not vary with the number of pages printed. The variable costs are paper and ink, as both vary with the number of pages printed.
Cost of paper per page is $35/10,000 = $0.0035
Cost of ink per page is $30/300 = $0.10
Variable rate per page is $0.0035 + $0.10 = $0.1035
The cost formula is:

Total cost of printing = $25 + ($0.1035 × Number of pages)

2. Expected fixed cost for next month is $25.
Expected variable cost for next month is $0.1035 × 4,400 pages = $455.40
Expected total printing cost for next month is $25 + $455.40 = $480.40

Why:

Because knowing the variable and fixed-cost components of any cost is essential to being able to predict what the future costs will be.

The following example with the same data will be used for each of the methods so that comparisons can easily be made. The example focuses on materials handling cost for Swish Maintenance Limited, a Peterborough, Ontario–based manufacturer of household cleaning products. Materials handling involves moving materials from one area of the factory—say, the raw materials storeroom—to another area, such as workstation 6. Large, complex organizations have found that the cost of moving materials can be quite significant. Understanding the behaviour of this cost could be an important part of deciding how to reduce the cost.

Suppose Swish's controller has accumulated data for the materials handling activity. The plant manager believes that the number of material moves is a good cost driver for the activity. Assume that the accounting records of Swish disclose the following materials handling costs and number of material moves for the past nine months:

Month	Materials Handling Cost ($)	Number of Moves
January	2,000	**100**
February	3,090	125
March	2,780	175
April	1,990	200
May	7,500	**500**
June	5,300	300
July	3,800	250
August	6,300	400
September	5,600	475

The High–Low Method

From basic geometry, we know that two points are needed to determine a line. Once we know the two points on a line, then its equation can be determined. Recall that the fixed cost is the *intercept* of the total cost line and that the variable rate is the *slope* of the line. Given two points, the slope and the intercept can be determined. **The high–low method** is a method of separating mixed costs into fixed and variable components by using just the high and low data points. Four steps must be taken in the high–low method.

analytical Q&A

When working high–low problems, it helps to circle the high and low points so that you don't become confused. Right now, go to the data given for materials handling cost and number of moves, and circle the high activity point and the low activity point.

Answers on pages 734 to 738.

Step 1: Find the high point and the low point for a given data set. The *high point* is defined as the point at which the *highest activity or output level* occurs. The *low point* is defined as the point at which the lowest activity *or output level* occurs. It is important to note that the high and low points are identified by looking at the activity levels and not the costs. In some cases, the highest (or lowest) activity level may also be associated with the highest (or lowest) cost, whereas in other cases it may not be. Therefore, the management accountant must be careful to use the *activity level* in identifying the high and low data points for the analysis, regardless of whether or not the high (or low) activity level is associated with the high (or low) cost. In the data for materials handling cost, the high output occurred in May, with 500 material moves at a total cost of \$7,500. The low output was in January with 100 material moves at a total cost of \$2,000.

Step 2: Using the high and low points, calculate the variable rate. To perform this calculation, we realize that, by definition, the fixed cost is the same at each level of activity and the difference between the two costs is related to the variable rate, or slope of the line. Therefore, the variable rate is equal to the difference in total cost between the two points divided by the different levels of output between the two points.

$$\text{Variable rate} = \frac{\text{High point cost} - \text{Low point cost}}{\text{High point output} - \text{Low point output}}$$

Using the high and low points for our example, the variable rate would be as follows:

$$\text{Variable rate} = \frac{(\$7{,}500 - \$2{,}000)}{(500 - 100)} = \frac{\$5{,}500}{400} = \$13.75$$

Step 3: Calculate the fixed cost using the variable rate (from step 2) using either the high or low point.

$$\text{Fixed cost} = \text{Total cost at high point} - (\text{Variable rate} \times \text{Output at high point})$$

OR

$$\text{Fixed cost} = \text{Total cost at low point} - (\text{Variable rate} \times \text{Output at low point})$$

Let's use the high point to calculate fixed cost.

$$\text{Fixed cost} = \$7{,}500 - (\$13.75 \times 500) = \$625$$

Step 4: Formulate the cost formula for materials handling based on the high–low method.

$$\text{Total cost} = \$625 + (\$13.75 \times \text{Number of moves})$$

Once we have the cost formula, we can use it in budgeting and in performance evaluation. For example, suppose that the number of moves for November is expected to be 350. Budgeted materials handling cost would be \$5,437.50, or \$625 + (\$13.75 × 350). Cornerstone 3.2 shows how to use the high–low method to construct a cost formula.

CORNERSTONE 3.2

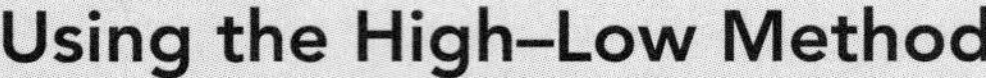

Information:

BlueDenim Company makes blue jeans. The company controller wants to calculate the fixed and variable costs associated with electricity used in the factory. Data for the past eight months were collected:

Month	Electricity Cost ($)	Machine Hours
January	3,255	460
February	3,485	500
March	4,100	600
April	3,300	470
May	3,312	470
June	2,575	350
July	3,910	570
August	4,200	590

Required:

Using the high–low method, calculate the fixed cost of electricity, calculate the variable rate per machine hour, and construct the cost formula for total electricity cost.

Solution:

Step 1—Find the high and low points: The high number of machine hours is in March, and the low number of machine hours is in June. (*Hint:* Did you notice that the high cost of $4,200 was for August? Yet August is not the high point because its number of machine hours is not the highest activity level. Remember, the high point is associated with the highest activity level; the low point is associated with the lowest activity level.)

Step 2—Calculate the variable rate:

$$\begin{aligned}\text{Variable rate} &= \frac{(\text{High cost} - \text{Low cost})}{(\text{High machine hours} - \text{Low machine hours})}\\ &= \frac{(\$4{,}100 - \$2{,}575)}{(600 - 350)}\\ &= \frac{\$1{,}525}{250}\\ &= \$6.10 \text{ per machine hour}\end{aligned}$$

Step 3—Calculate the fixed cost:

$$\text{Fixed cost} = \text{Total cost} - (\text{Variable rate} \times \text{Machine hours})$$

Let's choose the high point with cost of $4,100 and machine hours of 600.

$$\text{Fixed cost} = \$4{,}100 - (\$6.10 \times 600) = \$4{,}100 - \$3{,}660 = \$440$$

(*Hint:* Check your work by calculating fixed cost using the low point.)

Step 4—Construct a cost formula: If the variable rate is $6.10 per machine hour and fixed cost is $440 per month, then the formula for monthly electricity cost is:

$$\text{Total electricity cost} = \$440 + (\$6{:}10 \times \text{Machine hours})$$

Why:

Because separating fixed and variable costs is fundamental to predicting what costs will be at various levels of output and this is a simple, frequently used method to separate mixed costs into its variable and fixed components.

Alternatively, suppose that the controller wondered whether or not October's actual materials handling cost of $6,240 for 425 moves was reasonably close to what would have been predicted. Our cost formula would predict October's cost to be $6,469 (rounded). (This amount is found by multiplying $13.75 times the 425 actual moves and then adding fixed cost of $625.) The actual cost is just $229 (or 3.5 percent) different from the predicted cost and probably would be judged to be reasonably close to the budgeted cost.

Let's look at one last point. Notice that monthly data were used to find the high and low points and to calculate the fixed cost and variable rate. This means that the cost formula is the fixed cost *for the month*. Suppose, however, that the company wants to use that formula to predict cost for a different period of time—say, a year. In that case, the variable cost rate is just multiplied by the budgeted amount of the independent variable for the year. The intercept, or fixed cost, must be adjusted. To convert monthly fixed cost to yearly fixed cost, simply multiply the monthly fixed cost by 12 (because there are 12 months in a year). If weekly data were used to calculate the fixed and variable costs, one would multiply the weekly fixed cost by 52 to convert it to yearly fixed cost, and so on. Cornerstone 3.3 shows how to use the high–low method to calculate predicted total variable cost and total cost for budgeted output in which the time period differs from the data period.

analytical Q&A

Calculate the fixed cost by using the low point and the variable rate calculated in step 2. (You should get the same fixed cost, $625.)

Answers on pages 734 to 738.

Using the High–Low Method to Calculate Predicted Total Variable Cost and Total Cost for Budgeted Output

CORNERSTONE 3.3

Information:

Recall that BlueDenim Company constructed the following formula for monthly electricity cost. (Refer to Cornerstone 3.2 to see how the fixed cost per month and the variable rate were computed.)

Total electricity cost = $440 + ($6.10 × Machine hours)

Required:

Assume that 550 machine hours are budgeted for the month of September. Use the previous cost formula for the following calculations:

1. Calculate total variable electricity cost for September.
2. Calculate total electricity cost for September.

Solution:

1. Total variable electricity cost = Variable rate × Machine hours
   = $6.10 × 550
   = $3,355

2. Total electricity cost = Fixed cost + (Variable rate × Machine hours)
   = $440 + ($6.10 × 550)
   = $440 + $3,355
   = $3,795

Note that the fixed costs remain the same at all levels of output, within the relevant range.

(Continued)

CORNERSTONE

3.3

(Continued)

Required:

Assume that 6,500 machine hours are budgeted for the coming year. Use the previous cost formula to make the following calculations:

1. Calculate total variable electricity cost for the year.
2. Calculate total fixed electricity cost for the year.
3. Calculate total electricity cost for the coming year.

Solution:

1. Total variable electricity cost = Variable rate × Machine hours
   = $6.10 × 6,500
   = $39,650
2. There's a trick here; the cost formula is for the month, but we are being asked to budget electricity for the year. Thus we will need to multiply the fixed cost for the month by 12 (the number of months in a year).

   Total fixed electricity cost = Fixed cost × 12 months in a year
   = $440 × 12
   = $5,280
3. Total electricity cost = 12($440) + ($6.10 × 6,500)
   = $5,280 + $39,650
   = $44,930

Why:

Because the high–low method lends itself not only to assisting with separating mixed costs but also to using the cost formula as a prediction model for future variable and total costs.

The high–low method has several important advantages. One advantage is its objectivity. That is, any two people using the high–low method on a particular data set will arrive at the same answer. Also, the high–low method allows a manager to get a quick fix on a cost relationship by using a minimum of data. For example, a manager may have only two months of data. Sometimes this will be enough to get a crude approximation of the cost relationship. In addition, the high–low method is simple, inexpensive, and easily communicated to other individuals, even those who are not comfortable with numerical analyses. For these reasons, management accountants often use the high–low method.

However, the high–low method has several disadvantages that lead some managers to believe that it is not as good as the other methods for separating mixed costs into their fixed and variable components. Why? First, the high and low points often can be *outliers*, representing cost–activity relationships that are neither typical nor representative. For instance, if in the Swish example the high output had been 1,000 moves (rather than 500) due to some extremely unusual business activity during a given month, then this high point likely would have fallen outside of the company's relevant range of operations and, therefore, would have represented an outlier. In the case of outliers, the cost formula computed using these two points will not represent what usually takes place. The scattergraph method, explained in detail in the following section, can help a manager avoid this trap by selecting two points that appear to be representative of the general cost–activity pattern. Second, even if the high and low points are not outliers, other pairs of points may be more representative. To stress the likelihood of this possibility, a high–low analysis of 50 weeks of data would ignore 96 percent (i.e., 48 out of the 50 weeks) of the data! Again, the scattergraph method may allow for the choice of more representative points.

Scattergraph Method

The **scattergraph method** is a way to see the cost relationship by plotting the data points on a graph. The first step in applying the scattergraph method is to plot the data points so that the relationship between materials handling costs and activity output can be seen. This plot is referred to as a scattergraph and is shown in Exhibit 3.8A. The vertical axis is total cost (materials handling cost), and the horizontal axis is the driver or output measure (number of moves). Looking at Exhibit 3.8A, we see that the relationship between materials handling costs and number of moves is reasonably linear; cost goes up as the number of moves goes up, and vice versa.

EXHIBIT 3.8A

Swish's Materials Handling Cost Scattergraph Showing Data Points

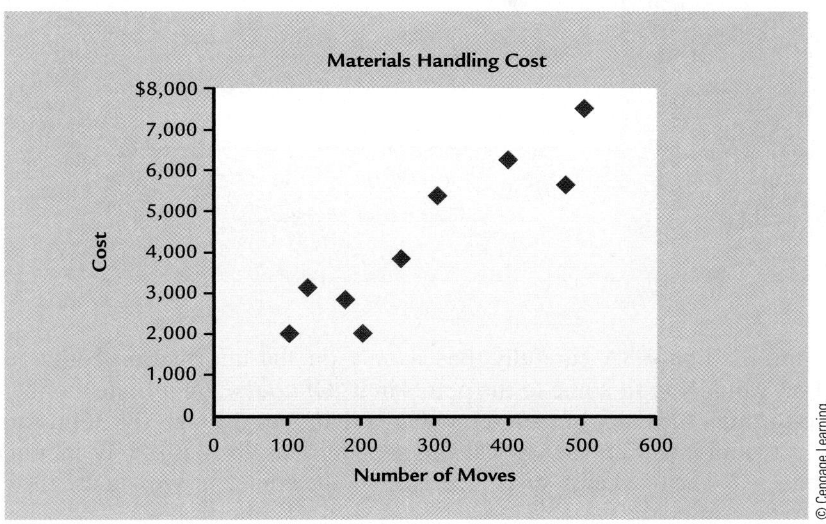

Now let's examine Exhibit 3.8B to see if the line determined by the high and low points is representative of the overall relationship. Of the nine points on the graph, two lie on the high–low line, the two values used in the high–low determination. Notice that three points lie above the high–low line and four lie below it, at different distances from the line. This realization does not give us confidence in the high–low results for fixed and variable costs. In particular, we might wonder if the variable cost (slope) calculated is somewhat higher than it should be and the fixed cost calculated is somewhat lower than it should be.

Thus, one purpose of a scattergraph is to see whether a straight line reasonably describes the cost relationship. Additionally, inspecting the scattergraph may reveal one or more points that do not seem to fit the general pattern of behaviour. Upon investigation, it may be discovered that these points (the outliers) were due to some irregular occurrences that are not expected to happen again. This knowledge might justify their elimination and perhaps lead to a better estimate of the underlying cost function.

We can use the scattergraph to visually fit a line to the data points on the graph. Of course, the manager or cost analyst will choose the line that appears to fit the points the best, and perhaps that choice will take into account past experience with the behaviour of the cost item. Experience may provide a good intuitive sense of how materials handling costs behave; the scattergraph then becomes a useful tool to quantify this intuition. Fitting a line to the points in this way is how the scattergraph method works best. Keep in mind that the scattergraph and other statistical aids are tools that can help managers improve their judgment. Using the tools does not restrict the manager from using judgment to alter any of the estimates produced by formal methods.

EXHIBIT 3.8B

Scattergraph with the High–Low Cost Line

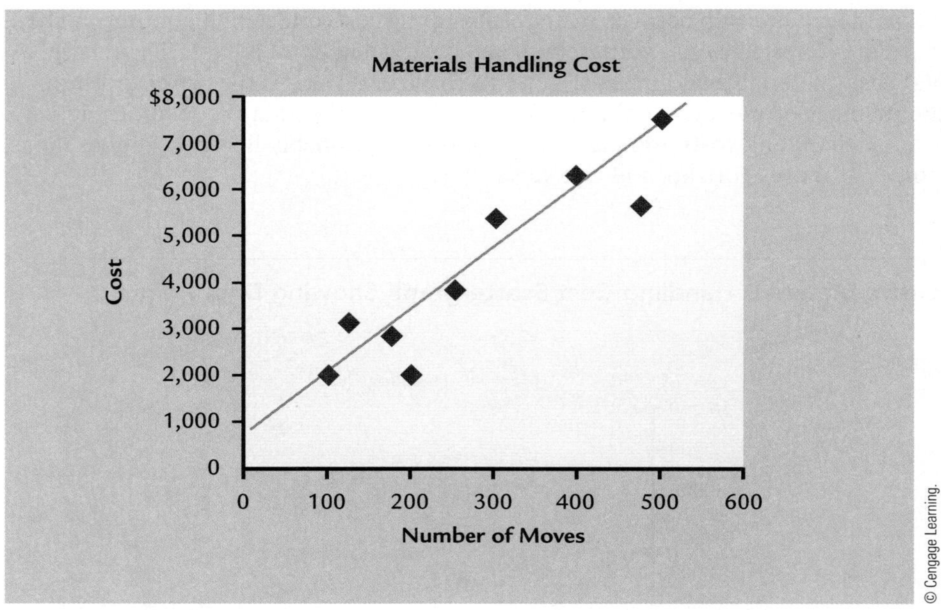

Examine Exhibit 3.8A carefully. Based only on the information contained in the graph, how would you fit a line to the points in it? Of course, an infinite number of lines might go through the data, but let's choose one that goes through the point for January (100, $2,000) and intersects the vertical axis at $800. This gives us the straight line shown in Exhibit 3.8C. The fixed cost, of course, is $800, the intercept. We can use the high–low method to determine the variable rate.

EXHIBIT 3.8C

Scattergraph with the Cost Line Fitted by Visual Inspection

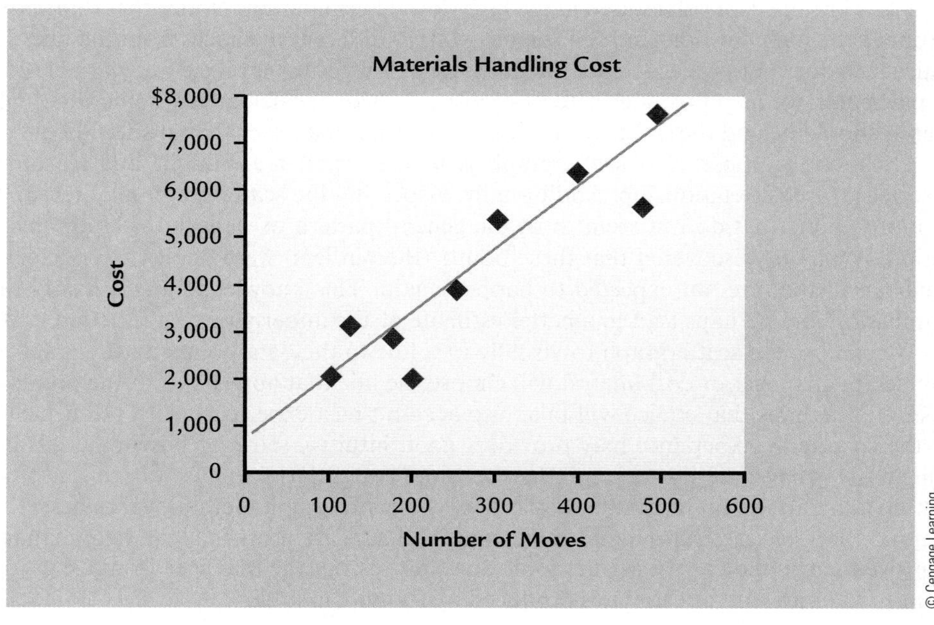

First, remember that our two points are (100, \$2,000) and (0, \$800). Next, use these two points to compute the variable rate (the slope):

$$\text{Variable rate} = \frac{\text{High point cost} - \text{Low point cost}}{\text{High point number of moves} - \text{Low point number of moves}}$$

$$= \frac{(\$2,000 - \$800)}{100 - 0}$$

$$= \frac{\$1,200}{100}$$

$$= \$12$$

Thus the variable rate is \$12 per material move.

The fixed cost and variable rate for materials handling cost have now been identified. The cost formula for the materials handling activity can be expressed as:

$$\text{Total cost} = \$800 + \$12 \times \text{Number of moves}$$

Using this formula, the total cost of materials handling for between 100 and 500 moves can be predicted and then separated between the fixed and variable components. For example, assume that 350 moves are planned for November. Using the cost formula, the predicted cost is \$5,000 [= \$800 + (\$12 × 350)]. Of this total cost, \$800 is fixed, and \$4,200 is variable.

The cost formula for materials handling was obtained by fitting a line to two points [(0, \$800) and (100, \$2,000)] in Exhibit 3.8C. Judgment was used to select the line. Whereas one person may decide that the best-fitting line is the one passing through those points, others, using their own judgment, may decide that the best line passes through other pairs of points.

The scattergraph method suffers from the lack of any objective criterion for choosing the best-fitting line. The quality of the cost formula depends on the quality of the subjective judgment of the analyst. The high–low method removes the subjectivity in the choice of the line. Regardless of who uses the high–low method, the same line will result.

Looking again at Exhibits 3.8B and 3.8C, we can compare the results of the scattergraph method with those of the high–low method. There is a difference between the fixed cost components and the variable rates. The predicted materials handling cost for 350 moves is \$5,000 according to the scattergraph method and \$5,438 according to the high–low method. Which is correct? Since the two methods can produce significantly different cost formulas, the question of which method is the best naturally arises. Ideally, a method is needed that is objective and, at the same time, produces the best-fitting line. In Appendix 3A, we will examine the method of least squares, which will overcome some of these disadvantages. The least squares (or regression) method allows us to calculate the cost formula using all of the data points, thus eliminating any subjective measures. As outlined in Appendix 3A, the complex mathematical calculations can be accomplished by using a spreadsheet program such as Microsoft Excel. Exhibit 3.9 summarizes and compares the three methods for separating mixed costs.

concept Q&A

In examining the results from the high–low method and the scattergraph method, we can conclude that the scattergraph method may give a more accurate indication of the fixed and variable components of a mixed cost. Why?

Answers on pages 734 to 738.

Managerial Judgment

Managerial judgment is critically important in determining cost behaviour and is by far the most widely used method in practice. Many managers simply use their experience and past observation of cost relationships to determine fixed and variable costs. This method may take a number of forms, however. Some managers simply assign some costs to the fixed category and others to the variable category. They ignore the possibility of mixed costs. Thus, a chemical firm may regard materials and utilities as strictly

EXHIBIT 3.9

Overview of Methods for Separating Mixed Costs into Fixed and Variable Components

Method	Overview	Advantages	Disadvantages
High–low method	A method for separating mixed costs into fixed and variable components by using just the low and high data points (Calculated as: Fixed cost \$625 + Variable cost \$13.75 per move)	• Objective • Quick • Simple • Inexpensive • Easily communicated to others	• Occurrence of outliers • Potential for misrepresentative data
Scattergraph method	A method for separating mixed costs into fixed and variable components by fitting a line to a set of data using two points that are selected by judgment (Calculated as: Fixed cost \$800 + Variable cost \$12.00 per move)	• Simple • Visual representation of the data	• Subjective (choosing the best-fitting line)
Method of least squares (regression)	A method for separating mixed costs into fixed and variable components by statistically finding the best-fitting line through a set of data points (Calculated as: Fixed cost \$789 + Variable cost \$12.38 per move)	• Objective • Regression packages can quickly and easily calculate the fixed cost and variable rate	• Complicated, lengthy process if done by hand

concept Q&A

Suppose that you own a small business with a photocopier that a neighbouring business owner asks to use occasionally. What is the average cost of copying one page? What cost items would you include? Now consider a FedEx Kinko's office and print centre. What cost items do you think it would include?

Answers on pages 734 to 738.

variable, with respect to kilograms of chemical produced, and all other costs as fixed. Even labour, the textbook example of a strictly variable cost, may be treated as fixed for this firm. The appeal of this method is its simplicity. Before opting for this method, however, management would do well to make sure that each cost is predominantly fixed or variable and that the decisions being made are not highly sensitive to errors in classifying costs between fixed or variable.

To illustrate the use of judgment in assessing cost behaviour, consider Elgin Sweeper Company, a leading manufacturer of motorized street sweepers and the distributor of Winnipeg-based Challenger Manufacturing Ltd.'s products in the United States. Using production volume as the measure of activity output, Elgin revised its chart of accounts to organize costs into fixed and variable components. Elgin's accountants used their knowledge of the company's operations to assign expenses to either a fixed or variable category, using a decision rule that categorized an expense as fixed if it was fixed at least 75 percent of the time and as variable if it was variable at least 75 percent of the time.[2]

Management may instead identify mixed costs and divide these costs into fixed and variable components by deciding what the fixed and variable parts are; that is, they may use experience to say that a certain amount of a cost is fixed and that the rest therefore must be variable. Suppose that a small business had a photocopier with a fixed cost of \$3,000 per year. The variable component could be computed by using one or more cost/volume data points.

Finally, management may use experience and judgment to refine statistical estimation results. Perhaps the experienced manager might "eyeball" the data and throw out several points as being highly unusual, or revise the results of estimation to take account of projected changes in cost structure or technology. For example, TECNOL Medical Products, Inc. radically changed its method of manufacturing medical face masks. Traditionally, face-mask production was labour intensive, requiring hand stitching. TECNOL developed its own highly automated equipment and became the industry's low-cost supplier—besting

[2] John P. Callan, Wesley N. Tredup, and Randy S. Wissinger, "Elgin Sweeper Company's Journey Toward Cost Management," *Management Accounting* (July 1991): 24–27.

both Johnson & Johnson and 3M. TECNOL's rapid expansion into new product lines and European markets means that historical data on costs and revenues are, for the most part, irrelevant. TECNOL's management must look forward, not back, to predict the impact of changes on profit.[3] Statistical techniques are highly accurate in depicting the past, but they cannot foresee the future, which, of course, is what management really wants.

The advantage of using managerial judgment to separate fixed and variable costs is its simplicity. In situations in which the manager has a deep understanding of the firm and its cost patterns, this method can give good results. However, if the manager does not have good judgment, errors will occur. Therefore, it is important to consider the experience of the manager, the potential for error, and the effect that error could have on related decisions.

Corporate and Social Responsibility

There are ethical implications to the use of managerial judgment. Managers use their knowledge of fixed and variable costs to make important decisions, such as whether to switch suppliers, expand or contract production, or lay workers off. These decisions affect the lives of workers, suppliers, and customers. The ethical manager will make sure that he or she has the best information possible when making these decisions. In addition, the manager will not let personal factors affect the use of cost information. For example, suppose that the purchasing department manager has a good friend who wants to supply some materials for production. The price of the materials is slightly lower than that of the current supplier; however, the friend's company cannot ensure 100 percent quality control—and that will lead to additional costs for rework and warranty repair. Before making a final decision, the ethical manager will include these additional costs along with the purchase price to calculate the full cost of purchasing from the friend's company.

YOU DECIDE Choosing a Cost Estimation Method

Assume that you work as a financial analyst for Four Seasons Hotels and Resorts, a Toronto-based company that operates some of the world's most luxurious hotels in many different countries. As an internal financial analyst, one of your most important tasks is to estimate the costs that Four Seasons will incur in opening and running a new hotel. The accuracy with which you predict Four Seasons' most important hotel-related costs will affect many of the strategic and operating decisions made by management. You are familiar with several common cost estimation methods, including scattergraph, high–low, and regression (see Appendix 3A). However, you also are aware that each method has its advantages and disadvantages.

Which cost estimation method should you employ?

If the scattergraph method were used, the analysis would be quite easy as you could employ Excel to quickly create a plot of the important costs against various potential cost drivers. However, this method does not involve quantitative analysis, which some believe is a significant weakness. If the high–low method were adopted, the analysis would be quantitative in nature and relatively easy to conduct and explain to management. However, this method can be subject to considerable inaccuracy if one or both of the two data points used to construct the cost formula is an outlier. Finally, regression overcomes many of the weaknesses of high–low because it incorporates all of the data into its estimate of the cost formula. Nevertheless, regression can require considerably more time than other methods to collect the necessary input data, ensure their accuracy, and explain the results to the ultimate users of the results.

To determine which method to employ, you would be wise to consult the managers who will be using your analysis. For example, does management need a general "ballpark" estimate or does it need the most accurate estimate possible? The results from your cost analysis, along with the competitive pressures facing Four Seasons, will affect important decisions such as how much to pay hotel employees to ensure a high–quality customer experience, the prices to charge customers to ensure affordability yet exclusivity, and the types and quantities of food, beverages, and shopping to offer in the hotel.

There is no obvious, one-size-fits-all answer as to the best cost estimation method to employ. Regardless of the cost estimation method ultimately selected, you likely will supplement the results with a dose of managerial judgment to help management make the best decisions possible.

[3] Stephanie Anderson Forest, "Who's Afraid of J&J and 3M?" *Business Week* (December 5, 1994): 66, 68.

APPENDIX 3A: USING REGRESSION ANALYSIS

The Method of Least Squares

OBJECTIVE 4

Separate mixed costs into their fixed and variable components using the method of least squares.

The **method of least squares (regression)** is a statistical way to find the *best-fitting* line through a set of data points. One advantage of the method of least squares is that for a given set of data, it will always produce the same cost formula. Basically, the best-fitting line is the one in which the data points are closer to the line than to any other line. What do we mean by *closer*? Let's take a look at Exhibit 3.10. Notice that there are a series of data points and a line—we'll assume that it is the regression line calculated by the method of least squares. The data points do not all lie directly on the line; this is typical. However, the regression line better describes the pattern of the data than other possible lines. This best description results because the squared deviations between the regression line and each data point are, in total, smaller than the sum of the squared deviations of the data points and any other line. The least squares statistical formulas can find the one line with the smallest sum of squared deviations. In other words, this method identifies the regression line that minimizes the cost prediction errors or differences between predicted costs (i.e., on the regression line) and actual costs (i.e., the actual data points). Given that the method of least squares generates the smallest possible cost prediction errors, many managers think of it as the most accurate method.

EXHIBIT 3.10

Line Deviations

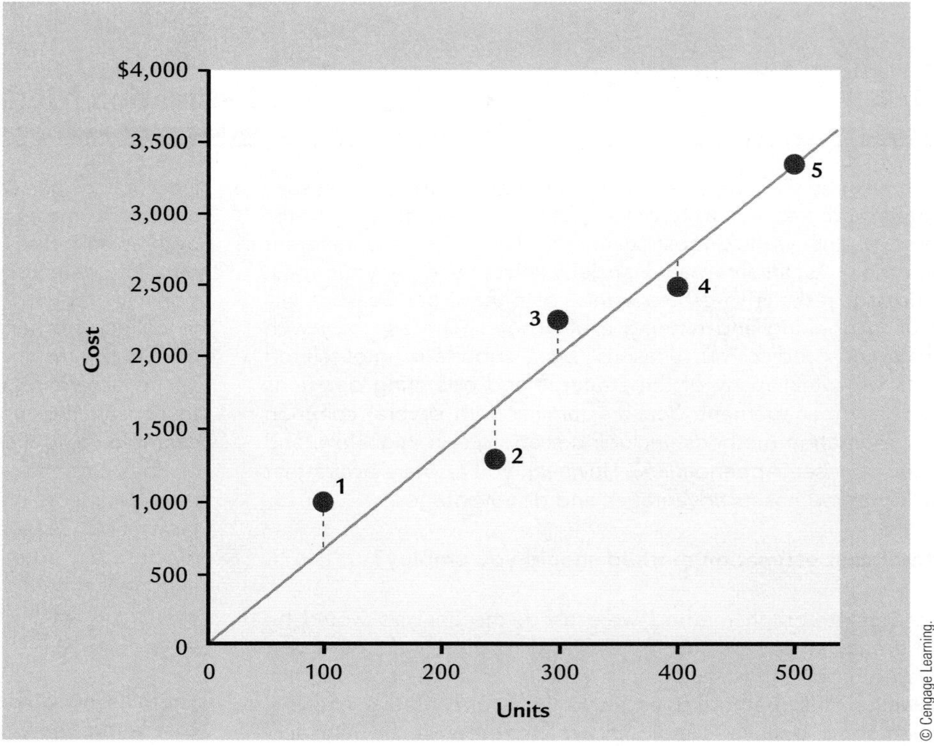

Formerly, the method of least squares had to be calculated by hand. It was a complicated and lengthy process. Today, spreadsheet programs for personal computers have regression packages built in. It is easy to use them to input data and to let the programs calculate the fixed cost and variable rate. Exhibit 3.11 shows a printout from a Microsoft

EXHIBIT 3.11

A Portion of the Summary Output from Excel for Swish

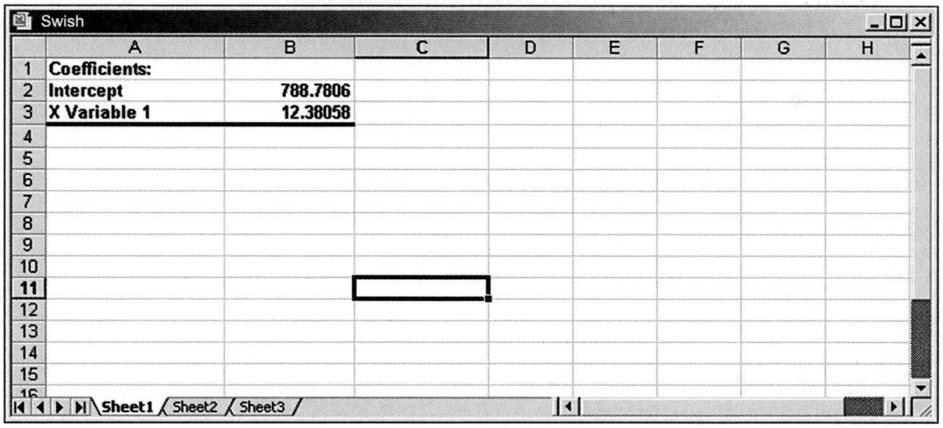

Swish

	A	B	C	D	E	F	G	H
1	**Coefficients:**							
2	**Intercept**	**788.7806**						
3	**X Variable 1**	**12.38058**						

Sheet1 Sheet2 Sheet3

Excel® spreadsheet regression analysis that was run on the data from Swish, which was used elsewhere in this chapter. Notice that the intercept term is the fixed cost, which is $789 (rounded). The variable rate is shown as "X Variable 1"; in other words, it is the first independent variable. So, the variable rate is $12.38 (rounded). We can use the output of regression in budgeting, control, and strategic planning in the same way that we used the results of the high–low and scattergraph methods.

Cornerstone 3.4 shows how to use results of regression to construct a cost formula.

- The method of least squares uses all of the data points (except outliers) on the scattergraph and produces a line that best fits all of the points.
- The method of least squares offers ways to assess the reliability of cost equations.

CORNERSTONE 3.4

Using the Regression Method to Calculate Fixed Cost and the Variable Rate, to Construct a Cost Formula, and to Determine Budgeted Cost

Information:

BlueDenim Company makes blue jeans. The company controller wants to calculate the fixed and variable costs associated with electricity used in the factory. Data for the past eight months are collected:

Month	Electricity Cost ($)	Machine Hours
January	3,255	460
February	3,485	500
March	4,100	600
April	3,300	470
May	3,312	470
June	2,575	350
July	3,910	570
August	4,200	590

CORNERSTONE VIDEO

(Continued)

CORNERSTONE
3.4

(Continued)

Coefficients shown by a regression program are:

Intercept	321
X Variable 1	6.38

Required:

Use the results of regression to perform the following.

1. Calculate the fixed cost of electricity and the variable rate per machine hour.
2. Construct the cost formula for total electricity cost.
3. Calculate the budgeted cost for next month, assuming that 550 machine hours are budgeted.

Solution:

1. The fixed cost and the variable rate are given directly by the regression results.

Fixed cost = \$321
Variable rate = \$6.38

2. The cost formula is:

Total electricity cost = \$321 + (\$6.38 × Machine hours)

3. Budgeted electricity cost = \$321 + (\$6.38 × 550) = \$3,830

Why:

Because the regression method uses an objective statistical formula that provides the best or most accurate cost estimates, it generates the smallest possible cost prediction errors.

Using the Regression Programs and Additional Information Provided

OBJECTIVE 5

Use a personal computer spreadsheet program to perform the method of least squares.

Computing the regression formula manually is tedious, even with only a few data points. As the number of data points increases, manual computation becomes impractical. Fortunately, spreadsheet packages such as Microsoft Excel have regression routines that will perform the computations. All you need to do is input the data. The spreadsheet regression program supplies more than the estimates of the coefficients. It also provides information that can be used to see how reliable the cost equation is—a feature that is not available for the scattergraph or the high–low methods.

The first step in using the computer to calculate regression coefficients is to enter the data. Exhibit 3.12 shows the computer screen that you would see if you entered the Swish data on moves into a spreadsheet. It is a good idea to label your variables as is done in the exhibit. That is, the months are labelled, as are column B for moving costs and column C for number of moves. The next step is to run the regression. In Excel, the regression routine is located under the Tools menu (located toward the top right of the screen). When you pull down the Tools menu, you will see other menu possibilities. Choose Add In, and then add the data analysis tools. When the data analysis tools have been added, Data Analysis will appear at the bottom of the tools menu; click on Data Analysis and then on Regression. If you are using Excel 2010 or later, you will have to add the Classic Menu feature to add in the analysis tool.

When the regression screen pops up, you can tell the program where the dependent and independent variables are located. Simply place the cursor at the beginning of the independent rectangle and then (again using the cursor) block the values under the independent variable column—in this case, cells C2 through C10. Then, move the cursor

EXHIBIT 3.12

Spreadsheet Data for Swish

Spreadsheet Data for Swish.xls

	A	B	C	D	E	F	G	H
1	Month	Cost	# Moves					
2	January	$2,000	100					
3	February	3,090	125					
4	March	2,780	175					
5	April	1,990	200					
6	May	7,500	500					
7	June	5,300	300					
8	July	3,800	250					
9	August	6,300	400					
10	September	5,600	475					
11								
12								
13								
14								

Sheet1 / Sheet2 / Sheet3

to the beginning of the dependent rectangle, and block the values in cells B2 through B10. Finally, you need to tell the computer where to place the output. Block a nice-size rectangle—say, cells A13 through F20—and click on OK. In a fraction of a second, the regression output is complete, as shown in Exhibit 3.13.

EXHIBIT 3.13

Regression Output for Swish

Regression Output for Swish.xls

	A	B	C	D	E	F	G	H
1	SUMMARY OUTPUT							
2								
3	*Regression Statistics*							
4	Multiple R	0.92436						
5	R Square	0.854442						
6	Standard Error	810.1969						
7	Observations	9						
8								
9								
10		*Coefficients*						
11	Intercept	788.7806						
12	X Variable 1	12.38058						
13								
14								
15								

Sheet1 / Sheet2 / Sheet3

Now, let's take a look at the output in Exhibit 3.13. First, let's locate the fixed cost and variable rate coefficients. At the bottom of the exhibit, the intercept and X Variable 1 are shown, and the next column gives their coefficients. Rounding, the fixed cost is 789 and the variable rate is 12.38. Now we can construct the cost formula for materials handling cost. It is:

Materials handling cost = $789 + ($12.38 × Number of moves)

We can use this formula to predict the materials handling cost for future months as we did with the formulas for the high–low and scattergraph methods.

Since the regression cost formula is the best-fitting line, it should produce better predictions of materials handling costs. Suppose that Swish expects the number of moves for November to be 350. Budgeted materials handling cost would be $5,122, or $789 (fixed) + ($12.38 × 350 (variable)). Using this prediction as a standard, the scattergraph line most closely approximates the least squares line.

Alternatively, suppose the controller wondered whether October's actual materials handling cost of $6,240 for 425 moves was reasonably close to what would have been predicted. Our cost formula would predict October cost of $6,051 (rounded). (This amount is found by multiplying $12.38 times the 425 actual moves and then adding the fixed cost of \$789.) The actual cost is just \$189 (or 3.1 percent) different from the predicted cost and probably would be judged to be reasonably close to the budgeted cost.

While the computer output in Exhibit 3.13 can give us the fixed and variable cost coefficients, its major usefulness lies in its ability to provide information about reliability of the estimated cost formula. This is a feature not provided by either the scattergraph or high–low method.

Goodness of Fit

Regression routines provide information on **goodness of fit**. Goodness of fit tells us how well the independent variable predicts the dependent variable. This information can be used to assess reliability of the estimated cost formula, a feature not provided by either the scattergraph or high–low method. The printout in Exhibit 3.13 provides a wealth of statistical information. However, we will look at just one more feature—the coefficient of determination, or R^2. (The remaining information is discussed in statistics classes and higher-level accounting classes.)

The Swish example suggests that the number of moves can explain changes in materials handling costs. The scattergraph shown in Exhibit 3.8A confirms this belief because it reveals that materials handling costs and activity output (as measured by number of moves) seem to move together. It is quite likely that a significant percentage of the total variability in cost is explained by our output variable. We can determine statistically just how much variability is explained by looking at the coefficient of determination. The percentage of variability in the dependent variable explained by an independent variable (in this case, a measure of activity output) is called the **coefficient of determination (R^2)**. The higher the percentage of cost variability explained, the better the job that the independent variable does of explaining the dependent variable. Since R^2 is the percentage of variability explained, it always has a value between 0 and 1.00. In the printout in Exhibit 3.13, the coefficient of determination is labelled R Square (R^2). The value given is 0.85 (rounded), which means that 85 percent of the variability in the materials handling cost is explained by the number of moves. How good is this result? There is no cutoff point for a good versus bad coefficient of determination. Clearly, the closer R^2 is to 1.00, the better. Is 85 percent good enough? How about 73 percent? Or even 46 percent? The answer is that it depends. If your cost equation yields a coefficient of determination of 75 percent, you know that your independent variable explains three-quarters of the variability in cost. You also know that some other factor or combination of factors explains the remaining one-quarter. Depending on your tolerance for error, you may want to improve the equation by trying different independent variables (e.g., materials handling hours worked rather than number of moves) or by trying multiple regression. (Multiple regression uses two or more independent variables. This topic is saved for more advanced courses.)

We note from the computer output in Exhibit 3.13 that the R^2 for materials handling cost is 0.85. In other words, material moves explain about 85 percent of the variability in the materials handling cost. This is not bad. However, something else explains the remaining 15 percent. Swish's controller may want to keep this in mind when using the regression results.

SUMMARY OF LEARNING OBJECTIVES

LO1. Explain the meaning of cost behaviour, and define and describe fixed and variable costs.

- Cost behaviour is the way a cost changes in relation to changes in activity output.
- Time horizon is important because costs can change from fixed to variable depending on whether the decision takes place over the short run or the long run.
- Variable costs change *in total* as the driver, or output measure, changes. Usually, we assume that variable costs increase in direct proportion to increases in activity output.
- Fixed costs do not change *in total* as activity output changes.

LO2. Define and describe mixed costs and step costs.

- Mixed costs have both a variable and a fixed component.
- Step costs remain at a constant level of cost for a range of output and then jump to a higher level of cost at some point, where they remain for a similar range of output.
- Cost objects that display a step cost behaviour must be purchased in chunks.
- The width of the step defines the range of output for which a particular amount of the resource applies.

LO3. Separate mixed costs into their fixed and variable components using the high–low method and the scattergraph method.

- In the high–low method, only two data points are used—the high point and the low point with respect to activity level. These two points then are used to compute the intercept (fixed cost) and the slope (variable rate) of the line on which they lie.
- The high–low method is objective and easy, but an unrepresentative high or low point will lead to an incorrectly estimated cost relationship.
- The scattergraph method involves inspecting a graph showing total mixed cost at various output levels and drawing a straight line that passes through one point and seems to represent the best approximation of best fit for all points on the graph. The intercept gives an estimate of the fixed cost component and the slope an estimate of the variable cost per unit of activity.
- The scattergraph method is a good way to identify nonlinearity, the presence of outliers, and the presence of a shift in the cost relationship. Its disadvantage is that it is subjective.
- Managers use their experience and knowledge of cost and activity-level relationships to identify outliers, understand structural shifts, and adjust parameters due to anticipated changing conditions.

LO4. (*Appendix 3A*) Separate mixed costs into their fixed and variable components using the method of least squares.

- The method of least squares is a mathematical approach that gives the best possible estimation of the relationship between fixed and variable costs.
- Not only does the method of least squares give an estimate of the fixed and variable costs, but it also indicates how accurate the estimate is.

LO5. (*Appendix 3A*) Use a personal computer spreadsheet program to perform the method of least squares.

- Most spreadsheet programs already have the method of least squares programmed in and therefore allow the computations to take place with little effort.

SUMMARY OF IMPORTANT EQUATIONS

1. Cost formula: Total cost = Total fixed cost + (Variable rate × Units of output)
2. Total variable cost = Variable rate × Units of output

CORNERSTONE 3.1	Creating and using a cost formula, page 87
CORNERSTONE 3.2	Using the high–low method, page 90
CORNERSTONE 3.3	Using the high–low method to calculate predicted total variable cost and total cost for budgeted output, page 91
CORNERSTONE 3.4	(*Appendix 3A*) Using the regression method to calculate fixed cost and the variable rate, to construct a cost formula, and to determine budgeted cost, page 99

GLOSSARY

Coefficient of determination (R^2) The percentage of total variability in a dependent variable that is explained by an independent variable. It assumes a value between 0 and 1.00. (p. 102)

Committed fixed costs Fixed costs that cannot be easily changed. (p. 81)

Cost behaviour The way in which a cost changes when the level of activity changes. (p. 78)

Cost driver A causal measurement that causes costs to change. (p. 79)

Dependent variable A variable whose value depends on the value of another variable. (p. 87)

Discretionary fixed costs Fixed costs that can be changed or avoided relatively easily at management's discretion. (p. 80)

Fixed costs Costs that, in total, are constant as the level of output increases or decreases. (p. 79)

Goodness of fit A measure of how well the independent variable predicts the dependent variable. (p. 102)

High–low method A method for separating mixed costs into fixed and variable components by using just the high and low data points. [*Note:* The high (low) data point corresponds to the high (low) output level.] (p. 89)

Independent variable A variable whose value does not depend on the value of another variable. (p. 87)

Intercept The fixed cost, representing the point where the cost formula intercepts the vertical axis. (p. 87)

Method of least squares (regression) A statistical method to find the best-fitting line through a set of data points. It is used to break out the fixed and variable components of a mixed cost. (p. 98)

Mixed costs Costs that have both a fixed and a variable component. (p. 82)

Relevant range The range of output over which an assumed cost relationship is valid for the normal operations of a firm. (p. 85)

Scattergraph method A method to fit a line to a set of data using two points that are selected by judgment. It is used to break out the fixed and variable components of a mixed cost. (p. 93)

Semi-variable costs Costs that have both a fixed and a variable component. (p. 82)

Slope The variable cost per unit of activity usage. (p. 87)

Step cost A cost that displays a constant level of cost for a range of output and then jumps to a higher level of cost at some point, where it remains for a similar range of output. (p. 83)

Variable costs Costs that, in total, vary in direct proportion to changes in output within the relevant range. (p. 81)

REVIEW PROBLEM

Fixed and Variable Costs

Kim Wilson, controller for Max Enterprises, has decided to estimate the fixed and variable components associated with the company's shipping activity. She has collected the following data for the past six months:

Packages Shipped	Total Shipping Costs ($)
10	800
20	1,100
15	900
12	900
18	1,050
25	1,250

Required:

1. Estimate the fixed and variable components for the shipping costs using the high–low method. Using the cost formula, predict the total cost of shipping if 14 packages are shipped.
2. (*Appendix 3A*) Estimate the fixed and variable components using the method of least squares. Using the cost formula, predict the total cost of shipping if 14 packages are shipped.
3. (*Appendix 3A*) For the method of least squares, explain what the coefficient of determination tells us.

Solution:

1. The estimate of fixed and variable costs using the high–low method is as follows:

$$\begin{aligned}
\text{Variable rate} &= \frac{(\$1{,}250 - \$800)}{(25 - 10)} \\
&= \frac{\$450}{15} \\
&= \$30 \text{ per package} \\
\text{Fixed amount} &= \$1{,}250 - \$30(25) = \$500 \\
\text{Total cost} &= \$500 + \$30X \\
&= \$500 + \$30(14) \\
&= \$920
\end{aligned}$$

2. The output of a spreadsheet regression routine is as follows: Regression output:

Constant	509.911894273125
Std Err of Y Est	32.1965672507378
R Squared	0.969285364659814
No. of Observations	6
Degrees of Freedom	4
X Coefficient(s)	29.4052863436125
Std Err of Coef	2.61723229918858

$Y = \$509.91 + \$29.41\ (14) = \$921.65$

3. The coefficient of determination (R^2) tells us that about 96.9 percent of total shipping cost is explained by the number of packages shipped.

DISCUSSION QUESTIONS

1. Why is knowledge of cost behaviour important for managerial decision making? Give an example to illustrate your answer.
2. What is a driver? Give an example of a cost and its corresponding output measure or driver.
3. Suppose a company finds that shipping cost is $3,560 each month plus $6.70 per package shipped. What is the cost formula for monthly shipping cost? Identify the independent variable, the dependent variable, the fixed cost per month, and the variable rate.
4. Some firms assign mixed costs to either the fixed or variable cost categories without using any formal methodology to separate them. Explain how this practice can be defended.
5. Explain the difference between committed and discretionary fixed costs. Give examples of each.
6. Explain why the concept of relevant range is important when dealing with step costs.
7. Why do mixed costs pose a problem when it comes to classifying costs into fixed and variable categories?
8. Describe the cost formula for a strictly fixed cost such as depreciation of $15,000 per year.

9. Describe the cost formula for a strictly variable cost such as electrical power cost of $1.15 per machine hour (i.e., every hour the machinery is run, electrical power cost goes up by $1.15).
10. What is the scattergraph method, and why is it used? Why is a scattergraph a good first step in separating mixed costs into their fixed and variable components?
11. Describe how the scattergraph method breaks out the fixed and variable costs from a mixed cost. Now describe how the high–low method works. How do the two methods differ?
12. What are the advantages of the scattergraph method over the high–low method? The high–low method over the scattergraph method?
13. Describe the method of least squares. Why is this method better than either the high–low method or the scattergraph method?
14. What is meant by *the best-fitting line*?
15. Explain the meaning of the coefficient of determination.

CORNERSTONE EXERCISES

OBJECTIVE 3
CORNERSTONE 3.1

Cornerstone Exercise 3-1 Creating and Using a Cost Formula

Big Thumbs Company manufactures portable flash drives for computers. Big Thumbs incurs monthly depreciation costs of $15,000 on its plant equipment and monthly advertising costs of $3,000 to place advertisements in magazines. Also, each drive requires materials and manufacturing overhead resources. On average, the company uses 280,000 grams of materials to manufacture 5,000 flash drives per month. Each gram of material costs $0.10. In addition, manufacturing overhead resources are driven by machine hours. On average, the company incurs $22,500 of manufacturing overhead resources to produce 5,000 flash drives per month.

Required:

1. Create a formula for the monthly cost of flash drives for Big Thumbs.
2. If the department expects to manufacture 6,000 flash drives next month, what is the expected fixed cost (assume that 6,000 units is within the company's current relevant range)? Total variable cost? Total manufacturing cost (i.e., both fixed and variable)?

OBJECTIVE 3
CORNERSTONE 3.2

Cornerstone Exercise 3-2 Using High–Low to Calculate Fixed Cost, Calculate the Variable Rate, and Construct a Cost Function

Pizza Vesuvio makes specialty pizzas. Vesuvio's controller wants to calculate the fixed and variable costs associated with labour used in the restaurant. Data for the past eight months were collected:

Month	Labour Cost ($)	Employee Hours
January	7,000	360
February	8,140	550
March	9,010	585
April	9,787	610
May	8,490	480
June	2,450	350
July	9,490	570
August	7,531	310

Required:

Using the high–low method, calculate the fixed cost of labour, calculate the variable rate per employee hour, and construct the cost formula for total labour cost.

Cornerstone Exercise 3-3 Using High–Low to Calculate Predicted Total Variable Cost and Total Cost for Budgeted Output

OBJECTIVE 3
CORNERSTONE 3.3

Refer to the Pizza Vesuvio company information in **Cornerstone Exercise 3-2**. Assume that Pizza Vesuvio used this information to construct the following formula for monthly labour cost.

Total labour cost = \$5,200 + (\$7.52 × Employee hours)

Required:

Assume that 675 employee hours are budgeted for the month of September. Use the total labour cost formula for the following calculations:

1. Total variable labour cost for September.
2. Total labour cost for September.

Cornerstone Exercise 3-4 Using High–Low to Calculate Predicted Total Variable Cost and Total Cost for a Time Period That Differs from the Data Period

OBJECTIVE 3
CORNERSTONE 3.3

Refer to the Pizza Vesuvio company information in **Cornerstone Exercise 3-2**. Assume that Pizza Vesuvio used this information to construct the following formula for monthly labour cost.

Total labour cost = \$5,200 + (\$7.52 × Employee hours)

Required:

Assume that 4,000 employee hours are budgeted for the coming year. Use the total labour cost formula to make the following calculations:

1. Total variable labour cost for the year.
2. Total fixed labour cost for the year.
3. Total labour cost for the coming year.

Cornerstone Exercise 3-5 (*Appendix 3A*) Using Regression to Calculate Fixed Cost, Calculate the Variable Rate, Construct a Cost Formula, and Determine Budgeted Cost

OBJECTIVE 3
CORNERSTONE 3.4

Refer to the Pizza Vesuvio company information in **Cornerstone Exercise 3-2**. Coefficients shown by a regression program for this data are:

Intercept	1,145
X Variable	13.82

Required:

Use the results of regression to do the following:

1. Calculate the fixed cost of labour and the variable rate per employee hour.
2. Construct the cost formula for total labour cost.
3. Calculate the budgeted cost for next month, assuming that 675 employee hours are budgeted. Round answers to the nearest dollar.

EXERCISES

Exercise 3-6 Variable and Fixed Costs

OBJECTIVE 1

What follows are a number of resources that are used by a manufacturer of futons. Assume that the output measure or cost driver is the number of futons produced. All direct labour is paid on an hourly basis, and hours worked can easily be changed by management. All other factory workers are salaried.

a. Power to operate a drill (to drill holes in the wooden frames of the futons)
b. Cloth to cover the futon mattress
c. Salary of the factory receptionist

(Continued)

d. Cost of food and decorations for the annual Canada Day party for all factory employees
e. Fuel for a forklift used to move materials in the factory
f. Depreciation on the factory
g. Depreciation on a forklift used to move partially completed goods
h. Wages paid to workers who assemble the futon frame
i. Wages paid to workers who maintain the factory equipment
j. Cloth rags used to wipe the excess stain off the wooden frames

Required:

Classify the resource costs as variable or fixed.

OBJECTIVE 1

Exercise 3-7 Cost Behaviour, Classification

Singh Concrete Company owns enough ready-mix trucks to deliver up to 100,000 cubic metres of concrete per year (considering each truck's capacity, weather, and distance to each job). Total truck depreciation is $200,000 per year. Raw materials (cement, gravel, and so on) cost $25 per cubic metre of cement.

Required:

1. Prepare a graph for truck depreciation. Use the vertical axis for cost and the horizontal axis for cubic metres of cement.
2. Prepare a graph for raw materials. Use the vertical axis for cost and the horizontal axis for cubic metres of cement.
3. Assume that the normal operating range for the company is 90,000 to 96,000 cubic metres per year. Classify truck depreciation and raw materials as variable or fixed costs.

OBJECTIVE 1

Exercise 3-8 Classifying Costs as Fixed or Variable in a Service Organization

Orangeville Community Hospital (OCH) has five laboratory technicians who are responsible for doing a series of standard blood tests. Each technician is paid a salary of $47,000. The lab facility represents a recent addition to the hospital and cost $450,000. It is expected to last 20 years. Equipment used for the testing cost $36,000 and has a life expectancy of five years. In addition to the salaries, facility, and equipment, OCH expects to spend $350,000 for chemicals, forms, power, and other supplies. This $350,000 is enough for 200,000 blood tests.

Required:

Assuming that the driver (measure of output) for each type of cost is the number of blood tests performed, classify the costs by completing the following table. Put a check mark in the appropriate box for variable cost, discretionary fixed cost, or committed fixed cost.

Cost Category	Variable Cost	Discretionary Fixed Cost	Committed Fixed Cost
Technician salaries			
Laboratory facility			
Laboratory equipment			
Chemicals and other supplies			

OBJECTIVE 1

Exercise 3-9 Cost Behaviour

Alisha Limited manufactures medical stents for use in heart bypass surgery. Based on past experience, Alisha has found that its total maintenance costs can be represented by the following formula:

$$\text{Maintenance cost} = \$460{,}000 + \$12.50X$$

where X = Number of heart stents. Last year, Alisha produced 150,000 stents. Actual maintenance costs for the year were as expected. Round all answers to two decimal places.

Required:

1. What is the total maintenance cost incurred by Alisha last year?
2. What is the total fixed maintenance cost incurred by Alisha last year?
3. What is the total variable maintenance cost incurred by Alisha last year?
4. What is the maintenance cost per unit produced?
5. What is the fixed maintenance cost per unit?
6. What is the variable maintenance cost per unit?

Exercise 3-10 Cost Behaviour

OBJECTIVE 1

Refer to the Alisha Limited information in **Exercise 3-9**. However, now assume that Alisha produced 80,000 stents (rather than 150,000). Round all answers to two decimal places.

Required:

1. What is the total maintenance cost incurred by Alisha last year?
2. What is the total fixed maintenance cost incurred by Alisha last year?
3. What is the total variable maintenance cost incurred by Alisha last year?
4. What is the maintenance cost per unit produced?
5. What is the fixed maintenance cost per unit?
6. What is the variable maintenance cost per unit?

Exercise 3-11 Step Costs, Relevant Range

OBJECTIVE 2

Keon Inc. produces large industrial machinery. Keon has a machining department and a group of direct labourers called machinists. Each machinist is paid $50,000 and can machine up to 500 units per year. Keon also hires supervisors to develop machine specification plans and to oversee production within the machining department. Given the planning and supervisory work, a supervisor can oversee, at most, three machinists. Keon's accounting and production history shows the following relationships between number of units produced and the costs of materials handling and supervision (measured on an annual basis):

Units Produced	Direct Labour ($)	Supervision ($)
0–500	36,000	40,000
501–1,000	72,000	40,000
1,001–1,500	108,000	40,000
1,501–2,000	144,000	80,000
2,001–2,500	180,000	80,000
2,501–3,000	216,000	80,000
3,001–3,500	252,000	120,000
3,501–4,000	288,000	120,000

Required:

1. Prepare a graph that illustrates the relationship between direct labour cost and number of units produced in the machining department. (Let cost be the vertical axis and number of units produced be the horizontal axis.) Would you classify this cost as a strictly variable cost, a fixed cost, or a step cost?
2. Prepare a graph that illustrates the relationship between the cost of supervision and the number of units produced. (Let cost be the vertical axis and number of units produced be the horizontal axis.) Would you classify this cost as a strictly variable cost, a fixed cost, or a step cost?
3. Suppose that the normal range of activity is between 1,400 and 1,500 units and that the exact number of machinists required to support this level of activity are currently employed. Further suppose that production for the next year is expected to increase by an additional 500 units. By how much will the cost of direct labour increase? Cost of supervision?

Exercise 3-12 Matching Cost Behavior Descriptions to Cost Behavior Graphs

Required:

Select the graph (A through K) that best matches the numbered (1 through 6) descriptions of various cost behavior. For each graph, the vertical (y) axis represents total dollars of cost, and the horizontal (x) axis represents output units during the period. The graphs may be used more than once.

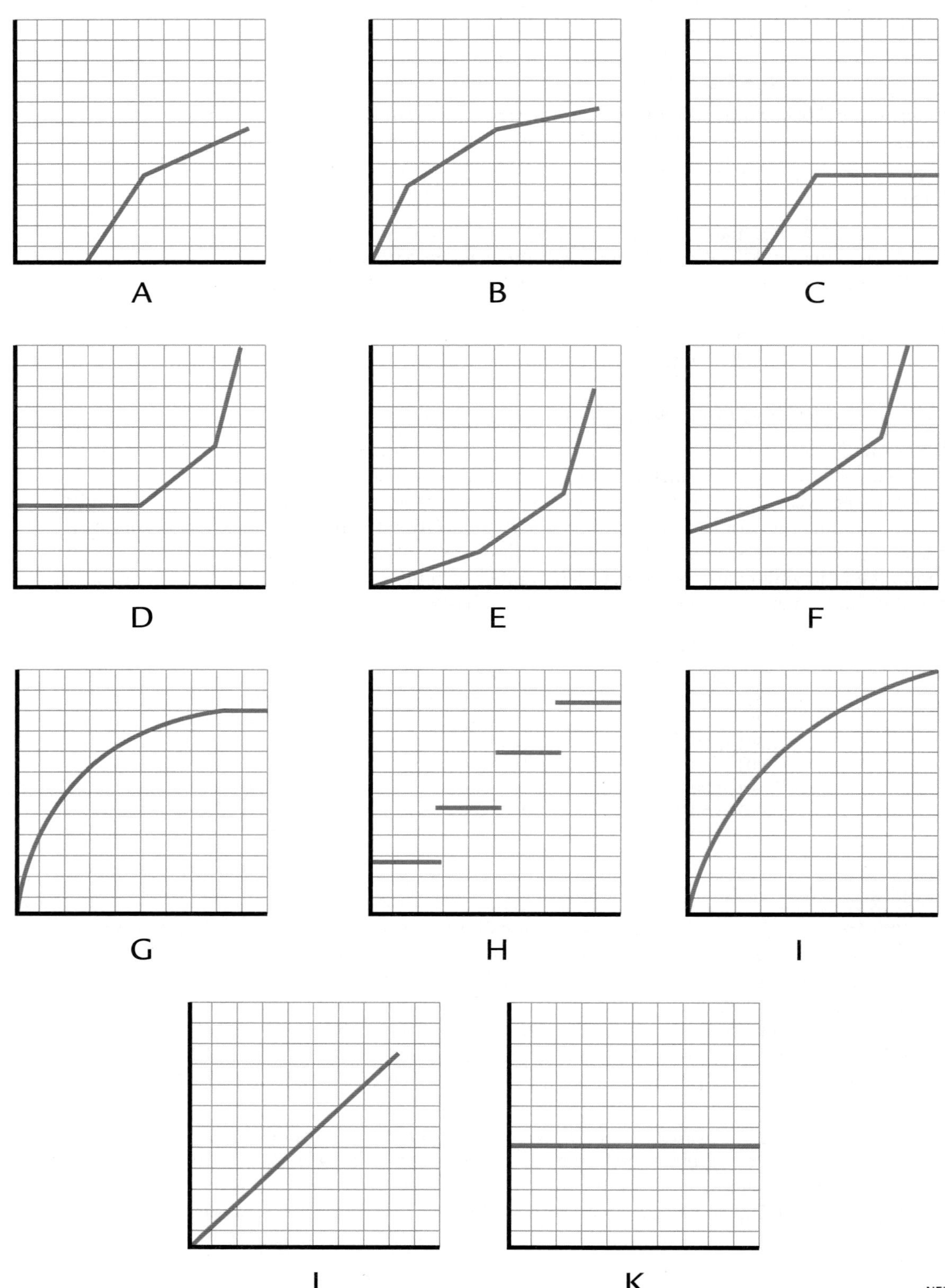

OBJECTIVE 2

1. The cost of depreciation on a large piece of production machinery equipment where the straight-line depreciation method is used. ____
2. The cost of operating a forklift to move work-in-process inventory across the factory floor where the forklift moves inventory in groups of 100 units. ____
3. The cost of direct materials where the first 2,000 kilograms of direct materials are free because they are donated by the local city government. After that, the direct materials cost consists of a per-unit amount that decreases after a threshold of 2,500 total kilograms is reached. ____
4. The cost of inspecting finished goods inventory. Each unit is inspected by a quality expert who is paid the same amount for each unit inspected. ____
5. The cost of product shipping for all output shipped in the period. The shipping cost per unit decreases with each unit shipped up to a certain number of units, at which time the shipping cost per unit remains constant. ____
6. An electric car plant manufactures car batteries. Part of the manufacturing process involves the emission of toxic chemicals into the environment, which is regulated by the Environmental Protection Agency in the form of a fee assessed on a per-unit manufactured basis. The per-unit cost of complying with these regulations increases with every fifth battery produced. ____

Exercise 3-13 Mixed Costs and Cost Formula

OBJECTIVE 2

Ivan Dimitrov owns an art gallery. He accepts paintings and sculptures on consignment and then receives 20 percent of the price of each piece as his fee. Space is limited, and there are costs involved, so Ivan is careful about accepting artists. When he does accept one, he arranges for an opening show (usually for three hours on a weekend night) and sends out invitations to his customer list. At the opening, he serves wine, soft drinks, and appetizers to create a comfortable environment for prospective customers to view the new works and to chat with the artist. On average, each opening costs $500. Ivan has given as many as 20 opening shows in a year. The total cost of running the gallery, including rent, furniture and fixtures, utilities, and a part-time assistant, amounts to $80,000 per year.

Required:

1. Prepare a graph that illustrates the relationship between the cost of giving opening shows and the number of opening shows given. (Let opening show cost be the vertical axis and number of opening shows given be the horizontal axis.) Would you classify this cost as a strictly variable cost, a fixed cost, or a mixed cost?
2. Prepare a graph that illustrates the relationship between the cost of running the gallery and the number of opening shows given. (Let gallery cost be the vertical axis and number of opening shows given be the horizontal axis.) Would you classify this cost as a strictly variable cost, a fixed cost, or a mixed cost?
3. Prepare a graph that illustrates the relationship between Ivan's total costs (the sum of the costs of giving opening shows and running the gallery) and the number of opening shows given. (Let total cost be the vertical axis and number of opening shows given be the horizontal axis.) Would you classify this cost as a strictly variable cost, a fixed cost, or a mixed cost?
4. Assume that the cost driver is number of opening shows. Develop the cost formula for the gallery's costs for a year.
5. Using the formula developed in Requirement 1, what is the total cost for Ivan in a year with 12 opening shows? With 14 opening shows?

Exercise 3-14 High–Low Method

OBJECTIVE 3

Holly Thompson has been operating a beauty shop in a university town for the past 10 years. Recently, Holly rented space next to her shop and opened a tanning salon. She anticipated that the

(Continued)

costs for the tanning service would primarily be fixed but found that tanning salon costs increased with the number of appointments. Costs for this service over the past eight months are as follows:

Month	Tanning Appointments	Total Cost ($)
January	1,400	3,516
February	4,000	4,280
March	6,200	5,580
April	5,000	4,800
May	3,000	3,600
June	4,600	4,550
July	2,300	4,400
August	6,000	5,280

Required:

1. Which month represents the high point? The low point?
2. Using the high–low method, compute the variable rate for tanning. Compute the fixed cost per month.
3. Using your answers to Requirement 2, write the cost formula for tanning services.
4. Calculate the total predicted cost of tanning services for September for 5,000 appointments using the formula found in Requirement 3. Of that total cost, how much is the total predicted fixed cost for September? How much is the total predicted variable cost for September?

OBJECTIVE 3

Exercise 3-15 Scattergraph Method

Refer to the Holly Thompson company information in **Exercise 3-14**.

Required:

Prepare a scattergraph based on Holly's data. Use cost for the vertical axis and number of tanning appointments for the horizontal. Based on an examination of the scattergraph, does there appear to be a linear relationship between the cost of tanning services and the number of appointments?

OBJECTIVE 4

Exercise 3-16 (*Appendix 3A*) Method of Least Squares

Refer to the Holly Thompson company information in **Exercise 3-14**.

Required:

1. Compute the cost formula for tanning services using the results from the method of least squares.
2. Using the formula computed in Requirement 1, what is the predicted cost of tanning services for September for 5,000 appointments?

Exercise 3-17 High–Low Method, Cost Formulas

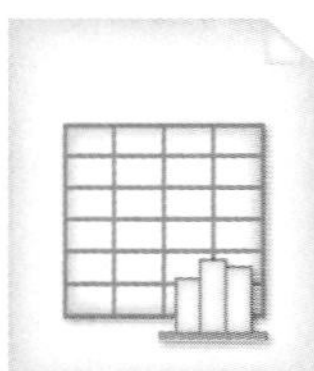

During the past year, the high and low use of three different resources for Wilson Trucking occurred in July and April. The resources are truck depreciation, fuel, and truck maintenance. The number of kilometres travelled is the driver. The total costs of the three resources and the related number of truck kilometres are as follows:

Resource	Truck Kilometres	Total Cost ($)
Truck depreciation:		
High	46,000,000	2,800,000
Low	32,400,000	2,800,000
Fuel:		
High	46,000,000	1,610,000
Low	32,400,000	1,134,000
Truck maintenance:		
High	46,000,000	1,797,200
Low	32,400,000	1,413,680

Required:

Use the high–low method to answer the following questions.

1. What is the variable rate for truck depreciation? The fixed cost?
2. What is the cost formula for truck depreciation?
3. What is the variable rate for fuel? The fixed cost?
4. What is the cost formula for fuel?
5. What is the variable rate for truck maintenance? The fixed cost?
6. What is the cost formula for truck maintenance?
7. Using the three cost formulas that you developed, predict the cost of each resource in a month with 36,000,000 kilometres travelled.
8. CONCEPTUAL CONNECTION Describe the difference between a fixed cost and a variable cost.

Exercise 3-18 Changing the Cost Formula for a Month to the Cost Formula for a Year

OBJECTIVE 

Refer to the Wilson Trucking company information in **Exercise 3-17**.

Required:

1. Develop annual cost formulas for truck depreciation, fuel, and truck maintenance.
2. Using the three annual cost formulas that you developed, predict the cost of each resource in a year with 480,000,000 truck miles.

Exercise 3-19 *(Appendix 3A)* Method of Least Squares, Developing and Using the Cost Formula

OBJECTIVE 4

The method of least squares was used to develop a cost equation to predict the cost of receiving parts in a manufacturing company; 96 data points from monthly data were used for the regression. The following computer output was received:

Intercept	106,327
Slope	193

The driver used was number of parts inspected.

Required:

1. What is the cost formula?
2. Using the cost formula from Requirement 1, identify each of the following: independent variable, dependent variable, variable rate, and fixed cost per month.
3. Using the cost formula, predict the cost of parts inspection for a month in which 2,500 parts are inspected.

Exercise 3-20 *(Appendix 3A)* Method of Least Squares; Budgeted Time Period Is Different from Time Period Used to Generate Results

OBJECTIVE 4

Refer to the company information in **Exercise 3-19**.

Required:

1. What is the cost formula for a year?
2. Using the cost formula from Requirement 1, predict the cost of parts inspection for a year in which 29,000 parts are inspected.

Exercise 3-21 Identifying the Parts of the Cost Formula; Calculating Monthly, Quarterly, and Yearly Costs Using a Cost Formula Based on Monthly Data

OBJECTIVE 

Gordon Company's controller, Eric Junior, estimated the following formula, based on monthly data, for overhead cost:

$$\text{Overhead cost} = \$109{,}743 + (\$80.75 \times \text{Direct labour hours})$$

(Continued)

Required:

1. Link each term in column A to the corresponding term in column B.

Column A	Column B
Overhead cost	Variable rate (slope)
$109,743	Independent variable
$80.75	Fixed cost (intercept)
Direct labour hours	Dependent variable

2. If next month's budgeted direct labour hours equal 5,000, what is the budgeted overhead cost?
3. If next quarter's budgeted direct labour hours equal 18,000, what is the budgeted overhead cost?
4. If next year's budgeted direct labour hours equal 58,000, what is the budgeted overhead cost?

OBJECTIVE 5

Exercise 3-22 (*Appendix 3A*) Method of Least Squares Using Computer Spreadsheet Program

The controller for Beckham Company believes that the number of direct labour hours is associated with overhead cost. He collected the following data on the number of direct labour hours and associated factory overhead cost for the months of January through August.

Month	Number of Direct Labour Hours	Overhead Cost ($)
January	1,378	55,500
February	1,400	55,900
March	1,440	56,500
April	1,380	55,700
May	1,360	55,700
June	1,180	54,100
July	1,500	57,200
August	1,350	56,080

Required:

1. Using a computer spreadsheet program such as Excel, run a regression on these data. Print out your results.
2. Using your results from Requirement 1, write the cost formula for overhead cost. (You may round the fixed cost to the nearest dollar and the variable rate to the nearest cent.)
3. What is R^2 based on your results? Do you think that the number of direct labour hours is a good predictor of factory overhead cost?
4. Assuming that expected September direct labour hours are 1,450, what is expected factory overhead cost using the cost formula in Requirement 2?

OBJECTIVE 5

Exercise 3-23 (*Appendix 3A*) Method of Least Squares Using Computer Spreadsheet Program

Susan Lewis, the owner of a flower shop, is interested in predicting the cost of delivering floral arrangements. She collected monthly data on the number of deliveries and the total monthly delivery cost (depreciation on the van, wages of the driver, and fuel) for the past year.

Month	Number of Deliveries	Delivery Cost ($)
January	100	1,200
February	550	1,800
March	85	1,100
April	115	1,050
May	160	1,190
June	590	1,980
July	500	1,800
August	520	1,700
September	100	1,100
October	200	1,275
November	260	1,400
December	450	2,200

Required:

1. Using a computer spreadsheet program such as Excel, run a regression on these data. Print out your results.
2. Using your results from Requirement 1, write the cost formula for delivery cost. (You may round the fixed cost to the nearest dollar and the variable rate to the nearest cent.)
3. What is R^2 based on your results? Do you think that the number of direct labour hours is a good predictor of delivery cost?
4. Using the cost formula in Requirement 2, what would predicted delivery cost be for a month with 300 deliveries?

PROBLEMS

Problem 3-24 Identifying Fixed, Variable, Mixed, and Step Costs

OBJECTIVE 1 2

Required:

For each of the following, independent scenarios, indicate the nature of the costs as variable, fixed, mixed, or step costs.

1. A cellphone contract where there is a minimum cost per month plus additional cost for usage.
2. The depreciation cost of a machine that is calculated on a straight-line basis.
3. The delivery cost for a courier where the costs include wages of an employee, depreciation of the vehicle, and fuel costs.
4. The cost of a sales manager in a situation where one manager can supervise 10 salespeople.
5. The cost of reimbursing employees for the use of their automobiles where they are paid on the basis of the number of kilometres driven each month.
6. The depreciation cost of a machine where the depreciation is based on the units-of-production method.
7. The cost of a babysitter who charges $6 per hour.
8. The cost of leasing an automobile where the lessee is granted a certain number of kilometres during the lease, then is charged extra beyond the maximum allowable.

Problem 3-25 Identifying Use of the High–Low, Scattergraph, and Least Squares Methods

OBJECTIVE 3 4

Consider each of the following independent situations:

a. Jennifer Reynolds just started her new job as controller for St. Matthias General Hospital. She wants to get a feel for the cost behaviour of various departments of the hospital. Jennifer first looks at the radiology department. She has annual data on total cost and the number of procedures that have been run for the past 15 years. However, she knows that the department upgraded its equipment substantially two years ago and is doing a wider variety of tests. So, Jennifer decides to use data for just the past two years.

b. Francis Hidalgo is a summer intern in the accounting department of a manufacturing firm. His boss assigned him a special project to determine the cost of manufacturing a special order. Francis needs information on variable and fixed overhead, so he gathers monthly data on overhead cost and machine hours for the past 60 months and enters them into his personal computer. A few keystrokes later, he has information on fixed and variable overhead costs.

c. Ron Wickstead sighed and studied his computer printout again. The results made no sense to him. He seemed to recall that sometimes it helped to visualize the cost relationships. He reached for some graph paper and a pencil.

d. Rikki Mohammad had hoped that she could find information on the actual cost of promoting new products. Unfortunately, she had spent the weekend going through the files and was only able to find data on the total cost of the sales department by month for the past three years. She was also able to figure out the number of new product launches by month for the same time period. Now, she had just 15 minutes before a staff meeting in which she needed to give the vice-president of sales an expected cost of the average new product launch. A light bulb went on in her head, and she reached for paper, a pencil, and a calculator.

Required:

Determine which of the following cost separation methods is being used: the high–low method, the scattergraph method, or the method of least squares.

OBJECTIVE 1

Problem 3-26 Identifying Variable Costs, Committed Fixed Costs, and Discretionary Fixed Costs

Required:

Classify each of the following costs for a jeans manufacturing company as a variable cost, committed fixed cost, or discretionary fixed cost.

1. The cost of buttons.
2. The cost to lease warehouse space for completed jeans. The lease contract runs for two years at $5,000 per year.
3. The salary of a summer intern.
4. The cost of landscaping and mowing the grass. The contract with a local mowing company runs from month to month.
5. Advertising in a national magazine for teenage girls.
6. Electricity to run the sewing machines.
7. Oil and spare needles for the sewing machines.
8. Quality training for employees—typically given for four hours at a time, every six months.
9. Food and beverages for the company Canada Day picnic.
10. Natural gas to heat the factory during the winter.

OBJECTIVE 3

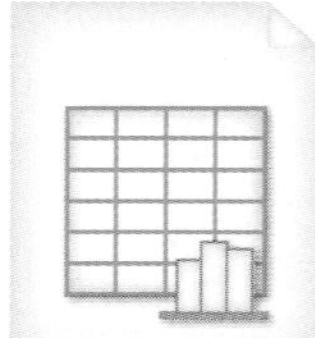

Problem 3-27 Scattergraph, High–Low Method, and Predicting Cost for a Different Time Period from the One Used to Develop a Cost Formula

Farnsworth Company has gathered data on its overhead activities and associated costs for the past 10 months. Tracy Heppler, a member of the controller's department, has convinced management that overhead costs can be better estimated and controlled if the fixed and variable components of each overhead activity are known. One such activity is receiving raw materials (unloading incoming goods, counting goods, and inspecting goods), which she believes is driven by the number of receiving orders. Ten months of data have been gathered for the receiving activity and are as follows:

Month	Receiving Orders	Receiving Cost ($)
1	1,000	27,000
2	700	22,500
3	1,500	42,000
4	1,200	25,500
5	1,300	37,500
6	1,100	31,500
7	1,600	43,500
8	1,400	36,000
9	1,700	40,500
10	900	24,000

Required:

1. Prepare a scattergraph based on the 10 months of data. Does the relationship appear to be linear?
2. Using the high–low method, prepare a cost formula for the receiving activity. Using this formula, what is the predicted cost of receiving for a month in which 1,450 receiving orders are processed?
3. Prepare a cost formula for the receiving activity for a quarter. Based on this formula, what is the predicted cost of receiving for a quarter in which 4,650 receiving orders are anticipated? Prepare a cost formula for the receiving activity for a year. Based on this formula, what is the predicted cost of receiving for a year in which 18,000 receiving orders are anticipated?

Check figures:

2. Fixed receiving cost = $9,900
3. Receiving cost for the year = $442,800

Problem 3-28 Method of Least Squares, Predicting Cost for Different Time Periods from the One Used to Develop a Cost Formula

OBJECTIVE 4

Refer to the Farnsworth Company information in **Problem 3-27**. However, now assume that Tracy has used the method of least squares on the receiving data and found the following results:

Intercept	4,818
Slope	22.73

Required:

1. Using the results from the method of least squares, prepare a cost formula for the receiving activity.
2. Using the formula from Requirement 1, what is the predicted cost of receiving for a month in which 1,450 receiving orders are processed? (Round your answer to the nearest dollar.)
3. Prepare a cost formula for the receiving activity for a quarter. Based on this formula, what is the predicted cost of receiving for a quarter in which 4,650 receiving orders are anticipated? Prepare a cost formula for the receiving activity for a year. Based on this formula, what is the predicted cost of receiving for a year in which 18,000 receiving orders are anticipated?

Check figure:
2. Receiving cost = $37,777

Problem 3-29 Cost Behaviour, High–Low Method, Pricing Decision

Rudolph, Donner, and Blitzen is a small, highly successful law firm in Markham, Ontario. The partners decide that they would like to give back to the community by opening a not-for-profit legal clinic in an economically disadvantaged neighbourhood. The services would provide low-income clients with an opportunity to get first-class service at a fraction of the normal cost. They decide to assign one of their more experienced juniors to the clinic, but are unsure of how to set the price that would result in the clinic breaking even. As a result, they decide to operate the clinic for two months, observe the costs, and then set the pricing for the long term.

For the month of January, they provided 120 hours of professional service; in February, this was 150 hours. The costs are summarized below:

	120 Hours ($)	150 Hours ($)
Salaries:		
Junior lawyer	4,500	4,500
Office assistant	1,800	1,800
Internet and software subscriptions	700	850
Consulting by senior partner	1,200	1,500
Depreciation (equipment)	2,400	2,400
Pamphlets and promotion	600	700
Supplies	905	1,100
Administration	500	500
Rent (offices)	2,000	2,000
Utilities	332	365

Required:

1. Classify each cost as fixed, variable, or mixed, using hours of professional service as the activity driver.
2. Use the high–low method to separate the mixed costs into their fixed and variable components.
3. Seth Jones, the chief accountant of the firm, has estimated that the clinic will average 140 professional hours per month. What would the total cost of operating the clinic be? How much is variable? How much is fixed?
4. If the clinic is to be operated as a not-for-profit organization, how much will it need to charge per professional hour?
5. Suppose the legal clinic averages 170 professional hours per month. How much would need to be charged per hour for the clinic to cover its costs? Explain why the per-hour charge decreased as the activity output increased.

Check figures:
3. Supplies variable rate = $6.50
4. Charge per hour = $110.39

Problem 3-30 Flexible and Committed Resources, Capacity Usage for a Service

Jana Morgan is about to sign up for cellphone service. She is primarily interested in the safety aspect of the phone; that is, she wants to have one available for emergencies. She does not want to use it as her primary phone. Jana has narrowed her options down to two plans:

	Plan 1	Plan 2
Monthly fee	\$20	\$30
Free local minutes	60	120
Additional charges per minute:		
Airtime (after free local minutes are used up)	\$0.40	\$0.30
Long distance	0.15	–
Regional roaming	0.60	–
National roaming	0.60	0.60

Both plans are subject to a \$25 activation fee and a \$120 cancellation fee if the service is cancelled before one year has passed. Jana's brother will give her a cellphone that he no longer needs. It is not the latest version (and is not Internet capable) but will work well with both plans.

Required:

1. Classify the charges associated with the cellphone service as (a) committed resources or (b) flexible resources.
2. Assume that Jana will use, on average, 45 minutes per month in local calling. For each plan, split her minute allotment into used and unused capacity. Which plan will be most cost effective? Why?
3. Assume that Jana loves her cellphone and ends up talking frequently with friends while travelling within her region. On average, she uses 60 local minutes a month and 30 regional minutes. For each plan, split her minute allotment into used and unused capacity. Which plan will be most cost effective? Why?
4. Analyze your own cellphone plan by comparing it with other possible options.

Check figures:

2. Plan 2 unused minutes = 75
3. Plan 2 minutes used = 90

Problem 3-31 Variable and Fixed Costs, Cost Formula, High–Low Method

Li Ming Yuan and Tiffany Shaden are the department heads for the accounting department and human resources department, respectively, at a Montreal insurance firm. They have just returned from an executive meeting at which the necessity of cutting costs and gaining efficiency has been stressed. After talking with Tiffany and some of her staff members, as well as his own staff members, Li Ming discovered that there were a number of costs associated with the claims processing activity. These costs included the salaries of the two paralegals who worked full-time on claims processing; the salary of the accountant who cut the cheques; the cost of claims forms, cheques, envelopes, and postage; and depreciation on the office equipment dedicated to the processing. Some of the paralegals' time is spent in the routine processing of uncontested claims, but much time is spent on the claims that have incomplete documentation or are contested. The accountant's time appears to vary with the number of claims processed.

Li Ming was able to separate the costs of processing claims from the costs of running the departments of accounting and human resources. He gathered the data on claims processing cost and the number of claims processed per month for the past six months. These data are as follows:

Month	Claims Processing Cost (\$)	Number of Claims Processed
February	34,907	5,700
March	31,260	4,900
April	37,950	6,100
May	38,250	6,500
June	44,895	7,930
July	44,055	7,514

Required:

1. Classify the claims processing costs that Li Ming identified as variable or fixed.
2. What is the independent variable? The dependent variable?
3. Use the high–low method to find the fixed cost per month and the variable rate. What is the cost formula?
4. Suppose that an outside company bids on the claims processing business. The bid price is $4.60 per claim. If Tiffany expects 75,600 claims next year, should she outsource the claims processing or continue to do it in-house?

Check figure:
3. Variable rate = $4.50

Problem 3-32 Cost Separation

OBJECTIVE 1 2

About eight years ago, North Shore Racquet Company faced the problem of rapidly increasing costs associated with workplace accidents. The costs included the following:

Insurance premiums	$100,000
Average cost per injury	$1,500
Number of injuries per year	15
Number of serious injuries	4
Number of workdays lost	30

A safety program was implemented with the following features: hiring a safety director, new employee orientation, stretching required four times a day, and systematic monitoring of adherence to the program by directors and supervisors. A year later, the indicators were as follows:

Insurance premiums	$50,000
Average cost per injury	$50
Number of injuries per year	10
Number of serious injuries	0
Number of workdays lost	0
Safety director's starting salary	$60,000

Required:

1. Discuss the safety-related costs listed. Are they variable or fixed with respect to units produced? With respect to other independent variables (describe)?
2. Did the safety program pay for itself? Discuss your reasoning.

Problem 3-33 *(Appendix 3A)* Method of Least Squares

OBJECTIVE 3 5

Refer to the Farnsworth Company information in **Problem 3-27** for the first 10 months of data on receiving orders and receiving cost. Now suppose that Tracy has gathered two more months of data:

Month	Receiving Orders	Receiving Cost ($)
11	1,200	42,000
12	950	26,250

For the following requirements, round the intercept terms to the nearest dollar and round the variable rates to the nearest cent.

Required:

1. Run two regressions using a computer spreadsheet program such as Excel. First, use the method of least squares on the first 10 months of data. Then, use the method of least squares on all 12 months of data. Record the results for the intercept, slope, and R2 for each regression. Compare the results.
2. Prepare a scattergraph using all 12 months of data. Do any points appear to be outliers? Suppose Tracy has learned that the factory suffered severe storm damage during month 11 that required extensive repairs to the receiving area—including major repairs on a forklift. These expenses, included in month 11 receiving costs, are not expected to recur. What step might Tracy, using her judgment, take to amend the results from the method of least squares?

(Continued)

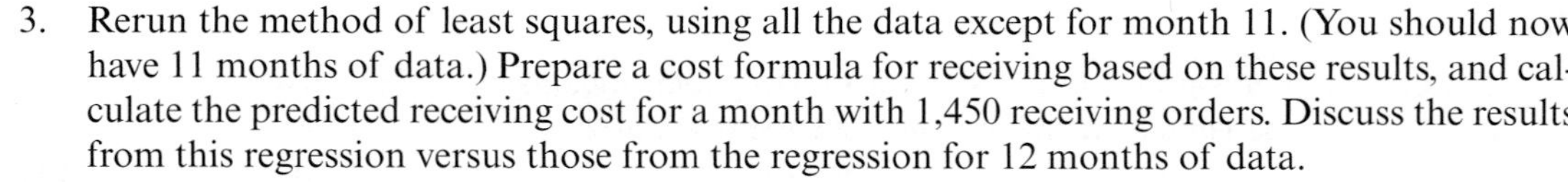

3. Rerun the method of least squares, using all the data except for month 11. (You should now have 11 months of data.) Prepare a cost formula for receiving based on these results, and calculate the predicted receiving cost for a month with 1,450 receiving orders. Discuss the results from this regression versus those from the regression for 12 months of data.

Check figure:

1. 10 months' data intercept = $4,818

OBJECTIVE 3 4

Problem 3-34 *(Appendix 3A)* Scattergraph, High–Low Method, Method of Least Squares, Use of Judgment

The management of Wheeler Company has decided to develop cost formulas for its major overhead activities. Wheeler uses a highly automated manufacturing process, and power costs are a significant manufacturing cost. Cost analysts have decided that power costs are mixed; thus, they must be broken into their fixed and variable elements so that the cost behaviour of the power usage activity can be properly described. Machine hours have been selected as the activity driver for power costs. The following data for the past eight quarters have been collected:

Quarter	Machine Hours	Power Cost ($)
1	20,000	39,000
2	25,000	57,000
3	30,000	63,750
4	22,000	55,500
5	21,000	51,000
6	18,000	43,500
7	24,000	54,000
8	28,000	60,000

For the following requirements, round the fixed cost to the nearest dollar and round the variable rates to the nearest cent.

Required:

1. Prepare a scattergraph by plotting power costs against machine hours. Does the scattergraph show a linear relationship between machine hours and power cost?
2. Using the high and low points, compute a power cost formula.
3. Use the method of least squares to compute a power cost formula. Evaluate the coefficient of determination.
4. Rerun the regression, and drop the point (20,000, $39,000) as an outlier. Compare the results from this regression to those for the regression in Requirement 3. Which is better?

Check figure:

2. Variable power cost = $1.69

OBJECTIVE 3 4

Problem 3-35 *(Appendix 3A)* Separating Fixed and Variable Costs, Service Setting

Ellen McGuire operates a local courier service with 10 vehicles. These vehicles pick up and deliver packages within the urban area. Ellen is very concerned about her delivery costs and wants to get a better idea of how to predict these costs in the future. She has gathered monthly data for the past year and has decided to try to categorize her costs by fixed and variable.

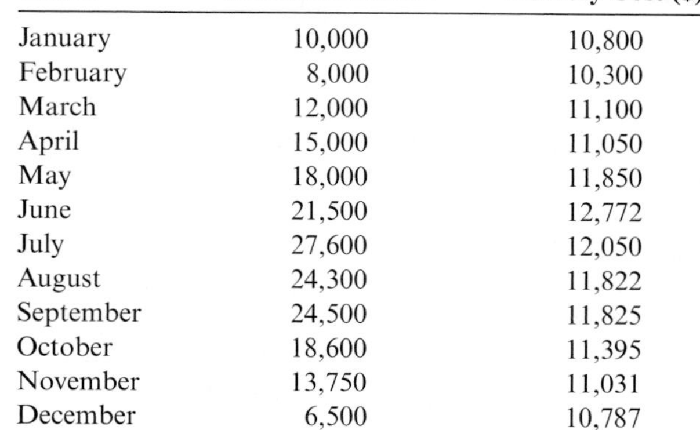

Month	Kilometres Driven	Delivery Cost ($)
January	10,000	10,800
February	8,000	10,300
March	12,000	11,100
April	15,000	11,050
May	18,000	11,850
June	21,500	12,772
July	27,600	12,050
August	24,300	11,822
September	24,500	11,825
October	18,600	11,395
November	13,750	11,031
December	6,500	10,787

Required:

1. Prepare a scattergraph to estimate the best fit for a cost line. Plot total cost on the vertical axis and kilometres driven on the horizontal axis.
2. Prepare a least squares analysis of the data.
3. What is the cost formula derived from the least squares analysis?
4. Does this result appear to be consistent with your scattergraph analysis?
5. CONCEPTUAL CONNECTION Which method do you prefer? Why?

Check figure:
2. Fixed rate = $10,010.22

OBJECTIVE 

Problem 3-36 *(Appendix 3A)* Separating Fixed and Variable Costs, Service Setting

Jiffy Print is a printing shop on a local college campus. In analyzing the costs over a two-year period, the following data was available for the printing jobs on the colour printer:

Month	Cost ($)	Jobs
January	1,588	175
February	2,143	295
March	2,005	260
April	1,908	245
May	2,163	305
June	1,478	155
July	1,458	145
August	1,613	175
September	1,708	195
October	1,348	205
November	1,428	225
December	1,638	255
January	1,840	230
February	1,728	285
March	1,543	265
April	1,940	250
May	1,860	230
June	1,590	220
July	1,513	225
August	1,633	235
September	1,928	265
October	2,028	285
November	1,850	300
December	2,038	275

Required:

1. Prepare a scattergraph based on these data. Plot cost on the vertical axis and number of jobs on the horizontal axis.
2. Compute the cost formula for print jobs using the method of least squares. Using the regression cost formula, what is the predicted cost for a month with 250 jobs?
3. Comment on the usefulness of the least squares approach in these circumstances and whether additional value has been added by using regression analysis.

Problem 3-37 *(Appendix 3A)* Separating Fixed and Variable Costs, Service Setting

A company has identified the following data with respect to a critical activity in its manufacturing process.

Month	Cost ($)	Activity
January	101,000	1,600
February	102,000	1,700
March	118,000	1,900
April	112,150	1,800

(Continued)

Month	Cost ($)	Activity
May	158,750	2,600
June	167,650	2,750
July	142,650	2,300
August	139,150	2,250
September	129,150	2,100
October	120,025	1,950
November	132,700	2,150
December	113,850	1,850
January	115,150	1,850
February	122,350	2,000
March	133,150	2,175
April	143,250	2,340
May	175,600	2,850
June	181,700	2,950
July	190,365	3,125
August	196,400	3,225
September	181,350	2,950
October	171,550	2,650
November	179,550	2,750
December	164,350	2,450

Management wants to ensure that it has a thorough understanding of how costs will behave in the future.

Required:

1. Prepare a scattergraph based on these data. Plot cost on the vertical axis and number of activities on the horizontal axis.
2. Identify the three outliers on the scattergraph.
3. Compute the cost formula using the method of least squares. Using the regression cost formula, what is the predicted cost for a month with 2,000 activities?
4. Recompute the least squares analysis after removing the outliers identified in Requirement 2.
5. Comment on the differences in the two regression analyses.

PROFESSIONAL EXAMINATION PROBLEM*

Professional Examination Problem 3-38 Cost Classification and Behaviour—Spark Electrical Company

Spark Electrical Company manufactures electrical components. Plant management has experienced difficulties with fluctuating monthly overhead costs. Management wants to be able to estimate overhead costs to plan its operations and financial needs. A trade association publication reports that for companies manufacturing electrical components, overhead tends to vary with machine hours.

Monthly data was gathered on machine hours and overhead costs for the past two years. There were no major changes in operations over this period of time. The raw data is:

Month Number	Machine Hours	Overhead Costs ($)
1	20,000	84,000
2	25,000	99,000
3	22,000	89,500
4	23,000	90,000
5	20,000	81,500
6	19,000	75,500

Month Number	Machine Hours	Overhead Costs ($)
7	14,000	70,500
8	10,000	64,500
9	12,000	69,000
10	17,000	75,000
11	16,000	71,500
12	19,000	78,000
13	21,000	86,000
14	24,000	93,000
15	23,000	93,000
16	22,000	87,000
17	20,000	80,000
18	18,000	76,500
19	12,000	67,500
20	13,000	71,000
21	15,000	73,500
22	17,000	72,500
23	15,000	71,000
24	18,000	75,000

The data was entered into Excel and a regression was run on the data. The following output was obtained:

R-square	0.91
Coefficients of the equation:	
Intercept	39,859
Independent variable (slope)	2.15

Required:

1. Use the high–low method to estimate the overhead costs.
2. Are the regression analysis results acceptable?
3. Use the results of both the high–low method and the regression to prepare the cost estimation equation and to prepare a cost estimate for 22,000 machine hours.

CASES

Case 3-39 *(Appendix 3A)* Cost Formulas, Single and Multiple Cost Drivers

OBJECTIVE 1 2 3 4 5

For the past five years, Velocity Manufacturing Company has had a policy of producing to meet customer demand. As a result, finished goods inventory is minimal, and for the most part, units produced equal units sold.

Recently, Velocity's industry entered a recession, and the company is producing well below capacity (and expects to continue doing so for the coming year). The president is willing to accept orders that at least cover their variable costs so that the company can keep its employees and avoid layoffs. Also, any orders above variable costs will increase overall profitability of the company. Toward that end, the president of Velocity implemented a policy that any special orders will be accepted if they cover the costs that the orders cause.

To help implement the policy, Velocity's controller developed the following cost formulas:

Direct material usage = $94X	$R^2 = 0.90$
Direct labour usage = $16X	$R^2 = 0.92$
Overhead = $80X	$R^2 = 0.56$
Selling costs = $7X	$R^2 = 0.86$

where X = direct labour hours

(Continued)

Required:

1. Compute the total unit variable cost. Suppose that Velocity has an opportunity to accept an order for 20,000 units at $212 per unit. Each unit uses one direct labour hour for production. Should Velocity accept the order? (The order would not displace any of Velocity's regular orders.)
2. (*Appendix 3A*) Explain the significance of the coefficient of determination measures for the cost formulas. Did these measures have a bearing on your answer in Requirement 1? Should they have a bearing? Why?
3. (*Appendix 3A*) Suppose that a multiple regression equation is developed for overhead costs: Y = $100,000 + $85X1 + $5,000X2 + $300X3, where X1 = Direct labour hours, X2 = Number of setups, and X3 = Engineering hours. The coefficient of determination for the equation is 0.89. Assume that the order of 20,000 units requires 12 setups and 600 engineering hours. Given this new information, should the company accept the special order referred to in Requirement 1? Is there any other information about cost behaviour that you would like to have? Explain.

Case 3-40 Service Organization Cost Classification

Max Foster sat in his office on a bright May morning contemplating a problem that had been bothering him for several weeks. Max was the managing partner of a relatively small consulting firm in Calgary that was experiencing substantial growth in its revenues. The firm consisted of three partners, 12 senior consultants, and 30 junior consultants. They specialized in the design of major drilling operations in difficult terrain.

The firm prided itself in compensating its consultants very well and giving them an opportunity to do very interesting work. Max was wrestling with an erosion of the profitability of the firm in recent months as revenue was increasing, a strange occurrence that he could not explain. He expected that the decline in profitability was due to very high fixed costs in a volatile market. The offices were in a magnificent building in downtown Calgary, which cost $3,000,000 per year in rent. The offices were fully furnished with all the latest office furniture and equipment, which was being depreciated at the rate of $250,000 per year. There were eight office staff and the full cost of administration was $360,000 annually. Each of the professional staff consumed supplies in doing their work at the rate of $10 per hour billed to clients.

The firm had lost some recent bids for business and Max worried that costs were not well understood. He wanted to change the way the firm accounted for costs and how consultants were compensated.

Each of the partners expected to earn $300,000 per year before profit sharing, while the senior consultants were paid between $125,000 and $150,000 per year. The junior consultants were paid about $75,000 per year, on average. The partners spent about 50 percent of their time promoting business and the balance actually doing consulting work. The rest of the consultants were not expected to do client promotion work but to concentrate fully on consulting.

Max's idea was to change the compensation package of every professional staff member, partner, senior consultant, and junior consultant to an arrangement whereby each person received a base salary and additional compensation calculated on the basis of the number of hours billed to clients. In addition, every professional staff member would receive an expense allowance based on the number of hours billed, to be used at their own discretion.

He would pay partners a base salary of $100,000 per year and $100 per hour of productive work, excluding client promotion. Senior consultants would be paid a base of $75,000 plus $50 per hour billed to clients, while junior consultants would be paid a $60,000 base salary and $10 per hour billed. The expense allowance would be $50 per partner per hour; senior consultants would get $6 per hour billed and the junior consultants would get $2 per hour billed.

Max believed that consultants should bill a minimum of 1,500 hours per year and would ideally bill 2,000 hours per year to clients.

Required:

1. Determine the cost formula for each category of expense that Max is contemplating.
2. Estimate the total cost of running the business if each professional bills an average of 1,500 hours per year and if each professional bills 2,000 hours per year.

Case 3-41 Suspicious Acquisition of Data, Ethical Issues

OBJECTIVE 1

Bill Taylor, vice-president of engineering for Hawthorne Construction, was working away in his office when Jacko McGuire, vice-president of sales of the company, came in to see him. The following conversation took place:

Jacko: Bill, you know that contract for the new office complex in the East End?

Bill: Yes, I do. I was deeply involved in the estimating of the costs for that project, as it is one of the most expensive bids that the company has considered.

Jacko: I know you were, and my team and I are trying to come up with the final price for the bid.

Bill: How has that been going? I've heard rumours that there is some disagreement about the risks involved.

Jacko: Yes, it seems that the finance team is concerned that the fixed costs appear to be very high and will only be covered if we are successful in landing the second phase of the project.

Bill: Yes, I recall that that was a major point of contention when we were involved in the costing process.

Jacko: Well, I'm certain that if we win phase one, we'll be a shoo-in for phases two, three, and four. With all four phases, we will be spectacularly profitable and the initial fixed costs will give us a huge advantage, but I can't get them to see it my way. They believe that the risks are too great because of the initial investment.

Bill: I can see their concern.

Jacko: When you were involved in the initial costing, I recall that the determination of the fixed costs was subject to some estimation on the part of your engineering team. Is that right?

Bill: Yes, it is. Like all estimation processes, especially on major contracts that run for several years, it is often difficult to estimate precisely the relationship between fixed and variable costs. Unfortunately, once fixed costs are incurred, you cannot get them back, while variable costs will only be incurred if the project continues forward into the future.

Jacko: That's what I thought. If you were to revisit the costing of the project, is it possible that a new estimate could be developed that showed the fixed costs as much lower, while variable costs were much higher? In this way, the analysts would be satisfied about the risks and we could prepare a bid that is sure to win.

Bill: But nothing has changed from our original estimates, so what's the issue?

Jacko: Bill, I'm not asking you to change the total estimated cost of the project, so everything would be very truthfully done. Just change your estimate of how much of the total cost is fixed and how much is variable.

Bill: I'm not sure I can do that, because there is far greater risk associated with incurring fixed costs rather than variable costs, and the decision would be based on assumptions that I believe are incorrect.

Jacko: But we would win the business and it would sustain us for many years to come.

Required:

What should Bill do? Elaborate on your answer to fully explain your reasoning.

4

Cost–Volume–Profit Analysis: A Managerial Planning Tool

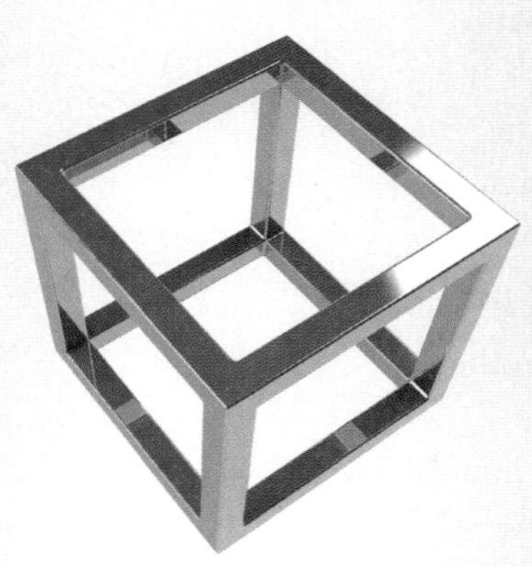

After studying Chapter 4, you should be able to:

1. Determine the break-even point in number of units sold and in total sales dollars.
2. Determine the number of units that must be sold, and the amount of revenue required, to earn a target profit.
3. Prepare a profit–volume graph and a cost–volume–profit graph, and explain the meaning of each.
4. Apply cost–volume–profit analysis in a multiple-product setting.
5. Explain the impact of risk, uncertainty, and changing variables on cost–volume–profit analysis.

Courtesy of Boyne Resorts

EXPERIENCE MANAGERIAL DECISIONS

with Boyne Resorts

When Alex Bilodeau won the gold medal in the men's mogul event at the 2010 Olympic Games, Canadians celebrated him not only as the winner of Canada's first gold medal of the 2010 games, but also as the first Canadian to win an Olympic gold medal on Canadian soil. The moguls event was held at Cypress Mountain near Vancouver, British Columbia.

Cypress Mountain is one of many ski resorts owned by Boyne Resorts, which has facilities in British Columbia, Washington, Montana, Maine, New Hampshire, Utah, and Michigan. Boyne earns a significant portion of its revenue from winter skiing. However, winter ski volume is heavily dependent on natural snowfall, which varies significantly from year to year. The business risk associated with such large snowfall variation is likely to continue into the foreseeable future as dramatic climatic changes, such as global warming, continue to occur. As a result, Boyne uses creative thinking along with various cost–volume–profit (CVP) analyses to develop activities that generate additional profit. Consider ski lifts at Cypress Mountain. Boyne develops a variety of lift ticket packages to accommodate as many snow skiers and snowboarders as possible. For example, lift tickets are interchangeable between multiple Boyne properties and can be used during night skiing in certain areas.

Like many ski resorts, Boyne markets spring, summer, and fall activities as well. For instance, many resorts promote mountain biking and hiking; participants purchase lift tickets for enclosed lifts, called gondolas, that carry them and their gear to the top of the mountain to begin their descent. Other ski resorts, such as Whistler–Blackcomb, build elaborate children's playgrounds, host mountain bike races, and plan numerous festivals and activities to generate additional summer business in ski areas that might otherwise be dormant during the off season. Still other resorts build elaborate mountaintop restaurants and entertainment areas that can be reached only via ski lifts or gondolas, thereby increasing both revenues and profits.

In analyzing the available opportunities, Boyne will estimate the additional revenues that can be generated by each alternative and the additional costs of the alternative. In most cases, the fixed cost increases will be minimal, so the focus is on the variable costs to be incurred. Using the CVP relationships, Boyne can determine in advance what impact each alternative will have on its operating profit. The main objective is to generate as much revenue as possible from the investments in fixed assets that it has already made (i.e., the chairlifts), which will, in turn, maximize profits. With careful CVP analysis and sound judgment, Boyne attempts to make the best decisions possible to increase its profitability and its reputation for fun.

BOYNE RESORTS
EXPERIENCE THE LIFESTYLE

COST–VOLUME–PROFIT RELATIONSHIPS

Managers are responsible for improving the profitable operation of their business in order to meet the needs of the shareholders (owners). One method of improving profits would be to increase revenues, but increasing revenues alone does not guarantee that profits will increase at all, much less enough to meet the needs of the shareholders.

In Chapter 3, we learned that costs behave in different ways, and understanding cost behaviour should help us predict how profits will change as revenues increase. It is important to remember that, within the relevant range, fixed costs will not change in total as the level of activity increases. At the same time, within the relevant range, variable costs per unit will remain constant.

These relationships will allow managers to analyze future operations of the business and to predict how changes in various factors will influence profitability. Ultimately, we want to know how much more profit we will earn as revenue increases. Since fixed costs will not increase, profit will increase by the difference between the increase in revenue and the increase in variable cost. We refer to the difference between revenue and variable cost as *contribution margin*, which represents the contribution made to cover fixed costs and profit.

Cost–volume–profit (CVP) analysis is one of the most valuable analytical tools that managers can use to understand the nature of the profitable performance of their business.

Determine the break-even point in number of units sold and in total sales dollars.

CVP analysis can address many other issues as well, such as the number of units that must be sold to break even, the impact of a given reduction in fixed costs on the break-even point, and the impact of an increase in price on profit. Additionally, CVP analysis allows managers to do sensitivity analysis by examining the impact of various price or cost levels on profit.

Using Operating Income in Cost–Volume–Profit Analysis

Remember from Chapter 2 that operating income is total revenue minus total expense. For the income statement, expenses were classified according to function—that is, the manufacturing (or service provision) function, the selling function, and the administrative function. For CVP analysis, however, it is much more useful to organize costs into the fixed and variable components. The focus is on the firm as a whole. Therefore, the costs refer to all costs of the company—production, selling, and administration. So variable costs are all costs that increase as more units are sold, including:

- direct materials
- direct labour
- variable factory overhead
- variable selling and administrative costs

Similarly, fixed costs include:

- fixed factory overhead
- fixed selling and administrative expenses

The income statement format that is based on the separation of costs into fixed and variable components is called the **contribution margin income statement**. Exhibit 4.1 illustrates an income statement prepared in a contribution margin format.

Contribution Margin

Contribution margin is defined as the excess of sales over variable costs:

$$\text{Contribution margin} = \text{Sales} - \text{Variable costs}$$

EXHIBIT 4.1

Contribution Margin Income Statement

Sales	(50,000 units × $20)	$1,000,0000
Variable costs	(50,000 units × $8)	400,000
Contribution margin	(50,000 units × $12)	600,000
Fixed costs		500,000
Income from operations		$ 100,000

Contribution margin refers to the amount left after the variable costs are covered to contribute toward satisfying the fixed costs. Once the fixed costs are paid, any additional contribution margin increases income from operations. As we saw in the Boyne Resorts example at the beginning of the chapter, the more contribution margin that can be generated, the more easily fixed costs can be covered.

Contribution margin is especially useful because it provides insight into the profit potential of a company. To illustrate, assume the following data:

Sales	50,000 units
Sales price per unit	$20 per unit
Variable cost per unit	$8 per unit
Fixed costs	$500,000

Contribution Margin Ratio

The contribution margin can also be expressed as a percentage. The **contribution margin ratio** indicates the percentage of each sales dollar available to cover fixed costs and to provide income from operations. The contribution margin ratio is computed as follows:

$$\text{Contribution margin ratio} = \frac{\text{Contribution margin}}{\text{Sales}}$$

The contribution margin ratio in the case referred to above is:

$$\frac{\$600,000}{\$1,000,000} = 60\%$$

The contribution margin ratio is most useful when the increase or decrease in sales volume is measured in sales dollars. In this case, the change in sales dollars multiplied by the contribution margin ratio equals the change in income from operations:

$$\text{Change in income from operations} = \text{Change in sales dollars} \times \text{Contribution margin ratio}$$

To illustrate, if the company adds $100,000 in sales orders, its income from operations will increase by:

$$\$100,000 \times 60\% = \$60,000$$

That is, income from operations will increase from $100,000 to $160,000 when sales increase from $1,000,000 to $1,100,000.

Variable costs as a percentage of sales are equal to 100 percent minus the contribution margin ratio. Thus, the variable costs in this illustration are 40 percent (= 100% − 60%) of sales, or, in absolute numbers, $440,000 (= $1,100,000 − $660,000). The total contribution margin, $660,000, can also be computed directly by multiplying the total sales by the contribution margin ratio ($1,100,000 × 60% = $660,000).

The contribution margin ratio is very useful in developing business strategies. For example, assume that a company has a high contribution margin ratio and is producing below 100 percent of capacity. In this case, a large increase in income from operations can be expected from an increase in sales volume. Therefore, the company might consider implementing a special sales campaign to increase sales. In contrast, a company with a small contribution margin ratio will probably want to reduce costs before attempting to promote sales.

Unit Contribution Margin

The unit contribution margin is also useful for analyzing the profit potential of proposed decisions. The **unit contribution margin** is computed as follows:

Unit contribution margin = Sales price per unit − Variable cost per unit

To illustrate, if the unit selling price is $20 and its variable cost per unit is $8, the unit contribution margin is $12, as shown below:

Sales price per unit − Variable cost per unit = $20 − $8
= $12

The unit contribution margin is most useful when the increase or decrease in sales volume is measured in sales units (quantities). In this case, the change in sales volume (units) multiplied by the unit contribution margin equals the change in income from operations:

Change in income from operations = Change in sales units × Unit contribution margin

To illustrate, assume that sales could be increased by 15,000 units, from 50,000 to 65,000. The company's income from operations would increase by $180,000, as shown:

Change in sales units × Unit contribution margin = Change in income from operations
15,000 × $12 = $180,000

Let's use Whittier Company, a Red Deer, Alberta–based manufacturer of mulching lawn mowers, as an example. Whittier's controller has budgeted the following production costs for the coming year:

Direct materials per mower	$ 180
Direct labour per mower	100
Variable factory overhead per mower	25
Total fixed factory overhead	15,000
Fixed selling and administrative expense	30,000
Sales commission, per mower sold	20

In the coming year, Whittier Company plans to produce and sell 1,000 mowers at a price of $400 each.

The total variable cost per mower includes direct materials, direct labour, variable factory overhead per unit, and the sales commission. Thus, variable cost per unit is $325 (= $180 + $100 + $25 + $20). The total fixed expense includes fixed factory overhead and fixed selling and administrative expense; the total fixed expense is $45,000 (= $15,000 + $30,000). Notice that both the variable cost per mower and the total fixed expense include all types of cost—both product and selling cost across the value chain.

The contribution margin income statement for Whittier Company for the coming year is shown in Cornerstone 4.1.

Preparing a Contribution Margin Income Statement

CORNERSTONE 4.1

Information:

Whittier Company plans to sell 1,000 mowers at $400 each in the coming year. Product costs include:

Direct materials per mower	$ 180
Direct labour per mower	100
Variable factory overhead per mower	25
Total fixed factory overhead	15,000
Variable selling and administrative per mower	20
Fixed selling and administrative expense	30,000

Required:

1. Calculate the total variable cost per unit.
2. Calculate the total fixed expense for the year.
3. Prepare a contribution margin income statement for Whittier Company for the coming year.

Solution:

1. Variable cost per unit
   = Direct materials + Direct labour + Variable factory overhead + Variable selling expense
   = $180 + $100 + $25 + $20
   = $325

2. Total fixed expense = Fixed factory overhead
   + Fixed selling and administrative expense
   = $15,000 + $30,000 = $45,000

3.

Whittier Company
Contribution Margin Income Statement
For the Coming Year

	Total	Per Unit
Sales ($400 × 1,000 mowers)	$400,000	$400
Total variable expense ($325 × 1,000)	325,000	325
Total contribution margin	75,000	$ 75
Total fixed expense	45,000	
Operating income	$ 30,000	

Why:

Because a contribution margin income statement provides some unique advantages over the conventional income statement, one of which is to facilitate the CVP analysis.

Notice that the contribution margin income statement in Cornerstone 4.1 shows a total contribution margin of $75,000. The per-unit contribution margin is $75 (= $400 − $325). That is, every mower sold contributes $75 toward fixed expense and operating income.

What does Whittier's contribution margin income statement show? First, of course, we notice that Whittier will more than break even at sales of 1,000 mowers. In fact, it expects an operating income of $30,000. Clearly, Whittier would just break even if total contribution margin equalled the total fixed cost. Let's see how to calculate the break-even point.

Break-Even Point in Units

Normally, CVP analysis starts with a break-even analysis. The **break-even point (BEP)** is the point where total revenue equals total cost (i.e., the point of zero profit). New start-up companies typically experience losses (negative operating income) initially and view their first break-even period as a significant milestone. For example, online retail pioneer Amazon.com was founded in 1994 but did not break even for the first time until the fourth quarter of 2001! Also, managers become very interested in CVP analysis during times of economic uncertainty. For example, to the dismay of many of its shareholders, Sirius Satellite Radio (now SiriusXM Radio) signed shock jock Howard Stern to a five-year, $500 million employment contract for joining the young company. As a result of Stern's monstrous contract cost, some analysts estimated that Sirius would need an additional 2.4 million subscribers (i.e., customers) to break even. CVP analysis can address many other issues as well.

If the contribution margin income statement is recast as an equation, it becomes more useful for solving CVP problems. The operating income equation is:

$$\text{Operating income} = \text{Sales} - \text{Total variable expenses} - \text{Total fixed expenses}$$

Notice that all we have done is remove the total contribution margin line from Exhibit 4.1, since it is identical to sales minus total variable expense. This equation is the basis of all our coming work on CVP. We can think of it as the basic CVP equation.

We can expand the operating income equation by expressing sales revenues and variable expenses in terms of unit dollar amounts and the number of units sold. Specifically, sales revenue is equal to the unit selling price times the number of units sold, and total variable costs are equal to the unit variable cost times the number of units sold. With these expressions, the operating income equation becomes:

$$\text{Operating income} = (\text{Price} \times \text{Number of units sold}) - (\text{Variable cost per unit} \times \text{Number of units sold}) - \text{Total fixed cost}$$

At the BEP, of course, operating income equals $0. Let's see how we can use the operating income equation to find the BEP in units for Whittier Company. Recall that Whittier sells mowers at $400 each, and variable cost per mower is $325. Total fixed cost equals $45,000.

$$(\$400 \times \text{Break-even units}) - (\$325 \times \text{Break-even units}) - \$45{,}000 = \$0$$

$$(\$75 \times \text{Break-even units}) - \$45{,}000 = \$0$$

$$\text{Break-even units} = \frac{\$45{,}000}{\$75}$$

$$\text{Break-even units} = 600$$

It is easy to see that a contribution margin income statement for Whittier Company, with sales of 600 mowers, does result in zero operating income.

Sales ($400 × 600 mowers)	$240,000
Total variable expense ($325 × 600)	195,000
Total contribution margin	45,000
Total fixed expense	45,000
Operating income	$ 0

When Whittier breaks even, total contribution margin equals total fixed cost. Exhibit 4.2 illustrates this important observation.

EXHIBIT 4.2

Contribution Margin and Fixed Cost at Break-Even for Whittier Company

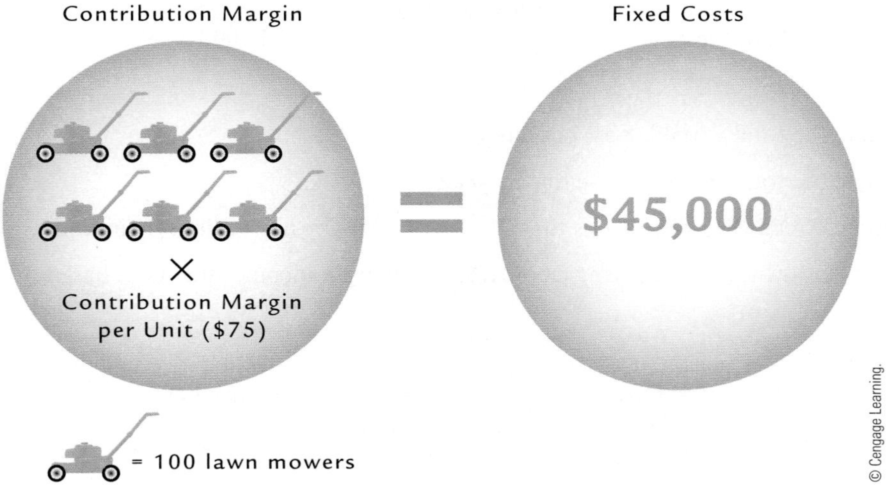

The operating income equation can be rearranged as follows to show the number of units at break-even:

$$\text{Break-even units} = \frac{\text{Total fixed cost}}{\text{Price} - \text{Variable cost per unit}}$$

In other words, the break-even units are equal to the fixed cost divided by the contribution margin per unit. So, if a company sells enough units for the contribution margin to just cover fixed costs, it will earn zero operating income. To express it differently, it will break even. It is quicker to solve break-even problems using this break-even version of the operating income equation than it is using the original operating income equation.

Cornerstone 4.2 shows how to use the break-even units equation to solve for the break-even point for Whittier Company.

Break-Even Point in Sales Dollars

In some cases when using CVP analysis, managers may prefer to use sales revenue as the measure of sales activity instead of units sold. This approach is especially useful in a multi-product environment. A units sold measure can be converted to a sales revenue measure by multiplying the unit selling price by the units sold. For example, the break-even point for Whittier Company is 600 mulching mowers. Since the selling price for each lawn mower is $400, the break-even volume in sales revenue is $240,000 (= $400 × 600).

Any answer expressed in units sold can easily be converted to one expressed in sales revenues, but the answer can be computed more directly by developing a separate formula

CORNERSTONE 4.2

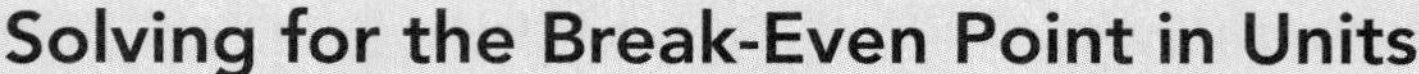

Solving for the Break-Even Point in Units

Information:

Whittier Company plans to sell 1,000 mowers at $400 each in the coming year. Product costs include:

Direct materials per mower	$ 180
Direct labour per mower	100
Variable factory overhead per mower	25
Total fixed factory overhead	15,000
Variable selling and administrative expense per mower	20
Fixed selling and administrative expense	30,000

Required:

1. Calculate the total variable cost per unit.
2. Calculate the total fixed expense for the year.
3. Calculate the number of mowers that Whittier Company must sell to break even.
4. Check your answer by preparing a contribution margin income statement based on the BEP.

Solution:

1. Variable cost per unit = Direct materials + Direct labour + Variable factory overhead + Variable selling expense
   = $180 + $100 + $25 + $20
   = $325

2. Total fixed expense = Fixed factory overhead + Fixed selling and administrative expense
   = $15,000 + $30,000 = $45,000

3. $$\text{Break-even number of mowers} = \frac{\text{Total fixed expense}}{(\text{Price} - \text{Variable cost})}$$
   $$= \frac{\$45{,}000}{(\$400 - \$325)} = 600$$

4. Contribution margin income statement based on 600 mowers.

Sales ($400 × 600 mowers)	$240,000
Total variable expense ($325 × 600)	195,000
Total contribution margin	45,000
Total fixed expense	45,000
Operating income	$ 0

Indeed, selling 600 units does yield a zero profit.

Why:

Because, as a starting point, a firm needs to know how many units need to be sold to break even.

for the sales revenue case. In this case, the important variable is sales dollars, so both the revenue and the variable costs must be expressed in dollars instead of units. Since sales revenue is always expressed in dollars, measuring that variable is no problem. Let's look more closely at variable costs and see how they can be expressed in terms of sales dollars.

To calculate the BEP in sales dollars, total variable costs are defined as a percentage of sales rather than as an amount per unit sold. For example, suppose that a company sells a product for \$10 per unit and incurs a variable cost of \$6 per unit. Of course, the remainder is contribution margin of \$4 (= \$10 − \$6). If 10 units are sold, total variable costs are \$60 (= \$6 × 10 units). Alternatively, since each unit sold earns \$10 of revenue and has \$6 of variable cost, one could say that 60 percent of each dollar of revenue earned is attributable to variable cost (\$6/\$10). Thus, sales revenues of \$100 would result in total variable costs of \$60 (= 0.60 × \$100).

This 60 percent is the variable cost ratio. The **variable cost ratio** is the proportion of each sales dollar that must be used to cover variable costs. The variable cost ratio can be computed using either total data or unit data. The percentage of sales dollars remaining after variable costs are covered is the contribution margin ratio.

The *contribution margin ratio* is the proportion of each sales dollar available to cover fixed costs and provide for profit. In this example, if the variable cost ratio is 60 percent of sales, then the contribution margin ratio must be the remaining 40 percent of sales. It makes sense that the complement of the variable cost ratio is the contribution margin ratio. After all, total variable costs and total contribution margin add up to sales revenue.

Just as the variable cost ratio can be computed using total or unit figures, the contribution margin ratio, 40 percent in our example, can also be computed in these two ways. That is, one can divide the total contribution margin by total sales (\$40/\$100), or one can use the unit contribution margin divided by price (\$4/\$10). Naturally, if the variable cost ratio is known, it can be subtracted from 1 to yield the contribution margin ratio (1 − 0.60 = 0.40). Cornerstone 4.3 shows how the income statement can be expanded to yield the variable cost ratio and the contribution margin ratio.

Calculating the Variable Cost Ratio and the Contribution Margin Ratio

CORNERSTONE 4.3

Information:

Whittier Company plans to sell 1,000 mowers at \$400 each in the coming year. As calculated in Cornerstones 4.1 and 4.2, total variable cost per unit is \$325 and total fixed cost is \$45,000.

Required:

1. Calculate the variable cost ratio.
2. Calculate the contribution margin ratio using unit figures.
3. Prepare a contribution margin income statement based on the budgeted figures for next year. In a column next to the income statement, show the percentages based on sales for sales, total variable costs, and total contribution margin.

Solution:

$$1.\ \text{Variable cost ratio} = \frac{\text{Variable cost per unit}}{\text{Price}}$$

$$= \frac{\$325}{\$400} = 0.8125, \text{ or } 81.25\%$$

(Continued)

CORNERSTONE
4.3

(Continued)

2. Contribution margin per unit = Price − Variable cost per unit
= $400 − $325 = $75

$$\text{Contribution margin ratio} = \frac{\text{Contribution margin per unit}}{\text{Price}}$$

$$= \frac{\$75}{\$400} = 0.1875, \text{ or } 18.75\%$$

3. Contribution margin income statement based on budgeted figures:

		Percent of Sales
Sales ($400 × 1,000 mowers)	$400,000	100.00
Total variable expense (0.8125 × $400,000)	325,000	81.25
Total contribution margin	75,000	18.75
Total fixed expense	45,000	
Operating income	$ 30,000	

Why:

Because it is useful to express the variable cost and contribution margin per unit not only in absolute dollars, but also as a percentage of selling price.

concept Q&A

1. If the contribution margin ratio is 30 percent, what is the variable cost ratio?
2. If the variable cost ratio is 77 percent, what is the contribution margin ratio?
3. Explain why the contribution margin ratio and the variable cost ratio always total 100 percent.

Answers on pages 734 to 738.

Notice in Cornerstone 4.3, Requirement 3, that sales revenue, variable costs, and contribution margin have been expressed as a percent of sales. The variable cost ratio is 0.8125 (= $325,000/$400,000); the contribution margin ratio is 0.1875 (computed as either 1 − 0.8125, or $75,000/$400,000).

How do fixed costs relate to the variable cost ratio and contribution margin ratio? Since the total contribution margin is the revenue remaining after total variable costs are covered, it must be the revenue available to cover fixed costs and contribute to profit. How does the relationship of fixed cost to contribution margin affect operating income? There are three possibilities: Fixed cost can equal contribution margin; fixed cost can be less than contribution margin; or fixed cost can be greater than contribution margin. *If fixed cost equals contribution margin, then operating income is $0 (the company is at break-even)*. If fixed cost is less than contribution margin, the company earns a positive operating income. Finally, if fixed cost is greater than contribution margin, then the company faces an operating loss.

Now, let's turn to the equation for calculating the BEP in sales dollars. One way of calculating break-even sales revenue is to multiply the break-even units by the price. However, often the company is a multiple-product firm, and it can be difficult to determine the BEP for each product sold. The operating income equation can be used to solve for break-even sales for Whittier as follows:

Operating income = Sales − Total variable expenses − Total fixed expenses

$$\$0 = \text{Break-even sales} - (0.8125 \times \text{Break-even sales}) - \$45{,}000$$

$$\$0 = \text{Break-even sales}\ (1.00 - 0.8125) - \$45{,}000$$

$$\text{Break-even sales} = \frac{\$45{,}000}{(1.00 - 0.8125)}$$

$$\text{Break-even sales} = \$240{,}000$$

So, Whittier Company has sales of $240,000 at the BEP.

Just as it was quicker to use an equation to calculate the break-even units directly, it is helpful to have an equation to calculate the break-even sales dollars. This equation is:

$$\text{Break-even sales} = \frac{\text{Total fixed expenses}}{\text{Contribution margin ratio}}$$

Cornerstone 4.4 shows how to obtain the BEP in sales dollars for Whittier Company.

Solving for the Break-Even Point in Sales Dollars

CORNERSTONE 4.4

Information:

Whittier Company plans to sell 1,000 mowers at $400 each in the coming year. As calculated in Cornerstones 4.1 and 4.2, total variable expense per unit is $325 and total fixed expense is $45,000.

Required:

1. Calculate the contribution margin ratio.
2. Calculate the sales revenue that Whittier Company must make to break even by using the BEP in sales dollars equation.
3. Check your answer by preparing a contribution margin income statement based on the BEP in sales dollars.

Solution:

1. Contribution margin per unit = Price − Variable expense per unit
$$= \$400 - \$325 = \$75$$

$$\text{Contribution margin ratio} = \frac{\text{Contribution margin per unit}}{\text{Price}}$$

$$= \frac{\$75}{\$400} = 0.1875, \text{ or } 18.75\%$$

[*Hint:* The contribution margin ratio comes out cleanly to four decimal places. Don't round it, and your BEP in sales dollars will yield an operating income of $0 (rather than being a few dollars off due to rounding).]

Notice that the variable cost ratio equals 0.8125, or the difference between 1.0000 and the contribution margin ratio.

2. Calculate the BEP in sales dollars:

$$\text{Break-even sales dollars} = \frac{\text{Total fixed expense}}{\text{Contribution margin ratio}}$$

$$= \frac{\$45{,}000}{0.1875} = \$240{,}000$$

(Continued)

CORNERSTONE

4.4

(Continued)

3. Contribution margin income statement based on sales of $240,000:

Sales	$240,000
Total variable expense (0.8125 × $240,000)	195,000
Total contribution margin	45,000
Total fixed expense	45,000
Operating income	$ 0

Indeed, having sales equal to $240,000 does yield a zero profit.

Why:

Because, in addition to knowing how many units it needs to break even, a firm needs to know what level of sales revenue is required.

Equation Formula Approach to Break-Even Analysis

The formula approach to break-even analysis uses an algebraic equation to calculate the BEP. The equation represents the variable costing income statement and shows the relationships among revenue, fixed cost, variable cost, volume, and profit. The income statement equation is:

$$\text{Sales} = VC + FC + Pr$$

$$\text{Break-even: } (P \times Q) = (Q \times VCU) + FC + 0$$

$$(P \times Q) - (Q \times VCU) = FC$$

$$Q(P - VCU) = FC$$

$$Q(CM) = FC$$

$$Q = \frac{FC}{CM}$$

Where

P = selling price per unit
Q = quantity (volume or number of units)
VCU = variable cost per unit
FC = total fixed cost

Thus, break-even volume equals total fixed cost divided by contribution margin per unit.

Because this equation is simply a formulaic representation of an income statement, profit can be set equal to zero to solve for the BEP. At the point where profit equals $0, total revenues are equal to total costs, and BEP in units can be found by solving the equation.

The BEP provides a starting point for planning future operations. However, managers want to earn operating profit rather than simply cover costs. Substituting an amount other than zero for the profit (Pr) term in the break-even formula converts break-even analysis into a profit planning analysis.

UNITS TO BE SOLD TO ACHIEVE A TARGET INCOME

OBJECTIVE 2

Determine the number of units that must be sold, and the amount of revenue required, to earn a target profit.

While the BEP is useful information and an important benchmark for relatively young companies, most companies would like to earn an acceptable level of operating income. CVP analysis gives us a way to determine how many units must be sold, or how much sales revenue must be generated, to earn a particular amount of target income. Let's look first at the number of units that must be sold to earn a target *operating* income.

Remember that at the BEP, operating income is $0. How can the equations used in our earlier break-even analyses be adjusted to find the number of units that must be sold to earn a target income? The answer is that we add the target income amount to the fixed costs. Let's try it in two different ways—with the operating income equation and with the basic break-even equation.

Remember that the equation for the operating income is:

$$\text{Operating income} = (\text{Price} \times \text{Units sold}) - (\text{Unit variable cost} \times \text{Units sold}) - \text{Fixed cost}$$

To solve for positive operating income, replace the operating income term with the target income. Recall that Whittier Company sells mowers at $400 each, incurs variable cost per unit of $325, and has total fixed expense of $45,000. Suppose that Whittier wants to make a target operating income of $37,500. The number of units that must be sold to achieve that target income is calculated as follows:

$$\$37{,}500 = (\$400 \times \text{Number of units}) - (\$325 \times \text{Number of units}) - \$45{,}000$$

$$\text{Number of units} = \frac{(\$37{,}500 + \$45{,}000)}{(\$400 - \$325)} = 1{,}100$$

Does the sale of 1,100 units really result in operating income of $37,500? The contribution margin income statement provides a good check.

Sales ($400 × 1,100)	$440,000
Total variable expense ($325 × 1,100)	357,500
Total contribution margin	82,500
Total fixed expense	45,000
Operating income	$ 37,500

Indeed, selling 1,100 units does yield operating income of $37,500.

The operating income equation can be used to find the number of units to sell to earn a target income. However, it is quicker to adjust the break-even units equation by adding target income to the fixed cost. This adjustment results in the following equation:

$$\text{Number of units to earn target income} = \frac{\text{Fixed cost} + \text{Target income}}{\text{Price} - \text{Variable cost per unit}}$$

This equation was used when calculating the 1,100 units needed to earn operating income of $37,500. Cornerstone 4.5 shows how Whittier Company can use this approach.

Another way to check the number of units to be sold to yield a target operating income is to use the BEP as a starting point. As shown in Cornerstone 4.5, Whittier must sell 1,100 lawn mowers, or 500 more than the break-even volume of 600 units, to earn a profit of $37,500. The contribution margin per lawn mower is $75. Multiplying $75 by the 500 lawn mowers above break-even produces the operating income of $37,500 (= $75 × 500). This outcome demonstrates that contribution margin per unit for each unit above break-even is equivalent to the operating income per unit above break-even. Since the break-even point had already been computed, the number of lawn mowers to be sold to yield a $37,500 operating income could have been calculated by dividing the unit contribution margin into the target income and adding the resulting amount to the break-even volume.

CORNERSTONE 4.5

Solving for the Number of Units to Be Sold to Earn a Target Operating Income

Information:

Whittier Company sells mulching mowers at $400 each. Variable cost per unit is $325, and total fixed costs are $45,000.

Required:

1. Calculate the number of units that Whittier Company must sell to earn operating income of $37,500.
2. Check your answer by preparing a contribution margin income statement based on the number of units calculated.

Solution:

1. $$\text{Number of units} = \frac{(\text{Fixed cost} + \text{Target income})}{(\text{Price} - \text{Variable cost per unit})} = \frac{(\$45{,}000 + \$37{,}500)}{(\$400 - \$325)} = 1{,}100$$

2. Contribution margin income statement based on sales of 1,100 units:

Sales ($400 × 1,100)	$440,000
Total variable expense ($325 × 1,100)	357,500
Total contribution margin	82,500
Total fixed expense	45,000
Operating income	$ 37,500

Indeed, selling 1,100 units does yield operating income of $37,500.

Why:

Because firms need not only to break even but also to generate an acceptable level of target profit. Finding how many units need to be sold to achieve this target profit is crucial to the success of the firm.

analytical Q&A

Lorna makes and sells decorative candles through gift shops. She knows she must sell 200 candles a month to break even. Every candle has a contribution margin of $1.50. So far this month, Lorna has sold 320 candles. How much has Lorna earned so far this month in operating income? If she sells 10 more candles, by how much will income increase?

Answers on pages 734 to 738.

In general, assuming that fixed costs remain the same, the impact on a firm's income resulting from a change in the number of units sold can be assessed by multiplying the unit contribution margin by the change in units sold. For example, if 1,400 lawn mowers instead of 1,100 are sold, how much more operating income will be earned? The change in units sold is an increase of 300 lawn mowers, and the unit contribution margin is $75. Thus, operating income will increase by $22,500 (= $75 × 300) over the $37,500 initially calculated, and total operating income will be $60,000.

Sales Revenue to Achieve a Target Income

Consider the following question: How much sales revenue must Whittier generate to earn an operating income of $37,500? This question is similar to the one we asked earlier in terms of units, but phrases the question directly in terms of sales revenue. To answer the question, add the target operating income of \$37,500 to the \$45,000 of fixed cost and divide by the contribution margin ratio. Then, the equation is the following:

$$\text{Sales dollars to earn target income} = \frac{\text{Fixed cost} + \text{Target income}}{\text{Contribution margin ratio}}$$

Cornerstone 4.6 shows how to calculate the sales revenue needed to earn a target operating income of \$37,500.

Solving for the Sales Needed to Earn a Target Operating Income

CORNERSTONE 4.6

Information:

Whittier Company sells mulching mowers at \$400 each. Variable cost per unit is \$325, and total fixed costs are \$45,000.

Required:

1. Calculate the contribution margin ratio.
2. Calculate the sales that Whittier Company must make to earn an operating income of \$37,500.
3. Check your answer by preparing a contribution margin income statement based on the sales dollars calculated.

Solution:

1. $\text{Contribution margin ratio} = \frac{(\$400 - \$325)}{\$400} = 0.1875$

2. $\text{Sales dollars} = \frac{(\text{Fixed cost} + \text{Target income})}{\text{Contribution margin ratio}}$

   $= \frac{(\$45{,}000 + \$37{,}500)}{0.1875} = \$440{,}000$

3. Contribution margin income statement based on sales revenue of \$440,000:

Sales	\$440,000
Total variable expense (0.8125 × \$440,000)	357,500
Total contribution margin	82,500
Total fixed expense	45,000
Operating income	\$ 37,500

Indeed, sales revenue of \$440,000 does yield operating income of \$37,500.

Why:

Because firms need to know what volume of sales revenue is necessary to achieve a target level of profit.

Whittier must earn revenues equal to \$440,000 to achieve a target profit of \$37,500. Since break-even sales equal \$240,000, additional sales of \$200,000 (= \$440,000 − \$240,000) must be earned above break-even. Notice that multiplying the contribution margin ratio by revenues above break-even yields the profit of \$37,500 (= 0.1875 × \$200,000). Above break-even, the contribution margin ratio is a profit ratio; therefore, it represents the proportion of each sales dollar attributable to profit. For Whittier Company, every sales dollar earned above break-even increases profits by \$0.1875.

In a diversified operation such as Boyne Resorts, concentration on total sales dollars to achieve a target profit makes more sense than simply focusing on unit sales.

In general, assuming that fixed costs remain unchanged, the contribution margin ratio can be used to find the profit impact of a change in sales revenue. To obtain the total change in profits from a change in revenue, multiply the contribution margin ratio times the change in sales revenue. For example, if sales revenue is \$400,000 instead of \$440,000, how will the expected profits be affected? A decrease in sales revenue of \$40,000 will cause a decrease in profits of \$7,500 (= 0.1875 × \$40,000).

Sales Revenue to Achieve a Target Income as Percentage of Sales

Many companies will express their target income not as a set amount but rather as a percentage of sales and so we must be able to calculate the desired sales revenue to achieve this goal. To do so, we will substitute the percentage of sales amount for the target profit in the previous equations.

$$\text{Unit sales to achieve target profit} = \frac{\text{Fixed cost} + (\text{Percent of sales revenue} \times \text{Sales revenue})}{(\text{Contribution margin per unit})}$$

We know that Whittier sells each mower for \$400, the variable costs are \$325, and fixed costs are \$45,000. Let's assume that the company wants to earn 10 percent of sales as its operating income. Then we can solve the equation above as follows:

$$X = \frac{\$45{,}000 + 0.10(\$400X)}{\$75}$$
$$\$75X - \$40X = \$45{,}000$$
$$X = 1{,}286^*$$

To prove this, we can apply the formula:

Revenue − Variable cost − Fixed cost = Operating income
(\$400 × 1,286) − (\$325 × 1,286) − \$45,000 = \$51,450,
which is 10 percent of the sales of \$514,500 (\$400 × 1,286) (rounded)

Income Taxes' Impact on Break-Even Analysis

Thus far we have ignored income taxes (as so many people would like to). However, in most countries, private enterprises are subject to income taxes. What is the impact of income taxes on break-even analysis? And how will changes in the structure of variable costs and fixed costs affect net income? We must remember that income taxes are calculated as a percentage of operating income.

* Rounded

The only change in the general break-even equation approach we have used all along would be on the right-hand side of the following equation:

$$\text{Target sales} - \text{Variable expenses} - \text{Fixed expenses} = \frac{\text{Target income after tax}}{(1 - \text{Tax rate})}$$

That is, the target income (earnings) after taxes is divided by (1 − Tax rate) to obtain the target earnings before taxes. As a shortcut to computing the effects of changes in sales volume on after-tax income, we use the following formula:

$$\text{Sales} = \frac{FC + NI/(1 - T)}{CM}$$

To illustrate, assume the following data:

Fixed costs	\$800,000
Target profit after tax	\$600,000
Unit selling price	\$90
Unit variable cost	\$50
Unit contribution margin	\$40
Tax rate	40%

In this way, we can transform after-tax profit to pre-tax profit [\$600,000/(1 − 0.40) = \$1,000,000] and add this to the fixed costs of \$800,000. Then, fixed costs plus after-tax profit is divided by contribution margin per unit [(\$800,000 + \$1,000,000)/\$40 = 45,000 units] to calculate the number of units needed to be sold to achieve the after-tax profit we are targeting.

$$\begin{aligned}\text{Sales} &= \frac{\$800{,}000 + \$600{,}000/(1 - 0.40)}{\$40}\\ &= \frac{\$800{,}000 + \$1{,}000{,}000}{\$40}\\ &= \frac{\$1{,}800{,}000}{\$40}\\ &= 45{,}000 \text{ units}\end{aligned}$$

Thus, instead of 20,000 units being necessary to break even (\$800,000/\$40 = 20,000), 45,000 units are needed to generate after-tax earnings of \$600,000. A total of 25,000 extra units need to be sold to generate a target profit of \$600,000 after paying the income taxes on the earnings.

Note that each unit beyond the BEP adds to after-tax net income at the unit contribution margin multiplied by (1 − Income tax rate). Also, the BEP itself does not change no matter what the income tax rate is. Why? Because there is no income tax at a level of zero profits.

THE PROFIT–VOLUME GRAPH

It may be helpful in understanding CVP relationships to see them portrayed visually. A graphical representation can help managers see the link between variable cost and break-even. It may also help them understand quickly what impact an increase or decrease in sales will have on profitability. Two basic graphs are the profit–volume graph and the cost–volume–profit graph.

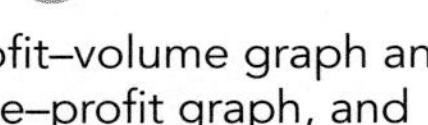

Prepare a profit–volume graph and a cost–volume–profit graph, and explain the meaning of each.

A **profit–volume graph** visually portrays the relationship between profits (operating income) and units sold. The profit–volume graph is the graph of the operating income equation

Operating income = (Price × Units) − (Unit variable cost × Units) − Total fixed cost

In this graph, operating income is the dependent variable, and the independent variable is units. Usually, values of the independent variable are measured along the horizontal axis, and values of the dependent variable are measured along the vertical axis.

To make this discussion more concrete, a simple set of data will be used. Assume that Tyson Company produces a single product with the following cost and price data:

Total fixed costs	$100
Variable costs per unit	5
Selling price per unit	10

Using these data, operating income can be expressed as:

Operating income = ($10 × Units) − ($5 × Units) − $100
= ($5 × Units) − $100

This relationship can be graphed by plotting units along the horizontal axis and operating income (or loss) along the vertical axis. When units sold are 0, Tyson experiences an operating loss of $100 (or an operating income of −$100). The point corresponding to zero sales volume, therefore, is (0, −$100). When no sales take place, the company suffers a loss equal to its total fixed costs. When operating income is $0, the units sold are equal to 20. The point corresponding to zero profits (break-even) is (20, $0). These two points, plotted in Exhibit 4.3, define the profit–volume graph.

EXHIBIT 4.3

Profit–Volume Graph

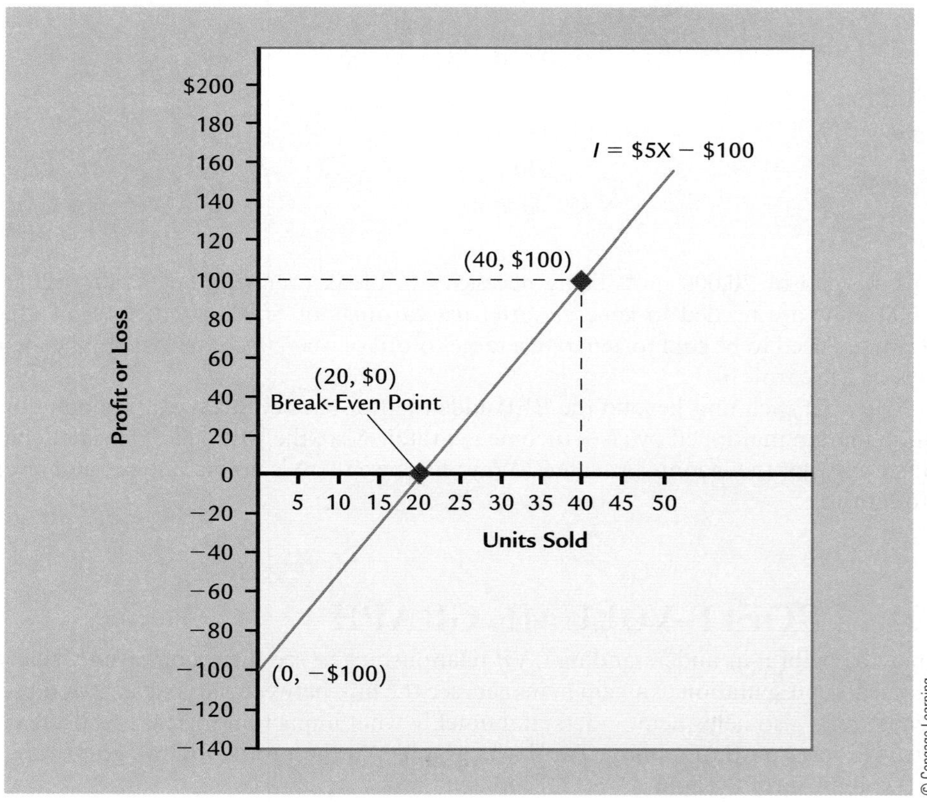

The graph in Exhibit 4.3 can be used to assess Tyson's profit (or loss) at any level of sales activity. For example, the profit associated with the sale of 40 units can be read from the graph by (1) drawing a vertical line from the horizontal axis to the profit line, and (2) drawing a horizontal line from the profit line to the vertical axis. As illustrated in Exhibit 4.3, the profit associated with sales of 40 units is $100. The profit–volume graph, while easy to interpret, fails to reveal how costs change as sales volume changes. An alternative approach to graphing can provide this detail.

The Cost–Volume–Profit Graph

The **cost–volume–profit graph** depicts the relationships among cost, volume, and profits (operating income) by plotting the total revenue line and the total cost line on a single graph. These two lines are represented by the following two equations:

Revenue = Price × Units
Total cost = (Unit variable cost × Units) + Fixed cost

Using the Tyson Company example, the revenue and cost equations are:

Revenue = $10 × Units
Total cost = ($5 × Units) + $100

To portray both equations in the same graph, the vertical axis is measured in dollars, and the horizontal axis is measured in units sold.

Again, two points are needed to graph each equation. For the revenue equation, setting number of units equal to 0 results in revenue of $0; setting number of units equal to 20 results in revenue of $200. Therefore, the two points for the revenue equation are (0, $0) and (20, $200). For the cost equation, units sold of 0 and units sold of 20 produce the points (0, $100) and (20, $200). The graph of each equation appears in Exhibit 4.4.

EXHIBIT 4.4

Cost–Volume–Profit Graph

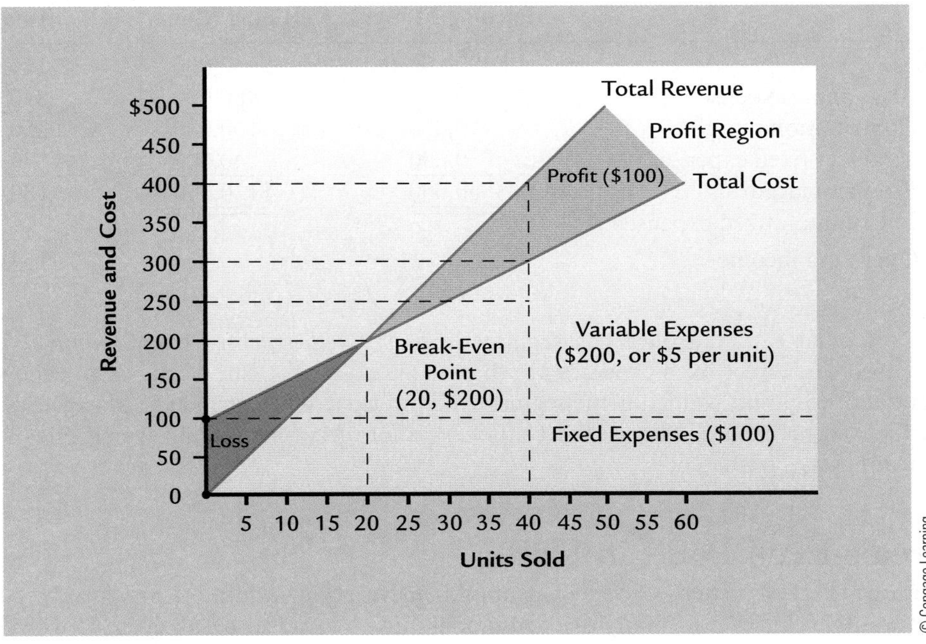

Notice that the total revenue line begins at the origin and rises with a slope equal to the selling price per unit (a slope of 10). The total cost line intercepts the vertical axis at a point equal to total fixed costs and rises with a slope equal to the variable cost per unit (a slope of 5). When the total revenue line lies below the total cost line, a loss region is defined. Similarly, when the total revenue line lies above the total cost line, a profit region is defined. The point where the total revenue line and the total cost line intersect is the BEP. To break even, Tyson Company must sell 20 units and, thus, receive $200 in total revenues.

Now, let's compare the information available from the CVP graph with that available from the profit–volume graph. To do so, consider the sale of 40 units. Recall that the profit–volume graph revealed that 40 units produced profits of $100. Examine Exhibit 4.4 again. The CVP graph also shows profits of $100, but it reveals more as well. The CVP graph discloses that total revenues of $400 and total costs of $300 are associated with the sale of 40 units. Furthermore, the total costs can be broken down into fixed costs of $100 and variable costs of $200. The CVP graph provides revenue and cost information not provided by the profit–volume graph. Unlike the profit–volume graph, some computation is needed to determine the profit associated with a given sales volume. Nonetheless, because of the greater information content, managers are likely to find the CVP graph a more useful tool.

MULTIPLE-PRODUCT ANALYSIS

Apply cost–volume–profit analysis in a multiple-product setting.

Cost–volume–profit analysis is fairly simple in the single-product setting. However, most firms produce and sell a number of products or services. Even though CVP analysis becomes more complex with multiple products, the operation is reasonably straightforward. Let's see how we can adapt the formulas used in a single-product setting to a multiple-product setting by expanding the Whittier Company example.

Whittier Company has decided to offer two models of lawn mowers: a mulching mower that sells for $400, and a riding mower that sells for $800. The marketing department is convinced that 1,200 mulching mowers and 800 riding mowers can be sold during the coming year. The controller has prepared the following projected income statement based on the sales forecast:

	Mulching Mower	Riding Mower	Total
Sales	$480,000	$640,000	$1,120,000
Less: Variable expenses	390,000	480,000	870,000
Contribution margin	90,000	160,000	250,000
Less: Direct fixed expenses	30,000	40,000	70,000
Product margin	$ 60,000	$120,000	180,000
Less: Common fixed expenses			26,250
Operating income			$ 153,750

Note that the controller has separated *direct fixed expenses* from *common fixed expenses*. The **direct fixed expenses** are those fixed costs that can be traced to each segment and would be avoided if the segment did not exist. The **common fixed expenses** are the fixed costs that are not traceable to the segments and would remain even if one of the segments was eliminated.

Break-Even Point in Units

The owner of Whittier is somewhat apprehensive about adding a new product line and wants to know how many of each model must be sold to break even. How would you answer this question? One possible response is to use the equation developed earlier in which fixed costs were divided by the contribution margin. This equation presents a problem, however: it was developed for single-product analysis. For two products, there are two prices and two variable costs per unit. The variable cost per unit is derived from the income statement. For the mulching mower, total variable costs are \$390,000 based on sales of 1,200 units, yielding a per-unit variable cost of \$325 (= \$390,000/1,200). For the riding mower, total variable costs are \$480,000 based on sales of 800 units, yielding a per-unit variable cost of \$600 (= \$480,000/800). Then, the mulching mower has a contribution margin per unit of \$75 (= \$400 − \$325); the riding mower has a contribution margin per unit of \$200 (= \$800 − \$600).

One possible solution is to apply the analysis separately to each product line. It is possible to obtain individual BEPs when income is defined as product margin. Break-even for the mulching mower is as follows:

concept Q&A

Suppose that the revenue line in Exhibit 4.4 had a steeper slope due to a higher price. What would that imply for the break-even point? For the amount of operating income (profit) for units sold above break-even? Now suppose that the revenue line remains unchanged, but that variable cost per unit increases. How would this increase affect the total cost line? What would this increase imply for the break-even point? For the amount of operating income (profit) for units sold above break-even?

Answers on pages 734 to 738.

$$\text{Mulching mower break-even units} = \frac{\text{Fixed cost}}{(\text{Price} - \text{Unit variable cost})} = \frac{\$30{,}000}{\$75} = 400 \text{ units}$$

Break-even for the riding mower can be computed as well:

$$\text{Riding mower break-even units} = \frac{\text{Fixed cost}}{(\text{Price} - \text{Unit variable cost})} = \frac{\$40{,}000}{\$200} = 200 \text{ units}$$

Thus, 400 mulching mowers and 200 riding mowers must be sold to achieve a break-even product margin. But a break-even product margin covers only direct fixed costs; the common fixed costs remain to be covered. Selling these numbers of lawn mowers would result in a loss equal to the common fixed costs. This level of sales is not the BEP for the firm as a whole; somehow the common fixed costs must be factored into the analysis.

Allocating the common fixed costs to each product line before computing a BEP may resolve this difficulty. The problem with this approach is that allocation of the common fixed costs is arbitrary. Thus, no meaningful break-even volume is readily apparent.

Another possible solution is to convert the multiple-product problem into a single-product problem. If this can be done, then all of the single-product CVP methodology can be applied directly. The key to this conversion is to identify the expected sales mix, in units, of the products being marketed. **Sales mix** is the relative combination of products being sold by a firm.

Determining the Sales Mix The sales mix is measured in units sold. For example, if Whittier plans on selling 1,200 mulching mowers and 800 riding mowers, then the sales mix in units is 1,200:800. Usually, the sales mix is reduced to the smallest possible whole numbers. Thus, the relative mix, 1,200:800, can be reduced to 12:8, and further reduced to 3:2. That is, Whittier expects that for every three mulching mowers sold, two riding mowers will be sold.

According to Whittier's marketing study, a sales mix of 3:2 can be expected. While we could examine a variety of sales mixes, and each one would result in a different break-even point, the expected sales mix is the ratio that should be used; all others can be ignored.

Sales Mix and Cost–Volume–Profit Analysis Defining a particular sales mix allows the conversion of a multiple-product problem into a single-product CVP format. Since Whittier expects to sell three mulching mowers for every two riding mowers, it can define the single product it sells as a package containing three mulching mowers and two riding mowers. By defining the product as a package, the multiple-product problem is converted into a single-product one. To use the approach of BEP in units, the package selling price and the variable cost per package must be known. To compute these package values, the sales mix, individual product prices, and individual variable costs are needed. Cornerstone 4.7 shows how the overall BEP for each product can be determined.

CORNERSTONE 4.7

Calculating the Break-Even Units for a Multiple-Product Firm

Information:

Recall that Whittier Company sells two products: mulching mowers priced at $400 and riding mowers priced at $800. The variable costs per unit are $325 per mulching mower and $600 per riding mower. Total fixed expense is $96,250 (direct fixed expense of $30,000 and $40,000, respectively, and common fixed expense of $26,250). Whittier's expected sales mix is three mulching mowers to two riding mowers.

Required:

1. Form a package of mulching and riding mowers based on the sales mix, and calculate the package contribution margin.
2. Calculate the BEP in units for mulching mowers and for riding mowers.
3. Check your answers by preparing a contribution margin income statement.

Solution:

1. Each package consists of three mulching mowers and two riding mowers:

Product	Price	Unit Variable Cost	Unit Contribution Margin	Sales Mix	Package Contribution Margin
Mulching	$400	$325	$ 75	3	$225
Riding	800	600	200	2	400
Package total					$625

The three mulching mowers in the package yield $225 (= 3 × $75) in contribution margin. The two riding mowers in the package yield $400 (= 2 × $200) in contribution margin. Thus, a package of five mowers (three mulching and two riding) has a total contribution margin of $625.

(Continued)

CORNERSTONE **4.7** *(Continued)*

2. $$\text{Break-even package} = \frac{\text{Fixed cost}}{\text{Package contribution margin}} = \frac{\$96{,}250}{\$625} = 154 \text{ packages}$$

   Mulching mower break-even units = 154 × 3 = 462
   Riding mower break-even units = 154 × 2 = 308

3. Income statement—break-even solution:

	Mulching Mower	Riding Mower	Total
Sales	$184,800	$246,400	$431,200
Less: Variable expenses	150,150	184,800	334,950
Contribution margin	$ 34,650	$ 61,600	96,250
Less: Total fixed expenses			96,250
Operating income			$ 0

Why:

Because, as in the case of a single-product firm, a multiple-product firm needs to know how many units of each product in the product mix must be sold to break even.

The complexity of the approach of BEP in units increases dramatically as the number of products increases. Imagine performing this analysis for a firm with several hundred products. This observation seems more overwhelming than it actually is. Computers can easily handle a problem with so much data. Furthermore, many firms simplify the problem by analyzing product groups rather than individual products. Another way to handle the increased complexity is to switch from the units sold approach to the sales revenue approach. This approach can accomplish a multiple-product CVP analysis using only the summary data found in an organization's income statement. The computational requirements are much simpler.

Break-Even Point in Sales Dollars

To illustrate the BEP in sales dollars, the same example will be used. However, the only information needed is the projected income statement for Whittier Company as a whole.

Sales	$1,120,000
Less: Variable costs	870,000
Contribution margin	250,000
Less: Fixed costs	96,250
Operating income	$ 153,750

Notice that this income statement corresponds to the total column of the more detailed income statement examined previously. The projected income statement rests on the assumption that 1,200 mulching mowers and 800 riding mowers will be sold (a 3:2 sales mix). The BEP in sales revenue also rests on the expected sales mix.

concept Q&A

Suppose a men's clothing store sells two brands of suits: designer suits with a contribution margin of $600 each and regular suits with a contribution margin of $500 each. At break-even, the store must sell a total of 100 suits a month. Last month, the store sold 100 suits in total but incurred an operating loss. There was no change in fixed cost, variable cost, or price. What happened?

Answers on pages 734 to 738.

With this income statement, the usual CVP questions can be addressed. For example, how much sales revenue must be earned to break even? Cornerstone 4.8 shows how to calculate the BEP in sales dollars for a multiple-product firm.

The BEP in sales dollars implicitly uses the assumed sales mix but avoids the requirement of building a package contribution margin. No knowledge of individual product data is needed. The computational effort is similar to that used in the single-product setting. Moreover, the answer is still expressed in sales revenue. Unlike the break-even point in units, the answer to CVP questions using sales dollars is still expressed in a single

CORNERSTONE 4.8

Calculating the Break-Even Sales Dollars for a Multiple-Product Firm

Information:

Recall that Whittier Company sells two products that are expected to produce total revenue next year of \$1,120,000 and total variable costs of \$870,000. Total fixed costs are expected to equal \$96,250.

Required:

1. Calculate the BEP in sales dollars for Whittier Company.
2. Check your answer by preparing a contribution margin income statement.

Solution:

1. $\text{Contribution margin ratio} = \dfrac{\$250{,}000}{\$1{,}120{,}000} = 0.22$

$$\text{Break-even sales} = \frac{\text{Fixed cost}}{\text{Contribution margin ratio}} = \frac{\$96{,}250}{0.22} = \$437{,}500$$

[*Note:* Total break-even sales differ slightly between Cornerstones 4.7 and 4.8 (\$431,200 vs. \$437,500) due to the rounding of the contribution margin ratio to only two decimal places (0.22). Had we used four decimal places, the difference due to rounding would have only been \$28.]

2. Income statement—break-even solution:

Sales	\$437,500
Less: Variable costs (0.78 × \$437,500)	341,250
Contribution margin	96,250
Less: Fixed costs	96,250
Operating income	\$ 0

Why:

Because, as in the case of a single-product firm, management needs to know the sales revenue necessary to break even, given an assumed sales mix.

summary measure. The sales revenue approach, however, does sacrifice information concerning individual product performance.

Underlying Assumptions of Cost–Volume–Profit Analysis

CVP analysis focuses on relationships among selling price, variable costs, fixed costs, volume, and profits. This model is a useful planning tool that can provide information about the impact on profits when changes are made in the cost structure or in the sales level. Several important but necessary assumptions are made in the CVP model. To begin with, the following assumptions can be stated about CVP analysis:

- It is a short-run decision making tool.
- It is based on historical costs and prices that are subject to change.
- It is better suited for single—not multiple—products.
- Productivity, efficiency, technology, and market conditions are constant (i.e., costs do not change).
- An accurate way has been devised to separate cost into variable and fixed components.
- Total fixed costs are constant within the relevant range. This assumption, in part, indicates that no capacity additions will be made during the period being considered.
- There is linearity between costs and revenue.
- Prices and costs are known with certainty.
- Sales mix is constant.
- Sales and production are equal; thus, there is no material fluctuation in inventory levels. This assumption is necessary because fixed cost can be allocated to inventory at a different rate each year. Because CVP and variable costing both focus on cost behaviour, they are distinctly compatible with each other.

Linear Cost and Revenue Functions CVP assumes that cost and revenue functions are linear; that is, they are straight lines. But, as was discussed in Chapter 3 on cost behaviour, these functions are often not linear. They may be curved or step functions. Fortunately, it is not necessary to consider all possible ranges of production and sales for a firm. Remember that CVP analysis is a short-run decision-making tool. (We know that it is short-run in orientation because some costs are fixed. In the long term, no costs are fixed.) It is only necessary for us to determine the current operating range, or relevant range, for which the linear cost and revenue relationships are valid. Once a relevant range has been identified, then the cost and price relationships are assumed to be known and constant.

Prices and Costs Known with Certainty In actuality, firms seldom know prices, variable costs, and fixed costs with certainty. A change in one variable usually affects the value of others. Often, there is a probability distribution to consider. Furthermore, there are formal ways of explicitly building uncertainty into the CVP model. These issues are explored in the section on incorporating risk and uncertainty into CVP analysis.

Constant Sales Mix In a single-product analysis, the sales mix is obviously constant—the one product accounts for 100 percent of sales. Multiple-product break-even analysis requires a constant sales mix. However, it is virtually impossible to predict the sales mix with certainty. Typically, this constraint is handled in practice through sensitivity analysis. By using the capabilities of spreadsheet analysis, the sensitivity of variables to a variety of sales mixes can be readily assessed.

Summary of Effects of Changes on Break-Even Point The BEP in sales changes in the *same* direction as changes in the variable cost per unit and fixed costs. In contrast, the BEP in sales changes in the *opposite* direction as changes in the unit selling price. These changes on the BEP in sales are summarized below.

Type of Change	Direction of Change	Effect of Change on Break-Even Sales
Fixed cost	Increase	Increase
	Decrease	Decrease
Unit variable cost	Increase	Increase
	Decrease	Decrease
Unit selling price	Increase	Decrease
	Decrease	Increase

YOUDECIDE Finding the Break-Even Point for a New Business

You are an accountant in private practice. A friend of yours, Michaela, recently started a novelty greeting card business. Michaela designs greeting cards that allow the sender to write in his or her own message. She uses heavy card stock, cut to size, and decorates the front of each card with bits of fabric, lace, and ribbon in seasonal motifs (e.g., a heart for Valentine's Day, a pine tree for Christmas). Michaela hired several friends to make the cards, according to Michaela's instructions, on a piece-work basis. (In piece work, the worker is paid on the basis of number of units produced.) The workers make the cards at their homes, meaning that no factory facilities are involved. Michaela designs the cards and travels around her four-city region to sell the completed cards on consignment. For the few months the company has been in existence, the cards have been selling well, but Michaela is operating at a loss.

What types of information do you need to find the BEP? How can the business owner use this information to make decisions?

In order to determine the BEP, you need to determine the prices and variable costs for the cards. Since creating a multi-product break-even analysis could be complex, it may be easier to determine the average price and the average variable cost for the cards, then find the total fixed cost, and tell Michaela how many cards she would need to sell to break even.

Suppose that the break-even number of cards is 250 per month, and that the average contribution margin per card is $0.80. Then, as soon as Michaela sells the 250th card, she knows she is in the black. From then on, every card sold adds $0.80 to her profit. This is very important information for Michaela—whose business losses are coming right out of her family's chequing account. Not only does Michaela have a sales goal for each month, but she also knows at any point in time how much income she has made.

Owners of small businesses find break-even analysis and concepts to be very helpful. A knowledge of contribution margin helps owners know how they are doing at any point in time.

COST–VOLUME–PROFIT ANALYSIS AND RISK AND UNCERTAINTY

OBJECTIVE 5

Explain the impact of risk, uncertainty, and changing variables on cost–volume–profit analysis.

Because firms operate in a dynamic world, they must be aware of changes in prices, variable costs, and fixed costs. They must also account for the effect of risk and uncertainty. The BEP can be affected by changes in price, unit contribution margin, and fixed cost. Managers can use CVP analysis to evaluate risk and uncertainty in the strategic planning process.

For example, in April 2014, Bombardier announced that it had 201 orders for its new C-series jet which would carry 100 to 149 passengers and compete directly with Airbus, Boeing, and Embraer. More than 200 orders were necessary to cover the more than $4 billion development costs for the plane. Speculation had been rampant that the company would encounter overruns in its development costs which would increase the number of planes needing to be sold to recover the development costs.[1]

For a given sales mix, CVP analysis can be used as if the firm were selling a single product. However, when the prices of individual products change, the sales mix can be

[1] Vladimir Karnozov, "Bombardier: CSeries Outsells in Its Segment," AINonline, http://www.ainonline.com/aviation-news/2014-04-08/bombardier-cseries-outsells-its-segment, accessed April 22, 2014.

affected because consumers may buy relatively more or less of each product. Keep in mind that a new sales mix will affect the units of each product that need to be sold in order to achieve a desired profit target. If the sales mix for the coming period is uncertain, it may be necessary to look at several different mixes. In this way, a manager can gain insight into the possible outcomes facing the firm.

Suppose that Whittier Company recently conducted a market study of the mulching lawn mower that revealed three different alternatives:

1. *Alternative 1:* If advertising expenditures increase by $8,000, then sales will increase from 1,600 units to 1,725 units.
2. *Alternative 2:* A price decrease from $400 to $375 per lawn mower will increase sales from 1,600 units to 1,900 units.
3. *Alternative 3:* Decreasing price to $375 *and* increasing advertising expenditures by $8,000 will increase sales from 1,600 units to 2,600 units.

Should Whittier maintain its current price and advertising policies, or should it select one of the three alternatives described by the marketing study?

The first alternative, increasing advertising costs by $8,000 with a resulting sales increase of 125 units, is summarized in Exhibit 4.5. This alternative can be analyzed by using the contribution margin per unit of $75. Since units sold increase by 125, the increase in total contribution margin is $9,375 (= $75 × 125 units). However, since fixed costs increase by $8,000, profits increase by $1,375 (= $9,375 − $8,000). Notice that we need to look only at the incremental increase in total contribution margin and fixed expenses to compute the increase in total operating income.

For the second alternative, the price is dropped to $375 (from $400), and the units sold increase to 1,900 (from 1,600). The effects of this alternative are summarized in Exhibit 4.6. Here, fixed expenses do not change, so only the change in total contribution margin is relevant. For the current price of $400, the contribution margin per unit is $75 (= $400 − $325), and the total contribution margin is $120,000 (= $75 × 1,600). For the new price, the contribution margin drops to $50 per unit (= $375 − $325). If 1,900 units are sold at the new price, then the new total contribution margin is $95,000 (= $50 × 1,900). Dropping the price results in a profit decline of $25,000 (= $120,000 − $95,000).

The third alternative calls for a decrease in the unit selling price and an increase in advertising costs. Like the first alternative, the profit impact can be assessed by looking

EXHIBIT 4.5

Summary of the Effects of Alternative 1

	Before the Increased Advertising	With the Increased Advertising
Units sold	1,600	1,725
Unit contribution margin	× $75	× $75
Total contribution margin	$120,000	$129,375
Less: Fixed expenses	45,000	53,000
Operating income	$ 75,000	$ 76,375

	Difference in Profit
Change in sales volume	125
Unit contribution margin	× $75
Change in contribution margin	$9,375
Less: Change in fixed expenses	8,000
Increase in operating income	$1,375

EXHIBIT 4.6

Summary of the Effects of Alternative 2

	Before the Proposed Price Decrease	With the Proposed Price Decrease
Units sold	1,600	1,900
Unit contribution margin	× $75	× $50
Total contribution margin	$120,000	$95,000
Less: Fixed expenses	45,000	45,000
Operating income	$ 75,000	$50,000
		Difference in Profit
Change in contribution margin ($95,000 − $120,000)		$(25,000)
Less: Change in fixed expenses		—
Decrease in operating income		$(25,000)

EXHIBIT 4.7

Summary of the Effects of Alternative 3

	Before the Proposed Price Decrease and Advertising Increase	With the Proposed Price Decrease and Advertising Increase
Units sold	1,600	2,600
Unit contribution margin	× $75	× $50
Total contribution margin	$120,000	$130,000
Less: Fixed expenses	45,000	53,000
Operating income	$ 75,000	$ 77,000
		Difference in Profit
Change in contribution margin ($130,000 − $120,000)		$10,000
Less: Change in fixed expenses ($53,000 − $45,000)		8,000
Increase in operating income		$ 2,000

at the incremental effects on contribution margin and fixed expenses. The incremental profit change can be found by (1) computing the incremental change in total contribution margin, (2) computing the incremental change in fixed expenses, and (3) combining the two results. As shown in Exhibit 4.7, the current total contribution margin (for 1,600 units sold) is $120,000. Since the new unit contribution margin is $50, the new total contribution margin is $130,000 (= $50 × 2,600 units). Thus, the incremental increase in total contribution margin is $10,000 (= $130,000 − $120,000). However, to achieve this incremental increase in contribution margin, an incremental increase of $8,000 in fixed costs is needed. The net effect is an incremental increase in operating income of $2,000.

Of the three alternatives identified by the marketing study, the third alternative promises the most benefit. It increases total operating income by $2,000. In contrast, the first alternative increases operating income by only $1,375, and the second *decreases* operating income by $25,000.

These examples are all based on the units sold approach. However, we could just as easily have applied the sales revenue approach. The answers would be the same.

Introducing Risk and Uncertainty

An important assumption of CVP analysis is that prices and costs are known with certainty. This assumption is seldom accurate. Risk and uncertainty are a part of business decision making and must be dealt with somehow. Formally, risk differs from uncertainty in that under risk, the probability distributions of the variables are known; under uncertainty, they are not known. For purposes of our CVP analysis, however, the terms will be used interchangeably.

How do managers deal with risk and uncertainty? There are a variety of methods. First, of course, is that management must realize the uncertain nature of future prices, costs, and quantities. Next, managers will move from consideration of a specific break-even point to what might be called a "break-even band." In other words, given the uncertain nature of the data, perhaps a firm might break even when 1,800 to 2,000 units are sold instead of using a single point estimate of 1,900 units. Furthermore, managers may engage in sensitivity or "what-if" analysis. In this instance, a computer spreadsheet is helpful, as managers set up the break-even (or target profit) relationships and then check to see the impact that varying costs and prices have on quantity sold. Two concepts useful to management are margin of safety and operating leverage. Both of these concepts may be considered measures of risk. Each requires knowledge of fixed and variable costs.

Margin of Safety

When making decisions about business opportunities and changes in sales mix, managers often consider the **margin of safety (MS)**, which is the excess of budgeted or actual sales over break-even sales. The margin of safety indicates the possible decrease in sales that may occur before an operating loss results. Thus, if the margin of safety is low, even a small decline in sales revenue may result in an operating loss. The margin of safety may be expressed in the following ways:

- dollars of sales
- units of sales
- percent of current sales

The following formulas are applicable:

$$\text{Margin of safety in units} = \text{Actual sales in units} - \text{Break-even sales in units}$$

$$\text{Margin of safety in dollars} = \text{Actual sales in dollars} - \text{Break-even sales in dollars}$$

$$\text{Margin of safety percentage} = \frac{\text{Margin of safety in units}}{\text{Actual unit sales}}$$

or

$$= \frac{\text{Margin of safety in dollars}}{\text{Actual sales in dollars}}$$

A margin of safety calculation allows management to determine how close the company is to operating at a "danger level" and, as such, provides an indication of risk. The lower the MS, the more carefully management must watch sales and control costs so that it will not generate a net loss. At low margins of safety, managers are less likely to take advantage of opportunities that, if incorrectly analyzed or forecasted, could send the company into a loss position. To illustrate, assume the following data:

Sales	$500,000
Sales at the break-even point	400,000
Unit selling price	25

The MS in dollars of sales is \$100,000 (= \$500,000 − \$400,000). The MS in units is 4,000 units (= \$100,000/\$25). The MS expressed as a percentage of current sales is 20 percent, as computed below:

$$\begin{aligned} MS &= \frac{\text{Sales} - \text{Sales at BEP}}{\text{Sales}} \\ &= \frac{\$500{,}000 - \$400{,}000}{\$500{,}000} \\ &= 20\% \end{aligned}$$

Therefore, the current sales may decline \$100,000, 4,000 units, or 20 percent before an operating loss occurs.

Exhibit 4.8 shows the calculation of the margin of safety and the margin of safety ratio. Cornerstone 4.9 shows the expected margin of safety for Whittier Company. The margin of safety can be viewed as a crude measure of risk. There are always events, unknown when plans are made, that can lower sales below the original expected level. In the event that sales take a downward turn, the risk of suffering losses is less if a firm's expected margin of safety is large than if the margin of safety is small. Managers who face a low margin of safety may wish to consider actions to lower their BEP, which would increase the margin of safety and lower the risk of incurring losses.

EXHIBIT 4.8

The Margin of Safety

CORNERSTONE 4.9

Computing the Margin of Safety

Information:

Recall that Whittier Company plans to sell 1,000 mowers at \$400 each in the coming year. Whittier has variable costs of \$325 and fixed costs of \$45,000. Break-even units were previously calculated as 600.

Required:

1. Calculate the margin of safety for Whittier Company in terms of the number of units.
2. Calculate the margin of safety for Whittier Company in terms of sales revenue.

(Continued)

CORNERSTONE

4.9

(Continued)

Solution:

1. Margin of safety in units = 1,000 − 600 = 400
2. Margin of safety in sales revenue = \$400(1,000) − \$400(600) = \$160,000

Why:

Because a firm should understand how vulnerable it is to possibly suffering losses. If the margin of safety is small, a small decline in sales may eliminate any projected profit and cause losses to occur.

Cost Structure Every company must weigh the trade-off between fixed costs and variable costs. If we assume that by increasing fixed costs we can reduce variable costs, and vice versa, then managers must choose the best combination of fixed and variable costs. As we have seen, higher fixed costs will result in a higher BEP. However, if as a result of incurring higher fixed costs our variable costs are lower, every dollar of revenue beyond break-even contributes more to operating profit. Higher fixed costs may create more risk in terms of breaking even, but will offer greater opportunity to achieve higher profits beyond break-even. The decision on cost structure will impact the risks incurred by a company.

Operating Leverage In physics, a lever is a simple device used to multiply force. Basically, the lever multiplies the force of the effort applied. The larger the load moved by a given amount of effort, the greater is the mechanical advantage of the lever. In financial terms, operating leverage relates to the relative mix of fixed costs and variable costs in an organization. It is sometimes possible to substitute fixed costs for variable costs. As variable costs decrease, the unit contribution margin increases, making the contribution of each unit sold that much greater. In such a case, fluctuations in sales have a magnified effect on profitability. Thus, firms that have realized lower variable costs by increasing the proportion of fixed costs to variable costs will benefit with greater increases in profits as sales increase than will firms with a lower proportion of fixed costs. Fixed costs are being used as leverage to increase profits. Unfortunately, it is also true that firms with a higher operating leverage will experience greater reductions in profits as sales decrease. **Operating leverage** is the use of fixed costs to extract higher percentage changes in profits as sales activity changes.

Automobile manufacturing companies typically have a very large investment in their manufacturing facilities, which are fixed costs. When demand falls, these facilities are not used to capacity but the costs are still incurred. In early 2011, General Motors reported that it earned a profit of \$4.7 billion in 2010, its first profit since 2004.[2] It attributed this resurgence to an increase of 12.2 percent in volume of sales. This is a clear indication that it had reached a point where all of its fixed costs were covered and the additional contribution margin went straight to the bottom line.

concept Q&A

Two companies have identical sales revenue of \$15 million. Is it true that both have the same operating income and the same margin of safety? Is it possible that one company has a higher margin of safety?

Answers on pages 734 to 738.

The **degree of operating leverage (DOL)** can be measured for a given level of sales by taking the ratio of contribution margin to operating income, as follows:

$$\text{Degree of operating leverage} = \frac{\text{Contribution margin}}{\text{Operating income}}$$

If fixed costs are increased to lower variable costs such that contribution margin increases and operating income decreases, then the degree of operating leverage

[2] Dominick Rushe, "General Motors Returns to Profit Two Years after Bankruptcy," *The Guardian*, http://www.theguardian.com/business/2011/feb/24/general-motors-back-in-profit-after-bankruptcy, February 24, 2011, accessed January 23, 2014.

CORNERSTONE 4.10 Computing the Degree of Operating Leverage

Information:

Recall that Whittier Company plans to sell 1,000 mowers at $400 each in the coming year. Whittier has variable costs of $325 and fixed costs of $45,000. Operating income at that level of sales was previously computed as $30,000.

Required:

Calculate the degree of operating leverage for Whittier Company.

Solution:

$$\text{Degree of operating leverage} = \frac{\text{Total contribution margin}}{\text{Operating income}}$$

$$= \frac{(\$400 - \$325)(1{,}000 \text{ units})}{\$30{,}000}$$

$$= 2.5$$

Why:

Because by calculating the DOL we can predict what will be the effect on operating income of a change in sales, and determine the risk to profits associated with fluctuations in sales levels as a result of the cost structure (proportion of fixed costs versus variable costs).

increases—signalling an increase in risk. Cornerstone 4.10 shows how to compute the degree of operating leverage for Whittier Company.

The greater the degree of operating leverage, the more that changes in sales will affect operating income. Because of this phenomenon, the mix of costs that an organization chooses can have a considerable influence on its operating risk and profitability. A company's mix of fixed costs relative to variable costs is referred to as its **cost structure**. Often, a company changes its cost structure by taking on more of one type of cost in exchange for reducing its amount of the other type of cost. For example, as Canadian companies try to compete more effectively with foreign competitors' significantly lower hourly labour costs (i.e., a variable cost), many are altering their cost structures by taking on more plant machine automation (i.e., a fixed cost) in exchange for using less labour.

To illustrate the impact of these concepts on management decision making, consider a firm that is planning to add a new product line that includes fabric. In adding the line, the firm can choose to rely heavily on automation by buying a cutting machine for the fabric, or rely on labour by having workers cut and piece the fabric. If the firm chooses to emphasize automation rather than labour, fixed costs will be higher, and unit variable costs will be lower. Relevant data for a sales level of 10,000 units follow:

	Automated System	Manual System
Sales	$1,000,000	$1,000,000
Less: Variable costs	500,000	800,000
Contribution margin	500,000	200,000
Less: Fixed costs	375,000	100,000
Operating income	$ 125,000	$ 100,000
Unit selling price	$ 100	$ 100
Unit variable cost	50	80
Unit contribution margin	50	20

After computing the new income statements, one may safely say that the automated system has a higher operating leverage simply because the fixed costs are higher than the fixed costs for the manual system.

The degree of operating leverage for the automated system is 4.0 (= $500,000/$125,000). The degree of operating leverage for the manual system is 2.0 (= $200,000/$100,000). What happens to profit in each system if sales increase by 40 percent? We can generate the following income statements to see:

	Automated System	Manual System
Sales	$1,400,000	$1,400,000
Less: Variable costs	700,000	1,120,000
Contribution margin	700,000	280,000
Less: Fixed costs	375,000	100,000
Operating income	$ 325,000	$ 180,000

Profits for the automated system would increase by $200,000 (= $325,000 − $125,000), for a 160 percent increase. In the manual system, profits increase by only $80,000 (= $180,000 − $100,000), for an 80 percent increase. The automated system has a greater percentage increase because it has a higher degree of operating leverage.

The degree of operating leverage can be used directly to calculate the change in operating income that would result from a given percentage change in sales.

Percentage change in operating income = DOL × Percentage change in sales

Since sales are predicted to increase by 40 percent, and the DOL for the automated system is 4.0, operating income increases by 160 percent. Since operating income based on the original sales level is $125,000, the operating income based on the increased sales level would be $325,000 [= $125,000 + ($125,000 × 1.6)]. Similarly, for the manual system, increased sales of 40 percent and DOL of 2.0 imply increased operating income of 80 percent. Therefore, operating income based on the increased sales level would be $180,000 [= $100,000 + ($100,000 × 0.8)]. Cornerstone 4.11 illustrates the impact of increased sales on operating income using the degree of operating leverage.

Computing the Impact of Increased Sales on Operating Income Using the DOL

CORNERSTONE 4.11

Information:

Recall that Whittier Company had expected to sell 1,000 mowers and earn operating income equal to $30,000 next year. Whittier's degree of operating leverage is equal to 2.5. The company plans to increase sales by 20 percent next year.

Required:

1. Calculate the percent change in operating income expected by Whittier Company for next year using the degree of operating leverage.
2. Calculate the operating income expected by Whittier Company next year using the percent change in operating income calculated in Requirement 1.

(Continued)

CORNERSTONE

4.11

(Continued)

Solution:

1. Percent change in operating income = DOL × Percent change in sales
   = 2.5 × 20% = 50%

2. Expected operating income = \$30,000 + (0.5 × \$30,000) = \$45,000

Why:

Because the DOL can be used to directly calculate the changes in operating income by simply multiplying DOL by the percentage change in sales without constructing a full income statement.

In choosing between the two systems, the effect of operating leverage is a valuable piece of information. Higher operating leverage multiplies the impact of increased sales on income. However, the effect is a two-edged sword. As sales decrease, the automated system will also show much higher percentage decreases in operating profits. Moreover, the increased operating leverage is available under the automated system because of the presence of increased fixed costs. The BEP for the automated system is 7,500 units (= \$375,000/\$50), whereas the BEP for the manual system is 5,000 units (= \$100,000/\$20). Thus, the automated system has greater operating risk. The increased risk, of course, provides a potentially higher profit level as long as units sold exceed 9,167. Why 9,167? Because that is the quantity for which the operating income for the automated system equals the operating income for the manual system.

The quantity at which two systems produce the same operating income is referred to as the **indifference point**. This number of units is computed by setting the operating income equations of the two systems equal and solving for number of units:

$$\$50(\text{Units}) - \$375{,}000 = \$20(\text{Units}) - \$100{,}000$$

$$\text{Units} = 9{,}167$$

In choosing between the automated and manual systems, the manager must consider the likelihood that sales will exceed 9,167 units. If after careful study there is a strong belief that sales will easily exceed this level, then the choice is obviously the automated system. On the other hand, if sales are unlikely to exceed 9,167 units, then the manual system is preferable as it reduces risk. Exhibit 4.9 summarizes the relative differences between the manual and automated systems in terms of some of the CVP concepts.

EXHIBIT 4.9

Differences between a Manual and an Automated System

	Manual System	Automated System
Selling price	Same	Same
Variable cost	Relatively higher	Relatively lower
Fixed cost	Relatively lower	Relatively higher
Contribution margin	Relatively lower	Relatively higher
Break-even point	Relatively lower	Relatively higher
Margin of safety	Relatively higher	Relatively lower

Sensitivity Analysis and Cost–Volume–Profit

The widespread use of personal computers and spreadsheets has placed sensitivity analysis within reach of most managers. An important tool, **sensitivity analysis** is a "what-if" technique that examines the impact of changes in underlying assumptions on a result. It is relatively simple to input data on prices, variable costs, fixed costs, and sales mix, and to set up formulas to calculate BEP and expected profits. Then, the data can be varied as desired to see how changes impact the expected profit.

In the example on operating leverage, a company analyzed the impact on profit of using an automated versus a manual system. The computations were essentially done by hand, so too much variation would be cumbersome. Using the power of a computer, it would be an easy matter to change the sales price in $1 increments between $75 and $125, with related assumptions about quantity sold. At the same time, variable and fixed costs could be adjusted. For example, suppose that the automated system has fixed costs of $375,000 but that those costs could easily double in the first year and come back down in the second and third years as bugs are worked out of the system and workers learn to use it. Again, the spreadsheet can effortlessly handle the many computations to give estimates of the results.

A spreadsheet, while wonderful for cranking out numerical answers, cannot do the most difficult job in CVP analysis: determining what data should be entered in the first place. The managerial accountant must be aware of the cost and price variations for the firm as well as of the impact of changing economic conditions on these variables. Determining the impact of uncertainty and understanding the potential risk associated with the unknown will give managers an appreciation of how important it is to carefully analyze the inputs as well as the outputs of their analysis.

Corporate and Social Responsibility

As you can see from the CVP analysis, the differentiation between fixed and variable costs will have a significant impact on the decisions being made. When a management accountant is preparing an analysis of a situation, the accountant cannot let personal biases enter into the determination of costs. As an example, if the management accountant wanted to influence the decision, he or she could estimate the costs as being either fixed or variable in a way that would ensure that the decision would go in the direction that the accountant wanted, rather than in a purely unbiased fashion. With the responsibility of preparing the analysis comes the requirement, as outlined in the Rules of Professional Conduct, to remain neutral so that the numbers tell the true story.

YOU DECIDE Using Contribution Margin Income Statements to Consider Varying Scenarios

You are the chief accountant for Boyne Resorts winter sports. Early in the year, you budgeted sales prices (lift tickets, restaurant prices), costs, and expected quantity to be sold. However, once the season starts, from week to week you will know more about the actual weather conditions.

How can you use this information about current weather conditions to better predict operating results for Boyne?

You can recast the budgeted statements according to how the weather will affect skiing. If the snow is good, some costs will go down. For example, you will lower the predicted cost of running the snow-making machines. However, good weather and more skiers will require additional seasonal hiring as more direct labour will be needed to run the lifts, operate ski equipment rental shops and restaurants, and so on. You can put together contribution margin budgeted income statements under various scenarios, increasing volume with good ski weather, and decreasing it with poor weather.

Having the ability to recast budgets will help managers respond quickly to the changing conditions and be able to raise or lower some prices as needed.

SUMMARY OF LEARNING OBJECTIVES

LO1. Determine the break-even point in number of units sold and in total sales dollars.

- At break-even, total costs (variable and fixed) equal total sales revenue.
- Break-even units equal total fixed costs divided by the contribution margin (price minus variable cost per unit).
- Break-even revenue equals total fixed costs divided by the contribution margin ratio.

LO2. Determine the number of units that must be sold, and the amount of revenue required, to earn a target profit.

- To earn a target (desired) profit, total costs (variable and fixed) plus the amount of target profit must equal total sales revenue.
- Units to earn target profit equal total fixed costs plus target profit divided by the contribution margin.
- Sales revenue to earn target profit equals total fixed costs plus target profit divided by the contribution margin ratio.

LO3. Prepare a profit–volume graph and a cost–volume–profit graph, and explain the meaning of each.

- CVP assumes linear revenue and cost functions, no finished goods ending inventories, constant sales mix, and that selling prices and fixed and variable costs are known with certainty.
- Profit–volume graphs plot the relationship between profit (operating income) and units sold. Break-even units are shown where the profit line crosses the horizontal axis.
- CVP graphs plot a line for total costs and a line for total sales revenue. The intersection of these two lines is the BEP in units.

LO4. Apply cost–volume–profit analysis in a multiple-product setting.

- Multiple-product analysis requires the determination of the expected sales mix.
- Break-even units for each product will change as the sales mix changes.
- Using the sales mix to establish a package of products enables us to apply the CVP equation to determine break-even.
- Using the sales revenue approach and the contribution margin ratio allows us to apply CVP analysis in complex situations to determine break-even.

LO5. Explain the impact of risk, uncertainty, and changing variables on cost–volume–profit analysis.

- Uncertainty regarding costs, prices, and sales mix will affect the BEP.
- Sensitivity analysis allows managers to vary costs, prices, and sales mix to show various possible BEPs.
- Margin of safety shows how far the company's actual sales and/or units are above or below the BEP.
- Operating leverage refers to the impact that a company's cost structure has on profitability as sales revenue increases or decreases.

SUMMARY OF IMPORTANT EQUATIONS

1. Sales revenue $=$ Price $\times$ Units sold
2. Operating income $=$ (Price $\times$ Units sold) $-$ (Unit variable cost $\times$ Units sold) $-$ Fixed cost
3. $$\text{Break-even point in units} = \frac{\text{Fixed cost}}{(\text{Price} - \text{Unit variable cost})}$$

4. $$\text{Contribution margin ratio} = \frac{\text{Total contribution margin}}{\text{Sales}}$$
or
$$= \frac{(\text{Price} - \text{Unit variable cost})}{\text{Price}}$$

5. $$\text{Variable cost ratio} = \frac{\text{Total variable cost}}{\text{Sales}}$$
or
$$= \frac{\text{Unit variable cost}}{\text{Price}}$$

6. $$\text{Break-even point in sales dollars} = \frac{\text{Fixed cost}}{\text{Contribution margin ratio}}$$
or
$$= \frac{\text{Fixed cost}}{1 - \text{Variable cost ratio}}$$

7. Margin of safety = Sales − Break-even sales

8. $$\text{Degree of operating leverage} = \frac{\text{Total contribution margin}}{\text{Operating income}}$$

9. Percentage change in profits = Degree of operating leverage × Percentage change in sales

CORNERSTONES

CORNERSTONE 4.1	Preparing a contribution margin income statement, page 131
CORNERSTONE 4.2	Solving for the break-even point in units, page 134
CORNERSTONE 4.3	Calculating the variable cost ratio and the contribution margin ratio, page 135
CORNERSTONE 4.4	Solving for the break-even point in sales dollars, page 137
CORNERSTONE 4.5	Solving for the number of units to be sold to earn a target operating income, page 140
CORNERSTONE 4.6	Solving for the sales needed to earn a target operating income, page 141
CORNERSTONE 4.7	Calculating the break-even units for a multiple-product firm, page 148
CORNERSTONE 4.8	Calculating the break-even sales dollars for a multiple-product firm, page 150
CORNERSTONE 4.9	Computing the margin of safety, page 156
CORNERSTONE 4.10	Computing the degree of operating leverage, page 158
CORNERSTONE 4.11	Computing the impact of increased sales on operating income using the DOL, page 159

GLOSSARY

Break-even point (BEP) The point where total sales revenue equals total cost; at this point, neither profit nor loss is earned. (p. 132)

Common fixed expenses Fixed expenses that cannot be directly traced to individual segments and that are unaffected by the elimination of any one segment. (p. 146)

Contribution margin Sales revenue minus total variable cost or price minus unit variable cost. (p. 128)

Contribution margin income statement The income statement format that is based on the separation of costs into fixed and variable components. (p. 128)

Contribution margin ratio Contribution margin divided by sales revenue. It is the proportion of each sales dollar available to cover fixed costs and provide for profit. (p. 129)

Cost structure A company's mix of fixed costs relative to variable costs. (p. 158)

Cost–volume–profit graph A graph that depicts the relationships among costs, volume, and profits. It consists of a total revenue line and a total cost line. (p. 145)

Degree of operating leverage (DOL) A measure of the sensitivity of profit changes to changes in sales volume. It helps to measure the percentage change in profits resulting from a percentage change in sales. (p. 157)

Direct fixed expenses Fixed costs that are directly traceable to a given segment and, consequently, disappear if the segment is eliminated. (p. 146)

Indifference point The quantity at which two systems produce the same operating income. (p. 160)

Margin of safety (MS) The units sold (or expected to be sold) or sales revenue earned (or expected to be earned) above the break-even volume. (p. 155)

Operating leverage The use of fixed costs to extract higher percentage changes in profits as sales activity changes. Leverage is achieved by increasing fixed costs while lowering variable costs. (p. 157)

Profit–volume graph A graphical portrayal of the relationship between profits and sales activity in units. (p. 144)

Sales mix The relative combination of products (or services) being sold by an organization. (p. 147)

Sensitivity analysis The "what-if" process of altering certain key variables to assess the effect on the original outcome. (p. 161)

Unit contribution margin Sales price per unit minus variable cost per unit. (p. 130)

Variable cost ratio Variable costs divided by sales revenues. It is the proportion of each sales dollar needed to cover variable costs. (p. 135)

REVIEW PROBLEMS

I. Single-Product Cost–Volume–Profit Analysis

Cutlass Company's projected profit for the coming year is as follows:

	Total	**Per Unit**
Sales	$200,000	$20
Less: Variable expenses	120,000	12
Contribution margin	80,000	$ 8
Less: Fixed expenses	64,000	
Operating income	$ 16,000	

Required:

1. Compute the variable cost ratio and the contribution margin ratio.
2. Compute the BEP in units.
3. Compute the BEP in sales dollars.
4. How many units must be sold to earn a profit of $30,000?
5. Using the contribution margin ratio, compute the additional profit that Cutlass would earn if sales were $25,000 more than expected.

6. For the projected level of sales, compute the margin of safety in units and in sales dollars.
7. Calculate the degree of operating leverage. Now suppose that Cutlass revises the forecast to show a 30 percent increase in sales over the original forecast. What is the percent change in operating income expected for the revised forecast? What is the total operating income expected by Cutlass after revising the sales forecast?

Solution:

1. $$\text{Variable cost ratio} = \frac{\text{Total variable cost}}{\text{Sales}} = \frac{\$120{,}000}{\$200{,}000} = 0.60, \text{ or } 60\%$$

$$\text{Contribution margin ratio} = \frac{\text{Contribution margin}}{\text{Sales}} = \frac{\$80{,}000}{\$200{,}000} = 0.40, \text{ or } 40\%$$

2. The BEP is computed as follows:

$$\text{Units} = \frac{\text{Fixed cost}}{(\text{Price} - \text{Unit variable cost})} = \frac{\$64{,}000}{(\$20 - \$12)} = \frac{\$64{,}000}{\$8} = 8{,}000 \text{ units}$$

3. The BEP in sales dollars is computed as follows:

$$\text{Break-even sales dollars} = \frac{\text{Fixed cost}}{\text{Contribution margin ratio}} = \frac{\$64{,}000}{0.40} = \$160{,}000$$

4. The number of units that must be sold to earn a profit of $30,000 is calculated as follows:

$$\text{Units} = \frac{(\$64{,}000 + \$30{,}000)}{\$8} = \frac{\$94{,}000}{\$8} = 11{,}750 \text{ units}$$

5. The additional contribution margin on additional sales of $25,000 would be 0.40 × $25,000 = $10,000.

6. Margin of safety in units = Projected units − Break-even units
= 10,000 − 8,000 = 2,000 units
Margin of safety in sales dollars = $200,000 − $160,000, or $40,000 in sales revenues

7. $$\text{Degree of operating leverage} = \frac{\text{Contribution margin}}{\text{Operating income}} = \frac{\$80{,}000}{\$16{,}000} = 5.0$$

$$\begin{aligned}\text{Percent change in operating income} &= \text{Degree of operating leverage} \times \text{Percent change in sales}\\ &= 5.0 \times 30\%\\ &= 150\%\\ \text{Expected operating income} &= \$16{,}000 + (1.5 \times \$16{,}000)\\ &= \$40{,}000\end{aligned}$$

II. Multiple-Product Cost–Volume–Profit Analysis

Alpha Company produces and sells two products: Alpha-Basic and Alpha-Deluxe. In the coming year, Alpha expects to sell 3,000 units of Alpha-Basic and 1,500 units of Alpha-Deluxe. Information on the two products is as follows:

	Alpha-Basic	Alpha-Deluxe
Price	$120	$200
Variable cost per unit	40	80

Total fixed costs are $140,000.

Required:

1. What is the sales mix of Alpha-Basic to Alpha-Deluxe?
2. Compute the break-even quantity of each product.

Solution:

1. The sales mix of Alpha-Basic to Alpha-Deluxe is 3,000:1,500 or 2:1.
2. Each package consists of two Alpha-Basic and one Alpha-Deluxe:

Product	Price	Unit Variable Cost	Unit Contribution Margin	Sales Mix	Package Unit Contribution Margin
Alpha-Basic	$120	$40	$ 80	2	$160
Alpha-Deluxe	200	80	120	1	120
Package total					$280

$$\begin{aligned}\text{Break-even packages} &= \frac{\text{Total fixed cost}}{\text{Package contribution margin}}\\ &= \frac{\$140{,}000}{\$280}\\ &= \$500 \text{ packages}\end{aligned}$$

Alpha-Basic break-even units = 500 × 2 = 1,000
Alpha-Deluxe break-even units = 500 × 1 = 500

DISCUSSION QUESTIONS

1. Explain how CVP analysis can be used for managerial planning.
2. Describe the difference between the units sold and the sales revenue approaches to CVP analysis.
3. Define the term *BEP*.
4. Explain why contribution margin per unit becomes profit per unit above the BEP.
5. What is the variable cost ratio? The contribution margin ratio? How are the two ratios related?
6. Suppose a firm with a contribution margin ratio of 0.3 increased its advertising expenses by $10,000 and found that sales increased by $30,000. Was it a good decision to increase advertising expenses? Suppose that the contribution margin ratio changes to 0.4. Is it a good decision to increase advertising expenses?

7. Define the term *sales mix*, and give an example to support your definition.
8. Explain how CVP analysis developed for single products can be used in a multiple-product setting.
9. "Since break-even analysis focuses on making zero profit, it is of no value in determining the units a firm must sell to earn a target profit." Do you agree or disagree with this statement? Why?
10. How does target profit enter into the break-even units equation?
11. Explain how a change in sales mix can change a company's BEP.
12. Define the term *margin of safety*. Explain how it can be used as a crude measure of operating risk.
13. Explain what is meant by the term *operating leverage*. What impact does increased leverage have on risk?
14. How can sensitivity analysis be used in conjunction with CVP analysis?
15. Why is a declining margin of safety over a period of time an issue of concern to managers?

CORNERSTONE EXERCISES

Cornerstone Exercise 4-1 Variable Cost, Fixed Cost, Contribution Margin Income Statement

OBJECTIVE 1
CORNERSTONE 4.1

Head-First Company plans to sell 5,000 bicycle helmets at $70 each in the coming year. Product costs include:

Direct materials per helmet	$ 30
Direct labour per helmet	5
Variable overhead per helmet	12
Total fixed factory overhead	14,000

Variable selling expense is a commission of $2 per helmet; fixed selling and administrative expense totals $15,400.

Required:

1. Calculate the total variable cost per unit.
2. Calculate the total fixed expense for the year.
3. Prepare a contribution margin income statement for Head-First Company for the coming year.

Cornerstone Exercise 4-2 Break-Even Point in Units

OBJECTIVE 1
CORNERSTONE 4.2

Head-First Company plans to sell 5,000 bicycle helmets at $70 each in the coming year. Unit variable cost is $49 (includes direct materials, direct labour, variable overhead, and variable selling expense). Total fixed cost equals $29,400 (includes fixed factory overhead and fixed selling and administrative expense).

Required:

1. Calculate the break-even number of helmets.
2. Check your answer by preparing a contribution margin income statement based on the break-even units.

Cornerstone Exercise 4-3 Variable Cost Ratio, Contribution Margin Ratio

Head-First Company plans to sell 5,000 bicycle helmets at $70 each in the coming year. Unit variable cost is $49 (includes direct materials, direct labour, variable overhead, and variable selling expense). Fixed factory overhead is $14,000 and fixed selling and administrative expense is $15,400.

(Continued)

Required:

1. Calculate the variable cost ratio.
2. Calculate the contribution margin ratio.
3. Prepare a contribution margin income statement based on the budgeted figures for next year. In a column next to the income statement, show the percentages based on sales for sales, total variable costs, and total contribution margin.

OBJECTIVE 1
CORNERSTONE 4.4

Cornerstone Exercise 4-4 Break-Even Point in Sales Dollars

Head-First Company plans to sell 5,000 bicycle helmets at $70 each in the coming year. Variable cost is 70 percent of the sales price; contribution margin is 30 percent of sales price. Total fixed cost equals $29,400 (includes fixed factory overhead and fixed selling and administrative expense).

Required:

1. Calculate the sales revenue that Head-First must make to break even by using the break-even point in sales equation.
2. Check your answer by preparing a contribution margin income statement based on the break-even point in sales dollars.

OBJECTIVE 2
CORNERSTONE 4.5

Cornerstone Exercise 4-5 Units to Earn Target Income

Head-First Company plans to sell 5,000 bicycle helmets at $70 each in the coming year. Unit variable cost is $49 (includes direct materials, direct labour, variable overhead, and variable selling expense). Total fixed cost equals $29,400 (includes fixed factory overhead and fixed selling and administrative expense).

Required:

1. Calculate the number of helmets Head-First must sell to earn operating income of $81,900.
2. Check your answer by preparing a contribution margin income statement based on the number of units calculated.

OBJECTIVE 2
CORNERSTONE 4.6

Cornerstone Exercise 4-6 Sales Needed to Earn Target Income

Head-First Company plans to sell 5,000 bicycle helmets at $70 each in the coming year. Variable cost is 70 percent of the sales price; contribution margin is 30 percent of sales price. Total fixed cost equals $29,400 (includes fixed factory overhead and fixed selling and administrative expense).

Required:

1. Calculate the sales revenue that Head-First must make to earn operating income of $81,900.
2. Check your answer by preparing a contribution margin income statement based on the sales dollars calculated in Requirement 1.
3. CONCEPTUAL CONNECTION How does a contribution margin income statement help managers make better decisions?

OBJECTIVE 4
CORNERSTONE 4.7

Cornerstone Exercise 4-7 Break-Even Point in Units for a Multiple-Product Firm

Suppose that Head-First Company now sells both bicycle helmets and motorcycle helmets. The bicycle helmets are priced at $70 and have variable costs of $49 each. The motorcycle helmets are priced at $220 and have variable costs of $143 each. Total fixed costs for Head-First as a whole equal $54,600 (includes all fixed factory overhead and fixed selling and administrative expense). Next year, Head-First expects to sell 5,000 bicycle helmets and 1,000 motorcycle helmets.

Required:

1. Form a package of bicycle and motorcycle helmets based on the sales mix expected for the coming year.
2. Calculate the BEP in units for bicycle helmets and for motorcycle helmets.
3. Check your answer by preparing a contribution margin income statement.

Cornerstone Exercise 4-8 **Break-Even Sales Dollars for a Multiple-Product Firm**

OBJECTIVE 4
CORNERSTONE 4.8

Head-First Company now sells both bicycle helmets and motorcycle helmets. Next year, Head-First expects to produce total revenue of $570,000 and total variable costs of $388,000. Total fixed costs are expected to be $54,600.

Required:

1. Calculate the BEP in sales dollars for Head-First. (Round the contribution margin ratio to four significant digits.)
2. Check your answer by preparing a contribution margin income statement.

Cornerstone Exercise 4-9 **Margin of Safety**

OBJECTIVE 5
CORNERSTONE 4.9

Head-First Company plans to sell 5,000 bicycle helmets at $70 each in the coming year. Unit variable cost is $49 (includes direct materials, direct labour, variable overhead, and variable selling expense). Total fixed cost equals $29,400 (includes fixed factory overhead and fixed selling and administrative expense). Break-even units equal 1,400.

Required:

1. Calculate the margin of safety in terms of the number of units.
2. Calculate the margin of safety in terms of sales revenue.

Cornerstone Exercise 4-10 **Degree of Operating Leverage**

OBJECTIVE 5
CORNERSTONE 4.10

Head-First Company plans to sell 5,000 bicycle helmets at $70 each in the coming year. Unit variable cost is $49 (includes direct materials, direct labour, variable overhead, and variable selling expense). Total fixed cost equals $29,400 (includes fixed factory overhead and fixed selling and administrative expense). Operating income at 5,000 units sold is $75,600.

Required:

Calculate the degree of operating leverage. (Round your answer to the nearest tenth.)

Cornerstone Exercise 4-11 **Impact of Increased Sales on Operating Income Using the Degree of Operating Leverage**

OBJECTIVE 5
CORNERSTONE 4.11

Head-First Company had planned to sell 5,000 bicycle helmets at $70 each in the coming year. Unit variable cost is $49 (includes direct materials, direct labour, variable overhead, and variable selling expense). Total fixed cost equals $29,400 (includes fixed factory overhead and fixed selling and administrative expense). Operating income at 5,000 units sold is $75,600. The degree of operating leverage is 1.4. Now Head-First expects to increase sales by 15 percent next year.

Required:

1. Calculate the percent change in operating income expected.
2. Calculate the operating income expected next year using the percent change in operating income calculated in Requirement 1.

EXERCISES

Exercise 4-12 **Basic Break-Even Calculations**

Suppose that Adams Company sells a product for $24. Unit costs are as follows:

Direct materials	$5.85
Direct labour	2.10
Variable overhead	3.15
Variable selling and administrative expense	2.40

Total fixed manufacturing overhead is $78,000 per year, and total fixed selling and administrative expense is $56,925.

Required:

1. Calculate the variable cost per unit and the contribution margin per unit.
2. Calculate the contribution margin ratio and the variable cost ratio.
3. Calculate the break-even units.
4. Prepare a contribution margin income statement at the break-even number of units.

OBJECTIVE 1

Exercise 4-13 Contribution Margin, Contribution Margin Ratio, Break-Even Point in Units, Break-Even Sales Revenue

Next year, Jefferson Company expects to sell 350,000 units at $19 each. Variable costs are 60 percent of sales price. Fixed costs total $874,000.

Required:

1. Calculate the contribution margin per unit.
2. Calculate the BEP in units.
3. Calculate the break-even sales revenue.
4. Prepare an income statement for Jefferson at break-even.
5. CONCEPTUAL CONNECTION Break-even operations always result in a profit of how much?

OBJECTIVE 1

Exercise 4-14 Contribution Margin Ratio, Variable Cost Ratio, Break-Even Sales Revenue

The controller of Dynamic Company prepared the following projected income statement:

Sales	$875,000
Less: Variable costs	393,750
Contribution margin	481,250
Less: Fixed costs	327,000
Operating income	$151,000

Required:

1. Calculate the contribution margin ratio.
2. Calculate the variable cost ratio.
3. Calculate the break-even sales revenue for Dynamic.

OBJECTIVE 2

Exercise 4-15 Income Statement, Break-Even Units, Units to Earn Target Income

Starfirst Company sold 37,500 units last year at $42 each. Variable cost was $32.60, and fixed costs were $183,300.

Required:

1. Prepare a contribution margin income statement for Starfirst Company for last year.
2. Calculate the BEP in units.
3. Calculate the units that Starfirst must sell to earn operating income of $200,000 next year.

OBJECTIVE 1

Exercise 4-16 Units Sold to Break Even, Unit Variable Cost, Unit Manufacturing Cost, Units to Earn Target Income

Prachi Company produces and sells disposable foil baking pans to retailers for $2.45 per pan. The variable costs per pan are as follows:

Direct materials	$0.27
Direct labour	0.58
Variable overhead	0.63
Variable selling	0.17

Fixed manufacturing costs total $131,650 per year. Fixed administrative costs total $18,350.

Required:

1. What is the unit variable cost? What is the unit variable manufacturing cost? Which is used in cost–volume–profit analysis and why?
2. Determine the number of pans that must be sold for Prachi to break even.
3. How many pans must be sold for Prachi to earn operating income of $12,600?
4. How much sales revenue must Prachi have to earn operating income of $12,600?

Exercise 4-17 Margin of Safety

OBJECTIVE 5

Chase Company produces and sells strings of colourful indoor/outdoor lights for holiday display to retailers for $11.75 per string. The variable costs per string are as follows:

Direct materials	$2.15
Direct labour	3.02
Variable overhead	1.04
Variable selling	0.37

Fixed manufacturing costs total $672,475 per year. Administrative costs (all fixed) total $827,962. Chase expects to sell 570,000 strings of lights next year.

Required:

1. Calculate the BEP in units.
2. Calculate the margin of safety in units.
3. Calculate the margin of safety in dollars.

Exercise 4-18 Contribution Margin, Unit Amounts, Break-Even Units

OBJECTIVE 1

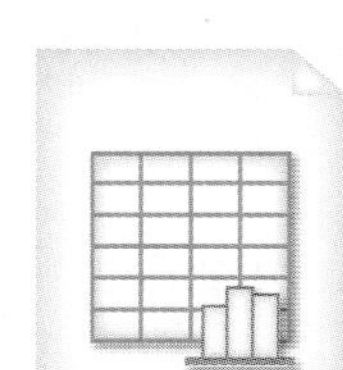

Information on four independent companies follows. Calculate the correct amount for each question mark. (Round your answers to two significant digits.)

	A	B	C	D
Sales	$15,000	$?	$?	$10,600
Total variable costs	5,000	11,700	9,750	?
Total contribution margin	10,000	3,900	?	?
Total fixed costs	?	4,000	?	4,452
Operating income (loss)	$ 500	$?	$ 364	$ 848

	A	B	C	D
Units sold	?	1,300	125	1,000
Price per unit	$5	?	$130	?
Variable cost per unit	?	$9	?	?
Contribution margin per unit	?	$3	?	?
Contribution margin ratio	?	?	40%	?
Break-even in units	?	?	?	?

Exercise 4-19 Sales Revenue Approach, Variable Cost Ratio, Contribution Margin Ratio

OBJECTIVE 1 2 5

Paragon Company's controller prepared the following budgeted income statement for the coming year:

Sales	$675,300
Less: Variable expenses	303,885
Contribution margin	371,415
Less: Fixed expenses	247,610
Operating income	$123,805

(Continued)

Required:

1. What is Paragon's variable cost ratio? What is its contribution margin ratio?
2. Suppose Paragon's actual revenues are $50,000 more than budgeted. By how much will operating income increase? Give the answer without preparing a new income statement.
3. How much sales revenue must Paragon earn to break even? Prepare a contribution margin income statement to verify your answer.
4. What is Paragon's expected margin of safety?
5. What is Paragon's margin of safety if sales revenue is $500,000?

OBJECTIVE 4

Exercise 4-20 Multiple-Product Break-Even

Switzer Company produces and sells yoga-training products: how-to DVDs and a basic equipment set (blocks, strap, and small pillows). Last year, Switzer sold 10,000 DVDs and 5,000 equipment sets. Information on the two products is as follows:

	DVDs	Equipment Sets
Price	$12	$15
Variable cost per unit	4	6

Total fixed costs are $70,000.

Required:

1. What is the sales mix of DVDs and equipment sets?
2. Compute the break-even quantity of each product.

Exercise 4-21 Multiple-Product Break-Even, Break-Even Sales Revenue

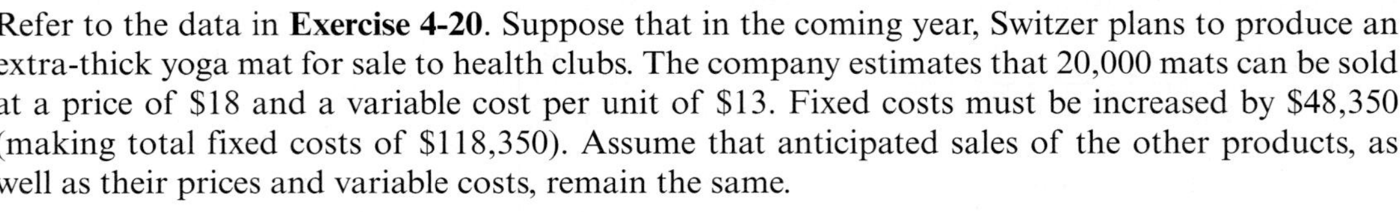

Refer to the data in **Exercise 4-20**. Suppose that in the coming year, Switzer plans to produce an extra-thick yoga mat for sale to health clubs. The company estimates that 20,000 mats can be sold at a price of $18 and a variable cost per unit of $13. Fixed costs must be increased by $48,350 (making total fixed costs of $118,350). Assume that anticipated sales of the other products, as well as their prices and variable costs, remain the same.

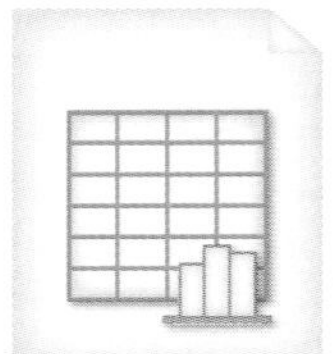

Required:

1. What is the sales mix of DVDs, equipment sets, and yoga mats?
2. Compute the break-even quantity of each product.
3. Prepare an income statement for Switzer for the coming year. What is the overall contribution margin ratio? The overall break-even sales revenue? (Round the contribution margin ratio to three significant digits; round the break-even sales revenue to the nearest dollar.)
4. Compute the margin of safety for the coming year in sales dollars.

OBJECTIVE 

Exercise 4-22 Contribution Margin Ratio, Break-Even Sales Revenue, and Margin of Safety for Multiple-Product Firm

Sonora Company produces and sells pottery chimineas (small clay outdoor fireplaces). The chimineas come in three models: small basic, large basic, and carved (ornately shaped and carved). In the coming year, Sonora expects to sell 30,000 small basic models, 50,000 large basic models, and 10,000 carved models. Information on the three models is as follows:

	Small	Large	Carved
Price	$180	$300	$525
Variable cost per unit	105	225	412

Total fixed costs are $669,750.

Required:

1. What is the sales mix of small basic to large basic to carved models?
2. Compute the break-even quantity of each product.
3. Prepare an income statement for Sonora for the coming year. What is the overall contribution margin ratio? The overall break-even sales revenue? (Round the contribution margin ratio to three significant digits; round the break-even sales revenue to the nearest dollar.)
4. Compute the margin of safety for the coming year.

OBJECTIVE 3

Exercise 4-23 Cost–Volume–Profit Graphs

Boudreau Company produces and sells one product. The selling price is $10, and the unit variable cost is $6. Total fixed costs are $10,000.

Required:

1. Prepare a CVP graph with "Units Sold" as the horizontal axis and "Revenue and Cost" as the vertical axis (similar to Exhibit 4.4). Label the BEP on the horizontal axis.
2. Prepare CVP graphs for each of the following independent scenarios:
   a. Fixed costs increase by $5,000.
   b. Unit variable cost increases to $7.
   c. Unit selling price increases to $12.
   d. Assume that fixed costs increase by $5,000 and unit variable cost is $7.

OBJECTIVE 1

Exercise 4-24 Basic Cost–Volume–Profit Concepts

Berry Company produces a single product. The projected income statement for the coming year is as follows:

Sales (24,000 units @ $75)	$1,800,000
Less: Variable costs	594,000
Contribution margin	1,206,000
Less: Fixed costs	984,025
Operating income	$ 221,975

Required:

1. Compute the unit contribution margin and the units that must be sold to break even.
2. Suppose 30,000 units are sold above break-even. What is the operating income?
3. Compute the contribution margin ratio and the BEP in dollars. Suppose that revenues are $500,000 more than expected for the coming year. What would the total operating income be?

OBJECTIVE 1 

Exercise 4-25 Margin of Safety and Operating Leverage

Maradona Company produces a single product. The projected income statement for the coming year is as follows:

Sales (50,000 units @ $90)	$4,500,000
Less: Variable costs	1,890,000
Contribution margin	2,610,000
Less: Fixed costs	1,833,300
Operating income	$ 776,700

(Round all dollar answers to the nearest dollar. Round fractional answers to two significant digits.)

Required:

1. Compute the break-even sales dollars.
2. Compute the margin of safety in sales dollars.

(Continued)

3. Compute the degree of operating leverage (rounded to two decimal places).
4. Compute the new operating income if sales are 20 percent higher than expected.

OBJECTIVE 1 4

Exercise 4-26 Multiple-Product Break-Even

Parker Pottery produces a line of vases and a line of ceramic figurines. Each line uses the same equipment and labour; hence, there are no traceable fixed costs. Common fixed costs equal \$75,000. Parker's accountant has begun to assess the profitability of the two lines and has gathered the following data for last year:

	Vases	Figurines
Price	\$100	\$175
Variable cost	75	105
Contribution margin	\$ 25	\$ 70
Number of units	1,000	500

Required:

1. Compute the number of vases and the number of figurines that must be sold for the company to break even.
2. Parker Pottery is considering upgrading its factory to improve the quality of its products. The upgrade will add \$13,150 per year to total fixed costs. If the upgrade is successful, the projected sales of vases will be 1,500, and figurine sales will increase to 1,000 units. What is the new BEP in units for each of the products?
3. CONCEPTUAL CONNECTION Why is it better to use the contribution margin ratio in determining break-even in a multi-product company?

Exercise 4-27 Break-Even Units, Contribution Margin Ratio, Multiple-Product Break-Even, Margin of Safety, Degree of Operating Leverage

Burton Inc.'s projected operating income (based on sales of 350,000 units) for the coming year is as follows:

	Total
Sales	\$8,400,000
Less: Variable expenses	6,720,000
Contribution margin	1,680,000
Less: Fixed expenses	1,512,000
Operating income	\$ 168,000

Required:

1. Compute:
   a. Variable cost per unit
   b. Contribution margin per unit
   c. Contribution margin ratio
   d. Break-even point in units
   e. Break-even point in sales dollars
2. How many units must be sold to earn operating income of \$300,000?
3. Compute the additional operating income that Burton would earn if sales were \$50,000 more than expected.
4. For the originally projected level of sales, compute the margin of safety in units, and then in sales dollars.
5. Compute the degree of operating leverage.
6. Compute the new operating income if sales are 10 percent higher than expected.

PROBLEMS

Problem 4-28 Break-Even Units, Contribution Margin Ratio, Margin of Safety

Chisholm Company's projected profit for the coming year is as follows:

	Total	Per Unit
Sales	$13,800,000	$60
Less: Variable expenses	8,970,000	39
Contribution margin	4,830,000	$21
Less: Fixed expenses	3,213,924	
Operating income	$ 1,616,076	

Check figures:
1. Break-even units = 153,044
2. Units for target profit = 281,616
4. Margin of safety in units = 76,956

Required:

1. Compute the BEP in units.
2. How many units must be sold to earn a profit of $2,700,000?
3. Compute the contribution margin ratio. Using that ratio, compute the additional profit that Chisholm would earn if sales were $300,000 more than expected.
4. For the projected level of sales, compute the margin of safety in units.

Problem 4-29 Break-Even Units, Operating Income, Margin of Safety

OBJECTIVE 1 5

Dorian Manufacturing Company produces T-shirts screen-printed with the logos of various sports teams. Each shirt is priced at $10 and has a unit variable cost of $5. Total fixed costs are $96,000.

Required:

1. Compute the BEP in units.
2. Suppose that Dorian could reduce its fixed costs by $13,500 by reducing the amount of setup and engineering time needed. How many units must be sold to break even in this case?
3. How does the reduction in fixed costs affect the BEP? Operating income? The margin of safety?

Check figure:
2. Break-even units = 16,500

Problem 4-30 Contribution Margin, Break-Even Units, Break-Even Sales, Margin of Safety, Degree of Operating Leverage

OBJECTIVE 

Cabrera Company produces a variety of chemicals. One division makes reagents for laboratories. The division's projected income statement for the coming year is:

Sales (384,000 units @ $50)	$19,200,000
Less: Variable expenses	13,440,000
Contribution margin	5,760,000
Less: Fixed expenses	3,000,000
Operating income	$ 2,760,000

Required:

1. Determine the contribution margin per unit, and the BEP in units. Calculate the contribution margin ratio and the break-even sales revenue.
2. The divisional manager has decided to increase the advertising budget by $300,000. This will increase sales revenues by $3 million. By how much will operating income increase or decrease as a result of this action?
3. Suppose sales revenues exceed the estimated amount on the income statement by $945,000. Without preparing a new income statement, by how much are profits underestimated?
4. CONCEPTUAL CONNECTION Why can we take the shortcut of simply focusing on the increased sales revenue to determine increased profitability?
5. Determine the margin of safety based on the original income statement.

Check figures:
1. Break-even sales = $10,000,000
3. $283,500
6. Percentage increase in operating income = 41.8%

6. Calculate the degree of operating leverage based on the original income statement. If sales revenues are 20 percent greater than expected, what is the percentage increase in operating income? (Round operating leverage to two decimal places.)

OBJECTIVE 2 4

Problem 4-31 Multiple-Product Analysis, Changes in Sales Mix, Sales to Earn Target Operating Income

Kenno Company produces two products: squares and circles. The projected income for the coming year, segmented by product line, follows:

	Squares	Circles	Total
Sales	$300,000	$2,500,000	$2,800,000
Less: Variable expenses	100,000	500,000	600,000
Contribution margin	200,000	2,000,000	2,200,000
Less: Direct fixed expenses	28,000	1,500,000	1,528,000
Product margin	$172,000	$ 500,000	$ 672,000
Less: Common fixed expenses			100,000
Operating income			$ 572,000

The selling prices are $30 for squares and $50 for circles.

Required:

1. Compute the number of units of each product that must be sold for Kenno Company to break even.
2. Assume that the marketing manager changes the sales mix of the two products so that the ratio is three squares to five circles. Repeat Requirement 1.
3. Refer to the original data. Suppose that Kenno can increase the sales of squares with increased advertising. The extra advertising would cost an additional $245,000, and some of the potential purchasers of circles would switch to squares. In total, sales of squares would increase by 25,000 units, and sales of circles would decrease by 5,000 units. Would Kenno be better off with this strategy?

Check figures:

2. Break-even circles = 31,310
3. Increase in total contribution margin = $300,000

Problem 4-32 Cost–Volume–Profit Equation, Basic Concepts, Solving for Unknowns

Goldilocks Company produces high-end combination shampoos and conditioners in individual-use bottles for hotels. Each bottle sells for $0.90. The variable costs for each bottle (materials, labour, and overhead) total $0.63. The total fixed costs are $210,600. During the most recent year, 830,000 bottles were sold.

Required:

1. What is the BEP in units for Goldilocks? What is the margin of safety in units for the most recent year?
2. Prepare an income statement for Goldilocks's most recent year.
3. How many units must be sold for Goldilocks to earn a profit of $40,500?
4. Using the contribution margin percentage approach, what is the level of sales dollars needed for Goldilocks to earn operating income of 20 percent of sales?

Check figures:

1. Margin of safety in units = 50,000 bottles
2. Operating income = $13,500
3. Units for target profit = 930,000 bottles

Problem 4-33 Contribution Margin Ratio, Break-Even Sales, Operating Leverage

Alonzo Company produces plastic mailboxes. The projected income statement for the coming year follows:

Sales	$560,400
Less: Variable costs	257,784
Contribution margin	302,616
Less: Fixed costs	150,000
Operating income	$152,616

Required:

1. Compute the contribution margin ratio for the mailboxes.
2. How much revenue must Alonzo earn in order to break even?
3. What is the effect on the contribution margin ratio if the unit selling price and unit variable cost each increase by 10 percent?
4. Suppose that management has decided to give a 3 percent commission on all sales. The projected income statement does not reflect this commission. Recompute the contribution margin ratio, assuming that the commission will be paid. What effect does this have on the break-even revenue?
5. If the commission is paid as described in Requirement 4, management expects sales revenues to increase by $80,000. How will this affect operating leverage? Is it a sound decision to implement the commission? Support your answer with appropriate computations.

Check figures:
2. $277,778
4. Break-even revenue = $294,118

Problem 4-34 Multiple Products, Break-Even Analysis, Operating Leverage

OBJECTIVE 

Carlyle Lighting Products produces two different types of lamps: a floor lamp and a desk lamp. Floor lamps sell for $30, and desk lamps sell for $20. The projected income statement for the coming year follows:

Sales	$600,000
Less: Variable costs	400,000
Contribution margin	200,000
Less: Fixed costs	150,000
Operating income	$ 50,000

The owner of Carlyle estimates that 60 percent of the sales revenues will be produced by floor lamps and the remaining 40 percent by desk lamps. Floor lamps are also responsible for 60 percent of the variable expenses. Of the fixed expenses, one-third are common to both products, and one-half are directly traceable to the floor lamp product line.

Required:

1. Compute the sales revenue that must be earned for Carlyle to break even.
2. Compute the number of floor lamps and desk lamps that must be sold for Carlyle to break even.
3. Compute the degree of operating leverage for Carlyle Lighting Products. Now assume that the actual revenues will be 40 percent higher than the projected revenues. By what percentage will profits increase with this change in sales volume?
4. CONCEPTUAL CONNECTION What is the theory behind the operating leverage concept?

Check figures:
1. Revenue = $450,000
2. Desk lamps = 8,998
3. Operating leverage = 4.0

Problem 4-35 Multiple-Product Break-Even

OBJECTIVE 

Polaris Inc. manufactures two types of metal stampings for the automobile industry: door handles and trim kits. Fixed costs equal $146,000. Each door handle sells for $12 and has variable costs of $9; each trim kit sells for $8 and has variable costs of $5.

Required:

1. What are the contribution margins per unit and the contribution margin ratios for door handles and for trim kits?
2. If Polaris sells 20,000 door handles and 40,000 trim kits, what is the operating income?
3. How many door handles and how many trim kits must be sold for Polaris to break even, assuming the same sales mix from Requirement 2?
4. Assume that Polaris has the opportunity to rearrange its plant to produce only trim kits. If this is done, fixed costs will decrease by $35,000, and 70,000 trim kits can be produced and sold. Is this a good idea? Explain.

Check figures:
2. Operating income = $34,000
3. Trim kits = 32,444

Problem 4-36 Cost–Volume–Profit, Margin of Safety

Victoria Company produces a single product. Last year's income statement is as follows:

Sales (36,000 units)	$1,512,000
Less: Variable costs	907,200
Contribution margin	604,800
Less: Fixed costs	504,000
Operating income	$ 100,800

Required:

1. Compute the BEP in units and sales dollars, using the contribution margin ratio.
2. What was the margin of safety for Victoria Company last year?
3. Suppose that Victoria Company is considering an investment in new technology that will increase fixed costs by $250,000 per year but will lower variable costs to 45 percent of sales. Units sold will remain unchanged. Prepare a budgeted income statement assuming that Victoria makes this investment. What is the new BEP in units and sales dollars, assuming that the investment is made?

Check figures:
1. Break-even units = 30,000 units
3. Operating income = $77,600

OBJECTIVE 1 5

Problem 4-37 Cost–Volume–Profit, Margin of Safety

Steven Kissick is a Kingston-based lawyer who has been in practice for several years. He knew that it would take some time to establish himself and hopefully generate enough revenue to make a decent living. His financial statements for his year ended June 30, 2018, are as follows:

Steven Kissick, Lawyer
Income Statement
For the year ended June 30, 2018

Revenue	$180,000
Direct costs of practice:	
Variable	66,000
Fixed	88,000
Gross margin	26,000
Indirect costs of practice:	
Variable	17,500
Fixed	110,000
Operating income/(loss)	(101,500)
Income tax (27.5%)	0
Net loss	$(101,500)

Check figures:
1. Break-even revenue = $369,334
2. Target revenue = $755,264

Required:

1. How much revenue must Kissick generate to break even?
2. How much revenue must Kissick generate to generate after-tax income of $150,000?
3. If his billing rate is $350 per hour, is the answer for Requirement 2 reasonable? Why or why not?

OBJECTIVE 1

Problem 4-38 Using the Break-Even Equations to Solve for Price and Variable Cost Per Unit

Solve the following independent problems, using the CVP relationships.

Required:

1. Mitch Company has a BEP of 27,500 units. Variable costs are $22,500; total fixed costs are $62,400. What price does Mitch charge?
2. Gillian Company generates $33,000 in operating income at a sales volume of $228,000. The variable cost margin is 65 percent. What are the fixed costs?
3. At break-even, Hollis Company has revenue of $800,000 and fixed costs of $220,000. What is its variable cost ratio?

Check figure:
1. Price = $3.09

Problem 4-39 Contribution Margin, Cost–Volume–Profit, Margin of Safety

OBJECTIVE   

Candyland Inc. produces particularly rich praline fudge. Each 300-gram box sells for $5.60. Variable unit costs are as follows:

Pecans	$0.70
Sugar	0.35
Butter	1.85
Other ingredients	0.34
Box, packing material	0.76
Selling commission	0.20

Fixed overhead cost is $32,300 per year. Fixed selling and administrative costs are $12,500 per year. Candyland sold 35,000 boxes last year.

Required:

1. What is the contribution margin per unit for a box of praline fudge? What is the contribution margin ratio?
2. How many boxes must be sold to break even? What is the break-even sales revenue?
3. What was Candyland's operating income last year?
4. What was the margin of safety?
5. Suppose that Candyland raises the price to $6.20 per box but anticipates a sales drop to 31,500 boxes. What will be the new BEP in units? Should Candyland raise the price? Explain.

Check figures:
1. Contribution margin ratio = 0.25
2. Break-even units = 32,000
4. Margin of safety = $16,800
5. New operating income = $18,200

Problem 4-40 Break-Even Sales, Operating Leverage, Change in Income

OBJECTIVE  

Income statements for two different companies in the same industry are as follows:

	Company A	Company B
Sales	$500,000	$500,000
Less: Variable costs	400,000	200,000
Contribution margin	100,000	300,000
Less: Fixed costs	50,000	250,000
Operating income	$ 50,000	$ 50,000

Required:

1. Compute the degree of operating leverage for each company.
2. Compute the BEP for each company. Explain why the BEP for Company B is higher.
3. Suppose that both companies experience a 50 percent increase in revenues. Compute the percentage change in profits for each company. Explain why the percentage increase in Company B's profits is so much larger than that of Company A.

Check figures:
1. Company B degree of operating leverage = 6
2. Company A break-even sales = $250,000
3. Company B increase in profits = 300%

Problem 4-41 Multi-Product Operation, Break-Even Sales, Target After-Tax Profit

OBJECTIVE  

Operating information for four different products sold by Kline Company follows:

	Product A	Product B	Product C	Product D
Units sold	1,000	600	300	100
Sales	$500,000	$1,080,000	$2,760,000	$3,600,000
Variable product costs	300,000	630,000	1,650,000	2,350,000
Identifiable fixed product costs	25,000	220,000	300,000	300,000
Variable selling/administrative	25,000	150,000	240,000	213,000
Identifiable fixed selling/administrative	64,200	50,000	50,000	150,000

Common fixed costs are $270,000 and the income tax rate is 35 percent.

(Continued)

Required:

1. Determine the revenues that Kline must achieve to break even.
2. Determine the number of units of each product that Kline must sell to break even, assuming the sales mix remains constant.
3. Determine the sales revenue needed to earn an after-tax profit of $1,625,000.
4. Determine the number of units of each product that must be sold for Kline to achieve an after-tax profit of $1,300,000.

   Note: Round all dollar values to the nearest dollar.

OBJECTIVE 1 2 4

Problem 4-42 Multi-Product Operation with a Change in Parameters

Operating information for four different products sold by Kline Company follows:

	Product A	Product B	Product C	Product D
Units sold	1,000	600	300	100
Sales	$500,000	$1,080,000	$2,760,000	$3,600,000
Variable product costs	300,000	630,000	1,650,000	2,350,000
Identifiable fixed product costs	25,000	220,000	300,000	300,000
Variable selling/administrative	25,000	150,000	240,000	213,000
Identifiable fixed selling/administrative	64,200	50,000	50,000	150,000

Common fixed costs are $270,000 and the income tax rate is 35 percent.

Required:

1. If all variable costs increased by 10 percent and the company incurred $1,000,000 in additional advertising costs, what is the new BEP in revenue dollars and units of each product?
2. How would your answer to Requirement 1 change if the expected unit sales changed to 900, 400, 500, and 200, respectively?
3. What two different levels of sales revenue would be required under the revised circumstances outlined in Requirements 1 and 2, respectively, for Kline to achieve an after-tax profit of $2,470,000?

   Note: Round all dollar values to the nearest dollar.

Problem 4-43 Contribution Margin, Break-Even Sales, Margin of Safety

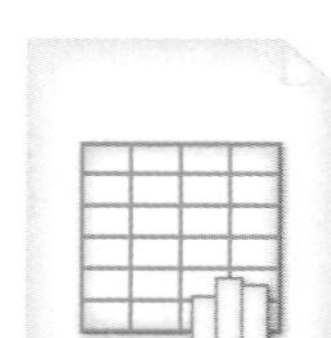

Suppose that Bissonette Company had the following sales and cost experience (in thousands of dollars) for May of the current year and for May of the prior year:

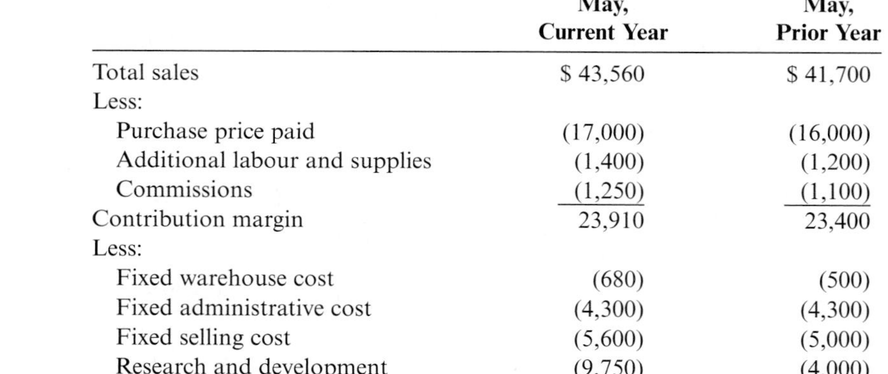

	May, Current Year	May, Prior Year
Total sales	$ 43,560	$ 41,700
Less:		
Purchase price paid	(17,000)	(16,000)
Additional labour and supplies	(1,400)	(1,200)
Commissions	(1,250)	(1,100)
Contribution margin	23,910	23,400
Less:		
Fixed warehouse cost	(680)	(500)
Fixed administrative cost	(4,300)	(4,300)
Fixed selling cost	(5,600)	(5,000)
Research and development	(9,750)	(4,000)
Operating income	$ 3,580	$ 9,600

In August of the prior year, Bissonette started an intensive quality program designed to enable it to build original equipment manufacturer (OEM) speaker systems for a major automobile company. The program was housed in research and development. The increased sales in the current year required additional warehouse space that Bissonette rented in town.

Required:

1. Calculate the contribution margin ratio for May of both years.
2. Calculate the BEP in sales dollars for both years.
3. Calculate the margin of safety in sales dollars for both years.
4. Analyze the differences shown by your calculations in Requirements 1, 2, and 3.

Check figures:
1. May current year contribution margin ratio = 0.549
2. May prior year break-even sales = $24,599
3. May current year margin of safety = $6,529

PROFESSIONAL EXAMINATION PROBLEM*

Professional Examination Problem 4-44 Cost–Volume–Profit Analysis—Attica Candy Company

Attica Candy Company is a wholesale distributor of candy. The company services grocery, convenience, and drug stores in a large metropolitan area. Attica has achieved modest but steady growth in sales over the past few years, while candy prices have been increasing. The company is formulating its plans for the coming fiscal year. Following is the data used to project the current year's after-tax net income of $110,400.

Average selling price	$ 4.00	per box
Average variable costs:		
Cost of candy	$ 2.00	per box
Selling expenses	0.40	per box
	$ 2.40	per box
Annual fixed costs:		
Selling	$ 160,000	
Administrative	280,000	
	$ 440,000	
Expected annual sales volume (390,000 boxes)	$1,560,000	
Tax rate	40%	

Manufacturers of candy have announced that they will increase prices of their products an average of 15 percent in the coming year due to increases in raw materials (sugar, cocoa, peanuts, etc.) and labour costs. Attica Candy Company expects all other costs will remain at the same rates or levels as the current year.

Required:

1. How was the $110,400 net income figure calculated?
2. What is Attica Candy Company's break-even in boxes of candy for the current year?
3. What selling price per box must Attica Candy Company charge to cover the 15 percent increase in the cost of candy and still maintain the current contribution margin ratio?
4. What volume of sales in dollars must Attica Candy Company achieve in the coming year to maintain the same net income after taxes as projected for the current year if the selling price of candy remains at $4 per box and the cost of candy increases 15 percent?
5. How many units would have to be sold next year to generate a net income equal to 10 percent of revenue?

CASES

Case 4-45 Cost–Volume–Profit with Multiple Products, Sales Mix Changes, Changes in Fixed and Variable Costs

OBJECTIVE 1 

Artistic Woodcrafting Inc. began several years ago as a one-person cabinet-making operation. Employees were added as the business expanded. Last year, sales volume totalled $850,000. Volume for the first five months of the current year totalled $600,000, and sales were expected to be $1.6 million for the entire year. Unfortunately, the cabinet business in the region where Artistic Woodcrafting is located is highly competitive. More than 200 cabinet shops are all competing for the same business.

Check figures:

1. Grade I sales = 224 units
2. Grade II break-even in units = 392 units
3. Increase in operating income = $29,602
4. Increase in operating income = $25,365

Artistic currently offers two different quality grades of cabinets: Grade I and Grade II, with Grade I being the higher quality. The average unit selling prices, unit variable costs, and direct fixed costs are as follows:

	Unit Price	Unit Variable Cost	Direct Fixed Cost
Grade I	$3,400	$2,686	$95,000
Grade II	1,600	1,328	95,000

Common fixed costs (fixed costs not traceable to either cabinet) are $35,000. Currently, for every three Grade I cabinets sold, seven Grade II cabinets are sold.

Required:

1. Calculate the number of Grade I and Grade II cabinets that are expected to be sold during the current year.
2. Calculate the number of Grade I and Grade II cabinets that must be sold for the company to break even.
3. Artistic Woodcrafting can buy computer-controlled machines that will make doors, drawers, and frames. If the machines are purchased, the variable costs for each type of cabinet will decrease by 9 percent, but common fixed costs will increase by $44,000 over the next seven months. Compute the effect on operating income, and also calculate the new BEP for the entire year. Assume the machines are purchased at the beginning of the sixth month. Fixed costs for the company are incurred uniformly throughout the year.
4. Refer to the original data and ignore the changes contemplated in Requirement 3 above. Artistic Woodcrafting is also considering adding a retail outlet. This will increase common fixed costs by $70,000 per year. As a result of adding the retail outlet, the additional publicity and emphasis on quality will allow the firm to change the sales mix to 1:1. The retail outlet is also expected to increase sales by 30 percent. Assume that the outlet is opened at the beginning of the sixth month. Calculate the effect on the company's expected profits for the current year, and calculate the new BEP for the entire year. Assume that fixed costs are incurred uniformly throughout the year.

OBJECTIVE 1 4

Case 4-46 Cost–Volume–Profit in a Multi-Product Situation

Five Rings Sports Limited was the brainchild of Adam Rinfrew, a third-year university student in Winnipeg. His idea was to produce T-shirts, sweatshirts, and fleece jackets with a logo that spoofed the Olympic rings. He felt that the Olympic spirit was a key sales motivator every two years, when the Olympics took place, but faded from the collective consciousness in the off-years. He believed that a spoof of the Olympic rings could sell every year, especially if he used high-quality materials in his products.

With this in mind, he began to develop a business plan to outline how his business would be run and how he could make it profitable in the long run. In analyzing the market, Adam determined that many small distributors would be very interested in carrying a product that took advantage of the Olympic spirit, but would sell every year, not just in Olympic years. His analysis indicated that by pricing his products very competitively to the distributors, the company could quickly build a critical mass of sales. Pricing the T-shirts at $6.50 each, the sweatshirts at $16.00, and the fleece jackets at $38.50 would provide a very good margin to the distributors and encourage them to buy his goods.

The next challenge was to source the high-quality materials that he believed would attract new customers and ensure repeat business. He was able to find a small mill that created high-quality materials at a reasonable price. The cost of materials for a T-shirt would be $1.50 each; a sweatshirt would cost $3.00; a fleece jacket would cost $12.00. These materials, because of their high quality, would make his labour force more efficient and he was convinced that producing his products in Canada would offer a moral advantage as long as the end product was profitable.

Finding a labour force that would be available and able to produce the high-quality garments that he wanted proved to be a difficult task. However, he was able to find an older gentleman who had worked all his life in the garment business and was interested in taking Adam under his wing to show him how to make it work. Together they identified a training program that would allow them to train young workers and, hopefully, instill in them the pride of workmanship that would be reflected in the end results. Between them, they worked on a manufacturing plan and plant layout to maximize efficiency and create a very favourable work environment. Estimated labour costs for the three products were $2.50 for a T-shirt, $3.00 for a sweatshirt, and $8.00 for a fleece jacket.

When all of the fixed manufacturing costs were estimated, including rent, machinery, and utilities, the manufacturing overhead for the factory would be $300,000. Adam was committed to being the main salesperson for the company, but he realized that he needed at least three salespeople, which would cost $50,000 each for base salary (including benefits) plus commissions of 10 percent of selling price. Based on the manner in which he intended to run the business as a "lean and mean" organization, he expected that all other costs of running the business, including advertising and administration, should be no more than $250,000.

His market analysis revealed that he should expect that T-shirts would make up 50 percent of overall unit sales, while sweatshirts should account for 30 percent of unit sales and the balance would be fleece jackets.

Required:

Adam has approached you to help him prepare the financial analysis of his business plan, since he is not very comfortable with numbers. He would like to know what revenues he must generate for each of the products to break even, assuming that he is right in his analysis of the mix of sales he has estimated. He also wants to know what revenues would be necessary for him to withdraw $140,000 per year for himself after paying 40 percent corporate income tax.

Case 4-47 Ethics and a Cost–Volume–Profit Application

Donna Wright, the marketing manager for a division that produces a variety of paper products, is considering the divisional manager's request for a sales forecast for a new line of paper napkins. The divisional manager has been gathering data so that he can choose between two different production processes. The first process would have a variable cost of $10 per case produced and fixed costs of $100,000. The second process would have a variable cost of $6 per case and fixed costs of $200,000. The selling price would be $30 per case. Donna has just completed a marketing analysis that projects annual sales of 30,000 cases.

Donna is reluctant to report the 30,000 forecast to the divisional manager. She knows that the first process would be labour intensive, whereas the second would be largely automated with little labour and no requirement for an additional production supervisor. If the first process is chosen, Hussan Khalil, her good friend, will be appointed as the line supervisor. If the second process is chosen, Jerry Brownlee and an entire line of labourers will be laid off. After some consideration, Donna revises the projected sales downward to 22,000 cases.

She believes that the revision downward is justified. Since it will lead the divisional manager to choose the manual system, it shows a sensitivity to the needs of current employees—a sensitivity that she is afraid her divisional manager does not possess. He is too focused on quantitative factors in his decision making and usually ignores the qualitative aspects.

Required:

1. Compute the BEP for each process.
2. Compute the sales volume for which the two processes are equally profitable. Identify the range of sales for which the manual process is more profitable than the automated process. Identify the range of sales for which the automated process is more profitable than the manual process. Why does the divisional manager want the sales forecast?
3. Discuss Donna's decision to alter the sales forecast. Do you agree with it? Is she acting ethically? Is her decision justified since it helps a number of employees retain their employment? Should the impact on employees be factored into decisions? In fact, is it unethical not to consider the impact of decisions on employees?

Check figures:
1. First process break-even = 5,000 cases
2. Units for equal profit = 25,000 cases

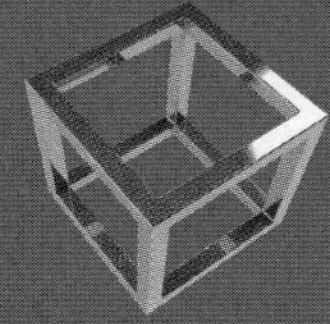

INTEGRATIVE CASE 1

Cost Behaviour and Cost–Volume–Profit Analysis for Many Glacier Hotel

Located on Swiftcurrent Lake in Glacier National Park, Many Glacier Hotel was built in 1915 by the Great Northern Railway. In an effort to supplement its lodging revenue, the hotel decided in 2001 to begin manufacturing and selling small wooden canoes decorated with symbols hand-painted by First Nations people living near the park. Due to the great success of the canoes, the hotel began manufacturing and selling paddles as well in 2003. Many hotel guests purchase a canoe and paddles for use in self-guided tours of Swiftcurrent Lake. Because production of the two products began in different years, the canoes and paddles are produced in separate production facilities and employ different labourers. Each canoe sells for $500, and each paddle sells for $50. A 2012 fire destroyed the hotel's accounting records. However, a new system put into place before the 2013 season provides the following aggregated data for the hotel's canoe and paddle manufacturing and marketing activities:

Manufacturing Data:

Year	Number of Canoes Manufactured	Total Canoe Manufacturing Costs	Year	Number of Paddles Manufactured	Total Paddle Manufacturing Costs
2018	250	$106,000	2018	900	$38,500
2017	275	115,000	2017	1,200	49,000
2016	240	108,000	2016	1,000	42,000
2015	310	122,000	2015	1,100	45,500
2014	350	130,000	2014	1,400	56,000
2013	400	140,000	2013	1,700	66,500

Marketing Data:

Year	Number of Canoes Sold	Total Canoe Marketing Costs	Year	Number of Paddles Sold	Total Paddle Marketing Costs
2018	250	$45,000	2018	900	$ 7,500
2017	275	47,500	2017	1,200	9,000
2016	240	44,000	2016	1,000	8,000
2015	310	51,000	2015	1,100	8,500
2014	350	55,000	2014	1,400	10,000
2013	400	60,000	2013	1,700	11,500

Required:

1. High–Low Cost Estimation Method
   a. Use the high–low method to estimate the per-unit variable costs and total fixed costs for the *canoe* product line.
   b. Use the high–low method to estimate the per-unit variable costs and total fixed costs for the *paddle* product line.

2. Cost–Volume–Profit Analysis, Single-Product Setting

   Use CVP analysis to calculate the break-even point in units for:

   a. The *canoe* product line *only* (i.e., single-product setting)
   b. The *paddle* product line *only* (i.e., single-product setting)

3. Cost–Volume–Profit Analysis, Multiple-Product Setting

   The hotel's accounting system data show an average sales mix of approximately 300 canoes and 1,200 paddles each season. Significantly more paddles are sold relative to canoes because some inexperienced canoe guests accidentally break one or more paddles, while other guests purchase additional paddles as presents for friends and relatives. In addition, for this multiple-product CVP analysis, assume the existence of an additional $30,000 of common fixed costs for a customer service hotline used for both canoe and paddle customers. Use CVP analysis to calculate the break-even point in units for both the canoe and paddle product lines combined (i.e., the multiple-product setting).

4. Cost Classification

   a. Classify the manufacturing costs, marketing costs, and customer service hotline costs either as production expenses or period expenses.
   b. For the period expenses, further classify them into either selling expenses or general and administrative expenses.

5. Sensitivity Cost–Volume–Profit Analysis and Production Versus Period Expenses, Multiple-Product Setting

   If both the variable and fixed *production* expenses (refer to your answer to part 1) associated with the *canoe* product line increased by 5 percent (beyond the estimate from the high–low analysis), how many canoes and paddles would need to be sold in order to earn a target income of $96,000? Assume the same sales mix and additional fixed costs as in part 3.

6. Margin of Safety

   Calculate the hotel's margin of safety (both in units and in sales dollars), assuming it sells 700 canoes and 2,500 paddles next year. Ignore the suggested change in expenses from part 5.

5

Job-Order Costing

After studying Chapter 5, you should be able to:

1. Describe the differences between job-order costing and process costing, and identify the types of firms that would use each method.
2. Compute the predetermined overhead rate, and use the rate to assign overhead to units produced or services provided.
3. Identify and set up the source documents used in job-order costing.
4. Describe the cost flows associated with job-order costing.
5. (*Appendix 5A*) Prepare the journal entries associated with job-order costing.
6. (*Appendix 5B*) Allocate support department costs to producing departments.

Wavebreakmediamicro/Dreamstime.com

EXPERIENCE MANAGERIAL DECISIONS

with Creating Dinners

Businesses that produce and sell fresh, fully cooked entrées have proliferated in recent years to help families and individuals—especially busy, dual-career families—with meal preparation. Creating Dinners of Dartmouth, Nova Scotia, is operated by husband-and-wife team Greg and Paula Dunn. Greg is the chef and Paula oversees the operations of the business. Creating Dinners prepares meals that are healthy and convenient for the family. Customers pay to have Creating Dinners do all the shopping and cooking for them. One can say that Creating Dinners is in the business of creating additional time for customers. The business takes on the stress and the time of menu planning, shopping, chopping, cooking, and cleaning up.

Creating Dinners runs a modern preparation facility designed to allow customers to buy nutritious and delicious, ready-to-cook meals that can be customized to each family's tastes. Customers view online monthly menus, choose the dates and times that are convenient for them, and place their orders on the Creating Dinners secure website.

How do Greg and Paula decide what price to charge for each meal? That is the purpose of job-order costing. Overpricing the meals would drive customers away from Creating Dinners to other alternatives. Underpricing would erode profit margins and risk business failure. In fact, it appears that Greg and Paula are already losing money. They have invested some $30,000 of their own money into the business, in addition to some government grants, and have already exhausted their line of credit.

Something needs to be done. Each meal is priced at $4 so that a family of four can eat for under $20. Is more promotion needed to bring extra customers to the store? Greg has been promoting the business as a celebrity chef with a cooking column in the local paper. Paula, who has a job at a local university besides being an MBA student and a mother, is thinking of leaving her job to dedicate herself full-time to the business. Before they do anything, they must determine what the exact costs are for every dinner and how to turn the business into a profit-making enterprise.

They are currently considering a number of questions: What is the cost of material, labour, and overhead of each meal cooked? Streamlining meal costs certainly would improve things, but how should the cost of each meal ordered be calculated? Once the exact costs are properly measured, is the price of $4 per meal adequate to be profitable?

Epilogue: Unfortunately for Greg and Paula, no matter how hard they worked, their business could not generate sufficient volume to allow it to succeed. They closed the business down and focused their efforts in different areas. However, this is a good example of why business analysis is important.

IMPORTANCE OF UNIT COSTING

Importance of Unit Costs to Manufacturing Firms

OBJECTIVE 1

Describe the differences between job-order costing and process costing, and identify the types of firms that would use each method.

Unit cost is a critical piece of information for any company, but especially for a manufacturer. Unit costs are essential for valuing inventory, determining income, and making a number of important strategic decisions.

Disclosing the cost of inventories and determining operating income are financial reporting requirements that a firm faces at the end of each period. In order to report the cost of its inventories, a firm must know the number of units on hand and the unit cost. The cost of goods sold (COGS), often the most significant cost used to determine operating income, also requires knowledge of the number of units sold and their cost.

From an operational perspective, unit costs are critical to evaluating performance on an ongoing basis, establishing a price for a product or service, and determining the long-term feasibility of a business strategy. In the long run, for any product to be viable, its price must cover all of its costs. Decisions to introduce a new product, to continue a current product, and to establish long-run prices are examples of important internal decisions that rely on unit cost information.

Importance of Unit Costs to Service Firms

Like manufacturing firms, service firms and not-for-profit organizations require unit cost information. Conceptually, the way companies accumulate and assign costs is the same irrespective of the manner in which they operate. A service firm must first identify the service "unit" being provided. A hospital would accumulate costs by patient, patient day, and type of procedure (e.g., X-ray, complete blood count test, etc.). A governmental agency must also identify the service provided. For example, city governments might provide household trash collection and calculate the cost by truck run or number of households served.

Service firms use costs in much the same way that manufacturing firms do to determine current profitability, evaluate the feasibility of introducing new services, and so on. However, since service firms do not produce physical products, they do not need to value finished goods (FG) inventories, as a manufacturer must.

Governmental agencies and not-for-profit firms have a fiduciary responsibility to use taxpayers' and donors' funds wisely. They must accurately track costs to ensure that they are providing their services in a cost-efficient manner. It is only through carefully determining unit cost that they can best fulfill their mandate.

A cost accounting system measures and assigns costs so that the unit cost of a product or service can be established. Bidding is a common requirement in the markets for specialized products and services (e.g., such as bids for special tools, audits, legal services, and medical tests and procedures). For example, it would be virtually impossible for Ernst & Young to submit a meaningful bid to one of its large audit clients without knowing the unit costs of the services to be provided. Because unit cost information is so vital, its accuracy is essential.

CHARACTERISTICS OF THE JOB-ORDER ENVIRONMENT

Companies can be divided into two major types, depending on whether or not their products or services are unique.

- Firms producing unique products or providing services require a job-order accounting system. A tailor making custom suits, a builder who remodels homes, an auto repair shop that fixes cars, and a lawyer who handles real estate transactions are examples that fall into this category.

- Firms producing identical products or services can use a process-costing accounting system. Petro-Canada, one of Canada's largest oil producers, falls into this category as its barrels of oil are indistinguishable from one another.

The characteristics of a company's actual production processes give rise to whether it needs a job-order or a process-costing accounting system.

Process Production and Costing

The cost of a product or service will consist of three key elements: direct materials, direct labour, and operational overhead. In some cases, the specific cost will be zero, but we should always consider these three elements when thinking of costs.

Firms in process industries mass-produce large quantities of similar or homogeneous products. The important point is that the cost of one unit of a product is identical to the cost of another. Examples of process manufacturers include food, cement, petroleum, and chemical firms. One litre of paint is the same as any other litre; one bottle of aspirin is the same as any other bottle. Some service firms can also use a process-costing approach. For example, cheque-clearing departments of banks incur a uniform cost to clear a cheque, no matter the size of the cheque or the name of the payee.

Process firms accumulate production costs by process or by department for a given period of time. The output for the process for that period of time is measured and unit costs are computed by dividing the process costs for the given period by the units of output of the period. This approach to cost accumulation is known as a **process-costing system** and is examined in detail in Chapter 6. A comparison of job-order costing and process costing is given in Exhibit 5.1.

EXHIBIT 5.1

Comparison of Job-Order and Process Costing

Job-Order Costing	Process Costing
1. Wide variety of distinct products	1. Homogeneous products
2. Costs accumulated by job	2. Costs accumulated by process or department
3. Unit cost computed by dividing total job costs by units produced for that job	3. Unit cost computed by dividing process costs for the period by the units produced in the period

Job-Order Production and Costing

Firms operating in job-order industries provide a wide variety of services or produce products that are quite distinct from one another. Customized or built-to-order products fit into this category, as do services that vary from customer to customer.

A **job**, then, is one distinct unit or set of units. For example, it may be a remodelling job for a specific family, or a set of 12 tables built for the children's reading room of the local library. Common job-order processes include printing, construction, furniture making, medical and dental services, automobile repair, and beauty services. Most often a job is associated with a particular order from a customer. The key feature of job-order costing is that the cost of one job differs from that of another and must be tracked separately.

Where costs are assigned and accumulated by job, the approach is called a **job-order costing system**. In a job-order firm, collecting costs by job provides vital information for management decision making. For example, prices frequently are based on costs incurred in a job-order environment.

We will use the variety of product-costing definitions discussed in Chapter 2, which apply to both job-order and process costing, to illustrate job-order costing procedures. Production costs consist of direct materials, direct labour, and manufacturing overhead. Direct materials and direct labour are usually quite easy to trace to individual jobs. In fact, this tracing will be considered later in this chapter in the section on source documents. It is manufacturing overhead that presents costing problems. By definition, manufacturing overhead is all production costs other than direct materials and direct labour, some of which might be easily traced to jobs, but most cannot. The dilemma is how to assign overhead cost to products produced or services rendered.

NORMAL COSTING AND OVERHEAD APPLICATION

OBJECTIVE 2

Compute the predetermined overhead rate, and use the rate to assign overhead to units produced or services provided.

Unit costs are very important because managers need accurate cost information on materials, labour, and overhead when making decisions. For example, PCL Construction Limited, an Edmonton-based, $6 billion international construction company, typically bills its clients at set points throughout construction. As a result, it is important to be able to generate the unit cost for each job in a timely fashion. Job-order costing using a normal cost system will give the company the unit cost information it needs for performance measurement and billing purposes.

Actual Costing versus Normal Costing

Two methods are commonly used to measure the costs associated with production: actual costing and normal costing.

Actual Costing In an **actual cost system**, only *actual* costs of direct materials, direct labour, and overhead are used to determine unit cost. Strict actual cost systems are rarely used because they cannot provide accurate unit cost information on a timely basis. Per unit computation of the direct materials and direct labour costs can be easily done. However, per unit overhead poses a serious problem: Overhead items are not incurred in direct relationship to units produced in the way that direct materials and direct labour are. Therefore a company would have to wait until the end of the accounting period to determine how much overhead should be applied to each job, which would be totally impractical if customers are to be charged when the job is completed.

One challenge is that many overhead costs are not incurred uniformly throughout the year. For example, actual repair cost occurs whenever a machine breaks down. This timing can make overhead costs in the month of a machine breakdown higher than in other months. Nonuniform production levels, a second challenge, can mean that low production in one month would result in higher unit overhead costs, while high production in another month would result in low unit overhead costs. Yet the production process and total overhead costs may remain unchanged, while output would have very different costs assigned to it. Clearly, one solution would be to wait until the end of the year to total the actual overhead costs and divide by the total actual production.

As you can appreciate, waiting until the end of the year to compute a unit overhead cost is unacceptable. A company needs unit cost information throughout the year, both for interim financial statements and to help managers make operational and strategic decisions such as pricing. Adjusting to changing conditions happens throughout the year and must be supported by accurate information.

concept Q&A

Give an example of a business in your community that would use job-order costing, and tell why it would be appropriate. Give an example of a business in your community that would use process costing and tell why it would be appropriate.

Answers on pages 734 to 738.

concept Q&A

The reality television show *What Not to Wear* chooses a contestant to participate in a makeover, including new make-up and hairstyling as well as the prime component, a new wardrobe. In the second half of the show, the contestant goes out shopping for clothes that are better suited to her style. The contestant is allowed to spend $5,000 on new clothes. Since this is the only price quoted, viewers might believe that this is the cost of the makeover. What is the true cost of the makeover?

Answers on pages 734 to 738.

EXHIBIT 5.2

Costing Systems and Inventory Valuation

Cost Accumulation System	Actual	Normal	Standard
Job order	Actual direct material Actual direct labour Actual overhead	Actual direct material Actual direct labour Overhead applied using predetermined rate (predetermined rate times actual input)	Standard direct material Standard direct labour Overhead applied using predetermined rate (predetermined rate times standard input)

Normal Costing Normal costing solves the problems associated with actual costing. A **normal cost system** determines unit cost by adding actual direct materials cost, actual direct labour cost, and estimated overhead cost to determine unit cost. Overhead can be applied by estimating the year's overhead cost and the anticipated output at the beginning of the year and then using a predetermined rate throughout the year to determine the unit cost for a product or service. Exhibit 5.2 shows how actual, normal, and standard costing systems value inventories.

Normal Costing and Estimating Overhead

In normal costing, overhead must be estimated and applied to output. The basics of overhead application can be described in three steps:

1. Calculate the predetermined overhead rate
2. Apply overhead to output throughout the year
3. Reconcile total actual overhead *incurred* during the year to total overhead *applied* to production

Step 1: Calculating the Predetermined Overhead Rate The **predetermined overhead rate** is calculated at the beginning of the year by dividing the total *estimated* annual overhead cost by the total *estimated* level of activity, or cost driver, for the year. Estimated overhead is simply the firm's best estimate of the amount of overhead (utilities, indirect labour, depreciation, etc.) to be incurred in the coming year.

The associated activity level depends on which activity is the best indication of changes in overhead amounts. Often, the activity chosen is the number of direct labour hours or the direct labour cost. This makes sense when the operation of the company relies heavily on direct labour. The number of machine hours could be a good choice for a company with highly automated production. The objective is to identify an activity, or a proxy, that can be traced to output which is closely related to the change in overhead costs. The estimated activity level is simply the number of direct labour hours, or machine hours, expected for the anticipated output in the coming year.

The predetermined overhead rate is calculated using the following formula:

$$\text{Predetermined overhead rate} = \frac{\text{Estimated annual overhead cost}}{\text{Estimated annual activity level}}$$

Notice that the predetermined overhead rate includes estimated amounts in *both* the numerator and the denominator. This estimation is necessary because the predetermined overhead rate is calculated in advance, usually at the beginning of the year. The actual levels are not known, and will not be known until the end of the period. Therefore, only estimated or budgeted amounts can be used in calculating the predetermined overhead rate.

Step 2: Applying Overhead to Production **Applied overhead** is found by multiplying the predetermined overhead rate by the actual use of the associated activity—the cost driver—for the period. Suppose that a company has an overhead rate of $5 per machine hour. In the first week of January, the company used 9,000 hours of machine time, so the overhead applied to the week's production is $45,000 (= $5 × 9,000). The total cost of product for that first week is the actual direct materials and direct labour plus the applied overhead. The concept is the same for any time period. So, if the company runs its machines for 50,000 hours in the month of January, applied overhead for January would be $250,000 (= $5 × 50,000). Cornerstone 5.1 shows how to calculate the predetermined overhead rate and how to use that rate to apply overhead to production.

CORNERSTONE 5.1

Calculating the Predetermined Overhead Rate and Applying Overhead to Production

Information:

At the beginning of the year, Argus Company estimated the following costs:

Overhead cost	$360,000
Direct labour cost	$720,000

Argus uses normal costing and applies overhead on the basis of direct labour cost. (Direct labour cost is equal to total direct labour hours worked multiplied by the wage rate.) For the month of February, direct labour cost was $56,000.

Required:

1. Calculate the predetermined overhead rate for the year.
2. Calculate the overhead applied to production in February.

Solution:

1. Predetermined overhead rate $= \frac{\$360{,}000}{\$720{,}000}$

$= 0.50$, or 50 percent of direct labour cost

2. Overhead applied to February production = 0.50 × $56,000 = $28,000

Why:

Because the predetermined overhead rate is needed in order to cost jobs as they are completed. With actual costing, the allocation rate cannot be known until all the costs are known, which is after the accounting period is completed.

Step 3: Reconciling Applied Overhead with Actual Overhead Recall that two types of overhead must be taken into consideration. One type is *actual* overhead; those costs are tracked throughout the year in the overhead account. The second type is *applied* overhead. Overhead is applied to production cost every time a unit of the cost driver is used. Overhead applied to production is computed throughout the year and is added to actual direct materials and actual direct labour to get total product cost. At the end of the year, however, we must reconcile any difference between actual and applied overhead and we must adjust the accounts to reflect actual overhead spending.

As was seen in the Creating Dinners example at the beginning of the chapter, covering the direct costs of a product or service is not enough. Overhead costs must be fully accounted for and recovered through our pricing formula to ensure success.

Since the predetermined overhead rate is based on estimated data, applied overhead will rarely equal actual overhead. If actual overhead is greater than applied overhead, then the difference is called **underapplied overhead**. If actual overhead is less than applied overhead, then the difference is called **overapplied overhead**. If overhead has been underapplied, then product cost has been understated; in this case, the cost appears lower than it really is. Conversely, if overhead has been overapplied, then product cost has been overstated; in this case, the cost appears higher than it really is.

Underapplied and Overapplied Overhead In order for the financial statements of a company to be presented as fairly as possible, we must ensure that any difference between *applied overhead* and *actual overhead* appears in the accounts of the company correctly. This entails determining how to deal with this difference (*the overhead variance*).

Suppose that Proto Company had incurred actual overhead costs of $400,000 for the year, but had only applied $390,000 to production. Since only $390,000 was applied in our example, the firm has *underapplied* overhead by $10,000. If applied overhead had been $410,000, then the firm would have *overapplied* overhead by $10,000. Exhibit 5.3 illustrates the concepts of over- and underapplied overhead.

EXHIBIT 5.3

Actual and Applied Overhead

These overhead variances, which are virtually inevitable, occur because it is impossible to estimate perfectly future overhead costs and production activity. At year-end, costs reported on the financial statements must be actual, not estimated, amounts; therefore, a correction is required. Most often, the entire overhead variance is assigned to COGS. This practice is justified on the basis that the amounts are not material to the fairness of the financial statements. Since the overhead variance is usually relatively small, the method of disposition is not a critical matter. All production costs will eventually appear in COGS. Thus, the underapplied overhead is added to COGS, and the overapplied overhead is subtracted from COGS.

For example, assume that Proto Company has an ending balance in its COGS account equal to $607,000. The underapplied overhead variance of $10,000 would be added to produce a new adjusted balance of $617,000. (Since applied overhead was $390,000, and actual overhead was $400,000, production costs were *understated* by $10,000. The COGS account must be increased to correct the problem.) If the variance had been overapplied, it would have been subtracted from COGS to produce a new balance of $597,000. Cornerstone 5.2 shows how to reconcile actual overhead with applied overhead for the Argus Company example.

CORNERSTONE 5.2 Reconciling Actual Overhead with Applied Overhead

Information:

At the beginning of the year, Argus Company estimated the following costs:

Overhead cost	\$360,000
Direct labour cost	\$720,000

By the end of the year, actual data are:

Overhead cost	\$375,400
Direct labour cost	\$750,000

Argus uses normal costing and applies overhead on the basis of direct labour cost. At the end of the year, cost of goods sold (before adjusting for any overhead variance) is \$632,000.

Required:

1. Calculate the overhead variance for the year.
2. Dispose of the overhead variance by adjusting cost of goods sold.

Solution:

1. Predetermined overhead rate $= \frac{\$360{,}000}{\$720{,}000} = 0.50$ of direct labour cost

Overhead applied for the year $= 0.50 \times \$750{,}000 = \$375{,}000$

Actual overhead	\$375,400
Applied overhead	375,000
Overhead variance—underapplied	\$ 400

2.

Unadjusted COGS	\$632,000
Add: Overhead variance—underapplied	400
Adjusted COGS	\$632,400

Why:

Because we must ensure that the financial statements at the end of the year reflect the true financial situation of the company. Any over- or underapplied overhead must be determined and properly accounted for.

If the overhead variance is material, and would distort the validity of the financial statements, the over- or underapplied overhead would be apportioned between the inventory accounts and COGS. The calculation is based on taking the balance in each of the Work-in-Process (WIP) Inventory, FG Inventory, and COGS accounts as a percentage of the total value of these accounts and dividing the over- or underapplied overhead between the individual accounts on this basis. This is referred to as a **pro rata application**.

As an example, if a company had underapplied overhead in the amount of $37,500 that was deemed to be a material amount, it would pro rate the amount. If COGS was $600,000, WIP was $125,000, and FG Inventory was $175,000, then the proportion of each would be: COGS, 0.6667 (= $600,000/$900,000); WIP, 0.1389 (= $125,000/$900,000); and FG, 0.1944 (= $175,000/$900,000). The underapplied overhead would be apportioned as follows: COGS, $25,000 (= 0.6667 × $37,500); WIP, $5,210 (= 0.1389 × $37,500); and FG, $7,290 (= 0.1944 × $37,500). In this case, each account would be increased by these amounts; had the overhead been overapplied, the accounts would be decreased by these amounts.

Plantwide and Departmental Overhead Rates

The description of overhead application so far has emphasized the plantwide overhead rate. A **plantwide overhead rate** is a single overhead rate calculated by using all estimated overhead for an entire factory divided by the estimated activity level across the entire factory. Cornerstone 5.3 shows how to calculate and apply overhead using a plantwide rate. However, it may be true that multiple overhead rates give more accurate costing information.

Calculating Plantwide Overhead Rate and Applying Overhead to Production

CORNERSTONE 5.3

Information:

At the beginning of the year, Sorrel Company estimated the following:

	Machining Department	Assembly Department	Total
Overhead	$240,000	$360,000	$600,000
Direct labour hours	135,000	240,000	375,000
Machine hours	200,000	—	200,000

Sorrel has decided to use a plantwide overhead rate based on direct labour hours. Actual data for the month of June are as follows:

	Machining Department	Assembly Department	Total
Overhead	$22,500	$30,750	$53,250
Direct labour hours	11,000	20,000	31,000
Machine hours	17,000	—	17,000

Required:

1. Calculate the predetermined plantwide overhead rate.
2. Calculate the overhead applied to production for the month of June.
3. Calculate the overhead variance for the month of June.

Solution:

1. Predetermined plantwide overhead rate $= \dfrac{\$600{,}000}{375{,}000}$

$= \$1.60$ per direct labour hour

(Continued)

CORNERSTONE
5.3
(Continued)

2. Overhead applied in June = $1.60 × 31,000 = $49,600

3. Overhead variance = Actual overhead − Applied overhead
= $53,250 − $49,600
= $3,650 underapplied

Why:

Because a plantwide overhead rate needs to be calculated at the beginning of the year to apply overhead to each job completed during the period. A plantwide rate ensures that all overhead is allocated to production.

A **departmental overhead rate** is simply the estimated overhead for a department divided by the estimated activity level for that same department. The steps involved in calculating and applying overhead are the same as those involved for one plantwide overhead rate. The company would have as many overhead rates as it has departments. Cornerstone 5.4 shows how to calculate and apply departmental overhead rates. Departmental overhead rates are often more accurate, especially when different jobs require different resources in different departments.

CORNERSTONE 5.4

Calculating Predetermined Departmental Overhead Rates and Applying Overhead to Production

Information:

At the beginning of the year, Sorrel Company estimated the following:

	Machining Department	Assembly Department	Total
Overhead cost	$240,000	$360,000	$600,000
Direct labour hours	135,000	240,000	375,000
Machine hours	200,000	—	200,000

Sorrel uses departmental overhead rates. In the machining department, overhead is applied on the basis of machine hours, while in the assembly department, overhead is applied on the basis of direct labour hours. Actual data for the month of June are as follows:

	Machining Department	Assembly Department	Total
Overhead	$22,500	$30,750	$53,250
Direct labour hours	11,000	20,000	31,000
Machine hours	17,000	—	17,000

Required:

1. Calculate the predetermined overhead rates for the machining and assembly departments.
2. Calculate the overhead applied to production in each department for the month of June.
3. By how much has each department's overhead been overapplied? Underapplied?

(Continued)

CORNERSTONE 5.4

(Continued)

Solution:

1. Machining department overhead rate $= \frac{\$240{,}000}{200{,}000}$
$= \$1.20$ per machine hour

Assembly department overhead rate $= \frac{\$360{,}000}{240{,}000}$
$= \$1.50$ per labour hour

2. Overhead applied by machining in June = $1.20 × 17,000 = $20,400

Overhead applied by assembly in June = $1.50 × 20,000 = $30,000

	Machining Department	Assembly Department
Actual overhead	$22,500	$30,750
Applied overhead	20,400	30,000
Underapplied overhead	$ 2,100	$ 750

Why:

Because, as in the case of a plantwide predetermined overhead rate, a departmental overhead rate needs to be calculated at the beginning of the year to apply overhead to each job completed during the year. Departmental rates are often a more accurate allocation of costs, especially when different jobs require different resources in different departments.

Considerable emphasis has been placed on describing how overhead costs are treated because this is the key to normal costing. Now it is time to see how normal costing is used to develop unit costs in the job-order costing system.

Unit Costs in the Job-Order System

In a job-order environment, predetermined overhead rates are always used because the cost information is needed on an ongoing basis and managers cannot wait until the end of the year to calculate them. Therefore, for the remainder of this chapter we will assume that normal costing is used unless otherwise specified.

The unit cost of a job is the total cost of the job (materials used on the job, labour worked on the job, and applied overhead for the job) divided by the number of units in the job. Although the concept is simple, the practical reality of the computation can be somewhat more complex because of the unique features of each job. Let's look at a simple example.

Suppose that Stan Johnson forms a new company, Johnson Leathergoods, which specializes in the production of custom leather products. Stan believes that there is a market for one-of-a-kind leather purses, briefcases, and backpacks. In January, his first month of operation, he obtains two orders: (1) 20 leather backpacks for a local sporting goods store; (2) 10 distinctively tooled briefcases for the coaches of a local university. Stan agrees to provide these orders at a price of cost plus 50 percent. The first order, the backpacks, will require direct materials (leather, thread, buckles), direct labour (cutting, sewing, assembling), and overhead. Assume that overhead is applied using direct labour hours. Suppose that the materials cost $1,000 and the direct labour costs $1,080 (= 120 hours at $9 per hour). If the predetermined overhead rate is $2 per direct labour hour, then the overhead applied to this job is $240 (= 120 hours at $2 per hour). The total cost of the backpacks is $2,320, and the unit cost is $116, computed as follows:

Direct materials	$1,000
Direct labour	1,080
Overhead	240
Total cost	$2,320
÷ Number of units	÷ 20
Unit cost	$ 116

Since cost is so closely linked to price in this case, it is easy to see that Stan will charge the sporting goods store $3,480 (cost of $2,320 plus 50 percent of $2,320), or $174 per backpack.

This is a simplified example of how Stan will arrive at the total cost of a single job. But how does he know that actual materials will cost $1,000 or that actual direct labour for this particular job will come to $1,080? In order to determine those figures, Stan will need to keep track of costs using a variety of source documents, which are described in the next section.

The Conversion Process

All organizations convert inputs (material, labour, and overhead) into outputs. In general, product costs are incurred in the production (conversion) area and period costs are incurred in all nonproduction areas.

The major distinction of retail firms relative to service and manufacturing firms is that retailers have a much lower degree of conversion than the other two types of firms.

KEEPING TRACK OF JOB COSTS WITH SOURCE DOCUMENTS

Identify and set up the source documents used in job-order costing.

Accounting for job-order production begins by preparing the source documents that are used to keep track of the costs of jobs. In a job-order firm, where price is so often based on cost, it is critically important to keep careful track of the costs of a job. Ethical issues arise when a firm adds costs from one job to the job-order sheet of another job. The first job is undercosted and underpriced, while the second job is overcosted and overpriced. Customers rely on the professionalism and honesty of the job-order firm in recordkeeping. Competition will also help to keep a company's recordkeeping in line.

Job-Order Cost Sheet

Every time a new job is started, a job-order cost sheet is prepared. The earlier computation of costs for Stan's backpack job, which lists the total cost of materials, labour, and overhead for that job, is the simplest example of a job-order cost sheet.

A **job-order cost sheet** is prepared for every job; it is subsidiary to the WIP account and is the primary document for accumulating all costs related to a particular job. Exhibit 5.4 illustrates a simple job-order cost sheet. The job-order cost sheet contains all information pertinent to a job. For a simple job, the job-order cost sheet is quite brief, containing only the job description (backpacks) and cost of materials, labour, and overhead added during the month.

EXHIBIT 5.4

Job-Order Cost Sheet

Johnson Leathergoods
Job-Order Cost Sheet

Job Name: Backpacks Date Started: Jan. 3, 2018 Date Completed: Jan. 29, 2018

Direct materials	$1,000
Direct labour	1,080
Applied overhead	240
Total cost	$2,320
÷ Number of units	÷ 20
Unit cost	$ 116

Johnson Leathergoods had only two jobs in January; these could easily be identified by calling them "Backpacks" and "Briefcases." Some companies may find that the customer's name is sufficient to identify a job. For example, a construction company may identify its custom houses as the "Kumar Residence" or the "Malkovich Residence."

As more and more jobs are produced, a company will usually find it most convenient to number them. For example, it may number them as Job 13, Job 22, or Job 44. Perhaps the job number starts with the year, so that the first job of 2018 is 2018-1, the second is 2018-2, and so on. The key point is that each job is unique and must have a unique identifier. This identifier, be it a name or a job number, heads the job-order sheet.

Work in process consists of all incomplete work. In a job-order system, this will be all of the unfinished jobs. The balance in WIP at the end of the month will be the total of all the job-order cost sheets for the incomplete jobs.

A job-order costing system must have the ability to identify the quantity of direct materials, direct labour, and overhead consumed by each job. In other words, documentation and procedures are needed to associate the manufacturing inputs used by a job with the job itself. This need is satisfied through the use of materials, requisitions for direct materials, time tickets for direct labour, and source documents for other activity drivers that might be used in applying overhead.

concept Q&A

Job-order cost sheets are subsidiary to the Work in Process account. Can you think of other accounts that have subsidiary accounts? (*Hint*: Consider Accounts Receivable or Accounts Payable. What might their respective subsidiary accounts be?)

Answers on pages 734 to 738.

Materials Requisitions

The cost of direct materials is assigned to a job by the use of a source document known as a **materials requisition form**, which is illustrated in Exhibit 5.5. Notice that the form asks for the type, quantity, and unit price of the direct materials issued and, most important, the identifier of the job. Using this form, the cost accounting department can enter the cost of direct materials onto the correct job-order cost sheet.

If the accounting system is automated, this posting may be made by directly entering the data at a computer terminal, using the materials requisition forms as source documents. A program enters the cost of direct materials into the record for each job. In addition to providing essential information for assigning direct materials costs to jobs, the materials requisition form may also include other data items, such as a requisition number, a date, and a signature. These items are useful for maintaining proper control over a firm's inventory of direct materials. The signature, for example, transfers responsibility for the materials from the storage area to the person receiving the materials, usually a production supervisor.

concept Q&A

Suppose that Johnson Leathergoods creates an automated tooling department and decides to track the number of machine hours used on each job. Design a source document for this purpose.

Answers on pages 734 to 738.

EXHIBIT 5.5

Materials Requisition Form

Materials Requisition Number: 012

Date: January 11, 2018
Department: Assembly
Job: Briefcases

Description	Quantity	Cost/Unit	Total Cost
Buckles	10	$3	$30

Authorized Signature Doug Lawson

No attempt is made to trace the cost of other materials—such as supplies, lubricants, and the like—to a particular job. You will recall that these indirect materials are assigned to jobs through the predetermined overhead rate.

Time Tickets

Direct labour must be associated with a specific job. The means by which direct labour costs are assigned to individual jobs is the source document known as a **time ticket** (Exhibit 5.6). Each day, the employee fills out a time ticket that identifies his or her name, wage rate, and hours worked on each job. These time tickets are collected and transferred to the cost accounting department, where the information is used to post the cost of direct labour to individual jobs. Again, in an automated system, posting involves entering the data into the computer.

Time tickets are used only for direct labourers. Since indirect labour is common to all jobs, these costs belong to overhead and are allocated using one or more predetermined overhead rates.

EXHIBIT 5.6

Time Ticket

Job Time Ticket #: 008

Employee Name: Bruce Wilson
Date: January 12, 2018

Start Time	Stop Time	Total Time	Hourly Rate	Amount	Job
8:00	10:00	2	$9	$18	Backpacks
10:00	11:00	1	9	9	Briefcases
11:00	12:00	1	9	9	Backpacks
1:00	5:00	4	9	36	Backpacks

Approved by: Doug Lawson
(Department Supervisor)

YOU DECIDE Creating Source Documents for Other Activities

You are the cost accounting manager for a company that provides photography services for special events such as weddings, bar mitzvahs, anniversary parties, convocations, and corporate functions. The cost of these services varies from job to job. The time of the photographers assigned to the job is already tracked using labour time tickets. However, your company now wants to reimburse the photographers for travel and may want to include an additional charge to clients for travel.

What type of source document could serve to accumulate the reported distance driven?

In this case, your company needs to know not only the number of kilometres each photographer drives, but also the job to which the travel pertains. A relatively simple travel log—listing the date, the client, the destination, starting odometer reading, ending odometer reading, and purpose of the trip—should suffice. This will allow you to compute the kilometres driven (ending odometer reading minus beginning odometer reading) and assign it to the specific photographic job. In addition, total kilometres for each photographer can be computed on a monthly basis and multiplied by your company's assigned rate for purposes of reimbursing each photographer for automotive operating costs.

Some companies might have other specific needs. For example, perhaps the company has a fleet of different vehicles and wants to compute different rates depending on the vehicle. Using a van might require a higher rate than using a small automobile. In this case, an additional column to record the type of vehicle or vehicle's licence plate would be necessary.

As a result, different firms may have different source documents to support their specialized needs for accounting information.

Source Documents for Other Activities

The company may use an overhead application base other than direct labour hours. In that case, other source documents will be required. For example, machine hours may be used to apply overhead. Then, a new document must be developed. A source document that will track the machine hours used by each job can be modelled on job time tickets.

All completed job-order cost sheets of a firm will serve as a subsidiary ledger for the FG inventory. Then, the WIP account consists of all of the job-order cost sheets for the unfinished jobs. The FG Inventory account consists of all the job-order cost sheets for jobs that are complete but not yet sold. As FG are sold and shipped, the cost records will be pulled (or deleted) from the FG inventory file. These records then form the basis for calculating a period's COGS. We will examine the flow of costs through these accounts next.

COST FLOW

OBJECTIVE 

Describe the cost flows associated with job-order costing.

Cost flow describes the way costs are accounted for from the point at which they are incurred to the point at which they are recognized as an expense on the income statement. The principal interest in a job-order costing system is the flow of manufacturing costs. Accordingly, we begin with a description of exactly how the three manufacturing cost elements—direct materials, direct labour, and overhead—flow through to WIP, into FG, and, finally, into COGS. The simplified job-shop environment provided by Johnson Leathergoods will continue to serve as an example. To start the business, Stan leased a small building and bought the necessary production equipment. Recall that he obtained two orders for January: one for 20 backpacks for a local sporting goods store and a second for 10 briefcases for the coaches of a local university. Both orders will be sold for manufacturing costs plus 50 percent. Stan expects to average two orders per month for the first year of operation.

Stan created two job-order cost sheets, one for each order. The first job-order cost sheet is for the backpacks; the second is for the briefcases.

Accounting for Materials Cost

Since the company is just starting business, it has no beginning inventories. To produce the backpacks and briefcases in January and to have a supply of materials on hand at the beginning of February, Stan purchases, on account, $2,500 of raw materials (leather, webbing for backpack straps, heavy-duty thread, buckles). Physically, the materials are put in a materials storeroom. In the accounting records, the Raw Materials and the Accounts Payable accounts are each increased by $2,500. Raw Materials is an inventory account (it appears on the balance sheet under current assets). It also is the controlling account for all raw materials. Any purchase increases the Raw Materials account.

When the production supervisor needs materials for a job, materials are removed from the storeroom. The cost of the materials is removed from the Raw Materials account and added to the WIP account. Of course, in a job-order environment, the materials moved from the storeroom to work stations on the factory floor must be "tagged" with the appropriate job identifier. Suppose that Stan needs $1,000 of materials for the backpacks and $500 for the briefcases. Then, the job-order cost sheet for the backpacks would show $1,000 for direct materials, and the job-order cost sheet for the briefcases would show $500 for direct materials. Exhibit 5.7 summarizes the raw materials cost flow into these two jobs.

EXHIBIT 5.7

Summary of Materials Cost Flows

	A	B	C	D	E	F	G	H
1	**Raw Materials Account**							
2	Beginning balance		$ 0					
3	Add: Purchases		2,500					
4	Less: Direct materials charged to jobs		1,500					
5	Ending balance		$1,000					
6								
7			**Work-in-Process Account**					
8	Job: Backpacks				Job: Briefcases			
9	Direct materials		$1,000		Direct materials		$500	
10	Direct labour				Direct labour			
11	Applied overhead				Applied overhead			
12	Total cost				Total cost			
13	Number of units		÷ 20		Number of units		÷ 10	
14	Unit cost*				Unit cost*			
15								

*Unit costs can only be calculated once all costs have been accumulated.

The Raw Materials account increased by $2,500 due to purchases and decreased by $1,500 as materials were withdrawn for use in production. So, what is the balance in the Raw Materials account after these two transactions? It is $1,000. This is calculated by taking the beginning balance in the Raw Materials account of $0, adding $2,500 of purchases, and subtracting $1,500 of materials used in production.

Accounting for Direct Labour Cost

Since two jobs were in progress during January, Stan must determine not only the total number of direct labour hours worked but also the time worked on each job. The backpacks required 120 hours at an average wage rate of $9 per hour, for a total direct labour cost of $1,080. For the briefcases, the total was $450, based on 50 hours at an average hourly wage of $9. These amounts are posted to each job's cost sheet. The summary of the labour cost flows is given in Exhibit 5.8. Notice that the direct labour costs assigned to the two jobs exactly equal the total labour costs assigned to WIP. Remember that the

EXHIBIT 5.8

Summary of Direct Labour Cost Flows

	A	B	C	D	E	F	G	H
1	**Wages Payable Account**							
2	Direct labour hours for backpacks		120					
3	Direct labour hours for briefcases		50					
4	Total direct labour hours		170					
5	Wage rate		× $9					
6	Total direct labour		$1,530					
7								
8	Work-in-Process Account							
9	Job: Backpacks				Job: Briefcases			
10	Direct materials		$1,000		Direct materials		$500	
11	Direct labour		1,080		Direct labour		450	
12	Applied overhead				Applied overhead			
13	Total cost				Total cost			
14	Number of units		÷ 20		Number of units		÷ 10	
15	Unit cost*				Unit cost*			
16								

*Unit costs can only be calculated once all costs have been accumulated.

labour cost flows reflect only direct labour cost. Indirect labour is assigned as part of overhead.

More accounts are involved in this transaction than meet the eye in Exhibit 5.8. Accounting for labour cost is a complex process because the company must keep track of Canada Pension Plan, Employment Insurance, income taxes, vacation time, and so on. We will concentrate on the concept that direct labour adds to the cost of the product or service and not on the details of the various labour-related accounts.

Accounting for Applied Overhead

The use of normal costing means that actual overhead costs are not assigned directly to jobs, so that overhead is applied to each job by using a predetermined rate. Actual overhead costs incurred must be accounted for as well, but on an overall (not a job-specific) basis.

Overhead costs can be assigned using a single plantwide overhead rate or departmental rates. Often, direct labour hours are the measure used to calculate a plantwide overhead rate, and departmental rates are based on drivers such as direct labour hours, machine hours, or direct materials dollars. The use of a plantwide rate has the virtue of being simple and reduces data collection requirements. To illustrate these two features, assume that total estimated overhead cost for Johnson Leathergoods is \$9,600, and the estimated direct labour hours total 4,800 hours. Accordingly, the predetermined overhead rate is:

$$\text{Overhead rate} = \frac{\$9{,}600}{4{,}800} = \$2 \text{ per direct labour hour}$$

For the backpacks, with a total of 120 hours worked, the amount of applied overhead cost posted to the job-order cost sheet is \$240 (= \$2 × 120). For the briefcases, the applied overhead cost is \$100 (= \$2 × 50). Note also that assigning overhead to jobs only requires a rate and the direct labour hours used by the job. Since direct labour hours are already being collected to assign direct labour costs to jobs, overhead assignment will not demand any additional data collection.

Accounting for Actual Overhead Costs

Overhead has been applied to the jobs, but what about the actual overhead incurred? To illustrate how actual overhead costs are recorded, assume that Johnson Leathergoods incurred the following indirect costs for January:

Lease payment	$200
Utilities	50
Equipment depreciation	100
Indirect labour	65
Total overhead costs	$415

It is important to understand that the actual overhead costs never enter the WIP account. The usual procedure is to record actual overhead to the Overhead Control account. Then, at the end of a period (typically a year), actual overhead is reconciled with applied overhead, and, if the variance is not material, it is closed to the COGS account.

For Johnson Leathergoods at the end of January, actual overhead incurred is $415, while applied overhead is $340. Therefore, the overhead variance of $75 (= $415 − $340) means that overhead is underapplied for the month of January.

The flow of overhead costs is summarized in Exhibit 5.9. Notice that the total overhead applied from all jobs is entered in the WIP account.

To recap, the cost of a job includes direct materials, direct labour, and applied overhead. These costs are entered on the job-order cost sheet. WIP, at any point in time, is the total of the costs on all open job-order cost sheets. When the job is complete, it must leave WIP and be entered into FG or COGS.

EXHIBIT 5.9

Summary of Overhead Cost Flows

	A	B	C	D	E	F	G	H
1	**Actual Overhead Account**				**Applied Overhead Account**			
2	Lease		$200		Direct labour hours		170	
3	Utilities		50		Overhead rate		× $2	
4	Equipment depreciation		100		Total applied overhead		$340	
5	Indirect labour		65					
6	Total actual overhead		$415					
7								
8			**Work-in-Process Account**					
9	**Job: Backpacks**				**Job: Briefcases**			
10	Direct materials		$1,000		Direct materials		$500	
11	Direct labour		1,080		Direct labour		450	
12	Applied overhead		240		Applied overhead		100	
13	Total cost		$2,320		Total cost		$1,050	
14	Number of units		÷ 20		Number of units		÷ 10	
15	Unit cost*				Unit cost*			
16								

*Unit costs can only be calculated once all costs have been accumulated.

Accounting for Finished Goods

When a job is complete, direct materials, direct labour, and applied overhead amounts are totalled to yield the manufacturing cost of the job. Simultaneously, the costs of the completed job are transferred from the WIP account to the FG account.

For example, assume that the backpacks were finished in January with the completed cost sheet shown in Exhibit 5.9. Since the backpacks are finished, the total manufacturing costs of $2,320 must be transferred from the WIP account to the FG account. A summary of the cost flows occurring when a job is finished is shown in Exhibit 5.10.

The completion of a job is an important step in the flow of manufacturing costs. The cost of the finished job must be removed from WIP, added to FG, and eventually added to the COGS on the income statement. To ensure accuracy in computing these costs, a cost of goods manufactured statement is prepared. The schedule of cost of goods manufactured presented in Exhibit 5.11 summarizes the production activity of Johnson Leathergoods for January. It is important to note that applied overhead is used to arrive at the cost of goods manufactured. Both WIP and FG inventories are carried at normal cost rather than actual cost.

EXHIBIT 5.10

Summary of Cost Flows from Work in Process to Finished Goods

	A	B	C	D	E	F	G	H
1	**Work-in-Process Account BEFORE Transfer of Backpacks to Finished Goods**							
2	**Job: Backpacks**				**Job: Briefcases**			
3	Direct materials		$1,000		Direct materials		$500	
4	Direct labour		1,080		Direct labour		450	
5	Applied overhead		240		Applied overhead		100	
6	Total cost		$2,320		Total cost		$1,050	
7	Number of units		÷ 20		Number of units			
8	Unit cost*		$ 116		Unit cost*			
9								
10	**Work-in-Process Account AFTER Transfer of Backpacks to Finished Goods**							
11	**Job: Briefcases**							
12	Direct materials		$ 500					
13	Direct labour		450					
14	Applied overhead		100					
15	Total cost		$1,050					
16	Number of units							
17	Unit cost							
18								
19	**Finished Goods Account**							
20	Beginning balance		$ 0					
21	Add: Completed backpacks		2,320					
22	Less: Jobs sold		0					
23	Ending balance		$2,320					
24								

*Unit cost information is included for backpacks because they are finished. The briefcases are still in process, so no unit cost is calculated.

Notice that ending WIP is $1,050. Where did this figure come from? Of the two jobs, the backpacks were finished and transferred to FG. The briefcases are still in process, however, and the manufacturing costs assigned thus far are direct materials, $500; direct labour, $450; and overhead applied, $100. The total of these costs gives the cost of ending WIP. You may want to check these figures against the job-order cost sheet for briefcases shown at the top right of Exhibit 5.10.

Accounting for Cost of Goods Sold

In a job-order firm, units can be produced for a particular customer, or they can be produced with the expectation of selling the units later. Usually the accounting is handled in

EXHIBIT 5.11

Schedule of Cost of Goods Manufactured

Johnson Leathergoods Schedule of Cost of Goods Manufactured For the Month of January		
Direct materials:		
Beginning raw materials inventory	$ 0	
Purchases of raw materials	2,500	
Total raw materials available	2,500	
Ending raw materials	1,000	
Total raw materials used		$ 1,500
Direct labour		1,530
Overhead:		
Overhead applied (170 direct labour hours × $2 per hour)		340
Current manufacturing costs		3,370
Add: Beginning work in process		0
Total manufacturing costs		3,370
Less: Ending work in process		1,050
Cost of goods manufactured		$2,320

the same way, using FG and then COGS. When the backpacks are finished, FG increases by $2,320, while WIP decreases by the same amount (the job is no longer incomplete, so its costs cannot stay in WIP). Then, the sale is recognized by increasing both Sales Revenue and Accounts Receivable by $3,480 (cost plus 50 percent of cost, or $2,320 + $1,160). Once the sale is recognized, COGS is increased by the cost of the goods, $2,320, and FG is decreased by the same amount.

A schedule of COGS is usually prepared at the end of each reporting period (e.g., monthly and quarterly). Exhibit 5.12 presents such a schedule for Johnson Leathergoods for January. Typically, the overhead variance is not material and, therefore, is closed to the COGS account.

The COGS before an adjustment for an overhead variance is called **normal cost of goods sold**. After the adjustment for the period's overhead variance takes place, the result is called the **adjusted cost of goods sold**. It is this latter figure that appears as an expense on the income statement.

However, closing the overhead variance to the COGS account is not usually done until the end of the year. Variances are expected each month because of nonuniform production and nonuniform actual overhead costs. As the year unfolds these monthly variances should, by and large, offset each other so that the year-end variance is small.

EXHIBIT 5.12

Statement of Cost of Goods Sold

Statement of Cost of Goods Sold	
Beginning finished goods inventory	$ 0
Cost of goods manufactured	2,320
Goods available for sale	2,320
Less: Ending finished goods inventory	0
Normal cost of goods sold	2,320
Add: Underapplied overhead	75
Adjusted cost of goods sold	$2,395

Nonetheless, to illustrate how the year-end overhead variance would be treated, we will close out the overhead variance experienced by Johnson Leathergoods in January.

Notice that there are two COGS figures in Exhibit 5.12. The first is normal COGS and is equal to actual direct materials, actual direct labour, and applied overhead for the jobs that were sold. The second figure is adjusted COGS. The adjusted COGS is equal to normal COGS plus or minus the overhead variance. In this case, overhead has been underapplied (actual overhead of $415 is $75 higher than the applied overhead of $340), so this amount is added to normal COGS. If the overhead variance shows overapplied overhead, then that amount will be subtracted from normal COGS.

Suppose that the backpacks had not been ordered by a customer but had been produced with the expectation that they could be sold through a subsequent marketing effort. Then, all 20 units might not be sold at the same time. Assume that on January 31, there were 15 backpacks sold. In this case, the COGS figure is the unit cost times the number of units sold ($116 × 15, or $1,740). The unit cost figure is found on the cost sheet in Exhibit 5.10.

Sometimes it is simpler to use a briefer version of the job-order cost sheet in order to calculate ending WIP, FG, and COGS. (This is particularly true when working homework and test questions.) Cornerstone 5.5 shows how to set up such a version to calculate account balances.

Preparing Brief Job-Order Cost Sheets

CORNERSTONE 5.5

Information:

At the beginning of June, Galway Company, a custom window manufacturer, had two jobs in process—Job 78 and Job 79—with the following accumulated cost information:

	Job 78	Job 79
Direct materials	$1,000	$ 800
Direct labour	600	1,000
Applied overhead	750	1,250
Balance, June 1	$2,350	$3,050

During June, two more jobs (80 and 81) were started. The following direct materials and direct labour costs were added to the four jobs during the month of June:

	Job 78	Job 79	Job 80	Job 81
Direct materials	$500	$1,110	$ 900	$100
Direct labour	400	1,400	2,000	320

At the end of June, Jobs 78, 79, and 80 were completed. Only Job 79 was sold. On June 1, the balance in Finished Goods was zero.

Required:

1. Calculate the overhead rate based on direct labour cost.
2. Prepare a brief job-order cost sheet for the four jobs. Show the balance as at June 1 as well as direct materials and direct labour added in June. Apply overhead to the four jobs for the month of June, and show the ending balances.

(Continued)

CORNERSTONE
5.5

(Continued)

3. Calculate the ending balances of Work in Process and Finished Goods as at June 30.
4. Calculate COGS for June.

Solution:

1. Ordinarily, the predetermined overhead rate is calculated using estimated overhead and, in this case, estimated direct labour cost. Those figures were not given. However, it is possible to work backward from the applied overhead at the beginning of June for Jobs 78 and 79.

$$\text{Applied overhead} = \text{Predetermined overhead rate} \times \text{Actual activity level for Job 78}$$

$$\$750 = \text{Predetermined overhead rate} \times \$600$$

$$\text{Predetermined overhead rate} = \frac{\$750}{\$600}$$

$$= 1.25\text{, or 125 percent of direct labour cost}$$

(The predetermined overhead rate using Job 79 is identical.)

2.

	Job 78	Job 79	Job 80	Job 81
Beginning balance, June 1	$2,350	$3,050	$ 0	$ 0
Direct materials	500	1,110	900	100
Direct labour	400	1,400	2,000	320
Applied overhead	500*	1,750*	2,500*	400*
Total, June 30	$3,750	$7,310	$5,400	$820

* $500 = $400 × 1.25; $1,750 = $1,400 × 1.25; $2,500 = $2,000 × 1.25; $400 = $320 × 1.25

3. By the end of June, Jobs 78, 79, and 80 have been transferred out of Work in Process. Therefore, the ending balance in Work in Process consists only of Job 81.

Work in process, June 30	$820

While three jobs (78, 79, and 80) were transferred out of Work in Process and into Finished Goods during June, only two jobs remain (Jobs 78 and 80).

Finished goods, June 1	$ 0
Job 78	3,750
Job 80	5,400
Finished goods, June 30	$9,150

4. One job, Job 79, was sold during June.

Cost of goods sold	$7,310

Why:

Because we need to determine the ending inventories of WIP and FG as well as COGS and preparing brief reports will save time.

Accounting for Nonmanufacturing Costs

Manufacturing costs are not the only costs experienced by a firm, however. Nonmanufacturing costs are also incurred. Recall that costs associated with selling and general administrative activities are period costs. Selling and administrative costs are never assigned to the product; they are not part of the manufacturing cost flows.

To illustrate how these costs are accounted for, assume Johnson Leathergoods had the following additional transactions in January:

Advertising circulars	\$ 75
Sales commission	125
Office salaries	500
Depreciation, office equipment	50

The first two transactions fall into the category of selling expense and the last two into the category of administrative expense. So, the selling expense account would increase by \$200 (= \$75 + \$125), and the administrative expense account would increase by \$550 (= \$500 + \$50).

Controlling accounts accumulate all of the selling and administrative expenses for a period. At the end of the period, all of these costs flow to the period's income statement. An income statement for Johnson Leathergoods is shown in Exhibit 5.13.

EXHIBIT 5.13

Income Statement

Johnson Leathergoods Income Statement For the Month Ended January 31, 2018		
Sales		\$3,480
Less: Cost of goods sold		2,395
Gross margin		1,085
Less selling and administrative expenses:		
Selling expenses	\$200	
Administrative expenses	550	750
Net operating income		\$ 335

With the preparation of the income statement, the flow of costs through the manufacturing, selling, and administrative expense accounts is complete. A more detailed look at the actual accounting for these cost flows is outlined in Appendix 5A to this chapter.

Job-Order Costing for Service Firms

A job-order costing system may be used for service firms as well. Architects, accountants, lawyers, tutors, physicians, and advertising agencies provide services to individual clients, students, or patients. In such cases, the client, student, or patient can be viewed as a job for which costs are accumulated and reported.

The primary product costs for a service business are direct labour and overhead. Any materials or supplies used in rendering services are normally insignificant. For that reason, materials and supply costs are included in the overhead cost. As in a manufacturing business, direct labour and overhead costs of rendering services to a client are accumulated in a WIP account. Each job/client has its own job cost sheet and WIP account.

When a job is completed and the client is billed, the costs are transferred to a Cost of Services account. Such an account is similar to the COG account for a merchandising or manufacturing business.

EXHIBIT 5.14

Cost Flow for a Service Firm

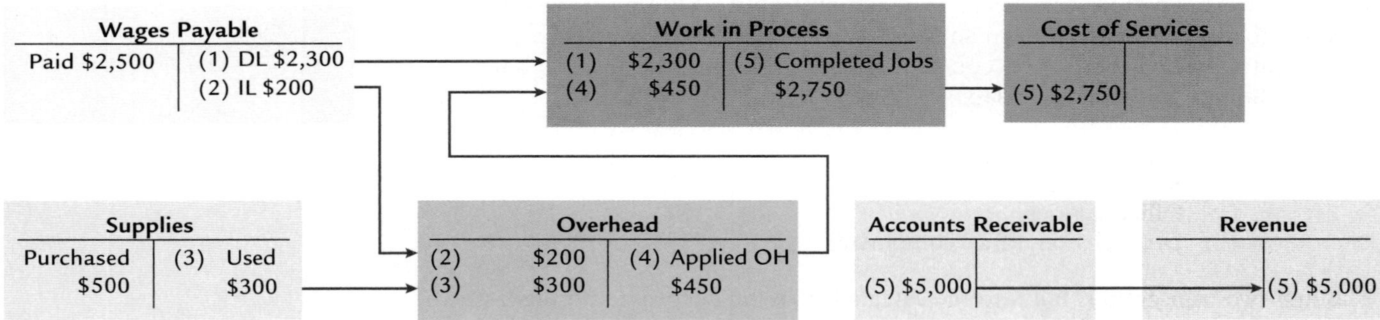

Transactions:
(1) Direct labour used in service jobs.
(2) Indirect labour (OH) incurred in providing service.
(3) Supplies used in providing service.
(4) OH applied to service jobs using the predetermined OH rate.
(5) Service job was completed and billed.

A FG account is not necessary, since the revenues for the services are recorded only after the services are provided.

In practice, other considerations unique to service businesses may need to be considered. For example, a service business may bill clients on a weekly or monthly basis rather than when a job is completed. In such cases, a portion of the costs related to each billing will be transferred from the WIP account to the Cost of Services account. A service business may also bill clients for services in advance; these would be accounted for as unearned revenue until the services are completed.

The cost flow for a service business using job-order costing is shown in Exhibit 5.14.

APPENDIX 5A: JOURNAL ENTRIES ASSOCIATED WITH JOB-ORDER COSTING

OBJECTIVE 5

Prepare the journal entries associated with job-order costing.

The transactions that flow through the accounts in job-order costing are entered into the accounting system by making journal entries and posting them to the accounts. Let's summarize the various transactions that occurred during the month of January for Johnson Leathergoods.

1. Purchased raw materials costing $2,500 on account.
2. Requisitioned materials costing $1,500 for use in production.
3. Recognized direct labour costing $1,530 (that is, it was not paid in cash but was shown as a liability in the Wages Payable account).
4. Applied overhead to production at the rate of $2 per direct labour hour. A total of 170 direct labour hours were worked.
5. Incurred actual overhead costs of $415.
6. Completed the backpack job and transferred it to Finished Goods.
7. Expensed the backpacks sold during the period.
8. Recorded revenues from the backpack job at cost plus 50 percent.
9. Closed underapplied overhead to COGS.

The journal entries for the above transactions are as follows:

		Debit	Credit
1.	Raw Materials	2,500	
	Accounts Payable		2,500
	To record purchase of materials		
2.	Work in Process	1,500	
	Raw Materials		1,500
	To record transfer of materials to factory for processing		
3.	Work in Process	1,530	
	Wages Payable		1,530
	To record wages for the period		
4.	Work in Process	340	
	Overhead Control		340
	To record overhead applied during the period		
5.	Overhead Control	415	
	Lease Payable		200
	Utilities Payable		50
	Accumulated Depreciation		100
	Wages Payable		65
	To record actual overhead costs incurred during the period		
6.	Finished Goods	2,320	
	Work in Process		2,320
	To record transfer of completed goods to Finished Goods Inventory		
7.	Cost of Goods Sold	2,320	
	Finished Goods		2,320
	To record cost of goods sold for the period		
8.	Accounts Receivable	3,480	
	Sales Revenue		3,480
	To record sale of goods for the period		
9.	Cost of Goods Sold	75	
	Overhead Control		75
	To record the disposition of the overhead variance for the period		

Journal entry 1 shows that the purchase of materials increases the Raw Materials account as well as the Accounts Payable account. In other words, the company has increased both assets (materials on hand) and liabilities (through Accounts Payable).

Entry 2 shows the transfer from the materials storeroom to the factory floor. In other words, the materials are no longer awaiting requisition; they are being used. Therefore, the WIP account goes up and the Raw Materials account goes down.

Entry 3 recognizes the contribution of direct labour. The amount of direct labour wages is added to WIP and also is added to the liability account, Wages Payable.

Entry 4 recognizes the application of overhead to the jobs. Since 170 hours of direct labour were worked, and the overhead rate is $2 per direct labour hour, then $340 of overhead has been applied to production. Notice that this overhead application increases the WIP account and shows as a credit to Overhead Control.

Entry 5 shows that the actual overhead incurred is debited to Overhead Control. The credit is to the various payable accounts and Accumulated Depreciation.

Entry 6 shows the transfer of the backpack job from WIP to FG. We find the appropriate cost by referring to the job-order cost sheet in Exhibit 5.10.

Entry 7 recognizes the cost of the backpack job that has been sold by debiting COGS for the cost and crediting FG, which mirrors the physical movement of the backpacks out of the warehouse and to the customer.

Entry 8 reflects the sale of the backpacks to the customer at the selling price of cost plus 50 percent.

Finally, in entry 9, we check the Overhead Control account. It has a debit balance of $75, indicating that the overhead variance is $75 underapplied. To bring the balance to zero, Overhead Control must be credited $75, and COGS must be debited $75.

Exhibit 5.15 summarizes these journal entries and posts them to the appropriate accounts.

EXHIBIT 5.15

Posting of Journal Entries to the Accounts

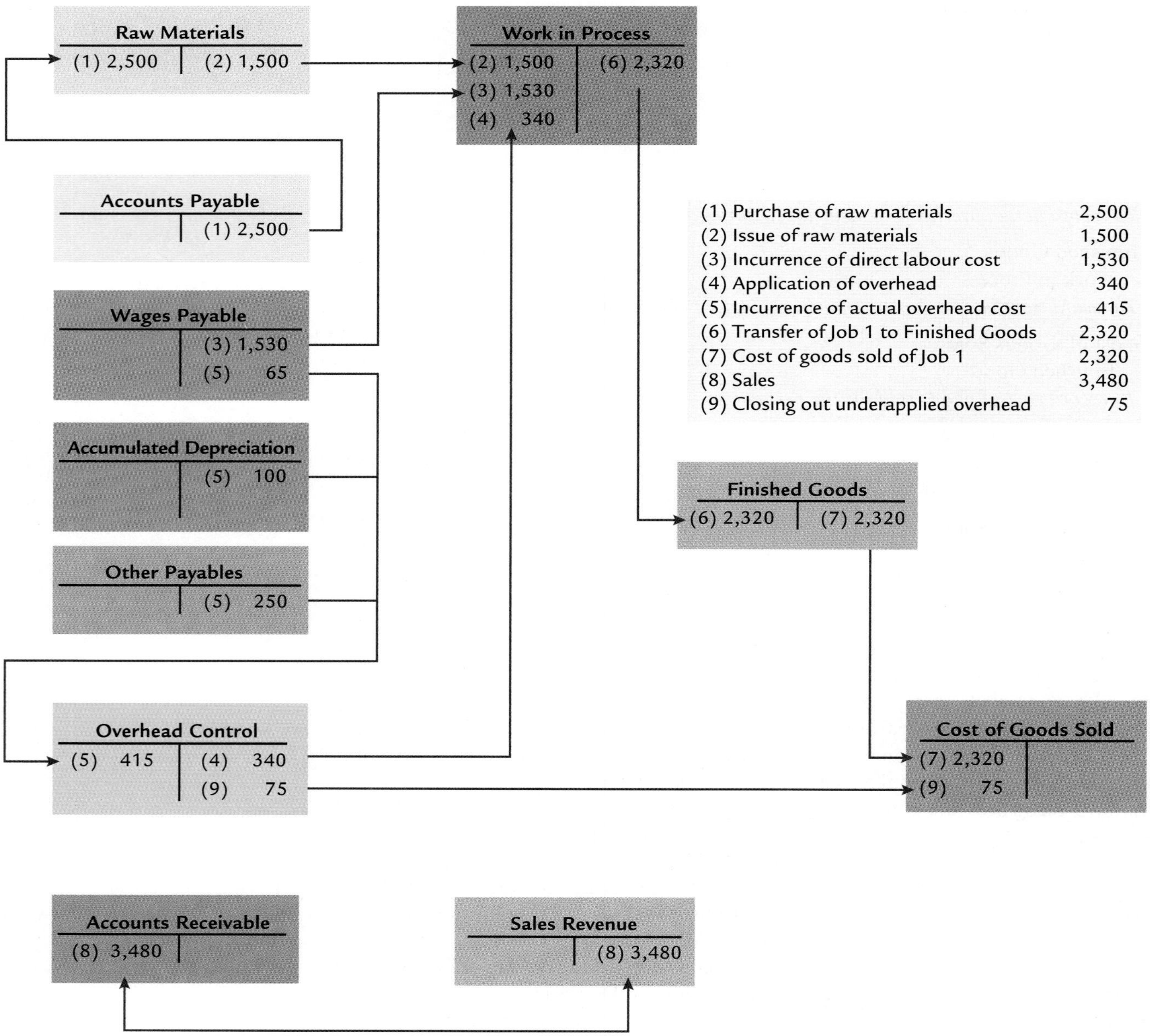
Raw Materials
(1) 2,500 | (2) 1,500
Work in Process
(2) 1,500 | (6) 2,320
(3) 1,530
(4) 340
Accounts Payable
(1) 2,500
Wages Payable
(3) 1,530
(5) 65
Accumulated Depreciation
(5) 100
Other Payables
(5) 250
Overhead Control
(5) 415 | (4) 340
(9) 75
Finished Goods
(6) 2,320 | (7) 2,320
Cost of Goods Sold
(7) 2,320
(9) 75
Accounts Receivable
(8) 3,480
Sales Revenue
(8) 3,480
(1) Purchase of raw materials 2,500
(2) Issue of raw materials 1,500
(3) Incurrence of direct labour cost 1,530
(4) Application of overhead 340
(5) Incurrence of actual overhead cost 415
(6) Transfer of Job 1 to Finished Goods 2,320
(7) Cost of goods sold of Job 1 2,320
(8) Sales 3,480
(9) Closing out underapplied overhead 75

APPENDIX 5B: SUPPORT DEPARTMENT COST ALLOCATION

OBJECTIVE 6

Allocate support department costs to producing departments.

The costs of resources shared by two or more services or products are referred to as **common costs**. For example, the cost of a maintenance department is shared by the producing departments that use these services. How to assign these shared costs to individual producing departments is the focus of this appendix.

Types of Departments

Nearly every company or factory has producing departments and support departments.

Producing departments are directly responsible for creating the products or services sold to customers. For example, a public accounting firm might have producing departments devoted to auditing, tax, and management advisory services. In a factory, producing departments are those that work directly on the products being manufactured, such as the grinding, machining, and assembly departments.

Support departments provide essential services for producing departments, but they do not actually make the product or service being sold. Examples include the maintenance, groundskeeping, engineering, housekeeping, personnel, and cafeteria departments.

Once producing and support departments have been identified, overhead costs that belong exclusively to each department are identified—these are direct overhead costs. For example, a factory cafeteria would have direct costs such as food, salaries of cooks and servers, depreciation on dishwashers and stoves, and supplies (e.g., dishwasher detergent, napkins, plastic forks). Direct overhead costs of a producing department would include supplies, supervisory salaries, and depreciation on equipment used in that department. Overhead that cannot easily be assigned to a producing or support department is assigned to a catchall department such as "general factory."

Once the direct overhead costs of each department are determined, the next step is to assign the support department costs to producing departments. These costs are assigned to producing departments by using **causal factors** (drivers) that measure the consumption of the services. Each producing department's share of the support department costs is added to that department's direct overhead cost. This total estimated overhead is then divided by a unit-level driver to obtain a predetermined overhead rate for each producing department. Overhead rates are calculated only for producing departments because products only pass through producing departments. Exhibit 5.16 summarizes the steps

EXHIBIT 5.16

Steps for Determining Product Costs by Using Predetermined Departmental Overhead Rates

1. Departmentalize the firm.
2. Classify each department as a support department or a producing department.
3. Trace all overhead costs in the firm to a support department or a producing department.
4. Assign support department costs to the producing departments using drivers that measure the consumption of support department services.
5. Calculate predetermined overhead rates for producing departments.
6. Assign overhead costs to the units of individual products using the predetermined overhead rates.

Corporate and Social Responsibility

Deliberations about strategic decisions within a company need to be kept confidential. For example, it may be tempting to use confidential information about the discontinuance of a support department to provide an unfair advantage to a friend or relative who may be the owner of an outside service firm that might be considered to replace the support department.

involved. Steps 1 through 4 are explained in this appendix; steps 5 and 6 are explained in Cornerstone 5.4 of this chapter.

Methods of Support Department Cost Allocation

A plantwide overhead rate adds together all of the direct overhead costs of the producing departments and all costs of any support departments to calculate a single plantwide overhead rate and assign overhead to units produced. However, many firms find that a single overhead rate does not accurately assign costs to various products. In that case, departmental overhead rates may be used. Then it is necessary to allocate support department costs to the producing departments in order to calculate meaningful departmental overhead rates.

The three methods of assigning costs of multiple support departments to producing departments are the *direct method*, the *sequential method*, and the *reciprocal method*.

- The direct method ignores interactions between support departments and assigns support department costs *directly* to producing departments. Ignoring these interactions and allocating service costs directly to producing departments may produce unfair and inaccurate cost assignments. For example, the power department, although a support department, may use 30 percent of the services of the maintenance department. By not assigning some maintenance costs to the power department, its costs are understated. As a result, a producing department that is a heavy user of power and an average or below-average user of maintenance will then receive, under the direct method, a cost allocation that is understated.
- The sequential method considers some of the interaction effects.
- The reciprocal method fully considers all interactions.

concept Q&A

What is the major disadvantage of the direct method?

Answers on pages 734 to 738.

In determining which support department cost allocation method to use, companies must determine the extent of support department interaction and weigh the individual costs and benefits of each method. In the next three sections, the *direct*, *sequential*, and *reciprocal* methods are discussed.

Direct Method The **direct method** assigns support department costs *only* to the producing departments. The direct method is the simplest and most straightforward way to assign support department costs.

Exhibit 5.17 illustrates the way support department costs are allocated to producing departments using the direct method. We see that by using the direct method, support department costs are assigned to producing departments only. No cost from one support department is given to another support department. Thus, no support department interaction is recognized. Cornerstone 5.6 shows how the direct method is used to assign the costs of two support departments to two producing departments.

EXHIBIT 5.17

Illustration of the Direct Method

Suppose there are two support departments, Power and Maintenance, and two producing departments, Grinding and Assembly, each with a "bucket" of directly traceable overhead cost.
Objective: Distribute all maintenance and power costs to Grinding and Assembly using the direct method.

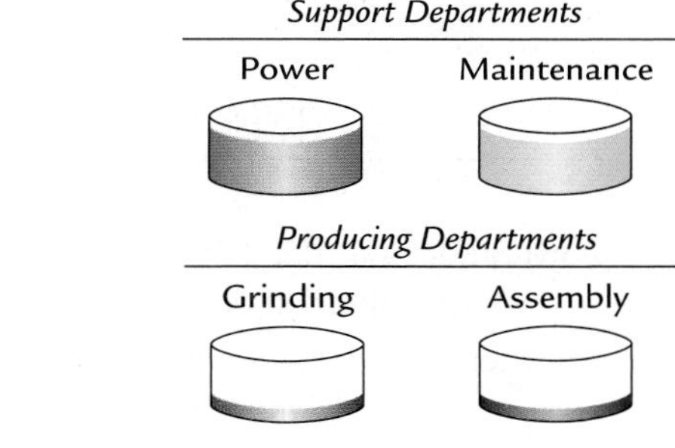

Direct method—Allocate maintenance and power costs only to Grinding and Assembly.

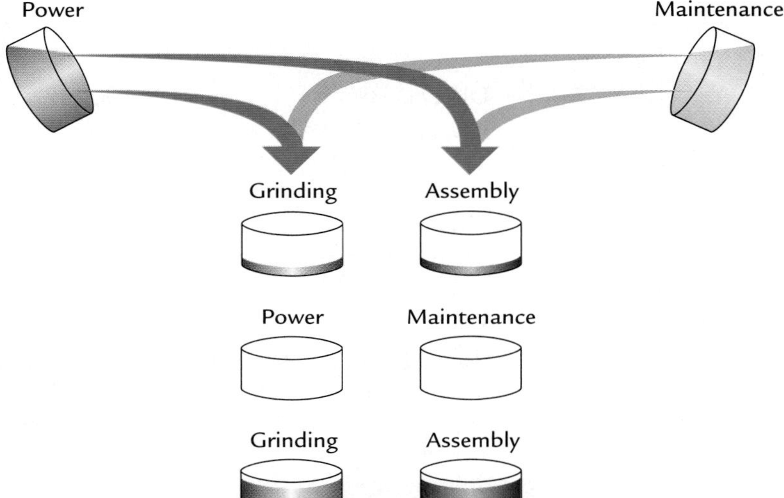

After allocation—Zero cost in Maintenance and Power; all overhead cost is in Grinding and Assembly.

Power Maintenance

Grinding Assembly

CORNERSTONE 5.6

Assigning Support Department Costs by Using the Direct Method

Information:

Departmental data:

	Support Departments		Producing Departments	
	Power	**Maintenance**	**Grinding**	**Assembly**
Direct overhead costs*	$250,000	$160,000	$100,000	$ 60,000
Expected activity:				
Kilowatt-hours	—	200,000	600,000	200,000
Maintenance hours	1,000	—	4,500	4,500

* Overhead costs that are directly traceable to the department.

(Continued)

CORNERSTONE

5.6

(Continued)

Required:

Using the direct method, assign the support department costs to the producing departments.

Solution:

Calculate usage or allocation ratios:

	Grinding	Assembly
Power: 600,000/(600,000 + 200,000)	0.75	—
200,000/(600,000 + 200,000)	—	0.25
Maintenance: 4,500/(4,500 + 4,500)	0.50	—
4,500/(4,500 + 4,500)	—	0.50

	Support Departments		Producing Departments	
	Power	**Maintenance**	**Grinding**	**Assembly**
Direct costs	$ 250,000	$ 160,000	$100,000	$ 60,000
Power[a]	(250,000)	—	187,500	62,500
Maintenance[b]	—	(160,000)	80,000	80,000
Total	$ 0	$ 0	$367,500	$202,500

[a] Using the allocation ratios for power: 0.75 × $250,000; 0.25 × $250,000.
[b] Using the allocation ratios for maintenance: 0.50 × $160,000; 0.50 × $160,000.

Why:

Because support department costs need to be absorbed by the producing departments as these are the only departments for which product costs can be calculated. Thus the production departments carry their own costs plus those of the support departments.

Sequential Method of Allocation The **sequential (or step) method** of allocation recognizes that interactions among support departments occur. Cost allocations are performed in a step-down (or sequential) fashion, following a predetermined ranking procedure. Usually, the sequence is defined by ranking the support departments in order of the amount of service rendered, from the greatest to the least, where degree of service is measured by the direct costs of each support department. However, the sequential method does not fully account for all support department interaction.

Exhibit 5.18 provides a visual portrayal of the sequential method. First, the support departments are ranked, usually in accordance with direct costs; here, the power department is first, then the maintenance department. Next, power costs are allocated to the maintenance department and the two producing departments. Finally, the costs of the maintenance department are allocated only to producing departments.

The costs of the support department rendering the greatest service are assigned to all support departments below it in the sequence and to all producing departments. The costs of the support department next in sequence are similarly allocated and so on. *In the sequential method, once a support department's costs are allocated, it never receives a subsequent allocation from another support department.* In other words, costs of a support department are never allocated to support departments

concept Q&A

Why is the sequential method considered to be more accurate than the direct method?

Answers on pages 734 to 738.

EXHIBIT 5.18

Illustration of the Sequential Method

Suppose there are two support departments, Power and Maintenance, and two producing departments, Grinding and Assembly, each with a "bucket" of directly traceable overhead cost.

Objective: Distribute all maintenance and power costs to Grinding and Assembly using the sequential method.

Step 1: Rank service departments—#1 Power, #2 Maintenance.

Step 2: Distribute power costs to Maintenance, Grinding, and Assembly.

Then, distribute maintenance to Grinding and Assembly.

After allocation—Zero cost in Maintenance and Power; all overhead cost is in Grinding and Assembly.

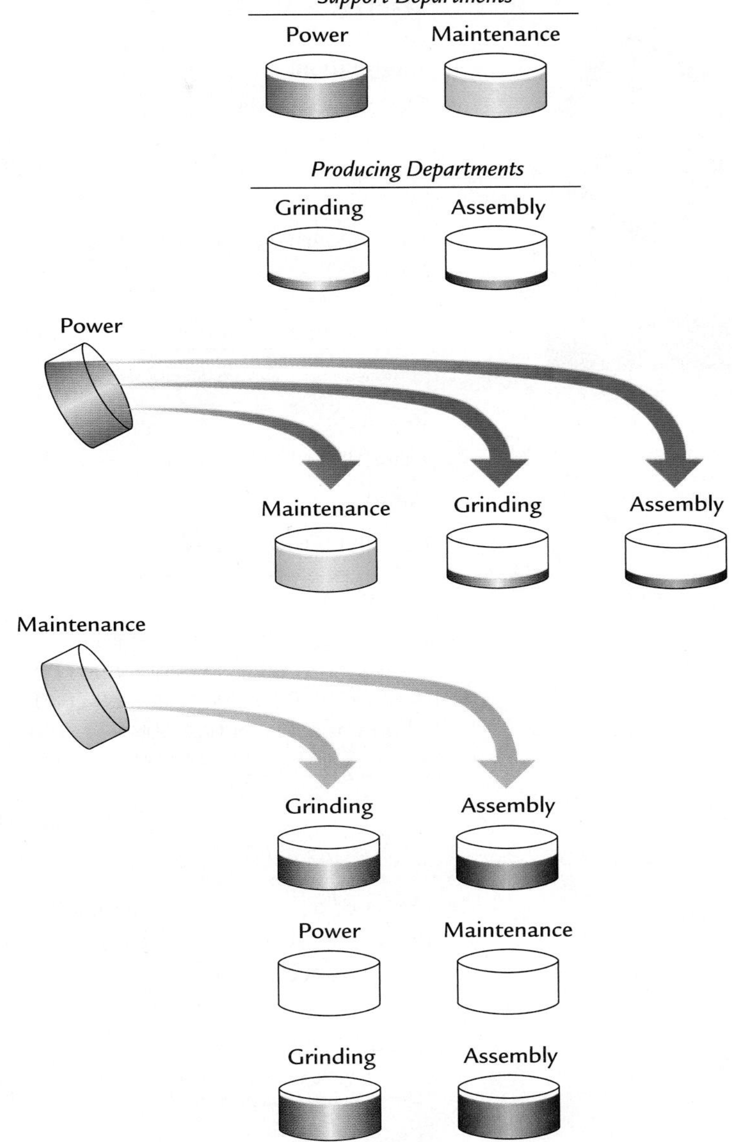

above it in the sequence. *Also, note that the costs allocated from a support department are its direct costs plus any costs it receives in allocations from other support departments.*

Cornerstone 5.7 shows how to assign support department costs to producing departments by using the sequential method. The power department will be allocated first since its direct cost is higher, followed by the maintenance department. Note that the allocation ratios for the maintenance department ignore the usage by the power department because power is above maintenance in the allocation sequence. Unlike the direct method, the sequential method recognizes some, but not all, interactions among the support departments. The reciprocal method corrects this deficiency.

CORNERSTONE 5.7

Assigning Support Department Costs by Using the Sequential Method

Information:

Departmental data:

	Support Departments		Producing Departments	
	Power	**Maintenance**	**Grinding**	**Assembly**
Direct overhead costs*	$250,000	$160,000	$100,000	$ 60,000
Expected activity:				
Kilowatt-hours	—	200,000	600,000	200,000
Maintenance hours	1,000	—	4,500	4,500

* Overhead costs that are directly traceable to the department.

Required:

Using the sequential method, assign the support department costs to the producing departments.

Solution:

Calculate usage ratios:

	Maintenance	**Grinding**	**Assembly**
Power: 200,000/(200,000 + 600,000 + 200,000)	0.20	—	—
600,000/(200,000 + 600,000 + 200,000)	—	0.60	—
200,000/(200,000 + 600,000 + 200,000)	—	—	0.20
Maintenance: 4,500/(4,500 + 4,500)	—	0.50	—
4,500/(4,500 + 4,500)	—	—	0.50

	Support Departments		Producing Departments	
	Power	**Maintenance**	**Grinding**	**Assembly**
Direct costs	$ 250,000	$ 160,000	$100,000	$ 60,000
Power[a]	(250,000)	50,000	150,000	50,000
Maintenance[b]	—	(210,000)	105,000	105,000
	$ 0	$ 0	$355,000	$215,000

[a] Using the usage ratios for power: 0.20 × $250,000; 0.60 × $250,000; 0.20 × $250,000.
[b] Using the usage ratios for maintenance: 0.50 × $210,000; 0.50 × $210,000.

Why:

Because support department costs need to be absorbed by the producing departments as these are the only departments for which product costs can be calculated. Thus the production departments carry their own costs plus those of the support departments. The sequential method recognizes some level of interaction between support departments.

Reciprocal Method of Allocation The **reciprocal method** of allocation recognizes all interactions among support departments (see Cornerstone 5.8). Under the reciprocal method, one support department's use by another figures in determining the total cost of each support department, where the total cost reflects interactions among all of the support departments. Then, the new total of support department costs is allocated to the producing departments. This method fully accounts for support department interaction by using a system of simultaneous linear equations. The reciprocal method is not widely used due to its complexity and limited value in providing more precise cost allocations.

Assigning Support Department Costs by Using the Reciprocal Method

CORNERSTONE 5.8

Information:

Baxter Company has two departments: human resources (HR) and custodial services (CS). It also has two producing departments: domestic sales and export sales.

The costs of the human resources department are allocated on the basis of the number of employees in each of the other departments. The costs of custodial services are allocated on the basis of floor area allocation. Baxter Company used the reciprocal method to allocate support department costs.

	Support Departments		Producing Departments	
	Human Resources	Custodial Services	Domestic Sales	Export Sales
Direct overhead costs	$150,000	$360,000	$125,000	$80,000
Number of employees	—	60	45	80
Floor area (square metres)	1,500	—	6,000	14,000

Required:

1. Develop a simultaneous equations system of total costs for the support departments. Solve for the total reciprocal costs of each support department (round reciprocated costs to the nearest dollar using four digits in the allocation ratios).
2. Using the reciprocal method, allocate the costs of human resources and custodial services to the producing departments (round to the nearest dollar).
3. What if the allocation ratios were rounded into six rather than four digits? How would that affect any rounding error in the allocation of costs?

Solution:

1. Percentage of employees in custodial services $= \dfrac{60}{(60 + 45 + 80)}$
$= 0.324$

Percentage of total floor area allocated to human resources

$$= \frac{1,500}{(1,500 + 6,000 + 14,000)} = 0.0698$$

Let HR = human resources and CS = custodial services

$HR = \$150,000 + 0.0698CS$

$CS = \$360,000 + 0.3243HR$

Solving for human resources:

$$\begin{aligned} HR &= \$150,000 + 0.0698CS \\ &= \$150,000 + 0.0698(\$360,000 + 0.3243HR) \\ &= \$150,000 + \$25,128 + 0.0226HR \\ 0.9774HR &= \$175,128 \\ HR &= \$179,177 \end{aligned}$$

(Continued)

CORNERSTONE
5.8
(Continued)

Solving for custodial services:

$$CS = \$360{,}000 + 0.3243HR$$
$$= \$360{,}000 + 0.3243(\$179{,}177) = \$418{,}107$$

2. Allocation ratios:

$$\text{Percentage of employees in custodial services} = \frac{60}{(60 + 45 + 80)} = 0.3243$$

$$\text{Percentage of employees in domestic sales} = \frac{45}{(60 + 45 + 80)} = 0.2432$$

$$\text{Percentage of employees in export sales} = \frac{80}{(60 + 45 + 80)} = 0.4324$$

$$\text{Percentage of total floor area in domestic sales} = \frac{6{,}000}{(1{,}500 + 6{,}000 + 14{,}000)} = 0.2791$$

$$\text{Percentage of total floor area in export sales} = \frac{14{,}000}{(1{,}500 + 6{,}000 + 14{,}000)} = 0.6512$$

$$\text{Percentage of total floor area in human resources} = \frac{1{,}500}{(1{,}500 + 6{,}000 + 14{,}000)} = 0.0698$$

	Percentage of driver used by			
	Human Resources	**Custodial Services**	**Domestic Sales**	**Export Sales**
Human resources	—	0.3243	0.2432	0.4324
Custodial services	0.0698	—	0.2791	0.6512

	Support Departments		**Producing Departments**	
	Human Resources	**Custodial Services**	**Domestic Sales**	**Export Sales**
Direct costs	$ 150,000	$ 360,000	$125,000	$ 80,000
Allocate:				
Human resources[1]	(179,177)	58,107	43,576	77,476
Custodial services[2]	29,184	(418,107)	116,694	272,271
Total after allocation	$ 7*	$ 0	$285,270	$429,747

[1] Custodial services = 0.3243 × $179,177 = $58,107; Domestic sales = 0.2432 × $179,177 = $43,576; Export sales = 0.4324 × $179,177 = $77,476

[2] Human resources = 0.0698 × $418,107 = $29,184; Domestic sales = 0.2791 × $418,107 = $116,694; Export sales = 0.6512 × $418,107 = $272,271

* Difference due to rounding.

3. Rounding the allocation ratios to six significant digits would produce a more precise allocation of costs and would reduce the rounding error. We can see that there is a $7 rounding error in human resources in Requirement 2. This is due to the rounding of the allocation ratios.

Why:

Because support department costs need to be absorbed by the producing departments as these are the only departments for which product costs can be calculated. Thus the production departments carry their own costs plus those of the support departments. Using the reciprocal method to allocate support department costs ensures that the amount of support department costs allocated to each of the producing departments most accurately reflects the true costs incurred by each producing department. It is preferable to the sequential method if there is a major difference in allocated costs between the two methods.

SUMMARY OF LEARNING OBJECTIVES

LO1. Describe the differences between job-order costing and process costing, and identify the types of firms that would use each method.

- Job-order firms collect costs by job.
- Job-order firms produce heterogeneous products/services—each unit or batch may have a different total cost.
- Job-order firms include construction, custom cabinetry, dentistry, medical services, and automotive repair.
- Process firms produce homogeneous products.
- In process firms, the cost of one batch or unit is the same as another batch or unit produced in the same period.
- Process firms include paint manufacturing, cheque clearing, and toy manufacturing.

LO2. Compute the predetermined overhead rate, and use the rate to assign overhead to units produced or services provided.

- Predetermined overhead is total budgeted overhead cost divided by total budgeted activity level.
- Overhead is applied by multiplying the predetermined rate by the actual activity usage.
- Applied overhead is added to total actual direct materials and direct labour cost to get total cost, which is divided by number of units to yield unit cost.

LO3. Identify and set up the source documents used in job-order costing.

- Job-order cost sheets summarize all costs associated with a job.
- Materials requisition forms are used to obtain direct materials for a job.
- Time tickets show the number of labour hours worked on a job.

LO4. Describe the cost flows associated with job-order costing.

- The job-order cost sheets are subsidiary to the WIP account.
- The balance in WIP consists of the sum of the balances of all the job-order cost sheets of the incomplete jobs.
- The cost of a finished job is transferred out of WIP and into FG.
- The costs of jobs sold are transferred out of FG and into COGS.

LO5. (*Appendix 5A*) Prepare the journal entries associated with job-order costing.

- Direct materials and direct labour are charged to WIP.
- Applied overhead costs are charged to WIP. Actual overhead costs are charged to Overhead Control.
- When units are completed, their total cost is debited to FG and credited to WIP.
- When units are sold, their total cost is debited to COGS and credited to FG.

LO6. (*Appendix 5B*) Allocate support department costs to producing departments.

- Producing departments actually make the products or services. Support departments provide service to the producing departments.
- When departmental overhead rates are used, the costs of support departments must be allocated to the producing departments.
- Three methods of support department cost allocation are the direct method, the sequential method, and the reciprocal method.

SUMMARY OF IMPORTANT EQUATIONS

1. $$\text{Predetermined overhead rate} = \frac{\text{Estimated annual overhead cost}}{\text{Estimated annual activity level}}$$

2. Applied overhead = Predetermined overhead rate × Actual activity usage

3. Overhead variance = Applied overhead − Actual overhead
4. Adjusted COGS = Unadjusted COGS ± Overhead variance
   (*Note*: Applied overhead > Actual overhead means overapplied overhead
   Applied overhead < Actual overhead means underapplied overhead)
5. $\text{Departmental overhead rate} = \dfrac{\text{Estimated departmental overhead}}{\text{Estimated departmental activity level}}$
6. Total product cost = Total direct materials + Total direct labour + Applied overhead
7. $\text{Unit product cost} = \dfrac{\text{Total product cost}}{\text{Number of units}}$

CORNERSTONES

CORNERSTONE 5.1 Calculating the predetermined overhead rate and applying overhead to production, page 192

CORNERSTONE 5.2 Reconciling actual overhead with applied overhead, page 194

CORNERSTONE 5.3 Calculating plantwide overhead rate and applying overhead to production, page 195

CORNERSTONE 5.4 Calculating predetermined departmental overhead rates and applying overhead to production, page 196

CORNERSTONE 5.5 Preparing brief job-order cost sheets, page 207

CORNERSTONE 5.6 (*Appendix 5B*) Assigning support department costs by using the direct method, page 215

CORNERSTONE 5.7 (*Appendix 5B*) Assigning support department costs by using the sequential method, page 218

CORNERSTONE 5.8 (*Appendix 5B*) Assigning support department costs by using the reciprocal method, page 219

GLOSSARY

Actual cost system An approach that assigns actual costs of direct materials, direct labour, and overhead to products. (p. 190)

Adjusted cost of goods sold The cost of goods sold after all adjustments for overhead variances are made. (p. 206)

Applied overhead Overhead assigned to production using predetermined rates. (p. 192)

Causal factors Activities or variables that invoke service costs. Generally, it is desirable to use causal factors as the basis for allocating service costs. (p. 213)

Common costs The costs of resources used in the output of two or more services or products. (p. 213)

Cost flow The way costs are accounted for from the point at which they are incurred to the point at which they are recognized as an expense on the income statement. (p. 201)

Departmental overhead rate Estimated overhead for a single department divided by the estimated activity level for that same department. (p. 196)

Direct method A method that allocates service costs directly to producing departments. This method ignores any interactions that may exist among support departments. (p. 214)

Job One distinct unit or set of units for which the costs of production must be assigned. (p. 189)

Job-order cost sheet A subsidiary account to the Work in Process account on which the total costs of materials, labour, and overhead for a single job are accumulated. (p. 198)

Job-order costing system A costing system in which costs are collected and assigned to units of production for each individual job. (p. 189)

Materials requisition form A source document that records the type, quantity, and unit price of the direct materials issued to each job. (p. 199)

Normal cost of goods sold The cost of goods sold before adjustment for any overhead variance. (p. 206)

Normal cost system An approach that assigns the actual costs of direct materials and direct labour to products, but uses a predetermined rate to assign overhead costs. (p. 191)

Overapplied overhead The amount by which applied overhead exceeds actual overhead. (p. 193)

Plantwide overhead rate A single overhead rate calculated using all estimated overhead for a factory divided by the estimated activity level across the entire factory. (p. 195)

Predetermined overhead rate An overhead rate computed using estimated data at the beginning of the year. (p. 191)

Pro rata application The process of allocating costs to various elements on the basis of the individual element cost to the total of all element costs. It is used when applying under- or overapplied overhead between cost of goods sold and inventory accounts. (p. 194)

Process-costing system A costing system that accumulates production costs by process or by department for a given period of time. (p. 189)

Producing departments Units within an organization responsible for producing the products or services that are sold to customers. (p. 213)

Reciprocal method A method that simultaneously allocates service costs to all user departments. It gives full consideration to interactions among support departments. (p. 218)

Sequential (or step) method A method that allocates service costs to user departments in a sequential manner. It gives partial consideration to interactions among support departments. (p. 216)

Support departments Units within an organization that provide essential support services for producing departments. (p. 213)

Time ticket A source document by which direct labour costs are assigned to individual jobs. (p. 200)

Underapplied overhead The amount by which actual overhead exceeds applied overhead. (p. 193)

REVIEW PROBLEMS

I. Job Cost Using Plantwide and Departmental Overhead Rates

Lindberg Company uses a normal job-order costing system. There are two departments, assembly and finishing, through which most jobs pass. Selected budgeted and actual data for the past year follow:

	Assembly	Finishing
Budgeted overhead	$330,000	$1,000,000
Actual overhead	$110,000	$520,000
Expected activity (direct labour hours)	150,000	25,000
Expected machine hours	25,000	125,000

(Continued)

During the year, several jobs were completed. Data pertaining to one such job, Job 330, follow:

Direct materials	$730,000
Direct labour cost:	
Assembly (5,000 hours @ $12/h)	$60,000
Finishing (400 hours @ $12/h)	$4,800
Machine hours used:	
Assembly	100
Finishing	1,200
Units produced	10,000

Lindberg Company uses a plantwide predetermined overhead rate based on direct labour hours (DLH) to assign overhead to jobs.

Required:

1. Compute the predetermined overhead rate.
2. Using the predetermined rate, compute the per-unit manufacturing cost for Job 330. (Round the unit cost to the nearest cent.)
3. Recalculate the unit manufacturing cost for Job 330 using departmental overhead rates. Use direct labour hours for assembly and machine hours for finishing.

Solution:

1. Predetermined overhead rate = $1,330,000/175,000 = $7.60 per DLH. Add the budgeted overhead for the two departments ($330,000 + $1,000,000), and divide by the total expected direct labour hours (DLH = 150,000 + 25,000).

2.

Direct materials	$730,000
Direct labour ($12 × 5,400)	64,800
Overhead ($7.60 × 5,400 DLH)	41,040
Total manufacturing costs	$835,840
Unit cost ($835,840/10,000)	$83.58

3. Predetermined rate for assembly $= \dfrac{\$330{,}000}{150{,}000} = \$2.20$ per DLH

Predetermined rate for finishing $= \dfrac{\$1{,}000{,}000}{125{,}000} = \$8$ per machine hour

Direct materials	$730,000
Direct labour	64,800
Overhead:	
Assembly ($2.20 × 5,000)	11,000
Finishing ($8 × 1,200)	9,600
Total manufacturing costs	$815,400
Unit cost ($815,400/10,000)	$81.54

II. Calculation of Work in Process and Cost of Goods Sold with Multiple Jobs

Olympia Kitchen and Bath (OKB) Company designs and installs upscale kitchens and bathrooms. On May 1, there were three jobs in process: Jobs 77, 78, and 79. During May, two more jobs were started: Jobs 80 and 81. By May 31, Jobs 77, 78, and 80 were completed and invoiced. The following data were gathered:

	Job 77	Job 78	Job 79	Job 80	Job 81
May 1 balance	$875	$1,140	$410	$ 0	$ 0
Direct materials	690	320	500	3,500	2,750
Direct labour	450	420	80	1,800	1,300

Overhead is applied at the rate of 150 percent of direct labour cost. Jobs are sold at cost plus 30 percent. Operating expenses for May totalled $2,700.

Required:

1. Prepare job-order cost sheets for each job as at May 31.
2. Calculate the ending balance in Work in Process (as at May 31) and Cost of Goods Sold for May.
3. Construct an income statement for OKB Company for the month of May.

Solution:

1.

	Job 77	Job 78	Job 79	Job 80	Job 81
May 1 balance	$ 875	$1,140	$ 410	$ 0	$ 0
Direct materials	690	320	500	3,500	2,750
Direct labour	450	420	80	1,800	1,300
Applied overhead	675	630	120	2,700	1,950
Totals	$2,690	$2,510	$1,110	$8,000	$6,000

2. Ending balance in Work in Process = Job 79 + Job 81
= $1,110 + $6,000
= $7,110

Cost of Goods Sold for May = Job 77 + Job 78 + Job 80
= $2,690 + $2,510 + $8,000
= $13,200

3.

OKB Company
Income Statement
For the Month Ended May 31

Sales*	$17,160
Cost of goods sold	13,200
Gross margin	3,960
Less: Operating expenses	2,700
Operating income	$ 1,260

* Sales = $13,200 + 0.30($13,200) = $17,160

III. Allocation: Direct and Sequential Methods

Baxter Manufacturing produces machine parts on a job-order basis. Most business is obtained through bidding. Most firms competing with Baxter bid full cost plus a 20 percent markup. Recently, with the hope of gaining more sales, Baxter reduced its markup from 25 percent to 20 percent of cost. The company operates two service departments and two producing departments. The budgeted costs and the normal activity levels for each department are given below.

	Service Departments		Producing Departments	
	A	B	C	D
Direct overhead costs	$100,000	$200,000	$100,000	$50,000
Number of employees	8	7	30	30
Maintenance hours	2,000	200	6,400	1,600
Machine hours	—	—	10,000	1,000
Labour hours	—	—	1,000	10,000

The direct costs of department A are allocated on the basis of employees; those of department B are allocated on the basis of maintenance hours. Departmental overhead rates are used to assign costs to products. Department C uses machine hours, and department D uses labour hours.

(Continued)

The firm is preparing to bid on a job (Job K) that requires three machine hours per unit produced in department C and no time in department D. The expected prime costs per unit are $67.

Required:

1. Allocate the service costs to the producing departments by using the direct method.
2. What will the bid be for Job K if the direct method of allocation is used?
3. Allocate the service costs to the producing departments by using the sequential method.
4. What will the bid be for Job K if the sequential method is used?

Solution:

1.

	Service Departments		Producing Departments	
	A	B	C	D
Direct overhead costs	$ 100,000	$ 200,000	$100,000	$ 50,000
Department A[a]	(100,000)	—	50,000	50,000
Department B[b]	—	(200,000)	160,000	40,000
Total	$ 0	$ 0	$310,000	$140,000

[a] Department A costs are allocated on the basis of the number of employees in the producing departments:
Proportion: Department C, 0.50 [= 30/(30 + 30)]
Department D, 0.50 [= 30/(30 + 30)]
Allocation: Department C, $50,000 (= 0.50 × $100,000)
Department D, $50,000 (= 0.50 × $100,000)

[b] Department B costs are allocated on the basis of maintenance hours used in the producing departments:
Proportion: Department C, 0.80 [= 6,400/(6,400 + 1,600)]
Department D, 0.20 [= 1,600/(6,400 + 1,600)]
Allocation: Department C, $160,000 (= 0.80 × $200,000)
Department D, $40,000 (= 0.20 × $200,000)

2. Department C: Overhead rate = $310,000/10,000 = $31 per machine hour. Product cost and bid price:

Prime cost	$ 67
Overhead (3 × $31)	93
Total unit cost	$160

Bid price = $160 × 1.2 = $192

3.

	Service Departments		Producing Departments	
	A	B	C	D
Direct overhead costs	$ 100,000	$ 200,000	$100,000	$ 50,000
Department B[a]	40,000	(200,000)	128,000	32,000
Department A[b]	(140,000)	—	70,000	70,000
Total	$ 0	$ 0	$298,000	$152,000

[a] Department B ranks first because its direct costs are higher than those of department A. Department B's costs are allocated on the basis of maintenance hours used in department A, and producing departments C and D.
Proportion: Department A, 0.20 [= 2,000/(2,000 + 6,400 + 1,600)]
Department C, 0.64 [= 6,400/(2,000 + 6,400 + 1,600)]
Department D, 0.16 [= 1,600/(2,000 + 6,400 + 1,600)]
Allocation: Department A, $40,000 (= 0.20 × $200,000)
Department C, $128,000 (= 0.64 × $200,000)
Department D, $32,000 (= 0.16 × $200,000)

[b] Department A's costs are allocated on the basis of number of employees in the producing departments, departments C and D.
Proportion: Department C, 0.50 [= 30/(30 + 30)]
Department D, 0.50 [= 30/(30 + 30)]
Allocation: Department C, $70,000 (= 0.50 × $140,000)
Department D, $70,000 (= 0.50 × $140,000)
(*Note:* The department A cost is no longer $100,000. It is $140,000 due to the $40,000 that was allocated from department B.)

4. Department C: Overhead rate = \$298,000/10,000 = \$29.80 per machine hour. Product cost and bid price:

Prime cost	\$ 67.00
Overhead (3 × \$29.80)	89.40
Total unit cost	\$156.40

Bid price = \$156.40 × 1.2 = \$187.68

DISCUSSION QUESTIONS

1. What are job-order costing and process costing? What types of firms use job-order costing? Process costing?
2. Give some examples of service firms that might use job-order costing, and explain why it is used in those firms.
3. What is normal costing? How does it differ from actual costing?
4. Why are actual overhead rates seldom used in practice?
5. Explain how overhead is assigned to production when a predetermined overhead rate is used.
6. What is underapplied overhead? When Cost of Goods Sold is adjusted for underapplied overhead, will the cost increase or decrease? Why?
7. What is overapplied overhead? When Cost of Goods Sold is adjusted for overapplied overhead, will the cost increase or decrease? Why?
8. Suppose that you and a friend decide to set up a lawn mowing service next summer. Describe the source documents that you would need to account for your activities.
9. Why might a company decide to use departmental overhead rates instead of a plantwide overhead rate?
10. What is the role of materials requisition forms in a job-order costing system? Time tickets? Predetermined overhead rates?
11. Carver Company uses a plantwide overhead rate based on direct labour cost. Suppose that during the year, Carver raises its wage rate for direct labour. How would that affect overhead applied? The total cost of jobs?
12. What is an overhead variance? How is it accounted for typically?
13. Is the cost of a job related to the price charged? Explain.
14. If a company decides to increase advertising expense by \$25,000, how will that affect the predetermined overhead rate? Eventual cost of goods sold?
15. How can a departmental overhead system be converted to a plantwide overhead system?
16. (*Appendix 5B*) Describe the difference between producing and support departments.
17. (*Appendix 5B*) Assume that a company has decided not to allocate any support department costs to producing departments. Describe the likely behaviour of the managers of the producing departments. Would this be good or bad? Explain why allocation would correct this type of behaviour.
18. (*Appendix 5B*) Why is it important to identify and use causal factors to allocate support department costs?
19. (*Appendix 5B*) Identify some possible causal factors for the following support departments:
    a. Cafeteria
    b. Custodial services
    c. Laundry
    d. Receiving, shipping, and storage

e. Maintenance
f. Personnel
g. Accounting

20. (*Appendix 5B*) Explain the difference between the direct method and the sequential method.

CORNERSTONE EXERCISES

OBJECTIVE 2
CORNERSTONE 5.1

Cornerstone Exercise 5-1 Predetermined Overhead Rate, Overhead Application

At the beginning of the year, Pryor Company estimated the following costs:

Overhead	$ 900,000
Direct labour cost	1,200,000

Pryor uses normal costing and applies overhead on the basis of direct labour cost. (Direct labour cost is equal to total direct labour hours worked multiplied by the wage rate.) For the month of December, direct labour cost was $77,800.

Required:

1. Calculate the predetermined overhead rate for the year.
2. Calculate the overhead applied to production in December.

OBJECTIVE 2
CORNERSTONE 5.2

Cornerstone Exercise 5-2 Overhead Variance (Over- or Underapplied), Closing to Cost of Goods Sold

At the end of the year, Pryor Company provided the following actual information:

Overhead	$ 913,000
Direct labour cost	1,214,400

Pryor uses normal costing and applies overhead at the rate of 75 percent of direct labour cost. At the end of the year, Cost of Goods Sold (before adjusting for any overhead variance) was $1,780,000.

Required:

1. Calculate the overhead variance for the year.
2. Dispose of the overhead variance by adjusting Cost of Goods Sold.

OBJECTIVE 2
CORNERSTONE 5.3

Cornerstone Exercise 5-3 Convert Departmental Data to Plantwide Data, Plantwide Overhead Rate, Apply Overhead to Production

At the beginning of the year, Badger Company estimated the following:

	Cutting Department	Sewing Department	Total
Overhead	$378,000	$450,000	$828,000
Direct labour hours	131,200	200,000	331,200
Machine hours	210,000	—	210,000

Badger has decided to use a plantwide overhead rate based on direct labour hours. Actual data for the month of June are as follows:

	Cutting Department	Sewing Department	Total
Overhead	$32,612	$35,750	$68,362
Direct labour hours	11,800	16,000	27,800
Machine hours	17,840	—	17,840

Required:

1. Calculate the predetermined plantwide overhead rate.
2. Calculate the overhead applied to production for the month of June.
3. Calculate the overhead variance for the month of June.

Cornerstone Exercise 5-4 Predetermined Departmental Overhead Rates, Applying Overhead to Production

OBJECTIVE 2
CORNERSTONE 5.4

At the beginning of the year, Badger Company estimated the following:

	Cutting Department	Sewing Department	Total
Overhead	$378,000	$450,000	$828,000
Direct labour hours	131,200	200,000	331,200
Machine hours	210,000	—	210,000

Badger uses departmental overhead rates. In the cutting department, overhead is applied on the basis of machine hours. In the sewing department, overhead is applied on the basis of direct labour hours. Actual data for the month of June are as follows:

	Cutting Department	Sewing Department	Total
Overhead	$32,612	$35,750	$68,362
Direct labour hours	11,800	16,000	27,800
Machine hours	17,840	—	17,840

Required:

1. Calculate the predetermined overhead rates for the cutting and sewing departments.
2. Calculate the overhead applied to production in each department for the month of June.
3. By how much has each department's overhead been overapplied? Underapplied?

Cornerstone Exercise 5-5 Prepare Job-Order Cost Sheets, Predetermined Overhead Rate, Ending Balance of Work in Process, Finished Goods, and Cost of Goods Sold

OBJECTIVE 4
CORNERSTONE 5.5

At the beginning of June, Donewell Company had two jobs in process—Job 44 and Job 45—with the following accumulated cost information:

	Job 44	Job 45
Direct materials	$13,800	$3,525
Direct labour	3,600	3,000
Applied overhead	2,250	1,875
Balance, June 1	$19,650	$8,400

During June, two more jobs (46 and 47) were started. The following direct materials and direct labour costs were added to the four jobs during the month of June:

	Job 44	Job 45	Job 46	Job 47
Direct materials	$4,500	$18,300	$2,400	$2,100
Direct labour	3,000	7,200	6,000	1,800

At the end of June, Jobs 44, 45, and 47 were completed. Only Job 45 was sold. On June 1, the balance in Finished Goods was zero.

(Continued)

Required:

1. Calculate the overhead rate based on direct labour cost.
2. Prepare a brief job-order cost sheet for the four jobs. Show the balance as at June 1 as well as direct materials and direct labour added in June. Apply overhead to the four jobs for the month of June, and show the ending balances.
3. Calculate the ending balances of Work in Process and Finished Goods as at June 30.
4. Calculate the Cost of Goods Sold for June.

OBJECTIVE 6
CORNERSTONE 5.6

Cornerstone Exercise 5-6 (*Appendix 5B*) Direct Method of Support Department Cost Allocation

The Pineapple Pen Company is divided into two operating divisions: pens and pencils. The company allocates the cost of the cafeteria and the maintenance department to each operating division using the direct method. Cafeteria costs are allocated on the basis of the number of employees in each department, and maintenance department costs on the basis of the number of square metres. Support department cost allocations using the direct method are based on the following data:

	Support Departments		Operating Divisions	
	Cafeteria	**Maintenance**	**Pens**	**Pencils**
Overhead costs	$1,050,000	$875,000	$1,800,000	$2,225,500
Number of employees	15	25	60	100
Square metres	15,000	5,000	100,000	125,000
Direct labour hours	—	—	108,000	135,000

Required:

1. Calculate the allocation ratios for the cafeteria and maintenance department. (Carry these calculations out to four significant digits.)
2. Allocate the support service costs to the producing departments.
3. Assume departmental overhead rates are based on direct labour hours. Calculate the overhead rate for the pen division and for the pencil division. (Round overhead rates to the nearest cent.)

OBJECTIVE 6
CORNERSTONE 5.7

Cornerstone Exercise 5-7 (*Appendix 5B*) Sequential Method of Support Department Cost Allocation

Refer to **Cornerstone Exercise 5-6** for data. Now assume that the Pineapple Pen Company uses the sequential method to allocate support department costs to the producing departments. Maintenance is allocated first in the sequential method for the company.

Required:

1. Calculate the allocation ratios for the cafeteria and the maintenance departments. (Carry these calculations out to four significant digits.)
2. Allocate the support service costs to the producing departments.
3. Assume departmental overhead rates are based on direct labour hours. Calculate the overhead rate for the pen division and for the pencil division (round overhead rates to the nearest cent).
4. CONCEPTUAL CONNECTION What is the difference between the direct method and the sequential method of allocating support centre costs? Which is better?

OBJECTIVE 6
CORNERSTONE 5.8

Cornerstone Exercise 5-8 (*Appendix 5B*) Reciprocal Method of Support Department Cost Allocation

Refer to **Cornerstone Exercise 5-6** for data. Now assume that the Pineapple Pen Company uses the reciprocal method to allocate support department costs to the producing departments.

Required:

1. Prepare the simultaneous equations to allocate the costs of the cafeteria and the maintenance department. (Carry these calculations out to four significant digits.)
2. Allocate the support service costs to the producing departments.
3. Assume departmental overhead rates are based on direct labour hours. Calculate the overhead rate for the pen division and for the pencil division (round overhead rates to the nearest cent).
4. CONCEPTUAL CONNECTION What is the difference between the sequential method and the reciprocal method of allocating support centre costs? Which is better?

EXERCISES

Exercise 5-9 Job-Order Costing versus Process Costing

OBJECTIVE 1

a. Paint manufacturing
b. Auto manufacturing
c. Toy manufacturing
d. Custom cabinet making
e. Airplane manufacturing (e.g., 767s)
f. Personal computer assembly
g. Furniture making
h. Custom furniture making
i. Dental services
j. Hospital services
k. Paper manufacturing
l. Auto repair
m. Architectural services
n. Landscape design services
o. Light bulb manufacturing

Required:

Identify each of these preceding types of businesses as being more likely to use either a job-order costing system or a process-costing system.

Exercise 5-10 Job-Order Costing versus Process Costing

OBJECTIVE 1

a. Auto manufacturing
b. Dental services
c. Auto repair
d. Costume making

Required:

1. For each of the given types of industries, give an example of a firm that would use job-order costing. Then, give an example of a firm that would use process costing.
2. CONCEPTUAL CONNECTION What differentiates a job-order costing environment from a process-costing environment?

Exercise 5-11 Calculating the Predetermined Overhead Rate, Applying Overhead to Production

OBJECTIVE 2

At the beginning of the year, Nature's Best estimated the following:

Overhead	$2,137,500
Direct labour hours	142,500

Nature's Best uses normal costing and applies overhead on the basis of direct labour hours. For the month of March, direct labour hours were 6,800.

(Continued)

Required:

1. Calculate the predetermined overhead rate for Nature's Best.
2. Calculate the overhead applied to production in March.

OBJECTIVE 2

Exercise 5-12 Calculating the Predetermined Overhead Rate, Applying Overhead to Production, Reconciling Overhead at the End of the Year, Adjusting Cost of Goods Sold for Under- and Overapplied Overhead

At the beginning of the year, Potter Company estimated the following:

Overhead	$864,000
Direct labour hours	320,000

Potter uses normal costing and applies overhead on the basis of direct labour hours. For the month of January, direct labour hours were 7,950. By the end of the year, Potter showed the following actual amounts:

Overhead	$904,000
Direct labour hours	330,400

Assume that unadjusted Cost of Goods Sold for Potter was $942,680.

Required:

1. Calculate the predetermined overhead rate for Potter.
2. Calculate the overhead applied to production in January.
3. Calculate the total applied overhead for the year. Was overhead over- or underapplied? By how much?
4. Calculate adjusted Cost of Goods Sold after adjusting for the overhead variance.
5. CONCEPTUAL CONNECTION What is meant by "overhead variance"? How is it calculated? What happens to it at the end of the accounting period?

Exercise 5-13 Calculating Departmental Overhead Rates and Applying Overhead to Production

At the beginning of the year, Videosym Company estimated the following:

	Assembly Department	Testing Department	Total
Overhead	$620,000	$180,000	$800,000
Direct labour hours	155,000	20,000	175,000
Machine hours	80,000	120,000	200,000

Videosym uses departmental overhead rates. In the assembly department, overhead is applied on the basis of direct labour hours. In the testing department, overhead is applied on the basis of machine hours. Actual data for the month of March are as follows:

	Assembly Department	Testing Department	Total
Overhead	$53,000	$15,500	$68,500
Direct labour hours	13,000	1,680	14,680
Machine hours	6,800	13,050	19,850

Required:

1. Calculate the predetermined overhead rates for the assembly and testing departments.
2. Calculate the overhead applied to production in each department for the month of March.
3. By how much has each department's overhead been overapplied? Underapplied?
4. CONCEPTUAL CONNECTION Why don't we simply leave the overhead variance in the overhead control account at the end of the accounting period?

Exercise 5-14 Job-Order Cost Sheet

OBJECTIVE 3

On June 1, Job 24 had a beginning balance of $330. During June, direct materials of $475 and direct labour of $280 were added to the job. Overhead is applied to production at the rate of 75 percent of direct labour cost.

Required:

1. Set up a simple job-order cost sheet for Job 24. What is the total cost of Job 24?
2. If Job 24 consisted of five units, what is the unit cost?

Exercise 5-15 Source Documents

OBJECTIVE 3

For each of the following independent situations, give the source document that would be referred to for the necessary information.

Required:

1. Direct materials costing $460 are requisitioned for use on a job.
2. Greiner's Garage uses a job-order costing system. Overhead is applied to jobs based on direct labour hours. Which source document gives the number of direct labour hours worked on Job 2018-276?
3. Lyon Investigative Services bills clients on a monthly basis for costs to date. Job 3-48 involved an investigator following the client's business partner for a week by automobile. Travel is billed at number of kilometres times $0.75.
4. The foreman on the Jackson job wonders what the actual direct materials cost was for that job.

Exercise 5-16 Applying Overhead to Jobs, Costing Jobs

OBJECTIVE 4

Herron Company designs and builds retaining walls for individual customers. On August 1, there were two jobs in process: Job 730 with a beginning balance of $12,600, and Job 731 with a beginning balance of $9,400. Herron applies overhead at the rate of $15 per direct labour hour. Direct labour wages average $20 per hour. Data on August costs for all jobs are as follows:

	Job 730	Job 731	Job 732	Job 733
Direct materials	$1,800	$12,000	$3,150	$4,500
Direct labour cost	3,600	8,000	4,000	1,600

During August, Jobs 732 and 733 were started. Job 730 was completed on August 17, and the client was billed at cost plus 60 percent. All other jobs remained in process.

Required:

1. Calculate the number of direct labour hours that were worked on each job in August.
2. Calculate the overhead applied to each job during the month of August.
3. Prepare job-order cost sheets for each job as at the end of August.
4. Calculate the balance in Work in Process as at August 31.
5. What is the price of Job 730?

Exercise 5-17 Applying Overhead to Jobs, Costing Jobs

OBJECTIVE 4

Brebeuf Company builds internal conveyor equipment to client specifications. On October 1, Job 877 was in process with a cost of $20,520 to date. During October, Jobs 878, 879, and 880 were started. Data on costs added during October for all jobs are as follows:

	Job 877	Job 878	Job 879	Job 880
Direct materials	$13,960	$ 7,000	$ 350	$4,800
Direct labour	13,800	10,000	1,500	4,000

(Continued)

Overhead is applied to production at the rate of 85 percent of direct labour cost. Job 878 was completed on October 28, and the client was billed at cost plus 50 percent. All other jobs remained in process.

Required:

1. Prepare a brief job-order cost sheet showing the October 1 balances of all four jobs, plus the direct materials and direct labour costs during October. (There is no need to calculate applied overhead at this point or to total the costs.)
2. Calculate the overhead applied during October.
3. Calculate the balance in Work in Process as at October 31.
4. What is the price of Job 878?

OBJECTIVE 4

Exercise 5-18 Balance of Work in Process and Finished Goods, Cost of Goods Sold

Hung Lee Company uses job-order costing. At the end of the month, the following information was gathered:

Job	Total Cost	Complete?	Sold?
301	$ 610	Yes	No
302	1,300	Yes	Yes
303	460	No	No
304	2,670	Yes	No
305	3,800	Yes	No
306	230	No	No
307	300	Yes	Yes
308	650	No	No
309	1,035	No	No
310	217	No	No

The beginning balance of Finished Goods was zero.

Required:

1. Calculate the balance in Work in Process at the end of the month.
2. Calculate the balance in Finished Goods at the end of the month.
3. Calculate Cost of Goods Sold for the month.

OBJECTIVE 4

Exercise 5-19 Job-Order Cost Sheets, Balance in Work in Process and Finished Goods

Berne Company, a job-order costing firm, worked on three jobs in July. Data are as follows:

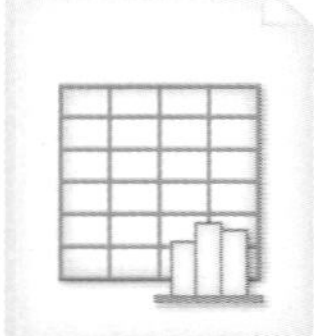

	Job 73	Job 74	Job 75
Balance, July 1	$8,450	$0	$0
Direct materials	$7,450	$12,300	$16,150
Direct labour	$12,000	$10,500	$23,000
Machine hours	400	350	1,000

Overhead is applied to jobs at the rate of $20 per machine hour. By July 31, Jobs 73 and 75 were completed. Jobs 70 and 73 were sold. Job 74 remained in process. On July 1, the balance in Finished Goods was $49,000 (consisting of Job 70 for $19,000 and Job 72 for $30,000).

Berne prices its jobs at cost plus 30 percent. During July, variable marketing expenses were 10 percent of sales, and fixed marketing expenses were $2,000; administrative expenses were $4,800.

Required:

1. Prepare job-order cost sheets for all jobs in process during July, showing all costs through July 31.

2. Calculate the balance in Work in Process as at July 31.
3. Calculate the balance in Finished Goods as at July 31.
4. Calculate Cost of Goods Sold for July.
5. Prepare an income statement for Berne Company for the month of July.

Exercise 5-20 Cost Flows

OBJECTIVE 4

Consider the following independent jobs. Overhead is applied in department 1 at the rate of $6 per direct labour hour. Overhead is applied in department 2 at the rate of $8 per machine hour. Direct labour wages average $10 per hour in each department.

	Job 213	Job 214	Job 217	Job 225
Total sales revenue	?	$4,375	$5,600	$1,150
Price per unit	$12	?	$14	$5
Materials used in production	$365	?	$488	$207
Department 1, direct labour cost	?	$700	$2,000	$230
Department 1, machine hours	15	35	50	12
Department 2, direct labour cost	$50	$100	?	$0
Department 2, machine hours	25	50	?	?
Department 1, overhead applied	$90	?	$1,200	$138
Department 2, overhead applied	?	$400	$160	$0
Total manufacturing cost	$855	$3,073	?	$575
Number of units	?	350	400	?
Unit cost	$8.55	?	$9.87	?

Required:

Fill in the missing data for each job.

Exercise 5-21 Job Cost Flows

OBJECTIVE 4

Venice Company uses a normal job-order costing system. The company has two departments through which most jobs pass. Overhead is applied using a plantwide overhead rate of $17 per direct labour hour. During the year, several jobs were completed. Data pertaining to one such job, Job 9-601, follow.

Direct materials	$54,000
Direct labour cost:	
Department A (12,000 hours @ $18)	$216,000
Department B (4,000 hours @ $18)	$72,000
Machine hours used:	
Department A	300
Department B	3,600
Units produced	25,000

For Requirements 3 and 4, assume that Venice uses departmental overhead rates. In department A, overhead is applied at the rate of $9 per direct labour hour. In department B, overhead is applied at the rate of $13 per machine hour.

Required:

1. Compute the total cost of Job 9-601.
2. Compute the per-unit manufacturing cost for Job 9-601.
3. Compute the total cost of Job 9-601.
4. Compute the per-unit manufacturing cost for Job 9-601.

OBJECTIVE 4

Exercise 5-22 Calculation of Work in Process and Cost of Goods Sold with Multiple Jobs

Greenthumb Landscape Design designs landscape plans and plants the material for clients. On April 1, there were three jobs in process: Jobs 68, 69, and 70. During April, two more jobs were started: Jobs 71 and 72. By April 30, Jobs 69, 70, and 72 were completed and sold. The following data were gathered:

	Job 68	Job 69	Job 70	Job 71	Job 72
Balance, April 1	$540	$1,230	$990	$ 0	$ 0
Direct materials	700	560	75	3,500	2,750
Direct labour	500	600	90	2,500	2,000

Overhead is applied at the rate of 120 percent of direct labour cost. Jobs are sold at cost plus 40 percent. Selling and administrative expenses for April totalled $3,670.

Required:

1. Prepare job-order cost sheets for each job as at April 30.
2. Calculate the ending balance in Work in Process (as at April 30) and Cost of Goods Sold for April.
3. Construct an income statement for Greenthumb Landscape Design for the month of April.

OBJECTIVE 5

Exercise 5-23 (*Appendix 5A*) Journal Entries

Garrity Inc. uses a job-order costing system. During the month of May, the following transactions occurred:

a. Purchased materials on account for $27,800.
b. Requisitioned materials totalling $21,000 for use in production. Of the total, $9,300 was for Job 58, $6,900 was for Job 59, and the remainder was for Job 60.
c. Incurred direct labour for the month of $27,000, with an average wage of $15 per hour. Job 58 used 800 hours; Job 59, 600 hours; and Job 60, 400 hours.
d. Incurred and paid actual overhead of $15,500 (credit Various Payables).
e. Charged overhead to production at the rate of $7.50 per direct labour hour.
f. Completed and transferred Jobs 58 and 59 to Finished Goods.
g. Sold Job 57 (see beginning balance of Finished Goods) and Job 58 to their respective clients on account for a price of cost plus 40 percent.

Beginning balances as of May 1 were:

Materials	$ 5,170
Work in Process	0
Finished Goods (Job 57)	31,400

Required:

1. Prepare the journal entries for transactions (a) through (g).
2. Prepare brief job-order cost sheets for Jobs 58, 59, and 60.
3. Calculate the ending balance of Raw Materials.
4. Calculate the ending balance of Work in Process.
5. Calculate the ending balance of Finished Goods.

OBJECTIVE 6

Exercise 5-24 (*Appendix 5B*) Direct Method of Support Department Cost Allocation

Dexter Company is divided into two operating divisions: battery and small motors. The company allocates power and human resources costs to each operating division using the direct method. Power costs are allocated on the basis of the number of machine hours, and human resources costs on the basis of the number of employees. Support department cost allocations using the direct method are based on the following data:

	Support Departments		Operating Divisions	
	Power	Human Resources	Battery	Small Motors
Overhead costs	$150,000	$365,000	$290,000	$127,500
Machine hours	2,500	2,500	7,500	4,500
Number of employees	35	45	25	75
Direct labour hours	—	—	25,000	115,000

Required:

1. Calculate the allocation ratios for power and human resources. (Carry these calculations out to three significant digits.)
2. Allocate the support service costs to the producing departments.
3. Assume departmental overhead rates are based on direct labour hours. Calculate the overhead rate for the battery division and for the small motors division. (Round overhead rates to the nearest cent.)

Exercise 5-25 (*Appendix 5B*) Sequential Method of Support Department Cost Allocation

OBJECTIVE 6

Refer to **Exercise 5-24** for data. Now assume that Dexter Company uses the sequential method to allocate support department costs to the producing departments. Human resources is allocated first in the sequential method for Dexter.

Required:

1. Calculate the allocation ratios for power and human resources. (Carry these calculations out to three significant digits.)
2. Allocate the support service costs to the producing departments.
3. Assume departmental overhead rates are based on direct labour hours. Calculate the overhead rate for the battery division and for the small motors division (round overhead rates to the nearest cent).
4. CONCEPTUAL CONNECTION What is the difference between the direct method and the sequential method of allocating support centre costs? Which is better?

PROBLEMS

Problem 5-26 Overhead Application and Job-Order Costing

Julian Company is a job-order costing firm that uses a plantwide overhead rate based on direct labour hours. Estimated information for the year is as follows:

Overhead	$665,000
Direct labour hours	100,000

Julian worked on five jobs in July. Data are as follows:

	Job 210	Job 211	Job 212	Job 213	Job 214
Balance, July 1	$32,780	$51,770	$29,600	$ 0	$ 0
Direct materials	$25,500	$39,800	$24,450	$13,600	$18,420
Direct labour cost	$60,000	$28,500	$41,500	$23,000	$21,300
Direct labour hours	4,000	1,900	2,700	1,500	1,400

By July 31, Jobs 210 and 212 were completed and sold. The remaining jobs were in process.

(Continued)

Check figures:

2. Total cost Job 212 = $113,505
4. Cost of goods sold = $258,385

Required:

1. Calculate the plantwide overhead rate for Julian Company.
2. Prepare job-order cost sheets for each job showing all costs through July 31.
3. Calculate the balance in Work in Process as at July 31.
4. Calculate Cost of Goods Sold for July.

OBJECTIVE 1 3

Problem 5-27 Job Cost, Source Documents

Marlowe Detective Agency performs investigative work for a variety of clients. Recently, Alban Insurance Company asked Marlowe to investigate a series of suspicious claims for whiplash. In each case, the claimant was driving on a highway and was suddenly rear-ended by an Alban-insured client. The claimants were all driving old, uninsured automobiles. The Alban clients reported that the claimants suddenly changed lanes in front of them, and the accidents were unavoidable. Alban suspected that these "accidents" were the result of insurance fraud. Basically, the claimants cruised the expressways in virtually worthless cars, attempting to cut in front of expensive late-model cars that would surely be insured. Alban believed that the injuries were faked.

Inspector Briant spent 37 hours shadowing the claimants and taking pictures as necessary. His surveillance methods located the office of a doctor used by all claimants. He also took pictures of claimants performing tasks that they had sworn were now impossible to perform due to whiplash injuries. Inspector Ackerman spent 48 hours using the Internet to research court records in adjoining provinces to locate the names of the claimants and their doctor. He found a pattern of similar insurance claims for each of the claimants.

Marlowe Detective Agency bills clients for detective time at $120 per hour. Transportation is charged at $0.50 per kilometre. The agency logged 510 kilometres on the Alban job. The miscellaneous costs of the job amounted to $120.

Required:

1. Prepare a job-order cost sheet for the Alban job.
2. Why is overhead not specified in the charges? How does Marlowe charge clients for the use of overhead (e.g., the ongoing costs of the office—supplies, paper for notes and reports, telephone, utilities)?
3. The kilometres are tallied from a source document. Design a source document for this use, and make up data for it that would total the 510 kilometres driven on the Alban job.

Check figure:

1. Total = $10,575

OBJECTIVE 4

Problem 5-28 Calculating Ending Work in Process, Income Statement

Kenno Prosthetics Company produces artificial limbs for individuals. Each prosthetic is unique. On January 1, three jobs (identified by the name of the person being fitted with the prosthetic) were in process with the following costs:

	Asher	Bryson	Cooper
Direct materials	$ 400	$1,360	$ 3,120
Direct labour	1,400	2,800	4,200
Applied overhead	1,120	2,240	3,360
Total	$2,920	$6,400	$10,680

During the month of January, two more jobs were started, for Davison and Egberts. Materials and labour costs incurred by each job in January are as follows:

	Materials	Direct Labour
Asher	$2,400	$1,200
Bryson	2,200	800
Cooper	3,440	1,000
Davison	5,240	6,600
Egberts	1,040	720

Cooper's and Davison's prosthetics were completed and sold by January 31.

Required:

1. If overhead is applied on the basis of direct labour dollars, what is the overhead rate?
2. Prepare simple job-order cost sheets for each of the five jobs in process during January.
3. What is the ending balance of Work in Process as at January 31? What is the Cost of Goods Sold in January?
4. Suppose that Kenno Prosthetics Company prices its jobs at cost plus 20 percent. In addition, during January, marketing and administrative costs of $3,400 were incurred. Prepare an income statement for the month of January.

Check figure:
3. Ending Work in Process January 31 = $19,856

Problem 5-29 Overhead Applied to Jobs, Departmental Overhead Rates

OBJECTIVE 

Watson Products Inc. uses a normal job-order costing system. Currently, a plantwide overhead rate based on machine hours is used. Marlon Burke, the plant manager, has heard that departmental overhead rates can offer significantly better cost assignments than a plantwide rate can offer. Watson has the following data for its two departments for the coming year:

	Department A	Department B
Overhead costs (estimated)	$2,660,000	$924,000
Normal activity (machine hours)	140,000	84,000

Required:

1. Calculate a predetermined overhead rate for the plant as a whole based on machine hours.
2. Compute predetermined overhead rates for each department using machine hours. (Carry your calculations out to three decimal places.)
3. Job 73 used 40 machine hours from department A and 60 machine hours from department B. Job 74 used 60 machine hours from department A and 40 machine hours from department B. Compute the overhead cost assigned to each job using the plantwide rate calculated in Requirement 1. Repeat the computation using the departmental rates found in Requirement 2. Which of the two approaches gives the fairer assignment? Why?
4. Repeat Requirement 3, assuming the expected overhead cost for department B is $1,596,000 (not $924,000). For this company, would you recommend departmental rates over a plantwide rate?
5. CONCEPTUAL CONNECTION In most instances, why would a departmental rate be preferable to a plantwide rate?

Check figures:
2. Dept A, $19 per machine hour; Dept B, $11 per machine hour
4. Plantwide rate, $19 per machine hour; Dept B, $19 per machine hour

Problem 5-30 Overhead Rates, Unit Costs

OBJECTIVE 

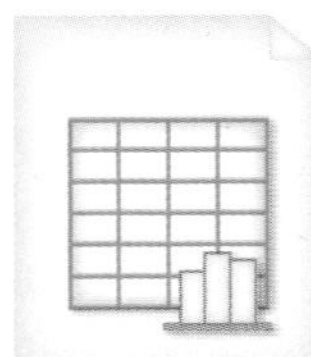

Xanning Company manufactures specialty tools to customer order. There are three producing departments. Departmental information on budgeted overhead and various activity measures for the coming year is as follows:

	Welding	Assembly	Finishing
Estimated overhead	$200,000	$22,000	$250,000
Direct labour hours	4,500	10,000	6,000
Direct labour cost	$90,000	$150,000	$120,000
Machine hours	5,000	1,000	2,000

Currently, overhead is applied on the basis of machine hours using a plantwide rate. However, Janine, the controller, has been wondering whether it might be worthwhile to use departmental overhead rates. She has analyzed the overhead costs and drivers for the various departments and decided that welding and finishing should base their overhead rates on machine hours and that assembly should base its overhead rate on direct labour hours.

(Continued)

Janine has been asked to prepare bids for two jobs with the following information:

	Job 1	Job 2
Direct materials	$4,500	$8,600
Direct labour cost	$1,000	$2,000
Direct labour hours:		
Welding	10	20
Assembly	60	20
Finishing	30	80
Number of machine hours:		
Welding	50	30
Assembly	40	5
Finishing	110	165

The typical bid price includes a 30 percent markup over full manufacturing cost.

Check figures:

2. Finishing department overhead rate = $125 per machine hour
2. Total manufacturing cost Job 2 = $32,469

Required:

1. Calculate a plantwide rate for Xanning Company based on machine hours. What is the bid price of each job using this rate?
2. Calculate departmental overhead rates for the producing departments. What is the bid price of each job using these rates? (Round all answers to the nearest dollar.)

OBJECTIVE 

Problem 5-31 Calculate Cost and Use It to Calculate Price

Morris, Leibowitz, and Guliani is a relatively new law firm that specializes in major accident injury cases. The partners have been reviewing their cost accumulation accounting system and are not confident that they are billing enough to their clients. Essentially, their work consists of three partners analyzing the merits of each case, preparing a lawsuit, and appearing in court on behalf of their clients.

Each partner is assisted by a junior lawyer and has an administrative assistant. The only other people employed by the firm are a receptionist, an accountant/office manager, and two clerks. The expenses related to the firm's operation are as follows:

	Junior Lawyer	Administrative Assistant	Depreciation on Equipment
Morris	$75,000	$45,000	$15,000
Leibowitz	90,000	40,000	26,000
Guliani	80,000	60,000	21,250

	Other Costs
Salaries	$360,000
Rent	180,000
Office expenses	120,000
Other	206,250

Each of the partners would like to earn $250,000 per year. They each expect to bill for 1,750 hours per year and to absorb the cost of their junior lawyers in their own billing.

Check figures:

Morris total cost: $673,750;
Morris per hour charge: $385

Required:

How much will each lawyer have to set as his/her hourly billing rate to accomplish the objectives set out?

Problem 5-32 (*Appendix 5A*) Unit Cost, Ending Work in Process, Journal Entries

OBJECTIVE 

During August, Pamell Inc. worked on two jobs. Data relating to these two jobs follow:

	Job 64	Job 65
Units in each order	500	1,000
Units sold	500	—
Materials requisitioned	$19,840	$15,760
Direct labour hours	900	1,260
Direct labour cost	$17,100	$23,940

Overhead is assigned on the basis of direct labour hours at a rate of $37. During August, Job 64 was completed and transferred to Finished Goods. Job 65 was the only unfinished job at the end of the month.

Required:

1. Calculate the per-unit cost of Job 64.
2. Compute the ending balance in the Work in Process account.
3. Prepare the journal entries reflecting the completion and sale on account of Job 64. The selling price is 160 percent of cost.

Check figure:
2. Ending Work in Process = $86,320

Problem 5-33 (*Appendix 5A*) Journal Entries, Job Costs

OBJECTIVE 4 5

The following transactions occurred during the month of April for Olakala Company:

a. Purchased materials costing $3,000 on account.
b. Requisitioned materials totalling $1,700 for use in production: $500 for Job 443 and the remainder for Job 444.
c. Recorded 50 hours of direct labour on Job 443 and 100 hours on Job 444 for the month. Direct labourers are paid at the rate of $8 per hour.
d. Applied overhead using a plantwide rate of $7.50 per direct labour hour.
e. Incurred and paid in cash actual overhead for the month of $1,230.
f. Completed and transferred Job 443 to Finished Goods.
g. Sold on account Job 442, which had been completed and transferred to Finished Goods in March, for cost ($2,000) plus 25 percent.

Required:

1. Prepare journal entries for transactions (a) through (e).
2. Prepare job-order cost sheets for Jobs 443 and 444. Prepare journal entries for transactions (f) and (g).
3. Prepare a statement of cost of goods manufactured for April. Assume that the beginning balance in the Raw Materials account was $1,400 and that the beginning balance in the Work in Process account was zero.

Check figure:
2. Total Job 444 = $2,750

Problem 5-34 (*Appendix 5A*) Predetermined Overhead Rates, Variances, Cost Flows

OBJECTIVE  

Playmore Costume Company, located in Toronto, sews costumes for plays and musicals. Playmore considers itself primarily a service firm, as it never produces costumes without a pre-existing order and only purchases materials to the specifications of the particular job. Any finished goods ending inventory is temporary and is zeroed out as soon as the show producer pays for the order. Overhead is applied on the basis of direct labour cost. During the first quarter of the year, the following activity took place in each of the accounts listed:

(Continued)

Work in Process

Bal.	17,000	Complete	245,000
DL	80,000		
OH	140,000		
DM	40,000		
Bal.	32,000		

Finished Goods

Bal.	40,000	Sold	210,000
Complete	245,000		
Bal.	75,000		

Overhead

	138,500		140,000
		Bal.	1,500

Cost of Goods Sold

210,000	

Job 32 was the only job in process at the end of the first quarter. A total of 1,000 direct labour hours at $10 per hour were charged to Job 32.

Required:

1. Assuming that overhead is applied on the basis of direct labour cost, what was the overhead rate used during the first quarter of the year?
2. What was the applied overhead for the first quarter? The actual overhead? The under- or overapplied overhead?
3. What was the cost of the goods manufactured for the quarter?
4. Assume that the overhead variance is closed to the Cost of Goods Sold account. Prepare the journal entry to close out the Overhead Control account. What is the adjusted balance in Cost of Goods Sold?
5. For Job 32, identify the costs incurred for direct materials, direct labour, and overhead.

Check figures:
1. Overhead rate = 175%
3. Cost of goods manufactured = $245,000

OBJECTIVE 2 4 5

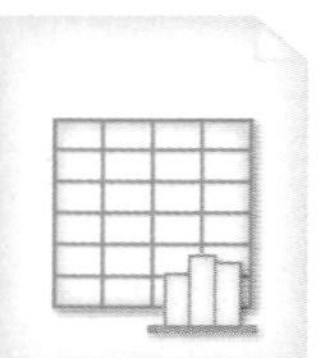

Problem 5-35 (*Appendix 5A*) Overhead Application, Journal Entries, Job Cost

At the beginning of the year, Dillon Company budgeted overhead of $180,000 as well as 15,000 direct labour hours. During the year, Job K456 was completed with the following information: direct materials cost, $2,340; direct labour cost, $3,600. The average wage for Dillon Company employees is $10 per hour.

By the end of the year, 15,400 direct labour hours had actually been worked, and Dillon Company incurred the following actual overhead costs for the year:

Equipment lease	$ 5,000
Depreciation on building	20,000
Indirect labour	100,000
Utilities	15,000
Other overhead	45,000

Required:

1. Calculate the overhead rate for the year.
2. Calculate the total cost of Job K456.
3. Prepare the journal entries to record actual overhead and to apply overhead to production for the year.
4. Is overhead overapplied or underapplied? By how much?
5. Assuming that the normal cost of goods sold for the year is $700,000, what is the adjusted cost of goods sold?

Check figures:
2. Applied overhead = $4,320
5. Adjusted cost of goods sold = $700,200

Problem 5-36 (*Appendix 5A*) Journal Entries, T-Accounts

OBJECTIVE 1 4 5

Lowder Inc. builds custom conveyor systems for warehouses and distribution centres. During the month of July, the following occurred:

a. Purchased materials on account for $117,360.
b. Requisitioned materials totalling $47,600 for use in production: $19,700 for Job 703 and the remainder for Job 704.
c. Recorded direct labour payroll for the month of $39,480 with an average wage of $21 per hour. Job 703 required 620 direct labour hours; Job 704 required 1,260 direct labour hours.
d. Incurred and paid actual overhead of $37,650.
e. Charged overhead to production at the rate of $18 per direct labour hour.
f. Completed Job 703 and transferred it to Finished Goods.
g. Kept Job 704, which was started during July, in process at the end of the month.
h. Sold Job 700, which had been completed in May, on account for cost plus 30 percent.

Beginning balances as at July 1 were:

Raw Materials	$ 9.652
Work in Process (for Job 703)	12,850
Finished Goods (for Job 700)	16,845

Required:

1. Prepare the journal entries for events (a) through (e).
2. Prepare simple job-order cost sheets for Jobs 703 and 704.
3. Prepare the journal entries for events (f) and (h).
4. Calculate the ending balances of the following:
   a. Raw Materials
   b. Work in Process
   c. Finished Goods

Check figures:
2. Total Job 703 = $57,730
4. Ending Work in Process = $76,040

Problem 5-37 (*Appendix 5B*) Support Department Cost Allocation

MedServices Inc. is divided into two operating departments: laboratory and tissue pathology. The company allocates delivery and accounting costs to each operating department. Delivery costs include the costs of a fleet of vans and drivers that drive throughout the province each day to clinics and doctors' offices to pick up samples and deliver them to the centrally located laboratory and tissue pathology offices. Delivery costs are allocated on the basis of the number of samples. Accounting costs are allocated on the basis of the number of transactions processed. No effort is made to separate fixed and variable costs; however, only budgeted costs are allocated. Allocations for the coming year are based on the following data:

	Support Departments		Producing Departments	
	Delivery	Accounting	Laboratory	Tissue Pathology
Overhead costs	$600,000	$675,000	$862,500	$1,140,000
Number of samples	—	—	175,500	117,000
Transactions processed	5,000	500	61,750	33,250

Check figures:
1. Laboratory costs: $1,661,250
2. Laboratory costs: $1,659,563

Required:

1. Assign the support department costs by using the direct method.
2. Assign the support department costs by using the sequential method.

Problem 5-38 (*Appendix 5B*) Support Department Cost Allocation: Comparison of Methods of Allocation

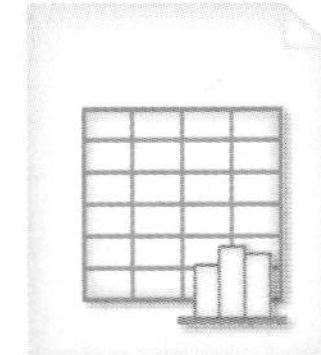

Bender Automotive Works Inc. manufactures a variety of front-end assemblies for automobiles. A front-end assembly is the unified front of an automobile that includes the headlamps, fender,

(Continued)

and surrounding metal/plastic. Bender has two producing departments: drilling and assembly. Usually, the front-end assemblies are ordered in batches of 100.

Two support departments provide support for Bender's operating units: maintenance and power. Budgeted data for the coming quarter follow. The company does not separate fixed and variable costs.

	Support Departments		Producing Departments	
	Maintenance	Power	Drilling	Assembly
Overhead costs	$475,000	$650,000	$197,000	$154,000
Machine hours	—	27,500	38,000	9,500
Kilowatt-hours	54,000	—	46,000	385,000
Direct labour hours	—	—	5,000	40,000

The predetermined overhead rate for drilling is computed on the basis of machine hours; direct labour hours are used for assembly. Maintenance costs are allocated based on machine hours and power costs are allocated based on kilowatt-hours.

Recently, a truck manufacturer requested a bid on a three-year contract that would supply front-end assemblies to a nearby factory. The prime costs for a batch of 100 front-end assemblies are $3,475. It takes two machine hours to produce a batch in the drilling department and 50 direct labour hours to assemble the 100 front-end assemblies in the assembly department.

Bender's policy is to bid full manufacturing cost, plus 15 percent.

Check figure:

1. Drilling rate = $17.01 per machine hour (direct); $13.83 (sequential)

Required:

1. Prepare bids for Bender Automotive Works by using each of the following allocation methods:
   a. Direct method.
   b. Sequential method (allocate maintenance department first).
2. Which method most accurately reflects the cost of producing the front-end assemblies? Why?

PROFESSIONAL EXAMINATION PROBLEMS*

Professional Examination Problem 5-39 Job Order Costing—ScaleDown Inc.

ScaleDown Inc. is a manufacturer of furnishings for infants and children. The company uses a normal job-order costing system. ScaleDown's WIP inventory at April 30, 2018, consisted of the following jobs:

Job Number	Items	Units	Accumulated Cost
CBS102	Cribs	20,000	$ 900,000
PLP086	Playpens	15,000	420,000
DRS114	Dressers	25,000	250,000
			$1,570,000

The company's finished goods inventory, using the FIFO method, consisted of five items:

Item	Quantity and Unit Cost	Accumulated Cost
Cribs	7,500 units @ $64	$ 480,000
Strollers	13,000 units @ $23	299,000
Carriages	11,200 units @ $102	1,142,400
Dressers	21,000 units @ $55	1,155,000
Playpens	19,400 units @ $35	679,000
		$3,755,400

ScaleDown applies factory overhead on the basis of direct labour hours. The company's factory overhead budget for the fiscal year ending May 31, 2018, totalled $4,500,000 and the company plans to expend 600,000 direct labour hours during this period. Through the first 11 months of the year, a total of 555,000 direct labour hours were worked and total factory overhead amounted to $4,273,500.

At the end of April, the balance in ScaleDown's raw materials inventory account, which includes both raw materials and purchased parts, was $668,000. Additions to and requisitions from raw materials inventory during the month of May included:

	Raw Materials	Purchased Parts
Additions	$242,000	$396,000
Requisitions:		
Job CBS102	51,000	104,000
Job PLP086	3,000	10,800
Job DRS114	124,000	87,000
Job STR077 (10,000 strollers)	2,000	81,000
Job CRG098 (5,000 carriages)	65,000	187,000

During the month of May, ScaleDown's factory payroll consisted of the following:

Account	Hours	Cost
CBS102	12,000	$122,400
PLP086	4,400	43,200
DRS114	19,500	200,500
STR077	3,500	30,000
CRG098	14,000	138,000
Indirect	3,000	29,400
Supervision		57,600
		$621,100

The following charts show jobs completed and units shipped for the month of May:

Job Number	Items	Quantity
CBS102	Cribs	20,000
PLP086	Playpens	15,000
STR077	Strollers	10,000
CRG098	Carriages	5,000

Items	Quantity Shipped
Cribs	17,500
Playpens	21,000
Strollers	14,000
Dressers	18,000
Carriages	6,000

Required:

1. Describe when it is appropriate for a company to use a job-order cost system.
2. Calculate the dollar balance in ScaleDown's WIP inventory account as at May 31, 2018.
3. Calculate the dollar amount related to the playpens in ScaleDown's finished goods inventory as at May 31, 2018.
4. Explain the proper accounting treatment for over- or underapplied overhead balances when using a job-order cost system.

Professional Examination Problem 5-40 (*Appendix 5B*) Departmental Costing and Cost Allocation—Corinth Ltd.

Corinth Ltd. consists of four departments: personnel and purchasing, which are service departments; and machining and painting, which are production departments. Budgeted data for the year consisted of the following:

Item	Personnel	Purchasing	Machining	Painting
Overhead costs	$40,000	$35,000	$128,000	$48,000
Number of employees	10	15	25	138
Machine hours	0	0	23,500	29
Direct labour costs	$0	$0	$32,000	$147,000
Purchase requisitions	6	0	2,650	450

Required:

1. Allocate the two service departments' costs using the sequential allocation method and develop departmental overhead rates for each of the production departments using the most logical base for each department.
2. Calculate and give the journal entry to record the total amount of under- or overapplied overhead for the company, assuming the following actual results for the year:

	Machining	Painting
Overhead costs	$173,000	$ 78,540
Direct labour costs	$ 38,300	$139,750
Machine hours	24,150	29

3. Briefly discuss reasons for allocating service department costs.

CASES

Case 5-41 Overhead Assignment: Actual and Normal Activity Compared

Reynolds Printing Company specializes in wedding announcements. Reynolds uses an actual job-order costing system. An actual overhead rate is calculated at the end of each month using actual direct labour hours and overhead for the month. Once the actual cost of a job is determined, the customer is billed at actual cost plus 50 percent.

During April, Mrs. Lucky, a good friend of owner Jane Reynolds, ordered three sets of wedding announcements to be delivered May 10, June 10, and July 10, respectively. Reynolds scheduled production for each order on May 7, June 7, and July 7, respectively. The orders were assigned job numbers 115, 116, and 117, respectively.

Reynolds assured Mrs. Lucky that she would attend each of her daughters' weddings. Out of sympathy and friendship, she also offered a lower price. Instead of cost plus 50 percent, she gave her a special price of cost plus 25 percent. Additionally, she agreed to wait until the final wedding to bill for the three jobs.

On August 15, Reynolds asked her accountant to bring her the completed job-order cost sheets for Jobs 115, 116, and 117. She also gave instructions to lower the price as had been agreed upon. The cost sheets revealed the following information:

	Job 115	Job 116	Job 117
Cost of direct materials	$250.00	$250.00	$250.00
Cost of direct labour (5 hours)	25.00	25.00	25.00
Cost of overhead	200.00	400.00	400.00
Total cost	$475.00	$675.00	$675.00
Total price	$593.75	$843.75	$843.75
Number of announcements	500	500	500

Reynolds could not understand why the overhead costs assigned to Jobs 116 and 117 were so much higher than those for Job 115. She asked for an overhead cost summary sheet for the months of May, June, and July, which showed that actual overhead costs were $20,000 each month. She also discovered that direct labour hours worked on all jobs were 500 hours in May and 250 hours each in June and July.

Required:

1. How do you think Mrs. Lucky will feel when she receives the bill for the three sets of wedding announcements?
2. Explain how the overhead costs were assigned to each job.
3. Assume that Reynolds's average activity is 500 hours per month and that the company usually experiences overhead costs of $240,000 each year. Can you recommend a better way to assign overhead costs to jobs? Recompute the cost of each job and its price given your method of overhead cost assignment. Which method do you think is best? Why?

Check figures:
2. May overhead assigned = $200
3. Total cost = $475

Case 5-42 Assigning Overhead to Jobs—Ethical Issues

Miroslav Klose, CMA and controller of the parts division of Matthaus Inc., was meeting with Franz Beckenbauer, manager of the division. The topic of discussion was the assignment of overhead costs to jobs and their impact on the division's pricing decisions. Their conversation was as follows:

Miroslav: Franz, as you know, about 25 percent of our business is based on government contracts, with the other 75 percent based on jobs from private sources won through bidding. During the past several years, our private business has declined. We have been losing more bids than usual. After some careful investigation, I have concluded that we are overpricing some jobs because of improper assignment of overhead costs. Some jobs are also being underpriced. Unfortunately, the jobs being overpriced are coming from our higher-volume, labour-intensive products; thus, we are losing business.

Franz: I think I understand. Jobs associated with our high-volume products are being assigned more overhead than they should be receiving. Then, when we add our standard 40 percent markup, we end up with a higher price than our competitors, who assign costs more accurately.

Miroslav: Exactly. We have two producing departments—one labour-intensive and the other machine-intensive. The labour-intensive department generates much less overhead than the machine-intensive department. Furthermore, virtually all of our high-volume jobs are labour-intensive. We have been using a plantwide rate based on direct labour hours to assign overhead to all jobs. As a result, the high-volume, labour-intensive jobs receive a greater share of the machine-intensive department's overhead than they deserve. This problem can be greatly alleviated by switching to departmental overhead rates. For example, an average high-volume job would be assigned $100,000 of overhead using a plantwide rate and only $70,000 using departmental rates. The change would lower our bidding price on high-volume jobs by an average of $42,000 per job. By increasing the accuracy of our product costing, we can make better pricing decisions and win back much of our private-sector business.

Franz: Sounds good. When can you implement the change in overhead rates?

Miroslav: It won't take long. I can have the new system working within four to six weeks—certainly by the start of the new fiscal year.

(Continued)

Franz: Hold it. I just thought of a possible complication. As I recall, most of our government contract work is done in the labour-intensive department. This new overhead assignment scheme will push down the cost on the government jobs, and we will lose revenues. They pay us full cost plus our standard markup. This business is not threatened by our current costing procedures, but we can't switch our rates for only the private business. Government auditors would question the lack of consistency in our costing procedures.

Miroslav: You do have a point. I thought of this issue also. According to my estimates, we will gain more revenues from the private sector than we will lose from our government contracts. Besides, the costs of our government jobs are distorted; in effect, we are overcharging the government.

Franz: They don't know that and never will unless we switch our overhead assignment procedures. I think I have the solution. Officially, let's keep our plantwide overhead rate. All of the official records will reflect this overhead costing approach for both our private and government business. Unofficially, I want you to develop a separate set of books that can be used to generate the information we need to prepare competitive bids for our private-sector business.

Required:

1. Do you believe that the solution proposed by Franz is ethical? Explain.
2. Suppose that Miroslav decides that Franz's solution is not right and objects strongly. Further suppose that, despite Miroslav's objections, Franz insists strongly on implementing the action. What should Miroslav do?

Case 5-43 Under- and Overapplied Overhead Disposition

Clifford Foster, the president of Quality Graphics, was meeting with his controller, Curtis Flavin, to discuss the results for their current fiscal year. Sales and production had been significantly lower than the previous year and the company had taken a major hit to cost of goods sold at year-end. Foster wanted to know what had happened and why.

Flavin explained that the overhead costs in the year were significantly greater than the overhead costs that had been applied to production during the period. The overhead costs were consistent with the previous year but, with such a fall in production, a large portion of these costs had remained unapplied. Also, because of the change in the market sector in which they competed, the company had dramatically increased its inventory levels, both in finished goods inventory and work-in-process.

Flavin indicated that they had always charged any unapplied overhead directly to Cost of Goods Sold at the end of the year because the financial statements that went to their bank must reflect the actual results. Clifford was very concerned that, due to the contraction of sales and the major reduction in profit, the bank might become unduly concerned about the future prospects of the business and either reduce their line of credit or call their loan.

He has asked you to examine the possibilities of mitigating the impact of the adjustment to cost of goods sold.

Required:

Write a memo to Clifford outlining the possible changes that could be made to the accounting for the adjustment.

Case 5-44 Plantwide Overhead Rates versus Departmental Overhead Rates

Steven Brown was in his office contemplating how to respond to his boss on a question he had been asked in a staff meeting that morning. Steven is the controller of Precision Parts Inc., a manufacturer of precision stainless steel parts for the nuclear industry. His boss, Ivayla Corovic, the vice-president of finance, had recently asked why Steven's department was spending so much time accumulating departmental information on the manufacturing process to be used to calculate departmental overhead rates when a simple plantwide rate would suffice.

The manufacturing operation has three departments: stamping, grinding, and finishing. The stamping department has three large machines; each was purchased for $5 million and is being operated by semi-skilled operators. The grinding department has a number of smaller machines; each was acquired for $100,000 and is being operated by highly skilled operators. The finishing department is staffed by a dozen very skilled individuals who are responsible for ensuring that the parts produced meet the very stringent specifications of the nuclear industry.

Steven developed a system for calculating overhead in each department based on the following: machine hours in the stamping department; direct labour hours in the grinding department; and direct labour hours in the finishing department. In the stamping department, each machine operates for 3,000 hours per year, while the three operators work 1,750 hours each per year. In the grinding department, the 12 operators work 1,500 hours each per year. In the finishing department, the operators work 1,750 hours each per year.

The two products that the company produces use different resources in the departments as follows:

	Product A	**Product B**
Stamping	0.1 machine hour	0.3 machine hour
Grinding	0.5 direct labour hour	0.2 direct labour hour
Finishing	0.2 direct labour hour	0.2 direct labour hour

The company produces three times as many of product B as of product A. Overhead costs for the three departments are $3 million, $5 million, and $2 million, respectively. Steven knew that Ivayla did not appreciate that the operations in each department were quite different, so he had to develop a very strong argument in support of his position on using departmental overhead rates rather than a single plantwide rate. Steven believed that departmental rates gave a better allocation of cost, but he had to give Ivayla a detailed answer.

Required:

Prepare a one-page memo supporting Steven's position. Be as specific as possible.

Case 5-45 Comprehensive Cost Allocation

Mercy Hospital is a regional hospital in Sault Ste. Marie, Ontario, which has recently completed a new building at a cost of $825 million. This building will be depreciated over a period of 30 years. With the new building and the expanded operation, the hospital wants to enter into discussions with the Ontario provincial government about a cost recovery formula that will ensure that the operating costs of the hospital are met on an ongoing basis.

The hospital is divided into three types of patient care areas: surgery, oncology, and internal medicine. The 1,000 beds of the hospital are divided between the three areas as follows: Surgery has 150 beds, oncology has 200 beds, and internal medicine has 650 beds. Nurses comprise one of the largest costs of the hospital and the various areas require nursing staff in proportion to the number of beds in the unit. Surgery requires an average of 8 nurses per bed, oncology 5 nurses per bed, and internal medicine 3 nurses per bed. On average, counting benefits and overtime premiums, nurses make about $82,500 per year.

In designing the new building, great care was taken to make the very best use of the facilities, and the staff are very pleased with the final outcome. The patient care areas make up 54 percent of the total floor area while the oncology treatment clinics make up 18 percent. Surgical operating rooms and internal medicine clinics each cover 10 percent of the space; the cafeteria takes 4 percent; administrative offices are 3 percent; and the pharmacy covers the remaining 1 percent.

The operating budget is composed of many different areas of the hospital and all costs must be recovered from an allocation from the province based on patient days. In calculating patient days, hospitals use 360 days per year and Mercy expects to achieve a 90 percent usage rate once it reaches full operations. Patient days for each department are calculated by multiplying the number of beds in the department by the estimated usage, which is 360 days multiplied by the usage rate.

The budgets for each area of the hospital, excluding nurses' salaries, are as follows: cafeteria, $60 million; internal medicine, $53.5 million; oncology, $26.5 million; surgery, $23.5 million; maintenance, $22.5 million; pharmacy, $12.5 million; and administration, $62.5 million. Cafeteria costs are allocated to the patient care areas on the basis of number of nurses in each patient care area; maintenance and building depreciation costs are allocated on the basis of occupancy and bed spaces; pharmacy and administration costs are allocated on the basis of number of beds in each patient care area.

Required:

You have been asked to recommend to the hospital directors the rate per patient day that the hospital should request for each area of patient care from the provincial government and to back up your recommendation with complete detail.

6

Process Costing

nagelestock.com/Alamy Stock Photo

After studying Chapter 6, you should be able to:

1. Describe the basic characteristics and cost flows associated with process manufacturing.
2. Define equivalent units and explain their role in process costing. Explain the differences between the weighted average method and the FIFO method of accounting for process costs.
3. Prepare a departmental production report using the weighted average method.
4. Explain how nonuniform inputs and multiple processing departments affect process costing.
5. (*Appendix 6A*) Examine how process costing may be used by service and manufacturing firms.
6. (*Appendix 6B*) Prepare a departmental production report using the FIFO method.

EXPERIENCE MANAGERIAL DECISIONS
with BP

The only consideration that most people give to gasoline is the price charged at the local pump. However, **BP**, one of the largest energy companies in the world, has been thinking about this issue and a lot more for quite a long time. BP was founded in 1901 after William D'Arcy obtained permission from the Shah of Persia to dig for oil in what is now the Iranian desert. BP drastically expanded its reach as it built a new refinery in Australia in 1924 and then established new exploration and excavation sites in places such as Canada, South America, Africa, and Europe, in addition to its Middle Eastern sites. As of the early 21st century, BP had active excavation and production occurring in 22 countries. BP runs its processes nonstop—24 hours a day, 365 days a year—to produce at full capacity, which represents 2.6 million barrels of oil each day or approximately 30 barrels every second! Producing that much of anything is a bit mind-boggling, which hints at the importance of BP's effective process-costing system in determining the costs associated with its numerous products, which include gasoline, heating fuel, greases, and asphalt.

In order to determine costs for a particular process, BP needs to know the total costs of production and the total number of units processed in a specified period of time. The costs include raw crude oil, which varies widely from sweet West Texas crude to heavier Canadian crude, plus labour and management overhead. Other costs include catalysts, which enhance the reactivity to make a molecule actually turn into something else, and chemicals, which become part of the final product. BP goes to a lot of trouble to combine its process-costing system outputs, current market prices, and a linear programming model in order to calculate the most profitable mix of products to produce from a given mix of raw crude materials.

Determining the costs associated with running a refinery with a continuous production process is complex. However, by calculating process costs and carefully setting production levels and product mixes, BP is able to manage this complex process at its facilities around the globe, thereby providing continued big profits for use in future energy discovery and distribution efforts and, to pay for extraordinary costs such as the cleanup, litigation, and reparations associated with the Gulf of Mexico oil spill in 2010 which, according to the final tally released in mid-2016, cost the company $61.6 billion.

CHARACTERISTICS OF PROCESS MANUFACTURING

OBJECTIVE 

Describe the basic characteristics and cost flows associated with process manufacturing.

A company's production process helps to determine the best way of accounting for its costs. Let's assume that a large number of similar products pass through an identical set of processes. Since each product within a product line passing through these processes would receive similar "doses" of materials, labour, and manufacturing overhead, the company's accountant would see no need to accumulate costs by batches (a job-order costing system). Instead, the accountant should recommend accumulating costs by process.

Process costing works well whenever relatively homogeneous products pass through a series of processes and receive similar amounts of manufacturing costs. Large manufacturing plants—such as those that produce chemicals, tires, and food—use process costing. For example, Americans purchase about 100 million bags of chocolate chips every year, many of which are made by Nestlè. The company accounts for the costs of its vast chocolate chip production by using a process-costing system.

Let's consider the process-costing environment of Health Blend Nutritional Supplements, a manufacturer of mineral and herbal supplements and vitamins. Health Blend uses the following three processes:

- **Picking:** In the picking department, direct labour selects the appropriate ingredients such as herbs, vitamins, minerals, and inert materials (typically some binder such as cornstarch) for the product to be manufactured. Then, the materials are measured and combined in a mixer to blend them thoroughly. The resulting mixture is sent to the encapsulating department.
- **Encapsulating:** In encapsulating, the completed mixture is loaded into a machine that fills one-half of a gelatin capsule. The filled half is inserted in the other half of the capsule, and a safety seal is applied. This process is entirely mechanized. Manufacturing overhead in this department consists of depreciation on machinery, maintenance of machinery, supervision, fringe benefits, lights, and power. Finally, the filled capsules are transferred to the bottling department.
- **Bottling:** In the bottling department, the filled capsules are loaded into a hopper, counted, and automatically dispensed into bottles that are then mechanically capped. The direct labour then manually packs the correct number of bottles into boxes to ship to retailers.

Types of Processes

Production at Health Blend Nutritional Supplements is an example of sequential processing. **Sequential processing** requires that units pass through one process before they can be worked on in later processes. Exhibit 6.1 shows the sequential pattern of the manufacture of Health Blend's supplements and vitamins.

To summarize, in a process firm, units typically pass through a series of manufacturing or producing departments; in each department or process is an operation that brings a product one step closer to completion. As well, in each department, materials, labour, and manufacturing overhead may be needed. Upon completion of a particular process, the partially completed goods are transferred to the next department. After passing through the final department, the goods are completed and transferred to the warehouse.

Parallel processing is another processing pattern that requires two or more sequential processes to produce a finished good. Partially completed units (e.g., two subcomponents) can be worked on simultaneously in different processes and then brought together in a final process for completion. Consider, for example, the manufacture of hard disc drives for personal computers. In one series of processes, write heads and cartridge disc drives are produced, assembled, and tested. In a second series of processes, printed circuit boards are produced and tested. These two major subcomponents then come together for assembly in the final process. Exhibit 6.2 portrays this type of process pattern. Notice that

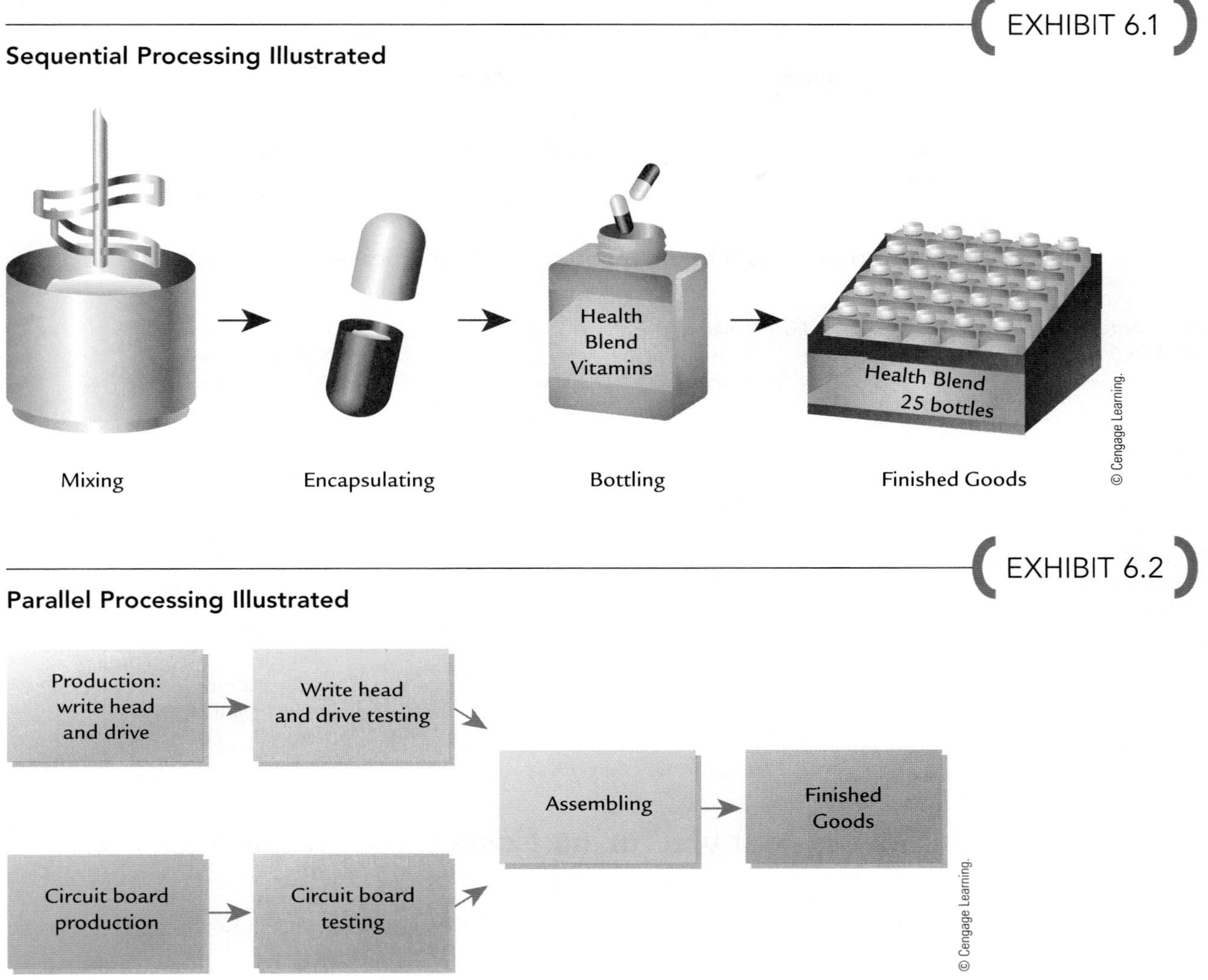

write head and cartridge disc drive production, assembly, and testing processes can occur independently of (or parallel to) circuit board production and testing processes.

Other forms of parallel processes also exist. However, regardless of which processing pattern exists within a firm, all units produced share a common property. Since units are homogeneous and subjected to the same operations for a given process, each unit produced in a period should receive the same unit cost. Understanding how unit costs are computed requires an understanding of the manufacturing cost flows that take place in a process-costing firm.

How Costs Flow through the Accounts in Process Costing

The manufacturing cost flows for a process-costing system are generally the same as those for a job-order system. As raw materials are purchased, the cost of these materials flows into a Raw Materials Inventory account. During production, raw materials, direct labour, and applied manufacturing overhead costs flow into a Work in Process (WIP) account. When goods are completed, the cost of the completed goods is transferred from WIP to the Finished Goods (FG) account. Finally, as goods are sold, the cost of the finished goods is transferred

> **concept Q&A**
>
> Will process costing be the same for sequential and parallel processing systems?
>
> Answers on pages 734 to 738.

to the Cost of Goods Sold (COGS) account. The journal entries required for a process-costing system generally parallel those described earlier for a job-order costing system.

Although job-order and process cost flows are generally similar, some differences exist. In process costing, each producing department has its own WIP account. As goods are completed in one department, they are transferred to the next department. Exhibit 6.3 illustrates this process for Health Blend. By the end of the process, all manufacturing costs end up in the final department (here, bottling) with the final product.

EXHIBIT 6.3

Flow of Manufacturing Costs through the Accounts of a Process-Costing Firm

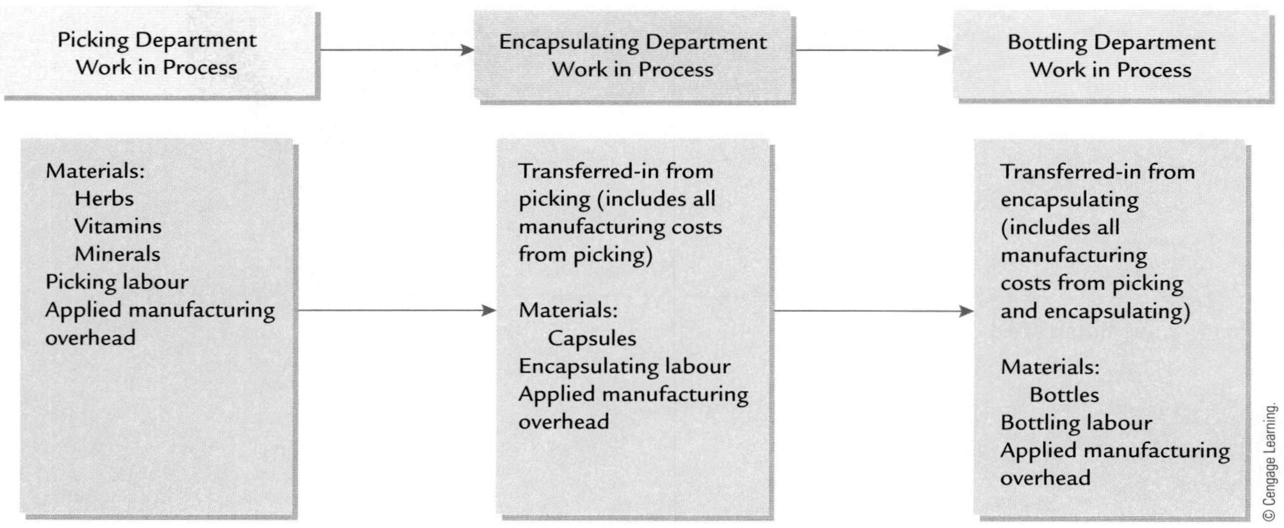

Flow of Manufacturing Costs through the Accounts of a Process-Costing Firm

Cornerstone 6.1 attaches costs to the various departments and shows how the costs flow from one department to the next.

CORNERSTONE 6.1

Calculating Cost Flows without Work in Process

Information:

Suppose that Health Blend decides to produce 2,000 bottles of multivitamins, all of which are started and completed in the current period, with the following costs:

	Picking Department	Encapsulating Department	Bottling Department
Direct materials	$1,700	$1,000	$800
Direct labour	50	60	300
Applied manufacturing overhead	450	500	600

Required:

1. Calculate the costs transferred out of each department.
2. Prepare journal entries that reflect these cost transfers.

(Continued)

CORNERSTONE 6.1

(Continued)

Solution:

1.

	Picking Department	Encapsulating Department	Bottling Department
Direct materials	$1,700	$1,000	$ 800
Direct labour	50	60	300
Applied manufacturing overhead	450	500	600
Costs added	2,200	1,560	1,700
Costs transferred in	0	2,200	3,760
Costs transferred out	$2,200	$3,760	$5,460

2. Journal entries:

Work in Process (Encapsulating)	2,200	
Work in Process (Picking)		2,200
Work in Process (Bottling)	3,760	
Work in Process (Encapsulating)		3,760
Finished Goods	5,460	
Work in Process (Bottling)		5,460

Why:

The purpose of cost accounting is to assign the costs of manufacturing products to the proper inventory accounts. Therefore, understanding how the costs flow through the system is essential to assigning such costs. Starting with the simple case allows us to focus on the critical elements without undue complications.

Cornerstone 6.1 shows that when the mixture is transferred from the picking department to the encapsulating department, it takes $2,200 of cost along with it. **Transferred-in costs** are costs transferred from a prior process to a subsequent process. From the viewpoint of the subsequent process, transferred-in costs are a type of raw material cost added at the beginning of production for the subsequent process and are always considered to be 100 percent complete. The same relationship exists between the encapsulating and bottling departments. The completed bottles are transferred to the FG warehouse at a total cost of $5,460.

Accumulating Costs in the Production Report

In process costing, costs are accumulated by department for a period of time. The **production report**, as seen later in Cornerstone 6.6, is the document that summarizes the manufacturing activity that takes place in a process department for a given period of time. A production report contains information on costs transferred in from prior departments, as well as costs added in the department such as direct materials, direct labour, and manufacturing overhead; it is subsidiary to the WIP account, just as the job-order cost sheet is subsidiary to the WIP account in a job-order costing system.

A production report provides information about the physical units processed in a department and also about the manufacturing costs associated with them. Thus, a production report is divided into a unit information

analytical Q&A

Suppose encapsulating transferred $5,000 of partially completed goods to bottling, and bottling added $3,000 of manufacturing cost and then transferred the completed goods to the finished goods warehouse. What two journal entries would be made for these transfers?

Answers on pages 734 to 738.

section and a cost information section. The unit information section has two major subdivisions: (1) units to account for, and (2) units accounted for. Similarly, the cost information section has two major subdivisions: (1) costs to account for, and (2) costs accounted for.

A production report traces the flow of units through a department, identifies the costs charged to the department, shows the computation of unit costs, and reveals the disposition of the department's costs for the reporting period.

THE IMPACT OF WORK-IN-PROCESS INVENTORIES ON PROCESS COSTING

OBJECTIVE 2

Define equivalent units and explain their role in process costing. Explain the differences between the weighted average method and the FIFO method of accounting for process costs.

The computation of unit cost for the work performed during a period is a key part of the production report. This unit cost is needed both to compute the cost of goods transferred out of a department and to value ending work-in-process (EWIP) inventory. Conceptually, calculating the unit cost is easy—just divide total cost by the number of units produced. However, the presence of WIP inventories causes two problems:

1. Defining the units produced can be difficult, given that some units produced during a period are complete, while those in ending WIP are not. This is handled through the concept of equivalent units of production.
2. How should the costs and work of beginning work-in-process (BWIP) inventory be treated? Should they be counted with the current period work and costs, or treated separately? Two methods have been developed to solve this problem: the weighted average method and the FIFO method.

analytical Q&A

In March, a company completed 8,000 tonnes of aluminum ingots and had 2,500 tonnes of ingots in EWIP, 60 percent complete. Calculate the equivalent units for March.

Answers on pages 734 to 738.

Equivalent Units of Production

By definition, EWIP is not complete. Thus, a unit completed and transferred out during the period is not identical (or equivalent) to one in EWIP inventory, and the cost attached to the two units should not be the same. In computing the unit cost, the output of the period must be defined. A major problem of process costing is making this definition.

To illustrate the output problem of process costing, assume that department A had the following data for October:

Units in BWIP	—
Units completed	1,000
Units in EWIP (25 percent complete)	600
Total manufacturing costs	$11,500

What is the output in October for this department? 1,000? 1,600? If the answer is 1,000 units, the effort expended on the units in EWIP is ignored. Furthermore, the manufacturing costs incurred in October belong both to the units completed and to the partially completed units in EWIP. On the other hand, if the answer is 1,600 units, the fact that the 600 units in EWIP are only partially completed is ignored. Somehow, output must be measured so that it reflects the effort expended on both completed and partially completed units.

The solution is to calculate equivalent units of output. **Equivalent units of output** are the complete units that could have been produced given the total amount of manufacturing effort expended for the period under consideration. Determining equivalent units of output for transferred-out units is easy; a unit would not be transferred out unless it was complete. Thus, every transferred-out unit is one equivalent unit. Units remaining in EWIP inventory, however, are not complete. Thus, someone in production must "eyeball" EWIP to estimate its average degree of completion. Cornerstone 6.2 illustrates how to calculate equivalent units of production, with the assumption that the degree of completion has been fairly assessed and stated.

Calculating Equivalent Units of Production: No Beginning Work in Process

CORNERSTONE 6.2

CORNERSTONE VIDEO

Concept:

100 units completed = 100 equivalent units

200 units, 50 percent complete = 100 equivalent units

Information:

October data: 1,000 units completed; 600 units, 25 percent complete

Required:

Calculate the equivalent units for October.

Solution:

1,000 units completed = 1,000 equivalent units

600 units × 0.25 = 150 equivalent units

October output = 1,150 equivalent units

Why:

Using equivalent units is the method whereby we can appropriately allocate costs among fully completed units and partially completed units in a fair manner. Since partially completed units should only attract the amount of costs in proportion to their average stage of completion, this is an essential step in determining cost allocation.

Corporate and Social Responsibility

Estimating the degree of completion is an act that requires judgment and, at the same time, ethical behaviour. For example, overestimating the degree of completion will increase the equivalent units of output and decrease per-unit costs. This outcome, in turn, would cause an increase both in net income (COGS will be less) and in assets (EWIP inventory will increase). Deliberately overestimating the degree of completion would clearly be in violation of ethical professional practice. In fact, manufacturing support costs can be a breeding ground for the manipulation of accounting numbers by deceptive managers eager to conceal their fraudulent activities (MacArthur, Waldrup, and Fane, 2004: 31): ". . . overhead costing is particularly susceptible to fraud because the costing is complex, the accounts have relatively large dollar values, and nonaccounting managers don't understand how they work. To nonaccountants, overhead accounts are a confusing 'black box' because accumulating and applying overhead is one of the least understood activities of the costing process."

Knowing the output for a period and the manufacturing costs for the department for that period, a unit cost can be calculated as:

$$\text{Unit cost} = \frac{\text{Total cost}}{\text{Equivalent units}}$$

The unit cost can then be used to determine the cost of units transferred out and the cost of the units in EWIP.

Cornerstone 6.3 shows how the calculations are done when there is no BWIP. In Cornerstone 6.3, the unit cost of \$10 is used to assign a cost of \$10,000 (= \$10 × 1,000) to the 1,000 units transferred out and a cost of \$1,500 (= \$10 × 150) to the 600 units in EWIP. Notice that the cost of the EWIP is obtained by multiplying the unit cost by the *equivalent* units, not the actual number of partially completed units.

CORNERSTONE 6.3

Measuring Output and Assigning Costs: No Beginning Work in Process

Information:

Manufacturing costs of the period, \$11,500; units transferred out, 1,000; units in EWIP, 600 (25 percent complete)

Required:

1. Calculate the unit cost.
2. Calculate the cost of goods transferred out and the cost of EWIP.

(Continued)

CORNERSTONE

6.3

(Continued)

Solution:

1. Unit cost:

Equivalent units:	
Units completed	1,000
Units in EWIP × 25 percent (600 × 0.25)	150
Equivalent units	1,150

$$\text{Cost per equivalent unit} = \frac{\$11{,}500}{1{,}150} = \$10$$

2. Cost assignment:

Cost of goods transferred out = \$10 per unit × 1,000 equivalent units = \$10,000

Cost of EWIP = \$10 per unit × 150 equivalent units = \$1,500

Why:

Knowing the costs and the equivalent units will enable the assignment of costs to the units in an appropriate and fair manner. Starting with no beginning inventory simplifies the process and allows us to focus on the critical elements of cost assignment.

Two Methods of Treating Beginning Work-in-Process Inventory

The calculations illustrated in Cornerstones 6.2 and 6.3 become more complicated when there are BWIP inventories. The work already done on these partially completed units represents prior-period work, and the costs assigned to them are prior-period costs, which appear on the balance sheet of the prior period. In computing a current-period unit cost for a department, two approaches have evolved for dealing with the prior-period output and prior-period costs found in BWIP: the weighted average method and the FIFO method.

- The **weighted average costing method** combines beginning inventory costs for work done in the previous period with current-period costs for work in the current period to calculate this period's unit cost. In essence, the costs carried over from the prior period are counted as if they belong to the current period. Thus, beginning inventory work and costs are pooled with current work and costs, and an average unit cost is computed and applied to both units transferred out and units remaining in ending inventory.
- The **FIFO costing method** separates costs of work on the equivalent units in beginning inventory from costs of work on the equivalent units produced during the current period. Only current costs on work are used to calculate this period's unit cost. It is assumed that units from beginning inventory are completed first and transferred out. The costs of these units include the costs of the work done in the prior period plus current-period costs necessary to complete the units. Units started in the current period are divided into two categories: units started and completed, and units started but not finished (EWIP). Units in both of these categories are valued using the current period's cost per equivalent unit.

If product costs do not change from period to period, or if there is no BWIP inventory, the FIFO and weighted average methods yield the same results. The weighted average method is discussed in more detail in the next section. Further discussion of the FIFO method is found later in the chapter.

analytical Q&A

During March, a moulding process transferred out 9,000 equivalent units to the grinding department and had 1,250 equivalent units in EWIP. The cost per equivalent unit for March was \$8.00. Calculate the cost of goods transferred out and the cost of the EWIP.

Answers on pages 734 to 738.

YOU DECIDE Estimating the Degree of Completion

You are the cost accounting manager for a plant that produces riding lawn mowers. The plant manager receives a bonus at the end of each quarter if the plant's income meets or exceeds the quarter's budgeted income. The plant had no WIP at the beginning of the quarter; however, it had 2,500 partially completed units at the end of the quarter. During the quarter, 4,000 units were completed and sold. Manufacturing costs for the quarter totalled $2,750,000. The production-line supervisors estimated that the units in process at the end of the quarter were 40 percent finished. Using this initial estimate, the income for the quarter was $190,000 less than the quarter's budgeted profit. After seeing this tentative result, the plant manager approaches you and argues that the average degree of the completion is underestimated and that it should be 60 percent rather than 40 percent. He explains that he personally examined the partially completed work and that 60 percent is his best guess. He would prefer that this new estimate be used.

What effect does the estimated degree of completion have on the quarter's income? Should you use the new estimate?

The two estimates produce significantly different unit costs, as illustrated below:

Measure	Equation	40% Degree of Completion	60% Degree of Completion
Total equivalent units	Equivalent units = Units completed + (Units in EWIP × Percentage complete)	4,000 + (0.40 × 2,500) = 5,000 equivalent units	4,000 + (0.60 × 2,500) = 5,500 equivalent units
Unit cost	$\text{Unit cost} = \frac{\text{Total cost}}{\text{Equivalent units}}$	$2,750,000/5,000 = $550	$2,750,000/5,500 = $500
Cost of goods sold	Cost of goods sold = Units sold × Unit cost	4,000 × $550 = $2,200,000	4,000 × $500 = $2,000,000

Compared to the 40 percent estimate, the 60 percent estimate increases income by $200,000.

As the cost accounting manager, whether you would feel comfortable using the new estimate depends on several factors. First, is the 60 percent estimate more valid than the 40 percent estimate? (Suppose that the line supervisors insist that their estimate is correct.) Second, does the plant manager regularly participate in estimating degree of completion? If not, what are his motives for doing so this time? Answers to these questions are important. The estimate by the plant manager allows income to increase by a sufficient amount to qualify him for a bonus. If evidence favours the 40 percent estimate and the plant manager's motive is the bonus, then an ethical dilemma exists. In this case, you would need to follow the organization's established policies on the resolution of such conflicts.

Estimating the degree of completion is a vital and important part of process costing and needs to be done with care and honesty.

WEIGHTED AVERAGE COSTING

OBJECTIVE 

Prepare a departmental production report using the weighted average method.

The weighted average costing method treats beginning inventory costs and the accompanying equivalent output as if they belong to the current period. This is done for costs by adding the manufacturing costs in BWIP to the manufacturing costs incurred during the current period. The total cost is treated as if it were the current period's total manufacturing cost. Similarly, beginning inventory output and current period output are merged in the calculation of equivalent units. Under the weighted average method, equivalent units of output are computed by adding units completed to equivalent units in EWIP. Notice that the equivalent units in BWIP are included in the computation. Consequently, these units are counted as part of the current period's equivalent units of output.

concept Q&A

What is the key difference between FIFO and the weighted average costing methods?

Answers on pages 734 to 738.

Overview of the Weighted Average Method

The essential conceptual and computational features of the weighted average method are illustrated in Cornerstone 6.4, which uses production data for Health Blend's picking department for July. The objective is to calculate a unit cost for July and to use this unit cost to value both goods transferred out and EWIP.

Cornerstone 6.4 illustrates that costs from BWIP are pooled with costs added to production during July. These total pooled costs ($13,650) are averaged and assigned to units transferred out and to units in EWIP. On the output side, it is necessary to concentrate on the degree of completion of all units at the end of the period. There is no need to be concerned with the percentage of completion of BWIP inventory. The only issue is whether these units are complete or not by the end of July. Thus, equivalent units are computed by pooling manufacturing efforts from June and July.

Measuring Output and Assigning Costs: Weighted Average Method

CORNERSTONE 6.4

CORNERSTONE VIDEO

Information:

Production:	
Units in process, July 1, 75 percent complete	20,000
Units completed and transferred out	50,000
Units in process, July 31, 25 percent complete	10,000
Costs:	
Work in process, July 1	$ 3,525
Costs added during July	10,125

Required:

1. Calculate an output measure for July.
2. Assign costs to units transferred out and EWIP using the weighted average method.

Solution:

1. Equivalent units:

Key: [■] = 10,000 units completed [□] = 10,000 units, 25% complete

Output for July:
60,000 total units ⟶ Become 52,500 equivalent units

Units completed:
BWIP:

[■][■] = 20,000

Units Started and Completed:

[■][■][■] = 30,000 50,000

+ EWIP, 25% complete:

[□] = 2,500

52,500

(Continued)

6.4

(Continued)

2. Cost assignment:

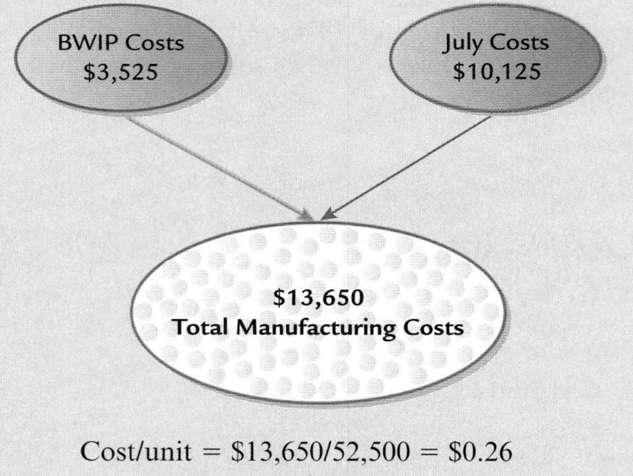

Cost/unit = $13,650/52,500 = $0.26

Transferred out ($0.26 × 50,000)	$13,000
EWIP ($0.26 × 2,500)	650
Total cost assigned	$13,650

Why:

The valuation of beginning inventory introduces a new complication as there are various methods of valuing inventory. If the weighted average method is used, each unit processed during the period will be valued using the same costs. In order to do the calculations, the cost of beginning work-in-process inventory is added to the current period costs; the total costs are then assigned to the output for the period, both the fully completed units and the partially completed units at the end of the period.

analytical Q&A

The weighted average cost per equivalent unit for April is $10. There were 3,800 units completed and transferred out during April and 750 units in EWIP, 40 percent complete. Calculate the cost of goods transferred out and the cost assigned to EWIP.

Answers on pages 734 to 738.

Five Steps in Preparing a Production Report

The elements of Cornerstone 6.4 are used to prepare a production report. Recall that the production report summarizes cost and manufacturing activity for a producing department for a given period of time. The production report is subsidiary to the WIP account for a department. The following five steps describe the general pattern of a process-costing production report:

1. Physical flow analysis
2. Calculation of equivalent units
3. Calculation of unit cost
4. Valuation of inventories (goods transferred out and EWIP)
5. Cost reconciliation

These five steps provide structure to the method of accounting for process costs.

Step 1: Physical Flow Analysis The purpose of step 1 is to trace the physical units of production. Physical units are not equivalent units; they are units that may be in any stage of completion. The **physical flow schedule**, like the one shown in Cornerstone 6.5 for Health

Preparing a Physical Flow Schedule

CORNERSTONE 6.5

Information:

Production:	
Units in process, July 1, 75 percent complete	20,000
Units completed and transferred out	50,000
Units in process, July 31, 25 percent complete	10,000

Required:

Prepare a physical flow schedule.

Solution:

Units started and completed = Units completed − Units in BWIP
= 50,000 − 20,000
= 30,000

Units started = Units started and completed + Units in EWIP
= 30,000 + 10,000
= 40,000

Physical flow schedule:

Units to account for:		
Units in BWIP (75 percent complete)	20,000	
Units started during the period	40,000	
Total units to account for	60,000	
Units accounted for:		
Units completed and transferred out:		
Started and completed	30,000	
From BWIP	20,000	50,000
Units in EWIP (25 percent complete)		10,000
Total units accounted for		60,000

Why:

In order to allocate the costs to the production units, we must understand how the physical units flow through the department and ensure that we have identified all units. These represent not equivalent units but the number of actual units to ensure that we have accounted for all of them at the end of the cost assignment process.

Blend's picking department, provides an analysis of the physical flow of units. To construct the schedule from the information given in the example, two calculations are needed:

Units started and completed = Total units completed − Units in BWIP
Units started = Units started and completed + Units in EWIP

Notice that the "Total units to account for" must equal the "Total units accounted for. " The physical flow schedule is important because it contains the information needed to calculate equivalent units (step 2).

Step 2: Calculation of Equivalent Units Given the information in the physical flow schedule, the weighted average equivalent units for July can be calculated as follows:

Units completed	50,000
Add: Units in ending work in process × Percentage complete	
(10,000 units × 25 percent)	2,500
Equivalent units of output	52,500

analytical Q&A

The following data are provided for the month of April:

Units in process, April 1, 40 percent complete	6,000 cases
Units completed and transferred out	20,000 cases

How many units were started and completed during April?

Answers on pages 734 to 738.

Notice that July's output is measured as 52,500 units, with 50,000 units completed and transferred out and 2,500 equivalent units from ending inventory (= 10,000 × 25 percent). What about beginning inventory? There were 20,000 units in beginning inventory, 75 percent complete. These units are included in the 50,000 units completed and transferred out during the month. Thus, the weighted average method treats beginning inventory units as if they were started and completed during the current period. Because of this, the equivalent unit schedule shown in step 2 shows only the total units completed. There is no need to show whether the units completed are from July or from BWIP, as was done in Cornerstone 6.4.

analytical Q&A

During June, 5,000 units were completed and transferred out, and there were 1,500 units in EWIP, 80 percent complete. How many equivalent units were completed in June, using the weighted average method?

Answers on pages 734 to 738.

Step 3: Calculation of Unit Cost In addition to July output, July manufacturing costs are needed to calculate a unit cost. The weighted average method rolls back and includes the manufacturing costs associated with the units in BWIP and counts these costs as if they belong to July. Thus, as Cornerstone 6.4 illustrated, these costs are pooled to define total manufacturing costs for July as:

Total manufacturing costs = BWIP for July + Costs added in July

Total manufacturing costs = \$3,525 + \$10,125 = \$13,650

The manufacturing costs carried over from the prior period (\$3,525) are treated as if they were current period costs. The unit cost for July is computed as follows:

Unit cost = Total costs/Equivalent units for July

$$\text{Unit cost} = \frac{\$13{,}650}{52{,}500}$$

$$= \$0.26 \text{ per equivalent unit}$$

Step 4: Valuation of Inventories Cornerstone 6.4 also showed how to value both goods transferred out and EWIP. Using the unit cost of \$0.26, we value the two inventories as follows:

- Cost of goods transferred to the encapsulating department is \$13,000 (= 50,000 units × \$0.26 per unit)
- Cost of EWIP is \$650 (= 2,500 equivalent units × \$0.26 per unit).

analytical Q&A

June had the following costs to account for:
BWIP: \$4,000
Incurred in June: \$27,000
There were 6,200 equivalent units produced in June. What is the unit cost for June using the weighted average method?

Answers on pages 734 to 738.

Notice that units completed (from step 1), equivalent units in EWIP (from step 2), and the unit cost (from step 3) were all needed to value both goods transferred out and EWIP.

Step 5: Cost Reconciliation The total manufacturing costs assigned to inventories are as follows:

Goods transferred out	\$13,000
Goods in EWIP	650
Total costs accounted for	\$13,650

The manufacturing costs to account for are also $13,650.

BWIP	$ 3,525
Incurred during the period	10,125
Total costs to account for	$13,650

Thus, the **cost reconciliation** checks to see if the costs to account for are exactly assigned to inventories. Remember, the total costs assigned to goods transferred out and to EWIP must be equal to the total costs in BWIP and the manufacturing costs incurred during the current period.

Production Report

Steps 1 through 5 provide all of the information needed to prepare a production report for the picking department for July. The method for preparing this report is shown in Cornerstone 6.6.

Preparing a Production Report: Weighted Average Method

CORNERSTONE 6.6

Information:

Steps 1 to 5 of the Health Blend example.

Required:

Prepare a production report.

Solution:

Health Blend
Picking Department Production Report
For July
(Weighted Average Method)

Unit Information

Physical Flow			
Units to account for:		Units accounted for:	
Units in beginning work in process	20,000	Units completed	50,000
Units started	40,000	Units in ending work in process	10,000
Total units to account for	60,000	Total units accounted for	60,000

Equivalent Units	
Units completed	50,000
Units in ending work in process	2,500
Total equivalent units	52,500

(Continued)

CORNERSTONE
6.6

(Continued)

Cost Information			
Costs to account for:			
Beginning work in process	$ 3,525		
Incurred during the period	10,125		
Total costs to account for	$13,650		
Cost per equivalent unit	$0.26 ($13,650/52,500)		

	Transferred Out	Ending Work in Process	Total
Costs accounted for:			
Goods transferred out ($0.26 × 50,000)	$13,000	$ —	$13,000
Goods in ending work in process ($0.26 × 2,500)	—	650	650
Total costs accounted for	$13,000	$650	$13,650

Why:

The production report brings together all five steps that we follow in calculating the costs of each type of inventory for the period. It allows us to ensure that all costs and all units are properly accounted for.

Evaluation of the Weighted Average Method

The major benefit of the weighted average method is simplicity. By treating units in BWIP as belonging to the current period, all equivalent units belong to the same category when it comes to calculating unit costs. Thus, unit cost computations are simplified. The main disadvantage of this method is reduced accuracy in computing unit costs for current period output and for units in BWIP. That is, since the weighted average method pools the manufacturing efforts of two periods, it is more difficult to accurately compute the unit costs for a single period. If the unit cost in a process is relatively stable from one period to the next, the weighted average method is reasonably accurate. However, if the price of manufacturing inputs increases significantly from one period to the next, the unit cost of current output is understated, and the unit cost of BWIP units is overstated. If greater accuracy in computing unit costs is desired, a company should use the FIFO method to determine unit costs.

MULTIPLE INPUTS, MULTIPLE DEPARTMENTS, AND HYBRID COSTING

OBJECTIVE 4

Explain how nonuniform inputs and multiple processing departments affect process costing.

Accounting for production under process costing is complicated by nonuniform application of manufacturing inputs and the presence of multiple processing departments. How process-costing methods address these complications will now be discussed.

Nonuniform Application of Manufacturing Inputs

Up to this point, we have assumed that WIP being 60 percent complete meant that 60 percent of materials, labour, and manufacturing overhead needed to complete the process have been used, and that another 40 percent are needed to finish the units. In other words, we have assumed that manufacturing inputs are applied uniformly as the manufacturing process unfolds.

Assuming uniform application of conversion costs (direct labour and manufacturing overhead) is not unreasonable. Direct labour input is usually needed throughout the process, and manufacturing overhead is normally assigned on the basis of direct labour hours. Direct materials, on the other hand, are not as likely to be applied uniformly. In many instances, materials are added at either the beginning or the end of the process, although materials may also be added at various stages of production.

Health Blend's three departments do not apply direct materials uniformly. In the picking and encapsulating departments, all materials are added at the beginning of the process. However, in the bottling department, materials are added both at the beginning (filled capsules and bottles) and at the end of the process (bottle caps and boxes).

WIP in the picking department that is 50 percent complete with respect to conversion inputs would be 100 percent complete with respect to the material inputs. But WIP in bottling that is 50 percent complete with respect to conversion would be 100 percent complete with respect to bottles and transferred-in capsules, but 0 percent complete with respect to bottle caps and boxes.

Different percentage completion figures for manufacturing inputs pose a problem for the calculation of equivalent units, unit cost, and valuation of EWIP (steps 2 to 4). Fortunately, the solution is relatively simple. Equivalent unit calculations are done for each category of manufacturing input. Thus, equivalent units are calculated for each category of materials and for conversion cost. Next, a unit cost for each category is computed. The individual category costs are then used in step 4 to cost out EWIP. The total unit cost is used to calculate the cost of goods transferred out in the same way as when there was only one input category. Cornerstone 6.7 shows how to calculate steps 2 through 4 with nonuniform inputs, using the weighted average method.

Calculating Equivalent Units and Unit Costs, and Valuing Inventories with Nonuniform Inputs

CORNERSTONE 6.7

CORNERSTONE VIDEO

Information:

The picking department of Health Blend has the following data for September:

Production:	
Units in process, September 1, 50 percent complete*	10,000
Units completed and transferred out	60,000
Units in process, September 30, 40 percent complete*	20,000
Costs:	
WIP, September 1:	
Materials	$ 1,600
Conversion costs	200
Total	$ 1,800
Current costs:	
Materials	$12,000
Conversion costs	3,200
Total	$15,200

* With respect to conversion costs, all materials are added at the beginning of the process.

(Continued)

CORNERSTONE
6.7

(Continued)

Required:

Perform steps 2 through 4 using the weighted average method.

Solution:

Step 2: Calculation of equivalent units, nonuniform application:

	Materials	Conversion
Units completed	60,000	60,000
Add: Units in EWIP × Percentage complete:		
= 20,000 × 100 percent	20,000	—
= 20,000 × 40 percent	—	8,000
Equivalent units of output	80,000	68,000

Step 3: Calculation of unit costs:

$$\text{Unit materials cost} = \frac{(\$1,600 + \$12,000)}{80,000}$$
$$= \$0.17$$

$$\text{Unit conversion cost} = \frac{(\$200 + \$3,200)}{68,000}$$
$$= \$0.05$$

$$\text{Total unit cost} = \text{Unit materials cost} + \text{Unit conversion cost}$$
$$= \$0.17 + \$0.05$$
$$= \$0.22 \text{ per completed unit}$$

Step 4: Valuation of EWIP and goods transferred out:

The cost of EWIP is as follows:

Materials: $0.17 × 20,000	$3,400
Conversion: $0.05 × 8,000	400
Total cost	$3,800

Valuation of goods transferred out:

Cost of goods transferred out = $0.22 × 60,000 = $13,200

Why:

In most manufacturing processes, the inputs are not added at the same rate over the entire process. Therefore, we must be able to distinguish among the inputs to account for the different rates at which the inputs are added. The equivalent units for each input will be the basis for allocating the cost of that input.

For illustrative purposes, a production report based on Cornerstone 6.7 is shown in Exhibit 6.4. As the example shows, applying manufacturing inputs at different stages of a process poses no serious problems. However, the effort required has increased.

Multiple Departments

In process manufacturing, some departments receive partially completed goods from prior departments. The usual approach is to treat transferred-in goods as a separate

EXHIBIT 6.4

Production Report: Weighted Average Method

Health Blend
Picking Department Production Report
For September
(Weighted Average Method)

Unit Information

Units to account for:		Units accounted for:	
Units in beginning work in process	10,000	Units completed	60,000
Units started during the period	70,000	Units in ending work in process	20,000
Total units to account for	80,000	Total units accounted for	80,000

	Equivalent Units	
	Materials	**Conversion Cost**
Units completed	60,000	60,000
Units in ending work in process	20,000[a]	8,000[b]
Total equivalent units	80,000	68,000

[a] 100% complete
[b] 40% complete

Cost Information

	Materials	**Conversion Cost**	**Total**
Costs to account for:			
Beginning work in process	$ 1,600	$ 200	$ 1,800
Incurred during the period	12,000	3,200	15,200
Total costs to account for	$13,600	$3,400	$17,000
Cost per equivalent unit	$ 0.17[c]	$ 0.05[d]	$0.22

[c] $13,600 ÷ 80,000 = $0.17
[d] $3,400 ÷ 68,000 = $0.05

	Transferred Out	**Ending Work in Process**	**Total**
Costs accounted for:			
Goods transferred out ($0.22 × 60,000)	$13,200	$ —	$13,200
Goods in ending work in process:			
Materials ($0.17 × 20,000)	—	3,400	3,400
Conversion ($0.05 × 8,000)	—	400	400
Total costs accounted for	$13,200	$3,800	$17,000

material category when calculating equivalent units. Thus, the department receiving transferred-in goods would have three input categories:

- transferred-in materials,
- materials added, and
- conversion costs.

In dealing with transferred-in goods, two important points should be remembered:

1. The cost of this material is the cost of the goods transferred out as calculated in the prior department.
2. The units started in the subsequent department correspond to the units transferred out from the prior department (assuming that there is a one-to-one relationship between the output measures of both departments).

Cornerstone 6.8 shows how to calculate the first three process-costing steps when there are transferred-in goods, where steps 2 and 3 are restricted to the transferred-in category.

CORNERSTONE 6.8

Calculating the Physical Flow Schedule, Equivalent Units, and Unit Costs for Transferred-In Goods

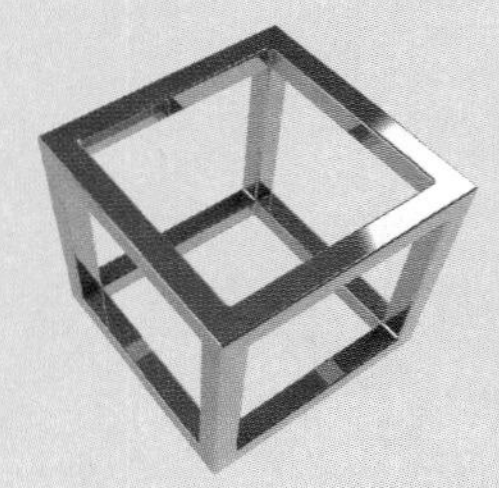

Information:

For September, Health Blend's encapsulating department had 15,000 units in beginning inventory (with transferred-in costs of $3,000) and completed 70,000 units during the month. Further, the picking department completed and transferred out 60,000 units at a cost of $13,200 in September.

Required:

1. Prepare a physical flow schedule for the encapsulating department.
2. Calculate equivalent units for the transferred-in category.
3. Calculate unit cost for the transferred-in category.

Solution:

1. In constructing a physical flow schedule for the encapsulating department, its dependence on the picking department must be considered:

Units to account for:	
Units in BWIP	15,000
Units transferred in during September	60,000
Total units to account for	75,000
Units accounted for:	
Units completed and transferred out:	
Started and completed	55,000
From BWIP	15,000
Units in EWIP	5,000
Total units accounted for	75,000

2. Equivalent units for the transferred-in category only:

Transferred in:	
Units completed	70,000
Add: Units in EWIP × Percentage complete (= 5,000 × 100 percent)*	5,000
Equivalent units of output	75,000

* Remember that the EWIP is 100 percent complete with respect to transferred-in costs, not to all costs of the encapsulating department.

3. To find the unit cost for the transferred-in category, we add the cost of the units transferred in from picking in September to the transferred-in costs in BWIP and divide by transferred-in equivalent units:

$$\text{Unit cost (transferred-in category)} = \frac{(\$13,200 + \$3,000)}{75,000} = \frac{\$16,200}{75,000} = \$0.216$$

(Continued)

Why:

The nature of manufacturing processes is that products move from department to department. As a product moves from one department to the next, the cost incurred in the previous department(s) must be included in the total cost of the units, but these costs represent fully completed units from the previous processes so they must be accounted for separately.

CORNERSTONE

6.8

(Continued)

The only additional complication introduced in the analysis for a subsequent department is the presence of the transferred-in category. As has just been shown, dealing with this category is similar to handling any other category. However, it must be remembered that the current cost of this special type of raw material is the cost of the units transferred in from the prior process and that the units transferred in are the units started.

analytical Q&A

A mixing process produced 200 equivalent units of material and 500 equivalent units of conversion activity during the month. If the materials cost was $400 and the conversion cost was $1,000, what is the cost per equivalent unit for the month?

Answers on pages 734 to 738.

Hybrid Costing

Hybrid costing is a combination of job-order costing (perhaps on a batch basis) and process costing. In some instances, a company will produce the basic product on a process costing basis and then add unique elements to certain products before they are completed. An example would be an automobile manufacturing plant, where the basic model is produced and then additional components, such as an upgraded stereo system or heavy-duty suspension, are added to the luxury version of the model. In these instances, elements of both process costing and job-order costing are used. Another example is the manufacture of refrigerators where the different models require different materials, yet manufacturing follows the same basic process. In this example, materials are applied to products on an individual basis while conversion costs (e.g., labour and overhead) are applied evenly to all refrigerators.

Why would a company use hybrid costing? A hybrid costing system is indicated when the cost of maintaining two separate costing systems is unreasonable, and yet the firm requires greater accuracy than is achieved by using either a job-order or process-costing system.

concept Q&A

How are transferred-in goods viewed and treated by the department receiving them?

Answers on pages 734 to 738.

APPENDIX 6A: SERVICE AND MANUFACTURING FIRMS

OBJECTIVE 

Examine how process costing may be used by service and manufacturing firms.

Any product or service that is basically homogeneous and repetitively produced can take advantage of a process-costing approach. Let's look at three possibilities:

1. Services
2. Manufacturing firms with a just-in-time (JIT) orientation
3. Traditional manufacturing firms

Services

Cheque processing in a bank, dental cleaning by a hygienist, air travel between Calgary and Vancouver, sorting mail by postal code, and laundering and pressing shirts are examples of homogeneous services that are repetitively produced. Although services cannot be stored, it is possible for firms engaged in service production to have WIP inventories. For example, a batch of tax returns can be partially completed at the end of a period. However, many services are provided so quickly that there are no WIP inventories. Dental cleanings, funerals, surgical operations, sonograms, and carpet cleanings are a few examples where WIP inventories would be virtually nonexistent. Therefore, process costing for services is relatively simple: The total costs for the period are divided by the number of services provided to compute unit cost.

$$\text{Unit cost} = \frac{\text{Total costs for the period}}{\text{Number of services provided}}$$

Manufacturing Firms with JIT Orientation

Manufacturing firms may also operate without significant WIP inventories. Specifically, firms that have adopted a just-in-time (JIT) approach to manufacturing view carrying unnecessary inventories as wasteful. These firms try to reduce WIP inventories to very low levels. Furthermore, JIT firms usually structure their manufacturing so that process costing can be used to determine product costs.

In many JIT firms, work cells are created that produce a product or subassembly from start to finish. Costs are collected by cell for a period of time, and output for the cell is measured for the same period. Unit costs are computed by dividing the costs of the period by output of the period.

$$\text{Unit cost} = \frac{\text{Total costs for the period}}{\text{Total output of the period}}$$

There is no ambiguity concerning what costs belong to the period and how output is measured. This simplification illustrates one of the significant benefits of JIT.

Traditional Manufacturing Firms

Finally, traditional manufacturing firms may have significant beginning and ending WIP inventories. This causes complications in process costing due to several factors, such as the presence of beginning and ending WIP inventories and different approaches to the treatment of beginning inventory cost. These complicating factors are explored in Appendix 6B.

APPENDIX 6B: PRODUCTION REPORT—FIRST-IN, FIRST-OUT COSTING

Prepare a departmental production report using the FIFO method.

Under the FIFO costing method, the equivalent units and manufacturing costs in BWIP are excluded from the current period unit cost calculation. This method recognizes that the work and costs carried over from the prior period legitimately belong to that period.

Differences between the First-In, First-Out and Weighted Average Methods

If changes occur in the prices of the manufacturing inputs from one period to the next, then FIFO produces a more accurate (i.e., more current) unit cost than does the weighted average method since the costs of each period are tracked separately. A more accurate unit cost means better cost control, better pricing decisions, and so on. Keep in mind that if the period is as short as a week or a month, the unit costs calculated under the two methods are not likely to differ much. In that case, the FIFO method has little value to offer over the weighted average method. Perhaps for this reason, many firms use the weighted average method.

Since FIFO excludes prior-period work and costs, it is necessary to create two categories of completed units:

1. BWIP units (FIFO assumes that units in BWIP are completed first, before any new units are started)
2. Units started and completed during the current period

For example, assume that a department had 20,000 units in BWIP and completed and transferred out a total of 50,000 units. Of the 50,000 completed units, 20,000 are the units initially found in WIP. The remaining 30,000 were started and completed during the current period.

These two categories of completed units are needed in the FIFO method so that each category can be costed correctly. For the units started and completed, the unit cost is obtained by dividing total current manufacturing costs by the current period equivalent units of output. However, for the BWIP units, the total associated manufacturing costs are the sum of the prior period costs plus the costs incurred in the current period to finish the units.

Example of the First-In, First-Out Method

Cornerstone 6.9 shows how FIFO handles output and cost calculations using the same Health Blend data used for the weighted average method (Cornerstone 6.4) to highlight the differences between the two methods. Cornerstone 6.9 shows that the equivalent unit calculation measures only the output for the current period.

Cornerstone 6.9 also reveals that costs from the current period and costs carried over from June (beginning inventory costs) are not pooled to calculate July's unit cost, as they would be when using the weighted average method. In the FIFO method, the unit cost calculation uses only July (current period) costs. The five steps used to determine production costs follow.

Calculating Output and Cost Assignments: First-In, First-Out Method

CORNERSTONE 6.9

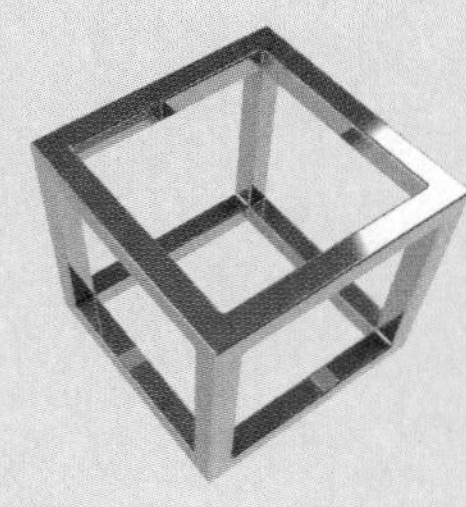

Information:

Production:	
Units in process, July 1, 75 percent complete	20,000
Units completed and transferred out	50,000
Units in process, July 31, 25 percent complete	10,000
Costs:	
Work in process, July 1	$ 3,525
Costs added during July	10,125

Required:

1. Calculate the output measure for July.
2. Assign costs to units transferred out and EWIP using the FIFO method.

(Continued)

CORNERSTONE **6.9**

(Continued)

Solution:

1. Equivalent units:

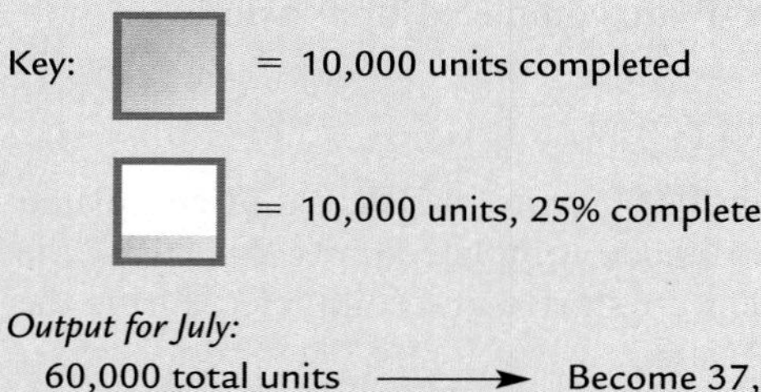

Output for July:

60,000 total units ⟶ Become 37,500 equivalent units

BWIP: To be completed (20,000 × 25%):

= 5,000

\+ Units started and completed:

= 30,000

\+ EWIP: Started but not completed

(10,000 × 0.25)

= 2,500

= 37,500

2. Cost assignment:
   Costs for July:

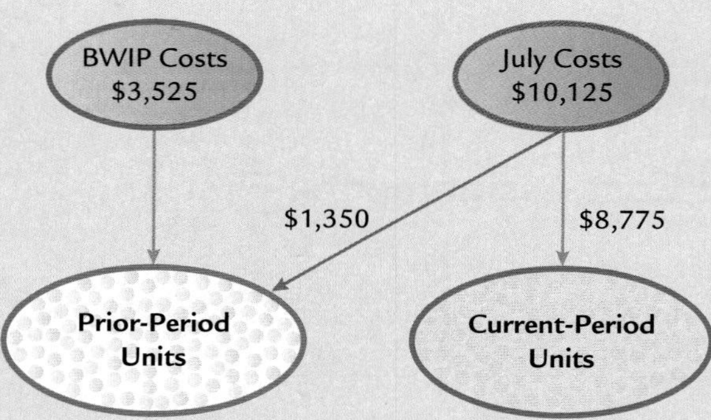

Cost/unit = $10,125/37,500 = $0.27

Transferred out:	
Cost from BWIP (prior period carryover)	$ 3,525
To complete BWIP ($0.27 × 5,000)	1,350
Started and completed ($0.27 × 30,000)	8,100
Total	12,975
EWIP ($0.27 × 2,500)	675
Total cost assigned	$13,650

(Continued)

Why:
Inventory can be measured on the first-in, first-out basis. Under this approach, the partially completed units in opening work in process will maintain the costs incurred in previous periods and the cost to complete these units in the current period will be added to calculate the total cost of these units. Therefore, units transferred out of the department in the current period could be valued at two different amounts depending on whether they were in process at the beginning of the period or were started and completed in the current period.

CORNERSTONE
6.9
(Continued)

Step 1: Physical Flow Analysis The purpose of step 1 is to trace the physical units of production. As with the weighted average method, in the FIFO method a physical flow schedule is prepared. This schedule is identical for both methods and for convenience is presented again in Exhibit 6.5. (See Cornerstone 6.5 for details on how to prepare this schedule.)

EXHIBIT 6.5

Physical Flow Schedule

Units to account for:		
Units in BWIP (75 percent complete)		20,000
Units started during the period		40,000
Total units to account for		60,000
Units accounted for:		
Units completed:		
Started and completed	30,000	
From BWIP	20,000	50,000
Units in EWIP (25 percent complete)		10,000
Total units accounted for		60,000

Step 2: Calculation of Equivalent Units Cornerstone 6.9 illustrates the calculation of equivalent units in the current period under the FIFO method and is summarized as follows without the graphic detail.

Units started and completed	30,000
Add: Units in BWIP × Percentage to be completed (= 20,000 × 25 percent)	5,000
Add: Units in EWIP × Percentage complete (=10,000 × 25 percent)	2,500
Equivalent units of output	37,500

From the equivalent unit computation, one difference between weighted average and FIFO becomes immediately apparent. Under FIFO, the equivalent units in BWIP (work done in the prior period) are not counted as part of the total equivalent work. Only the equivalent work to be completed this period is counted. The equivalent work to be completed in the current period for the units begun in the prior period is computed by multiplying the number of units in BWIP by the percentage of work remaining. Since in this example the percentage of work done in the prior period is 75 percent, the percentage left to be completed this period is 25 percent, or an equivalent of 5,000 additional units of work.

The effect of excluding prior period effort is to produce the current period equivalent output. Recall that under the weighted average method, 52,500

analytical Q&A

For August, there are 40,000 units in BWIP that are 30 percent complete and 20,000 units in EWIP that are 60 percent complete. There were 80,000 units started and completed. How many equivalent units were produced in August using the FIFO method?

Answers on pages 734 to 738.

equivalent units were computed for this month. Under FIFO, only 37,500 units are calculated for the same month. These 37,500 units represent current period output. The difference, of course, is explained by the fact that the weighted average method rolls back and counts the 15,000 equivalent units of prior period work (= 20,000 units BWIP × 75 percent) as belonging to this period.

Step 3: Calculation of Unit Cost The additional manufacturing costs incurred in the current period are $10,125. Thus, the current period unit manufacturing cost is $10,125/37,500, or $0.27. Notice that the costs of beginning inventory are excluded from this calculation. Only current period manufacturing costs are used.

Step 4: Valuation of Inventories Cornerstone 6.9 shows FIFO values for EWIP and goods transferred out. Since all equivalent units in EWIP are current period units, the cost of EWIP is simply $0.27 × 2,500, or $675. This differs from the cost of EWIP using the weighted average method, which is $0.26 × 2,500, or $650. In valuing goods transferred out, a significant difference between the weighted average method and FIFO can be observed. Under the weighted average method, the cost of goods transferred out is simply the unit cost times the units completed. Under FIFO, however, there are two sources of completed units:

- units started and completed (30,000)
- units from beginning inventory (20,000)

The cost of each source is computed separately and then summed to obtain the total cost of goods transferred out.

Cost of units started and completed = Unit cost × Units started and completed
= $0.27 × 30,000 = $8,100

The cost of the 30,000 units that were started and completed in the current period and transferred out is $8,100 (= $0.27 × 30,000). For these units, the use of the current period unit cost is entirely appropriate. However, the cost of the BWIP units that were transferred out is another matter. These units started the period with $3,525 of manufacturing costs already incurred and 15,000 units of equivalent output already completed. To finish these units, the equivalent of 5,000 units were needed. The cost of finishing the units in BWIP is:

Cost of finishing units in BWIP = Unit cost × Equivalent units to complete
= $0.27 × 5,000 = $1,350

Cost of finished units from BWIP = Prior period costs + Cost of finishing units in BWIP
= $3,525 + $1,350 = $4,875

The unit cost of these 20,000 units, then, is about $0.244 (= $4,875/20,000), a blend of both prior period and current period manufacturing costs.

Step 5: Cost Reconciliation The total manufacturing costs to account for during the period are:

BWIP	$ 3,525
Incurred during the period	10,125
Total costs to account for	$13,650

The total costs assigned to production are as follows:

Goods transferred out:	
Units from BWIP	$ 4,875
Units started and completed	8,100
Goods in EWIP	675
Total costs accounted for	$13,650

analytical Q&A

The FIFO cost per equivalent unit for July was $12. The BWIP had 25,000 units, 20 percent complete, with $50,000 of costs carried over from June. What is the total cost that these 25,000 units will contribute to the cost of goods transferred out?

Answers on pages 734 to 738.

Preparing a Production Report: First-In, First-Out Method

CORNERSTONE 6.10

Information:

Refer to steps 1 to 5 of the Health Blend example.

Required:

Prepare a production report for July (FIFO method).

Solution:

Health Blend
Picking Department Production Report
For July
(FIFO Method)

Unit Information

Units to account for:		
Units in beginning work in process	20,000	
Units started during the period	40,000	
Total units to account for	60,000	

	Physical Flow	Equivalent Units
Units accounted for:		
Units started and completed	30,000	30,000
Units completed from beginning work in process	20,000	5,000
Units in ending work in process	10,000	2,500
Total units accounted for	60,000	37,500

Cost Information

Costs to account for:	
Beginning work in process	$ 3,525
Incurred during the period	10,125
Total costs to account for	$13,650

Unit cost is calculated by using current period costs and the equivalent units of production in this period.

Cost per equivalent unit $0.27 (= $10,125/37,500)

	Transferred Out	Ending Work in Process	Total
Costs accounted for:			
Units in beginning work in process:			
From prior period	$ 3,525	$ —	$ 3,525
From current period (= $0.27 × 5,000)	1,350	—	1,350
Units started and completed (= $0.27 × 30,000)	8,100	—	8,100
Goods in ending work in process (= $0.27 × 2,500)	—	675	675
Total costs accounted for	$12,975	$675	$13,650

Why:

The production report brings together all five steps that we follow in calculating the costs of each type of inventory for the period. Under the FIFO method of inventory valuation, it isolates the costs assigned to completing the units that were in BWIP from the cost of units started and completed in the current period. It also allows us to ensure that all costs and all units are properly accounted for.

The costs assigned equal the costs to account for. With the completion of step 5, the production report can be prepared. Cornerstone 6.10 shows how to prepare this report for FIFO.

SUMMARY OF LEARNING OBJECTIVES

LO1. Describe the basic characteristics and cost flows associated with process manufacturing.

- Cost flows under process costing are similar to those under job-order costing.
- Raw materials are purchased and debited to the raw materials account.
- Direct materials used in production, direct labour, and applied manufacturing overhead are charged to the WIP account.
- In a production environment with several processes, there is a WIP account for each department or process. Goods completed in one department are transferred out to the next department.
- When units are completed in the final department or process, their cost is credited to WIP and is debited to FG.

LO2. Define equivalent units and explain their role in process costing. Explain the differences between the weighted average method and the FIFO method of accounting for process costs.

- Equivalent units of production are the complete units that could have been produced given the total amount of manufacturing effort expended during the period.
- The number of physical units is multiplied by the percentage of completion to calculate equivalent units.
- The weighted average costing method combines beginning inventory costs to compute unit costs.
- The FIFO costing method separates units in beginning inventory from those produced during the current period.

LO3. Prepare a departmental production report using the weighted average method.

- The production report summarizes the manufacturing activity occurring in a department for a given period.
- It discloses information concerning the physical flow of units, equivalent units, unit costs, and the disposition of the manufacturing costs associated with the period.

LO4. Explain how nonuniform inputs and multiple processing departments affect process costing.

- Nonuniform inputs and multiple departments are easily handled by process-costing methods.
- When inputs are added nonuniformly, equivalent units and unit cost are calculated for each separate input category.
- The adjustment for multiple departments is also relatively simple.
- The goods transferred from a prior department to a subsequent department are treated as a material added at the beginning of the process. Thus, there is a separate transferred-in materials category, where the equivalent units and unit cost are calculated.

LO5. (*Appendix 6A*) Examine how process costing may be used by service and manufacturing firms.

- Process costing may be appropriate for both service and manufacturing firms. The costing structure used by manufacturing firms is described in detail throughout Chapter 6 and is not entirely different from the structure used by service firms. For service firms, the unit cost can be calculated by dividing the total costs incurred in the period by the number of services provided. While some service industries (such as hospitality) may not have beginning or ending inventories, other industries (such as tax preparation) may have beginning and ending work in process (e.g., incomplete tax returns). Regardless, process costing may still be a reasonable costing system for those organizations.

LO6. (*Appendix 6B*) Prepare a departmental production report using the FIFO method.

- A production report prepared according to the FIFO method separates the cost of BWIP from the cost of the current period. BWIP is assumed to be completed and transferred out first. Costs from BWIP are not pooled with the current period costs in computing unit cost. Additionally, equivalent units of production exclude work done in the prior period. When calculating the cost of goods transferred out, the prior period costs are added to the costs of completing the units in BWIP, and then these costs are added to the costs of units started and completed.

SUMMARY OF IMPORTANT EQUATIONS

1. $\text{Unit cost} = \dfrac{\text{Total cost}}{\text{Equivalent units}}$
2. Units started and completed = Total units completed – Units in BWIP
3. Units started = Units started and completed + Units in EWIP
4. Total manufacturing costs = BWIP for period + Costs added in period
5. Cost of units started and completed = Unit cost × Units started and completed
6. Cost of finishing units in BWIP = Prior period costs + (Unit cost × Equivalent units to complete)
7. $\text{Unit cost} = \dfrac{\text{Total costs for the period}}{\text{Number of services provided}}$
8. $\text{Unit cost} = \dfrac{\text{Total costs for the period}}{\text{Total output of the period}}$

CORNERSTONES

CORNERSTONE 6.1	Calculating cost flows without work in process, page 256
CORNERSTONE 6.2	Calculating equivalent units of production: no beginning work in process, page 259
CORNERSTONE 6.3	Measuring output and assigning costs: no beginning work in process, page 260
CORNERSTONE 6.4	Measuring output and assigning costs: weighted average method, page 263
CORNERSTONE 6.5	Preparing a physical flow schedule, page 265
CORNERSTONE 6.6	Preparing a production report: weighted average method, page 267
CORNERSTONE 6.7	Calculating equivalent units and unit costs, and valuing inventories with nonuniform inputs, page 269
CORNERSTONE 6.8	Calculating the physical flow schedule, equivalent units, and unit costs for transferred-in goods, page 272
CORNERSTONE 6.9	(*Appendix 6B*) Calculating output and cost assignments: first-in, first-out method, page 275
CORNERSTONE 6.10	(*Appendix 6B*) Preparing a production report: first-in, first-out method, page 279

GLOSSARY

Cost reconciliation The final section of the production report that compares the costs to account for with the costs accounted for to ensure that they are equal. (p. 267)

Equivalent units of output Complete units that could have been produced given the total amount of manufacturing effort expended for the period. (p. 258)

FIFO costing method A process-costing method that separates units in beginning inventory from those produced during the current period. Unit costs include only current-period costs and production. (p. 261)

Parallel processing A processing pattern in which two or more sequential processes are required to produce a finished good. (p. 254)

Physical flow schedule A schedule that reconciles units to account for with units accounted for. The physical units are not adjusted for percent of completion. (p. 264)

Production report A document that summarizes the manufacturing activity that takes place in a process department for a given period of time. (p. 257)

Sequential processing A processing pattern in which units pass from one process to another in a set order. (p. 254)

Transferred-in costs Costs transferred from a prior process to a subsequent process. (p. 257)

Weighted average costing method A process-costing method that combines beginning inventory costs with current-period costs to compute unit costs. Costs and output from the current period and the previous period are averaged to compute unit costs. (p. 261)

REVIEW PROBLEMS

I. Process Costing

Springville Company, which uses the weighted average method, produces a product that passes through two departments: blending and cooking. In the blending department, all materials are added at the beginning of the process. All other manufacturing inputs are added uniformly. The following information pertains to the blending department for February:

a. WIP, February 1: 100,000 kilograms, 40 percent complete with respect to conversion costs. The costs assigned to this work are as follows:

Materials	$20,000
Labour	10,000
Overhead	30,000

b. WIP, February 28: 50,000 kilograms, 60 percent complete with respect to conversion costs.

c. Units completed and transferred out: 370,000 kilograms. The following costs were added during the month:

Materials	$211,000
Labour	100,000
Overhead	270,000

Required:

1. Prepare a physical flow schedule.
2. Prepare a schedule of equivalent units.
3. Compute the cost per equivalent unit.
4. Compute the cost of goods transferred out and the cost of EWIP.
5. Prepare a cost reconciliation.

Solution:

1. Physical flow schedule:

Units to account for:	
Units in BWIP	100,000
Units started	320,000
Total units to account for	420,000

Units accounted for:		
Units completed and transferred out:		
Started and completed	270,000	
From BWIP	100,000	370,000
Units in EWIP		50,000
Total units accounted for		420,000

2. Schedule of equivalent units:

	Materials	Conversion Costs
Units completed	370,000	370,000
Units in EWIP × Percent complete:		
Materials (50,000 × 100 percent)	50,000	—
Conversion costs (50,000 × 60 percent)	—	30,000
Equivalent units of output	420,000	400,000

3. Cost per equivalent unit:

$$\text{Materials unit cost} = \frac{(\$20{,}000 + \$211{,}000)}{420{,}000}$$
$$= \$0.55$$

$$\text{Conversion unit cost} = \frac{(\$40{,}000 + \$370{,}000)}{400{,}000}$$
$$= \$1.025$$

Total unit cost = $1.575 per equivalent unit

4. Cost of goods transferred out and cost of EWIP:

$$\text{Cost of goods transferred out} = \$1.575 \times 370{,}000 = \$582{,}750$$
$$\text{Cost of EWIP} = (\$0.55 \times 50{,}000) + (\$1.025 \times 30{,}000)$$
$$= \$58{,}250$$

5. Cost reconciliation:

Costs to account for:	
BWIP	$ 60,000
Incurred during the period	581,000
Total costs to account for	$641,000
Costs accounted for:	
Goods transferred out	$582,750
WIP	58,250
Total costs accounted for	$641,000

II. Process Costing

Now suppose that Springville Company uses the FIFO method for inventory valuations. Springville produces a product that passes through two departments: blending and cooking. In the blending department, all materials are added at the beginning of the process. All other manufacturing inputs are added uniformly. The following information pertains to the blending department for February:

a. WIP, February 1: 100,000 kilograms, 40 percent complete with respect to conversion costs. The costs assigned to this work are as follows:

Materials	$20,000
Labour	10,000
Overhead	30,000

(*Continued*)

b. WIP, February 28: 50,000 kilograms, 60 percent complete with respect to conversion costs.
c. Units completed and transferred out: 370,000 kilograms. The following costs were added during the month:

Materials	$211,000
Labour	100,000
Overhead	270,000

Required:

1. Prepare a physical flow schedule.
2. Prepare a schedule of equivalent units.
3. Calculate the cost per equivalent unit.
4. Determine the cost of goods transferred out and the cost of EWIP.

Solution:

1. Physical flow schedule:

Units to account for:		
Units in BWIP	100,000	
Units started	320,000	
Total units to account for	420,000	
Units accounted for:		
Units completed and transferred out:		
Started and completed	270,000	
From BWIP	100,000	370,000
Units in EWIP		50,000
Total units accounted for		420,000

2. Schedule of equivalent units:

	Materials	Conversion Costs
Units started and completed	270,000	270,000
Units in BWIP × Percentage to complete	—	60,000
Units in EWIP × Percentage complete:		
Materials (50,000 × 100 percent)	50,000	—
Conversion costs (50,000 × 60 percent)	—	30,000
Equivalent units of output	320,000	360,000

3. Cost per equivalent unit:

Materials unit cost $211,000/320,000	$0.659*
Conversion unit cost $370,000/360,000	1.028*
Total cost per equivalent unit	$1.687

* Rounded.

4. Cost of goods transferred out and cost of EWIP:

Cost of goods transferred out = ($1.687 × 270,000) + ($1.028 × 60,000) + $60,000 = $577,170
Cost of EWIP = ($0.659 × 50,000) + ($1.028 × 30,000)= $63,790

Note: Difference of $40 between total cost incurred ($60,000 + $581,000) and total cost assigned ($577,170 + $63,790) is due to rounding.

DISCUSSION QUESTIONS

1. Distinguish between sequential processing and parallel processing.
2. Describe the differences between process costing and job-order costing.
3. What are equivalent units? Why are they needed in a process-costing system?

4. Under the weighted average method, how are prior period costs and output treated? How are they treated under the FIFO method?
5. Under what conditions will the weighted average and FIFO methods give the same results?
6. How is the equivalent unit calculation affected when materials are added at the beginning or end of the process rather than uniformly throughout the process?
7. Explain why transferred-in costs are a special type of raw material for the receiving department.
8. What are the similarities and differences between the manufacturing cost flows for job-order firms and process firms?
9. What journal entry would be made as goods are transferred out from one department to another department? From the final department to the warehouse?
10. Describe the five steps in accounting for the manufacturing activity of a processing department, and explain how they interrelate.
11. What is a production report? What purpose does this report serve?
12. In assigning costs to goods transferred out, how do the weighted average and FIFO methods differ?
13. Describe the effect of automation on the process-costing accounting system.
14. How does the adoption of a JIT approach to manufacturing affect process costing?
15. How would process costing for services differ from process costing for manufactured goods?

CORNERSTONE EXERCISES

Cornerstone Exercise 6-1 Basic Cost Flows

OBJECTIVE 1
CORNERSTONE 6.1

Sabor Company produces 500-gram boxes of an oat cereal. Sabor uses three departments: mixing, cooking, and packaging. During the month of August, Sabor produced 150,000 boxes with the following costs:

	Mixing Department	Cooking Department	Packaging Department
Direct materials	$225,000	$75,000	$60,000
Direct labour	30,000	15,000	45,000
Applied overhead	45,000	22,500	67,500

Required:

1. Using the weighted average method, calculate the costs transferred out of each department.
2. Prepare journal entries that reflect these cost transfers.

Cornerstone Exercise 6-2 Equivalent Units, No Beginning Work in Process

OBJECTIVE 2
CORNERSTONE 6.2

Madaki Manufacturing produces cylinders used in internal combustion engines. During June, Madaki's welding department had the following data:

Units in BWIP	—
Units completed	30,000
Units in EWIP (40 percent complete)	2,000

Required:

Using the weighted average method, calculate June's output for the welding department in equivalent units of production.

Cornerstone Exercise 6-3 Unit Cost, Valuing Goods Transferred Out and EWIP

OBJECTIVE 2
CORNERSTONE 6.3

During the month of April, the moulding department of Khang Foundry completed and transferred out 34,000 units. At the end of April, there were 12,000 units in process, 60 percent complete. Khang incurred manufacturing costs totalling $618,000.

(Continued)

Required:

1. Using the weighted average method, calculate the unit cost.
2. Calculate the cost of goods transferred out and the cost of EWIP.

OBJECTIVE 3
CORNERSTONE 6.4

Cornerstone Exercise 6-4 Weighted Average Method, Unit Cost, Valuing Inventories

Nguyen Enterprises produces premium strawberry jam. Output is measured in litres. Nguyen uses the weighted average method. During January, the company had the following production data:

Units in process, January 1, 60 percent complete	10,000 litres
Units completed and transferred out	75,000 litres
Units in process, January 31, 40 percent complete	20,000 litres
Costs:	
Work in process, January 1	$ 44,000
Costs added during January	122,000

Required:

1. Using the weighted average method, calculate the equivalent units for January.
2. Calculate the unit cost for January.
3. Assign costs to units transferred out and EWIP.

OBJECTIVE 3
CORNERSTONE 6.5

Cornerstone Exercise 6-5 Physical Flow Schedule

Yeleshev Inc. just finished its second month of operations. Yeleshev mass produces integrated circuits. The following production information is provided for the month of November:

Units in process, November 1, 80 percent complete	75,000
Units completed and transferred out	450,000
Units in process, November 30, 60 percent complete	50,000

Required:

Prepare a physical flow schedule.

OBJECTIVE 3
CORNERSTONE 6.6

Cornerstone Exercise 6-6 Production Report, Weighted Average

Kinnamon Inc. manufactures bicycle frames in two departments: cutting and welding. Kinnamon uses the weighted average method. Manufacturing costs are added uniformly throughout the process. The following are cost and production data for the cutting department for October:

Production:	
Units in process, October 1, 40 percent complete	4,000
Units completed and transferred out	40,000
Units in process, October 31, 60 percent complete	8,000
Costs:	
WIP, October 1	$ 50,000
Costs added during October	756,400

Required:

Prepare a production report for the cutting department.

CORNERSTONE 6.7

Cornerstone Exercise 6-7 Nonuniform Inputs, Weighted Average

Jackson Inc. had the following production and cost information for its fabrication department during the month of March (materials are added at the beginning of the fabrication process):

Production:	
Units in process, March 1, 50 percent complete with respect to conversion	10,000
Units completed	65,200
Units in process, March 31, 40 percent complete	12,000

(Continued)

Costs:	
Work in process, March 1:	
Materials	$20,000
Conversion costs	15,000
Total	$35,000
Current costs:	
Materials	$125,000
Conversion costs	210,000
Total	$335,000

Jackson uses the weighted average method.

Required:

1. Using the weighted average method, prepare an equivalent units schedule.
2. Calculate the unit cost.
3. Calculate the cost of units transferred out and the cost of EWIP.

Cornerstone Exercise 6-8 Nonuniform Inputs, Weighted Average

Alcor Inc. is a small producer of high-quality ice cream. During production, the raw milk materials are added at the beginning of the process, while the flavouring materials are added when the ice cream is 60 percent complete. In April, the company reported the following production and cost information:

Production:	
Units in process, April 1, 70 percent complete	400
Units completed	4,950
Units in process, April 30, 20 percent complete	250
Costs:	
Work in process, April 1:	
Materials (raw milk)	$ 70
Materials (flavourings)	100
Conversion costs	375
Total	$ 545
Current costs:	
Materials (raw milk)	$ 970
Materials (flavourings)	1,880
Conversion costs	2,625
Total	$5,475

Alcor uses the weighted average method.

Required:

1. Using the weighted average method, prepare an equivalent units schedule.
2. Calculate the unit cost for conversion costs, materials (raw milk), and materials (flavourings).
3. Calculate the cost of units transferred out and the cost of EWIP.

Cornerstone Exercise 6-9 Weighted Average

OBJECTIVE 4
CORNERSTONE 6.8

Refroidir Co. produces refrigerators and has two manufacturing divisions: fabrication and assembly. Materials are added at the beginning of the process in each department. In September, the fabrication division reported the following:

Fabrication Division—Production:	
Units in process, September 1, 60 percent complete	400
Units completed	1,600
Units in process, September 30, 40 percent complete	200

(Continued)

Costs:	
Work in process, September 1:	
Materials	$ 94,000
Conversion costs	32,000
Total	$126,000
Current costs:	
Materials	$302,000
Conversion costs	94,000
Total	$396,000

Required:

1. Using the weighted average method, prepare an equivalent units schedule for the fabrication division.
2. Calculate the unit cost for the materials and conversion cost categories for the fabrication division.
3. Calculate the cost of units transferred out and the cost of EWIP for the fabrication division.

OBJECTIVE 4
CORNERSTONE 6.8

Cornerstone Exercise 6-10 Transferred-In Cost

In October, Refroidir Co.'s assembly division, in which materials are added at the beginning of the process, reported the following:

Assembly Division—Production:	
Units in process, October 1, 40 percent complete	200
Units completed	1,500
Units in process, October 31, 50 percent complete	300
Costs:	
Work in process, October 1:	
Transferred-in	$ 68,000
Materials	70,200
Conversion costs	129,000
Total	$267,200
Current costs:	
Transferred-in	$472,000
Materials	19,800
Conversion costs	44,250
Total	$536,050

Required:

1. Using the weighted average method, prepare an equivalent units schedule for the assembly division.
2. Calculate the unit cost for the materials and conversion cost categories for the assembly division.
3. Calculate the cost of units transferred out and the cost of EWIP for the assembly division.

OBJECTIVE 4
CORNERSTONE 6.8

Cornerstone Exercise 6-11 Transferred-In Cost

Energetics Inc. produces an energy drink and uses the weighted average method. The product is sold by the litre. The company has two departments: mixing and bottling. For July, the bottling department had 40,000 litres in beginning inventory (with transferred-in costs of $142,000) and completed 175,000 litres during the month. Further, the mixing department completed and transferred out 160,000 litres at a cost of $458,000 in July.

Required:

1. Prepare a physical flow schedule for the bottling department.
2. Calculate equivalent units for the transferred-in category.
3. Calculate the unit cost for the transferred-in category.

Cornerstone Exercise 6-12 First-In, First-Out Method; Equivalent Units

OBJECTIVE 6
CORNERSTONE 6.9

Bebida Inc. produces soft drinks. Mixing is the first department and its output is measured in litres. Bebida uses the FIFO method. All manufacturing costs are added uniformly. For August, the mixing department provided the following information:

Production:	
Units in process, August 1, 80 percent complete	10,000 litres
Units completed and transferred out	69,000 litres
Units in process, August 31, 75 percent complete	8,000 litres
Costs:	
Work in process, August 1	$ 9,600
Costs added during August	90,450

Required:

1. Calculate the equivalent units for August.
2. Calculate the unit cost.
3. Assign costs to units transferred out and EWIP using the FIFO method.

Cornerstone Exercise 6-13 FIFO; Production Report

OBJECTIVE 6
CORNERSTONE 6.10

Refer to the data in **Cornerstone Exercise 6-12**.

Required:

Prepare a cost of production report.

EXERCISES

Exercise 6-14 Basic Cost Flows

OBJECTIVE 1

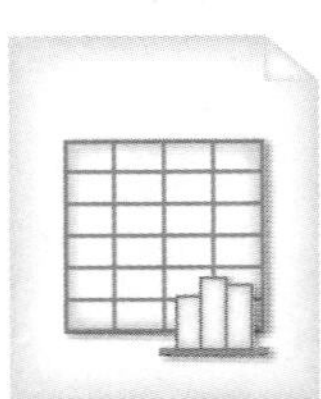

Huttunen Company produces a common machine component for industrial equipment. The component is produced in three departments: moulding, grinding, and finishing. The following data are available for the month of September:

	Moulding Department	Grinding Department	Finishing Department
Direct materials	$87,500	$10,200	$6,100
Direct labour	7,600	15,700	9,900
Applied overhead	9,700	67,900	9,600

During September, 6,000 components were completed. There is no beginning or ending WIP in any department.

Required:

1. Prepare a schedule showing, for each department, the cost of direct materials, direct labour, applied overhead, product transferred in from a prior department, and total manufacturing cost.
2. Calculate the unit cost.

Exercise 6-15 Journal Entries, Basic Cost Flows

OBJECTIVE 1

In October, Huttunen Company had the following cost flows:

	Moulding Department	Grinding Department	Finishing Department
Direct materials	$35,800	$ 5,000	$ 3,600
Direct labour	3,000	5,800	4,800
Applied overhead	3,200	29,200	4,600
Transferred-in cost:			
From moulding		42,000	
From grinding	—	—	82,000
Total cost	$42,000	$82,000	$95,000

(Continued)

Required:

1. Prepare the journal entries to transfer costs from (a) moulding to grinding, (b) grinding to finishing, and (c) finishing to finished goods.
2. CONCEPTUAL CONNECTION Explain how the journal entries differ from a job-order cost system.

OBJECTIVE 2

Exercise 6-16 Equivalent Units, Unit Cost, Valuation of Goods Transferred Out and Ending Work in Process

Using the weighted average method, the mixing department had the following data for the month of December:

Units in BWIP	—
Units completed	28,900
Units in EWIP (30 percent complete)	2,800
Total manufacturing costs	$68,750

Required:

1. What is the output in equivalent units for December?
2. What is the unit manufacturing cost for December?
3. Calculate the cost of goods transferred out for December.
4. Calculate the value of December's EWIP.

OBJECTIVE 3

Exercise 6-17 Weighted Average Method, Equivalent Units

Yeleshev Company produces a product where all manufacturing inputs are applied uniformly. The company produced the following physical flow schedule for March:

Units to account for:	
Units in BWIP (40 percent complete)	7,500
Units started	17,500
Total units to account for	25,000
Units accounted for:	
Units completed:	
From BWIP	5,000
Started and completed	16,000
	21,000
Units, EWIP (75 percent complete)	4,000
Total units accounted for	25,000

Required:

Prepare a schedule of equivalent units using the weighted average method.

OBJECTIVE 3

Exercise 6-18 Weighted Average Method, Unit Cost, Valuing Inventories

Garcia Inc. manufactures products that pass through two or more processes in which all manufacturing costs are incurred uniformly. During April, equivalent units were computed using the weighted average method:

Units completed	18,000
Units in EWIP × Percentage complete (12,000 × 60 percent)	7,200
Equivalent units of output	25,200
April's costs to account for are as follows:	
BWIP (40 percent complete)	$ 3,360
Materials	30,000
Conversion cost	12,000
Total	$45,360

Required:

1. Calculate the unit cost for April using the weighted average method.
2. Using the weighted average method, determine the cost of EWIP and the cost of the goods transferred out.
3. CONCEPTUAL CONNECTION Garcia had just finished implementing a series of measures designed to reduce the unit cost to $1.60, and was assured that this had been achieved and should be realized for June's production. Yet, upon seeing the unit cost for June, the president of the company was disappointed. Can you explain why the full effect of the cost reductions may not show up in June? What can you suggest to overcome this problem?

Exercise 6-19 Weighted Average Method, Unit Costs, Valuing Inventories

OBJECTIVE 3

Walser Inc. produces a product that passes through two processes. During February, equivalent units were calculated using the weighted average method:

Units completed	300,000
Add: Units in EWIP × Percentage complete (100,000 × 40 percent)	40,000
Equivalent units of output (weighted average)	340,000
Less: Units in BWIP × Percentage complete (50,000 × 70 percent)	35,000
Equivalent units of output (FIFO)	305,000

The costs that Walser had to account for during the month of February were as follows:

BWIP	$ 210,000
Costs added	1,986,000
Total	$2,196,000

Required:

1. Using the weighted average method, calculate unit cost.
2. Under the weighted average method, what is the total cost of units transferred out? What is the cost assigned to units in ending inventory?
3. CONCEPTUAL CONNECTION Daniel Tomic, the manager of Walser, is considering switching from weighted average to FIFO. Explain the key differences between the two approaches and make a recommendation to Daniel about which method should be used.

Exercise 6-20 Physical Flow Schedule

OBJECTIVE 3

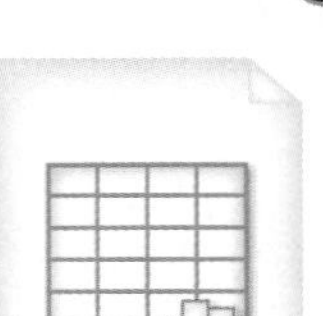

The following information was obtained for the first department of LPZ Company for April:

a. BWIP had 30,500 units, 30 percent complete with respect to manufacturing costs.
b. EWIP had 8,400 units, 25 percent complete with respect to manufacturing costs.
c. LPZ started 33,000 units in April.

Required:

Prepare a physical flow schedule.

Exercise 6-21 Physical Flow, Weighted Average Method

OBJECTIVE 3

Nelrok Company manufactures fertilizer. Department 1 mixes the chemicals required for the fertilizer. The following data are for the year:

BWIP (40 percent complete)	75,000
Units started	369,000
Units in EWIP (60 percent complete)	45,000

Required:

Prepare a physical flow schedule.

OBJECTIVE 3

Exercise 6-22 Production Report, Weighted Average

Mino Inc. manufactures chocolate syrup in three departments: mixing, cooking, and bottling. Mino uses the weighted average method. The following are cost and production data for the cooking department for April (assume that units are measured in litres):

Production:	
Units in process, April 1, 60 percent complete	20,000
Units completed and transferred out	50,000
Units in process, April 30, 20 percent complete	10,000
Costs:	
WIP, April 1	$ 93,600
Costs added during April	314,600

Required:

Prepare a production report for the cooking department.

OBJECTIVE 4

Exercise 6-23 Nonuniform Inputs, Equivalent Units

Terry Linens Inc. manufactures bed and bath linens. The bath linens department sews terry cloth into towels of various sizes. Terry uses the weighted average method. All materials are added at the beginning of the process. The following data are for the bath linens department for August:

Production:	
Units in process, August 1, 25 percent complete*	15,000
Units completed and transferred out	90,000
Units in process, August 31, 60 percent complete*	30,000

* With respect to conversion costs.

Required:

Calculate equivalent units of production for the bath linens department for August.

OBJECTIVE 4

Exercise 6-24 Unit Cost and Cost Assignment, Nonuniform Inputs

Loran Inc. uses the weighted average method and had the following equivalent units schedule and costs for its fabrication department during the month of September:

	Materials	Conversion
Units completed	360,000	360,000
Add: Units in ending WIP × Percentage complete (120,000 × 60%)	120,000	72,000
Equivalent units of output	480,000	432,000
Costs:		
Work in process, September 1:		
Materials	$ 294,000	
Conversion costs	15,750	
Total	$ 309,750	
Current costs:		
Materials	$2,106,000	
Conversion costs	472,410	
Total	$2,578,410	

Required:

1. Calculate the unit cost for materials, for conversion, and in total for the fabrication department for September.
2. Calculate the cost of units transferred out and the cost of EWIP.

Exercise 6-25 Nonuniform Inputs, Transferred-In Cost

OBJECTIVE 4

Drysdale Dairy produces a variety of dairy products and uses the weighted average method. In department 12, cream (transferred in from department 6) and other materials (sugar and flavourings) are mixed and churned to make ice cream. The following data are for department 12 for August:

Production:	
Units in process, August 1, 40 percent complete	175,000
Units completed and transferred out	697,000
Units in process, August 31, 25 percent complete	160,000

Required:

1. Prepare a physical flow schedule for August.
2. Calculate equivalent units for the following categories: transferred-in, materials, and conversion.

Exercise 6-26 Transferred-In Cost

OBJECTIVE 4

Goulas's finishing department uses the weighted average method and had the following data for the month of July:

	Transferred-In	Materials	Conversion
Units transferred out	60,000	60,000	60,000
Units in EWIP	15,000	15,000	9,000
Equivalent units	75,000	75,000	69,000
Costs:			
Work in process, July 1:			
Transferred-in from fabricating	$ 2,100		
Materials	1,500		
Conversion costs	3,000		
Total	$ 6,600		
Current costs:			
Transferred-in from fabricating	$30,900		
Materials	22,500		
Conversion costs	45,300		
Total	$98,700		

Required:

1. Calculate unit costs for the following categories: transferred-in, materials, and conversion.
2. Calculate total unit cost.

Exercise 6-27 First-In, First-Out Method; Equivalent Units

OBJECTIVE 6

Yeleshev Company produces a product where all manufacturing inputs are applied uniformly. The company produced the following physical flow schedule for March:

Units to account for:	
Units in BWIP (30 percent complete)	27,000
Units started	187,000
Total units to account for	214,000
Units accounted for:	
Units completed:	
From BWIP	27,000
Started and completed	168,000
	195,000
Units, EWIP (60 percent complete)	19,000
Total units accounted for	214,000

Required:

Prepare a schedule of equivalent units using the FIFO method.

OBJECTIVE 6

Exercise 6-28 First-In, First-Out Method; Unit Cost; Valuing Inventories

Loren Inc. manufactures products that pass through two or more processes. During April, equivalent units were computed using the FIFO method:

Units started and completed	4,600
Units in BWIP × Percentage to complete (60 percent)	840
Units in EWIP × Percentage complete (4,000 × 60 percent)	2,400
Equivalent units of output (FIFO)	7,840

April's costs to account for are as follows:	
BWIP (40 percent complete)	$ 1,120
Materials	10,000
Conversion cost	4,000
Total	$15,120

Required:

1. Calculate the unit cost for April using the FIFO method. Round to two decimal places.
2. Using the FIFO method, determine the cost of EWIP and the cost of the goods transferred out.

PROBLEMS

OBJECTIVE 

Problem 6-29 First-In, First-Out Method; Unit Cost; Valuing Inventories

The polishing department of Burgeo Tools operates a first-in, first-out process-costing system in which all direct materials are added when production in the department is 40 percent complete. In contrast, conversion costs are incurred evenly during processing. The following information pertains to the polishing department's March production activities:

	Physical Units	Direct Materials	Conversion Costs
Work in process at March 1 (60 percent complete)	400	$ 4,000	$ 7,000
Started during March	4,000		
Completed during March	3,600		
Work in process at March 31 (20 percent complete)	800		
Cost incurred during March		40,000	88,000

Required:

1. Prepare a physical flow analysis for the polishing department for March.
2. Calculate equivalent units of production for the polishing department for March.
3. Calculate the unit cost for the polishing department for March.
4. Calculate the cost of units transferred out and the cost of EWIP inventory.
5. Prepare a cost reconciliation for the polishing department for March.
6. CONCEPTUAL CONNECTION Kimberleigh Williams, the manager of the polishing department, is considering changing from a first-in, first-out system to a weighted average system. To help in her analysis, she has asked for your opinion. Prepare a brief memo outlining the advantages of a weighted average costing system.

OBJECTIVE 

Problem 6-30 Basic Flows, Equivalent Units

Karsen Company produces a pain medication that passes through two departments: mixing and tableting. Karsen uses the weighted average method. Data for November were as follows:

Mixing: BWIP was zero; EWIP had 2,400 units, 50 percent complete; and 28,000 units were started.

Tableting: BWIP was 1,600 units, 20 percent complete; and 800 units were in EWIP, 40 percent complete.

Required:

1. For mixing, calculate the following:
   a. Number of units transferred to tableting.
   b. Equivalent units of production.
2. For tableting, calculate the number of units transferred out to finished goods.
3. CONCEPTUAL CONNECTION Suppose that the units in the mixing department are measured in grams, while the units in the tableting department are measured in bottles of 100 tablets, with a total weight of eight grams (excluding the bottle). Decide how you would treat units that are measured differently, and then repeat Requirement 2 using this approach.

Check figures
1.b. Equivalent units = 26,800
2. Units transferred out = 26,400
3. Units transferred out = 3,300

Problem 6-31 Steps in Preparing a Cost of Production Report

OBJECTIVE   

Stilton Audio is a producer of speakers and amplifiers which are housed in plastic cabinets. Currently production of the plastic cabinets as well as final product assembly is completed in-house. For accounting purposes, Stilton Audio uses the weighted average method, where plastic cabinets and speaker and amplifier components are added at the beginning of the assembly process.

The following are cost and production data for the assembly process for April:

Production:	
Units in process, April 1, 60 percent complete	60,000
Units completed and transferred out	150,000
Units in process, April 30, 20 percent complete	30,000
Costs:	
WIP, April 1:	
Plastic cabinets	$ 1,200,000
Speaker and amplifier components	12,600,000
Conversion costs	5,400,000
Costs added during April:	
Plastic cabinets	2,400,000
Speaker and amplifier components	25,200,000
Conversion costs	8,640,000

Required:

1. Prepare a physical flow analysis for the assembly department for April.
2. Calculate equivalent units of production for the assembly department for April.
3. Calculate unit cost for the assembly department for April.
4. Calculate the cost of units transferred out and the cost of EWIP inventory.
5. Prepare a cost reconciliation for the assembly department for April.

Check figures:
1. Total units accounted for = 180,000
2. Equivalent units, conversion = 156,000
3. Unit cost = $320
4. Cost of EWIP = $7,440,000

Problem 6-32 Steps for a Cost of Production Report

OBJECTIVE 

Assume that Stilton Audio uses the weighted average method, where plastic cabinets, and speaker and amplifier components are added at the beginning of the assembly process. The following are cost and production data for the assembly process for April:

Production:	
Units in process, April 1, 20 percent complete	120,000
Units completed and transferred out	360,000
Units in process, April 30, 60 percent complete	75,000
Costs:	
WIP, April 1:	
Plastic cabinets	$ 450,000
Speaker and amplifier components	14,750,000
Conversion costs	7,640,000
Costs added during April:	
Plastic cabinets	$ 1,600,000
Speaker and amplifier components	29,680,000
Conversion costs	16,540,000

(*Continued*)

Required:

1. Prepare a cost of production report for the assembly department for April.
2. CONCEPTUAL CONNECTION Write a report that compares the purpose and content of the cost of production report with the job-order cost sheet.

Check figure:
1. Unit cost = $166.5543

Problem 6-33 Equivalent Units, Unit Cost, Weighted Average

Bonavista Quality Ltd. manufactures granite countertops for residential and commercial markets. The company operates two departments: mixing and packaging. This problem focuses strictly on the packaging department. The process-costing system at Bonavista has a single direct-cost category (direct materials) and a single indirect-cost category (conversion costs). The packaging department introduces all direct materials at the start of production. In contrast, conversion costs are added evenly during the packaging department's process.

The company relies on the weighted average method of process costing and reported the following production information pertaining to the packaging department for June:

	Physical Units	Transferred-In Costs	Direct Materials	Conversion Costs
Work in process, June 1	75	$ 270	$ 1,775	$ 135
Transferred in during June	550			
Completed and transferred out during June	500			
Work in process at June 30	125			
Total costs added during June		10,450	17,600	10,890

The WIP inventory at June 1 is 25 percent complete for conversion costs. The WIP inventory at June 30 is 40 percent complete for conversion costs.

Required:

1. Prepare a physical flow analysis for the packaging department for June.
2. Calculate equivalent units of production for the packaging department for June.
3. Calculate the unit cost for the packaging department for June.
4. Calculate the cost of units transferred out and the cost of EWIP inventory.
5. Prepare a cost reconciliation for the packaging department for June.

OBJECTIVE 

Problem 6-34 Equivalent Units, Unit Cost, Weighted Average

Fino Linens Inc. manufactures bed and bath linens. The bath linens department sews terry cloth into towels of various sizes. Fino uses the weighted average method. All manufacturing costs are added uniformly through the process. The following data are for the bath linens department for August:

Production:	
Units in process, August 1, 60 percent complete	20,000
Units completed and transferred out	60,000
Units in process, August 31, 60 percent complete	20,000
Costs:	
WIP, August 1	$11,520
Current costs	72,000
Total	$83,520

Check figures:
1. Total units to account for = 80,000
2. Equivalent units = 72,000
3. Unit conversion cost = $1.16

Required:

1. Prepare a physical flow analysis for the bath linens department for August.
2. Calculate equivalent units of production for the bath linens department for August.

3. Calculate the unit cost for the bath linens department for August.
4. Calculate the per unit cost using the FIFO method.

Problem 6-35 Cost of Production Report

OBJECTIVE 3

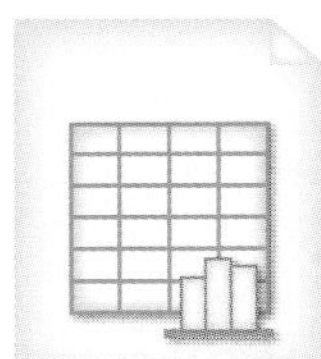

The owner of Fino Linens Inc., a manufacturer of bed and bath linens, insisted on a formal report that provided all the details of the weighted average method. In the manufacturing process, all materials are added at the beginning. The following data are for the bath linens department for August:

Production:		
Units in process, August 1, 40 percent complete	60,000	
Units completed and transferred out	480,000	
Units in process, August 31, 70 percent complete	40,000	
Costs:		
	Material	Conversion
WIP, August 1	$168,000	$ 49,300
Current costs	472,000	182,000
Total	$640,000	$231,300

Check figure:
Cost per equivalent unit = $1.6861

Required:

Prepare a cost of production report for the bath linens department for August using the weighted average method.

Problem 6-36 Weighted Average Method, Physical Flow, Equivalent Units, Unit Costs, Cost Assignment

OBJECTIVE 1  

Yomasca Inc. manufactures various Halloween masks. Each mask is shaped from a piece of rubber in the moulding department. The masks are then transferred to the finishing department, where they are painted and have elastic bands attached. Yomasca uses the weighted average method and materials are added uniformly through the process. In April, the moulding department reported the following data:

a. BWIP consisted of 6,000 units, 20 percent complete. Cost in beginning inventory totalled $552.
b. Costs added to production during the month were $8,698.
c. At the end of the month, 18,000 units were transferred out to the finishing department. Then, 2,000 units remained in EWIP, 25 percent complete.

Required:

1. Prepare a physical flow schedule.
2. Calculate equivalent units of production.
3. Compute unit cost.
4. Calculate the cost of goods transferred to finishing at the end of the month. Calculate the cost of ending inventory.
5. CONCEPTUAL CONNECTION Assume that the masks are inspected at the end of the moulding process. Of the 18,000 units inspected, 1,000 are rejected as faulty and are discarded. Thus, only 17,000 units are transferred to the finishing department. The manager of Yomasca considers all such spoilage abnormal and does not want to assign any of this cost to the 17,000 good units produced and transferred to the finishing department. Your task is to determine the cost of this spoilage of 1,000 units and then to discuss how you would account for this spoilage cost. Now suppose that the manager considers this spoilage cost just part of the cost of producing the good units transferred out. Therefore, he wants to assign this cost to the good production. Explain how this would be handled. (*Hint:* Spoiled units are a type of output, and equivalent units of spoilage can be calculated.)

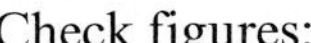

Check figures:
1. Units to account for = 20,000
2. Equivalent units = 18,500
3. Unit cost = $0.50
4. Cost of EWIP = $250
5. Spoilage cost = $500

OBJECTIVE 

Problem 6-37 Weighted Average Method, Single-Department Analysis

J Booth Company produces a product that passes through an assembly process and a finishing process. All manufacturing costs are added uniformly for both processes. The following information was obtained for the assembly department for March:

a. WIP, March 1, had 27,000 units (20 percent completed) and the following costs:

Direct materials	$357,600
Direct labour	217,500
Overhead applied	156,800

b. During March, 138,400 units were added to production, and the following costs were added to production:

Direct materials	$737,000
Direct labour	524,000
Overhead applied	468,000

c. On March 31, there were 31,700 partially completed units in process. These units were 40 percent complete.

Required:

Check figure: Unit cost = $16.8117

Prepare a production report for the assembly department for March using the weighted average method of costing.

OBJECTIVE  

Problem 6-38 First-In, First-Out Method; Single-Department Analysis; One Cost Category

J Booth Company produces a product that passes through an assembly process and a finishing process. All manufacturing costs are added uniformly for both processes. The following information was obtained for the assembly department for August:

a. WIP, August 1, had 48,000 units (60 percent completed) and the following costs:

Direct materials	$186,256
Direct labour	64,864
Overhead applied	34,400

b. During August, 138,400 units were completed and transferred to the finishing department, and the following costs were added to production:

Direct materials	$267,880
Direct labour	281,280
Overhead applied	117,144

Check figure: Cost per equivalent unit = $5.3424

c. On August 31, there were 21,600 partially completed units in process. These units were 70 percent complete.

Required:

Prepare a production report for the assembly department for August using the FIFO method of costing. (Carry the unit cost computation to four decimal places.)

OBJECTIVE 

Problem 6-39 Weighted Average Method, Separate Materials Cost

Da Silva Company produces a variety of stationery products. One product, sealing wax sticks, passes through two processes: blending and moulding. The weighted average method is used to account for the costs of production. After blending, the resulting product is sent to the moulding department, where it is poured into moulds and cooled. The following information relates to the blending process for August:

a. WIP, August 1, had 20,000 kilograms, 20 percent complete. Costs associated with partially completed units were:

Materials	$220,000
Direct labour	30,000
Overhead applied	10,000

b. WIP, August 31, had 30,000 kilograms, 70 percent complete.
c. Units completed and transferred out totalled 500,000 kilograms. All inputs are added uniformly, and costs added during the month were:

Materials	$5,610,000
Direct labour	3,877,500
Overhead applied	1,292,500

Required:

1. Prepare a physical flow schedule and an equivalent unit schedule.
2. Calculate the unit cost, rounded to two decimal places.
3. Determine the cost of EWIP and the cost of goods transferred out.
4. Prepare a cost reconciliation.
5. Suppose that the materials added uniformly in blending are paraffin and pigment and that the manager of the company wants to know how much each of these materials costs per equivalent unit produced. The costs of the materials in BWIP are as follows:

Paraffin	$120,000
Pigment	100,000

The costs of the materials added during the month are also given:

Paraffin	$3,060,000
Pigment	2,550,000

Prepare an equivalent unit schedule with cost categories for each material. Calculate the cost per unit for each type of material.

Check figures:
1. Total equivalent units = 521,000
2. Unit cost = $21.19
3. Cost of goods transferred out= $10,595,000
5. Unit paraffin cost = $6.10

Problem 6-40 Weighted Average Method, Journal Entries

OBJECTIVE   

Seacrest Company uses a process-costing system. The company manufactures a product that is processed in two departments, A and B. As work is completed in department A, it is transferred to department B. Materials are added uniformly throughout the process. The following summarizes the production activity and costs for November:

	Department A	Department B
Beginning inventories:		
Physical units	5,000	8,000
Costs:		
Transferred in	—	$160,720
Direct materials	$10,000	—
Conversion costs	$6,900	$16,800
Current production:		
Units started	25,000	?
Units transferred out	28,000	33,000
Costs:		
Transferred in	—	?
Direct materials	$57,800	$37,950
Conversion costs	$95,220	$128,100
Percentage completion:		
Beginning inventory	40%	50%
Ending inventory	80%	50%

Required:

1. Using the weighted average method, prepare the following for department A:
   a. A physical flow schedule.
   b. An equivalent unit calculation.

(Continued)

c. Calculation of unit costs, rounded to two decimal places.
d. Cost of EWIP and cost of goods transferred out.
e. A cost reconciliation.

2. CONCEPTUAL CONNECTION Prepare journal entries that show the flow of manufacturing costs for department A. Use a conversion cost control account for conversion costs. Many firms are now combining direct labour and manufacturing overhead costs into one category. They are not tracking direct labour separately. Offer some reasons for this practice.

Check figure:
1.c. Unit cost = $5.74

Problem 6-41 Weighted Average Method, Nonuniform Inputs, Multiple Departments

Benson Pharmaceuticals uses a process-costing system to compute the unit costs of the over-the-counter cold remedies that it produces. It has three departments: picking, encapsulating, and bottling. In the picking department, the ingredients for the cold capsules are added at the beginning of the process and measured, sifted, and blended. The blended mixture is transferred to the encapsulating department in litre containers. The encapsulating department fills capsules with the blended mixture, which is added at the beginning of the process. One litre of powdered mixture converts into 1,500 capsules. After the capsules are filled, sealed, and polished, they are transferred to the bottling department, where automated filling machines put them into bottles that are then affixed with a safety seal, lid, and label. Each bottle receives 50 capsules.

During March, the following results are available for the first two departments:

	Picking	Encapsulating
Beginning inventories:		
Physical units	10 litres	4,000
Costs:		
Materials	$252	$32
Labour	$282	$20
Overhead	?	?
Transferred in	—	$140
Current production:		
Transferred out	140 litres	208,000
Ending inventory	20 litres	6,000
Costs:		
Materials	$3,636	$1,573
Transferred in	—	?
Labour	$4,618	$1,944
Overhead	?	?
Percentage of completion:		
Beginning inventory	40%	50%
Ending inventory	50%	40%

Overhead in both departments is applied as a percentage of direct labour costs. In the picking department, overhead is 200 percent of direct labour. In the encapsulating department, the overhead rate is 150 percent of direct labour.

Required:

1. Prepare a production report for the picking department using the weighted average method. Follow the five steps outlined in the chapter. Round the unit cost to two decimal places.
2. Prepare a production report for the encapsulating department using the weighted average method. Follow the five steps outlined in the chapter. Round the unit cost to four decimal places.
3. CONCEPTUAL CONNECTION Explain why the weighted average method is easier to use than FIFO. Explain when weighted average will give about the same results as FIFO.

Check figures:
1. Cost of goods transferred out = $17,349
2. Cost of units transferred out = $23,400

Problem 6-42 Production Report, Ethical Behaviour

OBJECTIVE 3

Consider the following conversation between Gary Means, manager of a division that produces industrial machinery, and his controller, Donna Simpson, a chartered professional accountant:

Gary: Donna, we have a real problem. Our operating cash is dangerously low, and we are in desperate need of a loan. As you know, our financial position is marginal, and we need to come up with a way to show as much income as possible—and our assets will need bolstering as well.

Donna: I understand the problem, but I don't see what can be done at this point. This is the last week of the fiscal year, and it looks like we'll report income just slightly above break-even.

Gary: I understand all this. What we need is some creative accounting. I came up with an idea that might help us, and I wanted to get your opinion on it. I checked and we currently have 200 partially finished machines in process, averaging about 20 percent complete. That compares with the 1,000 units that we completed and sold during the year. When you calculated the per-unit cost, you used 1,040 equivalent units, giving us a manufacturing cost of $1,500 per unit. That per-unit cost gives us a COGS of $1.5 million and an EWIP of $60,000. The presence of the WIP gives us a chance to improve our financial position. If we report the units in WIP as 80 percent complete, instead of 20 percent, it will increase our equivalent units to 1,160. Our unit cost would reduce to about $1,345 and COGS to $1.345 million. The value of our WIP would increase to $215,200. With those financial stats, the loan would be a cinch.

Donna: Gary, I don't know. What you're suggesting is risky. It wouldn't take much auditing skill to catch this one.

Gary: You don't have to worry about that. The auditors won't be here for at least six to eight more weeks. By that time, we can have those partially completed units completed and sold. I can bury the labour cost by having some of our more loyal workers work overtime for some bonuses. The overtime will never be reported, and as you know, bonuses come out of the corporate budget and are assigned to overhead—next year's overhead. Donna, this will work. If we look good and get the loan to boot, corporate headquarters will treat us well. If we don't do this, we could lose our jobs.

Required:

1. Should Donna agree to Gary's proposal? Why or why not? To assist in deciding, review the Rules of Professional Conduct of CPA Ontario excerpted in Chapter 1. Do any apply?
2. Assume that Donna refuses to cooperate and that Gary accepts this decision and drops the matter. Does Donna have any obligation to report the divisional manager's behaviour to a superior? Explain.
3. Assume that Donna refuses to cooperate; however, Gary insists that the changes be made. Now what should she do? What would you do?
4. Suppose that Donna is aged 63 and that the prospects for employment elsewhere are bleak. Assume again that Gary insists that the changes be made. Donna also knows that his supervisor, the owner of the company, is his father-in-law. Under these circumstances, would your recommendations for Donna differ?

Problem 6-43 First-In, First-Out Method; Journal Entries

OBJECTIVE 1 2 4 6

Seacrest Company uses a process-costing system. The company manufactures a product that is processed in two departments, A and B, in which materials are added uniformly throughout the

(*Continued*)

process. As work is completed in department A , it is transferred to department B. The following summarizes the production activity and costs for November:

	Department A	Department B
Beginning inventories:		
Physical units	5,000	8,000
Costs:		
Transferred in	—	$160,940
Direct materials	$10,000	—
Conversion costs	$6,900	$16,800
Current production:		
Units started	25,000	?
Units transferred out	28,000	33,000
Costs:		
Transferred in	—	?
Direct materials	$57,800	$37,950
Conversion costs	$95,220	$128,100
Percentage completion:		
Beginning inventory	40%	50%
Ending inventory	80%	50%

Required:

1. Using the FIFO method, prepare the following for department A:
   a. A physical flow schedule.
   b. An equivalent unit calculation.
   c. Calculation of unit costs, rounded to two decimal places.
   d. Cost of EWIP and cost of goods transferred out.
   e. A cost reconciliation.
2. CONCEPTUAL CONNECTION Prepare journal entries that show the flow of manufacturing costs for department A. Use a conversion cost control account for conversion costs. Many firms are now combining direct labour and manufacturing overhead costs into one category. They are not tracking direct labour separately. Offer some reasons for this practice.

Check figure:
1.d. Cost of goods transferred out = $160,940

OBJECTIVE 6

Problem 6-44 First-In, First-Out Method

Benson Pharmaceuticals uses a process-costing system to determine the unit costs of the over-the-counter cold remedies that it produces. It has three departments: picking, encapsulating, and bottling. In the picking department, the ingredients for the cold capsules are added at the beginning of the process and measured, sifted, and blended. The blended mixture is transferred to the encapsulating department in litre containers. The encapsulating department fills capsules with the blended mixture, which is added at the beginning of the process. One litre of powdered mixture converts into 1,500 capsules. After the capsules are filled, sealed, and polished, they are transferred to the bottling department, where automated filling machines put them into bottles that are then affixed with a safety seal, lid, and label. Each bottle receives 50 capsules.

During August, the following results are available for the first two departments:

	Picking	Encapsulating
Beginning inventories:		
Physical units	20 litres	6,000
Costs:		
Materials	$575	$48
Labour	$610	$32
Overhead	?	?
Transferred in	—	$262
Current production:		
Transferred out	220 litres	320,000
Ending inventory	16 litres	3,000

(*Continued*)

Costs:		
Materials	$7,680	$1,275
Transferred in	—	?
Labour	$9,020	$3,076
Overhead	?	?
Percentage of completion:		
Beginning inventory	60%	40%
Ending inventory	75%	20%

Overhead in both departments is applied as a percentage of direct labour costs. In the picking department, overhead is 200 percent of direct labour. In the encapsulating department, the overhead rate is 150 percent of direct labour.

Check figures:

Cost of units started and completed in picking department = $15,573

Cost of units started and completed in encapsulating department = $23,174

Required:

Prepare a production report for each department using the FIFO method. (*Hint:* For the second department, you must convert litres to capsules.)

Problem 6-45 Weighted Average Cost Method, Nonuniform Inputs

OBJECTIVE 

Sherbrooke Toboggan Company manufactures toboggans for the Canadian market. The product goes through three manufacturing processes: forming, sealing, and assembly. In the forming department, the wood is shaped into the proper form; in the sealing department, a lacquer is applied to seal the wood and give it a satin finish; in the assembly department, the wood is assembled into the final product and cushions and rope are attached to the toboggan.

The company uses the weighted average cost method to calculate production costs, and materials are added in the sealing department at the beginning of the process. During August, the following information was determined for the sealing department:

BWIP:	
Units	2,000
Percentage complete	60%
Costs:	
Transferred in	$105,000
Materials	$3,950
Conversion	$12,350
Current production	
Units started	15,000
Costs:	
Transferred in	$750,000
Materials	$30,000
Conversion	$125,500
EWIP:	
Units	5,000
Percentage complete	35%

Required:

1. Prepare a cost of production report for the sealing department for August, including all five steps. (Take all calculations to four decimal places.)
2. Determine the unit cost in the previous period in the sealing department.

Check figure:

1. Cost of goods transferred out = $747,800

Problem 6-46 FIFO Cost Method, Nonuniform Inputs

OBJECTIVE 

Sherbrooke Toboggan Company manufactures toboggans for the Canadian market. The product goes through three manufacturing processes: forming, sealing, and assembly. In the forming department, the wood is shaped into the proper form; in the sealing department, a lacquer is applied to seal the wood and give it a satin finish; in the assembly department, the wood is assembled into the final product and cushions and rope are attached to the toboggan.

(Continued)

The company uses the FIFO method of costing to calculate production costs, and materials are added in the sealing department at the beginning of the process. During August, the following information was determined for the sealing department:

BWIP:	
Units	2,000
Percentage complete	60%
Costs:	
Transferred in	$105,000
Materials	$3,950
Conversion	$12,350
Current production	
Units started	15,000
Costs:	
Transferred in	$750,000
Materials	$30,000
Conversion	$125,500
EWIP:	
Units	5,000
Percentage complete	35%

Check figure:
1. Cost of EWIP = $277,500

Required:

1. Prepare a cost of production report for the sealing department for August, including all five steps. (Take all calculations to four decimal places.)
2. Explain how the calculations are different in this problem as compared to **Problem 6-45**.

OBJECTIVE 3 4

Problem 6-47 Weighted Average Cost Method, Multiple Processing Departments

Women's Entertainment television network features a TV show called *The Cupcake Girls*. This series follows best friends and business partners Heather and Lori in their hectic and entertaining journey to build a cupcake empire. In addition to the TV show, Heather and Lori bake cupcakes for retail customers for special occasions. The retail side of the business consists of two departments: the baking department and the packaging department. Within the baking department, the baking supplies (e.g., flour, sugar, eggs) are added at the beginning of the process; in contrast, the decorating supplies (e.g., icing, sprinkles) are added uniformly throughout the process. Within the packaging department, the costs of the packaging materials are added at the beginning of the process.

The following information relates to the baking department for February, an especially busy month because of Valentine's Day:

	Baking
BWIP:	
Units, 40 percent complete	750
Costs:	
Baking supplies	$985
Decorating supplies	$600
Conversion costs	$1,050
Current production	
Units started in February	7,400
Costs:	
Baking supplies	$11,825
Decorating supplies	$3,060
Conversion costs	$16,564
EWIP:	
Ending inventory, 80 percent complete	490

Required:

1. Prepare a production report for the baking department using the weighted average method.
2. For the packaging department, what is the number of units transferred in during February? What will be the transferred-in cost of those units?

PROFESSIONAL EXAMINATION PROBLEM*

Professional Examination Problem 6-48 Process Costing, Equivalent Units—Delphi Corporation

Delphi Corporation is a manufacturer that uses process costing to account for costs of production. Delphi manufactures a product in three separate departments: moulding, assembly, and finishing. The following information was obtained for the assembly department for the month of June:

Work-in-process, June 1—1,000 units made up of:

	Amount	Degree of Completion (%)
Moulding department costs transferred in	$32,000	100
Costs added by the assembly department		
Direct materials	20,000	100
Direct labour	7,200	60
Manufacturing overhead	5,500	50
Work-in-process, June 1	$64,700	

During the month of June, 5,000 units were transferred in from the moulding department at a cost of $160,000. The assembly department added the following $150,000 of costs:

Direct materials	$ 96,000
Direct labour	36,000
Manufacturing overhead	18,000
	$150,000

Four thousand units were completed and transferred to the finishing department.

At June 30, 2,000 units were still in WIP. The degree of completion of WIP at June 30 was:

Direct materials	90%
Direct labour	70
Manufacturing overhead	35

Required:

Calculate the cost of the units transferred out to the finishing department and the value of the ending WIP assuming that Delphi Corporation used: (a) the weighted average method; and (b) the FIFO method.

CASES

Case 6-49 Process Costing versus Alternative Costing Methods, Impact on Resource Allocation Decision

OBJECTIVE 1 2 3 4

Golding Manufacturing, a division of Farnsworth Sporting Inc., produces two different models of bows and eight models of knives. The bow-manufacturing process involves the production of two major subassemblies: the limbs and the handles. The limbs pass through four sequential processes before reaching final assembly: layup, moulding, fabricating, and finishing.

In the layup department, limbs are created by laminating layers of wood. In the moulding department, the limbs are heat-treated, under pressure, to become strong and resilient. In the fabricating department, any protruding glue or other processing residue is removed. Finally, in the finishing department, the limbs are cleaned with acetone, dried, and sprayed with the final finishes.

The handles pass through two processes before reaching final assembly: pattern and finishing. In the pattern department, blocks of wood are fed into a machine that is set to shape the handles. Different patterns are possible, depending on the machine's setting. After coming out of the machine, the handles are cleaned and smoothed. They then pass to the finishing department, where they are sprayed with the final finishes. In final assembly, the limbs and handles are assembled into different models using purchased parts such as pulley assemblies, weight-adjustment bolts, side plates, and string.

Golding, since its inception, has been using process costing to assign product costs. A predetermined overhead rate is used based on direct labour dollars (80 percent of direct labour dollars). Recently, Golding has hired a new controller, Karen Xu. After reviewing the product-costing procedures, Karen requested a meeting with the divisional manager, Aaron Suhr. The following is a transcript of their conversation.

Karen: Aaron, I have some concerns about our cost accounting system. We make two different models of bows and are treating them as if they were the same product. Now I know that the only real difference between the models is the handle. The processing of the handles is the same, but the handles differ significantly in the amount and quality of wood used. Our current costing does not reflect this difference in material input.

Aaron: Your predecessor is responsible for that decision. He believed that tracking the difference in material cost wasn't worth the effort. He simply didn't believe that it would make much difference in the unit cost of either model.

Karen: Well, he may have been right, but I have my doubts. If there is a significant difference, it could affect our views of which model is more important to the company. The additional bookkeeping isn't very difficult to implement. All we have to worry about is the pattern department. The other departments fit what I view as a process-costing pattern.

Aaron: Why don't you look into it? If there is a significant difference, go ahead and adjust the costing system.

After the meeting, Karen decided to collect cost data on the two models: the Deluxe model and the Econo model. She decided to track the costs for one week. At the end of the week, she had collected the following data from the pattern department:

a. A total of 2,500 bows were completed: 1,000 Deluxe models and 1,500 Econo models.
b. There was no BWIP; however, there were 300 units in EWIP: 200 Deluxe and 100 Econo models. Both models were 80 percent complete with respect to conversion costs and 100 percent complete with respect to materials.
c. The pattern department experienced the following costs:

Direct materials	$114,000
Direct labour	45,667

d. On an experimental basis, the requisition forms for materials were modified to identify the dollar value of the materials used by the Econo and Deluxe models:

Econo model	$30,000
Deluxe model	84,000

Required:

1. Determine the unit cost for the handles produced by the pattern department assuming that process costing is totally appropriate. Round the unit cost to two decimal places.

2. Calculate the unit cost of each handle using the separate cost information provided on materials. Round the unit cost to two decimal places.
3. Compare the unit costs computed in Requirements 1 and 2. Is Karen justified in her belief that a pure process-costing relationship is not appropriate? Describe the costing system that you would recommend.
4. In the past, the marketing manager has requested more money for advertising the Econo line. Aaron has repeatedly refused to grant any increase in this product's advertising budget because its per-unit profit (selling price less manufacturing cost) is so low. Given the results in Requirements 1 through 3, was Aaron justified in his position?

Case 6-50 Equivalent Units; Valuation of Work-In-Process Inventories; First-In, First-Out versus Weighted Average

OBJECTIVE 1 2 3 4

AKL Foundry manufactures metal components for different kinds of equipment used by the aerospace, commercial aircraft, medical equipment, and electronics industries. The company uses investment casting to produce the required components. Investment casting consists of creating, in wax, a replica of the final product and pouring a hard shell around it. After removing the wax, workers pour molten metal into the resulting cavity. What remains after the shell is broken is the desired metal object ready to be put to its designated use.

Metal components pass through eight processes: gating, shell creating, foundry work, cutoff, grinding, finishing, welding, and strengthening. Gating creates the wax mould and clusters the wax pattern around a sprue (a hole through which the molten metal will be poured through the gates into the mould in the foundry process), which is joined and supported by gates (flow channels) to form a tree of patterns. In the shell-creating process, the wax moulds are dipped alternately in a ceramic slurry and a fluidized bed of progressively coarser refractory grain until a sufficiently thick shell (or mould) completely encases the wax pattern. After drying, the mould is sent to the foundry process. Here, the wax is melted out of the mould, and the shell is fired, strengthened, and brought to the proper temperature. Molten metal is then poured into the dewaxed shell. Finally, the ceramic shell is removed, and the finished product is sent to the cutoff process, where the parts are separated from the tree by the use of a band saw. The parts are then sent to the grinding process, where the gates that allowed the molten metal to flow into the ceramic cavities are ground off using large abrasive grinders. In the finishing process, rough edges caused by the grinders are removed by small handheld pneumatic tools. Parts that are flawed at this point are sent to welding for corrective treatment. The last process uses heat to treat the parts to bring them to the desired strength.

Recently, the two partners who own AKL Foundry decided to split up and divide the business. In dissolving their business relationship, they are faced with the problem of dividing the business assets equitably. Since the company has two plants—one in Manitoba and one in Saskatchewan—a suggestion was made to split the business on the basis of geographic location. One partner would assume ownership of the plant in Manitoba, and the other would assume ownership of the plant in Saskatchewan. However, this arrangement has one major complication: the amount of WIP inventory located in the Saskatchewan plant.

The Saskatchewan facility has been in operation for more than a decade and is full of WIP. The Manitoba facility has been operational for only two years and has much smaller WIP inventories. The partner located in Manitoba has argued that to disregard the unequal values of the WIP inventories would be grossly unfair.

Unfortunately, during the entire business history of AKL Foundry, WIP inventories have never been assigned any value. In computing the COGS each year, the company has followed the policy of adding depreciation to the out-of-pocket costs of direct labour, direct materials, and overhead. Accruals for the company are nearly nonexistent, and there are hardly ever any ending inventories of materials.

Last year, the Saskatchewan plant had sales of $2,028,670. The COGS is itemized as follows:

Direct materials	$378,000
Direct labour	530,300
Overhead	643,518

Upon request, the owners of AKL have provided the following supplementary information (percentages are cumulative):

Costs Used by Each Process as a Percentage of Total Cost

	Direct Materials (%)	Direct Total Labour Cost (%)
Gating	23	35
Shell creating	70	50
Foundry work	100	70
Cutoff	100	72
Grinding	100	80
Finishing	100	90
Welding	100	93
Strengthening	100	100

Gating had 10,000 units in BWIP, 60 percent complete. Assume that all materials are added at the beginning of each process. During the year, 50,000 units were completed and transferred out. The ending inventory had 11,000 unfinished units, 60 percent complete.

Required:

1. The partners of AKL want a reasonable estimate of the cost of WIP inventories. Using the gating department's inventory as an example, prepare an estimate of the cost of the EWIP. What assumptions did you make? Did you use the FIFO or weighted average method? Why? Round the unit cost to two decimal places.
2. Assume that the shell-creating process has 8,000 units in BWIP, 20 percent complete. During the year, 50,000 units were completed and transferred out. (All 50,000 units were sold; no other units were sold.) The EWIP inventory had 8,000 units, 30 percent complete. Compute the value of the shell-creating department's EWIP. What additional assumptions had to be made?

Case 6-51 First-In, First-Out versus Weighted Average

Elise is the cost analyst at Canadian Steel Tube and Wire Company, which manufactures pup joints. Oil–country tubular goods pup joints are made of carbon or alloy steel; welded or seamless; heat-treated or not heat-treated; varyingly finished with an outside diameter from $2^3/_8$ inches to $4\frac{1}{2}$ inches (60.3 mm to 114.3 mm) and in lengths from 2 feet to 12 feet (61 cm to 366 cm).

On July 22, 2015, the Canada Border Services Agency (CBSA) received a written complaint from Canadian Steel Tube and Wire Company (hereafter, "the Complainant") alleging that imports of certain pup joints originating in or exported from the People's Republic of China (China) are being dumped and subsidized and causing injury to the Canadian industry.

On August 12, 2015, pursuant to subsection 32(1) of the *Special Import Measures Act* (SIMA), the CBSA informed the Complainant that the complaint was properly documented. The CBSA also notified the government of China (GOC) that a properly documented complaint had been received and provided the GOC with the non-confidential version of the subsidy portion of the complaint, which excluded sections dealing with normal value, export price, and margin of dumping.

The Complainant provided evidence to support the allegations that certain pup joints from China have been dumped and subsidized. The evidence also disclosed a reasonable indication that the dumping and subsidizing had caused injury and are threatening to cause injury to the Canadian industry producing these goods.

The CBSA has asked Canadian Steel Tube and Wire Company to provide further and more substantive evidence of injury caused by the dumping and subsidization of foreign manufactured pup joints. For the purpose of this investigation, injury can be demonstrated by evidence of lower production levels and/or proof of idle manufacturing assets, lower sales, lower profit, or employee downsizing.

Evidence of injury may have dramatic consequences because it will inform the CBSA investigation as to how much antidumping relief (in the form of tariff-based penalties on dumped and subsidized goods) it should award Canadian pup joint manufacturers for a period of five years. The greater the injury evidenced, the more the relief and the greater the economic advantage enjoyed by Canadian Steel Tube and Wire Company for the next five years.

On December 12, 2015, Elise is continuing to oversee the process-costing method using the FIFO method. Senior management, which has fixated upon providing injury evidence by showing lower profits, suspect that the FIFO method is hiding the extent of injury by understating the COGS and thereby overstating gross profit and net income.

Management is asking Elise to advise whether COGS would be increased or decreased by switching to weighted average process costing.

While all this is happening, due to the glut of pup joints caused by foreign dumping, demand for the manufacturing inputs for pup joints has fallen significantly by one-half. The drop in Canadian manufacturer demand for pup joint inputs has caused a similarly significant decline in the price of pup joint inputs. This drop in price has helped lower input costs for Canadian Steel Tube and Wire Company over the past year. However, due to slow sales, 75 percent of pup joint input raw materials on hand were purchased before the drop in prices.

Between September and November 2015, 30 percent of the pup joint input inventory on hand was used in the manufacture of completed and sold pup joints.

Required:

Given the information above, which process costing method would provide greater evidence of injury for Canadian Steel Tube and Wire Company?

7

Activity-Based Costing and Management

After studying Chapter 7, you should be able to:

1. Explain the potential for cost distortion using functional- or volume-based costing approaches.
2. Explain how an activity-based costing system works for product costing.
3. Describe activity-based customer costing and activity-based supplier costing.
4. Explain how activity-based management can be used for cost reduction.

Jim West/Alamy Stock Photo

EXPERIENCE MANAGERIAL DECISIONS

with Tim Hortons and Cold Stone Creamery

Experts believe that ice cream, as we currently know it, was invented in the 1600s and was popularized in part by Charles I of England, who made it a staple of the royal table. Ice cream remains as popular as ever today. However, trips to the local ice cream parlour have changed dramatically over the past quarter-century.

Tim Hortons, the popular Canadian doughnut store franchise, formed an international partnership with American ice cream store franchise giant Cold Stone Creamery, a division of Kahala Corp. The co-branding partnership between the two companies was established in 2009 when Tim Hortons franchises were added to 50 Cold Stone Creamery locations in the United States. In an effort to simplify its menu, Tim Hortons has decided not to continue the co-branding in Canada, but will continue this concept in the United States. The stores will be co-branded but not co-owned, in much the same way that the Tim Hortons partnership was created with the Wendy's hamburger franchise.

Cold Stone Creamery has helped lead this development with its innovative new business model focused on making ice cream buying an entertainment experience for the entire family. Cold Stone operates 1,500 stores worldwide, with another 1,000 new franchises in the works. Cold Stone executives must understand and control the company's complex cost structure in order to profitably manage its ice cream empire. For example, its most popular product line—ice cream with "Mix-Ins" ingredients—boasts eight basic flavours and some seasonal flavours of ice cream, with up to 30 different "Mix-Ins," and three sizes, which represents more than a thousand possible custom order combinations! The vast quantity of combinations is great for customers with varied tastes but is quite challenging for Cold Stone to manage given the different types of activities associated with the different types of product orders. Therefore, Cold Stone adopted activity-based costing (ABC), to identify the activities associated with each type of ice cream order that impact costs, and to estimate the costs of these activities.

Two important drivers of costs for Cold Stone are ingredients and time, both of which vary significantly across individual customer orders. With the insights gained from its ABC analysis, Cold Stone understands the cost of various orders' preparation times, which are measured in seconds. In addition to labour, Cold Stone's ABC system considers the costs associated with training, uniforms, and employee benefits when estimating the cost of each second required in making each product. When combined with other costs, the ABC analysis provides an estimate of profit margin by product type. If a particular product is not making its expected margin, Cold Stone managers know to explore and fine tune the activities involved in creating the product. Understanding its complex cost structure provides Cold Stone managers with a significant challenge. However, it is the mastery of this costing challenge that has provided Cold Stone Creamery with a valuable competitive advantage that has enabled it to become one of the most profitable and fastest-growing franchises in the world.

LIMITATIONS OF VOLUME-BASED COST ACCOUNTING SYSTEMS

Cost Drivers

Explain the potential for cost distortion using functional- or volume-based costing approaches.

Organizations engage in various activities that consume resources and cause costs. Every activity has a *cost driver*, a factor that drives or causes costs. Cost drivers may be volume related, such as labour or machine costs, or they may reflect the frequency of certain events, such as number of setups or kilometres driven. For example, setup costs are driven by the number of setups required as production moves from one kind of product to another. Similarly, distance travelled drives auto fuel costs. In most instances, more than one cost driver causes costs. Consider the insurance cost of a building. It can be driven by the value of the property, the value of plant and equipment in the building, the number of employees working in the building, the number of previous claims made, and so on. Usually the insurance company will take all of these factors into account when setting an insurance premium. The individual factors will be ranked in terms of importance. Traditionally, cost drivers have been at the unit level, in which case they are referred to as *unit-level drivers*. That single unit cost includes direct material, direct labour, and some traceable overhead. Products or services delivered in batches will have what are known as *batch-level drivers*. These include purchase orders, equipment maintenance, equipment depreciation, and quality control.

Overhead Rates

Plantwide and departmental overhead rates based on direct labour hours, machine hours, or other volume-based measures have been used for decades to assign overhead costs to products and continue to be used successfully by many organizations. However, for many settings, this approach to costing is equivalent to an averaging approach and may produce distorted or inaccurate costs. Distorted costs can be a real problem in extremely competitive environments like the automobile industry, where in 2007 General Motors, for the first time in 76 years, lost its spot as the world's largest automaker as a result of unrelenting competition from an increasing number of competitors like Toyota. To understand why average costing can cause difficulties, consider the case where two customers place orders with a supplier for a machine part. The first company orders 10 units of the part and the other orders 100 units of the part. Each order requires the same amount of time and effort to fill and under traditional cost accounting methods, each customer order would be charged the same amount per unit for the product. However, one can easily see that the order for 100 units costs less to fill on a per-unit basis than the order for 10 units. So using an average cost would underprice the 10-unit order and overprice the 100-unit order. The order-filling activity cost has no direct correlation to the number of units in an order.

In the same way, plantwide and departmental rates can produce average costs that severely understate or overstate individual product costs. Product cost distortions can be damaging, particularly for those firms whose business environment may be characterized by increasing competitive pressures (often on a worldwide level), decreasing profit margins, continuous improvement, total quality management (TQM), total customer satisfaction, or sophisticated technology. Firms operating in these types of business environments, in particular, need accurate cost information in order to make effective decisions and to stay competitive. In order to produce accurate cost information, it is important that the firm's cost system accurately reflect the firm's underlying business (or economic) reality. However, as firms operating in an intensely competitive environment adopt new strategies to achieve competitive excellence, their cost accounting systems must change to keep pace. Unfortunately, due to the time commitment and costs required to change cost systems, some firms do not change their systems when their business environments change. Due to the poor matching between the firm's dynamic business reality and the cost system's stagnant representation of that reality, cost distortions can result. Thus it is important that the management accountant continually ask the question, "How well does the cost system's *representation* of my business match the economic *reality* of my business?" If the answer is "Not very well," then it is likely that the cost system needs to be changed.

The need for more accurate product costs has forced many companies to take a serious look at their costing procedures. Two major factors can impair the ability of unit-based plantwide and departmental rates to assign overhead costs accurately:

- if the proportion of non-unit-related overhead costs to total overhead costs is large, or
- if the degree of product diversity is great.

Non-Unit-Related Overhead Costs

The use of either plantwide rates or departmental rates assumes that a product's consumption of overhead resources is related strictly to the number of units produced. For **unit-level activities**—activities that are performed each time a unit is produced—this assumption makes sense. Traditional, volume-based cost systems label the costs associated with these activities as variable in nature, because they increase or decrease in direct proportion to increases or decreases in the levels of these unit-level activities. All other costs (i.e., ones that are not unit-level) are considered fixed by volume-based cost systems.

But what if there are *non-unit-level activities*—activities that are not performed each time a unit of product is produced—that are variable in their nature? These costs vary with some other factor or factors, other than units, and identifying such factor(s) will be very helpful in predicting and managing these costs. Proponents of activity-based costing (ABC) support the view that costs are:

- *unit-level* (i.e., vary with output volume),
- *batch-level* (i.e., vary with the number of groups or batches that are run),
- *product-sustaining* (i.e., vary with the diversity of the product or service line), or
- *facility-sustaining* (i.e., do not vary with any factor but are necessary in operating the manufacturing facility).[1]

Exhibit 7.1 shows the ABC hierarchy. Activity-based costing is discussed in more detail later in this chapter, but the ABC cost hierarchy is identified at this point to illustrate its usefulness in helping managers realize that certain costs associated with non-unit-level activities are driven by other factors.

EXHIBIT 7.1

ABC Hierarchy

Type of Cost	Description of Cost Driver	Example
Unit-level	Varies with output volume (e. g., units); traditional variable costs	Cost of indirect materials for labelling each bottle of President's Choice ketchup
Batch-level	Varies with the number of batches produced	Cost of cleaning the bottling equipment for each batch of Steam Whistle beer
Product-sustaining	Varies with the number of product lines	Cost of product design and quality control of different garments produced by lululemon
Facility-sustaining	Necessary to operate the plant facility but does not vary with units, batches, or product lines	Cost of a Bombardier plant manager's salary

[1] R. Cooper, "Cost Classification in Unit-Based and Activity-Based Manufacturing Cost Systems," *Journal of Cost Management for the Manufacturing Industry* (Fall 1990): 4–14.

Consider the following two examples of non-unit-level activities: setting up equipment and re-engineering products. Often, the same equipment is used to produce different products. "Setting up equipment" means preparing it for the particular type of product being made. For example, a vat may be used to dye T-shirts. After a batch of 1,000 red T-shirts is completed, the vat must be carefully cleaned before a batch of 3,000 green T-shirts can be produced. Thus, setup costs are incurred each time a batch of products is produced. Whether a batch consists of 1,000 or 3,000 units, the cost of setup is the same. So as more batches are produced, setup costs increase. The number of setups (a batch-level cost), not the number of units produced (a unit-level cost), is a much better measure of the cost associated with the setup activity.

At times, based on customer feedback, firms face the necessity of redesigning their products. For example, Bombardier Recreational Products (BRP) may issue engineering work orders to improve the operating efficiency of its Ski-Doos or Sea-Doos. Product re-engineering costs may depend on the number of different engineering work orders (a product-sustaining cost) rather than on the units produced of any given product. Thus, *non-unit-level drivers* such as setups and engineering orders are needed for accurate cost assignment of non-unit-level activities. Also, JetBlue's decision to add a second type of jet, the Embraer 190, to its existing fleet of Airbus A320s caused it to incur significant additional product-sustaining costs that it would not have incurred had it stayed with only one type of plane. These additional product-sustaining costs included the costs for doubling the spare parts inventory, maintenance programs, and separate pilot-training tracks.[2] Therefore, **non-unit-level activity drivers** (i.e., batch, product-sustaining, and facility-sustaining activities) are factors that measure the consumption of non-unit-level activities by products and other cost objects, whereas **unit-level activity drivers** measure the consumption of unit-level activities. **Activity drivers**, then, are factors that measure the consumption of activities by products and other cost objects and can be classified as either *unit-level* or *non-unit-level*. By example, BRP may incur $350 of raw materials for each Sea-Doo it produces (unit-level), but the $1,000 setup cost to switch from Sea-Doo to Ski-Doo production is independent of the number of units produced in each batch after the setup charges are incurred (non-unit-level).[3]

Using only unit-based activity drivers to assign non-unit-related overhead costs can create distorted product costs. The severity of this distortion depends on what proportion of total overhead costs the non-unit-based costs represent. For many companies, this proportion can be significant. This possibility suggests that some care should be exercised in assigning non-unit-based overhead costs. If non-unit-based overhead costs are only a small proportion of total overhead costs, then the distortion of product costs will be quite small, and using unit-based activity drivers to assign overhead costs may be acceptable.

concept Q&A

One department inspects each product produced. A second department inspects only one unit of every 100 units in a batch. Which inspection activity is unit-level, and which is non-unit-level?

Answers on pages 734 to 738.

Product Diversity

The presence of significant non-unit overhead costs is a necessary but not a sufficient condition for plantwide and departmental rates to result in distorted costs. For example, if products consume the non-unit-level overhead activities in the same proportion as the unit-level overhead activities, then no product-costing distortion will occur if traditional overhead assignment methods are used. The presence of product diversity is also necessary for product cost distortion to occur. **Product diversity** means that products consume overhead activities in consistently different proportions. This may occur for several reasons. For example, differences in product size, product complexity, setup time, and batch size all can cause products to consume overhead at different rates. Regardless

[2] S. Carey, "Balancing Act: Amid JetBlue's Rapid Ascent, CEO Adopts Big Rivals' Traits," *The Wall Street Journal* (August 25, 2005).

[3] Numbers quoted are for illustrative purposes only and are not intended to represent the real costs, which are not known by the authors.

of the nature of the product diversity, under traditional approaches product costs will be distorted whenever the quantity of unit-based overhead that a product consumes does not vary in direct proportion to the quantity of non-unit-based overhead consumed. The proportion of each activity consumed by a product is defined as the **consumption ratio**.

Illustrating the Failure of Plantwide or Departmental Rates

To illustrate how traditional unit-based overhead rates can distort product costs, consider a plant that produces two models of washers: a deluxe and a regular model. The detailed data are provided in Exhibit 7.2. Because the quantity of the regular model produced is 10 times greater than that of the deluxe, we can label the regular model a high-volume product and the deluxe model a low-volume product. The models are produced in batches.

EXHIBIT 7.2

Product-Costing Data

	Activity Usage Measures		
	Deluxe	Regular	Total
Units produced	10	100	110
Prime costs	$800	$8,000	$8,800
Direct labour hours	20	80	100
Machine hours	10	40	50
Setup hours	3	1	4
Number of moves	6	4	10

Activity Cost Data

Activity	Activity Cost
Setting up equipment	$1,200
Moving goods	800
Machining	1,500
Assembly	1,500
Total	$5,000

Remember that prime costs represent direct materials and direct labour. Given that these costs are direct in nature, they can easily be traced to each individual unit produced. It is the indirect (or overhead) costs that must be treated differently in different types of cost systems. Usually, activity-based cost systems generate more accurate cost data than unit-based cost systems because of their more detailed treatment of overhead costs. For simplicity, only four types of overhead activities, performed by four distinct support departments, are assumed: setting up the equipment for each batch (different configurations are needed for the electronic components associated with each model), moving a batch, machining, and assembly. Assembly is performed after each department's operations.

Problems with Cost Distortion The activity usage data in Exhibit 7.2 reveal that some serious problems will emerge from using either plantwide or departmental rates for assigning overhead costs. The main problem with either procedure is the assumption that unit-level drivers such as machine hours or direct labour hours cause (or drive) all overhead costs.

From Exhibit 7.2, it can be seen that each batch of the regular model, the high-volume product, uses four times as many direct labour hours as the low-volume product

(80 hours vs. 20 hours). Thus, if a plantwide rate is used, the regular model will be assigned four times more overhead cost than the deluxe model. But is this reasonable? Do unit-based drivers explain the consumption of all overhead activities? In particular, is it reasonable to assume that each product's consumption of overhead increases in direct proportion to the direct labour hours used? Now consider the four overhead activities to see if the unit-level drivers accurately reflect the demands of regular and deluxe model production.

The data in Exhibit 7.2 suggest that a significant portion of overhead costs are not driven by direct labour hours. Each product's demands for setup and material-moving activities are more logically related to the setup hours and the number of moves, respectively. These non-unit activities represent 40 percent (= \$2,000/\$5,000) of the total overhead costs—a significant percentage. Notice that the low-volume product, the deluxe model, uses three times more setup hours than the regular model (3/1) and one and a half times as many moves (6/4) to produce one-tenth the number of units. However, using a plantwide rate based on direct labour hours, a unit-based activity driver assigns four times more setup and material moving costs to the regular model than to the deluxe. Thus, product diversity exists, and, using traditional overhead application methods, we should expect product cost distortion because the quantity of unit-based overhead that each product consumes does not vary in direct proportion to the quantity consumed of non-unit-based overhead.

Cornerstone 7.1 illustrates how to calculate the consumption ratios for the two batches of products. Consumption ratios represent the proportion

analytical Q&A

The activity driver for the receiving activity is the number of orders processed. Product A uses 10 orders and product B uses 30 orders. Calculate the consumption ratios for product A and product B.

Answers on pages 734 to 738.

CORNERSTONE 7.1 Calculating Consumption Ratios

Information:

Activity usage information, Exhibit 7.2

Required:

Calculate the consumption ratios for each product.

Solution:

First, we must identify the activity driver for each activity. Next, divide the amount of driver used for each product by the total driver quantity. We obtain the following:

	Consumption Ratios by Batch		
Overhead Activity	**Deluxe Model**	**Regular Model**	**Activity Driver**
Setting up equipment	0.75[a]	0.25[a]	Setup hours
Moving goods	0.60[b]	0.40[b]	Number of moves
Machining	0.20[c]	0.80[c]	Machine hours
Assembly	0.20[d]	0.80[d]	Direct labour hours

[a] 3/4 (deluxe) and 1/4 (regular)
[b] 6/10 (deluxe) and 4/10 (regular)
[c] 10/50 (deluxe) and 40/50 (regular)
[d] 20/100 (deluxe) and 80/100 (regular)

Why:

Because different products or services require different amounts of resources to be completed. Therefore one has to calculate the ratio (proportion) of each activity spent on each product/service produced.

of each activity consumed by a product. The consumption ratios suggest that a plantwide rate based on direct labour hours will overcost the regular model and undercost the deluxe model.

Solving the Problem of Cost Distortion The cost distortion just described can be solved by the use of activity rates. That is, rather than assigning the overhead costs by using a single, plantwide rate, why not calculate a rate for each overhead activity and then use these activity rates to assign overhead costs? Cornerstone 7.2 shows how to calculate these rates.

Calculating Activity Rates

CORNERSTONE 7.2

Information:

(from Exhibit 7.2)

Activity	Activity Cost ($)	Driver	Driver Quantity
Setting up equipment	1,200	Setup hours	4
Moving goods	800	Number of moves	10
Machining	1,500	Machine hours	50
Assembly	1,500	Direct labour hours	100

Required:

Calculate activity rates.

Solution:

The rates are obtained by dividing the activity cost by the total driver quantity:

Setup rate:	$1,200/4 setup hours = $300 per setup hour
Materials handling rate:	$800/10 moves = $80 per move
Machining rate:	$1,500/50 machine hours = $30 per machine hour
Assembly rate:	$1,500/100 direct labour hours = $15 per direct labour hour

Why:

Because different activities consume organizations' resources at different rates. It is important to determine the consumption rates for each activity a firm is involved with using different and pertinent drivers for each activity.

Because products consume these activities at different rates, to assign overhead costs, the amount of activity consumed by each product is needed along with the activity rates. Cornerstone 7.3 shows how to calculate the unit cost for each product by using activity rates. A visual summary is provided in Exhibit 7.3.

analytical Q&A

Inspecting provides 4,000 inspection hours and costs $80,000 per year. What is the activity rate for inspecting?

Answers on pages 734 to 738.

Comparison of Volume-Based and Activity-Based Product Costs A plantwide rate based on direct labour hours is calculated by dividing the total overhead costs by the total direct labour hours: $5,000/100 = $50 per

CORNERSTONE 7.3

Calculating Activity-Based Unit Costs

Information:

	Deluxe	Regular	Activity Rate($)
Units produced per year	10	100	
Prime costs	$800	$8,000	
Setup hours	3	1	300
Number of moves	6	4	80
Machine hours	10	40	30
Direct labour hours	20	80	15

Required:

Calculate the unit cost for the deluxe and the regular model.

Solution:

	Deluxe	Regular
Prime costs	$ 800	$ 8,000
Overhead costs:		
Setups:		
$300 × 3 setup hours	900	
$300 × 1 setup hour		300
Moving materials:		
$80 × 6 moves	480	
$80 × 4 moves		320
Machining:		
$30 × 10 machine hours	300	
$30 × 40 machine hours		1,200
Assembly:		
$15 × 20 direct labour hours	300	
$15 × 80 direct labour hours		1,200
Total manufacturing costs	$2,780	$11,020
Units produced	÷ 10	÷ 100
Unit cost (Total costs/Units)	$ 278	$110.20

Why:

Because a firm needs product/service cost per unit information to price inventories, price products competitively, prepare financial statements, and so on. Adding together the cost per unit of each activity and dividing it by the total number of units produced allows us to calculate the per-unit-of-product cost. Activity-based costing will usually provide more accurate costing information, especially if different products consume resources differently.

EXHIBIT 7.3

Visual Summary of Cornerstones 7.2 and 7.3

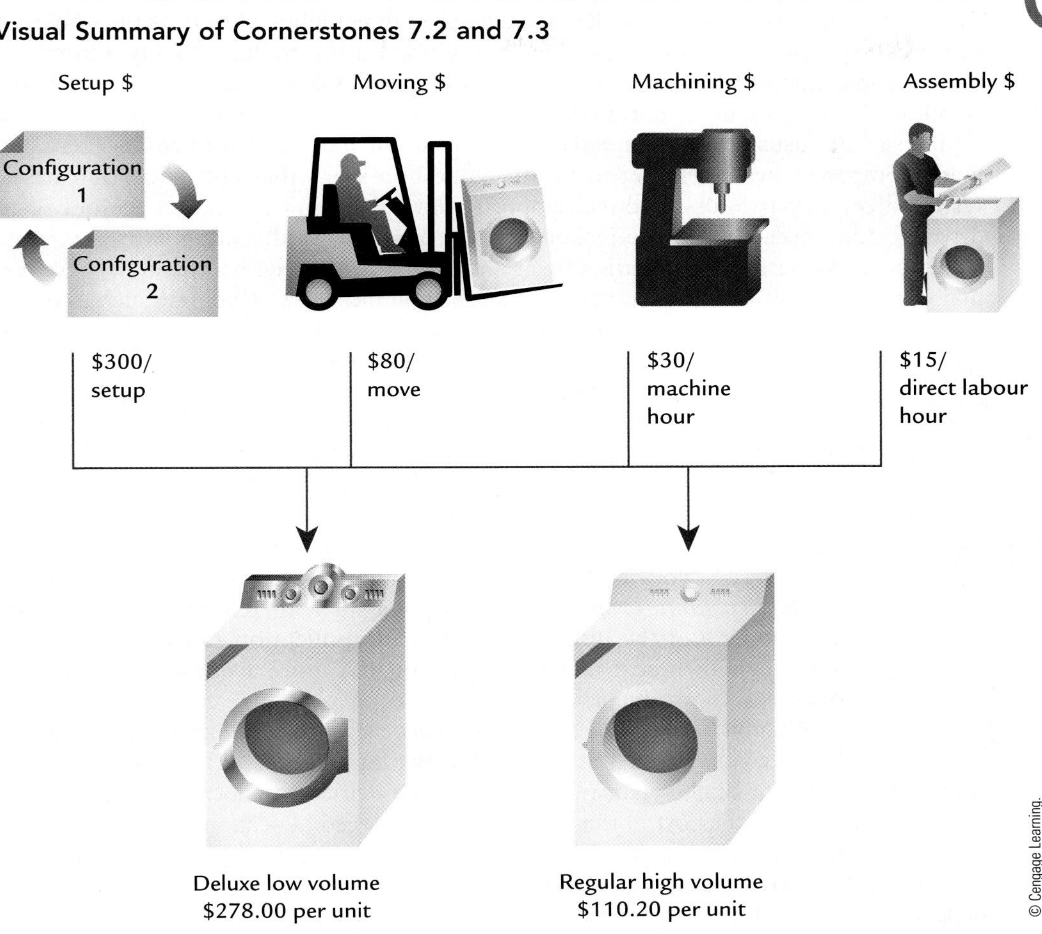

direct labour hour. The product cost for each product using this single unit-level overhead rate is calculated as follows:

	Deluxe	Regular
Prime costs	$ 800	$ 8,000
Overhead costs:		
$50 × 20	1,000	
$50 × 80		4,000
Total cost	$1,800	$12,000
Units produced	÷ 10	÷ 100
Unit cost	$ 180	$ 120

Now compare these product costs with the activity-based cost of Cornerstone 7.3. This comparison clearly illustrates the effects of using only unit-based activity drivers to assign overhead costs. The activity-based cost assignment reflects the pattern of overhead consumption and is, therefore, much more accurate. Activity-based product costing reveals that volume-based costing undercosts the low-volume deluxe model and overcosts the high-volume regular model. In fact, the ABC assignment increases the reported cost of the deluxe model by $98 per unit and decreases the reported cost of the regular model by almost $10 per unit—a movement in the right direction given the pattern of overhead consumption. This disparity in reported costs is typical of traditional costing methods versus activity-based costing methods. These discrepancies can lead to incorrect and expensive decisions, so it is important for the costing method chosen to reflect the most accurate costs possible.

ACTIVITY-BASED COSTING (ABC)

OBJECTIVE 2

Explain how an activity-based costing system works for product costing.

In the past, the vast majority of departments used direct labour hours as the only cost driver for applying costs to products and services. But in modern, highly automated organizations, direct labour hours are often not a good measure of the cause of costs. Labour-related costs in an automated system may be only a small percentage of the total costs and usually are not related to the causes of most overhead costs. Therefore, many companies are beginning to use machine hours or other cost-allocation bases. Using direct labour hours or direct labour dollars or machine hours as the only cost driver seldom meets the cause/effect criterion desired in cost allocation. However, most managers in modern manufacturing firms and automated service companies believe it is inappropriate to allocate all overhead costs based on measures of volume such as direct labour hours or direct labour dollars or machine hours. If many costs are caused by non-volume-based cost drivers, ABC should be considered.

> **analytical Q&A**
>
> Producing 5,000 units of a game console requires $150,000 of prime costs, uses 1,000 machine hours, and takes 600 setup hours. The activity rates are $20 per machine hour and $50 per setup hour. What is the unit cost of a game console?
>
> Answers on pages 734 to 738.

Activity-based costing is the process of assigning overhead costs to various cost categories related to the nature of the activity that causes (drives) these costs. By identifying costs by the activities that drive them, we can more accurately assign these costs to the products being produced. Each cost pool will have its own predetermined overhead application rate and will be assigned to products based on that specific cost driver. The types of costs will be categorized as *unit-level, batch-level, product-sustaining,* and *facility-sustaining*. The increase in the number of cost pools and the individual overhead application rates for each pool with their own cost drivers will result in a more accurate allocation of overhead to products.

Exhibit 7.4 draws a comparison between traditional costing and activity-based costing as it shows how the two approaches differ significantly. In traditional costing, a single, plantwide overhead rate is used to allocate all the indirect, or overhead, costs to the cost object. In ABC, a two-staged allocation takes place where the indirect or overhead costs are first allocated to individual cost pools based on activities. Then these costs are allocated to the cost object based on multiple allocation rates depending on different, and more accurate, cost drivers. The indirect costs represent all the

EXHIBIT 7.4

Traditional Cost Allocation vs. Activity-Based Costing Allocation

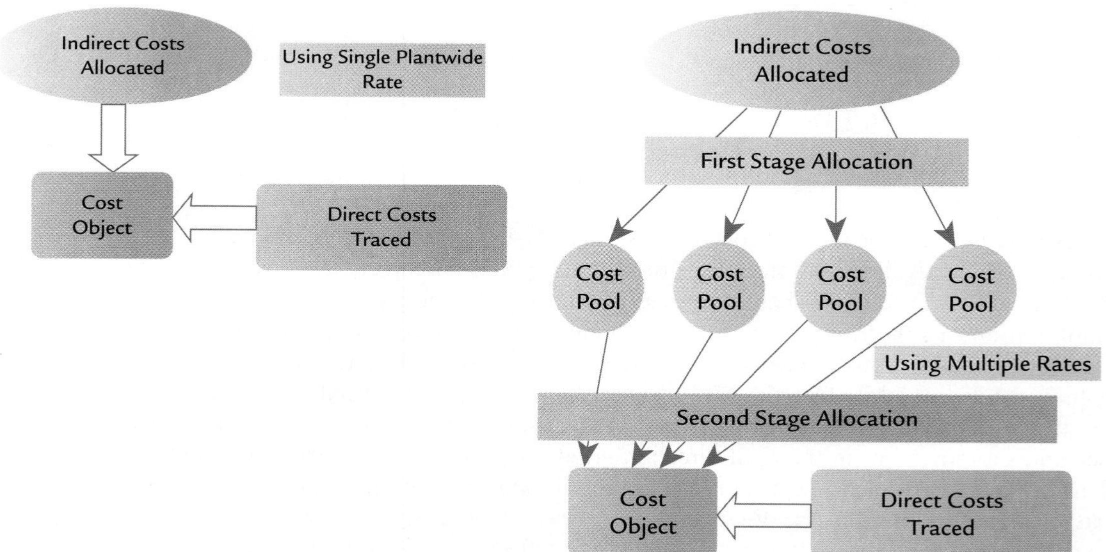

costs that are necessary for the manufacturing process but which cannot easily be traced to the end product or cost object. Direct costs, on the other hand, are those costs that can easily be traced to the cost object and, therefore, do not need an allocation rate. Exhibit 7.5 summarizes the steps for implementing ABC.

EXHIBIT 7.5

Steps for Implementing Activity-Based Costing

1. Identify activities (cost drivers), cost pools, and activity measures.
2. Assign overhead costs to activity cost pools.
3. Calculate activity rates for each cost pool.
4. Assign overhead costs to cost objects using the activity rates and activity measures.
5. Prepare management reports.

The goal is to reflect, as accurately as possible, how resources are consumed.

Corporate and Social Responsibility

One of the ethical standards of the Society of Management Accountants (which has carried forward under the new CPA alignment) requires that its members maintain professional expertise by continually developing knowledge and skills. An interesting issue is whether accounting professionals who resist learning different cost management methods are exhibiting ethical behaviour. At the very least, cost accounting professionals should learn about different approaches and assess whether the benefit–cost tradeoffs justify their use.

One can see from the Cold Stone Creamery example that a management accountant who did not keep up with new developments in the cost analysis area might be providing management with inadequate or inaccurate information that would prevent the company from competing with others in that business.

Activity-based costing accumulates overhead costs for each of the organization's activities and then assigns the costs of activities to the products, services, or other cost objects that caused those activities. To establish a cause/effect relationship between an activity and a cost object, cost drivers are identified for each activity. For example,

Activity	Cost Driver
Production setup	Number of production runs
Engineering	Number of engineering change orders
Maintenance	Number of machine hours
Power	Number of kilowatt-hours
Cleaning	Number of squares metres to be cleaned

Consider the billing department (BD) of a mobile phone company. The BD is engaged in providing account billing, account verification, account inquiries, and email correspondence.

Activity Centre	Cost Driver
Account billing	Number of lines
Account verification	Number of accounts verified
Account inquiry	Number of inquiries
Emails	Number of emails

Activity-based costing systems can turn many indirect manufacturing overhead costs into direct costs because each activity cost is caused by its cost drivers, and therefore costs can be traced to those activities (direct costs). Appropriate selection of activities and cost drivers allows managers to trace many manufacturing overhead costs to each activity. Because ABC systems classify more costs as direct than do traditional systems, managers have greater confidence in the costs of products and services that those systems report.

Consider the following visual explanation of ABC for a manufacturing company:

Visual Explanation of a Top-Down Structure and Activity-Based Costing

A. Business Functions

- Research and Development
- Product Design
- (Manufacturing)
- Marketing
- Distribution

B. Production Departments

The manufacturing function has three departments:

- Machining
- (Assembly)
- Forging

C. Activities

The assembly department involves four activities:

- Materials Handling
- Machine Inserting
- Testing
- Packaging

Once the organization structure is understood, one can begin the process of analyzing the activities in each area and the cost associated with them.

Set of Key Questions

Interview questions can be used to identify activities and activity attributes needed for costing purposes. The information derived from these questions serves as the basis for constructing an activity dictionary as well as providing data helpful for assigning resource costs to individual activities. The list is not exhaustive, but serves to illustrate the nature of the information gathering process.

Key Questions

1. How many employees are in your department? (Activities consume labour.)
2. Describe what they do. (Activities are people doing things for other people.)
3. Do customers outside your department use any equipment? (Activities also can be equipment working for other people. In other words, the equipment provides the service for someone by itself.)
4. What resources are used by each activity (equipment, materials, energy)? (Activities consume resources in addition to labour.)
5. What are the outputs of each activity? (This helps to identify activity drivers.)
6. Who or what uses the activity output? (This identifies the cost object: products, other activities, customers, etc.)

Key Questions (Continued)

7. How much time do workers spend on each activity? How much time does equipment spend on each activity? (Information is needed to assign the cost of labour and equipment to activities.)

Activity-based cost assignment consists of the following three steps:

1. *Identify and define activities using interviews and surveys*. Then build a list of activities (i.e., an **activity dictionary**). This dictionary lists **activity attributes**—that is, pieces of financial and nonfinancial information that describe the activities. For example:
   - Activity name—usually consists of an action verb and an object.
   - A description of the tasks that make up the activity.
   - Classification as a *primary activity* (activity consumed by a product or customer) or a *secondary activity* (activity consumed by other primary or secondary activities).
   - Activity driver—a measure of activity output.
2. *Assign costs to activities*. Determine the cost of resources (such as materials, labour, and capital) consumed by each activity:
   - If the resource is exclusive to the activity (such as materials), use direct tracing.
   - If the resource is shared by several activities, use drivers to trace and measure the consumption of resources by each activity.
   - The costs of secondary activities are ultimately assigned to primary activities using activity drivers.
3. *Assign costs to products*. After the cost of primary activities is calculated, assign the cost of these activities to products based on usage of the activity as measured by activity drivers. Costs assigned to products are calculated as follows:

Cost assigned to product = Predetermined activity rate × Actual usage of activity

ABC costing has several shortcomings. First, ABC does not conform to GAAP. ABC suggests that some nonproduct costs (such as those for R&D) *should* be allocated to products, whereas certain other product costs (such as factory building depreciation) should *not* be allocated to products. Therefore, most companies use ABC for internal reporting but continue to prepare their external financial statements with the more traditional system: job-order, using plantwide or departmental rates, or process costing. This dual costing system may incur additional costs. Second, ABC requires a significant amount of time and, thus, cost to implement. Substantial time is needed to properly identify and analyze the activities taking place, trace costs to those activities, and determine the cost drivers. Third, substantial support is needed throughout the firm to overcome a variety of barriers: individual (people need to learn new skills), organizational (people resist change), and environmental (regulatory agencies may not accept ABC data). Support for the status quo (i.e., traditional costing systems) may be strong.

To overcome these barriers, a firm must recognize that these barriers exist, investigate their causes, and communicate to all concerned why and how ABC is to be implemented. Those who work for the company must be educated in new terminology, concepts, and performance measurements. Top management must involve itself by providing support if the new system is to succeed.

As ABC systems become more accepted, more companies could choose to refine how ABC and GAAP determine product cost in order to make those definitions more compatible and thereby eliminate the need for two costing systems.

Companies attempting to implement ABC as a cure-all for sales volume declines or financial losses will quickly find that the system is ineffective for those purposes. However, companies that implement ABC as well as related approaches—such as TQM, just-in-time methods, and continuous improvement policies—will discover that they provide their customers with the best cost, price, quality, and service. This combination of changes should improve their competitive position. ABC systems help a company achieve the following:

- Identify activities that do not contribute to customer value (value-added vs. non-value-added activities).
- Identify the cost drivers that create or influence cost.
- Identify and monitor significant technology costs for activities.
- Trace many technology costs directly to products.
- Transform general company goals into specific activity goals.
- Analyze the utilization of activities across different business functions.
- Analyze performance problems.
- Promote standards of excellence.
- Increase profitability and market share.

ABC is a cost accounting tool that allocates overhead to products and services in a different way than traditional systems. ABC does not, merely by being implemented, reduce the amount of overhead a company incurs. However, implementing an activity-based focus can help identify and thereby reduce or eliminate non-value-added (NVA) activities and in that way help reduce overhead costs. ABC helps managers produce products and perform services more efficiently and effectively, thereby making them more competitive in the global business environment.

Activity-based costing provides better information for certain types of companies than can be generated under a traditional overhead allocation process, but it is not a panacea. As with any cost system, it does not provide exact cost information, nor does it ensure perfect decisions.

concept Q&A

What are some key differences between ABC and volume-based costing?

Answers on pages 734 to 738.

Illustrative Example: Implementing ABC in a Service Firm Suppose that a manager of a bank's credit card department is interviewed and presented with the set of key questions listed on page 322. Consider the purpose and response to each question in the order indicated.

Key Questions: Bank's Credit Card Department Manager

1. How many employees are in your department? (Activities consume labour.)	*There are five employees.*
2. Describe what they do. (Activities are people doing things for other people.)	*There are three major activities: processing credit card transactions, issuing customer statements, and answering customer questions.*
3. Do customers outside your department use any equipment? (Activities also can be equipment working for other people. In other words, the equipment provides the service for someone by itself.)	*Yes. Customers who require cash advances use automated teller machines (ATMs).*

Key Questions: Bank's Credit Card Department Manager	
4. What resources are used by each activity (equipment, materials, energy)? (Activities consume resources in addition to labour.)	*Each employee has his or her own computer, printer, and desk. Paper and other supplies are needed to operate the printers. Each employee has a telephone as well.*
5. What are the outputs of each activity? (This helps to identify activity drivers.)	*Processing transactions produces a posting for each transaction in our computer system and serves as a source for preparing the monthly statements. The number of monthly customer statements has to be the product for the issuing activity, and I suppose that customers served is the output for the answering activity. The number of cash advances measures the product of the ATM activity, although the ATM really generates more transactions for other products such as chequing accounts. So, perhaps the number of ATM transactions is the real output.*
6. Who or what uses the activity output? (This identifies the cost object: products, other activities, customers, etc.)	*We have three products: classic, gold, and platinum credit cards. Transactions are processed for these three types of cards, and statements are sent to clients holding these cards. Similarly, answers to questions are all directed to clients who hold these cards.*
7. How much time do workers spend on each activity? How much time does equipment spend on each activity? (Information is needed to assign the cost of labour and equipment to activities.)	*I just completed a work survey and have the percentage of time calculated for each worker. All five clerks work on each of the three departmental activities. About 40 percent of their time is spent processing transactions, with the rest of their time split evenly between preparing statements and answering questions. Phone time is used only for answering client questions, and computer time is 70 percent transaction processing, 20 percent statement preparation, and 10 percent answering questions. Furthermore, my own time and that of my computer are 100 percent administrative.*

Activity Analysis Based on the answers to the survey, an activity analysis chart can now be prepared. Exhibit 7.6 illustrates the activity analysis for the credit card department. The activity analysis describes the tasks that make up the activity, lists the users (cost objects), and identifies a measure of activity output (activity driver). The three products—classic, gold, and platinum credit cards—consume the activities. It is not unusual for a typical organization to produce an activity analysis containing 200–300 activities.

> **concept Q&A**
>
> What is the purpose of the interview questions?
>
> Answers on pages 734 to 738.

Assigning Costs to Activities Once activities are identified and described, the next task is to determine how much it costs to perform each activity. This determination requires identification of the resources being consumed by each activity. Some cost system experts consider this task to be the most difficult one in creating an accurate cost system. Activities consume resources such as labour, materials, energy, and capital. The cost of these resources is found in the general ledger, but the money spent on each activity is not

EXHIBIT 7.6

Activity Analysis: Credit Card Department

Activity Name	Activity Description	Cost Object(s)	Activity Driver
Processing	Sorting, keying, and verifying transactions	Credit cards	Number of transactions
Preparing statements	Reviewing, printing, stuffing, and mailing	Credit cards	Number of statements
Answering questions	Answering, logging, reviewing database, and making call backs	Credit cards	Number of calls
Providing ATM services	Accessing accounts, withdrawing funds	Credit cards, chequing and savings accounts	Number of ATM transactions

revealed. Thus, it becomes necessary to assign the resource costs to activities by using direct tracing and driver tracing. For labour resources, a *work distribution matrix* often is used. A work distribution matrix identifies the amount of labour consumed by each activity and is derived from the interview process (or a written survey). Exhibit 7.7 provides an example of a work distribution matrix supplied by the manager of the credit card department for individual activities (refer to the bank manager's answer to Question 7 on page 325).

EXHIBIT 7.7

Work Distribution Matrix

Activity	Percentage of Time on Each Activity
Processing transactions	40%
Preparing statements	30%
Answering questions	30%

We know that both direct tracing and driver tracing are used to assign resource costs to activities. For this example, the time spent on each activity is the basis for assigning the labour costs to the activity. If the time is 100 percent, then labour is exclusive to the activity, and the assignment method is direct tracing. If the resource is shared by several activities (as in the case of the clerical resource), then the assignment method is driver tracing, and the drivers are called *resource drivers*. **Resource drivers** are factors that measure the consumption of resources by activities. Once resource drivers are identified, then the costs of the resource can be assigned to the activity. Cornerstone 7.4 shows how resource drivers and direct tracing are used to assign labour cost to the credit department activities.

Of course, labour is not the only resource consumed by activities. Activities also consume materials, capital, and energy. The interview with the bank manager, for example, revealed that the activities within the credit card department use computers (capital), phones (capital), desks (capital), and paper (materials). The ATM activity uses the ATM (capital) and energy. The cost of these other resources must also be assigned to the various activities. They are assigned in the same way as was described for labour (using direct tracing and resource drivers). The cost of computers could be assigned by using direct tracing (for the supervising activity) and hours of usage for the remaining activities. From the interview, we know the relative usage of computers by each activity. The general ledger reveals that the cost per computer is $1,200 per year. Thus, an

Assigning Resource Costs to Activities by Using Direct Tracing and Resource Drivers

Information:

Assume that each clerk is paid a salary of $30,000 ($150,000 total clerical cost for five clerks). Refer also to the work distribution matrix of Exhibit 7.7.

Required:

Assign the cost of labour to each of the activities in the credit department.

Solution:

The amount of labour cost assigned to each activity is given below. The percentages come from the work distribution matrix.

Processing transactions	$60,000 (= 40% × $150,000)
Preparing statements	$45,000 (= 30% × $150,000)
Answering questions	$45,000 (= 30% × $150,000)

Why:

Costs are usually assigned by financial accounting entries to different categories, such as materials and labour costs, and each activity absorbs only a portion of these costs. Under activity-based costing, one has to determine what portion of, say, labour is used by each activity. Thus total labour cost is allocated or prorated to each activity according to how heavily it uses labour resources.

additional $6,000 (= 5 × $1,200) would be assigned to the three activities based on relative usage: 70 percent to processing transactions ($4,200), 20 percent to preparing statements ($1,200), and 10 percent to answering questions ($600). Repeating this process for all resources, the total cost of each activity can be calculated. Exhibit 7.8 gives the cost of the activities associated with the credit card department under the assumption that all resource costs have been assigned (these numbers are assumed because all resource data are not given for their calculation).

concept Q&A

How are resource costs assigned to activities?

Answers on pages 734 to 738.

EXHIBIT 7.8

Activity Costs, First Stage: Credit Card Department

Processing transactions	$130,000
Preparing statements	102,000
Answering questions	92,400
Providing ATMs	250,000

Assigning Costs to Products

From Cornerstone 7.3, we know that activity costs are assigned to products by multiplying a predetermined activity rate by the usage of the activity, as measured by activity drivers. Exhibit 7.6 identified the activity drivers for each of the four credit card activities: number of transactions for processing transactions, number of statements for preparing statements, number of calls for answering questions, and number of ATM transactions for the activity of providing ATMs. To calculate an activity rate, the practical or normal capacity of each activity must be determined. To assign costs, the amount of each activity consumed by each product must also be known. Assuming that the practical activity capacity is equal to the total activity usage by all products, the following actual data have been collected for the credit card example:

	Classic Card	Gold Card	Platinum Card	Total
Number of cards	5,000	3,000	2,000	10,000
Transactions processed	600,000	300,000	100,000	1,000,000
Number of statements	60,000	36,000	24,000	120,000
Number of calls	10,000	12,000	8,000	30,000
Number of ATM transactions	15,000	3,000	2,000	20,000

analytical Q&A

A company has three inspectors, each earning a salary of $50,000. One inspector works exclusively on inspecting parts received from outside suppliers, while the other two spend 30 percent of their time inspecting parts and 70 percent of their time inspecting final products. How much labour cost should be assigned to the activity of inspecting parts?

Answers on pages 734 to 738.

Applying Cornerstone 7.2 by using the data from Exhibit 7.8, the activity rates are calculated as follows:

Processing transactions:	$130,000/1,000,000 = $0.13 per transaction
Preparing statements:	$102,000/120,000 = $0.85 per statement
Answering questions:	$92,400/30,000 = $3.08 per call
Providing ATMs:	$250,000/200,000 = $1.25 per transaction

These rates provide the cost of each activity usage. Using these rates, costs are assigned as shown in Exhibit 7.9. Also, we now know the whole story behind the development of the activity rates and usage measures. Furthermore, the banking setting emphasizes the utility of ABC in service organizations.

EXHIBIT 7.9

Assigning Costs: Final Stage

	Classic	Gold	Platinum
Processing transactions:			
$0.13 × 600,000	$ 78,000		
$0.13 × 300,000		$ 39,000	
$0.13 × 100,000			$13,000
Preparing statements:			
$0.85 × 60,000	51,000		
$0.85 × 36,000		30,600	
$0.85 × 24,000			20,400
Answering questions:			
$3.08 × 10,000	30,800		
$3.08 × 12,000		36,960	
$3.08 × 8,000			24,640
Providing ATMs:			
$1.25 × 15,000	18,750		
$1.25 × 3,000		3,750	
$1.25 × 2,000			2,500
Total costs	$178,550	$110,310	$60,540
Units	÷ 5,000	÷ 3,000	÷ 2,000
Unit cost	$ 35.71	$ 36.77	$ 30.27

ACTIVITY-BASED CUSTOMER COSTING AND ACTIVITY-BASED SUPPLIER COSTING

OBJECTIVE 3

Describe activity-based customer costing and activity-based supplier costing.

ABC systems originally became popular for their ability to improve product-costing accuracy by tracing activity costs to the products that consume the activities. However, since the beginning of the 21st century, the use of ABC has expanded into areas upstream from production (i.e., before the production section of the value chain—research and development, prototyping, etc.) and downstream from production (i.e., after the production section of the value chain—marketing, distribution, customer service, etc.). Specifically, ABC often is used to determine more accurately the upstream costs of suppliers and the downstream costs of customers. Knowing the costs of suppliers and customers can be vital information for improving a company's profitability.

LSI Logic, a high-tech producer of semiconductors, implemented ABC customer costing and discovered that 10 percent of its customers were responsible for about 90 percent of its profits. LSI also discovered that it was actually losing money on about 50 percent of its customers. It worked to convert its unprofitable customers into profitable ones and invited those who would not provide a fair return to take their business elsewhere. As a consequence, LSI's sales decreased, but its profit tripled.[4] Exhibit 7.10 depicts this interesting yet common relationship between customers and their contributions to company profitability. Some managers refer to this graph as the "whale curve" of customer profitability, because of its resemblance to the shape of a whale breaching the water's surface. The important observation from the curve is that the customers to the left of the hump, or peak, increase the company's profitability, while the customers to the right decrease the company's profitability. Therefore, activity-based customer costing is helpful in determining where each customer falls on the curve and, subsequently, how each customer should therefore be treated given its position on the curve. Of particular interest are those customers to the far right because they severely decrease the company's profitability and need either to be terminated as unacceptably bad customers or altered in some way so as to become profitable customers for the company.

EXHIBIT 7.10

The Whale Curve of Cumulative Customer Profitability

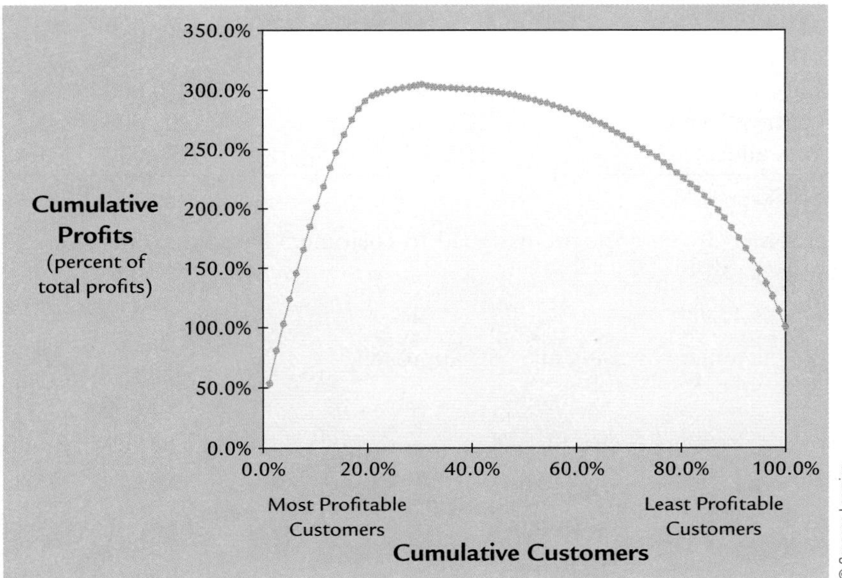

[4] Gary Cokins, "Are All of Your Customers Profitable (To You)?" (June 14, 2001): http://www.bettermanagment.com/Library (accessed January 2004).

Activity-Based Customer Costing

Customers are cost objects of fundamental interest. As the LSI Logic experience illustrates, customer management can produce significant gains in profit. It is possible to have customer diversity, just as it is possible to have product diversity. Customers can consume customer-driven activities in different proportions. Sources of customer diversity include order frequency, delivery frequency, geographic distance, sales and promotional support, and engineering support requirements. Knowing how much it costs to service different customers can be vital information for such purposes as setting pricing, determining customer mix, and improving profitability. Furthermore, because of diversity of customers, multiple drivers are needed to trace costs accurately. This outcome means that ABC can be useful to organizations that may have only one product, homogeneous products, or a just-in-time (JIT) structure where direct tracing diminishes the value of ABC for product costing.

Customer Costing versus Product Costing The costs of customer service are assigned to customers in the same way that manufacturing costs are assigned to products. Customer-driven activities such as order entry, order picking, shipping, making sales calls, and evaluating a client's credit are identified and listed in an activity dictionary. The cost of the resources consumed is assigned to activities, and the cost of the activities is assigned to individual customers. The same model and procedures that apply to products apply to customers as well. Cornerstone 7.5 illustrates how ABC assigns costs to customers.

CORNERSTONE 7.5

Calculating Activity-Based Customer Costs

Information:

Milan Company produces precision parts for 11 major buyers. Of its 11 customers, one accounts for 50 percent of the sales, with the remaining 10 accounting for the rest of the sales. The 10 smaller customers purchase parts in roughly equal quantities. Orders placed by the smaller customers are about the same size. Data concerning Milan's customer activity follow:

	Large Customer	Ten Smaller Customers
Units purchased	500,000	500,000
Orders placed	2	200
Number of sales calls	10	210
Manufacturing costs	$3,000,000	$3,000,000
Order filling costs allocated*	$202,000	$202,000
Sales force costs allocated*	$110,000	$110,000

*Allocated based on sales volume.

Currently, customer-driven costs are assigned to customers based on units sold, a unit-level driver.

Required:

Assign costs to customers by using an ABC approach.

Solution:

The appropriate drivers are orders placed and number of sales calls. The activity rates are:

$$\frac{\$404{,}000}{202 \text{ orders}} = \$2{,}000 \text{ per order}$$

$$\frac{\$220{,}000}{220 \text{ calls}} = \$1{,}000 \text{ per call}$$

(Continued)

CORNERSTONE

7.5

(Continued)

Using this information, the customer-driven costs can be assigned to each group of customers as follows:

	Large Customer	Ten Smaller Customers
Order filling costs:		
($2,000 × 2)	$ 4,000	
($2,000 × 200)		$400,000
Sales force costs:		
($1,000 × 10)	10,000	
($1,000 × 210)		210,000
	$14,000	$610,000

Why:

Because a typical firm has many unique customers. Some customers purchase a lot of the firm's products, while others only purchase a specific product; some place orders frequently, while others order only occasionally; some buy in large quantities, others in small quantities. Clearly, the costs per client are different, driven by the frequency and size of orders as well as the underlying product or service cost.

The activity-based cost assignments reveal a much different picture of the cost of servicing each type of customer. The smaller customer is costing more, attributable to smaller, more frequent orders and the evident need for the sales force to engage in more negotiations to make a sale.

What does this analysis tell management that it didn't know before? First, the large customer costs much less to service than the smaller customers and perhaps should be charged less. Second, it raises some significant questions relative to the smaller customers. For example, is it possible to encourage larger, less frequent orders? Perhaps offering discounts for larger orders would be appropriate. Why is it more difficult to sell to the smaller customers? Why are more calls needed? Are they less informed than the larger customer about the products? Can the company improve profits by influencing its customers to change their buying behaviour?

concept Q&A

How does ABC differ from traditional product costing?

Answers on pages 734 to 738.

YOUDECIDE Managing Customer Profitability

As a consultant, you recently implemented an activity-based customer-profitability system. In your written report to management, you classified the customers of the company into one of four categories based on current profitability and the potential for future profitability:[5]

1. High profitability, substantial future potential
2. Low profitability, substantial future potential
3. High profitability, limited future potential
4. Low profitability, limited future potential

After you discuss the report with the CEO, he asks you to answer the following question:

How would you manage the customers in each of the four categories?

For highly profitable customers, and especially those with long-term potential, special efforts should be made to retain these customers as it is much more expensive to attract new customers.

(Continued)

[5] Based on a classification in Gary Cokins, *Performance Management: Finding the Missing Pieces (to Close the Intelligence Gap)*. Wiley and SAS Business Series, March 29, 2004.

Offering these customers special discounts and new products and service lines coupled with managing their costs-to-serve to a lower level and improving business processes are ways to increase customer satisfaction while at the same time maintaining or increasing profitability. For customers with low profitability but substantial potential, the goal is to move these customers up to a high profitability state. Pricing policies or initiatives related to both the order and the transactions caused by the order are one way to increase profitability (e.g., activity-based pricing is based on the costs-to-serve, something clearly revealed by the ABC customer model). Another way is to lower the costs-to-serve by improving activity efficiency and eliminating non-value-added activities. Customers with low profitability and limited potential should be managed up or out—these customers need to be made profitable quickly or simply dropped.

Knowing customer profitability is important because not every revenue dollar contributes equally to overall profitability. Thus, it is critical for a manager to understand the net profit contribution that each customer makes to the company. Understanding individual customer profitability and the associated drivers allows managers to take actions to sustain and maintain profitable customers and transform unprofitable customers into profitable customers.[6]

Activity-Based Supplier Costing

ABC can also help a manager to identify the true cost of a firm's suppliers. The cost of a supplier is much more than the purchase price of the components or materials acquired. Just like customers, suppliers can affect many internal activities of a firm and significantly increase the cost of purchasing. A more correct view is one where the costs associated with quality, reliability, and late deliveries are added to the purchase costs. Managers are then required to evaluate suppliers based on total cost, not just purchase price. ABC is the key to tracing costs relating to purchases, as well as evaluating the quality, reliability, and delivery performance of suppliers.

Supplier Costing Methodology Assigning the costs of supplier-related activities to suppliers follows the same pattern as ABC product and customer costing. Supplier-driven activities such as purchasing, receiving, inspection of incoming components, reworking products (because of defective components), expediting products (because of late deliveries of suppliers), and warranty work (due to defective supplier components) are identified and listed in an activity dictionary. The cost of the resources consumed is assigned to these activities, and the cost of the activities is assigned to individual suppliers. Cornerstone 7.6 illustrates how to use ABC for supplier costing.

CORNERSTONE 7.6

Calculating Activity-Based Supplier Costs

Information:

Assume that a purchasing manager uses two suppliers, Murray Inc. and Plata Associates, as the source of two machine parts: part A1 and part B2. Consider two activities: repairing products (under warranty) and expediting products. Repairing products occurs because of part failure (bought from suppliers). Expediting products occurs because suppliers are late in delivering needed parts and require follow-up. Activity cost information and other data needed for supplier costing follow:

I. Activity Costs Caused by Suppliers (e.g., failed parts or late delivery)

Activity	Costs ($)
Repairing products	800,000
Expediting products	200,000

(Continued)

[6] Robert S. Kaplan and V. G. Narayanan, "Measuring and Managing Customer Profitability," *Journal of Cost Management* (September/October 2001): 5–15.

CORNERSTONE
7.6

(Continued)

II. Supplier Data

	Murray Inc.		Plata Associates	
	Part A1	**Part B2**	**Part A1**	**Part B2**
Unit purchase price	$20	$52	$24	$56
Units purchased	80,000	40,000	10,000	10,000
Failed units	1,600	380	10	10
Late shipments	60	40	0	0

Required:

Determine the cost of each supplier by using ABC.

Solution:

Using the above data, the activity rates for assigning costs to suppliers are computed as follows:

$$\text{Repair rate} = \frac{\$800{,}000}{2{,}000^{*}}$$
$$= \$400 \text{ per failed part}$$

* (1,600 + 380 + 10 + 10)

$$\text{Expediting rate} = \frac{\$200{,}000}{100^{**}}$$
$$= \$2{,}000 \text{ per late delivery}$$

** (60 + 40)

Using these rates and the activity data, the total purchasing cost per unit of each component is computed:

	Murray Inc.		Plata Associates	
	Part A1	**Part B2**	**Part A1**	**Part B2**
Purchase cost:				
$20 × 80,000	$1,600,000			
$52 × 40,000		$2,080,000		
$24 × 10,000			$240,000	
$56 × 10,000				$560,000
Repairing products:				
$400 × 1,600	640,000			
$400 × 380		152,000		
$400 × 10			4,000	
$400 × 10				4,000
Expediting products:				
$2,000 × 60	120,000			
$2,000 × 40		80,000		
Total costs	$2,360,000	$2,312,000	$244,000	$564,000
Units	÷ 80,000	÷ 40,000	÷ 10,000	÷ 10,000
Total unit cost	$ 29.50	$ 57.80	$ 24.40	$ 56.40

(Continued)

CORNERSTONE

7.6

(Continued)

Why:

Because not all suppliers are created equal. Some are more reliable than others, delivering orders when they promise (JIT delivery); others do so with undesirable delays. Such delays often necessitate extra expediting costs (e.g., expensive overnight delivery, extra shifts to complete work on time). Similarly, some suppliers produce higher quality products that result in lower warranty repair costs. The cost of a product from a supplier is not only the purchase price but also the cost of repair and the cost of expediting. It is sensible, then, for an organization to know the full cost per unit of every part it buys. The lowest cost per unit of such "failures" for each supplier can suggest the most desirable supplier.

concept Q&A

How are costs assigned to suppliers by using the ABC approach?

Answers on pages 734 to 738.

The example in Cornerstone 7.6 shows that Murray, the "low-cost" supplier (as measured by the purchase price of the two parts), actually costs more when the supplier-related activities of repairing and expediting are considered. If all costs are considered, then the choice becomes clear: Plata Associates is the better supplier with a higher-quality product, more on-time deliveries, and, consequently, a lower overall cost per unit. This analysis can be done throughout the value chain to achieve better results in all aspects of a company's operations.

PROCESS-VALUE ANALYSIS

OBJECTIVE 

Explain how activity-based management can be used for cost reduction.

Process-value analysis is fundamental to **activity-based management**. It focuses on cost reduction instead of cost assignment and emphasizes the maximization of systemwide performance. As the model in Exhibit 7.11 illustrates, process-value analysis is concerned with (1) *driver analysis*, (2) *activity analysis*, and (3) *performance analysis*.

EXHIBIT 7.11

Process-Value Analysis Model

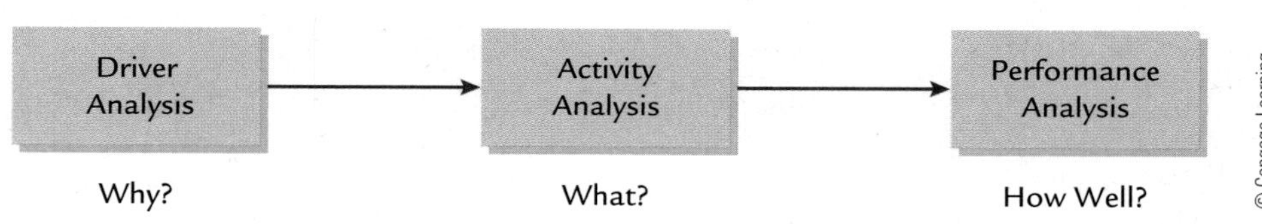

Driver Analysis: The Search for Root Causes

Managing activities requires an understanding of what causes activity costs. Every activity has inputs and outputs. **Activity inputs** are the resources consumed by the activity in producing its output. **Activity output** is the result or product of an activity. For example, if the activity is moving materials, the inputs would be such things as a forklift, a forklift driver, fuel (for the forklift), and crates. The output would be moved goods and materials. An **activity output measure** is the number of times the activity is performed. It is the quantifiable measure of the output. For example, the number of moves and distance moved are possible output measures for the material moving activity.

The output measure effectively is a measure of the demands placed on an activity and is what we have been calling an *activity driver*. As the demands for an activity change, the cost of the activity can change. For example, as the number of products increases and the number of trucks to be loaded increases, the activity in the warehouse must increase. However, output measures, such as the number of stores serviced, may not (and usually do not) correspond to the root causes of activity costs; rather, they are the consequences of the activity being performed. The purpose of driver analysis is to reveal root causes. Thus, **driver analysis** is the effort expended to identify those factors that are the root causes of activity costs. For example, an analysis may reveal that the root cause of the cost of moving materials is plant layout. Once the root cause is known, action can be taken to improve the activity. Specifically, reorganizing plant layout can reduce the cost of moving materials.

Often, the root cause of the cost of an activity is also the root cause of other related activities. For example, the costs of inspecting purchased parts and reordering may both be caused by poor quality parts from the supplier. By working with suppliers to reduce the number of defective components supplied (or choosing suppliers that provide fewer defective parts), the demand for both activities may then decrease, enabling the company to save money.

Activity Analysis: Identifying and Assessing Value Content

The heart of process-value analysis is activity analysis. **Activity analysis** is the process of identifying, describing, and evaluating the activities that an organization performs. Activity analysis should produce four outcomes:

1. What activities are done
2. How many people perform the activities
3. What time and resources are required to perform the activities; and
4. The value of the activities to the organization, including a recommendation to select and keep only those that add value.

Steps 1 through 3 have been described earlier and are common to the information needed for determining and assigning activity costs. Knowing how much an activity costs is clearly an important part of activity-based management. Step 4, determining the value-added content of activities, is concerned with cost reduction rather than cost assignment. Thus, some management accountants feel that this is the most important part of activity analysis. Activities can then be classified as *value-added* or *non-value-added*.

concept Q&A

What is the purpose of driver analysis?

Answers on pages 734 to 738.

Value-Added Activities and Non-Value-Added Activities

All activities require some resource consumption, and resource consumption inevitably drives costs higher. Higher costs cannot always be passed on to customers because most prices are set by the marketplace. This suggests that if prices are fixed, then in order to reduce costs, organizations that want to achieve higher profits have no choice but to reduce or eliminate activities. Well-run organizations try to identify those activities that do not improve their profitability.

A *value-added activity* increases the value to a customer of a product or service and is one for which the customer is willing to pay. To improve customer value and enhance profitability, value-added activities result in more efficient production methods, continuous operating improvements, better operational control, and reduced times for completing the operational cycle.

A *non-value-added (NVA) activity* increases the time spent on—or the cost of—a product or service, without increasing its worth to the customer. NVA activities may include warehousing materials or components until needed for production and/or recruiting and hiring employees with the necessary skills to make a product or provide a service. NVA activities may be necessary from a business perspective but not from a customer's

concept Q&A

What is a value-added activity?

Answers on pages 734 to 738.

perspective. Thus, every effort should be made to reduce or eliminate NVA activities in ways that do not affect the value or quality of the product or service.

Value-Added Activities Those activities necessary to remain in business are called **value-added activities**. Some activities—required activities—are necessary to comply with legal mandates. Activities needed to comply with the reporting requirements of the Ontario Securities Commission and the filing requirements of the Canada Revenue Agency are examples. These activities are value-added by *mandate*. The remaining activities in the firm are *discretionary*. A discretionary activity is classified as value-added provided it simultaneously satisfies three conditions: (1) the activity produces a change of state, (2) the change of state was not achievable by preceding activities, and (3) the activity enables other activities to be performed.

For example, consider the production of rods used in hydraulic cylinders. The first activity, cutting rods, cuts long rods into the correct lengths for the cylinders. Next, the cut rods are welded to cut plates. The cutting rod activity is value-added because (1) it causes a change of state—uncut rods become cut rods, (2) no prior activity was supposed to create this change of state, and (3) it enables the welding activity to be performed. Though the value-added properties are easy to see for an operational activity like cutting rods, what about a more general activity like supervising production workers? A managerial activity is specifically designed to manage other value-added activities—to ensure that they are performed in an efficient and timely manner. Supervision certainly satisfies the enabling condition. Is there a change in state? There are two ways of answering in the affirmative. First, supervising can be viewed as an enabling resource that is consumed by the operational activities that do produce a change of state. Thus, supervising is a secondary activity that serves as an input needed to help bring about the change of state expected for value-added primary activities. Second, it could be argued that the supervision brings order by changing the state from uncoordinated activities to coordinated activities. Once value-added activities are identified, we can define value-added costs. **Value-added costs** are the costs to perform value-added activities with perfect efficiency.

Non-Value-Added Activities All activities other than those that are absolutely essential to remain in business are referred to as **non-value-added activities**. A NVA activity can be identified by its failure to satisfy any one of the three previous defining conditions. Violation of the first two is the usual case for NVA activities. Inspecting cut rods (for correct length), for example, is a NVA activity. Inspection is a state-detection activity, not a state-changing activity (it tells us the state of the cut rod—whether it is the right length or not). Thus, it fails the first condition. Consider the activity of reworking goods or subassemblies. Rework is designed to bring a good from a nonconforming state to a conforming state. Thus, a change of state occurs. Yet the activity is NVA because it repeats work; it is doing something that should have been done by preceding activities (condition 2 is violated).

> **concept Q&A**
>
> How can a value-added activity have non-value-added costs?
>
> Answers on pages 734 to 738.

Non-value-added costs are costs that are caused either by NVA activities or by the inefficient performance of valued-added activities. For NVA activities, the NVA cost is the cost of the activity itself. For inefficient value-added activities, the activity cost must be broken into its value-added and non-value-added components. For example, if receiving should use 10,000 receiving orders but uses 20,000, then half the cost of receiving is value-added and half is NVA. The value-added component is the waste-free component of the value-added activity and is, therefore, the *value-added standard*. Due to increased competition, many firms are attempting to eliminate NVA activities because they add unnecessary cost and impede performance; firms are also striving to optimize value-added activities. Thus, activity analysis identifies and eventually eliminates all unnecessary activities and, simultaneously, increases the efficiency of necessary activities.

The theme of activity analysis is waste elimination. As waste is eliminated, costs are reduced. The cost reduction *follows* the elimination of waste. Note the value of managing the causes of the costs rather than the costs themselves. Though managing costs may increase the efficiency of an activity, if the activity is unnecessary, what does it matter if it's performed efficiently? An unnecessary activity is wasteful and should be eliminated. For example, moving raw materials and partially finished goods is often cited as a NVA activity. Installing an automated materials handling system may increase the efficiency of this activity, but changing to cellular manufacturing with on-site, just-in-time delivery of raw materials could virtually eliminate the activity. It's easy to see which is preferable.

Examples of Non-Value-Added Activities Reordering parts, expediting production, and rework because of defective parts are all examples of NVA activities. Other examples include warranty work, handling customer complaints, and reporting defects. NVA activities can exist anywhere in the organization. In the manufacturing operation, five major activities are often cited as wasteful and unnecessary:

1. *Scheduling* uses time and resources to determine when different products have access to processes (or when and how many setups must be done) and how much will be produced.
2. *Moving* uses time and resources to move raw materials, work in process, and finished goods from one department to another.
3. *Waiting* uses time and resources by keeping raw materials or work in process from moving to the next process.
4. *Inspecting* uses time and resources to ensure that the product meets specifications.
5. *Storing* uses time and resources while a good or raw material is held in inventory.

None of these activities adds any value for the customer. (Note that inspection would not be necessary if the product were produced correctly the first time and, therefore, adds no value for the customer.) The challenge of activity analysis is to find ways to produce the good without using any of these activities.

Cost Reduction Activity management carries with it the objective of cost reduction. Competitive conditions dictate that companies must deliver customer-desired products on time and at the lowest possible cost. These conditions mean that an organization must continually strive for cost improvement. Activity management can reduce costs in four ways:[7]

1. Activity elimination
2. Activity selection
3. Activity reduction
4. Activity sharing

Activity elimination focuses on NVA activities. Once activities that fail to add value are identified, measures can be taken to rid the organization of these activities. For example, the activity of inspecting incoming parts seems necessary to ensure that the product using the parts functions according to specifications. Use of a bad part can produce a bad final product. Yet this activity is necessary only because of the poor quality performance of the supplying firms. Selecting suppliers who are able to supply high-quality parts or who are willing to improve their quality performance to achieve this objective will eventually allow the elimination of incoming inspection. Cost reduction then follows.

[7] Peter B. B. Turney, "How Activity-Based Costing Helps Reduce Cost," *Journal of Cost Management* (Winter 1991): 29–35.

Activity selection involves choosing among different sets of activities that are caused by competing strategies. Different strategies cause different activities. Different product design strategies, for example, can require significantly different activities. Activities, in turn, cause costs. Each product design strategy has its own set of activities and associated costs. All other things being equal, the lowest-cost design strategy should be chosen. In a continuous improvement environment, redesign of existing products and processes can lead to a different, cheaper set of activities. Thus activity selection can have a significant effect on cost reduction.

Activity reduction decreases the time and resources required by an activity. This approach to cost reduction should be primarily aimed at improving the efficiency of necessary activities or at implementing a short-term strategy for improving NVA activities until they can be eliminated. Setup activity is a necessary activity that is often cited as an example for which less time and fewer resources need to be used. Finding ways to reduce setup time—and thus lower the cost of setups—is an example of the concept of gradual reductions in activity costs.

Activity sharing increases the efficiency of necessary activities by using economies of scale. Specifically, the quantity of the cost driver is increased without increasing the total cost of the activity itself. This lowers the per-unit cost of the cost driver and the amount of cost traceable to each product that consumes the activity. For example, a new product can be designed to use components already being used by other products. The activities associated with these components already exist, and the company avoids the creation of a whole new set of activities.

Cornerstone 7.7 shows how to determine the NVA cost of activities. Determining the cost is followed by a root-cause analysis and then by the selection of an approach to reduce the waste found in the activity. For example, defective products cause warranty work. Defective products, in turn, could be caused by such factors as defective internal processes, poor product design, and defective supplier components. Correcting the causes will lead to the elimination of the warranty activity. Inefficient purchasing can lead to systemic issues throughout a plant. Inefficient purchasing could be attributable to such root causes as poor product design (too many components), orders that are incorrectly filled out, and defective supplier components (producing additional orders). Correcting the causes will reduce the demand for the purchasing activity, and as the activity is reduced, cost reduction will follow.

CORNERSTONE 7.7

Assessing Non-Value-Added Costs

Information:

Consider the following two activities: (1) Performing warranty work, cost: $120,000. The warranty cost of the most efficient competitor is $20,000. (2) Purchasing components, cost: $200,000 (10,000 purchase orders). A benchmarking study reveals that the most efficient level will use 5,000 purchase orders and entail a cost of $110,000.

Required:

Determine the non-value-added cost of each activity.

Solution:

Is the activity non-value-added or value-added?

1. Performing warranty work is non-value-added; it is done to correct something that wasn't done right the first time. Thus, the non-value-added cost of performing warranty work is the full $120,000. The cost of the competitor is also non-value-added and has no bearing on this analysis. Root causes for warranty work are defective products.

(Continued)

CORNERSTONE **7.7** *(Continued)*

2. Purchasing components is necessary so that materials are available to produce products and, thus, is value-added. However, the activity is not performed efficiently, as revealed by the benchmarking study. The non-value-added cost is \$90,000 (= \$200,000 − \$110,000).

Why:

Because a firm engages in value-added and non-value-added activities. All costs that can be avoided if things are done right in the first place or done efficiently will improve a firm's profitability. So assessing the non-value-added costs is important, as they eat away an organization's profits and may in the long run render the firm uncompetitive.

REASONS FOR ADOPTING ABC COSTING

Because activity-based accounting systems are more complex and costly than traditional systems, not all companies use them. However, more and more organizations in both manufacturing and nonmanufacturing industries are adopting activity-based systems for a variety of reasons:

- Fierce global competition has resulted in shrinking profit margins. Companies may know their overall margin, but they often do not trust the accuracy of the margins for *individual* products or services. ABC costing better allows firms to trace the profitability for each product or service.
- There is wide diversity in the types of products and services, in customer classes, and in consumption of resources used by each product. ABC costing allows for better tracking of consumption of a company's shared resources among different products and customers.
- Indirect costs are far more important in today's modern business world, sometimes surpassing 50 percent of total cost. This promotes ABC costing, which turns overhead costs that are indirect under traditional costing methods into direct costs under ABC costing.
- Computer technology has reduced the costs of developing and operating cost systems, which allows for inexpensively tracking many activities and their costs.

LIMITATIONS OF ABC COSTING

ABC is a concept that can improve information and, hence, decision making within an organization. However, there are circumstances that may diminish the value of adopting ABC costing in certain circumstances. It would not be appropriate if:

- the products being produced were quite similar
- all products consumed resources in a similar manner
- the cost of developing individual cost pools was too great
- the cost of tracking appropriate cost drivers was too great
- resistance within the company was too great and would cause dissension among managers
- top management could not be convinced to support the project

Is ABC Costing Suitable for Your Company?

Direct labour hours or direct machine hours used in calculating plantwide overhead rates or departmental overhead rates provide inadequate cost information. A great deal of valuable information can be lost when activity and cost relationships are not properly considered. But does this mean that ABC is suitable for every organization? Some questions that companies must consider before adopting ABC include the following:

- Are the costs in each cost pool driven by and proportional to the company's activities?
- Are diverse products and/or services being produced?
- Do different products or services use resources differently?
- Do some products or services generate substantially higher overhead costs than others? (e.g., Do some require more advertising than others?)

One way or another, all organizations strive to eliminate NVA activities. Activity-based costing promotes understanding of cost drivers and identifies NVA activities; in this sense, continuous improvement and ABC costing go hand in hand.

ACTIVITY PERFORMANCE MEASUREMENT

Assessing how well activities (and processes) are performed is fundamental to management's efforts to improve profitability. Activity performance measures exist in both financial and nonfinancial forms. These measures are designed to assess how well an activity was performed and the results achieved. They are also designed to reveal if constant improvement is being realized. Measures of activity performance centre on three major dimensions: (1) efficiency, (2) quality, and (3) time.

Efficiency focuses on the relationship of activity inputs to activity outputs. For example, one way to improve activity efficiency is to produce the same activity output with lower cost for the inputs used. Thus cost and trends in cost become important measures of efficiency. *Quality* is concerned with doing the activity right the first time it is performed. If the activity output is defective, then the activity may need to be repeated, causing unnecessary cost and reduction in efficiency. Quality cost management is a major topical area and is discussed in more detail later in this chapter. The *time* required to perform an activity is also critical. Longer times usually mean more resource consumption and less ability to respond to customer demands. Time measures of performance tend to be nonfinancial, whereas efficiency and quality measures are both financial and nonfinancial.

> **concept Q&A**
>
> What are the three dimensions of performance for activities? Explain why they are important.
>
> Answers on pages 734 to 738.

Cycle time and *velocity* are two operational measures of time-based performance. Cycle time can be applied to any activity or process that produces an output, and it measures how long it takes to produce an output from start to finish. Consider the manufacturing process. In this case, **cycle time** is the length of time that it takes to produce a unit of output from the time raw materials are received (starting point of the cycle) until the good is delivered to finished goods inventory (finishing point of the cycle). Thus, cycle time is the time required to produce one unit of a product (time/units produced). **Velocity** is the number of units of output that can be produced in a given period of time (units produced/time). Notice that velocity is the reciprocal of cycle time. For the cycle time example, the velocity is two units per hour. Cornerstone 7.8 demonstrates how to compute cycle time and velocity.

Quality Cost Management

Activity-based management is also useful for understanding how quality costs can be managed. Quality costs can be substantial *in size* and a source of significant savings *if managed effectively*. Improving quality can produce significant improvements in profitability and overall efficiency. Quality improvement can increase profitability in two ways: (1) by increasing customer demand *and thus sales revenues* and (2) by decreasing costs. For example, when Toyota sold more cars and trucks than General Motors for the first time ever in 2007, some automotive industry experts attributed this crowning

Calculating Cycle Time and Velocity

Information:

Assume that a company takes 10,000 hours to produce 20,000 units of a product.

Required:

What is the velocity in hours? Cycle time in hours? Cycle time in minutes?

Solution:

$$\text{Velocity} = \frac{20{,}000 \text{ units}}{10{,}000 \text{ hours}} = 2 \text{ units per hour}$$

$$\text{Cycle time} = \frac{10{,}000 \text{ hours}}{20{,}000 \text{ units}} = \frac{1}{2} \text{ hour per unit}$$

$$\text{Cycle time} = \frac{(10{,}000 \text{ hours})(60 \text{ minutes/hour})}{20{,}000 \text{ units}} = 30 \text{ minutes per unit}$$

Why:

Because time is money. In managerial accounting, we assign value to time by calculating how long it takes to produce a product or deliver a service; the shorter the time, the better. Given the time constraints of a firm (e.g., eight hours per shift), one can calculate how many units can be produced given the capacity per hour. In addition, how long it takes (cycle time) from the beginning to the end to complete a product can be calculated.

achievement to Toyota's long-time commitment to quality-related issues, such as quality cost management.[8]

Quality-linked activities are those activities performed because poor quality may or does exist. The costs of performing these activities are referred to as **costs of quality**. Thus, the costs of quality are associated with two subcategories of quality-related activities: *control activities* and *failure activities*. **Control activities** are performed by an organization to prevent or detect poor quality (because poor quality may exist). **Control costs** are the costs of performing control activities. Control activities are made up of prevention and appraisal activities.

The definitions of *quality-related activities* also imply four categories of quality costs: (1) prevention costs, (2) appraisal costs, (3) internal failure costs, and (4) external failure costs.

Prevention costs are incurred to prevent poor quality in the products or services being produced. As prevention costs increase, we would expect the costs of failure to decrease. Examples of prevention costs are quality engineering, quality training programs, quality planning, quality reporting, supplier evaluation and selection, quality audits, quality circles, field trials, and design reviews.

Appraisal costs are incurred to determine whether products and services are conforming to their requirements or customer needs. Examples include raw materials inspection and testing, packaging inspection, appraisal activity supervision, product acceptance, process acceptance, measurement (inspection and testing) of equipment, and outside endorsements. The main objective of the appraisal function is to prevent nonconforming goods from being shipped to customers.

Failure activities are performed by an organization or its customers in response to poor quality (poor quality does exist). **Failure costs** are the costs incurred by an organization

[8] D. Jones, "Toyota's success pleases proponents of 'lean'," *USA Today* (May 3, 2007): 2B.

because failure activities are performed. Notice that the definitions of *failure activities* and *failure costs* imply that customer response to poor quality can impose costs on an organization.

Internal failure costs are incurred when products and services do not conform to specifications or customer needs. This nonconformance is detected *before* the bad products or services (nonconforming, unreliable, not durable, and so on) are shipped or delivered to outside parties. These are the failures detected by appraisal activities. Examples of internal failure costs are scrap, rework, downtime (due to defects), reinspection, retesting, and design changes. These costs disappear if no defects exist.

External failure costs are incurred when products and services fail to conform to requirements or satisfy customer needs *after* being delivered to customers. Of all the costs of quality, this category can be the most devastating. For example, costs of recalls can run into the hundreds of millions of dollars. Other examples include lost sales because of poor product performance, returns and allowances because of poor quality, warranties, repairs, product liability, customer dissatisfaction, lost market share, and complaint adjustment.

Environmental Cost Management

For many organizations, management of environmental costs is becoming a matter of high priority and a significant competitive issue. Many executives now believe that improving environmental quality may actually reduce environmental costs rather than increase them. For example, Toshiba reported that its environmental costs for fiscal 2012 were 43.1 billion yen (Cdn$1 = ¥93.85).[9] In the same report, it indicated that its environmental benefits were 83.2 billion yen divided between risk prevention (0.1 percent), customer benefits (49.0 percent), assumed benefits (39.8 percent), and actual benefits (11.1 percent).

Before environmental cost information can be provided to management, environmental costs must be defined. Various possibilities exist; however, an appealing approach is to adopt a definition consistent with a total environmental quality model. Accordingly, environmental costs can be referred to as *environmental quality costs*. Similar to product quality, environmentally linked activities are those activities performed because poor environmental quality may or does exist. The costs of performing these activities are referred to as *environmental costs*. As with quality costs, **environmental costs** are associated with two subcategories of environmentally related activities: *control activities* and *failure activities*. In other words, environmental costs are associated with the creation, detection, remediation, and prevention of environmental degradation. With this definition, environmental costs are also classified into four analogous categories: prevention costs, detection costs, internal failure costs, and external failure costs. External failure costs, in turn, can be subdivided into realized and unrealized categories.

Environmental prevention costs are the costs of activities carried out to prevent the production of contaminants and/or waste that could cause damage to the environment. Examples of prevention activities include the following: evaluating and selecting suppliers, evaluating and selecting equipment to control pollution, designing processes and products to reduce or eliminate contaminants, training employees, studying environmental impacts, auditing environmental risks, undertaking environmental research, developing environmental management systems, and recycling products.

Environmental detection costs are the costs of activities executed to determine if products, processes, and other activities within the firm are in compliance with appropriate environmental standards. The environmental standards and procedures that a firm seeks to follow are defined in three ways: (1) regulatory laws of governments, (2) voluntary standards developed by private organizations, and (3) environmental policies developed by management. Examples of detection activities are auditing environmental

[9] Toshiba website, http://www.toshiba.co.jp/env/en/management/account.htm (accessed April 2014).

activities, inspecting products and processes (for environmental compliance), developing environmental performance measures, carrying out contamination tests, verifying supplier environmental performance, and measuring levels of contamination.

Environmental internal failure costs are costs of activities performed because contaminants and waste have been produced but not discharged into the environment. Thus, internal failure costs are incurred to eliminate and manage contaminants or waste once produced. Internal failure activities have one of two goals: (1) to ensure that the contaminants and waste produced are not released to the environment or (2) to reduce the level of contaminants released to an amount that complies with environmental standards. Examples of internal failure activities include operating equipment to minimize or eliminate pollution, treating and disposing of toxic materials, maintaining pollution equipment, licensing facilities for producing contaminants, and recycling scrap.

Environmental external failure costs are the costs of activities performed after discharging contaminants and waste into the environment. **Realized external failure costs** are those incurred and paid for by the firm. **Unrealized external failure costs**, or **societal costs**, are caused by the firm but are incurred and paid for by parties outside the firm. Examples of realized external failure activities are cleaning up a polluted lake, cleaning up oil spills, cleaning up contaminated soil, using materials and energy inefficiently, settling personal injury claims from environmentally unsound practices, settling property damage claims, restoring land to its natural state, and losing sales from a bad environmental reputation. Examples of societal costs include receiving medical care because of polluted air (individual welfare), losing a lake for recreational use because of contamination (degradation), losing employment because of contamination (individual welfare), and damaging ecosystems from solid waste disposal (degradation).

concept Q&A

Why are there two categories of environmental external failure costs?

Answers on pages 734 to 738.

SUMMARY OF LEARNING OBJECTIVES

LO1. Explain the potential for cost distortion using functional- or volume-based costing approaches.

- Overhead costs have increased in significance over time and in many firms represent a much higher percentage of product costs than direct labour.
- Many overhead activities, and their associated costs, do not vary in proportion to units produced. Functional-based costing systems are not able to assign the costs of these non-unit-based overhead activities appropriately.
- Non-unit-based overhead activities often are consumed by products in different proportions than are unit-based overhead activities. Because of this imbalance, assigning overhead by using only unit-based drivers can distort product costs.
- If the non-unit-based overhead costs are a significant proportion of total overhead costs, the inaccuracy in cost assignments can be a serious matter.

LO2. Explain how an activity-based costing system works for product costing.

- Activities are identified and defined through the use of interviews and surveys. This information allows an activity dictionary to be constructed.
- The activity dictionary lists activities and potential activity drivers, classifies activities as primary or secondary, and provides any other attributes deemed to be important.
- Resource costs are assigned to activities by using direct tracing and resource drivers.
- The costs of secondary activities are ultimately assigned to primary activities by using activity drivers.
- Finally, the costs of primary activities are assigned to products, customers, and other cost objects using cost drivers.

- The cost assignment process is described by the following general steps: (1) identifying the major activities and building an activity dictionary, (2) determining the cost of each of those activities, (3) identifying a measure of consumption for each activity cost (activity drivers), (4) calculating an activity rate for each activity, (5) measuring the demands placed on each activity by each product, and (6) calculating product costs.

LO3. Describe activity-based customer costing and activity-based supplier costing.

- Tracing customer-driven costs to customers can provide significant information to managers.
- Accurate customer costs allow managers to make better pricing decisions, customer-mix decisions, and other customer-related decisions that will improve profitability.
- Tracing supplier-driven costs to suppliers, in addition to the actual cost of the item being supplied, can enable managers to choose the true low-cost suppliers, producing a stronger competitive position and increased profitability.

LO4. Explain how activity-based management can be used for cost reduction.

- Assigning costs accurately is vital for good decision making.
- Assigning the costs of an activity accurately does not address the issue of whether or not the activity should be performed or whether it is being performed efficiently.
- Activity-based management focuses on process-value analysis.
- Process-value analysis has three components: driver analysis, activity analysis, and performance evaluation. These three steps determine what activities are being done, why they are being done, and how well they are done.
- Understanding the root causes of activities provides the opportunities to manage activities so that costs can be reduced.
- Quality and environmental activities are particularly susceptible to activity-based management.
- Quality costs are costs that are incurred because poor product quality exists or may exist.
- Environmental costs are costs that are incurred because environmental degradation exists or may exist.

CORNERSTONES

CORNERSTONE 7.1	Calculating consumption ratios, page 316
CORNERSTONE 7.2	Calculating activity rates, page 317
CORNERSTONE 7.3	Calculating activity-based unit costs, page 318
CORNERSTONE 7.4	Assigning resource costs to activities by using direct tracing and resource drivers, page 327
CORNERSTONE 7.5	Calculating activity-based customer costs, page 330
CORNERSTONE 7.6	Calculating activity-based supplier costs, page 332
CORNERSTONE 7.7	Assessing non-value-added costs, page 338
CORNERSTONE 7.8	Calculating cycle time and velocity, page 341

GLOSSARY

Activity analysis The process of identifying, describing, and evaluating the activities an organization performs. (p. 335)

Activity attributes Nonfinancial and financial information that describes individual activities. (p. 323)

Activity-based management A systemwide, integrated approach that focuses management's attention on activities with the objective of improving customer value and the profit achieved by providing this value. It includes driver analysis, activity analysis, and performance evaluation, and draws on activity-based costing as a major source of information. (p. 334)

Activity dictionary A list of activities described by specific attributes such as name, definition, classification as primary or secondary, and activity driver. (p. 323)

Activity drivers Factors that measure the consumption of activities by products and other cost objects. (p. 314)

Activity elimination The process of eliminating non-value-added activities. (p. 337)

Activity inputs The resources consumed by an activity in producing its output (they are the factors that enable the activity to be performed). (p. 334)

Activity output The result or product of an activity. (p. 334)

Activity output measure The number of times an activity is performed. It is the quantifiable measure of the output. (p. 334)

Activity reduction Decreasing the time and resources required by an activity. (p. 338)

Activity selection The process of choosing among sets of activities caused by competing strategies. (p. 338)

Activity sharing Increasing the efficiency of necessary activities by using economies of scale. (p. 338)

Appraisal costs Costs incurred to determine whether products and services are conforming to requirements. (p. 341)

Consumption ratio The proportion of an overhead activity consumed by a product. (p. 315)

Control activities Activities performed by an organization to prevent or detect poor quality (because poor quality may exist). (p. 341)

Control costs Costs incurred from performing control activities. (p. 341)

Costs of quality Costs incurred because poor quality may exist or because poor quality does exist. (p. 341)

Cycle time The length of time required to produce one unit of a product. (p. 340)

Driver analysis The effort expended to identify those factors that are the root causes of activity costs. (p. 335)

Environmental costs Costs that are incurred because poor environmental quality exists or may exist. (p. 342)

Environmental detection costs Costs incurred to detect poor environmental performance. (p. 342)

Environmental external failure costs Costs incurred after contaminants are introduced into the environment. (p. 343)

Environmental internal failure costs Costs incurred after contaminants are produced, but before they are introduced into the environment. (p. 343)

Environmental prevention costs Costs incurred to prevent damage to the environment. (p. 342)

External failure costs Costs incurred because products fail to conform to requirements after being sold to outside parties. (p. 342)

Failure activities Activities performed by an organization or its customers in response to poor quality (poor quality does exist). (p. 341)

Failure costs The costs incurred by an organization because failure activities are performed. (p. 341)

Internal failure costs Costs incurred because products and services fail to conform to requirements where lack of conformity is discovered prior to external sale. (p. 342)

Non-unit-level activity drivers Factors that measure the consumption of non-unit-level activities by products and other cost objects. (p. 314)

Non-value-added activities All activities other than those that are absolutely essential to remain in business. (p. 336)

Non-value-added costs Costs that are caused either by non-value-added activities or by the inefficient performance of value-added activities. (p. 336)

Prevention costs Costs incurred to prevent defects in products or services being produced. (p. 341)

Process-value analysis An approach that focuses on processes and activities, and emphasizes systemwide performance instead of individual performance. (p. 334)

Product diversity The situation present when products consume overhead in different proportions. (p. 314)

Realized external failure costs Environmental costs caused by environmental degradation and paid for by the responsible organization. (p. 343)

Resource drivers Factors that measure the consumption of resources by activities. (p. 326)

Societal costs Environmental costs caused by an organization, but paid for by society; also called unrealized external failure costs. (p. 343)

Unit-level activities Activities that are performed each time a unit is produced. (p. 313)

Unit-level activity drivers Factors that measure the consumption of unit-level activities by products and other cost objects. (p. 314)

Unrealized external failure costs Environmental costs caused by an organization, but paid for by society; also called societal costs. (p. 343)

Value-added activities Activities that are necessary for a business to achieve corporate objectives and remain in business. (p. 336)

Value-added costs Costs caused by value-added activities. (p. 336)

Velocity The number of units that can be produced in a given period of time (e.g., output per hour). (p. 340)

REVIEW PROBLEMS

I. Plantwide Rates

Gee Company produces two types of stereo units: deluxe and regular. For the most recent year, Gee reports the following data:

Budgeted overhead	$180,000
Expected activity (in direct labour hours)	50,000
Actual activity (in direct labour hours)	51,000
Actual overhead	$200,000

	Deluxe	Regular
Units produced	5,000	50,000
Prime costs	$40,000	$300,000
Direct labour hours	5,000	46,000

Required:

1. Calculate a predetermined overhead rate based on direct labour hours.
2. What is the applied overhead?
3. What is the under- or overapplied overhead?
4. Calculate the unit cost of each stereo unit.

Solution:

1. $\text{Rate} = \dfrac{\$180{,}000}{50{,}000} = \$3.60$ per direct labour hour

2. Applied overhead = $3.60 × 51,000 = $183,600

3. Overhead variance = \$200,000 − \$183,600 = \$16,400 underapplied
4. Unit cost:

	Deluxe	Regular
Prime costs	\$40,000	\$300,000
Overhead costs:		
\$3.60 × 5,000	18,000	
\$3.60 × 46,000		165,600
Total manufacturing costs	\$58,000	\$465,600
Units produced	÷ 5,000	÷ 50,000
Unit cost (Total costs/Units)	\$ 11.60	\$ 9.31*

*Rounded.

II. Departmental Rates

Gee Company gathers the following departmental data of its operations. Two types of stereo units are produced: deluxe and regular.

	Fabrication	Assembly
Budgeted overhead	\$120,000	\$60,000
Expected and actual usage (direct labour hours):		
Deluxe	3,000	2,000
Regular	3,000	43,000
	6,000	45,000

	Fabrication	Assembly
Expected and actual usage (machine hours):		
Deluxe	2,000	5,000
Regular	18,000	5,000
	20,000	10,000

In addition to the departmental data, the following information is provided:

	Deluxe	Regular
Units produced	5,000	50,000
Prime costs	\$40,000	\$300,000

Required:

1. Calculate departmental overhead rates by using machine hours for fabrication and direct labour hours for assembly.
2. Calculate the applied overhead by department.
3. Calculate the applied overhead by product.
4. Calculate unit costs.

Solution:

1. Departmental rates:

$$\text{Fabrication: } \frac{\$120{,}000}{20{,}000} = \$6.00 \text{ per machine hour}$$

$$\text{Assembly: } \frac{\$60{,}000}{45{,}000} = \$1.33^{*} \text{ per direct labour hour}$$

*Rounded.

2. Applied overhead (by department):

Fabrication: \$6.00 × 20,000 = \$120,000
Assembly: \$1.33 × 45,000 = \$59,850

3. Applied overhead (by product):

Deluxe: ($6.00 × 2,000) + ($1.33 × 2,000) = $14,660
Regular: ($6.00 × 18,000) + ($1.33 × 43,000) = $165,190

4. Unit cost (rounded to the nearest cent):

$$\text{Deluxe: } \frac{(\$40{,}000 + \$14{,}660)}{5{,}000} = \$10.93$$

$$\text{Regular: } \frac{(\$300{,}000 + \$165{,}190)}{50{,}000} = \$9.30$$

III. Activity-Based Rates

Gee Company produces two types of stereo units: deluxe and regular. Activity data follow:

	Product-Costing Data		
Activity Usage Measures	**Deluxe**	**Regular**	**Total**
Units produced per year	5,000	50,000	55,000
Prime costs	$40,000	$300,000	$340,000
Direct labour hours	5,000	46,000	51,000
Machine hours	7,000	23,000	30,000
Production runs	10	5	15
Number of moves	120	60	180

Activity Cost Data (Overhead Activities)

Activity	Cost
Setups	$ 60,000
Materials handling	30,000
Power	50,000
Testing	40,000
Total	$180,000

Required:

1. Calculate the consumption ratios for each activity.
2. Group activities based on the consumption ratios.
3. Using the pool rates, calculate unit product costs.

Solution:

1. Consumption ratios:

Overhead Activity	Deluxe	Regular	Activity Driver
Setups	0.67[a]	0.33[a]	Production runs
Materials handling	0.67[b]	0.33[b]	Number of moves
Power	0.23[c]	0.77[c]	Machine hours
Testing	0.10[d]	0.90[d]	Direct labour hours

[a] 10/15 (deluxe) and 5/15 (regular)
[b] 120/180 (deluxe) and 60/180 (regular)
[c] 7,000/30,000 (deluxe) and 23,000/30,000 (regular)
[d] 5,000/51,000 (deluxe) and 46,000/51,000 (regular)

2. Batch-level: setups and materials handling
   Unit-level: power and testing

3. Unit Costs: Activity-Based Costing

	Deluxe	Regular
Prime costs	$ 40,000	$300,000
Overhead costs:		
Setups		
$60,000 × 0.67	40,200	
$60,000 × 0.33		19,800
Materials handling		
$30,000 × 0.67	20,100	
$30,000 × 0.33		9,900
Power		
$50,000 × 0.23	11,500	
$50,000 × 0.77		38,500
Testing		
$40,000 × 0.10	4,000	
$40,000 × 0.90		36,000
Total manufacturing costs	$115,800	$404,200
Units produced	÷ 5,000	÷ 50,000
Unit cost (Total costs/Units)	$ 23.16	$ 8.08

IV. Environmental Costs

At the beginning of 2018, Kleaner Company initiated a program to improve its environmental performance. Efforts were made to reduce the production and emission of contaminating gaseous, solid, and liquid residues. By the end of the year, in an executive meeting, the environmental manager indicated that the company had made significant improvement in its environmental performance, reducing the emission of contaminating residues of all types. The president of the company was pleased with the reported success, but wanted an assessment of the financial consequences of the environmental improvements. To satisfy this request, the following financial data were collected for 2017 and 2018 (all changes in costs are a result of environmental improvements):

	2017 ($)	2018 ($)
Sales	20,000,000	20,000,000
Evaluating and selecting suppliers	0	600,000
Treating and disposing of toxic materials	1,200,000	800,000
Inspecting processes (environmental objective)	200,000	300,000
Land restoration (annual fund contribution)	1,600,000	1,200,000
Maintaining pollution equipment	400,000	300,000
Testing for contaminants	150,000	100,000

Required:

Classify the costs as prevention, detection, internal failure, or external failure.

Solution:

Prevention costs: evaluating and selecting suppliers
Detection costs: testing for contaminants and inspecting processes
Internal failure costs: maintaining pollution equipment, and treating and disposing of toxic materials
External failure costs: land restoration

DISCUSSION QUESTIONS

1. Describe the two-stage process associated with plantwide overhead rates.
2. Describe the two-stage process for departmental overhead rates.
3. What are non-unit-level overhead activities? Non-unit-based cost drivers? Give some examples.
4. What is meant by "product diversity"?
5. What is an overhead consumption ratio?
6. What is activity-based product costing?
7. What is an activity dictionary?
8. Explain how costs are assigned to activities.
9. Describe the value of activity-based customer costing.
10. Explain how ABC can help a firm identify its true low-cost suppliers.
11. What is driver analysis? What role does it play in process-value analysis?
12. What are value-added activities? Value-added costs?
13. What are non-value-added activities? Non-value-added costs? Give an example of each.
14. Identify and define four different ways to manage activities so that costs can be reduced.
15. What is cycle time? Velocity?

CORNERSTONE EXERCISES

OBJECTIVE 1
CORNERSTONE 7.1

Cornerstone Exercise 7-1 Consumption Ratios

Rico Company produces two types of boots: cowboy and cowgirl. There are four activities associated with the two products. Drivers for the four activities are as follows:

	Cowboy	Cowgirl
Cutting hours	1,400	2,600
Assembly hours	1,000	1,500
Inspection hours	450	1,050
Rework hours	50	150

Required:

1. Calculate the consumption ratios for the four drivers.
2. Is there evidence of product diversity? Explain.

OBJECTIVE 1
CORNERSTONE 7.2

Cornerstone Exercise 7-2 Activity Rates

Refer to **Cornerstone Exercise 7-1**. The following activity data have been collected:

Cutting	$60,000
Assembling	25,000
Inspecting	12,000
Reworking	6,000

Required:

Calculate the activity rates that would be used to assign costs to each product.

OBJECTIVE 1
CORNERSTONE 7.3

Cornerstone Exercise 7-3 Calculating ABC Unit Costs

Credit Bank has collected the following information for four activities and two types of credit cards:

Activity	Driver	Classic	Gold	Activity Rate ($)
Processing transactions	Transactions processed	50,000	60,000	0.15
Preparing statements	Number of statements	5,000	20,000	0.90
Answering questions	Number of calls	10,000	25,000	3.00
Providing ATMs	ATM transactions	20,000	6,000	1.20

There are 5,000 holders of Classic cards and 20,000 holders of Gold cards.

Required:

Calculate the unit cost for Classic and Gold credit cards.

Cornerstone Exercise 7-4 Assigning Costs to Activities

Norrison Automotive produces brake systems for major automobile producers. The accounts payable department at Norrison has five clerks who process and pay supplier invoices. The total cost of their salaries is $250,000. The work distribution for the activities that they perform is as follows:

Activity	Percentage of Time on Each Activity
Comparing source documents	25%
Resolving discrepancies	45%
Processing payment	30%

Required:

Assign the cost of labour to each of the three activities in the accounts payable department.

Cornerstone Exercise 7-5 Activity-Based Customer Costing

Underwood Company produces sofas for 20 retail outlets. Of the 20 retail outlets, 19 are small, independently owned furniture stores and one is a retail chain. The retail chain buys 60 percent of the sofas produced. The 19 smaller customers purchase sofas in approximately equal quantities, where the orders are about the same size. Data concerning Underwood's customer activity are as follows:

	Large Retailer	Smaller Retailers
Units purchased	60,000	40,000
Orders placed	20	2,000
Number of sales calls	10	490
Manufacturing costs	$36,000,000	$24,000,000
Order filling costs allocated*	$1,212,000	$808,000
Sales force costs allocated*	$600,000	$400,000

* Allocated based on sales volume.

Currently, customer-driven costs are assigned to customers based on units sold, a unit-level driver.

Required:

Assign costs to customers by using an ABC approach.

OBJECTIVE 3
CORNERSTONE 7.6

Cornerstone Exercise 7-6 Activity-Based Supplier Costing

Webb Computers uses Alpha Electronics and Laval Company to buy two electronic components used in the manufacture of its computers: component 125X and component 30Y. Consider two activities: testing and reordering components. After the two components are inserted, testing is done to ensure that the two components in the computer are working properly. Reordering occurs because one or both of the components have failed the test and it is necessary to replenish component inventories. Activity cost information and other data needed for supplier costing are as follows:

I. Activity Costs Caused by Suppliers (testing failures and reordering as a result)

Activity	Costs ($)
Testing components	600,000
Reordering components	150,000

(*Continued*)

II. Supplier Data

	Alpha Electronics		Laval Company	
	125X	30Y	125X	30Y
Unit purchase price	$10	$26	$12	$28
Units purchased	60,000	30,000	7,500	7,500
Failed tests	600	390	5	5
Number of reorders	30	20	0	0

Required:

Determine the true unit cost from each supplier by using ABC.

OBJECTIVE 4
CORNERSTONE 7.7

Cornerstone Exercise 7-7 Non-Value-Added Costs

Dykes Inc. has the following two activities: (1) Retesting reworked products, cost: $160,000. The retesting cost of the most efficient competitor is $50,000. (2) Welding subassemblies, cost: $375,000 (15,000 welding hours). A benchmarking study reveals that the most efficient level for Dykes would use 12,000 welding hours and entail a cost of $240,000.

Required:

Determine the non-value-added cost of each activity.

OBJECTIVE 4
CORNERSTONE 7.8

Cornerstone Exercise 7-8 Velocity and Cycle Time

Kay Company takes 40,000 hours to produce 160,000 units of a product.

Required:

What is the velocity? Cycle time?

EXERCISES

OBJECTIVE 1

Exercise 7-9 Consumption Ratios; Activity Rates

Gladmark Company produces two types of get-well cards: scented and regular. Drivers for the four activities are as follows:

	Scented Cards	Regular Cards
Inspection hours	60	210
Setup hours	75	75
Machine hours	150	500
Number of moves	300	125

The following activity data have been collected:

Inspecting products	$12,500
Setting up equipment	6,250
Machining	24,000
Moving materials	2,975

Required:

1. Calculate the consumption ratios for the four drivers.
2. Is there evidence of product diversity? Explain.
3. Calculate the activity rates that would be used to assign costs to each product.
4. Suppose that the activity rate for inspecting products is $50 per inspection hour. How many hours of inspection are expected for the coming year?

Exercise 7-10 Activity Rates

Johansson Company uses ABC. Johansson manufactures outdoor water toys using two activities: plastic injection moulding and decal application. Johansson's 2018 total budgeted overhead costs for these two activities are $500,000 (70 percent for injection moulding and 30 percent for decal application). Moulding overhead costs are driven by the number of kilograms of plastic that are moulded together. Decal application overhead costs are driven by the number of decals applied to toys. The budgeted activity data for 2018 are as follows:

Kilograms of plastic moulded	3,500,000
Number of decals applied	375,000

Required:

1. Calculate the activity rate for the plastic injection moulding activity.
2. Calculate the activity rate for the decal application activity.

Exercise 7-11 Comparing ABC and Plantwide Overhead Cost Assignments

The Mackinaw Chocolate Company uses ABC. The controller identified two activities and their budgeted costs:

Setting up equipment	$ 76,300
Other overhead	175,000

Setting up equipment is based on setup hours, and other overhead is based on oven hours.

Mackinaw produces two products: fudge and cookies. Information on each product is as follows:

	Fudge	Cookies
Units produced	2,500	12,500
Setup hours	1,000	250
Oven hours	250	1,250

Required:

Round answers to four decimal places.

1. Calculate the activity rate for:
   a. setting up equipment
   b. other overhead
2. How much total overhead is assigned to fudge using ABC?
3. What is the unit overhead assigned to fudge using ABC?
4. Now, ignoring the ABC results, calculate the plantwide overhead rate, based on oven hours.
5. How much total overhead is assigned to fudge using the plantwide overhead rate?
6. Explain why the total overhead assigned to fudge is different under the ABC system (i.e., using the activity rates) than under the traditional system (i.e., using the plantwide rate).

Exercise 7-12 Activity-Based Product Costing

OBJECTIVE 1 2

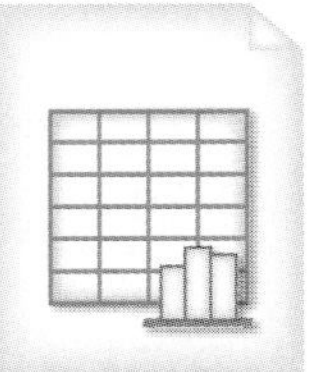

Suppose that a surgical ward has gathered the following information for four nursing activities and two types of patients:

	Driver	Patient Category: Normal	Patient Category: Intensive	Activity rate ($)
Treating patients	Treatments	4,000	20,000	8.00
Providing hygienic care	Hygienic hours	3,000	11,000	10.00
Responding to requests	Requests	20,000	50,000	4.00
Monitoring patients	Monitoring hours	15,000	180,000	1.50

(Continued)

Required:

1. Determine the total nursing costs assigned to each patient category.
2. Output is measured in patient days. Assuming that the normal patient category uses 10,000 patient days and that the intensive patient category uses 8,000 patient days, calculate the nursing cost per patient day for each type of patient.

OBJECTIVE 2

Exercise 7-13 Assigning Costs to Activities, Resource Drivers

Receiving has three activities: unloading, counting goods, and inspecting. Unloading uses a forklift that is leased for $18,000 per year. The forklift is used only for unloading. The fuel for the forklift is $3,600 per year. Other operating costs (maintenance) for the forklift total $2,000 per year. Inspection uses some special testing equipment that has a depreciation of $1,200 per year and an operating cost of $800. Receiving has three employees who have an average salary of $55,000 per year. The work distribution matrix for the receiving personnel is as follows:

Activity	Percentage of Time on Each Activity (%)
Unloading	40
Counting	25
Inspecting	35

No other resources are used for these activities.

Required:

1. Calculate the cost of each activity.
2. Explain the two methods used to assign costs to activities.

Exercise 7-14 Activity-Based Customer-Driven Costs

Suppose that Lone Star Designs has two classes of distributors: class A distributors and class B distributors. The class A distributor places small, frequent orders, and the class B distributor tends to place larger, less frequent orders. Both types of distributors are buying the same product. Lone Star provides the following information about customer-related activities and costs for the most recent quarter:

	Class A Distributors	Class B Distributors
Sales orders	1,000	100
Sales calls	100	100
Service calls	500	250
Average order size	2,500	25,000
Manufacturing cost/unit	$100	$100
Customer costs:		
Processing sales orders	$4,400,000	
Selling goods	1,600,000	
Servicing goods	1,500,000	
Total	$7,500,000	

Required:

1. Calculate the total revenues per distributor category, and assign the customer costs to each distributor type by using revenues as the allocation base. Selling price for one unit is $125.
2. Calculate the customer cost per distributor type using activity-based cost assignments. Discuss the merits of offering the class B distributors a $3 price decrease (assume that they are agitating for a price concession).
3. Assume that the class A distributors are simply imposing the frequent orders on Lone Star. No formal discussion has taken place between class A customers and Lone Star regarding the supply of goods on a very frequent basis. The sales pattern has evolved over time. As an independent consultant, what would you suggest to Lone Star's management?

Exercise 7-15 Activity-Based Supplier Costing

Seabrook Company manufactures heating systems. Seabrook produces all the parts necessary for its product except for one electronic component, which is purchased from two local suppliers: Wood Inc. and Forest Company. Both suppliers are reliable and seldom deliver late; however, Wood sells the component for $48 per unit, while Forest sells the same component for $43. Seabrook purchases 80 percent of its components from Forest because of its lower price. The total annual demand is 2,000,000 components.

To help assess the cost effect of the two components, the following data were collected for supplier-related activities and suppliers:

I. Activity Data

	Activity Cost ($)
Inspecting components (sampling only)	240,000
Reworking products (due to failed component)	3,042,000
Warranty work (due to failed component)	4,800,000

II. Supplier Data

	Wood Inc.	Forest Company
Unit purchase price	$48	$43
Units purchased	400,000	1,600,000
Sampling hours*	40	1,960
Rework hours	180	2,820
Warranty hours	400	7,600

* Sampling inspection for Wood's product has been reduced because the reject rate is so low.

Required:

1. Calculate the cost per component for each supplier, taking into consideration the costs of the supplier-related activities and using the current prices and sales volume. Round the unit cost to two decimal places.
2. Suppose that Seabrook loses $2,000,000 in sales per year because of the reputation effect of defective units attributable to failed components. Using warranty hours, assign the cost of lost sales to each supplier. By how much would this change the cost of each supplier's component?

Exercise 7-16 Non-Value-Added Costs

The following six situations are derived from different activity assessments and are not related.

a. A manual insertion process takes 30 minutes and 8 kilograms of material to produce a product. Automating the insertion process would require 15 minutes of machine time and 7.5 kilograms of material. The cost per labour hour is $12, the cost per machine hour is $8, and the cost per kilogram of materials is $10.
b. With its original design, a gear requires eight hours of setup time. By redesigning the gear so that the number of different grooves needed is reduced by 50 percent, the setup time is reduced by 75 percent. The cost per setup hour is $50.
c. A product currently requires six moves. By redesigning the manufacturing layout, the number of moves can be reduced from six to zero. The cost per move is $20.
d. Inspection time for a plant is 16,000 hours per year. The cost of inspection consists of salaries of eight inspectors, totalling $480,000. Inspection also uses supplies costing $5 per inspection hour. The company eliminated most defective components by eliminating low-quality suppliers. The number of production errors was reduced dramatically by installing a system of statistical process control. Further quality improvements were realized by redesigning the products, making them easier to manufacture. The net effect was to achieve a close to zero-defect state and eliminate the need for any inspection activity.

(Continued)

e. Each unit of a product requires six components. The average number of components is 6.5 due to component failure, requiring rework and extra components. Developing relations with the right suppliers and increasing the quality of the purchased component can reduce the average number of components to six components per unit. The cost per component is $500.
f. A plant produces 100 different electronic products. Each product requires an average of eight components that are purchased externally. The components are different for each part. By redesigning the products, it is possible to produce the 100 products so that they all have four components in common. This will reduce the demand for purchasing, receiving, and paying bills. Estimated savings from the reduced demand are $900,000 per year.

Required:

Estimate the non-value-added cost for each situation.

OBJECTIVE 4

Exercise 7-17 Driver Analysis

Refer to the six situations in Exercise 7-16.

Required:

For each situation, identify the possible root cause(s) of the activity cost (such as plant layout, process design, and product design).

OBJECTIVE 4

Exercise 7-18 Type of Activity Management

Refer to the six situations in Exercise 7-16.

Required:

For each situation, identify the cost reduction measure: activity elimination, activity reduction, activity sharing, or activity selection.

OBJECTIVE 4

Exercise 7-19 Cycle Time and Velocity

A manufacturing cell produces 90,000 stereo speakers per quarter. A total of 15,000 production hours are used within the cell per quarter.

Required:

1. Calculate the velocity (per hour).
2. Calculate the cycle time (minutes per unit produced).

OBJECTIVE 1 2

Exercise 7-20 Product-Costing Accuracy, Consumption Ratios

Singh Company produces two products: a mostly handcrafted soft leather briefcase sold under the label Elegant and a leather briefcase produced largely through automation and sold under the label Fina. The two products use two overhead activities, with the following costs:

Setting up equipment	$ 3,000
Machining	18,000

The controller has collected the following expected annual prime costs for each briefcase, the machine hours, the setup hours, and the expected production.

	Elegant	Fina
Direct labour	$9,000	$3,000
Direct materials	$3,000	$3,000
Units	3,000	3,000
Machine hours	500	4,500
Setup hours	100	100

Required:

1. Do you think that the direct labour costs and direct materials costs are accurately traced to each briefcase? Explain.
2. Calculate the consumption ratios for each activity.
3. Calculate the overhead cost per unit for each briefcase by using a plantwide rate based on direct labour costs. Comment on this approach to assigning overhead.
4. Calculate the overhead cost per unit for each briefcase by using overhead rates based on machine hours and setup hours. Explain why these assignments are more accurate than using the direct labour costs.

Exercise 7-21 Product-Costing Accuracy, Consumption Ratios, Activity Rates, Activity Costing

OBJECTIVE 1 2

Tristar Manufacturing produces two types of battery-operated toy soldiers: infantry and special forces. The soldiers are produced using one continuous process. Four activities have been identified: machining, setups, receiving, and packing. Resource drivers have been used to assign costs to each activity. The overhead activities, their costs, and the other related data are as follows:

Product	Machining (machine hours)	Setups (number of setups)	Receiving (number of orders)	Packing (number of orders)
Infantry	30,000	600	600	2,400
Special forces	30,000	200	75	1,200
Costs	$120,000	$52,000	$16,000	$50,000

Required:

1. Calculate the total overhead assigned to each product by using only machine hours to calculate a plantwide rate.
2. Calculate consumption ratios for each activity.
3. Calculate a rate for each activity by using the associated driver.
4. Assign the overhead costs to each product by using the activity rates computed in Requirement 3.
5. Comment on the difference between the assignment in Requirement 1 and the activity-based assignment.

Exercise 7-22 Formation of an Activity Analysis

A hospital is in the process of implementing an ABC system. A pilot study is being done to assess the effects of the costing changes on specific products. Of particular interest is the cost of caring for patients who receive in-patient recovery treatment for illness, surgery (noncardiac), and injury. These patients are housed on the third and fourth floors of the hospital (the floors are dedicated to patient care and have only nursing stations and patient rooms). A partial transcript of an interview with the hospital's nursing supervisor using the seven key questions is as follows:

1. How many nurses are in the hospital? — *There are 101 nurses, including me.*
2. Of the 100 nurses, excluding you, how many are assigned to the third and fourth floors? — *Fifty nurses in total are assigned to these two floors.*
3. What do these nurses do (please describe)? — *They provide nursing care for patients, which means answering questions, changing bandages, administering medicine, changing clothes, and many more similar activities.*
4. And what do you do? — *I supervise and coordinate all the nursing activity in the hospital. This includes surgery, maternity, the emergency room, and the two floors you mentioned.*
5. What other lodging and care activities are done for the third and fourth floors by persons other than the nurses? — *The patients must be fed. The hospital cafeteria delivers meals. The laundry department picks up dirty clothing and bedding once each shift. The floors also have a physical therapist assigned to provide care on a physician-directed basis.*

(*Continued*)

6. Do patients use any equipment?	*Yes. Mostly monitoring equipment.*
7. Who or what uses the activity output?	*Patients. But there are different kinds of patients. On these two floors, we classify patients into three categories according to severity: intensive care, intermediate care, and normal care. The more severe the illness, the more activity is used. Nurses spend much more time with intermediate care patients than with normal care. The more severe patients tend to use more of the laundry service as well. Their clothing and bedding need to be changed more frequently. On the other hand, severe patients use less food. They eat fewer meals. Typically, we measure each patient type by the number of days of hospital stay. And you have to keep in mind that every patient uses each type of activity to varying degrees.*

Required:

Prepare an activity analysis with three categories: activity name, activity description, and activity driver.

Exercise 7-23 Plantwide Rate and Activity-Based Costing

The controller for Crombie Inc. has established the following activity cost pools and cost drivers.

Activity Cost Pool	Budgeted Overhead Cost	Cost Driver	Budgeted Level for Cost Driver
Machine setups	$350,000	Number of setups	225
Materials handling	125,000	Weight of materials	25,000 kilograms
Waste control	75,000	Weight of chemicals	7,500 kilograms
Quality control	110,000	Number of inspections	400
Other overhead costs	400,000	Machine hours	30,000

Each order must be a minimum of 1,000 boxes of film chemicals.
The production requirements for each minimum order are as follows:

Machine setups	10 setups
Materials handling	2,500 kilograms
Waste control	300 kilograms
Quality control	4 inspections
Other overhead costs	750 machine hours

Required:

1. Calculate the overhead that should be assigned to each minimum order of film chemicals using the above data.
2. Calculate the overhead that should be assigned to each minimum order of film chemicals if Crombie decides to use a single predetermined overhead rate based on machine hours.

Exercise 7-24 Departmental Plantwide Rate

Britton Metals Inc. has two production departments with the following characteristics:

	Department A	Department B	Total
Direct labour hours per month	80,000	80,000	160,000
Machine hours per month	—	80,000	80,000
Floor space in square metres	8,000	232,000	240,000
Production equipment depreciation	—	$ 400,000	
Power cost	$ 800	$ 39,200	

Some of the company's products are produced exclusively in department A and others require activity only in department B. The following costs are budgeted for the month and form the basis for computing the predetermined overhead rate.

Building costs	$264,000
Power cost	40,000
Production equipment depreciation	400,000
Total	$704,000

Required:

1. Calculate a single predetermined overhead rate for the company, based on direct labour hours.
2. Calculate an overhead rate for each production department, based on two different cost drivers: direct labour hours in department A and machine hours in department B.
3. CONCEPTUAL CONNECTION Explain why the two calculations differ.

Exercise 7-25 Plantwide Rate and Activity-Based Costing

Mattawa Manufacturing Inc. has four categories of overhead. The expected overhead costs for each of the categories for the next year are as follows:

	Costs	Cost Driver	Expected Activity
Maintenance	$510,000	Machine hours	60,000
Materials handling	250,000	Material moves	20,000
Setups	60,000	Setups	3,000
Inspection	21,000	Inspections	12,000

Currently, the company applies overhead using a predetermined overhead rate based upon budgeted direct labour hours of 100,000. The company has been asked to submit a bid on a proposed job. Usually bids are based upon full manufacturing costs plus a markup of 60 percent. Estimates for the proposed job are as follows:

Direct materials	$30,000
Direct labour	$24,000
Number of direct labour hours	8,000
Number of material moves	100
Number of inspections	120
Number of setups	24
Number of machine hours	4,000

Required:

1. If the company used activity-based cost drivers to assign overhead, calculate the bid price of the proposed job.
2. If the company used direct labour hours as the cost driver, calculate the bid price of the proposed job.

Exercise 7-26 Plantwide Rate and Activity-Based Costing: Bid Price of Job

Potter Manufacturing Inc. has four categories of overhead. The expected overhead costs for each of the categories for the next year are as follows:

	Costs	Cost Driver	Expected Activity
Maintenance	$120,000	Machine hours	5,000
Materials handling	18,000	Material moves	600
Setups	16,000	Setups	200
Inspection	60,000	Inspections	1,000

Currently, the company applies overhead using a predetermined overhead rate based on budgeted direct labour hours of 20,000. The company has been asked to bid on a proposed job.

(Continued)

Usually bids are based on full manufacturing costs plus a markup of 35 percent. Estimates for the proposed job are as follows:

Direct materials	$2,000
Direct labour	$6,000
Number of direct labour hours	600
Number of material moves	4
Number of inspections	6
Number of setups	8
Number of machine hours	80

Required:

1. If the company used direct labour hours as the cost driver, calculate the bid price of the proposed job.
2. If the company used activity-based cost drivers to assign overhead, calculate the bid price of the proposed job.

OBJECTIVE 2

Exercise 7-27 Plantwide Rate and Activity-Based Costing

Rowland Textile Inc. manufactures two products: sweatshirts and T-shirts. The manufacturing process involves two activities: cutting and sewing. Expected overhead costs and cost drivers are as follows:

	Cutting	Sewing
Overhead costs	$320,000	$700,000
Machine hours	800,000	50,000
Direct labour hours	40,000	20,000

Required:

1. Calculate the activity-based overhead rates. Use machine hours for the cutting activity and direct labour hours for the sewing activity.
2. Calculate a plantwide overhead rate using direct labour hours as the cost driver.
3. Assume the activities for sweatshirts are as follows:

	Cutting	Sewing
Machine hours	4	2
Direct labour hours	2	4

   Calculate the overhead costs allocated to sweatshirts based on the activity-based overhead rates calculated in Requirement 1.
4. Using the assumptions given in Requirement 3, calculate the overhead costs allocated to sweatshirts using the plantwide overhead rate in Requirement 2.

Exercise 7-28 Plantwide Rate and Departmental Rates

Chan Inc. has two manufacturing departments: cutting and folding. The company has been using a plantwide predetermined rate based on direct labour cost. The following data are for the current year:

	Cutting	Folding	Total
Budgeted overhead	$480,000	$360,000	$840,000
Budgeted direct labour hours	30,000	12,000	42,000
Budgeted machine hours	9,000	10,000	19,000
Actual overhead	$440,000	$430,000	$870,000
Actual direct labour hours	31,000	13,000	44,000
Actual machine hours	9,000	11,000	20,000
Prime costs	$145,000	$155,000	$300,000

Required:

1. Calculate a plantwide predetermined overhead rate using direct labour hours.
2. Calculate applied overhead using the plantwide predetermined overhead rate.
3. Calculate the overhead variance and label the variance as under- or overapplied overhead.
4. Calculate separate departmental overhead rates using direct labour hours for cutting and machine hours for folding.
5. Calculate the total amount of applied overhead for each department, based on the activity-based overhead rates calculated in Requirement 4.

Exercise 7-29 Activity-Based Costing

OBJECTIVE 3

Wingli Corporation manufactures a variety of office chairs. The costing system was designed using an activity-based approach. The company produced two styles of chairs in December. The production data are as follows:

	Units	Direct Materials	Direct Labour Hours	Number of Parts
Style A	25,000	$3,000,000	37,500	500,000
Style B	500	125,000	2,500	17,500

Three activities have been identified. Resource drivers are used to assign costs to each activity. The overhead activities, activity costs, and other related data are as follows:

	Budgeted Costs	Cost Drivers	Cost Allocation Rate
Materials handling	1,000,000	Parts	0.25
Cutting	10,800,000	Parts	2.5
Assembly	10,000,000	Direct labour hours	25

There is no beginning or ending inventory. The direct labour rate is $30 per hour.

Required:

1. Calculate the December total manufacturing costs.
2. Calculate the unit costs for the style A and style B chairs.

Exercise 7-30 Activity-Based Costing

OBJECTIVE 3

Flex Company uses ABC to determine the costs of its products. The estimated total cost and expected activity for each of the company's three activity cost pools are as follows:

		Expected Activity		
Activity Cost Pools	**Estimated Costs**	**Product A**	**Product B**	**Total**
Receiving materials	$76,600	900	650	1,550
Inspecting goods	68,600	3,750	2,800	6,550
Shipping goods	27,500	875	720	1,595

Required:

Calculate the overhead that should be assigned to Product A and Product B.

Exercise 7-31 Activity Rates and Activity-Based Product Costing

OBJECTIVE 2

Hammer Company produces a variety of electronic equipment. One of its plants produces two laser printers: the deluxe and the regular. At the beginning of the year, the following data were prepared for this plant:

	Deluxe	Regular
Quantity	100,000	800,000
Selling price	$900	$750
Unit prime cost	$529	$483

Check figures:

2. Unit cost: Deluxe $763; Regular $565

(Continued)

In addition, the following information was provided so that overhead costs could be assigned to each product:

Activity Name	Activity Driver	Activity Cost ($)	Deluxe	Regular
Setups	Number of setups	2,000,000	300	200
Machining	Machine hours	80,000,000	100,000	300,000
Engineering	Engineering hours	6,000,000	50,000	100,000
Packing	Packing orders	1,000,000	100,000	400,000

Required:

1. Calculate the overhead rates for each activity.
2. Calculate the per-unit product cost for each product.

OBJECTIVE 4

Exercise 7-32 Value- and Non-Value-Added Costs

Waterfun Technology produces engines for recreational boats. Because of competitive pressures, the company was making an effort to reduce costs. As part of this effort, management implemented an activity-based management system and began focusing its attention on processes and activities. Purchasing was among the processes (activities) that were carefully studied. The study revealed that the number of purchase orders was a good driver for purchasing costs. During the past year, the company incurred fixed receiving costs of $630,000 (salaries of 15 employees). These fixed costs provide a capacity of processing 72,000 receiving orders (4,800 per employee at practical capacity). Management decided that the efficient level for purchasing should use 36,000 receiving orders, as much of the activity in the receiving department appears to be related to inefficient processes by either the purchasing department or the suppliers.

Required:

1. Explain why receiving would be viewed as a value-added activity. List all possible reasons. Also, list some possible reasons that explain why the demand for purchasing is more than the efficient level of 36,000 orders.
2. Break the cost of receiving into its value-added and non-value-added components.

PROBLEMS

Problem 7-33 Functional-Based versus Activity-Based Costing

For years, Sierra Grande Company produced only one product: backpacks. Recently, the company decided to add a line of duffel bags. With this addition, the company began assigning overhead costs by using departmental rates. (Prior to this, the company used a predetermined plantwide rate based on units produced.) Departmental rates meant that overhead costs had to be assigned to each producing department in order to create overhead pools so that predetermined departmental rates could be calculated. Surprisingly, after the addition of the duffel-bag line and the switch to departmental rates, the costs to produce the backpacks increased, and their profitability dropped.

The marketing manager and the production manager both complained about the increase in the production cost of backpacks. The marketing manager was concerned because the increase in unit costs led to pressure to increase the unit price of backpacks. She was resisting this pressure because she was certain that the increase would harm the company's market share. The production manager was receiving pressure to cut costs also, yet he was convinced that nothing different was being done in the way the backpacks were produced. He was also convinced that further efficiency in the manufacture of the backpacks was unlikely. After some discussion, the two managers decided that the problem had to be connected to the addition of the duffel-bag line.

Upon investigation, they were informed that the only real change in product costing procedures was in the way overhead costs were being assigned. A two-stage procedure was now in use. First, overhead costs were assigned to the two producing departments: patterns and finishing. Some overhead costs were assigned to the producing departments by using direct tracing, and some were assigned by using driver tracing. For example, the salaries of the producing department's supervisors were assigned by using direct tracing, whereas the costs of the factory's accounting department were assigned by using driver tracing (the driver being the number of transactions processed for each department). Second, the costs accumulated in the producing departments were assigned to the two products by using direct labour hours as a driver (the rate in each department is based on direct labour hours). The managers were assured that great care was taken to associate overhead costs with individual products. So that they could construct their own example of overhead cost assignment, the controller provided them with the information necessary to show how accounting costs were being assigned to products:

	Department		
	Patterns	**Finishing**	**Total**
Accounting cost	$48,000	$72,000	$120,000
Transactions processed	32,000	48,000	80,000
Total direct labour hours	10,000	20,000	30,000
Direct labour hours per backpack*	0.10	0.20	0.30
Direct labour hours per duffel bag*	0.40	0.80	1.20

* Hours required to produce one unit of each product.

The controller remarked that the cost of operating the accounting department had doubled with the addition of the new product line. The increase came because of the need to process additional transactions, which had also doubled in number.

During the first year of producing duffel bags, the company produced and sold 100,000 backpacks and 25,000 duffel bags. The 100,000 backpacks matched the prior year's output for that product.

Required:

1. Calculate the amount of accounting cost assigned to a backpack before the duffel-bag line was added by using a plantwide rate approach based on units produced. Is this assignment accurate? Explain.
2. Suppose that the company decided to assign the accounting costs directly to the product lines by using the number of transactions as the activity driver. What is the accounting cost per unit of backpacks? Per unit of duffel bags?
3. Calculate the amount of accounting cost assigned to each backpack and duffel bag by using departmental rates based on direct labour hours.
4. CONCEPTUAL CONNECTION Which way of assigning overhead does the best job—the functional-based approach by using departmental rates, or the activity-based approach by using transactions processed for each product? Explain. Discuss the value of ABC before the duffel-bag line was added.

Check figures:
2. Unit cost: Backpacks $0.60 per unit
3. Unit cost: Duffel bags $4.80

Problem 7-34 Plantwide versus Departmental Rates, Product-Costing Accuracy: Activity-Based Costing

OBJECTIVE 1 2

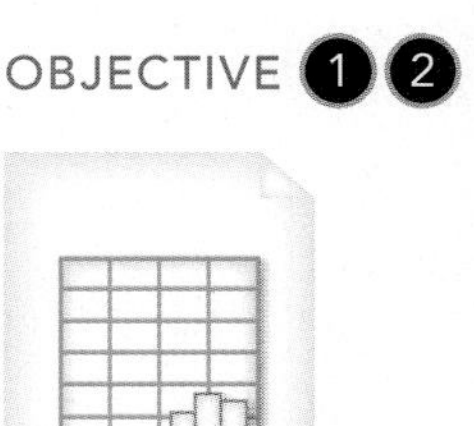

Ramsey Company produces speakers (model A and model B). Both products pass through two producing departments. Model A's production is much more labour-intensive than that of model B. Model B is also the more popular of the two speakers. The following data have been gathered for the two products:

	Product Data	
	Model A	**Model B**
Units produced per year	120,000	1,200,000
Prime costs	$600,000	$6,000,000
Direct labour hours	390,000	1,800,000

(Continued)

	Product Data	
	Model A	Model B
Machine hours	120,000	1,200,000
Production runs	240	360
Inspection hours	4,800	7,200
Maintenance hours	60,000	540,000
Overhead costs:		
Setup costs	$1,080,000	
Inspection costs	840,000	
Machining	960,000	
Maintenance	1,080,000	
Total	$3,960,000	

Required:

1. Calculate the overhead cost per unit for each product by using a plantwide rate based on direct labour hours. Round overhead rate to four decimal places and round overhead per unit to nearest cent.
2. Calculate the overhead cost per unit for each product by using ABC. Round rate to four decimal places. Round cost per unit to nearest cent.
3. Suppose that Ramsey decides to use departmental overhead rates. There are two departments: department 1 (machine intensive) with a rate of $2.33 per machine hour and department 2 (labour intensive) with a rate of $0.60 per direct labour hour. The consumption of these two drivers is as follows:

	Department 1 Machine Hours	Department 2 Direct Labour Hours
Model A	60,000	780,000
Model B	1,020,000	1,620,000

Calculate the overhead cost per unit for each product by using departmental rates. Round to two decimal places.

4. CONCEPTUAL CONNECTION Using the activity-based product costs as the standard, comment on the ability of departmental rates to improve the accuracy of product costing. (Did the departmental rates do better than the plantwide rate?)

Problem 7-35 Production-Based Costing versus Activity-Based Costing, Assigning Costs to Activities, Resource Drivers

Willow Company produces lawn mowers. One of its plants produces two versions of mowers: a basic model and a deluxe model. The deluxe model has a sturdier frame, a higher horsepower engine, a wider blade, and mulching capability. At the beginning of the year, the following data were prepared for this plant:

	Basic Model	Deluxe Model
Expected quantity	40,000	20,000
Selling price	$180	$360
Prime costs	$80	$160
Machine hours	5,000	5,000
Direct labour hours	10,000	10,000
Engineering support (hours)	1,500	4,500
Receiving (orders processed)	250	500
Materials handling (number of moves)	1,200	4,800
Purchasing (number of requisitions)	100	200
Maintenance (hours used)	1,000	3,000
Paying suppliers (invoices processed)	250	500
Setting up equipment (number of setups)	16	64

Additionally, the following overhead activity costs are reported:

Maintaining equipment	$114,000
Engineering support	120,000
Materials handling	?
Setting up equipment	96,000
Purchasing materials	60,000
Receiving goods	40,000
Paying suppliers	30,000
Providing space	20,000
Total	$?

Facility-level costs are allocated in proportion to machine hours (provides a measure of time the facility is used by each product). Materials handling uses three inputs: two forklifts, gasoline to operate the forklifts, and three operators. The three operators are paid a salary of $40,000 each. The operators spend 25 percent of their time on the receiving activity and 75 percent on moving goods (materials handling). Gasoline costs $3 per move. Depreciation amounts to $6,000 per forklift per year.

Required:

Round answers to two decimal places.

1. Calculate the cost of the materials handling activity. Label the cost assignments as driver tracing or direct tracing. Identify the resource drivers.
2. Calculate the cost per unit for each product by using direct labour hours to assign all overhead costs.
3. Calculate activity rates, and assign costs to each product. Calculate a unit cost for each product, and compare these costs with those calculated in Requirement 2.
4. Calculate consumption ratios for each activity.
5. Explain how the consumption ratios calculated in Requirement 4 can be used to reduce the number of rates. Calculate the rates that would apply under this approach.

Problem 7-36 Activity Costing, Assigning Resource Costs, Primary and Secondary Activities

OBJECTIVE 1 2

Trinity Clinic has identified three activities for daily maternity care: occupancy and feeding, nursing, and nursing supervision. The nursing supervisor oversees 150 nurses, 25 of whom are maternity nurses (the other nurses are located in other care areas such as the emergency room and intensive care). The nursing supervisor has three assistants, a secretary, several offices, computers, phones, and furniture. The three assistants spend 75 percent of their time on the supervising activity and 25 percent of their time as surgical nurses. They each receive a salary of $48,000. The nursing supervisor has a salary of $70,000. She spends 100 percent of her time supervising. The secretary receives a salary of $22,000 per year. Other costs directly traceable to the supervisory activity (depreciation, utilities, phone, etc.) average $100,000 per year.

Daily care output is measured as "patient days." The clinic has traditionally assigned the cost of daily care by using a daily rate (a rate per patient day). Different kinds of daily care are provided, and rates are structured to reflect these differences. For example, a higher daily rate is charged for an intensive care unit than for a maternity care unit. Within units, however, the daily rates are the same for all patients. Under the traditional, functional approach, the daily rate is computed by dividing the annual costs of occupancy and feeding, nursing, and a share of supervision by the unit's capacity expressed in patient days. The cost of supervision is assigned to each care area based on the number of nurses. A single driver (patient days) is used to assign the costs of daily care to each patient.

A pilot study has revealed that the demands for nursing care vary within the maternity unit, depending on the severity of a patient's case. Specifically, demand for nursing services per day increases with severity. Assume that the maternity unit has three levels of increasing severity:

(Continued)

normal patients, cesarean patients, and patients with complications. The pilot study provided the following activity and cost information:

Activity	Annual Cost ($)	Activity Driver	Annual Quantity
Occupancy and feeding	1,000,000	Patient days	10,000
Nursing care (maternity)	950,000	Hours of nursing care	50,000
Nursing supervision	?	Number of nurses	150

The pilot study also revealed the following information concerning the three types of patients and their annual demands:

Patient Type	Patient Days Demanded	Nursing Hours Demanded
Normal	7,000	17,500
Cesarean	2,000	12,500
Complications	1,000	20,000
Total	10,000	50,000

Check figures:
1. Cost per patient day $200
2. Cost per patient day Normal $150; Complications $500

Required:

1. Calculate the cost per patient day by using a functional-based approach.
2. Calculate the cost per patient day by using an activity-based approach.
3. The hospital processes 1,000,000 kilograms of laundry per year. The annual cost for the laundering activity is $500,000. In a functional-based cost system, the cost of the laundry department is assigned to each user department in proportion to the kilograms of laundry produced. Typically, maternity produces 200,000 kilograms per year. How much would this change the cost per patient day calculated in Requirement 1? Now, describe what information you would need to modify the calculation made in Requirement 2. Under what conditions would this activity calculation provide a more accurate cost assignment?

OBJECTIVE 1 2 3

Problem 7-37 Customers as a Cost Object

Security National Bank has requested an analysis of chequing account profitability by customer type. Customers are categorized according to the size of their account: low balances, medium balances, and high balances. The activities associated with the three different customer categories and their associated annual costs are as follows:

Opening and closing accounts	$ 300,000
Issuing monthly statements	500,000
Processing transactions	2,600,000
Customer inquiries	600,000
Providing automated teller machine (ATM) services	2,175,000
Total cost	$6,175,000

Additional data concerning the usage of the activities by the various customers are also provided:

	Account Balance		
	Low	Medium	High
Number of accounts opened/closed	25,000	5,000	3,500
Number of statements issued	650,000	150,000	75,000
Processing transactions	22,000,000	3,000,000	700,000
Number of telephone minutes	1,500,000	750,000	550,000
Number of ATM transactions	1,650,000	300,000	65,000
Number of chequing accounts	46,000	9,500	5,500

Required:

Round answers to two decimal places.

1. Calculate a cost per account per year by dividing the total cost of processing and maintaining chequing accounts by the total number of accounts. What is the average fee per month that the bank should charge to cover the costs incurred because of chequing accounts?

2. Calculate a cost per account by customer category by using activity rates.
3. Currently, the bank offers free chequing to all of its customers. The interest revenues average $90 per account; however, the interest revenues earned per account by category are $80, $100, and $165 for the low-, medium-, and high-balance accounts, respectively. Calculate the average profit per account (average revenue less average cost from Requirement 1). Then calculate the profit per account by using the revenue per customer type and the unit cost per customer type calculated in Requirement 2.
4. After the analysis in Requirement 3, a vice-president recommended eliminating the free chequing feature for low-balance customers. The bank president expressed reluctance to do so, arguing that the low-balance customers more than made up for the loss through cross-sales. He presented a survey that showed that 50 percent of the customers would switch banks if a chequing fee were imposed. Explain how you could verify the president's argument by using ABC.

Problem 7-38 Activity-Based Costing and Customer-Driven Costs

OBJECTIVE 2 3

Aero Manufacturing produces several types of bolts used in aircraft. The bolts are produced in batches according to customer orders. Although there are a variety of bolts, they can be grouped into three product families. Because the product families are used in different kinds of aircraft, customers also can be grouped into three categories, corresponding to the product family that they purchase. The number of units sold to each customer class is the same. The selling prices for the three product families range from $0.50 to $0.80 per unit. Historically, the costs of order entry, processing, and handling were expensed and not traced to individual customer groups. These costs are not trivial and totalled $4,500,000 for the most recent year. Furthermore, these costs had been increasing over time. Recently, the company started emphasizing a cost reduction strategy; however, any cost reduction decisions had to contribute to the creation of a competitive advantage.

Because of the magnitude and growth of order-filling costs, management decided to explore the causes of these costs. They discovered that order-filling costs were driven by the number of customer orders processed. Further investigation revealed the following cost behaviour for the order-filling activity:

Step-fixed cost component:	$50,000 per step (2,000 orders define a step)*
Variable cost component:	$20 per order

* Aero currently has sufficient steps to process 100,000 orders.

The expected customer orders for the year total 100,000. The expected usage of the order-filling activity and the average size of an order by customer category follow:

	Category I	Category II	Category III
Number of orders	50,000	30,000	20,000
Average order size	600	1,000	1,500

As a result of cost behaviour analysis, the marketing manager recommended the imposition of a charge per customer order. The president of the company concurred. The charge was implemented by adding the cost per order to the price of each order (computed by using the projected ordering costs and expected orders). This ordering cost was then reduced as the size of the order increased and was eliminated as the order size reached 2,000 units (the marketing manager indicated that any penalties imposed for orders greater than this size would lose sales from some of the smaller customers). Within a short period of communicating this new price information to customers, the average order size for all three product families increased to 2,000 units.

Required:

1. Aero traditionally has expensed order-filling costs. What is the most likely reason for this practice?
2. Calculate the cost per order for each customer category. Round to two decimal places.
3. CONCEPTUAL CONNECTION Calculate the reduction in order-filling costs produced by the change in pricing strategy (assume that resource spending is reduced as much as possible and that the total units sold remain unchanged). Explain how exploiting customer activity information produced this cost reduction. Would any other internal activities benefit from this pricing strategy?

Problem 7-39 Activity-Based Costing and Customer-Driven Costs

Lambo Auto Limited manufactures a limited edition luxury car that it sells through distributors. The company sells the cars to its distributors for $150,000 each and is very willing to accommodate the requirements of its distributors in order to increase volume. Even though the car sells for a high price, the small batch production methods result in only modest profits.

In addition to the normal manufacturing and operating costs that result in a margin on each auto sold of about $10,000, the company incurs some additional costs because of its close relationship to its distributors. These include sales and service calls ($3,500 each); engineering changes ($15,000 each); special packaging for overseas shipment ($15,000 each); and order processing costs ($3,500 each). While these costs seem quite high, the company believes that it controls the demands of its distributors to keep the costs low.

Below is a chart of the additional costs required by each of its distributors:

Distributor	Cars Sold	Sales/Service Calls	Changes Made	Packaging Requests	Orders Placed
Atkins	200	20	0	0	6
Brower	200	40	15	0	8
Caldwell	200	80	75	9	15
Driscoll	200	160	125	18	30

Required:

Determine the profitability of each customer and recommend action to the company.

Problem 7-40 Activity-Based Supplier Costing

Levy Inc. manufactures tractors for agricultural usage. Levy purchases the engines needed for its tractors from two sources: Johnson Engines and Watson Company. The Johnson engine is the more expensive of the two sources and has a price of $1,000. The Watson engine is $900 per unit. Levy produces and sells 22,000 tractors. Of the 22,000 engines needed for the tractors, 4,000 are purchased from Johnson Engines, and 18,000 are purchased from Watson Company. The production manager, Jamie Murray, prefers the Johnson engine. However, Jan Booth, purchasing manager, maintains that the price difference is too great to buy more than the 4,000 units currently purchased. Nevertheless, Jan still wants to maintain a significant connection with the Johnson source, just in case the less expensive source cannot supply the needed quantities. Even though Jamie understands the price argument, he is convinced that the quality of the Johnson engine is worth the price difference. Frank Wallace, the controller, has decided to use activity costing to resolve the issue. The following activity cost and supplier data have been collected:

Activity	Cost ($)
Replacing engines[a]	800,000
Expediting orders[b]	1,000,000
Repairing engines[c]	1,800,000

[a] All units are tested after assembly, and some are rejected because of engine failure. The failed engines are removed and replaced, with the supplier replacing any failed engine. The replaced engine is retested before being sold. Engine failure often causes collateral damage, and other parts often need to be replaced.

[b] Due to late or failed delivery of engines.

[c] Repair work is for units under warranty and almost invariably is due to engine failure. Repair usually means replacing the engine. This cost plus labour, transportation, and other costs make warranty work very expensive.

	Watson	Johnson
Engines replaced by source	1,980	20
Late or failed shipments	198	2
Warranty repairs (by source)	2,440	60

Required:

1. Calculate the activity-based supplier cost per engine (acquisition cost plus supplier-related activity costs). Which of the two suppliers is the low-cost supplier? Explain why this is a better measure of engine cost than the usual purchase costs assigned to the engines.
2. CONCEPTUAL CONNECTION Consider the supplier cost information obtained in Requirement 1. Suppose further that Johnson can only supply a total of 20,000 units. What actions would you advise Levy to undertake with its suppliers?

Problem 7-41 Activity-Based Management, Non-Value-Added Costs

OBJECTIVE 4

Danna Martin, president of Mays Electronics, was concerned about the year-end marketing report that she had just received. According to Larry Savage, marketing manager, a price decrease for the coming year was again needed to maintain the company's annual sales volume of integrated circuit boards (CBs). This would make a bad situation worse. The current selling price of $18 per unit was producing a $2-per-unit profit—half the customary $4-per-unit profit. Foreign competitors kept reducing their prices. To match the latest reduction would reduce the price from $18 to $14. This would put the price below the cost to produce and sell it. How could these firms sell for such a low price? Determined to find out if there were problems with the company's operations, Danna decided to hire a consultant to evaluate the way in which the CBs were produced and sold. After two weeks, the consultant had identified the following activities and costs:

Setting up equipment	$ 125,000
Materials handling	180,000
Inspecting products	122,000
Engineering support	120,000
Handling customer complaints	100,000
Filling warranties	170,000
Storing goods	80,000
Expediting goods	75,000
Using materials	500,000
Using power	48,000
Manual insertion labour[a]	250,000
Other direct labour	150,000
Total costs	$1,920,000[b]

[a] Diodes, resistors, and integrated circuits are inserted manually into the circuit board.
[b] This total cost produces a unit cost of $16 for last year's sales volume.

The consultant indicated that some preliminary activity analysis shows that per-unit costs can be reduced by at least $7. Since the marketing manager had indicated that the market share (sales volume) for the boards could be increased by 50 percent if the price could be reduced to $12, Danna became quite excited.

Required:

1. What is activity-based management? What phases of activity analysis did the consultant provide? What else remains to be done?
2. Identify as many non-value-added costs as possible. Calculate the cost savings per unit that would be realized if these costs were eliminated. Was the consultant correct in his preliminary cost reduction assessment? Discuss actions that the company can take to reduce or eliminate the non-value-added activities.
3. Calculate the unit cost required to maintain current market share, while earning a profit of $4 per unit. Now calculate the unit cost required to expand sales by 50 percent. How much cost reduction would be required to achieve each unit cost?
4. Assume that further activity analysis revealed the following: switching to automated insertion would save $60,000 of engineering support and $90,000 of direct labour. Now, what is the total potential cost reduction per unit available from activity analysis? With these

(Continued)

additional reductions, can Mays Electronics achieve the unit cost to maintain current sales? To increase it by 50 percent? What form of activity analysis is this: reduction, sharing, elimination, or selection?

5. Calculate income based on current sales, prices, and costs. Then calculate the income by using a $14 price and a $12 price, assuming that the maximum cost reduction possible is achieved (including Requirement 4's reduction). What price should be selected?

OBJECTIVE 3 4

Problem 7-42 Non-Value-Added Costs, Activity Costs, Activity Cost Reduction

John Thomas, vice-president of Mallett Company (a producer of a variety of plastic products), has been supervising the implementation of an ABC management system. One of John's objectives is to improve process efficiency by improving the activities that define the processes. To illustrate the potential of the new system to the president, John has decided to focus on two processes: production and customer service.

Within each process, one activity will be selected for improvement: materials usage for production and sustaining engineering for customer service (sustaining engineers are responsible for redesigning products based on customer needs and feedback). Value-added standards are identified for each activity (the level of efficiency so that no waste exists). For materials usage, the value-added standard calls for six kilograms per unit of output (although the plastic products differ in shape and function, their size—as measured by weight—is uniform). The value-added standard is based on the elimination of all waste due to defective moulds. The standard price of materials is $5 per kilogram. For sustaining engineering, the standard is 58 percent of current practical activity capacity. This standard is based on the fact that about 42 percent of the complaints have to do with design features that could have been avoided or anticipated by the company.

Current practical capacity (throughout 2018) is defined by the following requirements: 6,000 engineering hours for each product group that has been on the market or in development for five years or less and 2,400 hours per product group of more than five years. Four product groups have less than five years' experience, and 10 product groups have more. Each of the 24 engineers is paid a salary of $80,000. Each engineer can provide 2,000 hours of service per year. No other significant costs are incurred for the engineering activity.

Actual materials usage for 2018 was 25 percent above the level called for by the value-added standard; engineering usage was 35,400 hours. John and the operational managers have selected some improvement measures that promise to reduce NVA activity usage by 40 percent in 2019. Selected actual results for 2018 are as follows:

Units produced	80,000
Materials used	600,000

The actual prices paid for materials and engineering hours are identical to the standard or budgeted prices.

Required:

1. For 2018, calculate the non-value-added usage and costs for materials usage and sustaining engineering.
2. Using the budgeted improvements and assuming the same level of output for 2019, calculate the expected activity usage levels for 2019. Now, calculate the 2019 usage variances (the difference between the expected and actual values), expressed in both physical and financial measures, for materials and engineering. Comment on the company's ability to achieve its targeted reductions. In particular, discuss what measures the company must take to capture any realized reductions in resource usage.

OBJECTIVE 4

Problem 7-43 Cycle Time, Velocity, Product Costing

Goldman Company has structured its operations on a cell-based system. Each manufacturing cell is dedicated to the production of a single product or major subassembly. One cell, dedicated to the production of telescopes, has four operations: machining, finishing, assembly, and qualifying (testing).

For the coming year, the telescope cell has the following budgeted costs and cell time (both at theoretical capacity):

Budgeted conversion costs	$7,500,000
Budgeted raw materials	$9,000,000
Cell time	12,000 hours
Theoretical output	90,000 telescopes

During the year, the following actual results were obtained:

Actual conversion costs	$7,500,000
Actual raw materials	$7,800,000
Actual cell time	12,000 hours
Actual output	75,000 telescopes

Required:

1. Calculate the velocity (number of telescopes per hour) that the cell can theoretically achieve. Now, calculate the theoretical cycle time (number of hours or minutes per telescope) that it takes to produce one telescope.
2. Calculate the actual velocity and the actual cycle time.
3. Calculate the budgeted conversion costs per minute. Using this rate, calculate the conversion costs per telescope if theoretical output is achieved. Using this measure, calculate the conversion costs per telescope for actual output. Does this product costing approach provide an incentive for the cell manager to reduce cycle time? Explain.

Check figures:
1. Telescopes 7.5 per hour; 8 minutes
3. Potential reduction is $16.67 per telescope

Problem 7-44 Classification of Environmental Costs

OBJECTIVE 4

Consider the following independent environmental activities:

a. A company takes actions to reduce the amount of material in its packages.
b. After its useful life, a soft-drink producer returns the activated carbon used for purifying water for its beverages to the supplier. The supplier reactivates the carbon for a second use in nonfood applications. As a consequence, many tonnes of material are prevented from entering landfills.
c. An evaporator system is installed to treat wastewater and to collect usable solids for other uses.
d. The inks used to print snack packages (for chips) contain heavy metals.
e. Processes are inspected to ensure compliance with environmental standards.
f. Delivery boxes are used five times and then recycled. This prevents 50 million kilograms of cardboard from entering landfills and saves 2 million trees per year.
g. Scrubber equipment is installed to ensure that air emissions are less than the level permitted by law.
h. Local residents are incurring medical costs from illnesses caused by air pollution from automobile exhaust pollution.
i. As part of implementing an environmental perspective for a balanced performance measurement system, environmental performance measures are developed.
j. Because of liquid and solid residues being discharged into a local lake, it is no longer fit for swimming, fishing, and other recreational activities.
k. To reduce energy consumption, magnetic ballasts are replaced with electronic ballasts, and more efficient light bulbs and lighting sensors are installed. As a result, 2.3 million kilowatt-hours of electricity are saved per year.
l. Because of a legal settlement, a chemical company must spend $20,000,000 to clean up contaminated soil.
m. A soft-drink company uses the following practice: In all bottling plants, packages damaged during filling are collected and recycled (glass, plastic, and aluminum).
n. Processes are inspected to ensure that the gaseous emissions produced during operation follow legal and company guidelines.

(Continued)

o. Costs are incurred to operate pollution-control equipment.
p. An internal audit is conducted to verify that environmental policies are being followed.

Required:

Classify these environmental activities as prevention, detection, internal failure, or external failure costs. For external failure costs, classify the costs as societal or private. Also, label those activities that are compatible with sustainable development with "SD."

OBJECTIVE 4

Problem 7-45 Activity-Based Costing

Cairns Company has identified the following overhead activities, costs, and activity drivers for the coming year:

Activity	Expected Cost ($)	Activity Driver	Activity Capacity
Setting up	60,000	Number of setups	300
Inspecting	45,000	Inspection hours	4,500
Grinding	90,000	Machine hours	18,000
Receiving	25,000	Number of parts	50,000

The company produces several different machine subassemblies used by other manufacturers. Information on separate batches for two of these subassemblies follows:

	A	B
Direct materials	$850	$950
Direct labour	$600	$600
Units completed	100	50
Number of setups	1	1
Inspection hours	4	2
Machine hours	20	30
Parts used	20	40

The company's normal activity is 4,000 direct labour hours. Each batch uses 50 hours of direct labour.

Required:

1. Upon investigation, you discover that the receiving department employs one worker, who spends half her time on the receiving activity and half her time on inspecting products. Her salary is $40,000. Receiving also uses a forklift, at a cost of $5,000 per year for depreciation and fuel. The forklift is used only in receiving.
   a. Verify the cost of the receiving activity given above.
   b. What resource driver was used?
2. Determine the unit cost for each product using direct labour hours to apply overhead.
3. Determine the unit cost for each product using the four activity drivers.

OBJECTIVE 4

Problem 7-46 Activity-Based Costing

Mount Royal Company produces two types of jackets for equipment. Information concerning the two products follows:

	Jacket 1	Jacket 2
Units completed	150	75
Direct labour hours	60	90
Grinding hours	30	45
Number of setups	7	7
Inspection hours	6	3
Number of orders	23	40
Prime costs	$225,000	$240,000

Additionally, the following overhead costs are reported for the activities associated with the two products:

Setting up	$120,000
Inspecting	90,000
Grinding	180,000
Receiving	50,000
Total	$440,000

Required:

1. Calculate the total cost per unit of each jacket using a plantwide rate based on direct labour hours to assign overhead.
2. Calculate the total overhead of each jacket using ABC methods appropriate to the information provided.
3. CONCEPTUAL CONNECTION Which approach would you suggest that the company follow? Why?

Check figures:
1. Jacket 1 $2,673.33
2. Jacket 2 $6,263.28

PROFESSIONAL EXAMINATION PROBLEM*

Professional Examination Problem 7-47 Activity-Based Costing—Oineon Corporation

Oineon Corporation manufactures several different types of printed circuit boards; however, two of the boards account for the majority of the company's sales. The first board, a television circuit board, has been a standard in the industry for several years. The market for this type of board is competitive and, therefore, price sensitive. Oineon plans to sell 65,000 of the TV boards in 2019 at a price of $160 per unit. The second high-volume product, a personal computer (PC) circuit board, is a recent addition to Oineon's product line. Because the PC board incorporates the latest technology, it can be sold at a premium price; the 2019 plans include the sale of 40,000 PC boards at $325 per unit.

Oineon's management group is meeting to discuss strategies for 2019 and the current topic of conversation is how to spend the sales and promotion dollars for next year. The sales manager believes the market share for the TV board could be expanded by concentrating Oineon's promotional efforts in this area. In response to this suggestion, the production manager said, "Why don't you go after a bigger market for the PC board? The cost sheets I get show the contribution from the PC board is more than double the contribution from the TV board. I know we get a premium price for the PC board, so selling it should help overall profitability."

Oineon uses a standard cost system and the following data apply to the TV and PC boards.

	TV Board	PC Board
Direct material	$80	$140
Direct labour	1.5 hours	4 hours
Machine time	0.5 hours	1.5 hours

Variable factory overhead is applied on the basis of direct labour hours. For 2019, variable factory overhead is budgeted at $1,120,000 and direct labour hours are estimated at 280,000. The hourly rates for machine time and direct labour are $18 and $22, respectively. Oineon applies a materials handling charge at 10 percent of material cost. This materials handling charge is not included in variable factory overhead. Total 2019 expenditures for material are budgeted at $10,600,000.

Ed Welch, Oineon's controller, believes that before management proceeds with the discussion about allocating sales and promotional dollars to individual products, it might be worthwhile to look at the products on the basis of the activities involved in their production. As Welch explained to the group, "Activity-based costing integrates the cost of all activities, known as cost drivers,

(Continued)

into individual product costs rather than including these costs in overhead pools." Welch has prepared the following schedule to help management understand this concept.

	Budgeted Cost	Cost Driver	Annual Activity for Cost Driver
Material overhead:			
Procurement	$ 400,000	Number of parts	4,000,000 parts
Production scheduling	220,000	Number of boards	110,000 boards
Packaging and shipping	440,000	Number of boards	110,000 boards
	$1,060,000		
Variable overhead:			
Machine setup	$ 446,000	Number of setups	278,750 setups
Hazardous waste disposal	48,000	Kilograms of waste	16,000 kilograms
Quality control	560,000	Number of inspections	160,000 inspections
General supplies	66,000	Number of boards	110,000 boards
	$1,120,000		
Manufacturing:			
Machine insertion	$1,200,000	Number of parts	3,000,000 parts
Manual insertion	4,000,000	Number of parts	1,000,000 parts
Wave soldering	132,000	Number of boards	110,000 boards
	$5,332,000		

Required Per Unit	TV Board	PC Board
Parts	25	55
Machine insertions	24	35
Manual insertions	1	20
Machine setups	2	3
Hazardous waste	0.02 kg	0.35 kg
Inspections	1	2

"Using this information," Welch explained, "we can calculate an activity-based cost for each TV and PC board and then compare it to the standard cost we have been using. The only cost that remains the same for both cost methods is the cost of direct material. The cost drivers will replace the direct labour, machine time, and overhead costs in the standard cost."

Required:

Prepare an ABC report for the TV and PC boards, and comment on the differences with the current standard costs.

CASES

OBJECTIVE 2 3 4

Case 7-48 Activity-Based Costing, Customer Profitability

Lyle MacDonald owns a small local delivery company in Fredericton, New Brunswick. He started the business five years ago in an effort to create a balance in his life after a ten-year career in the finance industry. The company employs seven drivers at an average compensation of $40,000 each, including all benefits. The three-person administrative team of the company—consisting of a receptionist, a dispatcher and an accountant—average $50,000 each in compensation.

Lyle works with one other person as the sales team for the company and they each earn $60,000 in salary each year. The company pays no incentives on individual sales, but Lyle commits that 25 percent of pre-tax income will be set aside as a bonus pool to be shared by all employees. Unfortunately, the company has yet to earn a profit, so no additional compensation has been received by anyone within the company.

During a typical year, the company delivers about 120,000 packages for a variety of customers. Kyle instituted a single pricing policy of $10 per package no matter where it was being delivered or how many individual packages were delivered to a single location. In analyzing the pattern of activity for the company, Lyle determined that about three-quarters of the customers required deliveries of single packages to certain locations, while the remaining customers required deliveries of multiple packages to a single location. On average the latter customers sent three packages to a single location.

Lyle also determined that 60 percent of the deliveries were within two kilometres of the city centre, 20 percent were within a radius of five kilometres of the city centre but outside the two kilometre radius, and the balance were outside a five-kilometre radius. The farther the destination was from the city centre, the more time it took to deliver.

The company rents a facility on the outskirts of town at a cost of $180,000 per year. It spends $160,000 each year on gasoline and $125,000 on repairs to the automobiles. The final operating expense is for new uniforms for the drivers, replacement uniforms, and other miscellaneous driver-related costs, which total about $150,000 each year. The administrative expenses of the company are $75,000 per year and advertising is $100,000.

Lyle believes that the single rate for each package is perhaps the problem in achieving profitability, as delivering multiple packages to one customer at a single location is less expensive to handle than single packages. He also believes that covering different distances at the same cost is a mistake. He has asked you to help him analyze his costs and develop a system that will enable him to generate a pre-tax profit in the region of $250,000 per year so that he can share it with his employees and have a reasonable level of profit for himself.

Required:

Analyze the operations of the company and develop an approach to costing and pricing that will accomplish Lyle's objectives.

Case 7-49 Activity-Based Costing, Distorted Product Costs

OBJECTIVE  

Sharp Paper Inc. has three paper mills, one of which is located in Timmins, Ontario. The mill produces 300 different types of coated and uncoated specialty printing papers. This large variety of products was the result of a full-line marketing strategy adopted by Sharp's management. Management was convinced that the value of variety more than offset the extra costs of the increased complexity.

During 2015, the Timmins mill produced 120,000 tonnes of coated paper and 80,000 tonnes of uncoated paper. Of the 200,000 tonnes produced, 180,000 were sold. Sixty products account for 80 percent of the tonnes sold. Thus, 240 products are classified as low-volume products.

Lightweight lime hopsack in cartons (LLHC) is one of the low-volume products. LLHC is produced in rolls, converted into sheets of paper, and then sold in cartons. In 2018, the cost to produce and sell one tonne of LLHC was as follows:

Direct materials:		
Furnish (3 different pulps)	2,225 kilograms	$ 450
Additives (11 different items)	200 kilograms	500
Tub size	75 kilograms	10
Recycled scrap paper	(296 kilograms)	(20)
Total direct materials		940
Direct labour		450
Overhead:		
Paper machine ($100 per tonne × 1,250 kilograms)		125
Finishing machine ($120 per tonne × 1,250 kilograms)		150
Total overhead		275
Shipping and warehousing		30
Total manufacturing and selling cost		$1,695

Overhead is applied by using a two-stage process. First, overhead is allocated to the paper and finishing machines by using the direct method of allocation with carefully selected cost drivers. Second, the overhead assigned to each machine is divided by the budgeted tonnes of output. These rates are then multiplied by the number of kilograms required to produce one good tonne.

(Continued)

In 2018, LLHC sold for $2,400 per tonne, making it one of the most profitable products. A similar examination of some of the other low-volume products revealed that they also had very respectable profit margins. Unfortunately, the performance of the high-volume products was less impressive, with many showing losses or very low profit margins. This situation led Ryan Chesser to call a meeting with his marketing vice-president, Jennifer Woodruff, and his controller, Kaylin Penn.

Ryan: The above-average profitability of our low-volume specialty products and the poor profit performance of our high-volume products make me believe that we should switch our marketing emphasis to the low-volume line. Perhaps we should drop some of our high-volume products, particularly those showing a loss.

Jennifer: I'm not convinced that the solution you are proposing is the right one. I know our high-volume products are of high quality, and I am convinced that we are as efficient in our production as other firms. I think that somehow our costs are not being assigned correctly. For example, the shipping and warehousing costs are assigned by dividing these costs by the total tonnes of paper sold. Yet . . .

Kaylin: Jennifer, I hate to disagree, but the $30-per-tonne charge for shipping and warehousing seems reasonable. I know that our method to assign these costs is identical to a number of other paper companies.

Jennifer: Well, that may be true, but do these other companies have the variety of products that we have? Our low-volume products require special handling and processing, but when we assign shipping and warehousing costs, we average these special costs across our entire product line. Every tonne produced in our mill passes through our mill shipping department and is sent either directly to the customer or to our distribution centre and then eventually to customers. My records indicate quite clearly that virtually all of the high-volume products are sent directly to customers, whereas most of the low-volume products are sent to the distribution centre. Now, all of the products passing through the mill shipping department should receive a share of the $2,300,000 annual shipping costs. I am not convinced, however, that all products should receive a share of the receiving and shipping costs of the distribution centre as currently practised.

Ryan: Kaylin, is this true? Does our system allocate our shipping and warehousing costs in this way?

Kaylin: Yes, I'm afraid it does. Jennifer may have a point. Perhaps we need to re-evaluate our method to assign these costs to the product lines.

Ryan: Jennifer, do you have any suggestions concerning how the shipping and warehousing costs should be assigned?

Jennifer: It seems reasonable to make a distinction between products that spend time in the distribution centre and those that do not. We should also distinguish between the receiving and shipping activities at the distribution centre. All incoming shipments are packed on pallets and weigh one tonne each (there are 14 cartons of paper per pallet). In 2018, the receiving department processed 56,000 tonnes of paper. Receiving employs 15 people at an annual cost of $600,000. Other receiving costs totalled about $500,000. I would recommend that these costs be assigned by using tonnes processed.

Shipping, however, is different. There are two activities associated with shipping: picking the order from inventory and loading the paper. We employ 30 people for picking and 10 for loading, at an annual cost of $1,200,000. Other shipping costs totalled $1,100,000. Picking and loading are more concerned with the number of shipping items than with tonnage. That is, a shipping item may consist of two or three cartons instead of pallets. Accordingly, the shipping costs of the distribution centre should be assigned by using the number of items shipped. In 2018, for example, we handled 190,000 shipping items.

Ryan: These suggestions have merit. Kaylin, I would like to see what effect Jennifer's suggestions have on the per-unit assignment of shipping and warehousing for LLHC. If the effect is significant, then we will expand the analysis to include all products.

Kaylin: I'm willing to compute the effect, but I'd like to suggest one additional feature. Currently, we have a policy to carry about 25 tonnes of LLHC in inventory. Our current costing system totally ignores the cost of carrying this inventory. Since it costs us $1,665 to produce each tonne of this product, we are tying up a lot of money in inventory—money that could be invested in other productive opportunities. In fact, the return lost is about 16 percent per year. This cost should also be assigned to the units sold.

Ryan: Kaylin, this also sounds good to me. Go ahead and include the carrying cost in your computation.

To help in the analysis, Kaylin gathered the following data for LLHC for 2018:

Tonnes sold	10
Average cartons per shipment	2
Average shipments per tonne	7

Required:

1. Identify the flaws associated with the current method of assigning shipping and warehousing costs to Sharp's products.
2. Calculate the shipping and warehousing cost per tonne of LLHC sold by using the new method suggested by Jennifer and Kaylin.
3. Using the new costs computed in Requirement 2, calculate the profit per tonne of LLHC. Compare this with the profit per tonne computed by using the old method. Do you think that this same effect would be realized for other low-volume products? Explain.
4. CONCEPTUAL CONNECTION Comment on Ryan's proposal to drop some high-volume products and place more emphasis on low-volume products. Discuss the role of the accounting system in supporting this type of decision making.
5. After receiving the analysis of LLHC, Ryan decided to expand the analysis to all products. He also had Kaylin re-evaluate the way in which mill overhead was assigned to products. After the restructuring was completed, Ryan took the following actions: (a) the prices of most low-volume products were increased, (b) the prices of several high-volume products were decreased, and (c) some low-volume products were dropped. Explain why his strategy changed so dramatically.

Case 7-50 Activity-Based Product Costing and Ethical Behaviour

OBJECTIVE 2 3 4

Consider the following conversation between Leonard Bryner, president and manager of a firm engaged in job manufacturing, and Chuck Davis, chartered professional accountant, the firm's controller.

Leonard: Chuck, as you know, our firm has been losing market share over the past three years. We have been losing more and more bids, and I don't understand why. At first, I thought that other firms were undercutting simply to gain business, but after examining some of the public financial reports, I believe that they are making a reasonable rate of return. I am beginning to believe that our costs and costing methods are at fault.

Chuck: I can't agree with that. We have good control over our costs. Like most firms in our industry, we use a normal job-costing system. I really don't see any significant waste in the plant.

Leonard: After talking with some other managers at a recent industrial convention, I'm not so sure that waste by itself is the issue. They talked about activity-based management, activity-based costing, and continuous improvement. They mentioned the use of

(Continued)

something called "activity drivers" to assign overhead. They claimed that these new procedures can help to produce more efficiency in manufacturing, better control of overhead, and more accurate product costing. A big deal was made of eliminating activities that added no value. Maybe our bids are too high because these other firms have found ways to decrease their overhead costs and to increase the accuracy of their product costing.

Chuck: I doubt it. For one thing, I don't see how we can increase product costing accuracy. So many of our costs are indirect costs. Furthermore, everyone uses some measure of production activity to assign overhead costs. I imagine that what they are calling "activity drivers" is just some new buzzword for measures of production volume. Fads in costing come and go. I wouldn't worry about it. I'll bet that our problems with decreasing sales are temporary. You might recall that we experienced a similar problem about 12 years ago—it was two years before it straightened out.

Required:

1. Do you agree or disagree with Chuck and the advice that he gave Leonard? Explain.
2. Was there anything wrong or unethical in the behaviour that Chuck displayed? Explain your reasoning.
3. Do you think that Chuck was well informed—that he was aware of the accounting implications of ABC and that he knew what was meant by "activity drivers"? Should he have been well informed? Review (in Chapter 1) the standards of ethical conduct for professional accountants. Do any of these standards apply in Chuck's case?

OBJECTIVE 2 3 4

Case 7-51 Activity-Based Product Costing and Ethical Behaviour

Ethical behaviour is essential if a management team is to develop a trusting relationship that can be counted on when tough decisions have to be made. The use of ABC does not seem to create many areas where unethical behaviour can make a difference. However, like any other management activity, it is prone to misuse and favourable treatment for one group over another.

Required:

Comment on how ABC can distort the numbers within an organization and how some managers may be disadvantaged as a result.

8

Absorption and Variable Costing, and Inventory Management

After studying Chapter 8, you should be able to:

1. Explain the difference between absorption and variable costing.
2. Prepare segmented income statements.
3. (*Appendix 8A*) Discuss inventory management under the economic order quantity and just-in-time (JIT) models.

Courtesy of Lisa Peterson

EXPERIENCE MANAGERIAL DECISIONS

with the Ontario Securities Commission

It's déjà vu. At least, that's what the current debate swirling around non-GAAP measures and the use of adjusted numbers feels like in light of increased regulatory and media attention. Regulatory bodies around the world have been issuing new or updated guidance on what to do in order to ensure investors have the information they need and are not misled by non-GAAP measures. In Canada, for example, the Canadian Securities Administrators released Staff Notice 52-306 [Revised] – Non-GAAP Financial Measures in January 2016.

"Non-GAAP measures may be useful in highlighting particular aspects of financial performance or condition; however, poor use of them can result in a lack of transparency, comparability and consistency," says Gord Beal, vice-president of research, guidance and support at CPA Canada.

The Office of the Chief Accountant of the Ontario Securities Commission (OSC) published a staff notice in November 2016 that examines several financial reporting issues, including companies' use of non-standard accounting metrics, and indicates that the use of non-GAAP measures remains an "ongoing area of focus" for the regulator. Specifically, the OSC remains concerned about companies using non-GAAP numbers and giving non-GAAP measures greater prominence than more conventional accounting metrics, among other things.

All this regulatory activity is not new. Concern over non-GAAP measures and how they might mislead investors emerged as a hot topic in the 1990s. There is now a significant body of knowledge offering a foundation for understanding the broad spectrum of views surrounding the use of non-GAAP measures.

VARIABLE AND ABSORPTION INCOME STATEMENTS

OBJECTIVE 

Explain the difference between absorption and variable costing.

Many companies are composed of separate business units called profit centres. It is important for these companies to determine the performance of the individual profit centres, as well as the overall performance of the business. The overall income statement is useful for looking at overall company performance. However, this income statement is of little use for determining the viability of the individual business units or segments. Instead, it is important to develop a segmented income statement that shows performance of each profit centre. There are two methods of computing income: one is based on variable costing, and the other is based on full or absorption costing. These are costing methods because they refer to the way in which product costs are determined. Recall that product costs are inventoried; they include direct materials, direct labour, and factory overhead. Period costs, such as selling and administrative expense, are expensed in the period incurred. The difference between variable and absorption costing hinges on the treatment of one particular cost: fixed factory overhead.

Absorption costing assigns all manufacturing costs to the product. Direct materials, direct labour, variable overhead, and fixed overhead define the cost of a product. Thus, under absorption costing, fixed overhead is viewed as a product cost. Under this method, fixed overhead is assigned to the product through the use of a predetermined fixed overhead rate and is not expensed until the product is sold. In other words, fixed overhead is an inventoriable cost.

Variable costing assigns only variable manufacturing costs to the product; these costs include direct materials, direct labour, and variable overhead. Fixed overhead is treated as a period cost, is expensed in the period incurred, and is excluded from product cost. Variable costing stresses the difference between fixed and variable manufacturing costs. The rationale for this is that fixed overhead is a cost of capacity, or staying in business. Once the period is over, any benefits provided by capacity have expired and should not be inventoried. Under variable costing, fixed overhead of a period is seen as expiring in that period and is charged in total against the revenues of the period.

Generally accepted accounting principles (GAAP) require absorption costing for external reporting. Most regulatory bodies do not accept variable costing as a product-costing method for external reporting. The Canada Revenue Agency (CRA) does have a provision for the use of variable costing to value inventory only if this method provides a "truer picture" of the taxpayer's income. In most instances, the truer picture provision would not be met. Yet variable costing can supply vital cost information for decision making and control, information that is not supplied by absorption costing. For internal application, variable costing is an important managerial tool. When doing the CVP analysis in Chapter 4, we used the direct cost approach in which we focused on the difference between variable and fixed costs. Exhibit 8.1 shows how different costs are classified under the two approaches.

EXHIBIT 8.1

Classification of Costs under Absorption and Variable Costing as Product or Period Costs

	Absorption Costing	Variable Costing
Product costs	Direct materials Direct labour Variable overhead Fixed overhead	Direct materials Direct labour Variable overhead
Period costs	Selling expenses Administrative expenses	Fixed overhead Selling expenses Administrative expenses

Inventory Valuation

Inventory is valued at cost (product or manufacturing cost) and will *never* include the period costs of selling or administration. Under absorption costing, that product cost includes direct materials, direct labour, variable manufacturing overhead, and fixed manufacturing overhead. Cornerstone 8.1 shows how to compute inventory cost under absorption costing.

Computing Inventory Cost under Absorption Costing

CORNERSTONE 8.1

Information:

During the most recent year, Fairchild Company had the following data associated with the product it makes:

Units in beginning inventory	—
Units produced	10,000
Units sold ($300 per unit)	8,000
Variable costs per unit:	
Direct materials	$50
Direct labour	$100
Variable overhead	$50
Fixed costs:	
Fixed manufacturing overhead per unit produced	$25
Fixed selling and administrative	$100,000

Required:

1. How many units are in ending inventory?
2. Using absorption costing, calculate the per-unit product cost.
3. What is the value of ending inventory?

Solution:

1. Units in ending inventory = Units in beginning inventory + Units produced − Units sold
   = 0 + 10,000 − 8,000
   = 2,000

2. Absorption costing unit cost:

Direct materials	$ 50
Direct labour	100
Variable overhead	50
Fixed overhead	25
Unit product cost	$225

3. Value of ending inventory = Units in ending inventory × Absorption unit product cost
   = 2,000 × $225
   = $450,000

Why:

Because pricing the inventory is necessary to accurately state the total assets of a firm, the gross margin, and the net profit margin. Absorption costing is required for inventory valuation under GAAP for external reporting.

Notice that the inventory cost computed under absorption costing is the traditional product cost used for external financial statements and complies with GAAP. Each unit includes all variable manufacturing costs as well as a portion of fixed factory overhead.

Under variable costing, the product cost includes only direct materials, direct labour, and variable manufacturing overhead. Cornerstone 8.2 shows how to calculate inventory cost under variable costing.

CORNERSTONE 8.2 Computing Inventory Cost under Variable Costing

Information:

During the most recent year, Fairchild Company had the following data associated with the product it makes:

Units in beginning inventory	—
Units produced	10,000
Units sold ($300 per unit)	8,000
Variable costs per unit:	
Direct materials	$50
Direct labour	$100
Variable overhead	$50
Fixed costs:	
Fixed manufacturing overhead per unit produced	$25
Fixed selling and administrative	$100,000

Required:

1. How many units are in ending inventory?
2. Using variable costing, calculate the per-unit product cost.
3. What is the value of ending inventory?

Solution:

1. Units in ending inventory = Units in beginning inventory + Units produced − Units sold
   = 0 + 10,000 − 8,000
   = 2,000

2. Variable costing unit cost:

Direct materials	$ 50
Direct labour	100
Variable overhead	50
Unit product cost	$200

3. Value of ending inventory = Units in ending inventory × Variable unit product cost
   = 2,000 × $200
   = $400,000

Why:

Because valuing inventory under variable costing allows us to accurately calculate the variable cost of goods sold and the contribution margin for a firm by treating all fixed costs as period costs. This information can help managers to make more meaningful decisions.

Looking carefully at Cornerstones 8.1 and 8.2, we can see that the only difference between the two approaches is the treatment of fixed factory overhead. Thus, the unit product cost under absorption costing is always greater than the unit product cost under variable costing. Exhibit 8.2 shows this difference pictorially for a simplified example.

EXHIBIT 8.2

Product Cost under Absorption and Variable Costing

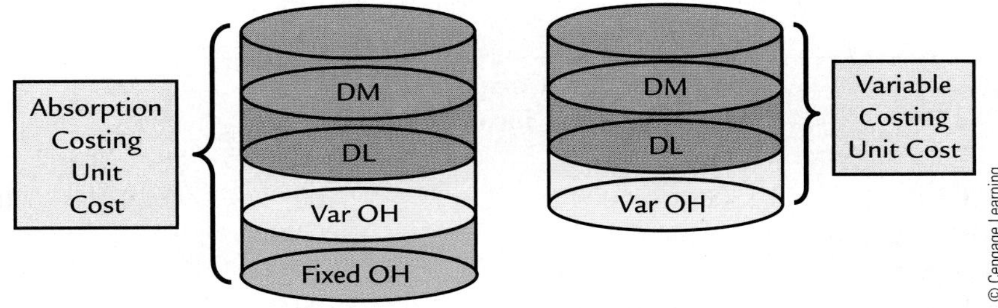

Income Statements Using Variable and Absorption Costing

Because unit product costs are the basis for determining cost of goods sold, the variable and absorption costing methods can lead to different operating income figures. The difference arises because the amount of fixed overhead recognized as an expense under the two methods may differ. Under absorption costing, fixed manufacturing overhead is expensed through cost of goods sold when the product, for which fixed manufacturing cost is a component of cost, is sold. Under variable costing, fixed manufacturing overhead is expensed in the period in which it is incurred, irrespective of the number of units sold. Cornerstone 8.3 shows how to develop cost of goods sold and income statements under absorption costing.

Preparing an Absorption-Costing Income Statement

CORNERSTONE 8.3

Information:

During the two most recent years, Fairchild Company had the following data:

	Year 1	Year 2
Units in beginning inventory	—	2,000
Units produced	10,000	10,000
Units sold ($300 per unit)	8,000	12,000
Variable costs per unit:		
Direct materials	$50	$50
Direct labour	$100	$100
Variable overhead	$50	$50
Fixed costs:		
Fixed manufacturing overhead per unit produced	$25	$25
Fixed selling and administrative	$100,000	$100,000

Required:

1. Calculate the cost of goods sold under absorption costing.
2. Prepare an income statement using absorption costing.

(Continued)

CORNERSTONE

8.3

(Continued)

Solution:

1. Cost of goods sold = Absorption unit product cost × Units sold

Year 1	Year 2
= $225 × 8,000	= $225 × 12,000
= $1,800,000	= $2,700,000

2.

Fairchild Company
Absorption-Costing Income Statement

	Year 1	Year 2
Sales ($300 × 8,000 and $300 × 12,000)	$2,400,000	$3,600,000
Less: Cost of goods sold	1,800,000	2,700,000
Gross margin	600,000	900,000
Less: Selling and administrative expenses	100,000	100,000
Operating income	$ 500,000	$ 800,000

Why:

Because absorption costing is required by GAAP for external reporting and most regulatory agencies will not accept any other approach.

As we see in Cornerstone 8.3, the cost of goods sold in Year 1 includes some, but not all, fixed factory overhead. Total fixed factory overhead is $250,000 (= $25 × 10,000 units produced). However, only $200,000 (= $25 × 8,000 units sold) of fixed overhead was expensed in cost of goods sold. The other $50,000 of fixed overhead is included in the cost of ending inventory.

Cornerstone 8.4 shows how to prepare a variable-costing income statement.

CORNERSTONE 8.4 Preparing a Variable-Costing Income Statement

Information:

During the two most recent years, Fairchild Company had the following data:

	Year 1	Year 2
Units in beginning inventory	—	2,000
Units produced	10,000	10,000
Units sold ($300 per unit)	8,000	12,000
Variable costs per unit:		
Direct materials	$50	$50
Direct labour	$100	$100
Variable overhead	$50	$50
Fixed costs:		
Fixed manufacturing overhead per unit produced	$25	$25
Fixed selling and administrative	$100,000	$100,000

(Continued)

CORNERSTONE
8.4
(Continued)

Required:

1. Calculate the cost of goods sold under variable costing.
2. Prepare an income statement using variable costing.

Solution:

1. Cost of goods sold = Variable unit product cost × Units sold

Year 1	Year 2
= $200 × 8,000	= $200 × 12,000
= $1,600,000	= $2,400,000

2.

Fairchild Company
Variable-Costing Income Statement

	Year 1	Year 2
Sales ($300 × 8,000 and $300 × 12,000)	$2,400,000	$3,600,000
Less variable expenses:		
Variable cost of goods sold	1,600,000	2,400,000
Contribution margin	800,000	1,200,000
Less fixed expenses:		
Fixed overhead ($250,000 + $100,000)	350,000	350,000
Operating income	$ 450,000	$ 850,000

Why:

Because a variable-costing income statement facilitates a better analysis of costs and their impact on profitability. From a strategic perspective, treating all fixed costs as period costs may provide better information.

Let's compare Cornerstones 8.3 and 8.4. Operating income under absorption costing for Year 1 is $500,000, whereas operating income under variable costing is only $450,000. Remember that $50,000 of current period product cost in fixed factory overhead went into inventory under absorption costing. However, all of the fixed factory overhead is included in the expenses under variable costing. Notice that selling and administrative expenses are not included in product cost under either method. They are always expensed on the income statement and will never appear on the balance sheet.

analytical Q&A

Suppose that unit production costs include direct materials of $6, direct labour of $7, and variable overhead of $2. Total fixed manufacturing overhead is $75,000 and typically 25,000 units are produced. What is the cost of one unit under variable costing? What is the cost of one unit under absorption costing?

Answers on pages 734 to 738.

Production, Sales, and Income Relationships

The relationship between variable-costing operating income and absorption-costing operating income changes as the relationship between production and sales changes. In the Fairchild example, more units were produced than sold in Year 1, and absorption-costing operating income was higher than operating income under variable costing. If more units are sold than the amount produced, variable-costing operating income would be greater than absorption-costing operating income. Selling more than was produced means that all units produced are being sold and, in addition, some beginning inventory units are sold. Under absorption costing, units coming out of inventory have fixed overhead from a prior period attached to them. In addition, units produced and sold in the current period have all of the current period's fixed overhead attached.

Thus, the amount of fixed overhead expensed by absorption costing is greater than the current period's fixed overhead by the amount of fixed overhead flowing out of beginning inventory. Accordingly, variable-costing income is greater than absorption-costing income by the amount of fixed overhead flowing out of beginning inventory under absorption costing.

If production and sales are equal, no difference exists between the two reported incomes. Since the units produced are all sold, absorption costing, like variable costing, will recognize the total fixed overhead of the period as an expense. No fixed overhead flows into or out of inventory.

The relationships between production, sales, and the two reported incomes are summarized in Exhibit 8.3. Note that if production is greater than sales, then inventory increases. If production is less than sales, then inventory decreases. If production is equal to sales, then the number of units in beginning inventory is equal to the number of units in ending inventory.

EXHIBIT 8.3

Production, Sales, and Income Relationships

If	Then
1. Production > Sales	Absorption net income > Variable net income
2. Production < Sales	Absorption net income < Variable net income
3. Production = Sales	Absorption net income = Variable net income

Reasons for Using Variable Costing One reason for using variable costing for internal purposes is that absorption-costing operating income is affected by production volume, while variable-costing operating income is not.

Suppose the evaluation of a manager's performance is based heavily on operating income. If the company uses the absorption-costing approach, a manager might be tempted to produce unneeded units just to increase reported operating income, as the increase in inventory would absorb some of the overhead costs (i.e., those costs would not be expensed). No such temptation exists with variable costing.

In Exhibit 8.4, we look at the Fairfield Company operating income statements for two years under the two types of costing—variable and absorption—and we see the difference in operating profits. In the first year, the company produces 10,000 units and sells 8,000 units, while in the second year, the company produces the same 10,000 units but sells 12,000 units. The difference in operating income shows the impact of producing for inventory. The $50,000 difference in operating profit is due to fixed manufacturing overhead being held in inventory under absorption costing but not in variable costing. Note that the total profit over the two years is the same, because the total number of products sold equals the total production over the two years. The difference is in the timing of the reported profit.

Comparing Variable and Absorption Costing

The contribution approach (variable or direct costing) is a method of internal reporting that emphasizes the distinction between variable and fixed costs for decision-making purposes. The income statement provides a contribution margin, which is computed after deducting all variable costs, including variable selling and administrative costs. This approach makes it easier to see the impact of changes in sales demand on operating income. It also is consistent with the cost–volume–profit analysis approach, which was introduced in Chapter 4.

The absorption approach (absorption or full costing) is the traditional approach used for external reporting. It considers all factory overhead, fixed and variable, to be product

EXHIBIT 8.4

Comparison of Operating Income under Both Income Statement Methods

Fairchild Company
Variable Costing Income Statements

	Year 1	Year 2
Sales Revenue	$2,400,000	$3,600,000
Less: Cost of Goods Sold	1,600,000	2,400,000
Contribution Margin	800,000	1,200,000
Less: Fixed Expenses		
Fixed Manufacturing Overhead	250,000	250,000
Fixed Selling and Administrative	100,000	100,000
Operating Income	$ 450,000	$ 850,000

Fairchild Company
Absorption Costing Income Statements

	Year 1	Year 2
Sales Revenue	$2,400,000	$3,600,000
Less: Cost of Goods Sold	1,800,000	2,700,000
Gross Margin	600,000	900,000
Less: Fixed Expenses		
Fixed Manufacturing Overhead	—	—
Fixed Selling and Administrative	100,000	100,000
Operating Income	$ 500,000	$ 800,000

costs and, therefore, inventoriable costs that will be expensed only when the products are sold. This is the approach taken by most companies.

For decision purposes, the major difference between the contribution approach and the absorption approach is that the former emphasizes the distinction between variable and fixed costs. Thus, costs are classified primarily by their cost behaviour patterns, fixed or variable, not by business functions.

In addition, variable costing operating income is affected only by the level of sales. Variable costs of goods sold and variable selling and administrative expense are a function of sales. Absorption costing operating income, by contrast, is a function of both sales and production (which includes production for inventory).

Gross Margin/Contribution Margin The growing use of the contribution approach in performance measurement and cost analysis has led to the increasing use of variable costing for internal reporting purposes. Keep in mind that advocates of the contribution approach do not maintain that fixed costs are unimportant or irrelevant; they simply stress that the distinctions between the behaviours of variable and fixed costs are crucial for certain decisions.

Variable costing for internal reporting requires that the company maintain two systems, since external reporting must be based on an absorption-costing approach. The difference between the gross margin (from the absorption approach) and the contribution margin (from the contribution approach) can be striking in manufacturing companies.

Despite the important differences between the two approaches, firms increasingly are less concerned with the choice between variable and absorption costing. The adoption of just-in-time production methods has sharply reduced inventory levels and, as a result, the difference in operating income levels under the two approaches is minimized as inventory levels shrink.

Reconciliation of Variable Costing and Absorption Costing Remember that the relationship between sales and production is what determines the difference between variable-costing and absorption-costing operating income. Whenever sales exceed production—that is, when inventory decreases—variable-costing income is greater than absorption-costing income. Whenever production exceeds sales—that is, when inventory increases—variable-costing income is less than absorption-costing income. See Exhibit 8.5. The difference in income also equals the difference in the total amount of fixed manufacturing overhead charged as an expense during a given year. The difference is explained by multiplying the fixed-overhead product-costing rate by the change in the total units in the beginning and ending inventories.

EXHIBIT 8.5

Variable and Absorption Costing Models

Variable Costing Model INCOME STATEMENT	
Revenue	XXXXXX
Less: Product costs (Variable cost of goods sold)	
Direct materials (DM)	XXXXXX
Direct labour (DL)	XXXXXX
Variable manufacturing overhead (VOH)	XXXXXX
Product contribution margin	XXXXXX
Less: Variable period costs	
Variable selling costs	XXXXXX
Variable administrative costs	XXXXXX
Total contribution margin	XXXXXX
Less: Fixed costs	
Fixed manufacturing overhead	XXXXXX
Fixed selling costs	XXXXXX
Fixed administrative costs	XXXXXX
Operating earnings before tax (EBT)	XXXXXX

Absorption Costing Model INCOME STATEMENT	
Revenue	XXXXXX
Less: Product costs (Absorption cost of goods sold)	
Direct materials (DM)	XXXXXX
Direct labour (DL)	XXXXXX
Variable manufacturing overhead (VOH)	XXXXXX
Fixed manufacturing overhead	XXXXXX
Gross margin	XXXXXX
Less: Period costs	
Selling costs	XXXXXX
Administrative costs	XXXXXX
Operating earnings before tax (EBT)	XXXXXX

Evaluating Profit-Centre Managers

The evaluation of managers, and their compensation, is often tied to the profitability of the units that they control. How income changes from one period to the next and how actual income compares with planned income are frequently used as signals of managerial ability. To be meaningful signals, however, income should reflect managerial effort.

For example, if a manager has worked hard and increased sales while holding costs in check, income should increase over the prior period, signalling success. In general terms, if income performance is expected to reflect managerial performance, then managers have the right to expect the following:

1. As sales revenue increases from one period to the next, all other things being equal, income should increase.
2. As sales revenue decreases from one period to the next, all other things being equal, income should decrease.
3. As sales revenue remains unchanged from one period to the next, all other things being equal, income should remain unchanged.

Variable costing ensures that the above relationships hold; however, absorption costing may not.

SEGMENTED INCOME STATEMENTS USING VARIABLE COSTING

OBJECTIVE 

Prepare segmented income statements.

A **segment** is a subunit of a company of sufficient importance to warrant the production of performance reports. Segments can be divisions, departments, product lines, customer classes, and so on. Variable costing is useful in preparing segmented income statements because it gives useful information on variable and fixed expenses.

In segmented income statements, fixed expenses are divided into two categories: direct fixed expenses and common fixed expenses. This additional subdivision highlights controllable versus noncontrollable costs and enhances the manager's ability to evaluate each segment's contribution to overall firm performance.

Direct fixed expenses are fixed expenses that are directly traceable to a segment. These are sometimes referred to as avoidable fixed expenses or traceable fixed expenses because they vanish if the segment is eliminated. For example, if the segments were sales regions, a direct fixed expense for each region would be the rent for the sales office, salary of the sales manager of each region, and so on. If one region were to be eliminated, then those fixed expenses would disappear.

Common fixed expenses are jointly caused by two or more segments. These expenses persist even if one of the segments to which they are common is eliminated. For example, depreciation on the corporate headquarters building, the salary of the CEO, and the cost of printing and distributing the annual report to shareholders are common fixed expenses for lululemon athletica inc. If lululemon were to open a new store or close an existing one, those common expenses would not be affected and would be reallocated to the remaining operations.

Often companies will analyze the segment profitability after deducting common fixed expenses and determine that, if segment contribution margin is negative, the segment should be closed down. Unfortunately, that may be the wrong decision, as the common fixed costs allocated to the segment that will be closed down must then be reallocated to the other parts of the business. The decision should be based on segment margin, before allocation of common fixed expenses, in order to maximize profits.

concept Q&A

Consider a department store. Suppose that the store decides to drop a department, such as the furniture department. What are the direct fixed costs involved? What are the common fixed costs that would not be reduced if the department is dropped?

Answers on pages 734 to 738.

Cornerstone 8.5 shows how to prepare a segmented income statement where the segments are product lines. In the example, Audiomatronics produces both MP3 players and game consoles.

Notice that Cornerstone 8.5 shows that both MP3 players and game consoles have large positive contribution margins ($181,000 for MP3 players and $77,000 for game consoles). Both products are providing revenue above variable costs that can be used to help cover the firm's fixed costs. However, some of the firm's fixed costs are caused by the

CORNERSTONE 8.5

Preparing a Segmented Income Statement

Audiomatronics Inc. produces MP3 players and game consoles in a single factory. The following information was provided for the coming year.

	MP3 Players	Game Consoles
Sales	$380,000	$220,000
Variable cost of goods sold	180,000	132,000
Direct fixed overhead	20,000	50,000

A sales commission of 5 percent of sales is paid for each of the two product lines. Direct fixed selling and administrative expense was estimated to be $5,000 for the MP3 line and $30,000 for the game consoles line.

Common fixed overhead for the factory was estimated to be $70,000; common selling and administrative expense was estimated to be $20,000.

Required:

Prepare a segmented income statement for Audiomatronics Inc. for the coming year, using variable costing, and comment on whether both products are contributing to overall company profit.

Solution:

Audiomatronics Inc.
Segmented Income Statement
For the Coming Year

	MP3 Players	Game Consoles	Total
Sales	$ 380,000	$ 220,000	$ 600,000
Variable cost of goods sold	(180,000)	(132,000)	(312,000)
Variable selling expense*	(19,000)	(11,000)	(30,000)
Contribution margin	181,000	77,000	258,000
Less direct fixed expenses:			
Direct fixed overhead	(20,000)	(50,000)	(70,000)
Direct selling and administrative	(5,000)	(30,000)	(35,000)
Segment margin	$ 156,000	$ (3,000)	153,000
Less common fixed expenses:			
Common fixed overhead			(70,000)
Common selling and administrative			(20,000)
Operating income			$ 63,000

* Variable selling expense for MP3 players = 0.05 × Sales = 0.05 × $380,000 = $19,000
Variable selling expense for game consoles = 0.05 × Sales = 0.05 × $220,000 = $11,000

The segmented income statement reveals that total company profit would be higher without the game consoles product.

Why:

Because it is often necessary to calculate net income per division or department and to evaluate segment performance.

segments themselves. Thus, the real measure of the profit contribution of each segment is what is left over after these direct fixed costs are covered.

The profit contribution each segment makes toward covering a firm's common fixed costs is called the **segment margin.** A segment should at least be able to cover both its own variable costs and direct fixed costs. A negative segment margin drags down the firm's total profit, making it time to consider dropping the product. Ignoring any effect a segment may have on the sales of other segments, the segment margin measures the change in a firm's profits that would occur if the segment were eliminated.

Segmented income statements are very useful in management decision making and strategic planning. The reason is that direct fixed costs are separated from common fixed costs. If common fixed costs are allocated to the segments, they can give a distorted picture of segment profitability. (See Exhibit 8.6.)

EXHIBIT 8.6

Comparison of Segmented Income Statement with and without Allocated Common Fixed Expense

Folsom Company provided the following information:

	Pens	Pencils	Markers
Units produced and sold	10,000	30,000	26,000
Price	$30	$25	$14
Variable cost per unit	$20	$18	$12
Direct fixed expense	$35,000	$38,000	$40,000

Common fixed expense was $100,000 and is allocated to each product line on the basis of relative sales for income statement A. Common fixed expense is not allocated to the segments for income statement B.

A. Segmented Income Statement with Allocation of Common Fixed Expense:

	Pens	Pencils	Markers	Total
Sales	$300,000	$750,000	$364,000	$1,414,000
Less: Variable cost	200,000	540,000	312,000	1,052,000
Contribution margin	100,000	210,000	52,000	362,000
Less: Direct fixed cost	35,000	38,000	40,000	113,000
Segment margin	65,000	172,000	12,000	249,000
Less: Allocated common cost*	21,220	53,040	25,740	100,000
Operating income	$ 43,780	$118,960	$ (13,740)	$ 149,000

* Rounded

B. Segmented Income Statement without Allocation of Common Fixed Expense:

	Pens	Pencils	Markers	Total
Sales	$300,000	$750,000	$364,000	$1,414,000
Less: Variable cost	200,000	540,000	312,000	1,052,000
Contribution margin	100,000	210,000	52,000	362,000
Less: Direct fixed cost	35,000	38,000	40,000	113,000
Segment margin	$ 65,000	$172,000	$ 12,000	249,000
Less: Common cost				100,000
Operating income				$ 149,000

YOU DECIDE Using Segmented Income Statements to Make Decisions

You are the vice-president of finance for Folsom Company, which sells three products: pens, pencils, and markers. You have just received the income statement shown in Panel A of Exhibit 8.6. Clearly, markers are unprofitable. In fact, the company is losing \$13,740 a year on markers.

Should you drop markers? Will income go up if you do?

Take a closer look at the income statement. Notice that both the direct fixed costs and the allocated common fixed costs are subtracted from each segment's contribution margin. This is misleading; it seems that dropping any segment would result in losing the operating income associated with the segment. However, if one segment is dropped, the allocated common fixed costs will remain.

A more useful income statement is presented in Panel B of Exhibit 8.6. Here, the segment margin for all three products is positive, as is overall income. While markers are not as profitable as pens and pencils, they are profitable. Dropping markers will result in a decrease in operating income of \$12,000, the amount of the segment margin.

Separating the direct fixed costs from the common fixed costs, and focusing on the segment margin, will give a truer picture of a segment's profitability.

APPENDIX 8A: INVENTORY MANAGEMENT

OBJECTIVE 

Discuss inventory management under the economic order quantity and just-in-time (JIT) models.

Inventory Management

Maintaining inventory is a necessary cost of doing business. Managing and minimizing the costs associated with inventory could have a significant impact on profitability. Apart from the product cost of inventory, there are other types of costs that relate to inventories of raw materials, work in process, and finished goods. For example, inventory must be bought, received, stored, and moved.

Inventory-Related Costs When the demand for a product or material is known with near certainty for a given period of time (usually a year), two major costs are associated with inventory. If the inventory is a material or good purchased from an outside source, then these inventory-related costs are known as ordering costs and carrying costs. (If the material or good is produced internally, then the costs are called setup costs and carrying costs.)

Ordering costs are the costs of placing and receiving an order. Examples include order processing costs (clerical costs and documents), the cost of insurance for the shipment, and unloading and receiving costs.

Carrying costs are the costs of keeping and storing inventory. Examples include insurance, obsolescence, the opportunity cost of funds tied up in inventory, handling costs, and storage space.

If demand is not known with certainty, then a third category of inventory costs—called stockout costs—exists. **Stockout costs** are the costs of not having a product available when demanded by a customer or the cost of not having a raw material available when needed for production. Examples are lost sales (both current and future), the costs of expediting (increased transportation charges, overtime, and so on), and the costs of interrupted production (e.g., idle workers).

It is important to realize that the purchase price of raw materials is not a part of the total cost associated with carrying inventory as that price must be paid anyway. Similarly, the product cost of units produced is not an inventory carrying cost.

Exhibit 8.7 summarizes the reasons typically offered for carrying inventory. It's important to realize that these reasons are given to justify carrying inventories. A host of other reasons can be offered that encourage the carrying of inventories. For example, performance measures such as measures of machine and labour efficiency may promote the buildup of inventories.

EXHIBIT 8.7

Traditional Reasons for Carrying Inventory

1. To balance ordering or setup costs and carrying costs
2. To satisfy customer demand (e.g., meet delivery dates)
3. To avoid shutting down manufacturing facilities because of:
   a. Machine failure
   b. Defective parts
   c. Unavailable parts
   d. Late delivery of parts
4. To buffer against unreliable production processes
5. To take advantage of discounts
6. To hedge against future price increases

Economic Order Quantity: The Traditional Inventory Model Once a company decides to carry inventory, two basic questions must be addressed:

1. How much should be ordered?
2. When should the order be placed?

The first question needs to be addressed before the second can be answered. Assume that demand is known. In choosing an order quantity, managers need to be concerned only with ordering and carrying costs. The formulas for calculating these are as follows:

concept Q&A

Has a store ever been out of an item that you wanted to buy? What did you do? What is the impact of the stockout on the store?

Answers on pages 734 to 738.

$$\text{Total inventory-related cost} = \text{Ordering cost} + \text{Carrying cost}$$

$$\text{Ordering cost} = \text{Number of orders per year} \times \text{Cost of placing an order}$$

$$\text{Average number of units in inventory} = \frac{\text{Units in order}}{2}$$

$$\text{Carrying cost} = \text{Average number of units in inventory} \times \text{Cost of carrying one unit in inventory}$$

The cost of carrying inventory can be computed for any organization that carries inventories, including retail, service, and manufacturing organizations. Cornerstone 8.6 illustrates the application for a service organization and shows how to calculate total ordering cost, carrying cost, and inventory cost.

The total carrying cost for the year is calculated by multiplying the average number of units on hand by the cost of carrying one unit in inventory for a year. But what is the average number of units on hand? Given the policy of ordering 1,000 units at a time, the maximum number on hand would be 1,000 units—the amount on hand just after an order is delivered. The minimum amount on hand would be zero, ideally, the amount seconds before the new order arrives. Therefore, the average amount in inventory is the maximum plus the minimum divided by two or, in this case, 500 units.

The total cost of Mall-o-Cars' current policy is $1,250 (= $250 + $1,000). An order quantity of 1,000 units with a total cost of $1,250, however, may not be the best choice. Some other order quantity may produce a lower total cost. The objective is to find the order quantity that minimizes the total cost. The number of units in the optimal size order quantity is called the **economic order quantity (EOQ)**.

CORNERSTONE 8.6

Calculating Ordering Cost, Carrying Cost, and Total Inventory-Related Cost

Information:

Mall-o-Cars Inc. sells a number of automotive brands and provides service after the sale for a variety of automotive makes and models. Part X7B is used in the repair of water pumps (the part is purchased from external suppliers). Each year, 10,000 units of part X7B are used; they are currently purchased in lots of 1,000 units. It costs Mall-o-Cars \$25 to place the order, and carrying cost is \$2 per part per year.

Required:

1. How many orders for part X7B does Mall-o-Cars place per year?
2. What is the total ordering cost of part X7B per year?
3. What is the total carrying cost of part X7B per year?
4. What is the total cost of Mall-o-Cars' inventory policy for part X7B per year?

Solution:

1. $$\text{Number of orders} = \frac{\text{Annual number of units used}}{\text{Number of units in an order}} = \frac{10{,}000}{1{,}000} = 10 \text{ orders per year}$$

2. $$\begin{aligned}\text{Total ordering cost} &= \text{Number of orders} \times \text{Cost per order}\\ &= 10 \text{ orders} \times \$25\\ &= \$250\end{aligned}$$

3. $$\begin{aligned}\text{Total carrying cost} &= \text{Average number of units in inventory} \times \text{Cost of carrying one unit in inventory}\\ &= \left(\frac{1{,}000}{2}\right) \times \$2\\ &= \$1{,}000\end{aligned}$$

4. $$\begin{aligned}\text{Total inventory-related cost} &= \text{Total ordering cost} + \text{Total carrying cost}\\ &= \$250 + \$1{,}000\\ &= \$1{,}250\end{aligned}$$

Why:

Because knowing the inventory-related costs allows for the efficient management of inventories and improvement of performance measures.

The Economic Order Quantity

Since EOQ is the quantity that minimizes total inventory-related costs, a formula[1] for computing it is as follows.

$$EOQ = \sqrt{\frac{2 \times CO \times D}{CC}}$$

[1] This formula is derived by using calculus. Its derivation is covered in statistics courses.

where:

EOQ = The optimal number of units to be ordered at one time
CO = The cost of placing one order
D = The annual demand for the item, in units
CC = The cost of carrying one unit in inventory for a year

Cornerstone 8.7 shows how to use the EOQ formula.

Calculating the Economic Order Quantity (EOQ)

CORNERSTONE 8.7

Information:

Mall-o-Cars Inc. sells a number of automotive brands and provides service after the sale for a variety of automotive makes and models. Part X7B is used in the repair of water pumps (the part is purchased from external suppliers). Each year, 10,000 units of part X7B are used; they are currently purchased in lots of 1,000 units. It costs Mall-o-Cars $25 to place the order, and carrying cost is $2 per part per year.

Required:

1. What is the EOQ for part X7B?
2. How many orders per year for part X7B will Mall-o-Cars place under the EOQ policy?
3. What is the total annual ordering cost of part X7B for a year under the EOQ policy?
4. What is the total annual carrying cost of part X7B per year under the EOQ policy?
5. What is the total annual inventory-related cost of part X7B under the EOQ?

Solution:

1. $EOQ = \sqrt{\frac{2 \times CO \times D}{CC}}$

$$EOQ = \sqrt{\frac{2 \times \$25 \times 10{,}000}{\$2}}$$
$$= \sqrt{\frac{500{,}000}{2}}$$
$$= 500 \text{ units}$$

2. $\text{Number of orders} = \frac{\text{Annual number of units used}}{\text{Number of units in an order}}$

$$= \frac{10{,}000}{500}$$
$$= 20 \text{ orders per year}$$

3. Total ordering cost = Number of orders × Cost per order
= 20 orders × $25
= $500

(Continued)

CORNERSTONE 8.7

(Continued)

4. Total carrying cost = Average number of units in inventory × Cost of carrying one unit in inventory

$$= \left(\frac{500}{2}\right) \times \$2$$

$$= \$500$$

5. Total inventory-related cost = Total ordering cost + Total carrying cost

$$= \$500 + \$500$$

$$= \$1{,}000$$

Why:

Because the EOQ determines the ideal order quantity that minimizes the inventory-related costs. Minimizing inventory-related costs will help improve profitability.

Look carefully at Cornerstone 8.7. Notice that at the EOQ, the carrying cost equals the ordering cost. This is always true for the simple EOQ model described here. Now compare Cornerstone 8.7 with Cornerstone 8.6. The EOQ order quantity of 500 units is less costly than an order quantity of 1,000 units ($1,000 vs. $1,250).

Reorder Point

The EOQ answers the question of how much to order (or produce). Knowing when to place an order (or set up for production) is also an essential part of any inventory policy. The **reorder point** is the point in time when a new order should be placed (or setup started). It is a function of the EOQ, the lead time, and the rate at which inventory is used. **Lead time** is the time required to receive the economic order quantity once an order is placed or a setup is started. To avoid stockout situations and the costs associated with them and to minimize carrying costs, an order should be placed so that it arrives just as the last item in inventory is used. Knowing the rate of usage and lead time allows us to compute the reorder point that accomplishes these objectives:

$$\text{Reorder point} = \text{Rate of usage} \times \text{Lead time}$$

Cornerstone 8.8 shows how to calculate the reorder point when usage is known with certainty.

CORNERSTONE 8.8

Calculating the Reorder Point

CORNERSTONE VIDEO

Information:

Mall-o-Cars Inc. sells a number of automotive brands and provides service after the sale for a variety of automotive makes and models. Part X7B is used in the repair of water pumps (the part is purchased from external suppliers). Each year, 10,000 units of part X7B are used, at the rate of 40 parts per day. It takes Mall-o-Cars five days from the time of order to the time of the arrival of the order.

Required:

Calculate the reorder point.

(Continued)

Solution:

Reorder point = Daily usage × Lead time
Reorder point = 40 parts per day × 5 days = 200 parts

Why:

Because it allows a firm to avoid stockout situations without carrying excess inventory. Thus, when Mall-o-Cars' supply of part X7B drops to 200 parts, it is time to reorder.

CORNERSTONE 8.8

(Continued)

If the demand for the part or product is not known with certainty, a stockout may occur even if orders are placed at the appropriate time. For example, if 45 units of the part were used per day instead of 40, the firm would use 200 parts after about four and a half days. Since the new order would not arrive until the end of the fifth day, production would be idle for half a day. To avoid this problem, organizations often choose to carry safety stock.

Safety stock is extra inventory carried to serve as insurance against changes in demand that may cause stockouts. Safety stock is computed by multiplying the lead time by the difference between the maximum rate of usage and the average rate of usage. Cornerstone 8.9 shows how to calculate safety stock and the reorder point with safety stock.

Calculating Safety Stock and the Reorder Point with Safety Stock

CORNERSTONE 8.9

Information:

Mall-o-Cars Inc. sells a number of automotive brands and provides service after the sale for a variety of automotive makes and models. Part X7B is used in the repair of water pumps (the part is purchased from external suppliers). Each year, 10,000 units of part X7B are used, at an average rate of 40 parts per day. However, some days, as many as 50 parts are used. It takes Mall-o-Cars five days from the time of order to the time of the arrival of the order.

Required:

1. Calculate the amount of safety stock.
2. Calculate the reorder point with safety stock.

Solution:

1. Safety stock = (Maximum daily usage − Average daily usage) × Lead time
   = (50 − 40) × 5 days
   = 50 parts

2. Reorder point = Maximum daily usage × Lead time
   Reorder point = 50 × 5 days = 250 parts

   OR

   Reorder point = (Average daily usage × Lead time) + Safety stock
   Reorder point = (40 × 5 days) + 50 = 250 parts

Why:

Because the safety stock calculation assists a firm in determining how to avoid the potential cost or lost sales from stockout situations.

Economic Order Quantity and Inventory Management

The EOQ model is very useful in identifying the optimal trade-off between inventory ordering costs and carrying costs. It also is useful in helping to deal with uncertainty by using safety stock. The historical importance of the EOQ model in many industries can be better appreciated by understanding the nature of the traditional manufacturing environment. This environment has been characterized by the mass production of a few standardized products that typically have a very high setup cost. The high setup cost encouraged a large batch size. Thus, production runs for these firms tended to be quite long, and the excess production was placed in inventory.

Just-in-Time Approach to Inventory Management

The economic environment for many traditional, large-batch, high-setup-cost firms has changed dramatically in the past 10 to 20 years. Advances in transportation and communications have contributed significantly to the ability of firms to compete globally, while advances in technology have contributed to shorter life cycles for products, and increased product diversity. These competitive pressures have led many firms to abandon the EOQ model in favour of a just-in-time (JIT) approach to reduce the costs of ordering and carrying inventory.

The **just-in-time (JIT)** approach is based on the premise that goods should be pulled through the system by present demand rather than being pushed through on a fixed schedule based on anticipated demand. Each operation produces only what is necessary to satisfy the demand of the succeeding operation. The materials or subassemblies arrive just in time for production to occur so that demand can be met.

Benefits of JIT

The hallmark of JIT is to reduce inventories to the lowest possible levels. Ordering costs are reduced by developing close and trusting relationships with suppliers. Negotiating long-term contracts for the supply of outside materials will reduce the number of orders and the associated ordering costs. Some retailers have reduced ordering costs by allowing the manufacturer to handle inventory management for the retailer. The manufacturer tells the retailer when and how much stock it should reorder. The retailer reviews the recommendation and approves the order if it makes sense. Hudson's Bay Company and Canadian Tire Corporation, for example, use this arrangement to reduce inventories as well as stockout problems.

Uncertainty in demand is approached by reducing setup times; then, manufacturers can literally produce to order. Most shutdowns occur for one of three reasons: machine failure, defective materials or subassemblies, and unavailability of raw materials or subassemblies. Holding inventories is one traditional solution to all three problems. Those espousing the JIT approach claim that inventories do not solve the problems of interrupted production due to machine failure, defective materials, or unavailability of materials but rather simply cover them up. JIT solves these three problems by emphasizing total preventive maintenance and total quality management, and by building the right kind of long-term relationships with suppliers.

JIT achieves the objective of minimizing purchase costs without carrying inventories by negotiating long-term contracts with a few chosen suppliers located as close to the production facility as possible and to establish more extensive supplier involvement. Suppliers are not selected on the basis of price alone. Performance—the quality of the component and the ability to deliver as needed—and commitment to JIT purchasing are vital considerations. Other benefits of long-term contracts exist. They stipulate prices and acceptable quality levels. Long-term contracts also dramatically reduce the number of orders placed, which helps drive down the ordering cost.

Some companies that use the JIT inventory approach also use **backflush costing** as a means to minimize recordkeeping in the manufacturing process. Under this approach, labour costs are added into the overhead costs and allocated to products so the only elements of cost that need to be accounted for are materials and overhead. In many instances, this will permit the company to avoid using work-in-process accounts and simply focus on finished goods inventory. The costs are fully accounted for, but record-keeping is substantially reduced.

Limitations of JIT

JIT is often referred to as a program of simplification—yet this does not mean that JIT is simple or easy to implement. Time is required, for example, to build sound relationships with suppliers. Insisting on immediate changes in delivery times and quality may not be realistic and may cause difficult confrontations between a company and its suppliers. Workers also may be affected by JIT. Studies have shown that sharp reductions in inventory buffers may cause a regimented workflow and high levels of stress among production workers. If the workers perceive JIT as a way of simply squeezing more out of them, then JIT efforts may be doomed. Perhaps a better strategy for JIT implementation is one where inventory reductions follow the process improvements that JIT offers.

The most glaring deficiency of JIT is the absence of inventory to buffer supply or production interruptions. Retailers who use JIT tactics also face the possibility of shortages. (JIT retailers order what they need now, not what they expect to sell; the idea is to flow goods through the channel as late as possible, keeping inventories low and decreasing the need for markdowns.) If demand increases well beyond the retailer's supply of inventory, then the retailer may be unable to make order adjustments quickly enough to avoid lost sales and irritated customers. The JIT manufacturing company is also willing to place current sales at risk to achieve assurance of future sales. This assurance comes from higher quality, quicker response time, and lower operating costs.

SUMMARY OF LEARNING OBJECTIVES

LO1. Explain the difference between absorption and variable costing.

- Absorption costing treats fixed factory overhead as a product cost. Unit product cost consists of direct materials, direct labour, variable factory overhead, and fixed factory overhead.
- The absorption-costing income statement groups expenses according to function:
  - Production cost—cost of goods sold, including variable and fixed product cost.
  - Selling expense—variable and fixed cost of selling and distributing product.
  - Administrative expense—variable and fixed cost of administration.
- Variable costing treats fixed factory overhead as a period expense. Unit product cost consists of direct materials, direct labour, and variable factory overhead.
- The variable-costing income statement groups expenses according to cost behaviour:
  - Variable expenses of manufacturing, selling, and administration.
  - Fixed expenses of manufacturing (fixed factory overhead), selling, and administration.
- Impact of units produced and units sold on absorption-costing income and variable-costing income:
  - If units produced > units sold, then absorption-costing net income > variable-costing net income.
  - If units produced < units sold, then absorption-costing net income < variable-costing net income.
  - If units produced = units sold, then absorption-costing net income = variable-costing net income.

LO2. Prepare segmented income statements.

- Segments are subunits of a firm large enough to affect income.
  - Products
  - Divisions
  - Geographical areas
  - Any other type of important subunit
- Using a variable-costing income statement gives managers important information.
- Fixed expenses are divided into two parts.
  - Direct fixed expenses (these would be eliminated if the segment is eliminated).
  - Common fixed expenses (apply to two or more subunits).
- Segment margin (contribution margin minus direct fixed expense) is important for evaluating the performance of subunits.

LO3. (*Appendix 8A*) Discuss inventory management under the economic order quantity and just-in-time (JIT) models.

- EOQ balances the cost of ordering inventory with the cost of carrying inventory.
- Ordering cost is the cost of placing an order.
- Carrying cost is the cost of holding one unit in inventory for a year.
- At the EOQ, ordering cost equals carrying cost.
- Safety stock protects against running out of inventory due to uncertainty in demand.
- The EOQ approach uses inventory to solve problems such as:
  - Uneven demand for the product
  - Avoiding shutdown of factories
  - Hedging against future price increases
  - Taking advantage of discounts
- JIT models solve problems such as uneven demand, production failures, and supply issues, without using inventory, through:
  - Long-term contracts
  - Supplier relationships
  - Reduced setup times to produce on demand
  - Creation of manufacturing cells
  - Maximizing quality and productivity

SUMMARY OF IMPORTANT EQUATIONS

1. Absorption costing product cost = Direct materials + Direct labour + Variable manufacturing overhead + Fixed overhead
2. Variable costing product cost = Direct materials + Direct labour + Variable manufacturing overhead
3. Total inventory-related cost = Ordering cost + Carrying cost
4. Ordering cost = Number of orders per year × Cost of placing one order
5. $\text{Average number of units in inventory} = \dfrac{\text{Units in order}}{2}$
6. Carrying cost = Average number of units in inventory × Cost of carrying one unit in inventory
7. $EOQ = \sqrt{\dfrac{2 \times CO \times D}{CC}}$
8. Reorder point without safety stock = Daily usage × Lead time
9. Safety stock = (Maximum daily usage − Average daily usage) × Lead time
10. Reorder point with safety stock = (Average daily usage + Safety stock) × Lead time

CORNERSTONES

GLOSSARY

Absorption costing A product-costing method that assigns all manufacturing costs to units of product: direct materials, direct labour, variable manufacturing overhead, and fixed manufacturing overhead. (p. 382)

Backflush costing A method of costing under which labour costs are added into overhead costs and allocated to products so that materials and overhead are the only elements of cost for which we need to account. (p. 400)

Carrying costs The costs of holding inventory. (p. 394)

Common fixed expenses Fixed expenses that cannot be directly traced to individual segments and that are unaffected by the elimination of any one segment. (p. 391)

Direct fixed expenses Fixed costs that are directly traceable to a given segment and, consequently, disappear if the segment is eliminated. (p. 391)

Economic order quantity (EOQ) The amount that should be ordered (or produced) to minimize the total ordering (or setup) and carrying costs. (p. 395)

Just-in-time (JIT) A demand-pull system whose objective is to eliminate waste by producing a product only when it is needed and only in the quantities demanded by customers. (p. 400)

Lead time The time required to receive the economic order quantity once an order is placed or a setup is started. (p. 398)

Ordering costs The costs of placing and receiving an order. (p. 394)

Reorder point The point in time when a new order should be placed (or setup started). (p. 398)

Safety stock Extra inventory carried to serve as insurance against changes in demand that may cause stockouts. Safety stock is computed by multiplying the lead time by the difference between the maximum rate of usage and the average rate of usage. (p. 399)

Segment A subunit of a company of sufficient importance to warrant the production of performance reports. (p. 391)

Segment margin The contribution a segment makes to cover common fixed costs and provide for profit after direct fixed costs and variable costs are deducted from the segment's sales revenue. (p. 393)

Stockout costs The costs of insufficient inventory. (p. 394)

Variable costing A product-costing method that assigns only variable manufacturing costs to production: direct materials, direct labour, and variable manufacturing overhead. Fixed manufacturing overhead is treated as a period cost. (p. 382)

REVIEW PROBLEMS

I. Absorption and Variable Costing; Segmented Income Statements

Fine Leathers Company produces a ladies' wallet and a men's wallet. Selected data for the past year follow:

	Ladies' Wallet	Men's Wallet
Production (units)	100,000	200,000
Sales (units)	90,000	210,000
Selling price	$5.50	$4.50
Direct labour hours	50,000	80,000
Manufacturing costs:		
Direct materials	$ 75,000	$100,000
Direct labour	250,000	400,000
Variable overhead	20,000	24,000
Fixed overhead:		
Direct	40,000	60,000
Common[a]	10,000	20,000
Nonmanufacturing costs:		
Variable selling	30,000	60,000
Direct fixed selling	35,000	40,000
Common fixed selling[b]	25,000	25,000

[a] Common fixed overhead totals $30,000 and is allocated between the two products in proportion to production.
[b] Common fixed selling costs total $50,000 and are divided equally between the two products.

Budgeted fixed overhead for the year of $130,000 equalled the actual fixed overhead. Fixed overhead is assigned to products using a plantwide rate based on expected direct labour hours, which were 130,000. The company had 10,000 men's wallets in inventory at the beginning of the year. These wallets had the same unit cost as the men's wallets produced during the year.

Required:

1. Compute the unit cost for the ladies' and men's wallets using the variable-costing method. Compute the unit cost using absorption costing.
2. Prepare an income statement using absorption costing.
3. Prepare an income statement using variable costing.
4. Prepare a segmented income statement using products as segments.

Solution:

1. The unit cost for the ladies' wallet is as follows:

$$\text{Direct materials} = \left(\frac{\$75{,}000}{100{,}000}\right) = \$0.75$$

$$\text{Direct labour} = \left(\frac{\$250{,}000}{100{,}000}\right) = \$2.50$$

$$\text{Variable overhead} = \left(\frac{\$20{,}000}{100{,}000}\right) = \$0.20$$

$$\text{Variable cost per unit} = \$3.45$$

$$\text{Fixed overhead} = \left[\frac{(50{,}000 \times \$1.00)}{100{,}000}\right] = \$0.50$$

Absorption cost per unit = $3.95

The unit cost for the men's wallet is as follows:

$$\text{Direct materials} = \left(\frac{\$100{,}000}{200{,}000}\right) = \$0.50$$

$$\text{Direct labour} = \left(\frac{\$400{,}000}{200{,}000}\right) = \$2.00$$

$$\text{Variable overhead} = \left(\frac{\$24{,}000}{200{,}000}\right) = \$0.12$$

Variable cost per unit = $2.62

$$\text{Fixed overhead} = \left[\frac{(80{,}000 \times \$1.00)}{200{,}000}\right] = \$0.40$$

Absorption cost per unit = $3.02

Notice that the only difference between the two unit costs is the assignment of the fixed overhead cost. Notice also that the fixed overhead unit cost is assigned using the predetermined fixed overhead rate ($130,000/130,000 hours = $1 per hour). For example, the ladies' wallets used 50,000 direct labour hours and so receive $1 × 50,000, or $50,000, of fixed overhead. This total, when divided by the units produced, gives the $0.50 per-unit fixed overhead cost. Finally, observe that variable nonmanufacturing costs are not part of the unit cost under variable costing. For both approaches, only manufacturing costs are used to compute the unit costs.

2. The income statement under absorption costing is as follows:

Sales [($5.50 × 90,000) + ($4.50 × 210,000)]	$1,440,000
Less: Cost of goods sold [($3.95 × 90,000) + ($3.02 × 210,000)]	989,700
Gross margin	450,300
Less: Selling expenses*	215,000
Operating income	$ 235,300

* The sum of selling expenses for both products.

3. The income statement under variable costing is as follows:

Sales [($5.50 × 90,000) + ($4.50 × 210,000)]	$1,440,000
Less variable expenses:	
Variable cost of goods sold [($3.45 × 90,000) + ($2.62 × 210,000)]	(860,700)
Variable selling expenses	(90,000)
Contribution margin	489,300
Less fixed expenses:	
Fixed overhead	(130,000)
Fixed selling	(125,000)
Operating income	$ 234,300

4. Segmented income statement:

	Ladies' Wallet	Men's Wallet	Total
Sales	$ 495,000	$ 945,000	$1,440,000
Less variable expenses:			
Variable cost of goods sold	(310,500)	(550,200)	(860,700)
Variable selling expenses	(30,000)	(60,000)	(90,000)
Contribution margin	154,500	334,800	489,300

(Continued)

	Ladies' Wallet	Men's Wallet	Total
Less direct fixed expenses:			
Direct fixed overhead	(40,000)	(60,000)	(100,000)
Direct selling expenses	(35,000)	(40,000)	(75,000)
Segment margin	$ 79,500	$ 234,800	314,300
Less common fixed expenses:			
Common fixed overhead			(30,000)
Common selling expenses			(50,000)
Operating income			$ 234,300

II. Inventory Costs, EOQ, Reorder Point

A local TV repair shop uses 36,000 units of a part each year (an average of 100 units per working day). It costs $20 to place and receive an order. The shop orders in lots of 400 units. It costs $4 to carry one unit per year in inventory.

Required:

1. Calculate the total annual ordering cost.
2. Calculate the total annual carrying cost.
3. Calculate the total annual inventory cost.
4. Calculate the EOQ.
5. Calculate the total annual inventory cost using the EOQ inventory policy.
6. How much is saved per year using the EOQ versus an order size of 400 units?
7. Compute the reorder point, assuming the lead time is three days.
8. Suppose that the usage of the part can be as much as 110 units per day. Calculate the safety stock and the new reorder point.

Solution:

1. $$\text{Ordering cost} = \text{Cost of placing an order} \times \left(\frac{\text{Demand in units}}{\text{Number of units in one order}}\right)$$
$$= \frac{\$20 \times 36{,}000}{400}$$
$$= \$1{,}800$$

2. $$\text{Carrying cost} = (\text{Carrying cost per unit} \times \text{Average units in inventory})$$
$$= \$4 \times \frac{400}{2}$$
$$= \$800$$

3. Total cost = Ordering cost + Carrying cost = $1,800 + $800 = $2,600

4. $$EOQ = \sqrt{\frac{2 \times CO \times D}{CC}}$$
$$= \sqrt{\frac{2 \times \$20 \times 36{,}000}{\$4}}$$
$$= \sqrt{360{,}000}$$
$$= 600 \text{ units}$$

5. $$\text{Total annual inventory cost} = \frac{(\text{Cost per order} \times \text{Total units})}{\text{Units per order}} + \frac{(\text{Carrying cost} \times \text{Units per order})}{2}$$
$$= \left[\frac{(\$20 \times 36{,}000)}{600}\right] + \left[\frac{(\$4 \times 600)}{2}\right]$$
$$= \$1{,}200 + \$1{,}200$$
$$= \$2{,}400$$

6. Savings = $2,600 − $2,400 = $200
7. Reorder point = 100 × 3 = 300 units
8. Safety stock = (110 − 100)3 = 30 units
9. Reorder point = 110 × 3 = 330 units or 300 + 30 = 330 units

DISCUSSION QUESTIONS

1. What is the difference between the unit cost of a product under absorption costing and variable costing?
2. If a company produces 10,000 units and sells 8,000 units during a period, which method of computing operating income (absorption costing or variable costing) will result in the higher operating income? Why?
3. What is a segment?
4. What is the difference between contribution margin and segment margin?
5. Does the purchase price of the part being ordered enter into the EOQ equation? Why or why not?
6. What are ordering costs? Carrying costs? Give examples of each.
7. What are stockout costs?
8. What are the reasons for carrying inventory?
9. Explain why, in the traditional view of inventory, carrying costs increase as ordering costs decrease.
10. What is the economic order quantity?
11. Explain how safety stock is used to deal with demand uncertainty.
12. What approach does JIT take to minimize total inventory costs?

CORNERSTONE EXERCISES

Cornerstone Exercise 8-1 **Inventory Valuation under Absorption Costing**

OBJECTIVE 1
CORNERSTONE 8.1

During the most recent year, Hampton Company had the following data associated with the product it makes:

Units in beginning inventory	550
Units produced	10,000
Units sold ($350 per unit)	9,800
Variable costs per unit:	
Direct materials	$27
Direct labour	$95
Variable overhead	$15
Fixed costs:	
Fixed overhead per unit produced	$35
Fixed selling and administrative	$120,000

Required:

1. How many units are in ending inventory?
2. Using absorption costing, calculate the per-unit product cost.
3. What is the value of ending inventory under absorption costing?

OBJECTIVE 1
CORNERSTONE 8.2

Cornerstone Exercise 8-2 Inventory Valuation under Variable Costing

During the most recent year, Hampton Company had the following data associated with the product it makes:

Units in beginning inventory	550
Units produced	10,000
Units sold ($350 per unit)	9,800
Variable costs per unit:	
Direct materials	$27
Direct labour	$95
Variable overhead	$15
Fixed costs:	
Fixed overhead per unit produced	$35
Fixed selling and administrative	$120,000

Required:

1. How many units are in ending inventory?
2. Using variable costing, calculate the per-unit product cost.
3. What is the value of ending inventory under variable costing?

OBJECTIVE 1
CORNERSTONE 8.3

Cornerstone Exercise 8-3 Absorption-Costing Income Statement

During the most recent year, Bennett Company had the following data:

Units in beginning inventory	—
Units produced	8,000
Units sold ($70 per unit)	7,500
Variable costs per unit:	
Direct materials	$20
Direct labour	$14
Variable overhead	$3
Fixed costs:	
Fixed overhead per unit produced	$5
Fixed selling and administrative	$142,000

Required:

1. Calculate the cost of goods sold under absorption costing.
2. Prepare an income statement using absorption costing.

OBJECTIVE 1
CORNERSTONE 8.4

Cornerstone Exercise 8-4 Variable-Costing Income Statement

During the most recent year, Bennett Company had the following data:

Units in beginning inventory	—
Units produced	8,000
Units sold ($70 per unit)	7,500
Variable costs per unit:	
Direct materials	$20
Direct labour	$14
Variable overhead	$3
Fixed costs:	
Fixed overhead per unit produced	$5
Fixed selling and administrative	$142,000

Required:

3. Calculate the cost of goods sold under variable costing.
4. Prepare an income statement using variable costing.
5. CONCEPTUAL CONNECTION Why are profits different under absorption costing and variable costing?

Cornerstone Exercise 8-5 Segmented Income Statement

OBJECTIVE 2
CORNERSTONE 8.5

Peninsula Garden Centres Inc. produces tomato plants and vines in a greenhouse/nursery operation. The following information was provided for the coming year.

	Tomatoes	Vines
Sales	$1,400,000	$3,500,000
Variable cost of goods sold	480,000	1,300,000
Direct fixed overhead	270,000	220,000

A sales commission of 4 percent of sales is paid for each of the two product lines. Direct fixed selling and administrative expense was estimated to be $135,000 for the tomato plants and $84,000 for the vines.

Common fixed overhead for the nursery operation was estimated to be $1,350,000; common selling and administrative expense was estimated to be $410,000.

Required:

Prepare a segmented income statement for Peninsula Garden Centres Inc. for the coming year, using variable costing.

Cornerstone Exercise 8-6 Ordering Cost, Carrying Cost, and Total Inventory-Related Cost

OBJECTIVE 3
CORNERSTONE 8.6

La Cucina Company sells kitchen supplies and housewares. Lava stone is used in production of *molcajetes* (mortars and pestles used in the making of guacamole) and is purchased from external suppliers. Each year, 2,500 kilograms of lava stone is used; it is currently purchased in lots of 500 kilograms. It costs La Cucina $4 to place the order, and carrying cost is $2 per kilogram per year.

Required:

1. How many orders for lava stone does La Cucina place per year?
2. What is the total ordering cost of lava stone per year?
3. What is the total carrying cost of lava stone per year?
4. What is the total cost of La Cucina's inventory policy for lava stone per year?

Cornerstone Exercise 8-7 Economic Order Quantity

OBJECTIVE 3
CORNERSTONE 8.7

La Cucina Company sells kitchen supplies and housewares. Lava stone is used in production of *molcajetes* (mortars and pestles used in the making of guacamole) and is purchased from external suppliers. Each year, 2,500 kilograms of lava stone is used; it is currently purchased in lots of 500 kilograms. It costs La Cucina $4 to place the order, and carrying cost is $2 per kilogram per year.

Required:

1. What is the EOQ for lava stone?
2. How many orders per year for lava stone will La Cucina place under the EOQ policy?
3. What is the total annual ordering cost of lava stone under the EOQ policy?
4. What is the total annual carrying cost of lava stone under the EOQ policy?
5. What is the total annual inventory-related cost of lava stone under the EOQ?

Cornerstone Exercise 8-8 Reorder Point

OBJECTIVE 3
CORNERSTONE 8.8

La Cucina Company sells kitchen supplies and housewares. Lava stone is used in production of *molcajetes* (mortars and pestles used in the making of guacamole) and is purchased from external suppliers. Each year, 2,500 kilograms of lava stone is used; it is used evenly at the rate of 10 kilograms per day. It takes La Cucina 4 days from the time of order to the time of arrival of the order.

Required:

Calculate the reorder point.

OBJECTIVE 3
CORNERSTONE 8.9

Cornerstone Exercise 8-9 Safety Stock and the Reorder Point with Safety Stock

La Cucina Company sells kitchen supplies and housewares. Lava stone is used in production of *molcajetes* (mortars and pestles used in the making of guacamole) and is purchased from external suppliers. Each year, 2,500 kilograms of lava stone is used; it is used evenly at the rate of 10 kilograms per day. However, some days as many as 15 kilograms are used. It takes La Cucina 4 days from the time of order to the time of arrival of the order.

Required:

1. Calculate the amount of safety stock.
2. Calculate the reorder point with safety stock.

EXERCISES

OBJECTIVE 1

Exercise 8-10 Inventory Valuation under Absorption Costing

Aerospar Company produced 16,000 units during its first year of operations and sold 14,200 at $24 per unit. The company chose practical activity—at 16,000 units—to compute its predetermined overhead rate. Manufacturing costs are as follows:

Direct materials	$ 87,200
Direct labour	120,000
Variable overhead	17,600
Fixed overhead	55,200

Required:

1. Calculate the unit cost for each of these four costs.
2. Calculate the cost of one unit of product under absorption costing.
3. How many units are in ending inventory?
4. Calculate the cost of ending inventory under absorption costing.

OBJECTIVE 1

Exercise 8-11 Inventory Valuation under Variable Costing

Astron Company produced 30,000 units during its first year of operations and sold 28,900 at $22 per unit. The company chose practical activity—at 30,000 units—to compute its predetermined overhead rate. Manufacturing costs are as follows:

Direct materials	$114,000
Direct labour	94,500
Variable overhead	20,400
Fixed overhead	51,000

Required:

1. Calculate the cost of one unit of product under variable costing.
2. Calculate the cost of ending inventory under variable costing.
3. CONCEPTUAL CONNECTION What is the difference in inventory valuation under absorption costing and under variable costing?

OBJECTIVE 1

Exercise 8-12 Inventory Valuation under Absorption and Variable Costing

San Remo Company produced 75,000 units last year. The company sold 74,600 units and there was no beginning inventory. The company chose practical activity—at 75,000 units—to compute its predetermined overhead rate. Manufacturing costs are as follows:

Direct materials	$615,000
Direct labour	105,000
Variable overhead	78,750
Fixed overhead	270,000

Required:

1. Calculate the cost of one unit of product under absorption costing.
2. Calculate the cost of one unit of product under variable costing.
3. Calculate the cost of ending inventory under absorption costing.
4. Calculate the cost of ending inventory under variable costing.

Exercise 8-13 Income Statements under Absorption and Variable Costing

In the coming year, Empire Company expects to sell 75,500 units at $33 each. Empire's controller provided the following information for the coming year.

Unit production	90,000
Unit direct materials	$8.75
Unit direct labour	$2.80
Unit variable overhead	$4.05
Unit fixed overhead*	$4.40
Unit selling expense (variable)	$2.10
Total fixed selling expense	$61,000
Total fixed administrative expense	$220,000

* The unit fixed overhead is based on 90,000 units produced.

Required:

1. Calculate the cost of one unit of product under absorption costing.
2. Calculate the cost of one unit of product under variable costing.
3. Calculate operating income under absorption costing for next year.
4. Calculate operating income under variable costing for next year.

Exercise 8-14 Inventory Valuation under Absorption and Variable Costing

OBJECTIVE 1

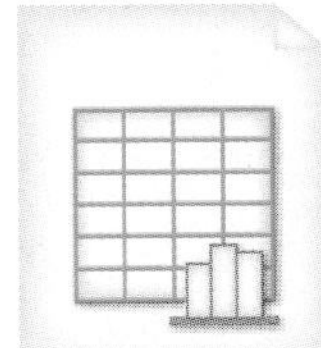

The following information pertains to Synergy Inc. for last year:

Beginning inventory in units	—
Units produced	20,000
Units sold	17,200
Costs per unit:	
Direct materials	$8.00
Direct labour	$4.00
Variable overhead	$1.50
Fixed overhead*	$4.15
Variable selling expenses	$3.00
Fixed selling and administrative costs	$24,300

* Fixed overhead totals $83,000 per year.

Required:

1. Calculate the cost of one unit of product under absorption costing.
2. Calculate the cost of one unit of product under variable costing.
3. How many units are in ending inventory?
4. Calculate the cost of ending inventory under absorption costing.
5. Calculate the cost of ending inventory under variable costing.

Exercise 8-15 Income Statements under Absorption and Variable Costing

The following information pertains to Synergy Inc. for last year:

Beginning inventory in units	—
Units produced	20,000
Units sold	17,200

(*Continued*)

Costs per unit:	
Direct materials	$8.00
Direct labour	$4.00
Variable overhead	$1.50
Fixed overhead*	$4.15
Variable selling expenses	$3.00
Fixed selling and administrative costs	$24,300

* Fixed overhead totals $83,000 per year.

Assume that the selling price is $32 per unit.

Required:

1. Prepare an income statement using absorption costing.
2. Prepare an income statement using variable costing.

OBJECTIVE 1

Exercise 8-16 Inventory Cost under Absorption and Variable Costing

During the most recent year, Durham Inc. had the following data associated with the product it makes:

Units in beginning inventory	—
Units produced	18,500
Units sold ($180 per unit)	15,000
Variable costs per unit:	
Direct materials	$33
Direct labour	$62
Variable overhead	$29
Fixed costs:	
Fixed manufacturing overhead per unit produced	$18
Fixed selling and administrative expense	$180,000

Required:

1. How many units are in ending inventory?
2. Using absorption costing, calculate the per-unit product cost. What is the value of ending inventory?
3. Using variable costing, calculate the per-unit product cost. What is the value of ending inventory?
4. Calculate operating income using absorption costing.
5. Calculate operating income using variable costing.

OBJECTIVE 2

Exercise 8-17 Segmented Income Statement

Trendy Inc. produces high-end sweaters and jackets in a single factory. The following information was provided for the coming year.

	Sweaters	Jackets
Sales	$300,000	$420,000
Variable cost of goods sold	180,000	200,000
Direct fixed overhead	25,000	40,000

A sales commission of 5 percent of sales is paid for each of the two product lines. Direct fixed selling and administrative expense was estimated to be $20,000 for the sweater line and $50,000 for the jacket line.

Common fixed overhead for the factory was estimated to be $45,000; common selling and administrative expense was estimated to be $15,000.

Required:

Prepare a segmented income statement for Trendy Inc. for the coming year, using variable costing.

Exercise 8-18 Segmented Income Statements, Inventory Valuation

OBJECTIVE 1 2

For the coming year, Archway Computers Inc. expects to produce and sell 200,000 computers. Of these, 80,000 will be consumer (personal) computers and 120,000 will be small business computers. Common fixed overhead is $700,000. Additional information for the coming year is as follows:

	Consumer Computers	Small Business Computers
Price	$ 780	$ 2,300
Unit direct materials	500	1,800
Unit direct labour	160	290
Unit variable overhead	40	75
Unit variable selling expense	75	70
Total direct fixed overhead	120,000	200,000

Fixed selling and administrative expense for Archway Computers Inc. is $3,460,000 per year.

Required:

1. Calculate the unit variable cost under variable costing. Is this cost the same as unit variable product cost? Why or why not?
2. Prepare a segmented variable-costing income statement for next year. The segments correspond to product lines: consumer computers and small business computers.

Exercise 8-19 Ordering Cost, Carrying Cost, and Total Inventory-Related Cost

OBJECTIVE 3

Franklin Company purchases 4,500 units of Widgelets each year in lots of 500 units per order. The cost of placing one order is $22, and the cost of carrying one unit of product in inventory for a year is $8.80.

Required:

1. How many orders for Widgelets does Franklin place per year?
2. What is the total ordering cost of Widgelets per year?
3. What is the total carrying cost of Widgelets per year?
4. What is the total cost of Franklin's inventory policy for Widgelets per year?

Exercise 8-20 EOQ, Ordering Cost, Carrying Cost, and Total Inventory-Related Cost

OBJECTIVE 3

Franklin Company purchases 4,500 units of Widgelets each year in lots of 500 units per order. The cost of placing one order is $22, and the cost of carrying one unit of product in inventory for a year is $8.80.

Required:

1. What is the EOQ for Widgelets?
2. How many orders for Widgelets will Franklin place per year under the EOQ policy?
3. What is the total annual ordering cost of Widgelets under the EOQ policy?
4. What is the total annual carrying cost of Widgelets under the EOQ policy?
5. What is the total annual cost of Franklin's inventory policy for Widgelets under the EOQ policy?

Exercise 8-21 Safety Stock; Reorder Point

OBJECTIVE 3

DaCosta Company makes a variety of household appliances, including dust-busters. Plastic handles used in making dust-busters are purchased from an outside supplier. Each year, 20,000 handles are used, at the rate of 80 handles per day. However, some days as many as 90 handles are used. It takes DaCosta 3 days from the time of order to the time of arrival of the order.

Required:

1. Calculate the reorder point without safety stock.
2. Calculate the amount of safety stock.
3. Calculate the reorder point with safety stock.

PROBLEMS

Problem 8-22 Variable- and Absorption-Costing Income

Bolton Company produces and sells recycled plastic boards that are used for building residential backyard decks. The operating costs for the past year were as follows:

Variable costs per unit:	
Direct materials	$ 5.60
Direct labour	3.20
Variable overhead	0.70
Variable selling	0.52
Fixed costs per year:	
Fixed overhead	360,000
Selling and administrative	210,000

During the year, Bolton produced 600,000 boards and sold 635,000 at $12.50 each. Bolton had 45,000 boards in beginning finished goods inventory; costs have not changed from last year to this year. An actual cost system is used for product costing.

Required:

Check figures:
2. Gross margin = $1,524,000
4. Operating income = $1,004,800
5. Absorption-costing income = $880,400

1. What is the per-unit inventory cost that will be reported on Bolton's balance sheet at the end of the year? How many units are in ending inventory? What is the total cost of ending inventory?
2. Calculate absorption-costing income.
3. What would the per-unit inventory cost be under variable costing? Does this differ from the unit cost computed in Requirement 1? Why?
4. Calculate variable-costing income.
5. Suppose that Bolton Company had sold 580,000 boards during the year. What would absorption-costing income have been? Variable-costing income?

OBJECTIVE 1 2

Problem 8-23 Variable Costing, Absorption Costing, Segmented Income Statements, Inventory Valuation

During its first year of operations, Aroma Inc. produced 55,000 jars of hand cream based on a formula containing 10 percent glycolic acid. Unit sales were 53,500 jars. Fixed overhead totalled $27,500 and was applied at the rate of $0.50 per unit produced. The results of the year's operations are as follows (on an absorption-costing basis):

Sales (53,500 units @ $8.50)	$454,750
Less: Cost of goods sold	160,500
Gross margin	294,250
Less: Selling and administrative (all fixed)	120,000
Operating income	$174,250

At the end of the first year of operations, Aroma is considering expanding its customer base. In its first year, it sold to small drugstores and supermarkets. Now, Aroma wants to add large discount stores and small beauty shops. Working together, the company controller and marketing manager have accumulated the following information:

a. Anticipated sales to discount stores would be 20,000 units at a discounted price of $6.75. Higher costs of shipping and return penalties would be incurred. Shipping would amount to $45,000 per year, and return penalties would average 1 percent of sales. In addition, a clerk would need to be hired solely to handle the discount stores' accounts. The clerk's salary and benefits would be $30,000 per year.
b. Anticipated sales to beauty shops would be 10,000 units at a price of $9. A commission of 10 percent of sales would be paid to independent jobbers who sell to the shops. In addition, an extra packing expense of $0.50 per unit would be incurred because the shops require fewer bottles per carton.

c. It is expected that the sales to drugstores and supermarkets would remain the same in the next year as in the past year.
d. The fixed overhead and selling and administrative expenses would remain unchanged and are treated as common costs.

Required:

1. Calculate the cost of Aroma's ending inventory at the end of the first year under absorption costing.
2. Calculate the cost of Aroma's ending inventory at the end of the first year under variable costing. What is operating income for the first year using variable costing?
3. Prepare a segmented variable-costing income statement for next year. The segments correspond to customer groups: drugstores and supermarkets, discount stores, and beauty shops.
4. Are all three customer groups profitable? Should Aroma expand its marketing base?

Check figures:
2. Ending inventory = $3,750
3. Segment margin beauty shops = $51,000

Problem 8-24 Segmented Income Statements, Product-Line Analysis

Walker Company produces blenders and coffee makers. During the past year, the company produced and sold 100,000 blenders and 25,000 coffee makers. Fixed costs for Walker totalled $250,000, of which $90,000 can be avoided if the blenders are not produced and $45,000 can be avoided if the coffee makers are not produced. Revenue and variable cost information follow:

	Blenders	Coffee Makers
Variable expenses per appliance	$20	$43
Selling price per appliance	22	45

Required:

1. Prepare segmented income statements. Separate direct and common fixed costs.
2. What would the effect be on Walker's profit if the coffee maker line was dropped? The blender line?
3. What would the effect be on firm profits if an additional 10,000 blenders could be produced (using existing capacity) and sold for $20.50 on a special-order basis? Existing sales would be unaffected by the special order.

Check figures:
1. Blender segment margin = $110,000
3. Blender segment margin = $115,000

OBJECTIVE 

Problem 8-25 Variable Costing, Absorption Costing, Inventory Valuation

Dynasty Company manufactures stackable plastic cubes that are used for storage in dorm rooms. In August 2018, Dynasty began producing multicoloured cubes. During the month of August, 9,000 were produced, and 8,800 were sold at $7.50 each. The following costs were incurred:

Direct materials	$10,800
Direct labour	6,750
Variable overhead	5,850
Fixed overhead	27,900

A selling commission of 10 percent of sales price was paid. Administrative expenses, all fixed, amounted to $23,000.

Required:

1. Calculate the unit cost and the cost of ending inventory under absorption costing.
2. Calculate the unit cost and the cost of ending inventory under variable costing.
3. What is the contribution margin per unit?
4. Dynasty believes that multicoloured cubes will really take off after one year of sales. Management thinks August 2019 sales will be twice as high as August 2018 sales. Prepare an income statement for August 2019 using the assumed higher level of sales. Which costing method should be used—absorption costing or variable costing?
5. CONCEPTUAL CONNECTION Explain the difference in the profitability measures between absorption and variable costing.

Check figures:
1. Unit cost = $5.70
3. Contribution margin per unit = $4.15
4. Operating income = $22,140

Problem 8-26 Segmented Income Statement, Management Decision Making

SushiFresh Company produces three lines of prepared dishes for a grocery store chain: Crispy Mango, Spicy Shrimp, and Yummy Rolls.

Segmented income statements for the past year are as follows:

	Crispy Mango	Spicy Shrimp	Yummy Rolls	Total
Sales	$86,000	$120,000	$145,000	$351,000
Less: Variable expenses	42,000	75,000	72,500	189,500
Contribution margin	44,000	45,000	72,500	161,500
Less: Direct fixed expenses	46,050	47,300	30,000	123,350
Segment margin	$ (2,050)	$ (2,300)	$ 42,500	38,150
Less: Common fixed expenses				38,100
Operating income				$ 50

Eito Sutoko, president of SushiFresh, is concerned about the financial performance of the firm and is seriously considering dropping both the Crispy Mango and Spicy Shrimp product lines. However, before making a final decision, he consults Jan Toff, SushiFresh's vice-president of marketing.

Check figures:
1. Spicy Shrimp segment margin = $(1,050)
2. Operating income (loss) = $(2,850)
3. Operating income = $2,100

Required:

1. Jan believes that by increasing advertising by $2,000 (= $1,000 each for the Crispy Mango and Spicy Shrimp product lines), sales of those two lines would increase by 5 percent. If you were Eito, how would you react to this information?
2. Jan warns Eito that eliminating the Crispy Mango and Spicy Shrimp product lines would lower the sales of the Yummy Rolls line by 10 percent. Given this information, would it be profitable to eliminate the Crispy Mango and Spicy Shrimp product lines?
3. Suppose that eliminating either line reduces sales of the Yummy Rolls line by 2 percent. Would a combination of increased advertising (the option described in Requirement 1) and eliminating one of the lines be beneficial? Identify the best combination for the firm.

Problem 8-27 Ordering and Carrying Costs, EOQ

Bonino Company uses 24,000 circuit boards each year in its production of stereo units. The cost of placing an order is $125. The cost of holding one unit of inventory for one year is $6. Currently, Bonino places 12 orders of 2,000 circuit boards per year.

Check figures:
3. $7,500
5. Carrying cost at EOQ = $3,000
7. Cost of ordering 1,000 units = $7,200

Required:

1. Compute the annual ordering cost.
2. Compute the annual carrying cost.
3. Compute the cost of Bonino's current inventory policy.
4. Compute the economic order quantity.
5. Compute the ordering cost and the carrying cost for the EOQ.
6. How much money does using the EOQ policy save the company over the policy of purchasing 2,000 circuit boards per order?
7. Suppose that the supplier charges an extra $0.05 per unit to purchase circuit boards in orders of 1,500 or fewer. Should Bonino switch to the EOQ policy or not?

Problem 8-28 Economic Order Quantity

Italia Pizzeria is a popular pizza restaurant near a university campus. Brandon Thayn, an accounting student, works for Italia Pizzeria. After several months at the restaurant, Brandon began to analyze the efficiency of the business, particularly inventory practices. He noticed that the owner had more than 50 items regularly carried in inventory. Of these items, the most expensive to buy and carry was cheese. Cheese was ordered in blocks at $17.50 per block. Annual usage totals 14,000 blocks.

Upon questioning the owner, Brandon discovered that the owner did not use any formal model for ordering cheese. It took five days to receive a new order when placed, which was done whenever the inventory of cheese dropped to 200 blocks. The size of the order was usually 400 blocks. The cost of carrying one block of cheese is 10 percent of its purchase price. It costs $40 to place and receive an order.

Italia Pizzeria stays open seven days a week and operates 50 weeks a year. The restaurant closes for the last two weeks of December.

Required:

1. Compute the total cost of ordering and carrying the cheese inventory under the current policy.
2. Compute the total cost of ordering and carrying cheese if the restaurant were to change to the EOQ. How much would the restaurant save per year by switching policies?
3. If the restaurant uses the EOQ, when should it place an order? (Assume that the amount of cheese used per day is the same throughout the year.) How does this compare with the current reorder policy?
4. Suppose that storage space allows a maximum of 600 blocks of cheese. Discuss the inventory policy that should be followed with this restriction.
5. Suppose that the maximum storage is 600 blocks of cheese and that cheese can be held for a maximum of 10 days. The owner will not hold cheese any longer than 10 days in order to ensure the right flavour and quality. Under these conditions, evaluate the owner's current inventory policy.

PROFESSIONAL EXAMINATION PROBLEM*

Professional Examination Problem 8-29 **Variable versus Absorption Costing**

Rhodes Inc. manufactures and sells a single product. Current year sales volume was 50,000 units at a selling price of $86 per unit. Direct materials and direct labour amount to $28 per unit. Variable manufacturing overhead costs were $13 per unit plus fixed costs of $455,000 per year. There were no beginning inventories and 65,000 units were produced during the year. Variable selling, general, and administrative costs were $4.50 per unit sold plus fixed costs of $765,000 for the year.

Required:

1. Prepare an absorption-costing income statement for the year.
2. Prepare a variable-costing income statement for the year.
3. Reconcile the difference between the two statements and explain why net income is different between the two costing approaches.

CASES

Case 8-30 **Absorption Costing, Performance Measurement** OBJECTIVE 1

Paul Vincelli was disturbed by a telephone call he had just received from an analyst with a major Bay Street investment firm. His company, Madison Avenue Fashions, had just released its third quarter results and finally the profit figures were beginning to look up. Profits had been languishing and Paul had tried everything to get costs down and profits up. Paul had been ill for several months and had left day-to-day operations to his trusted lieutenants.

He was pleased that his production people had seemed to have turned the corner on reducing costs of the various high-fashion items the company made. However, the analyst had just pointed out that, while gross margins had improved substantially, inventories seemed to have increased by about 40 percent. This observation had bothered Paul because he had been informed that any inventory increases were due to a shifting of orders from this quarter to the next quarter by

(Continued)

customers and were not under the control of the production people. However, as he took a closer look at the financial statements, he realized that order levels were consistent with prior periods.

Now he was even more perplexed. With lower unit costs and increased profits, Bay Street should be praising management, but exactly the opposite was happening. The analyst suggested that the company had been managing the earnings of the company by increasing production well over the requirements for the quarter.

Required:

Paul has asked you to explain in detail how something like this could alter the operating results of the company.

OBJECTIVE 1

Case 8-31 Ethical Issues, Absorption Costing, Performance Measurement

Ruth Swazey, divisional controller and chartered professional accountant, was upset by a recent memo she received from the divisional manager, Paul Chesser. Ruth was scheduled to present the division's financial performance at headquarters in one week. In the memo, Paul had given Ruth some instructions for this upcoming report. In particular, she had been told to emphasize the significant improvement in the division's profits over last year. Ruth, however, didn't believe that there was any real underlying improvement in the division's performance and was reluctant to say otherwise. She knew that the increase in profits was because of Paul's conscious decision to produce more inventory.

In an earlier meeting, Paul had convinced his plant managers to produce more than they knew they could sell. By doing so, more of the fixed factory overhead could be moved into inventory with the extra units produced. He argued that by deferring some of this period's fixed costs, reported profits would jump. He pointed out two significant benefits. First, by increasing profits, the division could exceed the minimum level needed so that all the managers would qualify for the annual bonus. Second, by meeting the budgeted profit level, the division would be better able to compete for much-needed capital. Ruth had objected but had been overruled. The most persuasive counterargument was that the increase in inventory could be liquidated in the coming year as the economy improved. However, Ruth considered this event unlikely. Based on past experience, she believed that it would take at least two years of improved market demand before the productive capacity of the division was exceeded.

Required:

1. Discuss the behaviour of Paul Chesser, the divisional manager. Was the decision to produce more inventory an ethical one?
2. What should Ruth Swazey do? Should she comply with the directive to emphasize the increase in profits? If not, what options does she have?
3. In Chapter 1, the Code of Professional Conduct for CPA Ontario was outlined. Identify any standards of behaviour that apply in this situation.

OBJECTIVE 3

Case 8-32 Ethical Issues, Absorption Costing, Performance Measurement

Mac Ericson and Irene Papas met at a CPA conference two months ago and began dating. Mac is the controller for Longley Enterprises, and Irene is a marketing manager for Sharp Products. Longley is a major supplier for Piura Products, a competitor of Sharp. Longley has entered into a long-term agreement to supply certain materials to Piura. Piura has been developing a JIT purchasing and manufacturing system. As part of its development, Piura and Longley have established electronic data interchange (EDI) capabilities. The following conversation between Mac and Irene took place during a lunch date:

Irene: Mac, I understand that you have EDI connections with Piura. Is that right?

Mac: Sure. It's part of the partners-in-profits arrangement that we have worked so hard to get. It's working really well. Knowing Piura's production schedule helps us stabilize our own schedule. It has actually cut some of our overhead costs. It has also decreased Piura's costs. I estimate that we both have decreased production costs by about 7 to 10 percent.

Irene: That's interesting. You know, I have a real chance of getting promoted to VP of marketing ...

Mac: Hey, that's great. When will you know?

Irene: It all depends on this deal that I am trying to cut with Balboa—if I win the contract, then I think I have it. My main problem is with Piura. If I knew what its production schedule was, I could get a pretty good idea as to how long it would take it to deliver. I could then make sure that we beat its delivery offer—even if we had to work overtime and do all kinds of expediting. I know that our delivery speed is very, very important to Balboa. Our quality is as good as Piura's, but it tends to beat us on delivery time. My boss would love to kick Piura. It has beaten us too many times recently. I am wondering if you would be willing to help me out.

Mac: Irene, you know that I would help if I could, but Piura's production schedule is confidential information. If word got out that I had leaked that kind of stuff to you, I would be history.

Irene: Well, no one would ever know. Besides, I have already had a chat with Tom Anderson, our CEO. Our VP of finance is retiring. He knows about you and your capabilities. I think he would be willing to hire you—especially if he knew that you helped swing this Balboa deal. You could increase your salary by 40 percent.

Mac: I don't know. I have my doubts about the propriety of all this. It might look kind of funny if I take over as VP of finance not long after Piura loses the Balboa deal. But a VP position and a big salary increase are tempting. It's unlikely that I'll ever have a shot at the VP position in my company.

Irene: Think it over. If you are interested, I'll arrange a dinner with Tom. He said he'd like to meet you. He knows a little about this. I'm sure that he has the ability to keep it quiet. I don't think there is much risk.

Required:

1. Based on this information, has Mac violated any of the rules of professional conduct? Explain.
2. Suppose that Mac decides to provide information in exchange for the VP position. Which CPA standards would he violate?

9

Budgeting, Production, Cash, and Master Budget

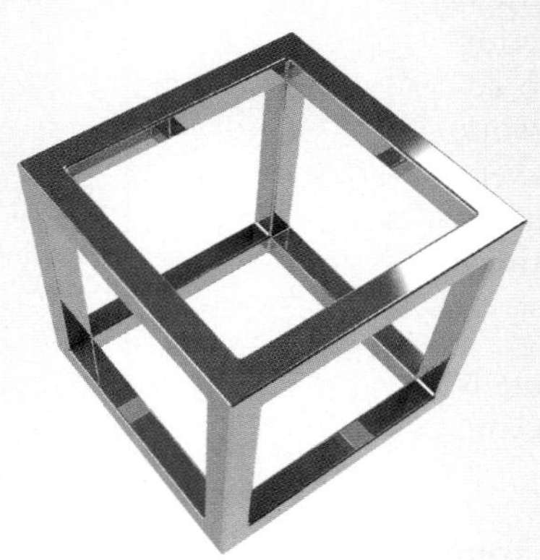

After studying Chapter 9, you should be able to:

1. Define budgeting, and discuss its role in planning, control, and decision making.
2. Define and prepare the operating budget, identify its major components, and explain the interrelationships of its various components.
3. Define and prepare the financial budget, identify its major components, and explain the interrelationships of its various components.
4. Describe the behavioural dimension of budgeting.

EXPERIENCE MANAGERIAL DECISIONS

with High Sierra

Have you ever wondered where that huge backpack you use to lug 20 kilograms of books, laptops, tablets, chargers, and headphones all over campus originated? If so, you might be surprised by the history behind the company. Right after the Second World War, an abundance of Army and Navy Surplus stores supplied consumers with tents, canteens, and canvas bags. One of these stores was Seaway Importing, a company founded by Harry Bernbaum. In 1978, Harry and his son Hank recognized the need to develop more durable products and founded High Sierra Sport Company.

Budgeting plays an important role in High Sierra's decision-making process. Throughout the 1980s, High Sierra developed its brand reputation as a manufacturer and supplier of numerous types of quality outdoor and foul weather gear, including backpacks, duffel bags, book bags, and hydration gear. During the mid-1990s, budgeting played a key role in helping High Sierra realize it needed to streamline its brand identity in order to keep its competitive edge in quality and price. High Sierra's management used its budgeting process to eliminate poorly performing products and to analyze new products, such as a winter sports product line that focused more directly on the company's brand and target market (e.g., alliances with the ski and snowboard associations). During the early 2000s, High Sierra's budgeting process showed management that it needed to expand operations by outsourcing some of its production overseas in order to remain cost competitive.

To ensure that its budgeting process continues to provide useful insights, High Sierra frequently adopts new and evolving techniques, such as participative budgeting and continuous budgeting. In summary, High Sierra uses budgeting as an effective planning and control tool to promote successful new product development that creates value for the company and keeps students buying those huge backpacks every year!

HIGH SIERRA®

DESCRIPTION OF BUDGETING

OBJECTIVE 

Define budgeting, and discuss its role in planning, control, and decision making.

All businesses should prepare budgets. Budgets help business owners and managers to plan ahead, and later, exercise control by comparing what actually happened to what was expected according to the budget. Budgets formalize managers' expectations regarding sales, prices, and costs. Even small businesses and non-profit entities can benefit from the planning and control provided by budgets.

Budgeting, Planning, and Control

Planning and control are linked. *Planning* is looking ahead to see what actions should be taken to realize particular goals. *Control* is looking backward, determining what actually happened, and comparing it with the previously planned outcomes. This comparison can then be used to adjust the budget, looking forward once more. Exhibit 9.1 illustrates the cycle of planning and control using budgets.

EXHIBIT 9.1

Budgeting, Planning, and Control

Planning Cycle

Control Cycle

Planning

Strategic Plan

Long-Term Objectives

Short-Term Objectives

Short-Term Plan

Budgets

Feedback

Execution

Monitoring of Actual Activity

Comparison of Actual with Planned

Investigation

Corrective Action

Budgets are financial plans for the future and are a key component of planning. They identify objectives and the actions needed to achieve them. Before a budget is prepared, an organization should develop a strategic plan. The **strategic plan** identifies strategies for future activities and operations, generally covering at least five years. The overall strategy is then translated into long- and short-term objectives that form the basis of the budget. The budget and the strategic plan should be tightly linked. Since budgets, especially one-year plans, are short-run in nature, this linkage is important because it helps management ensure that not all attention is focused on the short run.

For example, on June 28, 2013, the Ontario Teachers' Pension Plan (Teachers') completed the acquisition of majority stakes in three Australian telecommunications companies.[1] On April 24, 2013, Teachers' acquired SeaCube Container Leasing Ltd., a firm that owns, manages, and leases containers that are essential to international trade.[2]

[1] Ontario Teachers' Pension Plan website, http://www.otpp.com/news/article/-/article/693128, June 28, 2013, accessed on April 29, 2014.

[2] Ontario Teachers' Pension Plan website, http://www.otpp.com/news/article/-/article/688665, April 24, 2013, accessed on April 29, 2014.

The Teachers' Long-Term Equities group, which focuses on investments characterized by "steady cash flow, growth potential over the long-term horizon and low-to-moderate level or risk," motivated the acquisition and undoubtedly performed budgetary analyses of the firms' current and long-term earnings potential.

Advantages of Budgeting

A budgetary system gives an organization several advantages.

1. **Planning:** Budgeting forces management to plan for the future. It encourages managers to develop an overall direction for the organization, foresee problems, and develop future policies.
2. **Information for Decision Making:** Budgets improve decision making. For example, a restaurant owner who knows the expected revenues and the costs of meat, vegetables, cheeses, and so on might make menu changes that play up the less expensive items and reduce the use of more expensive ingredients. These better decisions, in turn, may keep customers happy while still providing a profitable living for the chefs, servers, and others who work at the restaurant.
3. **Standards for Performance Evaluation:** Budgets set standards that can control the use of a company's resources and motivate employees. A vital part of the budgetary system, **control** is achieved by comparing actual results with budgeted results on a periodic basis (e.g., monthly). A large difference between actual and planned results is feedback revealing that the system is out of control. Steps should be taken to find out why and then to correct the situation. For example, if a pizza restaurant knows how much cheese should be used on a pizza and what the cost should be, the owner can evaluate the amount of cheese actually used. If more cheese is being used than expected, the owner may discover that the workers are careless when preparing the pizzas such that some pizzas get less than their share of cheese and others get much more. Extra care in preparing the pizzas will produce savings and will convince customers that a consistent product will result each time. The same principle applies to other resources used by the restaurant. In total, the savings could be significant.
4. **Improved Communication and Coordination:** Budgets also serve to communicate and coordinate the plans of the organization to each employee. Accordingly, all employees should be aware of their particular role in achieving those objectives. Since budgets for the various areas and activities of the organization must all work together to achieve organizational objectives, coordination is promoted. Managers can see the needs of other areas and are encouraged to subordinate their individual interests to those of the organization. The role of communication and coordination becomes more significant as an organization grows.

For High Sierra, the budgeting process enabled the company to execute its plan as a producer of quality outdoor and foul weather gear. In the 1990s, information gathered through this process allowed High Sierra to identify underperforming products and eliminate those product lines from production. As a result, resources could be redirected to produce in-demand products. In the 2000s, this same information-gathering process helped High Sierra to remain cost competitive by identifying processes and products that could be outsourced. By comparing actual results to budgeted plans, High Sierra is able to identify areas where sales and expenses are higher or lower than expected and take corrective action where needed, and to communicate to managers and employees areas where improvements are required for the company to succeed.

concept Q&A

How can a budget help in planning and control?

Answers on pages 734 to 738.

The Master Budget

The **master budget** is the comprehensive financial plan for the organization as a whole. Typically, the master budget is for a one-year period, corresponding to the fiscal year of the company. Yearly budgets are broken down into quarterly and monthly budgets.

concept Q&A

What is the main objective of continuous budgeting?

Answers on pages 734 to 738.

The use of smaller time periods allows managers to compare actual data with budgeted data more frequently, so that problems may be noticed and resolved sooner.

Some organizations have developed a continuous budgeting philosophy. A **continuous budget** is a moving 12-month budget. As a month expires in the budget, an additional month in the future is added so that the company always has a 12-month plan on hand. Proponents of continuous budgeting maintain that it forces managers to plan ahead constantly.

Directing and Coordinating Most organizations prepare the master budget for the coming year during the last four or five months of the current year. The **budget committee** reviews the budget, provides policy guidelines and budgetary goals, resolves differences that arise as the budget is prepared, approves the final budget, and monitors the actual performance of the organization as the year unfolds. The president of the organization appoints the members of the committee, who are usually the president, vice-president of marketing, vice-president of manufacturing, other vice-presidents, and the controller. The controller usually serves as the **budget director**, the person responsible for directing and coordinating the organization's overall budgeting process.

Major Components of the Master Budget A master budget can be divided into operating and financial budgets.

- **Operating budgets** describe the income-generating activities of a firm: sales, production, and finished goods inventories. The ultimate outcome of the operating budgets is a pro forma or budgeted income statement.
- **Financial budgets** detail the inflows and outflows of cash and the overall financial position. Planned cash inflows and outflows appear in the cash budget. The expected financial position at the end of the budget period is shown in a pro forma or budgeted balance sheet.

Since many of the financing activities are not known until the operating budgets are known, the operating budget is prepared first. Describing and illustrating the individual budgets that make up the master budget will make apparent the interdependencies of the component budgets. A diagram displaying these interrelationships is shown in Exhibit 9.2. Details of the capital budget are covered in a separate chapter.

While this chapter describes the traditional approach to budgeting, it is important to note that many companies are finding it necessary to review and revise their budgets more frequently than once a year. For these firms, budgeting is not an annual process, but rather a continuous process that enables firms to gather timely information and respond quickly to events impacting firm performance, thus providing the firm with a competitive advantage.

PREPARING THE OPERATING BUDGET

Define and prepare the operating budget, identify its major components, and explain the interrelationships of its various components.

The operating budget consists of a budgeted income statement accompanied by the following supporting schedules:

1. Sales budget
2. Production budget or (for retail firms) merchandise purchasing budget
3. Direct materials purchases budget
4. Direct labour budget
5. Overhead budget
6. Ending finished goods inventory budget
7. Cost of goods sold budget
8. Selling and administrative expenses budget

EXHIBIT 9.2

The Master Budget and Its Interrelationships

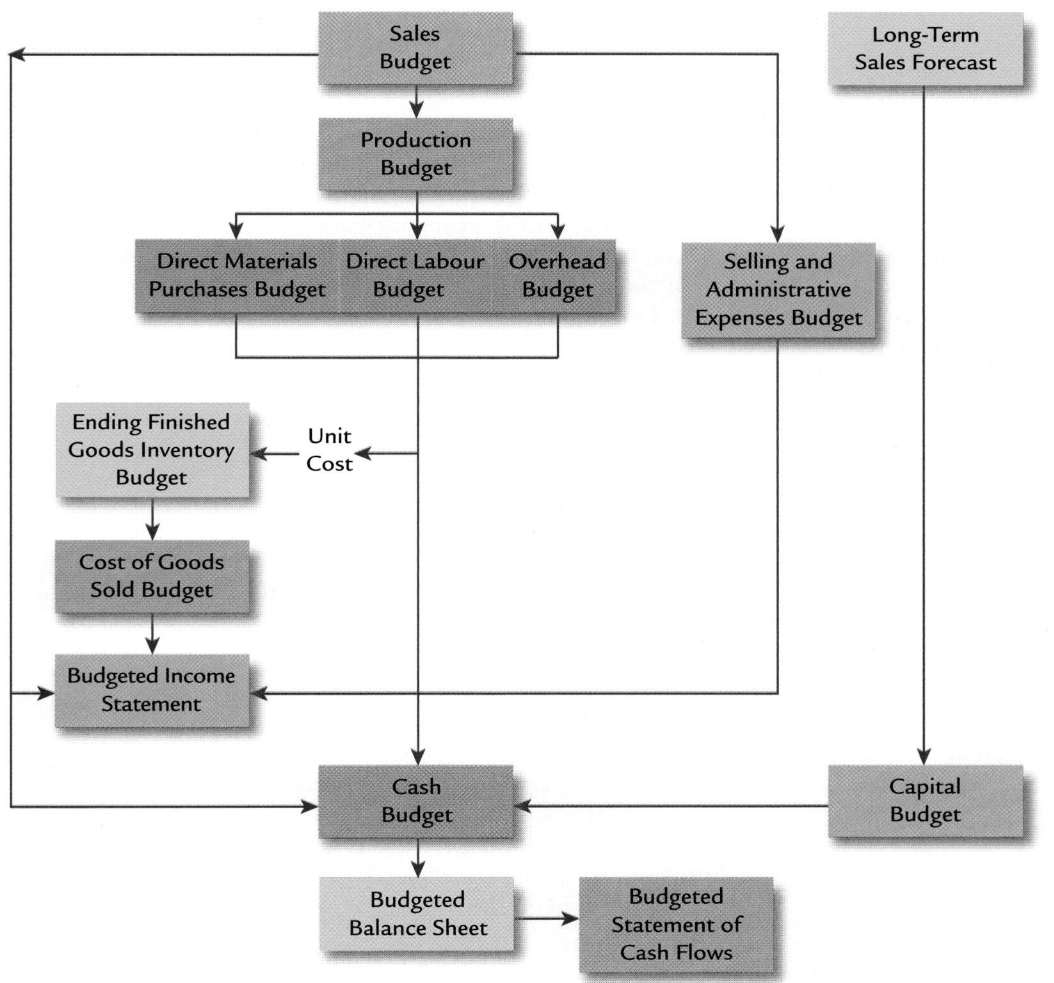

We illustrate the master budgeting process with an example based on the activities of Moose Patties Inc., a trendy restaurant in northern Ontario that sells T-shirts with the Moose Patties logo (a moose that engages in a variety of adventures while eating the hamburgers for which the restaurant is known). Moose Patties' production process involves purchasing from a supplier plain T-shirts, which it screen prints with its logo and sells to customers. In developing a master budget for Moose Patties' clothing manufacturing plant, we will first use the eight supporting schedules previously listed.

Sales Budget

The **sales budget** is approved by the budget committee and describes expected sales in units and dollars. Because the sales budget is the basis for all of the other operating budgets and most of the financial budgets, it is important that it be as accurate as possible.

The first step in creating a sales budget is to develop the sales forecast; this is usually the responsibility of the marketing department. One approach to forecasting sales is the *bottom-up approach*, which requires individual salespeople to submit sales predictions. These are aggregated to form a total sales forecast. The accuracy of this sales forecast may be improved by considering other factors such as the general economic climate, competition, advertising, pricing policies, and so on. Some companies use more formal approaches, such as time-series analysis, correlation analysis, and econometric modelling. For example, the regression technique studied in Appendix 3A can be applied to forecasting sales, in addition to costs.

The sales forecast is just the initial estimate, and it is often adjusted by the budget committee. The budget committee may decide that the forecast is too pessimistic or too optimistic and revise it appropriately.

For example, Brampton, Ontario–based Loblaws sales exceeded analyst forecasts in June 2013 by 8 percent despite strong US competition moving into Canada (e.g., Walmart). Consequently, Loblaws raised its 2013 annual earnings forecast from low-single digit growth to mid-single digit growth year-over-year.[3]

Cornerstone 9.1 shows how to prepare the sales budget for Moose Patties' standard T-shirt line. For simplicity, we assume that Moose Patties has only one product: a standard short-sleeved T-shirt with the Moose Patties logo screen-printed on the back. (For a multiple-product firm, the sales budget reflects sales for each product in units and sales dollars.)

CORNERSTONE 9.1 Preparing a Sales Budget

CORNERSTONE VIDEO

Information:

Budgeted units to be sold for each quarter of 2017: 1,000, 1,200, 1,500, and 2,000. Selling price is $10 per T-shirt.

Required:

Prepare a sales budget for each quarter and for the year.

Solution:

Moose Patties Inc.
Sales Budget
For the Year Ending December 31, 2017

	Quarter				
	1	**2**	**3**	**4**	**Year**
Units	1,000	1,200	1,500	2,000	5,700
Unit selling price	× $10	× $10	× $10	× $10	× $10
Budgeted sales	$10,000	$12,000	$15,000	$20,000	$57,000

Why:

Because the sales budget is the starting point for every budgeting exercise and all of the other budgets flow from this one set of assumptions.

concept Q&A

Why is the sales budget not necessarily the same as the sales forecast?

Answers on pages 734 to 738.

Notice that the sales budget in Cornerstone 9.1 reveals that Moose Patties' sales fluctuate seasonally. Most sales take place in the summer and fall quarters. This is due to the popularity of the T-shirts in the summer and the sales promotions that Moose Patties puts on for "back to school" and Christmas.

[3] Hollie Shaw, "Loblaw's Strong Food, Joe Fresh Sales in Second Quarter Help Boost Outlook," *The Financial Post*, http://business.financialpost.com/2013/07/24/loblaw-earnings-q2-2013/, July 24, 2013, accessed on April 29, 2014.

YOU DECIDE Budgeting in a Service Industry

You are the controller for a large downtown hotel affiliated with a Canada-wide chain. Since the hotel does not have its own parking garage, it rents—and designates as a parking area—a parcel of paved land across the street from the main entrance of the hotel. The hotel manager believes that hotel reviews will improve if the parcel currently rented is purchased and a parking structure with a covered skywalk traversing the street and connecting to the hotel is built. However, you are concerned that—while hotel reviews may improve—there may only be a trivial increase in parking revenues paired with a non-trivial increase in expenses. While parking revenues may increase incrementally, the capital expenditure and future maintenance costs may reduce cash available or increase debt. It is not clear whether the new parking structure, and the potentially better hotel reviews, will improve the hotel's occupancy rate and, in turn, translate into higher gross revenue.

What information do you need to forecast revenues and costs of the parking structure?

This is a two-part problem. The first question—What impact will the parking structure have on the hotel's revenues?—requires knowledge of the total number of hotel occupants per year and the proportion of these occupants who require and are willing to pay for parking availability. This information could come from the parking revenue line item from the income statement from the previous year. An adjustment may be required to account for revenue from the additional parking spots a multi-level parking structure will allow if any of the prior hotel occupants went without parking (or had to park at other parking locations nearby) due to parking space constraints. You may need to consult with the front desk manager to determine the extent, if any, of unmet parking demand. More adjustments may be required to account for local non-hotel-occupant related demand for downtown parking (e.g., revenue generated from daily commuters to the downtown core). A further adjustment is required to capture an estimate of the increase in the bottom line resulting from an increase in the occupancy rate, if any. You may need to check with the sales department to develop a better understanding of the link between parking availability (the new structure), access (the covered walkway), and hotel occupancy rates.

The second question—What impact will the parking structure have on the hotel's costs?—requires knowledge of the up-front and recurring costs. After determining the cost of purchasing the land and constructing the multi-level parking garage and walkway, there may be financing costs. Depending on the source of financing (e.g., internal cash holdings or debt financing), you may need to determine the amount of interest expected to be paid on a loan to finance the structure. This expense will be based on the total amount financed and the interest rate charged. You may need to check with the hotel's national headquarters to determine the interest rate available. Although borrowing costs are recurring, they will gradually fall over time as the debt is repaid. A second major expenditure is maintenance of the parking garage (e.g., security, cleaning, painting, and occasional repairs). This expense will be recurring and may rise over time. You may need to check with the hotel maintenance department to determine a reliable estimate for this maintenance expense. In addition to these expenses, the firm must also consider the opportunity cost, that is, the benefits forgone by selecting this particular course of action. For more detail on the role that opportunity costs play in decision-making, see Chapter 13.

Forecasts of sales revenues and costs are dependent on detailed information provided by sources such as maintenance, front desk and sales staff, national headquarters staff, and past accounting information.

Production Budget

The **production budget** tells how many units must be produced to meet sales needs and to satisfy ending inventory requirements. The Moose Patties' production budget would show how many T-shirts are needed to satisfy sales demand for each quarter and for the year. If there were no beginning or ending inventories, the T-shirts to be produced would exactly equal the units to be sold. This would be the case in a just-in-time (JIT) firm. However, many firms use inventories as a buffer against uncertainties in demand or production. Thus, they need to plan for inventory levels as well as sales.

To compute the units to be produced, both unit sales and units of beginning and ending finished goods inventory are needed:

Units to be produced = Expected unit sales
+ Units in desired ending inventory (EI)
− Units in beginning inventory (BI)

Cornerstone 9.2 shows how to prepare a production budget using this formula.

CORNERSTONE 9.2

Preparing a Production Budget

CORNERSTONE VIDEO

Information:

Budgeted units to be sold for each quarter of 2017: 1,000, 1,200, 1,500, and 2,000. Assume that company policy requires 20 percent of the next quarter's sales in ending inventory and that beginning inventory of T-shirts for the first quarter of the year was 180 units. Assume also that sales for the first quarter of 2018 are estimated at 1,000 units.

Required:

1. Calculate the desired ending inventory in units for each quarter of the year. What is the ending inventory in units for the year?
2. Prepare a production budget for each quarter and for the year.

Solution:

1. Ending inventory, quarter 1 = 0.20 × 1,200 units = 240 units
   Ending inventory, quarter 2 = 0.20 × 1,500 units = 300 units
   Ending inventory, quarter 3 = 0.20 × 2,000 units = 400 units
   Ending inventory, quarter 4 = 0.20 × 1,000 units = 200 units
   Ending inventory for the year = Ending inventory for quarter 4 = 200 units

2.

Moose Patties Inc.
Production Budget
For the Year Ending December 31, 2017

	Quarter				
	1	**2**	**3**	**4**	**Year**
Sales in units	1,000	1,200	1,500	2,000	5,700
Desired ending inventory*	240	300	400	200	200
Total needs	1,240	1,500	1,900	2,200	5,900
Less: Beginning inventory**	(180)	(240)	(300)	(400)	(180)
Units to be produced	1,060	1,260	1,600	1,800	5,720

* Ending inventory for each quarter is calculated in part 1.
** Recall that the beginning inventory for one quarter is equal to the ending inventory of the preceding quarter.

Why:

Because the production budget allows us to translate the requirements of the sales budget into the actual units that need to be produced to meet the needs of the company's operations, including inventory levels as set by corporate policy.

Consider the first column (quarter 1) of the budget in Cornerstone 9.2. Moose Patties anticipates sales of 1,000 T-shirts. In addition, the company wants 240 T-shirts in ending inventory at the end of the first quarter (0.20 × 1,200). Thus, 1,240 T-shirts are needed during the first quarter. Where will these 1,240 T-shirts come from? Beginning inventory can provide 180 of them, leaving 1,060 to be produced during the quarter. Notice that the production budget is expressed in terms of units.

Two important points should be emphasized.

1. The beginning inventory for one quarter is always equal to the ending inventory of the previous quarter. For quarter 2, the beginning inventory is 240 T-shirts, which is identical to the desired ending inventory for quarter 1.
2. The column for the year is not in all cases simply the addition of the amounts for the four quarters. Notice that the desired ending inventory for the year is 200 T-shirts, which is, of course, equal to the desired ending inventory for the fourth quarter.

analytical Q&A

Assume that the expected sales for January and February are 2,000 units and 2,500 units, respectively. The desired ending inventory is 20 percent of the next month's expected sales. If the inventory on hand at the beginning of January is 150 units, how many units should be budgeted for production in January?

Answers on pages 734 to 738.

Retail Firms—Merchandise Purchasing Budget

Since retail firms do not produce products for sale, retail firms do not require a production budget. Instead retail firms purchase products from manufacturers for resale to consumers and, therefore, use a merchandise purchasing budget. Similar to the production budget, the **merchandise purchasing budget** details how many units must be purchased to meet sales needs and to satisfy ending inventory requirements. Without any beginning or ending inventories, the number of units purchased would exactly equal the number of units sold. Due to uncertainty, most retail firms carry inventories as a buffer and, therefore, must plan for both expected unit sales and desired inventory levels.

To compute the units to be purchased, both unit sales and units of beginning and ending finished goods inventory are needed:

Units to be purchased = Expected unit sales + Units in desired ending inventory (EI)
− Units in beginning inventory (BI)

Cornerstone 9.3 shows how to prepare a merchandise purchasing budget using this formula.

Preparing a Merchandise Purchasing Budget

CORNERSTONE 9.3

Information:

Budgeted units to be sold for each quarter of 2017: 2,000, 2,400, 3,000, and 4,000. Assume that company policy requires 15 percent of the next quarter's sales in ending inventory and that beginning inventory for the first quarter of the year was 360 units. Assume also that sales for the first quarter of 2019 are estimated at 2,000 units.

Required:

1. Calculate the desired ending inventory in units for each quarter of the year. What is the ending inventory in units for the year?
2. Prepare a merchandise budget for each quarter and for the year.

Solution:

1. Ending inventory, quarter 1 = 0.15 × 2,400 units = 360 units
   Ending inventory, quarter 2 = 0.15 × 3,000 units = 450 units
   Ending inventory, quarter 3 = 0.15 × 4,000 units = 600 units
   Ending inventory, quarter 4 = 0.15 × 2,000 units = 300 units
   Ending inventory for the year = Ending inventory for quarter 4 = 300 units

(Continued)

CORNERSTONE

9.3

(Continued)

2.

Retail Firm
Merchandise Purchasing Budget
For the Year Ending December 31, 2017

	Quarter				
	1	**2**	**3**	**4**	**Year**
Sales in units	2,000	2,400	3,000	4,000	11,400
Desired ending inventory*	360	450	600	300	300
Total needs	2,360	2,850	3,600	4,300	11,700
Less: Beginning inventory**	(360)	(360)	(450)	(600)	(360)
Units to be produced	2,000	2,490	3,150	3,700	11,340

* Ending inventory for each quarter is calculated in part 1.
** Recall that the beginning inventory for one quarter is equal to the ending inventory of the preceding quarter.

Why:

Because the merchandise purchasing budget allows us to translate the requirements of the sales budget into the actual units that need to be purchased to meet the needs of the company's operations, including inventory levels as set by corporate policy.

Consider the first column (quarter 1) of the budget in Cornerstone 9.3. The retail firm anticipates sales of 2,000 units. In addition, the company wants 360 units in ending inventory at the end of the first quarter (0.15 × 2,400). Thus, 2,360 units are needed during the first quarter. Where will these 2,360 units come from? Beginning inventory can provide 360 of them, leaving 2,000 to be purchased during the quarter. As with the production budget, notice that the merchandise purchasing budget is expressed in terms of units.

Direct Materials Purchases Budget

After the production budget is completed, the budgets for direct materials, direct labour, and overhead can be prepared. The **direct materials purchases budget** shows the amount and cost of raw materials to be purchased in each time period; it depends on the expected use of materials in production and the raw materials inventory needs of the firm. The company needs to prepare a separate direct materials purchases budget for every type of raw material used. The formula used for calculating purchases is as follows:

Purchases = Direct materials needed for production
+ Direct materials in desired ending inventory (EI)
− Direct materials in beginning inventory (BI)

The quantity of direct materials in inventory is determined by the firm's inventory policy.

Moose Patties uses two types of raw materials: plain T-shirts and ink. The direct materials purchases budgets for each of these two materials are presented in Cornerstone 9.4.

Preparing a Direct Materials Purchases Budget

CORNERSTONE 9.4

Information:

Budgeted units to be produced for each quarter of 2017: 1,060, 1,260, 1,600, and 1,800. Plain T-shirts cost $3 each, and ink (for the screen-printing) costs $0.20 per gram. On a per-unit basis, the factory needs one plain T-shirt and five grams of ink for each logo T-shirt that it produces. Moose Patties' policy is to have 10 percent of the following quarter's production needs in ending inventory. The factory has 58 plain T-shirts and 390 grams of ink on hand on January 1, 2017. At the end of the year, the desired ending inventory is 106 plain T-shirts and 530 grams of ink.

Required:

1. Calculate the ending inventory of plain T-shirts and of ink for quarters 2 and 3.
2. Prepare a direct materials purchases budget for plain T-shirts and for ink.

Solution:

1. Ending inventory plain T-shirts, quarter 2 = 0.10 × (1,600 units × 1 T-shirt) = 160
   Ending inventory plain T-shirts, quarter 3 = 0.10 × (1,800 units × 1 T-shirt) = 180
   Ending inventory ink, quarter 2 = 0.10 × (1,600 units × 5 grams) = 800
   Ending inventory ink, quarter 3 = 0.10 × (1,800 units × 5 grams) = 900

2.

Moose Patties Inc.
Direct Materials Purchases Budget
For the Year Ending December 31, 2017

Plain T-shirts	**Quarter**				
	1	**2**	**3**	**4**	**Year**
Units to be produced	1,060	1,260	1,600	1,800	5,720
Direct materials per unit	× 1	× 1	× 1	× 1	× 1
Production needs	1,060	1,260	1,600	1,800	5,720
Desired ending inventory	126	160	180	106	106
Total needs	1,186	1,420	1,780	1,906	5,826
Less: Beginning inventory	(58)	(126)	(160)	(180)	(58)
Direct materials to be purchased	1,128	1,294	1,620	1,726	5,768
Cost per T-shirt	× $3	× $3	× $3	× $3	× $3
Total purchase cost plain T-shirts	$3,384	$3,882	$4,860	$5,178	$17,304

Ink	**Quarter**				
	1	**2**	**3**	**4**	**Year**
Units to be produced	1,060	1,260	1,600	1,800	5,720
Direct materials per unit	× 5	× 5	× 5	× 5	× 5
Production needs	5,300	6,300	8,000	9,000	28,600
Desired ending inventory	630	800	900	530	530
Total needs	5,930	7,100	8,900	9,530	29,130
Less: Beginning inventory	(390)	(630)	(800)	(900)	(390)
Direct materials to be purchased	5,540	6,470	8,100	8,630	28,740
Cost per gram	× $0.20	× $0.20	× $0.20	× $0.20	× $0.20
Total purchase cost of ink	$1,108	$1,294	$1,620	$1,726	$ 5,748
Total direct materials purchase cost	$4,492	$5,176	$6,480	$6,904	$23,052

(Continued)

CORNERSTONE 9.4

(Continued)

Why:

Because once the level of production has been established, these objectives must be expressed in terms of how much material needs to be purchased in order to allow the production operation to meet the goals.

Notice how similar the direct materials purchases budget is to the production budget. Consider the first quarter, starting with the plain T-shirts. It takes one plain T-shirt for every logo T-shirt, so the 1,060 logo T-shirts to be produced are multiplied by 1 to obtain the number of plain T-shirts needed for production. Next, the desired ending inventory of 126 (10 percent of the next quarter's production needs) is added. Thus, 1,186 plain T-shirts are needed during the first quarter. Of this total, 58 are already in beginning inventory, meaning that the remaining 1,128 must be purchased. Multiplying the 1,128 plain T-shirts by the cost of $3 each gives Moose Patties the $3,384 expected cost of plain T-shirt purchases for the first quarter of the year. The direct materials purchases budget for ink is done the same way as for the T-shirts, except that each T-shirt logo uses 5 grams of ink. Consequently, the total T-shirts to be produced must be multiplied by 5 to get the production needs of ink.

Direct Labour Budget

The **direct labour budget** shows the total direct labour hours and the direct labour cost needed for the number of units in the production budget. As with direct materials, the budgeted hours of direct labour are determined by the relationship between labour and output.

Suppose that it takes 0.12 direct labour hours to produce a single T-shirt, and that the average wage rate is $11.50 per direct labour hour. The direct labour budget for Moose Patties is shown in Cornerstone 9.5.

CORNERSTONE 9.5

Preparing a Direct Labour Budget

Information:

Recall from Cornerstone 9.2 that budgeted units to be produced for each quarter of 2017 are: 1,060, 1,260, 1,600, and 1,800. It takes 0.12 hour to produce one T-shirt. The average wage cost per hour is $11.50.

Required:

Prepare a direct labour budget.

Solution:

Moose Patties Inc.
Direct Labour Budget
For the Year Ending December 31, 2017

	Quarter				
	1	**2**	**3**	**4**	**Year**
Units to be produced	1,060	1,260	1,600	1,800	5,720
Direct labour time per unit in hours	× 0.12	× 0.12	× 0.12	× 0.12	× 0.12
Total hours needed	127.2	151.2	192.0	216.0	686.4
Average wage per hour	× $11.50	× $11.50	× $11.50	× $11.50	× $11.50
Total direct labour cost	$1,463	$1,739	$2,208	$2,484	$7,894

(Continued)

Why:

Because direct labour is a key component of the production operation and factory workers will have a target level of units to be produced for each hour of labour. These targets will then be translated into the number of direct labour hours needed to meet the production requirements established in the production budget, and the company will be able to ensure that it has the proper workforce available to meet its needs.

CORNERSTONE 9.5

(Continued)

While Cornerstone 9.5 demonstrates a practical approach to developing a direct labour budget, many organizations cannot use this approach. Given requirements negotiated in collective agreements in unionized environments or knowledge workers requiring a minimum number of employment hours, many firms cannot base the required number of direct labour hours on production volumes. For example, the income for salaried employees is stated in the employment contract and is independent of production output. For many firms, the direct labour budget will be dependent upon the agreed terms of employment with its employees.

Overhead Budget

The **overhead budget** shows the expected value of all production costs other than direct materials and direct labour, such as utilities and janitorial services. Many companies use direct labour hours as the driver for overhead. Then, costs that vary with direct labour hours are pooled and called variable overhead. The remaining overhead items are pooled into fixed overhead. The method for preparing an overhead budget using this approach to cost behaviour is shown in Cornerstone 9.6.

Preparing an Overhead Budget

CORNERSTONE 9.6

Information:

Refer to Cornerstone 9.5 for the direct labour budget. The variable overhead rate is $5 per direct labour hour; fixed overhead is budgeted at $1,645 per quarter (this amount includes $540 per quarter for depreciation).

Required:

Prepare an overhead budget.

Solution:

Moose Patties Inc.
Overhead Budget
For the Year Ending December 31, 2017

	Quarter				
	1	**2**	**3**	**4**	**Year**
Budgeted direct labour hours	127.2	151.2	192.0	216.0	686.4
Variable overhead rate	× $5	× $5	× $5	× $5	× $5
Budgeted variable overhead	$ 636	$ 756	$ 960	$1,080	$ 3,432
Budgeted fixed overhead*	1,645	1,645	1,645	1,645	6,580
Total overhead	$2,281	$2,401	$2,605	$2,725	$10,012

* Includes $540 of depreciation in each quarter.

(Continued)

CORNERSTONE
9.6

(Continued)

Why:

Because manufacturing overhead must be incurred in order to provide the appropriate level of support for the production operations. Being able to predict the overhead requirements will allow the company to ensure that it has arrangements in place to supply these requirements to the production process.

analytical Q&A

Assume that a product uses 2 hours of direct labour per unit. Expected production for the year is 1,250 units. The average wage cost per hour is $12. What is the budget for direct labour cost?

Answers on pages 734 to 738.

Ending Finished Goods Inventory Budget

The **ending finished goods inventory budget** supplies information needed for the balance sheet and also serves as an important input for the preparation of the cost of goods sold budget. To prepare this budget, the unit cost of producing each T-shirt must be calculated by using information from the direct materials, direct labour, and overhead budgets. The way to calculate the unit cost of a T-shirt and the cost of the planned ending inventory is shown in Cornerstone 9.7.

CORNERSTONE 9.7

Preparing an Ending Finished Goods Inventory Budget

Information:

Refer to Cornerstones 9.4, 9.5, and 9.6 for the direct materials, direct labour, and overhead budgets, respectively.

Required:

1. Calculate the unit product cost.
2. Prepare an ending finished goods inventory budget.

Solution:

1. Unit cost computation:

Direct materials:		
Plain T-shirt	$3.00	
Ink	1.00	$4.00
Direct labour (0.12 hr. @ $11.50)		1.38
Overhead:		
Variable (0.12 hr. @ $5)		0.60
Fixed (0.12 hr. @ $9.59*)		1.15
Total unit cost		$7.13

$$^* \frac{\text{Budgeted fixed overhead}}{\text{Budgeted direct labour hours}} = \frac{\$6{,}580}{686.4} = \$9.59$$

(Continued)

CORNERSTONE

9.7

(Continued)

2.

Moose Patties Inc.
Ending Finished Goods Inventory Budget
For the Year Ending December 31, 2017

Logo T-shirts	200
Unit cost	× $7.13
Total ending inventory	$1,426

Why:

Because part of the production budget calculation was a determination of the finished goods inventory in units throughout the process. At this point, we need to translate the units of finished goods inventory into a dollar value that represents the investment required by the company and that can be used in our GAAP compliant financial statement presentation.

Cost of Goods Sold Budget

Assuming that the beginning finished goods inventory is valued at $1,251, the budgeted cost of goods sold schedule can be prepared using information from Cornerstones 9.4 to 9.7. The **cost of goods sold budget** reveals the expected cost of the goods to be sold and is shown in Cornerstone 9.8.

Preparing a Cost of Goods Sold Budget

CORNERSTONE 9.8

Information:

Refer to Cornerstones 9.4 through 9.7 for the direct materials, direct labour, overhead, and ending finished goods budgets.

Required:

Prepare a cost of goods sold budget.

Solution:

Moose Patties Inc.
Cost of Goods Sold Budget
For the Year Ending December 31, 2017

Direct materials used (Cornerstone 9.4)*	$22,880
Direct labour used (Cornerstone 9.5)	7,894
Overhead (Cornerstone 9.6)	10,012
Budgeted manufacturing costs	40,786
Beginning finished goods	1,251
Goods available for sale	42,037
Less: Ending finished goods (Cornerstone 9.7)	(1,426)
Budgeted cost of goods sold	$40,611

* Production needs = (5,720 plain T-shirts × $3.00) + (28,600 grams ink × $0.20).

(Continued)

CORNERSTONE
9.8

(Continued)

Why:

Because the cost of goods sold is one of the fundamental amounts used to calculate corporate profitability. Certain financial ratios are calculated using cost of goods sold, and a company can determine whether it will meet its objectives in this area by looking at the draft budget.

analytical Q&A

Assume that the budget formula for overhead costs (OH) is OH = $2,000 + $3X, where X = total direct labour hours. If the company expects to work 5,000 direct labour hours, what is the budgeted variable overhead? Budgeted fixed overhead? Budgeted total overhead?

Answers on pages 734 to 738.

Selling and Administrative Expenses Budget

The next budget to be prepared, the **selling and administrative expenses budget**, outlines planned expenditures for nonmanufacturing activities. As with overhead, selling and administrative expenses can be broken down into fixed and variable components. Such items as sales commissions, freight, and supplies vary with sales activity. The selling and administrative expenses budget is illustrated in Cornerstone 9.9.

CORNERSTONE 9.9 Preparing a Selling and Administrative Expenses Budget

Information:

Refer to Cornerstone 9.1 for the sales budget. Variable expenses are $0.10 per unit sold. Salaries average $1,420 per quarter; utilities, $50 per quarter; and depreciation, $150 per quarter. Advertising for quarters 1 through 4 is $100, $200, $800, and $500, respectively.

Required:

Prepare a selling and administrative expenses budget.

Solution:

Moose Patties Inc.
Selling and Administrative Expenses Budget
For the Year Ending December 31, 2017

	Quarter				
	1	**2**	**3**	**4**	**Year**
Planned sales in units (Cornerstone 9.1)	1,000	1,200	1,500	2,000	5,700
Variable selling and administrative expenses per unit	× $0.10	× $0.10	× $0.10	× $0.10	× $0.10
Total variable expenses	$ 100	$ 120	$ 150	$ 200	$ 570
Fixed selling and administrative expenses:					
Salaries	1,420	1,420	1,420	1,420	5,680
Utilities	50	50	50	50	200
Advertising	100	200	800	500	1,600
Depreciation	150	150	150	150	600
Total fixed expenses	1,720	1,820	2,420	2,120	8,080
Total selling and administrative expenses	$ 1,820	$ 1,940	$ 2,570	$ 2,320	$ 8,650

(Continued)

Why:

Because the nature of the company's operations as determined in the previous budgets will determine the size and type of organization needed to meet its objectives. The company must ensure that it has or can acquire the resources to meet these needs.

CORNERSTONE 9.9

(Continued)

Budgeted Income Statement

With the completion of the budgeted cost of goods sold schedule and the budgeted selling and administrative expenses budget, Moose Patties has all the operating budgets needed to prepare an estimate of *operating* income. The way to prepare this budgeted income statement is shown in Cornerstone 9.10. The eight budgets already prepared, along with the budgeted operating income statement, define the operating budget for Moose Patties.

concept Q&A

What operating budgets are needed to calculate a budgeted unit cost?

Answers on pages 734 to 738.

Preparing a Budgeted Income Statement

CORNERSTONE 9.10

Information:

Refer to Cornerstones 9.1, 9.8, 9.9, and 9.13 for the sales budget, the cost of goods sold budget, the selling and administrative expenses budget, and the cash budget, respectively. Assume that the tax rate is 40 percent.

Required:

Prepare a budgeted income statement.

Solution:

Moose Patties Inc.
Budgeted Income Statement
For the Year Ending December 31, 2017

Sales (Cornerstone 9.1)	$ 57,000
Less: Cost of goods sold (Cornerstone 9.8)	(40,611)
Gross margin	16,389
Less: Selling and administrative expenses (Cornerstone 9.9)	(8,650)
Operating income	7,739
Less: Interest expense (Cornerstone 9.13)	(70)
Income before taxes	7,669
Less: Income taxes (0.40 × $7,669)	(3,068)
Net income	$ 4,601

Why:

Because the budgeted income statement can be prepared by reference to each of the component costs already calculated, together with interest expense from the cash budget. The budgeted income statement will indicate to the company's management whether the current budget assumptions will allow the company to achieve its financial targets. If not, the budgeting process will have to be reviewed and adjustments made.

analytical Q&A

Assume that the budgeted cost of goods sold is $700. There is no beginning finished goods inventory. Budgeted manufacturing costs are $1,000. What is the budgeted finished goods inventory?

Answers on pages 734 to 738.

analytical Q&A

Assume that sales agents are paid a commission of 2 percent of sales revenue. Further, the only fixed selling expense is advertising, which is expected to be $10,000. If sales revenue is budgeted at $500,000, what is the budgeted selling expense?

Answers on pages 734 to 738.

Operating income is *not* equivalent to the net income of a firm. To yield net income, interest expense and taxes must be subtracted from operating income. The interest expense deduction is taken from the cash budget for Moose Patties (Cornerstone 9.13), a budget discussed in the section on financial budgets. The taxes owed depend on the current federal and provincial tax laws. For simplicity, a combined rate of 40 percent is assumed.

PREPARING THE FINANCIAL BUDGET

The remaining budgets found in the master budget are the financial budgets. The usual financial budgets prepared are:

1. The cash budget
2. The budgeted balance sheet
3. The budget for capital expenditures

The master budget also contains a plan for acquiring long-term assets—that is, assets that have a time horizon that extends beyond the one-year operating period. Some of these assets may be purchased during the coming year; plans to purchase others may be detailed for future periods. This part of the master budget is typically referred to as the *capital budget*. Decision making for capital expenditures is considered in Chapter 14. Accordingly, only the cash budget and the budgeted balance sheet will be illustrated here.

OBJECTIVE 

Define and prepare the financial budget, identify its major components, and explain the interrelationships of its various components.

Cash Budget

Understanding cash flows is critical in managing a business. Often, a business successfully produces and sells products but fails because of timing problems associated with cash inflows and outflows. Examples include the smallest entrepreneurs, who are required by suppliers to pay cash up front but must sell to their customers on credit, as well as large corporations. As an example, more than 839 of Canada's 1,700 mining firms faced a cash crunch in early 2013 as metal prices declined while exploration and production prices soared.[4]

concept Q&A

Why is it not possible to prepare a budgeted income statement by using only operating budgets?

Answers on pages 734 to 738.

By knowing when cash inflows and outflows are likely to occur, a manager can plan to borrow cash when needed and to repay the loans during periods of excess cash. Because cash flow is the lifeblood of an organization, the cash budget is one of the most important budgets in the master budget. The basic structure of a **cash budget** includes cash receipts, disbursements, any excess or deficiency of cash, and financing. At its simplest, a cash budget is cash inflows minus cash outflows. Suppose, for example, that a company expects $3,000 in the cash account on June 1. During June, cash sales of $45,000 are predicted, as are cash disbursements of $39,000. The resulting cash budget for June is illustrated in Exhibit 9.3.

Cash available consists of the beginning cash balance and the expected cash receipts. Expected cash receipts include all sources of cash for the period being considered, principally from sales. Since a large proportion of sales is usually on account, a major task of an organization is to determine the pattern of collection for its accounts receivable. If a company has been in business for a while, it can use past experience in creating an expected accounts receivable aging schedule. In other words, the company can determine, on average, what percentages of its accounts receivable are paid in the months

[4] Allison Martell and Euan Rocha, "Hundreds of Struggling Junior Miners Face Delisting in Crisis That Could Choke Off Project Pipeline for Majors," *The Financial Post*, http://business.financialpost.com/2013/07/25/canada-junior-miners-crisis/, July 25, 2013, accessed on April 29, 2014.

EXHIBIT 9.3

The Cash Budget

Expected beginning balance	$ 3,000
Add cash receipts	45,000
Cash available	48,000
Less disbursements	39,000
Expected ending balance	$ 9,000

following sales. Cornerstone 9.11 shows how to create an accounts receivable aging schedule for Moose Patties.

While Moose Patties expects no bad debts expense, that may not be the case for all firms. If a firm expects less than 100 percent of the credit sales to be received in cash, then it expects some bad debts. For example, if a firm expects to be repaid 98 percent of credit sales, then it expects 2 percent bad debts. In other words, not everyone pays for their credit sales. This 2 percent is ignored for purposes of cash budgeting since it will never be received. Different firms have different accounts receivable repayment experiences.

CORNERSTONE 9.11

Preparing an Accounts Receivable Collections Schedule

Information:

Moose Patties expects that, on average, 25 percent of total sales are cash and 75 percent of total sales are on credit. Of the credit sales, Moose Patties expects that 90 percent will be paid in cash during the quarter of sale, and the remaining 10 percent will be paid in the following quarter. Recall from Cornerstone 9.1 that Moose Patties expects the following total sales:

Quarter 1	$10,000
Quarter 2	12,000
Quarter 3	15,000
Quarter 4	20,000

The balance in accounts receivable as of the last quarter of 2016 was $1,350. This will be collected in cash during the first quarter of 2017.

Required:

1. Calculate cash sales expected in each quarter of 2017.
2. Prepare a schedule showing cash receipts from sales expected in each quarter of 2017.

Solution:

1. Cash sales expected in Quarter 1 = $10,000 × 0.25 = $2,500
   Cash sales expected in Quarter 2 = $12,000 × 0.25 = $3,000
   Cash sales expected in Quarter 3 = $15,000 × 0.25 = $3,750
   Cash sales expected in Quarter 4 = $20,000 × 0.25 = $5,000

(Continued)

CORNERSTONE 9.11

(Continued)

2. Cash from credit sales:

Source	Quarter 1	2	3	4
Cash sales	$ 2,500	$ 3,000	$ 3,750	$ 5,000
Received on account from:				
Quarter 4, 2016	1,350			
Quarter 1, 2017	6,750[a]	750[b]		
Quarter 2, 2017		8,100[c]	900[d]	
Quarter 3, 2017			10,125[e]	1,125[f]
Quarter 4, 2017				13,500[g]
Total cash receipts	$10,600	$11,850	$14,775	$19,625

[a] ($10,000 × 0.75)(0.9)
[b] ($10,000 × 0.75)(0.1)
[c] ($12,000 × 0.75)(0.9)
[d] ($12,000 × 0.75)(0.1)
[e] ($15,000 × 0.75)(0.9)
[f] ($15,000 × 0.75)(0.1)
[g] ($20,000 × 0.75)(0.9)

Why:

Because cash collections from customers represent the primary source of cash to the company, and this is dependent on how long it takes the customers, on average, to pay their bills. Accounts receivable aging allows us to predict when amounts will be received.

The cash disbursements section lists all planned cash outlays for the period. All expenses that do not require a cash outlay are *excluded* from the list (e.g., depreciation is never included in the disbursements section). Just as sources of cash may require an accounts receivable aging schedule to calculate cash expected from credit sales, the disbursements section may require care in handling payments on account. Cornerstone 9.12 shows how to handle timing differences arising from paying for items on account.

CORNERSTONE 9.12

Determining Cash Payments on Accounts Payable

Information:

Moose Patties purchases all raw materials on account; 80 percent of purchases are paid for in the quarter of purchase. The remaining 20 percent are paid for in the following quarter. The purchases for the fourth quarter of 2016 were $5,000. Cornerstone 9.4 shows total expected purchases of raw materials for each quarter of 2017. These are shown here.

Quarter 1	$4,492
Quarter 2	5,176
Quarter 3	6,480
Quarter 4	6,904

(Continued)

CORNERSTONE
9.12

(Continued)

Required:

Prepare a schedule showing anticipated payments for accounts payable for materials.

Solution:

Cash needed for payments on account:

	Quarter			
Source	**1**	**2**	**3**	**4**
Quarter 4, 2016	$1,000[a]			
Quarter 1, 2017	3,594[b]	$ 898[c]		
Quarter 2, 2017		4,141[d]	$1,035[e]	
Quarter 3, 2017			5,184[f]	$1,296[g]
Quarter 4, 2017				5,523[h]
Total cash needed	$4,594	$5,039	$6,219	$6,819

[a] ($5,000 × 0.20)
[b] ($4,492 × 0.80)
[c] ($4,492 × 0.20)
[d] ($5,176 × 0.80)
[e] ($5,176 × 0.20)
[f] ($6,480 × 0.80)
[g] ($6,480 × 0.20)
[h] ($6,904 × 0.80)

Why:

Because, offsetting the cash receipts calculated previously, a company must make payments of various amounts to its suppliers. Establishing a policy of how suppliers will be paid allows a company to predict, with reasonable accuracy, how cash will be spent. These payments will represent the major cash outflows for the company.

A disbursement that is typically not included in the disbursements section is interest on short-term borrowing. This interest expenditure is reserved for the section on loan repayments.

Cash Excess or Deficiency The cash budget shown in Exhibit 9.3 is a very simple one. Often companies expand on this format, as is done with Moose Patties in Cornerstone 9.13, by adding lines to show any borrowing or repayment necessary to achieve a minimum desired cash amount. When this is done, the preliminary ending cash balance is called *cash excess* or *cash deficiency*. The cash excess or cash deficiency line is compared to the minimum cash balance required by company policy, which is simply the lowest amount of cash on hand the company finds acceptable.

Consider your own chequing account. You probably try to keep at least some cash in the account, perhaps because by having a minimum balance you avoid service charges, or because a minimum balance allows you to make an unplanned purchase. Similarly, companies also require minimum cash balances. The amount varies from firm to firm, and is determined by each company's particular needs and policies. If a deficiency exists, a short-term loan will be needed. On the other hand, with a cash excess, the firm has the ability to repay loans and perhaps to make some temporary investments.

concept Q&A

Why would a company want a minimum cash balance? Suppose that the minimum cash balance is $1,000 and that the projected cash surplus is $500. What would a company have to do to achieve the desired minimum?

Answers on pages 734 to 738.

In the summer of 2012, former Bank of Canada governor Mark Carney famously chided corporate Canada for sitting on mountains of "dead money," the idle dollars on balance sheets that could instead feed economic growth. Carney, in widely quoted August remarks to the Canadian Autoworkers, insisted companies should put their cash holdings into circulation, either by investing or by giving those funds back to their shareholders in the form of dividends. To him, those pools of cash represent an untapped—and possibly last-ditch—source of stimulus in a difficult economic environment where more public spending is politically untenable and lowering interest rates is financially unwise.[5]

Borrowing and Repayments The final section of the cash budget consists of borrowings and repayments. If there is a deficiency, this section shows the necessary amount to be borrowed. When excess cash is available, this section shows planned repayments, including interest expense.

Ending Cash Balance The last line of the cash budget is the planned ending cash balance. This line represents the planned amount of cash the company wishes to have on hand at the end of the period after all receipts and disbursements, including borrowings and repayments, are considered. As a result, the ending cash balance line must equal or exceed the minimum required level. The way to prepare a cash budget is illustrated in Cornerstone 9.13.

CORNERSTONE 9.13

Preparing a Cash Budget

Information:

Refer to Cornerstones 9.5, 9.6, 9.9, 9.10, 9.11, and 9.12 as well as the following details:

a. A $1,000 minimum cash balance is required for the end of each quarter. Interest is 12 percent per year on any amounts borrowed. Interest payments are made only for the amount of the principal being repaid. All borrowing takes place at the beginning of a quarter, and all repayment takes place at the end of a quarter.
b. Budgeted depreciation is $540 per quarter for overhead and $150 per quarter for selling and administrative expenses (Cornerstones 9.6 and 9.9).
c. The capital budget for 2017 revealed plans to purchase additional screen-printing equipment. The cash outlay for the equipment, $6,500, will take place in the first quarter. The company plans to finance the acquisition of the equipment with operating cash, supplementing it with short-term loans as necessary.
d. Corporate income taxes are approximately $3,068 and will be paid at the end of the fourth quarter (Cornerstone 9.10).
e. Beginning cash balance is $5,200.
f. All amounts in the budget are to be rounded to the nearest dollar.

Required:

Prepare a cash budget for Moose Patties.

(Continued)

[5] John Lorinc, "Dead Money," *Canadian Business*, http://www.canadianbusiness.com/economy/dead-money/, February 12, 2013, accessed on April 29, 2014.

Solution:

CORNERSTONE
9.13
(Continued)

Moose Patties Inc.
Cash Budget
For the Year Ending December 31, 2017

	Quarter 1	2	3	4	Year	Source*
Beginning cash balance	$ 5,200	$ 1,000	$ 1,183	$ 3,046	$ 5,200	e
Cash sales and collections on account:	10,600	11,850	14,775	19,625	56,850	11
Total cash available	15,800	12,850	15,958	22,671	62,050	
Less disbursements:						
Payments for:						
Raw materials	(4,594)	(5,039)	(6,219)	(6,819)	(22,671)	12
Direct labour	(1,463)	(1,739)	(2,208)	(2,484)	(7,894)	5
Overhead	(1,741)	(1,861)	(2,065)	(2,185)	(7,852)	b,6
Selling and administrative	(1,670)	(1,790)	(2,420)	(2,170)	(8,050)	b,9
Income taxes	—	—	—	(3,068)	(3,068)	d,10
Equipment	(6,500)	—	—	—	(6,500)	c
Total disbursements	(15,968)	(10,429)	(12,912)	(16,726)	(56,035)	
Excess (deficiency) of cash available over needs	(168)	2,421	3,046	5,945	6,015	
Financing:						
Borrowings	1,168	—	—	—	1,168	
Repayments	—	(1,168)	—	—	(1,168)	a
Interest**	—	(70)	—	—	(70)	a
Total financing	1,168	(1,238)	—	—	(70)	
Ending cash balance***	$ 1,000	$ 1,183	$ 3,046	$ 5,945	$ 5,945	

* Letters refer to the detailed information above. Numbers refer to Cornerstone schedules.
** Interest payment is $6/12 \times 0.12 \times \$1,168$. Since borrowings occur at the beginning of a quarter and repayments at the end of a quarter, the principal repayment takes place at the end of the second quarter.
*** Total cash available minus total disbursements plus (or minus) total financing.

Why:
The cash budget will indicate to the company when cash receipts will occur and when cash disbursements will be required. The compilation of all cash receipts and cash disbursements will allow a company to determine, in advance, when it might need to acquire additional cash resources from lenders and when these funds will be able to be repaid.

Cornerstone 9.13 reveals that much of the information needed to prepare the cash budget comes from the operating budgets and from the schedules for cash receipts on accounts receivable and cash payments on accounts payable.

The cash budget underscores the importance of breaking down the annual budget into smaller time periods. The cash budget for the year gives the impression that sufficient operating cash will be available to finance the acquisition of the new equipment. Quarterly information, however, shows the need for short-term borrowing ($1,168) because of both the acquisition of the new equipment and the timing of the firm's cash flows. Most firms prepare monthly cash budgets, and some even prepare weekly and daily budgets.

Another significant piece of information emerges from Moose Patties' cash budget. By the end of the third quarter, the firm has more cash ($2,046 more) than necessary to meet operating needs. Moose Patties' management should consider

concept Q&A

Sales for a month totalled $10,000. Cash receipts for the same month were $15,000. How is it possible for cash receipts to be more than sales?

Answers on pages 734 to 738.

investing the excess cash in an interest-bearing account. Once plans are finalized for use of the excess cash, the cash budget should be revised to reflect those plans. Budgeting is a dynamic process. As the budget is developed, new information becomes available, and better plans can be formulated.

Budgeted Balance Sheet

The budgeted balance sheet depends on information contained in the current balance sheet and in the other budgets in the master budget. Exhibit 9.4 shows the budgeted balance sheets as at December 31, 2016, and December 31, 2017. Explanations for the budgeted figures are provided in the footnotes.

YOUDECIDE Cash Budgeting for a Small Painting Company

You are the accountant for a number of small businesses in your town, one of which is Ramon's Paint and Plaster. Ramon has been through a tough year as construction in the town has been declining. However, new home construction is picking up and Ramon has been asked to bid on twice as many jobs in the past month as he was last year at this time. Ramon needs to know what his cash flow will be for the coming year. You are starting to amass information to help you forecast monthly cash inflows and outflows for the next six months.

What information do you need to forecast cash inflows and outflows for the paint and plaster business for the next six months?

This is a two-part problem. The first question, what inflows of cash are expected, depends on the number and size of the jobs Ramon can bid on successfully. Ramon's business has been primarily residential, so you'll need to know the number of housing starts (or the number of building permits applied for) and the number of remodelling jobs expected. You will also need to consider the price Ramon charges as well as the probability of prompt payment. Some builders have a good reputation for paying promptly in the first ten days of the month following work by Ramon's crew. Others lag behind. While you can encourage Ramon to work primarily with the better builders, he may be forced to accept some jobs with contractors who frequently pay later.

The second question requires a forecast of the potential cash outflows. Ramon has a crew of six workers and the hourly rate is known. He also can calculate the cost of the paint and plaster materials fairly accurately, once the size of the job is known. It will be difficult to forecast the cash inflows and outflows too far in advance. As a result, you will probably want to set up the cash budget for one to three months in advance and then update the forecasted numbers as the year progresses.

Forecasts of cash inflows and outflows depend on the economic conditions, the reputation of the payment patterns of the customers, and the prices charged both for the jobs obtained and for the supplies used. Information from the past year can be used as a baseline; however, changing economic conditions will affect future amounts.

OBJECTIVE 

Describe the behavioural dimension of budgeting.

Not-for-Profit Budgeting

Although this chapter has focused primarily on the budgeting process of profit-seeking firms, it is important to highlight that the budgeting process is equally important for not-for-profit organizations. Having practical budgets enables not-for-profit organizations to operationalize their mission and vision into a comprehensive plan. Similar to the sales budget that companies develop, a not-for-profit entity will have a budget detailing its expected revenue streams from donations, grants, endowments, and other sources. Other operating budgets will then be prepared based upon the nature of the activities performed by the not-for-profit organization. For example, some groups may be producing goods for sale where any profits are later transferred to beneficiaries. Consequently, these organizations would require a production budget, a direct materials budget, and a direct labour budget (assuming the workers are not volunteers). Other not-for-profit entities provide services, implying that they would require different operating budgets. Although there is no single template to use for not-for-profit organizations, budgeting remains an important responsibility for these entities.

EXHIBIT 9.4

Budgeted Balance Sheet

Moose Patties Inc. Balance Sheet December 31, 2016		
Assets		
Current assets:		
Cash	$ 5,200	
Accounts receivable	1,350	
Raw materials inventory	252	
Finished goods inventory	1,251	
Total current assets		$ 8,053
Property, plant, and equipment (PP&E):		
Land	1,100	
Building and equipment	30,000	
Accumulated depreciation	(5,000)	
Total PP&E		26,100
Total assets		$34,153
Liabilities and Shareholders' Equity		
Current liabilities:		
Accounts payable		$ 1,000
Shareholders' equity:		
Retained earnings		33,153
Total liabilities and shareholders' equity		$34,153

Moose Patties Inc. Budgeted Balance Sheet December 31, 2017		
Assets		
Current assets:		
Cash	$ 5,945[a]	
Accounts receivable	1,500[b]	
Raw materials inventory	424[c]	
Finished goods inventory	1,426[d]	
Total current assets		$ 9,295
Property, plant, and equipment (PP&E):		
Land	1,100[e]	
Building and equipment	36,500[f]	
Accumulated depreciation	(7,760)[g]	
Total PP&E		29,840
Total assets		$39,135
Liabilities and Shareholders' Equity		
Current liabilities:		
Accounts payable		$ 1,381[h]
Shareholders' equity:		
Retained earnings		37,754[i]
Total liabilities and shareholders' equity		$39,135

[a] Ending balance from Cornerstone 9.13.
[b] Ten percent of fourth-quarter credit sales (0.75 × $20,000)—see Cornerstones 9.1 and 9.11.
[c] From Cornerstone 9.4 [(106 × $3) + (530 × $0.20)].
[d] From Cornerstone 9.7.
[e] From the December 31, 2016, balance sheet.
[f] December 31, 2016, balance ($30,000) plus new equipment acquisition of $6,500 (see the 2016 ending balance sheet and Cornerstone 9.13).
[g] From the December 31, 2016, balance sheet, Cornerstone 9.6, and Cornerstone 9.9 ($5,000 + $2,160 + $600).
[h] Twenty percent of fourth-quarter purchases (0.20 × $6,904)—see Cornerstones 9.4 and 9.12.
i $33,153 + $4,601 (December 31, 2016, balance plus net income from Cornerstone 9.10).

concept Q&A

In the last quarter of the fiscal year, a divisional manager chose to delay budgeted preventive maintenance expenditures so that the budgeted income goals could be achieved. Is this an example of goal congruent behaviour or dysfunctional behaviour?

Answers on pages 734 to 738.

USING BUDGETS FOR PERFORMANCE EVALUATION

Budgets are often used to judge the performance of managers. Bonuses, salary increases, and promotions are all affected by a manager's ability to achieve or beat budgeted goals. Since a manager's financial status and career can be affected, budgets can have a significant behavioural effect. Whether that effect is positive or negative depends in large part on how budgets are used.

Positive behaviour occurs when the goals of each manager are aligned with the goals of the organization and each manager has the drive to achieve them. The alignment of managerial and organizational goals is often referred to as **goal congruence**. If the budget is improperly administered, subordinate managers may subvert the organization's goals. **Dysfunctional behaviour** is individual behaviour that is in basic conflict with the goals of the organization.

An ideal budgetary system is one that achieves complete goal congruence and, simultaneously, motivates managers to achieve the organization's goals in an ethical manner. While an ideal budgetary system probably does not exist, research and practice have identified some key features that promote a reasonable degree of positive behaviour. These features include:

- frequent feedback on performance
- monetary and nonmonetary incentives
- participative budgeting
- realistic standards
- controllability of costs
- multiple measures of performance

Frequent Feedback on Performance

Managers need to know how they are doing as the year progresses. Frequent, timely performance reports allow them to know how successful their efforts have been, to take corrective actions, and to change plans as necessary.

Monetary and Nonmonetary Incentives

A sound budgetary system encourages goal-congruent behaviour. **Incentives** are the means an organization uses to influence a manager to exert effort to achieve an organization's goals. Traditional organizational theory assumes that employees are primarily motivated by monetary rewards, that they resist work, and that they are inefficient and wasteful. Thus, **monetary incentives** are used to control a manager's tendency to shirk and waste resources by relating budgetary performance to salary increases, bonuses, and promotions. The threat of dismissal is the ultimate economic sanction for poor performance. Modern organizational theory asserts that employees are motivated by more than economic factors. Employees are also motivated by intrinsic psychological and social factors, such as the satisfaction of a job well done, recognition, responsibility, self-esteem, and the nature of the work itself. Thus **nonmonetary incentives**—including job enrichment, increased responsibility and autonomy, and recognition programs—can be used to enhance a budgetary control system.

Participative Budgeting

Rather than imposing budgets on subordinate managers, **participative budgeting** allows subordinate managers considerable say in how the budgets are established. Typically, overall objectives are communicated to the manager, who helps develop a budget that is intended to accomplish these objectives. Participative budgeting communicates a sense of responsibility to subordinate managers and fosters creativity. Since the subordinate manager creates the budget, its goals will more likely become the manager's personal goals, resulting in greater goal congruence. The increased responsibility and challenge inherent in the process provide nonmonetary incentives that lead to a higher level of performance.

Participative budgeting has three potential problems:

1. Setting standards that are either too high or too low
2. Building slack into the budget (often referred to as padding the budget)
3. Pseudoparticipation

concept Q&A

Assume that a company evaluates and rewards its managers based on their ability to achieve budgeted goals. Why would the same company ask its managers to participate in setting their budgeted standards?

Answers on pages 734 to 738.

Standard Setting Some managers may tend to set the budget either too loose or too tight. Since budgeted goals tend to become the manager's goals when participation is allowed, making this mistake in setting the budget can result in decreased performance levels. If goals are too easily achieved, then a manager may lose interest, and performance may actually drop. Feeling challenged is important to aggressive and creative individuals. Similarly, setting the goals too high ensures failure to achieve the standards and frustrates the manager. This frustration, too, can lead to poorer performance (see Exhibit 9.5). The trick is to get managers in a participative setting to set high but achievable goals.

The Art of Standard Setting

Standard set too loose;
goals too easily achieved

Standard set too tight;
frustration results

Budgetary Slack The second problem with participative budgeting is the opportunity for managers to build slack into the budget. **Budgetary slack** (or *padding the budget*) exists when a manager deliberately underestimates revenues or overestimates costs in an effort to make the future period appear less attractive in the budget than they think it will be in reality. Either approach increases the likelihood that the manager will achieve the budget and consequently reduces the risk that the manager faces. Top management should carefully review budgets proposed by subordinate managers and provide input, where needed, in order to decrease the effects of building slack into the budget.

Pseudoparticipation The third problem with participation occurs when top management assumes total control of the budgeting process, seeking only superficial participation from lower-level managers. This practice is termed **pseudoparticipation**. Top management is simply obtaining formal acceptance of the budget from subordinate managers, not seeking real input. Accordingly, none of the behavioural benefits of participation will be realized.

Corporate and Social Responsibility

The act of padding the budget is questionable when considering what is viewed as ethical professional practice. When budgets are used to evaluate the performance of managers, there is an inherent conflict of interest. For example, if a manager is rewarded for remaining under-budget, the manager may include excess funds in the budget, thereby providing an easy performance target to reach. Regrettably, budgetary slack distorts expectations for both the division and the manager and reduces the resources available for other departments to access. Additionally, the planning purpose of the budgeting process is undermined in these situations. Padding the budget is certainly not communicating information fairly and objectively and constitutes a violation of the credibility standard. The motive for such behaviour is also not consistent with the professional responsibility to exhibit integrity. While it might be useful to estimate some costs at a little higher amount than expected to factor in uncertainty, excessive padding is misrepresentation and can lead to failure to spend resources in other areas that may need them.

Realistic Standards

Budgeted objectives are used to gauge performance; accordingly, they should be based on realistic conditions and expectations. Budgets should reflect operating realities, including the following:

- *Actual Levels of Activity:* Flexible budgets are used to ensure that budgeted costs can be realistically compared with costs for actual levels of activity.
- *Seasonal Variations:* Interim budgets should reflect seasonal effects. Toys "R" Us, for example, would expect much higher sales in the quarter that includes Christmas than in other quarters.
- *Efficiencies:* Budgetary cuts should be based on *planned* increases in efficiency and not simply arbitrary across-the-board reductions. Across-the-board cuts without any formal evaluation may impair the ability of some units to carry out their missions.
- *General Economic Trends:* General economic conditions also need to be considered. Budgeting for a significant increase in sales when a recession is projected is not only foolish but also potentially dangerous.

Controllability of Costs

Ideally, managers are held accountable only for costs that they can control. **Controllable costs** are costs whose level a manager can influence. For example, divisional managers have no power to authorize such corporate-level costs as research and development and salaries of top managers. Therefore, they should not be held accountable for the incurrence of those costs. If noncontrollable costs are put in the budgets of subordinate managers to help them understand that these costs also need to be covered, then they should be separated from controllable costs and labelled as *noncontrollable*.

Multiple Measures of Performance

Often, organizations make the mistake of using budgets as their only measure of managerial performance. While financial measures of performance are important, overemphasis can lead to a form of dysfunctional behaviour called *milking the firm* or *myopia*. **Myopic behaviour** occurs when a manager takes actions that improve budgetary performance in the short run but bring long-run harm to the firm. For example, to meet budgeted cost objectives or profits, managers can delay promoting deserving employees or reduce expenditures for preventative maintenance, advertising, and new product development. While budgetary measures alone cannot prevent myopic behaviour, using measures that are both financial and nonfinancial and that are long-term and short-term can alleviate this problem.

Recently having won a $25-billion shipbuilding contract to build combat ships for the Canadian Navy, Halifax-based Irving Shipbuilding will spend $250,000 per year to operate the Irving Shipbuilding Centre of Excellence at Nova Scotia Community College,[6] which will serve to train and recruit local students.[7] When evaluating the success of the contract, financial measures will undoubtedly be an important metric to ensure there is good value for the money; however, there are clear nonfinancial intentions of this contract (e.g., the training and education of Canadians). Focusing solely on short-term financial objectives would not consider the full benefits this contract is expected to provide.

SUMMARY OF LEARNING OBJECTIVES

LO1. Define budgeting, and discuss its role in planning, control, and decision making.

- Budgeting is the creation of a plan of action expressed in financial terms.
- Budgeting plays a key role in planning, control, and decision making.
- Budgets also serve to improve communication and coordination, a role that becomes increasingly important as organizations grow in size.
- The master budget, which is the comprehensive financial plan of an organization, is made up of the operating and financial budgets.

LO2. Define and prepare the operating budget, identify its major components, and explain the interrelationships of its various components.

- The operating budget is the budgeted income statement and all supporting budgets.
- The sales budget consists of the anticipated quantity and price of all products to be sold. It is done first, and the results feed directly into the production budget.
- The production budget gives the expected production in units to meet forecasted sales and desired ending inventory goals; expected production is supplemented by beginning inventory. The results of the production budget are needed for the direct materials purchases budget and the direct labour budget.
- The direct materials purchases budget gives the necessary purchases during the year for every type of raw material to meet production and desired ending inventory goals.
- The direct labour budget shows the number of direct labour hours, and the direct labour cost needed to support production. The resulting direct labour hours are needed to prepare the overhead budget.
- The overhead budget may be broken down into fixed and variable components to facilitate preparation of the budget.
- The selling and administrative expenses budget gives the forecasted costs for these functions.
- The finished goods inventory budget and the cost of goods sold budget detail production costs for the expected ending inventory and the units sold, respectively.
- The budgeted income statement outlines the net income to be realized if budgeted plans come to fruition.

LO3. Define and prepare the financial budget, identify its major components, and explain the interrelationships of its various components.

- The financial budget includes the cash budget, the capital expenditures budget, and the budgeted balance sheet.
- The cash budget is the beginning balance in the cash account, plus anticipated receipts, minus anticipated disbursements, plus or minus any necessary borrowing.
- The budgeted (or pro forma) balance sheet gives the anticipated ending balances of the asset, liability, and equity accounts if budgeted plans hold.

[6] Government of Nova Scotia news release, "Nova Scotia Gets Ready to Build Ships," October 19, 2012, http://novascotia.ca/news/release/?id=20121019001, accessed on April 30, 2014.
[7] Barrie McKenna, "Why Training Workers in Canada Beats Importing Them from Abroad," *The Globe and Mail*, December 16, 2012, http://www.theglobeandmail.com/report-on-business/economy/canada-competes/why-training-workers-in-canada-beats-importing-them-from-abroad/article6460050/, accessed on May 1, 2014.

LO4. Describe the behavioural dimension of budgeting.

- The success of a budgetary system depends on how seriously human factors are considered.
- To discourage dysfunctional behaviour, organizations should avoid overemphasizing budgets as a control mechanism.
- Budgets can be improved as performance measures by using participative budgeting and other nonmonetary incentives, providing frequent feedback on performance, using flexible budgeting, ensuring that the budgetary objectives reflect reality, and holding managers accountable for only controllable costs.

SUMMARY OF IMPORTANT EQUATIONS

1. Units to be produced = Expected unit sales + Units in desired ending inventory (EI) − Units in beginning inventory (BI)
2. Purchases = Direct materials needed for production + Direct materials in desired ending inventory (EI) − Direct materials in beginning inventory (BI)
3. *For retail firms:* Units to be purchased = Expected unit sales + Units in desired ending inventory (EI) − Units in beginning inventory (BI)

CORNERSTONES

GLOSSARY

Budget committee A committee responsible for setting budgetary policies and goals, reviewing and approving the budget, and resolving any differences that may arise in the budgetary process. (p. 424)

Budget director The individual responsible for directing and coordinating the overall budgeting process. (p. 424)

Budgetary slack The process of padding the budget by overestimating costs and underestimating revenues. (p. 447)

Budgets Plans of action expressed in financial terms. (p. 422)

Cash budget A detailed plan that outlines all sources and uses of cash. (p. 438)

Continuous budget A moving 12-month budget with a future month added as the current month expires. (p. 424)

Control The process of setting standards, receiving feedback on actual performance, and taking corrective action whenever actual performance deviates significantly from planned performance. (p. 423)

Controllable costs Costs that managers have the power to influence. (p. 448)

Cost of goods sold budget The total product cost of goods expected to be sold during the period. (p. 435)

Direct labour budget A budget showing the total direct labour hours needed and the associated cost for the number of units in the production budget. (p. 432)

Direct materials purchases budget A budget that outlines the expected usage of materials production and purchases of the direct materials required. (p. 430)

Dysfunctional behaviour Individual behaviour that conflicts with the goals of the organization. (p. 446)

Ending finished goods inventory budget A budget that describes planned ending inventory of finished goods in units and dollars. (p. 434)

Financial budgets The portions of the master budget that include the cash budget, the budgeted balance sheet, the budgeted statement of cash flows, and the capital budget. (p. 424)

Goal congruence The alignment of an employee's personal goals with those of the organization. (p. 446)

Incentives The positive or negative measures taken by an organization to induce an employee to exert effort toward achieving the organization's goals. (p. 446)

Master budget The collection of all area and activity budgets representing a firm's comprehensive plan of action. (p. 423)

Merchandise purchasing budget A budget detailing how many units must be purchased to meet sales needs and to satisfy ending inventory requirements. (p. 429)

Monetary incentives The use of economic rewards to motivate managers. (p. 446)

Myopic behaviour Actions that improve budgetary performance in the short run, but which bring long-run harm to the firm. (p. 448)

Nonmonetary incentives The use of psychological and social rewards to motivate managers. (p. 446)

Operating budgets Budgets associated with the income-producing activities of an organization. (p. 424)

Overhead budget A budget that reveals the planned expenditures for all indirect manufacturing items. (p. 433)

Participative budgeting An approach to budgeting that allows employees who will be held accountable for budgetary performance to participate in the budget's development. (p. 446)

Production budget A budget that shows how many units must be produced to meet sales needs and to satisfy ending inventory requirements. (p. 427)

Pseudoparticipation A budgetary system in which top management solicits inputs from lower-level managers and then ignores those inputs. Thus, in reality, budgets are dictated from above. (p. 447)

Sales budget A budget that describes expected sales in units and dollars for the coming period. (p. 425)

Selling and administrative expenses budget A budget that outlines planned expenditures for non-manufacturing activities. (p. 436)

Strategic plan The long-term plan for future activities and operations, usually involving at least five years. (p. 422)

REVIEW PROBLEMS

I. Select Operational Budgets

Joven Products produces coat racks. The projected sales for the first quarter of the coming year and the beginning and ending inventory data are as follows:

Unit sales	100,000
Unit price	$15
Units in beginning inventory	8,000
Units in targeted ending inventory	12,000

The coat racks are moulded and then painted. Each rack requires four kilograms of metal, which costs $2.50 per kilogram. The beginning inventory of materials is 4,000 kilograms. Joven Products wants to have 6,000 kilograms of metal in inventory at the end of the quarter. Each rack produced requires 30 minutes of direct labour time, which is billed at $18 per hour.

Required:

1. Prepare a sales budget for the first quarter.
2. Prepare a production budget for the first quarter.
3. Prepare a direct materials purchases budget for the first quarter.
4. Prepare a direct labour budget for the first quarter.

Solution:

1.

Joven Products
Sales Budget
For the First Quarter

Units	100,000
Unit price	× $15
Sales	$1,500,000

2.

Joven Products
Production Budget
For the First Quarter

Sales (in units)	100,000
Desired ending inventory	12,000
Total needs	112,000
Less: Beginning inventory	8,000
Units to be produced	104,000

3.

Joven Products
Direct Materials Purchases Budget
For the First Quarter

Units to be produced	104,000
Direct materials per unit (kilograms)	× 4
Production needs (kilograms)	416,000
Desired ending inventory (kilograms)	6,000
Total needs (kilograms)	422,000
Less: Beginning inventory (kilograms)	4,000
Materials to be purchased (kilograms)	418,000
Cost per kilogram	× $2.50
Total purchase cost	$1,045,000

4.

Joven Products
Direct Labour Budget
For the First Quarter

Units to be produced	104,000
Labour: Hours per unit	× 0.5
Total hours needed	52,000
Cost per hour	× $18
Total direct labour cost	$936,000

II. Cash Budgeting

Kylles Inc. expects to receive cash from sales of $45,000 in March. In addition, Kylles expects to sell property worth $3,500. Payments for materials and supplies are expected to total $10,000, direct labour payroll will be $12,500, and other expenditures are budgeted at $14,900. On March 1, the cash account balance is $1,230.

Required:

1. Prepare a cash budget for Kylles Inc. for the month of March.
2. Assume that Kylles Inc. wanted a minimum cash balance of $15,000 and that it could borrow from the bank in multiples of $1,000 at an interest rate of 12 percent per year. Assume that all borrowings occur at the beginning of a month and that repayments occur at the end of a month. What would the adjusted ending balance for March be for Kylles? How much interest would Kylles owe in April, assuming that the entire amount borrowed in March would be paid back?

Solution:

1.

Kylles Inc.
Cash Budget
For the Month of March

Beginning cash balance	$ 1,230
Cash sales	45,000
Sale of property	3,500
Total cash available	49,730
Less disbursements:	
Materials and supplies	10,000
Direct labour payroll	12,500
Other expenditures	14,900
Total disbursements	37,400
Ending cash balance	$12,330

2.

Unadjusted ending balance	$12,330
Plus borrowing	3,000
Adjusted ending balance	$15,330

In April, interest owed would be (1/12 × 0.12 × $3,000 × 2 months) = $60.

DISCUSSION QUESTIONS

1. Define the term *budget*. How are budgets used in planning?
2. Define *control*. How are budgets used to control?
3. Explain how both small and large organizations can benefit from budgeting.
4. Discuss some reasons for budgeting.
5. What is a master budget? An operating budget? A financial budget?
6. Explain the role of a sales forecast in budgeting. What is the difference between a sales forecast and a sales budget?

7. "All budgets depend on the sales budget." Is this true? Explain.
8. Why is goal congruence important?
9. Why is it important for a manager to receive frequent feedback on his or her performance?
10. Discuss the roles of monetary and nonmonetary incentives. Do you believe that nonmonetary incentives are needed? Why?
11. What is participative budgeting? Discuss some of its advantages.
12. "A budget that is too easily achieved will lead to diminished performance." Do you agree? Explain why or why not.
13. What is the role of top management in participative budgeting?
14. Explain why a manager has an incentive to build slack into the budget.
15. Explain how a manager can milk the firm to improve budgetary performance.

CORNERSTONE EXERCISES

CORNERSTONE 9.1

Cornerstone Exercise 9-1 Preparing a Sales Budget

Memorsave Inc. makes and sells picture frames and expects the following units to be sold from July to September of the coming year:

July	56,000
August	59,000
September	61,000

The average price for a unit is $52.

Required:

Prepare a sales budget for the third quarter of the coming year, showing units and sales revenue by month and in total for the quarter.

CORNERSTONE 9.2

Cornerstone Exercise 9-2 Preparing a Production Budget

Memorsave Inc. makes and sells picture frames. From July to October of the coming year, Memorsave expects the following unit sales:

July	56,000
August	59,000
September	61,000
October	55,000

Memorsave's policy is to have 30 percent of next month's sales in ending inventory. On July 1, it is expected that there will be 7,400 units on hand.

Required:

Prepare a production budget for the third quarter of the year. Show the number of frames that should be produced each month as well as for the quarter in total.

OBJECTIVE 2

CORNERSTONE 9.1, 9.3

Cornerstone Exercise 9-3 Preparing a Sales Budget and a Merchandise Purchasing Budget

Adamis is a men's retailer of high-quality leather goods, primarily leather shoes and belts. The average selling price for a pair of shoes is $725 and the average selling price of a belt is $350. Planned sales for the months of October to January are as follows:

October	
Shoes (pairs)	875
Belts	640
November	
Shoes (pairs)	1,060
Belts	868

December	
Shoes (pairs)	1,835
Belts	1,246
January	
Shoes (pairs)	214
Belts	98

Adamis's policy is to have 25 percent of next month's sales in ending inventory. On October 1, it is expected that there will be 400 pairs of shoes and 100 belts on hand. On average, purchasing merchandise from suppliers costs Adamis $320 for a pair of leather shoes and $130 per belt.

Required:

1. Prepare a sales budget for the period of October to December for each product line, showing units and sales revenue by month and in total for the quarter.
2. Prepare a merchandise purchasing budget for the period of October to December. Show the number of shoes and belts that must be ordered each month as well as for the quarter in total and compute the cost for each product line for each month and a total for the quarter.

Cornerstone Exercise 9-4 Preparing a Direct Materials Purchases Budget

OBJECTIVE 2
CORNERSTONE 9.4

Selva Inc. makes keyboards for tablets, and packages them in crates containing 50 keyboards per crate. Planned production in units for the first three months of the coming year is:

January	43,800
February	41,000
March	50,250

Each keyboard requires two litres of chemicals and one plastic crate. Company policy requires that ending inventories of raw materials for each month be 15 percent of the next month's production needs. That policy was met for the ending inventory of December in the prior year. The cost of one litre of chemicals is $0.50. The cost of one crate is $1.60. (*Note:* Round all dollar amounts to the nearest dollar.)

Required:

1. Calculate the ending inventory of chemicals in litres for December of the prior year, and for January and February. What is the beginning inventory of chemicals for January?
2. Prepare a direct materials purchases budget for chemicals for the months of January and February.
3. Calculate the ending inventory of crates for December of the prior year, and for January and February. What is the beginning inventory of crates for January?
4. Prepare a direct materials purchases budget for crates for the months of January and February.

Cornerstone Exercise 9-5 Preparing a Direct Labour Budget

OBJECTIVE 2
CORNERSTONE 9.5

Selva Inc. makes keyboards for tablets. Planned production in units for the first three months of the coming year are:

January	43,800
February	41,000
March	50,250

Each crate takes 0.3 direct labour hours. The average wage is $18 per hour.

Required:

Prepare a direct labour budget for the months of January, February, and March, as well as the total for the first quarter.

OBJECTIVE 2
CORNERSTONE 9.6

Cornerstone Exercise 9-6 Preparing an Overhead Budget

Memorsave Inc. makes and sells picture frames. Budgeted direct labour hours for July to September of the coming year are:

July	15,200
August	16,350
September	17,100

The variable overhead rate is \$0.60 per direct labour hour; fixed overhead is budgeted at \$2,820 per month.

Required:

Prepare an overhead budget for the months of July, August, and September, as well as the total for the quarter. (*Note:* Round all dollar amounts to the nearest dollar.)

OBJECTIVE 2
CORNERSTONE 9.7

Cornerstone Exercise 9-7 Preparing an Ending Finished Goods Inventory Budget

Okeke Company manufactures a line of office chairs. Each chair takes \$14 of direct materials and uses 1.9 direct labour hours at \$16 per direct labour hour. The variable overhead rate is \$1.20 per direct labour hour and the fixed overhead rate is \$1.60 per direct labour hour. Okeke expects to have 675 chairs in ending inventory.

Required:

1. Calculate the unit product cost.
2. Calculate the cost of budgeted ending inventory.

OBJECTIVE 2
CORNERSTONE 9.8

Cornerstone Exercise 9-8 Preparing a Cost of Goods Sold Budget

Okeke Company manufactures a line of office chairs. Each chair takes \$14 of direct materials and uses 1.9 direct labour hours at \$16 per direct labour hour. The variable overhead rate is \$1.20 per direct labour hour and the fixed overhead rate is \$1.60 per direct labour hour. Okeke expects to produce 20,000 chairs next year and expects to have 675 chairs in ending inventory. There is no beginning inventory of office chairs.

Required:

Prepare a cost of goods sold budget for Okeke Company.

OBJECTIVE 2
CORNERSTONE 9.9

Cornerstone Exercise 9-9 Preparing a Selling and Administrative Expenses Budget

Fael Company makes and sells paper products. In the coming year, Fael expects total sales of \$19,730,000. There is a 3 percent commission on sales. In addition, fixed expenses of the sales and administrative offices include the following:

Salaries	\$ 960,000
Utilities	365,000
Office space	230,000
Advertising	1,200,000

Required:

Prepare a selling and administrative expenses budget for Fael Company for the coming year.

OBJECTIVE 2
CORNERSTONE 9.10

Cornerstone Exercise 9-10 Preparing a Budgeted Income Statement

Azizi Company provided the following information for the coming year:

Units produced and sold	160,000
Cost of goods sold per unit	\$6.30
Selling price	\$10.80
Variable selling and administrative expense per unit	\$1.10
Fixed selling and administrative expenses	\$423,000
Tax rate	35%

Required:

Prepare a budgeted income statement for Azizi Company for the coming year.

OBJECTIVE 3
CORNERSTONE 9.11

Cornerstone Exercise 9-11 **Preparing an Accounts Receivable Aging Schedule**

Bina Paudel and Company is a legal services firm. All sales of legal services are billed to clients (there are no cash sales). Bina Paudel expects that, on average, 20 percent will be paid in the month of billing, 50 percent will be paid in the month following billing, and 25 percent will be paid in the second month following billing. For the next five months, the following sales billings are expected:

May	$ 84,000
June	100,800
July	77,000
August	86,800
September	91,000

Required:

Prepare a schedule showing the cash expected in payments on accounts receivable in August and in September.

OBJECTIVE 3
CORNERSTONE 9.12

Cornerstone Exercise 9-12 **Preparing an Accounts Payable Schedule**

Demir Inc. purchases raw materials on account for use in production. The direct materials purchases budget shows the following expected purchases on account:

April	$374,400
May	411,200
June	416,000

Demir typically pays 20 percent on account in the month of billing and 80 percent in the next month.

Required:

1. How much cash is required for payments on account in May?
2. How much cash is expected for payments on account in June?

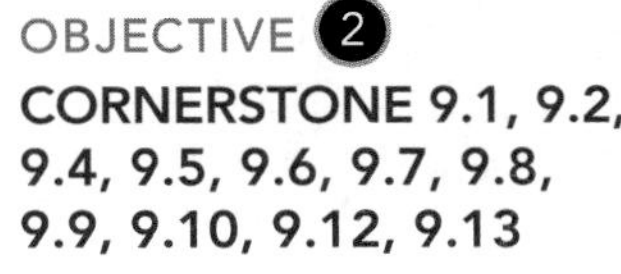

OBJECTIVE 2
CORNERSTONE 9.1, 9.2, 9.4, 9.5, 9.6, 9.7, 9.8, 9.9, 9.10, 9.12, 9.13

Cornerstone Exercise 9-13 **Operating Budget**

Royal Company is preparing budgets for the quarter ending June 30. The marketing department of Royal Company prepares the following information that will be used to prepare a budget for the quarter ending June 30. The selling price is $10.50 per unit. Budgeted sales for the next five months are:

April	10,000
May	30,000
June	25,000
July	17,000
August	17,500

- The management at Royal wants to minimize the probability of a stockout of inventory items. A policy has been implemented that requires the company to maintain ending inventory of 15 percent of the following month's budgeted sales. At the beginning of the quarter, Royal had 5,000 units in inventory.
- Each good unit of output requires 2 kilograms of direct material. Management does not want to run out of direct materials, so a policy has been established that materials on hand at the end of each month must equal 20 percent of the following month's production. At the beginning of the month, Royal has 13,000 kilograms of direct material on hand. Each kilogram of direct material costs 25 cents.

(Continued)

- At Royal, each unit of product requires 0.1 hours (6 minutes) of direct labour. The company pays employees a standard wage rate of $12 per hour.
- Royal applies overhead on the basis of direct labour hours. The variable manufacturing overhead rate is $12 per direct labour hour. The fixed overhead is $35,500 per month, of which $10,000 is noncash costs, primarily depreciation on the factory assets.
- Royal has a variable and fixed component to its selling and administrative expenses. The company estimates variable selling and administrative expenses at 50 cents per unit sold. Fixed selling and administrative expenses are estimated at $70,000 per month. Of this amount, $10,000 are noncash expenses, primarily depreciation.
- All sales at Royal are made on account. The company collects 70 percent of the sales revenue in the month of sale, and 30 percent in the following month. At the start of the quarter, Royal had $30,000 in accounts receivable that were deemed to be fully collectible.
- Recall that Royal pays 25 cents per kilogram of direct materials. The company pays for one-half of its purchases in the month of the purchase and one-half in the following month. At the beginning of the quarter, Royal owed creditors $12,000 for purchases of direct materials.
- For the cash budget, note the following information:
  - Maintains a 16 percent open line of credit for $75,000
  - Maintains a minimum cash balance of $30,000
  - Borrows on the first day of a month and repays loans on the last day of a month
  - Will pay cash dividend of $15,000 in June
  - Will purchase $43,700 of equipment in May and $12,250 in June (both purchases paid in cash)
  - Has an April 1 cash balance of $40,000
- Royal reported the following account balances prior to preparing its budgeted financial statements:
  - Land of $50,000
  - Common shares of $200,000
  - Retained earnings of $109,250
  - Equipment of $175,000
  - Accumulated depreciation of $60,000

Required:

1. Prepare a sales budget for each month and for the quarter.
2. Prepare the production budget for the months of April, May, and June, and for the quarter-end.
3. Prepare the direct materials purchases budget for the months of April, May, and June, and for the quarter-end.
4. Prepare the direct labour budget for the months of April, May, and June, and for the quarter-end.
5. Prepare the overhead budget for the months of April, May, and June, and for the quarter-end.
6. Prepare the ending finished goods inventory budget for the quarter ending June 30.
7. Prepare a cost of goods sold budget for the quarter ending June 30.
8. Prepare the selling and administrative expense budget for the months of April, May, and June, and for the quarter-end.
9. Prepare a budgeted income statement for the quarter-end.
10. Prepare the schedule of expected cash collections on sales for the months of April, May, and June, and for the quarter-end.
11. Prepare the schedule of expected cash disbursements for the months of April, May, and June, and for the quarter-end.
12. Prepare a cash budget for the months of April, May, and June, and for the quarter-end.
13. Prepare the budgeted balance sheet as at June 30, ignoring any depreciation charge.

Cornerstone Exercise 9-14 Preparing a Cash Budget

OBJECTIVE 3
CORNERSTONE 9.13

La Famiglia Pizzeria provided the following information for the month of October:

a. Sales are budgeted to be $157,000. About 85 percent of sales are cash; the remainder are on account.
b. La Famiglia expects that, on average, 70 percent of credit sales will be paid in the month of sale, and 28 percent will be paid in the following month.
c. Food and supplies purchases, all on account, are expected to be $116,000. La Famiglia pays 25 percent in the month of purchase and 75 percent in the month following purchase.
d. Most of the work is done by the owners, who typically withdraw $6,000 a month from the business as their salary. (*Note:* The $6,000 is a payment in total to the two owners, not per person.) Various part-time workers cost $7,300 per month. They are paid for their work weekly, so on average 90 percent of their wages are paid in the month incurred and the remaining 10 percent in the next month.
e. Utilities average $5,590 per month. Rent on the building is $4,100 per month.
f. Insurance is paid quarterly; the next payment of $1,200 is due in October.
g. September sales were $181,500 and purchases of food in September equalled $130,000.
h. The cash balance on October 1 is $2,147.

Required:

1. Calculate the cash receipts expected in October. (*Hint:* Remember to include both cash sales and payments from credit sales.)
2. Calculate the cash needed in October to pay for food purchases.
3. Prepare a cash budget for October.

EXERCISES

Exercise 9-15 Planning and Control

OBJECTIVE 1

a. To grow the existing business, the owner plans to expand the existing number of product lines.
b. SushiDate's owner wants to expand from a sit-down restaurant to become a supplier for grocery chain deli departments.
c. To improve cash, SushiDate's accountant will begin investing surplus cash more productively.
d. The owner expects to increase the pay of his four full-time and three part-time employees by 3 percent in the coming year.
e. The accountant plans to invest in marketable securities with a minimum credit rating of triple A to enhance returns on surplus cash.
f. The accountant creates revenue reports each month and compares this with monthly budgeted revenues. Revenues have been trending lower for the past two months.
g. The owner learns that a nearby sushi restaurant recently opened, leading him to believe that declining sales may be partly due to the new competitor.
h. The owner increased promotional efforts by distributing flyers door to door in surrounding neighbourhoods to generate additional interest in his restaurant. The accountant reported an increase in sales the following month.
i. The owner reduced the price on certain menu items to match the new competitor.

Required:

Match each statement with the following planning and control elements (a letter may be matched to more than one item):

1. Corrective action
2. Budgets
3. Feedback
4. Investigation
5. Short-term plan

(Continued)

6. Comparison of actual with planned
7. Monitoring of actual activity
8. Strategic plan
9. Short-term objectives
10. Long-term objectives

OBJECTIVE 

Exercise 9-16 Sales Budget

Imperial Doors produces two shower door models: Frosted23 and Frosted26. The Frosted23 sells for $250, and the Frosted26 sells for $375. Projected sales (number of doors) for the coming five quarters are as follows:

	Frosted23	Frosted26
First quarter, 2017	950	1,200
Second quarter, 2017	1,800	2,300
Third quarter, 2017	2,400	3,250
Fourth quarter, 2017	3,100	3,500
First quarter, 2018	1,010	1,480

The vice-president of sales believes that the projected sales are realistic and can be achieved by the company.

Required:

1. Prepare a sales budget for each quarter of 2017 and for the year in total. Show sales by product and in total for each time period.
2. CONCEPTUAL CONNECTION How will Imperial Doors use this sales budget?

OBJECTIVE 2

Exercise 9-17 Production Budget

Imperial Doors produces two shower door models: Frosted23 and Frosted26. Projected sales (number of doors) for the coming five quarters are as follows:

	Frosted23	Frosted26
First quarter, 2017	950	1,200
Second quarter, 2017	1,800	2,300
Third quarter, 2017	2,400	3,250
Fourth quarter, 2017	3,100	3,500
First quarter, 2018	1,010	1,480

The vice-president of sales believes that the projected sales are realistic and can be achieved by the company.

Imperial Doors needs a production budget for each product. Beginning inventory of Frosted23 for the first quarter of 2017 was 220 doors. The company's policy is to have 20 percent of the next quarter's sales of Frosted23 in ending inventory. Beginning inventory of Frosted26 was 170 doors. The company's policy is to have 10 percent of the next quarter's sales of Frosted26 in ending inventory.

Required:

Prepare a production budget for each quarter for 2017 and for the year in total.

OBJECTIVE 2

Exercise 9-18 Production Budget and Direct Materials Purchases Budgets

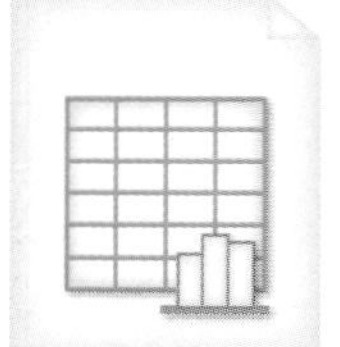

Peanut-Fresh Inc. produces all-natural organic peanut butter which is sold in 340-gram jars. The sales budget for the first four months of the year is as follows:

	Unit Sales	Dollar Sales ($)
January	48,000	100,800
February	46,000	96,600
March	55,000	121,000
April	58,000	125,200

Company policy requires that ending inventories for each month be 20 percent of next month's sales. At the beginning of January, the inventory of peanut butter is 14,500 jars.

Each jar of peanut butter needs two raw materials: 340 grams of peanuts and one jar. Company policy requires that ending inventories of raw materials for each month be 10 percent of the next month's production needs. That policy was met on January 1.

Required:

1. Prepare a production budget for the first quarter of the year. Show the number of jars that should be produced each month as well as for the quarter in total.
2. Prepare separate direct materials purchases budgets for jars and for peanuts for the months of January and February.

Exercise 9-19 Production Budget

De Silva Inc. produces submersible water pumps for ponds and cisterns. The unit sales for the first four months of the year for this product are as follows:

	Unit Sales
January	180,000
February	220,000
March	200,000
April	240,000

Company policy requires that ending inventories for each month be 25 percent of next month's sales. However, at the beginning of January, due to greater sales in December than anticipated, the beginning inventory of pumps is only 21,000.

Required:

Prepare a production budget for the first quarter of the year. Show the number of units that should be produced each month as well as for the quarter in total.

Exercise 9-20 Direct Materials Purchases Budget

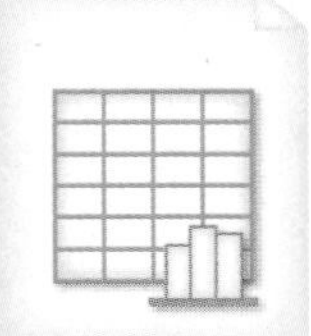

Tsiklauri Company produces plastic items, including plastic housing for humidifiers. Each housing requires 425 grams of plastic costing $0.34 per 10 grams. Tsiklauri moulds the plastic into the proper shape. Tsiklauri has budgeted production of the humidifiers for the next four months as follows:

	Units
March	3,500
April	4,400
May	4,900
June	6,300

Inventory policy requires that sufficient plastic be in ending monthly inventory to satisfy 20 percent of the following month's production needs. The inventory of plastic at the beginning of March equals exactly the amount needed to satisfy the inventory policy.

Required:

Prepare a direct materials purchases budget for March, April, and May, showing purchases in units and in dollars for each month and in total.

Exercise 9-21 Direct Labour Budget

Typefast Inc. manufactures computer keyboards. The following is Typefast's production budget for the fourth quarter of the calendar year:

	Units
October	35,000
November	42,000
December	51,000

(Continued)

On average each keyboard is expected to require 0.30 direct labour hours to produce. Direct labour costs the company $18 per hour.

Required:

Prepare a direct labour budget for October, November, and December, showing the hours needed and the direct labour cost for each month and in total.

OBJECTIVE 2

Exercise 9-22 Sales Budget

Abbasov Inc. manufactures six models of leaf blowers and weed eaters. Abbasov's budgeting team is finalizing the sales budget for the coming year. Sales in units and dollars for last year follow:

Product	Number Sold	Price ($)	Revenue
LB-1	14,700	32	$ 470,400
LB-2	18,000	20	360,000
WE-6	25,200	15	378,000
WE-7	16,200	10	162,000
WE-8	6,900	18	124,200
WE-9	4,000	22	88,000
Total			$1,582,600

In looking over the previous year's sales figures, Abbasov's sales budgeting team recalled the following:

a. Model LB-1 is a newer version of the leaf blower with a gasoline engine. The LB-1 is mounted on wheels instead of being carried. This model is designed for the commercial market and did better than expected in its first year. As a result, the number of units of model LB-1 to be sold was forecast at 250 percent of the previous year's units.
b. Models WE-8 and WE-9 were introduced on July 1 of last year. They are lighter versions of the traditional weed eater and are designed for smaller households or condo units. Abbasov estimates that demand for both models will continue at the previous year's rate.
c. A competitor has announced plans to introduce an improved version of model WE-6, Abbasov's traditional weed eater. Abbasov believes that the model WE-6 price must be cut 30 percent to maintain unit sales at the previous year's level.
d. It was assumed that unit sales of the other models would increase by 5 percent, prices remaining constant.

Required:

Prepare a sales budget by product and in total for Abbasov Inc. for the coming year.

OBJECTIVE 2

Exercise 9-23 Production Budget and Direct Materials Purchases Budget

Raylene Webber, owner of Raylene's Flowers and Gifts, produces gift baskets for various special occasions. Each gift basket includes fruit or assorted small gifts (e.g., a coffee mug, deck of cards, novelty cocoa mixes, scented soap) in a basket that is wrapped in colourful cellophane. Raylene has estimated the following unit sales of the standard gift basket for the coming five months:

September	250
October	200
November	230
December	380
January	100

Raylene likes to have 10 percent of the next month's sales needs on hand at the end of each month. This requirement was met on August 31.

Two materials are needed for each fruit basket:

Fruit	1 kilogram
Small gifts	6 items

The materials inventory policy is to have 5 percent of the next month's fruit needs on hand and 30 percent of the next month's production needs of small gifts. (The relatively low inventory amount for fruit is designed to prevent spoilage.) Materials inventory on September 1 met this company policy.

Required:

1. Prepare a production budget for September, October, November, and December for gift baskets.
2. Prepare a direct materials purchases budget for the two types of materials used in the production of gift baskets for the months of September, October, and November. (*Note:* Round answers to the nearest whole unit.)
3. CONCEPTUAL CONNECTION Why do you think there is such a big difference in budgeted units from November to December? Why did Raylene budget fewer units in January than in December?

Exercise 9-24 Accounts Receivable Aging Schedule and Cash Budget

OBJECTIVE 3

Bayco Wholesale Inc. found that about 45 percent of its sales are for cash. Bayco Wholesale has the following accounts receivable payment experience:

Percent paid in the month of sale	20
Percent paid in the month after the sale	76
Percent paid in the second month after the sale	3

Bayco Wholesale's anticipated sales for the next few months are as follows:

December	$375,000
January	340,000
February	318,000
March	325,000
April	332,000

Required:

1. Calculate credit sales for January, February, March, and April.
2. Prepare a schedule of cash receipts for March and April.

Exercise 9-25 Accounts Receivable Aging Schedule and Cash Budget

Janzen Inc. sells all of its product on account. Janzen has the following accounts receivable payment experience:

Percent paid in the month of sale	20
Percent paid in the month after the sale	55
Percent paid in the second month after the sale	23

To encourage payment in the month of sale, Janzen gives a 2 percent cash discount. Janzen's anticipated sales for the next few months are as follows:

April	$190,000
May	248,000
June	260,000
July	240,000
August	300,000

Required:

1. Prepare a schedule of cash receipts for July.
2. Prepare a schedule of cash receipts for August.

OBJECTIVE 3

Exercise 9-26 Cash Payments Schedule

Fein Company provided the following information relating to cash payments. Fein purchased direct materials on account in the following amounts:

June	$68,000
July	77,000
August	73,000

a. Fein pays 20 percent of accounts payable in the month of purchase and the remaining 80 percent in the following month.
b. In July, direct labour cost was $32,300. August direct labour cost was $35,400. The company finds that typically 90 percent of direct labour cost is paid in cash during the month, with the remainder paid in the following month.
c. August overhead amounted to $71,200, including $6,350 of depreciation.
d. Fein had taken out a loan of $15,000 on May 1. Interest, due with payment of principal, accrued at the rate of 9 percent per year. The loan and all interest was repaid on August 31. (*Note:* Use whole months to compute interest payment.)

Required:

Prepare a schedule of cash payments for Fein Company for August.

OBJECTIVE 3

Exercise 9-27 Cash Budget

The owner of a small mining supply company has requested a cash budget for June. After examining the records of the company, you find the following:

a. Cash balance on June 1 is $736.
b. Actual sales for April and May are as follows:

	April	May
Cash sales	$10,000	$18,000
Credit sales	28,900	35,000
Total sales	$38,900	$53,000

c. Credit sales are collected over a three-month period: 40 percent in the month of sale, 30 percent in the second month, and 20 percent in the third month. The sales collected in the third month are subject to a 2 percent late fee, which is paid by those customers in addition to what they owe. The remaining sales are uncollectible.
d. Inventory purchases average 64 percent of a month's total sales. Of those purchases, 20 percent are paid for in the month of purchase. The remaining 80 percent are paid for in the following month.
e. Salaries and wages total $11,750 per month, including a $4,500 salary paid to the owner.
f. Rent is $4,100 per month.
g. Taxes to be paid in June are $6,780.

The owner also tells you that he expects cash sales of $18,600 and credit sales of $54,000 for June. No minimum cash balance is required. The owner of the company does not have access to short-term loans.

Required:

1. Prepare a cash budget for June. Include supporting schedules for cash collections and cash payments.
2. CONCEPTUAL CONNECTION Did the business show a negative cash balance for June? Assuming that the owner has no hope of establishing a line of credit for the business, what recommendations would you give the owner for dealing with a negative cash balance?

PROBLEMS

Problem 9-28 Cash Budget

Noonan and Associates has found from past experience that 25 percent of its services are for cash. The remaining 75 percent are on credit. An aging schedule for accounts receivable reveals the following pattern:

a. 10 percent of fees on credit are paid in the month that service is rendered.
b. 60 percent of fees on credit are paid in the month following service.
c. 26 percent of fees on credit are paid in the second month following service.
d. 4 percent of fees on credit are never collected.

Fees (on credit) that have not been paid until the second month following performance of the service are considered overdue and are subject to a 3 percent late charge.

Noonan and Associates has developed the following forecast of fees:

May	$180,000
June	200,000
July	190,000
August	194,000
September	240,000

Check figure:
Total cash receipts, September = $203,462

Required:

Prepare a schedule of cash receipts for August and September.

Problem 9-29 Operating Budget, Comprehensive Analysis

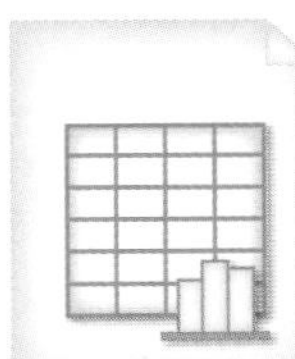

Hopewell Manufacturing produces dashboards used in the production of automobiles. The dashboard assembly is sold to a nearby automobile manufacturing plant. Projected sales in units for the coming five months follow:

January	80,000
February	90,000
March	95,000
April	96,000
May	92,000

The following data pertain to production policies and manufacturing specifications followed by Hopewell Manufacturing:

a. Finished goods inventory on January 1 is 38,000 units, each costing $274.69. The desired ending inventory for each month is 75 percent of the next month's sales.
b. The data on materials used are as follows:

Direct Materials	Per-Unit Usage (kilograms)	Unit Cost ($)
Plastix	12	16
Components	4	9

Inventory policy dictates that sufficient materials be on hand at the beginning of the month to produce 40 percent of that month's estimated sales. This is exactly the amount of materials on hand on January 1.

c. The direct labour used per unit of output is two hours. The average direct labour cost per hour is $18.50.
d. Overhead each month is estimated using a flexible budget formula. (*Note:* Activity is measured in direct labour hours.)

(Continued)

	Fixed-Cost Component ($)	Variable-Cost Component ($)
Supplies	—	1.20
Power	—	0.70
Maintenance	50,000	0.30
Supervision	24,000	—
Depreciation	230,000	—
Taxes	14,000	—
Other	90,000	0.60

e. Monthly selling and administrative expenses are also estimated using a flexible budgeting formula. (*Note:* Activity is measured in units sold.)

	Fixed Costs ($)	Variable Costs ($)
Salaries	70,000	—
Commissions	—	1.60
Depreciation	45,000	—
Shipping	—	0.75
Other	10,000	0.20

f. The unit selling price of the dashboard subassembly is $298.
g. All sales and purchases are for cash. The cash balance on January 1 is $4,600,000. The firm requires a minimum ending balance of $150,000. If the firm develops a cash shortage by the end of the month, sufficient cash is borrowed to cover the shortage. Any cash borrowed is repaid at the end of the month, as is the interest due (cash borrowed at the end of the month is repaid at the end of the following month). The interest rate is 6 percent per annum. No money is owed at the beginning of January.

Required:

1. Prepare a monthly operating budget for the first quarter with the following schedules. (*Note:* Assume that there is no change in work-in-process inventories.)
   a. Sales budget
   b. Production budget
   c. Direct materials purchases budget
   d. Direct labour budget
   e. Overhead budget
   f. Selling and administrative expenses budget
   g. Ending finished goods inventory budget
   h. Cost of goods sold budget
   i. Budgeted income statement
   j. Cash budget
2. CONCEPTUAL CONNECTION Form a group with two or three other students. Locate a manufacturing plant in your community that has headquarters elsewhere. Interview the controller for the plant regarding the master budgeting process. Ask when the process starts each year, what schedules and budgets are prepared at the plant level, how the controller forecasts the amounts, and how those schedules and budgets fit in with the overall corporate budget. Is the budgetary process participative? Also, find out how budgets are used for performance analysis. Write a summary of the interview.

Check figures:
1.i. Budgeted income = $5,125,310
1.j. Ending cash balance (March) = $2,713,818

OBJECTIVE 3

Problem 9-30 Pro Forma Income Statement

Victor Corporation is in the retail industry and purchases a product for resale. In November, the company is preparing pro forma statements for December. The company estimates that sales will be 240,000 units in December at a selling price of $12 per unit. Other forecasts are as follows:

Merchandise inventory, December 1	40,000 units
Desired ending inventory for December 31	60,000 units
Cost to purchase one unit	$8
Selling and administrative expenses	$225,000
Miscellaneous expenses (paid in cash)	$61,500
Opening cash balance, December 1	$60,000
October sales	$2,700,000
October purchases	$1,280,000
November sales	$2,220,000
November purchases	$1,568,000

a. Victor Company estimates that 60 percent of sales made in the current month are collected in the month of the sale, 30 percent are collected in the month after the sale, and 5 percent are collected in the second month after the sale.
b. The selling and administrative expenses include $45,000 of depreciation expense. The remaining balance is paid in cash in the month.
c. Victor Company pays for 70 percent of purchases in the month the purchase is made. The remaining 30 percent is paid in the month after the company has made the purchase.

Required:

1. How many units will Victor Company need to purchase in December? What is the cost of purchasing the units for December?
2. Complete a pro forma or budgeted income statement for the month ended December 31. (Ignore the impact of income taxes.)
3. Complete a pro forma statement of cash flows for the month ended December 31.
4. CONCEPTUAL CONNECTION Why is it important for companies to have accurate sales forecasts? What problems can occur when sales forecasts are inaccurate?

Problem 9-31 Cash Budget, Pro Forma Balance Sheet

OBJECTIVE 3

George Hatamleh, controller for Attar Retailers, has assembled the following data to assist in the preparation of a cash budget for the third quarter of 2017:

a. Sales:

May (actual)	$100,000
June (actual)	120,000
July (estimated)	90,000
August (estimated)	100,000
September (estimated)	135,000
October (estimated)	110,000

b. Each month, 30 percent of sales are for cash and 70 percent are on credit. The collection pattern for credit sales is 20 percent in the month of sale, 50 percent in the following month, and 30 percent in the second month following the sale.
c. Each month, the ending inventory exactly equals 50 percent of the cost of next month's sales. The markup on goods is 25 percent of cost.
d. Inventory purchases are paid for in the month following the purchase.
e. Recurring monthly expenses are as follows:

Salaries and wages	$10,000
Depreciation on plant and equipment	4,000
Utilities	1,000
Other	1,700

f. Property taxes of $15,000 are due and payable on July 15, 2017.
g. Advertising fees of $6,000 must be paid on August 20, 2017.
h. A lease on a new storage facility is scheduled to begin on September 2, 2017. Monthly payments are $5,000.

(Continued)

i. The company has a policy to maintain a minimum cash balance of $10,000. If necessary, it will borrow to meet its short-term needs. All borrowing is done at the end of a month. All payments on principal and interest are also made at the end of a month. The annual interest rate is 9 percent. The company must borrow in multiples of $1,000.

j. A partially completed balance sheet as at June 30, 2017, follows. (*Note:* Accounts payable is for inventory purchases only.)

Cash	$?	
Accounts receivable	?	
Inventory	?	
Plant and equipment	425,000	
Accounts payable		$?
Common shares		210,000
Retained earnings		268,750
Total	$?	$?

Required:

1. Complete the balance sheet given in item j.
2. Prepare a cash budget for each month in the third quarter and for the quarter in total (the third quarter begins on July 1). Provide a supporting schedule of cash collections.
3. Prepare a pro forma balance sheet as at September 30, 2017.
4. CONCEPTUAL CONNECTION Form a group with two or three other students. Discuss why a bank might require a cash budget for businesses that are seeking short-term loans. Determine what other financial reports might be useful for a loan decision. Also, discuss how the reliability of cash budgets and other financial information can be determined.

Check figures:
1. Total assets = $562,750
2. Ending cash (Sept.) = $12,005
3. Total assets = $565,605

OBJECTIVE 

Problem 9-32 Participative Budgeting, Not-for-Profit Setting

Winston Churchill was the prime minister of the United Kingdom during much of the Second World War from 1940 to 1945. He was famously quoted as saying “Plans are of little importance, but planning is essential.” What do you think he meant by this? Consider his comment with respect to the master budget. Do you agree or disagree? Be sure to include the impact of the master budget on planning and control.

OBJECTIVE 

Problem 9-33 Cash Budget

The controller of Munishi Company is gathering data to prepare the cash budget for October. She plans to develop the budget from the following information:

a. Of all sales, 45 percent are cash sales.

b. Of credit sales, 35 percent are collected within the month of sale. Half of the credit sales collected within the month receive a 1 percent cash discount (for accounts paid within 12 days). Forty percent of credit sales are collected in the following month; 23 percent of credit sales are collected the month thereafter. Bad debts are accepted as a normal part of selling on credit.

c. Sales for the third and fourth quarters of the year follow. (*Note:* The first three months are actual sales, and the last three months are estimated sales.)

	Sales ($)
July	500,000
August	575,000
September	820,000
October	990,000
November	1,278,000
December	1,350,000

d. The company sells all that it produces each month. The cost of raw materials equals 32 percent of each sales dollar. The company requires a monthly ending inventory equal to the coming month’s production requirements. Of raw materials purchases, 50 percent are paid for in the month of purchase. The remaining 50 percent are paid for in the following month.

e. Wages total $110,000 each month and are paid in the month incurred.
f. Budgeted monthly operating expenses total $385,000, of which $50,000 is depreciation and $7,000 is expiration of prepaid insurance (the annual premium of $84,000 is paid on January 1).
g. Dividends of $115,000, declared on September 30, will be paid on October 15.
h. A new delivery truck will be purchased for $124,000 on October 9.
i. On October 12, an old truck will be sold for $12,500.
j. The company maintains a minimum cash balance of $10,000.
k. The cash balance on October 1 is $35,000.

Required:

Prepare a cash budget for October. Include a supporting schedule that details the cash collections from sales.

Check figure:
Cash required (borrowed) = $114,120

Problem 9-34 Master Budget, Comprehensive Review

OBJECTIVE  

Optima Company is a high-technology organization that produces a mass-storage system. The design of Optima's system is unique and represents a breakthrough in the industry. The units Optima produces combine positive features of both compact and hard disks. The company is completing its fifth year of operations and is preparing to build its master budget for the coming year (2017). The budget will detail each quarter's activity and the activity for the year in total. The master budget will be based on the following information:

a. Fourth-quarter sales for 2016 are 55,000 units.
b. Unit sales by quarter (for 2017) are projected as follows:

First quarter	65,000
Second quarter	70,000
Third quarter	75,000
Fourth quarter	90,000

The selling price is $400 per unit. All sales are credit sales. Optima collects 85 percent of all sales within the quarter in which they are realized; the other 15 percent is collected in the following quarter. There are no bad debts.

c. There is no beginning inventory of finished goods. Optima is planning the following ending finished goods inventories for each quarter:

First quarter	13,000 units
Second quarter	15,000 units
Third quarter	20,000 units
Fourth quarter	10,000 units

d. Each mass-storage unit uses five hours of direct labour and three units of direct materials. Labourers are paid $10 per hour, and one unit of direct materials costs $80.
e. There are 65,700 units of direct materials in beginning inventory as at January 1, 2017. At the end of each quarter, Optima plans to have 30 percent of the direct materials needed based on next quarter's unit sales. Optima will end the year with the same amount of direct materials found in this year's beginning inventory.
f. Optima buys direct materials on account. Half of the purchases are paid for in the quarter of acquisition, and the remaining half are paid for in the following quarter. Wages and salaries are paid on the 15th and 30th of each month.
g. Fixed overhead totals $1 million each quarter. Of this total, $350,000 represents depreciation. All other fixed expenses are paid for in cash in the quarter incurred. The fixed overhead rate is computed by dividing the year's total fixed overhead by the year's expected actual units produced.
h. Variable overhead is budgeted at $6 per direct labour hour. All variable overhead expenses are paid for in the quarter incurred.

(Continued)

i. Fixed selling and administrative expenses total $250,000 per quarter, including $50,000 depreciation.
j. Variable selling and administrative expenses are budgeted at $10 per unit sold. All selling and administrative expenses are paid for in the quarter incurred.
k. The balance sheet as at December 31, 2016, is as follows:

Assets	
Cash	$ 250,000
Accounts receivable	3,300,000
Direct materials inventory	5,256,000
Plant and equipment	33,500,000
Total assets	$42,306,000

Liabilities and Shareholders' Equity	
Accounts payable	$ 7,248,000*
Common shares	27,000,000
Retained earnings	8,058,000
Total liabilities and shareholders' equity	$42,306,000

*For purchase of direct materials only.

l. Optima will pay quarterly dividends of $300,000. At the end of the fourth quarter, $2 million of equipment will be purchased.

Required:

Prepare a master budget for Optima Company for each quarter of 2017 and for the year in total. The following component budgets must be included:

1. Sales budget
2. Production budget
3. Direct materials purchases budget
4. Direct labour budget
5. Overhead budget
6. Selling and administrative expenses budget
7. Ending finished goods inventory budget
8. Cost of goods sold budget (*Note:* Assume that there is no change in work-in-process inventories.)
9. Cash budget
10. Pro forma income statement (using absorption costing) (*Note:* Ignore income taxes.)
11. Pro forma balance sheet (*Note:* Ignore income taxes.)

Check figure:
10. Income before taxes = $16,129,000

OBJECTIVE 2

Problem 9-35 Direct Materials and Direct Labour Budgets

Chistosa Company produces stuffed toy animals; one of these is Betty Rabbit. Each rabbit takes 0.2 metres of fabric and 6 grams of polyfibrefill. Fabric costs $3.50 per metre, and polyfibrefill is $0.05 per gram. Chistosa has budgeted production of stuffed rabbits for the next four months as follows:

	Units
October	20,000
November	40,000
December	25,000
January	30,000

Inventory policy requires that sufficient fabric be in ending monthly inventory to satisfy 15 percent of the following month's production needs and sufficient polyfibrefill be in inventory to satisfy 30 percent of the following month's production needs. Inventory of fabric and polyfibrefill at the beginning of October equals exactly the amount needed to satisfy the inventory policy.

Each rabbit produced requires (on average) 0.10 direct labour hours. The average cost of direct labour is $15.50 per hour.

Required:

1. Prepare a direct materials purchases budget of fabric for the last quarter of the year, showing purchases in units and in dollars for each month and for the quarter in total.
2. Prepare a direct materials purchases budget of polyfibrefill for the last quarter of the year, showing purchases in units and in dollars for each month and for the quarter in total.
3. Prepare a direct labour budget for the last quarter of the year, showing the hours needed and the direct labour cost for each month and for the quarter in total.

Check figure:

1. December materials to be purchased = 5,150 metres

OBJECTIVE 

Problem 9-36 Cash Budgeting

Shreva Parab owns The Eatery, an affordable restaurant located near tourist attractions in Toronto. Shreva accepts cash and cheques. Cheques are deposited immediately. The bank charges $0.50 per cheque; the amount per cheque averages $65. Bad cheques that Shreva cannot collect make up 2 percent of cheque revenue.

During a typical month, The Eatery has sales of $75,000. About 75 percent are cash sales. Estimated sales for the next three months are as follows:

July	$60,000
August	75,000
September	80,000

Shreva thinks that it may be time to refuse to accept cheques and to start accepting credit cards. She is negotiating with the credit card companies, and she would start the new policy on July 1. Shreva estimates that with the decrease in sales from the no-cheques policy and the increase in sales from the acceptance of credit cards, the net increase in sales will be 20 percent. The credit card processing service will charge no setup fee, however the following fees and conditions apply:

- Monthly gateway and statement fee totalling $19, paid on the first day of the month.
- Discount fee of 2 percent of the total sale. This is not paid separately; instead, the amount that Shreva receives from each credit sale is reduced by 2 percent. For example, on a credit card sale of $150, the processing company would take $3 and remit a net amount of $147 to Shreva's account.
- Transaction fee of $0.25 per transaction paid at the time of the transaction.

There will be a two-day delay between the date of the transaction and the date on which the net amount will be deposited into Shreva's account. On average, 94 percent of a month's net credit card sales will be deposited into her account that month. The remaining 6 percent will be deposited the next month.

If Shreva adds credit cards, she believes that cash sales will average just 5 percent of total sales, and that the average credit card transaction will be $50.

Required:

1. Prepare a schedule of cash receipts for August and September under the current policy of accepting cheques.
2. Assuming that Shreva decides to accept credit cards and refuse cheques:
   a. Calculate revised total sales, cash sales, and credit card sales by month for August and September.
   b. Calculate the total estimated number of credit card transactions for August and September.
3. Prepare a schedule of cash receipts for August and September that incorporates the changes in policy.

Check figure:

1. September total cash receipts = $79,446

OBJECTIVE 

Problem 9-37 Master Budget, Comprehensive Problem

Back Country Outfitters Inc., based in Nelson, British Columbia, assembles snowboards for the serious snowboarder. It buys the boards already cut to size and adds the various fittings required to make a first-class board. These boards sell for $500 each to distributors, who in turn sell them to the snowboarding enthusiast for prices ranging from $899.99 to $1,199.99, depending on location.

(Continued)

Back Country manages its inventory so that there are no in-process boards at the end of any quarter. The results for the past year are shown below:

Back Country Outfitters Inc.
Statement of Income
For the Year Ended June 30, 2017

Sales	$2,000,000
Cost of goods sold	940,000
Gross margin	1,060,000
Selling and administrative expenses	
Salaries	185,500
Sales commissions	100,000
Bad debt expense	36,000
Facilities rental	30,000
Advertising and promotion	25,000
Depreciation	18,000
Professional fees	15,000
Office expenses	15,000
Total selling and administrative	424,500
Net income before tax	635,500
Income tax expense	254,200
Net income	$ 381,300

The company expects unit sales to increase by 10 percent per year in each of the next two years and for the selling price to remain constant. Production costs are also expected to remain constant for the coming year. The following facts and policies have been stipulated for the company:

- Sales in 2017 followed a seasonal pattern so that first-quarter sales were 1,200 units, second-quarter sales were 1,600 units, third-quarter sales were 800 units, and fourth-quarter sales were 400 units. This pattern is expected to remain consistent into the future.
- Cash sales amount to only 10 percent of total sales. Collections of credit sales have followed a pattern of 30 percent collected in the quarter of sale; 60 percent collected in the quarter following sale; and 8 percent collected in the second quarter following sale.
- All purchases of materials are made on credit, but the suppliers have imposed strict credit policies on the company so that 80 percent of all purchases must be paid in the quarter of purchase and 20 percent in the quarter following purchase.
- The company requires that 25 percent of the following quarter's production requirement for each component be maintained in ending materials inventory. In planning ending inventory of components, the company predicts that production in the first quarter of fiscal 2019 will be 10 percent higher than in 2018.
- The company also requires that 30 percent of the following quarter's sales be maintained in ending finished goods inventory.
- Raw materials cost for the boards themselves is $142 per board, because the boards are specially formed and finished to very exacting specifications.
- The fittings for each board cost $50, representing the foot harnesses and other hardware.
- It takes one-half hour of direct labour to assemble each board with an average wage cost, including benefits, of $36 per hour.
- In 2017, manufacturing overhead costs consisted of $20 per direct labour hour of variable overhead and $60,000 of fixed overhead, including depreciation of $20,000.
- Fixed overhead is incurred evenly by quarter over the course of the year and is allocated to production at the rate of $30 per direct labour hour.
- Selling and administrative expenses, as shown in the income statement, are all fixed except for sales commissions and bad debt expense, which vary directly with sales.
- The tax rate remains the same as last year; taxes are paid in quarter 4.

- During 2018, the company will add $225,000 of equipment: $100,000 in the first quarter and $125,000 in the second quarter.
- At June 30, 2017, the company had $48,000 cash on hand, net accounts receivable of $151,200, and inventory of $150,525 (including 375 finished boards, 325 raw boards, and 325 fittings). Land amounted to $66,075, building and equipment to $148,000, accumulated depreciation to $68,700, accounts payable to $85,000, and shareholders' equity to $410,100.
- The company borrows any money that it needs on the first day of the quarter and repays any principal and interest on that principal on the last day of the quarter. The interest rate on all loans is 6 percent per year and is accessed in $100,000 increments.
- The company requires that a minimum of $100,000 be in the bank at the end of each quarter.

Required:

Prepare a master budget for fiscal 2018, with all of its components, including pro forma income statement and pro forma balance sheet, based on the above information.

Problem 9-38 Budgeting in the Government Sector, Internet Research

OBJECTIVE 1 2

Like companies do, the Canadian government must prepare a budget each year. However, unlike private, for-profit companies, the budget and its details are available to the public. The entire budgetary process is established by law. The government makes available a considerable amount of information concerning the federal budget. Most of this information can be found on the Internet. Using Internet resources (e.g., consider accessing the Department of Finance Canada at http://www.fin.gc.ca), answer the following questions.

Required:

1. When is the federal budget prepared?
2. Who is responsible for preparing the federal budget?
3. How is the final federal budget determined? Explain in detail how the government creates its budget.
4. What percentage of the gross domestic product (GDP) is represented by the federal budget?
5. What are the revenue sources for the federal budget? Indicate the percentage contribution of each of the major sources.
6. How does Canadian spending as a percentage of GDP compare with spending of other countries?
7. How are deficits financed?

PROFESSIONAL EXAMINATION PROBLEMS*

Professional Examination Problem 9-39 Budgeting—Delos Manufacturing Company

Delos Manufacturing Company makes two basic products, Cee and Dee. Data assembled by the managers is:

	Cee	Dee
Requirements for finished unit:		
Raw material 1	10 kg	8 kg
Raw material 2		4 kg
Raw material 3	2 units	1 unit
Direct labour	5 hours	8 hours
Sales price	$150	$200
Sales units	12,000	9,000
Estimated beginning inventory	400	150
Desired ending inventory	300	200

(Continued)

	Raw Materials		
	1	2	3
Cost	$ 2.00 per kilogram	$ 2.50 per kilogram	$ 0.50 per unit
Estimated beginning inventory	3,000	1,500	1,000
Desired ending inventory	4,000	1,000	1,500

The direct labour wage rate is $14 per hour. Overhead is applied on the basis of direct labour hours. The tax rate is 40 percent.

The budgeted sales level is divided into quarters. Delos estimates that 20 percent of the annual sales will be in the first quarter, 30 percent in the second, and 25 percent in the third and fourth quarters. The beginning inventory of finished products has the same cost per unit as the ending inventory. The work-in-process inventory is negligible.

Delos Manufacturing Company
Sales Forecasts by Products 2017

	Cee		Dee		
	Units	Dollars	Units	Dollars	Total Dollars
First quarter	2,400	$ 360,000	1,800	$ 360,000	$ 720,000
Second quarter	3,600	540,000	2,700	540,000	1,080,000
Third quarter	3,000	450,000	2,250	450,000	900,000
Fourth quarter	3,000	450,000	2,250	450,000	900,000
Total	12,000	$1,800,000	9,000	$1,800,000	$3,600,000

Factory Overhead Costs

Indirect materials	$ 10,000
Miscellaneous supplies and tools	5,000
Indirect labour	40,000
Supervision	20,000
Payroll taxes and fringe benefits	75,000
Maintenance costs—fixed	20,000
Maintenance costs—variable	10,000
Depreciation	70,000
Heat, light, and power—fixed	8,710
Heat, light, and power—variable	5,090
	$263,800

Selling and Administrative Expenses

Advertising	$ 60,000
Sales salaries	200,000
Travel and entertainment	60,000
Depreciation—warehouse	5,000
Office salaries	20,000
Executive salaries	250,000
Supplies	4,000
Depreciation—office	6,000
	$605,000

Required:

Prepare the following:

a. Production budget
b. Direct materials purchase budget
c. Direct labour budget
d. Cost of goods sold budget
e. Budgeted income statement

Note: Because you are given inventory values for the beginning and the end of the year, it is impossible to construct budgets by quarter. The budgets should be presented for the whole year.

Professional Examination Problem 9-40 **Budgeting—Calydon Corporation**

Calydon Corporation manufactures and distributes wooden baseball bats. This is a seasonal business with a large portion of its sales occurring in late winter and early spring. The production schedule for the last quarter of the year is heavy in order to build up inventory to meet expected sales volume.

The company experiences a temporary cash strain during this heavy production period. Payroll costs rise during the last quarter because overtime is scheduled to meet the increased production needs. Collections from customers are low because the fall season produces only modest sales. This year, the company's concern is intensified because prices are increasing during the current inflationary period. In addition, the sales department forecasts sales of fewer than 1 million bats for the first time in three years. This decrease in sales appears to be caused by the popularity of aluminum bats.

The cash account builds up during the first and second quarters as sales exceed production. The excess cash is invested in treasury bills and other commercial paper. During the last half of the year, the temporary investments are liquidated to meet the cash needs. In the early years of the company, short-term borrowing was used to supplement the funds released by selling investments, but this has not been necessary in recent years. Because costs are higher this year, the treasurer asks for a forecast for December to judge if the $40,000 in temporary investments will be adequate to carry the company through the month with a minimum balance of $10,000. Should this amount ($40,000) be insufficient, she wants to begin negotiations for a short-term loan.

The unit sales volume for the past two months and the estimate for the next four months are:

October (actual)	70,000
November (actual)	50,000
December (estimated)	50,000
January (estimated)	90,000
February (estimated)	90,000
March (estimated)	120,000

The bats are sold for $5 each. All sales are made on account. Half of the accounts are collected in the month of the sale, 40 percent are collected in the month following the sale, and the remaining 10 percent in the second month following the sale. Customers who pay in the month of the sale receive a 2 percent cash discount.

The production schedule for the six-month period beginning with October reflects the company's policy of maintaining a stable year-round workforce by scheduling overtime to meet the following production schedules:

October (actual)	90,000
November (actual)	90,000
December (estimated)	90,000
January (estimated)	90,000
February (estimated)	100,000
March (estimated)	100,000

The bats are made from wooden blocks that cost $6 each. Ten bats can be produced from each block. The blocks are acquired one year in advance so they can be properly aged. Calydon pays the supplier one-twelfth of the cost of this material each month until the obligation is retired. The monthly payment is $60,000.

The plant is normally scheduled for a 40-hour, five-day work week. During the busy production season, however, the work week may be increased to six 10-hour days. Workers can produce 7.5 bats per hour. Normal monthly output is 75,000 bats. Factory employees are paid $15 per hour for regular time and time and one-half for overtime.

Other manufacturing costs include variable overhead of $0.30 per unit and annual fixed overhead of $280,000. Depreciation charges totalling $40,000 are included among the fixed overhead. Selling expenses include variable costs of $0.20 per unit and annual fixed costs of $60,000.

(Continued)

Fixed administrative costs are $120,000 annually. All fixed costs are incurred uniformly throughout the year.

The controller has accumulated the following additional information:

a. The balances of selected accounts as at November 30, 2018, are:

Cash	$ 12,000
Marketable securities, at market value	40,000
Accounts receivable	96,000
Prepaid expenses	4,800
Accounts payable (arising from raw material purchases)	300,000
Accrued vacation pay	9,500
Equipment note payable	102,000
Accrued income taxes payable	50,000

b. Interest to be received from the company's temporary investments is estimated at $500 for December.

c. Prepaid expenses of $3,600 will expire during December and the balance of the prepaid account is estimated at $4,200 for the end of December.

d. Calydon purchased new machinery in 2018 as part of a plant modernization program. The machinery was financed by a 24-month note of $144,000. The terms call for equal principal payments over the next 24 months with interest paid at the rate of 1 percent per month on the unpaid balance at the first of the month. The first payment was made on May 1, 2018.

e. Old equipment, which has a book value of $8,000, is to be sold during December for $7,500.

f. Each month the company accrues $1,700 for vacation pay by charging vacation pay expense and crediting accrued vacation pay. The plant closes for two weeks in June when all plant employees take a vacation.

g. Quarterly dividends of $0.20 per share will be paid on December 15 to shareholders of record. Calydon Corporation has authorized 10,000 shares. The company has issued 7,000 shares.

h. The quarterly income taxes payment of $50,000 is due on December 15, 2018.

Required:

Prepare a schedule that forecasts the cash position at December 31, 2018. What action, if any, will be required to maintain a $10,000 cash balance?

CASES

Case 9-41 Budgeting

Rajvir, an owner of a quickly growing three-year-old small-sized manufacturing business employing 43 staff, storms into her offsite accountant's office.

Rajvir: That's it! I've had it with this budgeting process. Before the start of each year we spend months collecting the inputs and compiling the master budget and I get no value from it during the course of the year. It's disruptive, wastes my employees' time, and costs me money.

Isaiah: Rajvir, please sit down. I put a lot of effort into your budget; how is it possible you find it so unhelpful?

Rajvir: I don't know if it's this industry or our company, but every month we miss our targets by large margins—some months we're way over; some months we're way under—I can't afford to make decisions based on the master budget anymore. I think I'm going to quit the budgeting process. It's just not valuable.

Rajvir, frustrated, takes her leave. Moments later, Isaiah is contemplating Rajvir's lamentations, and says to himself, "Wow, about 35 percent of my billable hours are spent on this budget. If I can't convince Rajvir that it is a valuable undertaking, I will have a lot of idle time on my hands. What can I do to convince her of the merits of budgeting? I had better call in my partner to discuss this."

Required:

You are the partner. How would you advise Isaiah to reason with Rajvir? In coming up with your answer, consider the following questions.

1. How should Rajvir use the budget?
2. What are the merits of budgeting for a new firm in a highly volatile industry?
3. How can you, Isaiah, and Rajvir change or improve the process?

Case 9-42 Cash Budget

OBJECTIVE 1 3 4

Dr. Roger Jones is a successful dentist but he is experiencing recurring financial difficulties. For example, Dr. Jones owns his office building, which he leases to the professional corporation that houses his dental practice (he owns all shares in the corporation). However, Dr. Jones recently received a registered letter from the Canada Revenue Agency threatening to impound his business and sell its assets for the corporation's failure to pay payroll taxes for the past six months. Also, the corporation has had difficulty paying its suppliers, owing one of them over $200,000 plus interest. In the past, Dr. Jones solved similar problems by borrowing money on the equity in either his personal residence or his office building. Not surprisingly, Dr. Jones has grown weary of these recurring problems and has hired a local consultant for advice on how to fix his financial problems.

According to the analysis of the consultant, the financial difficulties facing Dr. Jones have been caused by the absence of proper planning and control. Budgetary control is sorely needed. To assist you in preparing a plan of action that will help his dental practice regain financial stability, Dr. Jones has made available the following financial information describing a typical month.

Revenues

	Average Fee ($)	Quantity
Fillings	50	90
Crowns	300	19
Root canals	170	8
Bridges	500	7
Extractions	45	30
Cleaning	25	108
X-rays	15	150

Costs

Salaries:		
Two dental assistants	$1,900	
Receptionist/bookkeeper	1,500	
Hygienist	1,800	
Public relations (Mrs. Jones)	1,000	
Personal salary	6,500	
Total salaries		$12,700
Benefits		1,344
Building lease		1,500
Dental supplies		1,200
Janitorial		300
Utilities		400
Phone		150
Office supplies		100
Lab fees		5,000
Loan payments		570
Interest payments		500
Miscellaneous		500
Depreciation		700
Total costs		$24,964

(Continued)

Benefits include Dr. Jones's share of a health insurance premium for all employees. Although all revenues billed in a month are not collected, the cash flowing into the business is approximately equal to the month's billings because of collections from prior months. The dental office is open Monday through Thursday from 8:30 a.m. to 4:00 p.m. and on Friday from 8:30 a.m. to 12:30 p.m. A total of 32 hours are worked each week. Additional hours could be worked, but Dr. Jones is reluctant to do so because of other personal endeavours that he enjoys.

Dr. Jones has noted that the two dental assistants and receptionist are not fully utilized. He estimates that they are busy about 70 percent of the time. Dr. Jones's wife spends about 5 hours each week on a monthly newsletter that is sent to all patients; she also maintains a birthday list and sends cards to patients on their birthdays.

Dr. Jones spends about $2,400 yearly on informational seminars. These seminars, targeted especially for dentists, teach them how to increase their revenues. It is from one of these seminars that Dr. Jones decided to invest in promotion and public relations (the newsletter and the birthday list).

Required:

1. Prepare a monthly cash budget for Dr. Jones. Does Dr. Jones have a significant cash flow problem? How would you use the budget to show Dr. Jones why he is having financial difficulties?
2. Using the cash budget prepared in Requirement 1 and the information given in the case, recommend actions to solve Dr. Jones's financial problems. Prepare a cash budget that reflects these recommendations and that demonstrates to Dr. Jones that the problems can be corrected. Do you think that Dr. Jones will accept your recommendations? Do any of the behavioural principles discussed in the chapter have a role in this type of setting? Explain.

OBJECTIVE 

Case 9-43 Budgetary Performance, Rewards, Ethical Behaviour

Linda Ellis, division manager, is evaluated and rewarded on the basis of budgetary performance. Linda, her assistants, and the plant managers are all eligible to receive a bonus if actual divisional profits are between budgeted profits and 120 percent of budgeted profits. The bonuses are based on a fixed percentage of actual profits. Profits above 120 percent of budgeted profits earn a bonus at the 120 percent level (in other words, there is an upper limit on possible bonus payments). If the actual profits are less than budgeted profits, no bonuses are awarded. Consider the following actions taken by Linda:

a. Linda tends to overestimate expenses and underestimate revenues. This approach facilitates the ability of the division to attain budgeted profits. Linda believes that the action is justified because it increases the likelihood of receiving bonuses and helps to keep the morale of the managers high.
b. Suppose that toward the end of the fiscal year, Linda saw that the division would not achieve budgeted profits. Accordingly, she instructed the sales department to defer the closing of a number of sales agreements to the following fiscal year. She also decided to write off some inventory that was nearly worthless. Deferring revenues to next year and writing off the inventory in a no-bonus year increased the chances of a bonus for next year.
c. Assume that toward the end of the year, Linda saw that actual profits would likely exceed the 120 percent limit and that she took actions similar to those described in item b.

Required:

1. Comment on the ethics of Linda's behaviour. Are her actions right or wrong? What role does the company play in encouraging her actions?
2. Suppose that you are the marketing manager for the division, and you receive instructions to defer the closing of sales until the next fiscal year. What would you do?

3. Suppose that you are a plant manager, and you know that your budget has been padded by the division manager. Further, suppose that the padding is common knowledge among the plant managers, who support it because it increases the ability to achieve the budget and receive a bonus. What would you do?
4. Suppose that you are the division controller, and you receive instructions from the division manager to accelerate the recognition of some expenses that legitimately belong to a future period. What would you do?

10

Standard Costing: A Managerial Control Tool

Larry MacDougal/Associated Press

After studying Chapter 10, you should be able to:

1. Explain how unit standards are set and why standard cost systems are adopted.
2. Explain the purpose of a standard cost sheet.
3. Describe the basic concepts underlying variance analysis, and explain when variances should be investigated.
4. Compute the materials variances, and explain how they are used for control.
5. Compute the labour variances, and explain how they are used for control.
6. *(Appendix 10A)* Prepare journal entries for materials and labour variances.

EXPERIENCE MANAGERIAL DECISIONS
with Agrium Inc.

Understanding an income statement is a relatively easy task. However, understanding the causes underlying net income represents a far more challenging task, especially for companies like Agrium Inc., a Canadian supplier of agricultural products and services, whose annual sales are typically in the neighbourhood of several billion dollars. Agrium uses variance analysis as an important tool for understanding the many causes of its income. This type of analysis helps managers at Agrium to learn which parts of the company are contributing to net income as expected and which parts are not contributing and, as such, will require careful attention to improve. For example, Agrium reported that its 2013 second quarter gross profit decreased by $129 million compared to the same period in 2012. If you were a manager in Agrium, what would you do after receiving this news?

Before Agrium's management took any rash action, it performed an in-depth variance analysis to understand what had caused the unfavourable variance between its actual profit at quarter-end 2013 and at quarter-end 2012. As you might expect, variance analysis revealed that the $129 million unfavourable variance comprised numerous smaller variances, some favourable and others unfavourable. For instance, the company was able to determine that the poor weather conditions in North America in the spring of 2013 largely contributed to the wholesale division's $166 million decrease in gross profit. More specifically, the weather factors reduced the selling prices for urea, potash, and phosphate, which had a direct impact on the wholesale division's income. Partially offsetting this decrease in gross profit, the retail division experienced a $38 million increase in gross profit by increasing the total sales of crop nutrients, crop protection products, and seeds.

Mike Wilson, Agrium's president and CEO, was quoted as saying:

> The cold, wet weather experienced in North America this spring resulted in a compressed spring application and Agrium rose to this challenge by delivering crop input products and services to our customers in a highly efficient manner. This highlights the strength of our production and distribution assets and our ability to deliver significant value to our customers.

Without variance analysis, Agrium would have a much harder time understanding the causes of its income and taking the appropriate action when components of income are different than expected.

UNIT STANDARDS

OBJECTIVE 1

Explain how unit standards are set and why standard cost systems are adopted.

Most operating managers recognize the need to control costs. Cost control often means the difference between success and failure, or between above-average profits and lesser profits. For example, as healthcare costs skyrocket due to the large and aging baby boomer generation, the growing complexity of medical treatments, and the growing number of uninsured patients, most healthcare facilities are desperately trying to budget and control costs more effectively. Usually, cost control means that managers must be cost conscious and assume responsibility for this important objective.

In Chapter 9, we learned that budgets set standards that are used to control and evaluate managerial performance. However, budgets are aggregate measures of performance; they identify the revenues and costs in total that an organization should experience if plans are executed as expected. By comparing the actual costs and actual revenues with the corresponding budgeted amounts at the same level of activity, a measure of managerial efficiency emerges.

Although the process just described provides significant information for control, developing standards for unit amounts—as well as for total amounts—can enhance control. To determine the unit standard cost for a particular input, two decisions must be made:

- *The quantity decision*—the amount of input that should be *used* per unit of output
- *The pricing decision*—the amount that should be paid for the quantity of the input to be used

The quantity decision produces **quantity standards**, and the pricing decision produces **price standards**. The unit standard cost can be computed by multiplying these two standards.

Standard cost per unit = Quantity standard × Price standard

analytical Q&A

If the unit quantity standard for a raw material is 10 kilograms per unit, and the cost per kilogram of this material is $8, what is the standard cost per unit of product for the material?

Answers on pages 734 to 738.

For example, a soft-drink bottling company may decide that 300 grams of fructose should be used for every 1 litre bottle of cola (the quantity standard), and the price of the fructose should be $0.20 per 100 grams (the price standard). The standard cost of the fructose per bottle of cola is then $0.60 (= 3 × $0.20). The standard cost per unit of fructose can be used to predict what the total cost of fructose should be as the activity level varies; thus, it becomes a flexible budget formula. If 10,000 bottles of cola are produced, then the total expected cost of fructose is $6,000 (= $0.60 × 10,000); if 15,000 bottles are produced, then the total expected cost of fructose is $9,000 (= $0.60 × 15,000).

How Standards Are Developed

Three potential sources of quantity standards are:

1. *Historical experience* Historical experience may provide an initial guideline for setting standards, but it should be used with caution. Often, processes are operating inefficiently; adopting input–output relationships from the past thus perpetuates these inefficiencies.
2. *Engineering studies* Engineering studies can determine the most efficient way to operate and can provide rigorous guidelines; however, engineered standards often are too rigorous. They may not be achievable by operating personnel.
3. *Input from operating personnel* Since operating personnel are accountable for meeting standards, they should have significant input in setting standards.

Price standards are the joint responsibility of operations, purchasing, personnel, and accounting. Operating personnel determine the quality of the inputs required; personnel and purchasing have responsibility for acquiring the labour and materials quality requested at the lowest price. Market forces limit the range of choices for price standards. In setting price standards, purchasing must consider discounts, freight, and quality; personnel, on the other hand, must consider payroll taxes, fringe benefits, and qualifications. Accounting is responsible for recording the price standards, as well as for preparing reports that compare actual performance with the standard.

concept Q&A

What is the difference between an ideal standard and a currently attainable standard?

Answers on pages 734 to 738.

Types of Standards

Standards are generally classified as either ideal or currently attainable.

- **Ideal standards** demand maximum efficiency and can be achieved only if everything operates perfectly. No machine breakdowns, slack, or lack of skill (even momentarily) are allowed.
- **Currently attainable standards** can be achieved under efficient operating conditions. Allowance is made for normal breakdowns, interruptions, less than perfect skill, and so on. These standards are demanding but achievable. Exhibit 10.1 provides a visual and conceptual portrayal of the two standards.

EXHIBIT 10.1

Types of Standards

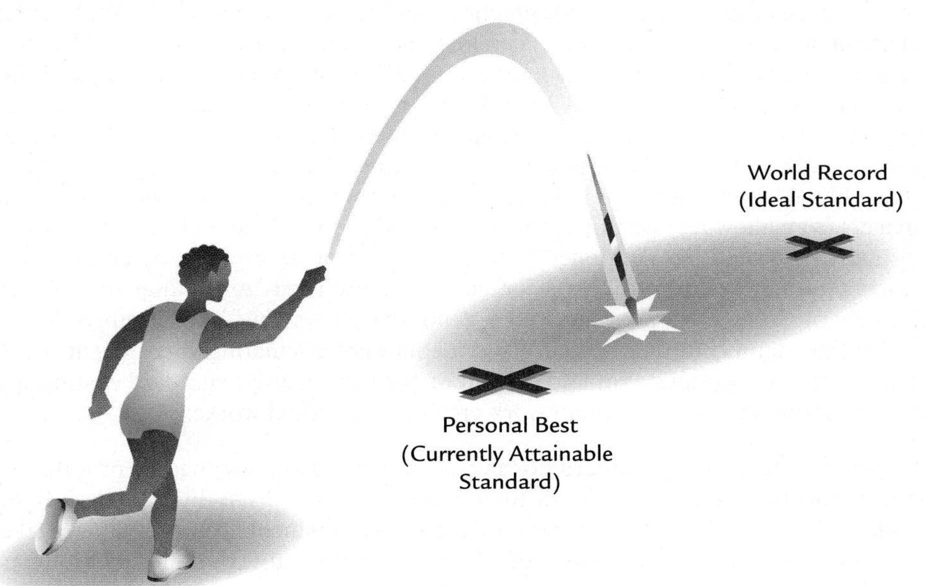

Of the two types, currently attainable standards offer the most behavioural benefits. If standards are too tight and never achievable, workers become frustrated and performance levels decline. However, challenging yet achievable standards tend to extract higher performance levels—particularly when the individuals subject to the standards have participated in their creation.

Why Standard Cost Systems Are Adopted

Two reasons for adopting a standard cost system are frequently mentioned: to improve planning and control, and to facilitate product costing.

Planning and Control Standard costing systems enhance planning and control and improve performance measurement. Unit standards are a fundamental requirement for a flexible budgeting system, which is a key feature of a meaningful planning and control system. Budgetary control systems compare actual costs with budgeted costs by computing variances, the difference between the actual and planned costs for the actual level of activity. By developing unit price and quantity standards, an overall variance can be further broken down into a price variance and a usage or efficiency variance which provide additional information to managers.

As an example, an unfavourable variance can show a manager whether there are discrepancies between planned prices and actual prices, between planned usage and actual usage, or between both prices and usage. For instance, variance analysis enabled Agrium to understand the impact of reduced selling prices of urea, potash, and phosphate on the wholesale division's operating income. Since operating managers have more control over the usage of inputs than over their prices, efficiency variances provide specific signals regarding the need for corrective action and where that action should be focused. Thus, in principle, the use of efficiency variances enhances operational control. Additionally, by breaking out the price variance, over which operating managers potentially have less control, the system provides an improved measure of managerial efficiency.

The benefits of operational control, however, may not extend to the manufacturing environments that are emphasizing continuous improvement and just-in-time (JIT) purchasing and manufacturing. The use of a standard cost system for operational control in these settings can produce dysfunctional behaviour. For example, materials price variance reporting may encourage the purchasing department to buy in large quantities in order to take advantage of discounts. Yet this practice might lead to holding significant inventories, something not desired by JIT firms. Therefore, the detailed computation of variances—at least at the operational level—is discouraged for JIT firms. Nonetheless, standards in this newer manufacturing environment are still useful for planning, such as in the creation of bids. Also, variances may still be computed and presented in reports to higher-level managers so that the financial dimension can be monitored. In addition, other incentives, such as a fee charged to managers for holding excessive inventories, can be created to discourage managers from allowing inventories to grow beyond the level desired by JIT systems.

Finally, it should be mentioned that many firms operate with conventional manufacturing systems; standard cost systems are widely used. According to one survey, 87 percent of the firms responding used a standard cost system.[1] Furthermore, the survey revealed that significant numbers of respondents were calculating variances at the operational level. For example, about 40 percent of the firms using a standard costing system reported labour variances for small work crews or individual workers.

Product Costing In a standard costing system, costs are assigned to products using quantity and price standards for all three manufacturing costs: direct materials, direct labour, and overhead. At the other end of the cost assignment spectrum, an actual costing system assigns the actual costs of all three manufacturing inputs to products. In the middle of this spectrum is a normal costing system, which predetermines overhead costs for the purpose of product costing but assigns direct materials and direct labour to products by using actual costs. Thus, a normal costing system assigns actual direct costs to products but allocates budgeted indirect costs to products using a budgeted rate and actual activity levels. Exhibit 10.2 summarizes these three cost assignment approaches.

Cost Assignment Approaches

Standard product costing has several advantages over normal costing and actual costing. One, of course, is the greater capacity for control. Standard costing systems also provide readily available unit cost information that can be used for pricing decisions at any time throughout the period because actual costs (either direct or indirect) do not need to be known. This ability is particularly helpful for companies that do a significant amount of bidding and that are paid on a cost-plus basis.

[1] Bruce R. Gaumnitz and Felix P. Kollaritsch, "Manufacturing Variances: Current Practice and Trends," *Journal of Cost Management* (Spring 1991): 59–64. Similar widespread usage is also reported by Carole B. Cheatham and Leo R. Cheatham, "Redesigning Cost Systems: Is Standard Costing Obsolete?" *Accounting Horizons* (December 1996): 23–31. Furthermore, a survey of UK firms revealed that 76 percent of them use a standard cost system; see Colin Drury, "Standard Costing: A Technique at Variance with Modern Management," *Management Accounting* (London, November 1999): 56–58.

EXHIBIT 10.2

Cost Assignment Approaches

	Manufacturing Costs		
	Direct Materials	Direct Labour	Overhead
Actual costing system	Actual	Actual	Actual
Normal costing system	Actual	Actual	Budgeted
Standard costing system	Standard	Standard	Standard

Other simplifications also are possible. For example, if a process-costing system uses standard costing to assign product costs, there is no need to compute a unit cost for each equivalent unit cost category since a standard unit cost would exist for each category. Additionally, there is no need to distinguish between the first-in, first-out (FIFO) and weighted average methods of accounting for beginning inventory costs. Usually, a standard process-costing system will follow the *equivalent unit* calculation of the FIFO approach. That is, current equivalent units of work are calculated using the FIFO approach. By calculating current equivalent work, current actual production costs can be compared with standard costs for control purposes.

concept Q&A

Why would a firm adopt a standard costing system?

Answers on pages 734 to 738.

STANDARD PRODUCT COSTS

OBJECTIVE 

Explain the purpose of a standard cost sheet.

In manufacturing firms, standard costs are developed for direct materials, direct labour, and overhead. Using these costs, the **standard cost per unit** is computed. The **standard cost sheet** provides the production data needed to calculate the standard unit cost. To illustrate, a standard cost sheet will be developed for a 500-gram bag of corn chips produced by Crunchy Chips Inc. The production of corn chips begins by steaming and soaking corn kernels overnight in a lime solution. This process softens the kernels so that they can be shaped into a sheet of dough. The dough is then cut into small triangular chips. Next, the chips are toasted in an oven and are dropped into a deep fryer. After cooking, the chips pass under a salting device and are inspected for quality. Substandard chips are sorted and discarded; the chips that pass inspection are bagged by a packaging machine. The bagged chips are manually packed into boxes for shipping.

Four materials are used to process corn chips: yellow corn, cooking oil, salt, and lime. The bag in which the chips are placed is also classified as a direct material. Crunchy Chips has two types of direct labourers: machine operators and inspectors (or sorters). Variable overhead is made up of three costs: gas, electricity, and water. Both variable and fixed overhead are applied by using direct labour hours. The standard cost sheet is given in Exhibit 10.3.

Note that it should cost \$1.61 to produce a 500-gram bag of corn chips. Also, notice that the company should use 550 grams of corn to produce a 500-gram bag of chips. There are two reasons for this 50-gram difference:

1. *Waste*: Some chips are discarded during the inspection process. The company plans on a normal amount of waste.
2. *Packaging*: The company wants to have slightly more than 500 grams in each bag to increase customer satisfaction with its product and to avoid any problems with fair packaging laws.

Exhibit 10.3 also reveals other important insights. The standard usage for variable and fixed overhead is tied to the direct labour standards. For variable overhead, the rate is \$4.00 per direct labour hour. Since one bag of corn chips should use 0.02 hours of direct labour per unit, the variable overhead cost assigned to a bag of corn chips is \$0.08 (= \$4.00 × 0.02).

EXHIBIT 10.3

Standard Cost Sheet for Corn Chips (500 g bag)

Description	Standard Price	Standard Usage	Standard Cost*	Subtotal
Direct materials:				
Yellow corn	$0.018**	550 g	$0.10	
Cooking oil	0.30**	50 g	0.15	
Salt	1.00**	25 g	0.25	
Lime	0.50**	100 g	0.50	
Bags	0.05	1 bag	0.05	
Total direct materials				$1.05
Direct labour:				
Inspection	8.00	0.01 hr.	0.08	
Machine operators	10.00	0.01 hr.	0.10	
Total direct labour				0.18
Overhead				
Variable overhead	4.00	0.02 hr.	0.08	
Fixed overhead	15.00	0.02 hr.	0.30	
Total overhead				0.38
Total standard unit cost				$1.61

* Calculated by multiplying price times usage. Yellow corn is rounded.
** Prices are per 100 grams.

analytical Q&A

A product is allowed 100 grams of silver per unit and 0.5 hour of labour. If 3,000 units are produced, what is the standard quantity of silver allowed? Standard quantity of labour?

Answers on pages 734 to 738.

For fixed overhead, the rate is $15.00 per direct labour hour, making the fixed overhead cost per bag of corn chips $0.30 (= $15.00 × 0.02). About 20 percent of the cost of production is fixed, indicating a capital-intensive production effort. Indeed, much of the operation is mechanized.

The standard cost sheet also indicates the quantity of each input that should be used to produce one unit of output. These unit quantity standards can then be used to compute the total amount of inputs allowed for the actual output. This computation is an essential component in computing efficiency variances. A manager should be able to compute the **standard quantity of materials allowed (SQ)** and the **standard hours allowed (SH)** for the actual output.

$$SQ = \text{Unit quantity standard} \times \text{Actual output}$$
$$SH = \text{Unit labour standard} \times \text{Actual output}$$

This computation must be done for every class of direct material and every class of direct labour. Cornerstone 10.1 shows how to compute these quantities by using one type of material and one class of labour.

CORNERSTONE 10.1 Computing Standard Quantities Allowed (*SQ* and *SH*)

Information:

Assume that 48,500 bags of corn chips are produced during the first week of March. The unit quantity standard is 550 grams of yellow corn per package (Exhibit 10.3). The unit quantity standard for machine operators is 0.01 hour per package produced (Exhibit 10.3).

(Continued)

Required:

How much yellow corn and how many operator hours should be used for the actual output of 48,500 packages?

CORNERSTONE

10.1

(Continued)

Solution:

Corn allowed:

SQ = Unit quantity standard × Actual output
= 550 × 48,500
= 26,675,000 grams

Operator hours allowed:

SH = Unit labour standard × Actual output
= 0.01 × 48,500
= 485 direct labour hours

Why:

Once quantity standards have been set for each unit of output, these must be translated into the quantities of units allowed for the level of output achieved, if the production operations were meeting the standards. These will be calculated for each component of input for the units produced.

VARIANCE ANALYSIS: GENERAL DESCRIPTION

OBJECTIVE 

Describe the basic concepts underlying variance analysis, and explain when variances should be investigated.

It is possible to calculate the costs that should have been incurred for the actual level of activity. This figure is obtained by multiplying the amount of input allowed (either materials or labour) for the actual output by the standard price of the input.

$$\text{Planned cost} = SP \times SQ$$

where

SP = Standard price per unit
SQ = Standard quantity of input allowed for the actual output

Actual input cost can be calculated as:

$$\text{Actual cost} = AP \times AQ$$

where

AP = Actual price per unit
AQ = Actual quantity of input used

The **total budget variance** is the difference between the actual cost of the input and its planned cost:

$$\begin{aligned}\text{Total budget variance} &= \text{Actual cost} - \text{Planned cost}\\ &= (AP \times AQ) - (SP \times SQ)\end{aligned}$$

As will be explained in Chapter 11, this variance is formally called the *static budget variance*. However, for now, the total budget variance will simply be called the *total variance*.

Because responsibility for deviations from planned prices tends to be located in the purchasing or personnel department and responsibility for deviations from planned usage of inputs tends to be located in the production department, it is important to separate the total variance into price and usage (quantity) variances.

Price and Usage Variances

Exhibit 10.4 provides a general model for calculating price and quantity variances for materials and labour.[2] For labour, the price variance is usually called a rate variance and is computed as the difference between the actual and standard unit price of an input multiplied by the number of inputs used:

$$\textbf{Price (rate) variance} = (AP - SP) \times AQ$$

The usage (quantity) variance is called an efficiency variance and is computed as the difference between the actual and standard quantities of inputs multiplied by the standard unit price of the input:

$$\textbf{Usage (efficiency) variance} = (AQ - SQ) \times SP$$

Unfavourable (U) variances occur whenever actual prices or actual usage of inputs are *greater* than standard prices or standard usage. When the opposite occurs, and actual prices or actual usage of inputs are *less* than standard prices or standard usage, **favourable (F) variances** are obtained. Favourable and unfavourable variances are not equivalent to good and bad variances. The terms merely indicate the relationship of the actual prices (or quantities) to the standard prices (or quantities). Whether the variances are good or bad depends on why they occurred. Determining the cause of a variance requires managers to do some investigation.

EXHIBIT 10.4

Variance Analysis: General Description

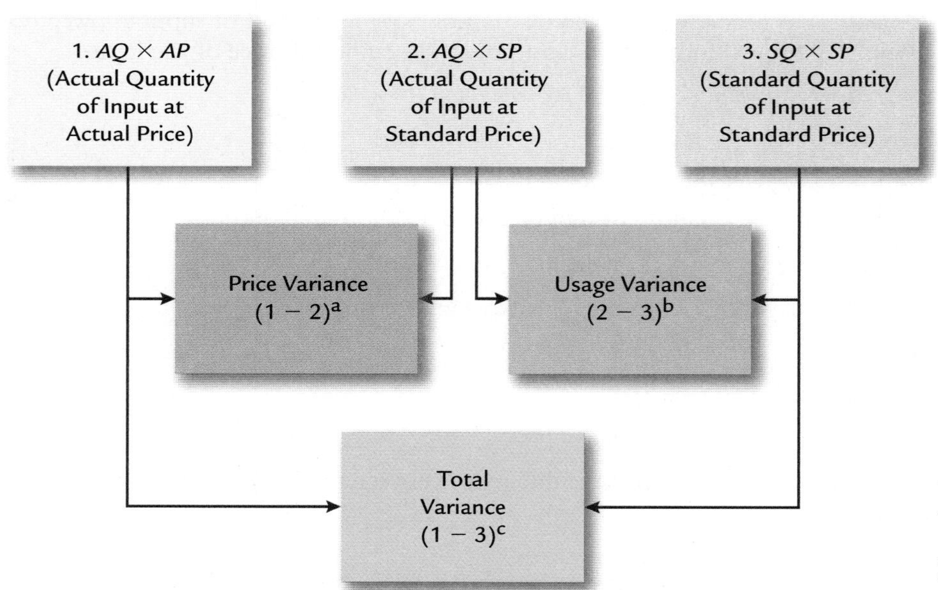

[a] Price variance = $(AQ \times AP) - (AQ \times SP) = (AP - SP)AQ$
[b] Usage variance = $(AQ \times SP) - (SQ \times SP) = (AQ - SQ)SP$
[c] Total variance = $(AQ \times AP) - (SQ \times SP)$

[2] Overhead variance analysis is discussed in Chapter 11.

The Decision to Investigate

Rarely will actual performance exactly meet the established standards, and management does not expect it to do so. Random variations around the standard are expected. As a result, management should have in mind an acceptable range of performance. When variances are within this range, they are assumed to be caused by random factors. When a variance falls outside of this range, the deviation is likely to be caused by nonrandom factors that managers may be able to control. In the noncontrollable case, managers need to revise the standard. In addition, it is possible that a variance too small to warrant investigation might be the result of two much larger but offsetting variances, which work in opposite directions. For example, a $5,000 unfavourable total variance for materials might comprise a $100,000 unfavourable price variance and a $95,000 favourable usage variance, both of which likely warrant investigation on their own. Detailed analysis allows managers to recognize such offsetting variance situations.

Two examples from the pharmaceutical industry may drive home the importance of variance investigation. Drugs must contain a certain amount of the active ingredient, plus or minus a small percent (e.g., aspirin claiming to have five grains per tablet must really have somewhere between 90 percent and 110 percent of the specified amount). In the United States, the Food and Drug Administration (FDA) is responsible for ensuring the safety and efficacy of drugs manufactured at home and abroad. An anonymous letter alerted the FDA to manufacturing problems with an antibiotic produced by a Canadian firm, Novopharm Ltd. Basically, the drug was too strong and could potentially destroy beneficial bacteria along with the harmful bacteria. Upon investigation, the FDA found the blending process to be "out of control." The result was that the firm stopped shipping that drug until the process could be corrected.[3]

In another situation from March 2013, pharmacists in an Ontario hospital noticed that a new supplier, Marchese Hospital Solutions, had provided diluted pre-mixed intravenous chemotherapy drugs. The previous supplier had provided the pre-mixed cancer drugs in bags with clear labelling detailing the total drug concentration, the total volume of saline, and the amount of active drug per millilitre of saline. As a result, pharmacists could administer the correct dosage for several patients from a single bag. Unaware that a single bag would be used for several patients, Marchese Hospital Solutions did not expect excess saline in each bag would be problematic. So long as a patient consumed the entire bag, the patient received the correct dosage. Unfortunately, due to the vague labelling, more than 1,200 people in Ontario and New Brunswick received the diluted cancer drugs.

Unlike for the Novopharm situation, the question of what to do about the company and the drug was not clear-cut. Since Marchese Hospital Solutions provided the drugs as contractually required, there were no clear rule violations. Instead, the example of Marchese Hospital Solutions highlighted a gap in quality control. While Health Canada requires drug manufacturers to follow strict quality control standards, companies providing pre-mixed drugs for hospitals do not have such tight controls. In response, Health Canada underwent a process to develop an oversight framework to reduce the likelihood of such an event occurring again.

concept Q&A

Suppose that the actual labour rate paid is $12 per hour, while the standard labour rate is $11.50. Will the labour rate variance be favourable or unfavourable?

Answers on pages 734 to 738.

Now that we understand why variance investigation is important, we need to understand when to investigate. Investigating the cause of variances and taking corrective action, like all activities, has associated costs. As a general principle, an investigation should be undertaken only if the expected benefits are greater than the expected costs. However, assessing the costs and benefits of a variance investigation is not an easy task. If a variance is likely to recur, the process may be permanently out of control, meaning that continuing savings may be achieved if corrective action is taken. But how is it possible to

[3] The FDA example given here is taken from an article by Christopher Drew, "Medicines from Afar Raise Safety Concerns," *The New York Times* (October 29, 1995): A1 and A16.

Corporate and Social Responsibility

The two pharmaceutical industry examples also illustrate the strong ethical content of variance analysis. Significant deviations from standards in these examples can cause physical harm to the users of the product, by being either too potent or not potent enough. In the most extreme situation, these deviations could have resulted in the loss of life. Therefore, it is critical that a strong control system be in place and function as intended. Competence is the guiding ethical standard. Clearly, the consumers of these products are concerned that those responsible individuals perform their professional duties in accordance with the relevant laws, regulations, and technical standards, and that the regulations are sufficient to protect the consumers. Organizations, professionals, consumers, and regulators all have an interest in maintaining high standards, as deviations from those expectations can have severe consequences.

know if the variance is going to recur unless an investigation is conducted? And how is it possible to know the cost of corrective action unless the cause of the variance is known?

Because it is difficult to assess the costs and benefits of variance analysis on a case-by-case basis, many firms adopt the general guideline of investigating variances only if they fall outside of an acceptable range. They are not investigated unless they are large enough to be of concern. They must be large enough to be caused by something other than random factors and large enough (on average) to justify the costs of investigating and taking corrective action.

How do managers determine whether variances are significant? How is the acceptable range established? The acceptable range is the standard, plus or minus an allowable deviation. The top and bottom measures of the allowable range are called the **control limits**. The upper control limit is the standard plus the allowable deviation, and the lower control limit is the standard minus the allowable deviation. Current practice sets the control limits subjectively. Based on past experience, intuition, and judgment, management determines the allowable deviation from standard.[4] The actual deviations from standard often are plotted over time against the upper and lower limits to allow managers to see the significance of the variance. Cornerstone 10.2 shows how control limits are used to trigger an investigation.

CORNERSTONE 10.2 Using Control Limits to Trigger a Variance Investigation

Information:

Standard cost is $100,000; allowable deviation is ±$10,000. The following are the actual costs for six months:

June	$ 97,500	September	$102,500
July	105,000	October	107,500
August	95,000	November	112,500

Required:

Plot the actual costs over time against the upper and lower control limits. Determine when a variance should be investigated.

(Continued)

[4] Bruce R. Gaumnitz and Felix P. Kollaritsch, "Manufacturing Variances: Current Practices and Trends," *Journal of Cost Management* (Spring 1991): 58–64. This article reports that about 45 to 47 percent of the firms use dollar or percentage control limits. Most of the remaining firms use judgment rather than any formal identification of limits.

CORNERSTONE 10.2

(Continued)

Solution:

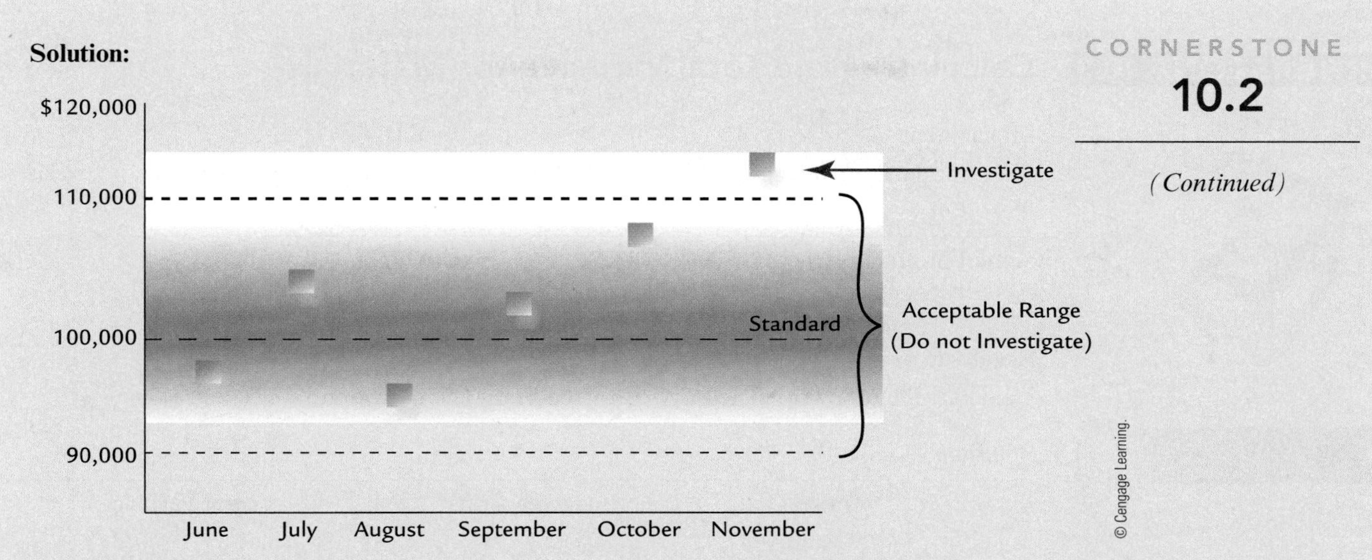

The control chart reveals that the last variance should be investigated. The chart also reveals a short-term increasing trend that suggests the process is moving out of control. A nongraphical approach is to calculate the difference between the actual cost and the upper or lower limit to determine if it exceeds $10,000.

Why:

Not all variances warrant a follow-up, so a mechanism must be established to determine which variances will be investigated further and which ones will not.

The control chart graphically illustrates the concept of control limits. The assumed standard is $100,000, and the allowable deviation is plus or minus $10,000; therefore, the upper limit is $110,000 and the lower limit is $90,000. Investigation occurs whenever an observation falls outside of these limits (as would be the case for the sixth observation). Trends can also be important.

The control limits often are expressed both as a percentage of the standard and as an absolute dollar amount. For example, the allowable deviation may be expressed as the lesser of 10 percent of the standard amount, and $10,000. In other words, management will investigate a deviation of more than $10,000 even if that deviation is less than 10 percent of the standard. Alternatively, even if the dollar amount is less than $10,000, an investigation is required if the deviation is more than 10 percent of the standard amount.

concept Q&A

Refer to the control chart in Cornerstone 10.2. What action would you take for an actual value of $89,750?

Answers on pages 734 to 738.

VARIANCE ANALYSIS: MATERIALS

OBJECTIVE 4

Compute the materials variances, and explain how they are used for control.

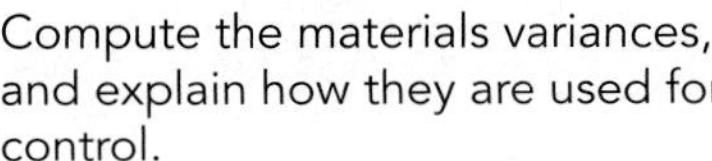

The total variance for materials measures the difference between the actual costs of materials and their budgeted costs for the actual level of activity.

$$\text{Total materials variance} = \text{Actual cost} - \text{Planned cost}$$
$$= (AP \times AQ) - (SP \times SQ)$$

Cornerstone 10.3 illustrates how to calculate the total variance for materials by using selected data from Crunchy Chips for the first week of March. To keep the example simple, only one material (corn) is illustrated.

CORNERSTONE 10.3

Calculating the Total Variance for Materials

Information:

Unit standards are from Exhibit 10.3. The following are the actual results for the first week in March:

Actual production	48,500 bags of corn chips
Actual cost of corn	26,000,000 grams at $0.02 per 100 g = $5,200

Required:

Calculate the total variance for corn for the first week in March.

Solution:

	Actual Costs $AQ \times AP$	Budgeted Costs* $SQ \times SP$	Total Variance $(AQ \times AP) - (SQ \times SP)$
Corn	$5,200	$4,801.50	$398.50 U

* The standard quantities for materials and labour are computed as unit quantity standards from Exhibit 10.3:

Corn: $SQ = 550 \times 48{,}500 = 26{,}675{,}000$ grams

Multiplying these standard quantities by the unit standard prices given in Exhibit 10.3 produces the budgeted amounts appearing in this column:

Corn: $0.018 per 100 g × 266,750 = $4,801.50

Why:

Calculating the total variance allows us to see that the actual results differ from the expected results. Further variance analysis of the total variance will allow us to understand what caused the total variance, such as a price or usage variance, or both.

Direct Materials Variances

To help control the cost of materials, price and usage variances are calculated. However, the sum of the price and usage variances will add up to the total materials variance calculated in Cornerstone 10.3 only if the materials purchased equal the materials used. The materials price variance (MPV) is computed by using the actual quantity of materials purchased, and the materials usage variance (MUV) is computed by using the actual quantity of materials used.

Since it is better to have information on variances earlier rather than later, the materials price variance uses the actual quantity of materials purchased rather than the actual quantity of materials used. The more timely the information, the more likely that proper managerial action can be taken. Materials may sit in inventory for weeks or months before they are needed in production. By the time the materials price variance is computed, signalling a problem, it may be too late to take corrective action. Or, even if corrective action is still possible, the delay may cost the company thousands of dollars. For example, suppose a new purchasing agent is unaware of the availability of a quantity discount on a raw material. If the materials price variance is computed when a new purchase is made, the resulting unfavourable signal will lead to quick corrective action. (In this case, the action would be to pursue the discount for future purchases.) If the materials price variance is not computed until the materials are issued to production, it may be several weeks or even months before the issue is discovered.

concept Q&A

When is the total materials variance the sum of the price variance and the usage variance?

Answers on pages 734 to 738.

Materials price and usage variances normally should be calculated using variance formulas. However, the three-pronged (columnar) approach is used when the materials purchased equal the materials used. Cornerstone 10.4 shows how to use the materials variance formulas, which we now specifically state and define.

Calculating Materials Variances: Formula and Columnar Approaches

CORNERSTONE 10.4

Information:

Unit standards are from Exhibit 10.3. The following are the actual results for the first week in March:

Actual production	48,500 bags of corn chips
Actual cost of corn	26,000,000 grams @ \$0.02 per 100 grams

Required:

Calculate the materials price and usage variances by using the three-pronged (columnar) and formula approaches.

Solution:

1. Formulas (recommended approach for materials variances because materials purchased may differ from materials used):

$$MPV = (AP - SP) \times AQ$$
$$= (\$0.02 - \$0.018) \times 260{,}000$$
$$= \$520 \text{ U}$$

$$MUV = (AQ - SQ) \times SP$$
$$= (260{,}000 - 266{,}750) \times \$0.018$$
$$= \$121.50 \text{ F}$$

2. Columnar (this approach is possible only if the materials purchased equal materials used):

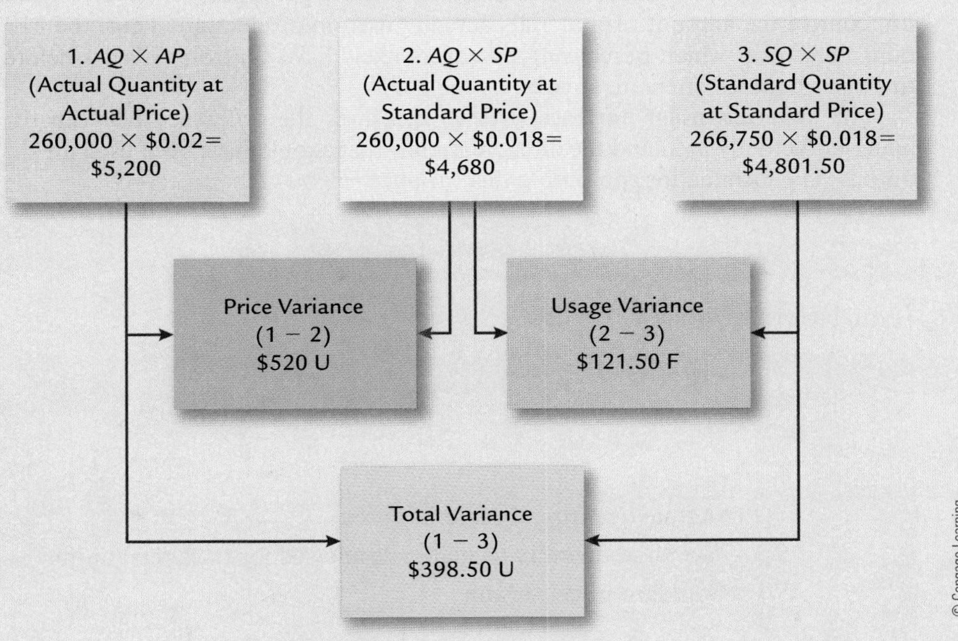

(Continued)

CORNERSTONE **10.4**

(Continued)

Why:

The total variance for materials is of limited value, so we must further analyze it into price and usage variances to be able to identify the specific type of corrective action that needs to be taken. There are two approaches that could be used.

The **materials price variance (MPV)** measures the difference between what should have been paid for raw materials and what was actually paid. The formula for computing this variance is:

$$MPV = (AP \times AQ) - (SP \times AQ)$$

or, factoring, we have:

$$MPV = (AP - SP) \times AQ$$

where

AP = Actual price per unit
SP = Standard price per unit
AQ = Actual quantity of materials purchased

It should be noted that the MPV formula uses the actual quantity purchased, rather than the standard amount that should have been purchased, because purchasing managers typically influence the amount of materials actually purchased. Likewise, the MPV uses materials purchased, rather than used, because purchasing managers typically do not control the amount of materials actually used in production. Thus, the MPV contains items over which purchasing managers likely have control, which is helpful given that their bonuses often are affected by the MPV.

The **materials usage variance (MUV)** measures the difference between the direct materials actually used and the direct materials that should have been used for the actual output. The formula for computing this variance is:

$$MUV = (SP \times AQ) - (SP \times SQ)$$

or, factoring:

$$MUV = (AQ - SQ) \times SP$$

where

AQ = Actual quantity of materials used
SQ = Standard quantity of materials allowed for the actual output
SP = Standard price per unit

It should be noted that the MUV formula uses the standard price that should have been paid, rather than the actual price that was paid, because production managers typically do not influence the actual price paid for materials. Using the standard price in the MUV—a variance for which production managers typically are held accountable—prevents them from unfairly being affected by the actual price.

> **analytical Q&A**
>
> Assume that $SP = \$3$ and $AP = \$2$. If 100 units are purchased, what is the materials price variance?
>
> Answers on pages 734 to 738.

Using Materials Variance Information

Calculating materials variances is only the first step. Using the variance information to exercise control is fundamental to a standard cost system. Responsibility must be assigned, variance significance must be assessed, and the variances must be accounted for and disposed of at the end of the year (see Appendix 10A for more information on the accounting for and disposition of variances).

Responsibility for the Materials Price Variance The responsibility for controlling the MPV usually belongs to the purchasing agent. Admittedly, the price of materials is largely beyond his or her control; however, the price variance can be influenced by such factors as quality, quantity discounts, distance of the source from the plant, and so on. These factors are often under the control of the agent.

Using the price variance to evaluate the performance of purchasing has some limitations. Emphasis on meeting or beating the standard can produce some undesirable outcomes. For example, if the purchasing agent feels pressured to produce favourable price variances, materials of lower quality than desired may be purchased or too much inventory may be acquired to take advantage of quantity discounts.

Analysis of the Materials Price Variance The first step in variance analysis is deciding whether or not the variance is significant. If it is judged insignificant, no further steps are needed. The MPV is $520 unfavourable, which is about 11 percent of standard cost (= $520/$4,801.50). Most managers would judge this variance to be significant. The next step is to find out why it occurred.

For the Crunchy Chips example, the investigation revealed that a higher-quality corn was purchased because of a shortage of the usual grade in the market. Once the reason is known, corrective action can be taken if necessary—and if possible. In this case, no corrective action is needed. The firm has no control over the supply shortage; it will simply have to wait until market conditions improve.

Responsibility for the Materials Usage Variance The production manager is generally responsible for materials usage. Minimizing scrap, waste, and rework are all ways in which the manager can ensure that the standard is met. However, at times, the cause of the variance is attributable to others outside of the production area, as the next section shows.

As with the price variance, using the usage variance to evaluate performance can lead to undesirable behaviour. For example, a production manager feeling pressure to produce a favourable usage variance might allow a defective unit to be transferred to finished goods (FG). While this transfer avoids the problem of wasted materials, it may create customer relations problems.

Analysis of the Materials Usage Variance The favourable MUV is 3 percent of standard cost (= $121.50/$4,801.50), implying that an investigation in this case is not justified. This favourable usage variance likely stems from the higher-quality corn acquired by the purchasing department. This variance is insignificant and would not be investigated.

The total materials variance is $398.50 unfavourable. This is the $520 unfavourable MPV being partly offset by the $121.50 favourable materials usage variance. From the company's perspective, purchasing higher-quality corn had a collective negative impact on profitability. Although the higher-quality corn appears to have enabled the company to be more efficient during production, this was more than offset by the unfavourable MPV. Consequently, the company should revert to purchasing regular corn when supply becomes available.

Accounting and Disposition of Materials Variances Recognizing the price variance for materials at the point of purchase also means that the raw materials inventory is carried at standard cost. In general, materials variances are not inventoried. Typically, materials variances are added to cost of goods sold (COGS) if unfavourable and are subtracted from COGS if favourable. The journal entries associated with the purchase and usage of raw materials for a standard cost system are illustrated in Appendix 10A.

YOU DECIDE Relationship between MPV and MUV

As plant manager, you have been approached by the purchasing manager and the production manager and have been provided with the following input. Fabio Borini, the production manager, is unhappy with the quality of the electronic components being purchased. He claims that the quality of the component from the current supplier makes it impossible to meet the materials usage standard of 1.05 components per unit produced (five components out of every hundred must be replaced before a good product is obtained). Laura Cisse, the purchasing manager, on the other hand, claims that there is only one supplier available that will sell the needed component for $2.00, which exactly meets the current price standard. There are two alternative suppliers that sell higher quality components, but the prices are higher.

To obtain more information, you ask Laura to buy the component from each of the alternative suppliers, one week at a time. That way, the MPV and MUV can be compared for all three suppliers. Laura provides the following results (there are no beginning or ending inventories of the component for any of the three suppliers):

Supplier	*AP*	*SP*	*AQ*	*SQ**	*MPV*	*MUV*
Current	$2.00	$2.00	11,000	10,500	$ 0	$1,000 U
Alternative 1	$2.05	$2.00	10,500	10,500	$ 525 U	$ 0
Alternative 2	$2.10	$2.00	10,010	10,500	$1,001 U	$ 980 F

* 1.05 × 10,000

As plant manager, how would you interpret these results? If they are expected to continue, what actions would you take?

There is a definite relationship between the MPV and MUV. Since the quality of materials purchased can affect the usage through rejects and waste, it is important to look at the tradeoffs for the two variances. Relative to the current standard, acquiring higher quality materials improves the MUV but causes the MPV to deteriorate. Adding the two together reveals the best outcome for the company:

Supplier	*MPV + MUV*
Current	$1,000 U
Alternative 1	525 U
Alternative 2	21 U

The best outcome is for the alternative 2 supplier. Thus, the purchasing manager should be instructed to buy from this supplier and the price standard should be changed to $2.10 and the unit materials standard to 1.001.

Managers often have to consider the perspectives of both the purchasing and production departments. It's important to understand how each department measures success (MPV versus MUV) in order to make the best decision for the company.

VARIANCE ANALYSIS: DIRECT LABOUR

OBJECTIVE 5

Compute the labour variances, and explain how they are used for control.

The total labour variance measures the difference between the actual costs of labour and their budgeted costs for the actual level of activity.

$$\text{Total labour variance} = (AR \times AH) - (SR \times SH)$$

where

AH = Actual direct labour hours used
SH = Standard hours allowed
AR = Actual hourly wage rate
SR = Standard hourly wage rate

Cornerstone 10.5 illustrates how to calculate the total variance for labour by using selected data from Crunchy Chips for the first week of March. To keep the example simple, only inspection labour is illustrated.

Calculating the Total Variance for Inspection Labour

CORNERSTONE 10.5

Information:

Unit standards are from Exhibit 10.3. The following are the actual results for the first week in March:

Actual production	48,500 bags of corn chips
Actual cost of inspection labour	360 hours @ \$8.35 = \$3,006

Required:

Calculate the total variance for inspection labour for the first week in March.

Solution:

	Actual Costs	Budgeted Costs*	Total Variance
	$AR \times AH$	$SR \times SH$	$(AR \times AH) - (SR \times SH)$
Inspection labour	\$3,006	\$3,880	\$874 F

* The standard quantities for inspection labour are computed as unit quantity standards from Exhibit 10.3:

Labour: $SH = 0.01 \times 48{,}500 = 485$ hours

Multiplying these standard quantities by the unit standard prices given in Exhibit 10.3 produces the budgeted amount appearing in this column:

Labour: \$8:00 × 485 = \$3,880

Why:

We must calculate the total variance for labour to help us explain why actual results are different from the expected results.

Direct Labour Variances

Labour hours cannot be purchased and stored for future use as can be done with materials (i.e., there can be no difference between the amount of labour purchased and the amount of labour used). Therefore, unlike the total materials variance, the labour rate and labour efficiency variances always will add up to the total labour variance, as calculated in Cornerstone 10.5. Thus, the rate (price) and efficiency (usage) variances for labour can be calculated by using either the columnar approach or the associated formulas. Which technique to use is a matter of preference. The formulas are adapted to reflect the specific terms used for labour prices (rates) and usage (efficiency).

The **labour rate variance (LRV)** computes the difference between what was paid to direct labourers and what should have been paid given the actual level of output:

$$LRV = (AR \times AH) - (SR \times AH)$$

or, factoring:

$$LRV = (AR - SR) \times AH$$

where

AR = Actual hourly wage rate
SR = Standard hourly wage rate
AH = Actual direct labour hours used

The **labour efficiency variance (LEV)** measures the difference between the labour hours that were actually used and the labour hours that should have been used:

$$LEV = (AH \times SR) - (SH \times SR)$$

or, factoring:

$$LEV = (AH - SH) \times SR$$

where

AH = Actual direct labour hours used
SH = Standard direct labour hours that should have been used
SR = Standard hourly wage rate

Cornerstone 10.6 shows how to calculate the labour rate and efficiency variances for the Crunchy Chips example (for inspection labour only), using both a columnar approach and a formula approach.

CORNERSTONE 10.6

Calculating Labour Variances: Formula and Columnar Approaches

Information:

Unit standards are from Exhibit 10.3. The following are the actual results for the first week in March:

Actual production	48,500 bags of corn chips
Actual cost of inspection labour	360 hours @ \$8.35 = \$3,006

(Continued)

CORNERSTONE

10.6

(Continued)

Required:

Calculate the labour rate and efficiency variances by using the three-pronged (columnar) and formula approaches.

Solution:

Formulas:

$$LRV = (AR - SR) \times AH$$
$$= (\$8.35 - \$8.00) \times 360$$
$$= \$126\ U$$

$$LEV = (AH - SH) \times SR$$
$$= (360 - 485) \times \$8.00$$
$$= \$1{,}000\ F$$

Columnar:

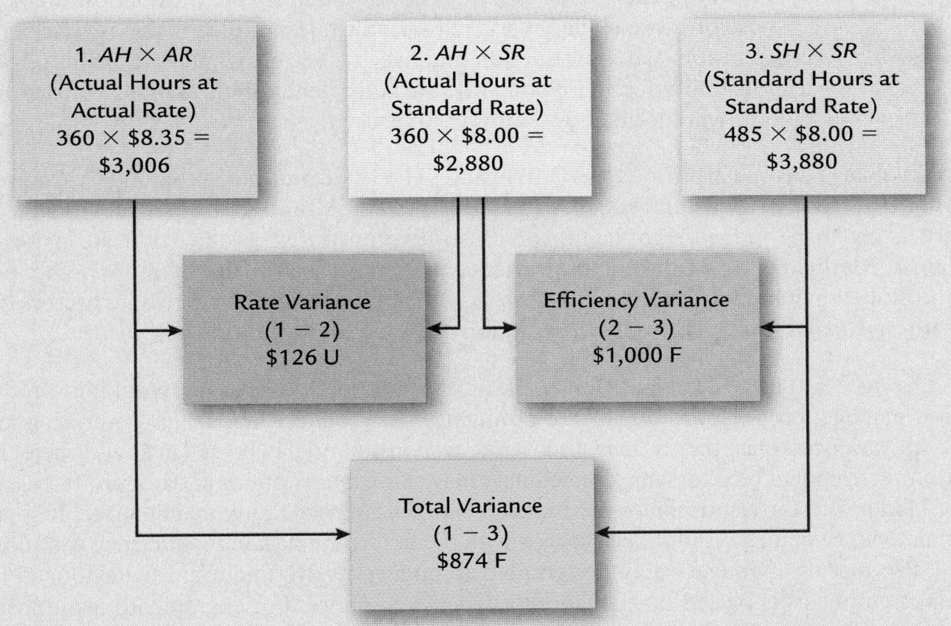

Why:

The total variance for labour is of limited value, so we must further analyze it into price and usage variances to be able to identify the specific type of corrective action that needs to be taken. There are two approaches that could be used.

Using Labour Variance Information

As with materials variances, calculating labour variances initiates the feedback process. Using the labour variance information to exercise control is fundamental. Responsibility must be assigned, variance significance must be assessed, and the variances must be accounted for and disposed of at the end of the year (see Appendix 10A for more information on the accounting for and disposition of variances).

Responsibility for the Labour Rate Variance Labour rates are largely determined by such external forces as labour market conditions and union contracts. The actual wage rate rarely departs from the standard rate. When labour rate variances do occur, they usually do so because:

- an average wage rate is used for the rate standard
- more skilled and more highly paid labourers are used for less-skilled tasks
- unexpected overtime was required

analytical Q&A

Assume that $AH = 100$ hours and $SH = 80$ hours, with $SR = \$10$. What is the labour efficiency variance?

Answers on pages 734 to 738.

Wage rates for a particular labour activity often differ among workers because of differing levels of seniority. Rather than selecting labour rate standards reflecting those different levels, often an average wage rate is chosen. As the seniority mix of workers changes, the average rate changes. This rate change will give rise to a labour rate variance; it also calls for a new standard to reflect the new seniority mix. Controllability is not assignable for this cause of a labour rate variance.

However, the use of labour is controllable by the production manager. The use of more-skilled workers to perform less-skilled tasks (or vice versa) is a decision that a production manager consciously makes. For this reason, responsibility for the labour rate variance generally is assigned to the individuals who decide how labour will be used.

Analysis of the Labour Rate Variance The unfavourable labour rate variance is only 3 percent of the standard cost (= $126/$3,880). Although a 3 percent variance is not likely to be judged significant, for illustrative purposes, assume that an investigation is conducted. The cause of the variance is found to be the use of more highly paid and skilled machine operators as inspectors, which occurred because two inspectors quit without formal notice. The corrective action is to hire and train two new inspectors.

Responsibility for the Labour Efficiency Variance Generally speaking, production managers are responsible for the productive use of direct labour. However, as is true of all variances, once the cause is discovered, responsibility may be assigned elsewhere. For example, frequent breakdowns of machinery may cause interruptions and nonproductive use of labour. But the responsibility for these breakdowns may be faulty maintenance. If so, the maintenance manager should be charged with the unfavourable labour efficiency variance.

Production managers may be tempted to engage in dysfunctional behaviour if too much emphasis is placed on the labour efficiency variance. For example, to avoid losing hours or using additional hours because of possible rework, a production manager could deliberately transfer defective units to FG.

Analysis of the Labour Efficiency Variance The labour efficiency variance is 26 percent of standard cost (= $1,000/$3,880). This favourable variance is judged to be significant, and an investigation is undertaken. Investigation reveals that inspections flowed more smoothly because of the higher-quality materials. This additional benefit should be factored into whether Crunchy should return to purchasing the normal-quality corn when it becomes available or whether the higher-quality material should again be purchased. In this case, it appears that the company can improve its profitability by continuing to purchase the higher-quality corn even when the normal quality material becomes available. Supporting this decision, the company's experience with using the higher-quality corn suggests that the $398.50 total unfavourable materials variance is more than offset by the $874 favourable labour variance.

Additional Cost Management Practices: Kaizen Costing and Target Costing

In addition to standard costing, some companies choose to employ other cost management practices, such as kaizen costing and target costing. Kaizen costing focuses on the continuous reduction of the manufacturing costs of existing products and processes. *Kaizen* is a

Japanese word meaning "continuous improvement." The philosophy in a *standard costing system* is that the budgeted expectation, or standard, should be met each period. However, as the phrase "continuous improvement" suggests, the philosophy in a *kaizen costing system* is that the budgeted expectation, or kaizen standard, of the current period should exceed the improvement accomplished the previous period. Using this philosophy, each period's kaizen standard is set based on prior periods' improvements, thereby locking in these improvements to push for even greater improvements in the future. Typically, continuous cost improvements are achieved by identifying a large number of relatively small cost-reducing opportunities (e.g., repositioning factory work space, placing or transporting work-in-process (WIP) inventory in such a way that the next worker can immediately access the inventory and begin working on it). For example, Honda uses kaizen costing practices to help its engineers implement the product design improvements identified by its shop floor workers.

Target costing focuses on the reduction of the design costs of existing and future products and processes. Increasingly, companies such as Toyota, Boeing, and Olympus are emphasizing cost management in the design stage as they begin to recognize that an astonishingly large percentage (somewhere between 75 and 90 percent) of a product's total costs are "locked in" or "committed to" by the time it finishes the design stage and moves into the manufacturing stage.[5] In target costing, the company will first determine a market price that reflects the product specifications or functions valued by the customer. From the market price, the company will deduct the desired per-unit profit which will leave the **target cost**—the difference between the sales price needed to capture a predetermined market share and the desired per-unit profit:

Target cost = Expected sales price per unit − Desired profit per unit

If the target cost is less than the current actual cost, then management must find cost reductions that decrease the actual cost to the target cost. Some managers refer to this process as closing the *cost gap*, which is the difference between current actual cost and the necessary target cost. Closing this cost gap is the principal challenge of target costing and usually requires the participation of suppliers and other business partners outside of the company over a period of several years. If this cost gap is not closed to zero (i.e., the actual cost is not reduced to the target cost) by the date the new product is planned to launch, then most target costing proponents will follow the cardinal rule of target costing and delay the product launch date until the gap is closed. The reason for the delay is that many managers feel that once the product launches, the incentive to reduce the actual cost falls significantly and, thus, the likelihood of the actual cost eventually decreasing to the target cost level necessary to generate the desired profit margin becomes unacceptably small. Caterpillar is famous for adhering to this rule even though the launch delay means that the company must forgo significant sales revenues during the delay period.

As you might have noticed, target costing is more than just cost control, because it includes expected sales revenues and desired profit margins in the calculation of the target cost. For this reason, target costing often is referred to as a profit-planning technique. In addition, target costing is more of a long-term approach to cost reduction, whereas kaizen costing is more of a continuous, short-term approach to cost reduction. Finally, given that target and kaizen costing practices focus on different segments of the value chain, they can serve as effective complements as an organization strives to reduce its costs along the entire value chain.

APPENDIX 10A: ACCOUNTING FOR VARIANCES

OBJECTIVE 6

Prepare journal entries for materials and labour variances.

To illustrate recording variances, we will assume that the MPV is computed at the time materials are purchased. With this assumption, we can state a general rule for a firm's inventory accounts: All inventories are carried at standard cost. As a result, actual costs

[5] See Julie H. Hertenstein and Marjorie B. Piatt, *Management Accounting*, April 1998, Vol. 79, Issue 10, p. 50 (6 pages).

are not entered into an inventory account; instead, applied standard costs flow through inventory and eventually to COGS. As illustrated in this appendix, the accounts containing the variances between applied standard costs and actual costs are closed, which allows the amount of actual costs to ultimately impact the final COGS number that appears in the financial statements. In recording variances, unfavourable variances are always debits, and favourable variances are always credits.

Entries for Direct Materials Variances

Materials Price Variance The entry to record the purchase of materials follows (assuming an unfavourable MPV and that AQ is materials purchased):

Materials	$SP \times AQ$	
Materials Price Variance	$(AP - SP)AQ$	
Accounts Payable		$AP \times AQ$

For example, if AP is \$0.0069 per gram of corn, SP is \$0.0060 per gram, and 780,000 grams of corn are purchased, the entry would be:

Materials	4,680	
Materials Price Variance	702	
Accounts Payable		5,382

Notice that the raw materials are carried in the inventory account at standard cost.

Materials Usage Variance The general form for the entry to record the issuance and usage of materials, assuming a favourable MUV, is as follows:

Work in Process	$SQ \times SP$	
Materials Usage Variance		$(AQ - SQ)SP$
Materials		$AQ \times SP$

Here, AQ is the materials issued and used, not necessarily equal to the materials purchased. Notice that only standard quantities and standard prices are used to assign costs to WIP; no actual costs enter this account.

For example, if AQ is 780,000 grams of corn, SQ is 873,000 grams, and SP is \$0.006, then the entry would be:

Work in Process	5,238	
Materials Usage Variance		558
Materials		4,680

Notice that the favourable usage variance appears as a credit entry.

Entries for Direct Labour Variances

Unlike the materials variances, the entry to record both types of labour variances is made simultaneously. The general form of this entry follows (assuming an unfavourable labour rate variance and an unfavourable labour efficiency variance).

Work in Process	$SH \times SR$	
Labour Rate Variance	$(AR - SR)AH$	
Labour Efficiency Variance	$(AH - SH)SR$	
Accrued Payroll		$AH \times AR$

Again, notice that only standard hours and standard rates are used to assign costs to WIP; actual prices or quantities are not used.

To give a specific example, assume that AH is 360 hours of inspection, SH is 339.5 hours, AR is \$7.35 per hour, and SR is \$7.00 per hour. The following journal entry would be made:

Work in Process	2,376.50	
Labour Rate Variance	126.00	
Labour Efficiency Variance	143.50	
Accrued Payroll		2,646.00

Disposition of Materials and Labour Variances

At the end of the year, the variances for materials and labour usually are closed to COGS. (This practice is acceptable provided that variances are not material in amount.) Using the previous data, the entries would take the following form:

Cost of Goods Sold	971.50	
Materials Price Variance		702.00
Labour Rate Variance		126.00
Labour Efficiency Variance		143.50
Materials Usage Variance	558.00	
Cost of Goods Sold		558.00

If the variances are material, they must be prorated among various accounts. For the MPV it is prorated among Materials Inventory, WIP, FG, and COGS. The remaining materials and labour variances are prorated among WIP, FG, and COGS. Typically, materials variances are prorated on the basis of the materials balances in each of these accounts and the labour variances on the basis of the labour balances in the accounts.

SUMMARY OF LEARNING OBJECTIVES

LO1. Explain how unit standards are set and why standard cost systems are adopted.

- A standard cost system budgets quantities and costs on a unit basis. These unit budgets are for labour, materials, and overhead. Standard costs, therefore, are the amount that should be expended to produce a product or service.
- Standards are set by using historical experience, engineering studies, and input from operating personnel, marketing, and accounting.
- Currently attainable standards are those that can be achieved under efficient operating conditions.
- Ideal standards are those achievable under maximum efficiency, or ideal operating conditions.
- Standard cost systems are adopted to improve planning and control, and to facilitate product costing. By comparing actual outcomes with standards and breaking the variance into price and quantity components, detailed feedback is provided to managers. This information allows managers to exercise a greater degree of cost control than that found in a normal or actual cost system.

LO2. Explain the purpose of a standard cost sheet.

- The standard cost sheet provides the details for computing the standard cost per unit. It shows the standard costs for materials, labour, and variable and fixed overhead.
- The standard cost sheet also reveals the quantity of each input that should be used to produce one unit of output. By using these unit quantity standards, the standard quantity of materials allowed and the standard hours allowed can be computed for the actual output.

LO3. Describe the basic concepts underlying variance analysis, and explain when variances should be investigated.

- The total variance is the difference between actual costs and planned costs.
- In a standard costing system, the total variance is broken down into price and usage variances. By breaking the total variances into price and usage variances, managers are better able to analyze and control the total variance.
- Variances should be investigated if they are material (i.e., significant) and if the benefits of corrective action are greater than the costs of investigation. Because of the difficulty of assessing costs and benefits on a case-by-case basis, many firms set up formal control limits—either a dollar amount, a percentage, or both. Other firms use judgment to assess the need to investigate.

LO4. Compute the materials variances, and explain how they are used for control.

- The materials price and usage variances are computed by using either a three-pronged (columnar) approach or formulas.
- The materials price variance is the difference between what was actually paid for materials (generally associated with the purchasing activity) and what should have been paid.
- The materials usage variance is the difference between the actual amount of materials used (generally associated with the production activity) and the amount of materials that should have been used.
- When a significant variance is signalled, an investigation is undertaken to find the cause. Corrective action is taken, if possible, to put the system back in control.

LO5. Compute the labour variances, and explain how they are used for control.

- The labour variances are computed by using either a three-pronged approach or formulas.
- The labour rate variance is caused by the actual wage rate differing from the standard wage rate. It is the difference between the wages that were paid and those that should have been paid.
- The labour efficiency variance is the difference between the actual amount of labour that was used and the amount of labour that should have been used.
- When a significant variance is signalled, investigation is called for, and corrective action should be taken, if possible, to put the system back in control.
- Kaizen costing focuses on continuous short-term improvements in manufacturing costs, while target costing focuses on long-term improvements in design costs. Target cost is the difference between the targeted revenue and the targeted profit.

LO6. (*Appendix 10A*) Prepare journal entries for materials and labour variances.

- Assuming that the materials price variance is computed at the point of purchase, all inventories are carried at standard cost.
- Actual costs are not entered into an inventory account. Instead, standard costs are applied to inventory and eventually flow through to cost of goods sold.
- Accounts are created for materials price and usage variances, and for labour rate and efficiency variances.
- Unfavourable variances are always debits; favourable variances are always credits.
- The closing of the variance accounts, which contain the difference between applied standard costs and actual costs, results in the amount of actual costs ultimately impacting cost of goods sold.

SUMMARY OF IMPORTANT EQUATIONS

1. $MPV = (AP - SP)AQ$
2. $MUV = (AQ - SQ)SP$
3. $LRV = (AR - SR)AH$
4. $LEV = (AH - SH)SR$

CORNERSTONES

GLOSSARY

Control limits The maximum allowable deviation from a standard. (p. 490)

Currently attainable standards Standards that reflect an efficient operating state; they are rigorous but achievable. (p. 483)

Favourable (F) variances Variances produced whenever the actual input amounts are less than the budgeted or standard allowances. (p. 488)

Ideal standards Standards that reflect perfect operating conditions. (p. 483)

Labour efficiency variance (LEV) The difference between the actual direct labour hours used and the standard direct labour hours allowed multiplied by the standard hourly wage rate. (p. 498)

Labour rate variance (LRV) The difference between the actual hourly rate paid and the standard hourly rate multiplied by the actual hours worked. (p. 498)

Materials price variance (MPV) The difference between the actual price paid per unit of materials and the standard price allowed per unit multiplied by the actual quantity of materials purchased. (p. 494)

Materials usage variance (MUV) The difference between the direct materials actually used and the direct materials allowed for the actual output multiplied by the standard price. (p. 494)

Price standards The price that should be paid per unit of input. (p. 482)

Price (rate) variance The difference between standard price and actual price multiplied by the actual quantity of inputs used. (p. 488)

Quantity standards The quantity of input allowed per unit of output. (p. 482)

Standard cost per unit The per-unit cost that should be achieved given materials, labour, and overhead standards. (p. 485)

Standard cost sheet A listing of the standard costs and standard quantities of direct materials, direct labour, and overhead that should apply to a single product. (p. 485)

Standard hours allowed (SH) The direct labour hours that should have been used to produce the actual output (Unit labour standard × Actual output). (p. 486)

Standard quantity of materials allowed (SQ) The quantity of materials that should have been used to produce the actual output (Unit materials standard × Actual output). (p. 486)

Target cost The difference between the sales price needed to achieve a projected market share and the desired per-unit profit. (p. 501)

Total budget variance The difference between the actual cost of an input and its planned cost. (p. 487)

Unfavourable (U) variances Variances produced whenever the actual input amounts are greater than the budgeted or standard allowances. (p. 488)

Usage (efficiency) variance The difference between standard quantities and actual quantities multiplied by standard price. (p. 488)

REVIEW PROBLEM

I. Materials, Labour, and Overhead Variances

Wilhelm Manufacturing has the following standards for one of its products:

Direct materials (2 metres @ $5)	$10
Direct labour (0.5 hr. @ $10)	5

During the most recent year, the following actual results were recorded:

Production	6,000 units
Direct materials (11,750 metres purchased and used)	$61,100
Direct labour (2,900 hrs.)	29,580

Required:

Compute the following variances:

1. Materials price and usage variances.
2. Labour rate and efficiency variances.

Solution:

1. Materials variances:

$$\begin{aligned} MPV &= (AP - SP)AQ \\ &= (\$5.20 - \$5.00)11{,}750 \\ &= \$2{,}350 \text{ U} \end{aligned}$$

$$\begin{aligned} MUV &= (AQ - SQ)SP \\ &= (11{,}750 - 12{,}000)\$5.00 \\ &= \$1{,}250 \text{ F} \end{aligned}$$

2. Labour variances:

$$\begin{aligned} LRV &= (AR - SR)AH \\ &= (\$10.20 - \$10.00)2{,}900 \\ &= \$580 \text{ U} \end{aligned}$$

$$\begin{aligned} LEV &= (AH - SH)SR \\ &= (2{,}900 - 3{,}000)\$10.00 \\ &= \$1{,}000 \text{ F} \end{aligned}$$

DISCUSSION QUESTIONS

1. Discuss the difference between budgets and standard costs.
2. Describe the relationship that unit standards have with flexible budgeting.
3. Why is historical experience often a poor basis for establishing standards?
4. What are ideal standards? Currently attainable standards? Of the two, which is usually adopted? Why?
5. Explain why standard costing systems are adopted.
6. How does standard costing improve the control function?
7. Discuss the differences among actual costing, normal costing, and standard costing.
8. What is the purpose of a standard cost sheet?

9. The budget variance for variable production costs is broken down into quantity and price variances. Explain why the quantity variance is more useful for control purposes than the price variance.
10. When should a standard cost variance be investigated?
11. What are control limits, and how are they set?
12. Explain why the materials price variance is often computed at the point of purchase rather than at the point of issuance.
13. "The materials usage variance is always the responsibility of the production supervisor." Do you agree or disagree? Why?
14. "The labour rate variance is never controllable." Do you agree or disagree? Why?
15. Suggest some possible causes of an unfavourable labour efficiency variance.
16. What is kaizen costing? On which part of the value chain does kaizen costing focus?
17. What is target costing? Describe how costs are reduced so that the target cost can be met.

CORNERSTONE EXERCISES

Cornerstone Exercise 10-1 **Standard Quantities Allowed of Labour and Materials**

OBJECTIVE 2
CORNERSTONE 10.1

Kolb Farms produces lemon yogurt. Each tub of lemon yogurt requires 80 grams of lemon powder (the unit quantity standard) and 0.06 labour hours (the unit labour standard). During the year, 900,000 tubs of lemon yogurt were produced.

Required:

1. Calculate the total amount of lemon powder allowed for the actual output.
2. Calculate the total amount of labour hours allowed for the actual output.

Cornerstone Exercise 10-2 **Control Limits**

OBJECTIVE 3
CORNERSTONE 10.2

During the past six weeks, the actual costs of materials were as follows:

Week 1	$47,500	Week 4	$50,000
Week 2	$52,500	Week 5	$60,000
Week 3	$60,000	Week 6	$65,000

The standard materials cost for each week was $50,000 with an allowable deviation of ±$5,000.

Required:

Plot the actual costs over time against the upper and lower limits. Comment on whether or not there is a need to investigate any of the variances.

Cornerstone Exercise 10-3 **Total Materials Variance**

OBJECTIVE 4
CORNERSTONE 10.3

Hockley Inc. produces plastic tubs. Production of 120-gram tubs has a standard unit quantity of 125 grams of plastic per tub. During the month of June, 40,000 tubs were produced using 5,100,000 grams of plastic. The actual cost of plastic was $0.31 per gram and the standard price was $0.30 per gram. There are no beginning or ending inventories of plastic.

Required:

Calculate the total variance for plastic for June.

Cornerstone Exercise 10-4 **Materials Price and Usage Variances**

OBJECTIVE 4
CORNERSTONE 10.4

Refer to the data provided in **Cornerstone Exercise 10-3**.

Required:

Calculate the materials price and usage variances using the columnar and formula approaches.

OBJECTIVE 5
CORNERSTONE 10.5

Cornerstone Exercise 10-5 Total Labour Variance

Hockley Inc. produces plastic tubs. Each tub has a standard labour requirement of 0.03 hours. During the month of June, 40,000 tubs were produced using 1,250 labour hours at $12.20. The standard wage rate is $13.00 per hour.

Required:

Calculate the total variance for production labour for June.

OBJECTIVE 5
CORNERSTONE 10.6

Cornerstone Exercise 10-6 Labour Rate and Efficiency Variances

Refer to the data provided in **Cornerstone Exercise 10-5**.

Required:

Calculate the labour rate and efficiency variances using the columnar and formula approaches.

EXERCISES

OBJECTIVE 2

Exercise 10-7 Investigation of Variances

Tasty Creations is a manufacturer of pumpkin pies. For September 2017, the company's operating budget included the following:

Sales (units—standard quantity)	500,000
Average selling price per pie	$ 4.50
Direct materials costs per pie	$ 1.75
Total fixed costs for the month	$350,000

Actual results were as follows:

Sales (units—actual quantity)	465,000
Average selling price per pie	$ 4.60
Direct materials costs per pie	$ 1.65
Total fixed costs for the month	$355,000

Tasty Creations' CEO observed that September's operating income was lower than anticipated and has asked you to prepare a report outlining the reasons for the discouraging results.

Required:

1. Calculate the total materials variance for September.
2. Calculate the materials price variance and materials usage variance for September, indicating whether the variances are favourable or unfavourable.
3. Prepare a brief memo for the CEO of Tasty Creations that discusses the reported operating income for September.

OBJECTIVE 3

Exercise 10-8 Investigation of Variances

Pasta Supreme uses the following rule to determine whether materials usage variances should be investigated: "A materials usage variance will be investigated any time the amount exceeds the lesser of $15,000 and 5 percent of the standard cost." Reports for the past five weeks provided the following information:

Week	MUV ($)	Standard Materials Cost ($)
1	14,000 F	260,000
2	11,200 U	240,000
3	13,100 F	245,000
4	15,500 U	252,000
5	9,200 U	210,000

Required:

1. Using the rule provided, identify the cases that will be investigated.
2. CONCEPTUAL CONNECTION Suppose investigation reveals that the cause of an unfavourable materials usage variance is the use of lower-quality materials than are normally used. Who is responsible? What corrective action would likely be taken?
3. CONCEPTUAL CONNECTION Suppose investigation reveals that the cause of a significant unfavourable materials usage variance is attributable to a new approach to manufacturing that takes less labour time but causes more material waste. Examination of the labour efficiency variance reveals that it is favourable and larger than the unfavourable materials usage variance. Who is responsible? What action should be taken?

Exercise 10-9 Budget Variances, Materials and Labour

OBJECTIVE 4 5

Mahn Corporation produces high-quality leather belts. The company uses a standard cost system and has set the following standards for materials and labour:

Leather (3 strips @ $4)	$12.00
Direct labour (0.75 hr. @ $12)	9.00
Total prime cost	$21.00

During the year, Mahn produced 92,000 belts. Actual leather purchased was 287,500 strips at $3.60 per strip. There were no beginning or ending inventories of leather. Actual direct labour was 78,200 hours at $12.50 per hour.

Required:

1. Compute the costs of leather and direct labour that should be incurred for the production of 92,000 leather belts.
2. Compute the total budget variances for materials and labour.
3. CONCEPTUAL CONNECTION Would you consider these variances material with a need for investigation? Explain.

Exercise 10-10 Materials Variances

Refer to the data provided in **Exercise 10-9**.

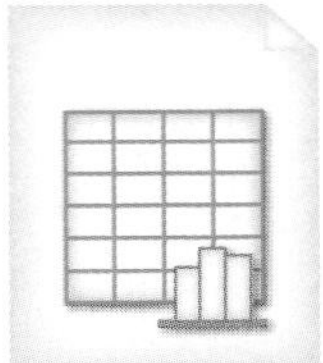

Required:

1. Break down the total variance for materials into a price variance and a usage variance using the columnar and formula approaches.
2. CONCEPTUAL CONNECTION Suppose the plant manager investigates the materials variances and is told by the purchasing manager that a cheaper source of leather strips had been discovered and that this is the reason for the favourable materials price variance. Quite pleased, the purchasing manager suggests that the materials price standard be updated to reflect this new, less expensive source of leather strips. Should the plant manager update the materials price standard as suggested? Why or why not?

Exercise 10-11 Labour Variances

OBJECTIVE 5

Refer to the data provided in **Exercise 10-9**.

Required:

1. Break down the total variance for labour into a rate variance and an efficiency variance using the columnar and formula approaches.
2. CONCEPTUAL CONNECTION As part of the investigation of the unfavourable variances, the plant manager interviews the production manager. The production manager complains strongly about the quality of the leather strips. He indicates that the strips are of lower quality than usual, so workers have to be more careful to avoid a belt with cracks and more time is

(Continued)

required. Also, even with extra care, many belts have to be discarded and new ones produced to replace the rejects. This replacement work has also produced some overtime demands. What corrective action should the plant manager take?

OBJECTIVE 4

Exercise 10-12 Materials Variances

Torres Company produces fruit juices, sold in litres. Recently, the company adopted the following material standard for one litre of its apple juice:

Direct materials (128 grams @ $0.05) = $6.40

During the first week of operation, the company experienced the following results:

a. Litre units produced: 20,000
b. Grams of materials purchased and used: 2,600,000 grams at $0.06
c. No beginning or ending inventories of raw materials

Required:

1. Compute the materials price variance.
2. Compute the materials usage variance.

OBJECTIVE 5
CORNERSTONE 10.6

Exercise 10-13 Labour Variances

Hobby Company produces sails for small recreational sailboats. During the year, 120,000 sails were produced. The actual labour used was 178,000 hours at $15.20 per hour. Hobby has the following labour standard: 1.5 hours at $14.80.

Required:

1. Compute the labour rate variance.
2. Compute the labour efficiency variance.

OBJECTIVE 4 5

Exercise 10-14 Materials and Labour Variances

At the beginning of the year, Shults Company had the following standard cost sheet for one of its plastic products:

Direct materials (5 kg @ $4.00)	$20,00
Direct labour (2 hrs. @ $11.25)	22.50
Standard prime cost per unit	$42.50

The actual results for the year are as follows:

a. Units produced: 175,000
b. Materials purchased: 930,000 kilograms @ $4.10
c. Materials used: 925,000 kilograms
d. Direct labour: 362,500 hours @ $11.15

Required:

1. Compute price and usage variances for materials.
2. Compute the labour rate and labour efficiency variances.

OBJECTIVE 1

Exercise 10-15 Variances, Evaluation, and Behaviour

Jackie Iverson was furious. She was about ready to fire Tom Rich, her purchasing agent. Just a month ago, she had given him a salary increase and a bonus for his performance. She had been especially pleased with his ability to meet or beat the price standards. But now, she found out that it was because of a huge purchase of raw materials. It would take months to use that inventory, and there was hardly space to store it. In the meantime, where could the other materials supplies be put that would be ordered and processed on a regular basis? Additionally, it was a lot of capital to tie up in inventory—money that could have been used to help finance the cash needs of the new product just coming on line.

Her interview with Tom was frustrating. He was defensive, arguing that he thought she wanted those standards met and that the means were not that important. He also pointed out that quantity purchases were the only way to meet the price standards. Otherwise, an unfavourable variance would have been realized.

Required:

1. Why did Tom Rich purchase the large quantity of raw materials? Do you think that this behaviour was the objective of the price standard? If not, what are the objectives?
2. Suppose that Tom is right and that the only way to meet the price standard is through the use of quantity discounts. Also, assume that using quantity discounts is not a desirable practice for this company. What would you do to solve this dilemma?
3. Should Tom be fired? Explain.

Exercise 10-16 Materials and Labour Variances

OBJECTIVE 4 5

QualiTech Company produces computer circuits in large batches. Materials for the circuits are formed and polished in specialized machines that require continuous maintenance and cleaning for each batch. After forming the materials for a set number of circuits, the machines are cleaned and prepared for the next batch of materials to be formed. The following standards for machine changeovers have been established:

Direct materials (15 litres @ $1.80)	$27.00
Direct labour (0.2 hr. @ $22.00)	4.40
Standard prime cost of a changeover	$31.40

During the year, 400,000 litres of material were purchased and used for the changeover activity. There were 25,000 batches produced, with the following actual prime costs:

Direct materials	$740,000
Direct labour	107,500 (for 6,300 hrs.)

Required:

1. Compute the materials and labour variances associated with the changeover activity, labelling each variance as favourable or unfavourable.
2. CONCEPTUAL CONNECTION What differentiates favourable variances and unfavourable variances?

Exercise 10-17 *(Appendix 10A)* Journal Entries

OBJECTIVE 6

Refer to the data provided in **Exercise 10-16**.

Required:

1. Prepare a journal entry for the purchase of raw materials.
2. Prepare a journal entry for the issuance of raw materials.
3. Prepare a journal entry for the addition of labour to Work in Process.
4. Prepare a journal entry for the closing of variances to Cost of Goods Sold.

Exercise 10-18 *(Appendix 10A)* Materials Variances, Journal Entries

Esteban Products produces instructional aids. Among the company's products are white boards, which use coloured markers instead of chalk. They are particularly popular for conference rooms in educational institutions and executive offices of large corporations. The standard cost of materials for this product is 12 kilograms at $8.25 per kilogram.

During the first month of the year, 3,200 boards were produced. Information concerning actual costs and usage of materials follows:

Materials purchased	38,000 kg @ $8.35
Materials used	37,500 kg

(Continued)

Required:

1. Compute the materials price and usage variances.
2. Prepare journal entries for all activity relating to materials.

OBJECTIVE 

Exercise 10-19 (*Appendix 10A*) Labour Variances, Journal Entries

Escuchar Products, a producer of DVD players, has established a labour standard for its product—direct labour: 2 hrs at $11.65 per hour. During January, Escuchar produced 25,400 players. The actual direct labour used was 48,900 hours at a total cost of $584,355.

Required:

1. Compute the labour rate and efficiency variances.
2. Prepare journal entries for all activities relating to labour.

PROBLEMS

OBJECTIVE 1

Problem 10-20 Setting Standards and Assigning Responsibility

Cabanarama Inc. designs and manufactures easy-to-set-up beach cabanas. The cabanas come in a kit that includes canvas, lacing, and aluminum support poles. Families can easily transport the cabanas to the beach, set them up, and have a protected place to change clothing, store picnic hampers, and so on. Cabanarama has expanded rapidly from a two-person operation to one involving over 100 employees. The founder and owner of Cabanarama, Frank Love, understands that a more formal approach to standard setting and control is needed to ensure that the consistent quality for which the company is known continues.

Frank and Annette Wilson, his financial vice-president, divided the company into departments and designated each department as a cost centre. Sales, quality control, and design report directly to Frank. Production, shipping, finance, and accounting report to Annette. In the production department, one of the supervisors was assigned the materials purchasing function; the job included purchasing all raw materials, overseeing inventory handling (receiving, storage, etc.), and tracking materials purchases and use.

Frank felt that control would be better achieved if there were a way for his employees to continue to perform in such a way that quality was maintained and cost reduction was achieved. Annette suggested that Cabanarama institute a standard costing system. Variances for materials and labour could then be calculated and reported directly to her, and she could alert Frank to any problems or opportunities for improvement.

Required:

1. a. CONCEPTUAL CONNECTION When Annette designs the standard costing system for Cabanarama, who should be involved in setting the standards for each cost component?
   b. CONCEPTUAL CONNECTION What factors should be considered in establishing the standards for each cost component?
2. CONCEPTUAL CONNECTION Assume that Cabanarama develops the standards for materials use, materials price, labour use, and labour wages. Who will be assigned responsibility for each and for any resulting variances? Why?

OBJECTIVE   

Problem 10-21 Basics of Variance Analysis, Variable Inputs

Durable Door Company replaces garage doors for residential customers. Because of the poor quality of materials used by its supplier, Durable Doors has had to replace many doors due to unacceptable performance or breakage. Two years ago, the company decided to manufacture its own vinyl doors as a cost-saving measure and to better control quality. A strategically located plant involved in this type of manufacturing was acquired. To help ensure cost efficiency, a standard cost system was installed in the plant. The following standards have been established for the product's variable inputs:

	Standard Quantity	Standard Price (rate in $)	Standard Cost ($)
Direct materials	42 kg	$ 3.85	$161.70
Direct labour	2.10 hrs.	16.00	33.60
Variable overhead	2.10 hrs.	2.60	5.46
Total			$200.76

The purchasing agent located a new source of slightly higher quality vinyl, and this material was used during the first week in January. Also, a new manufacturing process was implemented on a trial basis. The new process required a slightly lower level of skilled labour. The higher-quality material has no effect on labour utilization. However, the new manufacturing process was expected to reduce materials usage by 0.10 kilograms per door.

During the first week, the company had the following actual results:

Units produced	4,000
Actual labour costs	$134,725
Actual labour hours	8,500
Materials purchased and used	166,000 kg @ $4.05
Actual variable overhead costs	$39,750

Required:

1. CONCEPTUAL CONNECTION Compute the materials price and usage variances. Assume that the 0.10 kilogram per door reduction of materials occurred as expected and that the remaining effects are all attributable to the higher-quality material. Would you recommend that the purchasing agent continue to buy this quality, or should the usual quality be purchased? Assume that the quality of the end product is not affected significantly.
2. CONCEPTUAL CONNECTION Compute the labour rate and efficiency variances. Assuming that the labour variances are attributable to the new manufacturing process, should it be continued or discontinued? In answering, consider the new process's materials reduction effect as well. Explain your reasoning.
3. CONCEPTUAL CONNECTION Refer to Requirement 2. Suppose that the industrial engineer argued that the new process should not be evaluated after only one week. His reasoning was that it would take at least a week for the workers to become efficient with the new approach. Suppose that the production is the same the second week and that the actual labour hours were 7,400 and the labour cost was $117,290. Should the new process be adopted? Assume the variances are attributable to the new process. Assuming production of 4,000 units per week, what would be the projected annual savings? (Include the materials reduction effect.)

Check figures:
1. MUV = $7,700 F
2. LRV = $1,275 F
3. LEV = $16,000 F

Problem 10-22 Setting Standards, Materials and Labour Variances

OBJECTIVE 1  

Tom Belford and Tony Sorrentino own a small business devoted to kitchen and bath granite installations. Recently, building contractors have insisted on up-front bid prices for a house rather than the cost-plus system that Tom and Tony used. They worry because natural flaws in the granite make it impossible to tell in advance exactly how much granite will be used on a particular job. In addition, granite can be broken easily, meaning that Tom or Tony could ruin a slab and would need to start over with a new one. Sometimes the improperly cut pieces could be used for smaller installations, sometimes not. All their accounting is done by a local chartered professional accounting firm headed by Charlene Davenport. Charlene listened to their concerns and suggested that it might be time to implement tighter controls by setting up a standard costing system.

Charlene reviewed the invoices pertaining to a number of Tom and Tony's previous jobs to determine the average amount of granite and glue needed per square metre. She then updated

(Continued)

prices on both materials to reflect current conditions. The standards she developed for one square metre of counter installed were as follows:

Granite, per square metre	$50.00
Glue (5 g @ $0.03)	0.15
Direct labour hours:	
Cutting labour (0.10 hr. @ $15)	1.50
Installation labour (0.25 hr. @ $25)	6.25

These standards assumed that one seamless counter requires one sink cut (the space into which the sink will fit) as well as cutting the counter to fit the space available.

Charlene tracked the actual costs incurred by Tom and Tony for granite installation for the next six months. She found that they completed 50 jobs with an average of 32 square metres of granite installed in each one. The following information on actual amounts used and cost was gathered:

Granite purchased and used (1,640 sq. metres)	$79,048
Glue purchased and used (8,000 grams)	$400
Actual hours cutting labour	180
Actual hours installation labour	390

The actual wage rate for cutting and installation labour remained unchanged from the standard rate.

Required:

1. Calculate the materials price variances and materials usage variances for granite and for glue for the past six months.
2. Calculate the labour rate variances and labour efficiency variances for cutting labour and for installation labour for the past six months.
3. CONCEPTUAL CONNECTION Would it be worthwhile for Charlene to establish standards for atypical jobs (e.g., those with more than one sink cut or wider than normal)?

Check figure:
2. LEV, Cutting = $300 U

OBJECTIVE  

Problem 10-23 Basics of Variance Analysis, Variable Inputs

Kouloupáki Inc. is a gourmet cookie manufacturer. Cookies are sold by the kilogram for $10.65. Monthly production averages 200,000 kilograms. Each kilogram requires $1.75 of direct materials and 3 minutes of processing time at a cost of $20.50 per hour. In March 2017, Koulouráki reported the following actual results:

Units sold	225,000 kilograms
Total units produced	240,704 kilograms
Total direct materials	$481,408
Total direct labour	$224,964 for 10,415 hours

Required:

1. Calculate the materials price variance and materials usage variance for March.
2. Calculate the labour rate variance and labour efficiency variance for March.

OBJECTIVE 

Problem 10-24 Variance Analysis for a Service Company

Maid-Magic Ltd. provides household cleaning services for residential customers. With Claire Kenley as the manager for the past 10 years, the company has experienced steady growth by providing reliable, high-quality cleaning services. Despite the increase in business, the company has been experiencing reduced operating income and high employee turnover. Claire is confused and has asked you to look into the situation. Currently the company has five cleaning staff. On average, each staff member is paid $14 per hour and is expected to clean one house in 4 hours. The following information pertains to August 2018, when there were 23 working days per employee in the month:

	Budget	Actual
Houses cleaned	230	260
Revenues	$28,750	$32,500
Variable costs:		
Labour	12,880	16,965
Cost of cleaning supplies	520	585
Contribution margin	15,350	14,950
Fixed costs	2,400	2,400
Operating income	$12,950	$12,550

When investigating the company's operations, you have learned that employees are reporting an average of 4.5 hours per house. While the employees are paid by the hour, Maid-Magic charges customers a flat rate of $125 per household cleaning. As a result, any increases in operating costs are not directly passed along to the customer.

Required:

1. How many households did Claire budget for each employee? How many houses, on average, did each employee actually clean? How many hours were budgeted for each employee to work? On average, how many hours did each employee actually work? How many hours were actually worked by all employees?
2. Compute the labour rate variance and the labour efficiency variance.
3. Provide Claire with some advice on what she can do to motivate the cleaning staff to be more efficient.

Problem 10-25 Setting a Direct Labour Standard, Learning Curve Effects, Service Company

Mantenga Company provides routine maintenance services for heavy moving and transportation vehicles. Although the vehicles vary, the maintenance services provided follow a fairly standard pattern. Recently, a potential customer has approached the company, requesting a new maintenance service for a radically different type of vehicle. New servicing equipment and some new labour skills will be needed to provide the maintenance service. The customer is placing an initial order to service 150 vehicles and has indicated that if the service is satisfactory, several additional orders of the same size will be placed every three months over the next three to five years.

Mantenga uses a standard costing system and wants to develop a set of standards for the new service. The usage standards for direct materials such as oil, lubricants, and transmission fluids were easily established. The usage standard is 25 litres per servicing, with a standard cost of $4 per litre. Management has also decided on standard rates for labour and overhead: The standard labour rate is $15 per direct labour hour, the standard variable overhead rate is $8 per direct labour hour, and the standard fixed overhead rate is $12 per hour. The only remaining decision is the standard for labour usage. To assist in developing this standard, the engineering department has estimated the following relationship between units serviced and average direct labour hours used:

Units Serviced	Cumulative Average Time per Unit (hours)
40	2.500
80	2.000
160	1.600
320	1.280
640	1.024

As the workers learn more about servicing the new vehicles, they become more efficient, and the average time needed to service one unit declines. For example, the first 40 units take an average of 2.5 hours per unit, while the second 40 units take an average of 1.5 hours

(Continued)

per unit $\left(= \frac{(80 \times 2) - (40 \times 2.5)}{40} = 1.5 \right)$. Engineering estimates that all of the learning effects will be achieved by the time that 640 units are serviced. No further improvement will be realized past this level.

Required:

1. Assume that the average labour time is 0.768 hour per unit after the learning effects are achieved. Using this information, prepare a standard cost sheet that details the standard service cost per unit. Round costs to two decimal places.
2. CONCEPTUAL CONNECTION Given the per-unit labour standard, would you expect a favourable or an unfavourable labour efficiency? Explain your reasoning. Calculate the labour efficiency variance for servicing the first 640 units.
3. CONCEPTUAL CONNECTION Assuming no further improvement in labour time per unit is possible past 640 units, show that the standard labour time should be 0.768 hour per unit. Explain why this value is a good choice for the per-unit labour standard.

Check figures:

1. Standard cost per unit = \$126.88
2. LEV = \$2,457.60 U

OBJECTIVE 2 4 5

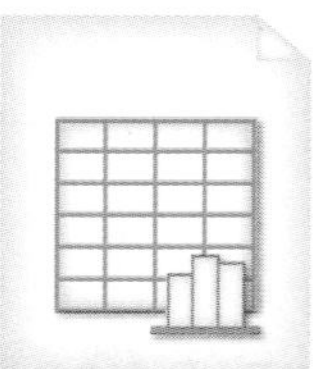

Problem 10-26 Unit Costs, Multiple Products, Variance Analysis, Service Setting

The maternity wing of the city hospital has two types of patients: natural and cesarean. The standard quantities of labour and materials per delivery for 2017 are:

	Natural	Cesarean
Direct materials (kilograms)	9	21
Nursing labour (hours)	2.5	5

The standard price paid per kilogram of direct materials is \$10. The standard rate for labour is \$16. Overhead is applied on the basis of direct labour hours. The variable overhead rate for maternity is \$30 per hour, and the fixed overhead rate is \$40 per hour.

Actual operating data for 2017 are as follows:

a. Patient days produced: natural, 4,000; cesarean, 8,000.
b. Direct materials purchased and used: 200,000 kilograms at \$9.85—35,000 for natural maternity patients and 165,000 for the cesarean patients; no beginning or ending raw materials inventories.
c. Nursing labour: 50,700 hours—10,200 hours for natural patients and 40,500 hours for the cesarean; total cost of labour, \$783,315.

Required:

1. Prepare a standard cost sheet showing the unit cost per patient day for each type of patient.
2. Compute the materials price and usage variances for each type of patient.
3. Compute the labour rate and efficiency variances.
4. CONCEPTUAL CONNECTION Assume that you know only the total direct materials used for both procedures and the total direct labour hours used for both procedures. Can you compute the total materials usage and labour efficiency variances? Explain.
5. CONCEPTUAL CONNECTION Standard costing concepts have been applied in the health care industry. For example, diagnosis-related groups (DRGs) are used for prospective payments for medicare patients. Select a search engine (such as Yahoo! or Google), and conduct a search to see what information you can obtain about DRGs. You might try "medicare DRGs" as a possible search term. Write a memo that answers the following questions:
   a. What is a DRG?
   b. How are DRGs established?
   c. How many DRGs are used?
   d. How does the DRG concept relate to standard costing concepts discussed in the chapter? Can hospitals use DRGs to control their costs? Explain.

Check figures:

1. Standard cost (natural) = \$305.00 per patient day
2. MUV cesarean = \$30,000 F
3. LRV natural = \$5,610 F
4. LEV = \$11,200 U

Problem 10-27 Control Limits, Variance Investigation

OBJECTIVE 3 4 5

Buenolorl Company produces a well-known cologne. The standard manufacturing cost of the cologne is described by the following standard cost sheet:

Direct materials:	
Liquids (4.5 decilitres @ $0.40)	$1.80
Bottles (1 @ $0.05)	0.05
Direct labour (0.2 hr. @ $15.00)	3.00
Variable overhead (0.2 hr. @ $5.00)	1.00
Fixed overhead (0.2 hr. @ $1.50)	0.30
Standard cost per unit	$6.15

Management has decided to investigate only those variances that exceed the lesser of 10 percent of the standard cost for each category and $20,000.

During the past quarter, 250,000 four-decilitre bottles of cologne were produced. Descriptions of actual activity for the quarter follow:

a. A total of 1.35 million decilitres of liquids were purchased, mixed, and processed. Evaporation was higher than expected (no inventories of liquids are maintained). The price paid per decilitre averaged $0.42.
b. Exactly 250,000 bottles were used. The price paid for each bottle was $0.048.
c. Direct labour hours totalled 48,250, with a total cost of $733,000.

Normal production volume for Buenolorl is 250,000 bottles per quarter. The standard overhead rates are computed by using normal volume. All overhead costs are incurred uniformly throughout the year.

Check figures:
1. UCL (labour) = $770,000
2. Total liquid variance = $117,000 U
3. LEV = $26,250 F

Required:

1. Calculate the upper and lower control limits for each manufacturing cost category.
2. Compute the total materials variances, and break them into price and usage variances. Would these variances be investigated?
3. Compute the total labour variance, and break it into rate and efficiency variances. Would these variances be investigated?

Problem 10-28 Control Limits, Variance Investigation

OBJECTIVE  

The management of Golding Company has determined that the cost to investigate a variance produced by its standard cost system ranges from $2,000 to $3,000. If a problem is discovered, the average benefit from taking corrective action usually outweighs the cost of investigation. Past experience from the investigation of variances has revealed that corrective action is rarely needed for deviations within 8 percent of the standard cost. Golding produces a single product, which has the following standards for materials and labour:

Direct materials (8 kg @ $0.25)	$2.00
Direct labour (0.4 hr. @ $14.50)	5.80

Actual production for the past three months with the associated actual usage and costs for materials and labour follow. There were no beginning or ending raw materials inventories.

	April	May	June
Production (units)	90,000	100,000	110,000
Direct materials:			
Cost	$189,000	$218,000	$230,000
Usage (kilograms)	723,000	870,000	885,000
Direct labour:			
Cost	$522,000	$623,920	$695,980
Usage (hours)	36,000	44,000	46,000

(Continued)

Required:

1. For each month, what upper and lower control limits would you use for materials variances? For labour variances?
2. Compute the materials and labour variances for April, May, and June. Identify those that would require investigation.
3. Let the horizontal axis be time and the vertical axis be variances measured as a percentage deviation from standard. Draw horizontal lines that identify upper and lower control limits. Plot the labour and material variances for April, May, and June. Prepare a separate graph for each type of variance. Explain how you would use these graphs (called control charts) to assist your analysis of variances.

Check figures:

1. June UCL (labour) = $51,040 (quantity standard)
2. May LRV = $14,080 F (2.2 percent of standard cost)

OBJECTIVE  

Problem 10-29 Standard Costing, Planned Variances

Ogundipe Company manufactures a plastic toy cell phone. The following standards have been established for the toy's materials and labour inputs:

	Standard Quantity	Standard Price (rate in $)	Standard Cost ($)
Direct materials	0.5 kg	1.50	0.75
Direct labour	0.15 hr.	10.00	1.50

During the first week of July, the company had the following results:

Units produced	90,000
Actual labour costs	$138,000
Actual labour hours	13,400
Materials purchased and used	44,250 kg @$1.55/kg

The purchasing agent located a new source of slightly higher-quality plastic, and this material was used during the first week in July. Also, a new manufacturing layout was implemented on a trial basis. The new layout required a slightly higher level of skilled labour. The higher-quality material has no effect on labour utilization. Similarly, the new manufacturing approach has no effect on material usage.

Required:

1. CONCEPTUAL CONNECTION Compute the materials price and usage variances. Assuming that the materials variances are essentially attributable to the higher quality of materials, would you recommend that the purchasing agent continue to buy this quality, or should the usual quality be purchased? Assume that the quality of the end product is not affected significantly.
2. CONCEPTUAL CONNECTION Compute the labour rate and efficiency variances. Assuming that the labour variances are attributable to the new manufacturing layout, should it be continued or discontinued? Explain your reasoning.
3. CONCEPTUAL CONNECTION Refer to Requirement 2. Suppose that the industrial engineer argued that the new layout should not be evaluated after only one week. His reasoning was that it would take at least a week for the workers to become efficient with the new approach. Suppose that the production is the same the second week and that the actual labour hours were 13,200 and the labour cost was $132,000. Should the new layout be adopted? Assume the variances are attributable to the new layout. If so, what would be the projected annual savings?

Check figures:

1. MPV = $2,213 U
2. LEV = $1,000 F
3. LRV = $0

OBJECTIVE 

Problem 10-30 Standard Costing

Whitecotton Company produces plastic bottles. The unit for costing purposes is a case of 18 bottles. The following standards for producing one case of bottles have been established:

Direct materials (4 kg @ $0.95)	$ 3.80
Direct labour (1.25 hours @ $15.00)	18.75
Standard prime cost	$22.55

During December, 78,000 kilograms of material were purchased and used in production. There were 15,000 cases produced, with the following actual prime costs:

Direct materials	$74,000
Direct labour	$315,000 (for 22,500 hrs.)

Required:

1. Compute the materials variances.
2. Compute the labour variances.
3. CONCEPTUAL CONNECTION What are the advantages and disadvantages that can result from the use of a standard costing system?

Check figures:
1. MUV = $17,100 U
2. LEV = $56,250 U

Problem 10-31 *(Appendix 10A)* Variance Analysis, Revision of Standards, Journal Entries

OBJECTIVE   6

Mannerist Statuary manufactures bronze bust statues of famous historical figures. All statues are the same size. Each unit requires the same amount of resources. For 2018, the standard quantities, standard prices, and standard unit costs for direct materials and direct manufacturing labour follow.

	Standard Quantity	Standard Price (rate in $)	Standard Unit Cost ($)
Direct materials	13 kg	11	143.00
Direct manufacturing labour	5.5 hours	35	192.50

During 2018, the actual number of units produced and sold was 5,000. Actual cost of direct materials used was $700,000, based on 56,000 kilograms purchased at $12.50 per kilogram. Direct manufacturing labour hours were 25,000, at the rate of $38 per hour. This resulted in actual direct manufacturing labour costs of $950,000. Actual fixed costs were $1,000,000. There was no beginning or ending inventory.

Required:

1. Calculate (a) the materials price variance, and (b) the materials efficiency variance, and (c) assess the manager's performance.
2. Calculate (a) the labour rate variance, and (b) the labour efficiency variance, and (c) assess the manager's performance.
3. Record journal entries for (a) the purchase of materials, (b) the issuance and usage of materials, and (c) the accrual for labour.
4. For simplicity, assume all of the variances are immaterial (though, they certainly are not). (a) Record the journal entries for the disposition of the variances, and (b) assess the manager's performance.

Problem 10-32 *(Appendix 10A)* Variance Analysis, Revision of Standards, Journal Entries

OBJECTIVE 

The Chatham plant of Morril's Small Motor Division produces a major subassembly for a 6.0 horsepower motor for lawn mowers. The plant uses a standard costing system for production costing and control. The standard cost sheet for the subassembly follows:

Direct materials (6.0 kg @ $5.00)	$30.00
Direct labour (1.6 hrs. @ $12.00)	19.20

During the year, the Chatham plant had the following actual production activity:

a. Production of motors totalled 50,000 units.
b. A total of 260,000 kilograms of raw materials were purchased at $4.70 per kilogram.
c. There were 60,000 kilograms of raw materials in beginning inventory (carried at $5 per kilogram). There was no ending inventory.
d. The company used 82,000 direct labour hours at a total cost of $1,066,000.
e. The Chatham plant's practical activity is 60,000 units per year. Standard overhead rates are computed based on practical activity measured in standard direct labour hours.

(Continued)

Required:

1. CONCEPTUAL CONNECTION Compute the materials price and usage variances. Of the two materials variances, which is viewed as the most controllable? To whom would you assign responsibility for the usage variance in this case? Explain your reasoning.
2. CONCEPTUAL CONNECTION Compute the labour rate and efficiency variances. Who is usually responsible for the labour efficiency variance? What are some possible causes for this variance?
3. CONCEPTUAL CONNECTION Assume that the purchasing agent for the small motors plant purchased a lower-quality raw material from a new supplier. Would you recommend that the plant continue to use this cheaper raw material? Briefly explain.
4. Prepare all possible journal entries.

Check figures:
1. MUV = $100,000 U
2. LEV = $24,000 U
3. Net effect = $46,000 U

PROFESSIONAL EXAMINATION PROBLEM*

Professional Examination Problem 10-33 Flexible Budget Variances—Pella Inc.

The controller of Pella Inc. created standards for variable costs for one of its products as:

	Per Unit
Direct material	$2.00
Direct labour	5.60
Variable overhead	1.25

At the beginning of the year, Pella Inc. estimated the average selling price to be $15 per unit and, at this price, estimated sales to be 70,000 units. Annual fixed costs were estimated to be $180,000.

Subsequent to year-end, the controller determined actual results to be sales of 75,000 units at an average price of $13.50 per unit. Total variable costs were $660,000 and total fixed costs were $192,000. There was no beginning or ending inventory.

Required:

Calculate the estimated results based on the revised estimated volume and compare them to the expected results using the original level of estimated sales. Compare the results.

CASES

Case 10-34 Establishment of Standards, Variance Analysis

Paul Golding and his wife, Nancy, established Crunchy Chips in 1938. (Nancy sold her piano to help raise capital to start the business.) Paul assumed responsibility for buying potatoes and selling chips to local grocers; Nancy assumed responsibility for production. Since Nancy was already known for her delicious thin potato chips, the business prospered.

Over the next 60 years, the company established distribution channels in all 10 provinces, with production facilities in British Columbia, Ontario, and Nova Scotia. In 1980, Paul died, and his son, Edward, took control of the business. By 2018, the company was facing stiff competition from multinational snack-food companies. Edward was advised that the company's plants needed to gain better control over production costs. To assist in achieving this objective, he hired a consultant to install a standard costing system. To help the consultant in establishing the necessary standards, Edward sent her the following memo:

To: Diana Craig, Chartered Professional Accountant
From: Edward Golding, President, Crunchy Chips
Subject: Description and Data Relating to the Production of Our Plain Potato Chips
Date: September 28, 2018

The manufacturing process for potato chips begins when the potatoes are placed into a large vat in which they are automatically washed. After washing, the potatoes flow directly to an automatic peeler. The peeled potatoes then pass by inspectors, who manually cut out deep eyes or other blemishes. After inspection, the potatoes are automatically sliced and then dropped into the cooking oil. The frying process is closely monitored by an employee. After the chips are cooked, they pass under a salting device and then pass by more inspectors, who sort out the unacceptable finished chips (those that are discoloured or too small). The chips then continue on the conveyor belt to a bagging machine that bags them in 500-gram bags. After bagging, the bags are placed in a box and shipped. The box holds 15 bags.

The raw potato pieces (eyes and blemishes), peelings, and rejected finished chips are sold to animal feed producers for $0.16 per kilogram. The company uses this revenue to reduce the cost of potatoes; we would like this reflected in the price standard relating to potatoes.

Crunchy Chips purchases high-quality potatoes at a cost of $0.245 per kilogram; each potato averages 135 grams. Under efficient operating conditions, it takes four potatoes to produce one 500-gram bag of plain chips. Although we label bags as containing 500 grams, we actually place 520 grams in each bag. We plan to continue this policy to ensure customer satisfaction. In addition to potatoes, other raw materials are the cooking oil, salt, bags, and boxes. Cooking oil costs $0.04 per gram, and we use 3.3 grams of oil per bag of chips. The cost of salt is so small that we add it to overhead. Bags cost $0.11 each and boxes $0.52 each.

Our plant produces 8.8 million bags of chips per year. A recent engineering study revealed that we would need the following direct labour hours to produce this quantity if our plant operates at peak efficiency:

Raw potato inspection	3,200
Finished chip inspection	12,000
Frying monitor	6,300
Boxing	16,600
Machine operators	6,300

I'm not sure that we can achieve the level of efficiency advocated by the study. In my opinion, the plant is operating efficiently for the level of output indicated if the hours allowed are about 10 percent higher.

The hourly labour rates agreed upon with the union are:

Raw potato inspectors	$15.20
Finished chip inspectors	10.30
Frying monitor	14.00
Boxing	11.00
Machine operators	13.00

Overhead is applied on the basis of direct labour dollars. We have found that variable overhead averages about 116 percent of our direct labour cost. Our fixed overhead is budgeted at $1,135,216 for the coming year.

Required:

1. Discuss the benefits of a standard costing system for Crunchy Chips.
2. Discuss the president's concern about using the result of the engineering study to set the labour standards. What standard would you recommend?
3. Form a group with two or three other students. Develop a standard cost sheet for one box of Crunchy Chips' plain potato chips.
4. Suppose that the level of production was 8.8 million bags of potato chips for the year as planned. If 4.8 million kilograms of potatoes were used, compute the materials usage variance for potatoes.

Case 10-35 Establishment of Standards, Variance Analysis

OBJECTIVE 1 2 4

Sudz'N'Bubbles Company owns and operates 10 car washes in Ontario. The general manager of each location reports to the company president, Christopher O'Donnell.

(*Continued*)

At the end of each quarter, Christopher evaluates the performance of each of the car wash locations and his evaluations determine the size of the bonus given to the staff at each location. If a location achieves its profit target, it receives $5,000 that is distributed among the staff who work at that location. The bonus increases by $5 for every $20 by which the location exceeded its profit target.

It is not uncommon for Christopher to make subjective adjustments to the bonus to take into account factors he deems outside the control of the staff at a location. For example, Christopher has made adjustments for the adverse effects on revenue of road construction in front of one location, downtime caused by vandalism at another location, and weather patterns that are significantly different from expected. In fact, weather is the largest uncontrollable factor that Christopher has to consider. Sales volumes tend to drop sharply when it rains but end up much closer to forecasts on good days when the sun is shining.

The budget for the Ottawa branch of Sudz'N'Bubbles, which is updated quarterly, was prepared on assumptions of hours of good weather. The average annual sunshine in Ottawa is 2,084 hours. Based on the wide-ranging variability of the weather, the assumptions are often wrong. During the 2018 spring quarter, it rained many more hours than were assumed in the budget, and actual profits for all the locations were far below the budget.

The financial results of the Ottawa location are shown in Table 1. Table 2 shows some operating assumptions and statistics for the Ottawa location. The budget was based on the assumption that the Ottawa location would be open every day, for 10 hours per day, when it was not raining. The car wash employees were paid a minimum hourly wage plus an amount for each car wash, so labour costs were partially variable with revenues.

Table 1: Variances for Ottawa Sudz'N'Bubbles for Spring 2018

	Budget	Actual	Variances
Revenue	$155,400	$149,500	–$5,900
Variable expenses (50% of revenue)	77,700	74,750	2,950
Fixed expenses	48,500	55,000	–6,500
Total expenses	126,200	129,750	–3,550
Profit	29,200	19,750	–9,450

Table 2: Operating Statistics for Ottawa Sudz'N'Bubbles for Spring 2018

	Budget Assumptions	Actual
Average number of vehicles washed in a good weather hour	21	25
Average revenue per vehicle	$10.00	$11.50
Total working hours in quarter	920	920
Hours of bad weather in quarter	180	400
Hours of good weather in quarter	740	520

Required:

Assume the role of Christopher and write a memo to the manager of the Ottawa location assessing the performance of the location. What bonus should be paid to the people working in the Ottawa Sudz'N'Bubbles? Explain your decision (be sure to include the selling price variance as part of this explanation).

Case 10-36 Standard Costing, Ethical Behaviour, Usefulness of Standard Costing

Pat James, the purchasing agent for a local plant of the Oakden Electronics Division, was considering the possible purchase of a component from a new supplier. The component's purchase price, $0.90, compared favourably with the standard price of $1.10. Given the quantity that would be purchased, Pat knew that the favourable price variance would help to offset an unfavourable variance for another component. By offsetting the unfavourable variance, his overall performance report would be impressive and good enough to help him qualify for the annual bonus. More importantly, a good performance rating this year would help him to secure a position at division headquarters at a significant salary increase.

Purchase of the part, however, presented Pat with a dilemma. Consistent with his past behaviour, Pat made inquiries regarding the reliability of the new supplier and the part's quality. Reports were basically negative. The supplier had a reputation for making the first two or three deliveries on schedule but being unreliable thereafter. Worse, the part itself was of questionable quality. The number of defective units was only slightly higher than that for other suppliers, but the life of the component was 25 percent less than what normal sources provided.

If the part were purchased, no problems with deliveries would surface for several months. The problem of shorter life would cause eventual customer dissatisfaction and perhaps some loss of sales, but the part would last at least 18 months after the final product began to be used. If all went well, Pat expected to be at headquarters within six months. He saw little personal risk associated with a decision to purchase the part from the new supplier. By the time any problems surfaced, they would belong to his successor. With this rationalization, Pat decided to purchase the component from the new supplier.

Required:

1. Do you agree with Pat's decision? Why or why not? How important was Pat's assessment of his personal risk in the decision? Should it be a factor?
2. Do you think that the use of standards and the practice of holding individuals accountable for their achievement played major roles in Pat's decision?
3. Review the discussion on corporate ethical standards in Chapter 1 and identify the standards that might apply to Pat's situation. Should every company adopt a set of ethical standards that apply to its employees, regardless of their specialty?
4. The usefulness of standard costing has been challenged in recent years. Some claim that its use is an impediment to the objective of continuous improvement (an objective that many feel is vital in today's competitive environment). Write a short paper (individually or in a small group with two or three other students) that analyzes the role and value of standard costing in today's manufacturing environment. Address the following questions:
   a. What are the major criticisms of standard costing?
   b. Will standard costing disappear, or is there still a role for it in the new manufacturing environment? If so, what is the role?
   c. Given the criticisms, can you explain why its use continues to be so prevalent? Will this use eventually change?

In preparing your paper, the following references may be useful; however, do not restrict your literature search to these references. They are simply to help you get started.

- Robin Cooper and Robert S. Kaplan, "Activity-Based Systems: Measuring the Costs of Resource Usage," *Accounting Horizons* (September 1992): 1–13.
- Forrest B. Green and Felix E. Amenkhienan, "Accounting Innovations: A Cross-Sectional Survey of Manufacturing Firms," *Journal of Cost Management* (Spring 1992): 59–64.
- Bruce R. Gaumnitz and Felix P. Kollaritsch, "Manufacturing Variances: Current Practice and Trends," *Journal of Cost Management* (Spring 1991): 59–64.
- Chris Guilding, Dane Lamminmaki, and Colin Drury, "Budgeting and Standard Costing Practices in New Zealand and the United Kingdom," *Journal of International Accounting,* Vol. 33, No. 5 (1998): 569–588.

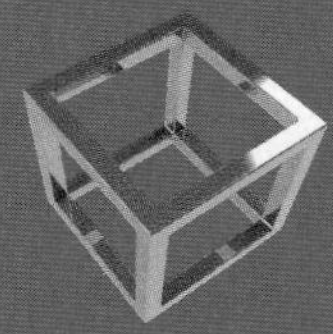

INTEGRATIVE CASE 2

The Two Cost Systems

Sacred Heart Hospital (SHH) faces skyrocketing nursing costs, all of which relate to its two biggest nursing service lines—the emergency room (ER) and the operating room (OR). SHH's current cost system assigns total nursing costs to the ER and OR based on the number of patients serviced by each line. Total hospital annual nursing costs for these two lines are expected to equal $300,000. The table below shows expected patient volume for both lines.

Measure	ER	OR	Total
Number of patients (ER visits; OR surgeries)	1,000	1,000	2,000
Number of vital signs checks	2,000	4,000	6,000
Number of nursing hours	10,000	5,000	15,000

Based on this information, the hospital-wide rate that SHH currently uses allocates $150 worth of nursing costs to each patient. Because the ER and OR provide care for equal numbers of patients, each service line is assigned $150,000 of the total hospital nursing costs. Given that the ER and OR require 10,000 and 5,000 nursing hours, this results in rates of $15 per ER hour and $30 per OR hour, respectively.

After speaking with several experienced nurses, Jack Bauer (SHH's accountant) decided that assigning nursing costs to the two service lines based on the number of times that nurses must check patients' vital signs might more closely match the underlying use of costly hospital resources. Therefore, for comparative purposes, Jack decided to develop a second cost system that assigns total nursing costs to the ER and OR based on the number of times nurses check patients' vital signs. This system is referred to as the *vital-signs costing system*.

Based on Jack's new line of thinking, the hospital-wide rate would allocate $50 worth of nursing costs each time a patient's vital signs are checked. In this case, because the activity levels differ between the ER and OR, the ER service line would be assigned $100,000 of the total hospital nursing costs and the OR service line would be assigned the remaining $200,000. Since the ER and OR require 10,000 and 5,000 nursing hours, this results in rates of $10 per ER hour and $40 per OR hour, respectively.

Budgeting and Variance Analysis

In an attempt to better plan for and control OR costs, SHH's management asked Jack to calculate the flexible budget variance (i.e., flexible budget costs less actual costs) for OR nursing costs, including the price variance and efficiency variance that make up the flexible budget variance for OR nursing costs. Given that Jack is interested in comparing the reported costs of both systems, he decided to prepare the requested OR variance analysis for both the current cost system and the vital-signs costing system. In addition, Jack chose to use each cost system's estimate of the cost per OR nursing hour as the standard cost per OR nursing hour. Jack collected the following additional information for use in preparing the flexible budget variance for both systems:

- Actual number of surgeries performed = 950
- Standard number of nursing hours allowed for each OR surgery = 5
- Actual number of OR nursing hours used = 5,000
- Actual OR nursing costs = $190,000

Jack is hoping that you will help him perform a budgeting and variance analysis for the OR service line. Jack believes that the information above will be sufficient to calculate the following: (1) flexible budget variance, (2) price variance, and (3) efficiency variance. He is hoping you will be able to do this for both the current cost system and the vital-signs costing system. (*Hint*: Use the cost per OR hour for each of the cost systems, provided above, as the standard cost per OR nursing hour.)

Since these systems are new and confusing to Jack, he is also hoping you might help him prepare a report to the leadership team at SHH. As mentioned at the beginning of this case, SHH faces skyrocketing nursing costs and is eager to get them under control.

Required:

1. Considering what Jack has told you about his discussion with experienced nurses regarding their use of hospital resources, and the reported costs that you calculated from each cost system, which cost system would you recommend? Provide some reasoning behind your choice so that Jack can include this in his report. Calculations should be provided to support your analysis.
2. Jack would also like your help in deciphering what each of the calculated variances means so that Jack knows what actions he should or should not take with respect to investigating and improving each variance. Briefly explain why the variances differ between the two cost systems.

11

Flexible Budgets and Overhead Analysis

After studying Chapter 11, you should be able to:

1. Prepare a flexible budget, and use it for performance reporting.
2. Calculate the variable overhead variances, and explain their meaning.
3. Calculate the fixed overhead variances, and explain their meaning.
4. (*Appendix 11A*) Prepare an activity-based flexible budget.

Courtesy of The Second City

EXPERIENCE MANAGERIAL DECISIONS
with The Second City

The Second City has been North America's premiere live improvisational and sketch comedy theatre company for the past 55 years. Many famous Canadian stars began their careers at The Second City, including John Candy, Mike Myers, Eugene Levy, Catherine O'Hara, Dave Thomas, Dan Aykroyd, Martin Short, and Rick Moranis. More than just The Second City Television (SCTV), The Second City includes training centres, national touring companies, media and entertainment offshoots, and a corporate communication division.

As you might imagine, The Second City is an entrepreneurial organization, as evidenced by its decision to provide comedy theatre aboard Norwegian Cruise Line ships. Given the nature of its businesses, The Second City is extremely dependent on overhead costs. These overhead costs must be allocated to each business to create accurate budgets, which is followed by variance analysis when actual overhead costs are very different from budgeted overhead costs. Its fixed overhead costs are associated with capacity and, as such, relate more to its resident stages and training centre facilities in Chicago, Toronto, and Hollywood. Examples of The Second City's fixed overhead costs include salaries, stage and other facilities' rent, facilities maintenance, depreciation, taxes, and insurance. These overhead costs then are assigned to individual business budgets by using allocation bases such as floor area, number of employees, and percentage of earnings. The Second City then uses overhead cost variances to "red flag" potential problems that might not be self-correcting and need managerial attention.

For example, The Second City Theatricals might have a slow year because the producers are too busy with other ventures to mount a new production, while at the same time, The Second City Training Centre might have a surge in enrollment. Such a scenario likely would lead The Second City financial executives to shift some assigned overhead costs from the theatrical business to the training centre business. Also, The Second City uses flexible budgeting to adjust budgets for its businesses that experience sporadic volumes, such as the seasonality present in some of its travelling and cruise activities. While the managerial accountants likely do not intentionally provide too many jokes, they do provide the critical function of budgeting and examining variances for overhead costs, which allows the comic talent of The Second City to continue to do what it does best—make us laugh!

USING BUDGETS FOR PERFORMANCE EVALUATION

OBJECTIVE 1

Prepare a flexible budget, and use it for performance reporting.

Budgets are useful for both planning and control, and are often used as benchmarks for performance evaluation. Determining how budgeted amounts should be compared with actual results is a major consideration that must be addressed.

Static Budgets versus Flexible Budgets

In Chapter 9, we learned how companies prepare a master budget based on their best estimate of the level of sales and production activity for the coming period. We also discussed some behavioural issues associated with performance reporting. In Chapter 10, we analyzed detailed variances at a unit level. However, no discussion was provided on how to prepare budgetary *performance reports*. A **performance report** compares actual costs with budgeted costs. There are two ways to make comparisons:

1. Compare actual costs with the budgeted costs for the budgeted level of activity.
2. Compare actual costs with the actual level of activity.

The first choice requires a report based on *static budgets*, whereas the second choice needs a report based on *flexible budgets*. The two approaches for variance calculation are illustrated in Exhibit 11.1. Notice the relationship between actual number of units produced (10,000) and the two types of budgets. The static budget compares actual costs for production of 10,000 units with the budgeted costs for 8,000 units. Unsurprisingly, the variance is unfavourable. The flexible budget, on the other hand, compares actual costs for production of 10,000 units with the budgeted costs for 10,000 units. This is a much more meaningful comparison. While used extensively by manufacturing firms, variance analysis is equally important for nonmanufacturing organizations, such as The Second City. Whenever an organization has a budget, there is an opportunity for variance analysis as a means of understanding where expectations were met, where the organization excelled, and where there are opportunities for improvement. As a result, variance analysis can be usefully employed by governmental agencies, not-for-profit organizations, retail firms, and firms operating in the service sector.

EXHIBIT 11.1

Static and Flexible Budget Variances

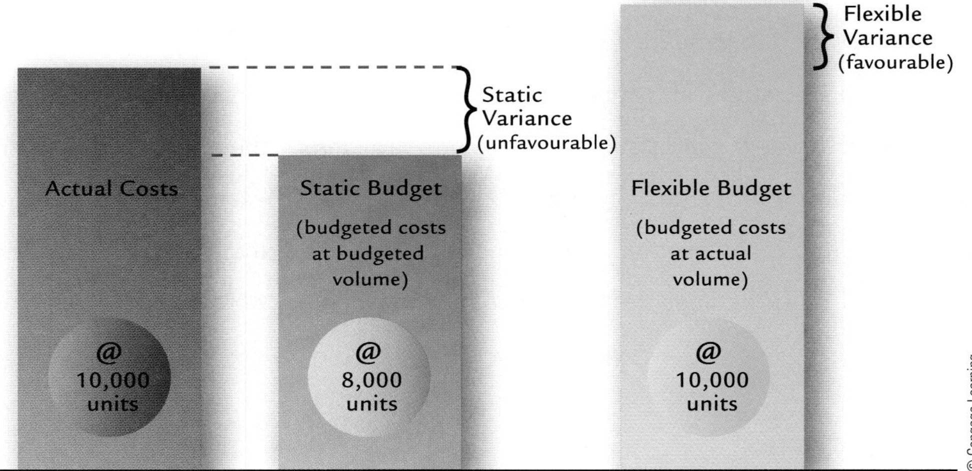

Static Budgets and Performance Reports A **static budget** is a budget prepared in advance based on a particular level of activity and is not adjusted or altered regardless of any subsequent changes in actual output, revenues, or costs. When the master budget is a static budget, a performance report can be prepared to compare the actual costs with the budgeted costs from the master budget. Using Cool-U in Cornerstone 11.1 as an example, the master budget was developed for the first quarter of the year when Cool-U expected to produce 1,060 pairs of shorts. At the end of the quarter, Cool-U found that it had actually produced 1,200 pairs of shorts.

Preparing a Performance Report Based on a Static Budget (Using Budgeted Production)

CORNERSTONE 11.1

Information:

Relationships from the Master Budget of Cool-U	Actual Data for Quarter 1
Budgeted production for Quarter 1: 1,060	Production: 1,200 units
Materials:	
1 plain pair of shorts @ $3.00	Materials cost: $4,830
5 grams of ink @ $0.20	
Labour: 0.12 hr. @ $10.00	Labour cost: $1,500
Variable overhead:	
Maintenance: 0.12 hr. @ $3.75	Maintenance cost: $535
Power: 0.12 hr. @ $1.25	Power cost: $170
Fixed overhead:	
Grounds keeping: $1,200 per quarter	Grounds keeping: $1,050
Depreciation: $600 per quarter	Depreciation: $600

Required:

Prepare a performance report using a budget based on expected production.

Solution:

	Actual	Budgeted	Variance
Units produced	1,200	1,060	140 F[a]
Direct materials cost	$4,830	$4,240[b]	$590 U[c]
Direct labour cost	1,500	1,272[d]	228 U
Variable overhead:			
Maintenance	535	477[e]	58 U
Power	170	159[f]	11 U
Fixed overhead:			
Grounds keeping	1,050	1,200	(150) F
Depreciation	600	600	0
Total	$8,685	$ 7,948	$ 737 U

[a] F means the variance is favourable.
[b] Budgeted units (shorts cost + ink cost) = 1,060[$3 + (5 g × $0.20)].
[c] U means the variance is unfavourable.
[d] Budgeted units (number of direct labour hours × cost per hour) = 1,060(0.12 × $10.00).
[e] Budgeted units (number of direct labour hours × variable maintenance rate) = 1,060(0.12 × $3.75).
[f] Budgeted units (number of direct labour hours × variable power rate) = 1,060(0.12 × $1.25).

Why:

The starting point for every budgeting exercise, the static budget, should be prepared before the accounting period begins. This budget, which is prepared using expected volumes of sales and output, is the budget that management usually identifies with, and we must be able to relate actual results to it.

Corporate and Social Responsibility

Companies that use static budgets as the benchmark for performance evaluation invite potential abuse by managers subject to this approach. Although unethical, a manager could manipulate the performance report by deliberately producing less than the planned output—producing, for example, 1,000 shorts instead of the planned 1,060. By producing less, the costs will be less than the budgeted amounts, creating a favourable performance outcome. Alternatively, an unethical manager could set a particularly low target for production knowing that the division will easily exceed the target, which can result in a favourable performance outcome. Using flexible budgeting allows the benchmark to be adjusted to reflect the expected costs for the actual level of output and, therefore, reduce the incentive for managers to act unethically.

According to Cornerstone 11.1, there were unfavourable variances for direct materials, direct labour, maintenance, and power. However, there is something fundamentally wrong with the report. Actual costs for production of 1,200 shorts are being compared with planned costs for production of 1,060. Because direct materials, direct labour, and variable overhead are variable costs, they should be greater at a higher level of production. Thus, even if cost control were perfect for the production of 1,200 units, unfavourable variances would be produced for at least some of the variable costs. To create a meaningful performance report, actual costs and expected costs must be compared at the *same* level of activity. Since actual output often differs from planned output, a method is needed to compute what the costs should have been for the actual output level.

Flexible Budgets

A **flexible budget** enables a firm to compute the expected costs per unit and then estimate costs for a range of activity levels or production volumes. The key to flexible budgeting is knowledge of fixed and variable costs. The two types of flexible budgets are:

1. *Before-the-fact*. This type of flexible budget gives the expected outcomes for a range of activity levels or production volumes. It can be used to generate financial results for a number of plausible scenarios.
2. *After-the-fact*. This flexible budget is based on the actual level of activity achieved in the period. This type of budget is used to compute what costs should have been for the actual level of activity or for the actual production volume. Those expected costs are then compared with the actual costs in order to assess performance.

concept Q&A

Why are static budgets usually not a good choice for benchmarks in preparing a performance report?

Answers on pages 734 to 738.

Flexible budgeting is the key to providing the frequent feedback that managers need to exercise control and effectively carry out the plans of an organization.

Suppose that the management of Cool-U wants to know the cost of producing 1,000 shorts, 1,200 shorts, and 1,400 shorts. To compute the expected cost for these different levels of output, the cost behaviour pattern of each item in the budget needs to be known. Knowing the variable cost per unit and the total fixed costs allows the calculation of the expected costs for various levels of activity. Cornerstone 11.2 shows how budgets can be prepared before-the-fact for different levels of activity within the relevant range.

Cornerstone 11.2 shows that total budgeted production costs increase as the production level increases. Budgeted costs change because total variable costs rise as output increases. Because of this, flexible budgets are sometimes referred to as **variable budgets**. Since Cool-U has a mix of variable and fixed costs, the overall cost of producing one pair of shorts goes *down* as production goes *up*. This makes sense: as production increases, there are more units over which to spread the fixed production costs.

Often flexible budget formulas are based on some level of input activity instead of units. For example, the variable cost formulas for variable overhead are $3.75 and

Preparing a Flexible Production Budget (Before the Fact)

CORNERSTONE 11.2

Information:

Levels of output: 1,000, 1,200, and 1,400.

Materials:
- 1 plain pair of shorts @ $3.00
- 5 grams of ink @ $0.20

Variable overhead:
- Maintenance: 0.12 hr. @ $3.75
- Power: 0.12 hr. @ $1.25

Labour:
- 0.12 hr. @ $10.00

Fixed overhead:
- Grounds keeping: $1,200 per quarter
- Depreciation: $600 per quarter

Required:

Prepare a budget for three levels of output: 1,000, 1,200, and 1,400 units.

Solution:

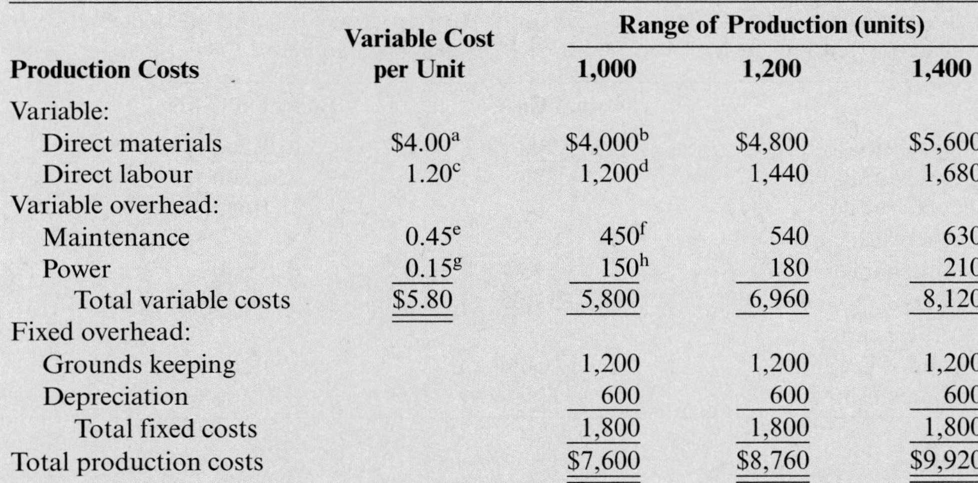

Production Costs	**Variable Cost per Unit**	**Range of Production (units)**		
		1,000	**1,200**	**1,400**
Variable:				
Direct materials	$4.00[a]	$4,000[b]	$4,800	$5,600
Direct labour	1.20[c]	1,200[d]	1,440	1,680
Variable overhead:				
Maintenance	0.45[e]	450[f]	540	630
Power	0.15[g]	150[h]	180	210
Total variable costs	$5.80	5,800	6,960	8,120
Fixed overhead:				
Grounds keeping		1,200	1,200	1,200
Depreciation		600	600	600
Total fixed costs		1,800	1,800	1,800
Total production costs		$7,600	$8,760	$9,920

[a] Shorts cost + Ink cost = [($3.00 × 1 pair of shorts) × ($0.20 × 5 g)]
[b] ($4 × 1,000 units)
[c] ($10.00 per direct labour hour × 0.12 direct labour hours per unit)
[d] ($1.20 × 1,000 units)
[e] ($3.75 per direct labour hour × 0.12 direct labour hours per unit)
[f] ($0.45 × 1,000 units)
[g] ($1.25 per direct labour hour × 0.12 direct labour hours per unit)
[h] ($0.15 × 1,000 units)

Why:

A flexible budget is a representation of the original budget, called the static budget, adjusted to reflect actual sales/output achieved. This prevents the distortions that would arise due to volume differences between the budgeted level of activity and the level actually achieved.

$1.25 per direct labour hour ($5.00 per direct labour hour in total) for maintenance and power, respectively. When standard hours are used, we need to convert units into direct labour hours. For the Cool-U example, the production of 1,000 budgeted units means that 120 direct labour hours will be needed (0.12 direct labour hours per unit × 1,000 budgeted units).

Flexible budgets are powerful control tools because they allow management to compute what the costs should be for the level of *output that actually occurred.* Recall that Cool-U thought that 1,060 units would be produced, and budgeted for that amount. However, actual production was 1,200 units. It does not make sense to compare the actual costs for 1,200 pairs of shorts to the budgeted costs for 1,060 pairs of shorts. Management will need a useful performance report, one that compares actual and budgeted costs for the actual level of activity. This is the second type of flexible budget, and preparation of this report is shown in Cornerstone 11.3. The revised performance report in Cornerstone 11.3 paints a much different picture than the one in Cornerstone 11.1. All of the variances are fairly small. Had they been larger, management would have searched for the cause and tried to correct the problems as necessary.

CORNERSTONE 11.3

Preparing a Performance Report Using a Flexible Budget (After the Fact)

Information:

For convenience, the actual costs for 1,200 units (Cornerstone 11.1) and the budgeted costs for the actual level of activity (Cornerstone 11.2) are repeated here.

	Actual Costs	Budgeted Costs
Units produced	1,200	1,200
Direct materials cost	$4,830	$4,800
Direct labour cost	1,500	1,440
Variable overhead:		
Maintenance	535	540
Power	170	180
Fixed overhead:		
Grounds keeping	1,050	1,200
Depreciation	600	600

Required:

Prepare a performance report using budgeted costs for the actual level of activity.

Solution:

	Actual	Budget	Variance
Units produced	1,200	1,200	—
Production costs:			
Direct materials	$ 4,830	$4,800	$ 30 U
Direct labour	1,500	1,440	60 U
Variable overhead:			
Maintenance	535	540	(5) F
Power	170	180	(10) F
Total variable costs	7,035	6,960	75 U
Fixed overhead:			
Grounds keeping	1,050	1,200	(150) F
Depreciation	600	600	—
Total fixed costs	1,650	1,800	(150) F
Total production costs	$ 8,685	$8,760	$ (75) F

(*Continued*)

Why:

The performance report, using flexible budget values that are based on actual activity levels achieved, will highlight the operational differences between expected performance and actual performance. This will assist us in identifying what explanations are required and, possibly, what corrective actions need to be taken.

CORNERSTONE

11.3

(Continued)

The difference between the actual amount and the flexible budget amount is the **flexible budget variance**. The flexible budget variance provides a measure of the efficiency of a manager; that is, how well did the manager control costs for the actual level of production? A static budget provides a measure of whether or not a manager accomplishes his or her goals and represents certain goals that the firm wants to achieve. A manager is effective if the goals described by the static budget are achieved or exceeded. In the Cool-U example, production volume was 140 units greater than the original budgeted amount; the manager exceeded the original budgeted goal. Therefore, the effectiveness of the manager is not in question.

analytical Q&A

What is the budgeted cost of maintenance if 2,000 pairs of shorts are produced?

Answers on pages 734 to 738.

YOU DECIDE Flexible Budgeting for Entertainment

You are the chief accountant for The Second City, the company described in the chapter opener. Your job includes budgeting for the live performances, including the national touring companies and the customized comedy shows put on by the company. (See www.secondcity.com for examples of the live performances.) At the beginning of each year, you must put together budgets for these performances based on projected demand for the shows and projected costs. As the year unfolds, you want to update the budgets in accordance with new information and create performance reports that compare the actual costs with projected costs.

What information will you need to create flexible budgets for the live performances?

You will need to consider the fixed and variable costs associated with putting on live performances away from The Second City's Toronto base. The variable costs will include travel and salary costs for the performers, stage and facilities rent for each venue, and other variable costs associated with the shows (e.g., costs of hiring ticket sellers and ushers, and supplies such as programs and tickets). Clearly, the variable costs will increase with an increase in the number of shows and venues. Some fixed costs must also be determined. These include the salaries of the writers, insurance, costs of props and costumes, and costs of marketing the shows to prospective customers including corporations and regional theatres.

Knowing the difference between the fixed and variable costs will enable you to create budgets that are useful to management in planning for the year ahead, as well as controlling costs as the year unfolds.

Flexible Budget Sales Variances

The sales component of a flexible budget will reveal the difference between the level of sales actually achieved and the level of sales indicated by the master budget. There can be several reasons for this difference, and only by isolating the differences as a result of the volume of units sold and the volume anticipated can the causes of the problem be understood. A sales price variance can be calculated by looking at the actual units sold and the expected (budgeted) revenues at that volume. Any difference will be explained by a selling price variance.

VARIABLE OVERHEAD ANALYSIS

OBJECTIVE 2

Calculate the variable overhead variances, and explain their meaning.

In Chapter 10, total variances for direct materials and direct labour were broken down into price and efficiency variances. In a standard cost system, the total overhead variance, which is the difference between applied and actual overhead, is also broken down into component variances. There are several methods of overhead variance analysis; the four-variance method is described in this chapter. First, overhead is divided into fixed and variable categories. Next, two variances are calculated for each category:

- Variable overhead variance
  - Variable overhead spending variance
  - Variable overhead efficiency variance
- Fixed overhead variance
  - Fixed overhead spending variance
  - Fixed overhead volume variance

Total Variable Overhead Variance

The total variable overhead variance is simply the difference between the total *actual variable overhead* and *applied variable overhead*. Variable overhead is applied by using hours allowed in a standard cost system. The total variable overhead variance can be divided into spending and efficiency variances. Variable overhead spending and efficiency variances can be calculated by using either the three-pronged (columnar) approach or formulas. The best approach is a matter of preference. However, the formulas first need to be expressed specifically for variable overhead.

Because the equations for variable overhead variances can be long if expressed in words, abbreviations are often used. Here are some common abbreviations that you will find in the rest of this section:

AH = actual direct labour hours
SH = standard direct labour hours that should have been worked for actual units produced
$AVOR$ = actual variable overhead rate
$SVOR$ = standard variable overhead rate

Cornerstone 11.4 illustrates how to calculate the total variable overhead variance using the first quarter data for Cool-U. The unit prices and quantities used for the flexible budget are assumed to be the standards associated with Cool-U's standard cost system.

CORNERSTONE 11.4

Calculating the Total Variable Overhead Variance

Information:

Standard variable overhead rate	$5.00 per direct labour hour
Actual variable overhead costs	$705
Standard hours allowed per unit	0.12 hour
Actual direct labour hours worked	150 hours
Actual production	1,200 units

(Continued)

CORNERSTONE

11.4

(Continued)

Required:

1. Calculate the actual variable overhead rate.
2. Calculate the total variable overhead variance.

Solution:

1. $$\text{Actual variable overhead rate} = \frac{\text{Actual variable overhead cost}}{\text{Actual direct labour hours}}$$

$$AVOR = \frac{\$705}{150 \text{ hours}}$$

$$AVOR = \$4.70$$

2.

Actual variable overhead ($AH \times AVOR$)	\$705
Applied variable overhead ($SH \times SVOR$)*	720
Total variable overhead variance [$(AH \times AVOR) - (SH \times SVOR)$]	\$(15) F

* $SH \times SVOR = 0.12 \times 1{,}200 \times \$5$

Why:

Overhead has become an increasingly important component of cost, and we must fully understand how we are incurring these overhead costs.

Variable Overhead Spending Variance The **variable overhead spending variance** measures the aggregate effect of differences between the actual variable overhead rate (AVOR) and the standard variable overhead rate (SVOR). The AVOR is computed as follows:

$$AVOR = \frac{\text{Actual variable overhead}}{\text{Actual hours}}$$

As shown by Cornerstone 11.4, this rate is \$4.70 per hour, computed as actual variable overhead cost of \$705 divided by 150 actual direct labour hours. The formula for computing the variable overhead spending variance is:

$$\text{Variable overhead spending variance} = (AVOR \times AH) - (SVOR \times AH)$$
$$= (AVOR - SVOR)AH$$

analytical Q&A

If actual hours equal 100, standard hours equal 90, and the standard variable overhead rate is \$6, what is the variable overhead efficiency variance?

Answers on pages 734 to 738.

Variable Overhead Efficiency Variance Variable overhead is assumed to vary as the production volume changes. Thus, variable overhead changes in proportion to changes in the direct labour hours used. The **variable overhead efficiency variance** measures the change in the actual variable overhead that occurs because of efficient (or inefficient) use of direct labour. The efficiency variance is computed by using the following formula:

$$\text{Variable overhead efficiency variance} = (AH - SH)SVOR$$

How to calculate the variable overhead variances using either a columnar or formula approach is shown for the Cool-U example in Cornerstone 11.5.

CORNERSTONE 11.5

Calculating Variable Overhead Spending and Efficiency Variances: Columnar and Formula Approaches

CORNERSTONE VIDEO

Information:

Standard variable overhead rate (SVOR)	$5.00 per direct labour hour
Actual variable overhead rate (AVOR)	$4.70
Actual hours worked (AH)	150 hours
Number of shorts produced	1,200 units
Hours allowed for production (SH)	144 hours[a]

[a] 0.12 × 1,200

Required:

Calculate the variable overhead spending and efficiency variances.

Solution:

Columnar:

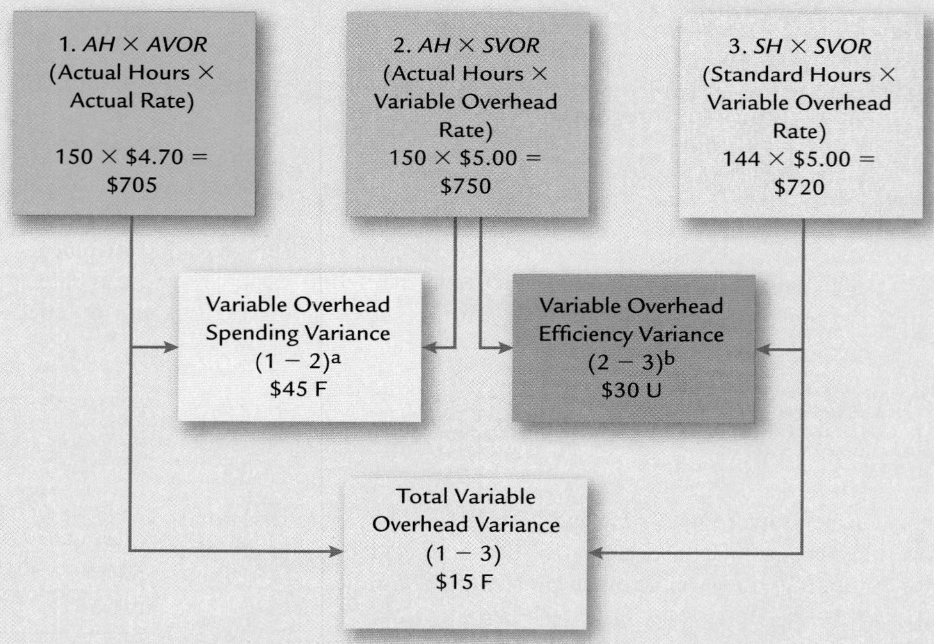

Formulas:

[a]*VOH* spending variance $= (AVOR - SVOR)AH$
$= (\$4.70 - \$5.00)150$
$= \$45$ F

[b]*VOH* efficiency variance $= (AH - SH)SVOR$
$= (150 - 144)(\$5.00)$
$= \$30$ U

Why:

Variable overhead is a key component of overhead costs and must be divided into understandable components: spending and efficiency variances. There are two approaches that will help us understand these variances: columnar and formula.

Comparison of the Variable Overhead Spending Variance with the Price Variances of Materials and Labour

The variable overhead spending variance is similar but not identical to the price variances of materials and labour; there are some conceptual differences. Variable overhead is not a single input—it is made up of a large number of individual items, such as indirect materials, indirect labour, electricity, maintenance, and so on. The SVOR represents the weighted cost per direct labour hour that should be incurred for all variable overhead items. The difference between what should have been spent per hour and what actually was spent per hour is a type of price variance.

One reason that variable overhead spending variances arise is because prices for individual variable overhead items have increased or decreased. Assume that the price changes of individual overhead items are the only cause of the spending variance. If the spending variance is unfavourable, price increases for individual variable overhead items are the cause; if the spending variance is favourable, price decreases are dominating.

concept Q&A

How does the variable overhead spending variance differ from the materials and labour price variances?

Answers on pages 734 to 738.

A second reason that variable overhead spending variances arise is due to the use of items that comprise variable overhead. Waste or inefficiency in the use of variable overhead increases the actual variable overhead cost that, in turn, is reflected in an increased AVOR. Thus, even if the actual prices of the individual overhead items were equal to the budgeted or standard prices, an unfavourable variable overhead spending variance could still take place. For example, more kilowatt-hours of power may be used than should be for the actual level of production. The result is an increase in the total cost of power and, thus, the total cost of variable overhead. Similarly, efficiency can decrease the actual variable overhead cost and decrease the AVOR. Efficient use of variable overhead items contributes to a favourable spending variance. If the waste effect dominates, then the net contribution will be unfavourable; if efficiency dominates, then the net contribution is favourable. Therefore, the variable overhead spending variance is the result of both price and efficiency.

Responsibility for the Variable Overhead Spending Variance

Many variable overhead items are affected by several responsibility centres. For example, utilities are a joint cost. To the extent that consumption of variable overhead can be traced to a responsibility centre, responsibility can be assigned. Consumption of indirect materials is an example of a traceable variable overhead cost.

Controllability is a prerequisite for assigning responsibility. Price changes of variable overhead items are essentially beyond the control of supervisors. If price changes are small (as they often are), then the spending variance is primarily a matter of the efficient use of overhead in production. This is controllable by production supervisors. Accordingly, responsibility for the variable overhead spending variance is generally assigned to production departments.

Responsibility for the Variable Overhead Efficiency Variance

The variable overhead efficiency variance is directly related to the direct labour efficiency or usage variance. If variable overhead is truly proportional to direct labour consumption then, like the labour usage variance, the variable overhead efficiency variance is caused by efficient or inefficient use of direct labour. If more (or fewer)

concept Q&A

Why are the labour efficiency and variable overhead efficiency variances similar in nature?

Answers on pages 734 to 738.

direct labour hours are used than the standard calls for, then the total variable overhead cost will increase (or decrease). The validity of the measure depends on the validity of the relationship between variable overhead costs and direct labour hours. In other words, do variable overhead costs really change in proportion to changes in direct labour hours? If so, responsibility for the variable overhead efficiency variance should be assigned to the individual who has responsibility for the use of direct labour: the production manager.

A Performance Report for the Variable Overhead Spending and Efficiency Variances

Cornerstone 11.5 showed a favourable $45 variable overhead spending variance and an unfavourable $30 variable overhead efficiency variance. The $45 F spending variance means that overall Cool-U spent less than expected on variable overhead. The reasons for the $30 U variable overhead efficiency variance are the same as those offered for an unfavourable labour usage variance. An unfavourable variance means that more hours were used than called for by the standard. Even if the total variable overhead spending and efficiency variances are insignificant, they reveal nothing about how well costs of *individual* variable overhead items were controlled. It is possible for two large variances of opposite sign to cancel each other out. Control of variable overhead requires line-by-line analysis for each item. Cornerstone 11.6 shows how to prepare a performance report that supplies the line-by-line information essential for detailed analysis of the variable overhead variances.

The analysis on a line-by-line basis reveals no unusual problems such as two large individual item variances with opposite signs. No individual item variance is greater than 10 percent of its budgeted amount. Thus, no variance at the individual item level appears to be of a large enough magnitude to be of concern.

CORNERSTONE 11.6

Preparing a Performance Report for the Variable Overhead Variances

Information:

Standard variable overhead rate	$5.00 per direct labour hour
Actual costs:	
Maintenance	$535
Power	$170
Actual hours worked (AH)	150 hours
Number of shorts produced	1,200 units
Hours allowed for production (SH)	144 hours[a]
Variable overhead:	
Maintenance	0.12 hr. @ $3.75
Power	0.12 hr. @ $1.25

[a] 0.12 × 1,200

Required:

Prepare a performance report that shows the variances on an item-by-item basis.

(Continued)

CORNERSTONE

11.6

(Continued)

Solution:

Performance Report
For the Quarter Ended March 31

Cost	Cost Formula[a]	Actual Costs	Budget for Actual Hours[b]	Spending Variance[c]	Budget for Standard Hours[d]	Efficiency Variance[e]
Maintenance	$3.75	$535	$562.50	$27.50 F	$540	$22.50 U
Power	1.25	170	187.50	17.50 F	180	7.50 U
Total	$5.00	$705	$750.00	$45.00 F	$720	$30.00 U

[a] Per direct labour hour
[b] Computed using the cost formula and 150 actual hours
[c] Spending variance = Actual costs − Budget for actual hours
[d] Computed using the cost formula and an activity level of 144 standard hours
[e] Efficiency variance = Budget for actual hours − Budget for standard hours

Why:

Reporting variable overhead variances will allow managers to understand where the potential problem areas are and who should be queried about their operations.

FIXED OVERHEAD ANALYSIS

OBJECTIVE 

Calculate the fixed overhead variances, and explain their meaning.

Fixed overhead costs are capacity costs that are acquired in advance of usage. Examples include the property, plant, and equipment needed to manufacture the product. Recall from Chapter 5 that the predetermined overhead rate is calculated at the beginning of the year by dividing budgeted overhead by the budgeted amount of the base (e.g., direct labour hours). Now, however, we need to divide that predetermined overhead rate into variable and fixed overhead rates. It was easy to find the variable overhead rate since that rate is unchanged even though the number of units produced, and thus direct labour hours, changes. However, the fixed overhead rate changes as the underlying activity changes. To keep a stable fixed overhead rate throughout the year, companies typically use practical capacity to determine the number of direct labour hours in the denominator of the fixed overhead rate. Since practical capacity does not tend to vary with levels of production, it is reasonable to use the static budget for variance analysis of fixed expenses (rather than a flexible budget). In using the static budget, this analysis involves comparing what was planned to what actually occurred without the additional complications of varying production outputs that we see in variable overhead variance analysis.

Assuming that Cool-U can produce 1,500 pairs of shorts per quarter under efficient operating conditions, then practical capacity measured in standard hours (SH_p) is calculated by the following formula:

$$SH_p = \text{Unit standard} \times \text{Units of practical capacity}$$

$$= 0.12 \times 1{,}500$$
$$= 180 \text{ hours}$$

Recall from Cornerstone 11.2 that Cool-U's total fixed costs per quarter equal $1,800. The standard fixed overhead rate (SFOR) is calculated as follows:

analytical Q&A

If the budgeted fixed overhead is $10,000 and the standard fixed overhead rate is $100 per direct labour hour (calculated using practical capacity), what is the practical capacity, measured in direct labour hours?

Answers on pages 734 to 738.

$$SFOR = \frac{\text{Budgeted fixed overhead costs}}{\text{Practical capacity}}$$

$$SFOR = \frac{\$1{,}800}{180}$$
$$= \$10 \text{ per direct labour hour}$$

Some firms use average or expected capacity instead of practical capacity to calculate fixed overhead rates. In this case, the standard hours used to calculate the fixed overhead rate will typically be less than the standard direct labour hours at practical capacity.

Total fixed overhead can be calculated by multiplying the fixed overhead rate by the number of direct labour hours at capacity (if direct labour hours are the overhead application base used).

Total Fixed Overhead Variances

The total fixed overhead variance is the difference between actual fixed overhead and applied fixed overhead, when applied fixed overhead is obtained by multiplying the standard fixed overhead rate times the standard hours allowed for the actual output. Thus, the applied fixed overhead is:

$$\text{Applied fixed overhead} = SFOR \times SH$$

The total fixed overhead variance is the difference between the actual fixed overhead and the applied fixed overhead:

$$\text{Total variance} = \text{Actual fixed overhead} - \text{Applied fixed overhead}$$

Cornerstone 11.7 illustrates how to calculate the total fixed overhead variance using the Cool-U example. The total fixed overhead variance can be divided into spending and volume variances. Spending and volume variances can be calculated by using either the three-pronged (columnar) approach or formulas. The best approach to use is a matter of preference. However, the formulas first need to be expressed specifically for fixed overhead.

CORNERSTONE 11.7 Calculating the Total Fixed Overhead Variance

Information:

Standard fixed overhead rate	$10.00 per direct labour hour
Actual fixed overhead costs	$1,650
Standard hours allowed per unit	0.12 hour
Actual production	1,200 units

Required:

1. Calculate the standard hours for actual units produced.
2. Calculate the total applied fixed overhead.
3. Calculate the total fixed overhead variance.

(Continued)

CORNERSTONE
11.7

(Continued)

Solution:

1. SH = Actual units × Standard hours allowed per unit
   = 1,200 units × 0.12 hour
   = 144 hours

2. Applied fixed overhead = $SH \times SFOR$
   = 144 × \$10
   = \$1,440

3.

Actual fixed overhead cost	\$1,650
Applied fixed overhead	1,440
Total variance	\$ 210 U

Why:

Fixed overhead is a critical component of overhead costs and must be analyzed separately from variable overhead costs. Since fixed costs do not vary irrespective of volume, there is no difference between the static budget amount for fixed overhead and the flexible budget amount for fixed overhead.

Fixed Overhead Spending Variance The **fixed overhead spending variance** is defined as the difference between the actual fixed overhead (AFOH) and the budgeted fixed overhead (BFOH):

$$FOH \text{ spending variance} = AFOH - BFOH$$

Fixed Overhead Volume Variance The **fixed overhead volume variance** is the difference between BFOH and applied fixed overhead:

$$\begin{aligned} FOH \text{ volume variance} &= BFOH - \text{Applied fixed overhead} \\ &= BFOH - (SH \times SFOR) \end{aligned}$$

The volume variance measures the effect of the actual output differing from the output used at the beginning of the year to compute the predetermined SFOR. If you think of the output used to calculate the fixed overhead rate as the capacity acquired (practical capacity) and the actual output as the capacity used, then the volume variance is the cost of unused capacity. Cornerstone 11.8 illustrates how to calculate the fixed overhead variances using either a columnar or a formula approach.

Responsibility for the Fixed Overhead Spending Variance

Fixed overhead is made up of items such as salaries, depreciation, taxes, and insurance. Many fixed overhead items—long-run investments, for instance—are not subject to change in the short run; consequently, fixed overhead costs are often beyond the immediate control of management. Since many fixed overhead costs are affected primarily by long-run decisions, and not by changes in production levels, the budget variance is usually small. For example, actual depreciation, salaries, taxes, and insurance costs are not likely to be much different from planned costs.

CORNERSTONE 11.8

Calculating Fixed Overhead Variances: Columnar and Formula Approaches

Information:

Standard fixed overhead rate (SFOR)	\$10.00 per direct labour hour
Budgeted fixed overhead (BFOH)	\$1,800
Number of shorts produced	1,200 units
Hours allowed for production (SH)	144 hours[a]

[a] 0.12 × 1,200

Required:

Calculate the fixed overhead spending and volume variances.

Solution:

Columnar:

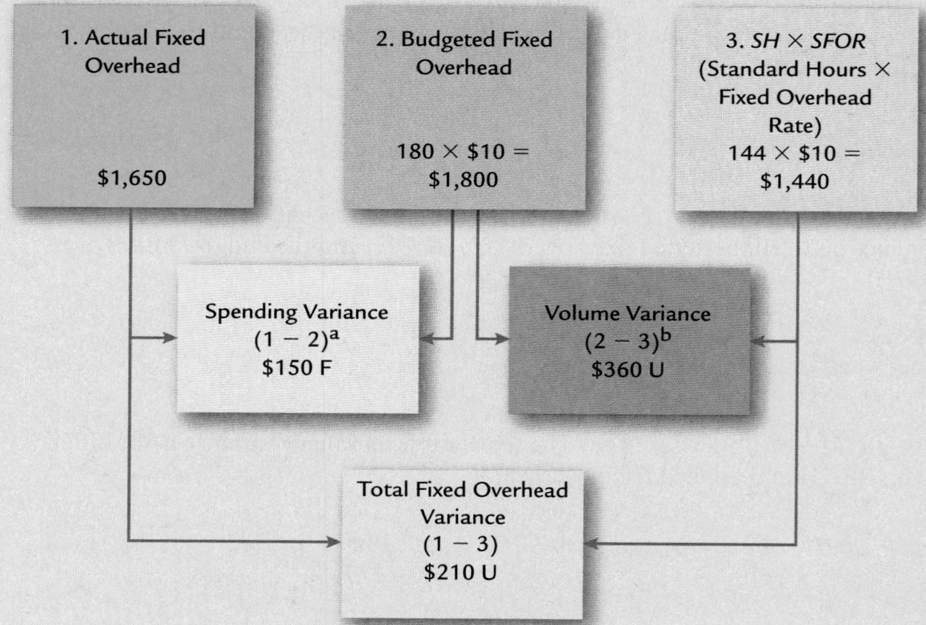

Formulas:

[a]*FOH* spending variance = Actual fixed overhead − Budgeted fixed overhead
= \$1,650 − \$1,800
= \$150 F

[b]*FOH* volume variance = Budgeted fixed overhead − Applied fixed overhead
= Budgeted fixed overhead − ($SH \times SFOR$)
= \$1,800 − (144 × \$10)
= \$1,800 − \$1,440
= \$360 U

Why:

Fixed overhead variances should be further divided into spending and volume variances to provide more useful information for further investigation. There are two approaches that can assist in this process: columnar and formula.

Analysis of the Fixed Overhead Spending Variance

Because fixed overhead is made up of many individual items, a line-by-line comparison of budgeted costs with actual costs provides more information concerning the causes of the spending variance. The fixed overhead section of Cornerstone 11.3 provides such a report. The report reveals that the fixed overhead spending variance is out of line with expectations. Less was spent on grounds keeping than expected. In fact, the entire spending variance is attributable to this one item. Since the amount is more than 10 percent of budget, it merits an investigation. An investigation might reveal, for example, that the weather was especially wet and thus reduced the cost of watering for the period involved. In this case, no action is needed, as a natural correction would be forthcoming.

Responsibility for the Fixed Overhead Volume Variance

The assumption that volume variance measures capacity utilization implies that the general responsibility for this variance should be assigned to the production department. At times, however, investigation into the reasons for a significant volume variance may reveal the cause to be factors beyond the control of production. In this instance, specific responsibility may be assigned elsewhere. For example, if the purchasing department buys lower-quality raw materials than usual, significant rework time may result. This will cause lower production and an unfavourable volume variance. In this case, responsibility for the variance rests with purchasing, not production.

Analysis of the Volume Variance

The $360 U volume variance (Cornerstone 11.8) occurs because the practical capacity is 180 hours and only 144 hours should have been used. Why the company failed to use all of its capacity is not known. Given that unused capacity is 20 percent of the total, investigation seems merited. Exhibit 11.2 graphically illustrates the volume variance.

EXHIBIT 11.2

Graphical Analysis of the Volume Variance

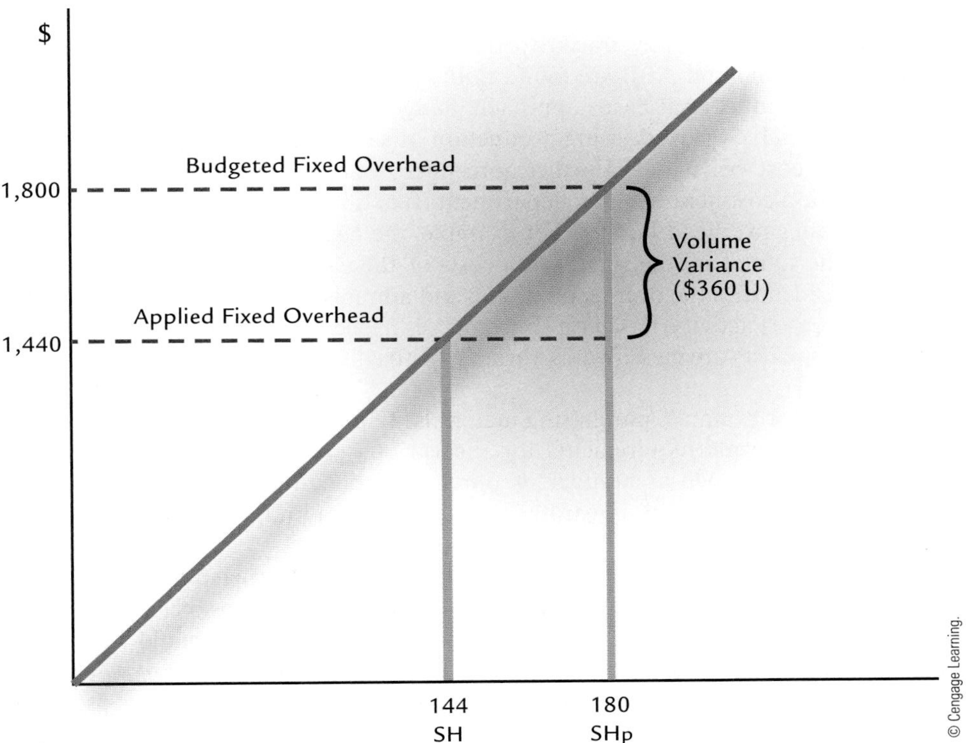

Notice that the volume variance occurs because fixed overhead is treated as if it were a variable cost. In reality, fixed costs do not change as activity changes, as a predetermined fixed overhead rate would imply.

APPENDIX 11A: ACTIVITY-BASED BUDGETING

Prepare an activity-based flexible budget.

The traditional approach to budgeting (explained in Chapter 9) emphasizes:

1. the estimation of revenues and costs by organizational units (e.g., departments, plants), and
2. the use of a single unit-based driver such as direct labour hours.

Companies that have implemented an activity-based costing (ABC) system may also wish to install an *activity-based budgeting system*. An **activity-based budgeting (ABB) system** focuses on:

1. estimating the costs of activities rather than the costs of departments and plants, and
2. the use of multiple drivers, both unit-based and non-unit-based.

The ABB approach supports continuous improvement and process management. Because activities consume resources (which cause costs), activity-based budgeting can be used to reduce costs through eliminating wasteful activities and improving the efficiency of necessary activities.

Static Activity Budgets

Assuming that ABC has been implemented, the major emphasis for ABB is estimating the workload (demand) for each activity and then determining the resources required for this workload. The workload for each activity must be set to support the sales and production activities expected for the coming period.

As with traditional budgeting, ABB begins with sales and production budgets. Direct materials and direct labour budgets are also compatible with an ABC framework because these inputs can be directly traced to the individual products. The major differences between functional and ABB are found in the overhead and selling and administration categories. In a functional-based approach, budgets within these categories are typically detailed as variable or fixed, using production or sales output measures as the basis for determining cost behaviour. Furthermore, these budgets are usually constructed by budgeting for a cost item within a department (function) and then rolling these items up into the master overhead budget. For example, the cost of supervision in an overhead budget is the sum of all the supervision costs of the various departments. ABB, on the other hand, identifies the overhead, selling, and administrative *activities* and then builds a budget for each activity, based on the resources needed to provide the required activity output levels. Costs are classified as variable or fixed with respect to the *activity* output measure.

Consider, for example, purchasing materials. The demand for this activity is a function of the materials requirements for the various products and services produced. An activity driver, such as number of purchase orders, measures the activity output demand. Cornerstone 11.9 illustrates how to prepare a budget at the activity level for the purchasing activity.

Of the resources consumed by the purchasing activity in Cornerstone 11.9, supplies is a variable cost, and the other resources are fixed costs (a step-fixed cost behaviour in the case of salaries and depreciation). However, one important difference should be mentioned: fixed and variable purchasing costs are defined with respect to the *number of purchase orders* and not measures of production output such as direct labour hours or units produced. In budgeting at the activity level, the cost behaviour of each activity is defined with respect to

Preparing a Static Budget for an Activity

CORNERSTONE 11.9

Information:

1. Demand for purchase orders based on materials requirements: 15,000 purchase orders.
2. Resources needed:
   a. Five purchasing agents, each capable of processing 3,000 orders per year; salary, $40,000 each.
   b. Supplies (forms, paper, stamps, envelopes, etc.), projected to cost $1.00 per purchase order.
   c. Desks and computers: depreciation, $5,000 per year.
   d. Office space, rent, and utilities, $6,000 per year.

Required:

Prepare a budget for the purchasing activity.

Solution:

Purchasing budget:

Salaries	$200,000
Depreciation	5,000
Supplies	15,000
Occupancy	6,000
Total	$226,000

Why:

Activity-based budgeting is an important tool for managers to use. Preparing a static budget for any activity will help managers understand the underlying principles used for the budgeting process.

its own output measure (which is often different from the production-based drivers used in functional-based budgeting). Knowing the output measure provides significant insights for controlling activity costs. In an activity framework, controlling costs results from managing activities. For example, by redesigning products so that they use more common components, the number of purchase orders can be decreased. Decreasing the number of purchase orders reduces the amount of resources used by the purchasing department. Furthermore, decreasing the number of purchase orders demanded also reduces the activity capacity needed. Thus, activity costs will decrease.

concept Q&A

What are the main differences between ABB and traditional budgeting?

Answers on pages 734 to 738.

Activity Flexible Budgeting

Understanding the relationship between changes in activity costs and changes in activity drivers allows managers to more carefully plan and monitor activity improvements. **Activity flexible budgeting** is the prediction of what activity costs will be as related output changes. Variance analysis within an activity framework makes it possible to improve traditional budgetary performance reporting, and enhances the ability to manage activities.

In a traditional-based approach, budgeted costs for the actual level of activity are obtained by assuming that a single unit-based driver (e.g., units of product or direct labour hours) drives all costs. A cost formula is developed for each cost item as a function of units produced or direct labour hours. Cornerstone 11.2 illustrated a traditional flexible budget for production based on direct labour hours. If, however, costs vary with respect to more than one cost driver, and the drivers are not highly correlated with direct labour hours, then the predicted costs can be misleading.

The solution is to build flexible budget formulas for more than one cost driver. Cost estimation procedures (high–low method, the method of least squares, and so on) can be used to estimate cost formulas for each activity. This multiple-formula approach allows managers to predict more accurately what costs should be for different levels of activity, as measured by the cost drivers. These costs can then be compared with the actual costs to help assess budgetary performance. Cornerstone 11.10 illustrates how to prepare an activity flexible budget. Notice that flexible budgets are computed for *each cost driver*.

CORNERSTONE 11.10 Preparing an Activity Flexible Budget

Information:

Information on five overhead activities for a company is given below.

Activity	Driver	Fixed Cost	Variable Rate
Maintenance	Machine hours	$ 20,000	$ 5.50
Machining	Machine hours	15,000	2.00
Setting up	Setups	—	1,800
Inspection	Setups	80,000	2,100
Purchasing	Purchase orders	211,000	1.00

Required:

Prepare an activity-based flexible budget for the following production levels:

Driver	32,000 units	64,000 units
Machine hours	8,000	16,000
Setups	25	30
Purchase orders	15,000	25,000

Solution:

Steps in developing the activity-based flexible budget include:

1. Prepare a table showing the activities under their related driver.
2. Calculate total activity cost by multiplying the variable rate times the driver level and adding the fixed amount. For example, at 8,000 machine hours,

   Maintenance = \$20,000 + (\$5.50 × 8,000 machine hours) = \$64,000

   And at 16,000 machine hours,

   Maintenance = \$20,000 + (\$5.50 × 16,000 machine hours) = \$108,000

			Required for	
			32,000 units	64,000 units
Driver: Machine Hours				
	Fixed	Variable	8,000	16,000
Maintenance	$20,000	$5.50	$64,000	$108,000
Machining	15,000	2.00	31,000	47,000
Subtotal	$35,000	$7.50	95,000	155,000

(Continued)

CORNERSTONE
11.10
(Continued)

Driver: Number of Setups

	Fixed	Variable	25	30
Setups	$ —	$1,800	45,000	54,000
Inspections	80,000	2,100	132,500	143,000
Subtotal	$80,000	$3,900	177,500	197,000

Driver: Number of Orders

	Fixed	Variable	15,000	25,000
Purchasing	$211,000	$1.00	226,000	236,000
Total			$498,500	$588,000

The flexible budget shown in Cornerstone 11.10 will be more accurate than one based on just a single unit-based driver. This will also give managers information that can be used in cost control because they can see what effect an increase or decrease in each driver has on total costs. An activity-based performance report is shown in Cornerstone 11.11. It compares the budgeted costs for the actual activity usage levels with the actual costs.

Preparing an Activity-Based Performance Report

CORNERSTONE 11.11

Information:

Actual activity level is the first activity column (32,000 units) for each activity listed in Cornerstone 11.10. For example, budgeted costs for maintenance would be based on 8,000 machine hours and would equal $64,000.

Actual costs:

Maintenance	$ 55,000
Machining	29,000
Setups	46,500
Inspections	125,500
Purchasing	220,000

Required:

Prepare an activity-based performance report.

Solution:

For this performance report, just input the actual costs as given above. Then input the budgeted costs for the activity levels required. The budget variance is the difference between the actual costs and the budgeted costs. If actual costs are greater than budgeted

(Continued)

CORNERSTONE
11.11
(Continued)

costs, the budget variance is unfavourable (U). If actual costs are less than budgeted costs, the budget variance is favourable (F).

	Actual Costs	Budgeted Costs	Budget Variance
Maintenance	$ 55,000	$ 64,000	$ 9,000 F
Machining	29,000	31,000	2,000 F
Setups	46,500	45,000	1,500 U
Inspections	125,500	132,500	7,000 F
Purchasing	220,000	226,000	6,000 F
Total	$476,000	$498,500	$22,500 F

Why:

Performance reports based on activity levels will help managers determine which activities need further attention.

concept Q&A

Why does activity-based flexible budgeting provide a more accurate prediction of costs?

Answers on pages 734 to 738.

Cornerstone 11.11 shows an activity-based performance report that compares the budgeted costs for the actual activity usage levels with the actual costs. The net outcome of the five items is a favourable variance of $22,500. The preparation of the performance report follows the pattern and approach in Cornerstone 11.3. The difference is that the comparison is for *each* activity.

One can also compare the actual fixed activity costs with the budgeted fixed activity costs and the actual variable activity costs with the budgeted variable activity costs. For example, assume that the actual fixed inspection costs are $82,000 (due to a midyear unexpected salary adjustment) and that the actual variable inspection costs are $43,500. The variable and fixed budget variances for the inspection activity are computed as follows:

Activity	Actual Cost	Budgeted Cost	Variance
Inspection			
Fixed	$ 82,000	$ 80,000	$2,000 U
Variable	43,500	52,500	9,000 F
Total	$125,500	$132,500	$7,000 F

Breaking each variance into fixed and variable components provides more insight into the source of the variation in planned and actual expenditures.

YOUDECIDE Activity Flexible Budgeting for Museums

Museums do much more than simply present art to the public: Today's art museums put on shows, provide access to the public to view the collections, sell art-related merchandise in the museum store and online, and may put on special events and performances. The annual budget for a museum can easily run into millions of dollars, so cost understanding and control are crucial. As an accountant for a large metropolitan museum, you would be responsible for budgeting and controlling costs.

(Continued)

Splitting costs into fixed and variable components would be a first step in budgeting. However, what driver would you use—the number of patrons going through the museum? That would be a good driver for a few costs, especially those related to printing tickets and explanatory materials (such as maps of the museum to help people navigate through the collections). However, the vast majority of costs would be fixed with respect to the number of people going through the museum. ABC and budgeting would give a much better view of the costs of running the various activities of the museum.

What type of information would you need to create activity-based budgets?

Your first step would be to determine the various activities of the museum. These might include providing access to the public, selling merchandise through the museum store, putting on special events (e.g., concerts, lectures, benefits), acquiring and cataloguing pieces of art, and so on. For example, the activity of cataloguing new art pieces would include the salaries of staff who catalogue the pieces or clean and restore them, insurance on the art, and so on. Many of these costs vary with the number of newly donated or purchased pieces. The activity of selling merchandise would have costs of staff to run the store, cost of the items purchased for sale, advertising, and so on. Those costs might vary with the number of items sold or with the revenue earned. Putting on special events would have a different set of costs attached and those might vary with the number of events and the number of attendees.

Recognizing the different activities associated with the museum and relating the costs to specific activity drivers will give you a much better idea of what costs to expect. This understanding can help the museum director exercise good stewardship of the funds donated and provide important services to the public.

SUMMARY OF LEARNING OBJECTIVES

LO1. Prepare a flexible budget, and use it for performance reporting.

- Static budgets provide expected cost for a given level of activity. If the actual level of activity differs from the level associated with the static budget level, then comparing actual costs with budgeted costs does not make any sense. The solution is flexible budgeting.
- Flexible budgets divide costs into those that vary with units of production (or direct labour hours) and those that are fixed with respect to these unit-level drivers. These relationships allow the identification of a cost formula for each item in the budget.
- Cost formulas are the means for calculating expected costs for various levels of activity. There are two applications of flexible budgets: before-the-fact and after-the-fact.
  - Before-the-fact applications allow managers to see what costs will be for different levels of activity (sensitivity analysis), thus helping in planning.
  - After-the-fact applications allow managers to see what the cost should have been for the actual level of activity achieved in the period. Knowing these after-the-fact expected or budgeted costs then provides the opportunity to evaluate efficiency by comparing actual costs with budgeted costs.

LO2. Calculate the variable overhead variances, and explain their meaning.

- Overhead costs are often a significant proportion of costs in a budget.
- Comparing actual variable and fixed overhead costs with applied overhead costs yields a total overhead variance.
- In a standard cost system, it is possible to break down these overhead variances into component variances.
- For variable overhead, the two component variances are the spending variance and the efficiency variance.
- The spending variance is the result of comparing the actual costs with budgeted costs.
- The variable overhead efficiency variance is the result of efficient or inefficient use of labour because variable overhead is assumed to vary with direct labour hours.

LO3. Calculate the fixed overhead variances, and explain their meaning.

- For fixed overhead, the two component variances are the spending variance and the volume variance.
- The spending variance is the result of comparing the actual costs with budgeted costs.
- The fixed overhead volume variance is the result of producing a level different from that used to calculate the predetermined fixed overhead rate. It can be interpreted as a measure of capacity utilization.

LO4. *(Appendix 11A)* Prepare an activity-based flexible budget.

- Activity-based budgeting is done at the activity level.
- First, demand for products is assessed.
- Next, the level of activity output needed to support the expected production level is estimated.
- Finally, the resources needed to support the required activity output are estimated. This then becomes the activity budget.
- Activity flexible budgets differ from traditional flexible budgets because the cost formulas are based on the activity drivers for the respective activities rather than being based only on a single unit-based driver, such as direct labour hours.

SUMMARY OF IMPORTANT EQUATIONS

Abbreviations:
AH = actual direct labour hours
SH = standard direct labour hours that *should have been worked* for actual units produced
AVOR = actual variable overhead rate
SVOR = standard variable overhead rate
SFOR = standard fixed overhead rate
BFOH = budgeted fixed overhead

1. Variable overhead spending variance $= (AVOR \times AH) - (SVOR \times AH)$
   $= (AVOR - SVOR)AH$
2. Variable overhead efficiency variance $= (AH - SH)SVOR$
3. $SFOR = \dfrac{\text{Budgeted fixed overhead costs}}{\text{Practical capacity}}$
4. Applied fixed overhead $= SFOR \times SH$
5. *FOH* spending variance = Actual fixed overhead − Budgeted fixed overhead
6. *FOH* volume variance = Budgeted fixed overhead − Applied fixed overhead
   $= BFOH - (SH \times SFOR)$

CORNERSTONES

GLOSSARY

Activity-based budgeting (ABB) system A budget system that focuses on estimating the costs of activities rather than the costs of departments and plants, and the use of multiple drivers, both unit-based and non-unit-based. (p. 544)

Activity flexible budgeting Predicting what activity costs will be as activity usage changes. (p. 545)

Fixed overhead spending variance The difference between actual fixed overhead and applied fixed overhead. (p. 541)

Fixed overhead volume variance The difference between budgeted fixed overhead and applied fixed overhead; it is a measure of capacity utilization. (p. 541)

Flexible budget A budget that can specify costs for a range of activity. (p. 530)

Flexible budget variance The sum of price variances and efficiency variances in a performance report comparing actual costs to expected costs predicted by a flexible budget. (p. 533)

Performance report A report that compares the actual data with planned data. (p. 528)

Static budget A budget for a particular level of activity. (p. 528)

Variable budgets Budgets that can specify costs for a range of activity. (p. 530)

Variable overhead efficiency variance The difference between the actual direct labour hours used and the standard hours allowed multiplied by the standard variable overhead rate. (p. 535)

Variable overhead spending variance The difference between the actual variable overhead and the budgeted variable overhead based on actual hours used to produce the actual output. (p. 535)

REVIEW PROBLEMS

I. Flexible Budgeting

Trina Hoyt, controller of Ferrel Company, wants to prepare a quarterly budget for three different levels of output (measured in units): 2,000, 2,500, and 3,000. The product uses the following inputs:

Materials:
  3 kilograms of plastic @ \$6
  4 grams of metal @ \$2
Labour:
  0.5 hr. @ \$10

(Continued)

Variable overhead:
Inspection: 0.2 hr. @ $10
Machining: 0.3 hr. @ $5
Fixed overhead:
Rent: $15,000 per quarter
Utilities: $3,000 per quarter

Required:

Prepare a budget for three levels of output: 2,000, 2,500, and 3,000 units.

Solution:

		Range of Production (units)		
Production Costs	**Variable Cost per Unit**	**2,000**	**2,500**	**3,000**
Variable:				
Direct materials	$26.00[a]	$52,000[b]	$ 65,000	$ 78,000
Direct labour	5.00[c]	10,000[d]	12,500	15,000
Variable overhead:				
Inspection	2.00[e]	4,000[f]	5,000	6,000
Machining	1.50[g]	3,000[h]	3,750	4,500
Total variable costs	$34.50	69,000	86,250	103,500
Fixed overhead:				
Rent		15,000	15,000	15,000
Utilities		3,000	3,000	3,000
Total fixed costs		18,000	18,000	18,000
Total production costs		$87,000	$104,250	$121,500

[a] (3 × $6) + (4 × $2)
[b] ($26 × 2,000)
[c] (0.5 × $10)
[d] ($5 × 2,000)
[e] (0.2 × $10)
[f] ($2 × 2,000)
[g] (0.3 × $5)
[h] ($1.50 × 2,000)

II. Overhead Variances

Klemmens Manufacturing has the following standard cost sheet for one of its products:

Direct materials (2 metres @ $5)	$10
Direct labour (0.5 hr. @ $10)	5
Fixed overhead (0.5 hr. @ $2)*	1
Variable overhead (0.5 hr. @ $4)	2
Standard unit cost	$18

* Rate based on budgeted fixed overhead of $5,000 and expected activity of 2,500 direct labour hours.

During the most recent year, the following actual results were recorded:

Production	6,000 units
Direct materials (11,750 metres purchased and used)	$61,100
Direct labour (2,900 hrs.)	29,580
Fixed overhead	6,000
Variable overhead	10,500

Required:

Compute the following variances for Klemmens Manufacturing:

1. Variable overhead spending and efficiency variances.
2. Fixed overhead spending and volume variances.

Solution:

1. Variable overhead variances:

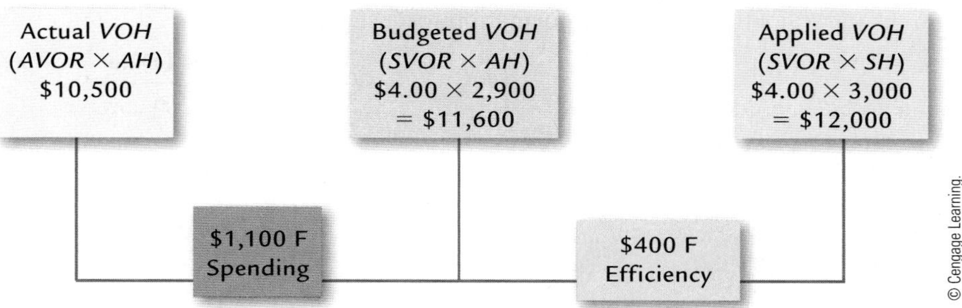

2. Fixed overhead variances:

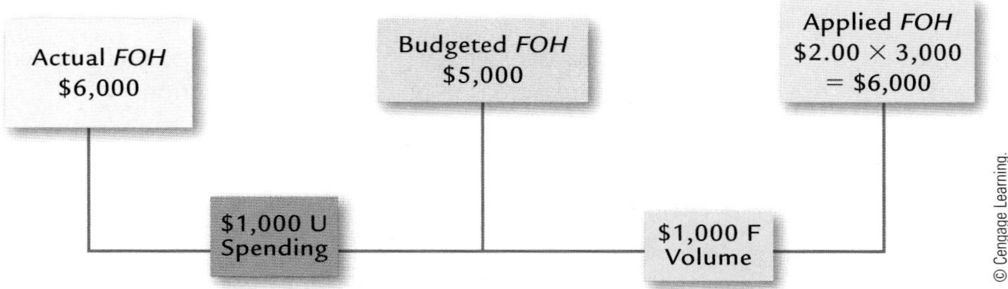

DISCUSSION QUESTIONS

1. Discuss the differences between static and flexible budgets.
2. Why are flexible budgets superior to static budgets for performance reporting?
3. Explain why mixed costs must be broken down into their fixed and variable components before a flexible budget can be developed.
4. What is the purpose of a before-the-fact flexible budget?
5. What is the purpose of an after-the-fact flexible budget?
6. Explain how an activity-based budget is prepared.
7. What is the difference between an activity flexible budget and a functional-based (traditional) flexible budget?
8. Why would an activity-based performance report be more accurate than a report based on a traditional flexible budget?
9. Explain why the variable overhead spending variance is not a pure price variance.
10. The variable overhead efficiency variance has nothing to do with efficient use of variable overhead. Do you agree or disagree? Why?
11. Describe the difference between the variable overhead efficiency variance and the labour efficiency variance.
12. Explain why the fixed overhead spending variance is usually very small.
13. What is the cause of an unfavourable volume variance?
14. Does the volume variance convey any meaningful information to managers?
15. Which do you think is more important for control of fixed overhead costs: the spending variance or the volume variance? Explain.

CORNERSTONE EXERCISES

OBJECTIVE 1
CORNERSTONE 11.1

Cornerstone Exercise 11-1 Performance Report

Propel Company provided the following information for last year.

Master Budget	Actual Data
Budgeted production 5,000 units	4,200 units
Direct materials:	
2 kilograms @ 0.75 per kilogram	$ 6,900
Direct labour:	
0.8 hr. @ $21.00 per hour	81,300
Variable overhead:	
0.8 hr. @ $2.45	9,500
Fixed overhead:	
Materials handling, $6,800	7,100
Depreciation, $3,200	3,200

Required:

1. Calculate the budgeted amounts for each cost category listed above for the 5,000 budgeted units.
2. Prepare a performance report using a budget based on expected production.

OBJECTIVE 1
CORNERSTONE 11.2

Cornerstone Exercise 11-2 Flexible Budget with Different Levels of Production

Propel Company budgeted the following amounts:

Variable costs of production:	
Direct materials	2 kilograms @ 0.75 per kilogram
Direct labour	0.8 hr. @ $21.00 per hour
Variable overhead	0.8 hr. @ $2.45
Fixed overhead:	
Materials handling	$6,800
Depreciation	$3,200

Required:

Prepare a flexible budget for 3,500 units, 4,000 units, and 4,500 units.

OBJECTIVE 1
CORNERSTONE 11.3

Cornerstone Exercise 11-3 Performance Report

Propel Company budgeted the following amounts:

Variable costs of production:	
Direct materials	2 kilograms @ 0.75 per kilogram
Direct labour	0.8 hr. @ $21.00 per hour
Variable overhead	0.8 hr. @ $2.45
Fixed overhead:	
Materials handling	$6,800
Depreciation	$3,200

At the end of the year, Propel had the following actual costs for production of 4,400 units:

Direct materials	$ 6,550
Direct labour	74,100
Variable overhead	8,722
Fixed overhead:	
Materials handling	6,890
Depreciation	3,200

Required:

Prepare a performance report using a budget based on the actual level of production.

Cornerstone Exercise 11-4 **Total Variable Overhead Variance**

OBJECTIVE 2
CORNERSTONE 11.4

Phan Company showed the following information for the year:

Standard variable overhead rate per direct labour hour	$3.70
Standard hours allowed per unit	4
Actual production in units	14,000
Actual variable overhead costs	$206,816
Actual direct labour hours worked	56,200

Required:

1. Calculate the actual variable overhead rate.
2. Calculate the applied variable overhead.
3. Calculate the total variable overhead variance.

Cornerstone Exercise 11-5 **Variable Overhead Spending and Efficiency Variances, Columnar and Formula Approaches**

OBJECTIVE 2
CORNERSTONE 11.5

Phan Company provided the following information:

Standard variable overhead rate per direct labour hour	$3.70
Actual variable overhead rate per direct labour hour	$3.68
Actual direct labour hours worked	56,200
Actual production in units	14,000
Standard hours allowed for actual units produced	56,000

Required:

1. Using the columnar approach, calculate the variable overhead spending and efficiency variances.
2. Using the formula approach, calculate the variable overhead spending variance.
3. Using the formula approach, calculate the variable overhead efficiency variance.
4. Calculate the total variable overhead variance.

Cornerstone Exercise 11-6 **Performance Report for Variable Variances**

OBJECTIVE 2
CORNERSTONE 11.6

Phan Company provided the following information:

Standard variable overhead rate per direct labour hour	$3.70
Actual variable overhead costs:	
Inspection	$112,300
Power	$94,516
Actual direct labour hours worked	56,200
Actual production in units	14,000
Standard hours allowed for actual units produced	56,000
Variable overhead:	
Inspection	4 hours @ $2.00
Power	4 hours @ $1.70

Required:

Prepare a performance report that shows the variances for each variable overhead item (inspection and power).

Cornerstone Exercise 11-7 **Total Fixed Overhead Variance**

OBJECTIVE 3
CORNERSTONE 11.7

Lukov Incorporated provided the following data:

Standard fixed overhead rate	$5 per direct labour hour
Actual fixed overhead costs	$282,686
Standard hours allowed per unit	4 hours
Actual production	14,000 units

(Continued)

Required:

1. Calculate the standard hours allowed for actual production.
2. Calculate the applied fixed overhead.
3. Calculate the total fixed overhead variance.

OBJECTIVE 3
CORNERSTONE 11.8

Cornerstone Exercise 11-8 Fixed Overhead Spending and Volume Variances, Columnar and Formula Approaches

Lukov Incorporated provided the following information:

Standard fixed overhead rate per direct labour hour	$5.00
Actual fixed overhead rate per direct labour hour	$5.03
Actual direct labour hours worked	56,200
Actual production in units	14,000
Standard hours allowed for actual units produced	56,000

Required:

1. Using the columnar approach, calculate the fixed overhead spending and volume variances.
2. Using the formula approach, calculate the fixed overhead spending variance.
3. Using the formula approach, calculate the fixed overhead volume variance.
4. Calculate the total fixed overhead variance.

OBJECTIVE 4
CORNERSTONE 11.9

Appendix 11A Cornerstone Exercise 11-9 Static Budget for an Activity

Gueye Company decided to look more closely at the inspection activity in its factory. The following information for a year was collected:

- Demand for inspections: 170,000
- Resources needed:
  - 6 inspectors, capable of inspecting 30,000 units per year. Salary is $32,000 each.
  - Supplies (small tools, oil, rags) expected to cost $0.70 per inspection.
  - Workbenches, computers, etc., depreciation: $18,300 per year.
  - Factory space for the inspection station, utilities: $12,600 per year.

Required:

Prepare a static budget for the inspection activity for the year.

OBJECTIVE 4
CORNERSTONE 11.10

Appendix 11A Cornerstone Exercise 11-10 Activity Flexible Budget

Cohlmia Company provided information on the following four overhead activities.

Activity	Driver	Fixed Cost	Variable Rate
Maintenance	Machine hours	$50,000	$1.80
Machining	Machine hours	25,000	3.00
Setting up	Setups	—	2,100
Purchasing	Purchase orders	75,000	7.00

Cohlmia has found that the following driver levels are associated with two different levels of production.

Driver	40,000 units	60,000 units
Machine hours	60,000	90,000
Setups	50	70
Purchase orders	12,000	18,000

Required:

Prepare an activity-based flexible budget.

Appendix 11A Cornerstone Exercise 11-11 Activity-Based Performance Report

OBJECTIVE 4
CORNERSTONE 11.11

Cohlmia Company produced 40,000 units last year. The information on the actual costs and budgeted costs at actual production of four activities is provided below.

Activity	Actual Cost	Budgeted Cost for Actual Production
Maintenance	$158,300	$158,000
Machining	205,400	205,000
Setting up	106,700	105,000
Purchasing	158,800	159,000

Required:

Prepare an activity-based performance report for the four activities for the past year.

EXERCISES

Exercise 11-12 Performance Report

OBJECTIVE 1

Master Budget	Actual Data
Budgeted production: 5,400 units	Actual production: 5,200 units
Materials: 4 metal plates @ $12.00	Materials cost: $258,800
Labour: 0.75 hr. @ $27.00	Labour cost: $108,500

Required:

1. Prepare a performance report using a budget based on expected production.
2. CONCEPTUAL CONNECTION Comment on the limitations of this report.

Exercise 11-13 Flexible Budget for Various Levels of Production

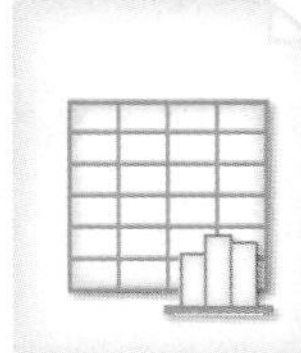

Kaya Inc. budgeted these amounts for the year:

Materials	2 leather strips @ $7.00
Labour	1.5 hr. @ $18.00
Variable overhead	1.5 hr. @ $1.20
Fixed overhead	$6,800

Required:

1. Prepare a flexible budget for 3,500, 4,000, and 4,500 units.
2. CONCEPTUAL CONNECTION Calculate the unit cost at 3,500, 4,000, and 4,500 units. (*Note:* Round to the nearest cent). What happens to unit cost as the number of units produced increases?

Exercise 11-14 Flexible Budget for Various Levels of Activity

OBJECTIVE 1

Hajiey Inc. produces a variety of toothpastes. Hajiey's controller has developed standard costs for the following four overhead items:

Overhead Item	Total Fixed Cost	Variable Rate per Direct Labour Hour
Maintenance	$ 86,000	$0.20
Power	—	0.45
Indirect labour	140,000	2.10
Rent	35,000	—

Next year, Hajiey expects production to require 90,000 direct labour hours.

Required:

1. Prepare an overhead budget for the expected level of direct labour hours for the coming year.
2. Prepare an overhead budget that reflects production that is 15 percent higher than expected, and for production that is 15 percent lower than expected.

OBJECTIVE 1

Exercise 11-15 Performance Report Based on Actual Production

Refer to the information provided in **Exercise 11-14.** Assume that Hajiey's actual production required 93,000 direct labour hours at standard. The actual overhead costs incurred were as follows:

Maintenance	$107,000
Power	41,200
Indirect labour	336,000
Rent	35,000

Required:

Prepare a performance report for the period based on actual production.

OBJECTIVE 2

Exercise 11-16 Variable Overhead Variances, Service Company

Travel Smooth Inc. operates a travel service for corporate clients. The corporation has a team of client advisors and has developed an online system to reserve and coordinate client travel plans efficiently. Travel Smooth has gathered the following actual data on last year's operations:

Client trip reservations	6,700
Direct labour	9,800 direct labour hours @ $20.00
Actual variable overhead	$103,640

Travel Smooth employs a standard costing system. During the year, a variable overhead rate of $9.80 per hour was used. The labour standard requires 1.4 hours per reservation.

Required:

1. Compute the standard hours allowed for actual reservations made last year.
2. Compute the variable overhead spending and efficiency variances.

OBJECTIVE 3

Exercise 11-17 Fixed Overhead Variances

Refer to **Exercise 11-16**. Assume that the actual fixed overhead was $199,600. Budgeted fixed overhead was $198,000, based on practical capacity of 11,000 direct labour hours.

Required:

1. Calculate the standard fixed overhead rate based on budgeted fixed overhead and practical capacity.
2. Compute the fixed overhead spending and volume variances.

OBJECTIVE 2 3

Exercise 11-18 Overhead Variances

At the beginning of the year, Raja Company had the following standard cost sheet for one of its chemical products:

Direct materials (4 kg @ $2.80)	$11.20
Direct labour (2 hrs. @ $18.00)	36.00
Fixed overhead (2 hrs. @ $5.20)	10.40
Variable overhead (2 hrs. @ $0.70)	1.40
Standard cost per unit	$59.00

Raja computes its overhead rates using practical volume, which is 80,000 units. The actual results for the year are as follows:

a. Units produced: 79,600
b. Direct labour: 158,900 hours at $18.10

c. Fixed overhead: $831,000
d. Variable overhead: $112,400

Required:

1. Compute the variable overhead spending and efficiency variances.
2. Compute the fixed overhead spending and volume variances.

Exercise 11-19 Overhead Application, Fixed and Variable Overhead Variances

Kojima Company is planning to produce 600,000 power drills for the coming year. The company uses direct labour hours to assign overhead to products. Each drill requires 0.75 standard hours of labour for completion. The total budgeted overhead was $1,777,500. The total fixed overhead budgeted for the coming year is $832,500. Predetermined overhead rates are calculated using expected production, measured in direct labour hours. Actual results for the year are:

Actual production (units)	594,000
Actual direct labour hours	446,000
Actual variable overhead	$928,000
Actual fixed overhead	$835,000

Required:

1. Compute the applied fixed overhead.
2. Compute the fixed overhead spending and volume variances.
3. Compute the applied variable overhead.
4. Compute the variable overhead spending and efficiency variances.

Exercise 11-20 Overhead Application, Fixed and Variable Overhead Variances

Wiarton Wood Products Ltd. is planning to produce 150,000 metal widgets for the coming year. Each unit requires 2 standard hours of direct labour for completion at a standard direct labour rate of $14.00 per hour, and a standard of 2.25 grams of direct material at a standard cost of $5 per gram. The company uses direct labour hours to assign overhead to products. The total overhead budgeted for the coming year is $1,200,000, and the standard fixed overhead rate is $3.50 per unit produced. Actual results for the year were:

Production (units)	142,000
Actual direct labour hours	270,000
Beginning direct materials inventory (units)	15,000
Ending direct materials inventory (units)	16,400
Direct materials purchases (units)	600,000
Cost of direct materials purchases	$2,900,000
Direct labour cost	$4,100,000
Actual variable overhead	$621,000
Actual fixed overhead	$490,000

Required:

1. Compute the variable overhead spending and efficiency variances. Label as favourable or unfavourable.
2. Compute the fixed overhead spending and volume variances. Label as favourable or unfavourable.

Exercise 11-21 Overhead Variances, Budgeted Amounts, Actual Units Produced, and Direct Labour Hours Worked

Last year, Tourna Company had planned to produce 140,000 units. However, 143,000 units were actually produced. The company uses direct labour hours to assign overhead to products. Each unit requires 0.9 standard hours of labour for completion. The fixed overhead rate was $11 per direct labour hour and the variable overhead rate was $6.36 per direct labour hour.

(Continued)

The following variances were computed:

Fixed overhead spending variance	$24,000 U
Fixed overhead volume variance	29,700 F
Variable overhead spending variance	9,196 U
Variable overhead efficiency variance	1,272 U

Required:

1. Calculate the total applied fixed overhead.
2. Calculate the budgeted fixed overhead.
3. Calculate the actual fixed overhead.
4. Calculate the total applied variable overhead.
5. Calculate the number of actual direct labour hours.
6. Calculate the actual variable overhead.

OBJECTIVE 

Exercise 11-22 Overhead Application, Fixed and Variable Overhead Variances

Raj Company is planning to produce 320,000 units for the coming year. The company uses direct labour hours to assign overhead to products. Each unit requires 1.2 standard hours of labour for completion. The total variable overhead budgeted was $921,600. The total fixed overhead budgeted for the coming year is $1,420,800. Predetermined overhead rates are calculated using direct labour hours based on expected production. Actual results for the year are:

Actual production (units)	328,000
Actual direct labour hours	426,400
Actual fixed overhead	$1,395,000
Actual variable overhead	$926,000

Required:

1. Compute the fixed overhead rate.
2. Compute the applied fixed overhead.
3. Compute the fixed overhead spending and volume variances.
4. Compute the applied variable overhead.
5. Compute the variable overhead spending and efficiency variances.

OBJECTIVE 

Exercise 11-23 Overhead Variances

Animal Days Incorporated operates a kennel designed to board and pamper up to 10 household cats and dogs while the pet owners are away. Pet owners pay a per-day fee. Variable indirect costs for the company include food, shampoo, and other miscellaneous supplies. Remaining expenses such as indirect labour, amortization, and rent are classified as fixed costs. Both variable and fixed costs are allocated to each pet based on the number of days the animal is with Animal Days. The following information was budgeted for March:

Animal guest days (10 animals × 31 days × 90 percent occupancy)	279
Variable overhead cost per guest day	$14.00
Fixed overhead rate per guest day	$21.00

Actual results for March are as follows:

Animal guest days	252
Variable overhead cost per guest day	$15.15
Fixed overhead rate per guest day	$22.95

Required:

1. Compute the variable overhead spending and efficiency variances and indicate whether each is favourable or unfavourable.
2. What factors might have caused the variable overhead spending variance? What factors might have caused the variable overhead efficiency variance?

3. Compute the fixed overhead spending variance and the fixed overhead volume variance and indicate whether each is favourable or unfavourable.
4. If fixed overhead is fixed, how could a company have a fixed overhead spending variance? Why might a company have a fixed overhead volume variance?

Exercise 11-24 Performance Report for Variable Overhead Variances

OBJECTIVE 1

Cobourg Company had the data below for its most recent year, ended December 31:

Actual Costs		Variable Overhead Standards	
Indirect labour	$50,000	Indirect labour	0.25 hr. @ $22.00
Supplies	$6,500	Supplies	0.25 hr. @ $3.20
Actual hours worked	2,220	Standard variable overhead rate	$18.50 per direct labour hour
Units produced	9,000 units		
Hours allowed for production	2,250 hours		

Required:

Prepare a performance report that shows the variances on an item-by-item basis.

Appendix 11A Exercise 11-25 Activity-Based Budgeting

OBJECTIVE 4

TopHat Company is more closely monitoring its purchasing department. The driver for purchasing is the number of purchase orders. The following information for a year was collected:

- Requirement for purchase orders: 90,000
- Resources needed:
  - 8 purchasing agents, capable of completing 12,000 purchase orders per year. (Preparation of a purchase order requires the determination of eligible suppliers from the approved supplier list and finding the optimum quality and price combination.) Salary is $35,000 for each purchasing agent.
  - Office supplies are expected to cost $1.20 per purchase order.
  - Desks, printers, computers, etc., depreciation: $12,400 per year.
  - Office space for the purchasing department, utilities, $14,100 per year.

Required:

1. Prepare a static budget for the purchasing activity for the year.
2. Calculate the cost per purchase order based on the annual requirement for purchase orders. (*Note:* Round to the nearest cent.)

Appendix 11A Exercise 11-26 Activity Flexible Budget

OBJECTIVE 4

Pulaski Company provided information on the following three overhead activities.

Activity	Driver	Fixed Cost	Variable Rate
Engineering	Engineering hours	$67,000	$5.50
Machining	Machine hours	36,000	1.40
Receiving	Receiving orders	51,000	3.75

Pulaski has found that the following driver levels are associated with two different levels of production.

Driver	40,000 units	50,000 units
Engineering hours	500	750
Machine hours	30,000	37,500
Receiving orders	9,000	12,000

Required:

Prepare an activity-based flexible budget for the two levels of activity.

OBJECTIVE 4

Appendix 11A Exercise 11-27 Activity-Based Performance Report

Angus Company produced 328,000 units during the past year. The information on the actual costs and budgeted costs at actual production of four activities follows.

Activity	Actual Cost	Budgeted Cost for Actual Production
Assembly	$185,800	$187,600
Maintenance	96,400	96,200
Setups	116,500	114,800
Purchasing	65,600	66,200

Required:

Prepare an activity-based performance report for the four activities for the past year.

PROBLEMS

OBJECTIVE 1

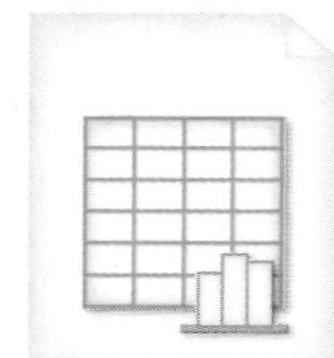

Problem 11-28 Overhead Budget for a Particular Level of Activity

Nadia Tamimi, controller for First-Aid-Care Company, has been instructed to develop a flexible budget for overhead costs. The company produces two types of bandages for hospitals: (1) Young-Ones, designed for children, and (2) Surga-Aid, designed for use on larger injuries. The two lines of bandages use common raw materials in different proportions. The company expects to produce 80,000 cartons of each product during the coming year. Young-Ones requires 0.20 direct labour hours per carton, and Surga-Aid requires 0.30 direct labour hours per carton. Nadia has developed the following fixed and variable costs for each of the four overhead items:

Overhead Item	Fixed Cost	Variable Rate per Direct Labour Hour
Maintenance	$57,250	$0.50
Power	—	0.40
Indirect labour	43,500	2.10
Rent	39,000	—

Check figures:
1. Direct labour hours = 40,000
2. Total variable overhead = $120,000

Required:

1. Calculate the total direct labour hours required for the production of 80,000 cartons of Young-Ones and 80,000 cartons of Surga-Aid.
2. Prepare an overhead budget for the expected activity level (calculated in Requirement 1) for the coming year.

OBJECTIVE 1

Problem 11-29 Flexible Budget for Various Production Levels

Refer to the information provided in **Problem 11-28**.

Check figures:
1. Direct labour hours for 20 percent lower = 32,000
2. Total overhead for 10 percent higher = $271,750

Required:

1. Calculate the direct labour hours required for production that is 10 percent higher than expected. Calculate the direct labour hours required for production that is 20 percent lower than expected.
2. Prepare an overhead budget that reflects production that is 10 percent higher than expected, and for production that is 20 percent lower than expected. (*Hint:* Use total direct labour hours calculated in Requirement 1.)

OBJECTIVE 1

Problem 11-30 Performance Report Based on Actual Production

Refer to the information provided in **Problem 11-28**. Assume that First-Aid-Care actually produced 100,000 cartons of Young-Ones and 90,000 cartons of Surga-Aid. The actual overhead costs incurred were as follows:

Maintenance	$ 81,300
Power	18,700
Indirect labour	143,600
Rent	39,000

Required:

1. Calculate the number of direct labour hours budgeted for actual production of the two products.
2. Prepare a performance report for the period based on actual production.
3. CONCEPTUAL CONNECTION Based on the report, would you judge any of the variances to be significant? Can you think of some possible reasons for the variances?

Check figure:
2. Total cost variance = $1,850 U

Problem 11-31 Overhead Budget, Flexible Budget

OBJECTIVE 

Visio Company manufactures eyeglasses and has developed the following flexible budget for overhead for the coming year. Activity level is measured in direct labour hours.

	Variable Cost Formula	Activity Level (hours)		
		6,000	8,000	10,000
Variable costs:				
Maintenance	$1.85	$ 11,100	$ 14,800	$ 18,500
Supplies	2.60	15,600	20,800	26,000
Power	0.05	300	400	500
Total variable costs	$4.50	27,000	36,000	45,000
Fixed costs:				
Depreciation		58,700	58,700	58,700
Salaries		65,600	65,600	65,600
Total fixed costs		124,300	124,300	124,300
Total overhead costs		$151,300	$160,300	$169,300

The company produces two different styles of glasses. The production budget for November is 9,000 units for style CA66, and 12,000 units for style CA88. Style CA66 requires 26 minutes of direct labour time, and CA88 requires 44 minutes. Fixed overhead costs are incurred uniformly throughout the year.

Required:

1. Calculate the number of direct labour hours needed in November to produce style CA66 and the number of direct labour hours needed in November to produce style CA88. What are the total direct labour hours budgeted for November?
2. Prepare an overhead budget for November. (*Hint:* The budgeted fixed costs given are for the year.)

Check figures:
1. Total direct labour hours = 12,700
2. Total overhead = $67,509

Problem 11-32 Flexible Budgeting

OBJECTIVE 

Quarterly budgeted overhead costs for two different levels of activity follow. The 2,000 level was the expected level from the master budget.

	Cost Formula ($)		Direct Labour Hours	
	Fixed	Variable	1,000 Hours	2,000 Hours
Maintenance	7,500	5.00	$12,500	$17,500
Depreciation	5,600	—	5,600	5,600
Supervision	22,000	—	22,000	22,000
Supplies	—	2.30	2,300	4,600
Power	—	0.60	600	1,200
Other	18,000	1.25	19,250	20,500

The actual activity level was 1,700 hours.

Required:

1. Prepare a flexible budget for an activity level of 1,700 direct labour hours.
2. Suppose that all of the formulas for each item are missing. You only have the budgeted costs for each level of activity. Show how you can obtain the formulas for each item by using the information given for the budgeted costs for the two levels.

(Continued)

Check figures:
1. Total = $68,655
2. Supplies, variable cost = $2.30 (× number of direct labour hours)

Problem 11-33 Flexible Budgeting

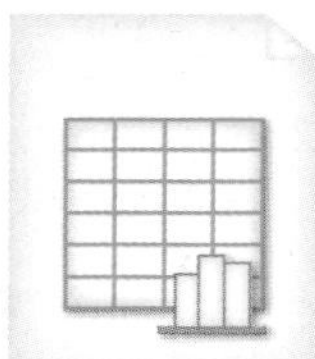

Fruta Inc. purchases fruit from numerous growers and packs fruit boxes and fruit baskets for sale. Fruta has developed the following flexible budget for overhead for the coming year. Activity level is measured in direct labour hours.

		Activity Level (hours)		
		2,000	**2,500**	**3,000**
Variable costs:				
Maintenance	$0.76	$ 1,520	$ 1,900	$ 2,280
Supplies	0.45	900	1,125	1,350
Power	0.20	400	500	600
Total variable costs	$1.41	2,820	3,525	4,230
Fixed costs:				
Depreciation		4,800	4,800	4,800
Salaries		24,500	24,500	24,500
Total fixed costs		29,300	29,300	29,300
Total overhead costs		$32,120	$32,825	$33,530

Required:

1. Prepare an overhead budget for May, using 200, 240, and 280 direct labour hours. (Round answers to the nearest cent).
2. CONCEPTUAL CONNECTION The Cushing High School Parent–Teacher Organization ordered 200 gift baskets from Fruta to be given to high school teachers and support staff as a token of appreciation for a successful school year. These gift baskets must be ready by May 31 and were not included in the original production budget for May. Describe how Fruta could adjust the total budgeted overhead for May to include the new order.

Check figure:
1. Total overhead = $2,836.47 for highest activity level

Problem 11-34 Performance Reporting

Pierre's is a small sandwich shop just off the Northern College campus. Customers enter off the street into a small counter area to order one of 10 varieties of sandwiches and a soft drink. All orders must be taken out because there is no space for dining in.

The owner of Pierre's is Serge Blouin, son of Pierre Blouin, who founded the shop. Serge is attempting to construct a series of budgets. He has accumulated the following information:

a. The average sandwich (which sells for $4.50) requires 1 roll, 100 grams of meat, 50 grams of cheese, 0.05 head of lettuce, 0.25 of a tomato, and a healthy squirt (25 millilitres) of secret sauce. (We can't reveal the recipe here, but it includes Serrano pepper and hoisin sauce.)
b. Each customer typically orders one soft drink (average price $1.50) consisting of a cup and 0.5 litres of pop. Refills on the pop are free, but this offer is seldom taken advantage of because the typical customer orders the sandwich and pop for take-out.
c. Use of paper supplies (napkins, bag, sandwich wrap, cups) varies somewhat from customer to customer but averages $1,650 per month.
d. Pierre's is open for two 4-hour shifts. The noon shift on Monday through Friday requires two workers earning $10 per hour. The evening shift is only worked on Friday, Saturday, and Sunday nights. The two evening shift employees also earn $10 per hour. There are 4.3 weeks in a month.
e. Rent is $575 per month. Other monthly cash expenses average $1,800.
f. Food costs are:

Meat	$14.00/kg
Cheese	$12.00/kg
Rolls	$28.80/gross
Lettuce (a box contains 24 heads)	$12.00/box
Tomatoes (a box contains 20 tomatoes)	$4/box
Secret sauce	$2.40/litre
Pop (syrup and carbonated water)	$0.56/litre

In a normal month when Northern College is in session, Pierre's sells 5,000 sandwiches and 5,000 cups of pop. In October, Northern College holds its homecoming celebration. Therefore, Serge figured that if he added a noon shift on Saturday and Sunday of homecoming weekend, October sales would be 30 percent higher than normal. To advertise his noon shifts during homecoming weekend, Serge bought cups emblazoned with the Northern College homecoming schedule. This added $200 to paper costs for the month. Last year, he added two additional shifts, and his sales goal was realized.

Required:

1. Prepare a flexible budget for a normal school month.
2. Prepare a flexible budget for October.
3. CONCEPTUAL CONNECTION Do you think it was worthwhile for Serge to add the additional shifts for homecoming weekend last October?

Check figure:
1. Total cost = $19,877

Problem 11-35 Functional versus Activity Flexible Budgeting

OBJECTIVE 

Darja Navitski, production manager, was upset with the latest performance report, which indicated that she was $100,000 over budget. Given the efforts that she and her workers had made, she was confident that they had met or beaten the budget. Now she was not only upset but also genuinely puzzled over the results. Three items—direct labour, power, and setups—were over budget. The actual costs for these three items follow:

Direct labour	$210,000
Power	135,000
Setups	140,000
Total	$485,000

Darja knew that her operation had produced more units than originally had been budgeted, so more power and labour had naturally been used. She also knew that the uncertainty in scheduling had led to more setups than planned. When she pointed this out to Jon Helguson, the controller, he assured her that the budgeted costs had been adjusted for the increase in productive activity. Curious, Darja questioned Jon about the methods used to make the adjustment.

Jon: If the actual level of activity differs from the original planned level, we adjust the budget by using budget formulas—formulas that allow us to predict the costs for different levels of activity.

Darja: The approach sounds reasonable. However, I'm sure something is wrong here. Tell me exactly how you adjusted the costs of direct labour, power, and setups.

Jon: First, we obtained formulas for the individual items in the budget by using the method of least squares. We assumed that cost variations could be explained by variations in productive activity where activity is measured by direct labour hours. Here is a list of the cost formulas for the three items you mentioned. The variable X is the number of direct labour hours.

$$\text{Direct labour cost} = \$10X$$
$$\text{Power cost} = \$5{,}000 + \$4X$$
$$\text{Setup cost} = \$100{,}000$$

Darja: I think I see the problem. Power costs don't have a lot to do with direct labour hours. They have more to do with machine hours. As production increases, machine hours increase more rapidly than direct labour hours.

Jon: You know, you have a point. The coefficient of determination for power cost is only about 50 percent. That leaves a lot of unexplained cost variation. The coefficient for labour, however, is much better—it explains about 96 percent of the cost variation. Setup costs, of course, are fixed.

Darja: Well, as I was about to say, setup costs also have little to do with direct labour hours. And I might add that they certainly are not fixed—at least not all of them. We had to do more setups than our original plan called for because of the scheduling changes.

And we have to pay our people when they work extra hours. It seems like we are always paying overtime. I wonder if we simply do not have enough people for the setup activity. Also, there are supplies that are used for each setup, and these are not cheap. Did you build these extra costs of increased setup activity into your budget?

Jon: No, we assumed that setup costs were fixed. I see now that some of them could vary as the number of setups increased. Darja, let me see if I can develop some cost formulas based on better explanatory variables. I'll get back to you in a few days.

After a few days' work, Jon developed the following cost formulas, all with a coefficient of determination greater than 90 percent:

Direct labour cost = $10X$, where X = direct labour hours
Power cost = $68,000 + $0.9Y$; where Y = machine hours
Setup cost = $98,000 + $400 Z; where Z = number of setups

The actual measure of each activity driver is as follows:

Direct labour hours	20,000
Machine hours	90,000
Number of setups	110

Required:

Check figures:
1. Total variance = $100,000 U
2. Total variance = $6,000 F

1. Prepare a performance report for direct labour, power, and setups using the direct labour-based formulas.
2. Prepare a performance report for direct labour, power, and setups using the multiple cost driver formulas that Jon developed.
3. CONCEPTUAL CONNECTION Of the two approaches, which provides the more accurate picture of Darja's performance? Why?

OBJECTIVE 

Appendix 11A Problem 11-36 Activity Flexible Budgeting

Jose Duarte, controller for Hermanus Inc., prepared the following budget for manufacturing costs at two different levels of activity for 2018:

	Level of Activity	
DIRECT LABOUR HOURS	**50,000**	**100,000**
Direct materials	$ 300,000	$ 600,000
Direct labour	200,000	400,000
Depreciation (plant)	100,000	100,000
Subtotal	600,000	1,100,000
MACHINE HOURS	**200,000**	**300,000**
Maintaining equipment	360,000	510,000
Machining	112,000	162,000
Subtotal	472,000	672,000
MATERIAL MOVES	**20,000**	**40,000**
Materials handling	165,000	290,000
NUMBER OF BATCHES INSPECTED	**100**	**200**
Inspecting products	125,000	225,000
Total	$1,362,000	$2,287,000

During 2014, Hermanus employees worked a total of 80,000 direct labour hours, used 250,000 machine hours, made 32,000 moves, and performed 120 batch inspections. The following actual costs were incurred:

Direct materials	$440,000
Direct labour	355,000
Depreciation	100,000
Maintenance	425,000
Machining	142,000
Materials handling	232,500
Inspecting products	160,000

Hermanus applies overhead using rates based on direct labour hours, machine hours, number of moves, and number of batches. The second level of activity (the far right column in the first table) is the practical level of activity (the available activity for resources acquired in advance of usage) and is used to compute predetermined overhead pool rates.

Required:

1. Prepare a performance report for Hermanus's manufacturing costs in 2018.
2. Assume that one of the products produced by Hermanus is budgeted to use 10,000 direct labour hours, 15,000 machine hours, and 500 moves and will be produced in five batches. A total of 10,000 units will be produced during the year. Calculate the budgeted unit manufacturing cost.
3. CONCEPTUAL CONNECTION One of Hermanus's managers said the following: "Budgeting at the activity level makes a lot of sense. It really helps us manage costs better. But this budget really needs to provide more detailed information. For example, I know that the materials handling activity involves the usage of forklifts and operators, and this information is lost with simply reporting the total cost of the activity for various levels of output. We have four forklifts, each capable of providing 10,000 moves per year. We lease these forklifts for five years, at $10,000 per year. Furthermore, for our two shifts, we need up to eight operators if we run all four forklifts. Each operator is paid a salary of $30,000 per year. Also, I know that fuel costs us about $0.25 per move." Based on these comments, explain how this additional information may help Hermanus to better manage its costs. Also, assuming that these are the only three items, expand the detail of the flexible budget for materials handling to reveal the cost of these three resource items for 20,000 moves and 40,000 moves, respectively. You may wish to review the concepts of flexible, committed, and discretionary resources found in Chapter 3.

Check figures:
1. Total variance = $2,500 F
2. Unit cost = $15.29
3. Total (20,000 moves) = $165,000

Problem 11-37 Flexible Budgeting

OBJECTIVE 

At the beginning of last year, Jade Kamm, controller for Jager Inc., prepared the following budget for conversion costs at two levels of activity for the coming year:

	Direct Labour Hours	
	100,000	**120,000**
Direct labour	$1,000,000	$1,200,000
Supervision	180,000	180,000
Utilities	18,000	21,000
Depreciation	225,000	225,000
Supplies	25,000	30,000
Maintenance	240,000	284,000
Rent	120,000	120,000
Other	60,000	70,000
Total manufacturing cost	$1,868,000	$2,130,000

(Continued)

During the year, the company worked a total of 112,000 direct labour hours and incurred the following actual costs:

Direct labour	$963,200
Supervision	190,000
Utilities	20,500
Depreciation	225,000
Supplies	24,640
Maintenance	237,000
Rent	120,000
Other	60,500

Jager applied overhead on the basis of direct labour hours. Normal volume of 120,000 direct labour hours is the activity level to be used to compute the predetermined overhead rate.

Required:

1. Determine the cost formula for each of Jager's conversion costs. (*Hint:* Use the high-low method.)
2. CONCEPTUAL CONNECTION Prepare a performance report for Jager's conversion costs for last year. Should any cost item be given special attention? Explain.

Check figure:

2. Total variance = $184,360 F

OBJECTIVE 2 3

Problem 11-38 Overhead Application, Overhead Variances

Tavera Company uses a standard cost system. The direct labour standard indicates that five direct labour hours should be used for every unit produced. Tavera produces one product. The normal production volume is 120,000 units of this product. The budgeted overhead for the coming year is as follows:

Fixed overhead	$2,160,000*
Variable overhead	1,440,000

* At normal volume

Tavera applies overhead on the basis of direct labour hours.

During the year, Tavera produced 118,600 units, worked 592,300 direct labour hours, and incurred actual fixed overhead costs of $2,150,400 and actual variable overhead costs of $1,422,800.

Required:

1. Calculate the standard fixed overhead rate and the standard variable overhead rate.
2. Compute the applied fixed overhead and the applied variable overhead. What is the total fixed overhead variance? Total variable overhead variance?
3. CONCEPTUAL CONNECTION Break down the total fixed overhead variance into a spending variance and a volume variance. Discuss the significance of each.
4. CONCEPTUAL CONNECTION Compute the variable overhead spending and efficiency variances. Discuss the significance of each.
5. Journal entries for overhead variances were not discussed in this chapter. Typically, the overhead variance entries happen at the end of the year. Assume that applied fixed (variable) overhead is accumulated on the credit side of the fixed (variable) overhead control account. Actual fixed (variable) overhead costs are accumulated on the debit side of the respective control accounts. At the end of the year, the balance in each control account is the total fixed (variable) variance. Create accounts for each of the four overhead variances and close out the total variances to each of these four variance accounts. These four variance accounts are then usually disposed of by closing them to Cost of Goods Sold (COGS). Form a group with two to four other students, and prepare the journal entries that isolate the four variances. Finally, prepare the journal entries that close these variances to COGS.

Check figures:

1. SFOR = $3.60; SVOR = $2.40
2. Total FOH variance = $15,600 U
3. FOH volume variance = $25,200 U
4. VOH efficiency variance = $1,680 F

Problem 11-39 Overhead Variance Analysis

OBJECTIVE 2 3

The Chatham plant of Morril's Small Motor Division produces a major subassembly for a 6.0 horsepower motor for lawn mowers. The plant uses a standard costing system for production costing and control. The standard cost sheet for the subassembly follows:

Direct materials (6.0 kg @ $5)	$30.00
Direct labour (1.6 hrs. @ $12)	19.20
Variable overhead (1.6 hrs. @ $10)	16.00
Fixed overhead (1.6 hrs. @ $6)	9.60
Standard unit cost	$74.80

During the year, the Chatham plant had the following actual production activity:

a. Production of motors totalled 50,000 units.
b. The company used 82,000 direct labour hours at a total cost of $1,066,000.
c. Actual fixed overhead totalled $556,000.
d. Actual variable overhead totalled $860,000.

The Chatham plant's practical activity is 60,000 units per year. Standard overhead rates are computed based on practical activity measured in standard direct labour hours.

Required:

1. Compute the variable overhead spending and efficiency variances.
2. CONCEPTUAL CONNECTION Compute the fixed overhead spending and volume variances. Interpret the volume variance. What can be done to reduce this variance?

Check figure:
1. VOH efficiency variance = $20,000 U

Problem 11-40 Overhead Variances

OBJECTIVE 2 

Extrim Company produces microwave ovens. Extrim's plant in Sault Ste. Marie uses a standard costing system. The standard costing system relies on direct labour hours to assign overhead costs to production. The direct labour standard indicates that four direct labour hours should be used for every microwave unit produced. (The Sault Ste. Marie plant produces only one model.) The normal production volume is 120,000 units. The budgeted overhead for the coming year is as follows:

Fixed overhead	$1,286,400*
Variable overhead	888,000

* At normal volume

Extrim applies overhead on the basis of direct labour hours.

During the year, Extrim produced 119,000 units, worked 487,900 direct labour hours, and incurred actual fixed overhead costs of $1.3 million and actual variable overhead costs of $927,010.

Required:

1. Calculate the standard fixed overhead rate and the standard variable overhead rate.
2. Compute the applied fixed overhead and the applied variable overhead. What is the total fixed overhead variance? Total variable overhead variance?
3. CONCEPTUAL CONNECTION Break down the total fixed overhead variance into a spending variance and a volume variance. Discuss the significance of each.
4. CONCEPTUAL CONNECTION Compute the variable overhead spending and efficiency variances. Discuss the significance of each.

Check figures:
1. Standard variable overhead rate = $1.85 per direct labour hour
3. Volume variance = $10,720 U
4. Efficiency variance = $22,015 U

Problem 11-41 Incomplete Data, Overhead Analysis

OBJECTIVE  

Lynwood Company produces surge protectors. To help control costs, Lynwood employs a standard costing system and uses a flexible budget to predict overhead costs at various levels of activity. For the most recent year, Lynwood used a standard overhead rate of $18 per direct labour hour. The rate was computed using practical capacity. Budgeted overhead costs are $396,000 for 18,000

(Continued)

direct labour hours and $540,000 for 30,000 direct labour hours. During the past year, Lynwood generated the following data:

a. Actual production: 100,000 units
b. Fixed overhead volume variance: $20,000 U
c. Variable overhead efficiency variance: $18,000 F
d. Actual fixed overhead costs: $200,000
e. Actual variable overhead costs: $310,000

Required:

Check figures:
3. VOH spending variance = $7,996 U
4. 0.26667 hours per unit

1. Calculate the fixed overhead rate.
2. Determine the fixed overhead spending variance.
3. Determine the variable overhead spending variance.
4. Determine the standard hours allowed per unit of product.

OBJECTIVE 

Problem 11-42 Flexible Budget, Overhead Variances

Shumaker Company manufactures a line of high-top basketball shoes. At the beginning of the year, the following plans for production and costs were revealed:

Pairs of shoes to be produced and sold	55,000
Standard cost per unit:	
Direct materials	$15
Direct labour	12
Variable overhead	6
Fixed overhead	3
Total unit cost	$ 36

During the year, a total of 50,000 units were produced and sold. The following actual costs were incurred:

Direct materials	$775,000
Direct labour	590,000
Variable overhead	310,000
Fixed overhead	180,000

There were no beginning or ending inventories of raw materials. In producing the 50,000 units, 63,000 hours were worked, 5 percent more hours than the standard allowed for the actual output. Overhead costs are applied to production using direct labour hours.

Check figures:
1. Total variance = $40,000 U
2.a. Volume variance = $15,000 U
2.b. Efficiency variance = $15,000 U

Required:

1. Using a flexible budget, prepare a performance report comparing expected costs for the actual production with actual costs.
2. Determine the following:
   a. Fixed overhead spending and volume variances.
   b. Variable overhead spending and efficiency variances.

PROFESSIONAL EXAMINATION PROBLEM*

Professional Examination Problem 11-43 Overhead Variances—Dion Glass Works

Dion Glass Works' production budget for the year ended November 30, 2018, in department C was based on 200,000 units. Each unit requires two standard hours of labour for completion.

Total overhead was budgeted at $900,000 for the year and the fixed overhead rate was estimated to be $3 per unit. Both fixed and variable overhead are applied to the product on the basis of direct labour hours. The actual data for the year ended November 30, 2018, are:

Actual production in units	198,000
Actual direct labour hours	440,000
Actual variable overhead	$352,000
Actual fixed overhead	$575,000

Required:

1. What were the standard hours allowed for actual production for the year ended November 30, 2018?
2. What was the VOH efficiency variance for the year?
3. What was the VOH spending variance for the year?
4. What was the FOH spending variance for the year?
5. What was the FOH applied to Dion's production for the year?
6. What was the FOH production volume variance for the year?

CASES

Case 11-44 Fixed Overhead Spending and Volume Variances, Capacity Management

OBJECTIVE 3

Lorale Company, a producer of recreational vehicles, recently decided to begin producing a major subassembly for jet skis. The subassembly would be used by Lorale's jet ski plants and also would be sold to other producers. The decision was made to lease two large buildings in two different locations: Red Deer, Alberta, and Bathurst, New Brunswick. The company agreed to an 11-year, renewable lease contract. The plants were of the same size, and each had 10 production lines. New equipment was purchased for each line and workers were hired to operate the equipment. The company also hired production line supervisors for each plant. A supervisor is capable of directing up to two production lines per shift. Two shifts are run for each plant. The practical production capacity of each plant is 300,000 subassemblies per year. Two standard direct labour hours are allowed for each subassembly. The costs for leasing, equipment depreciation, and supervision for a single plant are as follows (the costs are assumed to be the same for each plant):

Supervision (10 supervisors @ $50,000)	$ 500,000
Building lease (annual payment)	800,000
Equipment depreciation (annual)	1,100,000
Total fixed overhead costs*	$2,400,000

* For simplicity, assume these are the only fixed overhead costs.

After beginning operations, Lorale discovered that demand for the product in the region covered by the Red Deer plant was less than anticipated. At the end of the first year, only 240,000 units were sold. The Bathurst plant sold 300,000 units as expected. The actual fixed overhead costs at the end of the first year were $2,500,000 (for each plant).

Required:

1. Calculate a fixed overhead rate based on standard direct labour hours.
2. Calculate the fixed overhead spending and volume variances for the Red Deer and Bathurst plants. What is the most likely cause of the spending variance? Why are the volume variances different for the two plants?
3. Suppose that from now on the sales for the Red Deer plant are expected to be no more than 240,000 units. What actions would you take to manage the capacity costs (fixed overhead costs)?
4. Calculate the fixed overhead cost per subassembly for each plant. Do they differ? Should they differ? Explain. Do ABC concepts help in analyzing this issue?

OBJECTIVE 1 2 3

Case 11-45 Differing Unit Costs and Decision to Revise Costs

Powerhouse Corporation acquired Underling Corporation as of January 1, 2018. Powerhouse is a well-known manufacturer of netbook computers. Powerhouse has been in business since 2013 and although it has relatively sophisticated accounting information systems, significant growth in its business has prevented the company from always having the necessary time and energy to keep these systems perfectly up to date. Where Powerhouse once manufactured 20,000 netbooks per year, the recent 2017 year-end indicates just over 45,000 netbooks were manufactured and sold. This significant growth forced Powerhouse to open a second manufacturing plant. In the table below, Powerhouse has provided the standard production cost of a single netbook computer. In contrast, Underling Corporation is a newer organization, having entered the technology industry in 2016. The company's newness means that most of the equipment is also relatively new and that its accounting information systems were developed more recently. The table also includes the standard production cost of a single netbook computer made by Underling. Though Underling is a small netbook producer, having manufactured and sold 5,000 and 8,000 netbooks in 2016 and 2017 respectively, its strong growth and success also makes Underling a threat to competitors (most new entrants to the technology industry do not survive the first few years). Powerhouse's two plants and Underling's single plant are all similar in size. Powerhouse's second plant is nearing capacity, which is one of the motivating factors to acquire a company that has not reached capacity. For these reasons, Powerhouse Corporation bought Underling toward the end of 2017 and is laying the groundwork for merging their organizational structures, processes, and systems.

The leadership teams of Powerhouse and Underling recently met to discuss the future of the new conglomerate. The teams took little time in verifying that the netbooks each organization were producing are nearly identical (indeed, this was one of the advantages determined during Powerhouse's due diligence work). More specifically, the performance of the netbooks and the quality of the hardware were nearly indistinguishable. Shockingly, however, the standard production costs obtained from each organization's standard cost sheets were very different.

Production Cost	Powerhouse	Underling
Direct materials	$ 60	$ 80
Direct labour	48 (4 hours × $12/hour)	54 (3 hours × $18/hour)
Manufacturing overhead (allocated on the basis of machine hours)	22	39
Total unit cost	$130	$173

Required:

You have been hired as a consultant to prepare a report discussing the following:

1. Why are the standard product costs materially different?
2. For what reasons would Powerhouse want to revise *and* not revise the standards?

OBJECTIVE 1

Case 11-46 Ethical Considerations; Flexible Budgeting and the Environment

Ole Aburish, the chief financial officer of Ur Thrift Inc., a large retailer, had just finished a meeting with Filip Noga, the president of the large retailer, and Citlali Sandoval, its environmental officer. Over the years, Ole had overseen the development of a number of cost formulas that allowed Ur Thrift to budget the variable costs of a variety of items. For example, packaging for one of its private line of dolls had a cost formula of $Y = \$2.20\ X$, where X represented the number of dolls sold. The formula was used to calculate the expected packaging costs which were then compared with the actual packaging costs. Over the past several years, the actual costs and budgeted costs were virtually on target, prompting Ole to claim that packaging costs were well controlled.

Citlali Sandoval, however, argued that the packaging costs were not well controlled. In fact, she was adamant in her view that the packaging was excessive and that by reducing the packaging, costs could be reduced and the environmental impacts reduced as well. She argued that the company had an ethical obligation to reduce environmental impacts and that cost savings would also be captured, improving the profitability of the company. As another example, Citlali discussed the fleet of trucks used by Ur Thrift to move goods from its warehouses to retail outlets. The fuel cost formula was $3*X*, where *X* represented litres of fuel consumed. She pointed out that the performance data also revealed that fuel costs were in control. Yet her office had recently recommended the installation of an auxiliary power unit to heat and cool the cabs of the trucks during the mandatory 10-hour breaks required of its drivers, thus avoiding the need to have the engine idle during this rest period. She claimed that this would significantly reduce fuel costs and easily pay for the new auxiliary units in a short period of time.

Citlali had also made some comments that caused Ole to pause and do some soul searching. She noted that the financial officers of the company should be more concerned about reducing costs than simply predicting what they should be. Thus (according to her view), cost formulas are useful only to tell us where we currently are so that they can be used to assess how to reduce costs. The so-called flexible budgets are simply a means of enforcing static standards. She also said that the company's managers had an ethical obligation not to overconsume the resources of the planet. She urged both Ole and Filip to help position the company so that it could reduce its environmental impacts.

Required:

1. Do financial officers have an ethical obligation to help in reducing negative environmental impacts? Identify and discuss which of the Rules of Professional Conduct of CPA Ontario (see excerpts in Exhibit 1.6) might be used to sustain this point of view. Also, describe the role that flexible budgeting may play in reducing environmental impacts.
2. Suppose that Ole and Citlali embark on a cooperative effort to eliminate any excessive packaging. The projected results are impressive. The expected reductions will save $3 million in shipping costs ($0.50 per package), $2.4 million in packaging materials ($0.40 per package), 5,000 trees, and 1.25 million barrels of oil. Are there any ethical issues associated with these actions? What standards might apply?
3. Identify two potential ethical dilemmas that might surface in the use of flexible budgeting for performance evaluation (the dilemmas do not need to be connected with environmental activities).

12

Performance Evaluation and Decentralization

After studying Chapter 12, you should be able to:

1. Explain how and why firms choose to decentralize.
2. Compute and explain return on investment.
3. Compute and explain residual income and economic value added.
4. Explain the role of transfer pricing in a decentralized firm.
5. Explain the uses of the Balanced Scorecard, and compute cycle time, velocity, and manufacturing cycle efficiency.

Rawpixel.com/Shutterstock

EXPERIENCE MANAGERIAL DECISIONS
with T4G

Companies in growing, fast-paced, highly competitive industries look for every opportunity to gain an advantage. One potential source of advantage is organizational structure, and one company that understands this is T4G, a leading North American full-service, project-based technology service provider. The company has earned a place as one of the top 50 on the annual list of Best Workplaces in Canada for more than five consecutive years.

Flat organizational structures feature fewer layers of management. In flat organizational structures, employees are empowered and expected to take responsibility for a range of traditionally managerial decisions in their daily routines. Flat organizations decentralize decision making, thereby elevating employee responsibility and allowing more participation in decision making from all levels of an organization. Compared with taller organizational structures, in flat organizations communication can be faster, more reliable, and more effective. According to Geoff Flood, president of T4G, one contributing factor for earning recognition on the list of Best Workplaces in Canada is that "T4G is a flat, roles-based organization where business units and teams are managed in a 'federal' portfolio of talented professionals and teams which come together to build the best solutions."

DECENTRALIZATION AND RESPONSIBILITY CENTRES

OBJECTIVE 1

Explain how and why firms choose to decentralize.

In general, a company is organized along lines of responsibility. The traditional organizational chart illustrates the flow of responsibility from the chief executive officer down through the vice-presidents to middle-and lower-level managers. Today, most companies use a flattened hierarchy. This structure—emphasizing teams—is consistent with decentralization. Irving Oil, for example, is essentially a group of smaller businesses. A strong link exists between the structure of an organization and its responsibility accounting system. Ideally, the responsibility accounting system mirrors and supports the structure of an organization.

Firms with multiple responsibility centres usually choose one of two decision-making approaches to manage their diverse and complex activities:

- ***Centralized:*** In centralized decision making, decisions are made at the very top level, and lower-level managers are charged with implementing these decisions.
- ***Decentralized:*** Decentralized decision making allows managers at lower levels to make and implement key decisions pertaining to their areas of responsibility.

The practice of delegating decision-making authority to the lower levels of management in a company is called **decentralization**. Exhibit 12.1 illustrates the difference between centralized and decentralized companies.

EXHIBIT 12.1

Centralization and Decentralization

Centralization

Top Management

Information

Decisions

Responsibility Centres

Information

Decisions

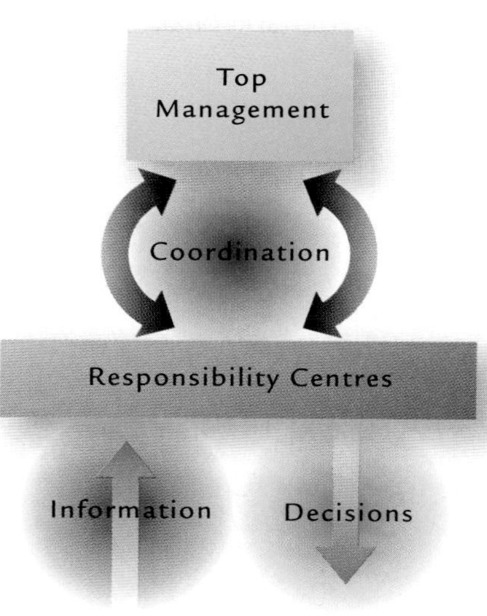

Organizations range from highly centralized to strongly decentralized. Most firms fall somewhere in between, with the majority tending toward decentralization. The reasons for the popularity of decentralization and the ways in which a company may choose to decentralize are discussed next.

Reasons for Decentralization

Firms decide to decentralize for several reasons, including:

1. gathering and using local information easily;
2. focusing central management;

3. training and motivating segment managers; and
4. enhancing competition, exposing segments to market forces.

Gathering and Using Local Information Easily The quality of decisions is affected by the quality of information available. As a firm grows in size and operates in different markets and regions, central management may not understand local conditions. Lower-level managers, however, are in contact with immediate operating conditions (such as the strength and nature of local competition, and the nature of the local labour force). As a result, they often are better positioned to make local decisions. For example, McDonald's has restaurants around the world. The tastes of people in China or France differ from those of people in Canada; so, McDonald's tailors its menu to different countries. The result is that the McDonald's in each country can differentiate to meet the needs of its local market.

Focusing Central Management By decentralizing the operating decisions, central management is free to engage in strategic planning and decision making. The long-run survival of the organization should be of more importance to central management than day-to-day operations.

Training and Motivating Segment Managers Organizations always need well-trained managers to replace higher-level managers who leave to take advantage of other opportunities. What better way to prepare a future generation of higher-level managers than by providing them with the opportunity to make significant decisions? These opportunities also enable top managers to evaluate local managers' capabilities and promote those who make the best decisions.

Enhancing Competition In a highly centralized company, overall profit margins can mask inefficiencies within the various subdivisions. Large companies may find that they cannot afford to keep a noncompetitive division. One of the best ways to improve performance of a division or factory is to expose it more fully to market forces. At Koch Industries, Inc., each unit is expected to act as an autonomous business unit and to set prices both externally and internally. Units whose services are not required by other Koch units may face possible elimination.

Divisions in the Decentralized Firm

Decentralization involves a cost–benefit tradeoff. As a firm becomes more decentralized, it passes more decision authority down the managerial hierarchy. As a result, managers in a decentralized firm make and implement more decisions than do managers in a centralized firm. The benefit of decentralization is that decisions are more likely to be made by managers who possess the specific local knowledge— not possessed by high-level managers—to use the firm's resources in the best way possible to maximize firm value. However, the cost of decentralization is that lower-level managers who have the knowledge to make the best decisions with the firm's resources are less likely to possess the same incentive as high-level managers to maximize firm value. Stated differently, as compared to high-level managers, lower-level managers are more likely to use the firm's resources for personal gain than for increasing the firm's share value. Therefore, decentralization requires the use of particular incentives, such as profit sharing and stock options, to motivate lower-level managers to make decisions that maximize firm value. Tim Hortons, for example, offers incentives such as health care benefits, life and disability insurances, and pension plans even to its part-time employees.[1] Providing these types of benefits for lower-level managers both increases the employee retention rate and reduces the incentives for individuals to make decisions maximizing their own personal gain at the expense of the organization. Successful decentralized firms manage this tradeoff effectively.

[1] Tim Hortons website, http://www.timhortons.com/ca/en/join/dist-trans-empl.html, accessed on May 2, 2014.

Decentralization usually is achieved by creating units called *divisions*. Divisions can be differentiated in a number of different ways, including:

- types of goods or services
- geographic lines, or
- responsibility centres.

Types of Goods or Services One way in which divisions are differentiated is by the types of goods or services produced. For example, divisions of PepsiCo include the Snack Ventures Europe Division (a joint venture with General Mills), Frito-Lay, Inc., and Tropicana, as well as its flagship soft-drink division. Exhibit 12.2 shows decentralized divisions of PepsiCo. These divisions are organized on the basis of product lines. Within PepsiCo, some divisions depend on other divisions. For example, PepsiCo spun off its restaurant divisions to YUMBrands. As a result, the pop you drink at Pizza Hut, Taco Bell, and KFC will be Pepsi—not Coke. In a decentralized setting, some interdependencies usually exist; otherwise, a company would merely be a collection of totally separate entities.

EXHIBIT 12.2

Decentralized Divisions

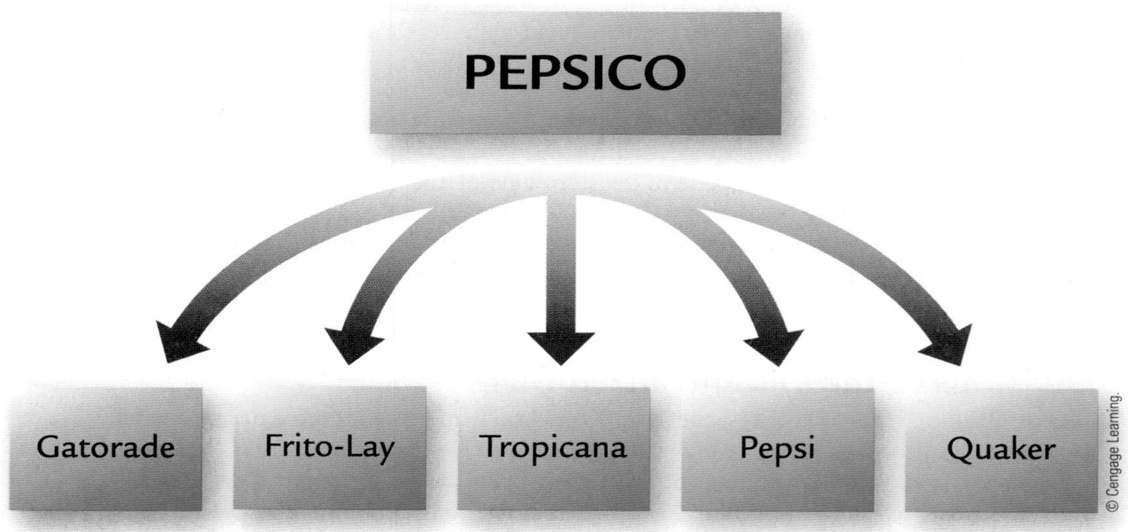

Geographic Lines Divisions may also be created along geographic lines. For example, North Bay, Ontario–based Redpath Mining has a number of regional divisions: Africa, Asia, Australia, Europe, North America, and South America. The presence of divisions spanning one or more regions creates the need for performance evaluation that can take into account differences in divisional environments.

> **concept Q&A**
>
> Think about jobs that you or your friends have held. To what extent did you or your friends work in a centralized or decentralized decision-making environment?
>
> Answers on pages 734 to 738.

Responsibility Centres A third way in which divisions differ is by the type of responsibility given to the divisional manager. As a firm grows, top management typically creates areas of responsibility, known as responsibility centres, and assigns subordinate managers to those areas. A **responsibility centre** is a segment of the business whose manager is accountable for specified sets of activities. The results of each responsibility centre can be measured according to the information that managers need to operate their centres. The four major types of responsibility centres are as follows:

1. **Cost centre**: A responsibility centre in which a manager is responsible only for costs.
2. **Revenue centre**: A responsibility centre in which a manager is responsible only for generating sales, or revenue.
3. **Profit centre**: A responsibility centre in which a manager is responsible for both revenues and costs.
4. **Investment centre**: A responsibility centre in which a manager is responsible for revenues, costs, and investments.

The choice of responsibility centre typically mirrors the actual situation and the type of information available to the manager. Information is the key to appropriately holding managers responsible for outcomes. For example, a production department manager is held responsible for departmental costs but not for sales. This responsibility choice occurs because the production department manager understands and directly controls some production costs but does not set selling prices. Any difference between actual and expected costs can best be explained at this level.

The marketing department manager sets the price and projected sales *revenue*. Therefore, the marketing department may be evaluated as a revenue centre. Direct costs of the marketing department and overall sales are the responsibility of the sales manager.

In some companies, plant managers are given the responsibility for manufacturing and marketing their products. These plant managers control both *costs* and *revenues*, putting them in control of a profit centre. Operating income is an important performance measure for profit centre managers.

Finally, divisions sometimes are cited as examples of investment centres. In addition to having control over cost and pricing decisions, divisional managers may have the power to make *investment* decisions such as plant closings and openings and decisions to keep or drop a product line. As a result, both operating income and some type of return on investment are important performance measures for investment centre managers. Exhibit 12.3 displays these centres along with the type of information that managers need in order to manage their operations. As the exhibit shows, investment centres represent the greatest degree of decentralization (followed by profit centres and finally by cost and revenue centres) because their managers have the freedom to make the greatest variety of decisions.

EXHIBIT 12.3

Types of Responsibility Centres and Accounting Information Used to Measure Performance

	Cost	Sales	Capital Investment	Other
Cost centre	X			
Revenue centre		X		
Profit centre	X	X		
Investment centre	X	X	X	X

It is important to realize that while the responsibility centre manager has responsibility only for the activities of that centre, decisions made by that manager can affect other responsibility centres. For example, the sales force at a floor care products firm routinely offers customers price discounts at the end of the month. Sales increase dramatically, which is good for revenue and the sales force. However, the factory is forced to institute overtime shifts to keep up with demand. These overtime shifts increase the costs of the factory as well as the cost per unit of product.

Organizing divisions as responsibility centres creates the opportunity to control the divisions through the use of responsibility accounting. Revenue centre control is achieved by evaluating the efficiency and the effectiveness of divisional managers on the basis of sales revenue. Cost centre control is based on control of costs and frequently employs variance analysis, as described in Chapters 10 and 11. This chapter will focus on the evaluation of profit centres and investment centres.

YOUDECIDE Organizational Structure

You are the CEO of a new hospital. One important early decision you face is determining the optimal level of decentralization for your various levels of supporting management.

What factors should you consider as you decide how best to structure the hospital management?

There is no easy, one-size-fits-all answer. However, some of the top-ranked hospitals in the world, such as Toronto's Hospital for Sick Children, recognize that much of the specific knowledge critically important for making the best patient care decisions resides with the hospital's physicians, surgeons, and nurses rather than with the chief executive officer or other "C-Suite" executives (e.g., chief financial officer, chief operations officer, chief integrity officer). Such hospitals choose a highly decentralized organizational structure so that many important decisions that affect patient treatment are made by individuals far removed from top management. The biggest challenge to effectively managing a highly decentralized decision-making structure like this one is to create quantitative performance measures for the decision makers—in this case, the physicians, surgeons, and nurses—to assess the quality of their decisions. Furthermore, these performance measures need to be used as part of the decision makers' compensation packages to reward (or punish) their wise (or unwise) decisions that hopefully are taken in the best interest of the patients and, ultimately, the hospital. A growing number of publicly traded companies in Canada, such as Suncor Energy Inc., offer all employees incentives such as profit-sharing and share purchase plans to take actions that are in the companies' best long-term interests.

In decentralized organizations, managerial accounting is important in designing effective performance measures and incentive systems to help ensure that lower-level managers use their decision-making authority to improve the organization's performance.

MEASURING THE PERFORMANCE OF INVESTMENT CENTRES BY USING RETURN ON INVESTMENT

OBJECTIVE 2

Compute and explain return on investment.

Typically, investment centres are evaluated on the basis of return on investment (ROI). Other measures, such as residual income and economic value added, are discussed in the following section.

Return on Investment

Divisions that are investment centres will have an income statement and a balance sheet. So, could those divisions be ranked on the basis of income? Suppose, for example, that a company has two divisions—Alpha and Beta. Alpha's operating income is $100,000, and Beta's operating income is $200,000. Did Beta perform better than Alpha? What if Alpha used an investment of $500,000 to produce the contribution of $100,000, while Beta used an investment of $2 million to produce the $200,000 contribution? Does your response change? Clearly, relating the reported operating profits to the assets used to produce them is a more meaningful measure of performance.

One way to relate operating profits to assets employed is to compute the **return on investment (ROI)**, which is the profit earned per dollar of investment. ROI is the most common measure of performance for an investment centre. It can be defined as follows:

$$ROI = \frac{\text{Operating income}}{\text{Average operating assets}}$$

Operating income refers to earnings before interest and taxes. **Operating assets** are all assets acquired to generate operating income, including cash, receivables, inventories, land, buildings, and equipment. The figure for average operating assets is computed as follows:

$$\text{Average operating assets} = \frac{(\text{Beginning assets} + \text{Ending assets})}{2}$$

Opinions vary regarding how long-term assets (plant and equipment) should be valued (e.g., gross book value vs. net book value, or historical cost vs. current cost). Most firms use historical cost and net book value.[2]

Returning to our example, Alpha's ROI is 0.20 (= \$100,000/\$500,000), while Beta's ROI is only 0.10 (= \$200,000/\$2,000,000). The formula for ROI is quick and easy to use. However, the decomposition of ROI into margin and turnover ratios gives additional information.

Margin and Turnover

A second way to calculate ROI is to separate the formula (Operating income ÷ Average operating assets) into margin and turnover.

$$ROI = \underbrace{\frac{\text{Operating income}}{\text{Sales}}}_{\textbf{Margin}} \times \underbrace{\frac{\text{Sales}}{\text{Average operating assets}}}_{\textbf{Turnover}}$$

Notice that "Sales" in the above formula can be cancelled out to yield the original ROI formula of (Operating income ÷ Average operating assets).

Margin is the ratio of operating income to sales. It tells how many cents of operating income result from each dollar of sales, and expresses the portion of sales that is available for interest, taxes, and profit. Some managers also refer to margin as return on sales. **Turnover** is a different measure; it is found by dividing sales by average operating assets. Turnover tells how many dollars of sales result from every dollar invested in operating assets, and shows how productively assets are being used to generate sales.

Suppose, for example, that Alpha had sales of \$400,000. Then, margin would be 0.25 (= \$100,000/\$400,000), and turnover would be 0.80 (= \$400,000/\$500,000). Alpha's ROI would still be 0.20 (= 0.25 × 0.80). Cornerstone 12.1 shows how to calculate these ratios.

Calculating Average Operating Assets, Margin, Turnover, and Return on Investment

CORNERSTONE 12.1

Information:

Celimar Company's Ontario division earned operating income last year as shown in the following income statement:

Sales	\$480,000
Cost of goods sold	222,000
Gross margin	258,000
Selling and administrative expense	210,000
Operating income	\$ 48,000

(Continued)

[2] There is no one correct way to calculate ROI. However, it is important to ensure that one method is applied consistently, which allows the company to compare the ROIs among divisions and over time.

CORNERSTONE

12.1

(Continued)

At the beginning of the year, the value of operating assets was $277,000. At the end of the year, the value of operating assets was $323,000.

Required:

For the Ontario division, calculate:

1. Average operating assets
2. Margin
3. Turnover
4. Return on investment

Solution:

1. $\text{Average operating assets} = \frac{(\text{Beginning assets} + \text{Ending assets})}{2}$

$$= \frac{(\$277{,}000 + \$323{,}000)}{2}$$

$$= \$300{,}000$$

2. $\text{Margin} = \frac{\text{Operating income}}{\text{Sales}}$

$$= \frac{\$48{,}000}{\$480{,}000}$$

$$= 0.10\text{, or 10 percent}$$

3. $\text{Turnover} = \frac{\text{Sales}}{\text{Average operating assets}} = \frac{\$480{,}000}{\$300{,}000} = 1.6$

4. $ROI = \text{Margin} \times \text{Turnover} = 0.10 \times 1.6 = 0.16\text{, or 16 percent}$

Alternatively,

$$ROI = \frac{\text{Operating income}}{\text{Average operating assets}}$$

$$= \frac{\$48{,}000}{\$300{,}000}$$

$$= 0.16\text{, or 16 percent}$$

Why:

Performance measures are critical to any system of management. Understanding how to calculate these important measures will enable managers to properly implement appropriate control measures.

While both approaches yield the same ROI, the calculation of margin and turnover gives a manager valuable information. To illustrate this additional information, consider the data presented in Exhibit 12.4. The electronics division improved its ROI from 18 percent in year 1 to 20 percent in year 2. The medical supplies division's ROI, however, dropped from 18 percent to 15 percent. Computing the margin and turnover ratios for each division provides more insight into what caused the change in rates. As with variance analysis, understanding the causes of managerial accounting measures (i.e., variances, margins, turnover, etc.) helps managers take actions to improve the division. These ratios also are presented in Exhibit 12.4. Notice that the margins for both divisions dropped from year 1 to year 2. In fact,

EXHIBIT 12.4

Comparison of Divisional Performance

	Comparison of ROI	
	Electronics Division	**Medical Supplies Division**
Year 1:		
Sales	$30,000,000	$117,000,000
Operating income	1,800,000	3,510,000
Average operating assets	10,000,000	19,500,000
ROI[a]	18%	18%
Year 2:		
Sales	$40,000,000	$117,000,000
Operating income	2,000,000	2,925,000
Average operating assets	10,000,000	19,500,000
ROI[a]	20%	15%

	Margin and Turnover Comparisons			
	Electronics Division		**Medical Supplies Division**	
	Year 1	**Year 2**	**Year 1**	**Year 2**
Margin[b]	6.0%	5.0%	3.0%	2.5%
Turnover[c]	× 3.0%	× 4.0%	× 6.0	× 6.0
	18.0%	20.0%	18.0%	15.0%

[a] Operating income divided by average operating assets.
[b] Operating income divided by sales.
[c] Sales divided by average operating assets.

the divisions experienced the *same* percentage of decline (16.67 percent). A declining margin could be explained by increasing expenses, by competitive pressures (forcing a decrease in selling prices), or both.

Despite the declining margin, the electronics division was able to increase its rate of return. The reason is that the increase in turnover more than compensated for the decline in margin. One explanation for the increased turnover could be a deliberate policy to reduce inventories. (Notice that the average assets employed remained the same for the electronics division even though sales increased by $10 million.)

The experience of the medical supplies division was less favourable. Because its turnover rate remained unchanged, its ROI dropped. This division, unlike the electronics division, could not overcome the decline in margin.

concept Q&A

Think about some stores in your town, such as a jewellery store, fast-food outlet, and grocery store. How do you suppose their margins and turnover ratios compare with each other? Explain your thinking.

Answers on pages 734 to 738.

Advantages of Return on Investment

At least three positive results stem from the use of ROI:

1. It encourages managers to focus on the relationships among sales, expenses, and investment, as should be the case for a manager of an investment centre.
2. It encourages managers to focus on cost efficiency.
3. It encourages managers to focus on operating asset efficiency.

These advantages are illustrated by the following three scenarios.

Focus on Return on Investment Relationships Della Barnes, manager of the plastics division, is mulling over a suggestion from her marketing vice-president to increase the advertising budget by $100,000. The marketing vice-president is confident that this increase will boost sales by $200,000. Della realizes that the increased sales will also raise expenses. She finds that the increased variable cost will be $80,000.

The division also will need to purchase additional machinery to handle the increased production. The equipment will cost $50,000 and will add $10,000 of depreciation expense. As a result, the proposal will add $10,000 (= $200,000 − $80,000 −$10,000 − $100,000) to operating income. Currently, the division has sales of $2 million, total expenses of $1,850,000, and operating income of $150,000. Operating assets equal $1 million.

	Without Increased Advertising	**With Increased Advertising**
Sales	$2,000,000	$2,200,000
Less: Expenses	1,850,000	2,040,000
Operating income	$ 150,000	$ 160,000
Average operating assets	$1,000,000	$1,050,000

ROI:

$$\frac{\$150,000}{\$1,000,000} = 0.15, \text{ or } 15 \text{ percent}$$

$$\frac{\$160,000}{\$1,050,000} = 0.1524, \text{ or } 15.24 \text{ percent}$$

The ROI without the additional advertising is 15 percent; the ROI with the additional advertising and $50,000 investment in assets is 15.24 percent. Since ROI is increased by the proposal, Della decides to authorize the increased advertising. In effect, the current ROI, without the proposal, is the *hurdle rate*. This term is frequently used to indicate the minimum ROI necessary to accept an investment.

Focus on Cost Efficiency Kyle Chugg, manager of Turner's battery division, groaned as he reviewed the projections for the last half of the current fiscal year. The recession was hurting his division's performance. Adding the projected operating income of $200,000 to the actual operating income of the first half produced expected annual earnings of $425,000. Kyle then divided the expected operating income by the division's average operating assets to obtain an expected ROI of 12.15 percent. "This is awful," muttered Kyle. "Last year, our ROI was 16 percent. And I'm looking at a couple more bad years before business returns to normal. Something has to be done to improve our performance."

Kyle directed all operating managers to identify and eliminate non-value-added activities. As a result, lower-level managers found ways to reduce costs by $150,000 for the remaining half of the year. This reduction increased the annual operating income from $425,000 to $575,000, increasing ROI from 12.15 percent to 16.43 percent as a result. Interestingly, Kyle found that some of the reductions could be maintained after business returned to normal.

Focus on Operating Asset Efficiency The electronic storage division prospered during its early years. In the beginning, the division developed portable external disk drives for storing data; sales and ROI were extraordinarily high. However, during the past several years, competitors had developed competing technology, and the division's ROI had plunged from 30 percent to 15 percent. Cost cutting had helped initially, but all of the excess had been removed, making further improvements from cost reductions impossible. Moreover, any increase in sales was unlikely—competition was too stiff. The divisional manager searched for some way to increase the ROI by at least 3–5 percent. Only by raising the ROI so that it compared favourably with that of the other divisions could the division expect to receive additional capital for research and development (R&D).

The divisional manager initiated an intensive program to reduce operating assets. Most of the gains were made in the area of inventory reductions; however, one plant was closed because of a long-term reduction in market share. By installing a just-in-time (JIT) purchasing and manufacturing system, the division was able to reduce its asset base without threatening its remaining market share. Finally, the reduction in operating assets meant that operating costs could be decreased still further. The end result was a 50 percent increase in the division's ROI, from 15 percent to more than 22 percent.

Disadvantages of the Return on Investment Measure

Overemphasis on ROI can produce myopic behaviour. Two negative aspects associated with ROI frequently are mentioned:

1. It can produce a narrow focus on divisional profitability at the expense of profitability for the overall firm.
2. It encourages managers to focus on the short run at the expense of the long run.

These disadvantages are illustrated by the following two scenarios.

Narrow Focus on Divisional Profitability A cleaning products division has the opportunity to invest in two projects for the coming year. The outlay required for each investment, the dollar returns, and the ROI are as follows:

	Project I	Project II
Investment	$10,000,000	$4,000,000
Operating income	1,300,000	640,000
ROI	13%	16%

The division currently earns ROI of 15 percent, with operating assets of $50 million and operating income on current investments of $7.5 million. The division has approval to request up to $15 million in new investment capital. Corporate headquarters requires that all investments earn at least 10 percent (this rate represents the corporation's cost of acquiring the capital). Any capital not used by a division is invested by headquarters, and it earns exactly 10 percent.

The division manager has four alternatives:

1. invest only in Project I;
2. invest only in Project II;
3. invest in both Project I and Project II; and
4. invest in neither project.

The divisional ROI was computed for each alternative.

	Alternatives			
	Select Project I	Select Project II	Select Both Projects	Select Neither Project
Operating income	$8,800,000	$8,140,000	$9,440,000	$7,500,000
Operating assets	$60,000,000	$54,000,000	$64,000,000	$50,000,000
ROI	14.67%	15.07%	14.75%	15.00%
Investment income	$500,000[a]	$1,100,000[b]	$100,000[c]	$1,500,000[d]
Operating income plus investment income	$9,300,000	$9,240,000	$9,540,000	$9,000,000

[a] ($15 million – $10 million) × 0.10 = $500,000
[b] ($15 million – $4 million) × 0.10 = $1,100,000
[c] ($15 million – $10 million – $4 million) × 0.10 = $100,000
[d] $15 million × 0.10 = $1,500,000

By choosing to invest only in Project II, the division manager boosts divisional ROI from 15 percent to 15.07 percent and increases division operating income by $640,000 (= $8,140,000 – $7,500,000). While the manager's choice maximizes divisional ROI, it does not maximize the profit the company could have earned. By quickly examining operating income plus investment income, we can clearly see that the company would have the most benefit by investing in both projects; however, by focusing narrowly on ROI, the divisional manger does not make a decision in the long-term best interests of the company.

Encourages Short-Run Optimization Ruth Lunsford, manager of the small tools division, was displeased with her division's performance during the first three quarters. Given the expected income for the fourth quarter, the ROI for the year would be 13 percent, at least two percentage points below where she had hoped to be. Such an ROI might not be strong enough to justify the early promotion she wanted. With only three months left, drastic action was needed. Increasing sales for the last quarter was unlikely. Most sales were booked at least two to three months in advance. Emphasizing extra sales activity would benefit next year's performance. What was needed were some ways to improve this year's performance.

After careful thought, Ruth decided to take the following actions:

1. Lay off five of the highest paid salespeople.
2. Cut the advertising budget for the fourth quarter by 50 percent.
3. Delay all promotions within the division for three months.
4. Reduce the preventive maintenance budget by 75 percent.
5. Use cheaper raw materials for fourth-quarter production.

In the aggregate, these steps would reduce expenses, increase income, and raise the ROI to about 15.2 percent for the current year.

While Ruth's actions increase the profits and ROI in the short run, they have some long-run negative consequences. Laying off the highest paid (and possibly the best) salespeople may harm the division's future sales-generating capabilities. Future sales could also be hurt by cutting back on advertising and using cheaper raw materials. Delaying promotions could hurt employee morale, which could, in turn, lower productivity and future sales. Finally, reducing preventive maintenance will likely increase downtime and decrease the life of the productive equipment.

Corporate and Social Responsibility

Corporate responsibility also comes into play when managers attempt to "game" ROI. In the previous example, Ruth's five top-earning salespeople probably were her best salespeople. Letting them go meant that sales would probably decrease, an outcome not in the best interests of the firm. Thus, her action is directly contrary to her obligation to take actions in the best interests of the company. The layoffs may also violate the implicit contract a company has with workers that outstanding work will lead to continued employment. When developing effective performance measures, companies must carefully consider their impact on the behaviour of managers and employees. Objectives that maximize income in the short term may hinder the long-term success of the company. For instance, delaying preventative maintenance will reduce current period expenses and, therefore, increase income; however, it increases the risk of producing poorer quality products that will need to be reworked, scrapped, or recalled if the products reach the consumers. In the long run, the cost of correcting quality problems can easily exceed the current period cost savings.

MEASURING THE PERFORMANCE OF INVESTMENT CENTRES BY USING RESIDUAL INCOME AND ECONOMIC VALUE ADDED

To compensate for the tendency of ROI to discourage investments that are profitable for the company but that lower a division's ROI, some companies have adopted alternative performance measures such as residual income and economic value added.

OBJECTIVE 3
Compute and explain residual income and economic value added.

Residual Income

Residual income is the difference between operating income and the minimum dollar return required on a company's operating assets:

Residual income = Operating income − (Minimum rate of return × Average operating assets)

Cornerstone 12.2 shows how to calculate residual income.

Calculating Residual Income

CORNERSTONE 12.2

Information:

Celimar Company's Ontario division earned operating income last year as shown in the following income statement:

Sales	$480,000
Cost of goods sold	222,000
Gross margin	258,000
Selling and administrative expense	210,000
Operating income	$ 48,000

At the beginning of the year, the value of operating assets was $277,000. At the end of the year, the value of operating assets was $323,000. Celimar Company requires a minimum rate of return of 12 percent.

Required:

For the Ontario division, calculate:

1. Average operating assets
2. Residual income

Solution:

1. Average operating assets $= \frac{\text{(Beginning assets + Ending assets)}}{2}$

$= \frac{(\$277{,}000 + \$323{,}000)}{2}$

$= \$300{,}000$

2. Residual income = Operating income − (Minimum rate of return × Average operating assets)

$= \$48{,}000 - (0.12 \times \$300{,}000)$

$= \$48{,}000 - \$36{,}000$

$= \$12{,}000$

(Continued)

CORNERSTONE
12.2

(Continued)

Why:
Residual income is a measure that many companies prefer to use to motivate managers to make the right decisions. It tends to correct some of the shortcomings of return on investment as a measurement tool.

The minimum rate of return is set by the company and is the same as the hurdle rate mentioned in the section on ROI. If residual income is greater than zero, then the division is earning more than the minimum required rate of return (or hurdle rate). If residual income is less than zero, then the division is earning less than the minimum required rate of return. Finally, if residual income equals zero, then the division is earning precisely the minimum required rate of return.

Advantage of Residual Income Recall that the manager of the cleaning products division rejected Project I because it would have reduced divisional ROI; however, that decision was not the most profitable from the company's perspective. The use of residual income as the performance measure would have prevented this loss. The residual income for each project is computed as follows:

Project I
Residual income = Operating income − (Minimum rate of return × Average operating assets)
= $1,300,000 − (0.10 × $10,000,000)
= $1,300,000 − $1,000,000
= $300,000

Project II
Residual income = $640,000 − (0.10 × $4,000,000)
= $640,000 − $400,000
= $240,000

Notice that both projects have positive residual income. For comparative purposes, the divisional residual income values for each of the four alternatives identified are as follows:

	Alternatives			
	Select Only Project I	**Select Only Project II**	**Select Both Projects**	**Select Neither Project**
Operating assets	$60,000,000	$54,000,000	$64,000,000	$50,000,000
Operating income	$ 8,800,000	$ 8,140,000	$ 9,440,000	$ 7,500,000
Minimum return*	6,000,000	5,400,000	6,400,000	5,000,000
Residual income	$ 2,800,000	$ 2,740,000	$ 3,040,000	$ 2,500,000

* 0.10 × Operating assets.

As shown above, selecting both projects produces the greatest increase in residual income. The use of residual income encourages managers to accept any project that earns a return that is above the minimum rate.

Disadvantages of Residual Income Residual income, like ROI, can encourage a short-run orientation. If Ruth Lunsford were being evaluated on the basis of residual income, she could have taken the same actions.

Another problem with residual income is that, unlike ROI, it is an absolute measure of profitability. Thus, direct comparison of the performance of two different investment centres becomes difficult, as the level of investment may differ. For example, consider the residual income computations for division A and division B, where the minimum required rate of return is 8 percent.

	Division A	**Division B**
Average operating assets	$15,000,000	$2,500,000
Operating income	$ 1,500,000	$ 300,000
Minimum return[a]	(1,200,000)	(200,000)
Residual income	$ 300,000	$ 100,000
Residual return[b]	2%	4%

[a] 0.08 × Operating assets.
[b] Residual income divided by operating assets.

It is tempting to claim that division A is outperforming division B since its residual income is three times higher. Notice, however, that division A is considerably larger than division B and has six times as many assets. One possible way to correct this disadvantage is to compute both ROI and residual income and to use both measures for performance evaluation. ROI could then be used for interdivisional comparisons.

Economic Value Added

Another financial performance measure that is similar to residual income is *economic value added*. **Economic value added (EVA)**[3] is after-tax operating income minus the dollar cost of capital employed. The dollar cost of capital employed is the actual percentage cost of capital[4] multiplied by the total capital employed. The equation for EVA is expressed as follows:

$$EVA = \text{After-tax operating income} - (\text{Actual percentage cost of capital} \times \text{Total capital employed})$$

Cornerstone 12.3 shows how to calculate EVA.

Calculating Economic Value Added

CORNERSTONE 12.3

Information:

Celimar Company's Ontario division earned net income last year as shown in the following income statement:

Sales	$480,000
Cost of goods sold	222,000
Gross margin	258,000
Selling and administrative expense	210,000
Operating income	48,000
Less: Income taxes (@ 30%)	14,400
Net income	$ 33,600

Total capital employed was $300,000. Celimar Company's actual cost of capital is 10 percent.

(Continued)

[3] EVA was developed by Stern Stewart & Co. in the 1990s. More information can be found on the firm's website, http://www.sternstewart.com.
[4] The computation of a company's actual cost of capital is reserved for advanced accounting courses.

CORNERSTONE

12.3

(Continued)

Required:

Calculate EVA for the Ontario division.

Solution:

$$\begin{aligned} EVA &= \text{After-tax operating income} - (\text{Actual percentage cost of capital} \\ &\quad \times \text{Total capital employed}) \\ &= \$33{,}600 - (0.10 \times \$300{,}000) \\ &= \$33{,}600 - \$30{,}000 \\ &= \$3{,}600 \end{aligned}$$

Why:

Economic value added is a measurement tool that some companies employ to reflect the actual cost of capital in the residual income type of calculation.

Basically, EVA is residual income with the minimum rate of return equal to the actual cost of capital for the firm (as opposed to some minimum rate of return desired by the company for other reasons). Companies have two sources of funding: debt and equity. When companies use debt for financing, lenders require companies to pay interest on the borrowed funds. When using equity financing, investors expect a return on their investment. For firms, regardless of the source of funding, there is a cost. By including the cost of capital in the EVA calculation, companies are able to determine if the return on an investment exceeds the cost of financing the investment opportunity. It is said that if EVA is positive, then the company has increased its wealth during the period; if EVA is negative, then the company has decreased its wealth during the period. Consider the old saying, "It takes money to make money." EVA helps the company to determine whether the money it makes is more than the money needed to make it. Over the long term, only those companies creating capital, or wealth, can survive.

As a form of residual income, EVA is a dollar figure, not a percentage rate of return. However, it does bear a resemblance to rates of return such as ROI because it links net income (return) to capital employed. The key feature of EVA is its emphasis on *after-tax* operating profit and the *actual* cost of capital. Residual income, on the other hand, uses a minimum expected rate of return. Investors like EVA because it relates profit to the amount of resources needed to achieve it. A number of companies have been evaluated on the basis of EVA. For example, companies such as General Electric, Walmart, Merck, IBM, Verizon Wireless, The Walt Disney Company, Pixar, and Jetblue Airways Corp. use EVA metrics in some capacity.

One important caveat for EVA metrics is that their calculation is not based on generally accepted accounting principles (GAAP). Different organizations will likely calculate EVA in different ways, making it difficult to compare the EVA metrics among companies.

concept Q&A

What are the differences and similarities between the basic residual income calculation and EVA?

Answers on pages 734 to 738.

Behavioural Aspects of Economic Value Added A number of companies have discovered that EVA helps to encourage the right kind of behaviour from their divisions in a way that emphasis on operating income alone cannot. Using EVA to understand the true cost of storing inventory enabled Herman Miller to quantify the long-term financial benefits of carrying less inventory and employing fewer fixed assets in its business. As a result, the company was able to go from reporting negative operating margins to near double-digit positive margins within a few years. The underlying reason is EVA's reliance on the actual cost of capital. In some companies, the responsibility for investment decisions rests with corporate management. As a result, the cost of capital is considered a corporate expense rather than an expense attributable to particular divisions. If a division builds inventories and investment, the cost of financing that investment is passed along to the overall income statement and does not show up as a reduction from that division's operating income as it would under an EVA analysis. Without an EVA analysis, the result is to make investment seem free to the divisions, and of course, they want more. Not surprisingly, research indicates that more firms continue to adopt EVA measures as part of their overall performance evaluation package.[5] It should be cautioned, however, that research also shows that some firms that collect EVA measures struggle to integrate these relatively complex measures into managerial decision making without considerable training for the managers.[6]

TRANSFER PRICING

OBJECTIVE 4

Explain the role of transfer pricing in a decentralized firm.

In many decentralized organizations, the output of one division is used as the input of another. For example, Cameco Corporation, a Saskatoon-based energy company, sells mined uranium to its wholly owned Switzerland-based subsidiary, Cameco Europe. In turn, Cameco Europe pursues the final sale to global customers.[7] This internal transfer between two divisions within Cameco Corporation raises an accounting issue: How is the transferred good valued? When divisions are treated as responsibility centres, they are evaluated on the basis of their contribution to costs, revenues, operating income, ROI, and residual income or EVA, depending on the particular centre type. As a result, the value of the transferred good is revenue to the selling division and cost to the buying division. This value, or internal price, is called the *transfer price*. In other words, a **transfer price** is the price charged for a component by the selling division to the buying division of the same company. Transfer pricing is a complex issue and has an impact on divisions and the company as a whole.

Impact of Transfer Pricing on Divisions and the Firm as a Whole

When one division of a company sells to another division, both divisions as well as the company as a whole are affected. The price charged for the transferred good affects (1) the costs of the buying division, and (2) the revenues of the selling division. Thus, the profits of both divisions, as well as the evaluation and compensation of their managers, are affected by the transfer price. Since profit-based performance measures of the two divisions are affected (for example, ROI and residual income), transfer pricing often can be an emotionally charged issue.

Exhibit 12.5 illustrates the effect of the transfer price on two divisions of ABC Inc. Division A produces a component and sells it to another division of the same company, division C. The $30 transfer price is revenue to division A; clearly, division A wants the price to be as high as possible. Conversely, the $30 transfer price is a cost to division C, just like the cost of any raw material. Division C prefers as low a transfer price as possible.

The actual transfer price nets out for the company *as a whole* in that total *pre-tax* income for the company is the same regardless of the transfer price. However, transfer pricing can affect the level of *after-tax* profits earned by a multinational company that

[5] Stern Stewart Research, "Stern Stewart's EVA Clients Outperform the Market and Their Peers," *Evaluation: Special Report* (October 2002).
[6] Alexander Mersereau, "Pushing the Art of Management Accounting," *CMA Management*, Volume 79, Issue 9 (February 1, 2006).
[7] David Milstead, "Cameco's $800-Million Tax Battle," *The Globe and Mail*, http://www.theglobeandmail.com/report-on-business/industry-news/energy-and-resources/camecos-800-million-tax-battle/article11665842/, accessed on May 2, 2014.

The Impact of Transfer Pricing on Transferring Divisions and the Company, ABC Inc., as a Whole

Division A	Division C
Produces component and transfers it to C for the transfer price of $30 per unit	Purchases component from A at the transfer price of $30 per unit and uses it in production of final product
Transfer price = $30 per unit	Transfer price = $30 per unit
Revenue to A	Cost to C
Increases income	Decreases income
Increases ROI	Decreases ROI

Note: Transfer price revenue = Transfer price cost; zero dollar impact on ABC Inc.

operates in multiple countries with different corporate tax rates and other legal requirements set by the countries in which the various divisions generate income. For example, if the selling division A operates in a low-tax country and the buying division B operates in a high-tax country, the transfer price may be set quite high. Then, the high transfer price (a revenue for A) would increase profit in the division in the low-tax country, and the high transfer price (a cost for B) would decrease profit in the division in the high-tax country. This transfer pricing strategy has the result of reducing overall corporate income taxes. The international transfer pricing situation is examined in detail in more advanced courses.

Transfer Pricing Policies

Recall that a decentralized company allows much more authority for decision making at lower management levels. It would be counterproductive for senior management of the decentralized company to then decide on the actual transfer prices between two divisions. As a result, top management usually sets the transfer pricing policy, but the divisions still decide whether or not to transfer. For example, top management at Verybig Inc. may set the corporate transfer pricing policy at full manufacturing cost. Then, if Mediumbig division wants to transfer a product to Somewhatbig division, the transfer price would be the product cost. However, neither division is forced to transfer the product internally. The transfer pricing policy only says that *if* the product is transferred, then it must be at cost.

Several transfer pricing policies are used in practice. These transfer pricing policies include:

- market price
- cost-based transfer prices
- negotiated transfer prices

Market Price If there is a competitive outside market for the transferred product, and the selling division can sell all that it can produce on the outside market, then the best transfer price is the market price. In such a case, divisional managers' actions will simultaneously optimize divisional profits and firmwide profits. Furthermore, no division can benefit at the expense of another. In this setting, top management will not be tempted to intervene.

Suppose that the furniture division of a corporation produces hide-a-beds. The mattress division of that same corporation produces mattresses, including a mattress model that fits into the hide-a-bed. If mattresses are transferred from the mattress division (the seller) to the furniture division (the buyer), a transfer pricing opportunity exists. Suppose that the mattresses can be sold to outside buyers at $50 each; this $50 is the market price.

Clearly, the mattress division would not sell the mattresses to the furniture division for less than $50 each and the furniture division would not pay more than $50 for the mattresses. Consequently, the transfer price is easily set at the market price.

If available, the market price is the best approach to transfer pricing. Will the two divisions transfer at the market price or transact on the open market? It really does not matter, since the divisions and the company as a whole will be as well off whether or not the transfer takes place internally.

Cost-Based Transfer Prices Frequently, an outside market does not exist for an internally transferred product. This might occur if, for instance, the transferred product uses patented designs owned by the parent company. If so, the company might use a cost-based transfer pricing approach. Suppose that the mattress company uses a high-density foam padding in the hide-a-bed mattress and that outside companies do not produce this type of mattress in the appropriate size. If the company has set a cost-based transfer pricing policy, then the mattress division will charge the full cost of producing the mattress. (Recall that full cost includes the cost of direct materials, direct labour, variable overhead, and a portion of fixed overhead.) Suppose that the full cost of the mattress is as follows:

Direct materials	$15
Direct labour	5
Variable overhead	3
Fixed overhead	5
Full cost	$28

Now, the transfer price is $28 per mattress, which is the amount to be paid to the mattress division by the furniture division. Notice that this transfer price does not allow for any profit for the selling division (here, the mattress division). A negative consequence of this pricing strategy is that the mattress division may well try to scale back production of the hide-a-bed mattress sold to the furniture division and increase production of mattresses available for sale to outside parties where the mattress division will earn a profit. To reduce this desire, top management may define cost as "cost plus." In this case, suppose that the company allows transfer pricing at cost plus 10 percent. Then, the transfer price is $30.80 [= $28 + (0.10 × $28)].

If the policy is cost-based transfer pricing, will the transfer take place? It depends. Suppose the furniture division wants to purchase lower-quality mattresses in the external market for $25 each. Then, no transfer will occur. Also, suppose the mattress division is producing at capacity and can sell the special mattresses for $40 each. The mattress division will refuse to transfer any mattresses to the furniture division and instead will sell all it can produce to outside parties. On the other hand, if the mattress division has excess capacity, the division manager may be willing to sell the mattresses to the furniture division for less than the full product cost. In this instance, the manager of the mattress division may be willing to transfer the mattresses for $23 (full product cost of $28 less the fixed overhead cost of $5).

Negotiated Transfer Prices Finally, top management may allow the selling and buying division managers to negotiate a transfer price. This approach is particularly useful in cases with market imperfections, such as the ability of an in-house division to avoid selling and distribution costs that external market participants would have to incur. Using a negotiated transfer price then allows the two divisions to share any cost savings resulting from avoided costs.

The fundamental overriding principle is that division managers in a decentralized organization will be empowered and required to make their own decisions. If the selling division is not operating at full capacity, then the manager of the selling division should be willing to sell at a price that covers all of the variable costs of producing and selling the product, yet does not include any amount for fixed overhead expenses.

Any amount greater than the variable cost of production would give the selling division extra profit.

Using the example of the mattress and furniture divisions, suppose that the hide-a-bed mattress typically sells for $50 and has full product cost of $28. Normally, a sales commission of $5 is paid to the salesperson, but that cost will not be incurred for any internal transfers. Now, a bargaining range exists for the two divisions to negotiate the transfer price, deciding how much of the cost savings will go to each division.

1. The minimum transfer price is the transfer price that would leave the selling division no worse off if the good were sold to an internal division than if the good were sold to an external party. This is sometimes referred to as the "floor" of the bargaining range.
2. The maximum transfer price is the transfer price that would leave the buying division no worse off if an input were purchased from an internal division than if the same good were purchased externally. This is sometimes referred to as the "ceiling" of the bargaining range.

In the example, the minimum transfer price is $45 (= $50 market price less the $5 selling commission that can be avoided on internal sales). The maximum transfer price is $50 (the price the furniture division would have to pay if the mattresses were bought externally). What is the actual transfer price? That depends on the negotiating skills of the mattress and furniture division managers. Any transfer price between $45 and $50 is possible. Cornerstone 12.4 shows how to calculate several types of transfer prices.

CORNERSTONE 12.4 Calculating Transfer Price

Information:

Omni Inc. has a number of divisions, including Alpha division, a producer of circuit boards, and Delta division, a heating and air-conditioning manufacturer.

Alpha division produces the cb-117 model, which can be used by Delta division in the production of thermostats that regulate the heating and air-conditioning systems. The market price of the cb-117 is $14, and the full cost of the circuit board is $9.

Required:

1. If Omni Inc. has a transfer pricing policy that requires transfer at full cost, what will the transfer price be? Do you suppose that the Alpha and Delta divisions would choose to transfer at that price?
2. If Omni Inc. has a transfer pricing policy that requires transfer at market price, what would the transfer price be? Do you suppose that the Alpha and Delta divisions would choose to transfer at that price?
3. Now suppose that Omni Inc. allows negotiated transfer pricing and that Alpha division can avoid $3 of selling expense by selling to Delta division. Which division sets the minimum transfer price, and what is it? Which division sets the maximum transfer price, and what is it? Do you suppose that the Alpha and Delta divisions would choose to transfer somewhere in the bargaining range?

Solution:

1.

Full cost	$9

(Continued)

CORNERSTONE

12.4

(Continued)

Delta division would be delighted to have the cb-117 transferred at a price of $9; however, the Alpha division would refuse to transfer for $9 since the division could sell the cb-117 to the outside market for $14 per unit.

2.

Market price	$14

Both Delta and Alpha divisions would be willing to transfer the cb-117 units at a price of $14 per unit since neither division would be worse off than if it bought/sold in the outside market.

3.

Market price	$14
Less: Avoidable selling expense	3
Minimum transfer price	$11

The minimum transfer price that Alpha division would accept is $11 per unit, while the maximum transfer price that Delta division would accept is $14 per unit. As a result, both divisions would be willing to accept a transfer price within the bargaining range. Precisely what the transfer price would be depends on the negotiating skills of the Alpha and Delta division managers.

Why:

Transfer pricing is a management tool that allows the transfer of products from one division to another at a price that is fair to both divisions. The calculations are important to ensure that both division managers are making decisions that will be in the best interests of the company.

THE BALANCED SCORECARD—BASIC CONCEPTS

OBJECTIVE 5

Explain the uses of the Balanced Scorecard, and compute cycle time, velocity, and manufacturing cycle efficiency.

Segment income, ROI, residual income, and EVA are important measures of managerial performance. As such, the temptation exists for managers to focus only on dollar figures. This focus may not tell the whole story for the company. In addition, lower-level managers and employees may feel helpless to affect income or investment. As a result, nonfinancial operating measures have been developed. For example, top management could look at such factors as market share, customer complaints, personnel turnover ratios, and personnel development. By letting lower-level managers know that attention to long-run factors is also vital, the tendency to overemphasize financial measures is reduced.

Managers in an advanced manufacturing environment are especially likely to use multiple measures of performance and to include nonfinancial as well as financial measures. For example, General Motors evaluated Robert Lutz, then head of product development, on the basis of 12 criteria that included how well he used existing parts in new vehicles and how many engineering hours he cut from the development process. In Canada, RCMP assistant commissioners and commanding officers use the Balanced Scorecard approach to better align internal processes with external reporting requirements.[8]

[8] Treasury Board of Canada Secretariat, "Royal Canadian Mounted Police—Report," http://www.tbs-sct.gc.ca/dpr-rmr/2009-2010/inst/rcm/rcm02-eng.asp, accessed on May 2, 2014.

The **Balanced Scorecard** is a strategic management system that defines a strategic-based responsibility accounting system. The Balanced Scorecard *translates* an organization's mission and strategy into operational objectives and performance measures for four different perspectives:

- The **financial perspective** describes the economic consequences of actions taken in the other three perspectives.
- The **customer perspective** defines the customer and market segments in which the business unit will compete.
- The **internal business process perspective** describes the internal processes needed to provide value for customers and owners.
- The **learning and growth (infrastructure) perspective** defines the capabilities that an organization needs to create long-term growth and improvement. This last perspective is concerned with three major *enabling factors:* employee capabilities, information systems capabilities, and employee attitudes (motivation, empowerment, and alignment).

Exhibit 12.6 shows a Balanced Scorecard for a typical hotel based on questionnaire data provided by a research survey of three- and four-star hotels. The scorecard includes the four basic scorecard categories and objectives with key measures for each category.

EXHIBIT 12.6

Balanced Scorecard for Ashley Hotel

Objective	Measure
	Financial Perspective
Operating revenues	• Total daily operating revenue • Revenue per available room
Operating costs	• Operating expenses relative to budget • Cost per occupant
	Customer Perspective
Customer satisfaction	• Customer satisfaction ratings • Number of monthly complaints
Customer loyalty	• Number of new reward club members • Percent of returning guests
	Internal Perspective
Employee turnover	• Employee turnover rate • Number of employee complaints
Response to customer complaints	• Percentage of complaints receiving response • Average response time
	Learning and Growth
New market identification	• Growth in reward club membership for new demographic segments
Employee training and advancement	• Percentage of employees participating in training courses • Survey scores pre- and post-training sessions

Source: N. Evans, "Assessing the Balanced Scorecard as a Management Tool for Hotels," *International Journal of Contemporary Hospitality Management*, Vol. 17 (Issue 4/5, 2005): 376–390.

Strategy Translation

Strategy, according to the creators of the Balanced Scorecard framework, is defined as:[9]

> *choosing the market and customer segments the business unit intends to serve, identifying the critical internal and business processes that the unit must excel at to deliver the value propositions to customers in the targeted market segments, and selecting the individual and organizational capabilities required for the internal, customer, and financial objectives.*

Strategy specifies management's desired relationships among the four perspectives and can be represented by a *strategy map* that links the strategic objectives among the four perspectives. *Strategy translation*, on the other hand, means specifying objectives, measures, targets, and initiatives for each perspective. Consider, for example, the financial perspective. For the financial perspective, a company's *objective* may be to grow revenues by introducing new products. The *performance measure* may be the percentage of revenues from the sale of new products. The *target* or *standard* for the coming year for the measure may be 20 percent (i.e., 20 percent of the total revenues for the coming year *must* be from the sale of new products). The *initiative* describes *how* this is to be accomplished. The "how," of course, involves the other three perspectives. The company must now identify the customer segments, internal processes, and individual and organizational capabilities that will permit the realization of the revenue growth objective. This illustrates the fact that the financial objectives serve as the focus for the objectives, measures, and initiatives of the other three perspectives.

The Role of Performance Measures The Balanced Scorecard is not simply a collection of critical performance measures. The performance measures are derived from a company's vision, strategy, and objectives. These measures must be *balanced* between:

- performance driver measures (i.e., lead indicators of future financial performance) and outcome measures (i.e., lagged indicators of financial performance)
- objective and subjective measures
- external and internal measures
- financial and nonfinancial measures

Using the Balanced Scorecard creates significant advantages for an organization. For example, each quarter, Analog Devices' senior managers gather to discuss Balanced Scorecard results for the various divisions. On one occasion, managers noted problems with their new-product ratios—used to measure the effectiveness of R&D spending. They quickly discovered that one division lagged in developing new products. The division's manager focused heavily on R&D by investing more money and exploring new market segments, new product sales, and marketing strategies. Analog Devices' corporate vice-president for marketing, quality, and planning noted that they would not have been able to catch the problem so early if they had just analyzed financial reports.[10] Other companies—such as Bank of Montreal, Hilton Hotels Corporation, Verizon Wireless, Duke University Children's Hospital, NatWest Bancorp, and AT&T Canada LDS—have had similar success.

The rapid and widespread adoption of this strategic management system is a strong testimonial to its worth. For example, companies such as General Electric, Verizon, and Microsoft have adapted their initial Balanced Scorecards into risk dashboards that contain key financial and nonfinancial measures pertaining to the important risks that threaten organizational success.[11] In addition, other organizations, such as Walmart, adapt their Balanced Scorecards to include measures that help their suppliers focus on

[9] Robert S. Kaplan and David P. Norton, *The Balanced Scorecard* (Boston: Harvard Business School Press, 1996), p. 37.
[10] Joel Kurtzman, "Is Your Company Off Course? Now You Can Find Out Why," *Fortune* (February 17, 1997), http://money.cnn.com/magazines/fortune/fortune_archive/1997/02/17/222180/index.htm (accessed on May 2, 2014).
[11] Ante Spencer, "Giving the Boss the Big Picture," *Business Week* (February 13, 2006).

increasingly important sustainability issues like using less packaging materials and more effective packaging techniques.[12]

Linking Performance Measures to Strategy Balancing outcome measures with performance drivers is essential to linking with the organization's strategy. Performance drivers make things happen and are indicators of how the outcomes are going to be realized. Thus, they tend to be unique to a particular strategy. Outcome measures are also important because they reveal whether the strategy is being implemented successfully with the desired economic consequences. For example, if the number of defective products is decreased, does this produce a greater market share? Does this, in turn, produce more revenues and profits? These questions suggest that the most important principle of linkage is the usage of cause-and-effect relationships. In fact, a **testable strategy** can be defined as a set of linked objectives aimed at an overall goal. The testability of the strategy is achieved by restating the strategy into a set of cause-and-effect hypotheses that are expressed by a sequence of if–then statements.[13] Consider, for example, the following sequence of if–then statements that link quality training with increased profitability:

- If design engineers receive quality training, then they can redesign products to reduce the number of defective units.
- If the number of defective units is reduced, then customer satisfaction will increase.
- If customer satisfaction increases, then market share will increase.
- If market share increases, then sales will increase.
- If sales increase, then profits will increase.

Exhibit 12.7 illustrates the quality improvement strategy described by a sequence of if–then statements. First, notice how each of the four perspectives is linked through the cause-and-effect relationships hypothesized. The learning and growth perspective

EXHIBIT 12.7

Testable Strategy Illustrated

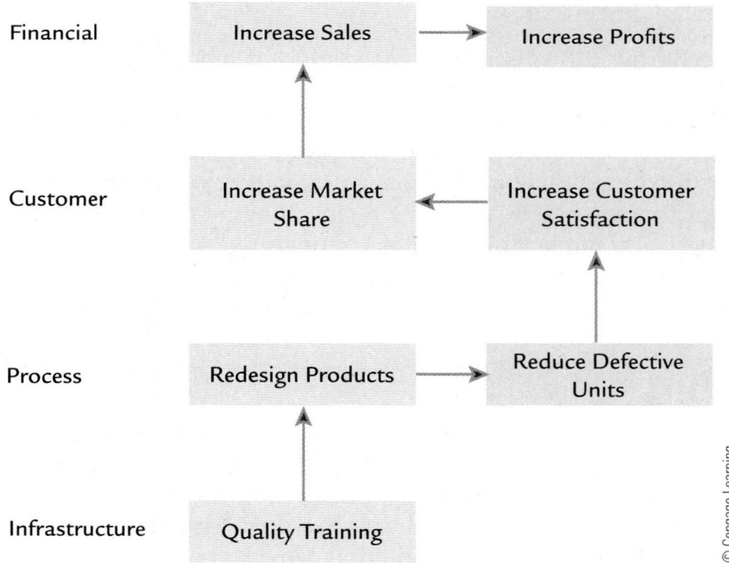

[12] "Getting Leaner—Ahead of the Pack: Suppliers Adjust to New Packaging Priorities," *Retailing Today*, Fourth Quarter, 2006: 16–18.
[13] Robert S. Kaplan and David P. Norton, *The Balanced Scorecard* (Boston: Harvard Business School Press, 1996), p. 149. (Kaplan and Norton describe the sequence of if–then statements only as a strategy. Calling it a testable strategy distinguishes it from the earlier, more general definition offered, and, in the authors' opinion, properly so.)

is present through the training dimension; the process perspective is represented by the redesign and manufacturing processes; the customer perspective is represented by customer satisfaction and market share; and, finally, the financial perspective is present because of revenues and profits. Second, viability of the strategy is testable. Strategic feedback is available that allows managers to test the reasonableness of the strategy. Hours of training, the number of products redesigned, the number of defective units, customer satisfaction, market share, revenues, and profits are all observable measures. Thus, the claimed relationships can be checked to see if the strategy produces the expected results. If not, it could be due to one of two causes: implementation problems, or an invalid strategy.

Implementation Problems It is possible that key *performance drivers* such as training and redesign of products did not achieve their targeted levels (i.e., fewer hours of training and fewer products redesigned than planned). In this case, the failure to produce the targeted *outcomes* for defects, customer satisfaction, market share, revenues, and profits could be merely an implementation problem.

Invalid Strategy If the targeted levels of performance drivers were achieved and the expected outcomes did not materialize, then the problem could very well lie with the strategy itself. This is an example of *double-loop feedback*. **Double-loop feedback** occurs whenever managers receive information about both the *effectiveness* of strategy implementation and the *validity* of the assumptions underlying the strategy. In a functional-based responsibility accounting system, typically only *single-loop feedback* is provided. **Single-loop feedback** emphasizes only effectiveness of implementation. In single-loop feedback, actual results deviating from planned results are a signal to take corrective action so that the plan (strategy) can be executed as intended. The validity of the assumptions underlying the plan is usually not questioned.

The Four Perspectives and Performance Measures

The four perspectives define the strategy of an organization. Furthermore, the example of if–then statements illustrates that the four perspectives provide the structure or framework for developing an integrated, cohesive set of performance measures. These measures, once developed, become the means for articulating and communicating the strategy of the organization to its employees and managers. The measures also serve the purpose of aligning individual objectives and actions with organizational objectives and initiatives. Given the role the four perspectives play in the development of performance measures, a more detailed examination of the perspectives is warranted.

The Financial Perspective The financial perspective establishes the long- and short-term financial performance objectives. The financial perspective is concerned with the global financial consequences of the other three perspectives. Thus, the objectives and measures of the other perspectives must be linked to the financial objectives. The financial perspective has three strategic themes—revenue growth, cost reduction, and asset utilization—that serve as the building blocks for the development of specific operational objectives and measures.

Revenue Growth Several possible objectives are associated with revenue growth, including:

- increase the number of new products
- create new applications for existing products
- develop new customers and markets, and
- adopt a new pricing strategy

Once operational objectives are known, performance measures can be designed. For example, possible measures for the above list of objectives (in the order given) are percentage of revenue from new products, percentage of revenue from new applications, percentage of revenue from new customers and market segments, and profitability by product or customer.

Cost Reduction Examples of cost reduction objectives are:

- reduce the cost per unit of product
- reduce the cost per customer, and
- reduce the cost per distribution channel

The appropriate measure is the cost per unit of the particular cost object. Trends in this measure will tell whether the costs are being reduced or not. For these objectives, the accuracy of cost assignments is especially important. Activity-based costing can play an essential measurement role, especially for selling and administrative costs—costs not usually assigned to cost objects like customers and distribution channels.

Asset Utilization Improving asset utilization is the principal objective. Financial measures such as ROI and EVA are used. The objectives and measures for the financial perspective are summarized in Exhibit 12.8.

EXHIBIT 12.8

Summary of Objectives and Measures: Financial Perspective

Objectives	Measures
Revenue Growth:	
Increase the number of new products	Percentage of revenue from new products
Create new applications	Percentage of revenue from new applications
Develop new customers and markets	Percentage of revenue from new sources
Adopt a new pricing strategy	Product and customer profitability
Cost Reduction:	
Reduce unit product cost	Unit product cost
Reduce unit customer cost	Unit customer cost
Reduce distribution channel cost	Cost per distribution channel
Asset Utilization:	
Improve asset utilization	Return on investment
	Economic value added

Customer Perspective The customer perspective is the source of the revenue component for the financial objectives. This perspective defines and selects the customer and market segments in which the company chooses to compete.

Core Objectives and Measures Once the customers and segments are defined, then *core objectives and measures* are developed. **Core objectives and measures** are those that are common across all organizations. The five key core objectives are as follows:

- increase market share
- increase customer retention
- increase customer acquisition
- increase customer satisfaction, and
- increase customer profitability

Possible core measures for these objectives, respectively, are market share (percentage of the market), percentage growth of business from existing customers and percentage of repeat customers, number of new customers, ratings from customer satisfaction surveys, and individual and segment profitability. Activity-based costing is a key tool in assessing customer profitability (Chapter 7). Notice that customer profitability is the only financial measure among the core measures. This measure, however, is critical because it emphasizes the importance of the *right* kind of customers. What good is it to have customers if they are not profitable? The obvious answer spells out the difference between being customer focused and customer obsessed.

Customer Value In addition to the core measures and objectives, measures are needed that drive the creation of *customer value* and, thus, drive the core outcomes. For example, increasing customer value builds customer loyalty (increases retention) and increases customer satisfaction. **Customer value** is the difference between realization and sacrifice, where realization is what the customer receives and sacrifice is what is given up in return. *Realization* includes such things as product functionality (features), product quality, reliability of delivery, delivery response time, image, and reputation. *Sacrifice* includes product price, time to learn to use the product, operating cost, maintenance cost, and disposal cost. The costs incurred by the customer *after* purchase are called **postpurchase costs**.

The attributes associated with the *realization* and *sacrifice* value propositions provide the basis for the objectives and measures that will lead to improving the core outcomes. The objectives for the sacrifice value proposition are the simplest: (1) decrease price, and (2) decrease postpurchase costs. Selling price and postpurchase costs are important measures of value creation. Decreasing these costs decreases customer sacrifice and, thus, increases customer value. Increasing customer value should impact favourably on most of the core objectives. Similar favourable effects can be obtained by increasing realization. Realization objectives, for example, would include the following:

- improve product functionality
- improve product quality
- increase delivery reliability, and
- improve product image and reputation

Possible measures for these objectives include, respectively, feature satisfaction ratings, percentage of returns, on-time delivery percentage, and product recognition ratings. Of these objectives and measures, delivery reliability will be used to illustrate how measures can affect managerial behaviour, indicating the need to be careful in the choice and use of performance measures.

Delivery reliability means that output is delivered on time. On-time delivery is a commonly used operational measure of reliability for which a firm sets delivery dates and then calculates on-time delivery performance by dividing the orders delivered on time by the total number of orders delivered. The goal, of course, is to achieve a ratio of 100 percent. Some, however, have found that use of this measure may produce undesirable behavioural consequences.[14] Specifically, plant managers were giving priority to filling orders not yet late over orders that were already late. The performance measure was encouraging managers to have one very late shipment rather than several moderately late shipments! A chart measuring the age of late deliveries could help mitigate this problem. Exhibit 12.9 summarizes the objectives and measures for the customer perspective.

Process Perspective The process perspective typically entails identifying the organization's core internal business processes needed to achieve the customer and financial objectives. To provide the framework needed for this perspective, a *process value chain* is defined. The **process value chain** comprises three processes:

- The **innovation process** anticipates the emerging and potential needs of customers and creates new products and services to satisfy those needs. It represents what is called the *long wave* of value creation.

[14] Joseph Fisher, "Nonfinancial Performance Measures," *Journal of Cost Management* (Spring 1992): 31–38.

EXHIBIT 12.9

Summary of Objectives and Measures: Customer Perspective

Objectives	Measures
Core:	
Increase market share	Market share (percentage of market)
Increase customer retention	Percentage growth of business from existing customers
	Percentage of repeat customers
Increase customer acquisition	Number of new customers
Increase customer satisfaction	Ratings from customer surveys
Increase customer profitability	Customer profitability
Performance Value:	
Decrease price	Price
Decrease postpurchase costs	Postpurchase costs
Improve product functionality	Ratings from customer surveys
Improve product quality	Percentage of returns
Increase delivery reliability	On-time delivery percentage
	Aging schedule
Improve product image and reputation	Ratings from customer surveys

- The **operations process** produces and delivers *existing* products and services to customers. It begins with a customer order and ends with the delivery of the product or service. It is the *short wave* of value creation.
- The **postsales service process** provides critical and responsive services to customers after the product or service has been delivered.

Innovation Process: Objectives and Measures Objectives for the innovation process include the following: (1) increase the number of new products, (2) increase the percentage of revenue from proprietary products, and (3) decrease the time to develop new products. Associated measures are actual new products developed versus planned products, percentage of total revenues from new products, percentage of revenues from proprietary products, and development cycle time (time to market).

Operations Process: Objectives and Measures The three operations process objectives that are almost always mentioned and emphasized are (1) increase process quality, (2) increase process efficiency, and (3) decrease process time. Examples of process quality measures are quality costs, output yields (good output/good input), and the percentage of defective units (good output/total output). Measures of process efficiency are concerned mainly with process cost and process productivity. Activity-based costing and process-value analysis facilitate measuring and tracking process costs. Common process time measures are cycle time and velocity, and manufacturing cycle effectiveness (MCE).

Cycle Time and Velocity The time to respond to a customer order is referred to as *responsiveness. Cycle time* and *velocity* are two operational measures of responsiveness. Cycle time is the length of time it takes to produce a unit of output from the time raw materials are received (starting point of the cycle) until the good is delivered to finished goods inventory (finishing point of the cycle). Thus, cycle time is the time required to produce a product (time/units produced). Velocity is the number of units of output that can be produced in a given period of time (units produced/time). Cornerstone 12.5 shows how to compute cycle time and velocity.

Computing Cycle Time and Velocity

CORNERSTONE 12.5

Information:

A company has the following data for one of its manufacturing cells:

a. Maximum units produced in a quarter (3-month period): 200,000 units
b. Actual units produced in a quarter: 160,000 units
c. Productive hours in one quarter: 40,000 hours

Required:

1. Compute the theoretical cycle time (in minutes).
2. Compute the actual cycle time (in minutes).
3. Compute the theoretical velocity in units per hour.
4. Compute the actual velocity in units per hour.

Solution:

1. $$\text{Theoretical cycle time} = \frac{(40{,}000 \text{ hours})(60 \text{ minutes per hour})}{200{,}000 \text{ units}}$$
$$= 12 \text{ minutes per unit}$$

2. $$\text{Actual cycle time} = \frac{(40{,}000 \text{ hours})(60 \text{ minutes per hour})}{160{,}000 \text{ units}}$$
$$= 15 \text{ minutes per unit}$$

3. $$\text{Theoretical velocity} = \frac{60 \text{ minutes per hour}}{12 \text{ minutes per unit}}$$
$$= 5 \text{ units per hour}$$

4. $$\text{Actual velocity} = \frac{60 \text{ minutes per hour}}{15 \text{ minutes per unit}}$$
$$= 4 \text{ units per hour}$$

Why:

Cycle time and velocity are two important concepts in analyzing a company's performance. These results can assist managers in understanding where the manufacturing process is performing well or poorly and can lead to corrective actions being taken as necessary.

Incentives can be used to encourage operational managers to reduce manufacturing cycle time or to increase velocity, thus improving delivery performance. A natural way to accomplish this objective is to tie product costs to cycle time and reward operational managers for reducing product costs. For example, in a JIT firm, conversion costs of the cell can be assigned to products on the basis of the time that it takes a product to move through the cell. Using the theoretical productive time available for a period (in minutes), a value-added standard cost per minute can be computed.

$$\text{Standard cost per minute} = \frac{\text{Cell conversion costs}}{\text{Minutes available}}$$

To obtain the conversion cost per unit, this standard cost per minute is multiplied by the actual cycle time used to produce the units during the period. By comparing the unit cost computed using the actual cycle time with the unit cost possible using the theoretical or optimal cycle time, a manager can assess the potential for improvement. Note that the more time it takes a product to move through the cell, the greater the unit product cost. With incentives to reduce product cost, this approach to product costing encourages operational managers and cell workers to find ways to decrease cycle time or increase velocity.

Manufacturing Cycle Efficiency Another time-based operational measure calculates **manufacturing cycle efficiency (MCE)**. MCE is measured as value-added time divided by total time. Total time includes both value-added time (the time spent efficiently producing the product) and non-value-added time (such as move time, inspection time, and waiting time). The formula for computing MCE is:

$$MCE = \frac{\text{Processing time}}{(\text{Processing time} + \text{Nonprocessing time})}$$

In this equation, processing time is the time that it takes to convert raw materials into a finished good. The other activities and their times are viewed as wasteful, and the goal is to reduce those times to zero. If this is accomplished, the value of MCE will be 1.0, or 100 percent. As MCE improves (moves toward 1.0), cycle time decreases. Furthermore, since the only way MCE can improve is by decreasing waste, cost reduction must also follow. Cornerstone 12.6 shows how to calculate MCE.

CORNERSTONE 12.6 Calculating Manufacturing Cycle Efficiency

Information:

A company provided the following information:

a. Maximum units produced in a quarter (3-month period): 200,000 units
b. Actual units produced in a quarter: 160,000 units
c. Productive hours in one quarter: 40,000 hours
d. Actual cycle time = 15 minutes
e. Theoretical cycle time = 12 minutes

Required:

1. Calculate the amount of processing time and the amount of nonprocessing time.
2. Calculate MCE.

Solution:

1. Processing time is equal to theoretical cycle time. That is, if everything goes smoothly and there is no wasted time, it takes 12 minutes to produce one unit. Nonprocessing time, therefore, must be the difference between actual cycle time (which includes some waste) and theoretical cycle time.

   Processing time = Theoretical cycle time = 12 minutes

   Nonprocessing time = Actual cycle time − Theoretical cycle time
   = 15 − 12 = 3 minutes

(Continued)

CORNERSTONE
12.6

(Continued)

2. $MCE = \frac{\text{Processing time}}{(\text{Processing time} + \text{Nonprocessing time})}$

$= \frac{12}{(12 + 3)}$

$= 0.8$, or 80 percent

Why:

Manufacturing cycle efficiency will tell us how closely we are tracking the objectives of the production process. This knowledge helps managers pinpoint problem areas.

Cornerstone 12.6 illustrates a fairly efficient process, as measured by MCE. Many manufacturing companies have MCEs less than 0.05.[15]

Postsales Service Process: Objectives and Measures Increasing quality, increasing efficiency, and decreasing process time are also objectives that apply to the postsales service process. Service quality, for example, can be measured by first-pass yields, where first-pass yields are defined as the percentage of customer requests resolved with a single service call. Efficiency can be measured by cost trends and productivity measures. Process time can be measured by cycle time, where the starting point of the cycle is defined as the receipt of a customer request, and the finishing point is when the customer's problem is solved. The objectives and measures for the process perspective are summarized in Exhibit 12.10.

EXHIBIT 12.10

Summary of Objectives and Measures: Process Perspective

Objectives	Measures
Innovation:	
Increase the number of new products	Number of new products vs. planned
Increase proprietary products	Percentage revenue from proprietary products
Decrease new product development time	Time to market (from start to finish)
Operations:	
Increase process quality	Quality costs
	Output yields
	Percentage of defective units
Increase process efficiency	Unit cost trends
	Output/input(s)
Decrease process time	Cycle time and velocity
	Manufacturing cycle efficiency
Postsales Service:	
Increase service quality	First-pass yields
Increase service efficiency	Cost trends
	Output/input(s)
Decrease service time	Cycle time

[15] Robert S. Kaplan and David P. Norton, *The Balanced Scorecard* (Boston: Harvard Business School Press, 1996), p. 117.

Learning and Growth Perspective The fourth and final category in a typical Balanced Scorecard is the learning and growth perspective, which represents the source of the capabilities that enable the accomplishment of the other three perspectives' objectives. This perspective has three major objectives:

- increase employee capabilities
- increase motivation, empowerment, and alignment, and
- increase information systems capabilities

Employee Capabilities Three core *outcome* measurements for employee capabilities are employee satisfaction ratings, employee turnover percentages, and employee productivity (e.g., revenue per employee). Examples of lead measures or performance drivers for employee capabilities are hours of training and strategic job coverage ratios (percentage of critical job requirements filled). As new processes are created, new skills are often required. Training and hiring are sources of these new skills. Furthermore, the percentage of the employees needed in certain key areas with the requisite skills signals the capability of the organization to meet the objectives of the other three perspectives.

Motivation, Empowerment, and Alignment Employees must have not only the necessary skills, but also the freedom, motivation, and initiative to use those skills effectively. The number of suggestions per employee and the number of suggestions implemented per employee are possible measures of motivation and empowerment. Suggestions per employee provide a measure of the degree of employee involvement, whereas suggestions implemented per employee signal the quality of the employee participation. The second measure also signals to employees whether or not their suggestions are being taken seriously.

Information Systems Capabilities Increasing information system capabilities means providing more accurate and timely information to employees so that they can improve processes and effectively execute new processes. Measures should be concerned with the *strategic information availability*. For example, possible measures include percentage of processes with real-time feedback capabilities and percentage of customer-facing employees with online access to customer and product information. Exhibit 12.11 summarizes the objectives and measures for the learning and growth perspective.

EXHIBIT 12.11

Summary of Objectives and Measures: Learning and Growth Perspective

Objectives	Measures
Increase employee capabilities	Employee satisfaction ratings Employee turnover percentages Employee productivity (revenue/employee) Hours of training Strategic job coverage ratio (percentage of critical job requirements filled)
Increase motivation and alignment	Suggestions per employee Suggestions implemented per employee
Increase information systems capabilities	Percentage of processes with real-time feedback capabilities Percentage of customer-facing employees with online access to customer and product information

SUMMARY OF LEARNING OBJECTIVES

LO1. Explain how and why firms choose to decentralize.

- In a decentralized organization, lower-level managers make and implement decisions. In a centralized organization, lower-level managers are responsible only for implementing decisions.
- Reasons why companies decentralize:
  - Local managers can make better decisions using local information.
  - Local managers can provide a more timely response.
  - It is impossible for any one central manager to be fully knowledgeable about all products and markets.
- Decentralization can train and motivate local managers and free top management from monitoring day-to-day operating conditions so that they can spend time on more long-range activities, such as strategic planning. Managerial accounting plays an important role in designing effective performance measures and incentive systems to help ensure that managers in a decentralized organization use their decision-making authority in a way that improves the organization's performance.
- Four types of responsibility centres are:
  - cost centres—the manager is responsible for costs
  - revenue centres—the manager is responsible for price and quantity sold
  - profit centres—the manager is responsible for costs and revenues
  - investment centres—the manager is responsible for costs, revenues, and investment

LO2. Compute and explain return on investment.

- ROI is the ratio of operating income to average operating assets or margin times turnover.
- Margin is operating income divided by sales.
- Turnover is sales divided by average operating assets.
- Advantage: ROI encourages managers to focus on improving sales, controlling costs, and using assets efficiently.
- Disadvantage: ROI can encourage managers to sacrifice long-run benefits for short-run benefits.

LO3. Compute and explain residual income and economic value added.

- Residual income is operating income minus a minimum percentage cost of capital times capital employed.
  - If residual income > 0, then the division is earning more than the minimum cost of capital.
  - If residual income < 0, then the division is earning less than the minimum cost of capital.
  - If residual income $= 0$, then the division is earning just the minimum cost of capital.
- Economic value added is after-tax operating profit minus the actual total annual cost of capital.
- If EVA > 0, then the company is creating wealth (or value).
- If EVA < 0, then the company is destroying wealth.

LO4. Explain the role of transfer pricing in a decentralized firm.

- Transfer price is charged by the selling division of a company to a buying division of the same company:
  - increases revenue to the selling division
  - increases cost to the buying division
- Common transfer pricing policies are:
  - cost based (e.g., total product cost)
  - market based (price charged in the outside market)
  - negotiated (between the buying and selling divisions' managers)

LO5. Explain the uses of the Balanced Scorecard, and compute cycle time, velocity, and manufacturing cycle efficiency.

- Balanced Scorecard is a strategic management system.
- Objectives and measures are developed for four perspectives:
  - financial perspective
  - customer perspective
  - process perspective
  - learning and growth perspective
- Velocity is the number of units produced in a period of time.
- Cycle time is the time needed to produce one unit.
- MCE is measured as value-added time divided by total time. The higher the MCE, the greater the firm's efficiency.

SUMMARY OF IMPORTANT EQUATIONS

1. $ROI = \frac{\text{Operating income}}{\text{Average operating assets}}$

   $ROI = \text{Margin} \times \text{Turnover}$
2. $\text{Average operating assets} = \frac{(\text{Beginning operating assets} + \text{Ending operating assets})}{2}$
3. $\text{Margin} = \frac{\text{Operating income}}{\text{Sales}}$
4. $\text{Turnover} = \frac{\text{Sales}}{\text{Average operating assets}}$
5. $\text{Residual income} = \text{Operating income} - (\text{Minimum rate of return} \times \text{Average operating assets})$
6. $EVA = \text{After-tax income} - (\text{Actual percentage cost of capital} \times \text{Total capital employed})$
7. $\text{Theoretical cycle time} = \frac{\text{Total time}}{\text{Number of units produced under ideal conditions}}$
8. $\text{Actual cycle time} = \frac{\text{Total time}}{\text{Actual number of units produced}}$
9. $\text{Theoretical velocity} = \frac{\text{Number of units produced under ideal conditions}}{\text{Total time}}$
10. $\text{Actual velocity} = \frac{\text{Actual numberof units produced}}{\text{Total time}}$
11. $\text{Standard cost per minute} = \frac{\text{Conversion cost}}{\text{Minutes available}}$
12. $MCE = \frac{\text{Processing time}}{(\text{Processing time} + \text{Nonprocessing time})}$

CORNERSTONES

GLOSSARY

Balanced Scorecard A strategic management system that defines a strategic-based responsibility accounting system. The Balanced Scorecard translates an organization's mission and strategy into operational objectives and performance measures for four different perspectives: the financial perspective, the customer perspective, the internal business process perspective, and the learning and growth (infrastructure) perspective. (p. 596)

Core objectives and measures Those objectives and measures common to most organizations. (p. 600)

Cost centre A division of a company that is evaluated on the basis of cost. (p. 579)

Customer perspective A Balanced Scorecard viewpoint that defines the customer and market segments in which the business will compete. (p. 596)

Customer value Realization less sacrifice, where realization is what the customer receives and sacrifice is what is given up. (p. 601)

Decentralization The granting of decision-making freedom to lower operating levels. (p. 576)

Double-loop feedback Information about both the effectiveness of strategy implementation and the validity of assumptions underlying the strategy. (p. 599)

Economic value added (EVA) A performance measure that is calculated by taking the after-tax operating profit minus the total annual cost of capital. (p. 589)

Financial perspective A Balanced Scorecard viewpoint that describes the financial consequences of actions taken in the other three perspectives. (p. 596)

Innovation process A process that anticipates the emerging and potential needs of customers and creates new products and services to satisfy those needs. (p. 601)

Internal business process perspective A Balanced Scorecard viewpoint that describes the internal processes needed to provide value for customers and owners. (p. 596)

Investment centre A division of a company that is evaluated on the basis of return on investment. (p. 579)

Learning and growth (infrastructure) perspective A Balanced Scorecard viewpoint that defines the capabilities that an organization needs to create long-term growth and improvement. (p. 596)

Manufacturing cycle efficiency (MCE) Measured as value-added time divided by total time. The result tells the company what percentage of total time spent is devoted to actual production. (p. 604)

Margin The ratio of net operating income to sales. (p. 581)

Operating assets Assets used to generate operating income, consisting usually of cash, inventories, receivables, and property, plant, and equipment. Average operating assets are found by adding together beginning operating assets and ending operating assets, and dividing the result by 2. (p. 581)

Operating income Revenues minus operating expenses from the firm's normal operations. Operating income is earnings before interest and taxes. (p. 581)

Operations process A process that produces and delivers existing products and services to customers. (p. 602)

Postpurchase costs The costs of using, maintaining, and disposing of the product. (p. 601)

Postsales service process A process that provides critical and responsive service to customers after the product or service has been delivered. (p. 602)

Process value chain The innovation, operations, and postsales service processes. (p. 601)

Profit centre A division of a company that is evaluated on the basis of operating income or profit. (p. 579)

Residual income The difference between operating income and the minimum dollar return required on a company's operating assets. (p. 587)

Responsibility centre A segment of the business whose manager is accountable for specified sets of activities. (p. 578)

Return on investment (ROI) The ratio of operating income to average operating assets. (p. 580)

Revenue centre A segment of the business that is evaluated on the basis of sales. (p. 579)

Single-loop feedback Information about the effectiveness of strategy implementation. (p. 599)

Strategy The process of choosing a business's market and customer segments, identifying its critical internal business processes, and selecting the individual and organizational capabilities needed to meet internal, customer, and financial objectives. (p. 597)

Testable strategy A set of linked objectives aimed at an overall goal that can be restated into a sequence of cause-and-effect hypotheses. (p. 598)

Transfer price The price charged for goods transferred from one division to another. (p. 591)

Turnover The ratio of sales to average operating assets. (p. 581)

REVIEW PROBLEMS

I. Return on Investment

Flip Flop Politics Inc. had gross margin of $550,000 and selling and administrative expense of $300,000 last year. Also, Flip Flop began last year with $1,400,000 of operating assets and ended the year with $1,100,000 of operating assets.

Required:

Calculate return on investment for Flip Flop Politics.

Solution:

Gross margin	$550,000
Selling and administrative expense	300,000
Operating income	$250,000

$$\text{Average operating assets} = \frac{(\text{Beginning operating assets} + \text{Ending operating assets})}{2}$$

$$= \frac{(\$1,400,000 + \$1,100,000)}{2}$$

$$= \frac{\$2,500,000}{2}$$

$$= \$1,250,000$$

$$\text{Return on investment} = \frac{\text{Operating income}}{\text{Average operating assets}}$$

$$= \frac{\$250,000}{\$1,250,000}$$

$$= 0.20, \text{ or } 20 \text{ percent}$$

II. Economic Value Added

Fabries Inc. had sales of $5,000,000, cost of goods sold of $3,500,000, and selling and administrative expense of $500,000 for its most recent year of operations. Fabries faces a tax rate of 40 percent. Also, Fabries employed $2,000,000 of debt capital and $4,000,000 of equity capital in generating its return. Finally, the company's actual cost of capital is 8 percent.

Required:

1. Calculate after-tax operating income for Fabries.
2. Calculate EVA for Fabries.

Solution:

1.

Sales	$5,000,000
Cost of goods sold	3,500,000
Gross margin	1,500,000
Selling and administrative expense	500,000
Operating income	1,000,000
Income taxes (@ 40%)	400,000
Net income	$ 600,000

2. EVA = After-tax operating income − (Actual percentage cost of capital × Total capital employed)
= $600,000 − [0.08 × ($2,000,000 + $4,000,000)]
= $600,000 − (0.08 × $6,000,000)
= $600,000 − $480,000
= $120,000

III. Transfer Pricing

The components division produces a part that is used by the goods division. The cost of manufacturing the part follows:

Direct materials	$10
Direct labour	2
Variable overhead	3
Fixed overhead*	5
Total cost	$20

* Based on a practical volume of 200,000 parts

Other costs incurred by the components division are as follows:

Fixed selling and administrative	$500,000
Variable selling (per unit)	1

The part usually sells for between $28 and $30 in the external market. Currently, the components division is selling it to external customers for $29. The division is capable of producing 200,000 units of the part per year; however, because of a weak economy, only 150,000 parts are expected to be sold during the coming year. The variable selling expenses are avoidable if the part is sold internally.

The goods division has been buying the same part from an external supplier for $28. It expects to use 50,000 units of the part during the coming year. The manager of the goods division has offered to buy 50,000 units from the components division for $18 per unit.

Required:

1. Determine the minimum transfer price that the components division would accept.
2. Determine the maximum transfer price that the manager of the goods division would pay.
3. Should an internal transfer take place? Why or why not? If you were the manager of the components division, would you sell the 50,000 components for $18 each? Explain.
4. Suppose that the average operating assets of the components division total $10 million. Compute the ROI for the coming year, assuming that the 50,000 units are transferred to the goods division for $21 each.

Solution:

1. The minimum transfer price is $15. The components division has idle capacity and so must cover only its incremental costs, which are the variable manufacturing costs. (Fixed costs are the same whether or not the internal transfer occurs; the variable selling expenses are avoidable.)
2. The maximum transfer price is $28. The goods division would not pay more for the part than it has to pay an external supplier.

3. Yes, an internal transfer should occur; the opportunity cost of the selling division is less than the opportunity cost of the buying division. The components division would earn an additional $150,000 profit (= $3 × 50,000). The total joint benefit, however, is $650,000 (= $13 × 50,000). The manager of the components division should attempt to negotiate a more favourable outcome for that division.
4. Income statement:

Sales [($29 × 150,000) + ($21 × 50,000)]	$ 5,400,000
Less: Variable cost of goods sold ($15 × 200,000)	(3,000,000)
Less: Variable selling expenses ($1 × 150,000)	(150,000)
Contribution margin	2,250,000
Less: Fixed overhead ($5 × 200,000)	(1,000,000)
Less: Fixed selling and administrative	(500,000)
Operating income	$ 750,000

$$ROI = \frac{\text{Operating income}}{\text{Average operating assets}}$$
$$= \frac{\$750{,}000}{\$10{,}000{,}000}$$
$$= 0.075 \text{ or } 7.5 \text{ percent}$$

DISCUSSION QUESTIONS

1. Discuss the differences between centralized and decentralized decision making.
2. What is decentralization?
3. Explain why firms choose to decentralize.
4. What are margin and turnover? Explain how these concepts can improve the evaluation of an investment centre.
5. What are the three benefits of ROI? Explain how each benefit can lead to improved profitability.
6. What is residual income? What is EVA? How does EVA differ from the general definition of residual income?
7. Can residual income or EVA ever be negative? What is the meaning of negative residual income or EVA?
8. What is a transfer price?
9. Briefly explain three common transfer pricing policies used by organizations.
10. What is the Balanced Scorecard?
11. Describe the four perspectives of the Balanced Scorecard.

CORNERSTONE EXERCISES

OBJECTIVE 2
CORNERSTONE 12.1

Cornerstone Exercise 12-1 Calculating Average Operating Assets, Margin, Turnover, and Return on Investment

Springmount earned operating income last year as shown in the following income statement:

Sales	$2,900,000
Cost of goods sold	2,100,000
Gross margin	800,000
Selling and administrative expense	650,000
Operating income	$ 150,000

At the beginning of the year, the value of operating assets was $1,450,000. At the end of the year, the value of operating assets was $1,050,000.

Required:

For Springmount, calculate:
1. Margin
2. Average operating assets
3. Turnover
4. Return on investment

OBJECTIVE 3
CORNERSTONE 12.2

Cornerstone Exercise 12-2 Calculating Residual Income

Springmount earned operating income last year as shown in the following income statement:

Sales	$2,900,000
Cost of goods sold	2,100,000
Gross margin	800,000
Selling and administrative expense	650,000
Operating income	$ 150,000

At the beginning of the year, the value of operating assets was $1,450,000. At the end of the year, the value of operating assets was $1,050,000. Springmount requires a minimum rate of return of 6 percent.

Required:

For Springmount, calculate:

1. Average operating assets
2. Residual income

OBJECTIVE 3
CORNERSTONE 12.3

Cornerstone Exercise 12-3 Calculating Economic Value Added

Springmount earned net income last year as shown in the following income statement:

Sales	$2,900,000
Cost of goods sold	2,100,000
Gross margin	800,000
Selling and administrative expense	650,000
Operating income	150,000
Less: Income taxes (@ $33\frac{1}{3}$%)	50,000
Net income	$ 100,000

Total capital employed equalled $900,000. Springmount's actual cost of capital is 5 percent.

Required:

Calculate the EVA for Springmount.

OBJECTIVE 4
CORNERSTONE 12.4

Cornerstone Exercise 12-4 Calculating Transfer Price

Lyubov Inc. has a number of divisions, including the Grad division (a producer of liquid pumps), and Vtori division (a manufacturer of boat engines). Grad division produces the h20-model pump that can be used by Vtori division in the production of motors that regulate the raising and lowering of the boat engine's stern drive unit. The market price of the h20-model is $1,440, and the full cost of the h20-model is $1,080.

Required:

1. If Lyubov Inc. has a transfer pricing policy that requires transfer at full cost, what will the transfer price be? Do you suppose that Grad and Vtori divisions will choose to transfer at that price?
2. If Lyubov Inc. has a transfer pricing policy that requires transfer at market price, what would the transfer price be? Do you suppose that Grad and Vtori divisions would choose to transfer at that price?

(Continued)

3. Now suppose that Lyubov Inc. allows negotiated transfer pricing and that Grad division can avoid $240 of selling expense by selling to Vtori division. Which division sets the minimum transfer price, and what is it? Which division sets the maximum transfer price, and what is it? Do you suppose that Grad and Vtori divisions would choose to transfer somewhere in the bargaining range?

OBJECTIVE 5
CORNERSTONE 12.5

Cornerstone Exercise 12-5 **Calculating Cycle Time and Velocity**

Sempel Company has the following data for one of its manufacturing plants:

a. Maximum units produced in a quarter (3-month period): 800,000 units
b. Actual units produced in a quarter (3-month period): 750,000 units
c. Productive hours in one quarter: 84,000 hours

Required:

1. Compute the theoretical cycle time (in minutes).
2. Compute the actual cycle time (in minutes).
3. Compute the theoretical velocity in units per hour.
4. Compute the actual velocity in units per hour.

OBJECTIVE 5
CORNERSTONE 12.6

Cornerstone Exercise 12-6 **Calculating Manufacturing Cycle Efficiency**

Cheval Company has the following data for one of its manufacturing plants:

a. Maximum units produced in a quarter (3-month period): 500,000 units
b. Actual units produced in a quarter (3-month period): 400,000 units
c. Productive hours in one quarter: 50,000 hours
d. Actual cycle time: 7.5 minutes
e. Theoretical cycle time: 6 minutes

Required:

1. Calculate the amount of processing time and the amount of nonprocessing time.
2. Calculate the MCE.

EXERCISES

Exercise 12-7 **Types of Responsibility Centres**

Consider each of the following independent scenarios:

a. Terrin Belson, plant manager for the laser printer factory of Compugear Inc., shook his head and sighed. December had been a bad month: two machines had broken down, and some factory production workers (all on salary) were idled for part of the month. Materials prices increased, and insurance premiums on the factory increased. There was no way out of it; costs were going up. He hoped that the marketing vice-president would be able to push through some price increases, but that really wasn't his department.
b. Joanna Pauly was delighted to see that her ROI figures had increased for the third straight year. She was sure that her campaign to lower costs and use machinery more efficiently (enabling her factories to sell several older machines) was the reason why. Joanna planned to take full credit for the improvements at her semiannual performance review.
c. Gil Caron, sales manager for Computer Works, was not pleased with a memo from headquarters detailing the recent cost increases for the laser printer line. Headquarters suggested raising prices. "Great," thought Gil, "an increase in price will kill sales and revenue will go down. Why can't the plant shape up and cut costs like every other company in Canada is doing? Why turn this into my problem?"
d. Susan Whitehorse looked at the quarterly profit/loss statement with disgust. Revenue was down, and cost was up—what a combination! Then she had an idea: If she cut back on

maintenance of equipment and let a product engineer go, expenses would decrease—perhaps enough to reverse the trend in income.

e. Shonna Lowry had just been hired to improve the fortunes of the southern division of ABC Inc. She met with top staff and hammered out a three-year plan to improve the situation. A centrepiece of the plan is the retirement of obsolete equipment and the purchase of state-of-the-art, computer-assisted machinery. The new machinery would take time for the workers to learn to use, but once that was done, waste would virtually be eliminated.

Required:

For each of the above independent scenarios, indicate the type of responsibility centre involved (cost, revenue, profit, or investment).

Exercise 12-8 Margin, Turnover, Return on Investment

OBJECTIVE 2

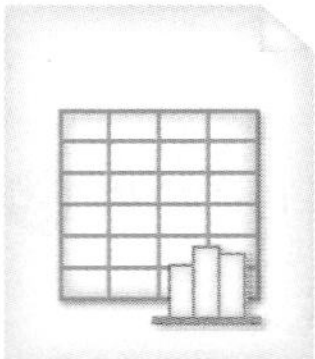

King Company had sales of $18,000,000, expenses of $12,375,000, and average operating assets of $7,200,000.

Required:

1. Compute the operating income.
2. Compute the margin and turnover ratios.
3. Compute the ROI.

Exercise 12-9 Margin, Turnover, Return on Investment, Average Operating Assets

OBJECTIVE 2

Liu Company provided the following income statement for last year:

Sales	$1,040,000
Less: Variable expenses	700,250
Contribution margin	339,750
Less: Fixed expenses	183,750
Operating income	$ 156,000

At the beginning of last year, Liu had $28,300 in operating assets. At the end of the year, Liu had $23,700 in operating assets.

Required:

1. Compute average operating assets.
2. Compute the margin and turnover ratios for last year.
3. Compute ROI.
4. CONCEPTUAL CONNECTION Briefly explain the meaning of ROI.
5. CONCEPTUAL CONNECTION Comment on why the ROI for Liu Company is relatively high (as compared to the lower ROI of a typical manufacturing company).

Exercise 12-10 Return on Investment, Margin, Turnover

Data follow for the Dogar division of Nanda Inc.:

	Year 1	Year 2
Sales	$148,500,000	$162,250,000
Operating income	8,910,000	8,112,500
Average operating assets	337,500,000	405,625,000

Required:

1. Compute the margin and turnover ratios for each year.
2. Compute the ROI for each year.

OBJECTIVE 3

Exercise 12-11 Residual Income

The Faber division of Fondori Company had operating income last year of $170,250 and operating assets of $3,625,000. Fondori's minimum acceptable rate of return is 5 percent.

Required:

1. Calculate the residual income for the Faber division.
2. Was the ROI for the Faber division greater than, less than, or equal to 5 percent?

OBJECTIVE 3

Exercise 12-12 Economic Value Added

Malik Company had net (after-tax) income last year of $12,375,400 and operating assets of $111,754,000. Malik's actual cost of capital was 9 percent.

Required:

1. Calculate the EVA for Malik Company.
2. CONCEPTUAL CONNECTION Is Malik creating or destroying wealth?

OBJECTIVE 3

Exercise 12-13 Economic Value Added

S.P.R. Company has two divisions: the Tana division and the Rabinur division. The following information pertains to last year's results:

	Tana Division	Rabinur Division
Net (after-tax) income	$ 907,500	$ 472,500
Operating assets	6,000,000	4,875,000

S.P.R.'s actual cost of capital was 12 percent.

Required:

1. Calculate the EVA for the Tana division.
2. Calculate the EVA for the Rabinur division.
3. CONCEPTUAL CONNECTION Is each division creating or destroying wealth?
4. CONCEPTUAL CONNECTION Describe generally the types of actions that S.P.R. Company's management team could take to increase Rabinur division's EVA.

OBJECTIVE 3

Exercise 12-14 Residual Income

Refer to the S.P.R. Company information in **Exercise 12-13**. In addition, S.P.R. Company's top management has set a minimum acceptable rate of return equal to 8 percent.

Required:

1. Calculate the residual income for the Tana division.
2. Calculate the residual income for the Rabinur division.

OBJECTIVE 4

Exercise 12-15 Transfer Pricing

Electromotion Inc. has a number of divisions, including an electric vehicle (EV) charger manufacturing division and an EV charger installation division. The installation division employs 30 electricians who are hired to install EV chargers in residential garages and small business locations. Each year, the installation division purchases EV chargers for installation at customer locations. Currently, it purchases EV chargers from an outside supplier for $400 each. The manager of the manufacturing division has approached the manager of the installation division about selling EV chargers directly. The full product cost to manufacture an EV charger is $290. The manufacturing division can sell all of the EV chargers it makes to outside installers for $400. The installation division needs 15,000 EV chargers per year; the manufacturing division has capacity to make up to 65,000 EV chargers per year.

Required:

1. Which division is motivated to set a maximum transfer price? Which division is motivated to set a minimum transfer price?
2. If company policy is that all internal transfers between division are at full cost, what is the transfer price?
3. CONCEPTUAL CONNECTION Do you think that the transfer will occur at the company-mandated transfer price (i.e., full cost)? Why or why not?

Exercise 12-16 Transfer Pricing

OBJECTIVE 4

Refer to the Electromotion Inc. company information shown in **Exercise 12-15**. Also, assume that the company policy is for all transfer prices to be negotiated by the divisions involved.

Required:

1. What is the maximum transfer price? Which division sets it?
2. What is the minimum transfer price? Which division sets it?
3. CONCEPTUAL CONNECTION If the transfer takes place, what will be the transfer price? Does it matter whether or not the transfer takes place?

Exercise 12-17 Transfer Pricing

OBJECTIVE 4

Refer to the Electromotion Inc. company information shown in **Exercise 12-15**. Also, although the manufacturing division has been operating at capacity (65,000 EV chargers per year), it expects to produce and sell only 50,000 EV chargers for $400 each next year. The manufacturing division incurs variable costs of $175 to produce each EV charger. The company policy is for all transfer prices to be negotiated by the divisions involved.

Required:

1. What is the maximum transfer price? Which division sets it?
2. What is the minimum transfer price? Which division sets it?
3. Suppose that the two divisions agree on a transfer price of $300. What is the change in operating income for the manufacturing division? For the installation division? For Electromotion as a whole?

Exercise 12-18 Calculating Transfer Price

OBJECTIVE 4

Jelkin Corporation is a processor of apples. The manufacturing facility has two divisions: the puree division and the finishing division. As apples arrive at the facility, the puree division cleans and purees the apples into a smooth sauce. The apple sauce may be packaged in the puree division and sold on the wholesale market for $22 a batch, or transferred to the finishing division where it is packaged in glass jars and sold to grocery stores for $35 per batch. Jelkin is able to produce 400,000 batches per year and reports the following costs per batch:

	Puree Division	Finishing Division
Direct material cost	$ 8.00	$ 6.00
Direct manufacturing labour cost	2.50	0.75
Variable overhead cost	3.25	1.50
Fixed overhead cost	1.25	2.75
Full manufacturing cost	$15.00	$11.00

Required:

1. What is the minimum transfer price the puree division manager would accept? What is the maximum transfer price the finishing division would accept? Briefly explain.
2. Assuming the 400,000 batches are transferred to the finishing division, compute the operating income for each division using: (a) market price for the transfer price, and (b) full manufacturing cost plus 10 percent for the transfer price.
3. If the division managers are awarded a bonus based on division operating income, briefly explain which transfer price each division manager would prefer.

OBJECTIVE 5

Exercise 12-19 Cycle Time and Velocity

Prakesh Company has the following data for one of its manufacturing cells:

a. Maximum units produced in a month: 150,000 units
b. Actual units produced in a month: 120,000 units
c. Hours of production labour in one month: 30,000 hours

Required:

1. Compute the theoretical cycle time (in minutes).
2. Compute the actual cycle time (in minutes).
3. Compute the theoretical velocity (in units per hour).
4. Compute the actual velocity (in units per hour).

OBJECTIVE 5

Exercise 12-20 Cycle Time and Velocity

Arnaud Company divided its tool production factory into manufacturing cells. Each cell produces one product. The cordless drill cell had the following data for last quarter:

a. Maximum units produced in a quarter: 270,000 units
b. Actual units produced in a quarter: 225,000 units
c. Hours of cell production labour in a quarter: 90,000 hours

Required:

1. Compute the theoretical cycle time (in minutes).
2. Compute the actual cycle time (in minutes).
3. Compute the theoretical velocity (in units per hour).
4. Compute the actual velocity (in units per hour).

OBJECTIVE 5

Exercise 12-21 Manufacturing Cycle Efficiency

Ventris Company found that one of its manufacturing cells had actual cycle time of 15 minutes per unit. The theoretical cycle time for this cell was 9 minutes per unit.

Required:

1. Calculate the amount of processing time per unit and the amount of nonprocessing time per unit.
2. Calculate the MCE.

OBJECTIVE 5

Exercise 12-22 Manufacturing Cycle Efficiency

Hemp Company provided the following information on one of its factories:

a. Maximum units produced in a quarter: 266,667 units
b. Actual units produced in a quarter: 240,000 units
c. Hours of production labour in a quarter: 80,000 hours
d. Theoretical cycle time: 18 minutes per unit
e. Actual cycle time: 20 minutes per unit

Required:

1. Calculate the amount of processing time per unit and the amount of nonprocessing time per unit.
2. Calculate the MCE.

PROBLEMS

OBJECTIVE 2

Problem 12-23 Calculating Return on Investment

Cucina Corporation operates using a decentralized organization structure where the two service divisions—the Marche division and the Aversa division—are investment centres. The company requires a minimum rate of return of 8 percent and evaluates all managers on the basis of division ROI. Recently, each division was approached to consider different investment opportunities.

Marche division was asked to consider an investment that requires $600,000 in capital and will provide a return of $60,000. Currently the Marche division has $180,000 in operating income and has $1 million in average operating assets.

Aversa division was asked to consider an investment that requires $800,000 in capital and provides a return of $56,000. Currently the Aversa division has $62,500 in operating income and has $1.25 million in average operating assets.

For Cucina Corporation, all managers are evaluated based upon division income.

Required:

For Marche division:

1. Compute the ROI of the investment.
2. Would the Marche division manager accept the investment? Why or why not? Do you agree with the manager's decision?

For Aversa division:

1. Compute the ROI of the investment.
2. Would the Aversa division manager accept the investment? Why or why not? Do you agree with the manager's decision?
3. What are the advantages and disadvantages of using ROI to evaluate investment opportunities?

Problem 12-24 Return on Investment and Investment Decisions

OBJECTIVE 2 3

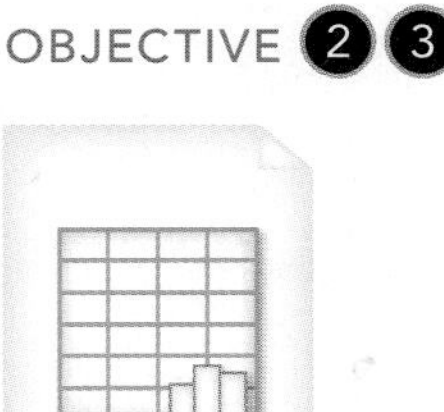

Ibrahima Duncan was debating the merits of a new product. Currently, the budgeted income of the manufacturing division was $1,450,000 with operating assets of $7,250,000. The proposed investment would add income of $1,280,000 and would require an additional investment in equipment of $8,000,000. The minimum required ROI for the company is 12 percent. Round all numbers to two decimal places.

Required:

1. Compute the ROI of:
   a. The division if the project is not undertaken.
   b. The project alone.
   c. The division if the project is undertaken.
2. Compute the residual income of:
   a. The division if the project is not undertaken.
   b. The project alone.
   c. The division if the project is undertaken.
3. CONCEPTUAL CONNECTION Do you suppose that Ibrahima will decide to invest in the new project? Why or why not?

Check figures:
1.b. 0.16, or 16%
2.c. $900,000

Problem 12-25 Return on Investment, Residual Income, and Economic Value Added Calculations

OBJECTIVE 

FunFund operates as two profit centres: an amusement park based in Ontario, and a second amusement park based in New Brunswick. Consider the following data for the two geographical divisions of FunFund.

	Ontario	New Brunswick
Total assets	$6,000,000	$2,500,000
Current liabilities	2,800,000	500,000
Operating income	840,000	200,000
After-tax income	510,000	140,000
Total capital employed	3,750,000	1,500,000

(Continued)

Required:

1. Calculate the ROI for each division using operating income as the measure of income and using total assets as the measure of investment.
2. FunFund has used residual income as a measure of management success, the variable it wants a manager to maximize. Using this criterion, what is the residual income for each division using operating income and total assets if the required rate of return on investment is 10 percent?
3. FunFund is considering the use of EVA as a measure of management success. Compute the EVA for each division, assuming the company has an 8 percent cost of capital.
4. Which of the measures calculated in Requirements 1, 2, and 3 would you recommend FunFund use and why? Explain briefly.

OBJECTIVE 2

Problem 12-26 Return on Investment, Margin, Turnover

Kamir Lumber is facing stiff competition from imported goods. Its operating income margin has been declining steadily for the past several years; the company has been forced to lower prices so that it can maintain its market share. The operating results for the past three years are as follows:

	Year 1	Year 2	Year 3
Sales	$5,000,000	$4,750,000	$4,500,000
Operating income	600,000	522,500	472,500
Average assets	7,500,000	7,500,000	7,500,000

For the coming year, Kamir's president plans to install a JIT purchasing and manufacturing system. She estimates that inventories will be reduced by 70 percent during the first year of operations, producing a 20 percent reduction in the average operating assets of the company, which would remain unchanged without the JIT system. She also estimates that sales and operating income will be restored to year 1 levels because of simultaneous reductions in per-unit operating expenses and selling prices. Lower selling prices will allow Kamir to expand its market share.

Required:

1. Compute the ROI, margin, and turnover for years 1, 2, and 3.
2. CONCEPTUAL CONNECTION Suppose that in year 4 the sales and operating income were achieved as expected, but inventories remained at the same level as in year 3. Compute the expected ROI, margin, and turnover. Explain why the ROI increased over the year 3 level.
3. CONCEPTUAL CONNECTION Suppose that the sales and net operating income for year 4 remained the same as in year 3 but inventory reductions were achieved as projected. Compute the ROI, margin, and turnover. Explain why the ROI exceeded the year 3 level.
4. CONCEPTUAL CONNECTION Assume that all expectations for year 4 were realized. Compute the expected ROI, margin, and turnover. Explain why the ROI increased over the year 3 level.

Check figures:
1. ROI year 3 = 6.30%
2. Turnover = 0.67
3. Turnover = 0.75

OBJECTIVE 

Problem 12-27 Return on Investment for Multiple Investments, Residual Income

The manager of a division that produces add-on products for the automobile industry has just been presented the opportunity to invest in two independent projects. The first is an air conditioner for the back seats of vans and minivans. The second is a turbocharger. Without the investments, the division will have average assets for the coming year of $28.9 million and expected operating income of $4.335 million. The outlay required for each investment and the expected operating incomes are as follows:

	Air Conditioner	Turbocharger
Outlay	$750,000	$540,000
Operating income	90,000	82,080

Required:

1. Compute the ROI for each investment project.
2. Compute the budgeted divisional ROI for each of the following four alternatives:
   a. The air conditioner investment is made.
   b. The turbocharger investment is made.
   c. Both investments are made.
   d. Neither additional investment is made.
3. CONCEPTUAL CONNECTION Assuming that divisional managers are evaluated and rewarded on the basis of ROI performance, which alternative do you think the divisional manager will choose?
4. CONCEPTUAL CONNECTION Suppose that the company sets a minimum required rate of return equal to 14 percent. Calculate the residual income for each of the following four alternatives:
   a. The air conditioner investment is made.
   b. The turbocharger investment is made.
   c. Both investments are made.
   d. Neither additional investment is made.
   Which option will the manager choose based on residual income? Explain.
5. CONCEPTUAL CONNECTION Suppose that the company sets a minimum required rate of return equal to 10 percent. Calculate the residual income for each of the following four alternatives:
   a. The air conditioner investment is made.
   b. The turbocharger investment is made.
   c. Both investments are made.
   d. Neither additional investment is made.
   Based on residual income, are the investments profitable? Why does your answer differ from your answer in Requirement 3?

Check figures:
1. Turbocharger ROI = 15.2%
5.d. Residual income with neither investment = $1,445,000

Problem 12-28 Return on Investment and Economic Value Added Calculations with Varying Assumptions

OBJECTIVE  

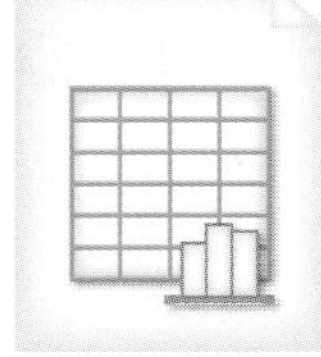

Asan Products is a division of Omar Fabrics Inc. During the coming year, it expects to earn income of $310,000 based on sales of $3.45 million; without any new investments, the division will have average operating assets of $3 million. The division is considering a capital investment project—adding knitting machines to produce gaiters—that requires an additional investment of $600,000 and increases net income by $57,500 (sales would increase by $575,000). If made, the investment would increase beginning operating assets by $600,000 and ending operating assets by $400,000. Assume that the actual cost of capital for the company is 7 percent.

Required:

1. Compute the ROI for the division without the investment.
2. Compute the margin and turnover ratios without the investment. Show that the product of the margin and turnover ratios equals the ROI computed in Requirement 1.
3. CONCEPTUAL CONNECTION Compute the ROI for the division with the new investment. Do you think the divisional manager will approve the investment?
4. CONCEPTUAL CONNECTION Compute the margin and turnover ratios for the division with the new investment. Compare these with the old ratios.
5. CONCEPTUAL CONNECTION Compute the EVA of the division with and without the investment. Should the manager decide to make the knitting machine investment?

Check figures:
2. ROI = 10.34%
4. Margin = 9.13%
5. EVA with investment = $122,500

Problem 12-29 Transfer Pricing

OBJECTIVE 

Ultimate Watercraft Ltd. provides small watercraft to the Canadian market. It has three divisions that produce the small boats: the leisure division, the amateur sport division, and the expert whitewater products division. Each division produces the body of the boat and buys accessories from outside suppliers. Recently, the amateur sport division of Ultimate Watercraft acquired a manufacturer of plastic seats that are common to all of the boats sold by all divisions. Company policy permits each manager to decide whether to buy or sell internally. Each divisional manager is evaluated on the basis of ROI and EVA.

The leisure division had bought its plastic seats from a vendor in Mexico. The average price paid was $55 per seat. However, the acquisition of the seat manufacturer made Fred Floatsum, manager of the leisure division, wonder whether a more favourable price could be arranged. He decided to approach Patricia Paddle, manager of the amateur sport division, to see if she wanted to offer a better price for an internal transfer. He suggested a transfer of 12,000 seats at $45 per seat to his leisure division.

Patricia gathered the following information regarding the cost of the plastic seats:

Direct materials	$24
Direct labour	4
Variable overhead	6
Fixed overhead*	8
Total unit cost	$42

* Fixed overhead is based on $480,000/60,000 seats.

Selling price	$55
Production capacity	60,000 seats

Required:

1. CONCEPTUAL CONNECTION Suppose that the seat factory is producing at capacity and can sell all that it produces to outside customers. How should Patricia respond to Fred's request for a lower transfer price?
2. CONCEPTUAL CONNECTION Now assume that the seat factory is currently selling 45,000 seats. What are the minimum and maximum transfer prices? Should Patricia consider the transfer at $45 per seat?
3. CONCEPTUAL CONNECTION Suppose that Ultimate Watercraft's policy is that all transfer prices be set at full cost plus 35 percent. Would the transfer take place? Why or why not?

Check figure:
2. Minimum price = $34

Problem 12-30 Setting Transfer Prices—Market Price versus Full Cost

Red Deer Electronics Inc. manufactures a variety of printers, scanners, and fax machines in its two divisions: the PSF division and the components division. The components division produces electronic components that can be used by the PSF division. All of the components that this division produces can be sold to outside customers; however, from the beginning, nearly 90 percent of its output has been used internally. The current policy requires that all internal transfers of components be made at full cost.

Recently, Cam DeVonn, the chief executive officer of Red Deer Electronics, decided to investigate the transfer pricing policy. He was concerned that the current method of pricing internal transfers might force decisions by divisional managers that would be suboptimal for the firm. As part of his inquiry, he gathered some information concerning component Y34, which is used by the PSF division in its production of a basic scanner, model SC67.

The PSF division sells 40,000 units of model SC67 each year at a unit price of $42. Given current market conditions, this is the maximum price that the division can charge for model SC67. The cost of manufacturing the scanner follows:

Component Y34	$ 6.50
Direct materials	12.50
Direct labour	3.00
Variable overhead	1.00
Fixed overhead	15.00
Total unit cost	$38.00

The scanner is produced efficiently, and no further reduction in manufacturing costs is possible.

The manager of the components division indicated that she could sell 40,000 units (the division's capacity for this part) of component Y34 to outside buyers at $12 per unit. The PSF division could also buy the part for $12 from external suppliers. She supplied the following details on the manufacturing cost of the component:

Direct materials	$2.50
Direct labour	0.50
Variable overhead	1.00
Fixed overhead	2.50
Total unit cost	$6.50

Required:

1. Compute the firmwide contribution margin associated with component Y34 and model SC67. Also, compute the contribution margin earned by each division.
2. Suppose that Cam DeVonn abolishes the current transfer pricing policy and gives divisions autonomy in setting transfer prices. Can you predict what transfer price the manager of the components division will set? What should be the minimum transfer price for this part? The maximum transfer price?
3. CONCEPTUAL CONNECTION Given the new transfer pricing policy, predict how this will affect the production decision of the PSF division manager for model SC67. How many units of component Y34 will the manager of the PSF division purchase, either internally or externally?
4. CONCEPTUAL CONNECTION Given the new transfer price set by the components division and your answer to Requirement 3, how many units of Y34 will be sold externally?
5. CONCEPTUAL CONNECTION Given your answers to Requirements 3 and 4, compute the firmwide contribution margin. What has happened? Was Cam's decision to grant additional decentralization good or bad?

Check figures:
1. Model SC67 contribution margin = $760,000
5. Contribution margin = $320,000

Problem 12-31 Full Cost-Plus Pricing and Negotiation

OBJECTIVE 

Technovia Inc. has two divisions: auxiliary components and audio systems. Divisional managers are encouraged to maximize ROI and EVA. Managers are essentially free to determine whether goods will be transferred internally and what the internal transfer prices will be. Headquarters has directed that all internal prices be expressed on a full cost-plus basis. The markup in the full cost pricing arrangement, however, is left to the discretion of the divisional managers. Recently, the two divisional managers met to discuss a pricing agreement for a subwoofer that would be sold with a personal computer system. Production of the subwoofers is at capacity. Subwoofers can be sold for $31 to outside customers. The audio systems division can also buy the subwoofer from external sources for the same price; however, the manager of this division is hoping to obtain a price concession by buying internally. The full cost of manufacturing the subwoofer is $20. If the manager of the auxiliary components division sells the subwoofer internally, $5 of selling and distribution costs can be avoided. The volume of business would be 250,000 units per year, which is well within the capacity of the producing division.

After some discussion, the two managers agreed on a full cost-plus pricing scheme that would be reviewed annually. Any increase in the outside selling price would be added to the transfer price by simply increasing the markup by an appropriate amount. Any major changes in the factors that led to the agreement could initiate a new round of negotiation; otherwise, the full cost-plus arrangement would continue in force for subsequent years.

Required:

1. Calculate the minimum and maximum transfer prices.
2. Assume that the transfer price agreed on between the two managers is halfway between the minimum and maximum transfer prices. Calculate this transfer price. What markup over full cost is implied by this transfer price?
3. Refer to Requirement 2. Assume that in the following year, the outside price of subwoofers increases to $32. What is the new full cost-plus transfer price?

(Continued)

Check figure:
2. Markup percentage = 42.5%

4. CONCEPTUAL CONNECTION Assume that two years after the initial agreement, the market for subwoofers has softened considerably, causing excess capacity for the auxiliary components division. Would you expect a renegotiation of the full cost-plus pricing arrangement for the coming year? Explain.

OBJECTIVE 5

Problem 12-32 Cycle Time, Velocity, Conversion Cost

The theoretical cycle time for a product is 30 minutes per unit. The budgeted conversion costs for the manufacturing cell are $2,700,000 per year. The total labour minutes available are 600,000. During the year, the cell was able to produce 1.5 units of the product per hour. Suppose also that production incentives exist to minimize unit product costs.

Required:

1. Compute the theoretical conversion cost per unit.
2. Compute the applied conversion cost per unit (the amount of conversion cost actually assigned to the product).
3. CONCEPTUAL CONNECTION Discuss how this approach to assigning conversion costs can improve delivery time performance.

Check figure:
1. Theoretical conversion cost per unit = $135

OBJECTIVE 5

Problem 12-33 Balanced Scorecard

The following list gives a number of measures associated with the Balanced Scorecard:

- Number of new customers
- Percentage of customer complaints resolved with one contact
- Unit product cost
- Cost per distribution channel
- Suggestions per employee
- Warranty repair costs
- Consumer satisfaction (from surveys)
- Cycle time for solving a customer problem
- Strategic job coverage ratio
- On-time delivery percentage
- Percentage of revenues from new products

Required:

1. Classify each performance measure as belonging to one of the following perspectives: financial, customer, internal business process, or learning and growth.
2. Suggest an additional measure for each of the four perspectives.

PROFESSIONAL EXAMINATION PROBLEMS*

Professional Examination Problem 12-34 Performance Evaluation and Decentralization—Messene Corporation

The Alpha division of Messene Corporation produces one product, a universal control that can be utilized in most hydraulic systems. Variable manufacturing costs are $16 and the fixed costs associated with operating the factory are $380,000 for 40,000 units. The selling price is $34 per unit. The division has net operating assets of $2,250,000 and the capacity to produce 50,000 units. Corporate management has a target rate of return of 16 percent on investment.

The Beta division of Messene is now buying 8,000 similar controls from outside suppliers at $30 each, but would like to purchase the same number of universal controls from the Alpha division if the price was $30. The manager of the Alpha division refuses to sell at that price since it would lower her ROI. She has produced the following figures to prove her point:

Selling price per unit		$30.00
Variable cost	$16.00	
Fixed cost ($380,000/40,000)	9.50	25.50
Margin per unit		$ 4.50

Required:

1. What profit margin percentage must the Alpha division achieve in order to meet the desired ROI of 16 percent, assuming a selling price of $34?
2. Calculate the Alpha division's current ROI and future ROI if the offer is accepted. Explain the behaviour of the manager of the Alpha division.

Professional Examination Problem 12-35 **Transfer Pricing—Ajax Division**

The Ajax division of Pylos Corporation, operating at capacity, has been asked by the Naxos division to supply it with part 123. Ajax sells this part to its customers for $7.50 each. Naxos, operating at 50 percent capacity, is willing to pay $5.00 for each unit. Naxos will put the unit into an assembly that it will manufacture on a cost-plus basis for an outside manufacturer if it wins the bid. Naxos has no other source of supply for part 123.

Ajax has a variable cost of producing part 123 of $4.25. The cost of the assembly being built by Naxos is:

Purchased parts—outside vendors	$22.50
Pay Ajax for part 123	5.00
Other variable costs	14.00
Fixed overhead	8.00
Total cost	$49.50

Naxos believes $49.50 is the maximum price that can be included in the bid.

Required:

1. As controller of Ajax, would you recommend that Ajax supply Naxos with part 123?
2. Would it be to the short-run advantage of Pylos for Ajax to supply Naxos?

CASES

Case 12-36 **Return on Investment, Ethical Considerations**

Jason Kemp had conflicting emotions. On the one hand, things were going so well. He had just completed six months as the assistant financial manager in the electronics division of Med-Products Inc. The pay was good, he enjoyed his co-workers, and he felt that he was part of a team that was making a difference in Canadian health care. On the other hand, his latest assignment was causing some sleepless nights.

Mel Cravens, his boss, had asked him to "refine" the figures on the division's latest project—a portable imaging device code-named ZM. The original estimates called for investment of $15.6 million and projected annual income of $1.87 million. Med-Products required an ROI of at least 15 percent for new project approval; so far, ZM's rate of return was nowhere near

(Continued)

that hurdle rate. Mel encouraged him to show increased sales and decreased expenses in order to get the projected income above $2.34 million. Jason asked for a meeting with Mel to voice his concerns.

Jason: Mel, I've gone over the figures for the new project and can't find any way to get the income above $1.9 million. The salespeople have given me the most likely revenue figures, and production feels that the expense figures are solid.

Mel: Jason, those figures are just projections. Sales doesn't really know what the revenue will be. In fact, when I talked with Sue Harris, our sales vice-president, she said that sales could range from $1.5 million to $2.5 million. Use the higher figure. I'm sure this product will justify our confidence in it!

Jason: I know the range of sales was that broad, but Sue felt the $2.5 million estimate was pretty unlikely. She thought that, during the first five years or so, ZM sales would stay in the lower end of the range.

Mel: Again, Sue doesn't know for sure. She's just estimating. Let's go with the higher estimate. We really need this product to expand our line and to give our division a chance to qualify for sales-based bonuses. If ZM sells at all, our revenue will go up, and we'll all share in the bonus pool!

Jason: I don't know, Mel. I feel pretty bad signing off on ROI projections that I have so little confidence in.

Mel: (frustrated) Look, Jason, just prepare the report. I'll back you up.

Required:

1. What is the ROI of project ZM based on the initial estimates? What would ROI be if the income rose to $2.34 million?
2. CONCEPTUAL CONNECTION Do you agree that Jason has an ethical dilemma? Explain. Is there any way that Mel could ethically justify raising the sales estimates and/or lowering expense estimates?
3. What do you think Jason should do? Explain.

OBJECTIVE 

Case 12-37 Balanced Scorecard

Karen is the executive director for a nonprofit daycare organization called Kids-Can-Play. There is an emerging trend in daycare organizations to replace traditional curriculum delivery (i.e., formalized learning via pre-planned themes, activities, and schedules) with play-based learning. Rather than force structured learning on young children, play-based learning leverages the natural curiosity of children by allowing them to lead the direction of learning activities. For example, if a child's curiosity is piqued by an excavator passing by the daycare site, the early childhood educator (ECE) should be spontaneous and work the excavator into the day's lessons. Perhaps children first discuss what excavators do, then they might draw their own versions of an excavator, followed by reading a storybook that features an excavator. Following this, the children (with careful guidance from the ECE) might lead their learning into something related such as how homes are built, or what other objects share the same colour or size. While the organization implements this change, Kids-Can-Play would also like to offer more innovative options for parents to accommodate their unique schedules (e.g., shift work) and to offer other convenient options (e.g., weekend daycare while parents do grocery shopping or other errands).

Karen has heard that the Balanced Scorecard is a valuable strategic management system that can help an organization translate its mission and strategy into operational objectives and performance measures, but is unsure about how to construct one for Kids-Can-Play. Karen has asked you to draft a Balanced Scorecard to facilitate Kids-Can-Play's transition from traditional curriculum delivery to play-based learning, as well as the organization's desire to offer more innovative options to parents. Karen is hoping that Kids-Can-Play can make both changes concurrently, and so she is hoping you will be able to suggest a relatively simple (i.e., two objectives for each perspective) scorecard that accounts for both changes. She is also worried that as a non-profit organization faced with the financial constraints common to not-for-profits, she is at risk of investing significant time and money into a product that will end up deep in a file drawer. She has asked that in addition to drafting a scorecard for the organization, you provide some guidance on how she can ensure the successful implementation and use of the Balanced Scorecard in Kids-Can-Play.

Required:

Develop a Balanced Scorecard to meet Karen's needs.

13

Short-Run Decision Making: Relevant Costing

After studying Chapter 13, you should be able to:

1. Describe the short-run decision-making model, and explain how cost behaviour affects the information used to make decisions.
2. Apply relevant costing and decision-making concepts in a variety of business situations.
3. Choose the optimal product mix when faced with one constrained resource.
4. Explain the impact of cost on pricing decisions.

Courtesy of Navistar

EXPERIENCE MANAGERIAL DECISIONS

with Navistar

Relevant decision analysis represents one of the most exciting and widely applicable managerial accounting tools in existence. One big proponent of relevant analysis is Navistar International Truck and Engine Corporation. Navistar manufactures components and electronics for a wide variety of vehicles—including buses, tractor-trailers, military vehicles, and trucks—for its diverse customers all around the world. When faced with additional important long-term growth issues, Navistar used relevant analysis to decide whether to expand axle production at its truck assembly plant in Chatham, Ontario, or to outsource its extra axle production requirements to an outside supplier.

Before the analysis could be conducted, Navistar's managerial accountants had to identify all relevant factors, both quantitative and qualitative, as well as the short-term and long-term impacts of these factors. Some factors were relatively easy to identify and measure, such as the labour cost that would be required if the additional axles were made in-house, or the cost of acquiring the extra factory space needed to produce the additional axles in-house. However, other factors complicated the analysis for Navistar, such as the need to eliminate bottlenecks that would be created from in-house production of the additional axles. In addition, if Navistar decided to make the additional axles in-house, it would require significant capacity-related capital expenditures, which carried a risk associated with the possibility that the current demand for additional axles might not persist in the long term. In this case, Navistar would be stuck with the cost of the additional capacity without the business to generate additional revenues to cover those costs. On the other hand, if the additional axle production were outsourced, Navistar would have to ensure that its new axle supplier partnered with the Canadian Auto Workers union (CAW) to minimize the outsourcing effect on Navistar's existing workforce-labour agreements. Furthermore, suppliers would have to be trained to deliver parts and subassemblies in sequence with Navistar's demanding schedule. This training represented a considerable outsourcing cost to Navistar.

In the end, the relevant costing analysis helped Navistar's executives decide to outsource its additional axle production, resulting in an annual cost savings of over $3 million! Further operational improvements soon followed, with Navistar consolidating its motor coach production and closing both its Chatham facility and Union City, Indiana, subsidiary. As a result, the company expected savings of $20 million to $30 million per year.

INTERNATIONAL

Navistar

Decision making is a key management responsibility. Often, it is useful to consider decision making as either long-run or short-run. Long-run decision making, often involving investment in property, plant, and equipment, is referred to as capital budgeting. That topic is covered in Chapter 14. The use of cost and revenue data in making short-run decisions, such as the acceptance of special orders or choosing to outsource the production of parts rather than make them in-house, is the focus of this chapter.

SHORT-RUN DECISION MAKING

OBJECTIVE 

Describe the short-run decision-making model, and explain how cost behaviour affects the information used to make decisions.

Short-run decision making consists of choosing among alternatives with an immediate or limited timeframe. Accepting a special order for less than the normal selling price to utilize idle capacity and to increase this year's profits is an example. Thus, some decisions tend to be short-run in nature; however, it should be emphasized that short-run decisions often have long-run consequences. Consider a second example. Suppose that a company is thinking about producing a component instead of buying it from suppliers. The immediate objective may be to lower the cost of making the main product. Yet this decision may be a small part of the overall strategy of establishing a cost leadership position for the firm. Therefore, short-run decisions can be small-scale actions that serve a larger purpose.

The Decision-Making Model

How does a company go about making good short-run decisions? A **decision model** (a specific set of procedures that lead to a decision) can be used to structure the decision maker's thinking and to organize the information to make optimal decisions. The following is an outline of one decision-making model.

1. Recognize and define the problem.
2. Identify alternatives as possible solutions to the problem; eliminate alternatives that are clearly not feasible.
3. Identify the costs and benefits associated with each feasible alternative. Classify costs and benefits as relevant or irrelevant, and eliminate irrelevant costs from consideration.
4. Estimate the relevant costs and benefits for each alternative.
5. Assess qualitative factors.
6. Make the decision by selecting the alternative with the greatest overall net benefit.

The decision-making model described has six steps, but nothing is special about this particular listing. You may find it more useful to break the steps into eight or ten segments. Alternatively, you may find it useful to aggregate them into a shorter list. For example, you could use a three-step model: (1) identify the decision, (2) identify alternatives and their associated relevant costs, and (3) make the decision. The key point is to find a comfortable way for you to remember the important steps in the decision-making model.

To illustrate the decision-making model, consider Audio-Blast Inc., a company that manufactures speaker systems for new automobiles. Recently, Audio-Blast was approached by a major automobile manufacturer about the possibility of purchasing 20,000 of Audio-Blast's main product—the mega-blast speaker system—for installation by the manufacturer into its new sports car. That way, Audio-Blast speakers would be installed at the factory. Suppose that Audio-Blast decides to pursue the speaker order from the automobile manufacturer. Currently, the company does not have sufficient productive and storage capacity to fulfill the order. How might the decision-making model help Audio-Blast find the best way of obtaining the needed capacity?

Step 1: Define the Problem The first step is to recognize and define a specific problem. For example, the members of Audio-Blast's management team recognized the need for additional productive capacity as well as increased space for raw materials and finished goods inventories. The number of workers and the amount of space needed, the reasons for the need, and how the additional space would be used are all important dimensions of the problem. However, the central question is *how* to acquire the additional capacity.

Step 2: Identify the Alternatives The second step is to list and consider possible solutions, which Audio-Blast's production head and consulting engineer determined to be:

1. Build a new factory with sufficient capacity to handle current and foreseeable needs.
2. Lease a larger facility, and sublease its current facility.
3. Lease an additional, similar facility.
4. Institute a second shift in the main factory, and lease an additional building that would be used for storage of raw materials and finished goods inventories only, thereby freeing up space for expanded production.
5. Outsource production to another company, and resell the speakers to the auto manufacturer.

As part of this step, Audio-Blast's upper management team met to discuss and eliminate alternatives that clearly were not feasible.

- Alternative 1—to build a new factory—was eliminated because it carried too much risk for the company. The order had not even been secured, and the popularity of the new sports car model was not proven. Audio-Blast's president refused to "bet the company" on such a risky proposition.
- Alternative 2—to lease a larger facility and sublease its current premises—was rejected because the economy in Audio-Blast's small town was such that subleasing a facility of its size was not possible.
- Alternative 3—to lease a second facility—was eliminated because it went too far in solving the space problem and, presumably, was too expensive.
- Alternatives 4 and 5—instituting a second shift and leasing a new storage site, or outsourcing production—were feasible; they were within the cost and risk constraints and solved the needs of the company.

Notice that the president linked the short-run decision (increase productive capacity) to the company's overall growth strategy by rejecting alternatives that involved too much risk at this stage of the company's development.

Step 3: Identify the Costs and Benefits Associated with Each Feasible Alternative In the third step, the costs and benefits associated with each feasible alternative are identified. At this point, clearly irrelevant costs can be eliminated from consideration. (It is fine to include irrelevant costs and benefits in the analysis as long as they are included for all alternatives. Since these costs and benefits are irrelevant, they will not impact the financial analysis, as will be shown in Step 4. The reason we usually do not include them is that focusing only on the relevant costs and benefits reduces the amount of data to be collected.) Typically, the controller is responsible for gathering the necessary data.

Assume Audio-Blast determines that the costs of making the 20,000 speakers include the following:

Direct materials	$ 60,000
Direct labour	110,000
Variable overhead	10,000
Total variable production cost	$180,000

In addition, a second shift must be put in place and a warehouse must be leased to store raw materials and finished goods inventories if Audio-Blast continues to manufacture the speakers internally. Additional costs of the second shift, including a production supervisor and part-time maintenance and engineering, amount to $90,000 per year. A building that could serve as a warehouse is sitting empty across the street and can be rented for $20,000 per year. Costs of operating the building for inventory storage—including telephone and Internet access as well as salaries of materials handlers—would amount to $80,000 per year. The second alternative is to purchase the speakers externally and use the freed-up production space for inventory. An outside supplier has offered to supply sufficient volume for $360,000 per year.

It should be mentioned that when the cash flow patterns become complicated for competing alternatives, more sophisticated procedures can and should be used for the analysis than those shown above. These procedures are discussed in Chapter 14, which deals with the long-run investment decisions referred to as capital expenditure decisions.

Step 4: Estimate the Relevant Costs and Benefits for Each Feasible Alternative

We now see that alternative 4—continuing to produce internally and leasing more space—costs $370,000, while alternative 5—purchasing outside and using internal space—costs $360,000. The comparison follows:

Alternative 4		**Alternative 5**	
Variable cost of production	$180,000	Purchase price	$360,000
Added second shift costs	90,000		
Building lease and operating costs	100,000		
Total	$370,000		

The **differential cost** is the difference between the summed costs of two alternatives in a decision. Notice that the differential cost is $10,000 in favour of alternative 5. Typically, a differential cost compares the sum of each alternative's *relevant* costs only, as in the differential cost comparison of alternatives 4 and 5. Emphasis on differential cost allows decision makers to occasionally include irrelevant costs in the alternatives if they choose to do so.

As noted earlier in the chapter, the inclusion of irrelevant costs is acceptable *only if all irrelevant costs are included for each alternative*. For example, suppose that the controller had included fixed manufacturing cost of $150,000 that must be paid whether the speakers are made internally or externally. Then, the total cost of each alternative would increase by $150,000—alternative 4 would total $520,000 and alternative 5 would total $510,000. However, the differential cost would still be $10,000.The inclusion of irrelevant costs often adds unnecessary data collection expenses and confusion in communicating additional information that is not relevant to the given analysis, therefore it is recommended to compare only relevant costs.

Step 5: Assess the Qualitative Factors While the costs and revenues associated with the alternatives are important, they do not tell the whole story. Qualitative factors—simply, those factors that are hard to put a value on, including things like political pressure and product safety—can significantly affect the manager's decision.

- *Political pressure*: Companies like Ford Motor Company and Levi's that relocate some or all of their North American manufacturing facilities to countries with cheaper labour often face stiff political pressure at home as a result of such offshoring decisions. Recently, the Royal Bank of Canada (RBC) revised its supplier code of conduct, which had permitted the outsourcing of Canadian jobs to companies that used temporary foreign workers. As a result of public outcry, RBC no longer outsources jobs offshore when the primary purpose is a savings in salaries. Some managers worry that such political pressure from customers can have long-term negative effects on sales that more than offset the labour cost savings that spurred the decision to outsource.
- *Product safety*: Product safety represents another key qualitative factor for outsourcing organizations, as illustrated by the trouble Mattel encountered when it was discovered that its Chinese suppliers used illegal lead paint on thousands of its toys.

Returning to Audio-Blast, its president likely would be concerned with qualitative considerations such as the quality of the speakers purchased externally, the reliability of supply sources, the expected stability of prices over the next several years, labour relations, community image, and so on. To illustrate the possible impact of qualitative factors on Audio-Blast's decision, consider the first two factors: quality and reliability of supply.

- *Quality*: If the quality of speakers is significantly less when purchased externally from what is available internally, then the quantitative advantage from purchasing may be more fictitious than real. Reselling lower-quality speakers to such a high-profile buyer could permanently damage Audio-Blast's reputation. Because of this possibility, Audio-Blast may choose to continue to produce the speakers internally.
- *Reliability of supply*: If supply sources are not reliable, production schedules could be interrupted, and customer orders could arrive late. These factors can increase labour costs and overhead, and hurt sales. Again, depending on the perceived trade-offs, Audio-Blast may decide that producing the speakers internally is better than purchasing them, even if relevant cost analysis gives the initial advantage to purchasing.

How should qualitative factors be handled in the decision-making process? First, they must be identified. Second, the decision maker should try to quantify them; often, qualitative factors are simply more difficult to quantify, not impossible. For example, possible unreliability of the outside supplier might be quantified as the probable number of late delivery days multiplied by the penalty Audio-Blast would be charged by the auto manufacturer for late delivery. More difficult measurement challenges exist. For example, Mobil Corporation decided to implement a strategic change of focusing on a new target audience, including "road warriors" (employees who drive a lot), "true blues" (affluent, loyal customers), and generation F3 (yuppies on the go who want *fuel*, want *food*, and want them *fast*).[1] However, successful implementation required that the company find a way to measure the experience of new target customers at newly designed Mobil gas pumps and convenience stores. After considerable thought, an innovative manager developed one of the first recognized "secret shopper" programs in which Mobil employees dressed as customers in order to live the Mobil gas station "experience." These secret shoppers then recorded numerous aspects of their experience on quantitative scales for feedback to station managers. Without such evaluative data, it would have been extremely difficult for Mobil managers to assess the causes of success or failure of the new strategy implementation. Finally, truly qualitative factors, such as the impact of late orders on customer relations, must be taken into consideration in the final step of the decision-making model—the selection of the alternative with the greatest overall benefit.

concept Q&A

Apply the decision-making model outlined in this section to a problem you have faced. For example, the problem might be whether to go to university, or which car to buy. Include all of the steps. Will the application of the decision-making model help you to make the decision? Why or why not?

Answers on pages 734 to 738.

Step 6: Make the Decision Once all relevant costs and benefits for each alternative have been assessed and the qualitative factors weighed, a decision can be made.

Corporate and Social Responsibility

Ethical concerns revolve around the way in which decisions are implemented and the possible sacrifice of long-run objectives for short-run gain. Relevant costs are used in making short-run decisions, however, decision makers should always maintain an ethical framework: Reaching objectives is important, but how you get there is perhaps more important. Unfortunately, many managers have the opposite view. Part of the reason for the problem is the extreme pressure to perform that many managers face. Often, the individual who is not a top performer may be laid off or demoted. Under such conditions, the temptation is often great to engage in questionable behaviour today and to let the future take care of itself.

Unfortunately, as the historic banking regulatory upheaval demonstrates, many U.S. financial services institutions in the mid-2000s yielded to unethical temptations to lend excessive amounts of money to prospective homeowners who, in the end, could not afford such loans. Leading up to the

(Continued)

[1] Marc Epstein and Bill Birchard, *Counting What Counts: Turning Corporate Accountability to Competitive Advantage.* Perseus Books, New York, NY. 2000.

financial crisis in the mid-2000s was a period of low-interest loans from U.S. financial institutions that fueled demand for housing, resulting in higher housing prices. When the housing bubble burst, housing prices began to fall and many consumers found the value of their house to be much lower than their mortgage debt. As homeowners defaulted on their loans, losses were suffered by financial institutions, many of which did not have a sufficient financial cushion to absorb the large quantity of losses. To help stabilize the financial markets, the U.S. Federal Reserve negotiated with the largest financial institutions to save the companies from complete failure and to help bring the U.S. economy out of the worst financial crisis since the 1930s' Great Depression.

Whenever relevant costing is used, it is important to include all costs that are relevant—including those involving ethical ramifications.

Relevant Costs Defined

The decision-making approach just described emphasized the importance of identifying and using relevant costs. **Relevant costs** possess two characteristics: (1) they are future costs and (2) they differ across alternatives. All pending decisions relate to the future; accordingly, only future costs can be relevant to decisions. However, to be relevant, a cost must not only be a future cost but also differ from one alternative to another. If a future cost is the same for more than one alternative, then it has no effect on the decision. Such a cost is irrelevant. The same relevance characteristics also apply to benefits. One alternative may produce an amount of future benefits different from another alternative (e.g., differences in future revenues). If future benefits differ across alternatives, then they are relevant and should be included in the analysis. The ability to identify relevant and irrelevant costs (and revenues) is a very important decision-making skill.

Relevant Costs Illustrated To illustrate the concept of relevant costs, consider Audio-Blast's make-or-buy alternatives. The cost of direct labour to produce the additional 20,000 speakers is $110,000. Is the direct labour cost a future cost that differs across the two alternatives? It is certainly a future cost. Producing the speakers for the auto manufacturer requires the services of direct labourers who must be paid. But does it differ across the two alternatives? If the speakers are purchased from an external supplier, then a second shift, with its direct labour, will not be needed. Thus, the cost of direct labour differs across alternatives ($110,000 for the make alternative and $0 for the buy alternative). Therefore, it is a relevant cost.

Implicit in this analysis is the use of a past cost to estimate a future cost. The most recent cost of direct labour has averaged $5.50 per speaker; for 20,000 speakers, the direct labour will cost $110,000. This past cost was used as the estimate of next year's cost. Although past costs are never relevant, they are often used to predict what future costs will be.

Another type of relevant cost is **opportunity cost**: the benefit sacrificed or forgone when one alternative is chosen over another. Therefore, an opportunity cost is relevant because it is both a future cost and one that differs across alternatives. While an opportunity cost is never an accounting cost, because accountants do not record the cost of what might happen in the future (i.e., it does not appear in financial statements), it is an important consideration in decision making. For example, if you are deciding whether to work full-time or to go to school full-time, the opportunity cost of going to school would be the wages you sacrifice by not working. Companies also include opportunity costs in many of their decision analyses. When Ernst & Young estimates the net benefit of sending thousands of its accountants to week-long training courses, it includes the opportunity cost of the tens of millions of dollars in lost revenue that it forgoes by not being able to bill clients for the services of those accountants. Opportunity costs are often quite challenging to estimate. However, their inclusion can change the final result of the analysis, such as whether or not to accept a special sales opportunity or to outsource a product rather than make it in-house. Therefore, managerial accountants have the ability to add significant value to relevant decision making by finding ways to measure particularly challenging opportunity costs.

Irrelevant Past Cost Illustrated Audio-Blast uses large power saws to cut the lumber that forms the housings for speakers. These saws were purchased three years ago and are being depreciated at an annual rate of $25,000. Is this $25,000 a relevant cost? In other words, is depreciation a future cost that differs across the two alternatives?

Depreciation represents an allocation of a cost already incurred. It is a **sunk cost**, a cost that cannot be affected by any future action. Although we allocate this sunk cost to future periods and call that allocation depreciation, none of the original cost is avoidable. Sunk costs are always the same across alternatives and, therefore, always irrelevant.

Thus, depreciation costs, like all sunk costs, fail to possess the two characteristics required of relevant costs and, therefore, always are irrelevant. In choosing between the two alternatives, the original cost of the power saws and their associated depreciation are not relevant factors. However, it should be noted that salvage value of the machinery is a relevant cost for certain decisions. For example, if Audio-Blast decides to transform itself into a distributor—not a producer—of speakers, the amount that can be realized from the sale of the power equipment will be relevant and will be included as a benefit of the switch to distributor status.

Finally, it is important to note the psychology behind managers' treatment of sunk costs. Although managers should ignore sunk costs when making decisions, such as whether to continue funding a particular product in the future, it unfortunately is human nature to allow sunk costs to affect these decisions. For example, Toshiba and its HD DVD product team engaged in a fierce, multi-year battle with Sony and its Blu-ray product team for recognition as the universally accepted format in the growing next-generation high-definition DVD market. Throughout the battle, both sides spent millions of dollars developing, manufacturing, and advertising their own formats. However, Sony's Blu-ray sales trounced Toshiba's HD DVD sales one Christmas shopping season, which prompted Hollywood giant Warner Bros. to decide to release its films only on Sony's Blu-ray format, rather than on both formats as it had done previously (the other major production companies had already sided with Sony as well). Around the same time, Blockbuster Video announced that it would only carry DVDs with the Blu-ray format. To objective entertainment business experts outside of Toshiba, these decisions by Warner Bros. and Blockbuster were the final blow to Toshiba's format and it was obvious that the HD DVD product line should be discontinued immediately to cut its losses and stop the financial bleeding. However, rather than ignore its significant sunk costs by cutting its future losses, Toshiba announced that it was "unwilling to concede defeat in the next-generation-DVD battle" and decided to launch an "aggressive advertising campaign to promote its [Toshiba's] HD DVD players and slash prices about 50%."[2] Therefore, not only did Toshiba continue to spend money developing, manufacturing, and marketing its failed product, but it expected to earn only about half of the regular sales revenue per unit sold! Eventually, even Toshiba recognized the handwriting on the wall and dropped its HD DVD format, but only after throwing away a considerable amount of money on a product that most experts believed should have been dropped much earlier.

Another classic example of inappropriately honouring sunk costs is Coca-Cola's New Coke debacle in the mid-1980s. The development and launching of New Coke was very costly and also an undeniably huge failure. However, Coca-Cola unwisely elected to continue to spend money to advertise and maintain its failed new product simply because it had already spent so much money on the product in the past. As business experts repeatedly noted, no amount of advertising was going to change the company's past expenditures to develop and launch New Coke and the company would have been far better off to scrap New Coke as soon as its failure became apparent.

The Concorde supersonic jet, over a period of 20 years, is another example of a company that failed to cut its losses and drop its product or service and instead continued to pour money into past failed ideas because of their large associated sunk costs. At its peak in the 1980s, British Airways was reporting profit of approximately €70 million per year operating the Concorde.[3] However, with only 20 aircraft built, the development of the

[2] Michelle Kessler, "Toshiba Turns Up Heat in DVD War," *USA Today* (January 15, 2008): 4B.

[3] European Commission, "Concorde Killed by Mounting Competition and Costs," http://ec.europa.eu/research/transport/news/items/concorde_killed_by_mounting_competition_and_costs_en.htm, February 20, 2012, accessed on May 7, 2012.

aircraft was considered an economic loss. Facing increasing fuel and maintenance costs, the Concorde was retired in 2003 after 27 years in operation.

Irrelevant Future Cost Illustrated Suppose that Audio-Blast currently pays an Internet provider $5,000 per year to store its website on the server. Since Audio-Blast intends to keep the webpage no matter what is decided regarding the potential speaker order, that cost is not relevant to the decision.

The same concepts apply to benefits. One alternative may produce an amount of future benefits different from another alternative (e.g., differences in future revenues). If future benefits are the same across alternatives, then they are irrelevant and should not be included in the analysis.

Cost Behaviour and Relevant Costs

Most short-run decisions require extensive consideration of cost behaviour. It is easy to fall into the trap of believing that variable costs are relevant and fixed costs are not, but this assumption is untrue. For example, the variable costs of production were relevant to Audio-Blast's decision. The fixed costs associated with the existing factory were not relevant. However, the additional fixed cost of the supervisor for a second shift was relevant to the decision.

The key point is that a change in price may occur as a result of changes in supply and demand for resources and this must be considered when assessing relevance. If changes in demand and supply for resources across alternatives bring about changes in spending, then the changes in resource spending are the relevant costs that should be used in assessing the relative desirability of the two alternatives.

Flexible resources can easily be purchased in the amount needed and at the time of use. For example, electricity used to run stoves that boil fruit in the production of jelly is a resource that can be acquired as used and needed. Thus, if the jelly manufacturer wants to increase production of jelly, electricity will increase just enough to satisfy that demand. This type of resource is typically referred to as a strictly variable cost.

Some resources are purchased before they are used. Clearly, investment in a factory of a particular size falls into this category; so does a year-to-year lease of office space or equipment. These costs usually are treated as fixed costs. If the decision covers a situation shorter than the time period for which the resource is fixed, then this cost usually is irrelevant.

Still other resources are acquired in advance of usage through implicit contracting; they are usually acquired in irregular amounts. In Chapter 3, these costs were shown as step costs. This category may include an organization's salaried and hourly employees. The implicit understanding is that the organization will maintain employment levels even though there may be temporary downturns in the quantity of an activity used. This understanding means that an activity may have unused capacity available. Recall that the relevant range is important in considering step costs. As long as a company remains within the relevant range, it will not go up or down a step, so the cost is fixed for all intents and purposes. For example, assume that a company has three purchasing agents who can each process 15,000 purchase orders a year. This assumption means that the existing staff can handle 45,000 purchase orders a year. If the company is processing only 40,000 purchase orders, then there is some unused capacity in purchasing. If the company is considering a special order that will require an additional 2,000 purchase orders, then there is no increased cost to purchasing. However, if the company considers an expansion that will require an additional 8,000 purchase orders per year, then additional staffing will be needed in purchasing.

SOME COMMON RELEVANT COST APPLICATIONS

OBJECTIVE 2

Apply relevant costing and decision-making concepts in a variety of business situations.

Relevant costing is of value in solving many different types of problems. Traditionally, these applications include decisions:

- to outsource services or production
- to accept a special order at less than the usual price

- to keep or drop a segment or product line
- to further process joint products or sell them at the split-off point

Though by no means an exhaustive list, many of the same decision-making principles apply to a variety of problems.

Outsourcing Decisions

Managers are often faced with the decision of whether to purchase a particular service or product from an outside supplier. A manager of a service firm may need to decide whether to provide a service in-house or to outsource it, while a manufacturer may need to consider whether to make or buy components used in manufacturing. Many services traditionally performed within the company—such as payroll processing, individual income tax form preparation, and human resources—are now being outsourced. Cornerstone 13.1 shows how to structure this outsourcing services problem.

Structuring an Outsourcing Services Problem

CORNERSTONE 13.1

Information:

Noah Services is a large charitable organization deciding whether to outsource its accounting and tax requirements to another organization, which would enable the charity to concentrate its efforts on fundraising. Cost information on internally completing the accounting and tax requirements on an annual basis includes the following:

	Total Cost
Direct labour	$11,000
Variable overhead	3,000
Fixed overhead	16,000
Total	$30,000

Fixed overhead will continue whether Noah outsources the work or not. An outside consulting firm has agreed to complete the accounting and tax services for $15,000 per year. No additional costs of purchasing the services will be incurred beyond the purchase price.

Required:

1. What are the alternatives for Noah?
2. List the relevant cost(s) of internally providing the services and externally purchasing them from another organization.
3. Which alternative is more cost effective and by how much?
4. Now assume that the fixed overhead includes $5,000 of cost that can be avoided if the services are purchased externally. Which alternative is more cost effective and by how much?

Solution:

1. There are two alternatives: complete the accounting and tax requirements in-house or purchase the services externally.
2. Relevant costs of providing the services in-house include direct labour and variable overhead. Relevant costs of purchasing the services externally include the purchase price from the other organization.

(Continued)

CORNERSTONE
13.1
(Continued)

3.

	Alternatives		
	In-house	**Outsource**	**Differential Cost**
Direct labour	$11,000	$ —	$11,000
Variable overhead	3,000	—	3,000
Purchase cost	—	15,000	(15,000)
Total relevant cost	$14,000	$15,000	$ (1,000)

It is cheaper to complete the accounting and tax services in-house. This alternative is cheaper by $1,000.

4.

	Alternatives		
	In-house	**Outsource**	**Differential Cost**
Direct labour	$11,000	$ —	$ 11,000
Variable overhead	3,000	—	3,000
Avoidable fixed overhead	5,000	—	5,000
Purchase cost	—	15,000	(15,000)
Total relevant cost	$19,000	$15,000	$ 4,000

Now it is cheaper to purchase the services. This alternative is cheaper by $4,000.

Why:

Outsourcing services decisions are among the most common decisions faced by management, and structuring the analysis of such a decision is critical to arriving at the most appropriate one. If the problem is not structured properly, the result can be faulty or overcomplicated analysis.

Make-or-buy decisions are those decisions involving a choice between internal and external production. Exhibit 13.1 illustrates the make-or-buy decision. To illustrate more fully the cost analysis of a make-or-buy problem, assume that Swasey Manufacturing currently produces an electronic component used in one of its printers. In one year, Swasey will switch production to another type of printer, and the electronic component will not be used. However, for the coming year, Swasey must produce 10,000 of these parts to support the production requirements for the old printer.

A potential supplier has approached Swasey about the component. The supplier will build the electronic component to Swasey's specifications for $4.75 per unit. The offer

EXHIBIT 13.1

Make or Buy

sounds very attractive since the full manufacturing cost per unit is $8.20. Should Swasey Manufacturing make or buy the component?

The problem and the feasible alternatives are both readily identifiable. Since the horizon for the decision is only one period, there is no need to be concerned about periodically recurring costs. Relevant costing is particularly useful for short-run analysis. We simply need to identify the relevant costs, total them, and make a choice (assuming no overriding qualitative concerns).

The full absorption cost of the component is computed as follows:

	Total Cost	Unit Cost
Direct materials	$10,000	$1.00
Direct labour	20,000	2.00
Variable overhead	8,000	0.80
Fixed overhead	44,000	4.40
Total	$82,000	$8.20

Fixed overhead consists of common factory costs that are allocated to each product line. No matter what happens to the component line, overall fixed overhead will not be affected. As a result, the fixed overhead is irrelevant; it can be safely ignored in structuring the problem.

All other costs are relevant. The costs of direct materials and direct labour are relevant because they will not be needed if the part is bought externally. Similarly, variable overhead is relevant, because its cost would not be incurred if the component were bought externally.

Now, what about the purchase of the component? Of course, the purchase price is relevant. If the component were made, this cost would not be incurred. Are there any other costs associated with an outside purchase? A check with the purchasing department and receiving dock confirmed that there was sufficient slack in the system to handle the additional purchase easily. Cornerstone 13.2 shows how to structure this make-or-buy problem.

Structuring a Make-or-Buy Problem

CORNERSTONE 13.2

Information:

Swasey Manufacturing needs to determine if it will be cheaper to make 10,000 units of a component in-house or to purchase them from an outside supplier for $4.75 each. Cost information on internal production includes the following:

	Total Cost	Unit Cost
Direct materials	$10,000	$1.00
Direct labour	20,000	2.00
Variable overhead	8,000	0.80
Fixed overhead	44,000	4.40
Total	$82,000	$8.20

Fixed overhead will continue whether the component is produced internally or externally. No additional costs of purchasing will be incurred beyond the purchase price.

Required:

1. What are the alternatives for Swasey Manufacturing?
2. List the relevant cost(s) of internal production and of external purchase.
3. Which alternative is more cost effective and by how much?

(Continued)

CORNERSTONE

13.2

(Continued)

4. Now assume that the fixed overhead includes $10,000 of cost that can be avoided if the component is purchased externally. Which alternative is more cost effective and by how much?

Solution:

1. There are two alternatives: make the component in-house or purchase it externally.
2. Relevant costs of making the component in-house include direct materials, direct labour, and variable overhead. Relevant costs of purchasing the component externally include the purchase price.
3.

	Alternatives		Differential
	Make	**Buy**	**Cost to Make**
Direct materials	$10,000	$ —	$10,000
Direct labour	20,000	—	20,000
Variable overhead	8,000	—	8,000
Purchase cost	—	47,500	(47,500)
Total relevant cost	$38,000	$47,500	$ 9,500

It is cheaper to make the component in-house. This alternative is cheaper by $9,500.

4.

	Alternatives		Differential
	Make	**Buy**	**Cost to Make**
Direct materials	$10,000	$ —	$10,000
Direct labour	20,000	—	20,000
Variable overhead	8,000	—	8,000
Avoidable fixed overhead	10,000	—	10,000
Purchase cost	—	47,500	(47,500)
Total relevant cost	$48,000	$47,500	$ 500

Now it is cheaper to purchase the component. This alternative is cheaper by $500.

Why:

Make-or-buy decisions are among the most common decisions faced by management, and structuring the analysis of such a decision is critical to arriving at the most appropriate one. If the problem is not structured properly, the result can be faulty or overcomplicated analysis.

Be sure to read the analysis in Cornerstone 13.2 carefully. At first, the fixed overhead remains whether or not the component is made internally. In this case, fixed overhead is not relevant, and making the product is $9,500 cheaper than buying it. Later, in Requirement 4, part of the fixed overhead is avoidable. This condition means that purchasing the component externally will save $10,000 in fixed cost (i.e., Swasey can avoid $10,000 of fixed overhead if it buys the component). Now, the $10,000 of fixed cost is relevant—it is a future cost and it differs between the two alternatives—and the offer of the supplier should be accepted; it is $500 cheaper to buy the component.

Corporate and Social Responsibility

One type of relevant cost that is becoming increasingly large due to globalization and the green environmental movement concerns the disposal costs associated with electronic waste (or e-waste). Increasingly, government agencies are charging manufacturers of computers, televisions, digital music devices, etc., a costly fee at production to cover product disposal costs that public landfills eventually incur once the products reach the end of their life cycle, become obsolete, and are discarded, when they begin to pollute the environment. Hewlett-Packard Co. has taken a strategic leadership position by recycling approximately 10 percent of its sales as a more cost-effective means than incurring the aforementioned governmental fees at production.[4] The failure to include relevant life-cycle costs can cause the make side of the make-or-buy analysis to appear more attractive (i.e., less costly) than it is in reality.

The same analysis can be performed on a unit-cost basis. Once the relevant costs are identified, relevant unit costs can be compared. For this example, these costs are $3.80 (= $38,000/10,000) for the make alternative and $4.75 (= $47,500/10,000) for the buy alternative.

concept Q&A

You also deal with make-or-buy decisions. For example, do you change the oil in your car yourself, or do you take it to the shop? Do you make your own clothing, or do you buy ready-to-wear garments from stores? Choose one such decision, and explain why you have chosen to "make it" or "buy it." What factors could influence you to change your mind?

Answers on pages 734 to 738.

Special-Order Decisions

From time to time, a company may consider offering a product or service at a price that is different from its usual price. For example, bid prices can vary for customers in the same market, and firms often have the opportunity to consider special orders from potential customers in markets not ordinarily served. For example, General Motors contracted with the U.S. Pentagon to use excess production capacity to manufacture its popular four-wheel-drive pickup truck for use by U.S. troops in desert combat situations, except that these trucks were altered to include bulletproof windows, mounts for machine guns, and night vision capability. A potentially important qualitative factor in this example is that certain customer segments might hold strong opinions about General Motors' association with combat activities. Such opinions might help or hurt regular sales, but their effect should be estimated and included in the relevant analysis if they are deemed to be significant. **Special-order decisions** focus on whether a specially priced order should be accepted or rejected. These orders often can be attractive, especially when the firm is operating below its maximum productive capacity. Exhibit 13.2 illustrates the special-order decision.

EXHIBIT 13.2

Accept or Reject a Special Order

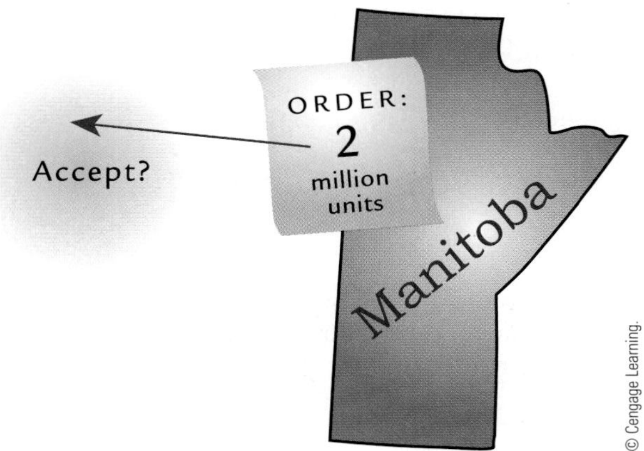

[4] Lorraine Woellert, "HP Wants Your Old PCs Back," *BusinessWeek* Online (April 10, 2006).

Suppose, for example, Cool-Treats is an ice cream company that produces only premium ice cream. Its factory has a capacity of 20 million 1-litre units but only plans to produce 16 million units. The total costs associated with producing and selling 16 million units are as follows (in thousands of dollars):

	Total	Unit Cost
Variable costs:		
Ingredients	$15,200	$0.950
Packaging	3,200	0.200
Direct labour	4,000	0.250
Variable overhead	1,280	0.080
Selling commission	320	0.020
Total variable costs	24,000	1.500
Total fixed costs	1,552	0.097
Total costs	$25,552	$1.597
Selling price		$ 2.00

An ice cream distributor from a geographic region not normally served by the company has offered to buy 2 million units at $1.55 per unit, provided its own label can be attached to the product. Since the distributor approached the company directly, there is no sales commission. As the manager of the ice cream company, would you accept or reject this order?

The offer of $1.55 is well below the normal selling price of $2.00; in fact, it is even below the total unit cost. Even so, accepting the order may be profitable. The company has idle capacity, and the order will not replace, or cannibalize, other units being produced to sell at the normal price. Additionally, many of the costs are not relevant; fixed costs will continue regardless of whether the order is accepted or rejected.

If the order is accepted, an incremental benefit of $1.55 per unit will be realized. However, all of the variable costs except for commissions ($0.02) also will be incurred, producing a cost of $1.48 per unit. The net benefit is $0.07 (= $1.55 − $1.48) per unit. The relevant cost analysis can be summarized as follows:

	Accept	Reject	Differential Benefit to Accept
Revenues	$ 3,100,000	$—	$ 3,100,000
Ingredients	(1,900,000)	—	(1,900,000)
Packaging	(400,000)	—	(400,000)
Direct labour	(500,000)	—	(500,000)
Variable overhead	(160,000)	—	(160,000)
Profit	$ 140,000	$ 0	$ 140,000

We see that for this company, accepting the special order will increase profits by $140,000 (= $0.07 × 2,000,000).

Cornerstone 13.3 shows how to apply relevant costing to a special-order problem.

CORNERSTONE 13.3 Structuring a Special-Order Problem

Information:

Cool-Treats Inc. manufactures premium ice cream at its factory, which has a capacity of 20 million 1-litre units. At the current production level of 16 million units, its production and selling costs (in thousands of dollars) are:

(Continued)

CORNERSTONE
13.3

(Continued)

	Total	Unit Cost
Variable costs:		
Ingredients	$15,200	$0.950
Packaging	3,200	0.200
Direct labour	4,000	0.250
Variable overhead	1,280	0.080
Selling commission	320	0.020
Total variable costs	24,000	1.500
Total fixed costs	1,552	0.097
Total costs	$25,552	$1.597
Selling price		$ 2.00

Cool-Treats has been approached by a new customer with an offer to purchase 6 million litres for a price of $1.75 per litre; however, since the company approached Cool-Treats, there is no sales commission. Since current production is 16 million litres with maximum capacity of 20 million, the company cannot sell to all the usual customers and accept this order. As a result, Cool-Treats must consider the following options: (1) refuse the offer from the new customer, (2) accept the offer and deny sales to some existing customers, or (3) accept the offer and temporarily increase capacity at a cost of $500,000 to meet the order without impacting sales to existing customers.

Required:

1. What are the relevant costs and benefits of the three alternatives?
2. By how much will operating income increase or decrease if the order is accepted?

Solution:

1. Relevant costs and benefits of option (2) include the sales price of $1.75, direct materials, direct labour, and variable overhead. Relevant costs and benefits of option (3) include the direct materials, direct labour, variable overhead, and additional fixed costs of $500,000. No relevant costs or benefits are attached to rejecting the order.

2.

	(1) Reject	(2) Accept (deny sales to customers)	(3) Accept (temporarily increase capacity)
Revenues	$—	$ 6,500,000[a]	$10,500,000
Ingredients	—	(3,800,000)[b]	(5,700,000)
Packaging	—	(800,000)[c]	(1,200,000)
Direct labour	—	(1,000,000)[d]	(1,500,000)
Variable overhead	—	(320,000)[e]	(480,000)
Additional fixed costs	—	—	(500,000)
Profit	$ 0	$ 580,000	$ 1,120,000

[a] ($1.75 × 6,000,000) − ($2.00 × 2,000,000)
[b] ($0.95 × 6,000,000) − ($0.95 × 2,000,000)
[c] ($0.20 × 6,000,000) − ($0.20 × 2,000,000)
[d] ($0.25 × 6,000,000) − ($0.25 × 2,000,000)
[e] ($0.08 × 6,000,000) − ($0.08 × 2,000,000)

Operating income will increase by $580,000 if the special order is accepted and Cool-Treats forgoes sales of 2 million litres to existing customers rather than reject the offer

CORNERSTONE
13.3

(Continued)

entirely. By far the better option is for Cool-Treats to temporarily increase capacity, which will permit the company to sell to existing customers and the new customer for an increase in operating income of $1,120,000 over rejecting the offer.

Why:

Special-order situations require careful analysis. Many different factors must be considered before the decision is made, so we must structure the analysis to consider all decision factors properly. In addition to considering the financial analysis, Cool-Treats will also need to consider nonfinancial factors, such as the possibility that existing customers might be upset to learn that Cool-Treats is willing to sell the ice cream for less to another company. Those existing customers might demand the same selling price or begin purchasing ice cream from a competitor—both scenarios could threaten the long-term survival of Cool-Treats.

Keep-or-Drop Decisions

Often, a manager needs to determine whether a segment, such as a product line, should be kept or dropped. **Keep-or-drop decisions** can be relatively small-scale in nature, such as when Bauer, a leading Canadian manufacturer of ice hockey equipment, decides what to do with particular existing celebrity- and athlete-sponsored clothing or equipment lines. On the other hand, these decisions can be very large-scale in nature, such as when Ford Motor Company contemplated the sale of its luxury Jaguar and Land Rover automobile lines. Segmented reports prepared on a variable-costing basis provide valuable information for these keep-or-drop decisions. Both the segment's contribution margin and its segment margin are useful in evaluating the performance of segments. However, while segmented reports provide useful information for keep-or-drop decisions, relevant costing describes how the information should be used to arrive at a decision.

To illustrate, consider Dongbei Materials Inc., which produces concrete blocks, bricks, and roofing tile. The controller has prepared the following estimated segment income statement for next year (in thousands of dollars):

	Concrete Blocks	Bricks	Roofing Tile	Total
Sales revenue	$500	$800	$ 150	$1,450
Less: Variable expenses	250	480	140	870
Contribution margin	250	320	10	580
Less direct fixed expenses:				
Advertising	(10)	(10)	(10)	(30)
Salaries	(37)	(40)	(35)	(112)
Depreciation	(53)	(40)	(10)	(103)
Segment margin	$150	$230	$ (45)	$ 335

The projected performance of the roofing tile line shows a negative segment margin. This occurrence would be the third consecutive year of poor performance for that line. The president of Dongbei Materials, Ping Zhang, is concerned about this poor performance and is trying to decide whether to drop or keep the roofing tile line.

His first reaction is to try to increase the sales revenue of roofing tiles, possibly through an aggressive sales promotion coupled with an increase in the selling price. The marketing manager thinks that this approach would be fruitless since the market is saturated, and the level of competition is too keen to hold out any hope for increasing the firm's market share.

Increasing the product line's profits through cost cutting is not feasible either. Costs were cut the past two years to reduce the loss to its present anticipated level. Any further reductions would lower the quality of the product and adversely affect sales.

With no realistic hope for improving the profit performance of the line beyond its projected level, Zhang has decided to drop it. He reasons that the firm will lose a total of $10,000 in contribution margin but will save $45,000 by dismissing the line's supervisor and eliminating its advertising budget. (The depreciation cost of $10,000 is not relevant because it represents an allocation of a sunk cost.) Thus, dropping the product line has a $35,000 advantage over keeping it. Cornerstone 13.4 shows how to structure this information as a keep-or-drop product line problem.

Structuring a Keep-or-Drop Product Line Problem

CORNERSTONE 13.4

CORNERSTONE VIDEO

Information:

Shown below is a segmented income statement for Dongbei Materials Inc.'s three product lines:

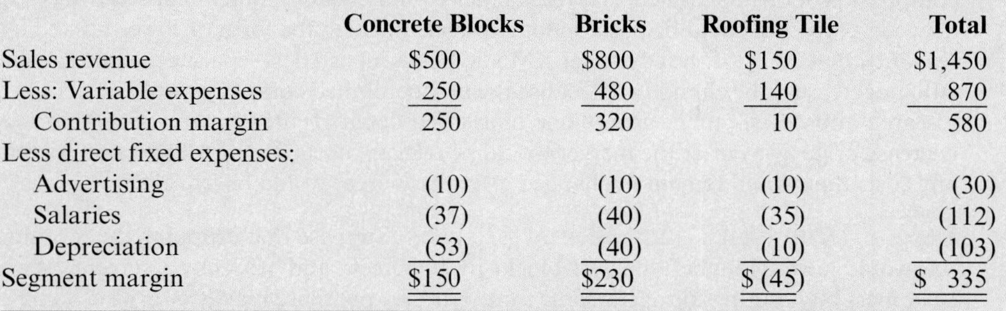

	Concrete Blocks	Bricks	Roofing Tile	Total
Sales revenue	$500	$800	$150	$1,450
Less: Variable expenses	250	480	140	870
Contribution margin	250	320	10	580
Less direct fixed expenses:				
Advertising	(10)	(10)	(10)	(30)
Salaries	(37)	(40)	(35)	(112)
Depreciation	(53)	(40)	(10)	(103)
Segment margin	$150	$230	$ (45)	$ 335

The roofing tile line has a contribution margin of $10,000 (sales of $150,000 less total variable costs of $140,000). All variable costs are relevant. Relevant fixed costs associated with this line include $10,000 in advertising and $35,000 in supervision.

Required:

1. List the alternatives being considered with respect to the roofing tile line.
2. List the relevant benefits and costs for each alternative.
3. Which alternative is more cost effective and by how much?

Solution:

1. The two alternatives are to keep the roofing tile line or to drop it.
2. The relevant benefits and costs of keeping the roofing tile line include sales of $150,000, variable costs of $140,000, advertising cost of $10,000, and supervision cost of $35,000. None of the relevant benefits and costs of keeping the roofing tile line would occur under the drop alternative.
3.

	Keep	Drop	Differential Amount to Keep
Sales	$150,000	$—	$150,000
Less: Variable expenses	140,000	—	140,000
Contribution margin	10,000	—	10,000
Less: Advertising	(10,000)	—	(10,000)
Cost of supervision	(35,000)	—	(35,000)
Total relevant benefit (loss)	$(35,000)	$ 0	$(35,000)

The difference is $35,000 in favour of dropping the roofing tile line.

(Continued)

CORNERSTONE

13.4

(Continued)

Why:

Every company faces the question of whether it should keep or drop a particular product or division. The analysis must consider a variety of factors, especially since the conclusions are not readily available from the raw data.

A merger between companies is another type of keep-or-drop decision that requires managerial accountants to estimate relevant costs, such as which costs would go away when two companies merge and which costs would remain. For example, when XM Satellite Radio and Sirius Satellite Radio considered merging into one giant satellite radio company, proponents argued that the merger would create significant cost savings to the new company that could be passed along to consumers in the form of lower prices.[5] They reasoned that many of the costs that XM and Sirius incurred as separate companies would either decrease or be eliminated because the new combined company would need only one research and development group, one marketing department, etc. Any costs that would decrease or go away after the merger would be relevant costs for the merger analysis, while any costs that would remain unchanged after the merger would be irrelevant.

Keep or Drop with Complementary Effects Suppose that dropping the roofing tile line would lower Dongbei's sales of blocks by 10 percent and bricks by 8 percent, as many customers buy roofing tile at the same time that they purchase blocks or bricks. Some customers will go elsewhere if they cannot buy both products at the same location. How does this information affect the keep-or-drop decision? Cornerstone 13.5 shows the impact on all product lines.

CORNERSTONE 13.5

Structuring a Keep-or-Drop Product Line Problem with Complementary Effects

Information:

Refer to Dongbei Materials' segmented income statement in Cornerstone 13.4. Assume that dropping the product line reduces sales of blocks by 10 percent and sales of bricks by 8 percent. All other information remains the same.

Required:

1. If the roofing tile line is dropped, what is the contribution margin for the block line? For the brick line?
2. Which alternative (keep or drop the roofing tile line) is now more cost effective and by how much?

Solution:

1. The previous contribution margin generated by blocks was $250,000. A 10 percent decrease in sales implies a 10 percent decrease in total variable costs, so the contribution margin decreases by 10 percent.

(Continued)

[5] Kim Peterson, "XM Plus Sirius Doesn't Equal Monopoly?" (March 24, 2008): accessed on April 5, 2008, from http://blogs.moneycentral.msn.com/topstocks/archive/2008/03/24/xm-plus-sirius-doesn-t-equal-monopoly-feds-say.aspx.

CORNERSTONE

13.5

(Continued)

New contribution margin for blocks = \$250,000 − 0.10(\$250,000) = \$225,000

The reasoning is the same for the brick line, but the decrease is 8 percent.

New contribution margin for bricks = \$320,000 − 0.08(\$320,000) = \$294,400

Therefore, if the roofing tile product line were dropped, the resulting total contribution margin for Dongbei would equal = \$519,400 (= \$225,000 + \$294,400).

2.

	Keep	Drop	Differential Amount to Keep
Contribution margin	\$ 580,000	\$ 519,400	\$ 60,600
Less: Advertising	(30,000)	(20,000)	(10,000)
Cost of supervision	(112,000)	(77,000)	(35,000)
Total	\$ 438,000	\$ 422,400	\$ 15,600

Notice that the contribution margin for the drop alternative equals the new contribution margins of the block and brick lines (\$225,000 + \$294,400). Also, advertising and supervision remain relevant across these alternatives.

Now the analysis favours keeping the roofing tile line. In fact, company income will be \$15,600 higher if all three lines are kept as opposed to dropping the roofing tile line.

Why:

A complication of any keep-or-drop question is the implications such a decision may have on other aspects of the business. We must analyze these implications carefully before making a final decision.

The example provides some insights beyond the simple application of the decision model. The initial analysis, which focused on two feasible alternatives, led to a tentative decision to drop the product line. Additional information provided by the marketing manager led to a reversal of the first decision. Perhaps other feasible alternatives exist as well. These additional alternatives would require still more analyses.

YOUDECIDE Relevant Decision Making

You are an elected official in a major city that is considering whether to move forward with a proposed plan to demolish the city's existing professional sports stadium and build an elaborate new stadium. One of the most difficult aspects of this decision is estimating the new stadium's incremental revenues and costs that would result if it were built, and the incremental economic benefit to the city.

What specific types of relevant revenues and costs would you consider in making this important decision?

There are many stadium events for which the associated relevant revenues and costs must be estimated accurately if the correct decision is to be made. These stadium events (and their relevant revenues and costs) include:

1. Main attraction sporting events (e.g., ticket revenues from baseball, basketball, and/or football games for which the stadium would be built; additional staffing, cleanup, and insurance costs)
2. Concessions and other sales (e.g., contribution margins or fees earned from product and service sales—most new stadiums boast as many high-end shopping opportunities as an upscale mall!)
3. Television contract terms (e.g., the amount and percentage of revenue brought in by *additional* games being televised in the new stadium, perhaps in primetime slots)
4. Offseason events (e.g., the ticket revenue from boxing matches, music concerts, etc.).

For stadium decisions, estimating the relevant revenues might be even more difficult than estimating the relevant costs. For instance, projecting how many *more* people will want to attend games in a new stadium can be unclear, as well as how much money they would be willing to spend for various seats

(Continued)

located around the stadium. A key question is whether the stadium will attract out-of-towners and persuade locals to spend more money on leisure. An economically neutral outcome would follow from locals simply re-allocating their leisure budget from one local spectator sport to another.

Several operators of stadiums in Canada have experienced tremendous difficulty in accurately estimating these amounts. For example, it took three decades for Quebec taxpayers to repay the $1.5 billion debt stemming from the construction of Olympic Stadium for the 1976 Summer Games in Montreal.[6] After the Olympics, the 58,500-seat stadium became the home of a Major League Baseball team until it was sold in 2004, causing related revenues to steeply fall thereafter. Moreover, premature wear at Olympic Stadium made the economic situation even worse. For example, rips and tears that were supposed to appear gradually in the roof's membrane have more than doubled since 2012. These tears have led to the cancellation of a number of games in recent years.[7]

A contemporary example can be found in Edmonton, Alberta, which has approved a deal with the owner of the Edmonton Oilers for a proposed $480 million downtown arena.[8] In Markham, Ontario, a $325 million stadium has been proposed. Stadiums are built over several years and decision makers struggle to reliably estimate how economic conditions, and the cost of labour and other inputs, will change during that time. Migrating host teams, unforeseen wear-and-tear, and debt-financing costs further complicate the process. As an elected official, you are concerned that it is often the municipality that is left with the bill when the project goes over budget.[9]

Another major issue is that some citizens object to such large amounts of money being spent on replacing existing fully functional sporting facilities with gargantuan sports palaces. They argue that these large sums could be better spent on different causes. Such sentiments, whether you agree or disagree with them, represent potentially important qualitative factors and quantitative opportunity costs that effective managerial accountants should consider when performing relevant analyses for proposed new stadiums. It is important to keep in mind that these citizens represent taxpayers or potential fans the stadium builders count on for purchasing expensive tickets in the future.

When making such an important decision, relevant costs for things like sporting events, concessions, television contracts, and off-season events must be considered in addition to qualitative factors like citizen sentiment.

Further Processing of Joint Products

Joint products have common processes and costs of production up to a split-off point. At that point, they become distinguishable as separately identifiable products. For example, certain minerals such as copper and gold may both be found in a given ore, which must be mined, crushed, and treated before the copper and gold are separated. The point of separation is called the **split-off point**. The costs of mining, crushing, and treatment are common to both products.

Many joint products are sold at the split-off point. However, sometimes it is more profitable to process a joint product further, beyond the split-off point, prior to selling it. A **sell-or-process-further decision** is an important relevant decision that a manager must make. Typically, analysis is limited to an evaluation of whether the increased revenues generated from processing further exceed the additional processing costs.

To illustrate, consider Appletime Corporation, a large corporate farm that specializes in growing apples. Each plot produces approximately one tonne of apples. The trees in each plot must be sprayed, fertilized, watered, and pruned. When the apples have ripened, workers are hired to pick them. The apples are then transported to a warehouse, where they are washed and sorted. The approximate cost of all these activities (including processing) is $300 per tonne per year.

Apples are sorted into three grades (A, B, and C), determined by size and blemishes, and are placed in separate bins. Every tonne of apples produces, on average, 400 kilograms of Grade A, 300 kilograms of Grade B, and 300 kilograms of Grade C.

- *Grade A*: Large apples without blemishes (bruises, cuts, wormholes, and so on). These apples are sold to large supermarkets for $0.80 per kilogram.

[6] Armina Ligaya, "Why Funding New Sports Stadiums Can Be a Losing Bet," CBC News, February 1, 2013, http://www.cbc.ca/news/canada/why-funding-new-sports-stadiums-can-be-a-losing-bet-1.1378210, accessed on May 7, 2014.
[7] Stadium Database, "Canada: Almost 3000 Rips and Tears Already on Montreal Olympic Stadium's Roof," July 29, 2013, http://stadiumdb.com/news/2013/07/canada_almost_3000_rips_and_tears_already_on_montreal_olympic_stadiums_roof, accessed on May 7, 2014.
[8] "Agreement for Edmonton Arena Passed by Council," CBC News, January 23, 2013, http://www.cbc.ca/news/canada/edmonton/agreement-for-edmonton-arena-passed-by-council-1.1327892, accessed on May 7, 2014.
[9] Armina Ligaya, "Why Funding New Sports Stadiums Can Be a Losing Bet," CBC News, February 1, 2013, http://www.cbc.ca/news/canada/why-funding-new-sports-stadiums-can-be-a-losing-bet-1.1378210, accessed on May 7, 2014.

- *Grade B*: Small apples without blemishes. These apples are packaged in 2-kilogram bags and sold to supermarkets for $1.25 per bag.
- *Grade C*: All remaining apples; Grade C apples are processed further and made into apple sauce. The sauce is sold in 0.5-kilogram cans for $0.75 each. The cost of processing is $0.10 per kilogram of apples. The final output is 500 cans weighing 0.5-kilogram each.

A large supermarket chain recently requested that Appletime supply 0.5-kilogram cans of apple pie filling for which the chain is willing to pay $0.90 per can. Appletime determined that the Grade B apples would be suitable for this purpose and estimated that it would cost $0.24 per can to process the apples into pie filling. The output would be 500 cans. Exhibit 13.3 illustrates the decision to sell Grade B apples at the split-off point or to process them further into pie filling.

EXHIBIT 13.3

Further Processing of Joint Products

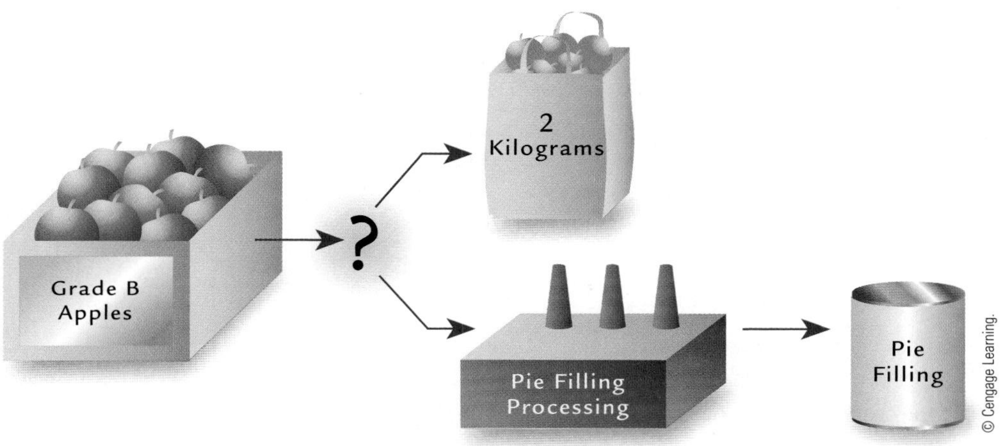

In deciding whether to sell Grade B apples at split-off or to process them further and sell them as pie filling, the common costs of spraying, pruning, and so on are not relevant. The company must pay the $300 per tonne for these activities regardless of whether it sells at split-off or processes further. However, the revenues earned at split-off are likely to differ from the revenues that would be received if the Grade B apples were further processed and sold as pie filling. Therefore, revenues are a relevant consideration. Similarly, the processing costs occur only if further processing takes place. Hence, processing costs are relevant. Cornerstone 13.6 shows how to structure the sell-or-process-further decision for the Grade B apples.

Structuring the Sell-or-Process-Further Decision

CORNERSTONE 13.6

Information:

Appletime grows apples and then sorts them into one of three grades, A, B, or C, based on their condition. Appletime must decide whether to sell the Grade B apples at split-off or to process them into apple pie filling. The company normally sells the Grade B apples in 150 two-kilogram bags at a per-unit price of $1.25. If the apples are processed into pie filling, the result will be 500 cans of filling with additional costs of $0.24 per can. The buyer will pay $0.90 per can.

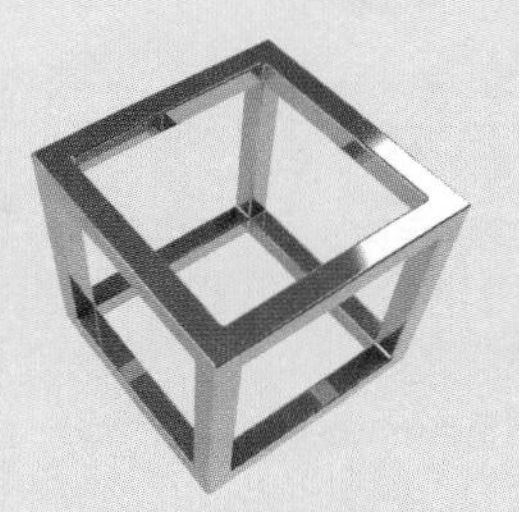

(Continued)

CORNERSTONE

13.6

(Continued)

Required:

1. What is the contribution to income from selling the Grade B apples in two-kilogram bags?
2. What is the contribution to income from processing the Grade B apples into pie filling?
3. Should Appletime continue to sell the Grade B apples in bags or process them further into pie filling?

Solution:

	Grade A: Large and unblemished	Grade B: Small and unblemished	Grade C: Remaining apples
Production from 1 tonne of apples	400 kg	300 kg	300 kg
Finished quantity	400 kg	150 bags	500 cans
Selling price	\$0.80/kg	\$1.25 per 2-kg bag	\$0.75 per 0.5-kg can
Revenue	\$320[a]	\$187.50[b]	\$375[c]
Further processing costs	—	\$120[d]	—
Revenue from processing further	—	\$450[e]	

[a] \$0.80 × 400
[b] \$1.25 × 150
[c] \$0.75 × 500
[d] \$0.24 × 500
[e] \$0.90 × 500

1. Revenue from apples in bags = \$1.25 × 150 = \$187.50
2. Revenue from further processing = \$0.90 × 500 = \$450
   Further processing cost = \$0.24 × 500 = \$120
   Income from further processing = \$450 − \$120 = \$330
3. Appletime should process the Grade B apples into pie filling because the company will make \$330 versus the \$187.50 it would make by selling the apples in bags.

Why:

Products that share common processes at the initial stages must be analyzed separately as to whether they should be processed further or sold at the split-off point. The overriding principle is that action should be taken that maximizes company profit.

PRODUCT MIX DECISIONS

OBJECTIVE 

Choose the optimal product mix when faced with one constrained resource.

Most of the time, organizations have wide flexibility in choosing their product mix. Decisions about product mix can have a significant impact on an organization's profitability.

Each mix represents an alternative that carries with it an associated profit level. A manager should choose the alternative that maximizes total profits. Since fixed costs do not vary with activity level, the total fixed costs of a firm will be the same for all possible mixes and, therefore, are not relevant to the decision. Thus, a manager needs to choose the alternative that maximizes total contribution margin.

Assume, for example, that Jorgenson Company produces two types of gears, X and Y, with unit contribution margins of $25 and $10, respectively. If the firm possesses unlimited resources and the demand for each product is unlimited, then the product mix decision is simple—produce an infinite number of each product. Unfortunately, every firm faces limited resources and limited demand for each product. These limitations are called **constraints**. A manager must choose the optimal mix given the constraints found within the firm.

Assuming that Jorgenson can sell all that is produced, some individuals might argue that only Gear X should be produced and sold—it has the larger contribution margin. However, this solution is not necessarily the best choice. The selection of the optimal mix can be significantly affected by the relationships of the constrained resources to the individual products. These relationships affect the quantity of each product that can be produced and, consequently, the total contribution margin that can be earned. This point is most vividly illustrated when faced with one resource constraint. Cornerstone 13.7 shows how to determine the optimal product mix with one constrained resource.

Determining the Optimal Product Mix with One Constrained Resource

CORNERSTONE 13.7

Information:

Jorgenson Company produces two types of gears, X and Y, with unit contribution margins of $25 and $10, respectively. Each gear must be notched by a special machine. The firm owns eight machines that together provide 40,000 hours of machine time per year. Gear X requires two hours of machine time, and Gear Y requires 0.5 hour of machine time. There are no other constraints.

Required:

1. What is the contribution margin per hour of machine time for each gear?
2. What is the optimal mix of gears?
3. What is the total contribution margin earned for the optimal mix?

Solution:

1.

	Gear X	Gear Y
Contribution margin per unit	$25.00	$10
Required machine time per unit	÷ 2	÷ 0.5
Contribution margin per hour of machine time	$12.50	$ 20

2. Since Gear Y yields $20 of contribution margin per hour of machine time, all machine time should be devoted to the production of Gear Y.

   Units Gear Y = 40,000 total hours/0.5 hour per Gear Y = 80,000 units

   The optimal mix is Gear Y—80,000 units and Gear X—0 units.

3. Total contribution margin of optimal mix = (80,000 units Gear Y) × $10
   = $800,000

Why:

A company often faces a situation where one of its processes (or resources) cannot handle all the demands placed on it. Therefore, the company must decide how best to allocate this scarce resource to production operations in order to maximize company profit.

concept Q&A

Consider your, or a friend's, cell phone plan. Often, there are different types of minutes, priced at different levels. For example, a plan might include 300 "anytime" minutes and 1,000 "night and weekend minutes." Discuss these different types of minutes as constraints. What do they constrain? Do these constraints affect the decision to call a friend?

Answers on pages 734 to 738.

Cornerstone 13.7 clearly illustrates a fundamentally important point involving relevant decision making with a constrained resource: The contribution margin per unit *of each product* is not the critical concern when deciding how much of each product type to produce and sell. Instead, the contribution margin per unit of the scarce resource is the deciding factor, which means that the product yielding the highest contribution margin per unit of the scarce resource should be selected. Returning to Cornerstone 13.7, Gear X earns a contribution margin per unit of $25, which is 2.5 times greater than the $10 contribution margin per unit earned by Gear Y. However, each Gear X unit requires more than 2.5 times as much machine time (the constrained factor) to produce than does each Gear Y unit, thereby making Gear Y more attractive financially than Gear X. Specifically, Gear X earns $12.50 of contribution margin per machine hour ($25 ÷ 2), but Gear Y earns $20 of contribution margin per machine hour ($10 ÷ 0.5). Thus, Gear Y is the more attractive product and the optimal mix is 80,000 units of Gear Y and no units of Gear X.

Suppose, however, that there is also a demand constraint. Only 60,000 units of Gear Y can be sold. Cornerstone 13.8 shows how to incorporate this additional constraint. Coffee chain Caribou Coffee and other retail businesses pay careful attention to profitability and sales per square metre of cafe floor space, which often is the most important constrained resource. The importance of this metric explains why fast-food restaurants like McDonald's push their drive-through service—customers using the drive-through option do not require any internal store floor space. In fact, some restaurants generate more than 80 percent of sales from this service!

CORNERSTONE 13.8 Determining the Optimal Product Mix with One Constrained Resource and a Sales Constraint

Information:

Jorgenson Company produces two types of gears, X and Y, with unit contribution margins of $25 and $10, respectively. Each gear must be notched by a special machine. The firm owns eight machines that together provide 40,000 hours of machine time per year. Gear X requires two hours of machine time, and Gear Y requires 0.5 hour of machine time. A maximum of 60,000 units of each gear can be sold.

Required:

1. What is the contribution margin per hour of machine time for each gear?
2. What is the optimal mix of gears?
3. What is the total contribution margin earned for the optimal mix?

Solution:

1.

	Gear X	Gear Y
Contribution margin per unit	$25.00	$ 10
Required machine time per unit	÷ 2	÷ 0.5
Contribution margin per hour of machine time	$12.50	$ 20

(Continued)

CORNERSTONE
13.8

(Continued)

2. Since Gear Y yields \$20 of contribution margin per hour of machine time, the first priority is to produce all of Gear Y that the market will take (i.e., demands).

   Machine time required for maximum amount of Gear Y = 60,000 × 0.5 machine hours required for each Gear Y unit
   = 30,000 hours needed to manufacture 60,000 Gear Y units

   Remaining machine time for Gear X = 40,000 − 30,000
   = 10,000 hours

   Units of Gear X to be produced in remaining 10,000 hours = 10,000/2
   = 5,000 units

   Now the optimal mix is 60,000 units of Gear Y and 5,000 units of Gear X. This mix will precisely exhaust the machine time available.

3. Total contribution margin of optimal mix = (60,000 units Gear Y × \$10)
   + (5,000 units Gear X × \$25)
   = \$725,000

Why:

A complication of the scarce resource question arises when there is also a sales constraint that indicates the maximum sales that can be achieved. Keeping both the constrained resource and the sales constraint in mind is essential if the best decision is to be made.

Multiple Constrained Resources

The presence of only one constrained resource might not be realistic. Organizations often face multiple constraints: limitations of raw materials, limitations of skilled labour, limited demand for each product, and so on. The solution of the product mix problem in the presence of multiple constraints is considerably more complicated and requires the use of a specialized mathematical technique known as linear programming, which is reserved for advanced cost management courses.

THE USE OF COSTS IN PRICING DECISIONS

OBJECTIVE 4
Explain the impact of cost on pricing decisions.

One of the more difficult decisions faced by a company is pricing. This section examines the impact of cost on price and the role of the accountant in gathering the needed information.

Cost-Based Pricing

Demand is one side of the pricing equation; supply is the other side. Since revenue must cover all costs for the firm to make a profit, many companies start with cost to determine price. That is, they calculate product cost and add the desired profit. The mechanics of this approach are straightforward. Usually, there is some base cost and a markup. The **markup** is a percentage applied to the base cost and is calculated as follows:

Price using markup = Cost per unit + (Cost per unit × Markup percentage)

It includes desired profit and any costs not included in the base cost. Companies that bid for jobs routinely base bid price on cost. Law firms and public accounting firms are service organizations that use cost-plus pricing to bid for clients. Cornerstone 13.9 shows how to apply a markup percentage to cost to obtain price.

CORNERSTONE 13.9

Calculating Price by Applying a Markup Percentage to Cost

Information:

Elvin Company assembles and installs computers to customer specifications. Elvin has decided to price its jobs at the cost of direct materials and direct labour plus 20 percent. The job for a local vocational–technical school included the following costs:

Direct materials	$65,000
Direct labour (assembly and installation)	4,000

Required:

Calculate the price charged by Elvin Company to the vocational–technical school.

Solution:

Price = Cost + Markup percentage × Cost
= $69,000 + 0.20($69,000)
= $69,000 + $13,800
= $82,800

Why:

Many companies try to achieve consistent gross margins on their products by applying a consistent markup percentage to the cost of each product. This greatly simplifies pricing formulas and enables pricing decisions to be made at various levels in the organization.

Notice in Cornerstone 13.9 that the markup of 20 percent is not pure profit. Instead, it includes other costs not specified, such as overhead (including Elvin's offices and management salaries) as well as any marketing and administrative expenses. The ease in using a cost-plus approach is that companies do not need to allocate overhead or support costs in determining the product cost for pricing purposes. Instead, the company can easily trace direct costs and use those amounts as the basis for determining the markup percentage. As long as the markup covers all costs that are not included in the formula (e.g., overhead), the pricing strategy is appropriate. The markup percentage can be calculated using a variety of bases.

Retail stores often use markup pricing, and typical markup is 100 percent of cost. Thus, if Graham Department Store purchases a sweater for $24, the retail price marked is $48 [= $24 + (1.00 × $24)]. Again, the 100 percent markup is not pure profit—it goes toward the salaries of the clerks, payment for space and equipment (e.g., cash registers, furniture, and fixtures), utilities, advertising, and so on. A major advantage of markup pricing is that standard markups are easy to apply. Consider the difficulty of setting a price for

concept Q&A

Consider a situation in which you want to buy something, but it is quite expensive. Suppose the salesperson says that the price of the item is high because the cost to the store is high. (That is, price is related to cost.) Suppose, on the other hand, that the salesperson says the price is high because the demand for the item is strong. (That is, price is not related to cost.) Which explanation would make you happier to buy the item?

Answers on pages 734 to 738.

every piece of merchandise in a hardware or department store. It is much simpler to apply a uniform markup to cost and then to adjust prices upward (or downward) if demand is more (or less) than anticipated.

Several important observations are in order at this point concerning the relationship between the base cost, the markup percentage, and the firm's cost system. First, when the firm includes relatively few costs in the base cost (rather than a large number of costs), it usually becomes very important for the firm to select a large enough markup percentage to ensure that the markup covers all of the remaining costs not included in the base cost. Covering more costs with the markup requires significant judgment and cost estimation. Second, on a related note, the effectiveness of cost-plus pricing relies heavily on the accuracy of the cost system and pricing managers' understanding of the firm's cost structure. For example, assume that a firm marks up only its direct manufacturing costs and does not understand the behaviour of its indirect manufacturing costs or its nonmanufacturing costs (e.g., research and development costs, distribution costs, and customer service costs). In this case, it is likely that the firm will encounter problems in setting prices either too high (and will be undercut by competitors with more appropriate lower prices) or too low (and will not cover all costs, thereby resulting in a net loss).

Target Costing and Pricing

Many North American and European firms set the price of a new product as the sum of the costs and the desired profit. The rationale is that the company must earn sufficient revenues to cover all costs and yield a profit. Peter Drucker writes, "This is true but irrelevant: Customers do not see it as their job to ensure manufacturers a profit. The only sound way to price is to start out with what the market is willing to pay."[10]

Target costing is a method of determining the cost of a product or service based on the price (target price) that customers are willing to pay. The marketing department determines what characteristics and price for a product are most acceptable to consumers; then, it is the job of the company's engineers to design and develop the product such that cost and profit can be covered by that price. Japanese firms have been doing this for years; North American companies are beginning to use target costing. For example, Olympus, Toyota, Boeing, Nissan, and Caterpillar have used a value chain perspective to implement target costing. Target costing recognizes that between 75 and 90 percent of a product's cost becomes "committed" or "locked in" by the time it finishes the design stage.[11] Therefore, it is most effective to make such large changes in the design and development stage of the product life cycle because at this point the features of the product, as well as its costs, are still fairly easy to adjust. Typical target costing efforts to reduce costs focus on redesigning the product to require fewer or less costly materials, labour, and processes during production, delivery, and customer service. Mercedes, for instance, used target costing extensively in the design of its popular M-class sport–utility vehicle series, which made its public debut in the blockbuster movie *Jurassic Park*.

Consider the target costing experience used by Digitime Company in developing a wristwatch that incorporates a PDA (personal digital assistant). The "cool factor" on this item is high, but actually inputting data on the watch is difficult. So, the company expects to be able to charge a premium price to a relatively small number of early adopters. The marketing vice-president's price estimate is $200. Digitime's management requires a 15 percent profit on new products. Therefore, target cost is calculated using the following equation:

$$\text{Target cost} = \text{Target price} - \text{Desired profit}$$

[10] Peter Drucker, "The Five Deadly Business Sins," *The Wall Street Journal* (October 21, 1993): A22.
[11] Antonio Davila and Marc Wouters, "Designing Cost-Competitive Technology Products through Cost Management," *Accounting Horizons*, Vol. 18, No. 1 (2004): 13–26.

Cornerstone 13.10 shows how to calculate a target cost.

CORNERSTONE 13.10 Calculating a Target Cost

Information:

Digitime manufactures wristwatches and is designing a new watch model that incorporates a PDA (personal digital assistant), which Digitime hopes consumers will view as a cool and valuable design feature. As such, the new PDA watch has a target price of $200. Management requires a 15 percent profit on new products.

Required:

1. Calculate the amount of desired profit.
2. Calculate the target cost.

Solution:

1. Desired profit = 0.15 × Target price
   = 0.15 × $200
   = $30
2. Target cost = Target price − Desired profit
   = $200 − $30 = $170

Why:

Some organizations determine prices based on market factors and must achieve certain target prices for the purchase or manufacture of their products in order to achieve consistent gross margins on sales. Target pricing allows them to calculate what must be accomplished to achieve this objective.

Target costing involves much more upfront work than cost-based pricing. If Digitime cannot make the watch for $170, then the engineers and designers will have to go back to the drawing board and find a way to get it done on budget. However, let's not forget the additional work that must be done if the cost-based price turns out to be higher than what customers will accept. Then, the arduous task of bringing costs into line to support a lower price, or the opportunity cost of missing the market altogether, begins. For example, in the 1980s, the U.S. consumer electronics market became virtually nonexistent because cost-based pricing led to increasingly higher prices. Japanese (and later Korean) firms practising target costing offered lower prices and just the features wanted by consumers to win the market.

Target costing can be used most effectively in the design and development stage of the product life cycle. At that point, the features of the product as well as its costs are still fairly easy to adjust.

SUMMARY OF LEARNING OBJECTIVES

LO1. Describe the short-run decision-making model, and explain how cost behaviour affects the information used to make decisions.

- Six steps of the decision-making model are:
  - Recognize and define the problem.
  - Identify feasible alternatives.

- Identify costs and benefits for each feasible alternative.
- Estimate the relevant costs and benefits for each alternative.
- Assess qualitative factors.
- Make the decision and select the alternative with the greatest overall net benefit.

- Relevant costs are:
  - future costs that differ across alternatives
  - frequently variable costs—called flexible resources

LO2. Apply relevant costing and decision-making concepts in a variety of business situations.

- Outsourcing decision
- Special-order decision
- Keep-or-drop decision
- Further processing of joint products

LO3. Choose the optimal product mix when faced with one constrained resource.

- Single constraint leads to production of the product with the greatest contribution margin per unit of scarce resource.
- Multiple constraints require linear programming.

LO4. Explain the impact of cost on pricing decisions.

- Markup costing applies markup to cost to determine price.
- Target costing works backward from desired price to find allowable cost.

SUMMARY OF IMPORTANT EQUATIONS

1. $$\text{Contribution margin per unit of scarce resource} = \frac{\text{Contribution margin per unit}}{\text{Amount of scarce resource to make one unit}}$$
2. Price using markup = Cost per unit + (Cost per unit × Markup percentage)
3. Target cost = Target price − Desired profit

CORNERSTONES

GLOSSARY

Constraints Mathematical expressions that express resource limitations. (p. 651)

Decision model A specific set of procedures that lead to a decision. (p. 630)

Differential cost The difference in total cost between the alternatives in a decision. (p. 632)

Joint products Products that are inseparable prior to a split-off point. All manufacturing costs up to the split-off point are joint costs. (p. 648)

Keep-or-drop decisions Relevant costing analyses that focus on keeping or dropping a segment of a business. (p. 644)

Make-or-buy decisions Relevant costing analyses that focus on whether a component should be made internally or purchased externally. (p. 638)

Markup The percentage applied to a base cost; it includes desired profit and any costs not included in the base cost. (p. 653)

Opportunity cost The benefit given up or sacrificed when one alternative is chosen over another. (p. 634)

Relevant costs Future costs that change across alternatives. (p. 634)

Sell-or-process-further decision Relevant costing analysis that focuses on whether a product should be processed beyond the split-off point. (p. 648)

Special-order decisions Relevant costing analyses that focus on whether a specially priced order should be accepted or rejected. (p. 641)

Split-off point The point at which products become distinguishable after passing through a common process. (p. 648)

Sunk cost A cost for which the outlay has already been made and that cannot be affected by a future decision. (p. 635)

Target costing A method of determining the cost of a product or service based on the price (target price) that customers are willing to pay. (p. 655)

REVIEW PROBLEMS

I. Special-Order Decision

Pastin Company produces a light-weight travel raincoat with the following unit cost:

Direct materials	$4.00
Direct labour	1.00
Variable overhead	1.75
Fixed overhead	2.00
Unit cost	$8.75

While production capacity is 200,000 units per year, Pastin expects to produce only 170,000 raincoats for the coming year. The fixed selling costs total $85,000 per year, and variable selling costs are $0.50 per unit sold. The raincoats normally sell for $12 each.

At the beginning of the year, a customer from a geographic region outside the area normally served by the company offered to buy 20,000 raincoats for $8 each. The customer would pay all transportation costs, and there would be no variable selling costs.

Required:

Should the company accept the order? Provide both qualitative and quantitative justification for your decision. Assume that no other orders are expected beyond the regular business and the special order.

Solution:

The company expects idle capacity. Accepting the special order would bring production up to near capacity. The two options are to accept or reject the order. If the order is accepted, then the company could avoid laying off employees and would enhance and maintain its community image. However, the order is considerably below the normal selling price of $12. Because the price is so low, the company needs to assess the potential impact of the sale on its regular customers and on the profitability of the firm. Considering the fact that the customer is located in a region not usually served by the company, the likelihood of an adverse impact on regular business is not high. Thus, the qualitative factors seem to favour acceptance.

To assess profitability, the firm should identify the relevant costs and benefits of each alternative. This analysis is as follows:

	Accept	Reject
Revenues	$160,000	$ —
Direct materials	(80,000)	—
Direct labour	(20,000)	—
Variable overhead	(35,000)	—
Total benefits	$ 25,000	$ 0

Accepting the order would increase profits by $25,000. (The fixed overhead and selling costs are all irrelevant because they are the same across both alternatives.) Conclusion: The order should be accepted because both qualitative and quantitative factors favour it.

II. Optimal Mix

Two types of gears are produced: A and B. Gear A has a unit contribution margin of $200, and Gear B has a unit contribution margin of $400. Gear A uses two hours of grinding time, and Gear B uses five hours of grinding time. There are 200 hours of grinding time available per week. This is the only constraint.

Required:

1. Is the grinding constraint an internal constraint or an external constraint?
2. Determine the optimal mix. What is the total contribution margin?
3. Suppose that there is an additional demand constraint: Market conditions will allow the sale of only 80 units of each gear. Now, what is the optimal mix? The total contribution margin?

Solution:

1. Grinding time is an internal constraint.
2. Gear A: $200/2 = $100 per grinding hour
   Gear B: $400/5 = $80 per grinding hour

   Since Gear A earns more contribution margin per unit of scarce resource than Gear B, only Gear A should be produced and sold (this is based on the fact that we can sell all we want of each product).

   Optimal mix: Gear A = 100 units* and Gear B = 0

   Total contribution margin = $200 × 100 = $20,000 per week
3. Now, we should sell 80 units of Gear A using 160 hours (2 hours × 80) and 8 units of Gear B (= 40/5).

   Total contribution margin = (80 × $200) + (8 × $400) = $19,200 per week

* 200/2 = 100 units of A can be produced per week.

DISCUSSION QUESTIONS

1. What is the difference between tactical and strategic decisions?
2. Explain why depreciation on an existing asset is always irrelevant.
3. Give an example of a future cost that is not relevant.
4. What role do past costs play in relevant costing decisions?
5. Can direct materials ever be irrelevant in a make-or-buy decision? Explain.
6. Discuss the importance of complementary effects in a keep-or-drop decision.
7. What are some ways that a manager can identify the feasible set of alternatives?
8. Should joint costs be considered in a sell-or-process-further decision? Explain.
9. Suppose that a product can be sold at split-off for $5,000 or processed further at a cost of $1,000 and then sold for $6,400. Should the product be processed further?
10. Suppose that a firm produces two products. Should the firm always place the most emphasis on the product with the largest contribution margin per unit? Explain.
11. Why would a firm ever offer a price on a product that is below its full cost?

CORNERSTONE EXERCISES

Cornerstone Exercise 13-1 Structuring an Outsourcing Problem

Recently, Claude Manufacturing was approached by a firm that is offering to provide accounting and tax services for $500,000 annually. Historically, Claude Manufacturing has completed these tasks in-house and must now decide if the company should continue with this process or accept the supplier's offer. By accepting the firm's offer, Claude Manufacturing can save 60 percent of fixed expenses in addition to relevant labour and variable expenses. To evaluate this decision, Claude Manufacturing gathered the following annual cost information for the accounting and tax services department:

	Total Cost
Direct labour	$225,000
Variable overhead	62,500
Fixed overhead	325,250
Total	$612,750

Required:

1. List the relevant cost(s) of internally providing the services and externally purchasing from another organization.
2. Which alternative is more cost effective and by how much?
3. At what cost of outsourcing would Claude Manufacturing be indifferent between providing the services in-house and outsourcing to another company?
4. What other factors should Claude Manufacturing consider before deciding to outsource these services?

Cornerstone Exercise 13-2 Structuring a Make-or-Buy Problem

Leather Products, a manufacturer of wallets and purses, is considering whether to produce 3,000 units of a new leather phone pouch or purchase them from an outside supplier for $15 each. Cost information on internal production includes the following:

	Total Cost	Unit Cost
Direct materials	$19,500	$ 6.50
Direct labour	10,500	3.50
Variable manufacturing overhead	7,500	2.50
Variable marketing overhead	4,500	1.50
Fixed plant overhead	15,000	5.00
Total	$57,000	$19.00

Fixed overhead will continue whether the pouch is produced internally or externally. No additional costs of purchasing will be incurred beyond the purchase price.

Required:

1. What are the alternatives for Leather Products?
2. List the relevant cost(s) of internal production and of external purchase.
3. Which alternative is more cost effective and by how much?
4. Now assume that 45 percent of the fixed overhead can be avoided if the units are purchased externally. Which alternative is more cost effective and by how much?

Cornerstone Exercise 13-3 **Structuring a Special-Order Problem**

OBJECTIVE 2
CORNERSTONE 13.3

Recently Wang Company was approached by a new customer with an offer to purchase 10,000 units of its model IJ4 at a price of $4 each. Normally Wang Company produces 75,000 units of the IJ4, which the company sells for $12 per unit. In the coming year, the company expects to produce and sell only 60,000 units. Accepting this offer will not affect sales to the company's other customers. Unit cost information for the normal level of activity is as follows:

Direct materials	$1.50
Direct labour	2.00
Variable overhead	1.00
Fixed overhead	3.25
Total	$7.75

Fixed overhead will not be affected by whether or not the special order is accepted.

Required:

1. What are the relevant costs and benefits of the two alternatives (accept or reject the special order)?
2. By how much will operating income increase or decrease if the order is accepted?

Cornerstone Exercise 13-4 **Structuring a Keep-or-Drop Product Line Problem**

A segmented income statement is shown below for snow shovel producer SnoGo Company in thousands of dollars:

	Ergo	Slider	Lite Lift	Total
Sales revenue	$350	$290	$250	$890
Less: Variable expenses	300	210	175	685
Contribution margin	50	80	75	205
Less direct fixed expenses:				
Machine rent	(20)	(10)	(8)	(38)
Supervision	(8)	(5)	(2)	(15)
Depreciation	(26)	(12)	(10)	(48)
Segment margin	$ (4)	$ 53	$ 55	$104

SnoGo's Ergo product line has a contribution margin of $50,000 (sales of $350,000 less total variable costs of $300,000). All variable costs are relevant. Relevant fixed costs associated with this line include $20,000 in machine rent and $8,000 in supervision salaries.

(Continued)

Required:

1. List the alternatives that could be considered with respect to the Ergo line (assuming outsourcing is not an option).
2. List the relevant benefits and costs for each alternative.
3. Which alternative is more cost effective and by how much?

OBJECTIVE 2
CORNERSTONE 13.5

Cornerstone Exercise 13-5 Structuring a Keep-or-Drop Product Line Problem with Complementary Effects

Refer to SnoGo's segmented income statement in **Cornerstone Exercise 13-4**. Assume that dropping the Ergo product line would reduce sales of the Slider line by 20 percent and sales of the Lite Lift line by 15 percent. All other information remains the same.

Required:

1. If the Ergo product line is dropped, what is the contribution margin for the Slider line? For the Lite Lift line?
2. Which alternative (keep or drop the Ergo product line) is now more cost effective and by how much?

OBJECTIVE 2
CORNERSTONE 13.6

Cornerstone Exercise 13-6 Structuring the Sell-or-Process-Further Decision

Pepin's Lumber Yard receives 8,000 large trees each period that it subsequently processes into rough logs which the company can sell (for use in log cabin construction) for a total of $500. Alternatively, the company can process the rough logs further into refined lumber (for use in regular construction framing), which produces 800 feet of lumber at an additional cost of $0.05 per foot and then sells for $0.75 per foot.

Required:

1. What is the contribution to income from selling the logs for log cabin construction?
2. What is the contribution to income from processing the logs into lumber?
3. Should Pepin's continue to sell the logs or process them further into lumber?

OBJECTIVE 3
CORNERSTONE 13.6

Cornerstone Exercise 13-7 Determining the Optimal Product Mix with One Constrained Resource

Comfy Fit Company manufactures two types of university sweatshirts, the Swoop and the Rufus, with unit contribution margins of $5 and $15, respectively. Regardless of type, each sweatshirt must be fed through a stitching machine to affix the appropriate university logo. The firm leases seven machines that each provide 1,000 hours of machine time per year. Each Swoop sweatshirt requires 6 minutes of machine time, and each Rufus sweatshirt requires 30 minutes of machine time. There are no other constraints.

Required:

1. What is the contribution margin per hour of machine time for each type of sweatshirt?
2. What is the optimal mix of sweatshirts?
3. What is the total contribution margin earned for the optimal mix?

OBJECTIVE 3
CORNERSTONE 13.8

Cornerstone Exercise 13-8 Determining the Optimal Product Mix with One Constrained Resource and a Sales Constraint

Comfy Fit Company manufactures two types of university sweatshirts, the Swoop and the Rufus, with unit contribution margins of $5 and $15, respectively. Regardless of type, each sweatshirt must be fed through a stitching machine to affix the appropriate university logo. The firm leases seven machines that each provide 1,000 hours of machine time per year. Each Swoop sweatshirt requires 6 minutes of machine time, and each Rufus sweatshirt requires 30 minutes of machine time. A maximum of 50,000 units of each sweatshirt can be sold.

Required:

1. What is the contribution margin per hour of machine time for each type of sweatshirt?
2. What is the optimal mix of sweatshirts?
3. What is the total contribution margin earned for the optimal mix?

Cornerstone Exercise 13-9 Calculating Price by Applying a Markup Percentage to Cost

OBJECTIVE 4
CORNERSTONE 13.9

Maksim's Financial Services provides various financial planning and investment training seminars and has decided to price its jobs at the total variable costs of the job plus 20 percent. The job for a two-hour seminar for a client includes the following costs:

Direct materials	$ 1,500
Direct labour (preparation and presentations)	2,800
Depreciation (using straight-line method) on Maksim's office building	40,000

Required:

Calculate the price charged by Maksim's Financial Services to the client.

Cornerstone Exercise 13-10 Calculating a Target Cost

OBJECTIVE 4
CORNERSTONE 13.10

Yuhu manufactures cell phones and is developing a new model with a feature (aptly named Don't Drink and Dial) that prevents the phone from dialing an owner-defined list of phone numbers between the hours of midnight and 6:00 a.m. The new phone model has a target price of $350. Management requires a 10 percent profit on new products.

Required:

1. Calculate the amount of desired profit.
2. Calculate the target cost.

EXERCISES

Exercise 13-11 Model for Making Tactical Decisions

OBJECTIVE 1

The model for making tactical decisions described in the text has six steps. These steps are listed, out of order, below.

1. Select the alternative with the greatest overall benefit.
2. Identify the costs and benefits associated with each feasible alternative.
3. Assess qualitative factors.
4. Recognize and define the problem.
5. Identify alternatives as possible solutions to the problem.
6. Total the relevant costs and benefits for each alternative.

Required:

Put the steps in the correct order.

Exercise 13-12 Model for Making Tactical Decisions

OBJECTIVE 1

Austin Saliu is an undergraduate student at Small Maritime University (SMU). He is considering whether to continue at this university or to transfer to one with a nationally recognized engineering program. Austin's decision-making process included the following:

a. He surfed the web to check out the sites of a number of universities with engineering programs.
b. Austin wrote to five of the universities to obtain information on their engineering programs, tuition and room and board costs, the likelihood of being accepted, and so on.
c. Austin compared costs of the five other schools with the cost of his present school. He totalled the balance in his chequing and savings accounts, estimated the earnings from his work-study job, and asked his parents whether they would be able to help him out.

(Continued)

d. Austin's high-school sweetheart had a long heart-to-heart talk with him about their future—specifically, that there might be no future if he left town.
e. Austin thought that while he enjoyed his present university, its engineering program did not have the national reputation that would enable him to get a good job in a major city. Working for a large company in a major city was an important dream of his.
f. Austin's major advisor agreed that a school with a national reputation would make job hunting easier. However, he reminded Austin that graduates of small universities had occasionally gotten the kinds of jobs that Austin wanted.
g. Austin had a number of good friends at SMU, and they were encouraging him to stay.
h. A friend of Austin's from high school returned home for a long weekend. She attends a prestigious university and told Austin of the fun and opportunities available at her school. She encouraged Austin to check out the possibilities elsewhere.
i. A friendly professor outside of Austin's major area ran into him at the student union. She listened to his thinking and reminded him that a degree from SMU would easily get him into a good graduate program. Perhaps he should consider postponing the job hunt until he had his master's degree in hand.
j. Two of the three prestigious universities accepted Austin and offered financial aid. The third one rejected his application.
k. Austin made his decision.

Required:

Classify the events (a) through (k) under the six steps of the model for making tactical decisions described in the text.

OBJECTIVE 2

Exercise 13-13 Special-Order Problem

Stade Company has been presented with an offer from a new customer to purchase 15,000 units of model F201 at a price of $15 each. In terms of proximity, the new customer is far enough away from the company's other customers that existing sales are not expected to be affected. Stade normally produces 80,000 units of F201 per year but only plans to produce and sell 60,000 in the coming year. The normal sales price is $19 per unit. Unit cost information for the normal level of activity is as follows:

Direct materials	$ 6.00
Direct labour	3.50
Variable overhead	2.20
Fixed overhead	4.50
Total	$16.20

Fixed overhead will not be affected by whether or not the special order is accepted.

Required:

1. What are the relevant costs and benefits of the two alternatives (accept or reject the special order)?
2. By how much will operating income increase or decrease if the order is accepted?

OBJECTIVE 1 

Exercise 13-14 Make-or-Buy Decision

Zion Manufacturing had always made its components in-house. However, Bryce Component Works had recently offered to supply one component, K2, at a price of $25 each. Zion uses 10,000 units of component K2 each year. The cost per unit of this component is as follows:

Direct materials	$12.00
Direct labour	8.25
Variable overhead	3.50
Fixed overhead	2.00
Total	$25.75

The fixed overhead is an allocated expense; none of it would be eliminated if production of component K2 stopped.

Required:

1. What are the alternatives facing Zion Manufacturing with respect to production of component K2?
2. List the relevant costs for each alternative.
3. CONCEPTUAL CONNECTION If Zion decides to purchase the component from Bryce, by how much will operating income increase or decrease? Which alternative is better?

Exercise 13-15 Make-or-Buy Decision

OBJECTIVE 2

Zion Manufacturing had always made its components in-house. However, Bryce Component Works had recently offered to supply one component, K2, at a price of $25 each. Zion uses 10,000 units of component K2 each year. The cost per unit of this component is as follows:

Direct materials	$12.00
Direct labour	8.25
Variable overhead	3.50
Fixed overhead	2.00
Total	$25.75

Assume that 75 percent of Zion Manufacturing's fixed overhead for component K2 would be eliminated if that component were no longer produced.

Required:

CONCEPTUAL CONNECTION If Zion decides to purchase the component from Bryce, by how much will operating income increase or decrease? Which alternative is better?

Exercise 13-16 Special-Order Decision

OBJECTIVE 2

Smooth Move Company manufactures professional paperweights and has been approached by a new customer with an offer to purchase 15,000 units at a per-unit price of $7. The new customer is geographically separated from Smooth Move's other customers, and existing sales will not be affected. Smooth Move normally produces 82,000 units but plans to produce and sell only 65,000 in the coming year. The normal sales price is $12 per unit. Unit cost information is as follows:

Direct materials	$3.00
Direct labour	2.25
Variable overhead	1.15
Fixed overhead	1.80
Total	$8.20

If Smooth Move accepts the order, no fixed manufacturing activities will be affected because there is sufficient excess capacity.

Required:

1. What are the alternatives for Smooth Move?
2. CONCEPTUAL CONNECTION Should Smooth Move accept the special order? By how much will profit increase or decrease if the order is accepted?

Exercise 13-17 Special Order

OBJECTIVE 2

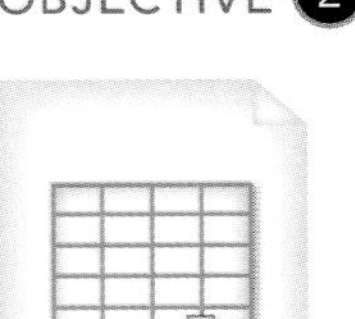

SolarGlo Company manufactures solar powered garden lights and has been approached by a new customer with an offer to purchase 20,000 units at a per-unit price of $20. The new customer is geographically separated from SolarGlo's other customers, and existing sales will not be affected.

(Continued)

SolarGlo normally produces 165,000 units but plans to produce and sell only 140,000 in the coming year. The normal sales price is $28 per unit. Unit cost information is as follows:

Direct materials	$12.00
Direct labour	3.75
Variable overhead	3.50
Fixed overhead	2.50
Total	$21.75

The customer wants to have its company logo affixed to each solar light using a label. SolarGlo would have to purchase a special logo labelling machine for this order that would cost $22,000. The machine would be able to label all 20,000 units and then it would be scrapped (with no further value). No other fixed overhead activities would be affected.

Required:

CONCEPTUAL CONNECTION Should SolarGlo accept the special order? By how much will profit increase or decrease if the order is accepted?

Exercise 13-18 Keep-or-Drop Decision

Petoskey Company produces three products: Alanson, Boyne, and Conway. A segmented income statement, with amounts given in thousands, follows:

	Alanson	Boyne	Conway	Total
Sales revenue	$1,280	$185	$300	$1,765
Less: Variable expenses	1,115	45	225	1,385
Contribution margin	165	140	75	380
Less direct fixed expenses:				
Depreciation	50	15	10	75
Salaries	95	85	80	260
Segment margin	$ 20	$ 40	$ (15)	$ 45

Direct fixed expenses consist of depreciation and plant supervisory salaries. All depreciation on the equipment is dedicated to the product lines. None of the equipment can be sold. Also, each of the three products has a different supervisor whose position would remain if the associated product were dropped.

Required:

CONCEPTUAL CONNECTION Estimate the impact on profit that would result from dropping Conway. Explain why Petoskey should keep or drop Conway.

Exercise 13-19 Keep-or-Drop Decision

Petoskey Company produces three products: Alanson, Boyne, and Conway. A segmented income statement, with amounts given in thousands, follows:

	Alanson	Boyne	Conway	Total
Sales revenue	$1,280	$185	$300	$1,765
Less: Variable expenses	1,115	45	225	1,385
Contribution margin	165	140	75	380
Less direct fixed expenses:				
Depreciation	50	15	10	75
Salaries	95	85	80	260
Segment margin	$ 20	$ 40	$ (15)	$ 45

Direct fixed expenses consist of depreciation and plant supervisory salaries. All depreciation on the equipment is dedicated to the product lines. None of the equipment can be sold. Also, each of the three products has a different supervisor whose position would be eliminated if the associated product were dropped.

Required:

CONCEPTUAL CONNECTION Estimate the impact on profit that would result from dropping Conway. Explain why Petoskey should keep or drop Conway.

Exercise 13-20 Keep-or-Drop Decision

OBJECTIVE 2

Refer to the Petoskey Company information provided in **Exercise 13-19**. In addition, assume that 20 percent of the Alanson customers choose to buy from Petoskey because it offers a full range of products, including Conway. If Conway were no longer available from Petoskey, these customers would go elsewhere to purchase Alanson.

Required:

CONCEPTUAL CONNECTION Estimate the impact on profit that would result from dropping Conway. Explain why Petoskey should keep or drop Conway.

Exercise 13-21 Sell at Split-Off or Process Further

OBJECTIVE 2

Chirp Inc. manufactures two products from a joint production process. The joint process costs $150,000 and yields 10,000 kilograms of PEROX compound and 32,000 kilograms of EPTOL compound. PEROX can be sold at split-off for $40 per kilogram. EPTOL can be sold at split-off for $6 per kilogram. A buyer of EPTOL asked Chirp Inc. to process EPTOL further into CHLOR compound. If EPTOL were processed further, it would cost $205,000 to turn 32,000 kilograms of EPTOL into 9,000 kilograms of CHLOR. The CHLOR would sell for $60 per kilogram.

Required:

1. What is the contribution to income from selling the 32,000 kilograms of EPTOL at split-off?
2. CONCEPTUAL CONNECTION What is the contribution to income from processing the 32,000 kilograms of EPTOL into 9,000 kilograms of CHLOR? Should Chirp Inc. continue to sell the EPTOL at split-off or process it further into CHLOR?

Exercise 13-22 Choosing the Optimal Product Mix with One Constrained Resource

OBJECTIVE 3

Vancouver Company produces two products, Product Whistler and Product Blackcomb. Each product goes through its own assembly and finishing departments. However, both of them must go through the painting department. The painting department has capacity of 2,460 hours per year. Product Whistler has a unit contribution margin of $120 and requires 5 hours of painting department time. Product Blackcomb has a unit contribution margin of $75 and requires 3 hours of painting department time. There are no other constraints.

Required:

1. What is the contribution margin per hour of painting department time for each product?
2. What is the optimal mix of products?
3. What is the total contribution margin earned for the optimal mix?

Exercise 13-23 Choosing the Optimal Product Mix with a Constrained Resource and a Demand Constraint

OBJECTIVE 3

Refer to the Vancouver Company information provided in **Exercise 13-22**. Also, assume that only 500 units of each product can be sold.

Required:

1. What is the optimal mix of products?
2. What is the total contribution margin earned for the optimal mix?

Exercise 13-24 Calculating Price Using a Markup Percentage of Cost

OBJECTIVE 4

Philips Company has decided to price the soccer balls that it sells at cost plus 60 percent. One type of standard soccer ball costs $24, and the smaller-sized kids' ball costs $9.50 each.

(Continued)

Required:

1. What price will Philips Company charge for the standard soccer ball?
2. What price will Philips Company charge for the kids' soccer ball?
3. CONCEPTUAL CONNECTION Briefly explain two specific challenges that the financial manager of Philips Company might encounter in employing this cost-plus pricing approach.

OBJECTIVE 2

Exercise 13-25 Discard or Process Further

Tembec buys pine logs and saws them into boards of two grades: A and B. The grade is determined by factors such as the number of knotholes and quality of the grain. Bark and shavings are also produced as a result of the sawing operation. On average, a log yields 35 percent A-grade boards, 55 percent B-grade boards, and 10 percent bark and shavings. Charles Merchant, the owner, just received the income statement for the sawmill, shown below, which represents a typical month's operations. Charles expects similar results in the foreseeable future.

Sawing costs include wages, depreciation, and other non-itemized costs of running the sawmill. The costs of logs and of sawing were allocated according to volume (35 percent, 55 percent, 10 percent). Trimming, sanding, and shipping costs were direct and avoidable. Charles was disturbed at the results. He told an employee, "The bark and shavings are really hurting me. I'd be better off throwing the stuff out."

	Grade A	Grade B	Bark and Shavings	Total
Sales	$36,000	$41,000	$ 3,000	$80,000
Costs:				
Logs	14,700	23,100	4,200	42,000
Sawing	5,950	9,350	1,700	17,000
Trimming	2,340	860	0	3,200
Sanding	4,320	3,380	0	7,700
Shipping	1,550	2,430	520	4,500
Total costs	28,860	39,120	6,420	74,400
Income (loss)	$ 7,140	$ 1,880	$ (3,420)	$ 5,600

Required:

1. Should Charles throw away the bark and shavings? Provide a financial analysis of the effect on Charles's profit if the bark and shavings are thrown out rather than sold.
2. Identify other considerations that would be relevant to Charles's decision.

OBJECTIVE 

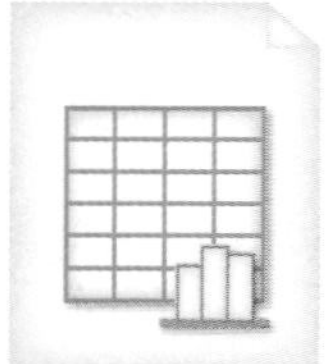

Exercise 13-26 Target Costing

M. Munir Company would like to design, produce, and sell versatile toasters for the home kitchen market. The toaster will have four slots that adjust in thickness to accommodate both slim slices of bread and oversized bagels. The target price is $75. Munir requires that new products be priced such that 25 percent of the price is profit.

Required:

1. Calculate the amount of desired profit per unit of the new toaster.
2. Calculate the target cost per unit of the new toaster.

OBJECTIVE 

Exercise 13-27 Keep or Buy, Sunk Costs

Dan Dunkard purchased a previously owned, five-year-old all terrain vehicle (ATV) for $7,500. Since purchasing the vehicle, he has spent the following amounts on parts and labour:

Rack and storage system	$ 900
1,600-kilogram winch	700
Tires	350
Total	$1,950

Unfortunately, the four-wheel drive system rarely engages and makes it impossible to haul the heavy loads the machine was purchased to move. Apparently, the ATV needs a considerable amount of work to make it useable equipment. Dan estimates that the needed repairs include the following:

Transmission overhaul	$1,800
Gear replacements	650
Labour	700
Total	$3,150

In a visit to a dealership, Dan has found a one-year-old utility tractor in mint condition for $8,500 that is sure to be capable of performing the required work. Dan has advertised and found that he can sell the ATV for only $5,950. If he buys the tractor, he will pay cash, but he would need to sell the ATV.

Required:

1. CONCEPTUAL CONNECTION In trying to decide whether to restore the ATV or to buy the tractor, Dan is distressed because he has already spent $9,450 on the ATV. The investment seems too much to give up. How would you react to his concern?
2. CONCEPTUAL CONNECTION Assuming that Dan would be equally happy with the ATV or the tractor, should he buy the tractor, or should he restore the ATV?

Exercise 13-28 Make or Buy

OBJECTIVE 2

Loro Company is currently manufacturing part Q108, producing 35,000 units annually. The part is used in the production of several products made by Loro. The cost per unit for Q108 is as follows:

Direct materials	$ 6.00
Direct labour	2.00
Variable overhead	1.50
Fixed overhead	3.50
Total	$13.00

Of the total fixed overhead assigned to Q108, $77,000 is direct fixed overhead (the lease of production machinery and salary of a production line supervisor—neither of which will be needed if the line is dropped). The remaining fixed overhead is common fixed overhead. An outside supplier has offered to sell the part to Loro for $11. There is no alternative use for the facilities currently used to produce the part.

Required:

1. CONCEPTUAL CONNECTION Should Loro Company make or buy part Q108?
2. What is the most that Loro would be willing to pay an outside supplier?
3. If Loro buys the part, by how much will income increase or decrease?

Exercise 13-29 Make or Buy

OBJECTIVE 1 2

Loro Company is currently manufacturing part Q108, producing 35,000 units annually. The part is used in the production of several products made by Loro. The cost per unit for Q108 is as follows:

Direct materials	$ 6.00
Direct labour	2.00
Variable overhead	1.50
Fixed overhead	3.50
Total	$13.00

All of the fixed overhead is common fixed overhead. An outside supplier has offered to sell the part to Loro for $11. There is no alternative use for the facilities currently used to produce the part.

(Continued)

Required:

1. CONCEPTUAL CONNECTION Should Loro Company make or buy part Q108?
2. What is the most Loro would be willing to pay an outside supplier?
3. If Loro buys the part, by how much will income increase or decrease?

PROBLEMS

OBJECTIVE 

Problem 13-30 Special-Order Decision

Rianne Company produces a light fixture with the following unit cost:

Direct materials	$2
Direct labour	1
Variable overhead	3
Fixed overhead	2
Unit cost	$8

The production capacity is 300,000 units per year. Because of a depressed housing market, the company expects to produce only 180,000 fixtures for the coming year. The company also has fixed selling costs totalling $500,000 per year and variable selling costs of $1 per unit sold. The fixtures normally sell for $12 each.

At the beginning of the year, a customer from a geographic region outside the area normally served by the company offered to buy 100,000 fixtures for $7 each. The customer also offered to pay all transportation costs. Since there would be no sales commissions involved, this order would not have any variable selling costs.

Required:

Check figure:
1. Total net benefit = $100,000

1. CONCEPTUAL CONNECTION Based on a quantitative (numerical) analysis, should the company accept the order?
2. CONCEPTUAL CONNECTION What qualitative factors might impact the decision? Assume that no other orders are expected beyond the regular business and the special order.

OBJECTIVE 

Problem 13-31 Make or Buy, Qualitative Considerations

Howarth Dental is a large dental practice. Currently, Howarth has its own dental laboratory to produce porcelain and gold crowns. The unit costs to produce the crowns are as follows:

	Porcelain	Gold
Raw materials	$125	$160
Direct labour	35	35
Variable overhead	12	12
Fixed overhead	26	26
Total	$198	$233

Fixed overhead is detailed as follows:

Salary (supervisor)	$32,000
Depreciation	6,000
Rent (lab facility)	34,000

Overhead is applied on the basis of direct labour hours. These rates were computed by using 6,200 direct labour hours.

A local dental laboratory has offered to supply Howarth all the crowns it needs. Its price is $190 for porcelain crowns and $205 for gold crowns; however, the offer is conditional on supplying both types of crowns—it will not supply just one type for the price indicated. If the offer is accepted, the equipment used by Howarth's laboratory would be scrapped (it is old and has no market value), and the lab facility would be closed. Howarth uses 2,400 porcelain crowns and 650 gold crowns per year.

Required:

1. CONCEPTUAL CONNECTION Should Howarth continue to make its own crowns, or should they be purchased from the external supplier? What is the dollar effect of purchasing?
2. CONCEPTUAL CONNECTION What qualitative factors should Howarth consider in making this decision?
3. CONCEPTUAL CONNECTION Suppose that the lab facility is owned rather than rented and that the $34,000 is depreciation rather than rent (assume lab space is not usable for any other purpose). What effect does this have on the analysis in Requirement 1?
4. CONCEPTUAL CONNECTION Refer to the original data. Assume that the volume of crowns used is 4,200 porcelain and 650 gold. Should Howarth make or buy the crowns? Explain the outcome.

Check figures:
1. Cost to make = $613,350
4. Cost to make = $922,950

Problem 13-32 Sell or Process Further

OBJECTIVE 1 2

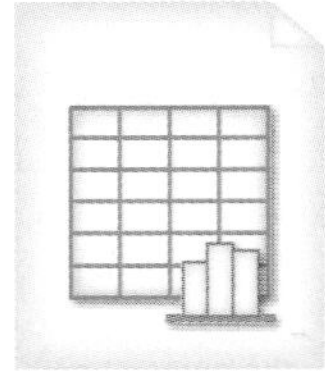

Zanda Drug Corporation buys three chemicals that are processed to produce two types of analgesics used as ingredients for popular over-the-counter drugs. The purchased chemicals are blended for 2-3 hours and then heated for 15 minutes. The results of the process are two separate analgesics, depryl and pencol, which are sent to a drying room until their moisture content is reduced to 6–8 percent. For every 1,300 kilograms of chemicals used, 600 kilograms of depryl and 600 kilograms of pencol are produced. After drying, depryl and pencol are sold to companies that process them into their final form. The selling prices are $12 per kilogram for depryl and $30 per kilogram for pencol. The costs to produce 600 kilograms of each analgesic are as follows:

Chemicals	$8,500
Direct labour	6,735
Overhead	9,900

The analgesics are packaged in 20-kilogram bags and shipped. The cost of each bag is $1.30. Shipping costs $0.10 per kilogram.

Zanda could process depryl further by grinding it into a fine powder and then moulding the powder into tablets. The tablets can be sold directly to retail drug stores as a generic brand. If this route were taken, the revenue received per bottle of tablets would be $4.00, with 10 bottles produced from every kilogram of depryl. The costs of grinding and tableting total $2.50 per kilogram of depryl. Bottles cost $0.40 each and are shipped in boxes that hold 25 bottles at a shipping cost of $1.60 per box.

Required:

1. CONCEPTUAL CONNECTION Should Zanda sell depryl at split-off, or should depryl be processed and sold as tablets?
2. CONCEPTUAL CONNECTION If Zanda normally sells 265,000 kilograms of depryl per year, what will be the difference in profits if depryl is processed further?

Check figure:
2. Additional income per kilogram = $21.025

Problem 13-33 Keep or Drop

OBJECTIVE  

AudioMart is a retailer of radios, stereos, and televisions. The store carries two portable sound systems that have radios, CD players, and speakers. System A, of slightly higher quality than system B, costs $20 more. With rare exceptions, the store also sells a headset when a system is sold. The headset can be used with either system. Variable-costing income statements for the three products follow:

	System A	System B	Headset
Sales	$45,000	$ 32,500	$8,000
Less: Variable expenses	20,000	25,500	3,200
Contribution margin	25,000	7,000	4,800
Less: Fixed costs*	10,000	18,000	2,700
Operating income	$15,000	$(11,000)	$2,100

* This includes common fixed costs totalling $18,000, allocated to each product in proportion to its revenues.

(*Continued*)

The owner of the store is concerned about the profit performance of system B and is considering dropping it. If the product is dropped, sales of system A will increase by 30 percent, and sales of headsets will drop by 25 percent.

Required:

1. Prepare segmented income statements for the three products using a better format.
2. CONCEPTUAL CONNECTION Prepare segmented income statements for system A and the headsets assuming that system B is dropped. Should system B be dropped?
3. CONCEPTUAL CONNECTION Suppose that a third system, system C, with a similar quality to system B, could be acquired. Assume that with C the sales of A would remain unchanged; however, C would produce only 80 percent of the revenues of B, and sales of the headsets would drop by 10 percent. The contribution margin ratio of C is 50 percent, and its direct fixed costs would be identical to those of B. Should system B be dropped and replaced with system C?

Check figures:

1. Operating income = $6,100
2. Operating income = $16,558
3. Total segment margin = $29,620

OBJECTIVE 1 2

Problem 13-34 Accept or Reject a Special Order

Steve Murningham, manager of an electronics division, was considering an offer by Pat Sellers, manager of a sister division. Pat's division was operating below capacity and had just been given an opportunity to produce 8,000 units of one of its products for a customer in a market not normally served. The opportunity involves a product that uses an electrical component produced by Steve's division. Each unit that Pat's division produces requires two of the components. However, the price that the customer is willing to pay is well below the price that is usually charged; to make a reasonable profit on the order, Pat needs a price concession from Steve's division. Pat had offered to pay full manufacturing cost for the parts. So Steve would know that everything was above board, Pat supplied the following unit cost and price information concerning the special order, excluding the cost of the electrical component:

Selling price	$32
Less costs:	
Direct materials	17
Direct labour	7
Variable overhead	2
Fixed overhead	3
Operating profit	$ 3

The normal selling price of the electrical component is $2.30 per unit; its full manufacturing cost is $1.85 (= $1.05 variable + $0.80 fixed). Pat argued that paying $2.30 per component would wipe out the operating profit and result in her division showing a loss. Steve was interested in the offer because his division was also operating below capacity (the order would not use all of the excess capacity).

Required:

1. CONCEPTUAL CONNECTION Should Steve accept the order at a selling price of $1.85 per unit? By how much will his division's profits be changed if the order is accepted? By how much will the profits of Pat's division change if Steve agrees to supply the part at full cost?
2. CONCEPTUAL CONNECTION Suppose that Steve offers to supply the component at $2. In offering this price, Steve says that it is a firm offer, not subject to negotiation. Should Pat accept this price and produce the special order? If Pat accepts the price, what is the change in profits for Steve's division?
3. CONCEPTUAL CONNECTION Assume that Steve's division is operating at full capacity and that Steve refuses to supply the part for less than the full price. Should Pat still accept the special order? Explain.

Check figures:

1. Increase Pat's income = $18,400
2. Increase Steve's income = $15,200

Problem 13-35 Accept or Reject a Special Order

Cyclo Company is a manufacturer of bicycle reflectors. Currently the company is able to produce 40,000 reflectors per month, although actual production averages 34,000 per month. Recently, the company was approached by an international bicycle manufacturer with an offer—the manufacturer would like to purchase 8,000 reflectors at a reduced selling price of $1.55 per reflector. However, since the bicycle manufacturer approached Cyclo, variable selling costs will not be incurred with this order.

Accepting the order will mean that Cyclo will be unable to sell all of the usual 34,000 reflectors to its existing customers. Instead, the company will only be able to provide 32,000 reflectors to those customers.

Normal per-unit data is as follows:

Selling price	$1.80
Direct materials	0.65
Direct labour	0.30
Variable selling cost	0.02
Variable overhead	0.20
Fixed overhead	0.45

Required:

1. How much will income increase or decrease by accepting the order?
2. What nonfinancial factors should Cyclo consider before accepting a special order?

Problem 13-36 Cost-Based Pricing Decision

OBJECTIVE 4

Jeremy Costa, owner of Costa Cabinets Inc., is preparing a bid on a job that requires $1,800 of direct materials, $1,600 of direct labour, and $800 of overhead. Jeremy normally applies a standard markup based on cost of goods sold to arrive at an initial bid price. He then adjusts the price as necessary in light of other factors (e.g., competitive pressure). Last year's income statement is as follows:

Sales	$130,000
Cost of goods sold	48,100
Gross margin	81,900
Selling and administrative expenses	46,300
Operating income	$ 35,600

Required:

1. Calculate the markup that Jeremy will use.
2. What is Jeremy's initial bid price?

Check figure:
1. Markup = $7,151

Problem 13-37 Product Mix Decision, Single Constraint

Harish Company manufactures three types of filing storage units. Each of the three types requires the use of a special machine that has a total operating capacity of 15,000 hours per year. Information on the three types of storage units is as follows:

	Basic	Standard	Deluxe
Selling price	$9.00	$30.00	$35.00
Variable cost	$6.00	$20.00	$10.00
Machine hours required	0.10	0.50	0.75

Harish Company's marketing director has assessed demand for the three types of storage units and believes that the firm can sell as many units as it can produce.

(Continued)

Required:

Check figure:

1. Standard contribution margin per machine hour = $20

1. How many of each type of unit should be produced and sold to maximize the company's contribution margin? What is the total contribution margin for your selection?
2. Now suppose that Harish Company believes it can sell no more than 12,000 of the deluxe model but up to 50,000 each of the basic and standard models at the selling prices estimated. What product mix would you recommend, and what would be the total contribution margin?

Problem 13-38 Special-Order Decision, Qualitative Aspects

The manager of Specialty Paper Products Company was agonizing over an offer for an order requesting 5,000 calendars. Specialty Paper Products was operating at 70 percent of its capacity and could use the extra business; unfortunately, the order's offering price of $4.20 per calendar was below the cost to produce the calendars. The controller, Anatoly Nikolayev, was opposed to taking a loss on the deal. However, the personnel manager, Yatika Blaine, argued in favour of accepting the order even though a loss would be incurred; it would avoid the problem of layoffs and would help to maintain the company's community image. The full cost to produce a calendar follows:

Direct materials	$1.15
Direct labour	2.00
Variable overhead	1.10
Fixed overhead	1.00
Total	$5.25

Later that day, Anatoly and Yatika met over coffee. Anatoly sympathized with Yatika's concerns and suggested that the two of them rethink the special-order decision. He offered to determine relevant costs if Yatika would list the activities that would be affected by a layoff. Yatika eagerly agreed and came up with the following activities: an increase in the Employment Insurance rate from 1 to 2 percent of total payroll, notification costs to lay off approximately 20 employees, and increased costs of rehiring and retraining workers when the downturn was over. Anatoly determined the following amounts:

a. Total payroll is $1,460,000 per year.
b. Layoff paperwork is $25 per laid-off employee.
c. Rehiring and retraining is $150 per new employee.

Required:

Check figure:

1. Loss per calendar = $0.05

1. CONCEPTUAL CONNECTION Assume that the company will accept the order only if it increases total profits. Ignoring the new information on activity costs associated with the layoff, should the company accept or reject the order? Provide supporting computations.
2. CONCEPTUAL CONNECTION Consider the new information on activity costs associated with the layoff. Should the company accept or reject the order? Provide supporting computations.

Problem 13-39 Sell or Process Further, Basic Analysis

Shenista Inc. produces four products (Alpha, Beta, Gamma, and Delta) from a common input. The joint costs for a typical quarter follow:

Direct materials	$95,000
Direct labour	43,000
Overhead	85,000

The revenues from each product are as follows: Alpha, $100,000; Beta, $93,000; Gamma, $30,000; and Delta, $40,000.

Management is considering processing Delta beyond the split-off point, which would increase the sales value of Delta to $75,000. However, to process Delta further means that the company must rent some special equipment that costs $15,400 per quarter. Additional materials and labour also needed will cost $8,500 per quarter.

Required:

1. CONCEPTUAL CONNECTION What is the operating profit earned by the four products for one quarter?
2. CONCEPTUAL CONNECTION Should the division process Delta further or sell it at split-off? What is the effect of the decision on quarterly operating profit?

Check figure:
1. Operating profit = $40,000

OBJECTIVE 

Problem 13-40 Product Mix Decision, Single Constraint

Wu Company produces two products (Widlet and Budlet) that use the same material input. Widlet uses three kilograms of the material for every unit produced, and Budlet uses six kilograms. Currently, Wu has 12,000 kilograms of the material in inventory; all of the material is imported. For the coming year, Wu plans to import an additional 7,000 kilograms to produce 1,500 units of Widlet and 3,000 units of Budlet. The unit contribution margin is $27 for Widlet and $42 for Budlet.

Wu Company has received word that the source of the material has been lost due to trade restrictions. Consequently, the company will not be able to import the 7,000 kilograms it had planned to use in the coming year's production. There is no other source of the material.

Required:

1. CONCEPTUAL CONNECTION Compute the total contribution margin that the company would earn if it could manufacture 1,500 units of Widlet and 3,000 units of Budlet.
2. CONCEPTUAL CONNECTION Determine the optimal usage of the company's inventory of 12,000 kilograms of the material. Compute the total contribution margin for the product mix that you recommend.

Check figure:
1. $166,500

OBJECTIVE 2

Problem 13-41 Sell at Split-Off or Process Further

Eunice Company produces two products from a joint process. Joint costs are $70,000 for one batch, which yields 1,000 litres of germain and 4,000 litres of hastain. Germain can be sold at the split-off point for $24 or processed further, into geraiten, at a manufacturing cost of $4,100 (for the 1,000 litres) and sold for $33 per litre.

If geraiten is sold, additional distribution costs of $0.80 per litre and sales commissions of 10 percent of sales will be incurred. In addition, Eunice's legal department is concerned about potential liability issues with geraiten—issues that do not arise with germain.

Required:

1. CONCEPTUAL CONNECTION Considering only gross profit, should germain be sold at the split-off point or processed further?
2. CONCEPTUAL CONNECTION Taking a value-chain approach (by considering distribution, marketing, and after-the-sale costs), determine whether or not germain should be processed into geraiten.

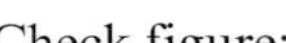

Check figure:
1. Differential amount to process further = $4,900

OBJECTIVE  

Problem 13-42 Differential Costing

For many years, the City of Blandford has conducted business with a local banking institution. When the bank's financial advisor left the bank for another job, the City of Blandford saw this as an opportunity to re-evaluate its banking relationship. Given the City of Blandford's strong financial position, the organization decided to take bids for its banking needs. As a result of the bidding process, the City of Blandford was pleased to have received three bids for consideration. The following information is needed with this analysis:

City of Blandford's Banking Requirements:

Chequing accounts needed: 6
Cheques per month:* 2,000
Foreign debits/credits on chequing accounts per month: 200
Deposits per month:* 300
Returned cheques:* 25 per month

* These are overall totals for the six accounts during a month.

(Continued)

Credit card charges per month: 4,000
Wire transfers per month: 100, of which 60 are to foreign bank accounts
Monthly credit needs (line of credit availability and cost): $100,000 average monthly usage

Internet banking services?
Knowledgeable loan officer?
Responsiveness of bank?

Ray Bank Bid:

Chequing accounts: $5 monthly maintenance fee per account, $0.10 foreign debit/credit, $0.50 earned for each deposit, $3 per returned cheque
Credit card fees: $0.50 per item

Wire transfers: $15 to domestic bank accounts, $50 to foreign bank accounts

Line of credit: Yes, this amount is available, interest charged at prime (4 percent) plus 2 percent, subject to a 6 percent minimum interest rate

Internet banking services: Yes, full online banking available: $15 one-time setup fee for each account, $20 monthly fee for software module

The financial advisor assigned to the potential City of Blandford account had 10 years of experience with medium to large business banking and showed an understanding of the needs of municipal governments.

Calcam Bank Bid:

Chequing accounts: No fees for the accounts, and no credits earned on deposits; $2.00 per returned cheque
Credit card fees: $0.50 per item, $7 per batch processed. Only manual processing was available, and the City of Blandford estimated 20 batches per month

Wire transfers: $30 per wire transfer

Line of credit: Yes, this amount is available, interest charged at prime (4 percent) plus 2 percent, subject to a 7 percent minimum interest rate

Internet banking services: Not currently available, but will be within the next six months

The financial advisor assigned to the potential City of Blandford account had four years of experience with medium to large business banking, none of which pertained to municipal governments.

Pestorn Bank Bid:

Chequing accounts: $5 monthly maintenance fee per account to be waived for the City of Blandford, $0.20 foreign debit/credit, $0.30 earned for each deposit, $3.80 per returned cheque
Credit card fees: $0.50 per item

Wire transfers: $10 to domestic bank accounts, $55 to foreign bank accounts

Line of credit: Yes, this amount is available, interest charged at prime (4 percent) plus 2 percent, subject to a 6.5 percent minimum interest rate

Internet banking services: Yes, full online banking available, one-time setup fee for each account waived for the City of Blandford, $20 monthly fee for software module

The financial advisor assigned to the potential City of Blandford account had two years of experience with large business banking. Another branch of the bank had expertise in dealings with municipal governments and would be willing to help as needed. This bank was the first one to submit a bid.

Required:

1. Calculate the predicted monthly cost of banking with each bank.
2. Suppose the City of Blandford felt that full online Internet banking was critical. How would that affect your analysis from Requirement 1? How would you incorporate the subjective factors (e.g., experience, access to expertise)?

PROFESSIONAL EXAMINATION PROBLEMS*

Professional Examination Problem 13-43 Relevant Costing—Special Orders—Eretria Inc.

Eretria Inc., a manufacturer, has received a special request for 1,000 units of its product, widgets, at a price of $52.50 per unit. The normal selling price for widgets is $60 per unit. Eretria Inc.'s annual capacity is 25,000 units and its current sales are 22,000 units per annum. To analyze this special order, Jim Blum, the sales manager, gathered the following budget information:

Direct materials per unit	$ 2.10
Direct labour per unit	1.75
Variable overhead per unit	0.96
Fixed manufacturing overhead per unit	1.10
Variable selling and administration per unit	10.96

The variable selling and administration costs per unit represent commissions and would not be incurred on this order.

Required:

1. Should Eretria Inc. accept this special order?
2. Assume Eretria Inc.'s annual sales are 25,000 units. Should Eretria Inc. accept this special order?

Professional Examination Problem 13-44 Relevant Costing—Buying Decision—Argos Company

Argos Company needs a total of 125 tonnes of sheet steel—50 tonnes of 2-inch width and 75 tonnes of 4-inch width—for a customer's job. Argos can purchase the sheet steel in these widths directly from a steel manufacturer (Actium Corporation) or it can purchase sheet steel from Actium that is 24 inches wide and have it slit into the desired widths by Heraclion Inc. Both vendors are local and have previously supplied materials to Argos.

Heraclion specializes in slitting sheet steel provided by a customer into any desired width. When negotiating a contract, Heraclion tells its customers there is a scrap loss in the slitting operation, but this loss has never exceeded 2.5 percent of input tonnes. Heraclion recommends if a customer has a specific tonnage requirement, it should supply an adequate amount of steel to yield the desired quantity. Heraclion's charges for steel slitting are based on good output, not input handled.

The 24-inch wide sheet steel is a regular stock item of Actium and can be shipped to Heraclion within five days after receipt of Argos's purchase order. If Actium is to do the slitting, shipment to Argos would be scheduled for 15 days after receipt of Argos's purchase order. Heraclion has quoted delivery at 10 days after receipt of the sheet steel. In prior dealings, Argos has found both Actium and Heraclion to be reliable vendors with high quality products.

Argos has received the following price quotations from Actium and Heraclion:

Actium Corporation Rates

Size	Gauge	Quantity	Cost Per Tonne
2-inch	14	50 tonnes	$210
4-inch	14	75 tonnes	200
24-inch	14	125 tonnes	180

* © CPA Ontario.

Heraclion Inc. Steel Slitting Rates

Size	Gauge	Quantity	Price Per Tonne of Output
2-inch	14	50 tonnes	$18
4-inch	14	75 tonnes	15

Freight and Handling Charges

Destination	Cost Per Tonne
Actium to Argos	$10.00
Actium to Heraclion	5.00
Heraclion to Argos	7.50

In addition, Heraclion informed Argos that if it purchases 100 output tonnes of each width, the per-tonne slitting rates would be reduced 12 percent. Argos knows the same customer will be placing a new order in the near future for the same material and estimates it would have to store the additional tonnage for an average of two months at a carrying cost of $1.50 per month for each tonne. There would be no change in Actium's prices for additional tonnes delivered to Heraclion.

Required:

1. Prepare an analysis that will show whether Argos Company should:
   a. Purchase the required slit steel directly from Actium Corporation.
   b. Purchase the 24-inch wide sheet steel from Actium and have it slit by Heraclion into 50 output tonnes 2 inches wide and 75 output tonnes 4 inches wide.
   c. Take advantage of Heraclion's reduced slitting rates by purchasing 100 output tonnes of each width.
2. Without prejudice to your answer to Requirement 1, present qualitative arguments why Argos Company may favour the purchase of the slit steel directly from Actium Corporation.

CASES

Case 13-45 Sell or Process Further

Paineze Drug Corporation buys three chemicals that are processed to produce two types of analgesic used as ingredients for popular over-the-counter drugs. The purchased chemicals are blended for 2-3 hours and then heated for 15 minutes. The results of the process are two separate analgesics, kyrtec and mobax, which are sent to a drying room until their moisture content is reduced to 6–8 percent. For every 1,100 kilograms of chemicals used, 500 kilograms of kyrtec and 500 kilograms of mobax are produced. After drying, kyrtec and mobax are sold to companies that process them into their final form. The selling prices are $10 per kilogram for kyrtec and $25 per kilogram for mobax. The total cost to produce 500 kilograms of each analgesic is as follows:

Chemicals	$5,500
Direct labour	4,500
Overhead	3,500

The analgesics are packaged in 25-kilogram bags and shipped. The cost of each bag is $0.75. Shipping costs are $0.10 per kilogram. Paineze could process kyrtec further by grinding it into a fine powder and then moulding the powder into tablets. The tablets could then be sold directly to retail drugstores as a generic brand. If this route is taken, the revenue received per bottle of tablets would be $3, with five bottles produced from every kilogram of kyrtec. The costs of grinding and tableting total $2.50 per kilogram of kyrtec. Bottles cost $0.20 each and are shipped in boxes that hold 25 at a shipping cost of $1.23 per box.

Paineze could also process mobax further by grinding it into a fine powder and then filling caplets with this powder. The caplets could then be sold directly to retail drugstores as a generic brand. If this route is taken, the revenue received per bottle of tablets would be $6, with five bottles produced from every kilogram of mobax. The costs of grinding and encapsulating total $5 per kilogram of mobax. Bottles cost $0.20 each and are shipped in boxes that hold 25 at a shipping cost of $1.23 per box.

Required:

Write a memo to the CEO of Paineze detailing the optimal path for maximizing profit. (*Hint:* Should Paineze continue to sell both kyrtec and mobax at the split-off point, process both kyrtec and mobax further, or a combination?). In your analysis to the CEO, be sure to confirm how much incremental profit will result from your recommendation. Recall that Paineze currently sells kyrtec and mobax at the split-off point, and assume that Paineze normally sells 295,000 kilograms each of kyrtec and mobax per year.

Case 13-46 Make or Buy: Ethical Considerations

OBJECTIVE 1 2

Pamela McDonald, chief management accountant and controller for Murray Manufacturing Ltd. was having lunch with Roger Branch, manager of the company's power department. Over the past six months, Pamela and Roger had developed a romantic relationship and were making plans for marriage. To keep company gossip at a minimum, Pamela and Roger had kept the relationship very quiet, and no one in the company was aware of it. During lunch, they were talking about a decision concerning the company's power department that Larry Johnson, president of the company, was about to make.

Pamela: Roger, in our last executive meeting, we were told that a local utility company offered to supply power and quoted a price per kilowatt-hour that they said would hold for the next three years. They even offered to enter into a contractual agreement with us.

Roger: This is news to me. Is the bid price a threat to my area? Can they sell us power cheaper than we make it? And why wasn't I informed about this matter? I should have some input. This burns me. I think I should give Larry a call this afternoon and lodge a strong complaint.

Pamela: Calm down, Roger. The last thing I want you to do is call Larry. Larry made us all promise to keep this whole deal quiet until a decision had been made. He did not want you involved because he wanted to make an unbiased decision. You know that the company is struggling somewhat, and they are looking for ways to save money.

Roger: Yeah, but at my expense? And at the expense of my department's workers? At my age, I doubt that I could find a job that pays as well and has the same benefits. How much of a threat is this offer?

Pamela: Jack Lacy, my assistant controller, prepared an analysis while I was on vacation. It showed that internal production is cheaper than buying, but not by much. Larry asked me to review the findings and submit a final recommendation for next Wednesday's meeting. I've reviewed Jack's analysis, and it's faulty. He overlooked the interactions of your department with other service departments. When these are considered, the analysis is overwhelmingly in favour of purchasing the power. The savings are about $300,000 per year.

Roger: If Larry hears that, my department's gone. Pam, you can't let this happen. I'm three years away from having a vested retirement. And my workers—they have home mortgages, kids in university, and families to support. No, it's not right. Pam, just tell him that your assistant's analysis is on target. He'll never know the difference.

Pamela: Roger, what you're suggesting doesn't sound right either. Would it be ethical for me to fail to disclose this information?

Roger: Ethical? Do you think it's right to lay off employees who have been loyal, faithful workers simply to fatten the pockets of the owners of this company? The Murrays already are so rich that they don't know what to do with their money. I think that it's even more unethical to penalize me and my workers. Why should we have to bear the consequences of some bad marketing decisions? Anyway, the effects of those decisions are about gone, and the company should be back to normal within a year or so.

Pamela: You may be right. Perhaps your and your workers' well-being are more important than saving $300,000 for the Murrays.

Required:

1. Should Pamela have told Roger about the impending decision concerning the power department? What do you think most corporate codes of ethics would say about this?
2. Should Pamela provide Larry with the correct data concerning the power department? Or should she protect its workers? What would you do if you were Pamela?

Case 13-47 Keep or Drop a Division

Jan Shumard, president and general manager of Gleason Company, was concerned about the future of one of the company's largest divisions. The division's most recent quarterly income statement follows:

Sales	$3,751,500
Less: Cost of goods sold	2,722,400
Gross profit	1,029,100
Less: Selling and administrative expenses	1,100,000
Operating loss	$ (70,900)

Jan is giving serious consideration to shutting down the division because this is the ninth consecutive quarter that it has shown a loss. To help him in his decision, the following additional information has been gathered:

a. The division produces one product at a selling price of $100 to outside parties.
b. The division sells 50 percent of its output to another division within the company for $83 per unit (full manufacturing cost plus 25 percent). The internal price is set by company policy. If the division is shut down, the user division will buy the part externally for $100 per unit.
c. The fixed overhead assigned per unit is $20.
d. There is no alternative use for the facilities if shut down. The facilities and equipment will be sold and the proceeds invested to produce an annuity of $100,000 per year. Of the fixed selling and administrative expenses, 30 percent represent allocated expenses from corporate headquarters.
e. Variable selling expenses are $5 per unit sold for units sold externally. These expenses are avoided for internal sales. No variable administrative expenses are incurred.

Required:

1. Prepare an income statement that more accurately reflects the division's profit performance.
2. Should the president shut down the division? What will be the effect on the company's profits if the division is closed?

Case 13-48 Internet Research, Group Case

OBJECTIVE 

Often, websites for major airlines contain news of current special fares and flights. A decision to run a brief "fare special" is an example of a tactical decision. Form a group with up to three other students. Have each member of the group choose one or two airlines and check their websites for recent examples of fare specials. Have the group collaborate in preparing a presentation to the class discussing the types of cost and revenue information that would go into making this type of tactical decision.

14

Capital Investment Decisions

After studying Chapter 14, you should be able to:

1. Explain the meaning of *capital investment decisions*, and distinguish between independent and mutually exclusive capital investment decisions.
2. Differentiate between present values and future values.
3. Compute the payback period and accounting rate of return for a proposed investment, and explain their roles in capital investment decisions.
4. Use net present value analysis and the profitability index for capital investment decisions involving independent projects.
5. Use the internal rate of return to assess the acceptability of independent projects.
6. Explain the role and value of postaudits.
7. Explain why net present value is better than internal rate of return for capital investment decisions involving mutually exclusive projects.
8. *(Appendix 14B)* Incorporate the tax shield into capital expenditure analysis.

Helen Sessions/Alamy Stock Photo

EXPERIENCE MANAGERIAL DECISIONS

with Hard Rock Cafe

Nearly everyone has visited, or at least seen T-shirts for, one of Hard Rock International's world-famous cafe restaurants launched in 1971 in London, England, and now located around the globe. What visitors likely appreciate most is Hard Rock's impressive collection of rock 'n' roll memorabilia and its tasty fare. However, for Hard Rock's managerial accountants and the readers of this textbook, what is most likely to be appreciated is Hard Rock's masterful use of effective capital budgeting techniques to make decisions on a very big scale that are critical to the company's continued success. One of those decisions concerns the opening of new cafes all over the world from Mumbai, India, to Ottawa, Ontario.

New cafes require advanced planning concerning anticipated cash flows, for both future costs and revenues. Future cost-related cash flow projections for the opening of a proposed cafe include items such as labour and materials from different countries, licensing laws, utilities, kitchen and bar equipment, computers, construction, and audio-visual equipment, which alone total just over $6 million! Future cash flows for food and beverage sales are even more difficult to project than costs because of uncertainties involving demographics, economic conditions, and competition. Another complicating factor is the challenge of estimating local awareness of the Hard Rock brand. Brand awareness is important because it drives Hard Rock's merchandise sales, which account for over 30 percent of its total revenue. Estimates of future cash flows for revenues and expenses are combined to calculate a proposed cafe's payback period and net present value (NPV). These metrics then are compared with Hard Rock's decision model requirements to help determine whether the proposed cafe is a wise decision.

Another capital investment decision for Hard Rock surrounds the buying and selling of its rock 'n' roll memorabilia. Hard Rock uses its memorabilia to generate food and merchandise revenues by attracting more customers into the cafe. The collection has grown from a single Eric Clapton guitar to more than 60,000 instruments, posters, costumes, photographs, platinum and gold LPs, and music and lyric sheets. Finally, Hard Rock uses capital budgeting techniques for its biggest project ever, a rock 'n' roll theme park requiring a $400 million venture—that represents the equivalent of approximately 70 new cafes! For this monstrous capital investment, Hard Rock relied heavily on input from a management team with experience and expertise in the theme park industry. Without effective capital budgeting practices, Hard Rock would be forced to "shoot from the hip and hope for the best" for its long-term investments. Such a strategy would not likely produce the impressive capital investment successes that Hard Rock has grown to expect in a very competitive market.

TYPES OF CAPITAL INVESTMENT DECISIONS

OBJECTIVE 

Explain the meaning of *capital investment decisions*, and distinguish between independent and mutually exclusive capital investment decisions.

Organizations often are faced with the opportunity (or need) to invest in assets or projects that represent long-term commitments. New production systems, new plants, new equipment, and new product development are examples of assets and projects that fit this category. Usually, many alternatives are available. For example, an organization may be faced with the decision of whether to invest in a new plant, or whether to invest in a flexible manufacturing system or to continue with an existing traditional manufacturing system. These long-range decisions are examples of *capital investment decisions*.

Capital investment decisions are concerned with the process of planning, setting goals and priorities, arranging financing, and using certain criteria to select long-term assets. Because capital investment decisions place large amounts of resources at risk for long periods of time and simultaneously affect the future development of the firm, they are among the most important decisions made by managers. Every organization has limited resources, which should be used to maintain or enhance its long-run profitability. Poor capital investment decisions can be disastrous. For example, a failure to invest in automated manufacturing when other competitors do so may result in significant losses in market share because of the inability to compete on the basis of quality, cost, and delivery time. Competitors with more modern facilities may produce more output at lower cost and higher quality. Thus, making the right capital investment decisions is absolutely essential for long-term survival.

The process of making capital investment decisions often is referred to as **capital budgeting**. Two types of capital budgeting projects will be considered: *independent projects* and *mutually exclusive projects*.

- **Independent projects** are projects that, if accepted or rejected, do not affect the cash flows of other projects. For example, a decision by Hard Rock to develop a new cafe in Canada is not affected by its decision to build a new cafe in Singapore. These are independent capital investment decisions.
- **Mutually exclusive projects** are those projects that, if accepted, preclude the acceptance of all other competing projects. For example, in early 2013, Alberta-based Ganotec West ULC considered automating its pipeline fabrication factory. In all likelihood, the company's decision process considered different types of automated systems. If three different automated systems were being evaluated, this would produce four alternatives: the current system plus the three potential new systems. One system must be chosen, and the other three excluded; therefore, they are mutually exclusive.

Capital investment decisions often are concerned with investments in long-term capital assets. With the exception of land, these assets depreciate over their lives, and the original investment is used up as the assets are employed. In general terms, a sound capital investment will earn back its original capital outlay over its life and, at the same time, provide a reasonable return on the original investment. Therefore, managers must decide whether a capital investment will earn back its original outlay and provide a reasonable return. By making this assessment, a manager can decide on the acceptability of independent projects and compare competing projects on the basis of their economic merits.

But what is meant by *reasonable return*? Generally, any new project must cover the opportunity cost of the funds invested. For example, if a company takes money from a money market fund that is earning 6 percent and invests it in a new project, then the project must provide at least a 6 percent return (the return that could have been earned had the money been left in the money market fund). In reality, funds for investment often come from different sources—with each representing a different opportunity cost. The return that must be earned is a blend of the opportunity costs of the different sources. Thus, if a company uses two sources of funds, one with an opportunity cost of 4 percent and the other with an opportunity cost of 6 percent, then the return that must be earned is somewhere between 4 and 6 percent, depending on the relative amounts used from each source. Furthermore, it is usually assumed that managers should select projects that promise to maximize the wealth of the firm's owners.

To make a capital investment decision, a manager must:

- estimate the quantity and timing of cash flows
- assess the risk of the investment
- consider the impact of the project on the firm's profits

Hard Rock has little difficulty estimating what a new cafe will cost (the investment required). However, estimating future cash flows is much more challenging. For example, Hard Rock projects sales for a new cafe by looking first at sales from existing cafes with a similar size and location. Next, local factors such as demographics, economic conditions, competition, and awareness of the Hard Rock brand are considered. After taking all these factors into account, two sets of sales estimates are made for a 10-year horizon: (1) a likely scenario, and (2) a worst-case scenario. Sales are also broken out into four sources: restaurant, catering, bar, and retail. This breakout is important because each revenue area has a different labour and materials cost structure. This facilitates the estimation of operating costs. Given the estimated revenues and costs, the future cash flows can then be calculated. Obviously, as the accuracy of cash flow forecasts increases, the reliability of the decision improves.

concept Q&A

What is the difference between independent and mutually exclusive investments?

Answers on pages 734 to 738.

Managers must set goals and priorities for capital investments. They also must identify some basic criteria for the acceptance or rejection of proposed investments. In this chapter, we will study four basic methods to guide managers in accepting or rejecting potential investments. The methods include both nondiscounting and discounting decision approaches (two methods are discussed for each approach). The discounting methods are applied to investment decisions involving both independent and mutually exclusive projects.

Although forecasting future cash flows is a critical part of the capital investment process, forecasting methods will not be considered here. Furthermore, the cash flows projected must be *after-tax cash flows*. Taxes have an important role in developing cash flow assessments. However, taxes will not be explicitly considered. Either tax effects are assumed away or the cash flows can be thought of as after-tax cash flows. Forecasting methodologies are issues that are left for more advanced studies. Consequently, after-tax cash flows are assumed to be known; the focus will be on making capital investment decisions given these cash flows.

PRESENT VALUE CONCEPTS

Differentiate between present values and future values.

An important feature of money is that it can be invested and can earn interest. A dollar today is not the same as a dollar tomorrow. This fundamental principle is the backbone of discounting methods, which rely on the relationships between current and future dollars. Thus, to use discounting methods, we must understand these relationships.

Future Value

Suppose that a bank advertises a 4 percent annual interest rate. If a customer invests \$100, he or she would receive, after one year, the original \$100 plus \$4 interest [\$100 + (0.04)(\$100)] = (1 + 0.04)\$100 = (1.04)(\$100) = \$104. This result can be expressed by the following equation, where F is the future amount, P is the initial or current outlay, and i is the interest rate:

$$F = P(1 + i)$$

For the example, $F = \$100(1 + 0.04) = \$100(1.04) = \$104$.

Now suppose that the same bank offers a 5 percent rate if the customer leaves the original deposit, plus any interest, on deposit for a total of two years. How much will the customer receive at the end of two years? Again assume that the customer invests \$100. Using the future value equation, the customer will earn \$105 at the end of year 1 [$F = \$100(1 + 0.05) = (\$100 \times 1.05) = \$105$]. If this amount is left in the account for a second year, this equation is used again with P now assumed to be \$105. At the end of the second year, then, the total is \$110.25 [$F = \$105(1 + 0.05) = (\$105 \times 1.05) = \$110.25$]. In the second year, interest is earned on both the original deposit and the interest earned in the first year. The earning of interest on interest is referred to as **compounding of interest**. The value that will accumulate by the end of an investment's life, assuming a specified compound return, is the **future value**. The future value of the \$100 deposit in the second example is \$110.25.

A more direct way to compute the future value is possible. Since the first application of the future value equation can be expressed as $F = \$105 = \$100(1.05)$, the second application can be expressed as $F = \$105(1.05) = \$100(1.05)(1.05) = \$100(1.05)^2 = P(1 + i)^2$. This suggests the following compounding interest formula for computing amounts for n periods into the future:

$$F = P(1 + i)^n$$

Present Value

Often, a manager needs to compute the amount that must be invested now in order to yield some given future value. The amount that must be invested now to produce the future value is known as the **present value** of the future amount. For example, how much must be invested now in order to yield \$363 two years from now, assuming that the interest rate is 10 percent? Or, put another way, what is the present value of \$363 to be received two years from now?

In this example, the future value, the years, and the interest rate are all known; we want to know the current outlay that will produce that future amount. In the compounding interest equation, the variable representing the current outlay (the present value of F) is P. Thus, to compute the present value of a future outlay, all we need to do is solve the compounding interest equation for P:

$$P = \frac{F}{(1 + i)^n}$$

Using this present value equation, we can compute the present value of \$363:

$$\begin{aligned} P &= \frac{\$363}{(1 + 0.1)^2} \\ &= \frac{\$363}{1.21} \\ &= \$300 \end{aligned}$$

The present value, \$300, is what the future amount of \$363 is worth today if it can be invested at 10 percent. All other things being equal, having \$300 today is the same as having \$363 two years from now. Put another way, if a firm requires a 10 percent rate of return, the most the firm would be willing to pay today is \$300 for any investment that yields \$363 two years from now.

The process of computing the present value of future cash flows is often referred to as **discounting**; thus, we say that we have discounted the future value of \$363 to its present value of \$300. The interest rate used to discount the future cash flow is the **discount rate**. The expression $1/(1 + i)^n$ in the present value equation is the **discount factor**. By letting the discount factor, called df, equal $1/(1 + i)^n$, the present value equation can be expressed as $P = F(df)$. To simplify the computation of present value, a table of discount factors is given for various combinations of i and n (refer to Exhibit 14A.1 in Appendix 14A).

For example, the discount factor for $i = 10$ percent and $n = 2$ is 0.82645 (go to the 10 percent column of the table and move down to the second row). With the discount factor, the present value of \$363 is computed as follows:

$$P = F(df)$$
$$= \$363 \times 0.82645$$
$$= \$300 \text{ (rounded)}$$

Present Value of an Uneven Series of Cash Flows

Exhibit 14A.1 can be used to compute the present value of any future cash flow or series of uneven future cash flows. The present value of an uneven series of cash flows is found by computing the present value of each future cash flow and then summing these values. For example, suppose that an investment is expected to produce the following annual cash flows: \$110, \$121, and \$133.10. Assuming a discount rate of 10 percent, the present value of this series of cash flows is computed in Exhibit 14.1.

EXHIBIT 14.1

Present Value of an Uneven Series of Cash Flows

Year	Cash Receipt	Discount Factor	Present Value*
1	$110.00	0.90909	$100.00
2	121.00	0.82645	100.00
3	133.10	0.75131	100.00
		2.48685	$300.00

* Rounded.

Present Value of an Annuity

If the series of cash flows is even, it is referred to as an **annuity**. The computation of the annuity's present value is simplified. For example, assume that an investment is expected to return \$100 per year for three years. Using Exhibit 14A.1 and assuming a discount rate of 10 percent, the present value of the annuity is computed in Exhibit 14.2.

EXHIBIT 14.2

Present Value of an Annuity

Year	Cash Receipt*	Discount Factor	Present Value*
1	$100	0.90909	$ 90.91
2	100	0.82645	82.65
3	100	0.75131	75.13
		2.48685	$248.69

* The annual cash flow of \$100 can be multiplied by the sum of the discount factors (2.48685) to obtain the present value of the uniform series (\$248.69).

As with the uneven series of cash flows, the present value in Exhibit 14.2 was computed by calculating the present value of each cash flow separately and then summing them. However, in the case of an annuity displaying uniform cash flows, the computations can be reduced from three to one as described in the footnote to the exhibit. The sum of the individual discount factors can be thought of as a discount factor for an annuity of uniform cash flows. A table of discount factors that can be used for an annuity of uniform cash flows is available in Exhibit 14A.2.

NONDISCOUNTING MODELS

OBJECTIVE 

Compute the payback period and accounting rate of return for a proposed investment, and explain their roles in capital investment decisions.

The basic capital investment decision models can be classified into two major categories: *nondiscounting models* and *discounting models*.

- **Nondiscounting models** ignore the time value of money.
- **Discounting models** explicitly consider the time value of money.

Although many accounting theorists disparage the nondiscounting models because they ignore the time value of money, many firms continue to use these models in making capital investment decisions. However, the use of discounting models has increased over the years, and few firms use only one model; indeed, most firms seem to use both types.[1] This pattern suggests that both categories—nondiscounted and discounted—supply useful information to managers as they optimize their capital investment decisions.

Payback Period

One type of nondiscounting model is the *payback period*. The **payback period** is the time required for a firm to recover its original investment. If the cash flows of a project are an equal amount each period, then the following formula can be used to compute its payback period:

$$\text{Payback period} = \frac{\text{Original investment}}{\text{Annual cash flow}}$$

If, however, the cash flows are unequal, the payback period is computed by adding the annual cash flows until such time as the original investment is recovered. If a fraction of a year is needed, it is assumed that cash flows occur evenly within each year. Cornerstone 14.1 shows how payback analysis is done for both even and uneven cash flows.

CORNERSTONE 14.1

Calculating Payback

CORNERSTONE VIDEO

Information:

Suppose that a new car wash facility requires an investment of $100,000 and either has:

a. Even cash flows of $50,000 per year or
b. The following expected annual cash flows: $30,000, $40,000, $50,000, $60,000, and $70,000.

Required:

Calculate the payback period for each case.

Solution:

a. Even cash flows:

$$\begin{aligned}\text{Payback period} &= \frac{\text{Original investment}}{\text{Annual cash flow}} \\ &= \frac{\$100{,}000}{\$50{,}000} \\ &= 2 \text{ years}\end{aligned}$$

(Continued)

[1] For example, John Graham and Campbell Harvey (*Journal of Applied Corporate Finance*, Volume 15, Spring 2002, pages 8–23) report that most firms rely on both discounting and nondiscounting techniques in evaluating investment proposals. Importantly, their evidence suggests that firm size plays a major role in shaping capital investment decisions: large firms are more likely to use discounting approaches such as NPV while small firms are more likely to use nondiscounting approaches such as the payback criterion.

b. Uneven cash flows:

Year	Unrecovered Investment ($) (beginning of year)	Annual Cash Flow ($)	Time Needed for Payback (years)
1	100,000	30,000	1.0
2	70,000	40,000	1.0
3	30,000	50,000	0.6*
4	0	60,000	0.0
5	0	70,000	0.0
			2.6

* At the beginning of year 3, $30,000 is needed to recover the investment. Since a net cash flow of $50,000 is expected, only 0.6 year (= $30,000/$50,000) is needed to recover the remaining $30,000, assuming a uniform cash inflow throughout the year.

CORNERSTONE

14.1

(Continued)

Why:

Payback is a simple concept that calculates how long it takes to recover the amount of money initially invested from the cash flow of a project. Sometimes it is the initial starting point in evaluating a project.

Using the Payback Period to Assess Risk One way to use the payback period is to set a maximum payback period for all projects and to reject any project that exceeds this level. Why would a firm use the payback period in this way? Some analysts suggest that the payback period can be used as a rough measure of risk, with the notion that the longer it takes for a project to pay for itself, the riskier it is. Also, firms with riskier cash flows in general could require a shorter payback period than normal. Additionally, firms with liquidity problems would be more interested in projects with quick paybacks. Another critical concern is obsolescence. In some industries, the risk of obsolescence is high; firms operating in these industries, such as computer and MP3 player manufacturers, would be interested in recovering funds rapidly.

analytical Q&A

Suppose that a project requires an investment of $30,000 and produces $8,000 cash per year. What is the payback period?

Answers on pages 734 to 738.

Corporate and Social Responsibility

Using the payback period to assess potential investments may cause managers to exhibit dysfunctional behaviours that are not in the best interests of the firm. Many managers in a position to make capital investment decisions may choose investments with quick payback periods out of self-interest. If a manager's performance is measured using short-run criteria, such as annual net income, he or she may choose projects with quick paybacks to show improved net income and cash flow as quickly as possible. Consider that divisional managers often are responsible for making capital investment decisions and are evaluated on divisional profit. The tenure of divisional managers, however, is typically short—three to five years, on average. Consequently, the incentive for such managers is to shy away from investments that promise healthy long-run returns but relatively meagre returns in the short run. New products and services that require time to develop a consumer following fit this description particularly well. Corporate budgeting policies and a budget review committee can address these problems by clearly communicating expected behaviours and carefully reviewing recommended capital investment decisions, as well as seeking information regarding alternative investments that were considered and rejected.

The payback period can be used to choose among competing alternatives. Under this approach, the investment with the shortest payback period is preferred over investments with longer payback periods. However, this use of the payback period is less defensible because this measure suffers from two major deficiencies:

- It ignores the cash flow performance of the investments beyond the payback period.
- It ignores the time value of money.

These two significant deficiencies are easily illustrated. Assume that an engineering firm is considering two different types of computer-aided design (CAD) systems: CAD-A and CAD-B. Each system requires an initial outlay of $150,000, has a five-year life, and generates the following annual cash flows:

Investment	Year 1	Year 2	Year 3	Year 4	Year 5
CAD-A	$90,000	$ 60,000	$50,000	$50,000	$50,000
CAD-B	40,000	110,000	25,000	25,000	25,000

Both investments have payback periods of two years. In other words, if a manager uses the payback period to choose among competing investments, the two investments would be equally desirable. In reality, however, the CAD-A system should be preferred over the CAD-B system for two reasons:

- The CAD-A system provides a much larger dollar return for the years three, four, and five beyond the payback period ($150,000 vs. $75,000).
- The CAD-A system returns $90,000 in the first year, while B returns only $40,000. The extra $50,000 that the CAD-A system provides in the first year could be put to productive use, such as investing in another project. It is better to have a dollar now than to have it one year from now, because the dollar on hand can be invested to provide a return one year from now.

In summary, the payback period provides information to managers that can be used as follows:

1. To help control the risks associated with the uncertainty of future cash flows.
2. To help minimize the impact of an investment on a firm's liquidity problems.
3. To help control the risk of obsolescence.
4. To help control the effect of the investment on performance measures.

However, the method suffers significant deficiencies: It ignores a project's total profitability and the time value of money. While the computation of the payback period may be useful to a manager, relying on it solely for a capital investment decision would be imprudent.

Accounting Rate of Return

The *accounting rate of return* is the second commonly used nondiscounting model. The **accounting rate of return (ARR)** measures the return on a project in terms of income, as opposed to using a project's cash flow. Several formulas for the accounting rate of return can be found, however a common formula is:

$$\text{Accounting rate of return} = \frac{\text{Average income}}{\text{Initial investment}}$$

Income is not equivalent to cash flows because of accruals and deferrals used in its computation. The average income of a project is obtained by adding the net income for each year of the project and then dividing this total by the number of years. Cornerstone 14.2 shows how to calculate the ARR.

Calculating the Accounting Rate of Return

CORNERSTONE 14.2

Information:

An investment requires an initial outlay of $100,000 and has a five-year life with no salvage value. The yearly net income amounts (before depreciation) are $50,000, $50,000, $60,000, $50,000, and $70,000.

Required:

1. Calculate the annual net income for each of the five years.
2. Calculate the accounting rate of return.

Solution:

1. $$\text{Yearly depreciation expense} = \frac{(\$100{,}000 - 0)}{5 \text{ years}} = \$20{,}000$$

   Annual net income = Net income − Depreciation expense
   Year 1 net income = $50,000 − $20,000 = $30,000
   Year 2 net income = $50,000 − $20,000 = $30,000
   Year 3 net income = $60,000 − $20,000 = $40,000
   Year 4 net income = $50,000 − $20,000 = $30,000
   Year 5 net income = $70,000 − $20,000 = $50,000

2. Total net income (five years) = $180,000

   $$\text{Average net income} = \frac{\$180{,}000}{5} = \$36{,}000$$

   $$\text{Accounting rate of return} = \frac{\$36{,}000}{\$100{,}000} = 0.36$$

Why:

The accounting rate of return is a simple concept used to evaluate a project by looking at the average annual return, calculated on an accounting basis. It is often used as a preliminary tool to assess a project.

Limitation of Accounting Rate of Return Unlike the payback period, the ARR does consider a project's profitability. However, the ARR has other potential drawbacks, including:

- *Ignoring the time value of money*: Like the payback period, it ignores the time value of money. Ignoring the time value of money is a critical deficiency in this method as well; it can lead a manager to choose investments that do not maximize returns. The ARR and payback models are referred to as *nondiscounting models* because they ignore the time value of money.
- *Dependency on net income*: ARR is dependent upon net income, which is the financial measure most likely to be manipulated by managers. Some of the reasons for manipulating net income include debt contracts (i.e., debt covenants) and bonuses. Often, debt contracts require that a firm maintain certain financial accounting ratios, which can be affected by the income reported and by the level of long-term assets. Accordingly, the ARR may be used as a screening measure to ensure that any new investment will not adversely affect these ratios.
- *Managers' incentives:* Because bonuses to managers often are based on accounting income or return on assets, managers may have a personal interest in ensuring that any new investment contributes significantly to net income.

concept Q&A

Why would a manager choose only investments that return the highest income per dollar invested?

Answers on pages 734 to 738.

A manager seeking to maximize personal income is likely to select investments that return the highest net income per dollar invested, even if the selected investments are not the ones that produce the greatest cash flows and return to the firm in the long-run.

DISCOUNTING MODELS: THE NET PRESENT VALUE METHOD

OBJECTIVE 

Use net present value analysis and the profitability index for capital investment decisions involving independent projects.

Discounting models use **discounted cash flows**, which are future cash flows expressed in terms of their present value. Three discounting models will be considered: *net present value* (NPV), profitability index, and *internal rate of return* (IRR). In practice, each of these methods is widely used. For instance, Hard Rock Cafe will use NPV calculations to estimate the expected profitability of an investment, such as opening a new store. Using these calculations also assists companies in selecting among several investment opportunities by identifying which are the most profitable over the life of the investment.

Net Present Value Defined

Net present value (NPV) is the difference between the present values of the cash inflows and outflows associated with a project:

$$
\begin{aligned}
NPV &= \left[\sum CF_t/(1+i)^t\right] - I \\
&= \left[\sum CF_t df_t\right] - I \\
&= P - I
\end{aligned}
$$

where

I = the present value of the project's cost (usually the initial cash outlay)
CF_t = the cash inflow to be received in period t, with $t = 1, \ldots, n$
i = the required rate of return
t = the time period
P = the present value of the project's future cash inflows
$df_t = 1/(1+i)^t$, the discount factor

Note: Σ means "the sum of," as in "the sum of all cash flows."

Net present value measures the profitability of an investment. A positive NPV indicates that the investment increases the firm's wealth. To use the NPV method, a *required rate of return* must be defined. The **required rate of return** or **cost of capital** is the minimum acceptable rate of return. It also is referred to as the *discount rate*, or *hurdle rate*. Given that future cash flows are uncertain, managers occasionally choose a discount rate that exceeds the cost of capital when uncertainty is unusually high. However, if the rate chosen is excessively high, it will bias the selection process toward short-term investments. Because of the risk of being overly conservative, it may be better to use the cost of capital as the discount rate and find other approaches to deal with uncertainty.

Once the NPV for a project is computed, it can be used to determine whether to accept an investment:

- If the NPV is positive, it signals that (1) the initial investment has been recovered, (2) the required rate of return has been recovered, and (3) a return in excess of (1) and (2) has been received. Thus, if the NPV is greater than zero, the investment is acceptable.
- If the NPV equals zero, the decision maker will be indifferent between accepting and rejecting the investment.
- If the NPV is less than zero, the investment should be rejected. In this case, it is earning less than the required rate of return.

concept Q&A

Suppose that the NPV of an investment is $2,000. Why does this mean that the investment should be accepted?

Answers on pages 734 to 738.

An Example Illustrating Net Present Value

Wong Company has developed new earphones for portable MP3 players that it believes are superior to other products on the market. The earphones have a projected product life cycle of five years. Although the marketing manager is excited about the new product's prospects, a decision to manufacture the new product depends on whether it can earn a positive NPV given the company's required rate of return of 12 percent. In order to make a decision regarding the earphones, two steps must be taken: (1) Identify the cash flows for each year, and (2) compute the NPV using the cash flows from step 1. Cornerstone 14.3 shows how to calculate the NPV.

In Cornerstone 14.3, notice that step 2 offers two approaches for computing NPV. Step 2A computes NPV by using discount factors from Exhibit 14A.1. Step 2B simplifies

Assessing Cash Flows and Calculating Net Present Value

CORNERSTONE 14.3

Information:

A detailed market study revealed expected annual revenues of $300,000 for new earphones. Equipment to produce the earphones will cost $320,000. After five years, the equipment can be sold for $40,000. In addition to equipment, working capital is expected to increase by $40,000 because of increases in inventories and receivables. The firm expects to recover the investment in working capital at the end of the project's life. Annual cash operating expenses are estimated at $180,000. The required rate of return is 12 percent.

Required:

Estimate the annual cash flows, and calculate the NPV.

Solution:

STEP 1. CASH FLOW IDENTIFICATION

Year	Item	Cash Flow
0	Equipment	$(320,000)
	Working capital	(40,000)
	Total	$(360,000)
1–4	Revenues	$ 300,000
	Operating expenses	(180,000)
	Total	$ 120,000
5	Revenues	$ 300,000
	Operating expenses	(180,000)
	Salvage	40,000
	Recovery of working capital	40,000
	Total	$ 200,000

STEP 2A. NPV ANALYSIS

Year	Cash Flow[a]	Discount Factor[b]	Present Value
0	$(360,000)	1.00000	$(360,000)
1	120,000	0.89286	107,143
2	120,000	0.79719	95,663
3	120,000	0.71178	85,414
4	120,000	0.63552	76,262
5	200,000	0.56743	113,486
Net present value			$ 117,968

(Continued)

CORNERSTONE

14.3

(Continued)

STEP 2B. NPV ANALYSIS

Year	Cash Flow	Discount Factor[c]	Present Value
0	$(360,000)	1.00000	$(360,000)
1–4	120,000	3.03735	364,482
5	200,000	0.56743	113,486
Net present value			$ 117,968

[a] From step 1.
[b] From Exhibit 14A.1.
[c] Years 1–4 from Exhibit 14A.2; year 5 from Exhibit 14A.1.

Why:

Cash flows and net present value are approaches that incorporate more sophisticated measures of the value of a project. These tools are generally regarded as a more reliable method of evaluating a project's value.

the computation by using a single discount factor from Exhibit 14A.2 for the even cash flows occurring in years 1 through 4.

Profitability Index

Another discounting method for evaluating a potential investment is the **profitability index (PI)**, which is calculated as follows:

$$\text{Profitability index} = \frac{\text{PV of future cash flows}}{\text{Initial investment}}$$

Given this formula, one of the three following instances will occur:

1. $PI > 1$: The investment should be accepted since the future cash flows exceed the original cost of the investment.
2. $PI = 1$: This indicates the investment will break even.
3. $PI < 1$: The investment should be rejected because the future cash flows are less than the original cost of the investment. That is, the investor will not recover the initial investment cost during the life of the investment.

Also, PI can be used to rank multiple independent investments in a limited resource environment, investments with a higher PI will be chosen first. Advantages of the PI are that it is easy to explain to users and that it incorporates the time value of money. Unfortunately, PI must be used with caution as the calculation is risky. PI ignores the length of time it takes for investments to be recovered and the rate of return used to discount the future cash flows cannot be predicted with absolute certainty. As with NPV calculations, it may be advisable to use the cost of capital for the discount rate.

INTERNAL RATE OF RETURN

OBJECTIVE 5

Use the internal rate of return to assess the acceptability of independent projects.

Another discounting model is the *internal rate of return* method. The **internal rate of return** (IRR) is defined as the interest rate that sets the present value of a project's cash inflows equal to the present value of the project's cost. In other words, it is the interest rate that sets the project's NPV at zero. The following equation can be used to determine a project's IRR:

$$I = \frac{\sum CF_t}{(1 + i)^t}$$

where $t = 1, \ldots, n$

The right-hand side of this equation is the present value of future cash flows, and the left-hand side is the investment. I, CF_t, and t are known. Thus, the IRR (the interest rate, i, in the equation) can be found using trial and error. Once the IRR for a project is computed, it is compared with the firm's required rate of return.

- If the IRR is greater than the required rate, the project is deemed acceptable.
- If the IRR is less than the required rate of return, the project is rejected.
- If the IRR is equal to the required rate of return, the firm is indifferent between accepting and rejecting the investment proposal.

The IRR is the most widely used of the capital investment techniques.[2] One reason for its popularity may be that it is a rate of return, a concept that managers are comfortable with using. Another possibility is that managers may believe that the IRR is the true or actual compounded rate of return being earned by the initial investment. Whatever the reasons for its popularity, a basic understanding of the IRR is necessary.

Example: Multiple-Period Setting with Uniform Cash Flows

Assume initially that the investment produces a series of uniform cash flows. Since the series of cash flows is uniform, a single discount factor from Exhibit 14A.2 can be used to compute the present value of the annuity. Letting *df* be this discount factor and *CF* be the annual cash flow, the IRR equation assumes the following form:

$$I = CF(df)$$

Solving for *df*, we obtain:

$$df = \frac{I}{CF} = \frac{\text{Investment}}{\text{Annual cash flow}}$$

Assume that the investment (I) is \$100 and that it produces a single-period cash flow of \$110. The discount factor is I/CF = \$100/\$110 = 0.90909. Looking in Exhibit 14A.2, a discount factor of 0.90909 for a single period corresponds to a rate of 10 percent, which is the IRR. In general, once the discount factor is computed, go to Exhibit 14A.2 and find the row corresponding to the life of the project, then move across that row until the computed discount factor is found. The interest rate corresponding to this discount factor is the IRR. Cornerstone 14.4 illustrates how to calculate the IRR for multiple-period uniform cash flows.

Calculating Internal Rate of Return with Uniform Cash Flows

CORNERSTONE 14.4

Information:

Assume that a hospital has the opportunity to invest \$205,570.50 in a new ultrasound system that will produce net cash inflows of \$50,000 at the end of each of the next six years.

(Continued)

[2] See John Graham and Campbell Harvey, "How Do CFOs Make Capital Budgeting and Capital Structure Decisions?" *Journal of Applied Corporate Finance*, Volume 15, Spring 2002, pages 8–23.

CORNERSTONE

14.4

(Continued)

Required:

Calculate the IRR for the ultrasound system.

Solution:

$$df = \frac{I}{CF}$$

$$= \frac{\$205,570.50}{\$50,000}$$

$$= 4.11141$$

Since the life of the investment is six years, find the sixth row in Exhibit 14.2A and then move across this row until $df = 4.11141$ is found. The interest rate corresponding to 4.11141 is 12 percent, which is the IRR.

Why:

The internal rate of return allows us to evaluate a variety of projects and compare them. It incorporates present value calculations, which are viewed as the most reliable indicators of value to a company.

YOUDECIDE IRR and Uncertainty in Estimates of Cash Savings and Project Life

As a manager of a plant producing cooking oils and margarines, you are concerned about the emission of contaminated water effluents. On a regular basis, your plant violates its discharge permit and dumps many times the allowable waste (organic solids) into a local river. This practice is beginning to draw increased attention and criticism from the provincial environmental agency. You are considering the acquisition and installation of a zero-discharge, closed-loop system with an expected life of 10 years and a required investment of $250,000. The new system is expected to produce the following expected annual savings:

Water (from the ability to recycle the water)	$20,000
Materials (from the ability to use extracted materials)	5,000
Avoidance of fines and penalties	15,000
Reduction in demand for laboratory analysis	10,000
Total savings	$50,000

To accept any project, the IRR must be greater than the cost of capital, which is 10 percent. Upon calculating the IRR, you find that it is about 15 percent, significantly greater than the 10 percent benchmark rate. However, upon seeking approval for the project from the divisional manager, you are asked how certain you are about the projected cash savings. He also questions the estimated life, arguing that based on his experience the expected life of the particular closed-loop system is usually closer to eight years than ten.

How would you address the divisional manager's concerns about projected cash savings and estimated life?

The concerns of the divisional manager relate to the uncertainty surrounding both the cash flow and project life estimates. The savings from recycling water and the fines and penalties probably have very little uncertainty attached to them. The same may also be true of the lab costs, especially if the analysis is outsourced. The major source of uncertainty probably is attached to the quantity of organic solids that, once extracted, can be used to produce additional margarines and cooking oils. Assuming that the extraction process does not produce any usable organic solids, the annual savings would be $45,000 (= $50,000 − $5,000), yielding the worst-case scenario for cash flows. This uncertainty in the cash flows can be dealt with by first calculating the minimum annual cash savings that must be realized to earn a rate equal to the firm's cost of capital, and then comparing this minimum cash savings with the cash flows of the worst-case scenario ($45,000). Calculating this minimum cash flow for an eight-year life simultaneously addresses the project life issue.

The minimum cash flow is calculated as follows (where *df* is the discount factor for eight years and 10 percent, from Exhibit 14.2A):

$$I = CF(df)$$

$$CF = \frac{I}{df}$$

$$= \frac{\$250,000}{5.33493}$$

$$= \$46,861 \text{ (rounded)}$$

(Continued)

In the worst-case scenario, the project will not meet the minimum cash savings requirement. The cash savings from the extraction of organic solids can be off by about 60 percent to retain project viability. As a plant manager, you might argue that there is a likely *underestimation* of future fines and penalties resulting from the increased political attention to polluting of the local river. Also, there may be a positive benefit, not included in the savings, of a more favourable public image (e.g., increased sales because of the favourable environmental action). Taken together, you should have a strong position for winning approval of the project.

Sensitivity analysis thus provides a powerful tool for assessing the impact of uncertainty in capital investment analysis.

Exhibit 14A.2 does not provide discount factors for every possible interest rate. To illustrate, assume that in Cornerstone 14.4 the annual cash inflows expected by the hospital are $51,000 instead of $50,000. The new discount factor is 4.03079 (= $205,570.50/$51,000). Returning to the sixth row in Exhibit 14A.2, it is clear that the discount factor—and thus the IRR—lies between 12 percent and 14 percent. It is straightforward to approximate the IRR by interpolation using the range for the IRR as indicated by the table values. Additionally, business calculators or spreadsheet programs like Excel can provide the values of IRR without the use of tables such as Exhibit 14A.2.

analytical Q&A

Suppose that an investment of $169 produces an annual cash flow of $100 for two years. What is the IRR?

Answers on pages 734 to 738.

Multiple-Period Setting: Uneven Cash Flows

If the cash flows are not uniform, then the IRR equation must be used. For a multiple-period setting, this equation can be solved by trial and error, or by using a business calculator or a spreadsheet program. To illustrate solution by trial and error, assume that a $10,000 investment in a PC system produces clerical savings of $6,000 and $7,200, respectively, for the two years. The IRR is the interest rate that sets the present value of these two cash inflows equal to $10,000:

$$P = \left[\frac{\$6{,}000}{(1+i)}\right] + \left[\frac{\$7{,}200}{(1+i)^2}\right]$$
$$= \$10{,}000$$

To solve this equation by trial and error, start by selecting a possible value for i. Given this first guess, compute the present value of the future cash flows and then compare with the initial investment. If the present value is greater than the initial investment, then the interest rate is too low; if the present value is less than the initial investment, then the interest rate is too high. The next guess is adjusted accordingly.

Assume that the first guess is 18 percent. Using i equal to 0.18, Exhibit 14A.1 yields the following discount factors: 0.84746 and 0.71818. These discount factors produce the following present value for the two cash inflows:

$$P = (0.84746 \times \$6{,}000) + (0.71818 \times \$7{,}200)$$
$$= \$10{,}256$$

Since P is greater than $10,000, the interest rate selected is too low. A higher guess is needed. If the next guess is 20 percent, we obtain the following:

$$P = (0.83333 \times \$6{,}000) + (0.69444 \times \$7{,}200)$$
$$= \$9{,}999.95$$

Since this value is very close to $10,000, we can say that the IRR is 20 percent. (The IRR is, in fact, exactly 20 percent; the present value is slightly less than the investment because the discount factors found in Exhibit 14A.1 have been rounded to five decimal places.)

POSTAUDIT OF CAPITAL PROJECTS

OBJECTIVE 6

Explain the role and value of postaudits.

A key element in the capital investment process is a follow-up analysis of a capital project once it has been implemented. This analysis is called a *postaudit*. A **postaudit** compares the actual benefits with the estimated benefits, and actual operating costs with estimated operating costs; it evaluates the overall outcome of the investment and proposes corrective action if needed. The following case illustrates the usefulness of a postaudit activity.

Honley Medical Company: An Illustrative Application

Naveen Chandar and Polina Kruk were discussing a persistent and irritating problem present in the process of producing intravenous (IV) needles. Both Naveen and Polina are employed by Honley Medical, which specializes in the production of medical products and has three divisions: the IV products division, the critical care monitoring division, and the specialty products division. Naveen and Polina both work with the IV products division—Naveen as the senior production engineer and Polina as the marketing manager.

The IV products division produces needles of five different sizes. During one stage of the manufacturing process, the needle itself is inserted into a plastic hub and is bonded by using epoxy glue. According to Polina, the use of epoxy to bond the needles was causing the division all kinds of problems. In many cases, the epoxy was not bonding correctly. The rejects were high and the division was receiving a large number of complaints from its customers. Corrective action was needed to avoid losing sales. After some discussion and analysis, a recommendation was made to use induction welding in lieu of epoxy bonding. In induction welding, the needles are inserted into the plastic hub, and an RF generator is used to heat the needles. The RF generator works on the same principle as a microwave oven. As the needles get hot, the plastic melts and the needles are bonded.

Switching to induction welding required an investment in RF generators and the associated tooling; the investment was justified by the IV products division based on the savings associated with the new system. Induction welding promised to reduce the cost of direct materials, eliminating the need to buy and use epoxy. Savings of direct labour costs also were predicted because the welding process is much more automated. Adding to these savings were the avoidance of daily cleanup costs and the reduction in rejects. Naveen presented a formal NPV analysis showing that the welding system was superior to the epoxy system. Headquarters approved its purchase.

One Year Later

Polina: Naveen, I'm quite pleased with induction welding for bonding needles. In the year since the new process was implemented, we've had virtually no complaints from our customers. The needles are firmly bonded.

Naveen: I wish that positive experience were true for all other areas as well. Unfortunately, implementing the process has uncovered some rather sticky and expensive problems that I didn't anticipate. The internal audit department recently completed a postaudit of the project, and now my feet are being held to the fire.

Polina: That's too bad. What's the problem?

Naveen: You mean *problems*. Let me list a few for you. One is that the RF generators interfered with the operation of other equipment. To eliminate this interference, we had to install filtering equipment. But that's not all. We also discovered that the average maintenance person doesn't know how to maintain the new equipment. Now we are faced with the need to initiate a training program to upgrade the skills of our maintenance people. Upgrading skills also implies higher wages. Although the RF bonding process is less messy, it is more complex. The manufacturing people complained to the internal auditors about that. They maintain that a simple process, even if messy, is preferred—especially now that demand for the product is increasing by leaps and bounds.

Polina: What did the internal auditors conclude?

Naveen: They concluded that many of the predicted savings did take place but that some significant costs were not foreseen. Because of these unforeseen problems, they have recommended that I look carefully at the possibility of moving back to using epoxy. They indicated that NPV analysis using actual data appears to favour that process. With production expanding, the acquisition of additional RF generators and filtering equipment plus the necessary training is simply not as attractive as returning to epoxy bonding. This conclusion is reinforced by the fact that the epoxy process is simpler and by the auditors' conclusion that the mixing of the epoxy can be automated, avoiding the quality problem that we had in the first place.

Polina: Well, Naveen, you can't really blame yourself. You had a real problem and took action to solve it. It's difficult to foresee all the problems and hidden costs of a new process.

Naveen: Unfortunately, the internal auditors don't totally agree. In fact, neither do I. I probably jumped too quickly. In the future, I intend to think through new projects more carefully.

Benefits of a Postaudit

In the case of the RF bonding decision, some of the estimated capital investment benefits did materialize: complaints from customers decreased, the number of rejects fell, and direct labour and materials costs decreased. However, the investment was greater than expected because filtering equipment was needed, and actual operating costs were much higher because of the increased maintenance cost and the increased complexity of the process. Overall, the internal auditors concluded that the investment was a poor decision. The corrective action that they recommended was to abandon the new process and return to epoxy bonding. Based on this recommendation, the firm abandoned inductive welding and returned to epoxy bonding, which was improved by automating the mix.

Firms that perform postaudits of capital projects experience a number of benefits, including:

- *Resource allocation*. By evaluating profitability, postaudits ensure that resources are used wisely. If the project is doing well, it may call for additional funds and additional attention. If the project is not doing well, corrective action may be needed to improve performance or it may recommend abandoning the project.
- *Positive impact on managers' behaviour*. If managers are held accountable for the results of a capital investment decision, they are more likely to make such decisions in the best interests of the firm. Additionally, postaudits supply feedback to managers that should help to improve future decision making. Consider Naveen's reaction to the postaudit of the RF bonding process. Certainly, we would expect him to be more careful and more thorough in making future investment recommendations. In the future, Naveen will probably consider more than one alternative, such as automating the mixing of the epoxy. Also, for those alternatives being considered, he will probably be especially alert to the possibility of hidden costs, such as increased training requirements for a new process.
- *Independence perspective*. The case also reveals that the postaudit was performed by the internal audit staff. Generally, more objective results are obtainable if the postaudit is done by an independent party. Since considerable effort is expended to ensure as much independence as possible for the internal audit staff, that group is usually the best choice for this task.

concept Q&A

Why do a postaudit?

Answers on pages 734 to 738.

Postaudit Limitations

Postaudits are costly. Moreover, even though they may provide significant benefits, they have other limitations. Most obvious is the fact that the assumptions driving the original analysis may often be invalidated by changes in the actual operating environment. Accountability must be qualified to some extent by the impossibility of foreseeing every possible outcome.

MUTUALLY EXCLUSIVE PROJECTS

OBJECTIVE 7

Explain why net present value is better than internal rate of return for capital investment decisions involving mutually exclusive projects.

Up to this point, we have focused on independent projects. However, many capital investment decisions deal with mutually exclusive projects. How NPV analysis and IRR are used to choose among competing projects is an interesting question. An even more interesting question to consider is whether NPV and IRR differ in their ability to help managers make wealth-maximizing decisions in the presence of competing alternatives. For example, we already know that the nondiscounting models can produce erroneous choices because they ignore the time value of money. Because of this deficiency, the discounting models are judged superior. Similarly, it can be shown that the NPV model is generally preferred to the IRR model when choosing among mutually exclusive alternatives.

Net Present Value Compared with Internal Rate of Return

NPV and IRR both yield the same decision for independent projects. For example, if the NPV is greater than zero, then the IRR is also greater than the required rate of return; both models signal the correct decision. However, for competing projects, the two methods can produce different results. Intuitively, we believe that for mutually exclusive projects, the project with the highest NPV or the highest IRR should be chosen. Since it is possible for the two methods to produce different rankings of mutually exclusive projects, the method that consistently reveals the wealth-maximizing project is preferred. It should be noted that financial factors are not the only factors for consideration. For instance, a project with strong positive financial benefits may not be pursued if the investment will compromise human safety.

NPV differs from IRR in two major ways:

1. The NPV assumes that each cash inflow received is reinvested at the required rate of return, whereas the IRR method assumes that each cash inflow is reinvested at the computed IRR. Reinvesting at the required rate of return is more realistic and produces more reliable results when comparing mutually exclusive projects.
2. The NPV method measures profitability in absolute terms, whereas the IRR method measures it in relative terms. NPV measures the amount by which the value of the firm changes.

These differences are summarized in Exhibit 14.3.

Since NPV measures the impact that competing projects have on the value of the firm, choosing the project with the largest NPV is consistent with maximizing the wealth of shareholders. On the other hand, IRR does not consistently result in choices that maximize wealth. IRR, as a relative measure of profitability, has the virtue of accurately measuring the rate of return of funds that remain internally invested. However, maximizing IRR will not necessarily maximize the wealth of firm owners because it cannot, by nature, consider the absolute dollar contributions of projects. In the final analysis, what counts are the total dollars earned—the absolute profits—not the relative profits. Accordingly, NPV—not IRR—should be used for choosing among competing, mutually exclusive projects or competing projects when capital funds are limited.

concept Q&A

Why is NPV better than IRR for choosing among competing projects?

Answers on pages 734 to 738.

EXHIBIT 14.3

Net Present Value Compared with Internal Rate of Return

	NPV	IRR
Type of measure	***Absolute*** dollars	***Relative*** percentage
Cash flow reinvestment assumption	At required rate of return	At internal rate of return

An independent project is acceptable if its NPV is positive. For mutually exclusive projects, the project with the largest NPV is chosen. There are three steps in selecting the best project from several competing projects:

1. Assess the cash flow pattern for each project.
2. Compute the NPV for each project.
3. Identify the project with the greatest NPV.

Example: Mutually Exclusive Projects

Thant Corporation has committed to improving its environmental performance. One environmental project identified a manufacturing process as being the source of both liquid and gaseous residues. After six months of research activity, the engineering department announced that it is possible to redesign the process to prevent the production of contaminating residues. Two different process designs (A and B) are being considered that prevent the production of contaminants. Both process designs are more expensive to operate than the current process; however, because the designs prevent production of contaminants, significant annual benefits are created. These benefits stem from eliminating the need to operate and maintain expensive pollution control equipment, treat and dispose of toxic liquid wastes, and pay the annual fines for exceeding allowable contaminant releases. Increased sales to environmentally conscious customers also are factored into the benefit estimates. Cornerstone 14.5 shows how NPV and IRR analyses are carried out for this setting.

Calculating Net Present Value and Internal Rate of Return for Mutually Exclusive Projects

Information:

Consider two pollution prevention designs: A and B. Both designs have a project life of five years. Design A requires an initial outlay of $180,000 and has a net annual after-tax cash inflow of $60,000 (revenues of $180,000 minus costs of $120,000). Design B, with an initial outlay of $210,000, has a net annual cash inflow of $70,000 (= $240,000 − $170,000). The after-tax cash flows are summarized as follows:

(Continued)

CORNERSTONE
14.5

(Continued)

CASH FLOW PATTERN

Year	Design A	Design B
0	$(180,000)	$(210,000)
1	60,000	70,000
2	60,000	70,000
3	60,000	70,000
4	60,000	70,000
5	60,000	70,000

The cost of capital for the company is 12 percent.

Required:

Calculate the NPV and the IRR for each project.

Solution:

DESIGN A: NPV ANALYSIS

Year	Cash Flow	Discount Factor*	Present Value
0	$(180,000)	1.00000	$(180,000)
1–5	60,000	3.60478	216,287
Net present value			$ 36,287

DESIGN A: IRR ANALYSIS

$$\text{Discount factor} = \frac{\text{Initial investment}}{\text{Annual cash flow}}$$
$$= \frac{\$180,000}{\$60,000}$$
$$= 3.00000$$

From Exhibit 14A.2, *df* = 3.00000 for five years implies that IRR = 20 percent.

DESIGN B: NPV ANALYSIS

Year	Cash Flow	Discount Factor	Present Value
0	$(210,000)	1.00000	$(210,000)
1–5	70,000	3.60478	252,335
Net present value			$ 42,335

DESIGN B: IRR ANALYSIS

$$\text{Discount factor} = \frac{\text{Initial investment}}{\text{Annual cash flow}}$$
$$= \frac{\$210,000}{\$70,000}$$
$$= 3.00000$$

From Exhibit 14A.2, *df* = 3.00000 for five years implies that IRR = 20 percent.

* From Exhibit 14A.2.

Why:

When a company is faced with projects of which only one will be accepted, we can evaluate them using either net present value analysis or internal rate of return. Often we will get conflicting results, so we must have a method of choosing among the projects. Both these alternatives use present value calculations, which will allow better decision making.

Based on NPV analysis in Cornerstone 14.5, design B is more profitable; it has the larger NPV. Accordingly, the company should select design B over design A. Interestingly, designs A and B have identical internal rates of return. As shown by Cornerstone 14.5, both designs have a discount factor of 3.00000. From Exhibit 14A.2, it is easily seen that a discount factor of 3.00000 and a life of five years yields an IRR of about 20 percent. Even though both projects have an IRR of 20 percent, the firm should not consider the two designs to be equally desirable. The analysis demonstrates that design B produces a larger NPV and, therefore, will increase the value of the firm more than design A. Design B should be chosen. This illustrates the conceptual superiority of NPV over IRR for analysis of competing projects.

Special Considerations for the Advanced Manufacturing Environment

How Investment Differs Investment in automated manufacturing processes is much more complex than investment in the standard manufacturing equipment of the past. For standard equipment, the direct costs of acquisition represent virtually the entire investment. For automated manufacturing, the direct costs can represent as little as 50–60 percent of the total investment; software, engineering, training, and implementation are a significant percentage of the total costs. Thus, great care must be exercised to assess the actual cost of an automated system. It is easy to overlook the peripheral costs, which can be substantial.

How Estimates of Operating Cash Flows Differ Estimates of operating cash flows from investments in standard equipment typically have relied on directly identifiable tangible benefits, such as direct savings from labour, power, and scrap. However, when investing in automated systems, the intangible and indirect benefits can be material and critical to the viability of the project. Greater quality, more reliability, reduced lead time, improved customer satisfaction, and an enhanced ability to maintain market share all are important intangible benefits of an advanced manufacturing system. Reduction of labour in support areas such as production scheduling and stores are indirect benefits. More effort is needed to measure these intangible and indirect benefits in order to assess more accurately the potential value of investments.

An example can be used to illustrate the importance of considering intangible and indirect benefits. Consider a company that is evaluating a potential investment in a flexible manufacturing system (FMS). The choice facing the company is to continue producing with its traditional equipment, expected to last 10 years, or to switch to the new system, which also is expected to have a useful life of 10 years. The company's discount rate is 12 percent. The data pertaining to the investment are presented in Exhibit 14.4. Notice that, for this example, the *incremental cash flows* are used to compare the new project with the old. Instead of calculating the NPV for each alternative and comparing them, an equivalent approach is to calculate the NPV of the incremental cash flows of the new system (cash flows of new system less cash flows of old system). If the NPV for the incremental cash flows is positive, then the new equipment is preferred to the old.

Using the incremental data in Exhibit 14.4, the NPV of the proposed system can be computed as follows:

Present value ($4,000,000 × 5.65022*)	$22,600,880
Investment	18,000,000
NPV	$ 4,600,880

* This number is the discount factor for an interest rate of 12 percent and a life of 10 years (see Exhibit 14A.2).

The NPV is positive and large in magnitude, and it clearly signals the acceptability of the FMS. This outcome, however, is strongly dependent on explicit recognition of both

EXHIBIT 14.4

Investment Data; Direct, Intangible, and Indirect Benefits

	FMS	Status Quo
Investment (current outlay)		
Direct costs	$10,000,000	—
Software, engineering	8,000,000	—
Total current outlay	$18,000,000	$ 0
Net after-tax cash flow	$ 5,000,000	$1,000,000
Less: After-tax cash flows for status quo	1,000,000	n/a
Incremental benefit	$ 4,000,000	n/a
Incremental Benefit Explained		
Direct benefits		
Direct labour	$1,500,000	
Scrap reduction	500,000	
Setups	200,000	
	2,200,000	
Intangible benefits (quality savings)		
Rework	200,000	
Warranties	400,000	
Maintenance of competitive position	1,000,000	
	1,600,000	
Indirect benefits		
Production scheduling	110,000	
Payroll	90,000	
	200,000	
Total	$4,000,000	

intangible and indirect benefits. If those benefits are eliminated, then the direct savings total $2.2 million, and the NPV is negative:

Present value ($2,200,000 × 5.65022)	$ 12,430,484
Investment	18,000,000
NPV	$ (5,569,516)

The rise of activity-based costing has made identifying indirect benefits easier with the use of cost drivers. Once they are identified, they can be included in the analysis if they are material.

Examination of Exhibit 14.4 reveals the importance of intangible benefits. One of the most important intangible benefits is maintaining or improving a firm's competitive position. A key question is what will happen to the cash flows of the firm if the investment is not made. That is, if the company chooses to forgo an investment in technologically advanced equipment, will it be able to continue to compete with other firms on the basis of quality, delivery, and cost? (The question becomes especially relevant if competitors choose to invest in advanced equipment.) If its competitive position deteriorates, the company's current cash flows will decrease.

If cash flows will decrease if the investment is not made, this decrease should show up as an incremental benefit for the advanced technology. In Exhibit 14.4, the company estimates this competitive benefit as $1,000,000. Estimating this benefit requires some serious strategic planning and analysis, but its effect can be critical. If this benefit had been ignored or overlooked, then the NPV would have been negative and the investment alternative rejected:

Present value ($3,000,000 × 5.65022)	$16,950,660
Investment	18,000,000
NPV	$ (1,049,340)

APPENDIX 14A: PRESENT VALUE TABLES

The present value tables are found in Exhibits 14A.1 and 14A.2.

EXHIBIT 14A.1

Discount Factors—Present Value of a Single Amount*

n/i	1%	2%	3%	4%	5%	6%	7%	8%	9%	10%	12%	14%	16%	18%	20%	25%	30%
1	0.99010	0.98039	0.97087	0.96154	0.95238	0.94340	0.93458	0.92593	0.91743	0.90909	0.89286	0.87719	0.86207	0.84746	0.83333	0.80000	0.76923
2	0.98030	0.96117	0.94260	0.92456	0.90703	0.89000	0.87344	0.85734	0.84168	0.82645	0.79719	0.76947	0.74316	0.71818	0.69444	0.64000	0.59172
3	0.97059	0.94232	0.91514	0.88900	0.86384	0.83962	0.81630	0.79383	0.77218	0.75131	0.71178	0.67497	0.64066	0.60863	0.57870	0.51200	0.45517
4	0.96098	0.92385	0.88849	0.85480	0.82270	0.79209	0.76290	0.73503	0.70843	0.68301	0.63552	0.59208	0.55229	0.51579	0.48225	0.40960	0.35013
5	0.95147	0.90573	0.86261	0.82193	0.78353	0.74726	0.71299	0.68058	0.64993	0.62092	0.56743	0.51937	0.47611	0.43711	0.40188	0.32768	0.26933
6	0.94205	0.88797	0.83748	0.79031	0.74622	0.70496	0.66634	0.63017	0.59627	0.56447	0.50663	0.45559	0.41044	0.37043	0.33490	0.26214	0.20718
7	0.93272	0.87056	0.81309	0.75992	0.71068	0.66506	0.62275	0.58349	0.54703	0.51316	0.45235	0.39964	0.35383	0.31393	0.27908	0.20972	0.15937
8	0.92348	0.85349	0.78941	0.73069	0.67684	0.62741	0.58201	0.54027	0.50187	0.46651	0.40388	0.35056	0.30503	0.26604	0.23257	0.16777	0.12259
9	0.91434	0.83676	0.76642	0.70259	0.64461	0.59190	0.54393	0.50025	0.46043	0.42410	0.36061	0.30751	0.26295	0.22546	0.19381	0.13422	0.09430
10	0.90529	0.82035	0.74409	0.67556	0.61391	0.55839	0.50835	0.46319	0.42241	0.38554	0.32197	0.26974	0.22668	0.19106	0.16151	0.10737	0.07254
11	0.89632	0.80426	0.72242	0.64958	0.58468	0.52679	0.47509	0.42888	0.38753	0.35049	0.28748	0.23662	0.19542	0.16192	0.13459	0.08590	0.05580
12	0.88745	0.78849	0.70138	0.62460	0.55684	0.49697	0.44401	0.39711	0.35553	0.31863	0.25668	0.20756	0.16846	0.13722	0.11216	0.06872	0.04292
13	0.87866	0.77303	0.68095	0.60057	0.53032	0.46884	0.41496	0.36770	0.32618	0.28966	0.22917	0.18207	0.14523	0.11629	0.09346	0.05498	0.03302
14	0.86996	0.75788	0.66112	0.57748	0.50507	0.44230	0.38782	0.34046	0.29925	0.26333	0.20462	0.15971	0.12520	0.09855	0.07789	0.04398	0.02540
15	0.86135	0.74301	0.64186	0.55526	0.48102	0.41727	0.36245	0.31524	0.27454	0.23939	0.18270	0.14010	0.10793	0.08352	0.06491	0.03518	0.01954
16	0.85282	0.72845	0.62317	0.53391	0.45811	0.39365	0.33873	0.29189	0.25187	0.21763	0.16312	0.12289	0.09304	0.07078	0.05409	0.02815	0.01503
17	0.84438	0.71416	0.60502	0.51337	0.43630	0.37136	0.31657	0.27027	0.23107	0.19784	0.14564	0.10780	0.08021	0.05998	0.04507	0.02252	0.01156
18	0.83602	0.70016	0.58739	0.49363	0.41552	0.35034	0.29586	0.25025	0.21199	0.17986	0.13004	0.09456	0.06914	0.05083	0.03756	0.01801	0.00889
19	0.82774	0.68643	0.57029	0.47464	0.39573	0.33051	0.27651	0.23171	0.19449	0.16351	0.11611	0.08295	0.05961	0.04308	0.03130	0.01441	0.00684
20	0.81954	0.67297	0.55368	0.45639	0.37689	0.31180	0.25842	0.21455	0.17843	0.14864	0.10367	0.07276	0.05139	0.03651	0.02608	0.01153	0.00526
21	0.81143	0.65978	0.53755	0.43883	0.35894	0.29416	0.24151	0.19866	0.16370	0.13513	0.09256	0.06383	0.04430	0.03094	0.02174	0.00922	0.00405
22	0.80340	0.64684	0.52189	0.42196	0.34185	0.27751	0.22571	0.18394	0.15018	0.12285	0.08264	0.05599	0.03819	0.02622	0.01811	0.00738	0.00311
23	0.79544	0.63416	0.50669	0.40573	0.32557	0.26180	0.21095	0.17032	0.13778	0.11168	0.07379	0.04911	0.03292	0.02222	0.01509	0.00590	0.00239
24	0.78757	0.62172	0.49193	0.39012	0.31007	0.24698	0.19715	0.15770	0.12640	0.10153	0.06588	0.04308	0.02838	0.01883	0.01258	0.00472	0.00184
25	0.77977	0.60953	0.47761	0.37512	0.29530	0.23300	0.18425	0.14602	0.11597	0.09230	0.05882	0.03779	0.02447	0.01596	0.01048	0.00378	0.00142
26	0.77205	0.59758	0.46369	0.36069	0.28124	0.21981	0.17220	0.13520	0.10639	0.08391	0.05252	0.03315	0.02109	0.01352	0.00874	0.00302	0.00109
27	0.76440	0.58586	0.45019	0.34682	0.26785	0.20737	0.16093	0.12519	0.09761	0.07628	0.04689	0.02908	0.01818	0.01146	0.00728	0.00242	0.00084
28	0.75684	0.57437	0.43708	0.33348	0.25509	0.19563	0.15040	0.11591	0.08955	0.06934	0.04187	0.02551	0.01567	0.00971	0.00607	0.00193	0.00065
29	0.74934	0.56311	0.42435	0.32065	0.24295	0.18456	0.14056	0.10733	0.08215	0.06304	0.03738	0.02237	0.01351	0.00823	0.00506	0.00155	0.00050
30	0.74192	0.55207	0.41199	0.30832	0.23138	0.17411	0.13137	0.09938.	0.07537	0.05731	0.03338	0.01963	0.01165	0.00697	0.00421	0.00124	0.00038

* $df = 1/(1 + i)^n$

EXHIBIT 14A.2

Discount Factors—Present Value of an Annuity*

n/i	1%	2%	3%	4%	5%	6%	7%	8%	9%	10%	12%	14%	16%	18%	20%	25%	30%
1	0.99010	0.98039	0.97087	0.96154	0.95238	0.94340	0.93458	0.92593	0.91743	0.90909	0.89286	0.87719	0.86207	0.84746	0.83333	0.80000	0.76923
2	1.97040	1.94156	1.91347	1.88609	1.85941	1.83339	1.80802	1.78326	1.75911	1.73554	1.69005	1.64666	1.60523	1.56564	1.52778	1.44000	1.36095
3	2.94099	2.88388	2.82861	2.77509	2.72325	2.67301	2.62432	2.57710	2.53129	2.48685	2.40183	2.32163	2.24589	2.17427	2.10648	1.95200	1.81611
4	3.90197	3.80773	3.71710	3.62990	3.54595	3.46511	3.38721	3.31213	3.23972	3.16987	3.03735	2.91371	2.79818	2.69006	2.58873	2.36160	2.16624
5	4.85343	4.71346	4.57971	4.45182	4.32948	4.21236	4.10020	3.99271	3.88965	3.79079	3.60478	3.43308	3.27429	3.12717	2.99061	2.68928	2.43557
6	5.79548	5.60143	5.41719	5.24214	5.07569	4.91732	4.76654	4.62288	4.48592	4.35526	4.11141	3.88867	3.68474	3.49760	3.32551	2.95142	2.64275
7	6.72819	6.47199	6.23028	6.00205	5.78637	5.58238	5.38929	5.20637	5.03295	4.86842	4.56376	4.28830	4.03857	3.81153	3.60459	3.16114	2.80211
8	7.65168	7.32548	7.01969	6.73274	6.46321	6.20979	5.97130	5.74664	5.53482	5.33493	4.96764	4.63886	4.34359	4.07757	3.83716	3.32891	2.92470
9	8.56602	8.16224	7.78611	7.43533	7.10782	6.80169	6.51523	6.24689	5.99525	5.75902	5.32825	4.94637	4.60654	4.30302	4.03097	3.46313	3.01900
10	9.47130	8.98259	8.53020	8.11090	7.72173	7.36009	7.02358	6.71008	6.41766	6.14457	5.65022	5.21612	4.83323	4.49409	4.19247	3.57050	3.09154
11	10.36763	9.78685	9.25262	8.76048	8.30641	7.88687	7.49867	7.13896	6.80519	6.49506	5.93770	5.45273	5.02864	4.65601	4.32706	3.65640	3.14734
12	11.25508	10.57534	9.95400	9.38507	8.86325	8.38384	7.94269	7.53608	7.16073	6.81369	6.19437	5.66029	5.19711	4.79322	4.43922	3.72512	3.19026
13	12.13374	11.34837	10.63496	9.98565	9.39357	8.85268	8.35765	7.90378	7.48690	7.10336	6.42355	5.84236	5.34233	4.90951	4.53268	3.78010	3.22328
14	13.00370	12.10625	11.29607	10.56312	9.89864	9.29498	8.74547	8.24424	7.78615	7.36669	6.62817	6.00207	5.46753	5.00806	4.61057	3.82408	3.24867
15	13.86505	12.84926	11.93794	11.11839	10.37966	9.71225	9.10791	8.55948	8.06069	7.60608	6.81086	6.14217	5.57546	5.09158	4.67547	3.85926	3.26821
16	14.71787	13.57771	12.56110	11.65230	10.83777	10.10590	9.44665	8.85137	8.31256	7.82371	6.97399	6.26506	5.66850	5.16235	4.72956	3.88741	3.28324
17	15.56225	14.29187	13.16612	12.16567	11.27407	10.47726	9.76322	9.12164	8.54363	8.02155	7.11963	6.37286	5.74870	5.22233	4.77463	3.90993	3.29480
18	16.39827	14.99203	13.75351	12.65930	11.68959	10.82760	10.05909	9.37189	8.75563	8.20141	7.24967	6.46742	5.81785	5.27316	4.81219	3.92794	3.30369
19	17.22601	15.67846	14.32380	13.13394	12.08532	11.15812	10.33560	9.60360	8.95011	8.36492	7.36578	6.55037	5.87746	5.31624	4.84350	3.94235	3.31053
20	18.04555	16.35143	14.87747	13.59033	12.46221	11.46992	10.59401	9.81815	9.12855	8.51356	7.46944	6.62313	5.92884	5.35275	4.86958	3.95388	3.31579
21	18.85698	17.01121	15.41502	14.02916	12.82115	11.76408	10.83553	10.01680	9.29224	8.64869	7.56200	6.68696	5.97314	5.38368	4.89132	3.96311	3.31984
22	19.66038	17.65805	15.93692	14.45112	13.16300	12.04158	11.06124	10.20074	9.44243	8.77154	7.64465	6.74294	6.01133	5.40990	4.90943	3.97049	3.32296
23	20.45582	18.29220	16.44361	14.85684	13.48857	12.30338	11.27219	10.37106	9.58021	8.88322	7.71843	6.79206	6.04425	5.43212	4.92453	3.97639	3.32535
24	21.24339	18.91393	16.93554	15.24696	13.79864	12.55036	11.46933	10.52876	9.70661	8.98474	7.78432	6.83514	6.07263	5.45095	4.93710	3.98111	3.32719
25	22.02316	19.52346	17.41315	15.62208	14.09394	12.78336	11.65358	10.67478	9.82258	9.07704	7.84314	6.87293	6.09709	5.46691	4.94759	3.98489	3.32861
26	22.79520	20.12104	17.87684	15.98277	14.37519	13.00317	11.82578	10.80998	9.92897	9.16095	7.89566	6.90608	6.11818	5.48043	4.95632	3.98791	3.32970
27	23.55961	20.70690	18.32703	16.32959	14.64303	13.21053	11.98671	10.93516	10.02658	9.23722	7.94255	6.93515	6.13636	5.49189	4.96360	3.99033	3.33054
28	24.31644	21.28127	18.76411	16.66306	14.89813	13.40616	12.13711	11.05108	10.11613	9.30657	7.98442	6.96066	6.15204	5.50160	4.96967	3.99226	3.33118
29	25.06579	21.84438	19.18845	16.98371	15.14107	13.59072	12.27767	11.15841	10.19828	9.36961	8.02181	6.98304	6.16555	5.50983	4.97472	3.99381	3.33168
30	25.80771	22.39646	19.60044	17.29203	15.37245	13.76483	12.40904	11.25778	10.27365	9.42691	8.05518	7.00266	6.17720	5.51681	4.97894	3.99505	3.33206

* $df = [1 - 1/(1 + i)^n]/i$

APPENDIX 14B: INCOME TAX CONSIDERATIONS IN CAPITAL BUDGETING

Introduction to Income Taxes

OBJECTIVE 

Incorporate the tax shield into capital expenditure analysis.

To this point in the chapter, we have considered the cash inflows and outflows of capital budgeting decisions without taking into account the income tax considerations. Now we will introduce this complication into our analysis.

The *Income Tax Act* (ITA) is specific legislation that deals with how Canadian taxpayers (both personal and corporate) will calculate how much they must pay the federal and provincial governments each year. For income tax purposes, companies must calculate their net income according to generally accepted accounting principles, except where the ITA specifically indicates how revenues or expenses must be calculated.

We must remember that the governments do not necessarily follow generally accepted accounting principles in determining how companies should calculate their net income for tax purposes, as the legislation is intended to reflect government policy. Governments will use the legislation to encourage or discourage investment in certain sectors and will use it to eliminate, wherever possible, the discretion that managers have to alter their net income.

This is especially true when it comes to the depreciation of capital assets. As you will recall from financial accounting, in determining the depreciation policies to be used, a company will estimate the useful life of an asset and estimate its salvage value at the end of its useful life. Changing either or both of these estimates will result in significant differences in the annual expense for depreciation.

To eliminate this discretion, the ITA specifies that, for tax purposes, the expense related to using an asset will be calculated, in almost all cases, on the declining balance basis, and the maximum rates used will be as specified in Schedule II of the regulations. In the ITA, this annual expense is referred to as capital cost allowance (CCA), and the balance remaining after deducting the CCA from the original cost of the asset is the undepreciated capital cost (UCC). Each year, the CCA rate is applied to the UCC to determine the maximum expense allowed for tax purposes.

A sample of these classes and rates is as follows:

Class 8	Office Equipment	20%
Class 10	Computer Equipment and Vehicles	30%
Class 43	Manufacturing Equipment	30%

Furthermore, all assets of the same class are pooled together into groups of assets for which CCA is calculated. On disposition of an asset in any class, the proceeds of disposition are deducted from the balance of the asset class before calculating the CCA in any year. This results in a taxable gain or loss on disposition of an asset only if the asset being disposed of represents the last asset in the class or the UCC becomes negative. This is referred to as a *terminal gain* or a *terminal loss*. Otherwise, accounting gains or losses on disposal are not taxable.

An additional complication is that the ITA specifies that a taxpayer can only deduct one-half of the normal CCA in the year of acquisition (the half-year rule). Since an asset will be disposed of during a year, it will not be depreciated for tax purposes in the year of disposal.

The government frequently changes the rates applicable to the classes of assets to be consistent with its then-current economic policy, so use up-to-date information when making a decision.

Impact on Capital Budgeting Decisions

When analyzing a capital project, we must focus on the actual cash flow to the company if we are to provide an accurate analysis of the project. To do so, we must adjust the cash inflows and outflows for the impact of taxation on those cash flows, and must understand how the cash inflows and outflows will be taxed, if at all.

As we have seen above, income tax is a very complicated area, so we must make several simplifying assumptions that will allow us to concentrate on the core principles involved. The first simplifying assumption is that companies are taxed at a flat rate of tax on all incremental income being generated. Second, we will assume that net income before tax for accounting purposes equals taxable income as reported on our tax return.

After-Tax Cash Flows When we report net income from a project, we must adjust it for the additional tax that will have to be paid if we decide to pursue the project. In simple terms, if we increase our net income before tax by $1,000, shareholders will not realize a $1,000 increase in value; they will realize an increase in value determined by the after-tax amount of the net income. At a 30 percent tax rate, shareholders would realize an increase in value of $700 (= $1,000 minus the tax on $1,000 of $300).

Similarly, if the company incurs a tax-deductible expense, shareholders will not see their value diminished by the full amount of the expense but rather by the amount of the expense less the reduction in income taxes related to that expense. If the expense were $500, the income tax would be reduced by $150, so the net impact on the shareholder would be a reduction in value of $350.

The after-tax impact of cash inflows and outflows, if they are taxable, can be achieved by multiplying the amount by 1 minus the tax rate $(1 - t)$.

However, we must be mindful that not all cash inflows and outflows are taxable or tax deductible, whichever the case may be. The original investment will be expensed over time through the use of depreciation, so the original investment will not be a tax deductible expense. Likewise, the investment of working capital will not be a tax-deductible expense.

On the other hand, the cash inflows from the project and the cash outflows representing expenses incurred as a result of the project will be tax-affected items and must be adjusted to their after-tax values to give us an accurate picture of the viability of the project.

Capital Cost Allowance As noted earlier, the tax department allows a company to deduct a certain amount for CCA (tax depreciation) when calculating its income tax obligation. While the CCA deduction is not a cash inflow to the company directly, it does allow the company to reduce the amount of income tax it must pay. Therefore, while the CCA deduction is not a cash inflow, the saving of tax is a cash inflow and must be recognized.

The amount of the reduction in tax is complicated by the half-year rule, so we must determine, over the course of the project, the net impact of the CCA deduction. One additional complication is that when a piece of equipment is disposed of, and the proceeds are deducted from the balance remaining in the class of asset, this amount is not taxable unless the asset being disposed of represents the last asset in the class or the UCC becomes negative. If the asset is the last asset in the class or the UCC becomes negative, the company will realize taxable income (terminal gain) or a tax deductible expense (terminal loss).

For our purposes, we will assume that any dispositions do not result in either a terminal gain or a terminal loss.

CCA Tax Shield Since the reduction of our net income for tax purposes is allowed through CCA deductions, this creates a reduction in income taxes payable. This fact is often referred to as a **tax shield**, since the deduction *shields* income that would otherwise result in a tax expense.

Since the CCA is available each year on an investment, and since the amount of the CCA will diminish each year under the declining balance method of calculation, we must use a formula to determine the present value of the tax shield for the investment. This formula is:

$$PV = \frac{Cdt}{d + k} \times \frac{1 + 0.5k}{1 + k}$$

where C represents the cost of the asset, d represents the CCA rate for the asset, and k represents the minimum acceptable rate of return.

The final term, $(1 + 0.5k) \div (1 + k)$, is required to adjust for *the half-year rule*.

Using the example outlined in Cornerstone 14.3, we can adjust the project analysis to show the tax implications, assuming a 12 percent required rate of return, a 30 percent tax rate, and a 40 percent CCA rate, as follows:

Cash Flow Identification

Year	Item	Cash Flow	Factor (1-30%)	After-Tax Cash Flow
0	Equipment	$ (320,000)	N/A	$(320,000)
	Working capital	(40,000)	N/A	(40,000)
	Total	$ (360,000)		$(360,000)
1–4	Revenues	$ 300,000	0.7	$ 210,000
	Operating expenses	(180,000)	0.7	(126,000)
	Total	$ 120,000		$ 84,000
5	Revenues	$ 300,000	0.7	$ 210,000
	Operating expenses	(180,000)	0.7	(126,000)
	Salvage (disposal)	40,000		40,000
	Recovery of working capital	40,000		40,000
	Total	$ 200,000		$ 164,000

NPV Analysis

Year	Cash Flow	Discount Factor	Present Value
0	$(360,000)	1.00000	$(360,000)
1–4	$84,000	3.03735	255,137
5	$164,000	0.56743	93,059
5	PV of CCA tax shield		69,890
			$ 58,086

Consequently, when compared to the analysis without taking income taxes into consideration, the NPV of the project is considerably different ($117,968, compared to $58,086). In some cases, the income tax considerations will render a project unacceptable, even if the project appeared acceptable before taking income taxes into consideration.

SUMMARY OF LEARNING OBJECTIVES

LO1. Explain the meaning of *capital investment decisions,* and distinguish between independent and mutually exclusive capital investment decisions.

- Capital investment decisions are concerned with the acquisition of long-term assets and usually involve a significant outlay of funds.
- The two types of capital investment projects are independent and mutually exclusive.
- Independent projects are projects that, whether accepted or rejected, do not affect the cash flows of other projects.
- Mutually exclusive projects are those projects that, if accepted, preclude the acceptance of all other competing projects.

LO2. Differentiate between present values and future values.

- A dollar today is worth more than a dollar in one year's time. Money can be invested and discounted future values can enable managers to evaluate capital investment decisions.
- The future value of an investment is the value that will accumulate by the end of an investment's life, assuming a specified compound return.
- The amount that must be invested now to produce the future value is known as the present value of the future amount Discounting is the process of computing the present value of future cash flows.
- A series of future cash flows is called an annuity. Annuity payments may be either uniform or nonuniform cash flows. Uniform cash flows are easy to compute, as was shown in this chapter. Nonuniform cash flows can be computed using NPV analysis.

LO3. Compute the payback period and accounting rate of return for a proposed investment, and explain their roles in capital investment decisions.

- Managers make capital investment decisions by using formal models to decide whether to accept or reject proposed projects.
- These decision models are classified as nondiscounting and discounting, depending on whether they address the question of the time value of money.
- The two nondiscounting models are the payback period and the ARR.
- The payback period is the time required for a firm to recover its initial investment. For even cash flows, it is calculated by dividing the investment by the annual cash flow. For uneven cash flows, the cash flows are summed until the investment is recovered. If only a fraction of a year is needed, then it is assumed that the cash flows occur evenly within each year.
- The payback period ignores the time value of money and the profitability of projects because it does not consider the cash inflows available beyond the payback period. However, it does supply some useful information. The payback period is useful for assessing and controlling risk, minimizing the impact of an investment on a firm's liquidity, and controlling the risk of obsolescence.
- The ARR is computed by dividing the average income expected from an investment by either the original or average investment.
- Unlike the payback period, the ARR does consider the profitability of a project; however, it ignores the time value of money.
- The ARR may be useful to managers for screening new investments to ensure that certain accounting ratios are not adversely affected (specifically, accounting ratios that may be monitored to ensure compliance with debt covenants).

LO4. Use net present value analysis and the profitability index for capital investment decisions involving independent projects.

- NPV is the difference between the present value of future cash flows and the initial investment outlay.
- To use the NPV model, a required rate of return must be identified (usually the cost of capital). The NPV method uses the required rate of return to compute the present value of a project's cash inflows and outflows.
- If the present value of the inflows is greater than the present value of the outflows, then the NPV is greater than zero, and the project is profitable. If the NPV is less than zero, then the project is not profitable and should be rejected.
- The profitability index is used to evaluate capital investments by dividing the present value of future cash flows by the initial investment. If the PI is greater than 1, the investment recovers the initial investment. If the PI equals 1, the investment breaks even. If the PI is less than 1, the investment does not recover the initial investment and should be rejected.

LO5. Use the internal rate of return to assess the acceptability of independent projects.

- The IRR is computed by finding the interest rate that equates the present value of a project's cash inflows with the present value of its cash outflows.

- If the IRR is greater than the required rate of return (cost of capital), then the project is acceptable. If the IRR is less than the required rate of return, then the project should be rejected.

LO6. Explain the role and value of postaudits.

- Postauditing of capital projects is an important step in capital investment.
- Postaudits evaluate the actual performance of a project in relation to its expected performance.
- A postaudit may lead to corrective action to improve the performance of the project or to abandon it.
- Postaudits also serve as an incentive for managers to make capital investment decisions prudently.

LO7. Explain why net present value is better than internal rate of return for capital investment decisions involving mutually exclusive projects.

- In evaluating mutually exclusive or competing projects, managers have a choice of using NPV or IRR.
- When choosing among competing projects, the NPV model correctly identifies the best investment alternative.
- IRR, at times, may choose an inferior project. Thus, since NPV always provides the correct signal, it should be used.

LO8. (*Appendix 14B*) Incorporate the tax shield into capital expenditure analysis.

- Taxes are an inevitable fact of life and must be considered in any investment calculation.
- After-tax cash flows must be calculated.
- While claiming tax depreciation (CCA) does not result in a cash inflow, it does result in a lowering of the income taxes to be paid, thereby reducing the cash outflow from income taxes.

SUMMARY OF IMPORTANT EQUATIONS

1. $$NPV = \left[\sum CF_t/(1+i)^t\right] - I$$
$$= \left[\sum CF_t df_t\right] - I$$
$$= P - I$$

2. $$I = \frac{\sum CF_t}{(1+i)^t}\text{, where } i \text{ is the IRR.}$$

3. $$PV = \frac{Cdt}{d+k} \times \frac{1+0.5k}{1+k}$$

CORNERSTONES

CORNERSTONE 14.1 Calculating payback, page 688

CORNERSTONE 14.2 Calculating the accounting rate of return, page 691

CORNERSTONE 14.3 Assessing cash flows and calculating net present value, page 693

CORNERSTONE 14.4 Calculating internal rate of return with uniform cash flows, page 695

CORNERSTONE 14.5 Calculating net present value and internal rate of return for mutually exclusive projects, page 701

GLOSSARY

Accounting rate of return (ARR) The rate of return obtained by dividing the average accounting net income by the original investment (or by average investment). (p. 690)

Annuity A series of future cash flows. (p. 687)

Capital budgeting The process of making capital investment decisions. (p. 684)

Capital investment decisions The process of planning, setting goals and priorities, arranging financing, and identifying criteria for making long-term investments. (p. 684)

Compounding of interest Paying interest on interest. (p. 686)

Cost of capital The cost of investment funds, usually viewed as a weighted average of the costs of funds from all sources. (p. 692)

Discount factor The factor used to convert a future cash flow to its present value. (p. 686)

Discount rate The rate of return used to compute the present value of future cash flows. (p. 686)

Discounted cash flows Future cash flows expressed in present-value terms. (p. 692)

Discounting The act of finding the present value of future cash flows. (p. 686)

Discounting models Capital investment models that explicitly consider the time value of money in identifying criteria for accepting and rejecting proposed projects. (p. 688)

Future value The value that will accumulate by the end of an investment's life if the investment earns a specified compounded return. (p. 686)

Independent projects Projects that, if accepted or rejected, will not affect the cash flows of another project. (p. 684)

Internal rate of return (IRR) The rate of return that equates the present value of a project's cash inflows with the present value of its cash outflows (i.e., it sets the NPV equal to zero). Also, the rate of return being earned on funds that remain internally invested in a project. (p. 694)

Mutually exclusive projects Projects that, if accepted, preclude the acceptance of competing projects. (p. 684)

Net present value (NPV) The difference between the present value of a project's cash inflows and the present value of its cash outflows. (p. 692)

Nondiscounting models Capital investment models that identify criteria for accepting or rejecting projects without considering the time value of money. (p. 688)

Payback period The time required for a project to return its investment. (p. 688)

Postaudit A follow-up analysis of an investment decision, comparing actual benefits and costs with expected benefits and costs. (p. 698)

Present value The current value of a future cash flow. It represents the amount that must be invested now if the future cash flow is to be received assuming compounding at a given rate of interest. (p. 686)

Profitability index (PI) A discounting method that divides the present value of future cash flows by the initial investment. (p. 694)

Required rate of return The minimum rate of return that a project must earn in order to be acceptable. Usually corresponds to the cost of capital. (p. 692)

Tax shield A legal way to reduce net income for tax purposes, creating a reduction in income taxes payable. (p. 708)

REVIEW PROBLEMS

I. Basics of Capital Investment

Kenn Day, manager of Day Laboratory, is investigating the possibility of acquiring some new test equipment. To acquire the equipment requires an initial outlay of $300,000. To raise the capital, Kenn will sell shares valued at $200,000 (the shares pay dividends of $24,000 per year) and borrow

$100,000. The loan for $100,000 would carry an interest rate of 6 percent. Kenn figures that his weighted average cost of capital is 10 percent [= (2/3 × 0.12) + (1/3 × 0.06)]. This weighted average cost of capital is the discount rate that will be used for capital investment decisions.

Kenn estimates that the new test equipment will produce a cash inflow of $50,000 per year. Kenn expects the equipment to last for 20 years.

Required:

1. Compute the payback period.
2. Assuming that depreciation is $14,000 per year, compute the ARR (on total investment).
3. Compute the NPV of the test equipment.
4. Compute the IRR of the test equipment.
5. Should Kenn buy the equipment?

Solution:

1. The payback period is $300,000/$50,000, or six years.
2. The ARR is ($50,000 − $14,000)/$300,000, or 12 percent.
3. From Exhibit 14A.2, the discount factor for an annuity with *i* at 10 percent and *n* at 20 years is 8.51356. Thus, the NPV is (8.51356 × $50,000) − $300,000, or $125,678.
4. The discount factor associated with the IRR is 6.00 (= $300,000/$50,000). From Exhibit 14A.2, the IRR is between 14 percent and 16 percent (using the row corresponding to period 20). Using a business calculator, the IRR is 15.78 percent.
5. Since the NPV is positive and the IRR is greater than Kenn's cost of capital, the test equipment is a sound investment. This, of course, assumes that the cash flow projections are accurate.

II. Capital Investments with Competing Projects

A hospital is considering the possibility of two new purchases: new X-ray equipment or new biopsy equipment. Each project would require an investment of $750,000. The expected life for each is five years with no expected salvage value. The net cash inflows associated with the two independent projects are as follows:

Year	X-Ray Equipment	Biopsy Equipment
1	$375,000	$ 75,000
2	150,000	75,000
3	300,000	525,000
4	150,000	600,000
5	75,000	675,000

Required:

1. Compute the net present value of each project, assuming a required rate of 12 percent.
2. Compute the payback period for each project. Assume that the manager of the hospital accepts only projects with a payback period of three years or less. Offer some reasons why this may be a rational strategy even though the NPV computed in Requirement 1 may indicate otherwise.

Solution:

1. X-ray equipment:

Year	Cash Flow	Discount Factor	Present Value
0	$(750,000)	1.00000	$(750,000)
1	375,000	0.89286	334,823
2	150,000	0.79719	119,579
3	300,000	0.71178	213,534
4	150,000	0.63552	95,328
5	75,000	0.56743	42,557
NPV			$ 55,821

Biopsy equipment:

Year	Cash Flow	Discount Factor	Present Value
0	$(750,000)	1.00000	$(750,000)
1	75,000	0.89286	66,965
2	75,000	0.79719	59,789
3	525,000	0.71178	373,685
4	600,000	0.63552	381,312
5	675,000	0.56743	383,015
NPV			$ 514,766

2. X-ray equipment:

Payback period =	$375,000	1.00 year
	150,000	1.00
	225,000	0.75 ($225,000/$300,000)
	$750,000	2.75 years

Biopsy equipment:

Payback period =	$ 75,000	1.00 year
	75,000	1.00
	525,000	1.00
	75,000	0.13 (= $75,000/$600,000)
	$750,000	3.13 years

This might be a reasonable strategy because payback is a rough measure of risk. The assumption is that the longer it takes a project to pay for itself, the riskier the project is. Other reasons might be that the firm might have liquidity problems, the cash flows might be risky, or there might be a high risk of obsolescence.

DISCUSSION QUESTIONS

1. Explain the difference between independent projects and mutually exclusive projects.
2. Explain why the timing and quantity of cash flows are important in capital investment decisions.
3. The time value of money is ignored by the payback period and the ARR. Explain why this is a major deficiency in these two models.
4. What is the payback period? Compute the payback period for an investment requiring an initial outlay of $80,000 with expected annual cash inflows of $30,000.
5. Name and discuss three possible reasons that the payback period is used to help make capital investment decisions.
6. What is the accounting rate of return? Compute the ARR for an investment that requires an initial outlay of $300,000 and promises an average net income of $100,000.
7. "The net present value is the same as the profit of a project expressed in present dollars." Do you agree? Explain.
8. Explain the relationship between NPV and a firm's value.
9. What is the cost of capital? What role does it play in capital investment decisions?
10. What is the role that the required rate of return plays in the NPV model? In the IRR model?
11. Explain how the NPV is used to determine whether a project should be accepted or rejected.
12. "The IRR is the true or actual rate of return being earned by the project." Do you agree or disagree? Discuss.

13. Explain what a postaudit is and how it can provide useful input for future capital investment decisions, especially those involving advanced technology.
14. Explain why NPV is generally preferred over IRR when choosing among competing or mutually exclusive projects. Why would managers continue to use IRR to choose among mutually exclusive projects?
15. Suppose that a firm must choose between two mutually exclusive projects, both of which have negative NPVs. Explain how a firm can legitimately choose between two such projects.

CORNERSTONE EXERCISES

Cornerstone Exercise 14-1 **Payback Period**

OBJECTIVE 3
CORNERSTONE 14.1

McNeill Manufacturing is considering an investment in a new automated manufacturing system. The new system requires an investment of $4,500,000 and either has:

a. Even cash flows of $900,000 per year *or*
b. The following expected annual cash flows: $625,000, $650,000, $1,250,000, $925,000, $800,000, and $250,000.

Required:

Calculate the payback period for each case.

Cornerstone Exercise 14-2 **Accounting Rate of Return**

OBJECTIVE 3
CORNERSTONE 14.2

Thanda Company invested $7,500,000 in a new product line. The life cycle of the product is projected to be seven years with the following net income stream: $300,000, $300,000, $500,000, $900,000, $1,000,000, $2,100,000, and $1,200,000.

Required:

Calculate the accounting rate of return.

Cornerstone Exercise 14-3 **Net Present Value**

OBJECTIVE 4
CORNERSTONE 14.3

Chene Inc. has just developed a new drill. The new product is expected to produce annual revenues of $1,350,000. To produce the drill requires an investment in new equipment costing $1,440,000 and with a projected life cycle of five years. After five years, the equipment can be sold for $180,000. Working capital is also expected to increase by $180,000, which Chene will recover by the end of the new product's life cycle. Annual cash operating expenses are estimated at $810,000. The required rate of return is 8 percent.

Required:

1. Prepare a schedule of the projected annual cash flows.
2. Calculate the NPV using only discount factors from Exhibit 14A.1.
3. Calculate the NPV using discount factors from both Exhibits 14A.1 and 14A.2.

Cornerstone Exercise 14-4 **Internal Rate of Return**

OBJECTIVE 5
CORNERSTONE 14.4

Spirit Rock Company is examining the possibility of investing in a new production system that will reduce operating costs of the current system. The new system will require a cash investment of $3,044,151 and will produce net cash savings of $550,000 per year. The system has a projected life of eight years.

Required:

Calculate the internal rate of return for the new production system.

OBJECTIVE 7
CORNERSTONE 14.5

Cornerstone Exercise 14-5 NPV and IRR, Mutually Exclusive Projects

Cuccoco Inc. intends to invest in one of two competing types of computer-aided manufacturing equipment, built by two different manufacturers: CAM X and CAM Y. Both CAM X and CAM Y models have a project life of 10 years. The purchase price of the CAM X model is $2,400,000 and it has a net annual after-tax cash inflow of $600,000. The CAM Y model is more expensive, selling for $2,800,000, but will produce a net annual after-tax cash inflow of $700,000. The cost of capital for the company is 10 percent.

Required:

1. Calculate the NPV for each project. Which model would you recommend?
2. Calculate the IRR for each project. Which model would you recommend?

EXERCISES

OBJECTIVE 1 2 3

Exercise 14-6 Payback Period

Each of the following situations is independent. Assume that all cash flows are after-tax cash flows.

a. Carolina Teranova has just invested $350,000 in a hair styling business. She expects to receive a cash income of $76,200 per year from the investment.
b. Ray Noble has just invested $2,200,000 in a new wearable technology device. He expects to receive the following cash flows over the next five years: $50,000, $230,000, $1,300,000, $1,800,000, and $2,400,000.
c. Raphael Turpay invested in a project that has a payback period of five years. The project brings in $740,000 per year.
d. Josée Rodrigue invested $1,800,000 in a project that pays her the same amount per year for six years. The payback period is 4.5 years.

Required:

1. What is the payback period for Carolina?
2. What is the payback period for Ray?
3. How much did Raphael invest in the project?
4. How much cash does Josée receive each year?

OBJECTIVE 1 2 3

Exercise 14-7 Accounting Rate of Return

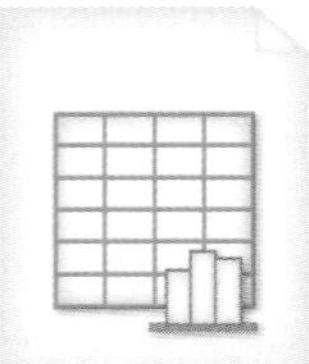

Each of the following scenarios is independent. Assume that all cash flows are after-tax cash flows.

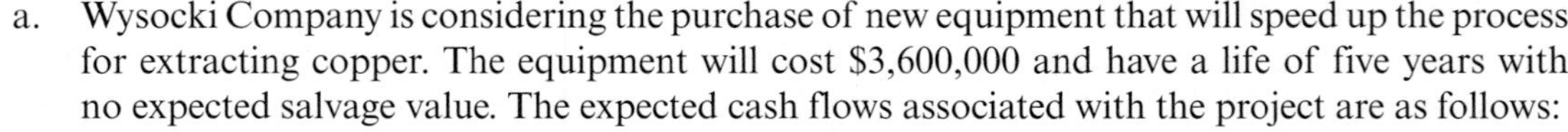

a. Wysocki Company is considering the purchase of new equipment that will speed up the process for extracting copper. The equipment will cost $3,600,000 and have a life of five years with no expected salvage value. The expected cash flows associated with the project are as follows:

Year	Cash Revenues	Cash Expenses
1	$6,000,000	$4,800,000
2	6,000,000	4,800,000
3	6,000,000	4,800,000
4	6,000,000	4,800,000
5	6,000,000	4,800,000

b. Marlene Straithe is considering investing in one of the following two projects. Either project will require an investment of $75,000. The expected revenues less cash expenses for the two projects follow. Assume each project is depreciable.

Year	Project A	Project B
1	$22,500	$22,500
2	30,000	30,000
3	45,000	45,000
4	71,250	22,500
5	71,250	22,500

c. Suppose that a project has an accounting rate of return of 30 percent (based on initial investment) and that the average net income of the project is $120,000.
d. Suppose that a project has an accounting rate of return of 50 percent and that the investment is $150,000.

Required:

1. Compute the ARR on the new equipment that Wysocki Company is considering.
2. CONCEPTUAL CONNECTION Which project should Marlene Straithe choose based on the ARR? Notice that the payback period is the same for both investments (thus equally preferred). Unlike the payback period, explain why ARR correctly signals that one project should be preferred over the other.
3. How much did the company in scenario (c) invest in the project?
4. What is the average income earned by the project in scenario (d)?

Exercise 14-8 Net Present Value

Each of the following scenarios is independent. Assume that all cash flows are after-tax cash flows.

a. Carlos Manufacturing is considering the purchase of a new welding system. The cash benefits will be $400,000 per year. The system costs $2,250,000 and will last 10 years.
b. Kokila Sarkar is interested in investing in a women's specialty shop. The cost of the investment is $180,000. She estimates that the return from owning her own shop will be $35,000 per year. She estimates that the shop will have a useful life of six years.
c. Mahelona Company calculated the NPV of a project and found it to be $21,300. The project's life was estimated to be eight years. The required rate of return used for the NPV calculation was 10 percent. The project was expected to produce annual after-tax cash flows of $45,000.

Required:

1. Compute the NPV for Carlos Manufacturing, assuming a discount rate of 12 percent. Should the company buy the new welding system?
2. CONCEPTUAL CONNECTION Assuming a required rate of return of 8 percent, calculate the NPV for Kokila Sarkar's investment. Should she invest? What if the estimated return was $45,000 per year? Would this affect the decision? What does this tell you about your analysis?
3. What was the required investment for Mahelona Company's project?

Exercise 14-9 Net Present Value and Competing Projects

Sulk Ltd. is considering investing in a new machine and has reduced the options to one of two types of machinery. Both machines will have a six-year life and have zero salvage value at the end of six years. Sulk has a 12 percent cost of capital.

	Machine A	Machine B
Initial investment in machinery	$280,000	$470,000
Annual cost savings	75,000	125,000

Required:

1. Compute the net present value for each machine. Which machine do you recommend Sulk purchase based on the NPV?
2. Compute the profitability index for each machine. Which machine do you recommend Sulk purchase based on the PI?
3. Why do the rankings of the machines differ in Requirements 1 and 2? Considering the results from Requirements 1 and 2, which machine do you recommend that Sulk purchase? Briefly discuss your recommendation.

Exercise 14-10 Internal Rate of Return

Each of the following scenarios is independent. Assume that all cash flows are after-tax cash flows.

a. Zenteno Company is considering the purchase of new equipment that will speed up the process for producing flash drives. The equipment will cost $7,200,000 and have a life of five years with no expected salvage value. The expected cash flows associated with the project follow:

Year	Cash Revenues	Cash Expenses
1	$8,000,000	$6,000,000
2	8,000,000	6,000,000
3	8,000,000	6,000,000
4	8,000,000	6,000,000
5	8,000,000	6,000,000

b. Nadine Fanger is evaluating an investment in an information system that will save $240,000 per year. She estimates that the system will last 10 years. The system will cost $1,248,000. Her company's cost of capital is 10 percent.

c. Castle Dale Enterprises just announced that a new plant would be built in Cold Lake, Alberta. Castle Dale told its shareholders that the plant has an expected life of 15 years and an expected IRR equal to 25 percent. The cost of building the plant is expected to be $2,880,000.

Required:

1. Calculate the IRR for Zenteno Company. The company's cost of capital is 16 percent. Should the new equipment be purchased?
2. Calculate Nadine Fanger's IRR. Should she acquire the new system?
3. What should be Castle Dale Enterprises' expected annual cash flow from the plant?

Exercise 14-11 Net Present Value and Competing Projects

Luana Hospital is investigating the possibility of investing in new dialysis equipment. Two local manufacturers of this equipment are being considered as sources of the equipment. After-tax cash inflows for the two competing projects are as follows:

Year	Limpio Equipment	Salman Equipment
1	$320,000	$120,000
2	280,000	120,000
3	240,000	320,000
4	160,000	400,000
5	120,000	440,000

Both projects require an initial investment of $560,000. In both cases, assume that the equipment has a life of five years with no salvage value.

Required:

1. Assuming a discount rate of 12 percent, compute the net present value of each piece of equipment.
2. A third option has surfaced for equipment purchased from an out-of-province supplier. The cost is also $560,000, but this equipment will produce even cash flows over its five-year life. What must the annual cash flow be for this equipment to be selected over the other two? Assume a 12 percent discount rate.

Exercise 14-12 Payback, Accounting Rate of Return, Net Present Value, Internal Rate of Return

Peters Company wants to buy a new machine costing $840,000. The equipment will last five years with no expected salvage value. The expected after-tax cash flows associated with the project follow:

Year	Cash Revenues	Cash Expenses
1	$1,150,000	$750,000
2	1,150,000	750,000
3	1,150,000	750,000
4	1,150,000	750,000
5	1,150,000	750,000

Required:

1. Compute the payback period for the equipment.
2. Compute the equipment's ARR.
3. Compute the investment's NPV, assuming a required rate of return of 9 percent.
4. Compute the investment's IRR.

Exercise 14-13 Net Present Value and Comparison of Projects

OBJECTIVE 1 4

Higa Corporation is planning to build a new facility in Regina, Saskatchewan. A local Regina contractor has offered to build the facility and has proposed two alternative payment options, as follows:

- **Payment Option 1:** Payment of $1,000,000 at the signing of the contract and $1,800,000 due at the end of the project in two years, *or*
- **Payment Option 2:** Payment of $500,000 due at the signing of the contract, $1,000,000 after one year, and another $1,000,000 due in two years.

  Higa requires a 10 percent rate of return.

Required:

Compute the NPV for each payment option. Which payment option should Higa choose?

Exercise 14-14 Payback, Accounting Rate of Return, Present Value, Net Present Value, Internal Rate of Return

All four parts are independent of all other parts. Assume that all cash flows are after-tax cash flows.

a. Isaac Ramos is considering investing in one of the following two projects. Either project will require an investment of $20,000. The expected cash flows for the two projects follow. Assume that each project is depreciable.

Year	Project A	Project B
1	$ 6,000	$ 6,000
2	8,000	8,000
3	10,000	10,000
4	10,000	3,000
5	10,000	3,000

b. Inka Laine is retiring and has the option to take her retirement as a lump sum of $450,000 or to receive $30,000 per year for 20 years. Inka's required rate of return is 6 percent.

c. Ahmad Sajadi is interested in investing in some tools and equipment so that he can do independent drywalling. The cost of the tools and equipment is $30,000. He estimates that the return from owning his own equipment will be $9,000 per year. The tools and equipment will last six years.

d. Patsy Folson is evaluating what appears to be an attractive opportunity. She is currently the owner of a small manufacturing company and has the opportunity to acquire another small company's equipment that would provide production of a part currently purchased externally. She estimates that the savings from internal production will be $75,000 per year. She estimates that the equipment will last 10 years. The owner is asking $400,000 for the equipment. Her company's cost of capital is 8 percent.

Required:

1. What is the payback period for each of Isaac Ramos's projects? If rapid payback is important, which project should be chosen? Which would you choose?
2. Which of Isaac's projects should be chosen based on the ARR?
3. Assuming that Inka Laine will live for another 20 years, should she take the lump sum or the annuity?
4. Assuming a required rate of return of 8 percent for Ahmad Sajadi, calculate the NPV of the investment. Should Ahmad invest?
5. Calculate the IRR for Patsy Folson's project. Should Patsy acquire the equipment?

OBJECTIVE 4

Exercise 14-15 Net Present Value, Basic Concepts

Roboto Company is considering an investment that requires an outlay of $450,000 and promises an after-tax cash inflow one year from now of $505,029. The company's cost of capital is 8 percent.

Required:

1. Break the $505,029 future cash inflow into three components: (a) the return of the original investment, (b) the cost of capital, and (c) the profit earned on the investment. Now compute the present value of the profit earned on the investment.
2. Compute the NPV of the investment. Compare this with the present value of the profit computed in Requirement 1. What does this tell you about the meaning of NPV?

OBJECTIVE 

Exercise 14-16 Solving for Unknowns

Each of the following cases is independent. Assume that all cash flows are after-tax cash flows.

a. Thomas Company is investing $120,000 in a project that will yield a uniform series of cash inflows over the next four years.
b. Video Repair has decided to invest in some new electronic equipment. The equipment will have a three-year life and will produce a uniform series of cash savings. The NPV of the equipment is $1,750, using a discount rate of 8 percent. The IRR is 12 percent.
c. A new lathe costing $60,096 will produce savings of $12,000 per year.
d. The NPV of a project is $3,927. The cost of the project is two times the cash flow produced in year 4. The discount rate is 10 percent. The project has a life of four years and produces the following cash flows.

Year 1	$10,000	Year 3	$15,000
Year 2	$12,000	Year 4	?

Required:

1. If the internal rate of return is 14 percent for Thomas Company, how much cash inflow per year can be expected?
2. Determine the investment and the amount of cash savings realized each year for Video Repair.
3. For scenario (c), how many years must the lathe last if an IRR of 18 percent is realized?
4. For scenario (d), find the cost of the project and the cash flow for year 4.

OBJECTIVE 7

Exercise 14-17 Net Present Value Versus Internal Rate of Return

A company is thinking about two different modifications to its current manufacturing process. The after-tax cash flows associated with the two investments follow:

Year	Project I	Project II
0	$(100,000)	$(100,000)
1	—	63,857
2	134,560	63,857

The company's cost of capital is 10 percent.

Required:

1. Compute the NPV and the IRR for each investment.
2. CONCEPTUAL CONNECTION Explain why the project with the larger NPV is the correct choice for the company.

PROBLEMS

Problem 14-18 Basic Net Present Value Analysis

OBJECTIVE 1 4

Peter Solway has redesigned company process equipment with improved environmental performance, using his skills as an environmental engineer. Peter knows the new process must also be economically attractive. The process design requires new equipment and an infusion of working capital. The equipment will cost $1,400,000, and its cash operating expenses will total $320,000 per year. The equipment will last for eight years but will need a major overhaul costing $110,000 at the end of the fifth year. At the end of eight years, the equipment will be sold for $88,000. An increase in working capital totalling $95,000 will also be needed at the beginning. This will be recovered at the end of the eight years.

On the positive side, Peter estimates that the new process will save $460,000 per year in environmental costs (fines and cleanup costs avoided). The cost of capital is 10 percent.

Required:

1. Prepare a schedule of cash flows for the proposed project. Assume that there are no income taxes.
2. Compute the NPV of the project. Should the new process design be accepted?

Check figure:
2. NPV = $(731,040)

Problem 14-19 Net Present Value Analysis

OBJECTIVE 1 4

Uintah Communications Company is considering the production and marketing of a communications system that will increase the efficiency of messaging for small businesses or branch offices of large companies. Each unit hooked into the system is assigned a mailbox number, which can be matched to a telephone extension number, providing access to messages 24 hours a day. Up to 20 units can be hooked into the system, allowing the delivery of the same message to as many as 20 people. Personal codes can be used to make messages confidential. Furthermore, messages can be reviewed, recorded, cancelled, replied to, or deleted all during the same phone call. Indicators wired to the telephone blink whenever new messages are present.

To produce this product, a $1.75 million investment in new equipment is required. The equipment will last 10 years but will need major maintenance costing $150,000 at the end of its sixth year. The salvage value of the equipment at the end of 10 years is estimated to be $100,000. If this new system is produced, working capital must also be increased by $90,000. This capital will be restored at the end of the product's life cycle, which is estimated to be 10 years. Revenues from the sale of the product are estimated at $1.65 million per year; cash operating expenses are estimated at $1.32 million per year.

Required:

1. Prepare a schedule of cash flows for the proposed project. Assume that there are no income taxes.
2. Assuming that Uintah's cost of capital is 12 percent, compute the project's NPV. Should the product be produced?

Check figure:
2. NPV = $9,751

Problem 14-20 Basic Internal Rate of Return Analysis

OBJECTIVE 

Hayma Sayama, owner of Baker Company, was approached by a local dealer of air-conditioning units. The dealer proposed replacing Baker's old cooling system with a modern, more efficient system. The cost of the new system was quoted at $339,000, but it would save $60,000 per year in energy costs. The estimated life of the new system is 10 years, with no salvage value expected. Excited over the possibility of saving $60,000 per year and having a more reliable unit, Hayma requested an analysis of the project's economic viability. All capital projects are required to earn at least the firm's cost of capital, which is 8 percent. There are no income taxes.

Required:

Check figures:
1. IRR = 0.12
2. Cash flow = $50,521
3. Minimum cash flow = $58,991

1. Calculate the project's IRR. Should the company acquire the new cooling system?
2. Suppose that energy savings are less than claimed. Calculate the minimum annual cash savings that must be realized for the project to earn a rate equal to the firm's cost of capital.
3. Suppose that the life of the new system is overestimated by two years. Repeat Requirements 1 and 2 under this assumption.
4. CONCEPTUAL CONNECTION Explain the implications of the answers from Requirements 1, 2, and 3.

OBJECTIVE 1 4

Problem 14-21 Net Present Value, Uncertainty

Maskel Airlines is considering the acquisition of a new aircraft to service a new route from Sarnia to Sudbury. The aircraft will fly one round trip daily except for scheduled maintenance days. There are 22 maintenance days scheduled each year. The seating capacity of the aircraft is 125. Flights are expected to be fully booked. The average revenue per passenger per flight (one-way) is $345. Annual operating costs of the aircraft follow:

Fuel	$2,900,000
Flight personnel	1,400,000
Food and beverages	140,000
Maintenance	800,000
Other	110,000
Total	$5,350,000

The aircraft will cost $140,000,000 and has an expected life of 20 years. The company requires a 12 percent return. Assume there are no income taxes.

Required:

Check figures:
1. NPV = $41,012,542
2. NPV = $(14,230,966)
3. Seating rate = 81.4%
4. Seating rate = 74.0%

1. Calculate the NPV for the aircraft. Should the company buy it?
2. In discussing the proposal, the marketing manager for the airline states that the assumption of 100 percent booking is unrealistic. He believes that the booking rate will be somewhere between 65 percent and 85 percent, with the most likely rate being 75 percent. Recalculate the NPV using a 75 percent seating capacity. Should the aircraft be purchased?
3. Calculate the average seating rate that would be needed so that NPV will equal zero.
4. CONCEPTUAL CONNECTION Suppose that the price per passenger could be increased by 10 percent without any effect on demand. What is the average seating rate now needed to achieve an NPV equal to zero? What would you now recommend?

OBJECTIVE 1 2 3 4 5

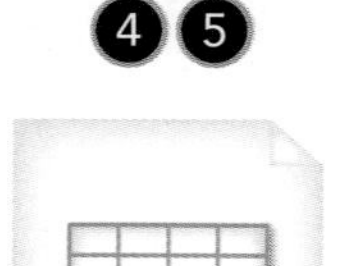

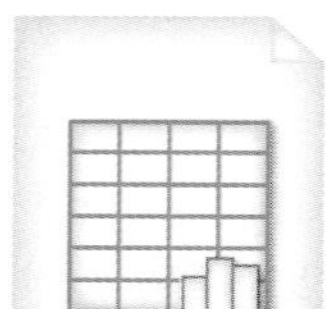

Problem 14-22 Review of Basic Capital Budgeting Procedures

Dr. Whitley Avard, a plastic surgeon, had just returned from a conference in which she learned of a new surgical procedure for removing wrinkles around the eyes, reducing the time to perform the normal procedure by 50 percent. Given her patient-load pressures, Dr. Avard is excited to try out the new technique. By decreasing the time spent on eye treatments or procedures, she can increase her total revenues by performing more services within a work period. Unfortunately, in order to implement the new procedure, special equipment costing $74,000 is needed. The equipment has an expected life of four years, with a salvage value of $6,000. Dr. Avard estimates that her cash revenues will increase by the following amounts:

Year	Revenue Increases
1	$19,800
2	27,000
3	32,400
4	32,400

She also expects additional cash expenses amounting to $3,000 per year. The cost of capital is 12 percent. Assume that there are no income taxes.

Required:

1. Compute the payback period for the new equipment.
2. Compute the ARR.
3. CONCEPTUAL CONNECTION Compute the NPV and IRR for the project. Should Dr. Avard purchase the new equipment? Should she be concerned about payback or the ARR in making this decision?
4. CONCEPTUAL CONNECTION Before finalizing her decision, Dr. Avard decided to call two plastic surgeons who have been using the new procedure for the past six months. The conversations revealed a somewhat less glowing report than she received at the conference. The new procedure reduced the time required by about 25 percent rather than the advertised 50 percent. Dr. Avard estimated that the net operating cash flows of the procedure would be cut by one-third because of the extra time and cost involved (salvage value would be unaffected). Using this information, recompute the NPV of the project. What would you now recommend?

Check figures:
1. Payback = 3.13 years
2. ARR = 10.68%
3. IRR = 14% (approximately)
4. NPV = $(21,025)

Problem 14-23 Basic Net Present Value Analysis, Competing Projects

Kildare Medical Centre, a for-profit hospital, has three investment opportunities: (1) adding a wing for in-patient treatment of substance abuse, (2) adding a pathology laboratory, and (3) expanding the outpatient surgery wing. The initial investments and the NPVs for the three alternatives are as follows:

	Substance Abuse	Laboratory	Outpatient Surgery
Investment	$1,500,000	$500,000	$1,000,000
NPV	150,000	140,000	135,000

Although the hospital would like to invest in all three alternatives, only $1.5 million is available.

Required:

1. Rank the projects on the basis of NPV, and allocate the funds in order of this ranking. What project or projects were selected? What is the total NPV realized by Kildare using this approach?
2. CONCEPTUAL CONNECTION Assume that the size of the lot on which the hospital is located makes the substance abuse wing and the outpatient surgery wing mutually exclusive. With unlimited capital, which projects would be chosen? With limited capital of $1.5 million, which projects would be chosen?
3. CONCEPTUAL CONNECTION Form a group with two to four other students, and discuss qualitative considerations that should be considered in capital budgeting evaluations. Identify three such considerations.

Problem 14-24 Payback, Net Present Value, Internal Rate of Return, Intangible Benefits, Inflation Adjustment

Max Company wants to buy a new machine to be used in production that will replace an existing manual system. The outlay required is $2,990,000. The equipment will last six years with no expected salvage value. The expected incremental after-tax cash flows (cash flows of the equipment less cash flows of the old equipment) associated with the project follow:

Year	Cash Benefits	Cash Expenses
1	$1,600,000	$950,000
2	1,600,000	950,000
3	1,600,000	950,000
4	1,600,000	950,000
5	1,600,000	950,000
6	1,600,000	950,000

Max has a cost of capital equal to 12 percent. The above cash flows are expressed without any consideration of inflation.

(Continued)

Required:

1. Compute the payback period.
2. Calculate the NPV and IRR of the proposed project.
3. CONCEPTUAL CONNECTION Inflation is expected to be 5 percent per year for the next six years. The discount rate of 12 percent is composed of two elements: the real rate and the inflationary element. Since the discount rate has an inflationary component, the projected cash flows should also be adjusted to account for inflation. Make this adjustment, and recalculate the NPV. Comment on the importance of adjusting cash flows for inflationary effects.

Check figures:
1. Payback = 4.6 years
2. NPV = $(317,584)
3. NPV = $140,393

OBJECTIVE 4

Problem 14-25 Net Present Value Capital Investment Decision

Quicken Iron and Soldering (Quicken), based in Montreal, is considering the purchase of several soldering torches. Each of the 60 industrial torches costs $4,000 and is expected to last six years. While the salesperson advertises net income potential of $1,200 per year per torch, prior experience suggests that 1 out of 15 torches fail at the end of the first year and 2 more out of 15 fail at the end of the second year. The remainder last their advertised lifetime. A warranty is provided for the first year only and Quicken will receive a new torch to replace each torch that fails within one year; the replacements are guaranteed to last the advertised timeframe.

Required:

Should Quicken proceed with the purchase if the expected inflation rate is 2 percent and the real rate of return demanded is 12 percent? (*Hint:* Compute the NPV.)

OBJECTIVE 4

Problem 14-26 Cost of Capital, Net Present Value

Leakam Company's product engineering department has developed a new product that has a three-year life cycle. Production of the product requires development of a new process that requires a current $100,000 capital outlay. The $100,000 will be raised by issuing $60,000 of bonds and selling shares for $40,000. The $60,000 in bonds will have net (after-tax) interest payments of $3,000 at the end of each of the three years, with the principal being repaid at the end of year 3. The share issue carries with it an expectation of a 17.5 percent return, expressed in the form of dividends at the end of each year ($7,000 in dividends is expected for each of the next three years). The sources of capital for this investment represent the same proportion and costs that the company typically has. Finally, the project will produce after-tax cash inflows of $50,000 per year for the next three years.

Required:

1. Compute the cost of capital for the project. (*Hint:* The cost of capital is a weighted average of the two sources of capital where the weights are the proportion of capital from each source.)
2. CONCEPTUAL CONNECTION Compute the NPV for the project. Explain why it is not necessary to subtract the interest payments and the dividend payments from the inflow of $50,000 in carrying out this computation.

Check figures:
1. Cost of capital = 0.10
2. NPV = $24,344

OBJECTIVE  

Problem 14-27 Capital Investment, Advanced Manufacturing Environment

"I know that it's the thing to do," insisted Pamela Kincaid, vice-president of finance for Colgate Manufacturing. "If we are going to be competitive, we need to build this completely automated plant."

"I'm not so sure," replied Bill Thomas, CEO of Colgate. "The savings from labour reductions and increased productivity are only $4 million per year. The price tag for this factory is $45 million. That gives a payback period of more than 11 years. That's a long time to put the company's money at risk."

"Yeah, but you're overlooking the savings that we'll get from the increase in quality," interjected John Simpson, production manager. "With this system, we can decrease our waste and our rework time significantly. Those savings are worth another million dollars per year."

"Another million will only cut the payback to about nine years," retorted Bill. "Tracy, you're the marketing manager—do you have any insights?"

"Well, there are other factors to consider, such as service quality and market share. I think that increasing our product quality and improving our delivery service will make us a lot more competitive. I know for a fact that two of our competitors have decided against automation. That'll give us a shot at their customers, provided our product is of higher quality and we can deliver it faster. I estimate that it'll increase our net cash benefits by another $2.4 million."

"Wow! Now that's impressive," Bill exclaimed, nearly convinced. "The payback is now getting down to a reasonable level."

"I agree," said Pamela, "but we do need to be sure that it's a sound investment. I know that estimates for construction of the facility have gone as high as $48 million. I also know that the expected residual value, after the 20 years of service we expect to get, is $5 million. I think I had better see if this project can cover our 14 percent cost of capital."

"Now wait a minute, Pamela," Bill demanded. "You know that I usually insist on a 20 percent rate of return, especially for a project of this magnitude."

Required:

1. Compute the NPV of the project by using the original savings and investment figures. Calculate by using discount rates of 14 percent and 20 percent. Include salvage value in the computation.
2. Compute the NPV of the project using the additional benefits noted by the production and marketing managers. Also, use the original cost estimate of $45 million. Again, calculate for both possible discount rates.
3. Compute the NPV of the project using all estimates of cash flows, including the possible initial outlay of $48 million. Calculate by using discount rates of 14 percent and 20 percent.
4. CONCEPTUAL CONNECTION If you were making the decision, what would you do? Explain.

Check figures:
1. NPV (14%) = $(18,143,680)
2. NPV (14%) = $4,374,962
3. NPV (14%) = $1,374,962

Problem 14-28 Postaudit, Sensitivity Analysis

OBJECTIVE 6 

Newmarge Products Inc. is evaluating a new design for one of its manufacturing processes. The new design will eliminate the production of a toxic solid residue. The initial cost of the system is estimated at $860,000 and includes computerized equipment, software, and installation. There is no expected salvage value. The new system has a useful life of eight years and is projected to produce cash operating savings of $225,000 per year over the old system (reducing labour costs and costs of processing and disposing of toxic waste). The cost of capital is 16 percent.

Required:

1. Compute the NPV of the new system.
2. One year after implementation, the internal audit staff noted the following about the new system: (1) the cost of acquiring the system was $60,000 more than expected due to higher installation costs, and (2) the annual cost savings were $20,000 less than expected because more labour cost was needed than anticipated. Using the changes in expected costs and benefits, compute the NPV as if this information had been available one year ago. Did the company make the right decision?
3. CONCEPTUAL CONNECTION Upon reporting the results mentioned in the postaudit, the marketing manager responded in a memo to the internal auditing department indicating that gross margin savings (revenues less cost of goods sold) had increased by $60,000 per year because of increased purchases by environmentally sensitive customers. Describe the effect that this has on the analysis in Requirement 2.
4. CONCEPTUAL CONNECTION Why is a postaudit beneficial to a firm?

Check figures:
1. NPV = $117,308
2. NPV = $(29,564)
3. NPV = $231,051

Problem 14-29 Discount Rates, Automated Manufacturing, Competing Investments

OBJECTIVE 

A company is considering two competing investments: (1) a standard piece of production equipment, or (2) computer-aided manufacturing (CAM) equipment. The investment and after-tax operating cash flows follow:

(Continued)

Year	Standard Equipment	CAM Equipment
0	$(650,000)	$(2,300,000)
1	330,000	110,000
2	220,000	220,000
3	110,000	330,000
4	110,000	440,000
5	110,000	440,000
6	110,000	440,000
7	110,000	550,000
8	110,000	1,200,000
9	110,000	1,200,000
10	110,000	1,200,000

Check figures:
1. NPV (standard) = $70,892
2. NPV (CAM) = $513,244

The company uses a discount rate of 20 percent for all of its investments. The company's cost of capital is 12 percent.

Required:

1. Calculate the NPV for each investment using a discount rate of 20 percent.
2. Calculate the NPV for each investment using a discount rate of 12 percent.
3. CONCEPTUAL CONNECTION Which rate should the company use to compute the NPV? Explain.

OBJECTIVE 7

Problem 14-30 Quality, Market Share, Automated Manufacturing Environment

A company is considering two competing investments: (1) a standard piece of production equipment, or (2) computer-aided manufacturing (CAM) equipment. The investment and after-tax operating cash flows follow:

Year	Standard Equipment	CAM Equipment
0	$(500,000)	$(2,000,000)
1	300,000	100,000
2	200,000	200,000
3	100,000	300,000
4	100,000	400,000
5	100,000	400,000
6	100,000	400,000
7	100,000	500,000
8	100,000	1,000,000
9	100,000	1,000,000
10	100,000	1,000,000

Assume that the company's cost of capital is 14 percent.

Required:

Check figures:
1. NPV (CAM) = $198,560
2. NPV (standard) = $95,524

1. Calculate the NPV of each alternative using the 14 percent rate.
2. CONCEPTUAL CONNECTION Now assume that if the standard equipment is purchased, the competitive position of the firm will deteriorate because of lower quality (relative to competitors who did automate). Marketing estimates that the loss in market share will decrease the projected net cash inflows by 50 percent for years 3 through 10. Recalculate the NPV of the standard equipment given this outcome. What is the decision now? Discuss the importance of assessing the effect of intangible benefits.

OBJECTIVE 6

Problem 14-31 Capital Budgeting Income Tax

Trudeau Analytical Services Inc. has the opportunity to increase its services of evaluating drilling results for exploration companies drilling for oil in the northern reaches of the Arctic. The additional services will generate about $1.2 million in additional annual revenues, with related cash expenditures of $800,000 per year.

In order to engage in these services, the company will require additional, very sophisticated testing equipment that will cost $1.5 million and will have a useful life of 20 years, at which time it can be sold for $150,000. This equipment will be categorized for tax purposes as Class 10 Equipment, with a CCA rate of 30 percent per year.

In addition to the equipment purchase, Trudeau will require $100,000 of additional working capital to support this venture. At the end of each five-year period, the company will be required to do maintenance on the new analyzing equipment at a cost of $50,000 each time.

Trudeau is subject to a combined federal and provincial income tax rate of 40 percent and expects a minimum after-tax return of 12 percent on any project that it engages in.

Required:

1. Prepare a memo outlining your recommendations to the management of the company as to whether the company should enter this new line of business. Show all calculations, and be very specific in your recommendation.
2. At what level of investment in the equipment would this project not be acceptable? Ignore the impact of the increased investment on the CCA tax shield.
3. Referring to the original facts, at what level of pre-tax income would this project not be acceptable?

Check figure:
1. NPV = $592,033

PROFESSIONAL EXAMINATION PROBLEM*

Professional Examination Problem 14-32 **Capital Budgeting—Knossos Limited**

Knossos Limited is a manufacturer of standard and custom-designed bottling equipment. Early in December 2017, Larissa Company asked Knossos to quote a price for a custom-designed bottling machine to be delivered on April 1, 2018. Larissa intends to make a decision on the purchase of such a machine by January 1, so Knossos would have the entire first quarter of 2018 to build the equipment.

Knossos's standard pricing policy for custom-designed equipment is 50 percent markup on full cost. Larissa's specifications for the equipment have been reviewed by Knossos's engineering and cost accounting departments, and they made the following estimates for raw materials and direct labour:

Direct materials	$256,000
Direct labour (11,000 hours at $15)	165,000

Manufacturing overhead is applied on the basis of direct labour hours. Knossos normally plans to run its plant with 15,000 direct labour hours per month and assigns overhead on the basis of 180,000 direct labour hours per year. The overhead application rate for 2018 of $9 per direct labour hour is based on the following budgeted manufacturing overhead costs for 2018:

Variable manufacturing overhead	$ 972,000
Fixed manufacturing overhead	648,000
	$1,620,000

The Knossos production schedule calls for 12,000 direct labour hours per month during the first quarter. If Knossos is awarded the contract for the Larissa equipment, production of one of its standard products will have to be reduced. This is necessary because production levels can only be increased to 15,000 direct labour hours each month on short notice. Furthermore, Knossos's employees are unwilling to work overtime.

Sales of the standard product equal to the reduced production will be lost, but there will be no permanent loss of future sales or customers. The standard product, whose production schedule will be reduced, has a unit sales price of $12,000 and the following cost structure:

(Continued)

Raw materials	$2,500
Direct labour (250 hours at $15)	3,750
Overhead (250 hours at $9)	2,250
	$8,500

Larissa needs the custom-designed equipment to increase its bottle-making capacity so that it will not have to buy bottles from an outside supplier. Larissa Company requires 5,000,000 bottles annually. Its present equipment has a maximum capacity of 4,500,000 bottles with a directly traceable cash outlay of $0.15 per bottle. Thus, Larissa has had to purchase 500,000 bottles from a supplier at $0.40 each. The new equipment would allow Larissa to manufacture its entire annual demand for bottles at a raw material cost savings of $0.01 for each bottle manufactured. Knossos estimates that Larissa's annual bottle demand will continue to be 5,000,000 bottles over the next five years, the estimated economic life of the special-purpose equipment. Knossos further estimates that Larissa has an after-tax cost of capital of 15 percent and is subject to a 40 percent marginal income tax rate, the same rates as Knossos.

Required:

1. Knossos Limited plans to submit a bid to Larissa Company for the manufacture of the special-purpose bottling equipment.
   a. Calculate the bid Knossos would submit if it follows its standard pricing policy for special-purpose equipment.
   b. Calculate the minimum bid Knossos would be willing to submit on the Larissa equipment that would result in the same profits as planned for the first quarter.
2. What is the maximum price Larissa Company would likely pay for the machine? In your answer, assume that the equipment will be depreciated for tax purposes as a Class 8 asset (20 percent declining balance) and that it will have a salvage value of $100,000 at the end of its useful life.

CASES

OBJECTIVE 4

Case 14-33 Net Present Value Capital Investment

Gallant Guitars is considering several possible projects; each project requires an outlay of $2,000,000 and yields an indefinite stream of cash flow. The projects differ in the level of riskiness (i.e., the certainty of future cash flows varies). After investigating this issue, management has learned that each project has the same NPV and, accordingly, the managers are indifferent concerning which project to pursue.

Project	Investment	Cash Flow	Years of Cash Flow	Risk-Level
A	$2,000,000	$150,000	Indefinite	No Risk
B	2,000,000	250,000	Indefinite	Low Risk
C	2,000,000	350,000	Indefinite	Medium Risk
D	2,000,000	450,000	Indefinite	High Risk

The discount rate for project A is 7.5 percent.

Required:

1. What is the discount rate necessary for projects B, C, and D such that the NPVs of all projects are equal?
2. What is the difference between the discount rates for projects B, C, and D, and the discount rate for project A?
3. How can this difference be interpreted?
4. Which project would you choose to pursue? Why?
5. What variety of factors influenced your decision?

Case 14-34 Capital Investment and Ethical Behaviour

OBJECTIVE 4

Manny Carson, certified management accountant and controller of Wakeman Enterprises, had been given permission to acquire a new computer and software for the company's accounting system. The capital investment analysis showed an NPV of $100,000; however, the initial estimates of acquisition and installation costs were made on the basis of tentative costs without any formal bids. Manny now has two formal bids: one that would allow the firm to meet or beat the original projected NPV, and one that would reduce the projected NPV by $50,000. The second bid involves a system that would increase both the initial cost and the operating cost.

Normally, Manny would take the first bid without hesitation. However, Todd Downing, the owner of the firm presenting the second bid, is a close friend. Manny called Todd and explained the situation, offering Todd an opportunity to alter his bid and win the job. Todd thanked Manny and then made a counteroffer.

Todd: Listen, Manny, this job at the original price is the key to a successful year for me. The revenues will help me gain approval for the loan I need for renovation and expansion. If I don't get that loan, I see hard times ahead. The financial stats for the loan approval are so marginal that reducing the bid price may blow my chances.

Manny: Losing the bid altogether would be even worse, don't you think?

Todd: True. However, I have a suggestion. If you grant me the job, I will have the capability of adding personnel. I know that your son is looking for a job, and I can offer him a good salary and a promising future. Additionally, I'll be able to take you and your wife on that vacation to Hawaii that we have been talking about.

Manny: Well, you have a point. My son is having an awful time finding a job, and he has a wife and three kids to support. My wife is tired of having them live with us. She and I could use a vacation. I doubt that the other bidder would make any fuss if we turned it down. Its offices are out of province, after all.

Todd: Out of province? All the more reason to turn it down. Given the province's economy, it seems almost criminal to take business outside. Those are the kinds of business decisions that cause problems for people like your son.

Required:

Is Manny behaving ethically? Should Manny have called Todd in the first place? What if Todd had agreed to meet the lower bid price—would there have been any problems? Identify the rules of professional conduct (listed in Chapter 1) that Manny may be violating, if any.

Case 14-35 Payback, Net Present Value, Internal Rate of Return, Effects of Differences in Sales on Project Viability

Shaftel Ready Mix is a processor and supplier of concrete, aggregate, and rock products. The company operates in the prairie provinces. Currently, Shaftel has 14 cement-processing plants and a labour force of more than 375 employees. With the exception of cement powder, all materials (e.g., aggregates and sand) are produced internally by the company. The demand for concrete and aggregates has been growing steadily nationally, and on the prairies, the growth rate has been above the national average. Because of this growth, Shaftel has more than tripled its gross revenues over the past 10 years.

Of the prairie provinces, Saskatchewan has been experiencing the most growth. Processing plants have been added over the past several years, and the company is considering the addition of yet another plant to be located in Regina. A major advantage of another plant in Saskatchewan is the ability to operate year round, a feature not found in the northern reaches of Alberta or Manitoba.

In setting up the new plant, land would have to be purchased and a small building constructed. Equipment and furniture would not need to be purchased; these items would be transferred from

(*Continued*)

a plant that opened in Winnipeg during the building boom period and closed a few years after the end of that boom. However, the equipment needs some repair and modifications before it can be used. It has a book value of $200,000, and the furniture has a book value of $30,000. Neither has any outside market value. Other costs, such as the installation of a silo, well, electrical hookups, and so on, will be incurred. No salvage value is expected. The summary of the initial investment costs by category is as follows:

Land	$ 20,000
Building	135,000
Equipment:	
Book value	200,000
Modifications	20,000
Furniture (book value)	30,000
Silo	20,000
Well	80,000
Electrical hookups	27,000
General setup	50,000
Total	$582,000

Estimates concerning the operation of the Regina plant follow:

Life of plant and equipment	10 years
Expected annual sales (in cubic metres of cement)	35,000
Selling price (per cubic metre of cement)	$ 45.00
Variable costs (per cubic metre of cement):	
Cement	$ 12.94
Sand/gravel	6.42
Fly ash	1.13
Admixture	1.53
Driver labour	3.24
Mechanics	1.43
Plant operations (batching and cleanup)	1.39
Loader operator	0.50
Truck parts	1.75
Fuel	1.48
Other	3.27
Total variable costs	$ 35.08
Fixed costs (annual):	
Salaries	$135,000
Insurance	75,000
Telephone	5,000
Depreciation	56,200*
Utilities	25,000
Total fixed costs	$296,200

* Straight-line depreciation is calculated by using all initial investment costs, excluding land, over a 10-year period assuming no salvage value.

After reviewing these data, Karl Flemming, vice-president of operations, argued against the proposed plant. Karl was concerned because the plant would earn significantly less than the normal 8.3 percent return on sales. All other plants in the company were earning between 7.5 percent and 8.5 percent on sales. Karl also noted that it would take more than five years to recover the total initial outlay of $582,000. In the past, the company had always insisted that payback be no more than four years. The company's cost of capital is 10 percent. Assume that there are no income taxes.

Required:

1. Prepare a variable-costing income statement for the proposed plant. Compute the ratio of net income to sales. Is Karl correct that the return on sales is significantly lower than the company average?
2. Compute the payback period for the proposed plant. Is Karl right that the payback period is greater than five years? Explain. Suppose you were told that the equipment being transferred from Winnipeg could be sold for its book value. Would this affect your answer?
3. Compute the NPV and the IRR for the proposed plant. Would your answer be affected if you were told that the furniture and equipment could be sold for their book values? If so, repeat the analysis with this effect considered.
4. Compute the cubic metres of cement that must be sold for the new plant to break even. Using this break-even volume, compute the NPV and the IRR. Would the investment be acceptable? Explain why an investment that promises to do nothing more than break even can be viewed as acceptable.
5. Compute the volume of cement that must be sold for the IRR to equal the firm's cost of capital. Using this volume, compute the firm's expected annual income.

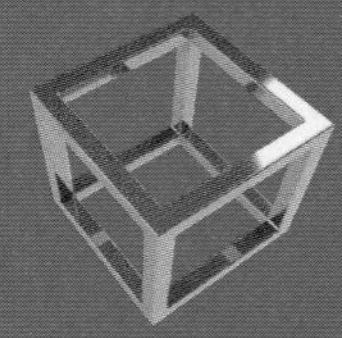

INTEGRATIVE CASE 3

Special Sales Offer

NoFat manufactures one product, olestra, and sells it to large potato chip manufacturers as the key ingredient in non-fat snack foods, including Ruffles, Lays, Doritos, and Tostitos brand products. For each of the past three years, sales of olestra have been far less than the expected annual volume of 125,000 kilograms. Therefore, the company has ended each year with significant unused capacity. Due to a short shelf life, NoFat must sell every kilogram of olestra that it produces each year. As a result, NoFat's controller, Allyson Ashley, has decided to seek out potential special sales offers from other companies. One company, Patterson Union (PU)—a toxic waste cleanup company—offered to buy 10,000 kilograms of olestra from NoFat during December for a price of $3.50 per kilogram. PU discovered through its research that olestra has proven to be very effective in cleaning up toxic waste locations designated as Superfund Sites by the U.S. Environmental Protection Agency.[1] Allyson was excited, noting that, "This is another way to use our expensive olestra plant!"

The annual costs incurred by NoFat to produce and sell 100,000 kilograms of olestra are as follows:

Variable costs per kilogram	
Direct materials	$1.00
Variable manufacturing overhead	0.75
Sales commissions	0.50
Direct manufacturing labour	0.25
Total fixed costs:	
Advertising	3,000
Customer hotline service	4,000
Machine setups	40,000
Plant machinery lease	12,000

In addition, Allyson met with several of NoFat's key production managers and discovered the following information:

- The special order could be produced without incurring any additional marketing or customer service costs.
- NoFat owns the aging plant facility that it uses to manufacture olestra.
- NoFat incurs costs to set up and clean its machines for each production run, or batch, of olestra that it produces. The total setup costs shown in the previous table represent the production of 20 batches during the year.
- NoFat leases its plant machinery. The lease agreement is negotiated and signed on the first day of each year. NoFat currently leases enough machinery to produce 125,000 kilograms of olestra.
- PU requires that an independent quality team must inspect any facility from which it makes purchases. The terms of the special sales offer would require NoFat to bear the $1,000 cost of the inspection team.

Allyson is uncertain whether NoFat should accept this special order offer, and has asked you for your help in evaluating it.

[1] This exercise is based on facts reported in the business press (e.g., Nanci Hellmich and Bruce Horovitz, "Fat Substitute Olestra Eyed as Hazardous Waste Cleaner: Potato Chips Sales Fall Short," *USA TODAY* (May 31, 2001): 1A).

Downsizing Alternative

After conducting a traditional, short-term relevant analysis, Allyson wonders whether it might be more profitable over the long term to downsize the company by reducing its manufacturing capacity (i.e., its plant machinery and plant facility). She is aware that downsizing requires a multiyear time horizon because companies usually cannot increase or decrease fixed plant assets every year. Therefore, Allyson has decided to use a five-year time horizon in her long-term decision analysis. She has identified the following information regarding capacity downsizing:

- The plant facility consists of several buildings. If it chooses to downsize its capacity, NoFat can immediately sell one of the buildings to an adjacent business for $30,000.
- If it chooses to downsize its capacity, NoFat's annual lease cost for plant machinery will decrease to $9,000.

Allyson is contemplating whether downsizing is the better option, and has asked you for your help in evaluating it.

Required:

1. Help Allyson evaluate both of NoFat's options by performing (1) a relevant analysis of the special sales offer compared to (2) an evaluation of the downsizing alternative. Assume that NoFat pays for all costs with cash. Also, assume a 10 percent discount rate, a five-year time horizon, and that all cash flows occur at the end of the year.
2. Allyson is looking to provide NoFat with a recommendation based on a long-term comparison of the alternatives. In your recommendation, describe some of the qualitative factors that NoFat should consider, in addition to the financial factors.

Q&A BOXES: ANSWERS

Chapter 2

Concept Q&A p. 36

Answers will vary.

Concept Q&A p. 39

Answers will vary.

Analytical Q&A p. 39

(1)	Total prime cost	=	Direct materials + Direct labour
		=	\$4,000 + \$5,000 = \$9,000
(2)	Conversion cost per unit	=	(Direct labour + Overhead)/ Number of units
		=	(\$5,000 + \$10,000)/1,000
		=	\$15

Analytical Q & A p. 52

No, the \$25 markup is not profit (operating income). The \$50 price is included in revenue; the \$25 original cost is included in cost of goods sold; and the \$25 over and above the cost to the store is gross margin.

Chapter 3

Analytical Q&A p. 80

The new line is above and parallel to the original one. The new line intersects the vertical axis at \$34,000.

Concept Q&A p. 81

Often, the number of guests is the output measure for a wedding reception. The cost of food and drinks varies with the number of guests. The relevant range for a wedding might be the approximate size—perhaps small (fewer than 100 guests), medium (100–200 guests), and large (200+ guests). Within a relevant range, fixed costs might include rental of the facility, flowers, and the cake.

Analytical Q&A p. 89

The high point is May, with cost of \$7,500 and 500 moves; the low point is January, with cost of \$2,000 and 100 moves.

Analytical Q&A p. 91

Fixed cost = \$2,000 − \$13.75(100) = \$625

Concept Q&A p. 95

The scattergraph method gives us a visual impression of the accuracy of the estimate using all the data points, while the high–low method only uses two points in making an estimate.

Concept Q&A p. 96

If the neighbouring business owner only rarely needed a copy, you might consider it a favour and not charge at all. If it happened several times a month, you might charge the variable cost of paper and toner. Finally, if the neighbouring business owner used your copier frequently, you might charge 10–20 cents per page—a price similar to that of an outside photocopying shop. Alternatively, the neighbour might buy you a ream of paper from time to time. Kinko's must include all costs in determining the cost of copies, including paper, toner, depreciation on equipment, cost of electricity and other utilities, and wages of staff.

Chapter 4

Concept Q&A p. 136

1. Variable cost ratio = 1.00 − 0.30 = 0.70, or 70 percent
2. Contribution margin ratio = 1.00 − 0.77 = 0.23, or 23 percent
3. The contribution margin ratio and the variable cost ratio always equal 100 percent of sales revenue because, by definition, sales revenue minus variable cost equals contribution margin. Therefore, it is a mathematical certainty that contribution margin plus variable cost will equal sales revenue.

Analytical Q&A p. 140

320 candles sold – 200 candles at break-even = 120 candles sold above break-even, 120 × \$1.50 = \$180. Lorna has earned operating income of \$180 so far during the month. An additional 10 candles will contribute \$15 to operating income (\$1.50 × 10).

Concept Q&A p. 147

A steeper revenue line would intersect the total cost line sooner. Thus, the break-even point would be lower; operating income above break-even would be higher. (*Hint:* Draw a steeper total revenue line on the exhibit to check this reasoning. Remember, revenue still starts at the origin; zero units sold means zero total revenue.) Increased variable cost per unit means a steeper slope for the total cost line. Thus, the break-even point would be higher, and the operating income above break-even would be lower.

Concept Q&A p. 149

Probably, the sales mix shifted toward the relatively lower-contribution-margin suits. For example, suppose that the break-even point, based on the assumed sales mix, for regular suits was 80, and the break-even point for designer suits was 20. If the mix shifted to 90 regular and 10 designer, it is easy to see that less total contribution margin (and, hence, operating income) would be realized.

Concept Q&A p. 157

It is not necessarily true that the two companies will achieve the same operating income simply because they have the same level of revenue. If one company has lower variable costs per unit and/or a lower total fixed cost, then its operating income would be higher. The differences in variable cost per unit and total fixed cost would lead to different break-even revenues. Of course, the company with the lower break-even sales would have a higher margin of safety.

Chapter 5

Concept Q&A p. 190

Answers will vary. One possible example: A tax accounting firm would keep track of costs by job because some tax returns are relatively simple, while others are complex and require time to fill out additional forms and to do necessary research. A "while you wait" oil change shop would use process costing (but cost the oil separately) since each car would take about the same amount of time and shop supplies to perform the oil change.

Concept Q&A p. 190

Under job order costing we would look at the total cost of the "makeover" as the job for which costs must be accumulated. The $5,000 only covers the clothes acquired. The true cost of the makeover includes the time of the make-up artists and the hairdresser, as well as the wardrobe consultants, who have spent considerable time coaching the contestant in appropriate styles. One could never duplicate the results for only $5,000.

Concept Q&A p. 199

Accounts Receivable is a control account; its subsidiary accounts are named (or numbered) by customers having an account with the company. Similarly, Accounts Payable has subsidiary accounts for each person/company to whom money is owed.

Concept Q&A p. 199

The form might be similar to the time ticket shown in Exhibit 5.6. However, the hourly rate and amount columns could be deleted and a column added for the initials of the worker entering the information.

Concept Q&A p. 214

The direct method ignores the interactions that may exist among support departments.

Concept Q&A p. 216

The sequential method considers some of the interactions among service departments in allocating support department costs.

Chapter 6

Concept Q&A p. 255

Yes. Process-costing procedures are the same for both process settings. Costs are collected by process and are assigned to units produced by the process. Each process undergoes this costing action regardless of whether it is a member of a sequential or a parallel processing system. Once goods are costed, they are transferred out to the next process.

Analytical Q&A p. 257

Work in Process (Bottling)	5,000	
Work in Process (Encapsulating)		5,000
Finished Goods	8,000	
Work in Process (Bottling)		8,000

Analytical Q&A p. 258

Equivalent units = 8,000 + (0.6 × 2,500) = 9,500

Analytical Q&A p. 261

Cost of goods transferred out: $8.00 × 9,000 = $72,000
EWIP: $8.00 × 1,250 = $10,000

Concept Q&A p. 262

FIFO treats work and costs in BWIP separately from the work and costs of the current period. Weighted average rolls back and picks up the work and costs of BWIP and counts them as if they belong to the current period's work and costs.

Analytical Q&A p. 264

Cost of goods transferred out: $10 × 3,800 = $38,000
EWIP: $10 × 0.4 × 750 = $3,000

Analytical Q&A p. 266

Units started and completed: 20,000 − 6,000 = 14,000

Analytical Q&A p. 266

Equivalent units = 5,000 + (0.8 × 1,500) = 6,200

Analytical Q&A p. 266

Unit cost = $31,000/6,200 = $5.00

Analytical Q&A p. 273

Unit cost = Unit materials cost + Unit conversion cost = ($400/200) + ($1,000/500) = $2 + $2 = $4

Concept Q&A p. 273

Transferred-in goods are viewed as materials added at the beginning of the process. They are treated as a separate input category, and equivalent units and a unit cost are calculated for transferred-in materials.

Analytical Q&A p. 277

Equivalent units = 80,000 + (0.70 × 40,000) + (0.60 × 20,000) = 120,000

Analytical Q&A p. 278

Total cost contributed to goods transferred out = ($12 × 25,000 × 0.8) + $50,000 = $290,000

Chapter 7

Concept Q&A p. 314

A unit-level activity is performed each time a unit is produced, whereas a non-unit-level activity is performed at times that do not correspond to individual unit production. Thus, inspection is unit-level for the first department and non-unit-level for the second department.

Analytical Q&A p. 316

Product A = 10/40 = 0.25
Product B = 30/40 = 0.75

Analytical Q&A p. 317

Rate = \$80,000/4,000 inspection hours = \$20 per inspection hour

Analytical Q&A p. 320

Unit cost = [\$150,000 + (\$20 × 1,000) + (\$50 × 600)]/5,000 = \$40

Concept Q&A p. 324

ABC uses cause-and-effect relationships to assign overhead costs. Volume-based costing uses unit-based drivers such as direct labour hours, which often have nothing to do with the actual amount of overhead resources consumed by a product.

Concept Q&A p. 325

The purpose of the interview questions is to identify activities, drivers, and other important attributes essential for ABC.

Concept Q&A p. 327

Resource costs are assigned by using both direct tracing (for exclusive direct resources) and driver tracing (for shared indirect resources).

Analytical Q&A p. 328

Cost assigned = \$50,000 + (30% × \$50,000) + (30% × \$50,000) = \$80,000

Concept Q&A p. 331

In traditional or volume costing, costs are assigned to products based on a single overhead application rate or a few overhead application rates, usually based on a single cost driver. In ABC, costs are assigned to products based on the nature of the activities that give rise to the costs in the company. In ABC there will be many different cost pools, each with its own cost driver and its own unique overhead application rate. This multiplicity of cost pools and application rates makes the assignment of overhead to products much more accurate.

Concept Q&A p. 334

Costs are traced to activities and are then assigned to suppliers based on a cause-and-effect relationship.

Concept Q&A p. 335

The objective of driver analysis is to find the root causes of activity costs. By knowing root causes, costs can be managed more effectively.

Concept Q&A p. 335

A value-added activity is one that must be performed for the firm to remain in business.

Concept Q&A p. 336

If a value-added activity is performed inefficiently, the inefficient component is waste and is the non-value-added cost.

Concept Q&A p. 340

Efficiency, quality, and time are the three performance dimensions for activities. All three relate to the ability of a manager to reduce activity cost.

Concept Q&A p. 343

One category of environmental external failure costs represents those costs that the firm causes and pays for, and the other category is those costs caused by the firm but paid for by parties outside the firm.

Chapter 8

Analytical Q&A p. 387

The cost of one unit under variable costing equals \$15 (= \$6 + \$7 + \$2). Only the unit costs of direct materials, direct labour, and variable overhead are included. Under absorption costing, the fixed overhead per unit must be computed. Thus, fixed overhead per unit = \$75,000/25,000 = \$3. Then, the cost of one unit under absorption costing equals \$18 (= \$6 + \$7 + \$2 + \$3).

Concept Q&A p. 391

The direct fixed costs of the furniture department include the wages of the clerks working in that department, the special fixtures that might be required to display some items (e.g., bedding), and the cost of display samples. Common fixed costs include utilities for the store as a whole, the cost of advertising a special storewide sales event, and the cost of the overall store manager.

Concept Q&A p. 395

You might have gone to another store, or tried to buy the item from a catalogue or online. The stockout cost for the first store is not only the profit to be made from selling to you, but also, potentially, your future business.

Chapter 9

Concept Q&A p. 423

A budget requires a plan. It also sets benchmarks that can be used to evaluate performance.

Concept Q&A p. 424

Continuous budgeting forces managers to plan ahead constantly—something especially needed when firms operate in rapidly changing environments.

Concept Q&A p. 426

The sales forecast is a starting point and an important input to the budgetary process; however, it is usually adjusted up or down, depending on the strategic objectives and plans of management.

Analytical Q&A p. 429

Budgeted units = Sales + EI − BI = 2,000 + (0.20 × 2,500) − 150 = 2,350

Analytical Q&A p. 434

Budget = (2 × 1,250) × \$12 = \$30,000

Analytical Q&A p. 436

Variable overhead = $3 × 5,000 = $15,000; Fixed overhead = $2,000
Total budgeted overhead = $15,000 + $2,000 = $17,000

Concept Q&A p. 437

Materials, labour, and overhead budgets are needed to calculate a budgeted unit cost. It could be argued that sales and production budgets are needed also because the three budgets listed cannot be developed until the sales and production budgets are known.

Analytical Q&A p. 438

Ending finished goods	=	Goods available for sale − Cost of goods sold
	=	$1,000 − $700 = $300

Analytical Q&A p. 438

Budgeted selling expense = $10,000 + (0.02 × $500,000) = $20,000

Concept Q&A p. 438

Interest expense comes from the financial budgets. Only operating income can be computed by using operating budgets.

Concept Q&A p. 442

A minimum cash balance is needed to reduce the risk of insufficient funds and satisfy account agreements with the banks. In the event of a shortage, it is necessary to borrow the difference of $500.

Concept Q&A p. 443

Money can be collected from credit sales of prior month(s).

Concept Q&A p. 446

Assuming that the budgeted maintenance expenditures were well specified, the manager is sacrificing the long-run well-being of the division to achieve a short-run benefit (dysfunctional behaviour).

Concept Q&A p. 447

Participation encourages managers to internalize the goals and make them their own, leading to improved performance.

Chapter 10

Analytical Q&A p. 482

Standard cost per unit = 10 × $8 = $80

Concept Q&A p. 483

An ideal standard is a standard of perfection—absolute efficiency is required. A currently attainable standard is rigorous but achievable and reflects a reasonable level of efficiency.

Concept Q&A p. 485

Standard costing enhances planning and control, and improves performance evaluation. It also simplifies product costing. Having a readily available product cost facilitates pricing decisions.

Analytical Q&A p. 486

SQ = 100 × 3,000 = 300,000 grams
SH = 0.5 × 3,000 = 1,500 direct labour hours

Concept Q&A p. 489

The labour rate variance will be unfavourable because the rate actually paid is more than the rate allowed.

Concept Q&A p. 491

An actual value of $89,750 would produce a value below the lower control limit, so there should be an investigation to find the cause or causes of the deviation. Corrective action could then be taken.

Concept Q&A p. 492

The total materials variance is the sum of the price variance and the usage variance when the materials purchased equal the materials used.

Analytical Q&A p. 495

MPV = ($2.00 − $3.00)100 = $100 F

Analytical Q&A p. 500

LEV = (AH − SH) × SR = (100 − 80) × $10 = $200 U

Chapter 11

Concept Q&A p. 530

The actual output may differ from the budgeted output, thus causing significant differences in cost. Comparing planned costs for one level of activity with the actual costs of a different level of activity does not provide good control information.

Analytical Q&A p. 533

Budgeted cost of maintenance = $0.45 × 2,000 = $900

Analytical Q&A p. 535

Variable overhead efficiency variance = (AH − SH) × SVOR = (100 − 90) × $6 = $60 U

Concept Q&A p. 537

The variable overhead spending variance is affected by price changes of individual items as well as efficiency issues.

Concept Q&A p. 538

Both the labour efficiency and variable overhead efficiency variances depend on the difference between actual and standard direct labour hours.

Analytical Q&A p. 539

Practical capacity = $10,000/$100 = 100 direct labour hours

Concept Q&A p. 545

ABB differs primarily from traditional budgeting in the overhead and selling and administrative budgets. ABB builds a budget for each activity based on the demands of the activity for resources, whereas traditional budgeting focuses on cost items required by organizational units such as departments.

Concept Q&A p. 548

Activity-based flexible budgeting is more accurate if costs vary with more than one driver and the drivers are not highly correlated with direct labour hours (which is often the case).

Chapter 12

Concept Q&A p. 578

If you worked at a Taco Bell or Pizza Hut, you were working for a decentralized company called YUM. This company owns many Taco Bells and Pizza Huts. Some decision making is pushed down to lower-level managers. On the other hand, suppose you worked for a small law or accounting firm that has only the local office. Then you were working for a centralized company, and the owner probably made all important operating and financial decisions.

Concept Q&A p. 583

Fast-food outlets and grocery stores probably have low margins and high turnover. These financial characteristics exist because they deal in perishables and must have continual turnover or the food will go bad. A jewellery store, on the other hand, has high margin and relatively low turnover. These financial characteristics exist because the goods are not perishable and there is relatively less competition in this market. (The existence of competition, of course, changes as more jewellery stores enter a market and as consumers become more confident about buying jewellery online.)

Concept Q&A p. 590

Residual income can use either before-tax income (operating income) or after-tax income. In addition, residual income uses a minimum required rate of return set by upper management. EVA, on the other hand, uses after-tax income and requires the company to compute its actual cost of capital.

Chapter 13

Concept Q&A p. 633

Answers will vary.

Concept Q&A p. 641

Suppose that you choose the oil-change decision. You might decide to change it yourself because (1) you know how to, (2) you have the appropriate tools to do the job, (3) you have the time, and (4) you don't mind messing around under the hood. Alternatively, you might decide to have it done in a shop because (1) you don't have confidence in your ability to do it, (2) you don't own the equipment (nozzle, pan to hold oil), (3) you are unsure which oil to choose, or (4) you don't want to do the job. A factor that could influence your decision from changing your own oil to taking your car to a shop might be that you have graduated from university and are working full time and really don't want to mess with oil changes in the few hours of free time that you do have.

Concept Q&A p. 652

The different types of minutes constrain the amount of time that you can talk per month. Early in the month, you might phone friends regularly. Later in the month, you might try to figure out how many minutes you have left and try harder to time your calls. For example, calls that must be made at a particular time may use "anytime minutes" (e.g., to set up a job interview appointment between 9 a.m. and 5 p.m.). Calls to friends and family might be postponed to the evening or the weekend.

Concept Q&A p. 654

You would probably be more likely to buy the item when the reason for the high price is high cost to the store. This situation makes the high price seem "fairer" to you, since the store is not gouging you but is simply trying to make a normal profit.

Chapter 14

Concept Q&A p. 685

Acceptance or rejection of an independent investment does not affect the cash flows of other investments. Acceptance of a mutually exclusive investment precludes the acceptance of any competing project.

Analytical Q&A p. 689

Payback period = $30,000/$8,000 = 3.75 years

Concept Q&A p. 691

Choosing only investments that return the highest income per dollar invested might be an action that helps the company comply with debt covenants. It also might have something to do with the manager's incentive compensation.

Concept Q&A p. 692

NPV greater than zero means that the investment recovers its capital while simultaneously earning a return in excess of the required rate.

Analytical Q&A p. 697

IRR = 12.00 percent

Concept Q&A p. 699

Postaudits allow a company to assess the quality of capital investment decisions and also produce corrective actions where some of the initial assumptions prove to be wrong. They also encourage managerial accountability and provide useful information for improving future capital budgeting decisions.

Concept Q&A p. 700

NPV uses a more realistic reinvestment assumption, and its signal is consistent with maximizing the wealth of firm owners (IRR does not measure absolute profits).

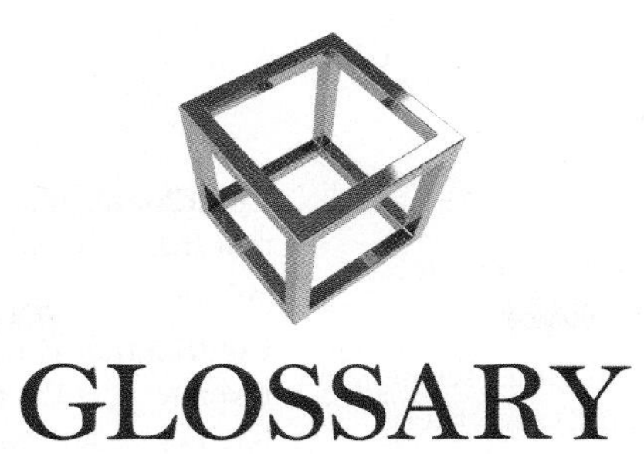

GLOSSARY

A

Absorption costing A product-costing method that assigns all manufacturing costs to units of product: direct materials, direct labour, variable manufacturing overhead, and fixed manufacturing overhead. (p. 382)

Accounting rate of return (ARR) The rate of return obtained by dividing the average accounting net income by the original investment (or by average investment). (p. 690)

Accumulating costs The way that costs are measured and recorded. (p. 32)

Activity analysis The process of identifying, describing, and evaluating the activities an organization performs. (p. 335)

Activity attributes Nonfinancial and financial information that describes individual activities. (p. 323)

Activity-based budgeting (ABB) system A budget system that focuses on estimating the costs of activities rather than the costs of departments and plants, and the use of multiple drivers, both unit-based and non-unit-based. (p. 544)

Activity-based costing (ABC) A method of costing goods and services that emphasizes the cost of the many activities or tasks that must be done to produce a product or offer a service. (p. 9)

Activity-based management A systemwide, integrated approach that focuses management's attention on activities with the objective of improving customer value and the profit achieved by providing this value. It includes driver analysis, activity analysis, and performance evaluation, and draws on activity-based costing as a major source of information. (p. 334)

Activity dictionary A list of activities described by specific attributes such as name, definition, classification as primary or secondary, and activity driver. (p. 323)

Activity drivers Factors that measure the consumption of activities by products and other cost objects. (p. 314)

Activity elimination The process of eliminating non-value-added activities. (p. 337)

Activity flexible budgeting Predicting what activity costs will be as activity usage changes. (p. 545)

Activity inputs The resources consumed by an activity in producing its output (they are the factors that enable the activity to be performed). (p. 334)

Activity output The result or product of an activity. (p. 334)

Activity output measure The number of times an activity is performed. It is the quantifiable measure of the output. (p. 334)

Activity reduction Decreasing the time and resources required by an activity. (p. 338)

Activity selection The process of choosing among sets of activities caused by competing strategies. (p. 338)

Activity sharing Increasing the efficiency of necessary activities by using economies of scale. (p. 338)

Actual cost system An approach that assigns actual costs of direct materials, direct labour, and overhead to products. (p. 190)

Adjusted cost of goods sold The cost of goods sold after all adjustments for overhead variances are made. (p. 206)

Administrative costs All costs associated with research, development, and general administration of the organization that cannot reasonably be assigned to either selling or production. (p. 42)

Allocation When an indirect cost is assigned to a cost object using a reasonable and convenient method. (p. 36)

Annuity A series of future cash flows. (p. 687)

Applied overhead Overhead assigned to production using predetermined rates. (p. 192)

Appraisal costs Costs incurred to determine whether products and services are conforming to requirements. (p. 341)

Assigning costs The way that a cost is linked to some cost object. (p. 33)

B

Backflush costing A method of costing under which labour costs are added into overhead costs and allocated to products so that materials and overhead are the only elements of cost for which we need to account. (p. 400)

Balanced Scorecard A strategic management system that defines a strategic-based responsibility accounting system. The Balanced Scorecard translates an organization's mission and strategy into operational objectives and performance measures for four different perspectives: the financial perspective, the customer perspective, the internal business process perspective, and the learning and growth (infrastructure) perspective. (p. 596)

Break-even point (BEP) The point where total sales revenue equals total cost; at this point, neither profit nor loss is earned. (p. 132)

Budget committee A committee responsible for setting budgetary policies and goals, reviewing and approving the budget, and resolving any differences that may arise in the budgetary process. (p. 424)

Budget director The individual responsible for directing and coordinating the overall budgeting process. (p. 424)

Budgetary slack The process of padding the budget by overestimating costs and underestimating revenues. (p. 447)

Budgets Plans of action expressed in financial terms. (p. 422)

C

Capital budgeting The process of making capital investment decisions. (p. 684)

Capital investment decisions The process of planning, setting goals and priorities, arranging financing, and identifying criteria for making long-term investments. (p. 684)

Carrying costs The costs of holding inventory. (p. 394)

Cash budget A detailed plan that outlines all sources and uses of cash. (p. 438)

Causal factors Activities or variables that invoke service costs. Generally, it is desirable to use causal factors as the basis for allocating service costs. (p. 213)

Certified General Accountant (CGA) A certified accountant who is permitted (by law) to serve as an external auditor. (p. 20)

Certified Management Accountant (CMA) A certified management accountant who has passed a rigorous qualifying examination, has met an experience requirement, and participates in continuing education. (p. 20)

Chartered Accountant (CA) An accountant who works as a business professional in public practice, industry, government, or education. CAs must pass a rigorous national examination and be licensed by the province in which they practise. (p. 20)

Chartered Professional Accountant (CPA) CPA is the designation for professional accountants in Canada. Recently, all three professional bodies for accountants in Canada merged into a single body to accredit professional accountants as CPAs. CPAs must pass a national examination and be licensed by the province in which they practise. (p. 22)

Coefficient of determination (R^2) The percentage of total variability in a dependent variable that is explained by an independent variable. It assumes a value between 0 and 1.00. (p. 102)

Committed fixed costs Fixed costs that cannot be easily changed. (p. 81)

Common costs The costs of resources used in the output of two or more services or products. (p. 213)

Common fixed expenses Fixed expenses that cannot be directly traced to individual segments and that are unaffected by the elimination of any one segment. (pp. 146, 391)

Compounding of interest Paying interest on interest. (p. 686)

Constraints Mathematical expressions that express resource limitations. (p. 651)

Consumption ratio The proportion of an overhead activity consumed by a product. (p. 315)

Continuous budget A moving 12-month budget with a future month added as the current month expires. (p. 424)

Continuous improvement Searching for ways to increase the overall efficiency and productivity of activities by reducing waste, increasing quality, and managing costs. (p. 12)

Contribution margin Sales revenue minus total variable cost or price minus unit variable cost. (p. 128)

Contribution margin income statement The income statement format that is based on the separation of costs into fixed and variable components. (p. 128)

Contribution margin ratio Contribution margin divided by sales revenue. It is the proportion of each sales dollar available to cover fixed costs and provide for profit. (p. 129)

Control The process of setting standards, receiving feedback on actual performance, and taking corrective action whenever actual performance deviates significantly from planned performance. (p. 423)

Control activities Activities performed by an organization to prevent or detect poor quality (because poor quality may exist). (p. 341)

Control costs Costs incurred from performing control activities. (p. 341)

Control limits The maximum allowable deviation from a standard. (p. 490)

Controllable costs Costs that managers have the power to influence. (p. 448)

Controller The chief accounting officer in an organization. (p. 16)

Controlling The managerial activity of monitoring a plan's implementation and taking corrective action as needed. (p. 5)

Conversion cost The sum of direct labour cost and overhead cost. (p. 40)

Core objectives and measures Those objectives and measures common to most organizations. (p. 600)

Cost The amount of cash or cash equivalent sacrificed for goods and/or services that are expected to bring a current or future benefit to the organization. (p. 32)

Cost behaviour The way in which a cost changes when the level of activity changes. (p. 78)

Cost centre A division of a company that is evaluated on the basis of cost. (p. 579)

Cost driver A causal measurement that causes costs to change. (p. 79)

Cost flow The way costs are accounted for from the point at which they are incurred to the point at which they are recognized as an expense on the income statement. (p. 201)

Cost object Any item such as a product, customer, department, project, and so on, for which costs are measured and assigned. (p. 33)

Cost of capital The cost of investment funds, usually viewed as a weighted average of the costs of funds from all sources. (p. 692)

Cost of goods manufactured The total product cost of goods completed during the current period. (p. 45)

Cost of goods sold The total product cost of goods sold during the period. (p. 47)

Cost of goods sold budget The total product cost of goods expected to be sold during the period. (p. 435)

Cost reconciliation The final section of the production report that compares the costs to account for with the costs accounted for to ensure that they are equal. (p. 267)

Cost structure A company's mix of fixed costs relative to variable costs. (p. 158)

Cost–volume–profit graph A graph that depicts the relationships among costs, volume, and profits. It consists of a total revenue line and a total cost line. (p. 145)

Costs of quality Costs incurred because poor quality may exist or because poor quality does exist. (p. 341)

CPA Canada As of June 2014, the body that brings together all three professional accounting groups across Canada and confers on members the designation of Chartered Professional Accountant (CPA) through its provincial or territorial counterparts. (p. 22)

Cross-functional perspective Seeing the interrelation in the disciplines of managerial accounting, marketing, management, engineering, finance, and other business functions. (p. 12)

Currently attainable standards Standards that reflect an efficient operating state; they are rigorous but achievable. (p. 483)

Customer perspective A Balanced Scorecard viewpoint that defines the customer and market segments in which the business will compete. (p. 596)

Customer value Realization less sacrifice, where realization is what the customer receives and sacrifice is what is given up. (p. 601)

Cycle time The length of time required to produce one unit of a product. (p. 340)

D

Decentralization The granting of decision-making freedom to lower operating levels. (p. 576)

Decision making The process of choosing among competing alternatives. (p. 5)

Decision model A specific set of procedures that lead to a decision. (p. 630)

Degree of operating leverage (DOL) A measure of the sensitivity of profit changes to changes in sales volume. It helps to measure the percentage change in profits resulting from a percentage change in sales. (p. 157)

Departmental overhead rate Estimated overhead for a single department divided by the estimated activity level for that same department. (p. 196)

Dependent variable A variable whose value depends on the value of another variable. (p. 87)

Differential cost The difference in total cost between the alternatives in a decision. (p. 632)

Direct costs Costs that can be easily and accurately traced to a cost object. (p. 35)

Direct fixed expenses Fixed costs that are directly traceable to a given segment and, consequently, disappear if the segment is eliminated. (pp. 146, 391)

Direct labour The labour that can be directly traced to the goods or services being produced. (p. 39)

Direct labour budget A budget showing the total direct labour hours needed and the associated cost for the number of units in the production budget. (p. 432)

Direct labour cost The wages of employees who are integral to the finished product. (p. 44)

Direct materials Materials that are a part of the final product and can be directly traced to the goods or services being produced. (p. 39)

Direct materials cost The cost of any materials that are an integral part of the finished product. (p. 43)

Direct materials purchases budget A budget that outlines the expected usage of materials production and purchases of the direct materials required. (p. 430)

Direct method A method that allocates service costs directly to producing departments. This method ignores any interactions that may exist among support departments. (p. 214)

Discount factor The factor used to convert a future cash flow to its present value. (p. 686)

Discount rate The rate of return used to compute the present value of future cash flows. (p. 686)

Discounted cash flows Future cash flows expressed in present-value terms. (p. 692)

Discounting The act of finding the present value of future cash flows. (p. 686)

Discounting models Capital investment models that explicitly consider the time value of money in identifying criteria for accepting and rejecting proposed projects. (p. 688)

Discretionary fixed costs Fixed costs that can be changed or avoided relatively easily at management's discretion. (p. 80)

Double-loop feedback Information about both the effectiveness of strategy implementation and the validity of assumptions underlying the strategy. (p. 599)

Driver analysis The effort expended to identify those factors that are the root causes of activity costs. (p. 335)

Dysfunctional behaviour Individual behaviour that conflicts with the goals of the organization. (p. 446)

E

Economic order quantity (EOQ) The amount that should be ordered (or produced) to minimize the total ordering (or setup) and carrying costs. (p. 395)

Economic value added (EVA) A performance measure that is calculated by taking the after-tax operating profit minus the total annual cost of capital. (p. 589)

Ending finished goods inventory budget A budget that describes planned ending inventory of finished goods in units and dollars. (p. 434)

Environmental costs Costs that are incurred because poor environmental quality exists or may exist. (p. 342)

Environmental detection costs Costs incurred to detect poor environmental performance. (p. 342)

Environmental external failure costs Costs incurred after contaminants are introduced into the environment. (p. 343)

Environmental internal failure costs Costs incurred after contaminants are produced, but before they are introduced into the environment. (p. 343)

Environmental prevention costs Costs incurred to prevent damage to the environment. (p. 342)

Equivalent units of output Complete units that could have been produced given the total amount of manufacturing effort expended for the period. (p. 258)

Ethical behaviour Choosing actions that are right, proper, and just. (p. 17)

Expenses Costs that are used up (expired) in the production of revenue. (p. 32)

External failure costs Costs incurred because products fail to conform to requirements after being sold to outside parties. (p. 342)

F

Failure activities Activities performed by an organization or its customers in response to poor quality (poor quality does exist). (p. 341)

Failure costs The costs incurred by an organization because failure activities are performed. (p. 341)

Favourable (F) variances Variances produced whenever the actual input amounts are less than the budgeted or standard allowances. (p. 488)

FIFO costing method A process-costing method that separates units in beginning inventory from those produced during the current period. Unit costs include only current-period costs and production. (p. 261)

Financial accounting A type of accounting that is primarily concerned with producing information for external users. (p. 6)

Financial budgets The portions of the master budget that include the cash budget, the budgeted balance sheet, the budgeted statement of cash flows, and the capital budget. (p. 424)

Financial perspective A Balanced Scorecard viewpoint that describes the financial consequences of actions taken in the other three perspectives. (p. 596)

Finished goods inventory Completed products that have not yet been sold. (p. 44)

Fixed cost Cost that, in total, is constant as the level of output increases or decreases. (p. 36)

Fixed costs Costs that, in total, are constant within the relevant range as the level of output increases or decreases. (p. 79)

Fixed overhead spending variance The difference between actual fixed overhead and applied fixed overhead. (p. 541)

Fixed overhead volume variance The difference between budgeted fixed overhead and applied fixed overhead; it is a measure of capacity utilization. (p. 541)

Flexible budget A budget that can specify costs for a range of activity. (p. 530)

Flexible budget variance The sum of price variances and efficiency variances in a performance report comparing actual costs to expected costs predicted by a flexible budget. (p. 533)

Future value The value that will accumulate by the end of an investment's life if the investment earns a specified compounded return. (p. 686)

G

Goal congruence The alignment of an employee's personal goals with those of the organization. (p. 446)

Goodness of fit A measure of how well the independent variable predicts the dependent variable. (p. 102)

Gross margin The difference between sales revenue and cost of goods sold. (p. 51)

H

High–low method A method for separating mixed costs into fixed and variable components by using just the high and low data points. [*Note:* The high (low) data point corresponds to the high (low) output level.] (p. 89)

I

Ideal standards Standards that reflect perfect operating conditions. (p. 483)

Incentives The positive or negative measures taken by an organization to induce an employee to exert effort toward achieving the organization's goals. (p. 446)

Independent projects Projects that, if accepted or rejected, will not affect the cash flows of another project. (p. 684)

Independent variable A variable whose value does not depend on the value of another variable. (p. 87)

Indifference point The quantity at which two systems produce the same operating income. (p. 160)

Indirect costs Costs that cannot be easily and accurately traced to a cost object. (p. 35)

Indirect labour Labour costs incurred in the manufacturing process that cannot easily be traced to a product and are, therefore, part of manufacturing overhead and are allocated to products as part of manufacturing overhead. (p. 44)

Indirect materials Materials that are consumed in the manufacturing process that cannot be easily traced to a product and are included in manufacturing overhead and allocated to the product. (p. 43)

Innovation process A process that anticipates the emerging and potential needs of customers and creates new products and services to satisfy those needs. (p. 601)

Intercept The fixed cost, representing the point where the cost formula intercepts the vertical axis. (p. 87)

Internal business process perspective A Balanced Scorecard viewpoint that describes the internal processes needed to provide value for customers and owners. (p. 596)

Internal failure costs Costs incurred because products and services fail to conform to requirements where lack of conformity is discovered prior to external sale. (p. 342)

Internal rate of return (IRR) The rate of return that equates the present value of a project's cash inflows with the present value of its cash outflows (i.e., it sets the NPV equal to zero). Also, the rate of return being earned on funds that remain internally invested in a project. (p. 694)

Investment centre A division of a company that is evaluated on the basis of return on investment. (p. 579)

J

Job One distinct unit or set of units for which the costs of production must be assigned. (p. 189)

Job-order cost sheet A subsidiary account to the Work in Process account on which the total costs of materials, labour, and overhead for a single job are accumulated. (p. 198)

Job-order costing system A costing system in which costs are collected and assigned to units of production for each individual job. (p. 189)

Joint products Products that are inseparable prior to a split-off point. All manufacturing costs up to the split-off point are joint costs. (p. 648)

Just-in-time (JIT) A demand-pull system whose objective is to eliminate waste by producing a product only when it is needed and only in the quantities demanded by customers. (p. 400)

K

Keep-or-drop decisions Relevant costing analyses that focus on keeping or dropping a segment of a business. (p. 644)

L

Labour efficiency variance (LEV) The difference between the actual direct labour hours used and the standard direct labour hours allowed multiplied by the standard hourly wage rate. (p. 498)

Labour rate variance (LRV) The difference between the actual hourly rate paid and the standard hourly rate multiplied by the actual hours worked. (p. 498)

Lead time The time required to receive the economic order quantity once an order is placed or a setup is started. (p. 398)

Lean accounting An accounting practice that organizes costs according to the value chain by focusing primarily on the elimination of waste. The objective is to provide information to managers that supports this effort and to provide financial statements that better reflect overall performance, using financial and nonfinancial information. (p. 13)

Learning and growth (infrastructure) perspective A Balanced Scorecard viewpoint that defines the capabilities that an organization needs to create long-term growth and improvement. (p. 596)

Line positions Positions that have direct responsibility for the basic objectives of an organization. (p. 15)

M

Make-or-buy decisions Relevant costing analyses that focus on whether a component should be made internally or purchased externally. (p. 638)

Managerial accounting The provision of accounting information for a company's internal users. (p. 4)

Manufacturing costs The total product cost of goods completed during the current period, equal to direct materials cost plus direct labour cost plus factory overhead cost. (p. 44)

Manufacturing cycle efficiency (MCE) Measured as value-added time divided by total time. The result tells the company what percentage of total time spent is devoted to actual production. (p. 604)

Manufacturing organizations Organizations that produce products. (p. 37)

Manufacturing overhead All product costs other than direct materials and direct labour. In a manufacturing firm, manufacturing overhead is also known as *factory burden* or *indirect* manufacturing costs. Costs are included in manufacturing overhead if they cannot be traced to the cost object of interest (e.g., unit of product). (p. 39)

Manufacturing overhead cost Combined costs that are incurred in the manufacturing process other than direct materials cost and direct labour cost. (p. 44)

Margin The ratio of net operating income to sales. (p. 581)

Margin of safety (MS) The units sold (or expected to be sold) or sales revenue earned (or expected to be earned) above the break-even volume. (p. 155)

Markup The percentage applied to a base cost; it includes desired profit and any costs not included in the base cost. (p. 653)

Master budget The collection of all area and activity budgets representing a firm's comprehensive plan of action. (p. 423)

Materials inventory The costs of direct and indirect materials that have not entered the manufacturing process. (p. 44)

Materials price variance (MPV) The difference between the actual price paid per unit of materials and the standard price allowed per unit multiplied by the actual quantity of materials purchased. (p. 494)

Materials requisition form A source document that records the type, quantity, and unit price of the direct materials issued to each job. (p. 199)

Materials usage variance (MUV) The difference between the direct materials actually used and the direct materials allowed for the actual output multiplied by the standard price. (p. 494)

Merchandise purchasing budget A budget detailing how many units must be purchased to meet sales needs and to satisfy ending inventory requirements. (p. 429)

Method of least squares (regression) A statistical method to find the best-fitting line through a set of data points. It is used to break out the fixed and variable components of a mixed cost. (p. 98)

Mixed costs Costs that have both a fixed and a variable component. (p. 82)

Monetary incentives The use of economic rewards to motivate managers. (p. 446)

Mutually exclusive projects Projects that, if accepted, preclude the acceptance of competing projects. (p. 684)

Myopic behaviour Actions that improve budgetary performance in the short run, but which bring long-run harm to the firm. (p. 448)

N

Net present value The difference between the present value of a project's cash inflows and the present value of its cash outflows. (p. 692)

Non-unit-level activity drivers Factors that measure the consumption of non-unit-level activities by products and other cost objects. (p. 314)

Non-value-added activities All activities other than those that are absolutely essential to remain in business. (p. 336)

Non-value-added costs Costs that are caused either by non-value-added activities or by the inefficient performance of value-added activities. (p. 336)

Nondiscounting models Capital investment models that identify criteria for accepting or rejecting projects without considering the time value of money. (p. 688)

Nonmonetary incentives The use of psychological and social rewards to motivate managers. (p. 446)

Normal cost of goods sold The cost of goods sold before adjustment for any overhead variance. (p. 206)

Normal cost system An approach that assigns the actual costs of direct materials and direct labour to products, but uses a predetermined rate to assign overhead costs. (p. 191)

O

Ontario Bill 198 A bill passed by the Ontario Legislature in response to a variety of financial scandals in Canada and the United States. It enacts legislation similar to the Sarbanes-Oxley Act in the United States. (p. 16)

Operating assets Assets used to generate operating income, consisting usually of cash, inventories, receivables, and property, plant, and equipment. Average operating assets are found by adding together beginning operating assets and ending operating assets, and dividing the result by 2. (p. 581)

Operating budgets Budgets associated with the income-producing activities of an organization. (p. 424)

Operating income Revenues minus operating expenses from the firm's normal operations. Operating income is earnings before interest and taxes. (p. 581)

Operating leverage The use of fixed costs to extract higher percentage changes in profits as sales activity changes. Leverage is achieved by increasing fixed costs while lowering variable costs. (p. 157)

Operations process A process that produces and delivers existing products and services to customers. (p. 602)

Opportunity cost The benefit given up or sacrificed when one alternative is chosen over another. (pp. 33, 634)

Ordering costs The costs of placing and receiving an order. (p. 394)

Overapplied overhead The amount by which applied overhead exceeds actual overhead. (p. 193)

Overhead budget A budget that reveals the planned expenditures for all indirect manufacturing items. (p. 433)

P

Parallel processing A processing pattern in which two or more sequential processes are required to produce a finished good. (p. 254)

Participative budgeting An approach to budgeting that allows employees who will be held accountable for budgetary performance to participate in the budget's development. (p. 446)

Payback period The time required for a project to return its investment. (p. 688)

Performance report A report that compares the actual data with planned data. (p. 528)

Period costs Costs that are expensed in the period in which they are incurred; they are not inventoried. (p. 41)

Physical flow schedule A schedule that reconciles units to account for with units accounted for. The physical units are not adjusted for percent of completion. (p. 264)

Planning A management activity that involves the detailed formulation of action to achieve a particular end. (p. 5)

Plantwide overhead rate A single overhead rate calculated using all estimated overhead for a factory divided by the estimated activity level across the entire factory. (p. 195)

Postaudit A follow-up analysis of an investment decision, comparing actual benefits and costs with expected benefits and costs. (p. 698)

Postpurchase costs The costs of using, maintaining, and disposing of the product. (p. 601)

Postsales service process A process that provides critical and responsive service to customers after the product or service has been delivered. (p. 602)

Predetermined overhead rate An overhead rate computed using estimated data. (p. 191)

Present value The current value of a future cash flow. It represents the amount that must be invested now if the future cash flow is to be received assuming compounding at a given rate of interest. (p. 686)

Prevention costs Costs incurred to prevent defects in products or services being produced. (p. 341)

Price The revenue per unit. (p. 32)

Price standards The price that should be paid per unit of input. (p. 482)

Price (rate) variance The difference between standard price and actual price multiplied by the actual quantity of inputs used. (p. 488)

Prime cost The sum of direct materials cost and direct labour cost. (p. 40)

Pro rata application The process of allocating costs to various elements on the basis of the individual element cost to the total of all element costs. It is used when applying under- or overapplied overhead between cost of goods sold and inventory accounts. (p. 194)

Process-costing system A costing system that accumulates production costs by process or by department for a given period of time. (p. 189)

Process-value analysis An approach that focuses on processes and activities, and emphasizes systemwide performance instead of individual performance. (p. 334)

Process value chain The innovation, operations, and postsales service processes. (p. 601)

Producing departments Units within an organization responsible for producing the products or services that are sold to customers. (p. 213)

Product (manufacturing) costs Costs associated with the manufacture of goods or the provision of services. Product costs include direct materials, direct labour, and overhead. (p. 38)

Product diversity The situation present when products consume overhead in different proportions. (p. 314)

Product life cycle New products' series of stages: conception, introduction into the market, growth, maturity, and decline and eventual withdrawal from the market. (p. 9)

Production budget A budget that shows how many units must be produced to meet sales needs and to satisfy ending inventory requirements. (p. 427)

Production report A document that summarizes the manufacturing activity that takes place in a process department for a given period of time. (p. 257)

Products Goods produced by converting raw materials through the use of labour and indirect manufacturing resources, such as the manufacturing plant, land, and machinery. (p. 37)

Profit centre A division of a company that is evaluated on the basis of operating income or profit. (p. 579)

Profit–volume graph A graphical portrayal of the relationship between profits and sales activity in units. (p. 144)

Profitability index (PI) A discounting method that divides the present value of future cash flows by the initial investment. (p. 694)

Pseudoparticipation A budgetary system in which top management solicits inputs from lower-level managers and then ignores those inputs. Thus, in reality, budgets are dictated from above. (p. 447)

Publicly traded companies Companies that issue shares traded on a stock exchange which are subject to regulation. (p. 16)

Q

Quantity standards The quantity of input allowed per unit of output. (p. 482)

R

Realized external failure costs Environmental costs caused by environmental degradation and paid for by the responsible organization. (p. 343)

Reciprocal method A method that simultaneously allocates service costs to all user departments. It gives full consideration to interactions among support departments. (p. 218)

Relevant costs Future costs that change across alternatives. (p. 634)

Relevant range The range of output over which an assumed cost relationship is valid for the normal operations of a firm. (p. 85)

Reorder point The point in time when a new order should be placed (or setup started). (p. 398)

Required rate of return The minimum rate of return that a project must earn in order to be acceptable. Usually corresponds to the cost of capital. (p. 692)

Residual income The difference between operating income and the minimum dollar return required on a company's operating assets. (p. 587)

Resource drivers Factors that measure the consumption of resources by activities. (p. 326)

Responsibility centre A segment of the business whose manager is accountable for specified sets of activities. (p. 578)

Return on investment (ROI) The ratio of operating income to average operating assets. (p. 580)

Revenue centre A segment of the business that is evaluated on the basis of sales. (p. 579)

S

Safety stock Extra inventory carried to serve as insurance against changes in demand that may cause stockouts. Safety stock is computed by multiplying the lead time by the difference between the maximum rate of usage and the average rate of usage. (p. 399)

Sales budget A budget that describes expected sales in units and dollars for the coming period. (p. 425)

Sales mix The relative combination of products (or services) being sold by an organization. (p. 147)

Sarbanes-Oxley Act (SOX) Passed in 2002 in response to revelations of misconduct and fraud by several well-known firms, this legislation established stronger governmental control and regulation of public companies in the United States, from enhanced oversight (PCAOB), to increased auditor independence and tightened regulation of corporate governance. (p. 16)

Scattergraph method A method to fit a line to a set of data using two points that are selected by judgment. It is used to break out the fixed and variable components of a mixed cost. (p. 93)

Segment A subunit of a company of sufficient importance to warrant the production of performance reports. (p. 391)

Segment margin The contribution a segment makes to cover common fixed costs and provide for profit after direct fixed costs and variable costs are deducted from the segment's sales revenue. (p. 393)

Sell-or-process-further decision Relevant costing analysis that focuses on whether a product should be processed beyond the split-off point. (p. 648)

Selling and administrative expenses budget A budget that outlines planned expenditures for nonmanufacturing activities. (p. 436)

Selling costs Those costs necessary to market, distribute, and service a product or service. (p. 42)

Semi-variable costs Costs that have both a fixed and a variable component (p. 82)

Sensitivity analysis The "what-if" process of altering certain key variables to assess the effect on the original outcome. (p. 161)

Sequential (or step) method A method that allocates service costs to user departments in a sequential manner. It gives partial consideration to interactions among support departments. (p. 216)

Sequential processing A processing pattern in which units pass from one process to another in a set order. (p. 254)

Service organizations Organizations that produce intangible products. (p. 37)

Services Tasks or activities performed for a customer, or an activity performed by a customer using an organization's products or facilities. (p. 37)

Single-loop feedback Information about the effectiveness of strategy implementation. (p. 599)

Slope The variable cost per unit of activity usage. (p. 87)

Societal costs Environmental costs caused by an organization, but paid for by society; also called unrealized external failure costs. (p. 343)

Special-order decisions Relevant costing analyses that focus on whether a specially priced order should be accepted or rejected. (p. 641)

Split-off point The point at which products become distinguishable after passing through a common process. (p. 648)

Staff positions Positions that are supportive in nature and have only indirect responsibility for an organization's basic objectives. (p. 15)

Standard cost per unit The per-unit cost that should be achieved given materials, labour, and overhead standards. (p. 485)

Standard cost sheet A listing of the standard costs and standard quantities of direct materials, direct labour, and overhead that should apply to a single product. (p. 485)

Standard hours allowed (SH) The direct labour hours that should have been used to produce the actual output (Unit labour standard × Actual output). (p. 486)

Standard quantity of materials allowed (SQ) The quantity of materials that should have been used to produce the actual output (Unit materials standard × Actual output). (p. 486)

Static budget A budget for a particular level of activity. (p. 528)

Step cost A cost that displays a constant level of cost for a range of output and then jumps to a higher level of cost at some point, where it remains for a similar range of output. (p. 83)

Stockout costs The costs of insufficient inventory. (p. 394)

Strategic plan The long-term plan for future activities and operations, usually involving at least five years. (p. 422)

Strategy The process of choosing a business's market and customer segments, identifying its critical internal business processes, and selecting the individual and organizational capabilities needed to meet internal, customer, and financial objectives. (p. 597)

Sunk cost A cost for which the outlay has already been made and that cannot be affected by a future decision. (p. 635)

Support departments Units within an organization that provide essential support services for producing departments. (p. 213)

T

Target cost The difference between the sales price needed to achieve a projected market share and the desired per-unit profit. (p. 501)

Target costing A method of determining the cost of a product or service based on the price (target price) that customers are willing to pay. (p. 655)

Tax shield A legal way to reduce net income for tax purposes, creating a reduction in income taxes payable. (p. 708)

Testable strategy A set of linked objectives aimed at an overall goal that can be restated into a sequence of cause-and-effect hypotheses. (p. 598)

Time ticket A source document by which direct labour costs are assigned to individual jobs. (p. 200)

Total budget variance The difference between the actual cost of an input and its planned cost. (p. 487)

Total quality management A management philosophy in which manufacturers strive to create an environment that will enable workers to manufacture perfect (zero-defect) products. (p. 13)

Transfer price The price charged for goods transferred from one division to another. (p. 591)

Transferred-in costs Costs transferred from a prior process to a subsequent process. (p. 257)

Treasurer The individual responsible for the finance function; raises capital and manages cash and investments. (p. 16)

Triple Bottom Line Performance measures for companies that include financial, social, and environmental factors. (p. 7)

Turnover The ratio of sales to average operating assets. (p. 581)

U

Underapplied overhead The amount by which actual overhead exceeds applied overhead. (p. 193)

Unfavourable (U) variances Variances produced whenever the actual input amounts are greater than the budgeted or standard allowances. (p. 488)

Unit contribution margin Sales price per unit minus variable cost per unit. (p. 130)

Unit-level activities Activities that are performed each time a unit is produced. (p. 313)

Unit-level activity drivers Factors that measure the consumption of unit-level activities by products and other cost objects. (p. 314)

Unrealized external failure costs Environmental costs caused by an organization, but paid for by society; also called societal costs. (p. 343)

Usage (efficiency) variance The difference between standard quantities and actual quantities multiplied by standard price. (p. 488)

V

Value chain The set of activities required to design, develop, produce, market, and deliver products and services to customers. (p. 10)

Value-added activities Activities that are necessary for a business to achieve corporate objectives and remain in business. (p. 336)

Value-added costs Costs caused by value-added activities. (p. 336)

Variable budgets Budgets that can specify costs for a range of activity. (p. 530)

Variable cost Cost that, in total, varies in direct proportion to changes in output. (p. 36)

Variable cost ratio Variable costs divided by sales revenues. It is the proportion of each sales dollar needed to cover variable costs. (p. 135)

Variable costing A product-costing method that assigns only variable manufacturing costs to production: direct materials, direct labour, and variable manufacturing overhead. Fixed manufacturing overhead is treated as a period cost. (p. 382)

Variable costs Costs that, in total, vary in direct proportion to changes in output within the relevant range. (p. 81)

Variable overhead efficiency variance The difference between the actual direct labour hours used and the standard hours allowed multiplied by the standard variable overhead rate. (p. 535)

Variable overhead spending variance The difference between the actual variable overhead and the budgeted variable overhead based on actual hours used to produce the actual output. (p. 535)

Velocity The number of units that can be produced in a given period of time (e.g., output per hour). (p. 340)

W

Weighted average costing method A process-costing method that combines beginning inventory costs with current-period costs to compute unit costs. Costs and output from the current period and the previous period are averaged to compute unit costs. (p. 261)

Work-in-process (WIP) inventory The cost of the partially completed goods that are still being worked on at the end of a time period. (p. 44)

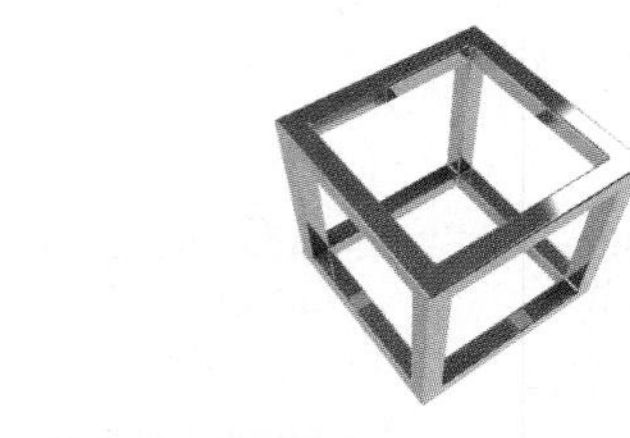

SUBJECT INDEX

C

D

O

P

W

Y

COMPANY INDEX

SUMMARY OF IMPORTANT EQUATIONS

Chapter 2

1. Total product cost = Direct materials + Direct labour + Manufacturing overhead
2. $\text{Unit product cost} = \dfrac{\text{Total product cost}}{\text{Number of units}}$
3. Prime cost = Direct materials + Direct labour
4. Conversion cost = Direct labour + Manufacturing overhead
5. Direct materials used in production = Beginning inventory of materials + Purchases − Ending inventory of materials
6. Cost of goods manufactured = Direct materials used in production + Direct labour used in production + Manufacturing overhead costs used in production + Beginning WIP inventory − Ending WIP inventory
7. Cost of goods sold = Beginning finished goods inventory + Cost of goods manufactured − Ending finished goods inventory

Chapter 3

1. Cost formula: Total cost = Total fixed cost + (Variable rate × Units of output)
2. Total variable cost = Variable rate × Units of output

Chapter 4

1. Sales revenue = Price × Units sold
2. Operating income = (Price × Units sold) − (Unit variable cost × Units sold) − Fixed cost
3. $\text{Break-even point in units} = \dfrac{\text{Fixed cost}}{(\text{Price} - \text{Unit variable cost})}$
4. $\text{Contribution margin ratio} = \dfrac{\text{Total contribution margin}}{\text{Sales}}$ or $= \dfrac{(\text{Price} - \text{Unit variable cost})}{\text{Price}}$
5. $\text{Variable cost ratio} = \dfrac{\text{Total variable cost}}{\text{Sales}}$ or $= \dfrac{\text{Unit variable cost}}{\text{Price}}$
6. $\text{Break-even point in sales dollars} = \dfrac{\text{Fixed cost}}{\text{Contribution margin ratio}}$ or $= \dfrac{\text{Fixed cost}}{1 - \text{Variable cost ratio}}$
7. Margin of safety = Sales − Break-even sales
8. $\text{Degree of operating leverage} = \dfrac{\text{Total contribution margin}}{\text{Operating income}}$
9. Percentage change in profits = Degree of operating leverage × Percentage change in sales

Chapter 5

1. $\text{Predetermined overhead rate} = \dfrac{\text{Estimated annual overhead cost}}{\text{Estimated annual activity level}}$
2. Applied overhead = Predetermined overhead rate × Actual activity usage
3. Overhead variance = Applied overhead − Actual overhead
4. Adjusted COGS = Unadjusted COGS ± Overhead variance
   (*Note:* Applied overhead > Actual overhead means overapplied overhead
   Applied overhead < Actual overhead means underapplied overhead)
5. $\text{Departmental overhead rate} = \dfrac{\text{Estimated departmental overhead}}{\text{Estimated departmental activity level}}$
6. Total product cost = Total direct materials + Total direct labour + Applied overhead
7. $\text{Unit product cost} = \dfrac{\text{Total product cost}}{\text{Number of units}}$

Chapter 6

1. $\text{Unit cost} = \dfrac{\text{Total cost}}{\text{Equivalent units}}$
2. Units started and completed = Total units completed − Units in BWIP
3. Units started = Units started and completed + Units in EWIP
4. Total manufacturing costs = BWIP for period + Costs added in period
5. Cost of units started and completed = Unit cost × Units started and completed
6. Cost of finishing units in BWIP = Prior period costs + (Unit cost × Equivalent units to complete)
7. $\text{Unit cost} = \dfrac{\text{Total costs for the period}}{\text{Number of services provided}}$
8. $\text{Unit cost} = \dfrac{\text{Total costs for the period}}{\text{Total output of the period}}$

Chapter 8

1. Absorption costing product cost = Direct materials + Direct labour + Variable manufacturing overhead + Fixed overhead
2. Variable costing product cost = Direct materials + Direct labour + Variable manufacturing overhead
3. Total inventory-related cost = Ordering cost + Carrying cost
4. Ordering cost = Number of orders per year × Cost of placing one order
5. $\text{Average number of units in inventory} = \dfrac{\text{Units in order}}{2}$
6. Carrying cost = Average number of units in inventory × Cost of carrying one unit of inventory
7. $EOQ = \sqrt{\dfrac{2 \times CO \times D}{CC}}$
8. Reorder point without safety stock = Daily usage × Lead time
9. Safety stock = (Maximum daily usage − Average daily usage) × Lead time
10. Reorder point with safety stock = (Average daily usage + Safety stock) × Lead time

Chapter 9

1. Units to be produced = Expected unit sales + Units in desired ending inventory (EI) − Units in beginning inventory (BI)
2. Purchases = Direct materials needed for production + Direct materials in desired ending inventory (EI) − Direct materials in beginning inventory (BI)
3. For retail firms: Units to be purchased = Expected unit sales + Units in desired ending inventory (EI) − Units in beginning inventory (BI)

Chapter 10

1. $MPV = (AP - SP)AQ$
2. $MUV = (AQ - SQ)SP$
3. $LRV = (AR - SR)AH$
4. $LEV = (AH - SH)SR$